Psychology: The Science of Mind and Behaviour

Psychology: The Science of Mind and Behaviour

Nigel Holt, Andy Bremner, Ed Sutherland, Michael Vliek, Michael W. Passer and Ronald E. Smith

London   Boston   Burr Ridge,IL   Dubuque, IA   Madison, WI   New York   San Francisco
St. Louis   Bangkok   Bogotá   Caracas   Kuala Lumpur   Lisbon   Madrid   Mexico City   Milan   Montreal
New Delhi   Santiago   Seoul   Singapore   Sydney   Taipei   Toronto

Psychology: The Science of Mind and Behaviour

Nigel Holt, Andy Bremner, Ed Sutherland, Michael Vliek, Michael W. Passer and Ronald E. Smith

ISBN-13 9780077169848

ISBN-10 0077169840

Published by McGraw-Hill Education
Shoppenhangers Road
Maidenhead
Berkshire
SL6 2QL
Telephone: 44 (0) 1628 502 500
Fax: 44 (0) 1628 770 224
Website: www.mheducation.co.uk

British Library Cataloguing in Publication Data
A catalogue record for this book is available from the British Library

Library of Congress Cataloguing in Publication Data
The Library of Congress data for this book has been applied for from the Library of Congress

Content Acquisitions Manager: Tom Hill
Product Developer: Rosie Churchill
Senior Content Product Manager: Jessica Moody
Marketing Manager: Geeta Kumar

Text Design by: Ian Youngs

Cover design by: Adam Renvoize

Printed and bound in the UK by Bell & Bain

ISBN-13 9780077169848

ISBN-10 0077169840

Dedication

Nigel Holl
To Katie

Andy Bremner
To Bea, Ed, Gavin, Joe, Maggie, Miranda and Theo

Ed Sutherland
To Siobhan, Samuel and Elayna and also to Bruce and Janice

Michael Vliek
To Ina, Leo, Martin and Daniela for their love and support

Brief table of contents

Detailed table of contents

Preface

Mind and behaviour: it is difficult to think of anything more fascinating. But we didn't all recognize this when we began university and we'd put money on many of you having a similar experience. Nigel Holt entered university to study Economics, whereas Michael Vliek and Andy Bremner turned up at university having chosen Psychology but weren't really sure why. Ed Sutherland had more of an inkling, having become hooked on Psychology during A levels. But each of us took an introductory psychology course, and suddenly our life-paths changed. Because of our teachers and lecturers who brought the subject to life, we were hooked, and that initial enthusiasm has never left us. The principles we have learned over the years, the skills of observation, critique, evaluation and our general awareness of the principles of behaviour have given us a strong foundation for our professional and personal lives and we hope you too will have similar experiences.

Through this textbook, we have the pleasure and privilege to share our enthusiasm with today's lecturers and students. Lecturers like nothing more than the sound of their own voice and the chance to express themselves in print and so this book holds in it our passions and personalities –we hope this comes through when you read it. In the earlier editions of the book we worked hard to help it find its own voice, to become a useful and indeed vital part of any well-designed psychology course. We received many positive and enthusiastic comments about these earlier editions and have built on them here, making the book relevant and up to date, ensuring both instructors and students find what they need. It's important that our updates reflect the nature of both psychology and education at that time: to ensure that the product supports teaching needs and allows incorporation of both the challenges psychology is facing and the baseline from which is continues to develop; and to ensure that we are effectively supporting the learning needs and expectations of students in today's universities.

The examples and research are geared towards an international audience. We want to help students to experience, as we did, the intellectual excitement of studying the science of mind and behaviour. We are also seeking to help students sharpen their critical-thinking skills and dispel commonly held myths. All of this is done within the simple conceptual framework begun in the earlier editions all those years ago.

THE THIRD EDITION

The original version of this textbook was written by Michael Passer and Ronald Smith to be relevant to North American students, and to facilitate the type of courses which their instructors would convene. Many teachers outside the USA saw the great strengths of Michael and Ronald's approach and were using the American version of the text in their universities across Europe, South Africa and Australasia. However, teaching and learning is better facilitated by using examples and research which are more relevant to the students' and teachers' cultures. And so, with this goal in mind, we developed an adaptation to be more relevant to an international audience of students and teachers.. This aim continues to be a key objective of the adaptation, ensuring relevance for teachers and students alike. However, the product has also evolved to take on a life of its own, beyond the original adaptation, responding to the current needs and changes within the Psychology discipline and within the Higher Education environment. This is evident through our continued desire to revise and hone the content, structure and research included in this product, whilst also ensuring a rich pedagogical experience tailored towards student needs. As teaching and learning evolve, so too does this pedagogical experience; moving beyond just the printed book and expanding into digital versions of the text and interactive and engaging learning materials via our Connect and LearnSmart products.

Content Updates

For this third edition, we have continued to listen to what teachers and students in Europe and South Africa had to say about the text, and have taken on board their comments; we have introduced new topics and recent research, as well as making changes to the book's features and layout. A few of the changes for this new edition include:

- The new field of epigenetics is now addressed and there is enhanced coverage of the role of evolution in psychology with guest co-author Debbie Custance (Chapter 3)
- Updated coverage of neuroscience methods (Chapter 4)
- Attention continues to be discussed in increasing detail alongside consciousness (Chapter 6)
- The chapter on physical and cognitive development presents recent work on developmental cognitive neuroscience (Chapter 12)
- Coverage of attachment has been expanded and enhanced (Chapter 13)
- Mass panic has been included as a social phenomenon (Chapter 14)
- The growing field of positive psychology is discussed in relation to health and optimism (Chapter 16)
- CBT is given more prominence and coverage as a major cognitive therapy (Chapter 18)
- Updated research is included throughout all the chapters and our pedagogy has been revised to provide the most effective selection we can provide:
  - Current topic boxes have been updated throughout to ensure they are topical and representative of the current field of psychology.
  - Research close-up boxes have been revised and updated to ensure a continued representation of both classic and contemporary research in a detailed and accessible manner.
  - Recommended reading, both classic and contemporary, has been newly added to each chapter to provide a springboard for further study.

THE BIG PICTURE: A SIMPLE UNIFYING FRAMEWORK THAT EASILY ADAPTS TO THE INSTRUCTOR'S PREFERENCES

Psychology is a vibrant but sprawling discipline, and the tremendous diversity of issues covered in the introductory course can lead students to perceive psychology as a collection of unrelated topics. To reduce this tendency and also help students become more sophisticated in their everyday understanding of behaviour, we present a simple unifying framework that is applied throughout the book. This framework, called 'Levels of analysis' (LOA), emphasizes how psychologists examine *biological, psychological* and *environmental factors* in their quest to understand behaviour. The LOA framework is easy for students to understand and remember; is consistently applied in every chapter; accurately portrays the focus of modern psychology; supports critical thinking; and also helps students understand how biological, psychological and environmental factors are related to one another.

Although we carry the LOA framework throughout the book in textual discussion and schematics, we are careful to apply it selectively so that it does not become overly repetitious for students or confining for instructors. Indeed, one of the beauties of the LOA framework is that it stands on its own and thus instructors can easily adapt it to their personal teaching preferences.

READABILITY, RIGOUR AND RELEVANCE

Textbooks like this have a surprisingly long shelf-life. We all remember the introductory book we used as undergraduates and more often than not they become like old friends, well-read first stops when we need to find something quickly and conveniently. We hope you have a similarly long and productive relationship with this book. We have made every attempt to use clear prose, careful explanations, engaging and relevant examples, and supporting artwork to make the book and multimedia accessible to our readers. The students at our own institutions form a fairly representative cross-section of those who may use the book. And so, as we wrote with our own students in mind, we hope that this will mean that those who read it will find the approach helpful. More broadly, we hope to portray psychology as the rigorous and keenly relevant discipline that it is. The following elements support these goals.

FOCUS ON SCIENTIFIC PSYCHOLOGY

The language of science can sometimes be intimidating. Throughout the narrative we portray *psychology as a contemporary science* without becoming excessively formal or terminological. And because we live in an era in which students (along with everyone else) are bombarded with scientific information and misinformation, we focus not only on principles derived from research, but also on how good research is done.

FOCUS ON RELATIONS BETWEEN BASIC SCIENCE AND PERSONAL AND SOCIETAL APPLICATIONS

Whether in the context of their personal lives or of larger societal issues, we emphasize that many questions studied from a basic science perspective are inspired by real-world questions and issues, and that basic research findings often guide solutions to individual and societal problems. We know from experience that everyday illustrative examples can help readers connect with what might otherwise seem like difficult concepts.

FOCUS ON HELPING STUDENTS TO THINK CRITICALLY AND DISPEL MISCONCEPTIONS

Critical thinking as a skill for students to learn and practice. We repeatedly address basic critical-thinking issues, such as the importance of identifying alternative explanations and recognizing that correlation does not establish causation. We emphasize that many faulty inferences – in everyday life as well as in science – are made by failing to pay attention to basic critical-thinking principles.

FOCUS ON ACCESSIBILITY

The design of the book has been streamlined over the years to make it easier to navigate between the main narrative and learning features. The book is designed to be accessible for students, in its presentation of both the written content and the visual content.

FOCUS ON RESEARCH

For many students, this will be their first experience of accessing psychological research. It can be overwhelming at first and require an adjustment to get used to the format and style, and also to engage with this new type of information. The book combats this through integrating research in a variety of ways. Our 'Research close-up' boxes present real studies in a format consistent with journal articles; this helps students prepare for reading real articles and familiarises them with style and format. The text also integrates research examples through the main narrative and this edition is rich in these discussions of research. We have also incorporated new references throughout, with hundreds of the book's citations from the years 2010 to 2014; a good deal of the cited research reflects the research interests of the countries in which the audience work and study.

We hope that you enjoy studying psychology and choose to embark on further explorations of the subject, as we did. Alternatively, we hope you find this book a useful and accessible resource to teach from.

Nigel Holt
Andy Bremner
Ed Sutherland
Michael Vliek

Guided tour

Focus arrows

These appear in the margins of the book adjacent to important material. They are designed to function as study guides, retrieval cues, and self-tests.

Key terms and concepts

These are highlighted and defined in the margins, with a summary at the end of each chapter so that they can be found quickly and easily. An ideal tool for last minute revision or to check definitions as you read.

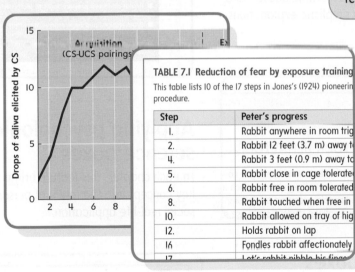

TABLE 7.I Reduction of fear by exposure training
This table lists I0 of the I7 steps in Jones's (I924) pioneerin procedure.

Step	Peter's progress
I.	Rabbit anywhere in room trig
2.	Rabbit I2 feet (3.7 m) away t
4.	Rabbit 3 feet (0.9 m) away to
5.	Rabbit close in cage tolerate
6.	Rabbit free in room tolerated
8.	Rabbit touched when free in
I0.	Rabbit allowed on tray of hig
I2.	Holds rabbit on lap
I6	Fondles rabbit affectionately
I7	Let's rabbit nibble his finger

Figures and tables

Each chapter provides a number of figures, illustrations and photos to help you to visualize key psychological theories and studies.

In review boxes

These boxes provide quick recaps of material presented throughout the chapter, to consolidate your understanding as you work through the book.

 In review

- The brain's ability to adapt and mo
- No single part of the brain regulate experience reward. The cerebellum
- Studies examining the brains of pe experiments with animals, support

Research close-up

USING SOCIAL-COGNITIVE THEORY TO H

Source: K. Ball, A. MacFarlane, D. Crawford, G. Savige, N. A
socioeconomic variations in eating behaviours? A mediation an

INTRODUCTION

Eating properly is very important to maintain health, and to a
something we see our governments working to avoid more an
years where children form habits and a palate associated with

Research close-up boxes

In each chapter, this feature uses a scientific-journal format to provide an inside look at a research study and engage students in a process of critical thinking about the research question.

Levels of analysis

The book's basic LOA framework emphasizes how psychologists carefully study behaviour from diverse angles, reinforces the core concept that behaviour typically has multiple causes, and encourages you to be wary of overly simplistic explanations.

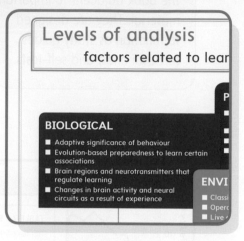

Levels of analysis
factors related to lear

BIOLOGICAL
- Adaptive significance of behaviour
- Evolution-based preparedness to learn certain associations
- Brain regions and neurotransmitters that regulate learning
- Changes in brain activity and neural circuits as a result of experience

ENVI
- Classi
- Opera
- Live

Applying psychological science

USING OPERANT PRINCIPLES TO MODIFY YOUR BEHAVIOUR

People often blame the inability to overcome bad habits or maladaptive behaviours on vague con
Behaviourists prefer the more optimistic assumption that we can acquire *self-regulation*, which i
our behaviour (Kanfer & Goldstein, 1991). This approach has helped people overcome addictions,
and improve their lives in many other ways. Let us examine how a college student could use

Applying psychological science boxes

In each chapter, this feature brings a key concept into the realm of personal or social real-life application.

Current topic boxes

This feature presents discussion topics for each chapter, looking at the key debates and unresolved questions raised by current psychologists.

Current topic

IMITATION: BABIES' BRAINS RES

As discussed in this chapter, we know from a grea
observational learning that various species emplo
observation in a special way – through imitation –
neurologically.

If you get a chance, spend a little time watch
people and unlike us they are not just being nosey

Making the connections

Chapter 14, Page 569

These are highlighted and provide a link in the margins to relevant information discussed in other chapters. They provide a chapter and page reference for quick cross-referencing.

CONNECT®
| PSYCHOLOGY

McGraw-Hill Connect Psychology is a learning and teaching environment that improves student performance and outcomes whilst promoting engagement and comprehension of content.

You can utilize publisher-provided materials, or add your own content to design a complete course to help your students achieve higher outcomes.

PROVEN EFFECTIVE

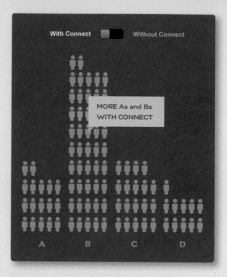

With Connect   Without Connect

MORE As and Bs
WITH CONNECT

A   B   C   D

INSTRUCTORS

With McGraw-Hill Connect Plus Psychology, instructors get:

- Simple **assignment management,** allowing you to spend more time teaching.

- **Auto-graded** assignments, quizzes and tests.

- **Detailed visual reporting** where students and section results can be viewed and analysed.

- Sophisticated **online testing** capability.

- A **filtering and reporting** function that allows you to easily assign and report on materials that are correlated to learning outcomes, topics, level of difficulty, and more. Reports can be accessed for individual students or the whole class, as well as offering the ability to drill into individual assignments, questions or categories.

- **Instructor materials** to help supplement your course.

STUDENTS

With McGraw-Hill Connect Plus Psychology, students get:

Assigned content

- Easy **online access** to homework, tests and quizzes.
- **Immediate feedback** and 24-hour tech support.

eBook

A fully searchable **eBook** allows you to brush up on your reading, allowing for **anytime, anywhere** access to the text-book with the ability to **highlight, note-take** and **bookmark** content. This media rich eBook contains **embedded videos and interactives** to support learning on core concepts. A powerful **search function** pinpoints and connects key concepts and provides **dynamic links** between assigned material and the location in the eBook where that content is covered.

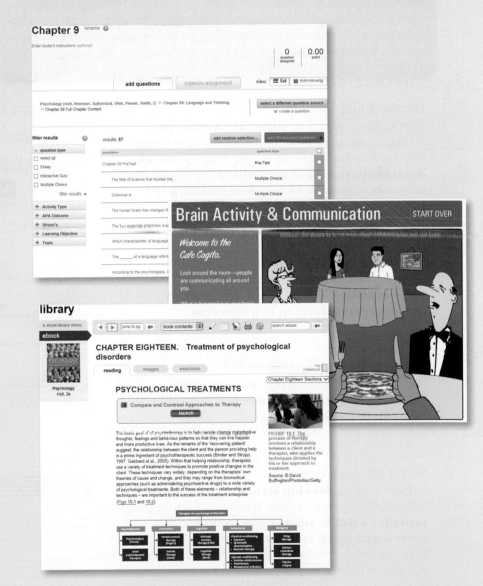

If your instructor is **not** prescribing Connect as part of your course, you can still access a full range of student support resources on our Self Study platform at http://connect.mcgraw-hill.com/selfstudy.

ACCESS OPTIONS

|PSYCHOLOGY

> Is an online assignment and assessment solution that offers a number of powerful tools and features that make managing assignments easier, so faculty can spend more time teaching. With Connect Psychology, students can engage with their coursework anytime and anywhere, making the learning process more accessible and efficient.

Interactives

Encourage students to **illustrate a concept** in an engaging and stimulating activity format with step-by-step guidance, to ensure **conceptual understanding** is tested, applied and reinforced. The activities provide **seamless assignability** and **automatic grading** capabilities.

Videos

Promote **engagement** and **student understanding**, offering content in a **fresh format** and **reinforcing key concepts**.

Multiple Choice Questions

Check students' knowledge and conceptual understanding. **Quick to answer** and gives students **immediate feedback**.

Short-answer questions

Ensure students **develop strong writing skills** with short-answer and essay questions. Each question **provides a guide answer** and allows you to **review and mark student responses**. These questions are clearly marked as being manually graded, so you can include or skip these as you see fit.

Pre-built assignments

Assign all of the **end of chapter or test bank material** as a **ready-made assignment** with the simple click of a button.

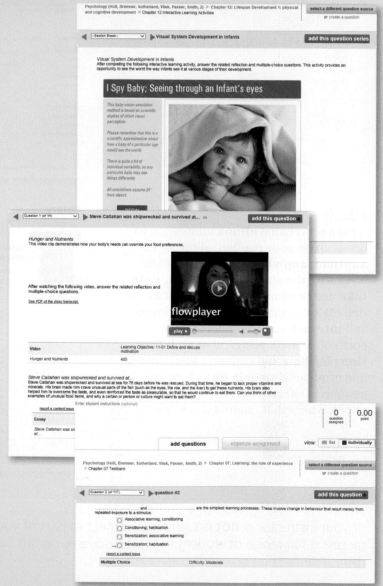

Online learning centre

| PSYCHOLOGY

LearnSmart™

McGraw-Hill LearnSmart is an adaptive learning program that identifies what an individual student knows and doesn't know. LearnSmart's adaptive learning path helps students learn faster, study more efficiently, and retain more knowledge. Reports available for both students and instructors indicate where students need to study more and assess their success rate in retaining knowledge.

SmartBook™

Fueled by LearnSmart—the most widely used and intelligent adaptive learning resource—SmartBook is the first and only adaptive reading experience available today. Distinguishing what a student knows from what they don't, and honing in on concepts they are most likely to forget, SmartBook personalizes content for each student in a continuously adapting reading experience. Valuable reports provide instructors insight as to how students are progressing through textbook content, and are useful for shaping in-class time or assessment.

customers (who want a high-quality product or service), and employees (who desire interesting work and reasonable compensation for their services). The community, which wants the company to contribute to activities and projects and minimize pollution of the environment, is also an important stakeholder.

Measuring Performance to Stakeholders: The Balanced Scorecard. The **balanced scorecard** gives managers an indication of the performance of a company based on the degree to which stakeholder needs are satisfied; it depicts the company from the perspective of internal and external customers, employees, and shareholders.[74] The balanced scorecard is important because it brings together most of the features that a company needs to focus on to be competitive. These include being customer-focused, improving quality, emphasizing teamwork, reducing new product and service development times, and managing for the long term.

The balanced scorecard differs from traditional measures of company performance by emphasizing that the critical indicators chosen are based on the company's business strategy and competitive demands. Companies need to customize their balanced scorecards based on different market situations, products, and competitive environments.

The balanced scorecard should be used to (1) link human resource management activities to the company's business strategy and (2) evaluate the extent to which the HRM function is helping the company meet its strategic objectives. Communicating the scorecard to employees gives them a framework that helps them see the goals and strategies of the company, how these goals and strategies are measured, and how they influence the critical indicators. Measures of HRM practices primarily relate to productivity, people, and process.[75] Productivity measures involve determining output per employee (such as revenue per employee). Measuring people includes assessing employees' behavior, attitudes, or knowledge. Process measures focus on assessing employees' satisfaction with people systems within the company. People systems can include the performance management system, the com-

Balanced Scorecard
A means of performance measurement that gives managers a chance to look at their company from the perspectives of internal and external customers, employees, and shareholders.

LO 1-3
Discuss how human resource management affects a company's balanced scorecard.

The balanced scorecard depicts a company's performance from whose perspective(s)?

Do you know the answer?   📖 Read about this

| I KNOW IT | THINK SO | UNSURE | NO IDEA |

Online learning centre

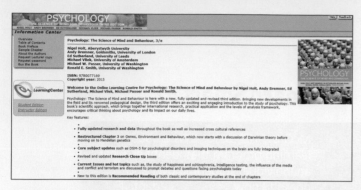

Lecturer support- Helping you to help your students

In addition to the assignments, questions, problems and activities McGraw-Hill Education provides within Connect, we also offer a host of resources to support your teaching.

- **Faster course preparation**—time-saving support for your module
- **High-calibre content to support your students**—resources written by your academic peers, who understand your need for rigorous and reliable content
- **Flexibility**—edit, adapt or repurpose; test in Connect or test through EZ Test. The choice is yours.

The materials created specifically for lecturers adopting this textbook include:

- Lecturer's Manual to support your module preparation, with case notes, guide answers, teaching tips and more
- PowerPoint presentations to use in lecture presentations
- Image library of artwork from the textbook
- Seminar material
- BPS course matching guidelines

To request your password to access these resources, contact your McGraw-Hill Education representative or visit:

www.mheducation.co.uk/textbooks/holt

Test Bank available in McGraw-Hill EZ Test Online

A test bank of hundreds of questions is available to lecturers adopting this book for their module. For flexibility, this is available for adopters of this book to use through Connect or through the EZ Test online website. For each chapter you will find:

- A range of multiple choice, true or false, short-answer or essay questions
- Questions identified by type, difficulty, and topic to help you to select questions that best suit your needs

McGraw-Hill EZ Test Online is:

- **Accessible** anywhere with an internet connection – your unique login provides you access to all your tests and material in any location
- **Simple** to set up and easy to use
- **Flexible**, offering a choice from question banks associated with your adopted textbook or allowing you to create your own questions
- **Comprehensive**, with access to hundreds of banks and thousands of questions created for other McGraw-Hill titles
- **Compatible** with Blackboard and other course management systems
- **Time-saving**—students' tests can be immediately marked and results and feedback delivered directly to your students to help them to monitor their progress.

To register for this FREE resource, visit www.eztestonline.com

 # create

Let us help make our content your solution

At McGraw-Hill Education our aim is to help lecturers to find the most suitable content for their needs delivered to their students in the most appropriate way. Our custom publishing solutions offer the ideal combination of content delivered in the way which best suits lecturer and students.

Our custom publishing programme offers lecturers the opportunity to select just the chapters or sections of material they wish to deliver to their students from a database called CREATE™ at

www.create.mheducation.com/uk/

CREATE™ contains over two million pages of content from:

- textbooks
- professional books
- case books – Harvard Articles, Insead, Ivey, Darden, Thunderbird and BusinessWeek
- Taking Sides – debate materials

Across the following imprints:

- McGraw-Hill Education
- Open University Press
- Harvard Business Publishing
- US and European material

There is also the option to include additional material authored by lecturers in the custom product – this does not necessarily have to be in English.

We will take care of everything from start to finish in the process of developing and delivering a custom product to ensure that lecturers and students receive exactly the material needed in the most suitable way.

With a Custom Publishing Solution, students enjoy the best selection of material deemed to be the most suitable for learning everything they need for their courses – something of real value to support their learning. Teachers are able to use exactly the material they want, in the way they want, to support their teaching on the course.

Please contact your local McGraw-Hill Education representative with any questions or alternatively contact Warren Eels: warren.eels@mheducation.com

Make the grade!

Acknowledgements

Our thanks go to the following reviewers for their comments at various stages in the text's development:

Verena Pritchard, University of Wales

Oliver Robinson, University of Greenwich

Ian Fairholm, University of Bath

David Tod, Aberystwyth University

René van der Veer, Leiden University

Adrian Parker, University of Gothenburg

Kiran Sarma, National University of Ireland Galway

Deborah Custance, Goldsmiths College, University of London

Pascal Wilhelm, University of Twente

Henrik Levinsson, Lund University

Robin Bergh, Uppsala University

Anna O'Reilly Trace, University College Cork

Martijn Meeter, Vrije University

Philip Higham, University of Southampton

Tom Frijns, Utrecht University

Christine Linehan, University College Dublin

Stuart Wilson, Queen Margaret University

Simon Goodman, Coventry University

Chris McVittie, Queen Margaret University

Tim Fosker, Queens University Belfast

Frederic Vallee, Kingston University

Roger Donaldson, Karlstad University

Ulrik Terp, Karlstad University

Adrian Brock, University College Dublin

We would also like to thank Eamon Fulcher for the material he has provided for this textbook and its accompanying online resources.

Our thanks also go to the following contributors for the work they have done on the online resources:

Jason Bohan, University of Glasgow

Adrian Brock, University College Dublin

Thanks to the students who continue to raise tricky and interesting questions. Countless researchers and academics have given their time freely and have been at the end of a telephone when information and clarification were needed at short notice, and we would like to thank them for their help. These include the academics of the Department of Psychology at Goldsmiths, Bath Spa, Leeds and the University of Amsterdam, Anna Weighall at Sheffield Hallam, Philip Beaman at Reading, Ian Walker at Bath, Ken Manktelow at Wolverhampton and Siobhan Hugh-Jones at Leeds who have all been very helpful. Michael Banissy, Andy Cooper, Alice Jones and Madoka Kumashiro at the Department of Psychology, Goldsmiths, University of London, have been, as always, incredibly helpful and knowledgeable colleagues. Debbie Custance in particular at Goldsmiths took the lead in adapting Chapter 3 for this new edition, and we are very grateful for her expert input. Special thanks also to Luke Williams, Michael Banissy and Caroline Catmur for their input into chapter 4. Also, Dr John Kennedy for putting up with Nigel's distraction in the closing stages of the book's development. At McGraw-Hill, we'd like to thank Natalie Jacobs for overseeing the project once again, and Tom Hill and Rosie Churchill's hard work on this new edition.

About the authors

NIGEL J. HOLT, DPhil

Nigel Holt is Head of the Department of Psychology at Aberystwyth University in Wales. Dr Holt's first degree from the University of Reading was followed by a DPhil from the University of York, where he investigated the perceptual lateralization of audio-visual stimuli. A brief spell in industry provided him with clear evidence that teaching and research in a university environment was the place for him. His current post followed a postdoctorate in speech perception, and a lectureship in England but he has now returned to his roots and lives on the very beautiful Aeron coast, a stone's throw from the beach in West Wales. He has examined at a senior level for a major examination board and is an external university examiner at various universities throughout the world. In between writing other books, he does his best to find time to research speech perception and how sound and other areas of cognition interact with potentially dangerous activities such as cycling and motorcycling. He himself is entirely risk averse, preferring his greenhouse to motorcycles, and a nice sit down and a cup of tea to anything even vaguely resembling a dangerous sport which should, he believes, be left to those younger and less prone to damage than he.

ANDY BREMNER, DPhil

Andy completed his first degree in experimental psychology at the University of Oxford and then decided to stay and submit a DPhil (three years later) on 'Object representation in infancy and early childhood' under the supervision of Professor Peter Bryant. Following two postdoctoral appointments in London and Brussels in which he undertook further research into cognitive development in early life, Andy took up a job in the Department of Psychology at Goldsmiths, University of London where he is now a senior lecturer. Andy conducts research into a variety of questions surrounding perceptual and cognitive development and cognitive neuroscience. Particular research interests include object recognition in infancy, the development of memory and cognitive control in the early preschool years, the development of spatial representations of the body and the environment in infancy and childhood, and the development of multi-sensory perceptual processes. Andy is Associate Editor of the *British Journal of Developmental Psychology*, and is on the Editorial Board of *PLoS ONE*. In 2009 he was awarded a €1.2m grant by the European Research Council for a 5-year research project investigating 'Human Embodied Multisensory Development'.

ED SUTHERLAND, PhD

Ed completed his first degree at the University of Bangor and his PhD at the University of Wolverhampton under the supervision of Professor Ken Manktelow. He then filled the next few years with a research post at the University of Reading and his first lectureship at the University of Derby. He became a lecturer in cognitive psychology at the University of Leeds where he is now Director of Learning and Teaching. His current research interests are on the role of emotion in reasoning and the psychology of design. When not working he spends his time with his family and on the river bank in pursuit of his beloved barbel.

MICHAEL L. W. VLIEK, PhD

Michael is a lecturer at the University of Amsterdam. After finishing his Master's at the University of Amsterdam, he decided to stay there to work on his PhD thesis on the subject of social comparison processes, followed by a position as lecturer at the same university (where he has now been for over ten years). Michael has also been a visiting scholar at the University of Sussex, England. His main research interests include social comparison and the dynamics of self-evaluation, intra-group processes and the influence of time in motivational processes.

MICHAEL W. PASSER, PhD

Michael Passer coordinates the introductory psychology programme at the University of Washington, which enrolls about 2,500 students per year, and also is the faculty coordinator of training for new teaching assistants. He received his bachelor's degree from the University of Rochester and his PhD in psychology from the University of California, Los Angeles, with a specialization in social psychology. Dr Passer has been a faculty member at the University of Washington since 1977. A former Danforth Foundation Fellow and University of Washington Distinguished Teaching Award finalist, Dr Passer has had a career-long love of teaching. Each academic year he teaches introductory psychology twice and a required pre-major course on the Teaching of Psychology, which prepares students for careers in the college classroom, and also has taught courses in social psychology and attribution theory. He has published more than 20 scientific articles and chapters, primarily in the areas of attribution, stress, and anxiety, and is author of the textbook, *Research Methods: Concepts and Connections* (Worth Publishers). Dr Passer has taught the introductory psychology course for 25 years.

RONALD E. SMITH, PhD

Ronald E. Smith is Professor of Psychology and Director of Clinical Psychology Training at the University of Washington, where he also has served as Area Head of the Social Psychology and Personality area. He received his bachelor's degree from Marquette University and his PhD from Southern Illinois University, where he had dual specializations in clinical and physiological psychology. His major research interests are in anxiety, stress and coping, and in performance-enhancement research and intervention. Dr Smith is a Fellow of the American Psychological Association. He received a Distinguished Alumnus Award from the UCLA Neuropsychiatric Institute for his contributions to the field of mental health. He has published more than 200 scientific articles and book chapters in his areas of interest and has authored or coauthored 29 books on introductory psychology, human performance enhancement and personality. An award-winning teacher, he has more than 15 years of experience in teaching the introductory psychology course.

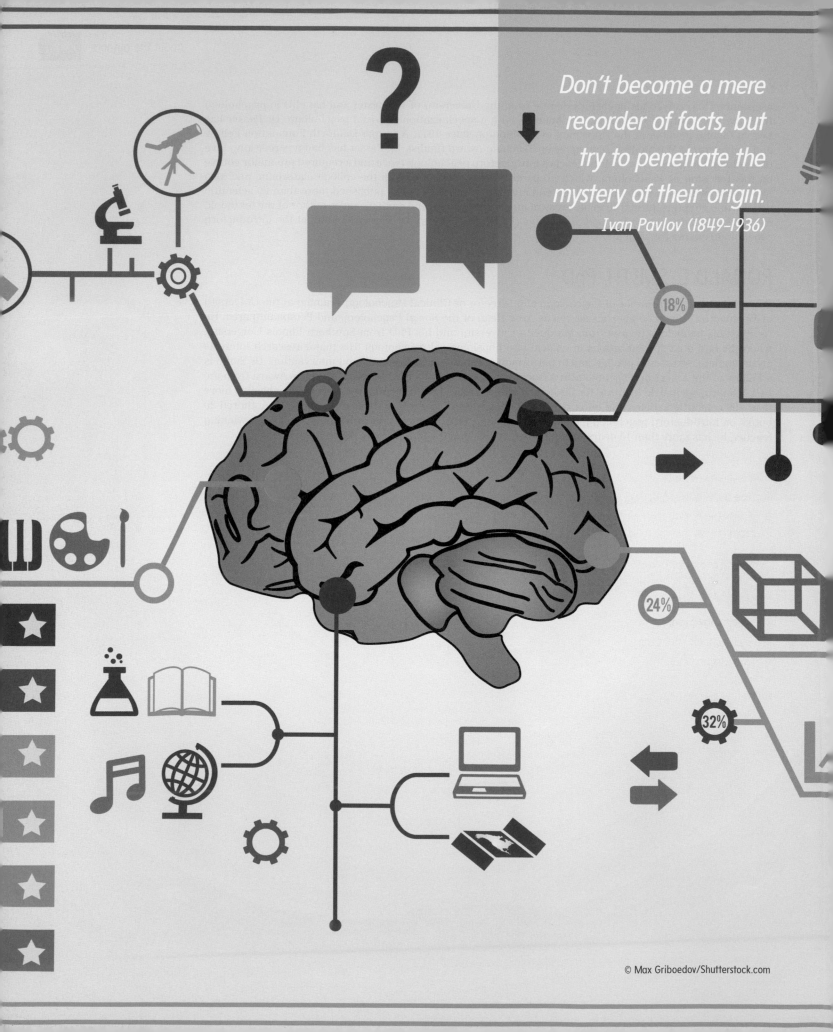

Don't become a mere recorder of facts, but try to penetrate the mystery of their origin.
Ivan Pavlov (1849–1936)

The science of psychology

1

Chapter Outline

In the early 1920s, a group of intrepid explorers, headed by Howard Carter, set off to Egypt to seek fame, fortune and the final resting place of one of history's most enigmatic kings. The expedition was funded by Lord Carnarvon and they were to discover the site of King Tutankhamun's tomb in the Valley of the Kings, near Luxor, opening it together on 17 February 1923. This was the beginning of a strange story of myth and legend, centring on a curse discovered in the tomb that those to disturb the resting place would suffer a swift death. Carnarvon died in the spring of 1923, bitten by a mosquito, and as he did so the lights of Cairo are said to have inexplicably gone out. The press exploded with stories of mysterious deaths of people, and animals, related to the expedition. Howard Carter's pet canary was allegedly bitten by a snake and died, and Carnarvon's dog is said to have dropped dead at 2 a.m. on the morning following his master's death. George Benedite of the Louvre in Paris and Arthur C. Mace from the Metropolitan Museum of Art in New York died shortly after exhibiting the contents of the tomb at their museums, and Howard Carter's secretary also died, as did his secretary's father. All these were blamed on the now legendary curse of the mummy's tomb.

THE NATURE OF PSYCHOLOGY

Why are some individuals shy and others outgoing? What causes people to become attracted to one another and fall in love? Can we predict which relationships will last? Why is it that we remember a first date from long ago yet forget information during a test that we studied for only hours before? Where in the brain are memories stored? Why do some people become depressed? In the case of Tutankhamun's 'curse', is it possible that a psychological factor – a culturally based belief in something akin to 'voodoo' – could have affected biological functioning and actually brought about the demise of the adventurers and their colleagues? We will return to the mystery of 'voodoo' later in the chapter. Psychology is the discipline that studies all of these questions and countless more. Attempting a definition of psychology is something we usually do in our first ever lesson and seminar, and it is quite a debate, but we usually end up at a consensus that involves the word 'mind' and hopefully 'science'. It follows from this that we define **psychology** as the scientific study of behaviour and the mind.

> **psychology**　the scientific study of behaviour and the mind

The term *behaviour* refers to actions and responses that we can directly observe, whereas the term *mind* refers to internal states and processes – such as thoughts and feelings – that cannot be seen directly and that must be inferred from observable, measurable responses. For example, we cannot directly see people's feelings of loneliness. Instead, we must infer how someone feels based on their behaviour and verbal statement that they are lonely.

Because behaviour is so rich and complex, its scientific study poses special challenges. As you become familiar with the kinds of evidence necessary to validate scientific conclusions, you will become a better-informed consumer of the many claims made in the name of psychology. The study of behaviour takes many forms, and psychology, like other disciplines, follows trends and fashions, with different schools in different countries and regions favouring and championing different approaches at different times in history. For instance, the biological basis of behaviours and the study of neuropsychology are driving research and explanations of behaviour in this, the beginning of the twenty-first century, whereas the psychodynamic school of Sigmund Freud and his followers still has its champions, but does not currently form the focus of much research in psychology.

> **Focus 1.1** What is psychology's focus? In science and daily life, what does critical thinking involve, and why is it important? (These focus questions will help you identify key concepts as you read, study and review; they also tie in with the 'Learning Objectives' in the digital supplements that accompany the text.)

The way you think about the subject is very important. You could consider it as learning to 'think psychologically' but the skills you pick up and sharpen within psychology are hugely useful elsewhere also. Critical thinking involves taking an active role in understanding the world around you, rather than merely receiving information. It is important to reflect on what that information means, how it fits in with your experiences, and its implications for your life and society. Critical thinking also means evaluating the validity of something presented to you as fact. For example, when someone tells you a new 'fact', ask yourself the following questions:

What exactly are you asking me to believe?

How do you know? What is the evidence?

Are there other possible explanations?

What is the most reasonable conclusion?

Why should you believe what you are told, and what you read?

The reason we tend to, of course, has its routes firmly in psychology. What gives people 'authority' for instance? Why is *their* knowledge any better than yours? You cannot possibly study everything from scratch and why would you want to? We can learn more and develop our subject better by starting from a position of knowledge in the first place, so we have to trust others' knowledge to some extent, but having a critical questioning approach is extremely useful.

SOCIAL CONSTRUCTIVISM

Constructivism is an approach in psychology in its own right. In the spirit of not believing what you read and in illustrating the merits of a different perspective we just briefly introduce the idea here.

Think for a moment about something we are all terribly familiar with. The idea of 'childhood' is a good example. We all know what it is, I imagine: it is something young people do while they are waiting to grow up. Take a moment though and think what defines a 'child'. Age certainly, legal rights, social rights, economic rights, educational level perhaps, or access to certain types of education maybe. All these things and more define what we know as 'child' and the period where these 'restrictions' apply.

Why do you know that these things make up the concept of a 'child'? You know it because you have been told it over the years and have just accepted it as a truth of some kind. All these things are, of course, culturally specific and what fits the bill for a child in one culture may not in another. We are so very certain that we 'know' what a child is that we might not actually look terribly carefully at what is actually a 'social construct' – a collection of characteristics and traits that are so often presented in society that their origins are lost in time and never questioned. We are left with the concept, the 'construct', and no longer question it.

One way to begin to question a 'construct' to allow us to better understand it might be to 'deconstruct' it. We can do this by identifying, as we have, the individual characteristics and building blocks that make up our construct. Next we can apply a different perspective to them. How about 'prison' as a perspective on childhood? The child is locked away from society at large, and her movements are guarded and restricted by parents (guards). Rights are removed until the sentence of childhood passes and the child has 'done their time'. When they do wrong they are punished, when they are good they are allowed certain privileges, perhaps some sweets, or some television time. Only when they leave the prison – become adults – can they take part in the things adults (those outside the prison) are able to. Only then can they earn real money, drive cars, drink alcohol, have sex and get married.

Of course, a perspective like this can only go so far, but I hope you can see how looking at something we once believed we knew all about can help us really think about it differently.

PSYCHOLOGY AS A BASIC AND APPLIED SCIENCE

Churchill said that the further backward you look the further forward you will see. Whereas that is not entirely the case with science, it is true that nothing in science goes to waste, and any work we do that builds on existing work will itself be further developed by those that come after us. It is as if we are part of a perpetual machine and we must acknowledge what has come before us. In psychology classic research is heavily drawn on not only by scientists developing new ideas and interventions, but also by politicians and practitioners in any number of fields from education to health who work to identify best practice in their own disciplines. It is for this reason that we include here and throughout the book research that has been done in the past but is still of great relevance to us today.

Science involves two types of research: **basic research**, which reflects the quest for knowledge purely for its own sake, and **applied research**, which is designed to solve specific, practical problems. For psychologists, most basic research examines how and why people behave, think and feel the way they do. Basic research may be carried out in laboratories or real-world settings, with human participants or other species. Psychologists who study other species usually attempt to discover principles that ultimately will shed light on human behaviour, but some study animal behaviour for its own sake. In applied research, psychologists often use basic scientific knowledge to design, implement and assess intervention programmes. Consider the following examples from psychology's past, but do not make the mistake of thinking they lack relevance today, they most certainly do not.

> **basic research** reflects the quest for knowledge purely for its own sake
>
> **applied research** is designed to solve specific, practical problems

> **Focus 1.2** How does basic and applied research differ? Explain how knowledge from basic research helps solve practical problems.

Classic Studies: Robber's Cave and the Jigsaw Classroom

How does hostility and prejudice develop between groups and what can be done to reduce it? In today's multicultural world, where religious and ethnic groups often clash, this question has great importance.

To provide an answer, psychologists conduct basic research on factors that increase and reduce intergroup hostility. In one experiment, researchers divided 11-year-old boys into two groups when the boys arrived at a summer camp in Robber's Cave, Oklahoma (Sherif, Harvey, White, Hood, & Sherif, 1961). The groups, named the 'Eagles' and 'Rattlers' lived in separate cabins but did all other activities together. Initially, they got along well.

To test the hypothesis that competition would breed intergroup hostility, the researchers began to pit the Eagles and Rattlers against one another in athletic and other contests. As predicted, hostility soon developed between the groups. Next the researchers examined whether conflict could be reduced by having the two groups share enjoyable activities, such as watching movies together. Surprisingly, these activities only bred more taunting and fighting. The researchers then created several small emergencies to test a final hypothesis – that placing hostile groups in situations requiring cooperation to attain important, common goals would reduce intergroup conflict. In one 'emergency', a heavy lorry bringing food to the hungry boys supposedly stalled, forcing the Eagles and Rattlers to pool their strength and tow it with a rope to get it started. This and other cooperative experiences gradually reduced hostility between the groups, and many new friendships developed.

The Robber's Cave study, which has since become a classic (that is, an older but widely known and influential study), represents basic research because its goal was to discover general principles of intergroup conflict, not to solve some pre-existing problem. Prejudice between the Eagles and Rattlers did not exist from the outset; rather, the researchers created it. They showed that hostility could be bred by competition and reduced by making hostile groups dependent on one another to reach a common goal. But could this principle, derived from basic research, also be applied to real-life situations?

Years later, psychologist Elliot Aronson and his co-workers (Aronson, Stephan, Sikes, & Snapp, 1978) developed and evaluated a classroom procedure called the 'jigsaw program'. The motivation for this programme was the desegregation of schools in the area. Ethnic groups were mixed in the classroom for the first time. This programme, which is now widely used to foster cooperation among children, involves creating multi-ethnic groups of five or six children who are assigned to prepare for an upcoming test on, for example, the life of Abraham Lincoln. Within the groups, each child is given a piece of the total knowledge to be learned. One child has information about Lincoln's childhood, another about his political career, and so on. To pass the test, group members must fit their knowledge pieces together as if working on a jigsaw puzzle. Each child must teach the others his or her piece of knowledge. Like the children at Robber's Cave, students learn that to succeed they must work together (Figure 1.1).

The jigsaw technique and other *cooperative learning programmes* have been evaluated in hundreds of classrooms, with encouraging results (Johnson, 2000). Children's liking for one another generally increases, prejudice decreases, and self-esteem and school achievement improve. Cooperative learning programmes show how basic research, such as the Robber's Cave experiment, provides a foundation for designing intervention programmes.

THE GOALS OF PSYCHOLOGY

As a science, psychology can be described as having five central goals:

1. To *describe* how people and other species behave.
2. To *understand* the causes of these behaviours.
3. To *predict* how people and animals will behave under certain conditions.
4. To *influence* behaviour through the control of its causes.
5. To *apply* psychological knowledge in ways that enhances human welfare.

In the Robber's Cave study, the researchers carefully observed the boys' behaviour under various conditions (description). They believed that competition would cause intergroup hostility and that cooperation could reduce it (tentative understanding). To test whether their understanding was correct, they predicted that competition would create hostility between the Eagles and Rattlers and that cooperation would reduce this conflict (prediction). Next they controlled the camp setting, first by pitting the Eagles and Rattlers against one another in contests, and then by arranging situations that forced the groups to cooperate (influence). As predicted, competition produced hostility and cooperation reduced it, suggesting that the researchers' understanding was correct. Later, when Aronson and his co-workers sought to reduce racial hostility within newly integrated schools, they had a scientific basis for predicting what might work. They were able to apply their knowledge successfully in the form of the jigsaw programme (application).

FIGURE I.I The jigsaw classroom, designed by psychologist Elliot Aronson, pictured here, was inspired by basic research that showed how mutual dependence and cooperation among hostile groups can reduce intergroup hostility. Aronson's applied research had similar positive effects within racially integrated classrooms.

Source: Guy Lasnier, University of California, Santa Cruz

> **Focus I.3** Identify the major goals of psychology.

PSYCHOLOGY'S BROAD SCOPE: A LEVELS-OF-ANALYSIS FRAMEWORK

The scope of modern psychology stretches from the borders of medicine and the biological sciences to those of the social sciences (Figure 1.2). Because we are biological creatures living in a complex social world, psychologists study an amazing array of factors to understand why people behave, think and feel as they do, including neuropsychological and biopsychological explanations. At times, this diversity of factors may seem a bit overwhelming, but we would like to provide you with a framework that will greatly simplify matters. We can call these levels *of analysis*: behaviour and its causes can be examined at the *biological level* (e.g., brain processes, genetic influences), the *psychological level* (e.g., our thoughts, feelings and motives) and the *environmental level* (e.g., past and current physical and social environments to which we are exposed).

Here is an example of how the levels-of-analysis framework can be applied.

Consider a rare and seemingly mysterious event, 'voodoo' death, or perhaps the curse of Tutankhamun. How can we explain something like this without invoking supernatural powers?

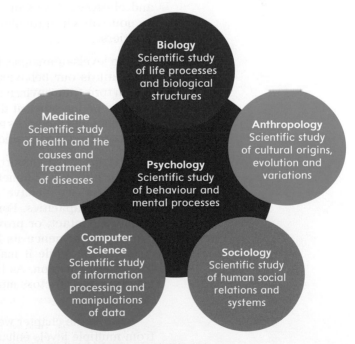

FIGURE I.2 Psychology as a scientific hub.

Psychology links with and overlaps many other sciences.

FIGURE I.3 Voodoo is a very real part of everyday life for many people in places like Haiti where it predates Christianity.

Source: © Robert Harding Picture Library Ltd/Alamy

Whereas the curse of Tutankhamun is a special case, voodoo-like practices (Figure 1.3) are common in several regions of the world. Decades ago, physiologist Walter Cannon (1942) suggested a possible mechanism for death by 'magic curses'. Cannon drew on his own research on severe stress responses in animals, as well as eyewitness reports by cultural anthropologists of deaths by magic curses. One such account described the practice of placing of a death curse by pointing a sacred bone at the victim and how the 'victim' reacts when this happens:

His cheeks blanch and his eyes become glassy . . . His body begins to tremble and the muscles twitch involuntarily . . . soon after he writhes as if in mortal agony. Unless help is forthcoming in the shape of a countercharm administered by the . . . medicine-man, his death is only a matter of a comparatively short time. (Basedow, 1925, pp. 178–179)

Cannon noted that in cases of death by magic curses, the victim firmly believed that he or she was doomed. For the victim, this belief represents the psychological level of analysis. At the environmental level, this belief was supported by the victim's family, friends, enemies and culture. At the biological level of analysis, Cannon speculated that the victim's beliefs triggered a profound and persistent stress response – a flood of stress hormones (chemicals released by glands in the body) – sending the victim into physiological shock. Cannon's research had shown that one aspect of such shock is a rapid and often fatal drop in blood pressure as stress hormones allow fluid to leak out of veins and capillaries. He noted that normal autopsy procedures would not detect this mechanism of death, making it appear that there was no natural cause.

Mind–Body and Nature–Nurture Interactions

Cannon's hypothesis is a plausible alternative to supernatural explanations and is consistent with research showing that negative thoughts about a stressful situation can quickly trigger the secretion of stress hormones (Ironson et al., 2014). This work illustrates what traditionally have been called *mind–body interactions* – the relations between mental processes in the brain and the functioning of other bodily systems. Mind–body interactions focus our attention on the fascinating interplay between the psychological and biological levels of analysis. This topic has a long history within psychology and, as you will see throughout the textbook, it remains one of psychology's most exciting frontiers.

The levels-of-analysis framework also addresses an issue that has been debated since antiquity: is our behaviour primarily shaped by nature (our biological endowment) or by nurture (our environment and learning history)? The pendulum has swung towards one end or the other at different times in history, but today growing interest in cultural influences and advances in genetics and brain research keep the nature–nurture pendulum in a more balanced position.

Perhaps most important, modern research increasingly reveals that nature and nurture interact (Zimmermann & Thompson, 2014). Just as our biological capacities affect how we behave and experience the world, our experiences influence our biological capacities. For humans and rats alike, continually depriving a newborn of physical contact, or providing a newborn with an enriched environment in which to grow, can influence its brain functioning and biological development (Rosenzweig, 1984). Thus, while it may be tempting to take sides, 'nature or nurture?' usually is the wrong question. As the levels-of-analysis framework implies, nature, nurture and psychological factors must all be taken into account to gain the fullest understanding of behaviour.

Later in the chapter we provide a more detailed example of how looking at behaviour from multiple levels enhances our understanding. For now, in concluding our discussion of psychology's scope, we would like you to think critically about Cannon's mind–body explanation for voodoo death.

In review

- *Psychology* is the scientific study of behaviour and the mind. The term *behaviour* refers to actions and responses that can be observed and measured directly. In contrast, mental processes such as thoughts and feelings must be inferred from directly observable responses.
- Basic research reflects the quest for knowledge for its own sake. Applied research focuses on solving practical problems.
- The primary goals of psychological science are to describe, understand, predict and influence behaviour, and to apply psychological knowledge to enhance human welfare.
- To understand more fully why people act, think and feel as they do, psychologists examine behaviour at the biological, the psychological and the environmental levels of analysis.

PERSPECTIVES ON BEHAVIOUR

The fact that psychologists study biological, psychological and environmental factors that influence behaviour is not new; it has been an integral part of psychology's history because psychology has roots in such varied disciplines as philosophy, medicine, and the biological and physical sciences. As a result, different ways of viewing people, called *perspectives*, became part of psychology's intellectual traditions. Perspectives serve as windows through which psychologists watch and interpret behaviour. In science, new perspectives provide us with a new window with a new view. Advances occur as existing beliefs are challenged, a debate ensues, and scientists seek new evidence to resolve the debate. Sometimes, the best-supported elements of contrasting perspectives are merged into a new framework, which in turn will be challenged by still newer viewpoints.

PSYCHOLOGY'S ROOTS

Humans have long sought to understand themselves, and at the centre of this quest lies an issue that has tested the best minds of the ages, the so-called *mind–body problem*. Is the mind – the inner agent of consciousness and thought – a spiritual entity separate from the body, or is it a part of the body's activities?

Many early philosophers held a position of **mind–body dualism**, the belief that the mind is a spiritual entity not subject to physical laws that govern the body. But if the mind is not composed of physical matter, how could it become aware of bodily sensations, and how could its thoughts exert control over bodily functions? French philosopher, mathematician and scientist René Descartes (1596–1650) proposed that the mind and body interact through the tiny pineal gland in the brain. Although Descartes placed the mind within the brain, he maintained that the mind was a spiritual, non-material entity. Dualism implies that no amount of research on the physical body (including the brain) could ever hope to unravel the mysteries of the non-physical mind.

An alternative view, **monism** (from the Greek word *monos*, meaning 'one'), holds the belief that mind and body are one and that the mind is not a separate spiritual entity. To monists, mental events are simply a product of physical events in the brain, a position advocated by English philosopher Thomas Hobbes (1588–1679). Monism helped set the stage for psychology because it implied that the mind could be studied by measuring physical processes within the brain. The stage was further set by John Locke (1632–1704) and other philosophers from the school of **empiricism**, which held that all ideas and knowledge are gained empirically – that is, through the senses. According to the empiricists, observation is a more valid approach to knowledge than is reason, because reason is fraught with the potential for error. This idea bolstered the development of modern science, whose methods are rooted in empirical observation.

Discoveries in physiology (an area of biology that examines bodily functioning) and medicine also paved the way for psychology's emergence. By 1870, European researchers

mind–body dualism the belief that the mind is a spiritual entity not subject to physical laws that govern the body

monism holds that mind and body are one and that the mind is not a separate spiritual entity

empiricism held that all ideas and knowledge are gained empirically – that is, through the senses

FIGURE 1.4 At the University of Leipzig in 1879, Wilhelm Wundt established the first laboratory of experimental psychology to study the structure of the mind.

Source: INTERFOTO/Alamy.

were electrically stimulating the brains of laboratory animals and mapping the surface areas that controlled various body movements. During this same period, medical reports linked damage in different areas of patients' brains with various behavioural and mental impairments. For example, damage to a specific region on the brain's left side impaired people's ability to speak fluently.

Mounting evidence of the relation between brain and behaviour supported the view that empirical methods of the natural sciences could also be used to study mental processes. Indeed, by the mid-1800s, German scientists were measuring people's sensory responses to many types of physical stimuli (for example, how the perceived loudness of a sound changes as its physical intensity increases). Their experiments established a new field called *psychophysics*, the study of how psychologically experienced sensations depend on the characteristics of physical stimuli.

Around this time, Charles Darwin's (1809–82) theory of evolution generated shock waves that are still felt today. His theory, which we discuss later, was vigorously opposed because it seemed to contradict philosophical and religious beliefs about the exalted nature of human beings. Evolution implied that the human mind was not a spiritual entity but, rather, the product of a biological continuity between humans and other species. Moreover, Darwin's theory implied that scientists might gain insight about human behaviour by studying other species. By the late 1800s, a convergence of intellectual forces provided the impetus for psychology's birth.

EARLY SCHOOLS: STRUCTURALISM AND FUNCTIONALISM

It is generally accepted that the science of psychology emerged in 1879, when Wilhelm Wundt (1832–1920) established the first experimental psychology laboratory at the University of Leipzig. Wundt wanted to model the study of the mind after the natural sciences (Figure 1.4). He believed that the mind could be studied by breaking it down into its basic components, as a chemist might do in studying a complex chemical compound. One of his graduate students, Englishman Edward Titchener (1867–1927), later established a psychology laboratory at Cornell University. Like Wundt, Titchener attempted to identify the basic building blocks, or structures, of the mind. Wundt and Titchener's approach came to be known as **structuralism**, the analysis of the mind in terms of its basic elements.

Structuralists used the method of *introspection* ('looking within') to study sensations, which they considered the basic elements of consciousness. They exposed participants to all sorts of sensory stimuli – lights, sounds, and tastes – and trained them to describe their inner experiences. Although this method of studying the mind was criticized and died out after a few decades, the structuralists left an important mark on the infant field of psychology by establishing a scientific tradition for the study of cognitive processes.

Structuralism eventually gave way to **functionalism**, which held that psychology should study the functions of consciousness rather than its structure. Here is a rough analogy to explain the difference between structuralism and functionalism: consider your arms and hands. A structuralist would try to explain their movement by studying how muscles, tendons and bones operate. In contrast, a functionalist would ask, 'Why do we have arms and hands? How do they help us adapt to our environment?' The functionalists asked similar questions about mental processes and behaviour. In part, they were influenced by Darwin's evolutionary theory, which stressed the importance of adaptation in helping organisms survive and reproduce in their environment. Functionalists did much of the early research on learning and problem-solving.

William James (1842–1910), a leader in the functionalist movement, taught courses in physiology, psychology and philosophy at Harvard University (Figure 1.5). James's broad approach helped widen the scope of psychology to include the study of various biological processes, mental processes and behaviours.

The tradition of functionalism endures in two modern-day fields: *cognitive psychology*, which studies mental processes, and *evolutionary psychology*, which emphasizes the adaptiveness of behaviour.

> **structuralism** the analysis of the mind in terms of its basic elements
>
> **functionalism** which held that psychology should study the functions of consciousness rather than its structure

> **Focus 1.4** Discuss psychology's philosophical and scientific roots, earliest schools of thought, and founders.

FIGURE I.5 William James (1842–1910), a leader of functionalism. His multivolume book *Principles of Psychology* (1950, first published 1890) greatly expanded the scope of psychology.

Source: Science Photo Library

FIGURE I.6 Melanie Klein (1882–1960), the great European psychoanalyst.

Source: Keystone-France/Gamma-Keystone via Getty Images

THE PSYCHODYNAMIC PERSPECTIVE: THE FORCES WITHIN

The **psychodynamic perspective** searches for the causes of behaviour within the inner workings of our personality (our unique pattern of traits, emotions and motives), emphasizing the role of unconscious processes. Pierre Janet (1859–1947) studied with Jean-Marc Chacot in Paris. He was a medic, a philosopher and professor of psychology at the Sorbonne where he first made the link between current events in a person's life and those in their past. Sigmund Freud (1856–1939) developed arguably the most influential psychodynamic theory. Freud's legacy was developed by others, including Melanie Klein (1882–1960) who began work as an analyst in the early part of the twentieth century (Figure 1.6).

Psychoanalysis: Freud's Great Challenge

Freud was intrigued by the workings of the brain. In his work as a physician he was confronted with patients who experienced physical symptoms such as blindness, pain or paralysis without any apparent bodily cause. Over time he treated patients who had other problems, such as *phobias* (intense unrealistic fears). No disease or bodily malfunction could explain these conditions, leading Freud to reason that the causes must be psychological. Moreover, if his patients were not producing their symptoms consciously, Freud reasoned that the causes must be hidden from awareness – they must be unconscious. Initially, Freud treated his patients with hypnosis. Later he used a technique called *free association*, in which the patient expressed any thoughts that came to mind. To Freud's surprise, his patients eventually described painful and long-'forgotten' childhood experiences, often sexual in nature. Often, after recalling and figuratively reliving these traumatic childhood experiences, the patients' symptoms improved.

Freud became convinced that an unconscious part of the mind profoundly influences behaviour, and he developed a theory and a form of psychotherapy called **psychoanalysis** – the analysis of internal and primarily unconscious psychological forces. He also proposed that humans have powerful inborn sexual and aggressive drives and that, because these desires are punished in childhood, we learn to fear them and become anxious when we are aware of their presence. This leads us to develop **defence mechanisms**, which are psychological techniques that help us cope with anxiety and the pain of traumatic experiences. Repression, a primary defence mechanism, protects us by keeping unacceptable impulses, feelings

psychodynamic perspective searches for the causes of behaviour within the inner workings of our personality (our unique pattern of traits, emotions and motives), emphasizing the role of unconscious processes

psychoanalysis the analysis of internal and primarily unconscious psychological forces

defence mechanisms psychological techniques that help us cope with anxiety and the pain of traumatic experiences and memories in the unconscious depths of the mind. All behaviour, whether normal or 'abnormal', reflects a largely unconscious and inevitable conflict between the defences and internal impulses. This ongoing psychological struggle between conflicting forces is dynamic in nature, hence the term *psychodynamic*. To explain a person's extreme shyness around the opposite sex for instance, Freud might have explored whether the person is unconsciously afraid of their sexual impulses and therefore avoids putting themselves into dating situations where they would have to confront those hidden impulses.

Freud's theory was almost immediately controversial. Some of his own followers strongly disagreed with aspects of the theory, especially its heavy emphasis on childhood sexuality. Other psychologists viewed the theory as difficult to test. Indeed, Freud opposed laboratory research on psychoanalytic theory, believing that his clinical observations were more valid. Nevertheless, Freud's ideas did stimulate research on topics such as dreams, memory, aggression and mental disorders. A review of more than 3,000 scientific studies examining Freud's ideas found support for some aspects of his theory, whereas other aspects were unsupported or contradicted (Fisher & Greenberg, 1996). Even where Freud's theory was not supported, the research it inspired led to important discoveries. Importantly, Freud's work provided a new perspective on the science of psychology and a new way of thinking about the study and treatment of psychological disorders.

Another prominent thinker in this area was Carl Jung (1875–1961), a student of Freud, who became a regular correspondent and friend. Their ways parted in the early 1900s as Jung began to disagree with Freud's focus on the libido and his views on religion, but Freud had greatly influenced Jung. Jung's contribution to psychoanalysis centred on his construction of what he called 'concepts', including the concepts of introversion and extroversion, and his idea of the 'complex'. By this he meant a build-up of feelings in the subconscious that analysis can help identify. It is this 'complex' that can account for a person's odd or difficult to understand behaviour. Jung courted controversy just before and during the Second World War, when he was labelled as having Nazi sympathies. Jung later denied this, and explained that his endorsement of Hitler's *Mein Kampf* as reading for psychoanalysts served to keep psychoanalysis, as a movement founded by Freud (a Jewish intellectual), alive during this dangerous time. He also made his friendship and respect for Freud very clear at the end of the war.

Modern Psychodynamic Theory

Modern psychodynamic theories continue to explore how unconscious and conscious aspects of personality influence behaviour. However, they downplay the role of hidden sexual and aggressive motives and focus more on how early family relationships, other social factors and our sense of 'self' shape our personality (Kohut, 1977). For example, psychodynamic **object relations theories** focus on how early experiences with caregivers shape the views that people form of themselves and others (Kernberg, 1984, 2000). In turn, these views unconsciously influence a person's relationships with other people throughout life. To explain a person's shyness, a modern psychodynamic psychologist might examine the person's conceptions of her/himself and their parents. The shyness may stem from a fear of rejection of which s/he is unaware. This fear may be based on conceptions that s/he developed of their parents as being rejecting and disapproving, views that now unconsciously shape her/his expectations of how relationships with people will be.

The psychodynamic perspective dominated thinking about personality, mental disorders and psychotherapy for the first half of the twentieth century, and it continues to influence applied and academic psychology. Psychoanalysis remains a major force in psychology, particularly in Europe, and is a prominent part of many therapists' weaponry throughout the world.

Links with psychodynamic concepts can be found within several areas of psychological science. For example, biologically oriented psychologists have identified brain mechanisms that can produce emotional reactions of which we are consciously unaware (Davidson, Pizzagalli, Nitschke, & Putnam, 2002), and cognitive scientists have shown that many aspects of information-processing occur outside of awareness (Chartrand & Bargh, 2002). Thus, while most contemporary psychological scientists reject Freud's version of the unconscious mind, many support the concept that behaviours can be triggered by non-conscious processes.

---

object relations theories
focus on how early experiences with caregivers shape the views that people form of themselves and others

Focus 1.5 Describe the psychodynamic perspective. Contrast Freud's psychoanalytic theory with modern psychodynamic theories.

THE BEHAVIOURAL PERSPECTIVE: THE POWER OF THE ENVIRONMENT

The **behavioural perspective** focuses on the role of the external environment in governing our actions. From this perspective, our behaviour is jointly determined by habits learned from previous life experiences and by stimuli in our immediate environment.

Origins of the Behavioural Perspective

The behavioural perspective is rooted in the philosophical school of empiricism, which held that all ideas and knowledge are gained through the senses. According to the early empiricist, John Locke, at birth the human mind is a *tabula rasa* – a 'blank tablet' or 'slate' – upon which experiences are written. In this view, human nature is shaped purely by the environment.

In the early 1900s, experiments by Russian physiologist Ivan Pavlov (1849–1936) revealed one way in which the environment shapes behaviour: through the association of events with one another. Pavlov found that dogs automatically learned to salivate to the sound of a new stimulus, such as a tone, if that stimulus was repeatedly paired with food. Meanwhile, Edward Thorndike (1874–1949) was examining how organisms learn through the consequences of their actions. According to Thorndike's (1911) *law of effect*, responses followed by satisfying consequences become more likely to recur, and those followed by unsatisfying consequences become less likely to recur. Thus learning is the key to understanding how experience moulds behaviour.

Behaviourism

Behaviourism, a school of thought that emphasizes environmental control of behaviour through learning, began to emerge in 1913. John B. Watson (1878–1958), who led the new movement, strongly opposed the 'mentalism' of the structuralists, functionalists and psychoanalysts. He argued that the proper subject matter of psychology was observable behaviour, not unobservable inner consciousness. Human beings, he said, are products of their learning experiences. So passionately did Watson hold this position that in 1924 he issued the following challenge:

> *Give me a dozen healthy infants, well-formed, and my own specialised world to bring them up in and I'll guarantee you to take any one of them at random and train him to become any type of specialist I might select – doctor, lawyer, artist, merchant-chief and, yes, even beggar man and thief, regardless of his talents, penchants, tendencies, abilities, vocations, and race of his ancestors.* (p. 82)

Behaviourists sought to discover the laws that govern learning, and in accord with Darwin's theory of evolution, they believed that the same basic principles of learning apply to all organisms. B.F. Skinner (1904–90) was the leading modern figure in behaviourism. Although Skinner did not deny that thoughts and feelings occur within us, he maintained that 'No account of what is happening inside the human body, no matter how complete, will explain the origins of human behaviour' (1989, p. 18). Skinner believed that the real causes of behaviour reside in the outer world and insisted that 'A person does not act upon the world, the world acts upon him' (1971, p. 211). His research, based largely on studies of rats and pigeons under controlled laboratory conditions, examined how behaviour is shaped by the rewarding and punishing consequences that it produces.

A behaviourist might explain a person's shyness, for instance, by examining their past experiences and whether their experiences with asking people out on dates were not good, perhaps repeatedly poor. Such punishment decreases the likelihood of a positive outcome and so the person may retreat from such dating behaviour.

It is not difficult to imagine why the investigation of such theories needs to be done with very careful ethical control. We have a responsibility to act responsibly in all our research where people or non-human animals might be affected in any way. Unfortunately there are reports from our subject where work is not carried out as ethically as we would hope and in some cases the work is ethically abhorrent. One

behavioural perspective focuses on the role of the external environment in governing our actions

behaviourism school of thought that emphasizes environmental control of behaviour through learning

Focus 1.6 What are the behavioural perspective's origins and focus? Contrast radical behaviourism with cognitive behaviourism.

FIGURE 1.7 Wendell Johnson – American psychologist who with his student Mary Tudor carried out in 1939 what has become known by many as 'the monster study'.

Source: Donald Miller/University of Iowa

cognitive behaviourism proposes that learning experiences and the environment influence our expectations and other thoughts, and in turn our thoughts influence how we behave

FIGURE 1.8 Albert Bandura has played a key role in developing cognitive behaviourism, which merges the behavioural and cognitive perspectives.

Source: Linda A. Cicero/Stanford News Service

such example has become known as *The Monster Study* and was carried out in 1939 by Wendell Johnson (Fig 1.7) and his students in Iowa. Johnson was interested in how behaviour might be influenced by positive or negative feedback in children. Wendell Johnson chose 22 orphan children, and stuttering as his target behaviour. His graduate student, Mary Tudor (unpublished thesis, 1939) delivered positive feedback to half of the children and negative feedback to the other half. In the positive feedback condition the children were praised for their speech at every turn. In the negative feedback condition students were berated for their poor speech, and told they were stutterers. What is important here is that the children did not have any speech problems at the start of the experiment; the intention was to induce stuttering. The overarching goal of the research was, arguably, well intentioned and was to look at how stuttering begins in children. The way the work was carried out was certainly not acceptable. Many of the children suffered for the rest of their lives psychologically; at least one of the orphans ran away from the orphanage to avoid the activity. The University of Iowa apologized officially in 2001 and a payment of just under a million dollars in compensation was paid to the men and women who suffered so badly as a result. What this study illustrates is that even though the means of proving or supporting a theory may well be available, carrying out the proposed activity should be done with great caution and with the correct safeguards put in place.

B.F. Skinner believed that society could harness the power of the environment to change behaviour in beneficial ways and that the chief barrier to creating a better world through 'social engineering' is an outmoded conception of people as free agents. Skinner's approach, known as *radical behaviourism*, was considered extreme by many psychologists, but he was esteemed for his scientific contributions and for focusing attention on how environmental forces could be used to enhance human welfare. In the 1960s, behaviourism inspired powerful techniques known collectively as *behaviour modification*. These techniques, aimed at decreasing problem behaviours and increasing positive behaviours by manipulating environmental factors, are still used widely today.

Behaviourism's insistence that psychology should focus only on observable stimuli and responses resonated with many who wanted this young science to model itself on the natural sciences. Behaviourism dominated much research on learning into the 1960s, and challenged psychodynamic views about the causes of psychological disorders, and led to highly effective treatments for some disorders. But radical behaviourism's influence waned after the 1970s as interest in studying mental processes expanded (Robins, Gosling, & Craik, 1999). Nevertheless, behaviourists continue to make important contributions to basic and applied psychology, and their discovery of basic laws of learning was one of the greatest contributions to psychology in the twentieth century.

Cognitive Behaviourism

In the 1960s and 1970s, a growing number of psychologists showed that cognitive processes such as attention and memory could be rigorously studied by using sophisticated experiments. This led some behaviourists to challenge radical behaviourism's view that mental life was off-limits as a topic for scientific study. They developed a modified view called **cognitive behaviourism**, which proposes that learning experiences and the environment influence our expectations and other thoughts, and in turn our thoughts influence how we behave (Bandura, 1969, 2002a, 2002b). Cognitive behaviourism remains an influential viewpoint to this day (Figure 1.8).

A cognitive behaviourist might say that past dating rejections are punishing and lead the person to expect that further attempts at romance would be doomed. In turn, these expectations of social rejection inhibited them from asking people out and even from making friends. Discussions with friends and family may help the person think about their situation in a new light enabling them to modify their behaviour, become more outgoing and improve their social relationships.

THE HUMANISTIC PERSPECTIVE: SELF-ACTUALIZATION AND POSITIVE PSYCHOLOGY

In the mid-twentieth century, as the psychodynamic and behavioural perspectives vied for intellectual dominance within psychology, a new viewpoint arose to challenge them both. Known as the **humanistic perspective** (or **humanism**), it emphasized free will, personal growth and the attempt to find meaning in one's existence.

Humanists rejected psychodynamic concepts of humans as being controlled by unconscious forces. They also denied behaviourism's view of humans as reactors moulded by the environment. Instead, humanistic theorists such as Abraham Maslow (1908–70) proposed that each of us has an inborn force towards *self-actualization*, the reaching of one's individual potential (Figure 1.9). When the human personality develops in a supportive environment, the positive inner nature of a person emerges. In contrast, misery and pathology occur when environments frustrate our innate tendency towards self-actualization. Humanists emphasized the importance of personal choice and responsibility, personality growth and positive feelings of self-worth. They insisted that the meaning of our existence resides squarely in our own hands.

Thinking about shyness and loneliness, a humanist might say that no matter how many rejections a person has had in the past, they must take personal responsibility for turning things around. A humanist also might wonder whether happiness and sense of self-worth may rest too heavily on a person's hope for a good romantic relationship. It may be more appropriate to build on a few friendships; to satisfy what Maslow (1954) called 'belongingness', our basic human need for social acceptance and companionship.

Few early humanists were scientists and, historically, humanism has had a more limited impact on mainstream psychological science than have other perspectives. Still, it has inspired important areas of research. Humanist Carl Rogers (1902–87) pioneered the scientific study of psychotherapy (Figure 1.10). In the 1940s and 1950s his research group was the first to audiotape counselling sessions and analyse their content. Rogers (1967) identified key processes that led to constructive changes in clients. As another example, psychologists have conducted many studies of self-concept over the past 30 years, and much of this work incorporates humanistic ideas (Verplanken & Holland, 2002).

Humanism's focus on self-actualization and growth is also seen in today's growing **positive psychology movement**, which emphasizes the study of human strengths, fulfilment and optimal living (Diener & Seligman, 2004). In contrast to psychology's long-standing focus on 'what's wrong with our world' (e.g., mental disorders, conflict, prejudice), positive psychology examines how we can nurture what is best within ourselves and society to create a happy and fulfilling life.

THE COGNITIVE PERSPECTIVE: THE THINKING HUMAN

Derived from the Latin word *cogitare* ('to think'), the **cognitive perspective** examines the nature of the mind and how mental processes influence behaviour. In this view, humans are information processors whose actions are governed by thought.

FIGURE 1.9 The humanistic perspective emphasizes the human ability to surmount obstacles in the drive towards self-actualization. Pictured here are Sir Edmund Hillary (left) and Sherpa Tenzing Norgay (right) after their magnificent ascent of Everest in 1953.

Source: Keystone/Getty Images

humanistic perspective (or **humanism**) emphasized free will, personal growth and the attempt to find meaning in one's existence

Focus 1.7 How does humanism's conception of human nature differ from that advanced by psychodynamic theory and behaviourism?

positive psychology movement emphasizes the study of human strengths, fulfilment and optimal living

cognitive perspective examines the nature of the mind and how mental processes influence behaviour

FIGURE 1.10 Carl Rogers (1902–87).

Source: Michael Rougier/The LIFE Picture Collection/Getty Images

Gestalt psychology examined how elements of experience are organized into wholes

FIGURE 1.11 This painting illustrates the Gestalt principle that the whole is greater than the sum of its parts. The individual elements are vegetables, but the whole is perceived as a portrait of a face. *Portrait with Vegetables –The Greengrocer,* by Arcimboldo, from Museo Civico Ala Ponzone, Cremona, Italy. Turning the image upside down makes the face disappear.

Source: The Art Archive/Alamy.

Origins of the Cognitive Perspective

As discussed earlier, structuralism and functionalism arose as two of psychology's earliest schools of thought. The structuralists attempted to identify the basic elements, or structure, of consciousness by using the method of introspection. In contrast, functionalists explored the purposes of consciousness. Other pioneering cognitive psychologists, such as Hermann Ebbinghaus (1850–1909), studied memory.

By the 1920s German scientists had formed a school of thought known as **Gestalt psychology**, which examined how elements of experience are organized into wholes. The word *gestalt* may be translated roughly as 'whole' or 'organization'. Instead of trying to break consciousness down into its elements, Gestalt psychologists argued that our perceptions are organized so that 'the whole is greater than the sum of its parts'. Consider the painting in Figure 1.11. Many people initially perceive it as a whole – as a portrait of a strange-looking person – rather than as a mosaic of vegetables. Gestalt psychology stimulated interest in cognitive topics such as perception and problem-solving. There is something interesting going on here, though, and we talk more about face processing later in the book, but try turning the image upside down. You'll notice that the face disappears. This is because faces are usually experienced the right way up, and Arcimbaldo's trick only really works in that orientation.

Renewed Interest in the Mind

Interest in cognition grew in a number of different areas. For example, a theory developed by Swiss psychologist Jean Piaget (1896–1980), which explained how children's thinking processes become more sophisticated with age, gained widespread recognition in the psychological community worldwide (Figure 1.12). Lev Semenovich Vygotsky (1886–1934) provided a slightly different, but just as important, perspective on cognitive development. Vygotsky was a Russian, studying in the then Soviet Republic, in the 1920s. He died, tragically, of tuberculosis, aged just 48, but his work has had a pronounced impact. Vygotsky believed that language and thought were closely linked. He also felt that the environment in which children developed, the social and cultural factors they were exposed to, had an important impact on their development.

In the 1950s several factors contributed to a renewed interest in studying cognitive processes. In part, this interest stemmed from psychologists' involvement during the Second World War in designing information displays, such as gauges in aeroplane cockpits that enabled military personnel (e.g., pilots) to recognize experiments that reflected an information-processing approach.

Computer technology, which was in its infancy at that time, provided new information-processing concepts and terminology that psychologists began to adapt to the study of memory and attention (Broadbent, 1958). A new metaphor was developing – the mind as a system that processes, stores and retrieves information. The information-processing approach to studying the mind continues to be influential.

On another front in the 1950s, a heated debate arose between behaviourists and linguists about how children acquire language. The behaviourists, led by B.F. Skinner, claimed that language is acquired through basic principles of learning. The linguists, led by Noam Chomsky (b. 1928), argued that humans are biologically 'pre-programmed' to acquire language and that children come to understand language as a set of 'mental rules' (Figure 1.13). This debate convinced many psychologists that language was

FIGURE 1.12 Swiss psychologist Jean Piaget was a master of observation. Many of his conclusions about cognitive development came from carefully watching children solve problems.

Source: AFP/Getty Images.

FIGURE 1.13 Noam Chomsky (b. 1928) argued that humans were born with the ability to acquire language.

Source: Bernal Revert/Alamy.

FIGURE 1.14 Cognitive psychologist Alan Baddeley (b. 1934) has provided important insights into the structure of memory

Source: Reprinted with permission of Alan Baddeley.

FIGURE 1.15 Perceptual scientist Sir Richard Gregory (1923–2010). His work in perception and most notably visual perception greatly influenced many thinkers in the field.

Source: Wellcome Library, London.

too complex to be explained by behavioural principles and that it needed to be examined from a more cognitive perspective. Overall, psychologists' interest in mental processes swelled by the 1960s and 1970s – a period that sometimes is referred to as the 'cognitive revolution'.

The Modern Cognitive Perspective

Cognitive psychology, which focuses on the study of mental processes, embodies the cognitive perspective. Cognitive psychologists study the processes by which people reason and make decisions, devise solutions to problems, form perceptions and mental images, and produce and understand language. They study the nature of knowledge and expertise. Some, such as Allan Baddeley have greatly expanded our understanding of memory and of factors that influence it (Figure 1.14), and Sir Richard Gregory's (1923–2010) work (Figure 1.15) in sensation and perception identified many now common examples of illusions and pioneered work in the area in Europe until his death in 2010. Cognitive psychologists continue to explore the nature of attention and consciousness, and have become increasingly interested in how non-conscious processes influence behaviour.

Cognitive neuroscience, which uses sophisticated electrical recording and brain-imaging techniques to examine brain activity while people engage in cognitive tasks, is a rapidly growing area that represents the intersection of cognitive psychology and the biological perspective within psychology. Cognitive neuroscientists seek to determine how the brain goes about its business of learning language, acquiring knowledge, forming memories, and performing other cognitive activities (Rajah & McIntosh, 2005). Advances in technology have played an important role in the advance of neuropsychology to its now prominent position within the discipline.

Social constructivism, an influential cognitive viewpoint, maintains that what we consider 'reality' is largely our own mental creation, from a shared way of thinking among members of social groups (Gergen, 2000). Constructivists would maintain, for example, that the long-standing conflict between Israeli Jews and Palestinian Arabs reflects immense differences in how they perceive God's plan for them and how they interpret the history of the land where they live (Rouhana & Bar-Tal, 1998).

From a cognitive perspective, we might examine someone's shyness in terms of how they pay attention to and process information, their perceptions and their memory. A person's interpretation of their past dating failures may also be based on faulty reasoning. The shy

cognitive psychology focuses on the study of mental processes and embodies the cognitive perspective

cognitive neuroscience uses sophisticated electrical recording and brain-imaging techniques to examine brain activity while people engage in cognitive tasks

social constructivism maintains that what we consider 'reality' is largely our own mental creation

Focus 1.8 Describe the focus and the origins of the cognitive perspective and some areas of modern cognitive science.

person may believe that their rejections are because of their personal qualities ('I'm not attractive or interesting enough') and therefore expects that future dating attempts will also be unsuccessful. If the person correctly attributed the rejections to some temporary or situational factor ('S/he was already interested in someone else'), then they would not necessarily expect other people to reject them in the future. A cognitive psychologist also might ask whether the person's memories of their past dating experiences are accurate or have become distorted over time. It is possible that the person may be remembering those events as much more unpleasant than they actually were.

THE SOCIOCULTURAL PERSPECTIVE: THE EMBEDDED HUMAN

Humans are social creatures. Embedded within a culture, each of us encounters ever-changing social settings that shape our actions and values, our sense of identity, our very conception of reality. The **sociocultural perspective** examines how the social environment and cultural learning influence our behaviour, thoughts and feelings.

Cultural Learning and Diversity

Culture refers to the enduring values, beliefs, behaviours and traditions that are shared by a large group of people and passed from one generation to the next. All cultural groups develop their own social **norms**, which are rules (often unwritten) that specify what behaviour is acceptable and expected for members of that group. Norms exist for all types of social behaviours, such as how to dress, respond to people of higher status, or act as a woman or man (Figure 1.16). For culture to endure, each new generation must internalize, or adopt, the norms and values of the group as their own. **Socialization** is the process by which culture is transmitted to new members and internalized by them.

In word if not in deed, psychologists have long recognized culture's impact in shaping who we are. The behaviourists, Miller and Dollard, noted in 1941 that:

> *no psychologist would venture to predict the behaviour of a rat without knowing [where in a maze] the feed or the shock is placed. It is no easier to predict the behaviour of a human being without knowing the conditions of his 'maze,' i.e. the structure of his social environment. Culture . . . is a statement of the design of the human maze, of the type of reward involved, and of what responses are to be rewarded.*
>
> (p. 5)

Subcultures or cultures within cultures are also bound by cultural norms. In certain subcultures unwritten rules exist that govern behaviour and the male readers will, perhaps be aware of one of these situations, the male urinal. With this situation in mind,

---

sociocultural perspective examines how the social environment and cultural learning influence our behaviour, thoughts and feelings

culture the enduring values, beliefs, behaviours and traditions that are shared by a large group of people and passed from one generation to the next

norms rules (often unwritten) that specify what behaviour is acceptable and expected for members of that group

socialization the process by which culture is transmitted to new members and internalized by them

---

Focus 1.9 Explain the sociocultural perspective. What are culture, norms, socialization and individualism-collectivism?

FIGURE 1.16 Social norms differ across cultures and over time within cultures.

The idea of women engaging in traditionally male-dominated pastimes such as football, or occupations such as pilot, would be less acceptable in some cultures and times than others.

Source: ©iStock.com/william87; ©iStock .com/strickke.

Middlemist, Knowles and Matter (1976) carried out some work that might, at first glance, appear to be questionable at best. The researchers were interested in how males respond in different 'social' conditions when using a urinal, most simply, how the distance to another person in the urinal influenced *micturition* (the start of urine flow) as well as the duration of urine flow. In the pilot condition, Middlemist tested the hypothesis that standing nearer a 'participant' would slow both micturition and duration of flow. He did this in the pilot by listening for a flow and timing it secretly with a stopwatch. Confident that there was something in the work, the team developed a looking device, a 'urinal periscope' where flow could be watched for onset time and flow duration using a device hidden among some books. In the procedure confederate researchers carefully positioned themselves at different distances from 'participants' and the 'observer' used the periscope to make the measurements. Findings revealed that the closer another person stands to a 'urinator' the slower the micturition and the duration of the flow. Isn't psychology just the most glamorous of subjects?

Yet despite acknowledging culture's importance, throughout much of the twentieth century psychological research largely ignored non-Western groups. Such cross-cultural work usually was left to anthropologists. Even within Western societies, for decades participants in psychological research typically were white and came from middle- or upper-class backgrounds. This situation was so common that in 1976, Robert Guthrie published a book titled *Even the rat was white: A historical view of psychology*. There were important exceptions, however, such as research by Kenneth Clark (1914–2005) and Mamie Clark (1917–83) and others, examining how discrimination and prejudice can influence the personality development (Clark & Clark, 1947; Figure 1.17).

FIGURE I.17 Psychologists Kenneth B. Clark and Mamie P. Clark studied the development of racial identity. Kenneth Clark also wrote books on the psychological impact of prejudice and discrimination.
Source: Library of Congress (PPOC)

Over time, psychologists increasingly began to study diverse ethnic and cultural groups. Today **cross-cultural psychology** explores how culture is transmitted to its members and examines psychological similarities and differences among people from diverse cultures.

One important difference among cultures is the extent to which they emphasize *individualism* versus *collectivism* (Triandis & Suh, 2002). Most industrialized cultures of northern Europe can be described as **individualistic**, with an emphasis on personal goals and self-identity based primarily on one's own attributes and achievements. In contrast, many cultures in Asia, Africa and South America are more **collectivist**, in which individual goals are subordinated to those of the group and personal identity is defined largely by the ties that bind one to the extended family and other social groups. This difference is created by social learning experiences that begin in childhood and continue in the form of social customs. In school, for example, Japanese children more often work in groups on a common assignment, whereas European children more often work alone on individual assignments.

The sociocultural perspective leads us to ask how our cultural upbringing and other social factors may contribute to a person's shy behaviour. For instance, throughout their teenage years, cultural norms for assertiveness, particularly in males, may have put pressure on men to perform in a certain way. Shyness may be evoked by teasing and other negative reactions from school peers, increasing a feeling of inadequacy by the time the person left school and reached university.

In each chapter of this book, we provide you with condensed, in-depth looks at important studies, paralleling the format of research articles published in psychological journals. We give you background information about the studies, describe their method and key results, and discuss and evaluate key aspects of the work. An example of these is 'Do dogs resemble their owners'. People have observed the phenomena and commented on it, but here we see psychology asking the (admittedly frivolous) question more formally. Although the research is clearly good fun, the point we make here is

cross-cultural psychology explores how culture is transmitted to its members and examines psychological similarities and differences among people from diverse cultures

individualistic an emphasis on personal goals and self-identity based primarily on one's own attributes and achievements

collectivist individual goals are subordinated to those of the group and personal identity is defined largely by the ties that bind one to the extended family and other social groups

Focus I.10 How does the 'Research close-up' illustrate cultural psychology's goals and importance?

very real. Careful science when done properly can help us address many questions and provide evidence to support views we may previously only have been able to express informally.

 Research close-up

DO OWNERS LOOK LIKE THEIR DOGS?

INTRODUCTION

Do people buy dogs that look like themselves in some way or do the dogs and owners grow to resemble one another over their years together? It could be that naturally healthy eaters tend to be more careful with food for their dogs and so have fitter leaner animals, and those of us who are happier on the couch with junk food have similarly lazy, less fit and perhaps overweight dogs. It's not just the condition of the body that people have recognized as similar though. Roy and Christenfeld (2004) have here formalized what many of us have observed informally, that dogs may in fact actually look like their owners, with similar hair and coats, similar face-shapes and similar body-types. As with all science, their work builds on clues and evidence from previous work. Zajonc, Adleman, Murphey and Niedenthal (1987) for instance, showed that the facial appearance of married couples appears to converge over time, and Coren (1999) showed that peoples taste in animals was related to their own appearance – women with long hair for insistence rating dogs with longer hair and floppier ears as more intelligent, attractive and friendly than other dogs.

METHOD

As much as possible, a good method should be as clear an uncomplicated as possible. The rule KIS (Keep It Simple) should apply in all cases when designing research. In this case the researchers kept the design very straightforward. Photographs of owners and photographs of their dogs (both purebred dogs and mixed breeds) were mixed up and participants asked to match dogs to owners. In total, 90 images were used, 45 (25 purebred, and 20 mixed breeds) dogs and 45 (24 men and 21 women) owners. In each case the background was different for dogs and their owners so participants could not use that as a cue.

RESULTS

The results were mixed. There was no evidence at all that mixed breed dogs looked like their owners. People could not match them to their owners successfully. However, of the purebred dogs, 16 out of the 25 – that's over half – could be successfully matched to their owners.

Next, the researchers looked at whether or not dogs and their owners 'grew' to be like one another over the years that they lived together. They looked at the amount of time the owners had had their pets and the success with which participants had successfully paired owner and their dogs. There was no correlation between the two.

To further investigate this finding, three new participants were asked to rate the appearance of the purebred dogs and their owners. Appearance was rated in terms of *hairiness, perceived friendliness, attractiveness, size, sharpness of features, and perceived energy levels. Initial* results showed strong inter-rater reliability – the three raters were consistently rating the dog's and the owner's attributes – showing that the ratings the three people gave of the owners and the ratings they gave of the dogs were not random, they were in close agreement with one another. However, when the researchers looked at how the ratings given to the dogs correlated with the ratings given to the owners very little agreement was found. In short, dogs did NOT look much like their owners on these categories. However, there was a trend for owners and their purebred pets to be rated similarly in 'friendliness'.

The final thing tested was whether hairstyle of owners (long or short) was related, as suggested by Coren (1999) to the floppiness of the dogs ears. No correlation was found.

DISCUSSION

The research showed that for some reason, those that chose the breed of their dog carefully (purebred) could be matched to their dogs quite successfully. There is then, some truth that in the case of the purebreds, owners and dogs did resemble one another in some way. However, the lack of correlation between the amount of time the dogs and their owners had been together suggests that they do not grow to be alike; rather the owners are choosing the dogs in the first place that resemble themselves in some way. What is really interesting here is that there is clearly some resemblance, but quite where that resemblance lies is unclear from these results. The only suggestion we have here is that the dogs and their owners seem to relate to one another in terms of ratings of 'friendliness'. The researchers concluded that just as in the case of selecting a spouse (as shown by Berscheid & Reis, 1998), that people choose a creature (in this case a dog) that is alike them in some way.

THE BIOLOGICAL PERSPECTIVE: THE BRAIN, GENES AND EVOLUTION

The **biological perspective** examines how brain processes and other bodily functions regulate behaviour. Biological psychology has always been a prominent part of the field, but its influence has increased dramatically over recent decades.

Behavioural Neuroscience

What brain regions, neural circuits and brain chemicals enable us to feel love, pleasure, fear and depression? To read, study and feel hunger? How do hormones influence behaviour? These questions are the province of **behavioural neuroscience** (also called *physiological psychology*), which examines brain processes and other physiological functions that underlie our behaviour, sensory experiences, emotions and thoughts (Robinson, Rennie, Rowe, O'Connor, & Gordon, 2005).

The study of brain–behaviour relations was in its infancy as psychology entered the twentieth century. Two pioneers of biological psychology, Karl Lashley (1890–1958) and Donald O. Hebb (1904–85), studied the brain's role in learning. Lashley trained rats to run through mazes and then measured how surgically produced lesions (damage) to various brain areas affected the rats' learning and memory. His research inspired other psychologists to map the brain regions involved in specific psychological functions (Figure 1.18).

Hebb (1949) proposed that changes in the connections between nerve cells in the brain provide the biological basis for learning, memory and perception. His influential theory inspired much research, continuing to this day, on how the brain's neural circuitry changes as we learn, remember and perceive. This research led to the discovery of **neurotransmitters**, which are chemicals released by nerve cells that allow them to communicate with one another. The study of neurotransmitters' role in normal behaviour and mental disorders represents an important area of current neuroscience research.

Because behavioural neuroscience focuses on processes that are largely invisible to the naked eye, using brain-imaging techniques and devices that record brainwaves, psychologists can watch activity in specific brain areas as people experience emotions, perceive stimuli and perform tasks (Figure 1.19). These advances have led to new areas of study that forge links between various psychological perspectives. For example, cognitive neuroscience – the study of brain processes that underlie attention, reasoning, problem-solving and so forth – represents an intersection of cognitive psychology and behavioural neuroscience. As a whole, however, behavioural neuroscience is broader than cognitive neuroscience. Behavioural neuroscientists, for example, also study the biology of hunger, thirst, sex, body-temperature regulation, emotion, movement, and sensory processes such as vision, hearing and taste. This area of research, more than any other, is gaining focus and popularity at this time. Advances in scanning technology are playing their part in driving forward this exciting area of research, with researchers in neuroscience forming part of the vanguard of the psychology of today.

Behaviour Genetics

Psychologists have had a long-standing interest in **behaviour genetics**, the study of how behavioural tendencies are influenced by genetic factors (Spinath & Johnson, 2011). As we all know, animals can be selectively bred for physical traits (Figure 1.20). But they can also be bred for behavioural traits such as aggression and intelligence. This is done by allowing highly aggressive or very bright males and females to mate with one another over generations. In Thailand, where gambling on fish fights is a national pastime, the selective breeding of winners has produced the highly aggressive Siamese fighting fish. The male of this species will instantly attack his own image in a mirror.

Human behaviour is also influenced by genetic factors. Identical twins, which result from the splitting of a fertilized egg and therefore have the same genetic make-up, are far more similar to one another on many behavioural traits than are fraternal twins, who result from two different fertilized eggs and therefore are no more similar genetically than are

FIGURE 1.18 Karl Lashley was a pioneer of physiological psychology (behavioural neuroscience). He examined how damage to various brain regions affected rats' ability to learn and remember.

Source: HUP Lashley, K. (2), Harvard University Archives.

biological perspective examines how brain processes and other bodily functions regulate behaviour

behavioural neuroscience examines brain processes and other physiological functions that underlie our behaviour, sensory experiences, emotions and thoughts

neurotransmitters chemicals released by nerve cells that allow them to communicate with one another

behaviour genetics the study of how behavioural tendencies are influenced by genetic factors

Focus 1.11 Describe the biological perspective and the focus of behavioural neuroscience and behaviour genetics.

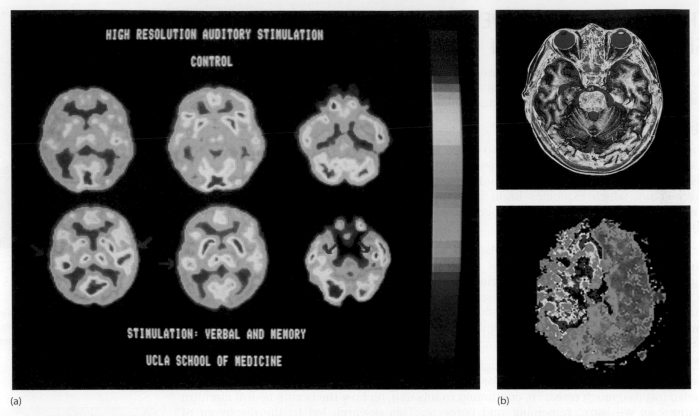

(a)   (b)

FIGURE 1.19 (a) Listening to and memorizing words. Coloured Positron Emission Tomography (PET) scan showing horizontal sections through a human brain during auditory stimulation. Successively deeper sections are seen from left to right. The top row "control" shows the brain not stimulated. The bottom row shows arrowed regions associated with verbal stimulation. At bottom left and centre, arrows highlight the auditory regions of the cerebrum that become active when words are listened to. At bottom right, arrows point to regions inside the temporal lobe that become active after words are heard and are associated with aspects of memory. (b) Magnetic resonance imaging (MRI) (*top*) provides detailed images of living brains, and functional magnetic resonance imaging (fMRI) (*bottom*) allows researchers to see how activity in the brain changes. This image shows the effect of a stroke on the brain.

Source: Science Photo Library

non-twin siblings. This greater degree of similarity is found even when the identical twins have been reared in different homes and dissimilar environments (Plomin & Caspi, 1999).

A behaviour geneticist would consider the extent to which heredity contributes to differences in many psychological attributes, including shyness. For instance, some infants display an extremely shy, inhibited emotional style that seems to be biologically based and persists through childhood into adulthood (Kagan, 1989; Newman, Caspi, Moffitt, & Silva, 1997).

Evolutionary Psychology

Charles Darwin published his theory of evolution in 1859 (Figure 1.21). He was not the first to suggest that organisms evolve, but his theory was the best documented. His ideas were stimulated by a five-year voyage aboard *The Beagle* – a research vessel that explored coastal regions around the globe. Darwin was struck by the numerous differences between seemingly similar species that lived in different environments. He began to view these differences as ways in which each species had adapted to its unique environment.

> **natural selection** if an inherited trait gives certain members an advantage over others these members will be more likely to survive and pass these characteristics on to their offspring

Darwin noted that the individual members of given species differ naturally in many ways. Some possess specific traits to a greater extent than other members do. Through a process he called **natural selection**, if an inherited trait gives certain members an advantage over others (such as increasing their ability to attract mates, escape danger or acquire food), these members will be more likely to survive and pass these characteristics on to their offspring. In this way, species evolve as the presence of adaptive traits increases

FIGURE I.20 Micropics were slectively bred to be tiny for medical research

Source: ©iStock.com/Patrick Heagney

FIGURE I.21 Charles Darwin formulated a theory of evolution that revolutionized scientific thinking.

Source: © GL Archive/Alamy

within the population over generations. In contrast, traits that put certain members at a disadvantage tend to become less common within a species over time because members having these traits will be less likely to survive and reproduce.

As the environment changes, the adaptiveness of a trait may increase or decrease. Thus, through natural selection, the biology of a species evolves in response to environmental conditions. Darwin assumed that the principle of natural selection could be applied to all living organisms, including humans.

Evolutionary psychology is a growing discipline that seeks to explain how evolution shaped modern human behaviour (Workman & Reader, 2008; Buss, 2013). Evolutionary psychologists stress that through natural selection, human mental abilities and behavioural tendencies evolved along with a changing body. Consider how the brain evolved over millions of years, with the greatest growth occurring in brain regions involving higher mental processes.

According to one theory, as our human-like ancestors developed new physical abilities (such as the ability to walk upright, thus freeing the use of the arms and hands), they began to use tools and weapons and to hunt and live in social groups (Buss, 2013). Certain psychological abilities – memory, thought, language and the capacity to learn and solve problems – became more important to survival as our ancestors had to adapt to new ways of living.

Within any generation, genetically based variations in brain structure and functioning occur among individuals. Ancestors whose brain characteristics better supported adaptive mental abilities were more likely to survive and reproduce. Thus, through natural selection, adaptations to new environmental demands contributed to the development of the brain, just as brain growth contributed to the further development of human behaviour.

Evolutionary psychologists also attempt to explain the evolution of human social behaviours. For example, consider marriage. As a species, why have we evolved to seek out a long-term bond with a mate? And why is it that across the world, on average, men desire a younger mate and attach greater importance than women to a potential mate's physical attractiveness, whereas women tend to seek an older mate and attach more importance than men to a potential mate's ambition? Whereas sociocultural psychologists argue that socialization and gender inequality in job opportunities cause most sex differences in mate preferences, some evolutionary psychologists propose that through natural selection men and women have become biologically predisposed to seek somewhat different qualities in a mate (Workman & Reader, 2008; Buss, 2013).

evolutionary psychology
a growing discipline that seeks to explain how evolution shaped modern human behaviour

Focus I.12 What is natural selection? Explain the focus of evolutionary psychology.

In review

- Psychology's intellectual roots lie in philosophy, biology and medicine. Several major perspectives have shaped psychology's scientific growth. In the late 1800s Wundt and James helped found psychology. Structuralism, which examined the basic components of consciousness, and functionalism, which focused on the purposes of consciousness, was psychology's two earliest schools of thought.

- The psychodynamic perspective calls attention to unconscious motives, conflicts, and defence mechanisms that influence our personality and behaviour. Freud emphasized how unconscious sexual and aggressive impulses and childhood experiences shape personality. Modern psychodynamic theories focus more on how early family relationships and our sense of self unconsciously influence our current behaviour.

- The behavioural perspective emphasizes how the external environment and learning shape behaviour. Behaviourists such as Watson and Skinner believed that psychology should only study observable stimuli and responses, not unobservable mental processes. Behaviourists discovered basic laws of learning through controlled research with laboratory animals and applied these principles to enhance human welfare. Cognitive behaviourists believe that learning experiences influence our thoughts, which in turn influence our behaviours.

- The humanistic perspective emphasizes personal freedom and choice, psychological growth and self-actualization. Humanism has contributed to research on the self, the process of psychotherapy and today's positive psychology movement.

- The cognitive perspective, embodied by the field of cognitive psychology, views humans as information processors who think, judge and solve problems. Its roots lie in the early schools of structuralism, functionalism and Gestalt psychology. Cognitive neuroscience examines the brain processes that occur as people perform mental tasks. Social constructivism maintains that much of what we call reality is a creation of our own mental processes.

- The sociocultural perspective examines how the social environment and cultural learning influence our behaviour and thoughts. Cultural psychologists study how culture is transmitted to its members and examine similarities and differences among people from various cultures. An orientation towards individualism versus collectivism represents one of many ways in which cultures vary.

- With roots in physiology, medicine and Darwin's theory of evolution, the biological perspective examines how bodily functions regulate behaviour. Behavioural neuroscientists study brain and hormonal processes that underlie our behaviour, sensations, emotions and thoughts. Behaviour geneticists study how behaviour is influenced by our genetic inheritance. Evolutionary psychologists examine the adaptive functions of behaviours and seek to explain how evolution has biologically predisposed modern humans towards certain ways of behaving.

USING LEVELS OF ANALYSIS TO INTEGRATE THE PERSPECTIVES

As summarized in Table 1.1, psychology's major perspectives (presented in the order we have discussed them) provide us with differing conceptions of human nature. Fortunately, we can distil the essence of these perspectives into the simple three-part framework that we briefly introduced earlier in the chapter: behaviour can be understood at biological, psychological and environmental levels of analysis.

First, we can analyse behaviour and its causes in terms of brain functioning and hormones, as well as genetic factors shaped over the course of evolution. This is the *biological level of analysis*. The biological level can tell us much, but not everything. For example, we may know that certain thoughts and emotions are associated with activity in particular brain regions, but this does not tell us what those thoughts are. Thus we must also examine the *psychological level of analysis*. Here we might look to the cognitive perspective and analyse how thought, memory and planning influence behaviour. Borrowing from the psychodynamic and humanistic perspectives, we also can examine how certain motives and personality traits influence behaviour. Finally, we must also consider the *environmental level of analysis*. Here we can use the behavioural and sociocultural perspectives to examine how stimuli in the physical and social environment shape our behaviour, thoughts and feelings.

TABLE 1.1 Comparison of six major perspectives on human behaviour

	Psychodynamic	Behavioural	Humanistic	Cognitive	Sociocultural	Biological
Conception of human nature	The human as controlled by inner forces and conflicts	The human as reactor to the environment	The human as free agent, seeking self-actualization	The human as thinker	The human as social being embedded in a culture	The human animal
Major causal factors in behaviour	Unconscious motives, conflicts, and defences; early childhood experiences and unresolved conflicts	Past learning experiences and the stimuli and behavioural consequences that exist in the current environment	Free will, choice and innate drive towards self-actualization; search for personal meaning of existence	Thoughts, anticipations, planning, perceptions, attention and memory processes	Social forces, including norms, social interactions, and group processes in one's culture and social environment	Genetic and evolutionary factors; brain and biochemical processes
Predominant focus and methods of discovery	Intensive observations of personality processes in clinical settings; some laboratory research	Study of learning processes in laboratory and real-world settings, with an emphasis on precise observation of stimuli and responses	Study of meaning, values and purpose in life; study of self-concept and its role in thought, emotion and behaviour	Study of cognitive processes, usually under highly controlled laboratory conditions	Study of behaviour and mental processes of people in different cultures; experiments examining people's responses to social stimuli	Study of brain-behaviour relations; role of hormones and biochemical factors in behaviour; behaviour genetics research

Realize that a full understanding of behaviour often moves us back and forth between these three levels. When we describe aspects of the culture in which they were raised, such as its religious values and social customs, we are operating at the environmental level of analysis. However, once we adopt the cultural values of the society in which we live as our own, those values became an essential part of our identities, which represent the psychological level of analysis. Similarly, we might describe a family environment as highly abusive, but an abused child's tendency to worry and feel anxious – and the chemical changes in the brain that underlie this anxiety – move us to the psychological and biological levels of analysis.

AN EXAMPLE: UNDERSTANDING DEPRESSION

To appreciate how the levels-of-analysis framework can help us understand behaviour, let us examine a common but complex psychological problem in our culture: depression. Most people experience sadness, grief or the blues at some time in their lives. It is not unusual for some students to feel lonely or homesick during their first year at university and they become mildly depressed for a short time. These feelings often are normal responses to significant negative events or losses that we have experienced. However, when these emotions are intense, persist over a long period, and are accompanied by thoughts of hopelessness and an inability to experience pleasure, we have crossed the boundary between a normal reaction and clinical depression.

To better understand depression, let us begin at the biological level of analysis. First, genetic factors appear to predispose some people towards developing depression (Neumeister, Young, & Stastny, 2004; Zavos, Rijsdijk, Gregory, & Eley, 2010). In one study, relatives of people who had developed major depression before age twenty were eight times more likely to become depressed at some point than were relatives of non-depressed people (Weissman et al., 1984).

Biochemical factors also play a role. Recall that neurotransmitters are chemicals that transmit signals between nerve cells within the brain. For many depressed people certain neurotransmitter systems do not operate normally, and the most effective antidepressant drugs restore neurotransmitter activity to more normal levels.

From an evolutionary perspective, ancestors who developed effective ways to cope with environmental threats increased their chances of surviving and passing on their genes. At times, the psychological and physical ability to withdraw and conserve one's resources was undoubtedly the most adaptive defence against an environmental stressor, such as an unavoidable defeat or personal loss. Some evolutionary theorists view depression (and its accompanying disengagement and sense of hopelessness) as an exaggerated form of this normally adaptive, genetically based withdrawal process (Gilbert, 2001).

Moving to a psychological level of analysis, we find that depression is associated with a thinking style in which the person interprets events pessimistically (Seligman & Isaacowitz, 2000). Depressed people can find the black cloud that surrounds every silver lining. They tend to blame themselves for negative things that occur and take little credit for the good things that happen in their lives; they generally view the future as bleak and may have perfectionist expectations that make them overly sensitive to how other people evaluate them (Bieling, Israeli, & Antony, 2004).

Are some personality patterns more prone to depression than others? Many psychodynamic theorists believe that severe losses, rejections or traumas in childhood help create a personality style that causes people to overreact to setbacks, setting the stage for future depression. In support of this notion, studies show that depressed people are more likely than non-depressed people to have experienced parental rejection, sexual abuse or the loss of a parent through death or separation during childhood (Bowlby, 2000).

Finally, at the environmental level of analysis, behaviourists propose that depression is a reaction to a non-rewarding environment. A vicious cycle begins when the environment provides fewer rewards for the person. As depression intensifies, some people feel so bad that they stop doing things that ordinarily give them pleasure, which decreases environmental rewards still further. To make things worse, depressed people may complain a lot and seek excessive support from others. These behaviours eventually begin to alienate other people, causing them to shy away from the depressed person. The net result is a worsening environment with fewer rewards, reduced support from others and hopeless pessimism (Lewinsohn, Hoberman, Teri, & Hantzinger, 1985; Nezlek, Hampton, & Shean, 2000).

Focus 1.13 Use the three-level framework to integrate psychology's perspectives and discuss causes of depression.

Sociocultural factors also affect depression. As noted above, abusive family environments and other traumatic social experiences increase children's risk for depression later in life. Moreover, although depression is found in virtually all cultures, its symptoms, causes and prevalence may reflect cultural differences (Kleinman, 2004). For reasons still unknown, in the USA, Canada and other western nations, women are twice as likely as men to report feeling depressed; no such sex difference is found in developing countries (Culbertson, 1997).

interaction the way in which one factor influences behaviour depends on the presence of another factor

The levels of analysis organize causal factors in depression into three classes: biological, psychological and environmental. Keep in mind, however, that the specific causes of depression and the way in which they combine or interact may differ from case to case. **Interaction** means that the way in which one factor influences behaviour depends on the presence of another factor. For example, someone who experiences a minor setback in life may become depressed if she or he has a strong biological predisposition for depression. The same setback might barely faze a person with a weak biological predisposition for depression; only a catastrophic loss might cause this other person to become depressed. Thus the intensity of life stress and strength of biological predisposition would interact to influence behaviour. Just as boiling water softens celery and hardens an egg, the same environment can affect two people differently.

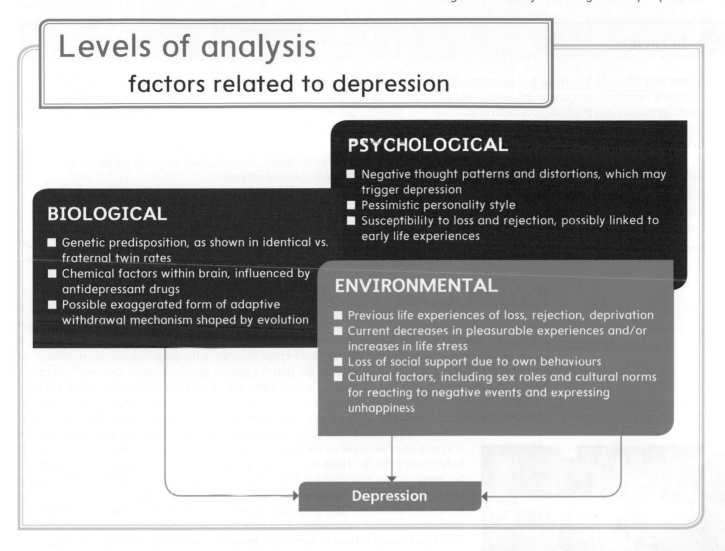

Levels of analysis
factors related to depression

PSYCHOLOGICAL
- Negative thought patterns and distortions, which may trigger depression
- Pessimistic personality style
- Susceptibility to loss and rejection, possibly linked to early life experiences

BIOLOGICAL
- Genetic predisposition, as shown in identical vs. fraternal twin rates
- Chemical factors within brain, influenced by antidepressant drugs
- Possible exaggerated form of adaptive withdrawal mechanism shaped by evolution

ENVIRONMENTAL
- Previous life experiences of loss, rejection, deprivation
- Current decreases in pleasurable experiences and/or increases in life stress
- Loss of social support due to own behaviours
- Cultural factors, including sex roles and cultural norms for reacting to negative events and expressing unhappiness

Depression

SUMMARY OF MAJOR THEMES

Our excursion through psychology's major perspectives and levels of analysis reveals several principles that you will encounter repeatedly as we explore the realm of behaviour:

1. As a science, psychology is empirical. It favours direct observation over pure intuition or reasoning as a means of attaining knowledge about behaviour.

2. Although committed to studying behaviour objectively, psychologists recognize that our personal experience of the world is subjective.

3. Behaviour is determined by multiple causal factors, including our biological endowment ('nature'), the environment and our past learning experiences ('nurture'), and psychological factors that include our thoughts and motives.

4. Behaviour is a means of adapting to environmental demands; capacities have evolved during each species' history because they facilitated adaptation and survival.

5. Behaviour and cognitive processes are affected by the social and cultural environments in which we develop and live.

Focus 1.14 Discuss five major themes identified in this chapter.

In review

■ Factors that influence behaviour can be organized into three broad levels of analysis. The biological level examines how brain processes, hormonal and genetic influences, and evolutionary adaptations underlie behaviour. The psychological level focuses on mental processes and psychological motives and how they influence behaviour. The environmental level examines physical and social stimuli, including cultural factors, that shape our behaviour and thoughts.

■ To understand behaviour, we often move back and forth between these levels of analysis. For example, when as children we are first exposed to cultural norms, those norms reflect a characteristic of our environment. However, once we adopt norms as our own, they become a part of our world view and now represent the psychological level of analysis.

■ Biological, psychological and environmental factors contribute to depression. These factors can also interact. A mild setback may trigger depression in a person who has a strong biological predisposition towards depression, whereas a person who has a weak biological predisposition may become depressed only after suffering a severe setback.

PSYCHOLOGY TODAY

To many people, when you say the word *psychologist*, the first image that comes to mind is that of a therapist. This is understandable, as a large number of psychologists are indeed *clinical psychologists*, who diagnose and treat people with psychological problems in clinics, hospitals and private practice. Yet many clinical psychologists also are scientists who conduct research on the causes of mental disorders and the effectiveness of various kinds of treatment. Moreover, there are many other types of psychologists who have no connection with therapy and instead work as basic or applied researchers. It is, however, misleading to think that psychology and the skills we learn as psychologists will not be of interest or useful in many areas. Notable here is the concept of behaviour change. How do we alter people's behaviours to those that might be deemed more desirable? For instance cycling is a desirable activity for a number of reasons. Environmentally it is not as damaging as driving and in terms of health, cycling provides exercise. How do we encourage people to engage in similar activities? The firm Volkswagen have an initiative called 'TheFunTheory' where behaviour change is encouraged imaginatively.

FIGURE I.22 'Piano Staircase' in Stockholm.
Source: DDB Stockholm and Volkswagen

For instance, in 'Piano Staircase' the stairs in a Stockholm metro station immediately adjacent to the escalator were replaced with a piano keyboard. Results showed that 66% more people used the 'stairs' in this case (Figure 1.22).

In another example a rubbish bin was fitted with a sound generator that presented the sound of a continued 'long drop' of the rubbish into the bin. This was called the 'world's deepest bin' – people were more likely to use it because it was fun.

A GLOBAL SCIENCE AND PROFESSION

As a science and a profession, psychology today is more diversified and robust than ever before. No psychologist can claim to be an expert on all aspects of behaviour because of the great breadth of the subject. As in other sciences, many areas of specialization have emerged. Table 1.2 describes some of psychology's major subfields, but note that psychological research often cuts across subfields. For example, developmental, social, clinical and physiological psychologists might all study the causes of antisocial behaviour among children.

Modern psychology is also geographically, ethnically and gender diversified. A century ago, psychological research was conducted almost entirely in Europe, North America and Russia by white males. Today these regions remain scientific powerhouses, but you will find women and men from diverse backgrounds conducting psychological research and providing psychological services around the globe. Founded in 1951 to support psychology worldwide, the International Union of Psychological Science consists of major

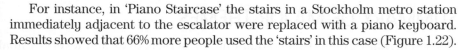

Focus I.15 Describe some of psychology's major subfields and professional organizations.

TABLE I.2 Key areas within psychology

Speciality	Subtopics
Biological psychology	Biological bases of behaviour, hormones and behaviour, behavioural genetics, neuropsychology, socio-biology and evolutionary psychology
Cognitive psychology	Perception, learning, memory, thinking, language, consciousness and cognitive neuropsychology
Developmental psychology	Childhood, adolescence and lifespan development, development of attachment, social relations, cognitive and language development, social and cultural contexts of development
Personality and individual differences	Abnormal and normal personality, psychological testing, intelligence, cognitive style, emotion, motivation and mood
Social psychology	Social cognition, attribution, attitudes, group processes and intergroup relations, close relationships and social constructionism
Research methods	Research design, the nature and appropriate statistical analysis of data, psychometrics and measurement techniques, and quantitative and qualitative methods

psychological organizations from 70 countries. Moreover, across the world, students are eagerly studying psychology both at university and, increasingly, in pre-university education. At university, students will learn about a number of key areas in psychology. Each of these key areas has subtopics that may or may not be included in the courses. Different professional bodies scrutinize the provision of psychology courses in their particular countries, and may require that certain topics are covered, maintaining parity and quality across institutions.

Besides its fascinating subject matter, psychology attracts many people with its rich variety of career options. Table 1.3 shows the major settings in which psychologists work. Many psychologists teach, engage in research or apply psychological principles and techniques to help solve personal or social problems. Practising as a psychologist depends partly on the type of psychology being conducted, and partly on the country in which the professional lives. For more information on careers in psychology, visit the Online Learning Centre (OLC) that accompanies this book.

TABLE I.3 Work settings of psychologists

Occupation	%
Administrative and secretarial	20.8
Managers and senior officials	7.4
Professional	16.2
Associate professional and technical	22.5
Personal and protective service	15.9
Sales and customer service	11.6
Others	5.6

Source: HESA Standard Occupational Classification (SOC) Psychology Graduates, 2003.

PSYCHOLOGY AND PUBLIC POLICY

Modern society faces a host of complex social problems. Psychology, as a science and profession, is poised to help solve them. Through basic research, psychologists provide knowledge about behaviour. In applied research, they use this knowledge to design, implement and assess intervention programmes (Rodham 2010). Together, basic research and applied research are pillars for *evidence-based public policies* that affect the lives of millions of people.

Psychologists can help influence national policy by helping politicians develop legislation dealing with a host of social issues, from preventing AIDS and obesity to enhancing childcare and attitudes to security, particularly in the wake of the post-9/11 terrorist activity, and discouraging smoking (Figure 1.23). School bullying, for example, is a serious problem in several countries. Norwegian psychologist, Dan Olweus, a leading researcher on bullying, developed a prevention programme that the Norwegian government makes available to all its public schools (Olweus, 2004).

Focus I.16 How can psychology help shape public policy?

CURRENT ISSUES IN PSYCHOLOGY

As you navigate through psychology you will quickly learn that some topics are currently in vogue, attracting more research and funding, and more prominent at the various departments around Europe than others. Freud's psychodynamic approach, for instance,

FIGURE 1.23 Warnings like these are common all over the world. You need not be able to read Swedish to know that this is a warning. It can be translated in English as 'Smoking can seriously harm yourself and others close to you'.

Source: Jonas Bergsten.

is less popular now among many than it once was, and the newer neuroscientific approach is more in vogue in many departments. That is, of course, not to say that just because something is not terribly 'fashionable' does not mean that it has merit, and we forget the work of our peers and forefathers at great peril.

Whereas approaches seem to change places in terms of their prominence, some debates remain with us. Of course, the debates we have in psychology are also subject to the science and the trends elsewhere that feed them, but some of the larger issues are always present. Our science, like any others, reflects the societies in which we live and so our work and theory development are driven by what we see around us. For instance, the global economic crisis has animated psychologists (Strack, 2009) and those interested in global warming (Swim et al., 2009) similarly. We must also look to relate sciences and approaches for trends and drivers in our work. *Human geography*, for instance, provides us with data on town and urban planning and this in turn drives and motivates research in the areas of psychology, notably applied cognition that are concerned with how people will engage with these cities, how they will travel, what choices they will make and how this will influence their health and quality of life. *Engineering* provides us with hugely exciting advances in motor vehicle technology, including almost silent electric vehicles – some psychologists are engaged in investigating how other road users, such as pedestrians and cyclists will engage with these vehicles and how our knowledge of human behaviour can be brought to bear in the development and deployment of these technologies. *Medicine* has enabled us to help people to live for longer, and engage in a fuller life – psychologists, reacting to this, are engaged with identifying how older people, an increasingly large portion of our society, can access what they need to maintain and improve their quality of life. In the book we will raise some of the issues related with these and other current issues and debates.

The concept of 'mindfulness' is a relatively new addition to theory and practice in psychology and is certainly a current topic. The idea is not, you will be unsurprised to hear, a new one. The origins of psychology are both within the traditionally pure sciences such as physics and biology, as well as within philosophy. One such philosophical approach is Buddhism. Mindfulness can be thought of as 'awareness' and in psychology we are learning that the approach teaches us to focus on what is happening in our immediate experience, and to think about it carefully and with definition. The concept has been used to help people become calm and focused through meditation, and the teaching here is not dissimilar.

Where a person is under pressure to complete many tasks, to manage different groups of people and to meet deadlines and demands of many employers, they may begin to lose focus. They may begin to lose sight of what they are doing and lack the focus required to complete any of their tasks successfully. Coupled with the demands of their personal lives things may well begin to suffer and when that happens the balance of their attention is shifted between one thing and the next, swinging often uncontrollably between problems that need fixing immediately before they can concentrate on the tasks in hand, be they work-based or home-based. This state could be thought of as one of 'mindlessness'. Mindfulness training is a meditative technique and there are a great many guides available for those that would like to learn some of the techniques. Jon Kabat-Zinn has written widely about the benefits of the approach since 1994, and his book *Wherever You Go, There You Are: Mindfulness Meditation in Everyday Life* is regarded by many as the starting point for the translation of mindfulness from Buddhism into mainstream psychology and thinking.

One very interesting way of thinking about mindfulness in relation to the world in which we live is in terms of habits and how we live a good deal of our lives on autopilot. Many decisions in our lives are made automatically with very little thought. The reasons for this are debatable, but it could be that we employ a form of heuristic, a rule that normally works, in many cases, and simply choose an approach that normally works. We do not question it, or think about the implications of our choice, we simply act. For instance, we choose food at the supermarket out of habit, our eating patterns are often habitual, the transport choices we make, usually to drive, are simply based on what normally works and convenience. In short, we are not mindful of many of the decisions we take and as such we are being driven by habit and are moving through many aspects of our lives on autopilot. One approach to mindfulness is that we should slow down, and 'wake up' as it were from a life lived on autopilot and think about what we are doing in the here and now.

A philosophy of how we might consider behaving is all well and good, but as scientists we should question the validity of any approach, and look for evidence of its efficacy. The scientific community is beginning to do this now, and material is appearing in the literature that shows that the approach is a positive one and that it can be measured. Hulbert-Williams, Nicholls, Joy and Hulbert-Williams (2013) have produced a Mindful Eating Scale, for instance, which drew on relevant principles and shows promising evaluations. The Mindful Assessment Awareness Scale (MAAS) is one of a number of tools that assess mindfulness. It has been used and validated in a number of situations and among a number of different cohorts, including children (Lawlor, Schonert-Reichl, Gadermann, & Zumbo, 2013) and Chinese populations (Deng, Tang, Zhu, Ryan, & Brown, 2012) showing its use, where used appropriately is valid cross culturally. The most important thing to note here is that the sales being used and under validation right now will allow us as psychologists to assess the effectiveness of mindfulness interventions on a number of different populations, sub-populations and levels. These will include psychological, behavioural and social levels. It will also allow us to make measurements of whether people are 'mindfully' disposed. By this I mean the scales, where designed and used appropriately will allow us to measure personality characteristics and traits associated with mindfulness, and so allow us to target appropriate interventions for people in different situations. If we know how likely a person is to respond to a mindfulness intervention, we can shape the intervention or packages of interventions accordingly.

Focus I.17 Describe scientifically based strategies that can enhance students' learning and academic performance.

PSYCHOLOGY AND YOUR LIFE

Many of you reading this are students, and so learning and studying is central to your lives. We can all learn to do this better, and our knowledge of psychology can help us improve our academic performance.

Applying psychological science

HOW TO ENHANCE YOUR ACADEMIC PERFORMANCE

University life presents many challenges, and work skills can be as important for meeting those challenges as working hard. The following strategies can help you increase your learning and academic performance (Figure I.24).

EFFECTIVE TIME MANAGEMENT

If you efficiently allocate the time needed for study, you will have a clear conscience when it is time for recreational activities and relaxation. First, *develop a written schedule.* This forces you to decide how to allocate your time and increases your commitment to the plan. Begin by writing down your class meetings, your seminars, your lectures and other responsibilities. Then block in periods of study, avoiding times when you are likely to be tired. Distribute study times throughout the week, and schedule some study times immediately before enjoyable activities, which you can use as rewards for studying.

Second, *prioritize your tasks.* Most of us tend to procrastinate by working on simple tasks while putting off the toughest tasks until later. This can result in never getting to the major tasks (such as writing a term paper or studying for an examination) until too little time remains. Ask yourself, each day, 'What is the most important thing to get done?' Do that task first, then move to the next most important task, and so on.

Third, *break large tasks into smaller parts* that can be completed at specific times. Important tasks often are too big to complete all at once, so break them down and define each part in terms of a specific but realistic goal (e.g., number of pages to be read or amount of material to be studied). Successfully completing each goal is rewarding, strengthens your study skills and increases your feelings of mastery.

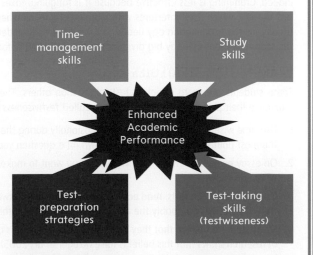

FIGURE I.24 Improving academic performance.

Academic performance-enhancement methods include strategies for managing time, studying more effectively, preparing for tests and taking tests.

STUDYING MORE EFFECTIVELY

After planning your study time, use that time effectively. *Choose a study place where there are no distractions and where you do nothing but study*, say, a quiet library rather than a busy cafeteria. In time, you will learn to associate that location with studying, and studying there will become even easier (Watson & Tharp, 1997).

How you study is vital to your academic success. Do not read material passively and hope that it will just soak in. Instead, *use an active approach to learning*. For example, when reading a textbook chapter, first look over the chapter outline, which will give you a good idea of the information you are going to be processing. As you read the material, think about how it applies to your life or how it relates to other information that you already know.

USE FOCUS QUESTIONS TO ENHANCE ACTIVE LEARNING

You can also increase active learning by using the focus questions that appear in the margins of this book. These questions call attention to major concepts and facts. Use them to help you anticipate key points before you read a section, and use them again after you have read each section to test your understanding of the material. This will require you to stop and think about the content. Research shows that responding to these types of questions promotes better recall (Moreland, Dansereau, & Chmielewski, 1997).

Realize that these questions focus on only a portion of the important material. We could have written more questions, but just because some sections do not have focus questions does not mean that you can skip the material. In fact, you will learn even more if you supplement our questions with ones of your own – especially for sections that do not already have focus questions. Answering the focus questions and writing questions of your own will require more effort than passive reading does, but it will result in better learning (Estes & Vaughn, 1985; Hamilton, 1985).

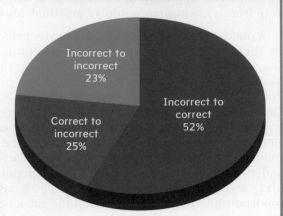

FIGURE 1.25 Changing answers on multiple-choice tests.

Researchers analysed the eraser marks on 6412 examinations taken by introductory psychology students. Contrary to popular wisdom, changing an answer was twice as likely to result in gaining points rather than losing points.

Source: Based on Kruger, Wirtz, & Miller, 2005.

PREPARING FOR TESTS AND EXAMINATIONS

Contrary to what some students believe, introductory psychology is not an easy course. It covers a lot of diverse material, and many new concepts must be mastered. Many students who are new to university do not realize that the academic demands far exceed those of secondary school. Moreover, many students do not realize how hard high achievers actually work. In one study, researchers found that failing students spent only one-third as many hours studying as did students who regularly achieved the highest grades (who studied about two hours for every hour spent in class). Yet the failing students *thought* they were studying as much as anyone else, and many wondered why they were not doing well (Watson & Tharp, 1997).

A written study schedule helps spread your test preparation over time and helps avoid last-minute cramming. There is something to say for cramming. If all else fails then cram for your life because squeezing vast amounts of information into your memory can mean that it may possibly be in there on the day of the examination. However, the chances of the information being there in any useful form for any real period of time are very slim indeed. Cramming is less effective because it is fatiguing, taxes your memory in a way that organized learning does not, and it may serve to increase test anxiety, which itself interferes with learning and recall when you want to remember the material you have crammed in (Sarason & Sarason, 1990). Ideally, as the examination day nears, you should already understand the material. Then use the time before the test to refine your knowledge. Using the focus questions can pay big dividends in the final days before an examination.

EXAMINATION STRATEGIES

Some students are more effective test-takers than others. They know how to approach different types of tests (e.g., multiple choice or essay) to maximize their performance. Such skills are called *testwiseness* (Fagley, 1987). Here are some strategies that test wise students use:

1. Use time wisely. Check your progress occasionally during the test. Answer the questions you know first (and, on essay examinations, the ones worth the most points). Do not get bogged down on a question you find difficult. Mark it and come back to it later.

2. On essay examinations, outline the points you want to make before you begin writing, then cover the key points in enough detail to communicate what you know.

3. On multiple-choice tests, read each question and try to answer it before reading the answer options. If you find your answer among the alternatives, that alternative is probably the correct one. Still, read all the other alternatives to make sure that you choose the best one.

4. Many students believe that they should not change answers on multiple-choice tests because the first guess is most likely to be correct. Eighty years of research shows that this belief is false (Kruger et al., 2005). As Figure 1.25 shows, changing an answer is far more likely to result in a wrong answer becoming a correct one than vice versa. Do not be reluctant to change an answer if you are fairly sure that the alternative is better.

5. Some multiple-choice questions have 'all of the above' as an alternative. If one of the other answers is clearly incorrect, eliminate the 'all of the above' option; if you are sure that at least two of the other answers are correct but are not sure about the third; choose 'all of the above'.

Time management, study skills, examination and test-preparation strategies and testwiseness are not acquired overnight; they require effort and practice.

In review

- Psychologists today conduct research and provide services around the globe.
- Psychologists specialize in various subfields and work in many settings. They teach, conduct research, perform therapy and counselling, and apply psychological principles to solve personal and social problems.
- You can use principles derived from psychological science to enhance your learning and increase your likelihood of performing well on tests. These include time-management principles, strategies for studying more effectively, test-preparation strategies, and techniques for taking tests.

What we hope to have shown you in this first of many chapters is that psychology is not perhaps what many people think it is. You will no doubt already have experienced other people's attitudes to our subject. When you tell people you are studying psychology their misconceptions become only too clear. Some people may even become nervous of speaking to you for fear of being analysed in some way. In the next chapter we will continue our journey into psychology by looking at ways of studying people scientifically – this is, after all, the science of mind and behaviour. When you are reading, try and begin to think like a psychologist – think about how different theories and ideas may relate to one another, take the skills you learn here into your everyday lives and look for patterns and examples of the ideas and theories you will encounter. If you do this, before you know it, it will become natural to you and the subject will begin to come alive as it does for many of us. When this happens you can really say you are well on the road to being a psychologist, and even if working in psychology is not for you, you can use these skills in your everyday life. People-watching in cafes, airports and on trains will be even more engaging than before as you think more deeply about the behaviours you observe. As you read, think particularly about *levels of analysis* and how they can help you think carefully and logically about the different ways of addressing and integrating the different perspectives we have begun to introduce here.

Psychology Timeline

Psychology is regarded by many as a boring science but its roots are very much in the planted in history. How a science grows and develops, what its cultural and historical perspectives and origins are can really help us understand the trends and motives within our subject.

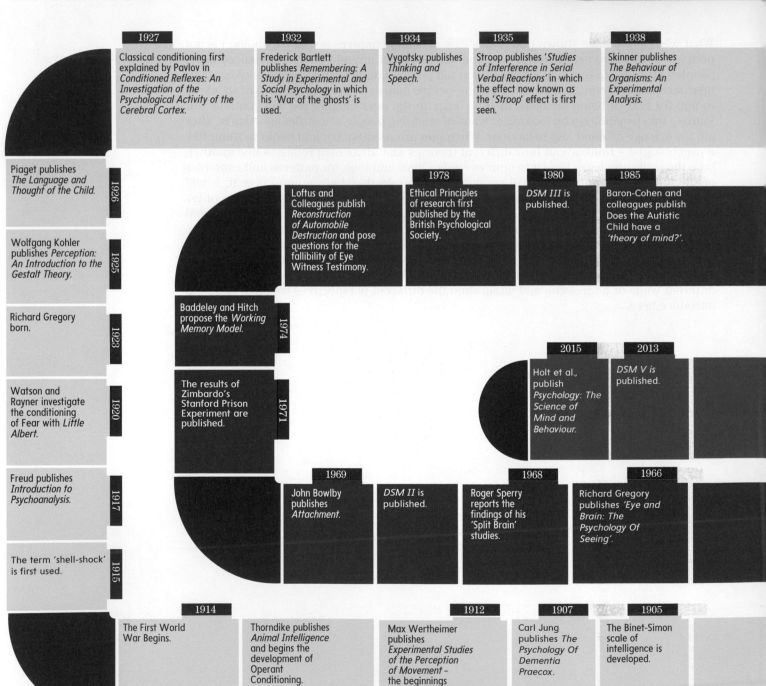

1650
René Descartes, founder of dualism, dies.

1927
Classical conditioning first explained by Pavlov in *Conditioned Reflexes: An Investigation of the Psychological Activity of the Cerebral Cortex.*

1932
Frederick Bartlett publishes *Remembering: A Study in Experimental and Social Psychology* in which his 'War of the ghosts' is used.

1934
Vygotsky publishes *Thinking and Speech.*

1935
Stroop publishes '*Studies of Interference in Serial Verbal Reactions*' in which the effect now known as the '*Stroop*' effect is first seen.

1938
Skinner publishes *The Behaviour of Organisms: An Experimental Analysis.*

1926
Piaget publishes *The Language and Thought of the Child.*

1925
Wolfgang Kohler publishes *Perception: An Introduction to the Gestalt Theory.*

1923
Richard Gregory born.

1920
Watson and Rayner investigate the conditioning of Fear with *Little Albert.*

1917
Freud publishes *Introduction to Psychoanalysis.*

1915
The term 'shell-shock' is first used.

1974
Baddeley and Hitch propose the *Working Memory Model.*

1971
The results of Zimbardo's Stanford Prison Experiment are published.

1978
Loftus and Colleagues publish *Reconstruction of Automobile Destruction* and pose questions for the fallibility of Eye Witness Testimony.

1980
DSM III is published.

1985
Baron-Cohen and colleagues publish Does the Autistic Child have a '*theory of mind?*'.

2015
Holt et al., publish *Psychology: The Science of Mind and Behaviour.*

2013
DSM V is published.

1969
John Bowlby publishes *Attachment.*

1968
DSM II is published.

1968
Roger Sperry reports the findings of his 'Split Brain' studies.

1966
Richard Gregory publishes '*Eye and Brain: The Psychology Of Seeing*'.

1914
The First World War Begins.

Thorndike publishes *Animal Intelligence* and begins the development of Operant Conditioning.

1912
Max Wertheimer publishes *Experimental Studies of the Perception of Movement –* the beginnings of Gestalt psychology.

1907
Carl Jung publishes *The Psychology Of Dementia Praecox.*

1905
The Binet-Simon scale of intelligence is developed.

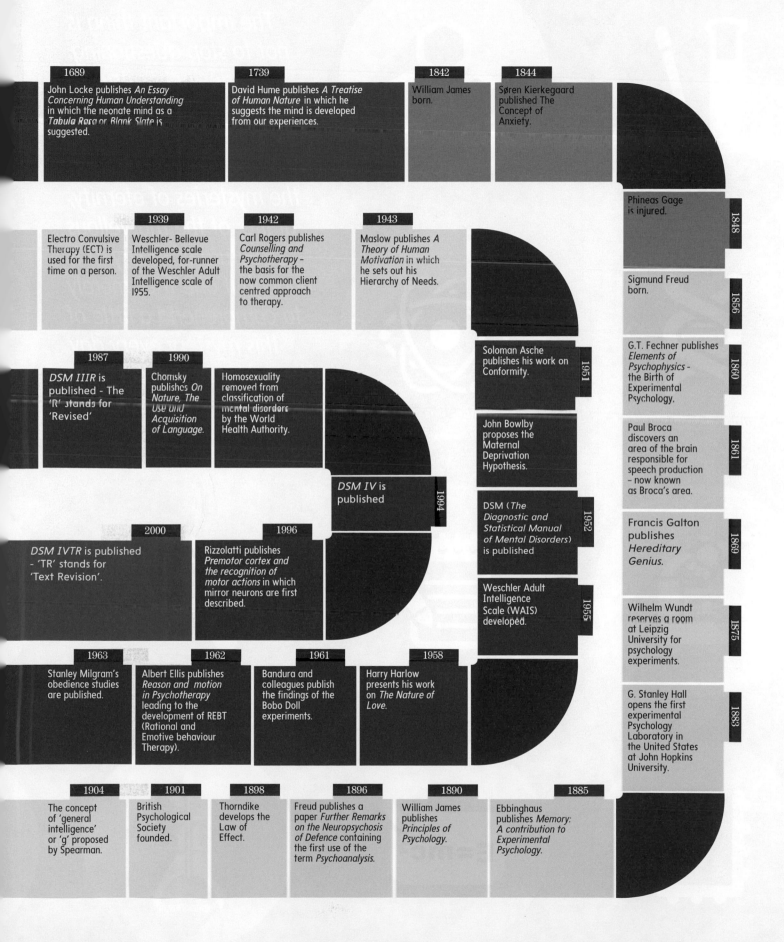

1689 — John Locke publishes *An Essay Concerning Human Understanding* in which the neonate mind as a *Tabula Rasa* or *Blank Slate* is suggested.

1739 — David Hume publishes *A Treatise of Human Nature* in which he suggests the mind is developed from our experiences.

1842 — William James born.

1844 — Søren Kierkegaard published The Concept of Anxiety.

1848 — Phineas Gage is injured.

1856 — Sigmund Freud born.

1860 — G.T. Fechner publishes *Elements of Psychophysics* – the Birth of Experimental Psychology.

1861 — Paul Broca discovers an area of the brain responsible for speech production – now known as Broca's area.

1869 — Francis Galton publishes *Hereditary Genius*.

1875 — Wilhelm Wundt reserves a room at Leipzig University for psychology experiments.

1883 — G. Stanley Hall opens the first experimental Psychology Laboratory in the United States at John Hopkins University.

1939 — Electro Convulsive Therapy (ECT) is used for the first time on a person.

1939 — Weschler-Bellevue Intelligence scale developed, for-runner of the Weschler Adult Intelligence scale of 1955.

1942 — Carl Rogers publishes *Counselling and Psychotherapy* – the basis for the now common client centred approach to therapy.

1943 — Maslow publishes *A Theory of Human Motivation* in which he sets out his Hierarchy of Needs.

1951 — Soloman Asche publishes his work on Conformity.

John Bowlby proposes the Maternal Deprivation Hypothesis.

1952 — DSM (*The Diagnostic and Statistical Manual of Mental Disorders*) is published

1955 — Weschler Adult Intelligence Scale (WAIS) developed.

1987 — *DSM IIIR* is published - The 'R' stands for 'Revised'

1990 — Chomsky publishes *On Nature, The Use and Acquisition of Language.*

Homosexuality removed from classification of mental disorders by the World Health Authority.

1994 — *DSM IV* is published

2000 — *DSM IVTR* is published - 'TR' stands for 'Text Revision'.

1996 — Rizzolatti publishes *Premotor cortex and the recognition of motor actions* in which mirror neurons are first described.

1963 — Stanley Milgram's obedience studies are published.

1962 — Albert Ellis publishes *Reason and motion in Psychotherapy* leading to the development of REBT (Rational and Emotive behaviour Therapy).

1961 — Bandura and colleagues publish the findings of the Bobo Doll experiments.

1958 — Harry Harlow presents his work on *The Nature of Love*.

1904 — The concept of 'general intelligence' or 'g' proposed by Spearman.

1901 — British Psychological Society founded.

1898 — Thorndike develops the Law of Effect.

1896 — Freud publishes a paper *Further Remarks on the Neuropsychosis of Defence* containing the first use of the term *Psychoanalysis*.

1890 — William James publishes *Principles of Psychology*.

1885 — Ebbinghaus publishes *Memory: A contribution to Experimental Psychology*.

The important thing is not to stop questioning. Curiosity has its own reason for existing. One cannot help but be in awe when he contemplates the mysteries of eternity, of life, of the marvellous structure of reality. It is enough if one tries merely to comprehend a little of this mystery every day. Never lose a holy curiosity.

Albert Einstein

$E=mc^2$

Studying behaviour scientifically

2

Chapter Outline

FIGURE 2.I What determines whether a bystander will help a victim?

Source: © Nikola Miljkovic.

On Friday 18 February 2011, a man chased and caught a gunman following an armed raid on a jeweller's shop in Peterborough, England. The man managed to knock the weapon from the hand of the robber as it was aimed at his head. The mystery man, believed to be in his twenties, disappeared without trace. (The story was reported in *The Telegraph*, 19 February 2011.)

In March 1964, 28-year-old Kitty Genovese was stabbed repeatedly and raped by a knife-wielding assailant as she returned from work to her New York City apartment at about 3 a.m. The attack lasted about 30 minutes, during which time her screams and pleas for help were heard by at least 38 neighbours. Many went to their windows to find out what was happening. Yet nobody assisted her, and by the time anyone called the police, she had died. The incident drew international attention from a shocked public, and commentators expressed outrage over 'bystander apathy' and people's refusal to 'get involved'.

Science frequently has all the mystery of a good detective story. Consider the psychological puzzle of bystander intervention. If you were in trouble and needed help from bystanders, would you receive it? Ordinary citizens often act decisively to help someone in need (Figure 2.1). However, people do not always come to the aid of others. Why do bystanders sometimes risk injury and death to assist a stranger yet at other times fail to intervene – even when helping or calling the police entails little personal risk?

In this chapter we explore principles and methods that form the foundation of psychological science. These principles also promote a way of thinking – critical thinking – that can serve you well in many aspects of your life.

SCIENTIFIC PRINCIPLES IN PSYCHOLOGY

Somewhere, something incredible is waiting to be known.   (Carl Sagan)

Science is about discovery – it is about finding things out, pursuing questions and riddles in the search for the truth. We learn about ourselves and the world in other ways: through philosophy, religion, art, music and literature, as well as through learning from loved ones. What distinguishes science from these approaches is that it is a process guided by certain principles.

SCIENTIFIC ATTITUDES

Nothing in life is to be feared, it is only to be understood. Now is the time to understand more, so that we may fear less.   (Marie Curie)

Curiosity, scepticism and open-mindedness are driving forces behind scientific inquiry. The good scientist has an insatiable curiosity, and is forever asking questions and reviewing and assessing the work done by other scientists in their pursuit. Many scientists will tell you that in their pursuit to solve a problem they often find more questions than they do answers and so their work goes on. Like a master detective, the good scientist is an incurable sceptic. Each claim is met with the reply, 'Show me your evidence'. Scientists also must remain open-minded to conclusions that are supported by facts, even if those conclusions refute their own beliefs. The mistake many people make is that they seem to think that science is something only scientists do. Not true. We all do it every day, but many of us just do not notice. When you add a little salt to your cooking, and taste it to see if it needs more or something else before you serve it, you are doing science. You are altering a system, your food, and testing it to see the effect your alteration had. You are manipulating a 'variable' and assessing the effect by measuring another variable. We will

discuss this more formally in this chapter. Science is, then, just a way of thinking about the world. We all do it, some of us more formally than others.

Science is a way of thinking much more than it is a body of knowledge.   (Carl Sagan)

Evidence-Based Practice

When we change our behaviour based on evidence we are engaging in evidence-based behaviour modifications. Good science is evidence based, changes are made and conclusions drawn on careful observation of how our manipulations have affected the object of our investigation. In psychology, evidence-based practice describes the preference for interventions in mental health treatment that have evidence to support their use. This evidence comes from the application of scientific principles that we will describe in this chapter. The importance of an evidence-based approach is mirrored in the scientist practitioner model of training that psychologists are often part of. This model maintains that the psychologist is primarily a scientist, going about their business with a careful, measured scientific approach that will inform their professional activities in an evidence-based approach. It is here that we see the pursuit of psychology most clearly defined as scientific. Psychology really is the *science* of mind and behaviour.

GATHERING EVIDENCE: STEPS IN THE SCIENTIFIC PROCESS

Figure 2.2 shows how scientific inquiry often proceeds.

Step I: Curiosity and the Research Question Sparks the First Step

We observe something noteworthy and ask a question about it. Following the Kitty Genovese murder, two psychologists, John Darley and Bibb Latané, met up and discussed

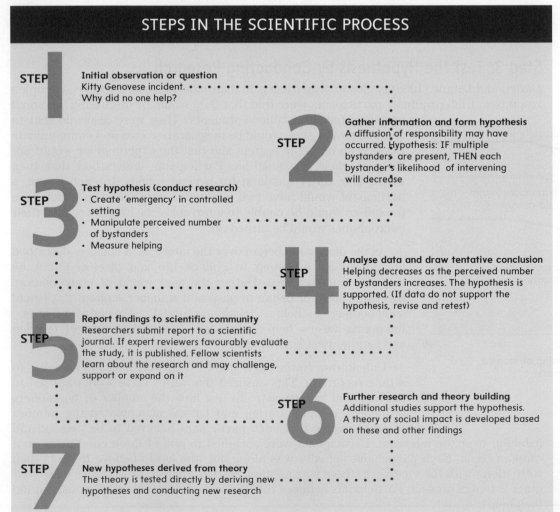

STEPS IN THE SCIENTIFIC PROCESS

STEP 1
Initial observation or question
Kitty Genovese incident.
Why did no one help?

STEP 2
Gather information and form hypothesis
A diffusion of responsibility may have occurred. Hypothesis: IF multiple bystanders are present, THEN each bystander's likelihood of intervening will decrease

STEP 3
Test hypothesis (conduct research)
• Create 'emergency' in controlled setting
• Manipulate perceived number of bystanders
• Measure helping

STEP 4
Analyse data and draw tentative conclusion
Helping decreases as the perceived number of bystanders increases. The hypothesis is supported. (If data do not support the hypothesis, revise and retest)

STEP 5
Report findings to scientific community
Researchers submit report to a scientific journal. If expert reviewers favourably evaluate the study, it is published. Fellow scientists learn about the research and may challenge, support or expand on it

STEP 6
Further research and theory building
Additional studies support the hypothesis. A theory of social impact is developed based on these and other findings

STEP 7
New hypotheses derived from theory
The theory is tested directly by deriving new hypotheses and conducting new research

FIGURE 2.2 Using the scientific method.

This sequence represents a common path through a scientific investigative process. In other cases, scientists begin with an observation or question, gather background information, and proceed directly to research without testing hypotheses or trying to build theories.

the curious case. They observed that nobody helped Kitty Genovese and then asked the question 'Why?' How was it that 38 people could witness a crime as violent as this and not call the police? Darley and Latané were not at all convinced by the 'bystander apathy' explanation the media offered in their reports. It was unlikely, in their opinion, that every one of the witnesses could have been apathetic to this degree. Their social psychological instincts told them that the social environment can powerfully influence behaviour. In their investigations of the incident they identified certain aspects of the case that were relevant psychologically. Importantly in this respect, the bystanders could see that others around them were looking out of their windows and had their lights turned on. It was clear to each of the bystanders that others were aware of the incident and so, even though they might have been concerned about Genovese, they may well have assumed that someone else would raise the alarm or go to her rescue. It is here that we arrive at our research question – the thing that drives us to investigate further. For Darley and Latané this question was a resounding one, and one that many of us reading the story will also have some to – 'Why did no one help?'

Step 2: Gather Information and Form a Hypothesis

Scientists examine whether any studies, theories and other information already exist that might help answer their question, and then they formulate a tentative explanation. Noting that many bystanders had been present and that each one probably knew that others were witnessing Genovese's plight, Darley and Latané combined these clues to arrive at a possible explanation: a diffusion of responsibility reduced the likelihood that any one bystander would feel responsible for helping. This tentative explanation is then translated into a **hypothesis**, a specific prediction about some phenomenon or other that often takes the form of an 'If–Then' statement: 'In an emergency, IF multiple bystanders are present, THEN the likelihood that any one bystander will intervene is reduced.'

> **hypothesis** a specific prediction about some phenomenon or other

Step 3: Test the Hypothesis by Conducting Research

Darley and Latané (1968) staged an 'emergency' in their laboratory and observed people's responses. Undergraduate participants were told that they would be discussing 'personal problems faced by college students'. They were also told that to ensure privacy, they would be in separate rooms and communicate through an intercom system and that the experimenter would not listen to their conversation. Participants understood that they would take turns speaking for several rounds. In each round, a participant would have two minutes to speak, during which time the others would be unable to interrupt or be heard, because their microphones would be turned off.

As the discussion began over the intercom, a speaker described his difficulties adjusting to college life and disclosed that he suffered from seizures. During the next round of conversation, this same speaker began to gasp and stammer, saying: '. . . Could somebody-er-er – help . . . [choking sounds] . . . I'm gonna die-er-er – I'm gonna die-er – help . . . seizure [chokes, then silence]' (Darley and Latané, 1968, p. 379).

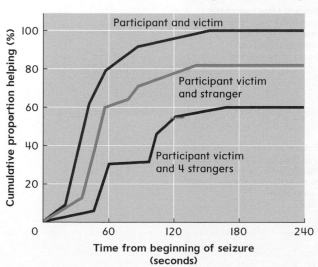

FIGURE 2.3 Helping in an emergency.
Source: Data from Darley and Latané, 1968.

Unbeknown to the participants, they were actually listening to a tape recording. This ensured that all of them were exposed to the identical 'emergency'. To test how the number of bystanders influences helping, Darley and Latané manipulated the number of other people that each participant believed to be present and listening over the intercom. Participants were assigned to one of three conditions on a random basis. Each participant actually was alone but was led to believe that (1) they were alone with the victim, (2) there was another listener present, or (3) there were four other listeners present. Participants believed that the seizure was real and serious. But did they help?

Step 4: Analyse Data, Draw Tentative Conclusions and Report Findings

Information (data) is collected and analysed. As Figure 2.3 shows, Darley and Latané found that all participants who thought they were alone with the victim helped within three minutes of the seizure. As the number of presumed bystanders increased, the proportion of actual participants who helped decreased, and those who helped took longer to respond. These findings support the diffusion-of-responsibility explanation and illustrate how research can contradict common-sense adages such as 'There's safety in numbers'. As you will see throughout this book, many common-sense beliefs have not survived the cutting edge of psychological research.

Step 5: Build a Body of Knowledge: Ask Further Questions, Conduct More Research, Develop and Test Theories

Scientists communicate their findings to the scientific community. Darley and Latané submitted to a scientific journal an article describing their research. Expert, peer reviewers favourably evaluated the quality and importance of their bystander research, so the journal published the article. Scientists may also present their research at professional conferences, in books and in journals designed specifically for use online, such as *Philica*. Disseminating research allows fellow scientists to learn about new ideas and findings, to scrutinize the research and to challenge or expand on it. As additional evidence comes in, scientists attempt to build theories. A **theory** is a set of formal statements that explains how and why certain events are related to one another. Theories are broader than hypotheses. For example, dozens of experiments revealed that diffusion of responsibility occurred across a range of situations. Latané then combined the principle of diffusion of responsibility with other principles of group behaviour to develop a broader *theory of social impact*, which others have since used to explain a variety of human social behaviours (Latané & Bourgeois, 2001).

> **theory** a set of formal statements that explains how and why certain events are related to one another

Theories are used to develop new hypotheses, which are then tested by conducting additional research and gathering new evidence. In this manner the scientific process becomes self-correcting. If research consistently supports the hypotheses derived from the theory, confidence in the theory becomes stronger. If the predictions made by the theory are not supported, then it will need to be modified or, ultimately, discarded. Accurately and carefully communicating the methodology applied in the research is a very important part of science. It allows others to replicate findings, extend their research and take it further. Replication of research is also an extremely important component in developing support for the hypothesis and developing confidence in the theory under investigation, and we describe this a little later in the chapter.

TWO APPROACHES TO UNDERSTANDING BEHAVIOUR

Humans have a strong desire to understand why things happen. Why do scientists favour the preceding step-by-step approach to understanding behaviour over the approach typically involved in everyday common sense: hindsight?

Hindsight (After-the-Fact Understanding)

> *Life is lived forwards, but understood backwards.*   (Søren Kierkegaard)

Many people erroneously believe that psychology is nothing more than common sense. It is always easy to arrive at an explanation to account for a statement you may hear. For instance, if you heard that when people wear seatbelts they drive more responsibly you might explain this by saying 'this is clearly because the seatbelt reminds them of the danger they and others are in, and so their driving reflects this'. When you are told that wearing seatbelts does *not* make a person drive more responsibly, but in fact there is contested evidence to suggest that it makes them drive *faster* then it is not difficult to arrive at just as suitable an explanation. You may, for instance say 'of course people drive faster. They feel safer wearing a seatbelt, so think they can drive faster and still be as safe as when they were not wearing one'.

Consider the following statements adapted from Stouffer et al. (Stouffer, Lumsdaine, Lumsdaine, & Williams, 1949a; Stouffer, Suchman, De Vinney, Star, & Williams, 1949b),

who looked at attitudes and behaviours of soldiers in the Second World War. How would you account for each of them?

1. Compared with white soldiers, black soldiers were less motivated to become officers.
2. During basic training, soldiers from rural areas had higher morale and adapted better than soldiers from large cities.
3. Soldiers were more motivated to return home while the fighting was going on than they were after the war ended.

You should have no difficulty explaining these results. Typical reasoning might go something like this: (1) owing to widespread prejudice, black soldiers knew that they had little chance of becoming officers. Why should they torment themselves wanting something that was unattainable? (2) It is obvious that the rigours of basic training would seem easier to people from farm settings, who were used to hard work and rising at the crack of dawn. (3) Any sane person would have wanted to go home while bullets were flying and people were dying.

What happens if we reverse the statements?

1. Compared to white soldiers, black soldiers were more motivated to become officers.
2. During basic training, soldiers from rural areas had lower morale and adapted worse than soldiers from large cities.
3. Soldiers less motivated to return home while the fighting was going on than they were after the war ended.

You should find that it is just as simple to arrive at explanations for the statements now as it was the first time you did it. After-the-fact explanations for almost any result are easy to arrive at.

The major limitation of relying solely on hindsight is that past events usually can be explained in many ways, and there is no sure way to know which – if any – of the explanations is correct. You may find the phrase *post hoc, ergo propter hoc* used in other textbooks and sometimes as a criticism of research findings. *Post hoc* means 'after the event', *ergo* means 'and so, or therefore' and *propter hoc* means 'resulting from the event'. Literally, the assumption is made, after the event, that because something is observed it must be a result of the event itself. A causal relationship has been assumed even though there may well be no causal relationship at all, one of the perils of 'post hoc' or 'after-the-fact' reasoning.

Despite this drawback, after-the-fact understanding can provide insights and is often the foundation on which further scientific inquiry is built. For example, Darley and Latané's diffusion-of-responsibility explanation was initially based on after-the-fact reasoning about the Kitty Genovese murder.

Understanding through Prediction, Control and Theory Building

Whenever possible, scientists prefer to test their understanding of 'what causes what' more directly. If we truly understand the causes of a given behaviour, then we should be able to predict the conditions under which that behaviour will occur in the future. Furthermore, if we can control those conditions (e.g., in the laboratory), then we should be able to produce that behaviour.

Darley and Latané's research illustrates this approach. They predicted that owing to a diffusion of responsibility, the presence of multiple bystanders during an emergency would reduce individual helping. Next, they carefully staged an emergency and controlled participants' beliefs about the number of bystanders present. Their prediction was supported. Understanding through prediction and control is a scientific alternative to after-the-fact understanding.

Theory building is the strongest test of scientific understanding, because good theories generate an integrated network of predictions. A good theory has several important characteristics.

1. It incorporates existing knowledge within a broad framework; that is, it organizes information in a meaningful way.
2. It is testable. It generates new hypotheses whose accuracy can be evaluated by gathering new evidence (Figure 2.4).
3. The predictions made by the theory are supported by the findings of new research.
4. It conforms to the *law of parsimony:* if two theories can explain and predict the same phenomenon equally well, the simpler theory is the preferred one.

Even when a theory is supported by many successful predictions, it is never to be regarded as an absolute (always happens) truth. There is always the possibility that some future observation will contradict it or that a newer and more accurate theory will take its place. The rather overused example is that of gravity. Gravity is a theory, not a fact. Given a set of assumptions and in a particular environment, what goes up, must come down. You can test this hypothesis over and over again, and you will find that throwing items into the air is followed by their returning to earth. There is a great deal of evidence to support this particular hypothesis. Many billions of items have returned to earth after being elevated in some way. However, it would take only a single item to remain 'up' when thrown skywards to disprove the hypothesis and we would have to start all over again with a new hypothesis. The displacement of old beliefs and theories by newer ones is the essence of scientific progress, and the process never stops. What we find out today, as scientists, will advance our understanding and further develop theories. Our work as scientists is never lost. It is here forever as part of the process.

Finally, although scientists use prediction as a test of 'understanding', this does not mean that prediction requires understanding. Based on experience, even a child can predict that thunder will follow lightning without knowing why it does so. But prediction based on understanding (i.e., theory building) has advantages: it satisfies our curiosity and generates principles that can be applied to new situations that we have not yet directly experienced.

DEFINING AND MEASURING VARIABLES

Psychologists study variables and the relations among them. A **variable**, quite simply, is any characteristic or factor that can vary (later in the chapter (page 58) we discuss the concepts of variables in a little more detail). Gender is a variable: some people are female, others male. People's age, weight and typing speed are variables, as are concepts such as intelligence and stress. There were three major variables in Darley and Latané's bystander experiment: (1) the number of other bystanders that the real participants thought were present, (2) whether a participant helped the victim or not, and (3) for those who helped, how many seconds passed before they responded.

Because any variable (such as stress) may mean different things to different people, scientists must define their terms clearly. When conducting research, scientists do this by defining variables operationally. An **operational definition** defines a variable in terms of the specific procedures used to produce or measure it. Operational definitions translate abstract terms into something observable and measurable that the rest of the scientific community can understand clearly.

For example, suppose we want to study the relation between stress and academic performance among university students. How shall we operationally define our concepts? 'Academic performance' could mean a single test score, a grade for a module, or one's overall average. So, for our study, let us define it as students' final examination scores in an introductory chemistry course. As for 'stress', before or during the examination we could measure students' levels of muscle tension or stress hormones, or ask them to report how worried they feel. During the test we might observe their frequency of nail biting. We also could define stress in terms of environmental conditions, such as whether the examination questions and grading scale are easy or difficult. The levels of analysis summarize how we might operationally define examination stress at the biological, psychological and environmental levels.

FIGURE 2.4 Is the statement 'Elixir of Life will let us live forever' a testable hypothesis?

Yes - if people drink it but still die at some point, then we have refuted the hypothesis therefore it is testable. It is, however, impossible to absolutely prove true. If a person drinks the potion, then no matter how long she or he lives - even a million years - she or he might die the next day. Thus we cannot prove that the potion can make you live forever.

Source: ©iStock.com/marioaguilar

> **Focus 2.1** Describe some characteristics of a good theory.

> **variable** any characteristic or factor that can vary
>
> **operational definition** defines a variable in terms of the specific procedures used to produce or measure it

To define a concept operationally, we must be able to measure it. Measurement is challenging because psychologists study incredibly varied and complex processes. Some processes are directly observable, but others are not. Fortunately, psychologists have numerous measurement techniques at their disposal. For instance, they may use self-report techniques, such as questionnaires and interviews, or physiological techniques, such as brain scanning, or behavioural techniques where behaviours are observed or measured in some way. There are often a number of different ways to operationalize a variable, and different members of the scientific community may have a preference for a particular method. For instance, a psychologist working in a biological field may choose to operationalize their variable differently from a psychologist investigating the same topic from a psychophysical perspective.

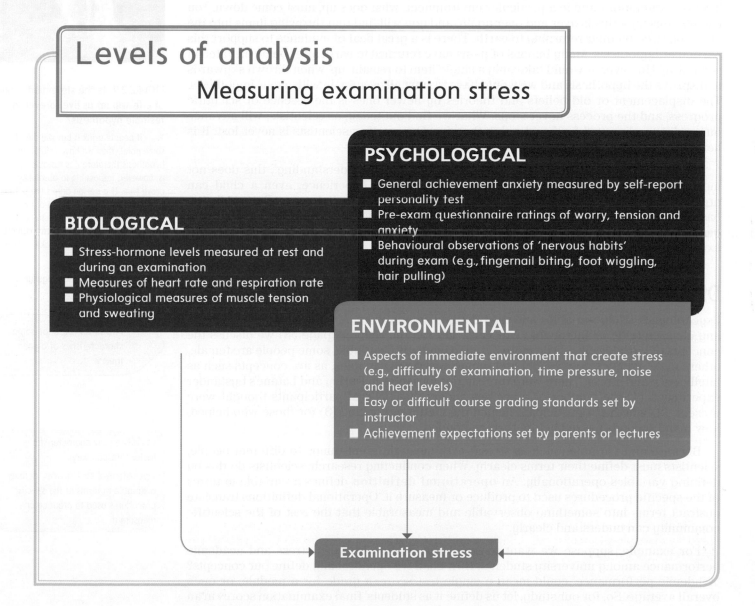

Levels of analysis
Measuring examination stress

BIOLOGICAL

- Stress-hormone levels measured at rest and during an examination
- Measures of heart rate and respiration rate
- Physiological measures of muscle tension and sweating

PSYCHOLOGICAL

- General achievement anxiety measured by self-report personality test
- Pre-exam questionnaire ratings of worry, tension and anxiety
- Behavioural observations of 'nervous habits' during exam (e.g., fingernail biting, foot wiggling, hair pulling)

ENVIRONMENTAL

- Aspects of immediate environment that create stress (e.g., difficulty of examination, time pressure, noise and heat levels)
- Easy or difficult course grading standards set by instructor
- Achievement expectations set by parents or lectures

Examination stress

Self-Reports and Reports by Others

Self-report measures ask people to report on their own knowledge, attitudes, feelings, experiences or behaviour. This information can be gathered in several ways, such as through interviews or questionnaires. The accuracy of self-reports hinges on people's ability and willingness to respond honestly. Especially when questions focus on sensitive topics, such

as sexual habits or drug use, self-reports may be distorted by *social desirability bias*, that is, the tendency to respond in a socially acceptable manner rather than according to how one truly feels or behaves. Researchers try to minimize this bias by allowing participants to respond confidentially or anonymously. Questionnaires can also be designed to reduce social desirability bias.

We also can get information about someone's behaviour by obtaining *reports made by other people*, such as parents, spouses, and teachers who know the person. University students might be asked to rate their classmates' personality traits, and job supervisors might be asked to rate a worker's competence. As with self-reports, researchers try to maximize participants' honesty in reporting about other people.

Observations of Behaviour

Another measurement approach is to *observe and record overt (i.e., directly visible) behaviour.* In an animal learning experiment, we might measure how often a rat follows the correct path in a maze. In Darley and Latané's (1968) bystander emergency experiment, they recorded whether college students helped a seizure victim. Psychologists also develop *coding systems* to record different categories of behaviour. If we observe how a parent behaves while a child performs a task, we might code each instance of parental behaviour into categories such as 'praises child', 'assists child', 'criticizes child', and so forth. Once a coding system is developed, observers are trained to use it properly so that their measurements will be *reliable* (i.e., consistent). If two observers watching the same behaviours repeatedly disagree in their coding (e.g., one says the parent 'praised' and another says the parent 'assisted'), then the data are unreliable and of little use. Ideally, a coder will be an independent in the data-gathering procedure, that is, they will be 'blind' to the aims and hypotheses under assessment thus ensuring their judgements are not influenced by their expectations of what they hope to, or might be expected to observe.

Humans and other animals may behave differently when they know they are being observed. To counter this problem, and if this is considered to be an issue in the design, researchers may choose to camouflage themselves or use **unobtrusive measures**, which record behaviour in a way that keeps participants unaware that they are being observed. A person's choice of words in a conversation may reveal something about them and something about their true feelings and meanings. Careful analysis of a discussion (called discourse analysis) is an example of an unobtrusive measure.

> **unobtrusive measure** records behaviour in a way that keeps participants unaware that they are being observed
>
> **archival measure** record or document that already exists

Psychologists also gather information about behaviour by using **archival measures**, which are records or documents that already exist. For example, researchers assessing a programme to reduce drunk driving could examine police records to measure how many people were arrested for driving while drunk before and after the programme was implemented.

Psychological Tests

Psychologists develop and use specialized tests to measure many types of variables. For example, *personality tests*, which assess people's personality traits, often contain series of questions that ask how a person typically feels or behaves (e.g., 'True or false: I prefer to be alone rather than in social gatherings.'). In essence, such tests are specialized self-reports. Other personality tests present a series of ambiguous stimuli (e.g., pictures that could have different meanings), and personality traits are judged based on how a person interprets these stimuli.

Other psychological tests consist of performance tasks. For example, *intelligence tests* may ask people to assemble objects or solve arithmetic problems. *Neuropsychological tests* help diagnose normal and abnormal brain functioning by measuring how well people perform mental and physical tasks, such as recalling lists of words or manipulating objects (Abramowitz & Caron, 2010).

> **Focus 2.2** Why are operational definitions important? Identify four major ways to measure behaviour and explain a limitation of each one.

Physiological Measures

Physiological responses can be recorded to assess what people are experiencing. Measures of heart rate, blood pressure, respiration rate, hormonal secretions, and electrical and

biochemical processes in the brain have long been the mainstay of researchers working within the biological perspective, but these measures have become increasingly important in many other areas of psychology. Physiological responses can have their own interpretive problems. For example, if a person shows increased heart rate and brain activity in a particular situation, what emotion or thought is being expressed? The links between specific patterns of physiological activity and particular mental events are far from being completely understood.

 In review

- Curiosity, scepticism and open-mindedness are key scientific attitudes. The scientific process proceeds through several steps: (1) asking questions based on some type of observation, (2) formulating a tentative explanation and a testable hypothesis, (3) conducting research to test the hypothesis, (4) analysing the data and drawing a tentative conclusion, (5) reporting one's findings to the scientific community, (6) building a theory and (7) using the theory to generate new hypotheses, which are tested by more research.

- In everyday life we typically use hindsight to explain behaviour. Hindsight is flawed because there may be many possible explanations and no way to assess which is correct. Psychologists prefer to test their understanding through prediction, control and theory building.

- A good theory organizes known facts, gives rise to additional hypotheses that are testable, is supported by the findings of new research and is parsimonious.

- An operational definition defines a concept or variable in terms of the specific procedures used to produce or measure it.

- To measure behaviour, psychologists obtain people's self-reports and reports from others who know the participants, directly observe behaviour, use unobtrusive measures, analyse archival data, administer psychological tests and measure physiological responses.

ETHICAL PRINCIPLES IN RESEARCH

FIGURE 2.5 Ethical standards are designed in part to protect the welfare of participants
Source: ANNABELLA BLUESKY/SCIENCE PHOTO LIBRARY

When conducting research, scientists must weigh the knowledge and possible applications to be gained against potential risks to research participants. To safeguard the rights of participants, researchers must adhere to ethical standards set by government regulations and national psychological organizations (Figure 2.5). Animal subjects must also be treated in accordance with established ethical guidelines. At academic and research institutions, it is a growing practice that special committees review the ethical issues involved in research proposals. If a proposed study is considered ethically questionable, it must be modified or the research cannot be conducted.

The national psychological associations are collectively described as 'the professional bodies'. Most countries, including Ireland, Holland, Denmark, Britain, Finland, Norway and South Africa all have one. The Scandinavian Psychological Society also covers many important ethical considerations relating to research. Even if not a member, and working in a university experimentally, adhering to the principles of ethical research identified by these bodies is a very important rule. There are subtle differences in the codes of ethical practice of the professional bodies, but essentially the codes all describe principles of conduct when conducting research in psychology.

The following principles are representative of those adopted by professional bodies across the world:

1. *Competence:* maintenance of high levels of training, and operation within boundaries of ability.
2. *Responsibility:* performing professional duties with utmost care.
3. *Integrity:* being honest and accurate.
4. *Respect:* respecting people's dignity and rights to confidentiality and self-determination.

ETHICAL STANDARDS IN HUMAN RESEARCH

These *ethics codes* also provide specific guidelines for psychological activities, including research.

Informed Consent

According to the ethical standard of **informed consent**, before people agree to participate in research they should be informed about:

- the study's purpose and procedures
- the study's potential benefits
- potential risks to participants
- the right to decline participation and withdraw at any time without penalty
- whether responses will be confidential and, if not, how privacy will be safeguarded.

> **informed consent** before people agree to participate in research they should be informed about: the study's purpose and procedures; the study's potential benefits; potential risks to participants; the right to decline participation and withdraw at any time without penalty; whether responses will be confidential and, if not, how privacy will be safeguarded

Working with Children or Vulnerable People

When children or other vulnerable people, such as those with mental illnesses, who cannot give true informed consent, are involved, consent must be obtained from parents, guardians or, in some cases, doctors. To safeguard a participant's right to privacy, researchers typically gather and report data in ways that keep participants' identity anonymous or confidential, often referring to specific cases or individuals by numbers or initials rather than names.

Distress, Stigma and Harm

Participants should not be made to feel bad in any way. They should not be distressed, or feel stigmatized at all. The origins of distress could be in the procedure or the subject matter under investigation, and this needs to be avoided. For instance, a psychologist may be interested in people's reactions to images of war, or to pornographic material. These may well cause offence and distress to some participants, and so very careful ethical consideration should be given to a proposal for this research. Walker, Holt, and Lewis (2010) point out a very simple, but subtle mistake than many researchers make where informed consent is concerned and related to another important issue of avoiding distress and stigma. Imagine a scenario where a lecturer, keen on collecting data quickly, hands out a set of questionnaires at the start of a lecture, asking participants to hand them in at the end. You, a student, may decide not to fill in the questionnaire because you just do not want to spare the time, or because you really do not want to hand over the information required. This refusal is obvious to the lecturer and everyone else in the room. You are singled out as a 'refuser', and this is not acceptable – your right to participate or not without penalty has been damaged.

It should really go without saying that a participant should not be harmed in any way during the procedure. Researching responses to pain is a good example here. Those interested in the relationship between pain and concentration are not allowed to cause pain simply by poking the participant in the leg with a sharp stick. One procedure they are allowed to use is called the cold-pressor test where a participant places their hand in iced

water. This is a surprisingly painful, but not damaging, procedure. If done correctly, the participant is in full control and able to remove their hand whenever they like. It has been used in the investigation of how certain procedures such as hypnosis can help with pain tolerance (**Chapter 6**).

Chapter 6, Page 260

Deception

Deception, which occurs when participants are misled about the nature of a study, is controversial. Consider the Darley and Latané (1968) bystander experiment. Participants were not told that the study was going to examine how they would respond to an emergency, nor were they informed that the procedure (someone presumably having a seizure) might cause them stress. Deception violates the principle of informed consent, but its proponents argue that when studying certain types of behaviours, deception is the only way to obtain natural, spontaneous responses from participants. Darley and Latané's participants, for example, had to believe that the emergency was significant and real. Guidelines may permit deception only when no other feasible alternative is available and the study has scientific, educational or applied benefits that clearly outweigh the ethical costs of deceiving participants. For instance, you may be interested in finding out whether distracting a person in some way means that they forget whether or not to carry out a task. The participant may be told at the very start of the session to remember to turn off the light when they leave the room 45 minutes later. You may then enter into a series of memory and physical tasks designed specifically to distract the participant from remembering to do this. The goal of the procedure is to investigate whether your tasks interfere with the original memory task, to turn out the light. Obviously, telling the participant this ('All the tasks you will do are largely irrelevant, we are only interested in whether you remember to turn out the light') will spoil your procedure, and so you must deceive them by not telling them the true nature of the task. When deception is used, however, the true purpose of the study should be explained to participants after it is over in a 'debriefing' procedure. The overwhelming majority of psychological studies do not involve deception of this or any other kind and, where they do; careful consideration is given to the proposal to carry out the research when the work is considered for ethical approval.

Privacy and Confidentiality

Those who take part in research should be able to do so with the assurance that their information will be kept private. This means that the data they provide in the study should not be linked to them publicly. Their confidentiality should be respected. They should not be identified in reports. In addition to this, their data should be carefully stored so that no one looking at it in the future can identify the individual. This is sometimes harder to achieve than you might expect, and those of us who conduct psychological research must provide workable solutions to this issue when proposing our ideas to ethics committees and authorities who might fund our research. One way in which this is done is for the participant to choose an acronym by which they are happy to be known for the course of the research. They may choose their initials for instance; the reason why they may need to do this is that their responses on different sessions of the research perhaps at different stages of treatment, or on different days, may need to be linked in some way. Initials or a number identifier will allow researchers to do this without recording the participant's name with their data.

Debriefing

This is a terribly important part of the research process. After the participant has completed their involvement in the data they would be provided with a document explaining the background to the research. The debrief also helps the researcher check carefully whether the participant has come to any harm during the procedure. The debriefing document may be replaced or augmented with a careful conversation with the researcher. A good debrief will provide information about where a participant may go for support should they feel they need it and should they feel any ill effects following the procedure. The real aim of the debrief is to return the participant to the state they were in at the start of the procedure.

At this stage the participant is encouraged to ask questions to reassure themselves of anything they may feel uncomfortable or curious about. Many researchers will tell you that a 30-minute procedure should be timetabled for an hour at least, to allow for a full and comprehensive debrief. In some cases participants are extremely interested in the work and often ask related questions in this period that researchers find very useful in the further development of their work. For instance, if taking part in a task requiring the differentiation of two sounds the participant may have applied some kind of strategy when making their decision. This information may be of use and interest to the researcher who will analyse and present the work on its completion.

ETHICAL STANDARDS IN ANIMAL RESEARCH

In a minority of experimental procedures in psychology, animals are used as subjects. This includes research done in the wild and in more controlled settings. Rodents and birds comprise 90% of the animals studied; non-human primates comprise another 5%.

Some psychologists study animals to discover principles that shed light on human behaviour, and some do so to learn more about other species. As in medical research, some studies expose animals to conditions considered too hazardous for humans. This topic is controversial, with some believing that animals should never be used in research. Many scientists feel that careful animal research is an important route to scientific progress in psychology.

Ethics guidelines require that animals be treated humanely and that the potential importance of the research clearly justify the risks to which they are exposed. This determination, however, is not always easy to make, and people often disagree. For example, should researchers be allowed to inject a drug into an animal in order to learn whether that drug might permanently impair memory? Before animal research can be conducted, it must be reviewed and approved by panels that often include non-scientists.

Animal research is debated both outside and within the psychological community (Herzog, 2005). Psychologists agree that it is morally wrong to subject animals to needless suffering. Many scientists, however, do not agree with anti-vivisectionists who maintain that animals should never be used in research 'which is not for the benefit of the animals involved' (Goodman, 1982, p. 61). Proponents point to important medical and psychological advances made possible by animal research. They might ask: 'Does the prospect of finding a cure for cancer or of identifying harmful drug effects or the causes of psychological disorders justify exposing some animals to harm?'

Other research using animals in captivity is focused on how animals behave. A healthy, psychologically sound animal is more likely to behave 'normally' and as such their welfare is extremely important. Legislation to ensure animal welfare of this kind is carefully monitored by groups such as the International Fund for Animal Welfare (IFAW). In 1956 the Treaty of Rome was signed to set up the European Union. The treaty did not include any legislation to account for animal welfare, but in 1997 it was amended to take this into account. The 'Treaty of Amsterdam' became effective in 1999.

Although animal research has declined slightly in recent decades, the ethical questions remain as vexing as ever. What is most encouraging is that the welfare of animals in research is receiving the careful attention it deserves.

A point often overlooked is the importance of animal welfare to good research. Consider a laboratory in which animals are kept in tiny, cramped, dirty conditions. The result would be that the animals' behaviour is unlikely to be 'normal' and likely to reflect the unpleasant surroundings in which they spend their lives. The stress they experience may well influence their behaviour when tested. As such it is in the interest of those whose job it is to look after laboratory animals to do so carefully and respectfully, not only because it is a duty to look after animals in this way, but because in not doing so they jeopardize the science to which the animals will contribute.

Focus 2.3 Identify major ethical issues in human and animal research.

Current topic

WHERE WE CAN'T TRUST THE DATA, WE CAN'T TRUST THE SUBJECT

Something else to consider when discussing ethics is the ethical behaviour of the researcher – or in some cases the lack of it. As we heard in Chapter 1 when we described the Monster Study (Tudor, 1939) – where stuttering was induced in orphaned children – the work itself may not be carried out ethically. There are occasions where scientists make up their data entirely. Where this comes to light, and it does in waves occasionally, their careers are either damaged or ruined and, more importantly for all of us, people's trust in our subject is damaged. Cyril Burt, for instance, worked with identical twins and claimed that his data showed that intelligence was inherited. Later however, his data was shown to have been fabricated. The problem here goes a good deal deeper. Although the findings have been discredited, and Burt's reputation among those of us that are aware of this black mark on our subject's history are fully aware of the issues, people do stumble on his work and findings occasionally and do not look further to find these shameful details. The work, then, continues to influence people's thinking and can still cause great problems to these contemporary researchers.

 Chapter I, Page 13

In a case that rocked psychology and science in general, the Dutch Social psychologist, Diederik Stapel, was accused and found guilty of serious scientific fraud. In September 2011 he was removed from his position as Professor of Social Psychology in Tilburg University as soon as the fraud was first identified. No one, though, was prepared for the scope of the problem Stapel had generated. His crime against psychology and science was inventing his data on a huge scale in over 50 published papers, doctoral theses and chapters. The scale of this dishonesty rocked psychology to its core. In an open email about the state of social psychology from Nobel Prize winner Daniel Kahneman, the impact on science and psychological research of Stapel's fraud is stated very clearly:

> Your field is now the poster child for doubts about the integrity of psychological research. Your problem is not with a few people who have actively challenged the validity of some priming results. It is with the much larger population of colleagues who in the past accepted your surprising results as facts when they were published. These people have now attached a question mark to the field, and it is your responsibility to remove it.

Removing the problem is not at all simple. Exorcizing published work in a digital age and in the many thousands of copies of journals containing it is no simple task. The scientific community and psychology in general are ashamed that this has happened and we must do all we can to be vigilant and to emphasize to our colleagues, peers and where we can our students, that this behaviour is at the very top of the list of things any self respecting scientist or student must never do – for their own sake, and for that of our subject and for the sake of science in general. We will pick Stapel's story up later in the chapter where we discuss the role of replication in science.

 In review

- Psychological research follows extensive ethical guidelines. In human research, key issues are the use of informed consent, the participants' right to privacy, potential risks to participants and the use of deception.

- Ethical guidelines require that animals be treated humanely and that the risks to which they are exposed be justified by the potential importance of the research. As in human research, before animal research can be conducted it must be reviewed and approved, often by ethics review boards that include non-scientists.

- Scientists have a responsibility to conduct themselves ethically both in the design and execution of their work as well as in the dissemination of their data. We as scientists have a responsibility to live up to the trust society puts in us. If we do not, we bring ourselves, science and psychology into disrepute.

METHODS OF RESEARCH

Like detectives searching for clues to solve a case, psychologists conduct research to gather evidence about behaviour and its causes. The research method chosen depends on the problem being studied, the investigator's objectives, and ethical principles.

descriptive research seeks to identify how humans and other animals behave, particularly in natural settings

DESCRIPTIVE RESEARCH: RECORDING EVENTS

Descriptive research seeks to identify how humans and other animals behave, particularly in natural settings. It provides valuable information about the diversity of behaviour, can

be used to test hypotheses and may yield clues about potential cause–effect relations that are later tested experimentally. Case studies, naturalistic observation and surveys are common descriptive methods.

Case Studies

A **case study** is an in-depth analysis of an individual, group, or event. By studying a single case in great detail, the researcher typically hopes to discover principles of behaviour that hold true for people or situations in general. Data may be gathered through observation, interviews, psychological tests, physiological recordings or task performance.

One advantage of a case study is that when a rare phenomenon occurs, this method enables scientists to study it closely. A second advantage is that a case study may challenge the validity of a theory or widely held scientific belief. Perhaps the biggest advantage of a case study is that it can be a vibrant source of new ideas that may subsequently be examined using other research methods. History is littered with famous case studies that have hugely influenced our understanding of science and behaviour. These case studies have often informed the progression of science. Later in the book (**Chapter 12**) we will hear about one of the most famous: the case of Victor, the wild boy of Aveyron.

> **case study** an in-depth analysis of an individual, group or event

 Chapter 12, Page 498

Naturalistic Observation: Chimpanzees, Tool Use and Cultural Learning

In **naturalistic observation**, the researcher observes behaviour as it occurs in a natural setting. Naturalistic observation is used extensively to study animal behaviour (Figure 2.6). Jane Goodall gained fame for her observations of African chimpanzees in the wild. Goodall (1986) and other researchers found that chimpanzees display behaviours, such as making and using tools, that were formerly believed to lie only within the human domain. Goodall's careful, detailed observations were vital in making her work accessible, and acceptable, to an initially sceptical scientific community.

> **naturalistic observation** the researcher observes behaviour as it occurs in a natural setting

Swiss researcher Christophe Boesch (1991) has observed a 'hammer/anvil' tool-use technique among wild African chimpanzees. A chimp places a nut on a hard surface (the anvil) and then hammers it several times with a stone or a fallen branch until it cracks. Some nuts with hard shells are tricky to open, and it may take several years for chimps to perfect their hammering. Especially fascinating is Boesch's observation that mothers seem to intentionally teach their young how to use this technique. Consider this interaction between a chimp named Ricci and her five-year-old daughter, Nina:

> *Nina . . . tried to open nuts with the only available hammer, which was of an irregular shape. As she struggled unsuccessfully . . . Ricci joined her and Nina immediately gave her the hammer . . . Ricci, in a very deliberate manner, slowly rotated the hammer into the best position with which to pound the nut effectively . . . With Nina watching her, she then proceeded to use the hammer to crack 10 nuts . . . then Ricci left and Nina resumed cracking. Now, by adopting the same hammer grip as her mother, she succeeded in opening four nuts in 15 min . . . In this example the mother corrected an error in her daughter's behaviour.(Boesch, 1991, p. 532)*

For evolutionary and cultural psychologists, such naturalistic observations can provide clues about the possible origins of human behaviour. As in human cultures, these chimpanzees developed a method for using tools and appeared to teach it to their young. These findings support the view that the mechanisms by which human cultures are formed – such as the intentional transmission of information across generations – may have an evolutionary basis (Workman & Reader, 2008).

Naturalistic observation can provide a rich description of behaviour and is also used to study human behaviour.

FIGURE 2.6 Researcher Jane Goodall uses naturalistic observation to study the behaviour of wild chimpanzees.

Source: Gerry Ellis/Getty Images

to happiness? These and countless other psychological questions ask about associations between naturally occurring events or variables. To examine such relationships, scientists typically conduct **correlational research**, which in its very simplest form has three components:

> **correlational research**
> measures one variable (X), measures a second variable (Y), and statistically determines whether X and Y are related

1. The researcher measures one variable (X), such as people's age.
2. The researcher measures a second variable (Y), such as self-reported daytime sleepiness.
3. The researcher statistically determines whether X and Y are related.

Keep in mind that correlational research involves *measuring* variables, not *manipulating* them.

> **Focus 2.6** Describe three components of correlational research and how they are illustrated by the study of very happy people.

Naturalistic observation and surveys are often used not only to describe events but also to study associations between variables. Imagine we needed to investigate the relationship between how the sale of ice cream changes with temperature. Our data may look something like those shown in Table 2.1. Here the *association* between the two variables (*temperature* and *volume of ice cream sold*) is shown as a positive relationship. As one variable increases (it gets hotter) more ice cream is sold. You might also use correlation in other types of research as our 'Research close-up' section illustrates.

 Research close-up

SEASONAL AFFECTIVE DISORDER

Source: P. P. A. Mersch, H. M. Middendorp, A. L. Bouhuys, D. G. M. Beersma & R. H. van den Hoofdakker (1999). Seasonal affective disorder and latitude: A review of the literature, *Journal of Affective Disorders*, 53, 35–48

INTRODUCTION

The long winter nights of Northern Europe give way to glorious sunshine (hopefully!) in April, May and June. We spend more time outside because the weather is warm and the days are longer. Spending time outside, and in the sunshine, for some reason makes us feel happy. A relaxing summer holiday on a wonderful beach in Greece or Spain perhaps, recharges our batteries, both physically and psychologically. The summer makes way to darker, shorter days in September and October. It rains more, and we spend more time indoors, huddled around our fires and television sets. We leave for our places of work or study in the dark in the morning, and arrive home in the dark in the evening.

For some reason, we feel less good in ourselves than we did in the summer. People have known this for a long time. *Seasonal affective disorder (SAD)*, described by Rosenthal et al. in 1984, indicates why some of us suffer more with these changes in happiness, or feelings of well-being, as the seasons change. Among those suffering with this problem, there appears to be a strong correlation between feeling of well-being and exposure to sunshine. In this paper, Mersch et al. have reviewed literature that looks at how the *latitude (how far north) at which we live* may influence our feeling of well-being, as measured here by incidence of seasonal affective disorder. Lower SAD means a generally better feeling among the population studied. Previous work from Lingjaerde, Bratlid, Hansen, and Gotestam (1986) in Norway and Potkin, Zetin, Stamenkovic, Kripke, and Bunney (1986) in the USA had shown just such a relationship, and a meta-analysis (see later in this chapter for an explanation of this term) of the available data would help Mersch et al. see any patterns that might reveal support for the hypothesis.

METHOD

Mersch et al. looked at many papers that investigated SAD in different seasons. These papers used different methods to assess SAD and were carried out on different samples and populations. By looking for patterns in the data Mersch et al. hoped to be able to either confirm or deny a relationship between latitude and incidence of SAD. To do this, two variables were collected: latitude and percentage of those with SAD symptoms. These were then plotted on a scatterplot, like those seen in Figure 2.8.

RESULTS

The results were a little confusing. Mersch et al. found that the relationship between latitude and SAD in the USA was significant. In Europe the relationship was not significant. In other words, people who live at the same latitude were more likely to show SAD symptoms if they lived in America than if they lived in Europe. How could this be?

DISCUSSION

It seems that the relationship between latitude and SAD is not clear. Something else may be playing a part in the incidence of SAD, or the level of well-being we feel. It makes perfect sense to think that living further north means that there is generally less sunshine and less light, and that this would account for the greater incidence of SAD. It seems, though, that a third variable may be playing a part, one which we may not have accounted for.

▶

Living in America, for whatever reason, seems to mean that SAD is more likely, when latitude is taken into consideration, than living in Europe. So what is going on here? Mersch et al. suggest that *climate* may be the mystery factor. Even though they are at the same latitude, Madrid and New York have very different climates. The weather in New York has extremes of cold and hot, and is much harsher than Madrid's weather pattern. They also point out that social and cultural patterns and factors should be considered. Admitting a psychological problem in a questionnaire or interview may be more acceptable in some cultures than others. Also, genetic factors may influence the data. It could be that a weakness to suffer from SAD may be passed genetically, and for some reason may become more prominent as the generations go by. It could be that Americans have a genetic predisposition to show these symptoms, whereas Europeans may not. Another issue in the prevalence of SAD may be the general knowledge of the diagnosis in the population. It may be that in the American surveys the samples used had a greater awareness that SAD existed than did the European samples, and would be more likely to answer positively if asked about symptoms. Finally, the difference in US and European data may have been something to do with the samples used in the original studies. It might be that the samples were not representative of the general population, and that the test used to measure whether the person showed SAD symptoms may not have been valid for all groups of people.

We can conclude, then, that the relationship between latitude and SAD is not terribly clear. It is different in the USA than in Europe and this may be due to all sorts of factors. A new study that collects new data rather than looking at existing data taking all the factors Mersch et al. identified would help us clear up this interesting area of research.

Correlation and Causation

It is tempting to conclude from studies of seasonal affective disorder that spending time outside in the sun causes people to have an increased feeling of well-being, but we have seen from Mersch et al.'s work that correlational research does not allow us to draw clear conclusions like this. First, the direction of causality could be just the opposite. Perhaps feeling good in ourselves causes people to want to get out more. In correlational research, you must consider the possibility that variable X (spending time outside) has caused variable Y (feeling of well-being), that Y has caused X, or that both variables have influenced each other. This interpretive problem is called the *bidirectionality* (i.e., *two-way causality*) *problem* (Figure 2.8b).

Second, the association between time spent outside and our feeling of well-being may be artificial, or what scientists call *spurious* (not genuine). Although the two are statistically related, it may be that neither variable has any causal effect on the other. A third variable, Z, may really be the cause of why some people spend time outside. In general, people with a more outgoing and agreeable 'personality tend' to worry less about how others perceive them. They may not think twice about putting on a swimsuit and strolling to the beach on a hot day, whereas shy people or those with a more negative body image would not experience the sunshine in the same way because of a lack of confidence.

TABLE 2.1 Ice cream sales and temperature

The relationship between sales of ice cream and the weather. Cf. Cohen, Doyle, Turner, Alper, & Skoner, 2003.

Temperature	Litres of ice cream sold
2 °C	5
22 °C	36
32 °C	52

Focus 2.7 Explain why scientists cannot draw causal conclusions from correlation research. Discuss an example.

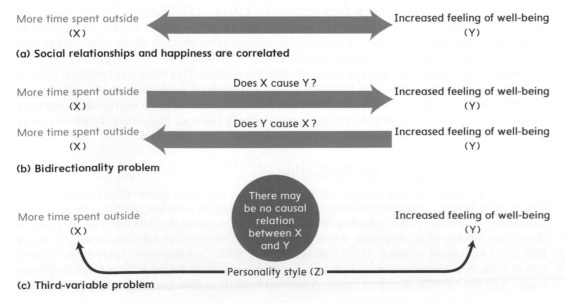

(a) Social relationships and happiness are correlated

(b) Bidirectionality problem

(c) Third-variable problem

FIGURE 2.8 Correlation and causation.

(a) Why does an association occur between spending more time outdoors and having an increased sense of well-being? (b) Spending more time outside could cause people to feel better or, conversely, feeling better in themselves could make people feel like going out more. This is the bidirectionality problem. (c) There may be no causal link at all. Other variables, such as personality traits, may be part of the true common origin of how we feel in ourselves, and whether we enjoy spending time outdoors. This is the third-variable problem.

In this case, it is a personality style that means that people enjoy more time outdoors, and experience more sunshine. At the same time, this style may help people soak up more joy from life and therefore feel happier in themselves. Thus, on the surface it looks as if time spent outside and a feeling of well-being are causally linked, but in reality this may only be due to Z (in this case, personality style).

This interpretive problem is called the *third-variable problem:* Z is responsible for what looks like a relation between X and Y (Figure 2.8c). As Z varies, it causes X to change. As Z varies, it also causes Y to change. The net result is that X and Y change in unison, but this is caused by Z – not by any direct effect of X or Y on each other. In sum, we cannot draw causal conclusions from correlational data, and this is the major disadvantage of correlational research. For instance, as ice-cream sales (X) increase so too do incidences of drowning (Y). There are possibly very rare incidences of people drowning in ice cream or gorging themselves insensible on the stuff, but we cannot really say that, as a rule, ice cream causes drowning. The third factor (Z) of 'temperature' is more likely to come into play. There is a tendency for people to gather near water on hot days. The increased likelihood of swimming means an increased likelihood of drowning – nothing at all to do with ice cream. A clear case of the 'post hoc ergo propter hoc' issue (see page 42).

The Correlation Coefficient

A **correlation coefficient** is a statistic that indicates the direction and strength of the relation between two variables. Generally speaking, it can only do correlations if you have numerical measures on two or more variables from a number of different individuals. The correlation coefficient is arrived at using some relatively straightforward mathematics. Variables can be correlated either positively or negatively. A **positive correlation** means that higher scores on one variable are associated with higher scores on a second variable. Thus social relationships and happiness are positively correlated such that more satisfying relationships are associated with higher levels of happiness. Similarly, people's height and weight are positively correlated (i.e., in general, taller people tend to weigh more), as are hours of daylight and average daily temperature (overall, the longer days of spring and summer have higher average temperatures than do the shorter days of autumn and winter).

A **negative correlation** occurs when higher scores on one variable are associated with lower scores on a second variable. Job satisfaction and job turnover are negatively correlated, which means that workers who are more satisfied with their jobs tend to have lower rates of turnover (e.g., quitting, being fired). Likewise, students' test anxiety and examination performance are negatively correlated (students with higher levels of test anxiety tend to perform more poorly in examinations), as are hours of daylight and time spent indoors (overall, on the longer days of the year we spend less time indoors).

Correlation coefficients range from values of +1.00 to −1.00. The plus or minus sign tells you the direction of a correlation (i.e., whether the variables are positively or negatively correlated). The absolute value of the statistic tells you the strength of the correlation. The closer the correlation is to +1.00 (a perfect positive correlation) or −1.00 (a perfect negative correlation), the more strongly the two variables are related. Therefore a correlation of −.59 indicates a stronger association between X and Y than does a correlation of +.37. A zero correlation (0.00) means that X and Y are not related statistically: as scores on X increase or decrease, scores on Y do not change in any orderly fashion. Figure 2.9 illustrates three **scatterplots**, graphs that show the correlation between two variables.

Correlation as a Basis for Prediction

Why conduct correlational research if it does not permit clear cause–effect conclusions? One benefit is that correlational research can help establish whether relations found in the laboratory generalize to the outside world. For example, suppose that laboratory experiments show that talking on a telephone while operating a driving simulator causes people to get into more simulated crashes. Correlational studies, while not demonstrating cause–effect, can at least establish whether there is a real-world association between driver mobile-phone usage and road-traffic-accident rates. A second benefit is that correlational research can

---

correlation coefficient a statistic that indicates the direction and strength of the relation between two variables

positive correlation higher scores on one variable are associated with higher scores on a second variable

negative correlation when higher scores on one variable are associated with lower scores on a second variable

scatterplots graphs that show the correlation between two variables

---

Focus 2.8 Explain positive and negative correlation coefficients and scatterplots. How does correlation facilitate prediction?

(a) A positive correlation

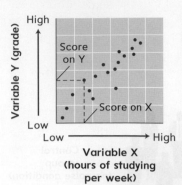

Variable Y (grade) — High / Low
Score on Y
Score on X

**Variable X
(hours of studying
per week)**

Low → High

(b) Zero correlation

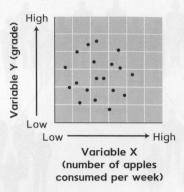

Variable Y (grade) — High / Low

**Variable X
(number of apples
consumed per week)**

Low → High

(c) A negative correlation

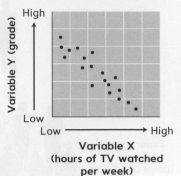

Variable Y (grade) — High / Low

**Variable X
(hours of TV watched
per week)**

Low → High

FIGURE 2.9 Scatterplots depicting correlations.

A scatterplot depicts the correlation between two variables. The horizontal axis represents variable X, the vertical axis variable Y. Each data point represents a specific pair of X and Y scores. The three scatterplots show (a) a strong positive correlation, (b) a zero correlation (0.00) and (c) a strong negative correlation for hypothetical sets of data.

be conducted before experiments to discover associations that can then be studied under controlled laboratory conditions. Third, for practical or ethical reasons some questions cannot be studied with experiments but can be examined correlationally. We cannot experimentally manipulate how religious someone is, but we can measure people's religiousness and determine if it is associated with other variables, such as personality traits.

Another benefit is that correlational data allow us to make predictions. If two variables are correlated, either positively or negatively, knowing the score of one variable helps us estimate the score on the other variable. For example, the space drivers afford to cyclists when overtaking them at different times of day (Walker, 2006, 2007), as the scatterplot in Figure 2.10 shows.

These data suggest that the later the time of day, the more room drivers give cyclists when overtaking (Walker, 2007). The scatterplot shows that this positive correlation is not perfect. Some drivers give cyclists more room than others early on in the day; conversely, some drivers give cyclists less space than others later in the day. Remember, we are not saying that the time of day causes drivers to give cyclists a certain amount of space when overtaking, only that the time of day helps us predict how much space will be given in an overtaking procedure.

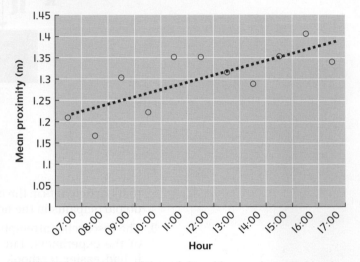

FIGURE 2.10 Correlation of time of day with space between bicycle and car in an overtaking procedure.

This scatterplot represents data for a sample of 50 students. The horizontal axis represents variable X, time of day. The vertical axis represents variable Y, space between car and bicycle in an overtaking procedure. Variables X and Y are moderately correlated.

EXPERIMENTS: EXAMINING CAUSE AND EFFECT

In contrast to descriptive and correlational methods, experiments are a powerful tool for examining cause-and-effect relations, and are carefully controlled trials in what could be described as a clinical setting. Suppose we conduct an experiment to examine whether noise influences university students' ability to learn new information. Each student is placed alone in a room, has 30 minutes to study five pages of textbook material, and then takes a 20-item multiple-choice test.

An **experiment** has three essential characteristics:

1. The researcher manipulates one or more variables. In the noise example, the researcher manipulates (i.e., controls) one variable – the amount of noise in the room. Some students (participants) are placed in a noisy room; others are placed in a quiet room. These would represent the groups (conditions) of the experiment (i.e., noise condition, no-noise condition).

2. The researcher measures whether this manipulation influences other variables (i.e., variables that represent the participants' responses). In the noise experiment, the researcher uses the multiple-choice test to measure whether the amount of learning differs in the noise condition versus the no-noise condition. We might find, for example,

> **experiment** in an experiment the experimenter manipulates one or more variables, measures whether this manipulation influences other variables and attempts to control extraneous factors that might influence the outcome of the procedure

> **Focus 2.9** What is the major advantage of experiments? Identify the key characteristics and logic of experiments.

FIGURE 2.11 The logic of designing an experiment.

The experimenter manipulates the amount of noise to which participants are exposed, measures their learning, and attempts to treat them equally in every other way. This creates an experimental group and a control group.

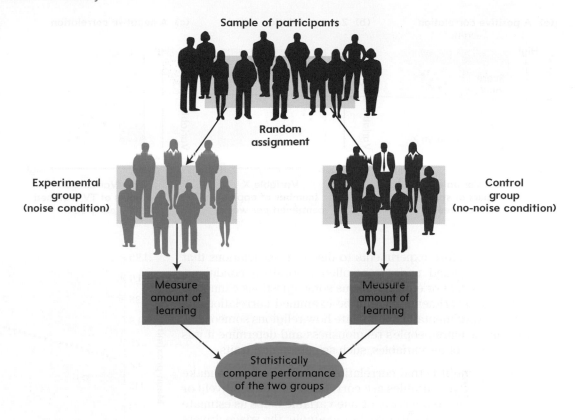

that participants in the noise condition perform less well on the multiple-choice test than do participants in the no-noise condition.

3. The researcher attempts to control extraneous factors that might influence the outcome of the experiment. For example, we would not want one group to do better because it had easier textbook material or test questions. So every participant will read the same material and take the same test. The room temperature and lighting will be kept constant, and the researcher will be courteous to everyone.

The logic behind this approach is straightforward:

1. Start out with equivalent groups of participants.
2. Treat them equally in all respects except for the variable that is of particular interest (in this case, noise).
3. Isolate this variable and manipulate it (creating the presence or absence of noise).
4. Measure how the groups respond (in this case, the amount they learn).

If the groups respond differently, then the most likely explanation is that these differences were caused by the manipulated variable (Figure 2.11).

Independent and Dependent Variables

The term **independent variable** refers to the factor that is manipulated by the experimenter. In our example, noise is the independent variable. The **dependent variable** is the factor that is measured by the experimenter and may be influenced by the independent variable. In this experiment, the amount of learning is the dependent variable.

An easy way to keep this distinction clear is to remember that the dependent variable *depends* on the independent variable. Presumably, students' learning will *depend* on whether they were in a noisy or quiet room. The independent variable is the cause (noise or no-noise), and the dependent variable is the effect (learning).

We have described the independent and dependent variables at a general level earlier on in the chapter, but recall that when doing research we must also define our variables operationally. 'Noise' could mean many things, from the roar of a jet engine to the annoying drip of a tap.

> **independent (predictor) variable** the factor that is manipulated by the experimenter
>
> **dependent (response, output, outcome) variable** the factor that is measured by the experimenter and may be influenced by the independent variable

TABLE 2.2 Operationally defining variables

	Independent variable (cause)	Dependent variable (effect)
Conceptual level	Noise	Learning
Operational level	Recording of street sounds played at 60 decibels for 30 minutes (versus quiet room)	Number of multiple-choice questions, based on five pages of text, answered correctly

'Learning' could mean anything from memorizing a list of words to acquiring the skill to ride a bicycle. In our experiment, we could operationally define our variables as in Table 2.2.

Our noise experiment thus far has only one dependent variable, but we could have many. We could measure how quickly participants read the material, their stress during the task, and so on. This way, we could gain more knowledge about how noise affects people.

Experimental and Control Groups

The terms *experimental group* and *control group* are often used when discussing experiments. An **experimental group** is the group that receives a treatment or an active level of the independent variable. A **control group** is not exposed to the treatment or receives a zero-level of the independent variable. The purpose of the control group is to provide a standard of behaviour with which the experimental group can be compared. In our experiment, the participants in the noise condition represent the experimental group (or experimental condition), and the participants in the no-noise condition represent the control group (or control condition).

Experiments often include several experimental groups. In our study on noise, we could play the recording of street sounds at three different volume levels, creating high-noise, moderate-noise, and low-noise experimental conditions. The no-noise condition would still represent the control group. In some experiments, however, the concept of a control group does not apply. For example, in a taste-test experiment in which participants taste and then rate how much they like Coca-Cola versus Pepsi, each drink represents an experimental condition, and participants simply make a direct comparison between the two drinks.

Two Basic Ways to Design an Experiment

One common way to design an experiment is to have different participants in each condition. To draw meaningful conclusions, the various groups of participants must be equivalent at the start of the study. For example, suppose that in our experiment the noise group performed substantially worse on the multiple-choice test than the no-noise group. If the students in the noise group, on average, happened to be poorer readers or more anxious than the students in the no-noise group, then these factors – not the noise – might have been why they performed more poorly.

To address this issue, researchers typically use **random assignment**, a procedure in which each participant has an equal likelihood of being assigned to any one group within an experiment. Thus a participant would have a 50% chance of being in the noise group and a 50% chance of being in the no-noise group; that determination would be made randomly. This procedure does not eliminate the fact that participants differ from one another in reading ability, anxiety or other characteristics. Instead, random assignment is used to balance these differences across the various conditions of the experiment. It increases our confidence that, at the start of an experiment, participants in the various conditions are equivalent overall.

A second way to design experiments is to expose each participant to all the conditions. We could measure how much the same people learn when exposed to noise and when placed in a quiet room. By doing so, factors such as the participants' reading ability and general anxiety are held constant across the no-noise and noise conditions, and therefore we can rule them out as alternative explanations for any results we obtain. However, this approach creates problems if not used properly.

experimental group the group that receives a treatment or an active level of the independent variable

control group is not exposed to the treatment or receives a zero level of the independent variable

Focus 2.10 What are independent and dependent variables? Experimental and control groups?

random assignment procedure in which each participant has an equal likelihood of being assigned to any one group within an experiment

counterbalancing procedure in which the order of conditions is varied so that no condition has an overall advantage relative to the others

Focus 2.11 How and why are random assignment and counterbalancing used to design experiments?

For one thing, it would make little sense to have our participants read the same textbook pages and take the same multiple-choice questions twice. Instead, we would have to develop two equally difficult reading tasks and have participants perform each task only once. Most important, suppose that every participant were exposed to the no-noise condition first. If they then learned more poorly in the noise condition, what would be the cause? The noise? Perhaps. But perhaps the participants were bored or fatigued by the time they performed the second task. To avoid this problem, researchers use **counterbalancing**, a procedure in which the order of conditions is varied so that no condition has an overall advantage relative to the others. Half the participants would be exposed to the no-noise condition first and the noise condition second. For the remaining participants, this order would be reversed.

Manipulating One Independent Variable: Effects of Environmental Stimulation on Brain Development

In a hospital, a massage therapist gently strokes a tiny premature baby who was exposed to cocaine while in its mother's womb. This procedure is repeated several times each day. Why?

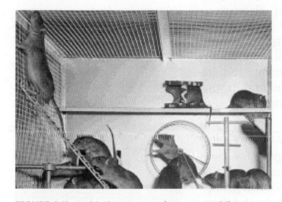

FIGURE 2.12 At birth, rat pups from several litters were randomly assigned to experimental and control groups. The experimental group was given toys and playmates. Control-group pups were raised alone in standard laboratory cages. In this experiment, the difference in the environmental conditions represented the independent variable. Brain development was the main dependent variable.

Source: AAAS

The answer partially lies in landmark experiments by physiological psychologist Mark Rosenzweig (1984) and his co-workers, who manipulated the degree of environmental stimulation to which infant rats (called 'pups') were exposed. This independent variable – environmental stimulation – was operationally defined by creating two conditions: an experimental condition in which some pups lived in a stimulating environment containing toys and other pups with whom they could interact, and a control condition in which other pups lived alone in standard cages (Figure 2.12). The pups came from several litters, so to create equivalent groups at the outset the researchers randomly assigned some pups from each litter to the enriched and standard environments.

After the rats had lived in these environments for several months, the dependent variable – brain development – was measured. Brain development was operationally defined by several measures, such as the weight of the rats' brains and the concentrations of brain chemicals involved in learning. The rats raised in the enriched environment were superior on each measure and performed better on learning tasks than did the control-group rats. More recent research found that physical stimulation and the environment in which the newborn rat lives can significantly influence its long-term development and behaviour (Pryce & Feldon, 2003). This evidence can be applied a little closer to home. A not insubstantial, and growing, body of research indicates that touch and massage can significantly influence a child's development, and improves a premature baby's health, so massage therapy is now often applied in hospitals as seen in Figure 2.13 (Field, 2001).

QUALITATIVE RESEARCH

Up to this point we have discussed research that might be described as 'quantitative'. This means that measures of variables are made with representative samples from the population. 'Qualitative' research is a slightly different approach, but one which is very popular in some areas, and one which is extremely useful in many areas of psychology. Consider market research for instance. Here we look at the underlying reasons behind people's behaviour and ask why people behave as they do and how. The samples we might choose for qualitative research use sample populations that might be from a particular group rather than a random sample. For instance, we may want to know the decision process involved in choosing a career as a firefighter. This risky, not terribly well-paid job attracts all sorts of people and we might want to know how to attract more. Careful qualitative research can help us try and find patterns in people's behaviour. A qualitative report focuses on these patterns. One way that you might think of the difference between

the two types of research is that qualitative research is exploratory, digging out patterns to reveal reasons why decisions were made. Quantitative research might be described as more conclusive, in that decisions about cause and effect are made more often (Denzin & Lincoln, 2005).

Another way to think of qualitative research is that it can involve the analysis of words in discussions or interviews, images in books or in a video, or even objects and artefacts. Quantitative research involves analysis of numbers. In qualitative research the experimenter has an idea of the area they wish to study, but the commentary in interviews may be a surprise, they may not know exactly the type of thing they are looking for when they start off on their exploration. In quantitative research the researchers know exactly what they are looking for, and are careful not to let anything spoil (confound) the relationship between their variables. In qualitative research the opinions of the participants are terribly important; the words of the participants are the data that inform the investigation. How they feel and their subjective decisions only add to the richness of the data.

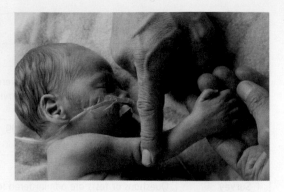

FIGURE 2.13 Experiments by psychologist Tiffany Field and others reveal that massage therapy improves the health and enhances the physical development of premature infants. It also shortens their hospital stay, thus reducing medical costs.

Source: Sarah Leen/ Getty Images

One problem with qualitative research is also one of its strengths. The subjective nature of the material available for analysis may be difficult to interpret, or different observers of the material may come to very different conclusions. For this reason the validity of the data may be at risk. The qualitative researcher must try and balance the need for rich subjective data with the problem associated with interpreting it.

If the research warrants it, and researchers decide to approach their topic qualitatively, a number of options are open to them. These include interviews, questionnaires, and analysis of text and video material. It is from the data gathered from the qualitative methods chosen that the researchers glean evidence upon which to draw conclusions and develop their research further. Whereas qualitative research is certainly exploratory, it is important to highlight the evidence-based quality of the process.

Questionnaires are used for all manner of topics. It is common for us to experience market research, or other work that may be questionnaire based, on almost a daily basis. Interviews may take a number of different forms. They can be unstructured, where the participant is encouraged to speak and present data in their own time and organized in any way they feel appropriate. The researcher organizes the topic, either recording responses electronically or taking notes. The interviews may be semi-structured, where there are no fixed questions, but the researcher guides the discussion, perhaps through a series of predetermined topics. Finally, the interview may be structured. In this case the researcher asks each participant the same set of carefully organized questions.

Analysing documents and media recordings of material can achieve extremely rich data. In these cases the researcher seeks to find evidence and data, usually with a predetermined set of research criteria. If the data are language based, perhaps political speeches or transcripts of conversations held in government debates, then the researcher can be said to be using discourse analysis. The relationships between the different speakers may be analysed, as well as many issues such as the use of language in developing a hierarchy or power structure.

In qualitative research the researchers themselves are an integral part of the analysis process. They decide on the way in which data will be collected, be it using questionnaires or interviews or other methods. They go on to design the questionnaires that go to participants. They conduct the long interviews, carefully guiding questions so as to help the interviewee develop a train of thought relevant to the research project. Once this is done, the researchers themselves analyse the data. They themselves take the answers in the completed questionnaires and interpret them; using criteria they themselves may have developed for the process. They take the videotapes or audio recordings of interviews and analyse the often subtle opinions expressed, forming patterns which they later develop into a series of concluding remarks. In short their input is central, and must be as objective as possible. This can be extremely hard to do well, and in recent years an exciting development in qualitative research has been in establishing methods that attempt

TABLE 2.3 An overview of research methods

Method	Primary features	Main advantages	Main disadvantages
Case study	An individual, group, or event is examined in detail, often using several techniques (e.g., observations, interviews, psychological tests)	Provides rich descriptive information, often suggesting hypotheses for further study. Can study rare phenomena in depth	Poor method for establishing cause–effect. The case may not be representative. Often relies on the researcher's subjective interpretations
Naturalistic observation	Behaviour is observed in the setting where it naturally occurs	Can provide detailed information about the nature, frequency, and context of naturally occurring behaviours	Poor method for establishing cause–effect relations. Observer's presence, if known, may influence participants' behaviour
Survey	Questions or tests are administered to a sample drawn from a larger population	A properly selected, representative sample typically yields accurate information about the broader population	Unrepresentative samples may yield misleading results. Interviewer bias and social desirability bias can distort the findings
Correlational study	Variables are measured and the strength of their association is determined. (Naturalistic observation and surveys are often used to examine associations between variables)	Correlation allows prediction. May help establish how well findings from experiments generalize to more natural settings. Can examine issues that cannot be studied ethically or practically in experiments	Correlation does not imply causation, due to the bidirectionality problem and the third-variable problem (which creates a confounding of variables)
Experiment	Independent variables are manipulated, and their effects on dependent variables are measured	Optimal method for examining cause–effect relations. Ability to control extraneous factors helps rule out alternative explanations	Confounding of variables, demand characteristics, placebo effects and experimenter expectancies can threaten the validity of causal conclusions
Qualitative study	More open data-gathering techniques, such as interviews, self-report questionnaires and analysis of video material, are used and analysed looking for patterns laid down by the researcher	The data are rich, unrestricted and unpredictable. The method allows for opinion and subjective commentary and may reveal patterns not identifiable with stricter, quantitative methods	The samples may be unrepresentative. Subjective opinions may be badly analysed with subjective misinterpretations

to set objective standards for the research process. In quantitative research the data are analysed following well-understood and agreed statistical procedures, and only then does the researcher engage in inferential remarks.

Table 2.3 summarizes key features of the research methods we have discussed, as well as some limitations which we discuss next.

MIXED-METHODS DESIGN

The researcher can take advantage of the various benefits of a qualitative or quantitative design by using both methods in their research. A mixed-methods approach employs aspects of both. Consider a situation where a new tablet-PC is being prepared for the marketplace. The designers will benefit from information about many things including the ease with which the tablet is navigated, and the speed that information can be found. This might be best done with a carefully designed quantitative approach, measuring speeds and search strategies employed by the tablet user, perhaps with an eye-tracker to record where they look. In addition to this, opinions of the user experience may be sought in an attempt to develop the product further and optimize user comfort and the gadget's desirability. This would be best done with a qualitative approach, perhaps as a focus group following a detailed questionnaire, or a structured interview used to carefully probe aspects of the user experience.

Finally, it is worth noting that often one type of design is not necessarily better than another, and there is usually more than one way of doing things. A good knowledge of both quantitative and qualitative approaches is the best way to access the most suitable method(s) of gathering your data. Each method and technique is a different tool in the psychologist's toolbox. Choosing the correct one or selection of tools will provide the evidence that will better inform us and other scientists in the future.

In review

- Descriptive research describes how organisms behave, particularly in natural settings. Case studies involve the detailed study of a person, group or event. They often suggest ideas for further research, but are a poor method for establishing cause–effect relations.

- Naturalistic observation gathers information about behaviour in real-life settings. It can yield rich descriptions of behaviour and allows the examination of relations between variables. Researchers must avoid influencing the participants that they observe.

- Surveys involve administering questionnaires or interviews to many people. Most surveys study a sample that is randomly drawn from the larger population in which the researcher is interested. Representative samples allow for reasonably accurate estimates of the opinions or behaviours of the entire population. Unrepresentative samples can lead to inaccurate estimates. Interviewer bias and bias in participants' self-reports can distort survey results.

- Correlational research measures the relation between naturally occurring variables. A positive correlation means that higher scores on one variable are associated with higher scores on a second variable. A negative correlation occurs when higher scores on one variable are associated with lower scores on a second variable.

- Causal conclusions cannot be drawn from correlational data. Variable X may cause Y, Y may cause X or some third variable (Z) may be the true cause of both X and Y. Nevertheless, if two variables are correlated, then knowing the scores of one variable will help predict the scores of the other.

- A well-designed experiment is the best way to examine cause–effect relations. Experiments have three essential characteristics: (1) one or more variables are manipulated, (2) their effects on other variables are measured, and (3) extraneous factors are eliminated or reduced so that cause–effect conclusions can be drawn.

- Manipulated variables are called independent variables. Dependent variables are measured, not manipulated. The independent variable is viewed as the cause, the dependent variable as the effect.

- The experimental group receives a treatment or an active level of the independent variable, whereas the control group does not.

- In some experiments different participants are randomly assigned to each condition. In other experiments the same participants are exposed to all the conditions, but the order in which the conditions are presented is counterbalanced.

- Researchers can study several causal factors within one experiment by simultaneously manipulating two or more independent variables. They assess the separate influence of each variable on behaviour and examine whether combinations of variables produce distinct effects.

THREATS TO THE VALIDITY OF RESEARCH

Although the experimental approach is a powerful tool for examining causality, researchers must avoid errors that can lead to faulty conclusions. **Internal validity** represents the degree to which an experiment supports clear causal conclusions. For example, because Darley and Latané's bystander experiment had proper controls, we can be confident that it was the independent variable (i.e., the number of bystanders) that caused the differences in the dependent variable (i.e., whether a bystander helped the victim). Thus the experiment had high internal validity. However, if an experiment contains important flaws it will have low internal validity because we can no longer be sure what caused the differences in the dependent variable.

> **internal validity** the degree to which an experiment supports clear causal conclusions

CONFOUNDING OF VARIABLES

Consider a fictitious experiment in which Dr Edelman examines how listening to different types of music influences people's feelings of relaxation. The independent variable is the type of music: classical, country or rock. Sixty university students are randomly assigned to listen to one of the three types of music for 20 minutes. Afterwards, they rate how relaxed they feel on a questionnaire.

Dr Edelman believes that the experiment will be more realistic if the classical music is played at a low volume, the country music at a moderate volume and the rock music at a loud volume. The results show that students who listened to the classical music felt most relaxed, while those who listened to the rock music felt least relaxed. Dr Edelman concludes that, of the three types of music, classical music is the most relaxing.

TABLE 2.4 Independent variables and possible confounding variables

	Group 1	Group 2	Group 3
Independent variable (type of music)	Classical	Country	Rock
Confounding variable (volume level)	Low	Moderate	High

confounding of variables two variables are intertwined in such a way that we cannot determine which one has influenced a dependent variable

FIGURE 2.14 Mice in a maze: Are we observing them or are they just showing us what we want or expect to see?

Source: Fer Gregory/Shutterstock

What is wrong with Dr Edelman's conclusion that the type of music caused the differences in how relaxed students felt? Stated differently, can you identify another major factor that could have produced these results? Perhaps students who listened to classical music felt most relaxed because their music was played at the lowest, most soothing volume. Had they listened to it at a high volume, maybe they would have felt no more relaxed than the students who listened to the rock music. We now have two variables that, like the strands of a rope, are intertwined: the independent variable (the type of music) that Dr Edelman really was interested in and a second variable (the volume level) that Dr Edelman was not interested in but foolishly did not keep constant (Table 2.4).

Confounding of variables means that two variables are intertwined in such a way that we cannot determine which one has influenced a dependent variable. In this experiment the music's volume level is called a *confound* or a *confounding variable*.

The key point to remember is that this confounding of variables prevents Dr Edelman from drawing clear causal conclusions, thereby ruining the internal validity of the experiment. Dr Edelman can eliminate this problem by keeping the volume level constant across the three music conditions.

Confounding, by the way, is a key reason why causal conclusions cannot be drawn from correlational research. Recall the 'third-variable' problem (see page 56). If variables X (e.g., feeling of well-being) and Y (e.g., time spent outside) are correlated, a third variable, Z (e.g., personality style) may be mixed up with X and Y, so we cannot tell what has caused what. Thus Z is just another type of confounding variable.

DEMAND CHARACTERISTICS

demand characteristics cues that participants pick up about the hypothesis of a study or about how they are supposed to behave

In unfamiliar situations, it is natural for us to search for clues about how we are expected to act. **Demand characteristics** are cues that participants pick up about the hypothesis of a study or about how they are supposed to behave (Orne, 1962). Consider an experiment looking at the relationship between alcohol consumption and sexual arousal. Some participants are told that they are drinking alcohol but in reality are given non-alcoholic drinks. Suppose that after a few drinks a participant does not feel intoxicated and concludes that the drinks are non-alcoholic. At this point the researchers' statement that the drinks are alcoholic is a cue – a demand characteristic – that may tip off the participant about the hypothesis being tested ('Hmm, maybe they're trying to see how I behave if I simply believe I'm drinking alcohol.'). This damages the experiment's internal validity because it can distort participants' true responses. Most people want to be good participants and may respond in ways that they think the experimenter wants (Figure 2.14).

Focus 2.12 What is internal validity? Why do confounding of variables and demand characteristics decrease internal validity?

Skilled researchers try to anticipate demand characteristics and design studies to avoid them. For example, if careful procedures are used, participants given non-alcoholic drinks can be convinced that they have consumed moderate to high amounts of alcohol (MacDonald, Uesiliana, & Hayne, 2000).

PLACEBO EFFECTS

placebo a substance that has no pharmacological effect

In medical research, the term **placebo** refers to a substance that has no pharmacological effect. In experiments testing the effectiveness of new drugs for treating diseases, one group of patients – the *treatment group* – receives the actual drug (e.g., through

pills or injections). A second group, the *placebo control group*, only receives a placebo (e.g., pills composed of inactive ingredients or injections of saline). Typically, participants are told that they will be given either a drug or a placebo, but they are not told which one.

The rationale for using placebos is that patients' symptoms may improve solely because they expect that a drug will help them. If 40% of patients receiving the actual drug improve but 37% of the placebo control patients show similar improvement, then we have evidence of a **placebo effect**: people receiving a treatment show a change in behaviour because of their expectations, not because the treatment itself had any specific benefit (Figure 2.15).

Placebo effects decrease internal validity by providing an alternative explanation for why responses change after exposure to a treatment. This problem applies to evaluating all types of treatments, not just those that test the effectiveness of drugs. For example, suppose that depressed patients improve (i.e., become less depressed) while receiving psychotherapy. Is this due to the specific procedures and content of the psychotherapy itself, or might it merely be a placebo effect resulting from their positive expectations that the therapy would help them? Experiments that include the proper control groups can examine this question, as we discuss in **Chapter 18**.

EXPERIMENTER EXPECTANCY EFFECTS

Researchers typically have a strong commitment to the hypothesis they are testing. In psychology, the term **experimenter expectancy effects** refers to the subtle and unintentional ways researchers influence their participants to respond in a manner that is consistent with the researcher's hypothesis. Scientists can take several steps to avoid experimenter expectancy effects. For example, researchers who interact with participants in a study or who record participants' responses are often kept blind to (i.e., not told about) the hypothesis or the specific condition to which a participant has been assigned. This makes it less likely that these researchers will develop expectations about how participants 'should' behave.

The **double-blind procedure**, in which both the participant and experimenter are kept blind as to which experimental condition the participant is in, simultaneously minimizes participant placebo effects and experimenter expectancy effects. In research testing drug effects, each participant receives either a real drug or a placebo but does not know which. People who interact with the participants (e.g., those who dispense the drugs or measure participants' symptoms) also are kept unaware of which participants receive the drug or placebo. This procedure minimizes the likelihood that the researchers will behave differently towards the two groups of participants, and it reduces the chance that participants' own expectations will influence the outcome of the experiment.

REPLICATING AND GENERALIZING THE FINDINGS

Let us return to our finding that university students in a noisy room learned textbook material more poorly than did students in a quiet room. Our study was done properly, therefore it has high internal validity, and thus we are confident that the noise, and not some other factor, caused students to perform more poorly. There remain, however, other questions that we must ask. Would the results be similar with other types of participants (e.g., children, adults not at university) or with different tasks (e.g., learning music or sports skills)? Does noise impair learning in real-world settings?

These questions focus on **external validity**, which is the degree to which the results of a study can be generalized to other populations, settings and conditions. Judgements about external validity typically do not focus on the exact responses of the participants. For example, the fact that students in noisy versus quiet rooms correctly answered, say, 48%

placebo effect people receiving a treatment show a change in behaviour because of their expectations, not because the treatment itself had any specific benefit

experimenter expectancy effects subtle and unintentional ways researchers influence their participants to respond in a manner that is consistent with the researcher's hypothesis

 Chapter 18, Page 807

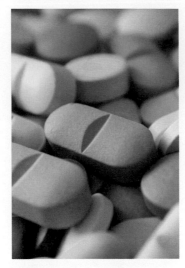

FIGURE 2.15 Placebo effects have fostered the commercial success of many products that had no proven physiological benefit. Do herbal medicines really work? The best way to answer this question is through experiments that include placebo control groups.

Source: © FotografiaBasica/iStock

double-blind procedure both the participant and experimenter are kept blind as to which experimental condition the participant is in

external validity the degree to which the results of a study can be generalized to other populations, settings and conditions

versus 83% of the questions is not the issue. Rather, *we are concerned about the external validity of the underlying principle:* does noise decrease learning?

Replication

To determine external validity, either we or other scientists will need to replicate our experiment. The importance of this component of the process cannot be underestimated. **Replication** is the process of repeating a study to determine whether the original findings can be duplicated. If our findings are successfully replicated – especially in experiments that study other types of participants (e.g., children), noise (e.g., aeroplanes flying overhead) and learning tasks (e.g., learning a sports skill) – we become more confident in concluding that noise impairs learning. Although straight replications are rarely published, lack of replication can eventually cast doubt on the claims of scientists. Replications are usually done as part of the process of extending the findings of one study into a new area or into a wider context.

> **replication** process of repeating a study to determine whether the original findings can be duplicated

Earlier in this chapter we reported the shocking behaviour of Diederik Stapel who fabricated a huge amount of his data, causing huge harm to himself, his co-authors, and students and to our subject as a whole. Where careful replication is undertaken such problems can be avoided. Where findings can be replicated the body of literature supporting the theories built on those findings is increased. The more replicable an effect is, the more confident we as scientists can be with the findings and the more confident we can be in reporting those findings to the rest of the world, to the large and growing community of interested press commentators and readers of psychology and science.

The importance of replication to the process should not be underplayed and leads us to another related issue concerning how we read research. Why *should* you believe what you are reading? For all you know another Stapel has been at work, making up data to further their career, to get ahead of others snapping at their academic heels. Part of the problem is that the success of a researcher, and so their ability to attract research funding, bigger and better jobs and research teams is largely based on their ability to produce and publish work, so the temptation for some to make this work up is huge. How are you and I, interested readers of psychology, supposed to know whether the paper in front of us at any one time is not part of someone's attempt to increase their published work? Well, one way you can do this is to look for replications, sometimes by the same authoring team, but better still by others who have found similar related results. A little digging in the literature and on electronic databases will allow you to do this by searching for other work that refers to, and cites the work in question. Replication then is a safeguard and part of the badge of quality we seek in good, reputable, trustworthy science.

Replication in related areas is part of the way we develop the ability to generalize work. Dianne van Hemert (2003) from Tilburg explains how careful analysis of cross-cultural data from many different sources and pieces of research can help us determine patterns. This type of analysis is called *meta-analysis* and we return to it later in this chapter. The patterns and similarities across cultures increase our confidence in the generalizability of our findings (Figure 2.16).

Research findings that fail to replicate often lead to important discoveries. For example, there is evidence that men believe that consuming a few alcoholic drinks (even

FIGURE 2.16 Workman and Reader (2008) report Ekman's research (Ekman and Friesen, 1967, 1969, 1971) describing the universality of emotional facial expressions. Cross-cultural patterns such as these provide evidence allowing us to generalize the hypothesis that there are six basic emotional expressions of the face: happiness, anger, sadness, fear, surprise, and disgust/contempt.

Source: (a) ©iStock.com/naran; (b) ©iStock.com/Muralinath; (c) ©iStock.com/Bartosz Hadyniak.

if the drinks are non-alcoholic) increases their sexual arousal to explicit sexual materials. But experiments have found that women's expectation of having consumed a few alcoholic drinks does not increase their sexual responsiveness (Crowe & George, 1989; Norris, 1994). Scientists are still exploring why this gender difference occurs.

In contrast, studies that consistently fail to replicate the original results of earlier research suggest that the original study may have been flawed or that the finding was a fluke. Even so, the scientific process has done its job and prevented us from getting caught in a blind alley.

SCIENCE, PSYCHICS AND THE PARANORMAL

Students are often surprised to find researchers in serious psychology departments who spend their time researching the paranormal (Figure 2.17). Paranormal experiences are described as those that conflict with the 'basic limiting principles' of science (Broad, 1953) and so they lend themselves to careful investigation applying the kinds of methods we have discussed in this chapter. This area is known as anomalistic psychology and is a very serious area of study, and includes investigations of such things as mental telepathy (transmitting thoughts between individuals) and precognition (foretelling the future). There is widespread belief in the paranormal the world over. Adopting a scientific attitude means we should approach this issue with open-minded scepticism; that is, we should apply rigorous standards of evaluation, as we do to all phenomena (Cardeña, Lynn, & Krippner, 2000). Replication of the experience or findings is a very important aspect of science and features strongly in investigations of paranormal experiences.

When tested under controlled conditions in well-designed experiments and replications, claims of psychic ability have failed to materialize. The Koestler Parapsychology unit at Edinburgh University investigates these beliefs with the scientific method. The unit consists of psychologists, other scientists, philosophers and those skilled in stage magic and illusion. To conclude that a phenomenon is psychic we must rule out presently known natural physical or psychological explanations and this involves very careful control of the environment and manipulation of variables, exactly the process used by scientists when investigating any phenomenon.

FIGURE 2.17 Many people believe in the paranormal. Careful scientific investigation can help identify whether paranormal experiences can be attributed to known psychological or physical explanations

Source: ©iStock.com/Renphoto

It was relatively common at the turn of the nineteenth century to attend a party where you might join in with a séance, or experience so-called 'psychic' phenomena such as 'table-tipping' where furniture moved apparently at the command of mysterious spirits. These psychics were revealed as fakes and charlatans, but there are still those in this day and age who claim psychic powers of the type alluded to all those years ago.

Even though the science shows that the claims cannot be attributed to psychic phenomena we must still treat each case on its merits and be careful not to be biased in our approaches. Careful consideration and investigation of each claim will form an investigation that may either expose the 'psychic' as a fraud, or show the existence of powers yet to be shown in a controlled environment.

Claiming psychic powers is no worse really than claiming any ability you do not have. It only becomes a problem when vulnerable people are taken advantage of. The Victorian 'table tippers' were taking money under false pretences, and so were criminally culpable. The human propensity to want to believe is still, apparently, a motivating force behind some criminal activity. In November 2005 the BBC reported a fraud where conmen in the Thames valley in the south of England were offering, for a small fee, to protect the public from 'evil' in the form of the paranormal.

In the 1990s a report in a major scientific journal provided evidence of mental telepathy from 11 studies using the *ganzfeld procedure* (Bem & Honorton, 1994). In this approach,

a participant (the 'receiver') listens to a hissing sound played through earphones and sees red light through translucent goggles. Parapsychologists believe this procedure makes the receiver more sensitive to mental telepathy signals. In another shielded room, the 'sender' concentrates on one of four different visual forms presented in random order. In these studies, the receivers reported the correct form on 32% of the trials, a statistically significant increase above the chance level of 25%.

Does the ganzfeld procedure – which involves many rigorous controls – provide the first solid evidence of psychic phenomenon? Some scientists suggest that the original ganzfeld studies may not have fully prevented the receivers from detecting extremely subtle cues that could have influenced their responses (Hyman, 1994). Although several parapsychology researchers have reported successful replications (Parker, 2000), psychologists Julie Milton and Richard Wiseman (1999) analysed 30 ganzfeld studies conducted by seven independent laboratories and concluded that 'the ganzfeld technique does not at present offer a replicable method for producing ESP in the laboratory' (p. 387). This is a very good example of how science progresses and works. New material is published that questions a theory, or supports a theory, and other researchers look carefully to see whether the claims made are valid and supported by the evidence. As newer studies and reviews are published, scientists will continue to debate the status of the ganzfeld and other findings within anomalistic psychology (Palmer, 2003).

Critical thinking requires us to have a reasoned scepticism that demands solid scientific evidence, arrived at by solid scientific investigation and the application of the scientific method, but not a blind scepticism that rejects the unknown as impossible. Researchers must keep an open mind and not enter into an investigation convinced that they will, or will not, find something. It is the opinion of this author that, at present there is no generally accepted scientific evidence to support the existence of paranormal phenomena, but that is not to say that others may well hold a different opinion. For instance, Schmeidler and Edge (1999) say that the meta-analysis of ganzfeld procedures carried out by Milton and Wiseman (1999) was not biased in its analysis, but it was in the studies it chose to include and exclude from the research. Were they to have altered the studies used, they would have arrived at a different conclusion. Research continues, and while the burden of proof lies with those who believe in the paranormal, evaluations of their claims should be based on scientific evidence rather than on preconceived positive or negative expectations.

Focus 2.13 What is external validity? Why is replication important? Apply these concepts to paranormal claims.

 In review

- An experiment has high internal validity when it is designed well and permits clear causal conclusions.
- Confounding occurs when the independent variable becomes mixed up with an uncontrolled variable. This ruins internal validity because we can no longer tell which variable caused the changes in the dependent variable.
- Internal validity is weakened by: (1) demand characteristics, which are cues that tip off participants as to how they should behave; (2) placebo effects, in which the mere expectation of receiving a treatment produces a change in behaviour; and (3) experimenter expectancy effects, which are the subtle ways a researcher's behaviour influences participants to behave in a manner consistent with the hypothesis being tested.
- The double-blind procedure prevents placebo effects and experimenter expectancy effects from biasing research results.
- External validity is the degree to which the findings of a study can be generalized to other populations, settings, and conditions. By replicating (repeating) a study under other circumstances, researchers can establish its external validity.

Focus 2.14 What are some things you can do to be a critical consumer of statistics?

ANALYSING AND INTERPRETING DATA

Around election time, do you feel like you are swimming in a sea of statistics from endless voter polls and political advertisements? As a student, you live in a world of grades and average marks. And in newspapers and television shows that cover sports and finances, you will find loads of statistics about athletes, teams, the economy and stock prices.

Current topic

CONSUMING STATISTICS

47 per cent of statistics are made up on the spot. (Steven Wright)

Statistics are woven into the fabric of modern life, and they are integral to psychological research. We need to know whether our observations and measurements really do support our predictions and hypotheses and we use statistics to do this. However, statistics are used and often abused by those who wish to tell a story or draw conclusions that place themselves and their research in a positive light. A (very often basic) knowledge of statistics can help us see through these attempts at deception. Suppose that a group in your home town wants your support for a new crime-watch programme. To convince you, the group quotes statistics from a nearby town, showing that this programme will reduce your chance of being robbed by a whopping 50%. Sounds impressive, but would you be impressed if you learned that in 2009 this town had two robberies and that after adopting the crime-watch programme in 2010 they had only one? Because the number of robberies was so low to begin with, this percentage change does not mean much. Conclusions based on statistics can change very significantly if information like the number of cases in the data is kept from the reader. For instance, some may be very interested to hear that children born at one hospital were three times more likely to be male than female. If the previously undisclosed information that only three children were born in that hospital in 2011 was provided, people may think quite differently. If you heard that the life expectancy in an area of Norway was 98 years old, you may go out of your way to move there, until you learn that only two people live there, an elderly couple, one of 99 the other 97. The examples need not be this abstract, however. On 24 February 2009, the BBC reported that 'Consuming one drink a day increased the risk of all types of cancer by 6 per cent'. This is clearly nonsense. If every drink increased the likelihood of something by 6% then a drink a day is very likely to result in the illness very quickly. The issue here is the 'percentage'. Six per cent of what exactly? The research was misrepresented simply because the statistics were, as they often are, misunderstood. Approximately 9% of women experience breast cancer before the age of 80. Drinking an extra drink a day increases this risk by 6%. Six per cent of nine is 0.54%. Having an extra drink every day therefore makes your risk 9.54%. It has increased, but not as catastrophically as the statistics and reporting led us to believe. You may not, therefore, be surprised that data and details of the generation of statistics are sometimes 'removed' when they become inconvenient or if their inclusion alters the desired conclusion.

Psychology is such that its graduates are often very well versed in statistics and a surprisingly large number work in data analysis, so watching out for these examples is an important part of our training as scientists. Not only is this a current topic, it is an extremely important one. The better informed we are as to how statistics may be used and abused, the less likely we are to be swindled and fooled by companies, charlatans and even governments. Some science writers, like Ben Goldacre (e.g. Goldacre, 2008), spend a good deal of their time publicizing poor practice in the area and you will find a number of examples in his book *Bad Science*. Dorothy Bishop, a neuroscientist from Oxford, offers a prize for 'journalistic misrepresentation' for a report in an English language national newspaper that has the most inaccurate report of a piece of academic work. Many of us see this sort of vigilance as an important part of our role as scientists and your training in psychology will provide you with the statistical knowledge to avoid being misled.

USING STATISTICS TO DESCRIBE DATA

In contrast to the information in Table 2.5, psychological research often involves a large number of measurements. Typically, it is difficult to make much sense out of the *data* (i.e., the information collected) by examining the individual scores of each participant. **Descriptive statistics** allow us to summarize and describe the characteristics of a set

> **descriptive statistics** allow us to summarize and describe the characteristics of a set (or distribution) of data

TABLE 2.5 Salaries of 10 consultants at Honest Al's Consulting firm

Consultant	Annual salary (€)	
Al's brother	263,000	mode – 263,000 (most frequent salary)
Al's sister	263,000	
Smith	30,500	
Rodriguez	29,500	
Müller	29,000	median – 28,500 (middle salary)
van-Noorden	28,000	
Johansson	27,500	
Carter	27,500	mean – 75,000 (mathematical average)
James	26,500	
Watson	26,000	Total salary
Total	*750,000*	Number of salaries

(or distribution) of data. You are already familiar with one descriptive statistic – the correlation coefficient, which we discussed on page 56. Now we introduce two other types of descriptive statistics.

Measures of Central Tendency

Given a set of data, *measures of central tendency* address the question, 'What's the typical score?' One measure, the mode, is the most frequently occurring score in a distribution. At Honest Al's the modal salary is €263,000. While the mode is easy to identify, it may not be the most representative score. Clearly, €263,000 is not the typical salary of the 10 consultants.

A second measure of central tendency is the median, the point that divides a distribution of scores in half when those scores are arranged in order from lowest to highest. Half of the scores lie above the median, half below it. In Table 2.5, because there is an even number of scores, the median is €28,500 – the point halfway between employee 5 (€29,000) and employee 6 (€28,000).

Finally, the mean is the arithmetic average of a set of scores. To determine the mean you simply add up all the scores in a distribution and divide by the number of scores. The €75,000 average that Honest Al quoted was the mean salary.

Note that the mean has a disadvantage: it is affected by extreme scores. The €263,000 salaries of Al's brother and sister inflate the mean, making it less representative of the typical salary. The median, in contrast, is not affected by extreme scores. Changing the top salary to €1 million does not change the median but further inflates the mean. Still, the mean has a key advantage over the median and mode: it captures information from every score. In Table 2.5, if Johansson and Rodriguez each received a €50,000 salary increase, the median and mode would not change. However, the mean would increase and reflect the fact that Honest Al was now paying some of his employees a better salary.

Because the mean takes all the information in a set of scores into account, it is the most commonly used measure of central tendency in research and perhaps in everyday life as well. But keep in mind that extreme scores will distort the mean. When you go for that job interview, also ask about the median and modal salaries. Although all these ways of measuring central tendency are well understood and agreed upon, there is no automatic decision procedure as to which is most appropriate. The researcher in the end has to use their knowledge of statistics to employ the best method of describing the data that makes a true statement and does not distort the picture they are trying to present.

Measures of Variability

To describe a set of data, we want to know not only the typical score, but also whether the scores cluster together or vary widely. *Measures of variability* capture the degree of variation, or spread, in a distribution of scores. Look at Table 2.6, which lists Honest Al's salaries alongside those of 10 consultants from Claire's consulting firm. The mean salary is the same at both firms, but notice how Claire's salaries are closer to one another – less variable – than are Al's. The simplest but least informative measure of variability is the range, which is the difference between the highest and lowest scores in a distribution. At Honest Al's, the salary range is €237,000; at Claire's the range is only €11,000.

A more important statistic, the standard deviation, takes into account how much each score in a distribution differs from the mean. At Honest Al's, the standard deviation is €94,009; at Claire's it is only €3,000. We need not be concerned here with how the standard deviation is calculated. Rather, the key point is that it uses information from every score, whereas the range only takes into account the highest and lowest scores.

USING STATISTICS TO MAKE INFERENCES

Descriptive statistics allow researchers to summarize data efficiently, but researchers typically want to go beyond mere description and draw *inferences* (conclusions) from their data. To illustrate, let us return to our experiment examining how noise affects students' learning. Suppose that 80 college students agree to participate in our study. We randomly assign 40 students to the noise condition and 40 to the quiet condition. They study the

---

mode the most frequently occurring score in a distribution

median the point that divides a distribution of scores in half when those scores are arranged in order from lowest to highest

mean the arithmetic average of a set of scores

---

range the difference between the highest and lowest scores in a distribution

standard deviation takes into account how much each score in a distribution differs from the mean

---

Focus 2.15 Describe three measures of central tendency and two measures of variability.

TABLE 2.6 Annual salaries of 10 consultants at two consulting firms (€)

Honest Al's firm		Claire's firm
263,000		81,000
263,000		78,000
30,500		76,000
29,500		76,000
29,000		76,000
28,000		75,000
27,500		73,000
27,000		73,000
26,500		72,000
26,000		70,000
75,000	Mean	75,000
237,000	Range	11,000
94,009	Standard deviation	3,000

identical textbook material for 30 minutes and then take a 20-item multiple-choice test. We find that, on average, students in the noisy room perform more poorly (mean = 8.20 correct answers) than students in the quiet room (mean = 12.50).

At this point we would like to make a general inference: noise impairs students' learning of textbook material. However, we must first wrestle with a key issue: even if our experiment had all the proper controls and there were no confounding variables, perhaps the noise really had no effect on performance, and our findings were merely a chance outcome. Perhaps, for example, just by random chance we happened to end up with 40 students in the noisy room who would have performed this poorly anyway, even if they had been in a quiet room.

For all types of research, **inferential statistics** allow us to make inferences about a population from data provided by a sample of that distribution. In our case, they help determine the probability that we would obtain similar results if our experiment were repeated over and over with other samples drawn from the same population of college students. Inferential statistics tell researchers whether their findings are *statistically significant*. **Statistical significance** means that it is very unlikely that a particular finding occurred by chance alone. Psychologists typically consider results to be statistically significant only if the results could have occurred by chance alone fewer than five times in 100.

Keep in mind that *statistical significance* does not mean that a finding is scientifically or socially important. If thousands of students took our 20-item test in either a noisy or quiet room, and if the variability (the standard deviation) within each condition was small, then even a tiny difference between the average test performances of these groups might be statistically significant but trivial for practical purposes. Yet a psychological technique that helps athletes run or swim faster by one-hundredth of a second might make the difference between winning the gold medal or no medal at the Olympics. Statistical significance only means it is unlikely that the results of study are due to chance. The scientific or social significance of the findings must be judged within a broader context.

inferential statistics allow us to make inferences about a population from data provided by a sample of that distribution

statistical significance is very unlikely that a particular finding occurred by chance alone

Focus 2.16 What is the purpose of inferential statistics? What is statistical significance?

META-ANALYSIS: COMBINING THE RESULTS OF MANY STUDIES

As research on a topic accumulates, scientists must reach overall conclusions about how variables are related. We described earlier how meta-analyses of this kind are a useful technique in cross-cultural psychology. Experts on a topic often will review the number and quality of studies that support, or fail to support a particular relation and then draw conclusions that they believe are best supported by the facts.

Increasingly, these expert reviews are being supplemented by **meta-analysis**, a statistical procedure for combining the results of different studies that examine the same

meta-analysis a statistical procedure for combining the results of different studies that examine the same topic

topic. In a typical research study, the responses of each participant are analysed. In a meta-analysis, however, each study is treated as a 'single participant', and its overall results are analysed with those of other studies. A meta-analysis will tell researchers about the direction and statistical strength of the relation between two variables.

For example, would you expect that exercising during the day helps people sleep better at night? One meta-analysis combined the results of 38 studies and concluded that the overall relation is weak (Youngstedt, O'Connor, & Dishman, 1997). On average, people slept only about 10 minutes longer when they had exercised that day, and they fell asleep only about 1 minute faster.

An important point can be made here about meta-analyses. Typically, a meta-analysis includes relevant papers on a phenomenon such as SAD earlier. Just because the results of a study do not necessarily agree with the majority of material published does not mean that they cannot find influence in a meta-analysis. However, such data cannot be included in a meta-analysis if it has not been published and so made public. The point here is that a great many experiments and studies are carried out and statistically about 95% of them will show a null-result – that is to say, their hypotheses must be rejected; only the statistically significant will be published and accepted for publication. This means that a huge amount of data is languishing in filing cabinets all over the world and because this is the case it cannot be included in relevant meta-analyses. This means that we may well be drawing conclusions that are false. Had we access to these unpublished data sets, meta-analyses would be more likely to be true representations of the data collected in the area and so conclusions based on their analyses would be more reliable. The take-home message here, then, is that we must be cautious in the conclusions we draw from meta-analyses like these. Since they draw on published work only, they necessarily lack data that may have influenced or indeed dramatically changed the conclusions of the analysis.

The term 'file-drawer' problem was coined by Robert Rosenthal in 1979 and is really a reflection of a bias in the traditional route to publication in academia. If the publication of data depends on whether they show support for a hypothesis then those that do not, where a null-result is shown, remain unpublished. More worryingly, it may be that the results are commercially sensitive, or their findings may not be what those that funded the work may like to see in the public domain, and so they too will remain in the file-drawer. For instance, it may be that research is sponsored by a well-known tobacco firm and the results of the research showed that the brand of tobacco was particularly dangerous to health. Publishing this work would be damaging to sales of the tobacco and therefore the results may be restricted. In an attempt to mediate this problem many journals now require authors to state publicly in their papers a statement of any conflict of interest and an indication of who funded the work so we the readers can make up our own minds.

Some open-access routes to publishing, such as *www.philica.com* allow review by a quite different route and so allow work to see publication even though more traditional routes may not have allowed the papers into their journals. Things are changing and more careful publication guidelines and safeguards, as well as more open-access routes are appearing each year. This may not be a definite solution to the file-drawer problem but it certainly is a step in the right direction.

Researchers who use meta-analysis must decide which studies to include and describe their common limitations. The authors of the meta-analysis on exercise and sleep cautioned that most studies only examined young adults who slept well. Many researchers consider meta-analysis to be the most objective way to integrate the findings of multiple studies and reach overall conclusions about behaviour.

An important addition to a meta-analysis should be a representation of *effect size*. This is a very misunderstood statistic by many people, but is actually rather a simple and eminently sensible concept. The effect size is a way of expressing the size of any differences between the groups being assessed in the analysis. Instead of just being able to say 'there is a difference here' we can say 'and the difference is this big'. Think of it like this. Our meta-analysis is of 30 or 40 sets of data each looking at the effectiveness of public policy on smoking reduction in children. Our analysis shows that there is indeed an effect, but we need to know how big that effect is so the strength of our analysis can be assessed. An effect size calculation will allow us to do that.

Focus 2.17 Describe the purpose of meta-analysis.

In review

- Statistics can be misleading if they are based on very few observations or are distorted by extreme scores. Understanding basic statistical concepts can help you be a smarter citizen and consumer.

- Descriptive statistics summarize the characteristics of a set of data.

- Measures of central tendency identify the typical score in a distribution. The mode is the most frequent score. The median is the halfway point in a distribution of scores arranged in numerical order; half of the scores are above and half are below. The mean is the arithmetic average of the scores.

- Measures of variability assess whether scores are clustered together or spread out. The range is the difference between the highest and lowest scores. The standard deviation takes into account how much each score differs from the mean.

- Inferential statistics allow researchers to determine whether their findings reflect a chance occurrence. The term *statistical significance* means that it is very unlikely that a particular finding occurred by chance alone.

- Meta-analysis statistically combines the results of many studies that examine the same variables. It calculates the direction and strength of the overall relation between those variables.

CRITICAL THINKING IN SCIENCE AND EVERYDAY LIFE

In today's world we are exposed to a great deal of information about human behaviour – some of which is accurate and much of which is not. Especially in the popular media, we encounter oversimplifications, overgeneralizations and *pseudoscientific misinformation* – nonsense and jargon that is made to sound scientific. To be an informed consumer, you must be able to critically evaluate research and identify factors that limit the validity of conclusions. Critical-thinking skills can also help you avoid being misled by claims made in everyday life, such as those in advertisements. Thus, enhancing your critical-thinking skills is an important benefit that you can derive from your psychology course.

> **Focus 2.18** What critical thinking questions can be used to evaluate claims made in everyday life?

Throughout this chapter you have seen how critical thinking, a healthy dose of scepticism and the scientific method help scientists solve puzzles of mind and behaviour. Refresh your knowledge of anomalistic psychology and ESP in particular; we covered it earlier in the chapter (page 67). The topics covered there lend themselves rather well to a critical thinking exercise. As critical thinkers, we should recognize that our beliefs and emotions can act as psychological blinders that allow us to accept inadequate evidence uncritically, especially when this evidence supports our current views. This does not mean that we should be so sceptical of everything that we end up believing nothing at all. Rather, we need to balance open-mindedness with a healthy scepticism and evaluate evidence for what it is worth (Figure 2.18).

FIGURE 2.18 Modern societies bombard us with scientific and pseudoscientific claims. Critical thinking often can help us tell good science from junk science. This journal, which promotes healthy scepticism and critical thinking, is published by the Committee for the Scientific Investigation of Claims of the Paranormal. Another organization, the Skeptics Society, publishes *Skeptic*.

Source: Used by permission of the *Skeptical Inquirer* magazine (www.ciscop.org).

Applying psychological science

EVALUATING CLAIMS ON RESEARCH AND EVERYDAY LIFE

To exercise your critical-thinking skills, read the following descriptions of a research study, an advertisement, and a newspaper article. Have some fun and see if you agree with the claims made.

Write down your answers and compare them with the answers provided at the end of the box. You can facilitate critical thinking by asking yourself the following questions:

1. What claim is being made?
2. What evidence is being presented to support this claim?
3. What is the quality of the evidence? Are there any other plausible explanations for the conclusions being drawn?
4. What additional evidence would be needed to reach a clearer conclusion?
5. What is the most reasonable conclusion to draw?

SOME INTERESTING CLAIMS

Example 1: a lot of bull

Deep inside the brain of humans and other mammals is a structure called the *caudate nucleus*. Years ago, a prominent researcher hypothesized that this part of the brain is responsible for turning off aggressive behaviour. The scientist was so confident in his hypothesis that he bet his life on it. A microelectrode was implanted inside the caudate nucleus of a large, aggressive bull. The researcher stood before the bull and, like a Spanish matador, waved a cape to incite the bull to charge. As the bull thundered towards him, the researcher pressed a button on a radio transmitter that he held in his other hand. This sent a signal that caused the microelectrode to stimulate the bull's caudate nucleus. Suddenly, the bull broke off its charge and stopped. Each time this sequence was repeated, the bull stopped its charge. The researcher concluded that the caudate nucleus was the 'aggression-off' centre of the brain.

Stimulating the caudate nucleus caused the bull to stop charging, but does this demonstrate that the caudate nucleus is an aggression-off centre? Why or why not? (*Hint:* What other bodily functions might the caudate nucleus help regulate that would cause the bull to stop charging?)

Example 2: holidays and burglaries

Consider the following scenario. A newspaper advertisement appeared in several countries. The headline 'While You Are Taking your Summer Holiday, Burglars Go to Work' was followed by this statement: 'According to police statistics, over 26 per cent of home burglaries take place between 1 June and 30 September.' The advertisement then offered a home security system at a special, summer-only price of €500, a reduction of €250. In sum, the advertisement implied that burglaries are particularly likely to occur while people are away on summer holiday. How do you feel about this claim and its supporting evidence?

Example 3: will staying up late cause you to forget what you have studied?

The headline of a newspaper article read, 'Best Way to Retain Complex Information? Sleep on It, Researcher Says'. The article began: 'Students who work hard from Monday to Friday and then party all night on weekends may lose much of what they learned during the week, according to a sleep researcher.' The researcher was then quoted as saying: 'It appears skewing the sleep cycle by just two hours can have this effect. Watching a long, late movie the night following a class and then sleeping in the next morning will make it so you're not learning what you thought. You'll not lose it all – just about 30 per cent.'

Next, the experiment was described. University students learned a complex logic game and then were assigned to one of four sleep conditions. Students in the control condition were allowed to have a normal night's sleep. Those in condition 2 were not allowed to have any sleep, whereas students in conditions 3 and 4 were awakened only when they went into a particular stage of sleep. (We learn about sleep stages in Chapter 5 page 228.) A week later everyone was tested again. Participants in conditions 3 and 4 performed 30% worse than the other two groups.

Re-examine the experimental conditions, then identify what's wrong with the claims in the first paragraph.

CRITICAL ANALYSES OF THE CLAIMS

Analysis 1: a lot of bull

Perhaps the caudate nucleus plays a role in vision, memory or movement, and stimulating it momentarily caused the bull either to become blind, to forget what it was doing or to alter its movement. Perhaps the bull simply became dizzy or experienced pain. These are all possible explanations for why the bull stopped charging. In fact, the caudate nucleus helps regulate movement; it is not an aggression-off centre in the brain.

Analysis 2: holidays and burglaries

First, how much is 'over 26 per cent'? We do not know for sure but can assume that it is less than 27%, because it would be to the advertiser's advantage to state the highest number possible. The key problem is that the time period between 1 June and 1 September typically represents about 25% of the days of the year. Therefore about 26% of burglaries occur during about 25% of the year. Wow! Technically the advert is correct: burglars do go to work in the summer while you are on holiday. But the advert also may have misled people. Burglars seem to be just as busy at other times of the year.

▶

◀ **Analysis 3: will staying up late cause you to forget what you have studied?**

It could be true that going to bed and waking up later than usual might cause you to forget more of what you have studied. However, the article does not provide evidence for this claim. Look at the four conditions carefully. To test this claim, an experiment would need to include a condition in which participants went to bed later than usual, slept through the night and then awakened later than usual. But in this experiment the control group slept normally, and the three experimental conditions examined only the effects of getting no sleep or losing certain types of sleep.

When you read newspaper or magazine articles, look beyond the headlines and think about whether the claims are truly supported by the evidence. Were you able to pick out some flaws in these claims before you read the analyses? Critical thinking requires practice, and you will get better at it if you keep asking yourself the five critical-thinking questions listed previously.

 In review

■ Critical thinking is an important life skill. We should also be open-minded to new ideas that are supported by solid evidence.

■ In science and everyday life, critical thinking can prevent us from developing false impressions about how the world operates and from being duped in everyday life by unsubstantiated claims.

■ When someone presents you with a claim, you should consider the quality of the evidence, whether there are other plausible explanations for the conclusions being drawn, and whether additional evidence is needed to reach a clearer conclusion. Then ask yourself whether the claim is the most reasonable conclusion to draw.

 Recommended reading

CLASSIC

Kellogg, W. N. & Kellogg, L. A. (1933). *The ape and the child: A comparative study of the environmental influence upon early behavior.* New York and London: Hafner Publishing.

Kuhn, T. S. (1962). *The structure of scientific revolutions,* (ist. ed.). Chicago: University of Chicago Press.

CONTEMPORARY

British Psychological Society (2009). Ethics and standards, http://www.bps.org.uk/what-we-do/ethics-standards/ethics-standards

Holt, N. J. & Walker, I. (2009). *Research with people: Plans and practicals.* Basingstoke: Palgrave Macmillan.

Retraction Watch (2013). Diederik Stapel, http://retractionwatch.com/category/by-author/diederik-stapel/

Wells, F. & Farthing, M. (Eds.) (2008). *Fraud and misconduct in biomedical research* (4th ed.). Boca Raton, FL: CRC Press.

The interaction of nature and circumstances is very close, and it is impossible to separate them with precision . . . (but) . . . we are perfectly justified in attempting to appraise their relative importance.

Sir Francis Galton

Evolution, genes, environment and behaviour

with Deborah Custance

3

Chapter Outline

On 20 June 2000, the American President, Bill Clinton, and the British Prime Minister, Tony Blair, made a joint announcement to the world's press. They declared the first survey of the mapping of the entire human genome. President Clinton stated that, 'Without a doubt, this is the most important, most wondrous map ever produced by human kind'.

On 18 December 2013, an international team of scientists revealed to the world that they had mapped the entire genome of a Siberian Neanderthal woman from her 130,000-year-old toe bone (Prüfer et al., 2014). Most scientists assume that Neanderthals (*Homo neanderthalensis*) were not the direct ancestors of modern humans (*Homo sapiens*). Instead, the fossil and DNA evidence suggests that they diverged from the human lineage between 700,000 and 370,000 years ago and went extinct around 60,000 years ago (Noonan et al., 2006). Although the recent Neanderthal genomic map supports such a view, there was also evidence of interbreeding between Neanderthals and humans. Neanderthals went extinct, but it seems that some of their genes survive in modern humans today. Thus, we not only carry our direct ancestor's evolutionary past with us in our genes, but also that of an extinct hominid relative.

In fact, the vast majority of species in the history of life on Earth have, like Neanderthals, ended as evolutionary dead ends, consigned to the dustbin of extinction. Only a fraction of all species that have ever existed has survived through to the present day. Every living creature can, in theory, trace his or her lineage back through the Tree of Life in an unbroken chain to the first self-replicating organism in the primordial soup (Figure 3.1). If even one of your ancestors had not behaved effectively enough to survive and reproduce, you would not be here to contemplate your existence. Thus, you are an evolutionary success story and your very existence is little short of a miracle. The biological units that have been bequeathed to you by your ancestors are genes, which are functional segments of a long molecule called deoxyribonucleic acid or DNA. As descendants of successful forebears, you carry within you genes that contributed to their adaptive and reproductive success. It seems that some of us are also carrying a few genetic hitchhikers from long-gone Neanderthals.

Why Should Psychologists Study Evolution and Genes?

Although undoubtedly a cause for fascination and awe, you might be wondering why psychologists should concern themselves with evolution and genes. Surely evolutionary theory is the proper subject of biology, not psychology? When one thinks of evolution, one tends to think of gradual *physiological* changes that occur over eons of time. In terms of human evolution, one thinks of hairy, heavy browed, knuckle-walking apes that changed over time into fine-featured, hairless bipeds (i.e., creatures that walk habitually on two legs). As the title of this book indicates, psychologists are primarily concerned with the science of mind and behaviour, not physiology. Yet, physiology is intimately related to cognition and behaviour. There can be no thinking and behaviour without the physical substrates of brain and body; and there can be no brain and body without genes. The particular set of genes an individual possesses came about in turn during the course of evolution. So to understand fully brain and behaviour, one must consider genes and their selection during the course of evolution.

Since the brain is the seat of all thought, it is naturally an object of fascination for psychologists. Yet the fossil evidence suggests that the human brain did not just pop into existence fully formed. The remains of crania from long dead hominids (i.e., the 20 or so species of bipedal ape, including modern humans, that diverged during the course of evolution away from the other great apes) suggest our ancestors' brains underwent a dramatic and rapid process of change. Early hominids such as *Australopithecus* had brains about the size of modern chimpanzees (Figure 3.2). What made them distinctly human was not their brain size so much as the fact that they were semi-bipedal. Over the course of one to two million years, from about 1.6 million to 100,000 years ago, the human brains tripled in size (Schwartz et al., 2004; Figure 3.2). No other species has undergone such a dramatically rapid expansion in brain size (Dorus et al., 2004). There must have been extraordinary selection pressures for the human brain to change so profoundly in such a relatively short period of time.

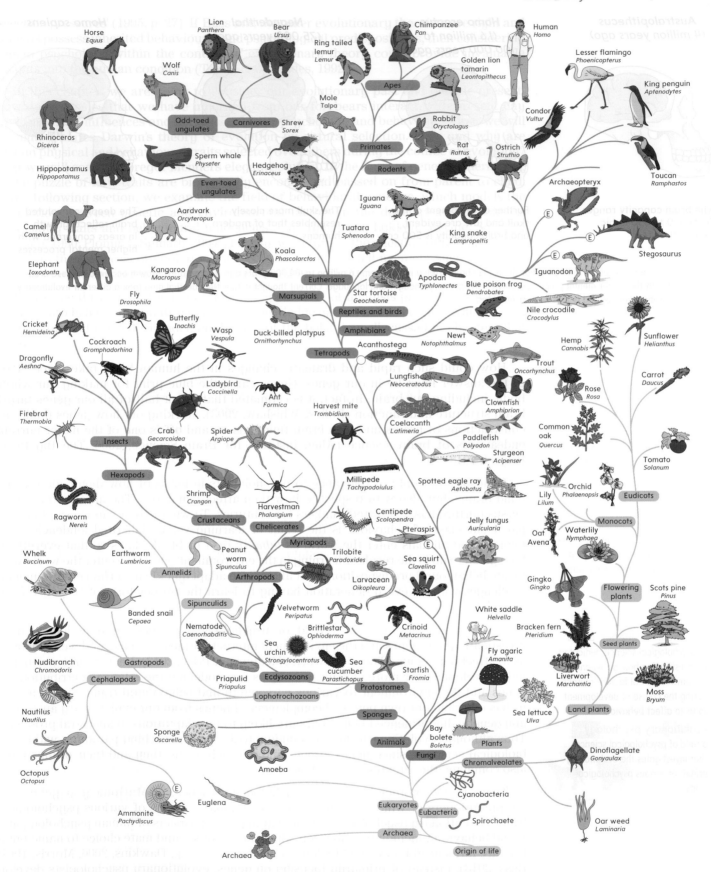

FIGURE 3.1 The Tree of Life

The branches culminating in extant (i.e. not extinct) species can be considered evolutionary success stories.

Source: Based on and adapted from The Tree of Life from The Open University

FIGURE 3.4 The thick coat of the Arctic wolf makes them well adapted to their cold, mountainous environment.

Source: ©iStock.com/Cybernesco

or 'blind' process based upon three factors: (1) biological variation; (2) high reproduction rates and the fact that not all members of a population survive; and (3) competition over limited resources (Lewin, 2005). The individuals of any given species biologically differ from one other. Some of those differences may convey an advantage in terms of survival and reproduction. For example, some members of a particular prey species may possess more acute hearing than others and hence be better able to detect and avoid predators. If those adaptive traits are heritable, that is, can be biologically passed on from parent to infant, then over time they will increase in frequency in the population.

It is easier to understand how natural selection works when one considers a concrete example. Imagine a population of wolves that live in a hot, dry climate. The wolves slightly differ from one another in their degree of furriness. Some of them are very thin-coated, while others have a slightly thicker covering of fur. Now imagine that the climate changes: it becomes considerably colder and as a consequence there is less to eat. Those wolves that are better insulated by their slightly thicker fur are more energy efficient and can survive on less food. If the furry trait is heritable then the offspring of the furriest survivors will also be better adapted to the climate and more likely to survive and reproduce in their turn. As a result, the next generation of wolves will be that bit furrier than the last. If the temperature continues to plummet, in future generations it is again the furriest individuals who are most likely to win through in the competition for food and mates. If the process continues from generation to generation, the final result may be a population of wolves that look very different from their thinly coated forebears. Indeed, in nature we find that thick-coated species of extant wolves, such as the Arctic wolf (*Canis lupus arctos*) live in cold climates (Figure 3.4), while thin-coated species such as the Indian Wolf (*Canis lupis pallipes*) live in hot climates (Figure 3.5). Notice also how the wolves differ not only in the thickness of their fur, but also their colour.

Natural selection not only affects physiological features such as degree of furriness, but also behavioural traits. We can again see this in dogs and wolves. When Axelsson et al. (2013) directly compared the genomes of dogs and wolves, the largest areas of difference were related to brain function and nervous system development. Research has shown that dogs and wolves differ in the way they interact with humans even when both have been raised in human households as pets. Hare, Brown, Williamson and Tomasello (2002) found that dogs followed a human's pointing and eye gaze cues to locate hidden food significantly better than wolves. When Miklosi, Kubinyi, Topal, Viranyi and Csanyi (2003) replicated these findings, they found that the crucial difference between the species was that wolves looked back at humans much less than domestic dogs do. We cannot easily explain these findings in terms of differences in learning or experience, since both species in these experiments had been raised in a similar manner. Thus it would seem that differences in quite surprisingly subtle behaviour such as visually orienting to humans are under the influence of inherited biological factors.

Although dogs and wolves provide a neat example of artificial and natural selection, there is a vital element missing in the above account. How do new traits emerge in a population? In the example of wolf evolution, where does the extra fur come from in each new generation? If organisms faithfully inherit parental characteristics, then the wolves should not exceed the furriness of the parental stock. Darwin was unable to answer such questions, since he was wholly ignorant of the mechanisms of inheritance; as were indeed all his peers except for one, the father of modern genetics, Gregor Mendel. The answer is related to genetic mutation. **Mutations** are random events and accidents in gene reproduction during the division of cells. If mutations occur in the cells that become sperm or eggs, the altered genes will be passed on to offspring. Mutations help create variation within a population's physical and behavioural characteristics. It is this genetic variation that makes evolution possible. Thus, to understand fully how evolution occurs one must take into account the role of genes.

> **Focus 3.1** Describe how natural selection might change a population of rabbits with relatively poor hearing into a population with very acute hearing. What change in the environment might trigger the selection of sharp-eared rabbits?

FIGURE 3.5 Indian wolves have a relatively thin coat of hair, which makes them well adapted to the hot Indian climate.

Source: ©iStock.com/yairleibo

mutations random events and accidents in gene reproduction during the division of cells

In review

- Biological evolution refers to gradual change in organic life that may culminate in the emergence of new species. Charles Darwin was the first person to suggest a viable mechanism by which evolution could occur: natural selection.
- Natural selection is based upon biological variation, high reproduction and mortality rates and competition over limited resources. If a biologically variable and heritable trait conveys an advantage in terms of higher reproductive success that trait will increase in frequency in a given population.
- Genetic mutation is necessary if biological variation is to exceed the sum of a trait found in the parental stock of a population.

MENDELLIAN GENETICS

Nowadays we know that genes are the means by which we inherit not only physiological, but also certain behavioural, perceptual and temperament or personality traits. Scientists in Darwin's day were fascinated by patterns of biological inheritance. Darwin himself became a keen pigeon-fancier in order to study their inherited differences due to selective breeding. To that end, he collected and bred every known breed of pigeon in Victorian Britain. He noted differences not just in terms of the pigeon's body shape and plumage, but also in their behaviour. Some of them cooed in distinctive ways and others flew in odd ways: the tumbler literally tumbles from the sky when it descends in flight. Just as domestic dogs are all derived from the gray wolf, all domestic pigeons are derived from one wild species of bird, the rock dove (*Columba livia*). All the observed physiological and behavioural differences in domestic pigeons must somehow be 'hidden' within the biology of rock doves. Although Darwin could control the breeding of his domestic birds and thereby vary some of these traits, he was at a complete loss as to explain the underlying biological mechanisms.

Actually, birds are particularly good subjects for considering the effects of biological inheritance on behaviour. Many species of bird perform elaborate and complex behaviour, such as constructing complicated nests or following long migration routes, even when they have been raised in captivity and had no opportunity to learn from other members of their own species (Jenson, 2009). Dilger (1962) performed cross-breeding experiments on lovebirds that showed the effects of inheritance on nesting behaviour. Lovebirds are small African parrots. They make nests by lining holes in trees with strips of bark. Fisher's lovebirds (*Agopornis fisheri*) carry single strips of bark in their beaks. Peach-faced lovebirds (*Agopornis roseicollis*) transport several pieces of bark at once by tucking them into their flank and rump feathers. Dilger cross-bred Fisher's and peach-faced lovebirds and found that the resultant offspring performed a confused and intermediate pattern of nesting behaviour. Young captive hybrid birds tore off strips of paper, tucked them into their rump and flank feathers, but then would not release them from their beaks and would take them out again, repeating these actions over and over. It was as if the two behaviours, 'carry in beak' and 'tuck in feathers', were both biologically preserved in the birds, but working in direct conflict with each another. Thus, it seems that quite specific behaviours can be subject to biological influence. Yet, what exactly was passed on biologically from parent to chick that could affect the young birds' behaviour in this way? Dilger knew that it was something to do with the birds' genes, but he could not study their pattern of inheritance systematically beyond the first generation since all the hybrid birds were sterile. Yet, Darwin and all his contemporaries (except for one, the father of modern genetics, Gregor Mendel) knew nothing of genes.

The lack of a satisfactory theory of biological inheritance constituted a gaping hole in Darwin's theory of evolution by natural selection. The most widely accepted model of inheritance during Darwin's lifetime, and the one he eventually subscribed to, was Blending Theory. Blending suggests that parental traits are blended together rather

like mixing white and red paint to produce pink. The problem with blending is that it is incompatible with natural selection (Jenkin, 1867). Blending traits eliminates variability. Thus, if one mixes all the paints in a paint box, one will end up with a murky uniform brown colour and lose the original wide array of colour choices. Without variability natural selection cannot operate because it has nothing to select among. Thus if blending were true for every inherited trait, be it physiological or psychological, one would eventually end up with the mean or average pattern. Everyone would have the same basic personality, the same intelligence, the same hair and eye colour and so on. Any differences in behaviour would be purely due to learning from the environment. Yet the very variety that emerges from selectively breeding pigeons and dogs belies blending. The great puzzle of inheritance was eventually solved in the 1860s by a relatively unknown Austrian monk, Gregor Mendel (see Henig, 2001). Unfortunately, the relevance of Mendel's work was not fully recognized until the early decades of the twentieth century.

Mendel, however, did not concentrate upon the inheritance of behavioural traits. He was trained in both physics and plant physiology and was renowned as a plant breeder. He worked out the laws of inheritance by conducting elegant experiments on pea plants. The pea plant offers a very simple model for understanding the laws of genetic inheritance. So although peas are of very little psychological relevance, we will study Mendel's classic experiments in order to help us understand the fundamentals of genetic inheritance. We will then explore how these simple laws that apply to peas can be used to explain the inheritance of certain psychological conditions in humans.

Mendel was fascinated with the variations he saw in plants of the same species. For example, the humble garden pea has several strictly dichotomous characteristics. It can produce either white or purple flowers; long or short stems; yellow or green pods with an inflated or constricted shape; and yellow or green seeds (or peas as they are more commonly called) with wrinkled or smooth skins (Figure 3.6). Best of all, from a research perspective, pea plants are very well suited to breeding experiments. They normally self-fertilize, but one can easily artificially control their fertilization so as to combine the dichotomous features one is interested in. In a series of elegantly controlled experiments, Mendel did exactly that, carefully recording the features of the resultant offspring. Let's consider his findings with respect to pea colour in more detail.

The variety of pea plant Mendel chose, *Pisum sativum*, produces either all green, all yellow or a mixture of green and yellow peas. First, Mendel grew plants that produced either all green or all yellow peas. When they had bred true for two years, that is, they only produced one or other of the two pea colours; they formed the baseline parent generation (P). Mendel prevented parental plants from self-fertilizing and manually cross-fertilized them. The resultant peas in the following generation (f1) were all yellow: the green characteristic had completely disappeared (see Figure 3.6). Mendel then planted those yellow peas and allowed the resultant plants to self-fertilize. When he opened up the pea pods of these plants (f2), he found that the green trait had re-emerged. There was an overall ratio of three yellow peas to one green pea inside the pods. He then planted these peas, let the plants self-fertilize, and examined the peas they produced (f3). The green peas grew into plants that only produced further green peas (see bottom far right of Figure 3.6). One third of plants grown from the yellow peas produced all yellow peas (see bottom far left of Figure 3.6). The remaining plants produced that magic ratio of three yellow peas to one green pea again.

The importance of Mendel's work was the elegant way in which he explained his findings. Since the cross-fertilized plants only produced yellow peas, Mendel proposed that yellow was a **dominant** trait while green was **recessive**. Yet, since the yellow peas from the cross-fertilized plants grew into plants that

> **dominant** the particular characteristic that it controls will be displayed
>
> **recessive** the characteristic will not show up unless the partner gene inherited from the other parent is also recessive

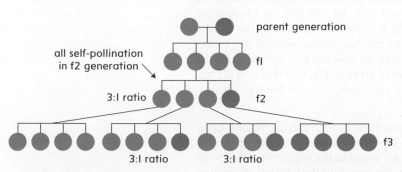

FIGURE 3.6 The pea colour ratios produced in Mendel's breeding experiments from one generation to the next.

produced both green and yellow peas, they must still have been carrying the green trait, but unexpressed. Mendel proposed that heredity factors, that is, genes, must come in double doses – each of which is called an allele. The particular combination of dominant and recessive alleles determines the outwardly expressed characteristic of an organism or its phenotype.

Geneticists use a standardized form of notation in which dominant alleles are represented by capital letters and recessive alleles are expressed in lower case. In terms of pea plants, peas that contain two dominant alleles (AA) produce plants that breed true for yellow peas. Peas that contain two recessive alleles (aa) produce plants that breed true for green peas. And peas that contain one dominant and one recessive allele (Aa), express the dominant yellow trait, but continue to carry the recessive allele within them. You can see that these traits are modular, at no point are they blended. Thus, Mendellian inheritance retains the biological variation needed for natural selection to operate.

Gametes or sex cells (eggs or sperm) differ from other cells in that they only carry one allele. The complementary pairs of alleles come together in different combinations during fertilization. Organisms that receive the same alleles, that is, two dominant or two recessive, for a trait are called homozygous and organisms with different forms of alleles, one dominant and one recessive, are called heterozygous.

Early in the twentieth century, geneticists made the important distinction between genotype, the complete genetic code of the individual, and phenotype, the individual's outwardly observable characteristics (Johannsen, 1911). Genotype is present from conception, but phenotype can be affected both by other genes and by the environment. The same phenotype can have different genotypes. As we saw in Mendel's peas, yellow peas can be based on a genotype of either AA or Aa. The same is true in humans. In humans, for example, brown eyes are dominant over blue eyes. A child will have blue eyes only if both parents have contributed recessive genes for blue eyes so that she is homozygous for the recessive trait (bb). If a child is heterozygous so that she inherits a dominant gene for brown eyes from one parent and a recessive gene for blue eyes from the other (Bb), she will have brown eyes and the blue-eyed trait will remain hidden in her genotype. Eventually, the brown-eyed child may pass the recessive gene for blue eyes to her own offspring (Klug, Cumings, Spencer, & Palladino, 2009). Just as the same phenotype can have different genotypes, the same genotype can have different phenotypes. Identical twins have the same genes, but if one eats more than the other they will differ in the phenotypic expression of body weight (Plomin et al., 2013). One helpful analogy might be to think of it as a genotype being like the software commands in your word-processing program that allow you to type an email; while phenotype is like the content of the email that appears on your computer screen.

The basic principles that govern the inheritance of seed colour in pea plants also govern human inheritance as we have already seen with respect to brown and blue eye colour. Now that you understand these basic principles we can use them to better understand directly psychologically relevant conditions. Phenylketonuria and Huntington's disease manifest themselves primarily in terms of psychological malfunctioning. They are both based upon the inheritance of specific combinations of the alleles from single genes.

Phenylketonuria

Phenylketonuria or PKU is associated with developmental delay and severe learning difficulties (Williams et al., 2008). It occurs at a rate of approximately one in 10,000 births. Before the biological cause of PKU was discovered, it is estimated that 1% of people placed in mental institutions were suffering from PKU (Plomin et al., 2013). It was a Norwegian biochemist, Ivar Følling, who in the 1930s discovered that PKU is due to an inability to metabolize the essential amino acid phenylalanine (Følling, 1934). Often parents of children with PKU do not exhibit the condition. Nonetheless, it does run in families and it tends to occur at a higher incidence in small, inbred communities: so that it is sometimes referred to as the Kissing Cousins Disease.

Just like with Mendel's green peas and human blue eyes, PKU is based upon the inheritance of a double dose of recessive alleles (pp). If a parent is homozygous for the

---

allele alternative forms of a gene that produce different characteristics

homozygous organisms that possess the same type of allele for a trait, either two dominant or two recessive

heterozygous organisms that possess different allele for a trait, one dominant and one recessive

genotype the specific and complete genetic make-up of the individual

phenotype the individual's outward observable characteristics

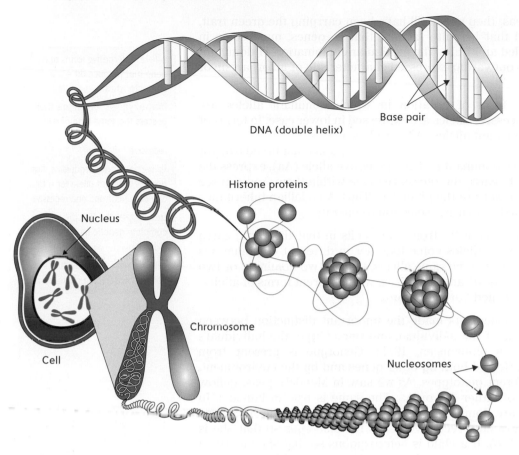

Base pair

DNA (double helix)

Histone proteins

Nucleus

Cell

Chromosome

Nucleosomes

FIGURE 3.7 Chromosomes and DNA.

Source: © Copyright University of Waikato, Science Learning Hub/Science Learning Hub

dominant allele (PP) he or she cannot pass on the disorder. If one parent is a carrier (Pp) and the other parent is not (PP), then although none of their children will develop the disorder, there is a 50% chance that they will still be a carrier (since they will always receive a dominant allele from the unaffected parent, but have a 50% chance of inheriting a copy of the affected parent's recessive allele). If both parents are carriers, they themselves will not have the disorder, but their offspring will have a 25% chance of inheriting two recessive alleles, one from each parent (.5 × .5 = .25), and if so they will be born with PKU. PKU occurs at a higher rate in small inbred communities because once it develops there is a higher chance of any given individual inheriting the recessive allele and hence a higher chance of them marrying and having children with a fellow carrier. Fortunately, nowadays, there exists a simple urine test for PKU that is routinely administered to newborns and if detected the condition can be treated via diet.

Huntington's Disease

Huntington's disease (HD) is a degenerative disorder in which the sufferer experiences personality changes along with decreasing mental, memory and movement functioning over time. It affects one in 20,000 people. The average age of onset is 40 years. Generally, one parent has the condition and his or her children have a 50% chance of passing it on to their children (Plomin et al., 2013).

HD is based upon the inheritance of a dominant allele; so that the inheritance of the condition is somewhat similar to that found with yellow peas. Unaffected individuals have two recessive alleles, while affected individuals have usually inherited one of the dominant alleles from their affected parent. It would be statistically very unlikely that two heterozygotes (Hh) for HD would meet and have children together. If this ever did occur, then on average each of their children would have a 75% chance of developing the disorder: since there would be a 50% chance of a child being heterozygous for the condition (Hh), a 25% chance of them inheriting a double dose of the dominant allele (HH) so that they and all their future offspring would inherit the condition and a 25% chance of being condition-free having inherited two recessive alleles (hh). HD remains in the population because of its late onset. Since the disorder does not begin to manifest itself until the affected individual is around 40 years of age, by that time he or she will often have had children. Those children will have a 50:50 chance of inheriting the dominant allele from their affected parent and so in turn eventually manifest the symptoms of HD. The Current Topic later in this chapter discusses in depth the emotional and moral quagmire related to genetic screening.

Focus 3.2 Since HD is based upon the inheritance of a dominant allele, why doesn't it slowly increase in the population? For a possible answer conduct a web search using the phrase 'Huntington's Disease and anticipation'.

GENES AND CHROMOSOMES

Although we have talked about genes and their pattern of inheritance a great deal so far, we have not discussed exactly what genes are and what they do. Mendel never actually used the word 'gene'. Instead, he used the phrase 'organic factors', but he had no idea at the molecular level what these factors were or how they worked. Answering these questions is one of the triumphs of twentieth-century science.

So what exactly are genes? **Genes** are functional segments of a long molecule called deoxyribonucleic acid or DNA. Each gene carries the chemical code for manufacturing specific proteins, as well as the codes for when and where in the body they will be made. Proteins can take many forms and functions, and they underlie every bodily structure and chemical process. For that reason, DNA has been described as the blueprint for the body. It used to be thought that humans had a total of around two million genes. However, ever since the mapping of the entire human genome that number has been shrinking. It is now thought that humans have around 20,000 genes (International Genome Sequencing Consortium 2004). The average gene has about 3,000 chemical base pairs, but sizes vary greatly; the largest gene has 2.4 million bases. It is estimated that about half of all genes target brain structure and functions (Kolb & Whishaw, 2003). Every moment of every day, the strands of DNA silently transmit their detailed instructions for cellular functioning.

DNA is not floating loose in the cell. Instead, it is wound up tightly in tiny rod-like structures called **chromosomes**, which are found only within a cell's nucleus (see Figure 3.7). Chromosomes take the form of a single string or rod (called a chromatid) until they copy themselves just prior to cell division, which is when they assume their iconic X-like shape. Chromosomes are comprised of proteins and DNA. Histone proteins are tiny structures around which the string of DNA is wound rather like thread on a cotton reel. If unravelled, the DNA molecule, although invisible to the naked eye, would be approximately 6 feet or 2 metres long (Masterpasqua, 2009).

Chromosomes come in pairs. All non-sex or **somatic** cells (except for red blood cells that have no nucleus) contain the **diploid** number of chromosomes, which constitutes the full complement with both members of each pair being present. Different species have different diploid numbers of chromosomes: humans have 46 made up of 23 pairs, whereas dogs, for example, have 78 with 39 pairs and fruit flies have 8 with 4 pairs. Sex cells or **gametes** (eggs and sperm) contain what is called the **haploid** number of chromosomes comprised of only one of each of the pairs from one or other of the parents, that is, 23 in humans. When the human egg and sperm combine, the fertilized egg or **zygote** contains all 46 chromosomes, with one of each pair coming from the father and its complementary pair from the mother. The fact that there are complementary pairs of chromosomes relates to alleles. Each gene is represented twice (i.e., as alleles) at the same locus (which is Latin for place; the plural is loci) on each of the chromosome pairs (Figure 3.8).

Chromosomes are made of two substances: nucleic acids and proteins. Proteins are much more varied than nucleic acids. They are molecules made of chains of approximately 100 amino acids. The precise order of amino acids along the chain determines the type of protein. There are 20 different kinds of amino acids, thus there are 20^{100} possibly combinations – 20^{100} is more than the total number of atoms in the universe (Patterson, 1998)! Since there are so many potential proteins, initially scientists thought that proteins must contain the heredity code. Instead, the code for life is found in the nucleic acid, DNA.

DNA has a distinctive structure, which was first discovered by Francis Crick and James Watson, largely based upon the experimental work of Maurice Wilkins and Rosalind Franklin, in the early 1950s. Its geometric shape is a double helix, which looks a bit like a twisted ladder. The rails of the ladder are made up of alternating sugar and phosphate molecules. The rungs are made up of pairs of four chemical or nitrogenous bases – adenine (A), thymine (T), guanine (G) and cytosine (C). It is as if the ladder

genes functional segments of the long molecule deoxyribonucleic acid or DNA that code for proteins

chromosome a single or double stranded structure comprised of proteins and deoxyribonucleic acid (DNA)

somatic cell is any cell forming the body of an organism. They do not contain reproductive cells

diploid number is a cell consisting of two sets of chromosomes

gametes are sex cells (eggs and sperm)

haploid number is half the number of chromosomes found in a gamete

zygote is a fertilized egg containing 46 pairs of chromosomes

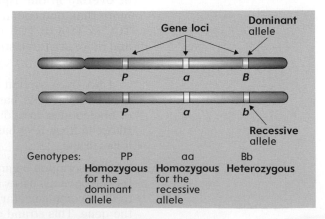

FIGURE 3.8 Alleles and gene loci on a pair of chromosomes.

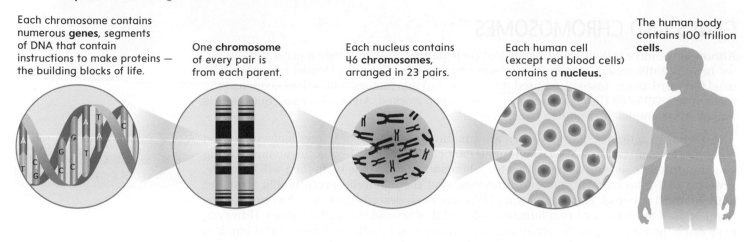

Each chromosome contains numerous **genes**, segments of DNA that contain instructions to make proteins — the building blocks of life.

One **chromosome** of every pair is from each parent.

Each nucleus contains 46 **chromosomes**, arranged in 23 pairs.

Each human cell (except red blood cells) contains a **nucleus**.

The human body contains 100 trillion **cells**.

FIGURE 3.9 The ladder of life.

Chromosomes consist of two long, twisted strands of DNA, the chemical that carries genetic information. With the exception of red blood cells, every cell in the body carries within its nucleus 23 pairs of chromosomes, each containing numerous genes that regulate every aspect of cellular functioning.

> nucleotides nitrogenous base, phosphate and sugar groups
>
> codon a non-overlapping triplet sequence of nucleotides

rungs are made of two halves locked together: the chemical base guanine (G) is always opposite cytosine (C) and adenine (A) is always opposite thymine (T). Figure 3.9 shows a very simplified model of the structure of DNA on the far left.

The beauty of DNA is that it allows for very accurate copying. During replication the two halves of the ladder split lengthways down the centre and each half can be used as a template to reconstruct the whole again. When the ladder is split, free-floating nucleotides (which are nitrogenous base, phosphate and sugar groups) in the cell are attracted to their complementary open bases on the DNA strand. It is rather like a self-assembling, four-piece, 3D jigsaw.

Human DNA has about 3 billion nitrogenous base pairs (Human Genome Project, 2007). The ordering of 99.9% of these bases is the same in all people. The sequence of the four letters of the DNA alphabet – A, T, G and C – creates the specific commands for every feature and function of your body. The basic unit of the genetic code is made up of non-overlapping triplet sequences of nucleotides each of which is called a codon. With four different 'letters' (i.e., nitrogenous bases) of the DNA alphabet being read in non-overlapping triplet sequences, there are 64 possible combinations or permutations, 4*4*4 (e.g., AAA, AAT, AAG, AAC, ATA, ATG, ATC etc.). There are two types of statement: one type specifies an amino acid and the other signals 'stop' in the sense that it stops the process of 'translating' a gene. With 20 types of amino acid and a stop sign, the total number of statements needed is 21. With 64 possible permutations, there is a great deal of overlap in the triplet code so that nearly every type of amino acid is specified by more than one codon. For instance, six codons code for the amino acid serine, TCT or TCC or TCA or TCG or AGT or AGT, two codons, TTT or TTC, code for phenylalanine and there are three stop codons, TAG, TGA or TAA (Griffiths, Miller, Suzuki, Lewontin, & Gelbart, 2000).

DNA transcription occurs with the help of another kind of nucleic acid: ribonucleic acid or RNA. RNA has a simpler structure than DNA. It is comprised of a single strand of nucleotides. In addition, instead of the sugar being deoxyribose as it is with DNA, it is ribose in RNA. RNA has the same nitrogenous bases as DNA except that instead of thymine it has uracil.

Transcription begins in the nucleus of the cell. A section of DNA unzips itself exposing the nitrogenous bases of a gene. The nucleotides of messenger RNA (mRNA) are attracted to their complementary bases and they form into a continuous strand along the length of the gene. This strand of mRNA then travels out of the nucleus into the cytoplasm of the cell. A large molecule called a ribose then travels along the length of the mRNA activating

its codons as it goes. When a codon is activated, transfer RNA (tRNA), which is floating loose in the cytoplasm, fixes itself to its complementary codon, rather like a three-pronged key fitting a lock. Specific amino acids are attached to the surface of particular types of tRNA. The amino acids from each tRNA bond together and form a chain. When the ribose reaches the stop codon, the chain of amino acids is released. This chain will fold into a particular shape depending on the order of the different types of amino acids along its length. The shape that the amino acids form determines the specific type of protein they become. Transcription is a very complex process and the description here is extremely simplified. The most important thing to understand is that the end product of genetic transcription is a protein.

Since genes are primarily code for proteins, it is not technically correct to state that there is a 'gene for' any particular phenotypic feature. Thus phrases such as 'a gene for autism' or 'a gene for eye colour' are technically incorrect. Genes influence phenotypic expression in a more indirect manner. Nonetheless, since proteins are involved in every structure of the body, including the brain, DNA has a profound effect on our cognitive processing, personality and behaviour.

Monogenic and Polygenic Effects

Most of the conditions or traits that we have discussed so far have been monogenic, that is, they are based upon the influence of one gene. However, in a great many instances, a number of gene pairs combine their influences to create a single phenotypic trait. This is known as **polygenic transmission**, and it complicates the straightforward picture that would occur if all characteristics were determined by one pair of genes. It also magnifies the number of possible variations in a trait that can occur. Despite the fact that about 99.9% of human genes are identical among people, it is estimated that the union of sperm and egg can result in about 70 trillion potential genotypes, accounting for the great diversity of characteristics that occurs even among siblings. The majority of traits that are of concern to psychologists such as intelligence and personality are most likely polygenic – assuming that genes influence them at all. Indeed, how do we scientifically establish whether any behavioural traits are under the influence of genes?

Focus 3.3 Although DNA allows for accurate copying, errors do occur. What effect do you think such errors have? Do you think all copying errors will always have bad effects? (As a hint, refer back to the passage on natural selection and mutations. p81-82)

polygenic transmission when a number of gene pairs combine their influences to create a single phenotypic trait

 In review

- Gregor Mendel showed how inheritance could occur without eliminating biological variation. In elegant breeding experiments with pea plants, he laid down the foundations of genetic science.
- Since Mendel, scientists have uncovered many of the details of the molecular and biochemical processes underlying genetic inheritance. We now know that genes are segments of deoxyribonucleic acid or DNA that encode for particular proteins.
- Some inherited traits are monogenic (based upon the influence of one gene). However, complex traits such as intelligence and personality are most probably polygenic (based upon the influence of many genes). However, all genetically influenced traits interact with environmental influences.

INHERITED BEHAVIOURAL ADAPTATIONS

One way to test whether a behaviour or trait is innate is to deny an organism the opportunity to learn from its environment and test to see if they exhibit the behaviour anyway. It is claimed that in an attempt to learn whether language is an innate ability, James IV of Scotland sent two babies to be raised by a mute woman on the remote island of Inchkeith. It was reported that at the end of the experiment they were found to speak perfect Hebrew (Lindsay, 1814).

Despite James IV's experiment, there is a long history of resistance within psychology to the suggestion that behaviour is based upon innate or inherited predispositions (see **Chapter 1**).

 Chapter 1, Page 15

Focus 3.4 Consider the human behaviour of playing badminton. Is it more the results of nature or nurture? Do not forget that one needs to be bipedal, possess good binocular vision and grasping hands to play badminton.

inherited behavioural adaptations traits that organisms are born with that help promote their chances of survival and reproductive success

fixed action pattern (FAP) an unlearned response automatically triggered by a particular stimulus

releasing stimuli external stimuli that trigger fixed action patterns

superstimulus an exaggerated version of a releasing stimulus that triggers a stronger response than the naturalistic model

Behaviourism dominated psychology from the early 1900s through to the 1960s. Behaviourists assumed that there are laws of learning that apply to virtually all organisms. For example, each species they studied – whether birds, reptiles, rats, monkeys or humans – responded in predictable ways to patterns of reward or punishment.

Behaviourists treated the organism as a *tabula rasa*, or 'blank slate', on which learning experiences were inscribed. Most of their research was conducted with non-human species in controlled laboratory settings. Behaviourists explained learning solely in terms of directly observable events and avoided speculating about an organism's mental state (as cognitive psychologists later did).

ETHOLOGY

While behaviourism flourished in early to mid-twentieth-century America, a specialty area called *ethology* arose in Europe within the discipline of biology (Lorenz, 1937; Tinbergen, 1951; Verhulst & Bolhuis, 2009). Ethologists focused on animal behaviour in the natural environment, viewing the organism as much more than a blank slate, and arguing that, because of evolution, every species comes into the world biologically prepared to act in certain ways. Thus, they possess **inherited behavioural adaptations** – traits that they are born with that promote their chances of survival and reproductive success.

An example of the kinds of behaviour studied by ethologists is that of young herring gulls' pecking behaviour. Newly hatched herring gulls beg for food by pecking at a red mark on the lower mandible of their parents' beaks. Parents respond by regurgitating partially digested fish, which the hatchlings ingest. Yet how do the chicks know to do this? Do they peck haphazardly and randomly at first until they by chance strike at the spot on their parent's beak and receive a food reward? If it was found that they did learn this way, it could be explained according to the principles of behaviourism. Yet, Niko Tinbergen suspected that the chicks enter the world with an innate **fixed action pattern** of pecking that could be triggered by pre-programmed **releasing stimuli**. He set out to test his ideas.

Tinbergen (1950) visited a wild colony of herring gulls and waited for the eggs to hatch. Before the newly hatched chicks had a chance to learn to peck at their parents' beaks, he collected them and presented them with various stimuli to see what would induce them to peck. The chicks did not peck at everything presented to them equally. First, the stimulus had to be moving; and second, it had to have contrasting foreground and background shades. Tinbergen found that the chicks pecked at flat templates cut in the shape of gull heads, as long as they had a distinctive spot at the end of the beak, as much as they pecked at a stuffed natural head. They pecked at black or blue spots as often as red spots. They pecked markedly less at beaks with white spots, no spot or a red spot painted just below the eye. The stimulus they pecked at most, even more than the natural head, was a pointed stick with contrasting red and white horizontal bands painted toward its point (Figure 3.10). Tinbergen called this a **superstimulus** since it worked better than the naturalistic model. Thus it seems that herring gull chicks do enter the world with a predisposition to respond to certain stimuli without needing to rely on learning.

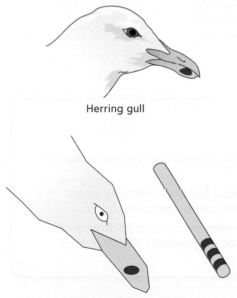

Herring gull

Inanimate releaser stimuli (model of gull face, rod)

FIGURE 3.10 A herring gull hatchling will peck most frequently at objects that are long and have contrasting foreground and background shades, even if they are inanimate models and do not look like adult gulls. This innate fixed action pattern is present from birth and does not require learning. The stimuli that trigger a fixed action pattern, such as the red markings on the inanimate objects and on the beak of the real herring gull shown here, are called releaser stimuli.

Source: Adapted from Hailman, 1969.

As ethology research proceeded, it became increasingly clear that even quite apparently rigid behaviour such as fixed actions patterns is subject to refinement by learning. For example, Hailman (1967) found that older laughing chicks learn what an adult gull looks like and within a relatively short time of hatching will not peck at an inanimate object unless it resembles the head of an adult gull. Another fascinating example is provided by the migratory behaviour of indigo buntings. The indigo bunting is a songbird that migrates between North and Central America. As if by pure instinct, it knows which direction to fly by using the North Star to navigate. (The North Star is the only stationary star in the Northern Hemisphere that maintains a fixed compass position.) In

autumn, the buntings migrate south by flying away from the North Star; they return in the spring by flying towards it. To study whether any learning was involved in the buntings' navigational behaviour, Emlen (1975) raised birds in a planetarium with either a true sky or a false sky in which a star other than the North Star was the only stationary one. In the autumn, the buntings became restless in their cages as migration time approached. When the birds raised in the planetarium with the true sky were released, they flew away in the direction opposite the North Star. In contrast, those exposed to the false sky ignored the North Star and instead flew away in the direction opposite the 'false' stationary star. Emlen concluded that although the indigo bunting is genetically pre-wired to navigate by a fixed star, it has to learn through experience in the environment which specific star in the night sky is stationary.

Focus 3.5 Do you think yawning is a fixed action pattern (FAP)? What social signal might act as a releasing stimulus for yawning? Why do you think there seem to be few obvious examples of FAPs in humans?

Shared and Unshared Environments

Measuring or estimating the effect of the environment is vital if we are to tease this apart from the effect of genetic influence. Environment is a very broad term, referring to everything from the prenatal world of the womb and the simplest physical environment to the complex social systems in which we interact with multiple people, places and things. Some of these environments, such as our family household or school classroom, are shared with other people, such as our siblings and classmates. This is called a **shared environment** because the people who reside in these experience many of their features in common. Siblings living in the same home are exposed to a common physical environment, the availability or unavailability of books, a television or a computer. They share the quality of food in the home, exposure to the attitudes and values transmitted by parents, and many other experiences. However, each of us also has experiences that are unique to us, or an **unshared environment**. Even children living in the same home have their own unique experiences, including distinct relationships with their parents and siblings.

shared environment the people who reside in these experience many of their features in common

unshared environment experiences that are unique to us

Twin studies (especially those that include twins raised together and apart) are particularly useful in estimating the extent to which genotype, shared environment and unshared environment contribute to group variance on a particular characteristic (see Figure 3.11). As we shall see, such studies have provided new insights on the factors that influence a wide range of human characteristics.

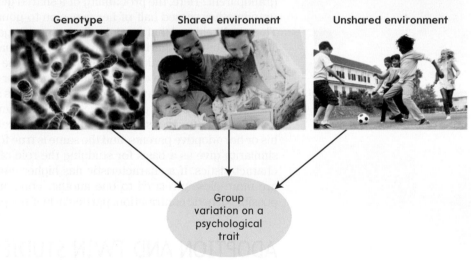

Genotype   **Shared environment**   **Unshared environment**

Group variation on a psychological trait

FIGURE 3.11 Behavioural genetics research methods permit the estimation of three sources of variation in a group's scores on any characteristics. It is therefore possible to estimate from results of twin and adoption studies the contributions of genetic factors and of shared and unshared-environmental factors.

Source: (a) ©iStock.com/BlackJack3D; (b) rSnapshotPhotos; (c) ©iStock.com/GlobalStock

In review

■ The environment exerts its effects largely through processes of learning that are made possible by innate biological mechanisms. Humans and other organisms can learn which stimuli are important and which responses are likely to result in goal attainment.

■ Since learning always occurs within environments, it is important to distinguish between different kinds of environments. Behavioural genetics researchers make an important distinction between shared and unshared environmental influences.

BEHAVIOURAL GENETICS

behavioural genetics how heredity and environmental factors influence psychological characteristics

degree of relatedness the number of genes we share with others by direct common descent

concordance co-occurrence

adoption study people who were adopted early in life are compared on some characteristic both with their biological parents, with whom they share genetic endowment, and with their adoptive parents, with whom they share no genes

Researchers in the field of **behavioural genetics** study how heredity and environmental factors influence psychological characteristics. In contrast to evolutionary psychologists who are interested in the genetic commonalities among people, behavioural geneticists try to determine the relative influence of genetic and environmental factors in accounting for individual differences in behaviour. For example, a behavioural geneticist might ask: 'How important are genetic factors in aggression, intelligence, personality characteristics and various types of psychological disorders?'

Genetic similarity can be expressed in two ways. First, we can take equivalent sections of DNA between different humans or different species and calculate the degree of similarity between base pairs. According to such comparisons, we share around 98–99% of our DNA code with chimpanzees (Venn, Turner, Mathieson, De Groot, Bontrop, & McVean, 2014) and about 99.9% with other unrelated humans. Second, we can express genetic difference in terms of the inheritance of specific alleles from our parents. We directly inherit half our alleles from our mother and the other half from our father. Thus, we receive 50% of each of our parents' genes by direct common descent. The **degree of relatedness** refers to the latter form of genetic comparison. Let's explore the concept of degree of relatedness a little further.

The probability of sharing any particular gene with one of your parents is 50%, or .50. If you have brothers and sisters, you also have a .50 probability of sharing the same gene by common decent with each of them, since they get their genetic material from the same parents. Identical twins share the same genotype (Figure 3.12). Thus, if you are an identical twin, you have a 1.00 probability of sharing any particular gene with your twin. And what about a grandparent? Here, the probability of a shared gene is .25 because, for example, your maternal grandmother passed half of her genes on to your mother, who passed half of hers on to you. Thus the likelihood that you inherited a specific gene from your grandmother is .50 × .50, or .25. The probability of sharing a gene is also .25 for half-siblings, who share half of their genes with the common biological parent but none with the other parent. If you have a first cousin, that is, the daughter or son of your mother's full sister or brother, you share .125 of your genes with him or her. This is because your mother' siblings shares .50 of their genes by common descent with your mother, thus you share .25 with your aunts and uncles and half of that, .125, with their children, your first cousins. An adopted child receives no genes by direct common descent from his or her adoptive parents, and the same is true for unrelated people. These facts about genetic similarity give us a basis for studying the role of genetic factors in physical and behavioural characteristics. If a characteristic has higher **concordance**, or co-occurrence, in people who are more closely related to one another compared to unrelated individuals, this points to a possible genetic contribution, particularly if the people have lived in different environments.

ADOPTION AND TWIN STUDIES

Knowing the degree of relatedness among family and kin provides a basis for estimating the relative contributions of heredity and environment to a physical or psychological characteristic (Kaprio & Silventoinen, 2011). Many studies have shown that the more similar people are genetically, the more similar they are likely to be psychologically, although this level of similarity differs depending on the characteristic in question.

One research method used to estimate the influence of genetic factors is the **adoption study,** in which people who were adopted early in life are compared on some characteristic with both their biological parents, with whom they share genetic endowment, and with their adoptive parents, with whom they share no genes by direct common descent. If adopted people are more similar to a biological parent (with whom they share 50% of their genes) than to an adoptive parent (with whom they share a common environment but no genes), a genetic influence on that trait is indicated. If they are more similar to their adoptive parents, environmental factors are judged to be more important for that particular characteristic.

In one such study, Kety and co-workers (Kety, Rosenthal, Wender, Schulsinger, & Jacobsen, 1978) identified adoptees who were diagnosed with schizophrenia in adulthood. They then examined the backgrounds of the biological and adoptive parents and relatives

to determine the rate of schizophrenia in the two sets of families. The researchers found that 12% of biological family members had also been diagnosed with schizophrenia, compared with a concordance rate of only 3% of adoptive family members, suggesting a hereditary link.

Twin studies, which compare trait similarities in identical and fraternal twins, are one of the more powerful techniques used in behavioural genetics (Boomsma, Busjahn, & Peltonen, 2002). Because *monozygotic*, or identical, twins develop from the same fertilized egg, they are genetically identical (Figure 3.12). Approximately one in 250 births produces identical twins. *Dizygotic*, or fraternal, twins develop from two fertilized eggs, so they share 50% of their genetic endowment, like any other set of brothers and sisters. Approximately one in 150 births produces fraternal twins.

Twins, like other siblings, are usually raised in the same familial environment. Thus, we can compare **concordance rates**, or trait similarity, in samples of identical and fraternal twins. We assume that if the identical twins are far more similar to one another than are the fraternal twins in a specific characteristic, a genetic factor is likely to be involved. Of course, the drawback is the possibility that because identical twins are more similar to one another in appearance than fraternal twins are, they are treated more alike and therefore share a more similar environment. This could partially account for greater behavioural similarity in identical twins.

To rule out this environmental explanation, behavioural geneticists have adopted an even more elegant research method. Sometimes researchers are able to find and compare sets of identical and fraternal twins who were separated very early in life and raised in *different* environments (Bouchard et al., 1990). By eliminating environmental similarity, this research design permits a better basis for evaluating the respective contributions of genes and environment.

Some of the similarities found between identical twins raised apart from infancy and reunited in adulthood are extraordinary. For example, Jim Lewis and Jim Springer first met in 1979 after 39 years of being separated. They had grown into adulthood oblivious to the existence of one another until Jim Lewis felt a need to learn more about his family of origin. When they met, Lewis described it as 'like looking into a mirror', but the similarities went far beyond their nearly identical appearance. Despite having been raised apart, they discovered that they shared some very surprising similarities. They both had childhood dogs named Toy. Both had been nail-biters and fretful sleepers, suffered from migraine headaches and had high blood-pressure. Both men married women named Linda, had been divorced and married second wives named Betty. Lewis named his first son James Allen, Springer named his James Alan. For years, they both had taken holidays at the same Florida beach. Both of the Jims worked as sheriff's deputies. They both drank the same kind of beer and smoked the same brand of cigarettes. Both loved and hated the same sports and left regular love notes to their wives, made doll's furniture in their basements, and had constructed unusual circular benches around the trees in their gardens (see Figure 3.13).

> **twin studies** compare trait similarities in identical and fraternal twins
>
> **concordance rates** statistical expression of the probability that two individuals with shared genes will share a particular trait to the same degree

> **Focus 3.6** Why are adoption and twin studies so useful when trying to estimate genetic and environmental influences upon behaviour?

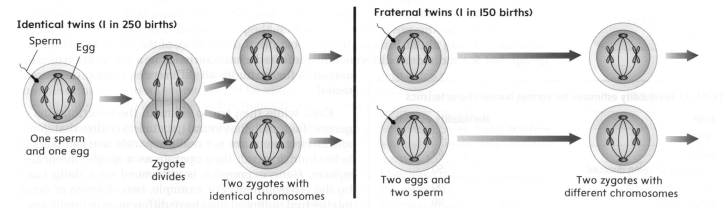

Identical twins (I in 250 births)

Sperm Egg

One sperm and one egg

Zygote divides

Two zygotes with identical chromosomes

Fraternal twins (I in I50 births)

Two eggs and two sperm

Two zygotes with different chromosomes

FIGURE 3.12 Genetics of twins.

Identical (monozygotic) twins come from a single egg and sperm as a result of a division of the zygote. They have all of their genes in common. Fraternal (dizygotic) twins result from two eggs fertilized by two sperm. They share only half of their genes as a result.

TABLE 3.2 Correlations in intelligence among people who differ in genetic similarity and who live together or apart

Relationship	Percentage of shared genes	Correlation of IQ scores
Identical twins reared together	100	.86
Identical twins reared apart	100	.75
Non-identical twins reared together	50	.57
Siblings reared together	50	.45
Siblings reared apart	50	.21
Biological parent – offspring reared by parent	50	.36
Biological parent – offspring not reared by parent	50	.20
Cousins	25	.25
Adopted child – adoptive parent	0	.19
Adopted children reared together	0	.32

Sources: Based on Bouchard & McGue, 1981; Bouchard et al., 1990; Scarr, 1992.

Focus 3.8 How large a factor is heritability in individual differences in intelligence?

Adoption studies are also instructive. As Table 3.2 shows, IQs of adopted children correlate as highly with their biological parents' IQs as they do with the IQs of the adoptive parents who reared them. Overall, the pattern is quite clear: the more genes people have in common, the more similar their IQs tend to be. This is very strong evidence that genes play a significant role in intelligence, accounting for 50 to 70% of group variation in IQ (Petrill, 2003; Plomin & Spinath, 2004). However, analysis of the human genome shows that there clearly is not a single 'intelligence' gene (Plomin & Craig, 2002). The diverse abilities measured by intelligence tests are undoubtedly influenced by large numbers of interacting genes, and different combinations seem to underlie specific abilities (Luciano, Wright, Smith, Geffen, Geffen, & Martin, 2001; Plomin & Spinath, 2004).

Environmental Determinants

Because genotype accounts for only 50 to 70% of the IQ variation among the individuals in these studies, genetics research provides a strong argument for the contribution of environmental factors to intelligence (Plomin & Spinath, 2004). Good places to look for such factors are in the home and school environments.

Shared family environment

How important to intelligence level is the shared environment of the home in which people are raised? If home environment is an important determinant of intelligence, then children who grow up together should be more similar than children who are reared apart. As Table 3.2 shows, siblings who were raised together were indeed more similar to one another than those reared apart, whether they were identical twins or biological siblings. Note also that there was a correlation of .32 between unrelated adopted children reared in the same home. Overall, it appears that between a quarter and a third of the individual differences in intelligence found in these particular groups could be attributed to shared-environmental factors.

The home environment clearly matters, but there may be an important additional factor. Recent research suggests that differences within home environments are much more important at lower socioeconomic levels than they are in upper-class families. This may be because lower socioeconomic families differ more among themselves in the intellectual richness of the home environment than do upper-class families (Turkheimer, Haley, Waldron, D'Onofrio, & Gottesman, 2003). Indeed, a lower-income family that has books in the house, cannot afford video games and encourages academic effort may be a very good environment for a child with good intellectual potential.

Environmental enrichment and deprivation

Another line of evidence for environmental effects comes from studies of children who are removed from deprived environments and placed in middle- or upper-class adoptive

homes. Typically, such children show a gradual increase in IQ in the order of 10 to 12 points (Scarr & Weinberg, 1977; Schiff & Lewontin, 1986). Conversely, when deprived children remain in their impoverished environments, they either show no improvement in IQ or they actually deteriorate intellectually over time (Serpell, 2000). Scores on general intelligence tests correlate around .40 with the socioeconomic status of the family in which a child is reared (Lubinski, 2004).

Educational experiences

As we might expect, educational experiences, perhaps best viewed as a non-shared variable, can also have a significant impact on intelligence. Many studies have shown that school attendance can raise IQ and that lack of attendance can lower it. A small decrease in IQ occurs over summer holidays, especially among low-income children. Intelligence quotient scores also drop when children are unable to start school on time owing to teacher shortages or strikes, natural disasters, or other reasons (Ceci & Williams, 1997). It appears that exposure to an environment in which children have the opportunity to practise mental skills is important in solidifying those skills.

Where intelligence is concerned, we have seen that genetic factors, shared environment and unique experiences all contribute to individual differences in intelligence. Do the same factors apply to personality differences?

> **Focus 3.9** Describe the shared and unshared environmental influences on intelligence.

GENES, ENVIRONMENT AND PERSONALITY

'Like father, like son' is a saying which young and even quite old men hear very often. But if this old saying has validity, what causes similarities in personality between fathers and sons (and mothers and daughters)? Is it genes, environment, or both?

Heritability of Personality

Behavioural genetics studies on personality have examined genetic and environmental influences on relatively broad personality traits (e.g., Schermer, Vernon, Maio, & Jany, 2011). One prominent personality trait theory is called the five factor model (see **Chapter 15**). Five factor theorists believe that individual differences in personality can be accounted for by variation along five broad personality dimensions or traits known as the Big Five: (1) *extraversion–introversion* (sociable, outgoing, adventuresome, spontaneous versus quiet, aloof, inhibited, solitary); (2) *agreeableness* (cooperative, helpful, good natured versus antagonistic, uncooperative, suspicious); (3) *conscientiousness* (responsible, goal-directed, dependable versus undependable, careless, irresponsible); (4) *neuroticism* (worrying, anxious, emotionally unstable versus well adjusted, secure, calm); and (5) *openness to experience* (imaginative, artistically sensitive, refined versus unreflective, crude and boorish, lacking in intellectual curiosity) (McCrae & Costa, 2003).

Chapter 15, Page 647

What results are obtained if we compare the Big Five traits in identical and fraternal twins who were raised together and those who were raised apart? Table 3.3 shows heritability estimates of the Big Five personality factors described above. These results are consistent with studies of other personality variables as well, indicating that between 40 and 50% of the personality variations among people included in these studies are attributable to genotype differences (Bouchard, 2004). Although personality characteristics do not show as high a level of heritability as the .70 figure found for intelligence, it is clear that genetic factors account for a significant amount of personality difference.

TABLE 3.3 Heritability of the big five personality factors based on twins studies

Trait	Heritability coefficient
Extraversion	.54
Neuroticism	.48
Conscientiousness	.49
Agreeableness	.42
Openness to experience	.57

Source: Bouchard, 2004.

Environment and Personality Development

If genetic differences in previous twins studies account for only about 40 to 50% of variations in personality (Bouchard, 2004), then surely environment is even more important than it is in the case of intelligence. Researchers expected that the shared environment might be even more important for personality than it is for intelligence. Over the years, virtually every theory of personality has embraced the

assumption that experiences within the family, such as the amount of love expressed by parents and other child-rearing practices, are critical determinants of personality development. Imagine, therefore, the shock waves generated by the findings from twin studies that shared features of the family environment account for little or no variance in major personality traits (Bouchard, Guillemette, & Landry-Léger, 2004; Plomin, 1997). The key finding was that twins raised together and apart, whether identical or fraternal, did not differ in their degree of personality similarity (although identical twins were always more similar to one another than were fraternal twins). In fact, researchers have found that pairs of children who are raised within the same family are as different from one another as are pairs of children who are randomly selected from the population (Plomin & Caspi, 1999).

Adoption studies support a similar conclusion. In adoption studies, the average correlation for personality variables between adopted siblings who are genetically dissimilar but do share much of their environment, including the parents who raise them, the schools they attend, the religious training they receive, and so on, is close to .00 (Plomin, Fulker, Corley, & DeFries, 1997). Except at child-rearing extremes, where children are abused or seriously neglected, parents probably get more credit when children turn out well personality-wise – and more blame when they do not – than they deserve (Scarr, 1992).

Focus 3.10 Since research has indicated that environment makes little contribution to individual differences in personality development, should parents not bother to try and influence their children's manners and morals?

However, the surprising findings concerning shared environments do not mean that experience is not important. Rather than the general family environment, it seems to be the individual's unique or unshared environment, such as his or her unique school experiences (for example, being in Mr Jones's classroom, where conscientiousness and openness to experience were stressed) and interactions with specific peers (such as Jeremy, who fostered extraverted relationships with others) that account for considerable personality variance. Even within the same family, we should realize, siblings have different experiences while growing up, and each child's relationship with his or her parents and siblings may vary in important ways. It is these unique experiences that help shape personality development. Whereas behavioural geneticists have found important shared-environment effects in intelligence, attitudes, religious beliefs, occupational preferences, notions of masculinity and femininity, political attitudes, and health behaviours such as smoking and drinking (Larsen & Buss, 2007), these shared-environment effects do not extend to general personality traits such as the Big Five. At this point, we do not know whether there are some crucial unshared-environmental variables that researchers have missed because of their preoccupation with shared-environmental factors, or whether there are countless small variables that make the difference. This question is of key importance to personality research.

In review

- Hereditary potential is carried in the genes, whose commands trigger the production of proteins that control body structures and processes. Genotype (genetic structure) and phenotype (outward appearance) are not identical, in part because some genes are dominant while others are recessive. Many characteristics are polygenic in origin, that is, they are influenced by the interactions of multiple genes.

- Behavioural geneticists study how genetic and environmental factors contribute to the development of psychological traits and behaviours. Adoption and twin studies are the major research methods used to disentangle hereditary and environmental factors. Especially useful is the study of identical and fraternal twins who were separated early in life and raised in different environments. Identical twins are more similar on a host of psychological characteristics, even when reared apart. Many psychological characteristics have appreciable heritability.

- Intelligence has a strong genetic basis, with heritability coefficients in the .50 to .70 range. Shared family environment is also important (particularly at lower socio-economic levels), as are educational experiences.

- Personality also has a genetic contribution, though not as strong as that for intelligence. In contrast to intelligence, shared family environment seems to have no impact on the development of personality traits. Unshared individual experiences are far more important environmental determinants.

GENE–ENVIRONMENT INTERACTIONS

Genes and environment both influence intelligence, personality and other human characteristics. But, as we have stressed throughout this chapter, they rarely operate independently. Even the prenatal environment can influence how genes express themselves, as when the mother's drug use or malnutrition retards gene-directed brain development. In the critical periods following birth, enriched environments, including the simple touching or massaging of newborns, can influence the unfolding development of premature infants (Field, 2001) and the future 'personality' of young monkeys (Harlow, 1958). Although they cannot modify the genotype itself, environmental conditions can influence how genetically based characteristics express themselves phenotypically throughout the course of development (Plomin et al., 2007).

Just as environmental effects influence phenotypic characteristics, genes can influence how the individual will experience the environment and respond to it (Hernandez & Blazer, 2007; Plomin & Spinath, 2004). Let us examine some of these interactions between genes and experience.

> **reaction range** the range of possibilities – the upper and lower limits – that the genetic code allows

HOW THE ENVIRONMENT CAN INFLUENCE GENE EXPRESSION

First, genes produce a range of potential outcomes. The concept of *reaction range* provides one useful framework for understanding gene–environmental interactions. The **reaction range** for a genetically influenced trait is the range of possibilities – the upper and lower limits – that the genetic code allows. For example, to say that intelligence is genetically influenced does not mean that intelligence is fixed at birth. Instead, it means that an individual inherits a *range* for potential intelligence that has upper and lower limits. Environmental effects will then determine where the person falls within these genetically determined boundaries.

At present, genetic reaction ranges cannot be measured directly, and we do not know if their sizes differ from one person to another. The concept has been applied most often in the study of intelligence. There, studies of IQ gains associated with environmental enrichment and adoption programmes suggest that the ranges could be as large as 15 to 20 points on the IQ scale (Dunn & Plomin, 1990). If this is indeed the case, then the influence of environmental factors on intelligence would be highly significant. A shift this large can move an individual from a below-average to an average intellectual level, or from an average IQ that would not predict college success to an above-average one that would predict success.

Some practical implications of the reaction range concept are illustrated in Figure 3.14. First, consider persons B and H. They have identical reaction ranges, but person B develops in a very deprived environment and H in an enriched environment with many cultural and educational advantages. Person H is able to realize her innate potential and has an IQ that is 20 points higher than person B's. Now compare persons C and I. Person C actually has greater intellectual potential than person I but ends up with a lower IQ as a result of living in an environment that does not allow that potential to develop. Finally, note person G, who was born with high genetic endowment and reared in an enriched environment. His slightly above-average IQ of 110 is lower than we would expect, suggesting that he did not take advantage of either his biological capacity or his environmental advantages. This serves to remind us that intellectual growth depends not only on genetic endowment and environmental advantage, but also on interests,

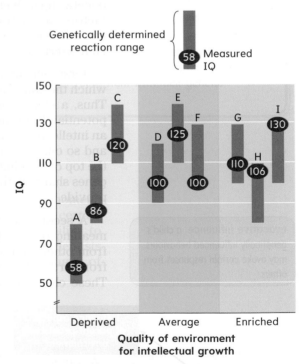

FIGURE 3.14 Reaction range is an example of how environmental factors can influence the phenotypic expression of genetic factors. Genetic endowment is believed to create a range of possibilities within which environment exerts its effects. Enriched environments are expected to allow a person's intelligence to develop to the upper region of his or her reaction range, whereas deprived environments may limit intelligence to the lower portion of the range. Where intelligence is concerned, the reaction range may cover as much as 15 to 20 points on the IQ scale.

we share a number of similarities – eyes for instance. The *Pax6* gene has been identified as responsible for eye development. If this gene is not switched on at the correct time, eyes do not develop. If the human *Pax6* gene is inserted into the side of the fruit fly an eye does indeed develop there, but not a human eye. Instead, a multifaceted, drosphylia eye, appropriate to the fly in which the gene was implanted develops. This, says Hartwell, Hood, Goldberg, Reynolds and Silver (2010) is an example of the importance of the biological environment in which the gene resides. It is not, then, only the DNA itself that is vital in the expression of the gene. Masterpasqua (2009) says that the physical environment in which the gene resides, as well as the social environment of the host, can be influential in changing molecular structures that are themselves responsible for regulating gene expression.

Gene-manipulation can be achieved in a number of ways. For instance, therapies can be developed to modify the structure of brain tissue. To do this, you first need to find a virus that can travel into the brain. Next you need to modify the genetic code of the virus before it is released into the host. Enzymes are used that can split threads of the DNA to be inserted into pieces, before combining it with the DNA of the virus, which then carries the inserted DNA to the brain. Similarly, the DNA of bacterium can be modified with pieces of DNA so that when inserted into a host the new bacterium subdivides to produce multiple copies of itself, spreading the DNA throughout the host.

knock-out procedure where a function of a gene is removed, or eliminated

knock-in procedure where a new gene is inserted into an animal at embryonic stage

Knock-Out and Knock-In Procedures

These are two methods of genetic modification, typically, and currently carried out in mice. In each case a component of the DNA is either removed (**knock-out procedure**) or new genetic material is inserted (**knock-in procedure**). In each case, a function of the gene is either removed or another function is inserted.

Current topic

TO KNOW OR NOT TO KNOW – GENETIC SCREENING

Our knowledge of human DNA and screening programmes to identify whether people may be susceptible to genetic diseases has already improved the amelioration of symptoms and improved the quality of life of a good many people through tests that help with diagnosis and targeted treatment. Genetic screening can also be used in identifying genetic illnesses in embryos, and so gives parents a choice whether to bring a child with a genetic problem into the world. This side of the debate, the protesting side, is very clear. Knowing you have or may contract a disease is vital in its treatment, or in avoiding environmental stimuli that may cause difficulties. Similarly, knowing that a disease may be contracted may allow a person to take protective steps by modifying their own behaviour. Where muscles or muscular control may be influenced by an illness for instance, the person may take time over a fitness programme specifically designed to target and strengthen areas of their body that may be affected by the disease, thereby improving their ability to deal with the symptoms.

Genetic testing of embryos typifies a very clear problem with this sort of therapy, and provokes a heated and emotional debate. Ethically, identifying a genetic illness can be extremely problematic. Some would argue that a life, be it one with issues relating to a genetic illness, is still a life and screening like this is something we should not be doing, Also of interest to those of this opinion would be that tests can sometimes give false results. Additionally, knowing that you might contract Alzheimer's or Huntington's disease is not the same as contracting it. Similarly, genetic modifications may in the future allow us to combat psychological problems such as schizophrenia or depression. It should be recognized, however, that environmental factors play a role and these should not be ignored. The psychological issues of knowing that you may contract a particular illness should not be underestimated. The character 'Thirteen' from the television series *House*, did all she could to avoid finding out whether she carried the gene for Huntington's disease, that killed the pioneering folk singer Woody Guthrie in 1967 (Figure 3.16). Many would say that knowing is best, but a similar number would not want to know the illness that may carry them off. The moral debates surrounding gene therapy look set to continue. No one can deny, however, that epigenetics looks set to play a very important role in all our futures.

To inform your debate, consider the following points where we summarize again a few of the more pertinent and controversial areas for discussion.

To summarize, three questions are important in thinking about genetic screening:

1. *What are the potential benefits of genetic screening?* There are at present more than 900 genetic tests available from testing laboratories (Human Genome Project, 2007). Proponents argue that screening can provide information that will benefit people. Early detection of a treatable condition can save lives. For example, were you to find through genetic screening that you have a predisposition to develop heart disease, you could alter your lifestyle with exercise and dietary measures to improve your chances of staying healthy. Screening could also affect reproductive decisions that reduce the probability of having children affected by a genetic disease. In a New York community, Hasidic Jews from Eastern Europe had a high incidence of Tay-Sachs disease, a fatal, genetically based neurological disorder. A genetic screening programme allowed rabbis to counsel against child-bearing in marriages involving two carriers of the abnormal allele, virtually eliminating the disease in offspring.

2. *How accurate are the screens?* Another issue is whether an inaccurate screen may result in fateful decisions. Although screens for various diseases exceed 90% accuracy, it is still possible that there can be a false positive result (an indication that a genetic predisposition to a disorder is present when it is not). Thus, a person may decide not to have children on the basis of an erroneous test that indicates a high risk of having a child with a particular problem. Alternatively, a false negative test may indicate that a predisposition is not present when in fact it is. Moreover, some tests, called *susceptibility tests*, simply tell you that you are more likely than others to develop a particular disorder, with no assurance that that will indeed occur.

3. *How should people be educated and counselled about test results?* Because of the importance of decisions that might be made on the basis of genetic screening, there is strong agreement that clients should be educated and counselled by specially trained counsellors. In the sickle-cell anaemia screening of the 1970s, follow-up education was inadequate, the result being that some African-American men who were informed that they were carriers of the sickle-cell allele elected to remain childless because they were not told that the disorder would not occur in their offspring if their mates were non-carriers of the allele. The genetic counsellor's role is to help the person, couple or family to decide whether to be screened, to help them to fully understand the meaning of the test results, and to assist them during what might well be a difficult and traumatic time.

> **Focus 3.13** Only about 10 to 20% of people at risk for HD choose to be genetically screened. Why do you think this is?

 In review

- Genetic and environmental factors interact in complex ways to influence phenotypic characteristics. Genetic reaction range sets upper and lower limits for the impact of environmental factors. Where intelligence is concerned, environmental factors may create differences as large as 20 IQ points. Genotype can influence the kind of environments to which children are exposed, as when intelligent parents create an enriched environment. Genetically influenced behaviour patterns also have an evocative influence, influencing how the environment responds to the person. Finally, people often select environments that match genetically influenced personal characteristics.

- Genetic manipulation allows scientists to duplicate and alter genetic material or, potentially, to repair dysfunctional genes. These procedures promise ground-breaking advances in understanding genetic mechanisms and in treating physical and psychological disorders. Moreover, our ability to analyse people's genotypes allows for genetic screening and raises a host of practical and ethical issues.

EVOLUTION AND HUMAN NATURE

The evidence from behavioural genetics has gone a long way to convincing people that human nature is indeed influenced by evolved predispositions. However, the application of principles of natural selection to psychology has not been without controversy. Indeed a healthy scepticism is to be recommended. There is a great danger in the misapplication of

Darwin's thinking. For example, Francis Galton argued that certain traits which might have been functional and useful in the past were not so in modern Victorian England. He coined the term 'eugenics' to describe a practice of improving the human race by encouraging 'desirable' human traits through selective breeding. Those who had these 'desirable' traits should be encouraged to have children; those who did not (such as criminals) should be discouraged or prevented. Bitter experience has taught us that the principles of eugenics can be taken even further with horrifying consequences; Hitler's attempts to improve society with eugenics resulted in the death of millions in Nazi Germany.

Eugenics placed an unmerited moral value on evolutionary **adaptations**, which are physical or behavioural changes that allow organisms to meet recurring environmental challenges to their survival. There is no 'should' or 'ought' in evolution – life just is the way it is. People sometimes ask questions such as, 'What is the point of a mosquito?' According to the dictates of evolution, this is a nonsensical question. Natural selection is a blind, mechanical, purposeless process. It is not directed toward any particular higher goal or value. It is based upon random genetic mutations. The name of the game is long-term genetic survival and there is no particular moral merit in that. Thus, one should not consider any particular extant species evolutionarily more worthy or advanced than any another. Humans, in evolutionary terms, are not better than cockroaches because we have evolved bigger brains and are capable of more complex behaviour. If humans were to wipe themselves out in a nuclear holocaust while cockroaches survived, cockroaches would be the evolutionary success story, not us. Similarly, if an inherited tendency toward criminality were to increase the possessors' reproductive success, then in evolutionary terms, these genes would be preferable to genes that promoted more law-abiding tendencies. By placing value judgements onto natural selection, eugenicists fundamentally misunderstood the logic of the principles underlying Darwinian evolution.

> **adaptations** physical or behavioural changes that allow organisms to meet recurring environmental challenges to their survival, thereby increasing their reproductive ability

FOR THE GOOD OF THE GENE

As we have seen, eugenicists proposed that we could improve the species by denying certain groups of people the right to reproduce. Yet, in *The Origin of Species*, Darwin clearly argued that natural selection does not work for 'the good of the species' or 'the good of the group'. Instead, he proposed that natural selection would always favour biological traits that promoted the reproductive success of individuals over and above what is good for the group or species. To understand why, let us consider the case of lemmings.

Lemmings are small rodents that live on the Arctic tundra. It is widely believed that when their population exceeds their food supply a large proportion of lemmings will selflessly commit mass suicide by leaping off cliffs thereby ensuring the survival of the rest of the group and in the long run the species as a whole. However, it is difficult to see how a genetic mutation that influences its carrier to commit selfless suicide could ever be selected in preference to individuals who lack these genes. Any 'selfish' individuals, who failed to sacrifice themselves by leaping off cliffs, would remain on the tundra and benefit from the reduced feeding competition. They would also continue to breed and very quickly their genes would become predominant in the population. Therefore, suicide for the good of the group or species is not an evolutionarily stable strategy: it could never establish itself as the modal trait within a population. So how do we explain the lemmings' behaviour? Actually, lemming mass suicides are a myth. There are no validated scientific observations of lemmings leaping off cliffs when their food supply runs short. Lemming populations do undergo a cyclical pattern of boom and bust (Chitty, 1996), but they do not commit suicide during the boom phases; rather some proportion of the population will serve their genetically selfish long-term individual interests by migrating.

Since natural selection does not operate for the good of the group or species, Darwinian theory seems to present a rather bleak view of existence. It seems to suggest a brutal world of ruthless competition, summed up in the infamous phrase, 'survival of the fittest' (which incidentally was first coined by Herbert Spencer not Darwin, though Darwin used and approved of it). Biological 'fitness' does not necessarily refer to the strongest or fastest or even longest-lived members of a population. If an organism lived for a thousand years, but died without doing anything to ensure that some biological part of it survived

after its death, it would be an evolutionary dead end. Darwin measured fitness in terms of the number of offspring an individual produces. However, we now know that the unit of inheritance is the gene. Thus, modern evolutionary theorists measure reproductive success in terms of the estimated number of copies of individual genes that survive into future generations (Dawkins, 2006).

Of course, as mentioned earlier, we do not just share a higher proportion of our genes with our offspring, but also our close family members. In light of this fact, William Hamilton (1963) put forward the concept of **kin selection**. He reasoned that since we share a high proportion of our genes with our close relatives, we could promote the survival of those genes by helping to ensure the survival and reproductive success of our kin. There are lots of examples in nature of animals risking or even sacrificing their lives in order to protect their kin and the genes they carry. For example, goffers or prairie dogs are more likely to risk their lives by giving predator alarm calls when close kin, rather than more distantly related individuals, are in the audience (Hoogland, 1995). Thus, the world created by natural selection is not as entirely dog-eat-dog as one might suppose.

Robert Trivers (1971) has even suggested a mechanism by which self-sacrifice for non-relatives could evolve. He called the mechanism **reciprocal altruism**. The tendency to perform an immediately selfless behaviour for the benefit of non-kin could be selected as long as at a later time the recipient reciprocates the favour resulting in a net benefit to both parties. To put it in more layperson's terms, it is a case of, 'I'll scratch your back now, if you scratch my back later' (Dawkins, 1989). One of the most well studied examples in nature comes from vampire bats (Wilkinson, 1984; Carter & Wilkinson, 2013). Vampire bats make a living by biting and drinking the blood of other living animals. Seven per cent of adults and 33% of juveniles (which are bats under two years of age) fail to feed on any given night. Failure to feed is very serious, since bats die after an average of only 70 hours of fasting. They can avoid starvation by begging from other bats in their colony, some of which will regurgitate a blood meal for their starving companion. Although bats most often regurgitate for family members, Wilkinson (1984) suspected that reciprocal relationships existed between non-relatives too. To test this, he formed two captive groups from natural vampire bat clusters so that the members in the experimental groups were non-relatives. He then removed bats and deprived them of food for one or two days. Under these conditions, reciprocal partnerships of blood sharing between pairs of unrelated bats were observed.

kin selection is an evolutionary strategy in which behaviours art selected which favour the reproductive success of an organism's relatives even if that is at a cost to that organism's our survival and reproduction

reciprocal altruism is a behaviour is an organism which reduces its fitness to survive and reproduce while increasing another organism's fitness, undertaken with the expectation that the favour will be returned later

 ## Applying Psychological Science

Darwinian evolution would seem to suggest that we have evolved to be ruthlessly competitive and selfish (Dawkins, 2006). However, as we have seen kin selection and reciprocal altruism provide mechanisms, which can select for more positive social behaviour. Recent research has suggests that human social emotions such as guilt, shame, righteous indignation and gratitude may also be based on evolved predispositions (Shiota et al., 2004). These emotions may be ways of monitoring and maintaining mutually beneficial social relationships.

In recent years, psychologists have been studying positive social emotions in more detail. Seligman (2002) studied the emotions related to generosity and gratitude. He found that people reported higher levels of happiness by showing generosity to others than when they just pleased themselves. Similarly, Dunn et al. (2008) found people were happier when in an experiment they were instructed to spend money on others versus themselves.

Seligman et al. (2005) also investigated the effect on levels of reported happiness in terms of expressing gratitude. Participants were asked to identify and think about someone whom they were grateful to but had never explicitly thanked. They wrote and read out loud to that person a gratitude letter. The participants' levels of self-reported happiness were measured before and after the delivery of the letter. The participants reported significantly higher levels of happiness up to a month after completing the gratitude exercise. It seems we have a strong predisposition to promote our social relationships, underpinned by strong social emotions.

Try it yourself. Think long and hard about someone you are grateful to. Write an approximately 300-word letter of gratitude to that person. Be specific in the letter: say what the person had done for you, how it has affected your life and how it has made you feel. Arrange to visit the person but don't tell them why. When you see them, read the letter out loud. It may feel a bit strange, even embarrassing, but the research has shown that not only will you make the recipient of your positive social act happier, but you seem to be biologically wired with emotions that mean you will be happier too.

Culturally Universal Characteristics

Although reciprocal altruism is rare in non-human species, it is a common feature of all human groups. Culturally universal aspects of behaviour are of particular interest to evolutionary psychologists. If nearly every single human culture, even those that are relatively isolated from all other human groups, expresses a certain characteristic it suggests the expression of inborn biological tendencies that have evolved through natural selection. There exists a vast catalogue of human culturally universal characteristics and capabilities that unfold in all normally developing human beings. Consider, for example, this brief preview of commonalities in human behaviour that are discussed in greater detail in later chapters.

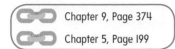

Chapter 9, Page 374

Chapter 5, Page 199

1. Infants are born with an ability to acquire any language spoken in the world (see **Chapter 9**). The specific languages learned depend on which ones they are exposed to. Deaf children have a similar ability to acquire any sign language, and their language acquisition pattern parallels the learning of spoken language. Language is central to human thought and communication.

2. Humans newborns are pre-wired to perceive specific stimuli (see **Chapter 5**). For example, they are more responsive to pictures of human faces than to pictures of the same facial features arranged in a random pattern (Johnson, Dziurawiec, Ellis, & Morton, 1991). They are also able to discriminate the odour of their mother's milk from that of other women (McFarlane, 1975). Facial perception and orientation may be an adaptation to promote human bonding with caregivers.

Focus 3.14 How have evolutionary principles been used to account for diverse cultures?

3. At one week of age, human neonates (i.e., babies less than one month old) show primitive mathematical skills, successfully discriminating between two and three objects. These abilities improve with age in the absence of any training. The brain seems designed to make 'greater than' and 'less than' judgements, which are clearly important in decision making (Geary, 2005).

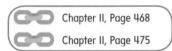

Chapter 11, Page 468

Chapter 11, Page 475

4. According to Robert Hogan (1983), establishing cooperative relationships with other group members was critical to individual survival and reproductive success in ancestral humans. Thus humans seem to have a need to belong and strongly fear being ostracized from the group (see **Chapter 11**). Social anxiety (fear of social disapproval) may be an adaptive mechanism to protect against doing things that will prompt group rejection (Baumeister & Tice, 1990).

Focus 3.15 Do genetically based diseases provide an argument against natural selection?

5. As we will see in **Chapter 11**, there is much evidence for a set of basic emotions that are universally recognized (Ekman, 1973). Smiling, for example, is a universal expression of happiness and goodwill that typically evokes positive reactions from others (Figure 3.16). Emotions are important means of social communication that trigger mental, emotional and behavioural mechanisms in others (Ketellar, 1995).

6. In virtually all cultures, males are more violent and more likely to kill others (particularly other males) than are females. The differences are striking, with male–male killings outnumbering female–female killings, on average, by about 30 to one (Daly & Wilson, 1988). Evolutionary researchers suggest that male–male violence is rooted in hunting, establishing dominance hierarchies and competing successfully for the most fertile mates, all of which enhanced personal and reproductive survival during the course of human evolution.

Having sampled from the wide range of behavioural phenomena that have been subjected to an evolutionary analysis, let us focus in greater detail on two areas of current theorizing that relate to both commonalities and differences among people – sex and self. Before doing so, however, we should emphasize a most important principle: *behaviour does not occur in a biological vacuum; it always involves a biological organism acting within (and often, in response to) an environment.* That environment may be inside the body in the form of interactions with other genes, influencing how genes and the protein molecules through which they operate express themselves. It may be inside the mother's womb, or it may be 'out there', in the form of a physical environment or a culture. Although everyone agrees

FIGURE 3.16 The human smile seems to be a universal expression of positive emotion and is universally perceived in that way. Evolutionary psychologists believe that expressions of basic emotions are hard-wired biological mechanisms that have adaptive value as methods of communication.

Source: © Aldo Murillo.

that biological and environmental factors interact with one another, most of the debates in evolutionary psychology concern two issues: (1) How general or specific are the biological mechanisms that have evolved? (2) How much are these mechanisms influenced in their expression by the environment?

EVOLUTIONARY APPROACHES TO HUMAN MATE CHOICE

The most direct way to ensure one's long-term genetic survival is to mate and produce offspring. We should not be surprised, therefore, that evolutionary theorists and researchers have devoted great attention to sexuality, differences between men and women, and mate-seeking. This topic also has generated considerable debate about the relative contributions of evolutionary and sociocultural factors to this domain of behaviour.

One of the most important and intimate ways that humans relate to one another is by seeking a mate. Marriage seems to be universal across the globe (Buss & Schmitt, 1993). In seeking mates, however, women and men display different mating strategies and preferences. Compared with women, men typically show more interest in short-term mating, prefer a greater number of short-term sexual partners, and have more permissive sexual attitudes and more sexual partners over their lifetimes (Schmitt, Shackelford, & Buss, 2001). In one study of 266 undergraduates, two-thirds of the women said that they desired only one sexual partner over the next 30 years, but only about half of the men shared that goal (Pedersen, Miller, Putcha-Bhagavatula, & Yang, 2002). These attitudinal differences also extend to behaviour. In research conducted at three different universities, Russell Clark and Elaine Hatfield (1989; Clark, 1990) sent male and female research assistants of average physical attractiveness out across the campus. Upon seeing an attractive person of the opposite sex, the assistant approached the person, said he or she found the person attractive, and asked, 'Would you go to bed with me tonight?' Women approached in this manner almost always reacted very negatively to the overture and frequently dismissed the assistants as 'sleaze' or 'pervert'. Not a single woman agreed to have sex. In contrast, three in every four men enthusiastically agreed, some asking why it was necessary to wait until that night. Other findings show that men think about sex about three times more often than women do, desire more frequent sex and initiate more sexual encounters than do women (Baumeister, Catanese, & Vohs, 2001; Laumann, Gagnon, Michael, & Michaels, 1994). Men also are much more likely to interpret a woman's friendliness as a sexual come-on, apparently projecting their own sexual desires onto the woman (Johnson, Wadsworth, Wellings, & Bradshaw, 1992).

Despite these differences, most men and women make a commitment at some point in their lives to a long-term mate. What qualities do women and men seek in such a mate? Once again, we see sex differences. Men typically prefer women somewhat younger than themselves, whereas women prefer somewhat older men. This tendency is exaggerated in the 'trophy wives' sometimes exhibited by wealthy and famous older men. In terms of personal qualities, Table 3.4 shows the overall results of a worldwide study of mate preferences in 37 cultures (Buss et al., 1990). Men and women again show considerable overall agreement, but some differences emerge. Men place

TABLE 3.4 Characteristics of a mate

Women and men rated each characteristic on a 4-point scale. From top to bottom, the following numbers represent the order (rank) of most highly rated to least highly rated items for Buss's worldwide sample. How would you rate their importance?

Characteristic desired in a mate	Rated by	
	Women	Men
Mutual attraction/love	1	1
Dependable character	2	2
Emotional stability/maturity	3	3
Pleasing disposition	4	4
Education/intelligence	5	6
Sociability	6	7
Good health	7	5
Desire for home/children	8	8
Ambition	9	11
Refinement	10	9
Similar education	11	14
Good financial prospect	12	13
Good looks	13	10
Social status	14	15
Good cook/housekeeper	15	12
Similar religion	16	17
Similar politics	17	18
Chastity	18	16

Source: Based on Buss et al., 1990.

greater value on a potential mate's physical attractiveness, whereas women place greater value on a potential mate's earning potential, status and ambitiousness. But why might this be? Evolutionary psychologists have an answer.

According to an evolutionary viewpoint called **sexual strategies theory** (and a related model called **parental investment theory**), mating strategies and preferences reflect inherited tendencies, shaped over the ages in response to different types of adaptive problems that men and women faced (Buss & Schmitt, 1993; Trivers, 1972). In evolutionary terms, our most successful ancestors were those who survived and passed down the greatest numbers of their genes to future generations. Men who had sex with more partners increased the likelihood of fathering more children, so they were interested in mating widely. Men also may have taken a woman's youth and attractive, healthy appearance as signs that she was fertile and had many years left to bear his children (Buss, 1989).

In contrast, ancestral women had little to gain and much to lose by mating with numerous men. They were interested in mating wisely, not widely. In humans and other mammals, females typically make a greater investment than males: they carry the foetus, incur health risks and possible birth-related death, and nourish the newborn. Engaging in short-term sexual relationships with multiple males can in the end create uncertainty about who is the father, thereby decreasing a male's willingness to commit resources to helping a mother raise the child. For these reasons, women maximized their reproductive success – and the survival chances of themselves and their offspring – by being selective and choosing mates who were willing and able to commit time, energy and other resources (e.g., food, shelter, protection) to the family. Women increased their likelihood of passing their genes into the future by mating wisely, and men by mating widely. Through natural selection, according to evolutionary psychologists, the differing qualities that maximized men's and women's reproductive success eventually became part of their biological nature (Buss, 2007).

Steven Gangestad, Martie Haselton and David Buss (2006) found that some of these mate preference patterns are more pronounced in parts of the world with historically high levels of pathogens (disease-causing germs) that endangered survival than in areas that had historically low levels of pathogens. Where diseases like malaria, plague and yellow fever are more prevalent, male factors such as physical attractiveness and robustness, intelligence and social dominance – all presumably signs of biological fitness – seem especially important to women even today. Gangestad et al. suggest that in such environments, women seem willing to sacrifice some degree of male investment in their offspring in favour of a mate who has a higher probability of giving them healthy children. To men, a woman's attractiveness and healthiness (and that of her family) also is more important in high-pathogen environments, presumably because these historically were signs of a woman who would be more likely to give birth to healthy children and live long enough to rear them.

Not all scientists have bought into this evolutionary explanation for human mating patterns and other social behaviours. Again, the disagreement revolves around the relative potency of interacting biological and environmental factors. In the case of mate selection, proponents of **social structure theory** maintain that men and women display different mating preferences not because nature impels them to do so, but because society guides them into different social roles (Eagly & Wood, 1999, 2006). Adaptive behaviour patterns may have been passed from parents to children not through genes but through learning. Social structure theorists point out that despite the shift over the past several decades towards greater gender equality, today's women still have generally less power, lower wages and less access to resources than do men. In a two-income marriage, the woman is more likely to be the partner who switches to part-time work or becomes a full-time homemaker after childbirth. Thus, society's division of labour still tends to socialize men into the breadwinner role and women into the homemaker role.

Given these power and resource disparities and the need to care for children, it makes sense for women to seek men who will be successful wage earners and for men to seek women who can have children and fulfil the domestic-worker role. An older male–younger female age gap is favourable because older men are likely to be further along in earning power and younger women are more economically dependent, and this state of affairs conforms to cultural expectations of marital roles. This division-of-labour hypothesis does not directly address why men emphasize a mate's physical attractiveness more than

sexual strategies theory (and a related model called **parental investment theory**) mating strategies and preferences reflect inherited tendencies, shaped over the ages in response to different types of adaptive problems that men and women faced

social structure theory men and women display different mating preferences not because nature impels them to do so, but because society guides them into different social roles

women do, but Alice Eagly and Wendy Wood (1999) speculate that attractiveness is viewed as part of what women 'exchange' in return for a male's earning capacity.

We now have two competing explanations for sex differences in mating behaviour: the evolution-based sexual strategies approach and the social structure view. Our 'Research close-up' looks at one attempt to compare predictions derived from the two theories.

Focus 3.16 Why should the mate choice criteria of men and women overlap so much?

 Research close-up

SEX DIFFERENCES IN THE IDEAL MATE: EVOLUTION OR SOCIAL ROLES?

Sources: D. M. Buss (1989). Sex differences in human mate preferences: Evolutionary hypotheses tested in 37 cultures. *Behavioral and Brain Sciences, 12,* 1–49; A. Eagly and W. Wood (1999). The origins of sex differences in human behavior: Evolved dispositions versus social roles. *American Psychologist, 54,* 408–423.

INTRODUCTION

How can we possibly test the hypothesis that, over the ages, evolution has shaped the psyches of men and women to be inherently different? Evolutionary psychologist David Buss proposes that, as a start, we can examine whether gender differences in mating preferences are similar across cultures. If they are, this would be consistent with the view that men and women follow universal, biologically based mating strategies that transcend culture. Based on principles of evolutionary psychology, Buss hypothesized that *across cultures*, men will prefer to marry younger women because such women have greater reproductive capacity; men will value a potential mate's attractiveness more than women will because men use attractiveness as a sign of health and fertility; and women will place greater value than men on a potential mate's earning potential because this provides survival advantages for the woman and her offspring.

METHOD

Buss's team of 50 scientists administered questionnaires to women and men from 37 cultures around the globe. Although random sampling could not be used, the sample of 10,047 participants was ethnically, religiously and socio-economically diverse. Participants reported the ideal ages at which they and a spouse would marry, rank-ordered (from 'most desirable' to 'least desirable') a list of 13 qualities that a potential mate might have, and rated the importance of 18 mate qualities on a second list (see Table 3.4).

Alice Eagly and Wendy Wood wondered if men's and women's mate preferences might be influenced by a third variable, namely, cultural differences in gender roles and power differentials. To find out, they re-analysed Buss's data, using the United Nations Gender Empowerment Measure to assess the degree of gender equality in each of the cultures. This measure reflects women's earned income relative to men's, seats in parliament, and share of administrative, managerial, professional and technical jobs.

RESULTS

In all 37 cultures, men wanted to marry younger women. Overall, they believed that the ideal ages for men and women to marry were 27.5 and 24.8 years, respectively. Similarly, women preferred older men, reporting on average an ideal marriage age of 28.8 for husbands and 25.4 for wives. In every culture, men valued having a physically attractive mate more than women did, and in 36 of 37 cultures, women attached more importance than men did to a mate's earning potential.

EVOLUTIONARY AND SOCIAL ROLES' INTERPRETATIONS

David Buss concluded that the findings strongly supported the predictions of evolutionary (sexual strategies) theory. Subsequently, Alice Eagly and Wendy Wood analysed Buss's data further in order to test two key predictions derived from their social structure theory:

1. Men place greater value than women on a mate's having good domestic skills because this is consistent with culturally defined gender roles.

2. If economic and power inequalities cause men and women to attach different values to a mate's age, earning potential and domestic skills, then these gender differences should be smaller in cultures where there is less inequality between men and women.

As reported by Buss, the potential-mate characteristic 'good cook/housekeeper' produced large overall gender differences, with men valuing it more highly. Could

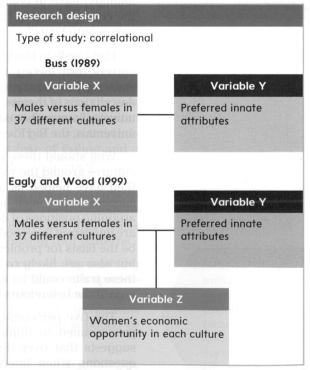

Research design

Type of study: correlational

Buss (1989)

Variable X	Variable Y
Males versus females in 37 different cultures	Preferred innate attributes

Eagly and Wood (1999)

Variable X	Variable Y
Males versus females in 37 different cultures	Preferred innate attributes

Variable Z

Women's economic opportunity in each culture

isolation, however, but in concert with environmental factors, some of which are created by nature and some of which are of human origin. Together, these forces have forged the human psychological capabilities and processes that are the focus of psychological science. Levels of analysis show how the causes of behaviour can be studied.

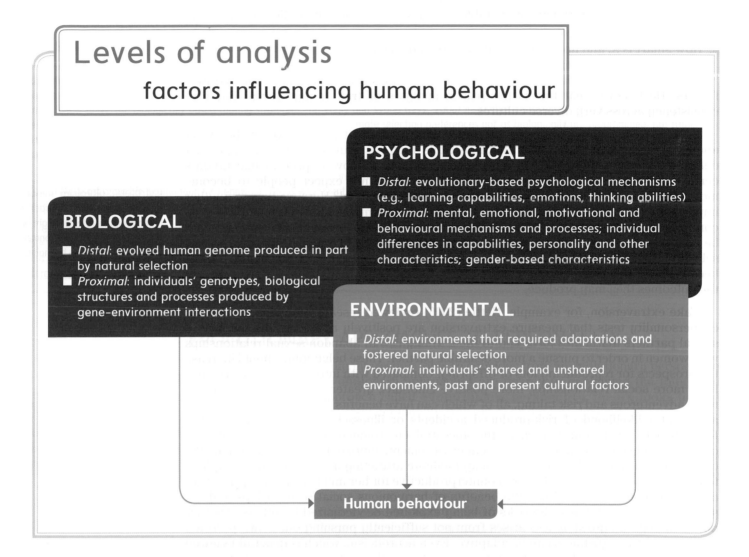

Levels of analysis
factors influencing human behaviour

PSYCHOLOGICAL
- *Distal*: evolutionary-based psychological mechanisms (e.g., learning capabilities, emotions, thinking abilities)
- *Proximal*: mental, emotional, motivational and behavioural mechanisms and processes; individual differences in capabilities, personality and other characteristics; gender-based characteristics

BIOLOGICAL
- *Distal*: evolved human genome produced in part by natural selection
- *Proximal*: individuals' genotypes, biological structures and processes produced by gene–environment interactions

ENVIRONMENTAL
- *Distal*: environments that required adaptations and fostered natural selection
- *Proximal*: individuals' shared and unshared environments, past and present cultural factors

Human behaviour

 In review

- Evolutionary psychology focuses on biologically based mechanisms sculpted by evolutionary forces as solutions to the problems of adaptation faced by species. Some of these genetically based mechanisms are general (e.g., the ability to learn from the consequences of our behaviour), whereas others are thought to be domain-specific, devoted to solving specific problems, such as mate selection.
- Evolution is a change over time in the frequency with which particular genes, and the characteristics they produce, occur within an interbreeding population. Evolution represents an interaction between biological and environmental factors.
- The cornerstone of Darwin's theory of evolution is the principle of natural selection. According to this principle, biologically based characteristics that contribute to survival and reproductive success increase in the population over time because those who lack the characteristics are less likely to pass on their genes.
- Among the aspects of human behaviour that have received evolutionary explanations are human mate selection and personality traits. In research on mate selection, evolutionary explanations have been tested against hypotheses derived from social structure theory, which emphasizes the role of cultural factors.

Recommended Reading

CONTEMPORARY

Plomin, R. Dearies, J.C., Knopik, V.S. & Neiderhiser,J.M. (2013). *Behavioural Genetics* (6th edn). New York: Worth.

Rutter, M. (2006). *Genes and behavior: Nature-nuture interplay explained.* Oxford: Blackwell.

CLASSIC

Dawkins, R. (1976). *The Selfish Gene.* New York: Oxford University Press.

Lorenz, K. (1961). *King Solomon's Ring* (Trans. M. Kerr Wilson). London: Methuen.

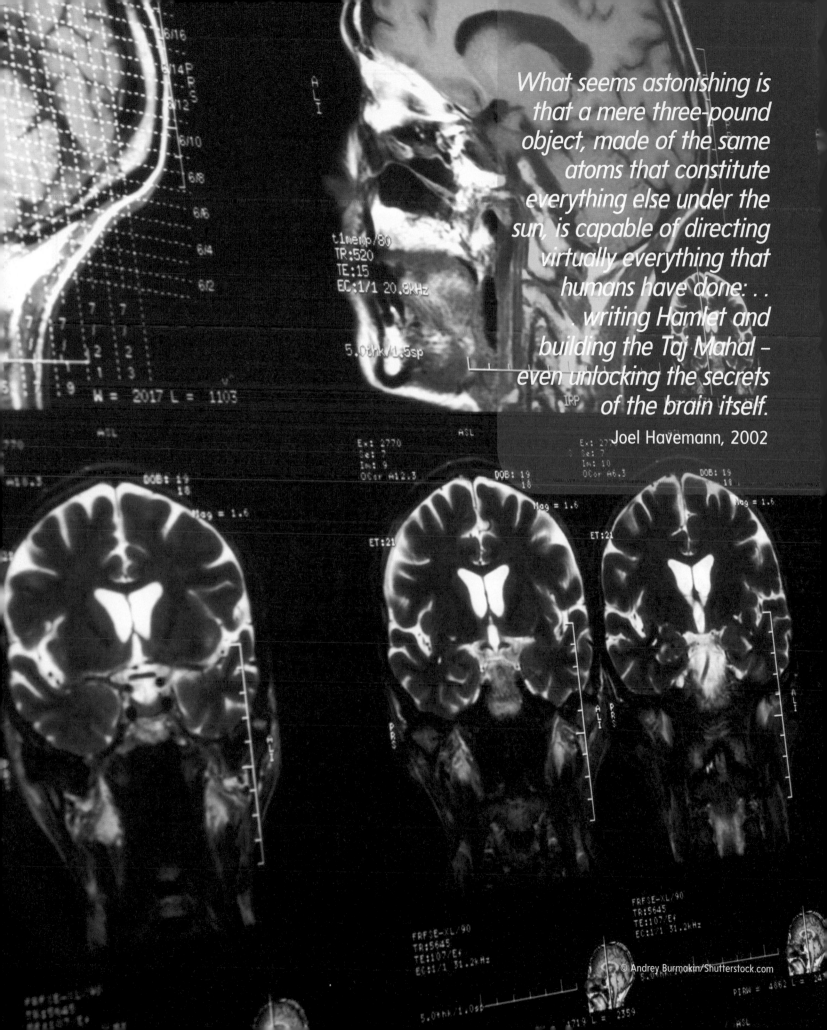

What seems astonishing is that a mere three-pound object, made of the same atoms that constitute everything else under the sun, is capable of directing virtually everything that humans have done: . . . writing Hamlet and building the Taj Mahal – even unlocking the secrets of the brain itself.

Joel Havemann, 2002

The brain and behaviour

4

Chapter Outline

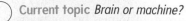

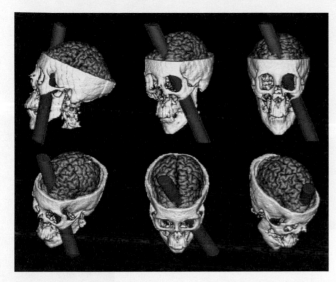

FIGURE 4.1 The brain damage suffered by Phineas Gage seemed to change him into a new person. The red image shows the path of the spike that shot through Gage's brain.

Source: PATRICK LANDMANN/SCIENCE PHOTO LIBRARY

The year was 1848 and a railway construction crew hurried to clear rocks so that a track could be laid before the winter set in. Phineas Gage, a 25-year-old foreman in a blasting crew, was using a 'tamping iron' to pack explosives into a hole before detonating it to blast away the rock. Gage, by mistake, started 'tamping' the hole before sand had been put in on top of the explosive powder, and the subsequent explosion propelled the tamping iron (a 5.9 kg spike of nearly a metre in length) through his head. The spike entered through his left cheek, passed through his brain, and emerged through the top of his skull (Figure 4.1).

Miraculously, Gage survived and his wounds healed. His personality, however, changed forever. Harlow (1868) reports an imbalance 'between his intellectual faculties and animal propensities'. He became foul-mouthed and at best indifferent to those around him. Harlow goes on to say that 'his friends and acquaintances say that he is "no longer Gage"' (Harlow, 1868, pp. 339–340). The story of Gage's miraculous but not without costs survival is so famous that it features in most textbooks like this one.

A word of caution, however; the case of Phineas Gage is often over-stated and badly represented. The evidence for the changes Gage experienced is taken from very limited resources and is not always clear. Nevertheless, his tragic story illustrates the intimate connection between brain, mind and behaviour. Is our personal identity so thoroughly locked inside our skull? Is who we are and what we do reducible to the electrochemical activities of the nervous system? Most neuroscientists would not hesitate to answer, 'Yes'.

Our understanding of the ways in which the brain functions has come on immeasurably in recent times. Since the twentieth century, neuropsychological studies of brain-injured patients and neurophysiological investigations of the functions of neurons (the cells which transmit nervous activity) have provided the foundations of our understanding of how the brain functions. The more recent developments in brain-mapping techniques have allowed neuroscientists to push forward even further our understanding of the biological basis of our psychological functions. As our understanding of how the brain and nervous system works improves, the more important and useful this biological perspective becomes in explaining psychological processes. In this chapter we will discuss what we know about the biological building blocks of psychology.

THE NERVOUS SYSTEM

The nervous system is the body's control centre. It is made up of two kinds of cell: neurons and glial cells. **Neurons** send a combination of electrical and chemical signals throughout the body. Some of these signals are simple and control automatic body functions like the heartbeat. Other signals are extremely complicated and involve a much larger network of neurons. It is the electrical and chemical signals of neurons which make up our mental activity. **Glial cells** are typically described as support and supply cells. They surround the neurons and hold them in place, manufacturing nutrients for the neurons and absorbing toxins.

The ways in which we think and process information are determined by the ways in which neurons pass electricity through the nervous system. The power of our mental processes is determined to a great extent by the numbers of these neurons and the numbers of connections (**synapses**) which can be made between different neurons. The average adult male brain contains 86 billion (86,000,000,000) neurons (Azevedo et al., 2009), which is something like the number of trees in the Amazonian rainforest. If we take it that each neuron possesses about 600 synapses with other neurons, then that gives us 51,600,000,000,000 neurons, which is something approaching the number of leaves on all of the trees in the Amazonian rainforest. The brain clearly has a lot of processing power.

neurons the functional building blocks of the nervous system. Cells which transmit the electrical activity which underlies psychological processes

glial cell from the Greek for 'glue'. Cells surrounding neurons, holding them in place, providing nutrients neurons need and isolating toxins that would harm the neuron

synapse a connection between neurons

Focus 4.1 What are the three major types of neurons in the nervous system? What are their functions?

Three major types of neurons carry out the system's input, output and integration functions. **Sensory neurons** carry input messages from the sense organs to the spinal cord and brain. **Motor neurons** transmit output impulses from the brain and spinal cord to the body's muscles and organs. Finally, there are neurons that link the input and output functions. These **interneurons**, which far outnumber sensory and motor neurons, perform connective or associative functions within the nervous system. For example, interneurons would allow us to recognize a friend by linking the sensory input from the visual system with the memory of that person's characteristics stored elsewhere in the brain. The activity of interneurons makes possible the complexity of our higher mental functions, emotions and behavioural capabilities.

The nervous system can be broken down into several interrelated subsystems (Figure 4.2). The two major divisions are the peripheral and central nervous systems.

THE PERIPHERAL NERVOUS SYSTEM

The **peripheral nervous system** contains all the neural structures that lie outside the brain and spinal cord. Its specialized neurons are mostly sensory and motor neurons, and help carry out: (1) the sensory input functions that enable us to sense what is going on inside and outside our bodies; and (2) the motor output functions that enable us to respond with our muscles and glands. The peripheral nervous system has two major divisions: the somatic nervous system and the autonomic nervous system.

The Somatic Nervous System

The **somatic nervous system** consists of sensory neurons that are specialized to transmit messages from the eyes, ears and other sensory receptors, and motor neurons that send messages from the brain and spinal cord to the muscles that control our voluntary movements. Sensory neurons group together like many strands of a rope to form sensory nerves, and motor neurons combine to form motor nerves. As you read this page, sensory neurons in your eyes are sending impulses into a complex network of specialized visual tracts that course through your brain. (Inside the brain and spinal cord, nerves are called tracts.) At the same time, motor neurons are stimulating the eye

sensory neurons carry input messages from the sense organs to the spinal cord and brain

motor neurons transmit output impulses from the brain and spinal cord to the body's muscles and organs

interneurons perform connective or associative functions within the nervous system

peripheral nervous system contains all the neural structures that lie outside the brain and spinal cord

somatic nervous system consists of sensory neurons that are specialized to transmit messages from the eyes, ears and other sensory receptors, and motor neurons that send messages from the brain and spinal cord to the muscles that control our voluntary movements

Focus 4.2 Name the two divisions of the peripheral nervous system. How does the autonomic system maintain homeostasis?

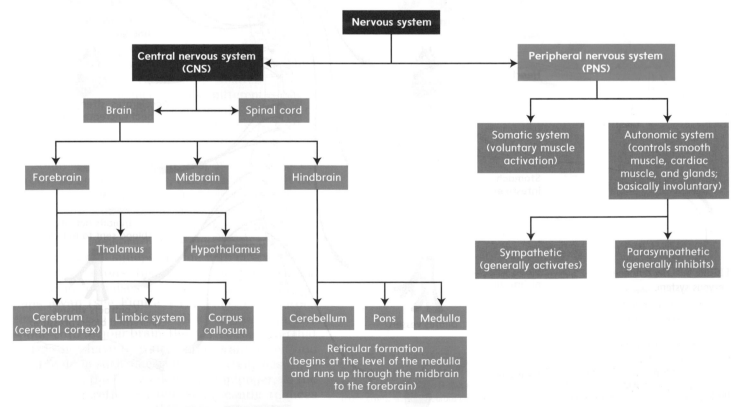

FIGURE 4.2 Structural organization of the nervous system.

FIGURE 4.5 White and grey matter in the brain.

The brain is composed of grey matter (neuron cell bodies) and white matter (the axons of neurons). In this figure we can see a slice through the brain which shows how the grey and white matter separate. This kind of section is called a coronal section.

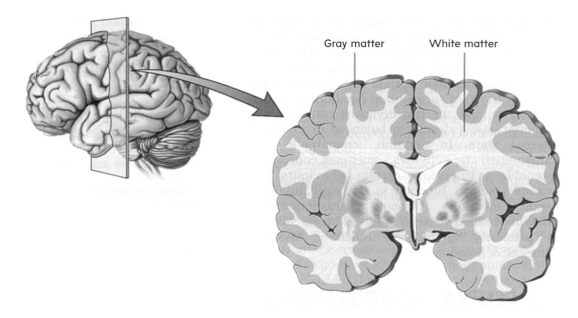

Gray matter   White matter

The Brain

Focus 4.3 What are the two main structures in the central nervous system?

As befits this biological marvel, your brain is the most active energy consumer of all your body organs. It accounts for only about 2% of your total body weight, but it consumes about 25% of your body's oxygen and 70% of its glucose. It never rests; its rate of energy metabolism is relatively constant day and night. In fact, when you dream, the brain's metabolic rate actually increases (Simon, 2007). The brain, like the spinal cord, is composed of grey matter and white matter (Figure 4.5), but this time the grey matter is on the outside of the brain, and the white matter is on the inside. The grey and white matter are composed of the different parts of the neurons which make up the brain and nervous system. The grey matter is made up of the cell bodies of neurons. The white matter is made up of the long connecting parts of neurons, the axons. The axons connect various levels of the brain and spinal cord with each other. In the next section we will describe the neuron and its various parts (including axons and cell bodies), and how these function to transmit neural signals. Later we will discuss how the different parts of the brain are specialized for different functions.

 In review

■ The nervous system contains sensory neurons, motor neurons and interneurons. Its two major divisions are the central nervous system, consisting of the brain and spinal cord, and the peripheral nervous system. The peripheral system is divided into the somatic system (which is responsible for sensory and motor functions) and the autonomic nervous system (which directs the activity of the body's internal organs and glands).

■ The autonomic nervous system consists of sympathetic and parasympathetic divisions. The sympathetic system has an arousal function and tends to act as a unit. The parasympathetic system slows down body processes and is more specific in its actions. Together, the two divisions maintain a state of homeostasis, or internal balance.

■ The spinal cord contains sensory neurons and motor neurons. Interneurons inside the spinal cord serve a connective function between the two. Simple stimulus–response sequences can occur as spinal reflexes.

■ The brain and spinal cord contain white and grey matter. Grey matter is where cells connect, and is comprised of the cell bodies and synapses of neurons. White matter is where signals are transmitted between different parts of the nervous system within the axons of neurons.

NEURONS

Specialized cells called neurons are the basic building blocks of the nervous system. The estimated 85 billion nerve cells in your brain and spinal cord are linked together in circuits, not unlike the electrical circuits in a computer. Neurons can vary greatly in size and shape. For instance, neurons found in the brain may be extremely short and only millimetres in length, but neurons situated in your spinal cord may have an axon that is long enough to extend to the tips of your fingers. Each neuron has three main parts: a cell body, dendrites and an axon (Figure 4.6). The cell bodies and dendrites make up the grey matter of the nervous system, and the axons make up the white matter. The cell body, or *soma*, contains the biochemical structures needed to keep the neuron alive, and its nucleus carries the genetic information that determines how the cell develops and functions. Emerging from the cell body are branch-like fibres called **dendrites** (from the Greek word meaning 'tree'), specialized receiving units like antennae that collect messages from neighbouring neurons and send them on to the cell body. There, the incoming information from all neighbouring cells is combined. The many branches of the dendrites can receive input from 1,000 or more neighbouring neurons. The surface of the cell body also has receptor areas that can be directly stimulated by other neurons. All parts of a neuron are covered by a cell membrane that controls the exchange of chemical substances between the inside and outside of the cell. These exchanges play a critical role in the electrical activities of nerve cells.

Extending from one side of the cell body is a single **axon**, which conducts electrical impulses away from the cell body to other neurons, muscles or glands. The axon branches out at its end to form a number of *axon terminals* – as many as several hundred in some cases. Each axon terminal may connect with dendrites from numerous neurons, making it possible for a single neuron to pass messages to many thousands of other neurons (Ward, 2010). Given the structure of the dendrites and axons, it is easy to see how there can be trillions of interconnections in the brain, making it capable of performing the complex activities that are of interest to psychologists.

> **dendrites** specialized receiving units like antennae that collect messages from neighbouring neurons and send them on to the cell body
>
> **axon** conducts electrical impulses away from the cell body to other neurons, muscles or glands

THE ELECTRICAL ACTIVITY OF NEURONS

Like tiny batteries, neurons generate electricity that creates nerve impulses. They also release chemicals that allow them to communicate with other neurons and with muscles and glands.

Nerve activation involves three basic steps:

1. When not involved in creating impulses the neuron maintains an electrical *resting potential* through the distribution of positively and negatively charged chemical ions inside and outside the neuron.

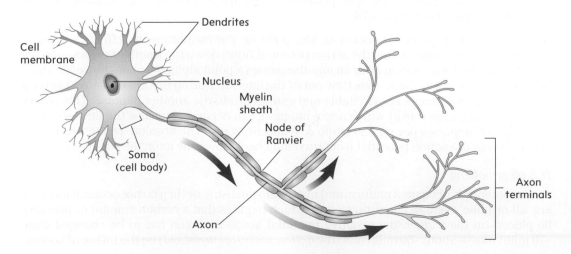

FIGURE 4.6 The neuron and its structural elements.

Stimulation received by the dendrites or soma (cell body) may trigger a nerve impulse, which travels down the axon to stimulate other neurons, muscles or glands. Some axons have a fatty myelin sheath interrupted at intervals by the nodes of Ranvier. The myelin sheath helps increase the speed of electrical conduction.

2. When stimulated by other neurons, a flow of ions in and out through the cell membrane depolarizes and reverses the electrical charge of the resting potential, producing an *action potential*, or neural impulse.

3. The resting potential is again restored.

Like other cells, neurons are surrounded by body fluids and separated from this liquid environment by a cell membrane. This cell membrane is a bit like a selective sieve, allowing certain substances in the body fluid to pass through *ion channels* into the cell, while refusing or limiting passage to other substances.

The chemical environment inside the neuron differs from its external environment in significant ways, and the process whereby a nerve impulse is created involves the exchange of electrically charged atoms called *ions*. In the salty fluid outside the neuron are positively charged sodium ions (Na^+) and negatively charged chloride ions (Cl^-). Inside the neurons are large negatively charged protein molecules (*anions*, or A^-) and positively charged potassium ions (K^+). The cell membrane actively maintains a high concentration of Na^+ ions in the fluid outside the cell via an ion pump, and this results in an uneven distribution of positive and negative ions that creates an electrical charge difference across the membrane with the interior of the cell negatively charged, and the exterior positively charged (Figure 4.7a). This difference of 70 millivolts (mV) is called the neuron's **resting potential**. In a way, calling this a 'resting' potential belies the fact that the cell actively expends energy in maintaining this balance of charge (also known as a state of *polarization*). This resting potential sets the stage allowing the neuron to fire off a communicative impulse – an action potential – when required.

Nerve Impulses: The Action Potential

Hodgkin and Huxley (1963), working with neurons from a squid, found that if they stimulated a neuron's axon with a mild electrical stimulus, the voltage difference across the membrane shifted instantaneously from –70 millivolts (negative inside the axon) to +40 millivolts (positive inside the axon). This electrical shift which lasts about a millisecond (1/1000 of a second) is called the **action potential**.

Hodgkin and Huxley found that the key mechanism underlying an action potential was the work of sodium and potassium ion channels in the cell membrane. Figure 4.7 shows what happens. In a resting state, the neuron's sodium and potassium channels are closed, and the concentration of Na^+ ions is 10 times higher outside the neuron than inside it (see Figure 4.7a). But when a neuron is stimulated sufficiently, nearby sodium channels open up. Attracted by the negative protein ions inside, positively charged sodium ions flood into the axon, creating a state of *depolarization* (see Figure 4.7b). In an instant, the interior now becomes positive (by about 40 millivolts) in relation to the outside, creating the action potential. In a reflex action to restore the resting potential, the cell closes its sodium channels, and positively charged potassium ions flow out through their channels, restoring the negative resting potential (see Figure 4.7c). Eventually, the excess sodium ions flow out of the neuron, and the escaped potassium ions are recovered. The resulting voltage changes are shown in Figure 4.7d.

Once an action potential occurs at any point on the membrane, its effects spread to adjacent sodium channels, and the action potential flows down the length of the axon to the axon terminals. Immediately after an impulse passes a point along the axon, however, there is a recovery period as the K^+ ions flow out of the interior. During this **absolute refractory period**, the membrane is not excitable and cannot discharge another impulse. This places an upper limit on the rate at which nerve impulses can occur. In humans, the limit seems to be about 300 impulses per second (Kolb & Whishaw, 2005). The absolute refractory period also prevents the action potential from travelling back down the axon the way it has come.

It is all or nothing

Action potentials occur at a uniform and maximum intensity, or they do not occur at all (they are 'all-or-none' events). Like firing a gun, which requires that a certain amount of pressure be placed on the trigger, the negative potential inside the axon has to be changed from –70 millivolts to about –50 millivolts (the *action potential threshold*) by the influx of sodium

---

resting potential internal difference of around 70 millivolts (mV)

action potential electrical shift across the neural membrane, which lasts about a millisecond (1/1000 of a second) and propagates electrical signals down an axon

Focus 4.4 What chemical actions create the neuron's resting potential? What chemical changes cause the action potential?

absolute refractory period period during which the membrane is not excitable and cannot discharge another impulse

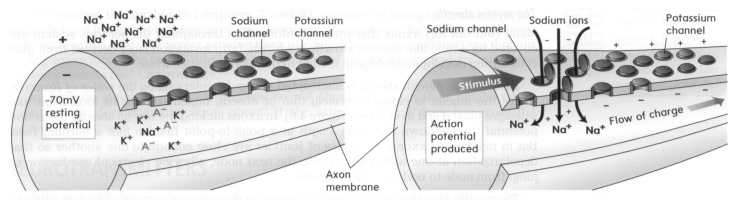

(a) The 10:1 concentration of sodium (Na⁺) ions outside the neuron and the negative protein (A⁻) ions inside contribute to a resting potential of –70mV.

(b) If the neuron is sufficiently stimulated, sodium channels open and sodium ions flood into the axon. Note that the potassium channels are still closed.

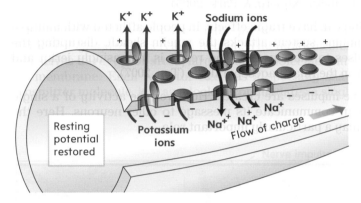

(c) Sodium channels that were open in (b) have now closed and potassium channels behind them are open, allowing potassium ions to exit and restoring the resting potential at that point. Sodium channels are opening at the next point as the action potential moves down the axon.

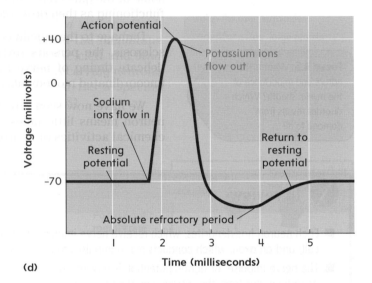

(d)

FIGURE 4.7 Neural impulses: from resting potential to action potential.

When a neuron is not being stimulated, a difference in electrical charge of about –70 millivolts (mV) exists between the interior and the surface of the neuron. (a) This resting potential is caused by the membrane actively maintaining an uneven distribution of positively and negatively charged ions across it, with a greater concentration of positively charged sodium ions kept outside the cell by closed sodium channels and the presence of negatively charged protein (A⁻) ions inside the cell. In addition, the action of sodium–potassium pumps helps maintain the negative interior by pumping out three sodium (Na⁺) ions for every two positively charged potassium (K⁺) ions drawn into the cell. (b) Sufficient stimulation of the neuron causes an action potential. Sodium channels open for an instant and Na⁺ ions flood into the axon, reversing the electrical potential from –70 mV to +40 mV. (c) Within a millisecond, the sodium channels close and many K⁺ ions flow out of the cell through open potassium channels, helping to restore the interior negative potential. As adjacent sodium channels are opened and the sequence in (b) and (c) is repeated, the action potential moves down the length of the axon. (d) Shown here are the changes in electrical potential that would be recorded from a particular point on the axon. After a brief absolute refractory period during which the neuron cannot be stimulated, another action potential can follow.

ions into the axon for the action potential to be triggered. Changes in the negative resting potential that do not reach the –50 millivolt action potential threshold are called **graded potentials**. Under certain circumstances, graded potentials caused by several neurons can add up to trigger an action potential in a postsynaptic neuron (Sherwood, 2011).

For a neuron to function properly, sodium and potassium ions must enter and leave the membrane at just the right rate. Drugs that alter this transit system can decrease or prevent neural functioning. For example, local anaesthetics such as Novocain and Xylocaine attach themselves to the sodium channels, stopping the flow of sodium ions into the neurons. This is how these anaesthetics stop pain impulses from being sent by neurons (Ray & Ksir, 2004). Here we see one example of how chemicals play a role in neural impulses. In the section below on synaptic transmission we will see how chemicals also play a crucial role at synapses between neurons.

graded potentials changes in the negative resting potential that do not reach the –50 millivolt action potential threshold

Focus 4.6 Describe five important steps in neurotransmitter function. How do transmitters produce excitation and inhibition? How are they deactivated?

When a transmitter molecule binds to a receptor site, a chemical reaction occurs and has two possible effects on the receiving neuron. When an *excitatory* transmitter is at work, the chemical reaction causes the postsynaptic neuron's sodium channels to open. As sodium ions flood into the cell and depolarize it, they create either a graded potential or an action potential as just described. An *inhibitory* neurotransmitter will do the opposite. It may cause positive potassium ions to flow out of the neuron or negative chloride ions from the exterior to flow into it through chloride channels in the membrane, increasing the neuron's negative potential and making it harder to fire the neuron. The action of an inhibitory neurotransmitter from one presynaptic neuron may prevent the postsynaptic neuron from firing an action potential even if it is receiving excitatory stimulation from other neurons at the same time.

If the nervous system is to function properly, it must maintain a fine-tuned balance between excitation and inhibition. Even such a simple act as bending your arm requires excitation of your biceps muscles and simultaneous inhibition of your triceps so those muscles can relax.

Once a neurotransmitter molecule binds to its receptor, it continues to excite or inhibit the neuron until it is *deactivated*, or shut off (Simon, 2007). Some transmitter molecules are deactivated by other chemicals located in the synaptic cleft that breaks them down into their chemical components. In other instances, the deactivation mechanism is **re-uptake**, in which the transmitter molecules are taken back into the presynaptic axon terminals. Some antidepressant medications inhibit re-uptake of the excitatory transmitter serotonin, allowing serotonin to continue to excite neurons and thereby reduce depression.

re-uptake the transmitter molecules are taken back into the presynaptic axon terminals

SPECIALIZED TRANSMITTER SYSTEMS

Through the use of chemical transmitters, nature has found an ingenious way of dividing up the brain into systems that are uniquely sensitive to certain messages. There is only one kind of electricity, but there are many shapes that can be assumed by transmitter molecules. Because the various systems in the brain recognize only certain chemical messengers, they are immune to neurotransmitters produced by different systems.

There are many different neurotransmitter substances, some of which can coexist within the same neuron. A given neuron may use one transmitter at one synapse and a different transmitter at another synapse. Moreover, different transmitters can be found within the same axon terminal or in the same synapse, adding another layer of complexity (Kolb & Whishaw, 2005). Each substance has a specific excitatory or inhibitory effect on certain neurons. Some neurotransmitters (for example, noradrenalin – see Table 4.1) can have either excitatory or inhibitory effects, depending on which receptor sites they bind to.

acetylcholine (ACh) a neurotransmitter involved in muscle activity and memory

Table 4.1 lists several of the more important neurotransmitters that have been linked to psychological phenomena. We will encounter all of these substances in this and future chapters. For the moment, we focus on **acetylcholine (ACh)**, a neurotransmitter involved in muscle activity and memory, to illustrate the diversity of neurotransmitter mechanisms.

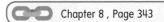 Chapter 8 , Page 343

Underproduction of ACh is an important factor in Alzheimer's disease (Morris & Becker, 2005). Alzheimer's disease is a neurodegenerative disorder which is the most common cause of dementia in adults over 65 years of age. The most well-known impairments in Alzheimer's disease are associated with memory (we discuss Alzheimer's disease in more detail in **Chapter 8**), but it also leads to difficulties in speech and movement. Reductions in acetylcholine weaken or deactivate neural circuitry that stores memories, creating profound memory impairments. Acetylcholine is also an excitatory transmitter at the synapses where neurons activate muscle cells, helping to account for some of motor impairments found in Alzheimer's disease.

Focus 4.7 Describe the roles played by acetylcholine and the consequences that occur when its functioning is disrupted.

TABLE 4.1 Some neurotransmitters and their effects

Neurotransmitter	Major function	Disorders associated with malfunctioning	Additional discussion
Acetylcholine (ACh), produced in numerous sites, including the Basal Forebrain	Excitatory at synapses involved in muscular movement and memory	Alzheimer's disease (undersupply); paralysis (absence); violent muscle contractions and convulsions (oversupply)	Chapter 8
Noradrenaline (known as norepinephrine in the USA), released from the adrenal medulla	Excitatory and inhibitory functions at various sites, involved in neural circuits controlling learning, memory, wakefulness and eating	Depression (undersupply); stress and panic disorders (over activity)	Chapters 6, 18
Serotonin, produced in the central nervous system and the intestines	Inhibitory or excitatory; involved in mood, sleep, eating and arousal, and may be an important transmitter underlying pleasure and pain	Depression; sleeping and eating disorders (undersupply); obsessive-compulsive disorder (over activity)	Chapters 6, 11, 14, 17, 18
Dopamine, produced in the substantia nigra	Excitatory; involved in voluntary movement, emotional arousal, learning, memory and experiencing pleasure or pain	Parkinson's disease and depression (undersupply); schizophrenia (over activity)	Chapters 6, 7, 11, 12, 17, 18
GABA (gamma-aminobutyric acid), produced widely throughout the body	Inhibitory transmitter in motor system	Destruction of GABA producing neurons in Huntington's disease produces tremors and loss of motor control, as well as personality changes	Chapters 6, 17, 18
Endorphin, produced by the hypothalamus and pituitary gland	Inhibits transmission of pain impulses (a neuromodulator)	Insensitivity to pain (oversupply); pain hypersensitivity, immune problems (undersupply)	Chapters 11, 16
Glutamate, better known as monosodium glutamate (MSG) – produced widely throughout the body	Excitatory, a mediator of excitatory information in the nervous system. Involved therefore in most aspects of brain function	(Oversupply) – neurotoxin, a contributor to a number of neurodegenerative disorders such as Alzheimer's disease; (undersupply) – seizures, tremors and insomnia	Chapters 6, 8, 17

Drugs that block the action of ACh can prevent muscle activation and cause paralysis. One example occurs in botulism, a serious type of food poisoning that can result from improperly canned food. The toxin formed by the **botulinum bacteria** blocks the release of ACh from the axon terminal, resulting in a potentially fatal paralysis of the muscles, including those of the respiratory system.

The opposite effect of ACh occurs with the bite of the black widow spider. The spider's venom triggers a torrent of ACh, resulting in violent muscle contractions, convulsions and possible death.

Most neurotransmitters have their excitatory or inhibitory effects only on specific neurons that have receptors for them. Others, called **neuromodulators**, have a more widespread and generalized influence on synaptic transmission. These substances circulate through the brain and either increase or decrease (i.e., modulate) the sensitivity of thousands, perhaps millions, of neurons to their specific transmitters. *Endorphins* are neuromodulators that travel through the brain's circulatory system and inhibit pain transmission while enhancing neural activity that produces pleasurable feelings. Other neuromodulators play important roles in a range of functions including eating, sleeping and coping with stress.

botulinum bacteria toxin-forming bacteria, a mild form of which is known commonly as botox

neuromodulators have a more widespread and generalized influence on synaptic transmission

Applying psychological science

UNDERSTANDING HOW DRUGS AFFECT YOUR BRAIN

psychoactive drugs chemicals that produce alterations in consciousness, emotion and behaviour

agonist a drug that increases the activity of a neurotransmitter

antagonist a drug that inhibits or decreases the action of a neurotransmitter

Knowledge about neurotransmitter systems helps us understand the mechanisms that underlie the effects of psychoactive drugs, chemicals that produce alterations in consciousness, emotion and behaviour. It is important to remember that many drugs we ingest are legal. If you have ever had a cup of coffee, taken an aspirin or smoked a cigarette, you have ingested a drug. However, a 2012 report from the Health and Social Care Information Centre (for England and Wales) describes how widespread illegal drug use is. The report provides statistics for drug use in a number of categories. In the year 2011–12, 36.5% of adults were estimated to have taken an illicit drug at some point in their life, and 5.2% of adults were estimated to have used an illicit drug in the last month; 6.9% of adults had used cannabis in the last year, 2.2% had taken cocaine, and 1.4% had taken ecstasy. In addition to this, in 81% of cases in which people received treatment for drug use were related to opioid (e.g. heroin) abuse. Perhaps you have wondered exactly how these various psychoactive drugs exert their diverse effects. As we will see, there is a diverse range of ways in which drugs can affect neural activity

Most psychoactive drugs produce their effects by either increasing or decreasing the synthesis, storage, release, binding or deactivation of neurotransmitters. An agonist is a drug that increases the activity of a neurotransmitter. Agonists may: (1) enhance a neuron's ability to synthesize, store or release neurotransmitters; (2) actually be a neurotransmitter, and thus bind with and stimulate postsynaptic receptor sites; (3) mimic the action of a neurotransmitter by binding with and stimulating postsynaptic receptor sites; or (4) make it more difficult for neurotransmitters to be stopped from activating the postsynaptic receptors, such as by inhibiting re-uptake.

An antagonist is a drug that inhibits or decreases the action of a neurotransmitter. An antagonist may: (1) reduce a neuron's ability to synthesize, store or release neurotransmitters; or (2) prevent a neurotransmitter from binding with the postsynaptic neuron by fitting into and blocking the receptor sites on the postsynaptic neuron.

With the distinction between agonist and antagonist functions in mind, let us consider how some commonly used drugs work within the brain. One of the most confusing things is that drugs can have a range of different effects on the brain simultaneously. Alcohol, for instance, is a depressant drug which has both agonist and antagonist effects. As an agonist, it stimulates the activity of the inhibitory transmitter GABA, thereby depressing neural activity. As an antagonist, it decreases the activity of glutamate, an excitatory transmitter (Levinthal, 2007). The double-barrelled effect of this is a neural slowdown that inhibits normal brain functions, including clear thinking, emotional control and motor coordination. Sedative drugs, including barbiturates and tranquillizers, also increase GABA activity, and taking them with alcohol can be deadly when their depressant effects on neural activity are combined with those of alcohol.

Caffeine is a stimulant drug that increases the activity of neurons and other cells. It is an antagonist for the transmitter adenosine. Adenosine inhibits the release of excitatory transmitters. By reducing adenosine activity, caffeine helps produce higher rates of cellular activity and more available energy. Although caffeine is a stimulant, it is important to note that contrary to popular belief, caffeine does *not* counteract the effects of alcohol and sober people up. What your drunken friend needs is a ride home with a driver who is sober – not a cup of coffee to help them drive themselves.

Nicotine is an agonist for the excitatory transmitter acetylcholine. Its chemical structure is similar enough to ACh to allow it to fit into ACh binding sites and create action potentials. At other receptor sites, nicotine stimulates dopamine activity, which seems to be an important chemical mediator of energy and pleasure. Researchers are working to develop medications that could wean people off cigarettes and other tobacco products by blocking or occupying the specific receptor sites that trigger dopamine release.

Amphetamines are stimulant drugs that boost arousal and mood by increasing the activity of the excitatory neurotransmitters dopamine and norepinephrine. They do so in two major ways. First, they cause presynaptic neurons to release greater amounts of these neurotransmitters. Second, they inhibit re-uptake, allowing dopamine and noradrenaline to keep stimulating postsynaptic neurons (Ksir, Hart, & Ray, 2008). Cocaine produces excitation, a sense of increased muscular strength and euphoria. Like amphetamines, cocaine increases the activity of noradrenaline and dopamine, but it does so in only one major way: it blocks their re-uptake. Thus amphetamines and cocaine have different mechanisms of action on the dopamine and noradrenaline transmitter systems, but both drugs produce highly stimulating effects on mood, thinking and behaviour.

Rohypnol (flunitrazepam) and GHB (gamma hydroxybutyrate) are so-called date rape drugs. Partygoers sometimes add these drugs to punch and other drinks in the hopes of lowering drinkers' inhibitions and facilitating sexual conquests, which of course in this context is non-consensual. These drugs are powerful sedatives that suppress general neural activity by enhancing the action of the inhibitory transmitter GABA (Lobina, Agabio, Reali, Gessa, & Colombo, 1999). In high doses or when mixed with alcohol or other drugs, these substances may lead to respiratory depression, loss of consciousness, and even coma and death. Rohypnol also affects neurotransmission in areas of the brain involved in memory, producing an amnesia effect that may prevent users from remembering the circumstances under which they ingested the drug or what happened to them afterwards.

So we have talked about the immediate effects that drugs have on the brain, but what is it about certain drugs which makes them so addictive? The answer to this question lies in so-called 'reward pathways' in the brain (Volkow, Wang, Fowler, & Tomasi, 2012). Reward pathways are actively involved ▶

in many of the processes which we find pleasurable such as eating, drinking, and sex. One particularly important pathway is the dopamine system which is located between parts of the brain known as the brainstem, nucleus accumbens, and the prefrontal cortex (Olds & Milner, 1954; George, Le Moal, & Koob, 2012). As its name suggests, this pathway is particularly stimulated by dopamine.

Although most recreational drugs activate reward pathways in the brain at some point, the most addictive drugs, such as cocaine, activate reward pathways directly leading to intense pleasure. This kind of heightened pleasure can lead to addiction through a range of ways. Once the pleasure is experienced, it leads to increased temptation to experience it again. However, with more frequent use the reward pathways become more tolerant to the effects of the drug, requiring more to be taken in order to gain the same level of pleasure. Furthermore, when the brain is repeatedly exposed to a drug, it responds by counteracting the drug's effects (in order to retain a balanced physiological state). Thus, if the drug is no longer present, these counteracting processes can produce the opposite of pleasure. This withdrawal response produces a strong signal for addicts to take the drug again.

FIGURE 4.9 Partying can alter brain activity.

Nicotine from cigarette smoke activates acetylcholine and dopamine neurons, increasing neural excitation. Alcohol stimulates the activity of the inhibitory transmitter GABA and decreases the activity of an excitatory transmitter, glutamate, thus depressing brain functions.

Source: ©iStock.com / tfoxfoto

 In review

- Neural transmission, or synaptic transmission, is a chemical process by which neurons send signals to each other.
- When an action potential arrives at an axon terminal this causes neurotransmitter chemicals to be released into the synaptic cleft. These neurotransmitter molecules in turn bind onto receptor sites on the dendrites of a post-synaptic neuron and cause membrane depolarization which can result in an action potential in the post-synaptic neuron.
- Psychoactive drugs such as caffeine, alcohol, nicotine and amphetamines produce their effects by either increasing or decreasing the action of neurotransmitters. Agonists can mimic or increase the action of neurotransmitters, whereas antagonists inhibit or decrease the action of neurotransmitters. Drugs are addictive because of their influences on the reward pathways in the brain.

UNLOCKING THE SECRETS OF THE BRAIN

Neuroscientists use a number of methods to study the brain's structures and activities.

NEUROPSYCHOLOGY

Another way to assess brain function, particularly in terms of research, is to investigate the effects of a brain lesion. The study of the effects of brain damage on mental functions is often referred to as **neuropsychology** (although some textbooks will give you a broader definition of what neuropsychology covers). The study of the effects of brain damage on psychological functioning, often in the form of individual case studies, has been one of the most productive methods for understanding the brain basis of psychological processes.

Focus 4.8 How do agonist and antagonist functions underlie the neural and behavioural effects of psychoactive drugs?

neuropsychology the study of the function of the brain by investigating the effects of brain damage on mental functions

TABLE 4.2 Different causes of brain injury

Cause of damage	Description
Vascular	Disruption to blood flow to the brain for a number of reasons including a blockage (stroke), partial blockage (ischemia) or an enlarged artery (aneurysm). The loss of function depends on the severity of the event and the position of the damage
Tumour	Also described as a neoplasm. A mass of tissue with no physiological function that grows and disrupts normal functioning. The tumour may cause vascular problems, or may destroy neurons. The severity of the tumour depends on its size, growth rate and position. Gliomas begin with abnormal glial cells. Meninglomas originate in the meninges, surrounding the brain. Metastic tumours originate elsewhere in the body but invade the bloodstream and so travel to the brain
Degenerative disease	A breakdown of neurological material. May be genetic, as in Huntington's, and influenced by environmental factors. Examples include Alzheimer's, Parkinson's and Korsakoff's diseases. May be cortical (in the cortex) or sub-cortical (beneath the cortex). Each disorder presents with different behavioural and neurological symptoms
Infectious disease	A virus may result in neurological symptoms. HIV and AIDS tend to result in sub-cortical damage, herpes attacks cortical structures
Trauma	A violent assault on the head, be it with a car or a weapon, can result in trauma to the brain. May be closed or open head, depending on whether the skull remains intact. The resulting damage may or may not be at the point of the impact. The trauma may also result in vascular problems
Epilepsy	A transient loss of consciousness resulting from excessive and often focused electrical activity in the brain. Investigated with EEG. Often triggered by a trauma, they disrupt activity across a wide area of the brain and so are hard to investigate cognitively

This method was particularly important in the mid-twentieth century, but despite the rise of modern brain imaging techniques, continues to be highly relevant today. Causes of brain injury are categorized in Table 4.2.

Neuropsychological Tests

Neuropsychologists use a variety of *neuropsychological tests* to measure verbal and non-verbal behaviours of people who may have suffered brain damage through accident or disease (Strauss, Sherman, & Spreen, 2006). As well as providing diagnostic tools, these tests are also important research tools. For example, Figure 4.10 shows a portion of a trail-making test, used to test memory and planning. Scores on the test give an indication of a person's type and severity of brain damage. Neuropsychological tests of this kind have provided much information about brain behaviour relations. They are also used to assess learning disabilities and developmental disorders.

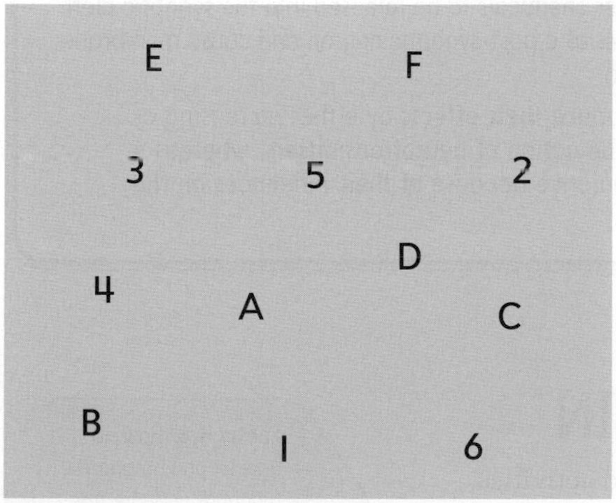

FIGURE 4.10 A neuropsychological test.

The trail-making test is used by psychologists to assess brain functioning. It consists of randomly scattered numbers and letters, which the patient must connect consecutively with a continuous line or 'trail' (i.e., A to I to B to 2 to C to 3, and so on). People with certain kinds of brain damage have trouble alternating between the numbers and letters because they cannot retain a plan in memory for long enough.

Neuropsychology: Single and Double Dissociation

By studying patterns of impairment and sparing of function on neuropsychological tests across brain-injured patients, neuropsychologists can draw inferences about how brain functions are related to one another in the brain. An important concept here is that of dissociation of function.

Put very simply, dissociation is a difference in performance between two tasks. For instance, if a patient or a group of patients with damage to a particular part of the brain performs poorly on verbal dexterity but well on comprehension then this provides some evidence that the damaged part of the brain is involved in verbal dexterity, but not comprehension. This kind of evidence is called a *single dissociation* (Table 4.3). The problem here is that the pattern of findings could also be explained by appealing to differences in the difficulties of the two tasks (dexterity and comprehension). If the brain damage under investigation has more generally disrupted cognitive performance, giving the patient more general problems with attention or concentration, then they are likely to show most impairment on the more difficult task. So, if verbal dexterity is more difficult than comprehension then a general impairment could explain the single dissociation without us needing to say that verbal dexterity and comprehension are separable functions sub-served by different parts of the brain.

TABLE 4.3 Single and double dissociations

A single dissociation	Comprehension performance (%)	Verbal task performance (%)
Patient A	95	12
A single dissociation	Comprehension performance (%)	Verbal task performance (%)
Patient A	95	12
Patient B	56	95

Stronger evidence of separation of function comes from *double dissociations*. In a double dissociation (as illustrated in Table 4.3), we see a pattern in which one patient is impaired on task A but spared on task B, whereas a second patient is impaired on task B but spared on task A. When we have a double dissociation like this, we can say much more confidently that the differences seen are due to the fact that these two tasks are sub-served by functionally separate systems in the brain.

Perhaps the most famous example of double dissociation of function is between Broca's and Wernicke's aphasias. Paul Broca and Carl Wernicke were two early neuropsychologists working at the end of the nineteenth century. On the basis of observations of brain damage, Broca and Wernicke identified two particular areas of the brain involved in language, known respectively as Broca's area and Wernicke's area. We will describe these areas in the brain in more detail in the next section, and you can see them labelled in Figure 4.16 later in this chapter. However, here it simply suffices to note that damage to these brain areas results in different patterns of impairment and sparing.

Damage to Wernicke's area in the temporal lobe of the brain (see Figure 4.16) typically leaves patients unable to understand written or spoken speech. Scott Moss, a psychologist who suffered temporary aphasia from a left-hemisphere stroke (blockage or bursting of blood vessels in the brain that resulted in death of neurons from lack of oxygen) described his experience: 'I recollect trying to read the headlines of the Chicago Tribune but they didn't make any sense to me at all. I didn't have any difficulty focusing, it was simply that the words, individually or in combination, didn't have meaning' (Moss, 1972, p. 4). However, patients with **Wernicke's aphasia** can typically produce speech, but due to the deficit in comprehension that speech tends to be jumbled.

Damage to Broca's area in the frontal lobe of the brain (see Figure 4.16), can lead to the opposite pattern. Whereas patients with **Broca's aphasia** are usually able to understand speech, their difficulties are in expressing speech with words and sentences. It is important to bear in mind that individual patients with Broca's and Wernicke's aphasias can vary in the extent to which they show pure impairments of production or comprehension (see Parkin, 1996), but this is a useful example for illustrating how evidence from brain damaged patients can help us understand how the brain underlies our different mental functions. Neuropsychological research not only helps us understand the functional architecture of the brain. It can also help greatly in targeted treatment or therapy.

> **Wernicke's aphasia** results from damage in the temporal lobe, and is primarily manifested as difficulties with speech comprehension
>
> **Broca's aphasia** results from damage in the frontal lobe and is primarily manifested as difficulties with the production of speech

Lesion Studies in Animals

Experimental lesion studies with animals are another useful method of learning about the brain (Tatlisumak & Fisher, 2006). Researchers can produce brain damage (lesions) in which specific nervous tissue is destroyed with electricity, with cold or heat, or with chemicals. They can also surgically remove some portion of the brain and study the consequences.

ELECTRICAL RECORDING

Because brain function consists partly of electrical activity scientists can eavesdrop on the electrical 'conversations' occurring within the brain by measuring that electrical activity. One method is to measure the activity of single neurons or small groups of neurons by

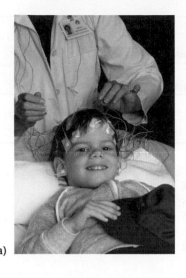
(a)

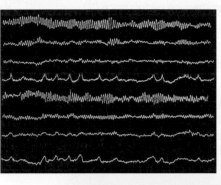
(b)

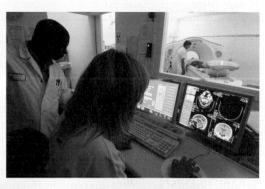
(c)

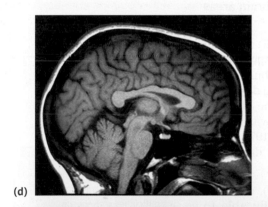
(d)

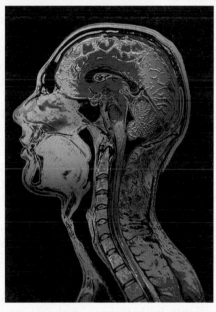
(e)

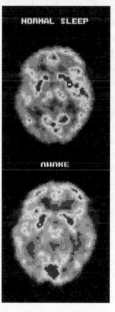

NORMAL SLEEP

AWAKE

(g)

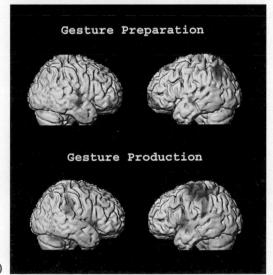

Gesture Preparation

Gesture Production

(f)

FIGURE 4.11 Measuring brain activity.

(a) EEG records the activity of large groups of neurons in the brain through a series of electrodes attached to the scalp. (b) EEG can be recordings from several electrodes at once. (c) MRI scanners produce vivid pictures of brain structures and can also measure brain function. (d) A structural MRI scan showing the anatomical structure of the brain in both 2D and 3D renderings. (e) A diffusion tensor image (DTI) showing the structure of white matter tracts in the brain. (f) A functional MRI (fMRI) scan showing patterns of oxygenated blood levels in the brain. (g) PET scans record the amount of radioactive substance that collects in various brain regions to assess brain activity.

Sources: (a) Larry Mulvehill/Science Photo Library; (b) Science Photo Library; (c) Gabrielle Voinot/ Look at Sciences/Science Photo Library; (d) Edward Kinsman/Science Photo Library; (e) Sovereign, Ism/Science Photo Library; (f) Dr. Scott T. Grafton, Visuals Unlimited /Science Photo Library. (g) Hank Morgan/Science Photo Library

inserting small electrodes in particular areas of the brain. Occasionally it is possible to do this kind of research in humans, usually when a participant is undergoing investigative surgery for epilepsy (e.g., Engel, Moll, Fried, & Ojemann, 2005; Jacobs & Kahana, 2010; Quiroga, 2012). However, the majority of such studies are conducted with animals. Some of the most important advances in our understanding of how neurons work together to underpin perceptual and cognitive functions have come from such animal studies. For instance, in 1981, the neurophysiologists David Hubel and Torsten Wiesel received the Nobel Prize for their work on how neurons in visual areas of the brain respond to different aspects of the visual world (Hubel & Wiesel, 1959, 1962).

In additional to measuring the activity of small numbers of neurons, neuroscientists can also measure the activity of much larger groups of neurons. One advantage of this method is that it is possible to measure the responses of large groups of neurons without an invasive procedure. We can record neural activity from the surface of the scalp. **Electroencephalography (EEG)** measures the activity of large groups of neurons through a series of electrodes placed on the scalp (Figure 4.11a and b). Although the EEG is a rather non-specific measure that taps the electrical activity of thousands of neurons in many parts of the brain, specific EEG patterns correspond to certain states of consciousness, such as wakefulness and sleep. As we will see in **Chapter 12**, this method has been particularly useful for studying neural responses in human infants. Clinicians also use the EEG to detect abnormal electrical patterns that signal the presence of brain disorders.

> **electroencephalography (EEG)** measures the activity of large groups of neurons through a series of large electrodes placed on the scalp

 Chapter 12, Page 514

BRAIN IMAGING

The most recent methods for investigating brain activity are imaging techniques that permit neuroscientists to peer into the living, functioning brain. The most important of these are magnetic resonance imaging (MRI), functional magnetic resonance imaging (fMRI) and Positron-Emission Tomography (PET).

In **magnetic resonance imaging (MRI)** a strong magnetic field is passed through the brain and pulsed on and off. This oscillating magnetic field causes the molecules and atoms in the brain (or any tissue) to respond. When the magnetic field is shut off, the molecules in the brain emit a radio signal which is then detected and mapped to provide images of the tissue.

A more recent method using MRI is **diffusion tensor imaging (DTI)**. DTI measures how water molecules diffuse in tissue. In the brain, water molecules are not free to move in any direction because of the shapes of the cells and structures which they inhabit. This means that we can get information about how structures and pathways or tracts in the brain are aligned. This has been particularly useful for providing pictures of how white matter tracts are arrayed in the brain, telling us about how the brain is structurally connected (see Figure 4.11e).

A particularly important advance in MRI technology is **functional MRI (fMRI)**. fMRI makes use of the fact that oxygenated and deoxygenated blood respond differently to the magnetic fields used with MRI scans. When there is neural activity more oxygenated blood is sent to that part of the brain. fMRI researchers thus investigate where the highest concentrations of oxygenated blood are being sent in the brain at any one time, and infer on that basis which parts of the brain are most active when a participant is undertaking a particular task (Huettel, Song, & McCarthy, 2005). If the patient is performing a reasoning task, for example, a researcher can tell from the fMRI which parts of the brain are most active during reasoning.

Positron-emission tomography (PET) scans have provided another way of measuring where blood flows to in the brain. Glucose, a natural sugar, is the major nutrient of neurons, so when neurons are active, they consume more glucose. To prepare a patient for a PET scan, a radioactive form of glucose is injected into the bloodstream and travels to the brain, where it circulates in the blood supply. The PET scan measures the energy emitted by the radioactive substance, and can thus map out which parts of the brain are most active. One of the disadvantages of PET involves the injection

> **diffusion tensor imaging (DTI)** mesures how water molecules diffuse in tissue
>
> **magnetic resonance imaging (MRI)** creates images based on how atoms in living tissue respond to a magnetic pulse delivered by the device
>
> **functional MRI (fMRI)** can produce pictures of blood flow in the brain taken less than a second apart
>
> **positron-emission tomography (PET) scans** measure brain activity, including metabolism, blood flow and neurotransmitter activity

> **Focus 4.9** Describe four methods used to study brain–behaviour relations.

of radioactive isotopes which can be harmful if applied frequently. This is one of the reasons why fMRI is a more popular method for imaging brain activity. However, one of the advantages of PET is that it is possible to use radioactive isotopes to label particular neurotransmitters. This means that PET is still an important method for investigating the role of particular neurotransmitters in brain function (Tomasi, 2012; Wong, Robert Brašić, Gean, & Nandi, 2013).

Functional near-infrared spectroscopy (fNIRS) is a relatively new method for investigating brain function. It involves shining a particular kind of light (near-infrared light) into the brain and measuring the ways in which it is reflected back. This method is completely non-invasive as near-infrared light (although we cannot see it) is naturally occurring and able to permeate biological tissue. In fact near-infrared light is likely shining into your brain right now. Because oxygenated and deoxygenated blood absorb near-infrared light to different extents it is possible to use fNIRS in a similar way to fMRI, measuring the signatures of blood flow to determine which parts of the brain are the most active. fNIRS is a little limited in comparison to fMRI as it gives less precise maps of the brain, and it can only really tell us about blood flow to areas close to the scalp (as near-infrared only illuminates a few centimetres into the brain). However, it has some important advantages. Firstly, it is a relatively inexpensive technique to use by comparison with fMRI. Secondly, whereas fMRI simply does not work if the participant moves, with fNIRS it is possible to image the brain of someone who is moving around and acting on their environment. This makes it particularly useful for examining the neural basis of motor behaviours, and also makes it very handy for using with participants who do not usually sit still –infants, for example (Lloyd-Fox, Blasi, & Elwell, 2010; Taga et al., 2011; see **Chapter 12**).

> Functional near-infrared spectroscopy (fNIRS) by shining near-infrared light into the brain and measuring the ways in which it is reflected, fNIRS can tell us about which parts of the brain are using most oxygen

> **Focus 4.10** How are MRIs produced, and what kinds of information does MRI and fMRI provide?

Chapter 12, Page 514

BRAIN STIMULATION

An alternative to measuring the activity of neurons is to stimulate them and see what happens as a result. The importance of brain stimulation techniques is that they can show us more directly about what processes brain activity drive. If we are gathering EEG or observing fMRI data while a person engages in a particular task we are always simply looking at what kinds of neural activity are correlated with a particular behaviour. It is more difficult to determine whether the activity we are observing actually causes the behaviours of interest. To look at causes, we can intervene directly in brain processes and measure the outcomes.

Many brain stimulation studies have been carried out experimentally with animals. In chemical stimulation, a tiny tube, or *cannula*, is inserted into a precise area of the brain so that chemicals, including neurotransmitters, can be delivered directly and their effects on behaviour studied. A specific region of the brain can also be stimulated by a mild electric current. Electrodes can be permanently implanted so that the region of interest can be stimulated repeatedly. Some electrodes are so tiny that they can stimulate individual neurons. An electric stimulation study conducted by Olds and Milner (1954) was one of the first studies to identify the reward centres of the brain (discussed earlier). Olds and Milner placed an electrode in and around the hypothalamus in a rat's brain. They found that, if given the opportunity, the rat would press a lever in order to stimulate themselves in this part of the brain, and they would do this repeatedly for long periods of time. This motivation to self-stimulate this particular brain region suggests that it is fundamentally involved in the same kinds of processes of reward which underlie addiction in humans. Humans who have had electrodes implanted in their brains to search for abnormal brain tissue have reported experiencing pleasure when these reward regions were electrically stimulated. One patient reportedly proposed marriage to the experimenter while being stimulated (Heath, 1972).

Electrical-stimulation studies are also possible in humans, often when electrodes are implanted in order to evaluate patients in advance of treatment for epilepsy. In the 1930s–50s, a neurosurgeon by the name of Wilder Penfield conducted several investigations of the effects of brain stimulation in epilepsy patients who were unconscious by locally anaesthetized on the operating table. From these studies (Penfield & Jasper, 1954) Penfield was able to make precise maps of the function of somatosensory cortex, the part of the

brain involved in sensing touches. When he stimulated a particular part of somatosensory cortex, the patients reported where they felt touch sensations. Penfield found that the whole body was mapped out over the somatosensory cortex in a regular organization of limbs and body parts – you will be able to see this later in the chapter (Figure 4.17). In another more recent study of this type, placement of electrodes on a specific region of the brain's outer surface above the right ear (the right angular gyrus) produced a surprising effect. A patient experienced herself as floating in the air above her body (Blanke, Ortigue, Landis, & Seeck, 2002). Neuroscientists thus argued that this area of the brain is intimately involved in the neural basis of bodily (and in this case out-of-body) experiences.

Transcranial Magnetic Stimulation (TMS)

Transcranial magnetic stimulation (TMS) offers researchers a way of stimulating the brain in a non-invasive way (Miniussi, Paulus, & Rossini, 2012). TMS researchers place an electromagnetic coil over the brain of a participant (see Figure 4.12). A large electrical current is passed through the coil, and this gives rise to a focused magnetic field which in turn induces an electrical current in the neural circuits of the brain. The main way in which TMS is used in research is in order to introduce temporary lesions in a kind of 'virtual neuropsychology' mimicking the effects of focal brain damage (Stewart & Walsh, 2000; Walsh & Cowey, 2000). TMS can temporarily disrupt function in the area of the brain over which it is placed, and so researchers can measure the effects of these temporary lesions on mental processes. For instance, applying TMS above part of the temporal cortex (known as BA37) disrupts picture naming (Stewart, Meyer, Frith, & Rothwell, 2001). Applying TMS over a brain area known as the interparietal sulcus impairs people's ability to make judgements about numbers (Cappelletti, Barth, Fregni, Spelke, & Pascual-Leone, 2007).

More recently researchers have begun investigating how brain stimulation can actually enhance mental performance. It has been found that both TMS (Luber & Lisanby, 2014) and another method which is gaining interest called **transcranial direct current stimulation (TDCS)** (Falcone, Coffman, Clark, & Parasuraman, 2012) can enhance mental processes and learning. For instance, Santiesteban, Banissy, Catmur and Bird (2012) recently showed that TDCS over an area of the brain called the temporoparietal junction (TPJ) improves people's ability to take different social perspectives. The application of these kinds of methods to treating psychological illnesses such as depression is garnering a lot of interest at present (Stagg & Nitsche, 2011).

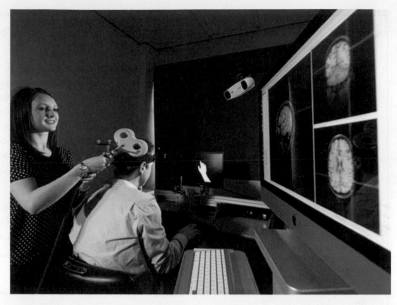

FIGURE 4.12 Transcranial magnetic stimulation.

A participant in a TMS experiment undertakes a task while a coil is used to apply magnetic pulses to his brain.

Credit: Richard Booth/University of Surrey

> **transcranial magnetic stimulation (TMS)** electrical stimulation of a targeted part of the brain via magnetic pulses sent from an electromagnetic coil
>
> **transcranial direct current stimulation (TDCS)** electrical stimulation of the brain by applying a low current to the scalp.

 Current topic

BRAIN OR MACHINE?

Are neural implants a solution that we should pursue or do they pose a unique case worthy of the very closest ethical scrutiny?

It may sound like science fiction, but devices already exist that help our brains and nervous systems to operate. Cochlear implants, for instance, are devices which can help people hear when damage to the inner ear would otherwise prevent this. In cochlear implants sound signals are presented electrically to the auditory nerve in the cochlear, simulating the impulses which would occur if the inner ear were functioning normally. Deep brain stimulation (DBS) is a method which can be used to control symptoms in several disorders including Parkinson's disease, depression and obsessive compulsive disorder (OCD). In DBS, electrical stimulators are surgically implanted into specific areas of the brain. These are then stimulated at high frequency via a neurostimulator device. This method has been particularly successful in treating the movement symptoms of Parkinson's disease ▶

◀including slowness of movement, stiffness and tremor. Brain machine interface-based motor prosthetics use neural implants that allow a person to control their own prosthetic limb movements.

Despite the benefits of these kinds of implants, there are concerns over some unwanted effects. Those undergoing DBS, for instance, present with mental illness at a higher frequency than those without it, and personality changes have also been seen. There are also wider social concerns. For instance, many in the non-hearing community have categorically rejected the use of cochlear implants. They feel that their culture, based around signing and lip-reading, is marginalized further by these devices. Blanke and Aspell (2009) offer an extremely interesting viewpoint on the rise of neural implants. They note that neural implants offer the possibility that external influences could control the regions of the brain responsible for our impressions of bodily self-consciousness. If this were to happen, for instance via a computer, then the line between human and robot would become significantly blurred. Not only that, but they argue that such external control could change human identity. Because brain signals underlying bodily self-consciousness are crucial components of the 'self' (Blanke & Metzinger, 2009), there is the theoretical possibility that neural prosthetics could fundamentally alter a person's sense of self.

With the rise of the neural implant, brain machine interfaces really are on the front line of brain science and so we should all watch developments with great interest. Blanke and Aspell (2009) suggest that although we should not welcome the benefits brought by introducing links between machine and brain, we should also pursue such research with great care and a mind to its wider-reaching implications.

In review

- Neuropsychologists study the effects of brain damage on mental functioning so that they can determine the role of the brain in behaviour. Neuropsychologists make use of a range of tests, and case study methods.
- Electrical recording and brain imaging methods have facilitated discoveries about brain–behaviour relations. The last 30 years have seen giant steps in methods for generating pictures of structures and processes within the living brain. These methods include MRI, DTI, fMRI and fNIRS.
- Brain stimulation methods provide a way of more directly determining how brain regions are involved in behaviours and psychological processes.

THE HIERARCHICAL BRAIN: STRUCTURES AND BEHAVIOURAL FUNCTIONS

The brain represents millions of years of evolutionary development. The human brain is like a living archaeological site, with the more recently developed structures built on top of structures from the distant evolutionary past (Striedter, 2005). The structures at the brain's core, which we share with all other vertebrates, govern the basic physiological functions that keep us alive, such as breathing and heart rate. Built upon these basic structures are newer systems that involve progressively more complex functions – sensing, emoting, wanting, thinking and reasoning. Evolutionary theorists believe that as genetic variation sculpted these newer structures over time, natural selection favoured their retention because animals that had them were more likely to survive within ever-changing environments.

The major structures of the human brain and their psychological functions are shown in Figure 4.13 and you will find much more detail of many aspects of neurology in the *Sylvius Interactive Brain Anatomy Dictionary*. The brain has traditionally been viewed as having three major subdivisions: the hindbrain, the midbrain, which lies above the hindbrain, and the forebrain.

THE HINDBRAIN

| hindbrain the lowest and most primitive level of the brain |

The **hindbrain** is the lowest and most primitive level of the brain. As the spinal cord enters the brain, it enlarges to form the structures that compose part of the stalk-like brain stem which also includes the midbrain. Attached to the hindbrain part of the brain stem is the other major portion of the hindbrain, the *cerebellum*.

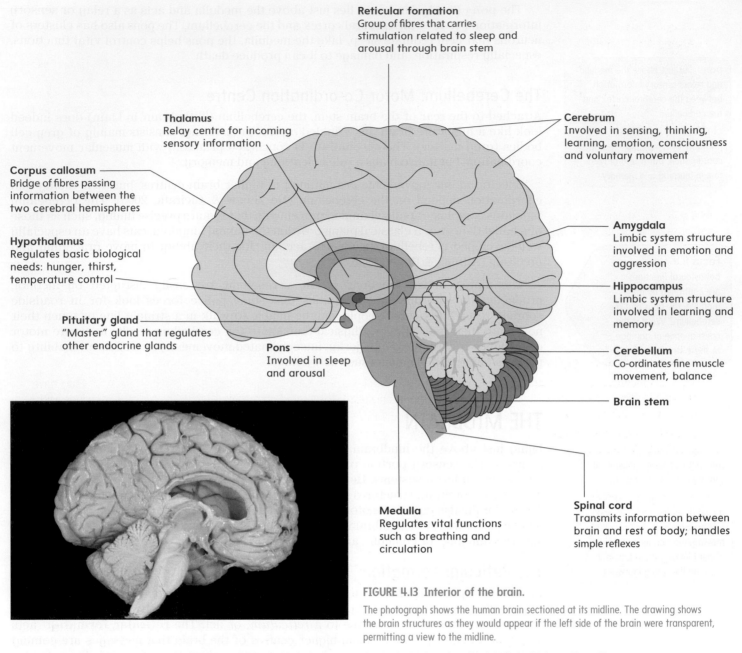

Reticular formation
Group of fibres that carries stimulation related to sleep and arousal through brain stem

Thalamus
Relay centre for incoming sensory information

Cerebrum
Involved in sensing, thinking, learning, emotion, consciousness and voluntary movement

Corpus callosum
Bridge of fibres passing information between the two cerebral hemispheres

Amygdala
Limbic system structure involved in emotion and aggression

Hypothalamus
Regulates basic biological needs: hunger, thirst, temperature control

Hippocampus
Limbic system structure involved in learning and memory

Pituitary gland
"Master" gland that regulates other endocrine glands

Pons
Involved in sleep and arousal

Cerebellum
Co-ordinates fine muscle movement, balance

Brain stem

Medulla
Regulates vital functions such as breathing and circulation

Spinal cord
Transmits information between brain and rest of body; handles simple reflexes

FIGURE 4.13 Interior of the brain.

The photograph shows the human brain sectioned at its midline. The drawing shows the brain structures as they would appear if the left side of the brain were transparent, permitting a view to the midline.

Source: Dr. Fred Hossler, Visuals Unlimited/Science Photo Library

The Medulla and Pons: Life-Support Systems

The structures of the **brain stem** support vital life functions. Included are the *medulla* and the *pons*. The 1.5-inch-long (3.8 cm) medulla is the first structure above the spinal cord. Well developed at birth, the **medulla** plays an important role in vital body functions such as heart rate and respiration. Because of your medulla, these functions occur automatically. Damage to the medulla usually results in death or, at best, the need to be maintained on life-support systems. Suppression of medulla activity can occur at high levels of alcohol intoxication, resulting in death by heart or respiratory failure (Blessing, 1997).

The medulla is also a two-way thoroughfare for all the sensory and motor nerve tracts coming up from the spinal cord and descending from the brain. Most of these tracts cross over within the medulla, so the left side of the brain receives sensory input from and exerts motor control over the right side of the body, and the right side of the brain serves the left side of the body. Why this crossover occurs is one of the unsolved mysteries of brain function.

> **brain stem** supports vital life functions
>
> **medulla** plays an important role in vital body functions such as heart rate and respiration

The **pons** ('bridge' in Latin) lies just above the medulla and acts as a relay or sensory information between the cerebral cortex and the cerebellum. The pons also has clusters of neurons that help regulate sleep. Like the medulla, the pons helps control vital functions, especially respiration, and damage to it can produce death.

pons lies just above the medulla and relays sensory information between the cerebral cortex and the cerebellum.

cerebellum concerned primarily with muscular movement coordination, but it also plays a role in learning and memory

The Cerebellum: Motor Co-ordination Centre

Attached to the rear of the brain stem, the cerebellum ('little brain' in Latin) does indeed look like a miniature brain. Its wrinkled *cortex*, or covering, consists mainly of grey cell bodies (grey matter). The **cerebellum** is concerned primarily with muscular movement coordination, but it also plays a role in learning and memory.

Specific motor movements are initiated in higher brain centres, but their timing and coordination depend on the cerebellum (De Zeeuw & Cicirata, 2005). The cerebellum regulates complex, rapidly changing movements that require precise timing, such as those of a ballet dancer or a classical pianist. Within the animal kingdom, cats have an especially well-developed cerebellum, helping to account for their ability to move gracefully and precisely (Altman & Bayer, 1996).

Focus 4.11 Which behavioural functions are controlled by the medulla, the pons and the cerebellum? What is the consequence of damage to these structures?

The motor-control functions of the cerebellum are easily disrupted by alcohol, producing the coordination difficulties that some police forces look for in roadside sobriety tests. Intoxicated people may be unable to walk in a straight line or touch their nose with their index finger. Physical damage to the cerebellum results in severe motor disturbances characterized by jerky, uncoordinated movements, as well as an inability to perform habitual movements such as walking.

THE MIDBRAIN

Lying just above the hindbrain, the **midbrain** contains clusters of sensory and motor neurons. The sensory portion of the midbrain contains important relay centres for the visual and auditory systems. Here, nerve impulses from the eyes and ears are organized and sent to forebrain structures involved in visual and auditory perception (Nolte, 2002). The midbrain also contains motor neurons that control eye movements. Some of the exotic named structures in the midbrain include the reticular formation, the tectum (including the superior and inferior colliculi), and the substantia nigra.

midbrain contains clusters of sensory and motor neurons

reticular formation acts as a kind of sentry, both alerting higher centres of the brain that messages are coming and then either blocking those messages or allowing them to go forward

The Reticular Formation: The Brain's Gatekeeper

Buried within the midbrain is a finger-shaped structure that extends from the hindbrain up into the lower portions of the forebrain. This structure receives its name from its resemblance under a microscope to a *reticulum*, or net. The **reticular formation** acts as a kind of sentry, both alerting higher centres of the brain that messages are coming and then either blocking those messages or allowing them to go forward. The reticular formation has an *ascending* part, which sends input to higher regions of the brain to alert it, and a *descending* portion, through which higher brain centres can either admit or block out sensory input.

The reticular formation plays a central role in consciousness, sleep and attention. Without reticular stimulation of higher brain regions, sensory messages do not register in conscious awareness even though the nerve impulses may reach the appropriate higher areas of the brain. It is as if the brain is not awake enough to notice them. In fact, some general anaesthetics work by deactivating neurons of the ascending reticular formation so that sensory impulses that ordinarily would be experienced as pain never register in the sensory areas of the brain (Simon, 2007).

The reticular formation also affects sleep and wakefulness. Researchers discovered that electrical stimulation of different portions of the reticular formation can produce instant sleep in a wakeful cat and sudden wakefulness in a sleeping animal (Marshall & Magoun, 1997). Severe damage to the reticular formation can produce a permanent coma (Pendlebury, 2007).

Attention (see **Chapter 6**) is an active process during which only important or meaningful sensory inputs get through to our consciousness. Other inputs have to be toned down or completely blocked out or we would be overwhelmed by stimulation. The descending reticular formation plays an important part in this process, serving as a kind of gate through which some inputs are admitted while others are blocked out by signals coming down from higher brain centres (Van Zomeren and Brouwer, 1994).

THE FOREBRAIN

The **forebrain** is the most recently evolved part of the brain. Its major structure, the **cerebrum**, consists of two large hemispheres, a left side and a right side, that wrap around the brain stem as the two halves of a cut grapefruit might wrap around a large spoon. The outer portion of the forebrain has a thin covering, or cortex. Within the cerebrum are a number of other important forebrain structures buried in the central regions of the hemispheres.

The Thalamus: The Brain's Sensory Switchboard

The *thalamus* is located above the midbrain. It resembles two small balls, one within each cerebral hemisphere (in Figure 4.14 you can only see one thalamus as the section projects sideways through the brain, taking in both balls of the thalamus at once). The **thalamus** has sometimes been likened to a switchboard that organizes inputs from sensory organs and routes them to the appropriate areas of the brain. The visual, auditory and body senses (balance and equilibrium) all have major relay stations in the thalamus (Jones, 2006).

Because the thalamus plays such a key role in routing sensory information to higher brain regions, it seems likely that individuals with disrupted functioning in the thalamus would experience sensory confusion. Disrupted function of the thalamus has been implicated especially in schizophrenia (Andreason, 1997; Ellison-Wright & Bullmore, 2009), and stroke damage in the thalamus often gives rise to schizophrenia-like symptoms (Cronenwett & Csernansky, 2010). It is possible that thalamic damage may lead to garbled sensory information being sent to the higher regions of the brain, creating the confusing sensory experiences and hallucinations reported by schizophrenia patients.

The Hypothalamus: Motivation and Emotion

The *hypothalamus* (literally, 'under the thalamus') consists of tiny groups of neuron cell bodies that lie at the base of the brain, above the roof of the mouth. The **hypothalamus** plays a major role in many aspects of motivation and emotion, including sexual behaviour, temperature regulation, sleeping, eating, drinking and aggression. Damage to the hypothalamus can disrupt all of these behaviours (Toy, 2007). For example, destruction of one area of a male's hypothalamus results in a complete loss of sex drive; damage to another portion produces an overwhelming urge to eat, resulting in extreme obesity (Morrison, 2006).

The hypothalamus has important connections with the *endocrine system*, the body's collection of hormone-producing glands (discussed later in this chapter). Through its connection with the nearby *pituitary gland* (the master gland that exerts control over the other glands of the endocrine system), the hypothalamus directly controls many hormonal secretions that regulate sexual development and sexual behaviour, metabolism and reactions to stress.

As we have already mentioned, the hypothalamus is also involved in our experiences of pleasure. You will recall Olds and Milner's (1954) study of electrical stimulation of rat hypothalamus. They found that rats would self-stimulate their brain via such an electrode with a voracious appetite. Stimulation of other nearby areas produced just the opposite effect – a tendency to stop performing any behaviour that was followed by stimulation, as if the animal had been punished. These findings indicate that the hypothalamus and surrounding structures are important in reward and punishment. As already mentioned, the reward areas are rich in neurons that release dopamine, which seems to be an important chemical mediator of pleasure (Kolb & Whishaw, 2005).

 Chapter 6, Page 217

Focus 4.12 Describe the roles played by the ascending and descending reticular formation. What occurs with damage to this structure?

forebrain the brain's most recently evolved portion

cerebrum the most superior part of the forebrain comprising the cerebral cortex and several more central structures.

thalamus has sometimes been likened to a switchboard that organizes inputs from sensory organs and routes them to the appropriate areas of the brain

hypothalamus plays a major role in many aspects of motivation and emotion, including sexual behaviour, temperature regulation, sleeping, eating, drinking and aggression

Focus 4.13 Describe the structural characteristics and functions of the thalamus and the hypothalamus.

The Limbic System: Memory, Emotion and Goal-Directed Behaviour

As we continue our journey up through the brain, we come to the *limbic system*, a set of structures lying deep within the cerebral hemispheres (Figure 4.14). The **limbic system** helps coordinate behaviours needed to satisfy motivational and emotional urges that arise in the hypothalamus. It is also involved in memory.

Two key structures in the limbic system are the *hippocampus* and the *amygdala*. The **hippocampus** is involved in forming and retrieving memories. Damage there can result in severe memory impairment for recent events (Isaacson, 2002). The **amygdala** (from the Greek word for 'almond') is involved in emotional behaviours, particularly those linked to aggression and fear (LeDoux, 1998). Electrically stimulating certain areas of the amygdala causes animals to snarl and assume aggressive postures (see Figure 4.14b), whereas stimulation of other areas results in a fearful inability to respond aggressively, even in self-defence. For example, a normally aggressive and hungry cat will cower in fear from a tiny mouse placed in its cage. The amygdala can also produce emotional responses without the higher centres of the brain 'knowing' that we are emotionally aroused, providing a possible explanation for unconscious emotional responses (LeDoux, 1998).

The amygdala is a key part of a larger control system for anger and fear that also involves other brain regions (Siegel, 2005). It has important interconnections with the hippocampus, and amygdala stimulation is important in the hippocampus's creation of emotional memories. Without amygdala activity, emotional memories are not well established.

As in the hypothalamus, other structures within the limbic system contain reward and punishment areas that have important motivational functions. Certain drugs, such as cocaine and marijuana, seem to induce pleasure by stimulating limbic reward areas that use dopamine as their neurotransmitter (LeMoal, 1999).

The Cerebral Cortex: Crown of the Brain

The **cerebral cortex**, the most recently evolved part of the forebrain is a 0.63 cm thick sheet, consisting primarily of grey matter (i.e., unmyelinated cell bodies). This is the outermost layer of the human brain. Fish and amphibians have no cerebral cortex, and

limbic system helps coordinate behaviours needed to satisfy motivational and emotional urges that arise in the hypothalamus. It is also involved in memory

hippocampus involved in forming and retrieving memories

amygdala underlies emotional behaviours, particularly those linked to aggression and fear

Focus 4.14 What roles do the hippocampus and amygdala play in psychological functions?

cerebral cortex 0.63 cm thick sheet, consisting primarily of grey matter

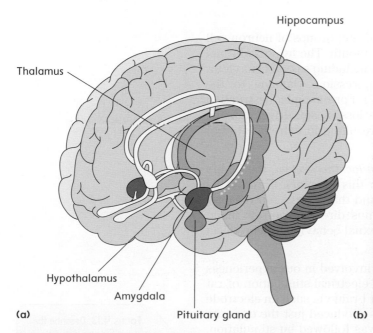

FIGURE 4.14 Limbic system structures.

(a) The amygdala and hippocampus are major structures of the limbic system. The hippocampus is important in the establishment of memories. (b) Electrical stimulation of the amygdala, which organizes emotional responses, can evoke an immediate aggressive response.

Source: © James L. Amos/Corbis

the progression from more primitive to more advanced mammals is marked by a dramatic increase in the proportion of cortical tissue. In humans, the cortex and its underlying white matter constitutes 80% of brain tissue (Simon, 2007).

The cerebral cortex is not essential for physical survival in the way that the brain stem structures are, but it is essential for human functioning. How much so is evident in this description of patients who, as a result of problems during prenatal development, were born without a cerebral cortex:

> *Some of these individuals may survive for years, in one case of mine for twenty years. From these cases, it appears that the human [lacking a cortex] sleeps and wakes; . . . reacts to hunger, loud sounds, and crude visual stimuli by movement of eyes, eyelids, and facial muscles; . . . may see and hear, . . . may be able to taste and smell, to reject the unpalatable and accept such food as it likes. . . . [They can] utter crude sounds, can cry and smile, showing displeasure when hungry and pleasure, in a babyish way, when being sung to; [they] may be able to perform spontaneously crude [limb] movements.* (Cairns, 1952, p. 109)

Because the cortex is wrinkled and convoluted, like a wadded-up piece of paper, a great amount of cortical tissue is compressed into a relatively small space inside the skull. If we could remove the cortex and smooth it out, the tissue would cover an area roughly the size of a pillowcase. Perhaps 75% of the cortex's total surface area lies within its *fissures*, the inward folds of the cortex which are not visible on the surface. Three of these fissures (also known as sulci) are important landmarks. One large fissure runs lengthwise across the top of the brain, dividing it into a right and a left hemisphere. This is called the *medial longitudinal fissure*. Within each hemisphere, the *central fissure* divides the cerebrum into front (anterior) and rear (posterior) halves, and a third fissure, the *sylvian fissure*, runs from front to rear along the side of each hemisphere. On the basis of these landmarks, neurologists have divided each hemisphere into four lobes: *frontal*, *parietal*, *occipital* and *temporal*. A fist made with your right hand (with the side of your thumb facing you) can serve as a rough orientation to these lobes. The bend in your fingers represents the frontal lobe, your knuckles the parietal lobe, your wrist area the occipital lobe and your thumb the temporal lobe of the left hemisphere (Figure 4.15).

FIGURE 4.15 Fist showing the rough orientation of the lobes.

Source: ©iStock.com/pink_cotton_candy

As shown in Figure 4.16, each of the cerebral lobes is associated with particular sensory and motor functions, as well as with speech understanding and speech production (Biller,

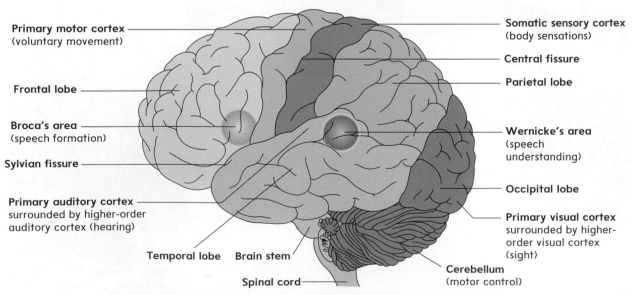

FIGURE 4.16 Lobes of the brain.

Division of the brain into frontal (blue), parietal (green), occipital (purple) and temporal (yellow) lobes, showing localization of sensory, motor and some important language functions in the cortex. The remainder is primarily association cortex, consisting of interneurons involved in complex psychological functions, such as perception and reasoning.

Brazis, & Masdeu, 2006). The large areas in Figure 4.16 that are not associated with sensory or motor functions (about three-fourths of the cortex) make up the *association cortex*, involved in mental processes such as thought, memory, and perception. (We discuss the association cortex in more detail shortly.)

The motor cortex

The **motor cortex** controls the 600 or more muscles involved in voluntary body movements. It lies at the rear of the frontal lobes adjacent to the central fissure. Because the nerve tracts from the motor cortex cross over at the level of the medulla, each hemisphere governs movement on the opposite side of the body. Thus severe damage to the right motor cortex would produce paralysis in the left side of the body. The left side of Figure 4.17 shows the relative organization of function within the motor cortex. As you can see, specific body areas are represented in upside-down fashion within the motor cortex, and the amount of cortex devoted to each area depends on the complexity of the movements that are carried out by the body part. For example, the amount of cortical tissue devoted to your fingers is far greater than that devoted to your torso, even though your torso is much larger. If we electrically stimulate a particular point on the motor cortex, movements occur in the muscles governed by that part of the cortex.

The sensory cortices

Specific areas of the cortex receive input from our sensory receptors. With the exception of taste and smell, at least one specific area in the cortex has been identified for each of the senses.

The **somatosensory cortex** receives sensory input that gives rise to our sensations of heat, touch and cold, and to our senses of balance and body movement (kinaesthesis). It lies at the front portion of the parietal lobe just behind the motor cortex, separated from the more anterior motor cortex by the central fissure. In a similar arrangement to

> **motor cortex** controls the 600 or more muscles involved in voluntary body movements
>
> **somatosensory cortex** receives sensory input that gives rise to our sensations of heat, touch and cold, and to our senses of balance and body movement (kinaesthesis)

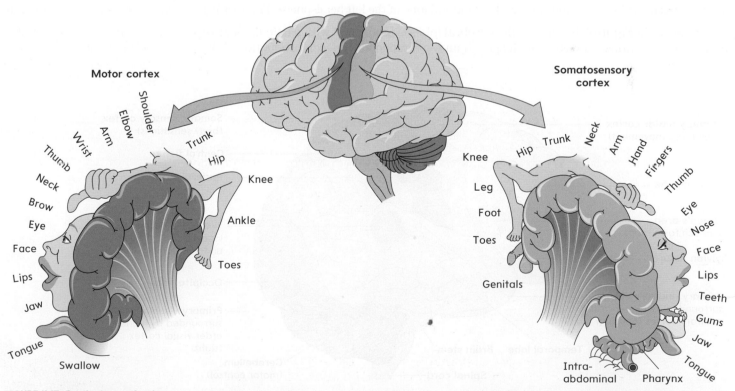

FIGURE 4.17 Cortical organization.

Both the motor cortex and the somatosensory (touch) cortex are highly specialized so that every site is associated with a particular part of the body. The amount of cortex devoted to each body part is proportional to the sensitivity of that area's motor or sensory functions. Both the motor cortex and somatosensory cortex are arranged in an upside-down fashion and serve the opposite side of the body.

the motor system, each side of the body sends sensory input to the opposite hemisphere. Like the motor area next to it, the somatosensory area is basically organized in an upside-down fashion, with the feet being represented near the top of the brain. Likewise, the amount of cortex devoted to each body area is directly proportional to that region's sensory sensitivity. The organization of the sensory cortex is shown on the right side of Figure 4.17, as is the proportion of cortex devoted to each body area. As far as your sensory cortex is concerned, you are mainly fingers, lips and tongue. Notice also that the organization of the sensory cortex is such that the body structures it serves lie side by side with those in the motor cortex, an arrangement that enhances sensory-motor interactions in the same body area.

The senses of hearing and sight are well represented in the cortex. As shown in Figure 4.16, the *primary auditory cortex* lies on the surface of the temporal lobe at the side of each hemisphere. Each ear sends messages to the auditory areas of both hemispheres, so the loss of one temporal lobe has little effect on hearing. The primary visual cortex lies at the rear of the occipital lobe. Here, messages from the eyes are analysed, integrated and translated into sight. As in the auditory system, each eye sends input to both hemispheres.

Within each sensory area, neurons are tuned to respond to particular aspects of the sensory stimulus; they are sensitive to specific aspects of the environment. Thus certain cells in the visual cortex fire only when we look at a particular kind of stimulus, such as a vertical line or a corner (Hubel & Wiesel, 1979). In the auditory cortex, some neurons fire only in response to high tones, whereas others respond only to tones having some other specific frequency. Many of these neuronal responses are present at birth, suggesting that we are pre-wired to perceive many aspects of our sensory environment (Noback, Strominger, & Ruggiero, 2005). Nonetheless, the sensory cortices, like other parts of the brain, is also sensitive to experience. For example, when people learn to read Braille, the area in the somatosensory cortex that receives input from the fingertips increases in size, making the person more sensitive to the tiny sets of raised dots (Pool, 1994).

Association cortex

The **association cortices** are involved in many important mental functions, including perception, language and thought. These areas are sometimes referred to as 'silent areas' because electrically stimulating them does not give rise to either sensory experiences or motor responses. Damage to specific parts of association cortex causes disruption or loss of functions such as speech, understanding, thinking and problem-solving. As we might expect, if the association cortex is involved in higher mental processes, the amount of association cortex increases dramatically as we move up the brain ladder from lower animals to human beings. It constitutes about 75% of the human cerebral cortex which presumably accounts for the human tendency to engage in more cognitive behaviours. One scientist has described our mass of association cortex as 'evolution's missing link' (Skoyles, 1997). He suggests that its flexibility and learning capacity have allowed us to acquire new mental skills specific to our human way of life, such as reading and mathematics, far more quickly than could have occurred through natural selection alone.

> **association cortex** is involved in many important mental functions, including perception, language and thought

One example of the importance of the association cortex is demonstrated in people who suffer from *agnosia*, the inability to identify familiar objects. One such case is described by the neurologist Oliver Sacks (1985).

Dr P (one of Sacks's patients) was a talented and accomplished musician whose behaviour was quite normal with one glaring exception: although his vision was perfect, he often had difficulty recognizing familiar people and objects. He would chat with pieces of furniture and wonder why they did not reply, or pat the tops of fire hydrants, thinking they were children. One day, while visiting Sacks's office for an examination, Dr P looked for his hat as he was ready to depart. Suddenly he reached out and grabbed his wife's head, trying to lift it. He had mistaken his wife for his hat! His wife smiled tolerantly as she had become accustomed to such actions on his part. Dr P had suffered brain damage that left him unable to connect the information sent to the visual cortex with information stored in other cortical areas that concerned the nature of objects. The associative neurons responsible for linking the two types of information no longer served him.

> **Focus 4.15** Describe the locations of the four lobes of the brain and the organization of the motor, sensory, and association cortexes.

The frontal lobes: the human difference

Some neuroscientists suggest that the entire period of human evolutionary existence could well be termed the age of the frontal lobe (Krasnegor, Lyon, & Goldman, 1997). This brain region hardly exists in mammals such as mice and rats. The frontal lobes compose about 3.5% of the cerebral cortex in the cat, 7% in the dog, and 17% in the chimpanzee. In a human, the frontal lobes constitute 29% of the cortex. The frontal lobes – the site of such human qualities as self-awareness, planning, initiative and responsibility – are certainly the most mysterious and least understood parts of the brain.

Much of what we know about the frontal lobes comes from detailed studies of patients who have experienced brain damage. Frontal-lobe damage results not so much in a loss of intellectual abilities as in an inability to plan and carry out a sequence of actions, even when patients can verbalize what they should do. This can result in an inability to correct actions that are clearly erroneous and self-defeating (Shallice & Burgess, 1991).

The frontal cortex is also involved in emotional experience. In people with normal brains, PET scans show increased activity in the frontal cortex when people are experiencing feelings of happiness, sadness or disgust (Lane, Reiman, Ahern, & Schwartz, 1997). In contrast, patients with frontal-lobe damage often exhibit attitudes of apathy and lack of concern. They simply do not seem to care about anything. Consider the following episode reported by a neurologist who was testing a patient with frontal-lobe damage:

> *Testing left-right discrimination was oddly difficult, because she said left or right indifferently. When I drew her attention to this, she said, 'Left/right. Right/left. Why the fuss?*
> *What's the difference?'*
> *'Is there a difference?' I asked.*
> *'Of course,' she said with a chemist's precision . . . 'But they mean nothing to me. They're no different for me. Hands . . . Doctors . . . Sisters,' she added, seeing my puzzlement. 'Don't you understand? They mean nothing – nothing to me. Nothing means anything, at least to me.'*
> *Mrs. B, though acute and intelligent, was somehow not present – 'desouled' – as a person.*
> (Sacks, 1985, p. 174)

A region of the frontal lobe has received increasing attention in recent years. The **prefrontal cortex**, located just behind the forehead, is the seat of the so-called executive functions. Executive functions are mental strategic planning and impulse control – which allow people to direct their behaviour in an adaptive fashion. Deficits in executive functions seem to underlie a number of problem behaviours. People with prefrontal cortex disorders seem oblivious to the future consequences of their actions and seem to be governed only by immediate consequences (Zald & Rauch, 2006). As you may remember, Phineas Gage, the railroad foreman described in our chapter-opening case, suffered massive prefrontal damage when the spike tore through his brain (see Figure 4.1). Thereafter he exhibited classic symptoms of disturbed executive functions, becoming behaviourally impulsive and losing his capacity for future planning.

A more ominous manifestation of prefrontal dysfunction – the capacity to kill – was recently discovered by researchers using PET technology. We describe this landmark study in the following 'Research close-up'.

HEMISPHERIC LATERALIZATION: THE LEFT AND RIGHT BRAINS

The left and right cerebral hemispheres are connected by a broad white band of myelinated nerve fibres. The **corpus callosum** is a neural bridge consisting of white matter tracts that acts as a major communication link between the two hemispheres and allows them to function as a single unit (see Figure 4.14). Despite the fact that they normally act in concert, there are important differences between the psychological functions of the two cerebral hemispheres (Hugdahl & Davidson, 2005). **Lateralization** refers to the relatively greater localization of a function in one hemisphere or the other.

---

prefrontal cortex located just behind the forehead, is the seat of the so-called executive functions

Focus 4.16 Describe the role of the frontal cortex in higher mental (including executive) functions.

corpus callosum is a neural bridge consisting of white matter tracts that acts as a major communication link between the two hemispheres and allows them to function together

lateralization refers to the relatively greater localization of a function in one hemisphere or the other

Medical studies of patients who suffered various types of brain damage provided the first clues that certain complex psychological functions were lateralized on one side of the brain or the other. The deficits observed in people with damage to either the left or right hemisphere suggested that for most people, verbal abilities and speech are localized in the left hemisphere, as are mathematical and logical abilities (Springer, 1997). When Broca's or Wernicke's speech areas in the left hemisphere are damaged, the result is aphasia, the partial or total loss of the ability to communicate. Depending on the location of the damage, the problem may lie in recognizing the meaning of words, in communicating verbally with others, or in both functions. We should note, however, that women are less likely to suffer aphasia when their left hemisphere is damaged, suggesting that for women, language is represented in both hemispheres to a greater extent than for men (Rossell, Bullmore, Williams, & David, 2002).

> **aphasia** the partial or total loss of the ability to communicate

 ## Research close-up

INSIDE THE BRAIN OF A PSYCHOPATH

Source: Y. Yang, A. Raine, T. Lencz, S. Bihrle, L. LaCasse & P. Colletti, (2005). Volume reduction in prefrontal grey matter in unsuccessful criminal psychopaths. *Biological Psychiatry, 57*, 1103–1108.

INTRODUCTION

What stops us from impulsively killing an irritating neighbour, a disloyal friend, or a total stranger wearing a coat we would like to own? The answer may lie, at least in part, in our frontal lobes. Much of what makes you a civilized person – self-control, judgement, foresight, reasoning, delaying gratification – is regulated by the executive functions of your prefrontal cortex. As seen in the case of Phineas Gage, damage in this region of the brain can reduce those civilizing inhibitions.

Until recently, researchers could only infer that impulsively violent people without obvious brain damage had reduced prefrontal activity, for they could not look directly into the brain and measure aspects of its function or measure how large different components were.

METHOD

An SCID (Structured Clinical Interview for DSM) was carried out on volunteer individuals, drawn from employment agencies, to allow a rich psychological diagnosis which included many relevant aspects such as IQ and histories of drug and alcohol abuse. The Psychopathy Checklist – Revised, PCL-R (Hare, 1991) was also administered, and a history of criminal activity given. Participants were split into three groups: successful psychopaths (scoring highly on the PCL-R, and whose crimes had remained undetected); unsuccessful psychopaths (high PCL-R scores, but convicted of crimes); and controls, who had low PCL-R scores and no criminal experience. Next, MRI scans were taken of the frontal lobes of each participant – Damasio, Tranel and Damasio (1990) have shown that damage to the prefrontal cortex is often linked with a psychopathic-like personality.

RESULTS

In total 52 participants were included, 16 unsuccessful psychopaths, 13 successful psychopaths and 23 controls. The volume of the prefrontal lobe was measured with MRI in each participant and the results showed that the scores on the PCL-R, that is to say, the total psychopathy scores, were associated with lower prefrontal cortex volume. The results are shown in Figure 4.18.

Unsuccessful psychopaths showed a lower volume of grey matter in the prefrontal cortex than do psychopaths, who in turn have less than controls. Compared with controls, the unsuccessful psychopaths had a 22.3% reduction in grey matter.

DISCUSSION

A good way to think about these results is in terms of an ability to control our actions. Damasio (1994) says that damage to the prefrontal cortex results in disrupted decision-making ability. The prefrontal lobes have been implicated in psychopathic behaviour for this reason for some time and these data add to that understanding. Also interesting here is the finding that unsuccessful psychopaths appear to have less prefrontal cortex white matter than successful psychopaths. This can be explained in terms of sensitivity to signals indicating danger. The psychological tests carried out in this research also showed that the unsuccessful psychopaths showed reduced

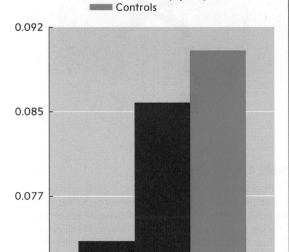

FIGURE 4.18 Prefrontal grey to whole brain ratio in successful and unsuccessful psychopaths and control participants.

Source: Data from Yang et al., 2005.

reactions to stress as well as control abilities. It may be that this reduced sensitivity to stress which may predict potential punishment coupled with a reduction in prefrontal grey matter may make unsuccessful psychopaths insensitive to the danger signs associated with their crimes and may make them susceptible to capture. Successful psychopaths, on the other hand, show more sensitivity to these danger signals and so avoid capture and their crimes go unpunished. The authors conclude that damage to the prefrontal lobes is not, in itself, sufficient to cause psychopathic behaviour. Instead, they conclude that the disruption of the prefrontal cortex predisposes the person to personality traits that may result in psychopathic behaviour. What is most important here is that the research shows an important distinction between successful and unsuccessful psychopaths.

Focus 4.17 What is hemispheric lateralization, and what functions are localized in the left and right hemispheres?

When the right hemisphere is damaged, the clinical picture is quite different. Language functions are not ordinarily affected, but the person has great difficulty perceiving spatial relations. A patient may have a hard time recognizing faces and may even forget a well-travelled route or, as in the case of Dr P, mistake his wife for a hat (Sacks, 1985). It appears that mental imagery, musical and artistic abilities, and the ability to perceive and understand spatial relations are primarily right-hemisphere functions (Biller et al., 2006).

The two hemispheres differ not only in the cognitive functions that reside there but also in their links with positive and negative emotions. EEG studies have shown that the right hemisphere is relatively more active when negative emotions such as sadness and anger are being experienced. Positive emotions such as joy and happiness are accompanied by relatively greater left-hemisphere activation (Marshall & Fox, 2000).

THE SPLIT BRAIN: DIVIDING THE HEMISPHERES

Despite the lateralization of specific functions in the two cerebral hemispheres, the brain normally functions as a unified whole because the two hemispheres communicate with one another through the corpus callosum. But what would happen if this communication link were cut? Would we, in effect, produce two different and largely independent minds in the same person? A series of Nobel Prize-winning studies by Roger Sperry (1970) and his associates addressed this question. Sperry and his co-workers studied people whose corpora callosa had been severed to stop epileptic seizures from spreading throughout the brain.

Split-brain research was made possible by the way in which our visual input to the brain is organized. To illustrate, extend your two hands straight out in front of you, separated by about 1 foot (30 cm). Now focus on the point between them. You will find that you can still see both hands in your peripheral vision and that you have a unified view of the scene. It therefore might surprise you to know that your left hand is being 'seen' only by your right hemisphere and your right hand only by your left hemisphere. To see how this occurs, examine Figure 4.19, which shows that some of the fibres of the optic nerve from each eye cross over at the *optic chiasm* and travel to the opposite brain hemisphere.

Despite this arrangement, we experience a unified visual world (as you did when you looked at your hands), rather than two half-worlds, because our hemispheres' visual areas are connected by the

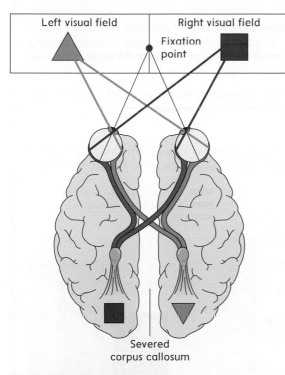

FIGURE 4.19 The split brain.

The visual system's anatomy made studies of split brain subjects possible. Images entering the eye are reversed by the lens, so that light waves from the right visual field fall on the left side of the retina and those from the left visual field fall on the right side of the retina. Optic nerve fibres from the inner portion of the retina (towards the nose) cross over at the optic chiasm, whereas the fibres from the outer portion of the retina do not. As a result, the right side of the visual field projects to the visual cortex of the left hemisphere, whereas the left visual field projects to the right hemisphere. When the corpus callosum is cut, the two hemispheres no longer communicate with each other. By presenting stimuli to either side of the visual fixation point, researchers can control which hemisphere receives the information.

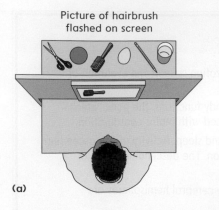

Picture of hairbrush flashed on screen

(a)

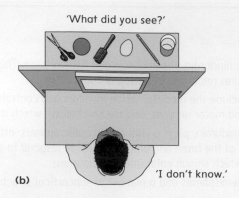

'What did you see?'

(b)

'I don't know.'

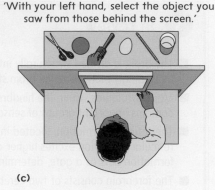

'With your left hand, select the object you saw from those behind the screen.'

(c)

FIGURE 4.20 A split-brain patient.

A split-brain patient focuses on the fixation point in the centre of the screen. (a) A picture of a hairbrush is briefly shown, meaning gaze could not be redirected to the object, and so limiting the projection to the left side of the visual field, thus sending the information to the right hemisphere. (b) The patient is asked to report what she saw. She cannot name the object. (c) She is then asked to select the object she saw and quickly finds it with her left hand. What would happen if the object were to be transferred to her right hand or if the word were to be projected to the right side of the visual field? In either case, the information would be sent to the language-rich left hemisphere, and she would be able to name the object.

corpus callosum. When the corpus callosum is cut, however, visual input to only one hemisphere can be accomplished by projecting the stimulus to either the right side of the visual field, in which case the image goes only to the left hemisphere, or to the left side of the visual field, which sends it to the right hemisphere.

In Sperry's experiments, split-brain patients basically did what you did with your hands: they focused on a fixation point, a dot on the centre of a screen, while slides containing visual stimuli (words, pictures, and so on) were flashed to the right or to the left side of the fixation point (Figure 4.20).

Sperry found that when words were flashed to the right side of the visual field, resulting in these being sent to the language-rich left hemisphere, patients could verbally describe what they had seen. They could also write what they had seen with their right hand (which is controlled by the left hemisphere). However, if words were flashed to the left side of the visual field and sent on to the right hemisphere, the patients could not describe what they had seen on the screen. This pattern of findings indicates that the right hemisphere does not have well-developed verbal expressive abilities.

The inability to describe stimuli verbally did not mean, however, that the right hemisphere was incapable of recognizing them. If a picture of an object (e.g., a hairbrush) was flashed to the right hemisphere and the left hand (controlled by the right hemisphere) was allowed to feel different objects behind the screen, the person's hand would immediately select the brush. As long as the person continued to hold the brush in the left hand, sending sensory input about the object to the 'non-verbal' right hemisphere, the person was unable to name it. However, if the brush was transferred to the right hand, the person could immediately name it. In other words, until the object was transferred to the right hand, the left hemisphere had no knowledge of what the right hemisphere was experiencing.

Later research showed the right hemisphere's definite superiority over the left in the recognition of patterns. In one study, three split-brain patients were presented with photographs of similar looking faces projected in either the left or right visual fields. On each trial, they were asked to select the photo they had just seen from a set of 10 cards. In this task, the spatially oriented right hemisphere was far more accurate than the linguistic left hemisphere in correctly identifying the photos. Apparently, the faces were too similar to one another to be differentiated very easily by left-hemisphere verbal descriptions, but the pattern-recognition abilities of the right hemisphere allowed discrimination among them (Gazzaniga & Smylie, 1983). Split-brain research firmly established the different abilities of the two hemispheres.

In review

- The brain is divided structurally into the hindbrain, the midbrain and the forebrain. This organization reflects the evolution of increasingly more complex brain structures related to behavioural capabilities.

- Major structures within the hindbrain include the medulla, which monitors and controls vital body functions; the pons, which contains important groups of sensory and motor neurons; and the cerebellum, which is concerned with motor coordination.

- The reticular formation, located in the midbrain, plays a vital role in consciousness, attention and sleep. Activity of the ascending reticular formation excites higher areas of the brain and prepares them to respond to stimulation. The descending reticular formation acts as a gate, determining which stimuli enter into consciousness.

- The forebrain consists of two cerebral hemispheres and a number of subcortical structures. The cerebral hemispheres are connected by the corpus callosum.

- The thalamus acts as a switchboard through which impulses originating in sense organs are routed to the appropriate sensory-projection areas. The hypothalamus plays a major role in many aspects of motivational and emotional behaviour. The limbic system seems to be involved in organizing the behaviours involved in motivation and emotion.

- The cerebral cortex is divided into frontal, parietal, occipital and temporal lobes. Some areas of the cerebral cortex receive sensory input, some control motor functions, and others (the association cortex) are involved in higher mental processes in humans. The frontal lobes are particularly important in such executive functions as planning, voluntary behaviour and self-awareness.

- Although the two cerebral hemispheres ordinarily work in coordination with one another, they appear to have different functions and abilities. Studies of split-brain patients, whose corpora callosa have been cut, indicate that the left hemisphere commands language and mathematical abilities, whereas the right hemisphere has well-developed spatial abilities but a generally limited ability to communicate through speech. Positive emotions are linked to relatively greater left hemisphere activation and negative emotions to relatively greater right-hemisphere involvement. Despite hemispheric localization, however, most behaviour involves interactions between both hemispheres; the brain normally operates as a highly integrated system.

PLASTICITY IN THE BRAIN: THE ROLE OF EXPERIENCE AND THE RECOVERY OF FUNCTION

Learn to walk, acquire speech, begin to read or fall in love, and your brain changes in ways that make you a different person from who you were before. Learning and practising a mental or physical skill may change the size or number of brain areas involved and alter the neural pathways used in the skill (Adams & Cox, 2002; Posner & Rothbart, 2007a). This process of brain alteration begins in the womb and continues throughout life. It is governed in important ways by genetic factors but is also strongly influenced by the environment.

neural plasticity the ability of neurons and brain areas and networks to change in structure and function

Neural plasticity refers to the ability of neurons and brain areas and networks to change in structure and function (Huttenlocher, 2002). Two aspects of neural plasticity – the effects of early experience on brain development and recovery from brain damage – are at the forefront of current research.

HOW EXPERIENCE CHANGES THE BRAIN

Brain development is programmed by complex commands from our genes, but how these genetic commands express themselves can be powerfully affected by the environment in which we develop, including the environment we are exposed to in the womb (Fenichel, 2006). Consider the following research findings:

1. Prematurely born human infants who were caressed and massaged on a regular basis showed faster neurological development than did those given normal care and human contact (Field et al., 1986).

2. Compared with those of normally reared rats, the brains of rat pups raised in a stimulating environment weighed more and had larger neurons, more dendritic branches and greater concentrations of acetylcholine, a neurotransmitter involved in motor control and in memory (Rosenzweig, 1984; Simpson & Kelly, 2011).

3. MRI recordings revealed that experienced violinists and other string-instrument players who do elaborate movements on the strings with their left hands had a larger right hemisphere somatosensory area devoted to these fingers than did non-musicians. The corresponding left-hemisphere (right-hand) cortical areas of the musicians and non-musicians did not differ. The earlier in life the musicians had started playing their instruments, the greater the cortical differences (Elbert, Pantev, Wienbruch, Rockstroh, & Taub, 1995).

4. Some theorists believe that life stress has a similar negative effect on neuron formation in the brain, thereby causing or maintaining clinical depression. Antidepressant medications increase serotonin action in the brain, and serotonin increases neuron production in the brain (Jacobs, 2004).

5. Cultural factors may affect brain development as well. For example, the Chinese language uses complex pictorial images (rather than words) to represent objects or concepts. Because pictorial stimuli are processed in the right hemisphere, we might expect less left hemisphere lateralization of language among speakers of Chinese than among people who speak English or other alphabet-based languages. There is evidence to support this hypothesis in the areas of reading and writing (Tzeng, Hung, Cohen, & Wang, 1979).

6. Even your job may cause changes in your brain. A study by Maguire and colleagues (2000; Woollett & Maguire, 2011) showed that London taxi drivers, who are required to have an encyclopaedic knowledge of London's streets, have larger posterior hippocampuses than control participants. The hippocampus is known to play an important role in spatial navigation (Burgess et al., 2002).

These and other findings show that in a very real sense, each person's brain goes through its own personal evolutionary process. In **Chapter 12** we will discuss the way experience influences brain development in more detail. For our purposes in this chapter, it suffices to note that the brain changes and adapts as it is sculpted by life experiences (Posner & Rothbart, 2007b). Furthermore, these changes are not restricted just to early life. Brain plasticity is a lifelong phenomenon.

Chapter 12, Page 499

Studies using the electron microscope help explain why such plasticity is possible early in life. As we will see in Chapter 12, the one- to two-year-old child has about 50% more brain synapses than mature adults do (Lomber & Eggermont, 2006). Some have argued that this greater availability of synapses in early life enables children to recover from brain damage more quickly and completely than adults. However, this argument does not go unchallenged. Other researchers have suggested that the greater availability of synapses may actually make the brain more vulnerable to injury in early life (Pascual-Leone, Amedi, Fregni, & Merabet, 2005), and this is a matter of much current debate (Anderson, Spencer-Smith, & Wood, 2011). Regardless of this debate, the days of synaptic riches do not last forever. Unused or weaker synapses are pruned away with age, so that the brain loses some of its plasticity (Huttenlocher, 2002). Moreover, cell death is programmed into every neuron by its genes, and what some neuroscientists refer to as the neuron's 'suicide apparatus' is activated by a lack of stimulation from other neurons and by many other factors that are not yet known. As a result, adults actually have fewer synapses than do children, despite their more advanced cognitive and motor capabilities. However, the remaining neurons form new connections in response to experiences and the formation of new memories. This plasticity, and ability to form new connections is extremely useful, but can be influenced. Nicotine, for example, has been shown to help concentration and cognition, and has been seen to show beneficial effects in those with Parkinson's disease, but findings have also shown that it actually reduces the plasticity of cells in the frontal lobes (Couey et al., 2007).

Focus 4.18 What is neural plasticity?

HEALING THE NERVOUS SYSTEM

When nerve tissue is destroyed or neurons die as part of the ageing process, surviving neurons can restore functioning by modifying themselves either structurally or

biochemically. They can alter their structure by sprouting enlarged networks of dendrites or by extending axons from surviving neurons to form new synapses (Shepherd, 1997). Surviving neurons may also make up for the loss by increasing the volume of neurotransmitters they release (Robinson, 1997). Moreover, research findings have disproved the long-standing assumption of brain scientists that dead neurons cannot be replaced in the mature brain (McMillan, Robertson, & Wilson, 1999). The production of new neurons in the nervous system is called **neurogenesis**. Neurogenesis occurs in both the immature and the adult brain. In the adult brain, the birth of new cells has been established only in the hippocampus so far, but it may occur in other areas as well. The study of neurogenesis is an exciting research frontier.

Ian Robertson's research group in Trinity, Dublin, is looking at a number of different strands of research surrounding rehabilitation and degeneration. Among a raft of other things, their work on brain plasticity has included investigations in Alzheimer's disease and traumatic brain injuries. They are also part of pioneering exciting work on another aspect of neuropsychology called cognitive neurogenomics. Cognitive neurogenomics refers to the genetic make-up of cognitive function. It typically involves the search for neuropsychological or biological markers for clinical disorders (i.e., attention deficit hyperactivity disorder (ADHD), autism, etc.) linked to known genetic patterns. For example, genetic variation within the DAT1 genotype that helps distribute the neurotransmitter dopamine, can influence the development of prefrontal cortex. It has been found that children possessing two copies of the DAT-associated risk allele had significantly poorer sustained attention than those ADHD children who did not possess this risk component. This is a high priority for the health service because drugs like Ritalin which are used to treat the symptoms of ADHD may only have an influence on a certain subset (proportion) of ADHD children who show the appropriate genotypic response to the drug. The research is providing exciting possibilities for combining focused drug treatments for disorders with behavioural and cognitive techniques that may significantly improve the quality of life of those with these neuropsychological problems.

One revolutionary neurogenesis technique involves the transplantation into the brain of **neural stem cells**, immature 'uncommitted' cells that can mature into any type of neuron or glial cell needed by the brain. These cells, found in both the developing and adult nervous systems, can be put into a liquid medium and injected directly into the brain. Once in the brain, they can travel to any of its regions, especially developing or degenerating areas. There they can detect defective or genetically impaired cells and somehow convert themselves into healthy forms of the defective cells. Stem cells have been successfully transplanted into the spinal cords of injured animals, where they have taken hold and organized themselves into neural networks (Tzeng, 1997). This success may herald an eventual ability to do what has never before been possible: repair the severed spinal cord.

The fact that transplanted stem cells can apparently go anywhere in the brain and become any kind of cell suggests the possibility of revolutionary treatments for diseases involving neural degeneration and dysfunction. These include Alzheimer's disease, multiple sclerosis, strokes, mental disorders and genetically based birth defects, all of which have serious psychological consequences (Wernig & Brustle, 2002). Stem cells may also hold the key to countering the effects of ageing on brain functioning. In one study, human stem cells transplanted into the brains of aged rats migrated to the hippocampus and cortex. Four weeks later, these rats showed improved performance in a water-maze task, suggesting improved learning and memory ability (Qu, Brannen, Kim, & Sugaya, 2001). Much more research is needed, but, at long last, we may be on the threshold of being able to heal the damaged brain and restore lost psychological functions (Brazel & Rao, 2004). A key to doing so will be to discover why it is that stem cells, which have the potential to produce new neurons and are found throughout the adult brain, are not utilized more widely by the brain to repair itself. It may be that altering stem cells through pharmacological or genetic interventions will increase their ability to repair the damaged brain (Kempermann, 2005).

neurogenesis the production of new neurons in the nervous system

neural stem cells immature 'uncommitted' cells that can mature into any type of neuron or glial cell needed by the brain

Focus 4.19 Describe the ways in which neural function can be restored following damage.

In review

- Neural plasticity refers to the ability of neurons to change in structure and function. Environmental factors, particularly early in life, have notable effects on brain development. There are often periods during which environmental factors have their greatest (or only) effects on plasticity.
- A person's ability to recover from brain damage depends on several factors. Other things being equal, recovery is greatest early in life and declines with age.
- When neurons die, surviving neurons can alter their structure and functions to recover the ability to send and receive nerve impulses. Neurons can also increase the amount of neurotransmitters they release. Recent findings suggest that the brains of mature primates and humans are capable of producing new neurons (neurogenesis).
- Current advances in the treatment of neurological disorders include experiments on neurogenesis and the injection of neural stem cells into the brain, where they find and replace diseased or dead neurons.

THE NERVOUS SYSTEM INTERACTS WITH THE ENDOCRINE AND IMMUNE SYSTEMS

The nervous system interacts with two other communication systems within the body, namely, the endocrine and immune systems. These interactions have major influences on behaviour and on psychological and physical well-being.

INTERACTIONS WITH THE ENDOCRINE SYSTEM

The **endocrine system** consists of numerous hormone-secreting glands distributed throughout the body (Figure 4.21). Like the nervous system, the endocrine system's function is to convey information from one area of the body to another. Rather than using nerve impulses, however, the endocrine system conveys information in the form of **hormones**, chemical messengers that are secreted from its glands into the bloodstream. Just as neurons have receptors for certain neurotransmitters, cells in the body (including neurons) have receptor molecules that respond to specific hormones from the endocrine glands (Porterfield & White, 2007). Many of the hormones secreted by these glands affect psychological development and functioning.

Endocrine messages trigger responses in the brain, and mental processes within the brain can affect endocrine functioning. For example, negative thoughts about a stressful situation can quickly trigger the secretion of stress hormones within the body (Borod, 2000).

The nervous system transmits information rapidly, with the speed of nerve impulses. In contrast, the endocrine system is much slower because the delivery of its messages depends on the rate of blood flow. Nonetheless, hormones travel throughout the body in the bloodstream and can reach billions of individual cells. Thus, when the brain has important information to transmit, it has the choice of sending it quickly and directly in the form of nerve impulses to a relatively small number of neurons or indirectly by means of hormones to a large number of cells. Often both communication networks are used, resulting in both immediate and prolonged stimulation.

Hormones begin to influence our development, capacities and behaviour long before we are born. In the third to fourth month of pregnancy, genetically programmed releases of sex hormones in the foetus determine sex organ development, as well as differences in the structure and function of several parts of the nervous system, including the hypothalamus. One area of the hypothalamus affected in this manner continues to influence hormonal release in later life, such as the cyclic pattern of hormonal release during the female menstrual cycle.

> **endocrine system** consists of numerous hormone-secreting glands distributed throughout the body
>
> **hormones** chemical messengers that are secreted from its glands into the bloodstream

> **Focus 4.20** How does the endocrine system differ from the nervous system? How do hormones affect development and behaviour?

FIGURE 4.21 The endocrine system.

The location of the glands that comprise the endocrine system and the effects of their hormones on bodily functions.

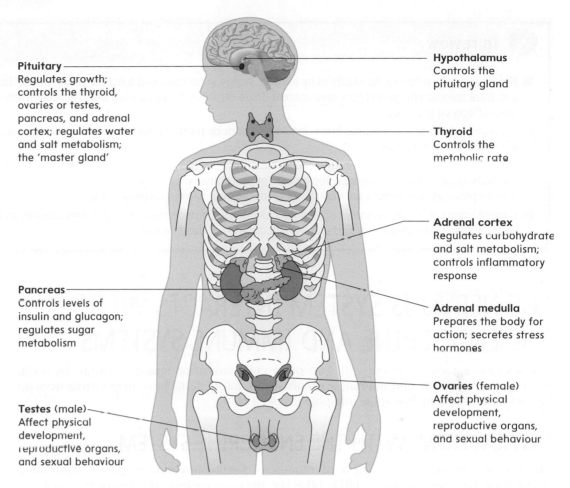

Pituitary
Regulates growth; controls the thyroid, ovaries or testes, pancreas, and adrenal cortex; regulates water and salt metabolism; the 'master gland'

Hypothalamus
Controls the pituitary gland

Thyroid
Controls the metabolic rate

Adrenal cortex
Regulates carbohydrate and salt metabolism; controls inflammatory response

Pancreas
Controls levels of insulin and glucagon; regulates sugar metabolism

Adrenal medulla
Prepares the body for action; secretes stress hormones

Ovaries (female)
Affect physical development, reproductive organs, and sexual behaviour

Testes (male)
Affect physical development, reproductive organs, and sexual behaviour

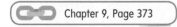 Chapter 9, Page 373

adrenal glands twin structures perched on top of the kidneys that serve, quite literally, as hormone factories, producing and secreting about 50 different hormones

Aside from reproductive structures and sexual behaviours, prenatal hormones affect a variety of other characteristics including sex differences in aggressiveness and longevity; males tend to be more aggressive than females, and females live longer than men (Nelson & Luciana, 2001). Prenatal hormones also produce differences in brain structures in males and females. Females have a greater density of neurons in language-relevant areas of the temporal lobe, which may contribute to the small overall superiority they manifest in verbal skills (Collins & Kimura, 1997). They also tend to have a relatively larger corpus callosum than males, which may help account for the fact that language functions are less localized in the left hemisphere in females (Rossell et al., 2002). These sex differences are discussed in greater detail in **Chapter 9**.

Of special interest to psychologists are the **adrenal glands** (see Figure 4.21), twin structures perched on top of the kidneys that serve, quite literally, as hormone factories, producing and secreting about 50 different hormones that regulate many metabolic processes within the brain and other parts of the body. The adrenals produce the neurotransmitter dopamine, as well as several stress hormones. In an emergency, the adrenal glands are activated by the sympathetic branch of the autonomic nervous system. Stress hormones are then secreted into the bloodstream, mobilizing the body's emergency response system. Because hormones remain in the bloodstream for some time, the action of these adrenal hormones is especially important under conditions of prolonged stress. If not for the long-term influence of hormones, the autonomic nervous system would have to produce a constant barrage of nerve impulses to the organs involved in responding to stress.

INTERACTIONS INVOLVING THE IMMUNE SYSTEM

The nervous and endocrine systems interact not only with one another but also with the immune system (Chrousos, Kaltsas, & Mastorakos, 2006). A normal, healthy immune

system is a wonder of nature. At this moment, microscopic soldiers patrol every part of your body, including your brain. They are on a search-and-destroy mission, seeking out biological invaders that could disable or kill you. Programmed into this legion of tiny defenders is an innate ability to recognize which substances belong to the body and which are foreign and must be destroyed. Such recognition occurs because foreign substances known as **antigens** (meaning *anti* body *gen*erators) trigger a biochemical response from the immune system. Bacteria, viruses, abnormal cells and many chemical molecules with antigenic properties start the wars that rage inside our bodies every moment of every day (Figure 4.22).

antigens foreign substances that trigger a biochemical response from the immune system

The immune system has a remarkable memory. Once it has encountered one of the millions of different antigens that enter the body, it will recognize the antigen immediately in the future and produce the biochemical weapons, or *antibodies*, needed to destroy it (Nossal & Hall, 1995). This memory is the basis for developing vaccines to protect people and animals from some diseases; it is also the reason we normally catch diseases such as mumps and chicken pox only once in our lives. Unfortunately, though the memory may be perfect, our body's defences may not be. Some bacteria and viruses evolve so rapidly that they can change just enough over time to slip past the sentinels in our immune system and give us this year's cold or flu.

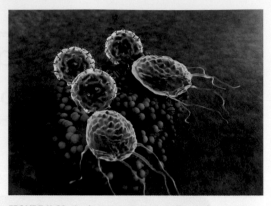

FIGURE 4.22 An immune-system cell reaches out to capture bacteria, shown here in yellow. The bacteria that have already been pulled to the surface of the cell will be engulfed and devoured.

Source: ©iStock.com/Ugreen

The immune system, like the nervous system, has an exquisite capacity to receive, interpret and respond to specific forms of stimulation. In many ways it behaves as if, like the nervous system, it senses, learns, remembers and reacts. Despite these similarities, research on the nervous and immune systems proceeded along independent paths for many years, with only a few visionaries suggesting that the two systems might be able to communicate and influence each other's activities. We now know that the nervous, endocrine and immune systems are all parts of a communication network that so completely underlies our every mental, emotional and physical action that neuroscientist Candace Pert (1986), one of the pioneers in this area of research, has dubbed this network 'bodymind'.

Pieces of this communication puzzle began to fall into place with several key discoveries. First, researchers found that electrical stimulation or destruction of certain sites in the hypothalamus and cerebral cortex resulted in immediate increases or decreases in immune-system activity. Conversely, activating the immune system by injecting antigens into the body resulted in increased electrical activity in several brain regions (Saphier, 1992). Clearly, the nervous and immune systems were communicating with and influencing one another.

Later research showed that the nervous and immune systems are chemically connected as well. Immune-system cells contain receptors keyed to specific neurotransmitter substances, meaning that the action of immune cells can be directly influenced by chemical messengers from the brain (Maier & Watkins, 1999). An equally startling discovery was that immune cells can actually produce hormones and neurotransmitters, allowing them to directly influence the brain and endocrine system (Felton & Maida, 2000). In sum, the brain, endocrine glands and immune system form a complete communication loop, with each having sensory and motor functions and each influencing and being influenced by one another.

Focus 4.21 What evidence exists that the nervous, endocrine and immune systems communicate with and influence one another?

Inspired by these findings, many researchers began to study psychological influences on the immune system. Scientific investigations soon revealed a host of psychosocial factors that can increase or decrease immunity. For example, chronic stress, depression and pessimistic thinking reduce immune functioning, whereas stress management skills, an optimistic outlook, a sense of humour and social support help preserve immunity (Kiecolt-Glaser, McGuire, Robles, & Glaser, 2002; Segerstrom & Miller, 2004). As the levels of analysis shows, immune functioning is now being studied at biological, psychological and environmental levels of analysis. We examine these findings and their applied implications in greater depth in **Chapter 16.**

 Chapter 16 , Page 681

And so it is clear that the brain and nervous system are involved with almost all levels of human functioning, from basic bodily processes, such as those governed by the

autonomic nervous system (and via the psychological influences on the immune system just discussed), to the processing and manipulation of complex patterns of information required by higher brain functions. As we gain greater understanding of the biological processes which underpin psychology and behaviour, the biological level of explanation becomes ever more relevant in the field of psychology.

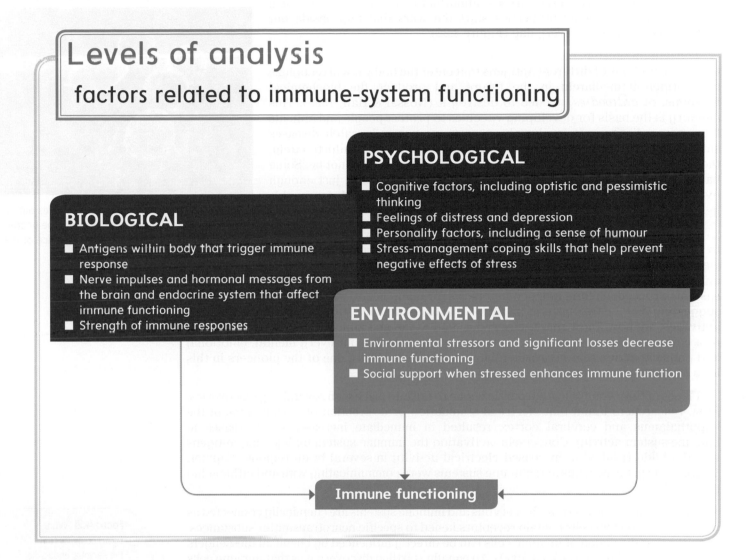

Levels of analysis
factors related to immune-system functioning

PSYCHOLOGICAL

- Cognitive factors, including optistic and pessimistic thinking
- Feelings of distress and depression
- Personality factors, including a sense of humour
- Stress-management coping skills that help prevent negative effects of stress

BIOLOGICAL

- Antigens within body that trigger immune response
- Nerve impulses and hormonal messages from the brain and endocrine system that affect immune functioning
- Strength of immune responses

ENVIRONMENTAL

- Environmental stressors and significant losses decrease immune functioning
- Social support when stressed enhances immune function

Immune functioning

 In review

- The nervous, endocrine and immune systems have extensive neural and chemical means of communication, and each is capable of affecting and being affected by the others.
- The endocrine system secretes hormones into the bloodstream. These chemical messengers affect many body processes, including those associated with the central and autonomic nervous systems. Because of the adrenal glands' relation to functions of the nervous system, they are of particular interest to psychologists. Hormonal effects in the womb may produce brain differences in males and females that influence sex differences in certain psychological functions.
- The immune system interacts extensively with the central and autonomic nervous systems and with the endocrine system. As a behaving entity, the immune system has the capacity to sense, interpret and respond to specific forms of stimulation.

Recommended Reading

CLASSIC

Kandel, E.R., Schwartz, J.H. & Jessell, T. M. (Eds.) (2000). Principles of neural science (Vol. 4, pp. 1227–1246). New York: McGraw-Hill.

Damasio, H. Grabowski, T. Frank, R. Galaburda, A. M. & Damasio, A. R. (1994). The return of Phineas Gage: Clues about the brain from the skull of a famous patient. *Science, 264* (5162), 1102–1105.

Posner, M. I. & Ruichle, M. E. (1994). *Images of mind. Scientific American.* Library/Scientific American Books.

CONTEMPORARY

Kolb, B. & Whishaw, I. Q. (2009). Fundamentals of human neuropsychology. New York. Macmillan.

Schwartz, J. M. & Begley, S. (2002). *The mind and the brain: Neuroplasticity and the power of mental force.* Regan Books/Harper Collins Publishers.

All our knowledge has its origins in our perceptions.
Leonardo Da Vinci

Like the image in Figure 5.49 on page 197 of this chapter, this picture, by Arcimbaldo is undeniably a rather odd face of a person. Turning the book upside down changes our perception of the picture very significantly.

Sensation and perception 5

Chapter Outline

SENSORY PROCESSES

- Stimulus detection: the absolute threshold
- Signal-detection theory
- The difference threshold
- Sensory adaptation

THE SENSORY SYSTEMS

- Vision
- Audition
- Taste and smell: the chemical senses
- The skin and body senses
- Current topic *Multi-modal perception*

 Applying psychological science *Sensory prosthetics: 'eyes' for the blind, 'ears' for the hearing impaired*

PERCEPTION: THE CREATION OF EXPERIENCE

- Perceptions have organization and structure
- Perception involves hypothesis testing
- Perception is influenced by expectations: perceptual set
- Stimuli are recognizable under changing conditions: perceptual constancies

PERCEPTION OF DEPTH, DISTANCE AND MOVEMENT

- Depth and distance perception

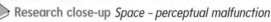 Research close-up *Space – perceptual malfunction*
- perception of movement

ILLUSIONS: FALSE PERCEPTUAL HYPOTHESES

Research close-up *stalking a deadly illusion*

FACE PERCEPTION

- The importance of 'features'
- Emotion
- Attractiveness
- Recognizing faces

EXPERIENCE, CRITICAL PERIODS AND PERCEPTUAL DEVELOPMENT

- Cross-cultural research in perception
- Current topic *Cross-cultural differences in multi-sensory perceptions*
- Critical periods: the role of early experience
- Restored sensory capacity

Sometimes, it is true, a sense of isolation enfolds me like a cold mist as I sit alone and wait at life's shut gate. Beyond, there is light, and music, and sweet companionship; but I may not enter. Fate, silent, pitiless, bars the way . . . Silence sits immense upon my soul.   *(Keller, 1955, p. 62)*

So wrote Helen Keller, deprived of both vision and hearing by an acute illness she suffered at the age of 19 months. For those of us who enjoy and take for granted the use of these senses, it is hard to imagine what it would be like to sink into a dark and silent universe, cut off from all sight and sound. Helen Keller worked closely with her teacher, Anne Sullivan, who tried day after day to communicate with her by tapping signs onto the little girl's palm. One day, Anne tapped *water* onto Helen's palm as she placed the child's hand under the gushing spout of a pump. Communication was at last possible.

That living word awakened my soul, gave it light, hope, joy, set it free! That was because I saw everything with a strange new sight that had come to me . . . It would have been difficult to find a happier child than I was.

(Keller, 1955, p. 103)

Helen Keller went on to write her celebrated book, *The Story of my Life* (1955). She became an inspirational advocate for people with disabilities.

Sensory-impaired people like Helen Keller provide glimpses into different aspects of how we sense and understand our world, as do those who are not impaired but experience synesthesia (discussed later in this chapter) where sensory information from different senses mixes together. These processes, previewed in Figure 5.1, begin when specific types of stimuli activate specialized sensory receptors. Whether the stimulus is light, sound waves, a chemical molecule or pressure, your sensory receptors must translate the information into nerve impulses. Once this translation occurs, specialized neurons break down and analyse the specific features of the stimulus. At the next stage, these numerous stimulus features are reconstructed into a neural representation that is then compared with previously stored information, such as our knowledge of how particular objects look, smell or feel. This matching of a new stimulus with our internal store of knowledge allows us to recognize the stimulus and give it meaning. We then consciously experience a perception.

In some ways, sensation and perception blend together so completely that they are difficult to separate, for the stimulation we receive through our sense organs is quickly organized and transformed into the experiences that we refer to as perceptions. There is, however, a distinction in psychology. **Sensation** is the stimulus detection process by which our sense organs respond to and translate environmental stimuli into nerve impulses that are sent to the brain. **Perception** involves making 'sense' of what our senses tell us. It is the active process of organizing this stimulus input and giving it meaning (Goldstein, 2007; Pashler & Yantis, 2002).

Because perception is an active and creative process, the same sensory input may be perceived in different ways at different times. For example, read the two sets of symbols in Figure 5.2. The middle symbols in both sets are exactly the same, and they sent identical input to your brain, but you probably perceived them differently. Your interpretation, or perception, of the characters was influenced by their context – that is, by the characters that preceded and followed them and by your learned expectation of what normally follows the letter A and the number 12. This is a simple illustration of how perception takes us a step beyond sensation.

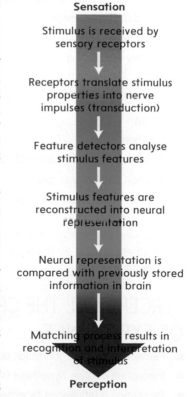

Sensation

Stimulus is received by sensory receptors

↓

Receptors translate stimulus properties into nerve impulses (transduction)

↓

Feature detectors analyse stimulus features

↓

Stimulus features are reconstructed into neural representation

↓

Neural representation is compared with previously stored information in brain

↓

Matching process results in recognition and interpretation of stimulus

Perception

FIGURE 5.1 Sensation becomes perception.

Sensory and perceptual processes proceed from the reception and translation of physical stimuli into nerve impulses. The brain then receives the nerve impulses, organizes and confers meaning on them, and constructs a perceptual experience.

sensation the stimulus detection process by which our sense organs respond to and translate environmental stimuli into nerve impulses that are sent to the brain

perception making 'sense' of what our senses tell us. It is the active process of organizing this stimulus input and giving it meaning

Focus 5.1 Describe the six stages in the sensory processing and perception of information. Differentiate between sensation and perception.

SENSORY PROCESSES

Your brain cannot 'understand' light waves, sound waves or the other types of stimuli that make up the language of the environment. Certain neurons have developed into specialized sensory receptors that can transform and translate these energy forms into the code language of nerve impulses that the brain can understand and work with.

As a starting point, we might ask how many senses there are. If you think about it, you might be surprised to reach the conclusion that there appear to be more than the five classical senses: vision, audition (hearing), gustation (taste), olfaction (smell) and touch. For example, there are senses that provide information about balance and body position. Also, the sense of touch can be subdivided into separate senses of pressure, pain and temperature. Receptors deep within the brain monitor the chemical composition of our blood.

Like those of other organisms, human sensory systems are designed to extract from the environment the information that we need to function and survive. Although our survival does not depend on having eyes like owls, noses like bloodhounds or ears as sensitive as cats', we do have specialized sensors that can detect many different kinds of stimuli with considerable sensitivity. The scientific area of **psychophysics**, which studies the relationship between the physical characteristics of stimuli and sensory capabilities, is concerned with *two* kinds of sensitivity. The first concerns the absolute limits of sensitivity – for example, the dimmest light, the faintest sound or the weakest salt solution that humans can detect. The second kind of sensitivity has to do with differences between stimuli – the smallest difference between two tones that we can detect or the tiniest difference between two shades of grey.

FIGURE 5.2 Context and perception.
Quickly read these two lines of symbols out loud. Your perception of the middle symbol in each line is influenced by the symbols that surround it.

> **psychophysics** studies the relationship between the physical characteristics of stimuli and sensory capabilities

STIMULUS DETECTION: THE ABSOLUTE THRESHOLD

How intense must a stimulus be before we can detect its presence? Researchers answer this question by systematically presenting stimuli of varying intensities to people and asking whether they can detect them. Researchers designate the **absolute threshold** as the lowest intensity at which a stimulus can be detected 50% of the time, thus the lower the absolute threshold, the greater the sensitivity. From studies of absolute thresholds, we can estimate the general limits of human sensitivity for the five major senses. Some examples are presented in Table 5.1. As you can see, many of our absolute thresholds are surprisingly low. Yet some other species have sensitivities that far surpass those of humans. For example, a female silkworm moth that is ready to mate needs to release only a billionth of an ounce of an attractant chemical molecule per second to attract every male silkworm moth within a mile (1.6 km) radius.

> **absolute threshold** the lowest intensity at which a stimulus can be detected 50% of the time

SIGNAL-DETECTION THEORY

Perhaps you can remember lying in bed as a child, in the dark after seeing a frightening film or reading a story that gave you a scare. You may recall straining your ears in an attempt to detect any unusual sound that might signal the presence of a monster or intruder in the house. You may even have detected the occasional faint and ominous sound that would have probably gone unnoticed had you just watched a comedy or read one of your school books.

At one time scientists thought that although some people have greater sensory acuity than others, each person has a more or less fixed level of sensitivity for each sense.

TABLE 5.1 Some approximate absolute thresholds for humans

Sensory modality	Absolute threshold
Vision	Candle flame seen at 50 kilometres on a clear, dark night
Hearing	Tick of a watch under quiet conditions at 20 feet (6 metres)
Taste	1 teaspoon of sugar in 7.5 litres of water
Smell	1 drop of perfume diffused into the entire volume of a large room
Touch	Wing of a fly or bee falling on a person's cheek from a distance of 1 centimetre

Source: Based on Galanter, 1962.

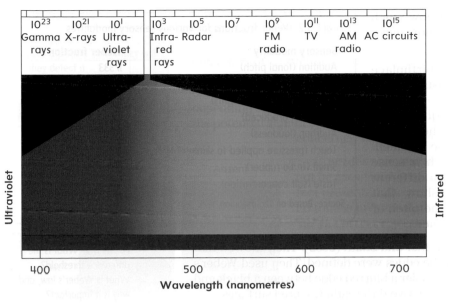

FIGURE 5.5 Light energy.

Of the full spectrum of electromagnetic radiation, only the narrow band between 400 and 700 nanometres (nm) is visible to the human eye. One nanometre equals one 1,000,000,000th of a metre.

We also produce three different types of purposive eye movements. *Saccades* are short; approximately 200 ms eye movements that occur all the time as we experience the visual field about us. *Saccades* may be purposive, where you shift vision quickly from one point to another, as you do when you skip from one part of a page to the next when reading or from one place on a painting to the next when looking at art. *Pursuit movements* are tracking movements. We use them when following an object such as a runner or a car as they move across our field of vision. *Conjugate movements* are those that allow us to keep the same image on the appropriate parts of the retina in each eye. If you hold a pencil up in front of you, imagine where on each retina the image is. Now, move the pencil towards you and away from you. The movements your eyes make to keep focus on the pencil, and to keep its image on corresponding parts of each retina are conjugate movements.

Although sensory adaptation may reduce our overall sensitivity, it is adaptive, for it frees our senses from the constant and the mundane, allowing them to pick up informative changes in the environment that could be important to our well-being or survival.

 In review

■ Sensation is the process by which our sense organs receive and transmit information, whereas perception involves the brain's processing and interpretation of the information.

■ The difference threshold, or just noticeable difference (jnd), is the amount by which two stimuli must differ for them to be perceived as different 50% of the time. Studies of the jnd led to Weber's law, which states that the jnd is proportional to the intensity of the original stimulus and is constant within a given sense modality.

■ Sensory systems are particularly responsive to changes in stimulation, and adaptation occurs in response to unchanging stimuli.

THE SENSORY SYSTEMS

> **transduction** the process whereby the characteristics of a stimulus are converted into nerve impulses

The particular stimuli to which different animals are sensitive vary considerably. The sensory equipment of any species is an adaptation to the environment in which it lives. Many species have senses that humans lack altogether. Sharks, for instance, sense electric currents leaking through the skins of fish hiding in undersea crevices. Whatever the source of stimulation, its energy must be converted into nerve impulses and transmitted to the appropriate parts of the brain. Transduction refers to the changing of one type of information into another. A microphone, for instance, transduces movement at a sensitive membrane at the tip of the microphone, into electricity, which can be understood by the amplifier. In this context, **transduction** is the process whereby the characteristics of a stimulus are converted into nerve impulses.

VISION

Light travels in waves of electromagnetic energy. These waves are measured in nanometres (nm), or one billionth of a metre. In addition to the tiny portion of light waves that humans can perceive, the electromagnetic spectrum encompasses X-rays, television and radio signals, and infrared and ultraviolet rays (Figure 5.5). Our visual system is sensitive to wavelengths extending from about 700 nanometres (red) down to about 400 nanometres (blue-violet).

The Human Eye

Light waves enter the eye through the *cornea*, a transparent protective structure at the front of the eye (Figure 5.6). Behind the cornea is the *pupil*, an adjustable opening that can dilate (get wider) or constrict to control the amount of light that enters the eye. The pupil's size is controlled by muscles in the coloured *iris* that surrounds the pupil. Low levels of illumination cause the pupil to dilate, letting more light into the eye to improve optical clarity; bright light makes the pupil constrict.

Behind the pupil is the **lens**, an elastic structure that becomes thinner to focus on distant objects and thicker to focus on nearby objects. The lens of the eye focuses the visual image on the **retina**, a multilayered light-sensitive tissue at the rear of the fluid-filled eyeball. As seen in Figure 5.8a, the lens reverses the image from right to left and top to bottom when it is projected upon the retina, but the brain reverses the visual input into the image that we perceive.

The ability to see clearly depends in part on the lens's ability to focus the image directly onto the retina (Pedrotti & Pedrotti, 1992) and is known as *accommodation*. If you have good vision for nearby objects but have difficulty seeing faraway objects, you probably suffer from *myopia* (nearsightedness). In near-sighted people, the lens focuses the visual image in front of the retina (or too near the lens), resulting in a blurred image for faraway objects. This condition generally occurs because the eyeball is longer (front to back) than normal. In contrast, some people have excellent distance vision but have difficulty

> **lens** an elastic structure that becomes thinner to focus on distant objects and thicker to focus on nearby objects
>
> **retina** multilayered light-sensitive tissue at the rear of the fluid-filled eyeball

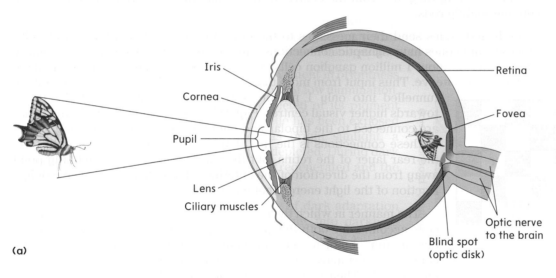

(a)

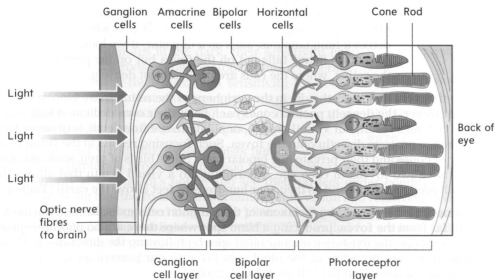

(b)

FIGURE 5.6 The human eye.

(a) The iris controls the size of the pupil. The ciliary muscles control the shape of the lens. The image entering the eye is reversed by the lens and cast on the retina, which contains the rod and cone photoreceptor cells. The optic disk, where the optic nerve exits the eye, has no receptors and produces a blind spot. (b) Photoreceptors in the retina, the rods and cones, synapse with bipolar cells, which in turn synapse with ganglion cells whose axons form the optic nerve. The horizontal and amacrine cells allow sideways integration of retinal activity across areas of the retina.

FIGURE 5.9 Sunset over
Gothenburg, Sweden.

Source: © Martin Wahlborg.

Colour Vision

We are blessed with a world rich in colour (Figure 5.9). The majesty of a glowing sunset, the rich blues and greens of our coasts and the brilliant colours of autumn are all visual delights.

Human vision is finely attuned to colour; our difference thresholds for light wavelengths are so small that we are able to distinguish an estimated 7.5 million hue variations (Backhaus, Kliegl, & Werner, 1998). Historically, two different theories of colour vision have tried to explain how this occurs.

The trichromatic theory

At the beginning of the nineteenth century it was discovered that any colour in the visible spectrum could be produced by some combination of the wavelengths that correspond to the colours blue, green and red in what is known as additive colour mixture (Figure 5.10a). In additive colour mixture, a beam of light of a specific wavelength directed onto a white surface is perceived as the colour that corresponds to that wavelength on the visible spectrum. If beams of light that fall at certain points within the blue, green or red colour range are directed together onto the surface in the correct proportions, a combined, or additive, mixture of wavelengths will result, with the possibility of producing any colour in the visible spectrum (including white at the point where all three colours intersect). The Young–Helmholtz trichromatic theory of colour vision assumes that colour perception results from the additive mixture of impulses from cones that are sensitive to blue, green and red.

In subtractive colour mixture (Figure 5.10b), mixing pigments or paints produces new colours by subtraction – that is, by removing (i.e., absorbing) other wavelengths. Paints absorb (subtract) colours different from themselves while reflecting their own colour. For example, blue paint mainly absorbs wavelengths that correspond to non-blue hues. Mixing blue paint with yellow paint (which absorbs wavelengths other than yellow) will produce a subtractive mixture that emits wavelengths between yellow and blue (i.e., green). Theoretically, certain wavelengths of the three primary colours of blue, yellow (not green, as in additive mixture) and red can produce the whole spectrum of colours by subtractive mixture.

Thus in additive colour mixture, the primary colours are blue, green and red; in subtractive colour mixture they are blue, yellow and red. This fact was the basis for an important trichromatic (three-colour) theory of colour vision advanced by the physicist,

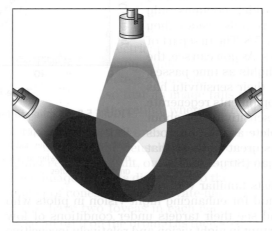

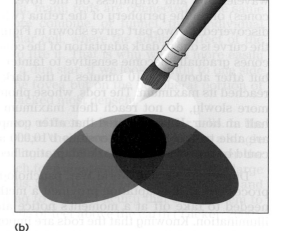

(a)   (b)

FIGURE 5.10 Two kinds of colour mixtures.

Additive and subtractive colour mixtures are different processes.

Thomas Young, and the physiologist, Hermann von Helmholtz. According to the **Young–Helmholtz trichromatic theory**, there are three types of colour receptors in the retina. Although all cones can be stimulated by most wavelengths to varying degrees, individual cones are most sensitive to wavelengths that correspond to blue, green or red (Figure 5.15). The ratio of activity in the three types of cones facilitates our experience of a particular hue, or colour. Presumably, each of these receptor classes sends messages to the brain, based on the extent to which they are activated by the light energy's wavelength. The visual system then combines the signals to recreate the original hue. If all three cones are equally activated, pure white is perceived (see the centre of Figure 5.10a).

Although the Young–Helmholtz theory was consistent with the laws of additive colour mixture, there are several facts that did not fit the theory. Take our perception of yellow, for example. According to the theory, yellow is produced by the activity of red and green receptors. Yet certain people with red–green colour blindness, who are unable to perceive either colour, are somehow able to experience yellow. A second phenomenon that posed problems for the trichromatic theory was the colour afterimage, in which an image in a different colour appears after a colour stimulus has been viewed steadily and then withdrawn. To experience an afterimage, follow the instructions for Figure 5.12. Trichromatic theory cannot account for what you will see.

Opponent-process theory

A second influential colour theory, formulated by Ewald Hering in 1870, also assumed that there are three types of cones. **Hering's opponent-process theory** proposed that each of the three cone types responds to two different wavelengths. One type responds to blue or yellow, another to red or green and a third to black or white. For example, a red–green cone responds with one chemical reaction to a green stimulus and with its other chemical reaction (opponent process) to a red stimulus (sees Figure 5.11). Each of the receptors can function in two possible ways, depending on the wavelength of the stimulus. Again, the pattern of activity in the receptors yields our perception of the hue. You have experienced one of the phenomena that support the existence of opponent processes if you did the exercise in Figure 5.12. The afterimage that you saw in the blank space contains the colours specified by opponent-process theory: the yellow portion of the flag appeared as blue, and the blue as yellow. According to opponent-process theory, as you stared at the blue and yellow colours, the neural processes that register those colours became fatigued. Then when you cast your gaze on the white surface, which reflects all wavelengths, a rebound opponent reaction occurred as each receptor responded with its opposing blue or yellow reactions.

Dual processes in colour transduction

Which theory – the trichromatic theory or the opponent-process theory – is correct? Two centuries of research have provided verifying evidence for each theory.

Young–Helmholtz trichromatic theory there are three types of colour receptors in the retina

Hering's opponent-process theory each of the three cone types responds to two different wavelengths

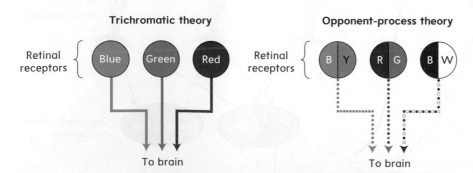

FIGURE 5.11 The Young–Helmholtz trichromatic theory and Hering's opponent-process theory.

The Young–Helmholtz trichromatic theory proposed three different receptors, one for blue, one for green and one for red.

FIGURE 5.12 Opponent Processes At Work.

Negative colour afterimages demonstrate opponent processes occurring in the visual system. Stare steadily at the centre of the flag for about a minute, and then look quickly at a blank piece of white paper. The opponent colours should appear.

Today's **dual-process theory** combines the trichromatic and opponent-process theories to account for the colour transduction process (Knoblauch, 2002).

The trichromatic theorists Young and Helmholtz were right about the cones. The cones do indeed contain one of three different protein photopigments that are most sensitive to wavelengths roughly corresponding to the colours blue, green and red (Abramov & Gordon, 1994). Different ratios of activity in the blue-, green- and red-sensitive cones can produce a pattern of neural activity that corresponds to any hue in the spectrum (Backhaus et al., 1998).

Hering's opponent-process theory was also partly correct, but opponent processes do not occur at the level of the cones, as he maintained. When researchers began to use microelectrodes to record from single cells in the visual system, they discovered that ganglion cells in the retina, as well as neurons in visual relay stations and the visual cortex, respond in an opponent-process fashion by altering their rate of firing (Knoblauch, 2002). For example, if a red light is shone on the retina, an opponent-process ganglion cell may respond with a high rate of firing, but a green light will cause the same cell to fire at a very low rate. Other neurons respond in a similar opponent fashion to blue and yellow stimuli.

The red–green opponent processes are triggered directly by input from the red- or green-sensitive cones in the retina (Figure 5.13). The blue–yellow opponent process is a bit more complex. Activity of blue-sensitive cones directly stimulates the blue process further along in the visual system. And yellow? The yellow opponent process is triggered not by a yellow-sensitive cone, as Hering proposed, but rather by simultaneous input from the red- and green-sensitive cones (Valberg, 2006).

Colour-deficient vision

People with normal colour vision are referred to as *trichromats*. They are sensitive to all three systems: blue–yellow, red–green and black–white. However, about 7% of the male population and 1% of the female population have a deficiency in the blue–yellow system, the red–green system or both. This deficiency is caused by an absence of hue-sensitive photo-pigment in certain cone types. A *dichromat* is a person who is colour-blind in only one of the systems (blue–yellow or red–green). A *monochromat* is sensitive only to the black–white system and is totally colour-blind. Most colour-deficient people are dichromats and have their deficiency in the red–green system. Typically, colour-blindness tests employ sets of coloured dots such as those in

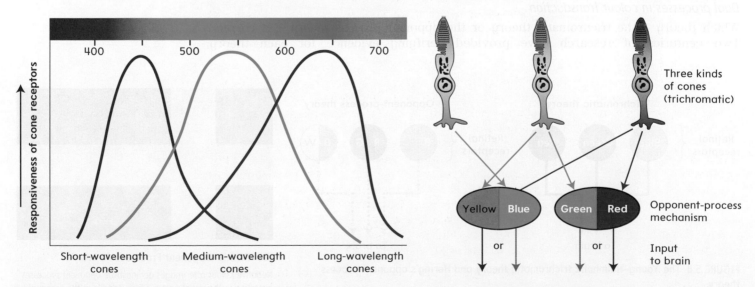

FIGURE 5.13 Dual colour vision processes.

Colour vision involves both trichromatic and opponent processes that occur at different places in the visual system. Consistent with trichromatic theory, three types of cones are maximally sensitive to short (blue), medium (green) and long (red) wavelengths, respectively. However, opponent processes occur further along in the visual system, as opponent cells in the retina, visual relay stations, and the visual cortex respond differentially to blue versus yellow, red versus green and black versus white stimuli. Shown here are the inputs from the cones that produce the blue-yellow and red-green opponent processes.

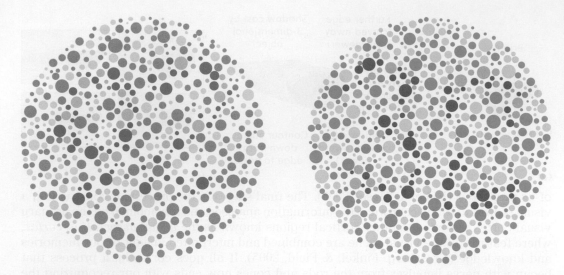

FIGURE 5.14 Test your colour vision.

These *Ishihara disks* are named after the Japanese scientist, *Shinobu Ishihara*. They were first published in 1917. The left one tests for blue–yellow colour blindness, the right one for red–green colour blindness. Because the dots in the picture are of equal lightness, colour is the only available cue for perceiving the numbers in the circles. Can you see them? You should be able to read '92' in the blue disk and '32' in the predominantly green disk.

Figure 5.14. Depending on the type of deficit, a colour-blind person cannot discern the number embedded in one of the two circles.

Analysis and Reconstruction of Visual Scenes

Once the transformation of light energy to nerve impulses occurs, the process of combining the messages received from the photoreceptors into the perception of a visual scene begins. As you read this page, nerve impulses from countless neurons are being analysed and the visual image that you perceive is being reconstructed. Moreover, you know what these black squiggles on the page mean. How does this occur?

From the retina, the optic nerve sends impulses to a visual relay station in the thalamus, the brain's sensory switchboard. From there, the input is routed to various parts of the cortex, particularly the primary visual cortex in the occipital lobe at the rear of the brain. Microelectrode studies have shown that there is a point-to-point correspondence between tiny regions of the retina and groups of neurons in the visual cortex. This is called retinotopic mapping. As you might expect, the fovea, where the one-to-one synapses of cones with bipolar cells produce high visual acuity, is represented by a disproportionately large area of the visual cortex. Somewhat more surprising is the fact that there is more than one retinotopic cortical map; there are many retinotopic maps and not all are exact duplicates of one another. This might be explained as some kind of insurance policy. If one goes wrong, or is damaged in some way then we have a number of spares to fall back on. It may also be that the multiple maps are used in the integration of visual input (Bullier, 2002).

Groups of neurons within the primary visual cortex are organized to receive and integrate sensory nerve impulses originating in specific regions of the retina. Some of these cells, known as **feature detectors**, fire selectively in response to visual stimuli that have specific characteristics (Kanwisher, 1998). Discovery of these feature detectors won David Hubel and Torsten Wiesel of Harvard University the 1981 Nobel Prize. Using tiny electrodes to record the activity of individual cells of the visual cortex of animals, Hubel and Wiesel found that certain neurons fired most frequently when lines of certain orientations were presented. One neuron might fire most frequently when a horizontal line was presented; another neuron in response to a line of a slightly different orientation; and so on 'around the clock'. For example, the letter A could be constructed from the response of feature detectors that responded to three different line orientations: /, \, and –. Within the cortex, this information is integrated and analysed by successively more complex feature-detector systems to produce our perception of objects (Palmer, 2002).

Other classes of feature detectors respond to colour, to depth, or to movement (Livingstone & Hubel, 1994a; Zanker, 2010). These feature-detector 'modules' subdivide a visual scene into its component dimensions and process them simultaneously. Thus, as a red, white and green beach ball sails towards you, separate but overlapping modules within the brain are simultaneously analysing its colours, shape, distance and movement by engaging in parallel processing of the information and constructing a unified image

feature detectors fire selectively in response to visual stimuli that have specific characteristics

Focus 5.8 What kinds of feature detectors exist in the visual system? What is parallel processing of sensory information?

FIGURE 5.15 Marr's computational model.

(a) Primal sketch - here edges of the object, a result of processing light and shade, are represented. (b) 2½D sketch - shading and texture provide more information, and binocular information is also used to give information about depth. (c) The final 3D model: all the information is combined. The viewpoint is irrelevant. The relationship between all the constituent parts of the object is considered and built into a rich 3D model.

Source: Redrawn from Marr, 1982.

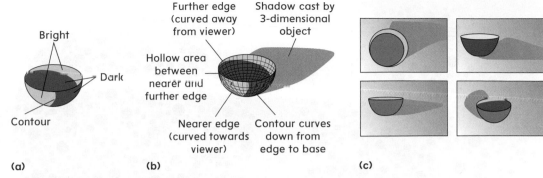

(a)   **(b)**   **(c)**

of its properties (Hubel & Wiesel, 2005). The final stages in the process of constructing a visual representation occur when the information analysed and recombined by the primary visual cortex is routed to other cortical regions known as the *visual association cortex*, where features of the visual scene are combined and interpreted in light of our memories and knowledge (Grossberg, Finkel, & Field, 2005). If all goes correctly, a process that began with nerve impulses from the rods and cones now ends with our recognizing the beach ball for what it is and catching it. Quite another conscious experience and response would probably occur if we interpreted the oncoming object as a water balloon.

Object Recognition

Recognizing the objects around us is an important goal of the visual perceptual process. You will not be surprised to hear that there are a number of theories that explain how this happens. In the next section we introduce two approaches. First, David Marr's ground-breaking computational model and, second, Biederman's recognition-by-components theory which followed it.

A Computational Model of Visual Processing

In 1982, David Marr produced an extremely influential model of visual perception. In his *computational model*, he proposes that vision is a three-stage process, which takes the perceiver from an extremely basic two-dimensional (2D) view of the item being perceived, through to a more complex, three-dimensional (3D) representation. You can see this illustrated in Figure 5.15.

The first thing we see is a basic or *primal sketch*. All we have of the object so far are patterns of light and shade, which once processed provide us with information about edges. Next, information is developed into what Marr calls a *2½D sketch*. Information from the shading is built into the new representation, providing information regarding relative distances from us of the different parts of the object. This is what the object actually looks like from our (the perceiver's) perspective. Finally we develop a *three-dimensional model*. Here we have internalized a visual model of the item we are observing, free of the constraints of viewpoint. We have developed an understanding of what the reverse of the object should look like for instance.

Recognition by Components

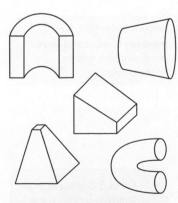

FIGURE 5.16 Geons: Biederman's (1987) recognition-by-components theory proposes that objects are made up of 36 basic shapes, which he calls *geons*. Here are five of them.

Biederman's (1987, 1990) *recognition-by-components* (RBC) theory can be seen as a development of Marr's work. Biederman describes the visual world as being made up of a number of basic shapes. Some examples of these shapes can be seen in Figure 5.16. These are called *geons*. Take a moment and look at the images in Figure 5.17 and identify the *geons* in each item.

The telephone, for instance, can be made up of a sausage shape laid on top of a wedge shape. A cup might be made up of a funnel shape with the sausage-shaped geon as the handle. Let us take a step back for a moment. We have the idea of geons and RBC theory, that items might be identified by how their component geons are arranged, but how do we identify the geons in the first place? Biederman indicates that *edge detection* is central to this theory. The first thing that must be done is to parse, or chop up, the object into geons, and we do this through information from the edges we can identify. Biederman identifies five invariant (unchanging) properties of edges, that in different combinations allow us to identify the different geons. These are *curvature* (points on the edge are on a curve), *parallel* (points are in parallel), *cotermination* (edges end at the same point), *symmetry* and *colinearity* (points are in a straight line).

(a)

(b)

(c)

(d)

FIGURE 5.17 Identify the geons seen in these pictures.

Sources: (a) ©iStock.com/Floortje; (b) ©iStock.com/kyoshino; (c) ©iStock.com/Les Palenik; (d) ©iStock.com/Justin Allfree.

This provides Biederman's theory with a real strength. Even though we may not be able to see the entire object, perhaps because it is obscured somehow, we know that these properties exist, and they do not change. We may only need to see a small part of an edge to know how it will behave for the rest of the partially obscured object. Only a small part of many objects needs to be seen at all to identify them, and as such much of the object is redundant anyway as far as its identity is concerned. This means that the viewpoint of the observer, so important in Marr's theory, becomes irrelevant here as long as the geons can be identified. Tarr and Bülthoff (1998), however, say that viewpoint is important in analysis of the visual scene. They showed that participants made more errors and were slower at recognizing familiar objects shown from unfamiliar viewpoints, indicating that viewpoint was very important, and thereby supporting Marr's computational model.

In summary, then, Marr's model gives us an understanding of how systematic processes might be used in the representation of our visual world. The computational theory begins from basics, and is in that sense a bottom-up process (see page 184). One criticism that might be made of the theory is that the role of expectation, a top-down component of perceptual processing, is not developed in the theory. Also, how we reach the 3D representation from the 21/2D stage is not well explained. Biederman's later RBC analysis indicates that visual objects can be made up of a combination of simple shapes, or geons. These geons can be identified simply from our knowledge of edges, and even if partially obscured, we should still be able to pick them out of the scene, eliminating the importance of the viewpoint of the observer. Tarr and Bülthoff (1998) show that viewpoint *is* an issue though. One criticism that has been levied at both theories is that neither allows subtle distinctions. They may allow us to identify a cup, or a mug or a cat, but neither allows us to identify whether the object we see is our favourite cup or mug, or whether the animal is our pet cat.

 In review

■ The senses may be classified in terms of the stimuli to which they respond. Through the process of transduction, these stimuli are transformed into nerve impulses.

■ The normal stimulus for vision is electromagnetic energy, or light waves. Light-sensitive visual receptor cells are located in the retina. The rods are brightness receptors, and the less numerous cones are colour receptors. Light energy striking the retina is converted into nerve impulses by chemical reactions in the photopigments of the rods and cones. Dark adaptation involves the gradual regeneration of photopigments that have been depleted by brighter illumination.

■ Colour vision is a two-stage process having both trichromatic and opponent-process components. The first stage involves the reactions of cones that are maximally sensitive to blue, green and red wavelengths. In the second stage, colour information from the cones is coded through an opponent-process mechanism further along in the visual system.

■ Visual stimuli are analysed by feature detectors in the primary visual cortex, and the stimulus elements are reconstructed and interpreted in light of input from the visual association cortex.

■ Marr and Biederman provide us with two influential theories that help explain how we identify and recognize objects. Marr's computational theory describes how simple representations are developed into more complex 3D models, and Biederman's recognition-by-components theory says that all objects can be made up of simple shapes called geons.

AUDITION

The stimuli for our sense of hearing are sound waves, a form of mechanical energy. What we call *sound* is actually pressure waves in air, water or some other conducting medium. When a stereo's volume is high enough, you can actually see cloth speaker covers moving in and out. If you balance a tiny piece of paper or a table tennis ball on a speaker cone, you will see it moving with the music, as the cone pushes it into the air. The resulting vibrations cause successive waves of compression and expansion among the air molecules surrounding the source of the sound. These sound waves have two characteristics: frequency and amplitude (Figure 5.18).

Frequency is the number of sound waves, or cycles, per second. **Hertz (Hz)** is the measure of cycles per second; 1 hertz equals 1 cycle per second. The sound waves' frequency (how often – how *frequent* the cycles are) is related to the perceived pitch of the sound; the higher the frequency (hertz), the higher the perceived pitch. Humans are capable of detecting sound frequencies from 20 to 20,000 hertz (20–20 kilohertz [kHz]). As a rule, the younger we are, the higher the frequency we can perceive. As we age we lose sensitivity at the higher end. Among musical instruments, the piano can play the widest range of frequencies, from 27.5 hertz at the low end of the keyboard to 4186 hertz at the high end.

Amplitude refers to the vertical size of the sound waves – the depth between the peaks and the troughs in the sound wave. The sound wave's amplitude is the primary determinant of the sound's perceived loudness. Differences in amplitude are expressed in **decibels (dB)**, a measure of the physical pressures that occur at the eardrum. Zero decibels is designated as our minimum absolute threshold, any quieter and we cannot hear it. Each increase of 10 decibels represents roughly a doubling in loudness. Table 5.3 shows various sounds scaled in decibels.

Auditory Transduction: From Pressure Waves to Nerve Impulses

The transduction system of the ear is made up of tiny bones, membranes and liquid-filled tubes designed to translate pressure waves into nerve impulses (Figure 5.19). The three sections of the system are the outer, middle and inner ear.

The *outer ear* is the visual part of the ear (*the pinna*) and the auditory canal, the part that contains wax, which many people use cotton-buds to remove. The role of the pinna is partly to catch the sound. If you cup your hand behind your pinna you will catch more sound, helping you to hear voices across a busy table, or in a noisy room. The pinna also has a role in sound localization which we will describe in a moment.

frequency the number of sound waves, or cycles, per second

hertz (Hz) the measure of cycles per second; 1 hertz equals 1 cycle per second

amplitude the vertical size of the sound waves – the depth between the peaks and the troughs in the sound wave

decibels (dB) measure of the physical pressures that occur at the eardrum

Focus 5.9 Describe the two physical characteristics of sound waves and their relation to auditory experience.

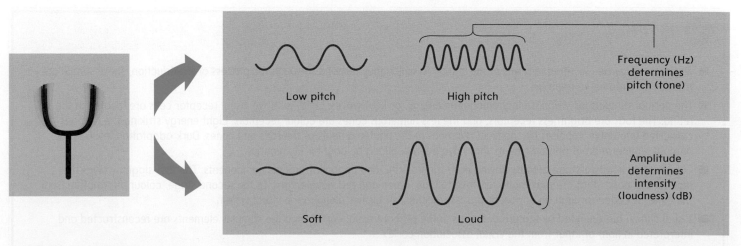

FIGURE 5.18 Auditory stimuli.

Sound waves are a form of mechanical energy. As the tuning fork vibrates, it produces successive waves of compression and expansion of air molecules. The number of maximum compressions per second (cycles per second) is its frequency, measured in hertz (Hz). The height of the wave *represents* the sound's amplitude. Frequency determines pitch; amplitude determines loudness, measured in decibels (dB).

TABLE 5.3 Decibel scaling of common sounds

Level in decibels (dB)	Common sounds	Threshold levels
140	Jet fighter taking off 25 metres away, Formula I car at I metre	Potential damage to auditory system
130	Loud metal workshop	Human pain threshold
120	Rock-and-roll band, jet aircraft at 166 metres overhead	
110	Car horn at I metre	
100	Crosscut saw at position of operator	
90	Kitchen blender	Hearing damage with prolonged exposure
80	Vacuum cleaner at I metre	
70	Motorway traffic	
60	A busy city street	
50	Restaurant	
40	Quiet suburban street	
30	Quiet bedroom or theatre	
20	Recording studio, whispered speech	
10	Breathing	
0	A fly at 3 metres	Minimum threshold of hearing

Note: The decibel scale relates a *physical quantity* – sound intensity – to *the human perception* of that quantity – sound loudness. It is a *logarithmic scale* – that is, each increment of 10dB represents a tenfold increase in loudness. The table indicates the decibel ranges of some common sounds as well as thresholds for hearing, hearing damage and pain.

Next is the *middle ear*, containing three tiny bones, called the hammer, anvil and stirrup – the ossicles. The role of the ossicles is something called *impedance matching*. Sound travels through air, which has very low *impedance* by which we mean that it does not impede the wave very much. It does not get in the way of the sound very much at all. The inner ear is extremely sensitive, so evolution has seen fit to put the ossicles between the air (low impedance) and the cochlea (extremely low impedance) to ensure that sound caught by the pinna does not damage the sensitive organ of Corti. The bones translate the sound, reducing it in energy and transferring it to the inner ear. The ossicles *match the impedance of the air to that of the cochlea*. They provide a safety mechanism to help avoid damage to the sensitive inner ear.

The *inner ear* contains the **cochlea**, a coiled, snail-shaped tube about 3.5 cm in length that contains the **basilar membrane**, a sheet of tissue that runs its length. Resting on the basilar membrane is the **organ of Corti**, which contains thousands of tiny hair cells that are the actual sound receptors. The tips of the hair cells contain even tinier protrusions called cilia, which lie beneath another membrane, the *tectorial membrane*, which overhangs the basilar membrane along the entire length of the cochlea. As the basilar membrane flexes, the hair cells also move. This movement in turn produces a movement of the cilia. It is this bending motion that causes the hair cell to fire. The hair cells pass information with the neurons of the auditory nerve, which in turn send impulses via the thalamus to the temporal lobe's auditory cortex (Ando, 2009).

In summary, sound waves strike the eardrum and pressure is created at the oval window by the ossicles. The waves that result vibrate the basilar membrane and the tectorial membrane, causing a bending of the hair cells in the organ of Corti (see Figure 5.19b). This bending of the hair cells results in nerve impulses that are sent to the brain. Within the auditory cortex are feature-detector neurons that respond to specific kinds of auditory input, much as occurs in the visual system (Goldstein, 2002).

cochlea coiled, snail-shaped tube about 3.5 cm in length

basilar membrane sheet of tissue that runs its length

organ of Corti contains thousands of tiny hair cells that are the actual sound receptors

Focus 5.10 Describe how the middle and inner ear structures are involved in the auditory transduction process.

Coding of Pitch and Loudness

The auditory system transforms the sensory qualities of wave amplitude and frequency (experienced by us as loudness and pitch) into nerve impulses. In the case of intensity, high-amplitude sound waves cause the hair cells to bend more and release more neurotransmitter substance at the point where the synapse connects with auditory nerve cells, resulting in a higher rate of firing within the auditory nerve. Also, certain receptor

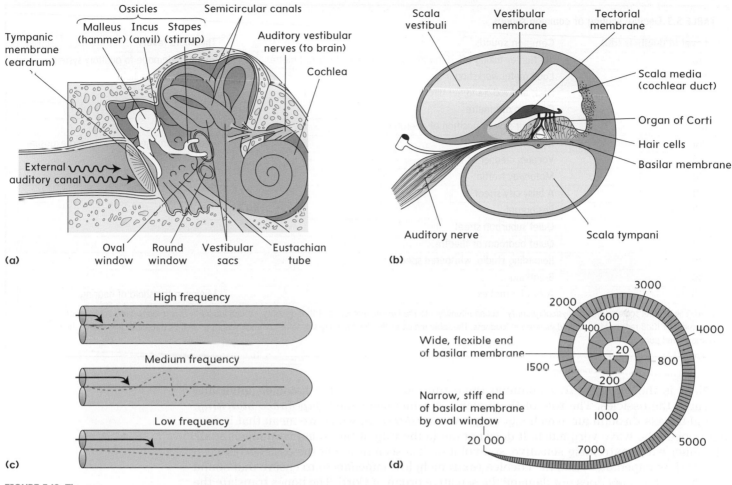

FIGURE 5.19 The ear.

(a) A cross-section of the ear shows the structures that transmit sound waves from the auditory canal to the cochlea. The semicircular canals and vestibular sacs of the inner ear contain components that provide us with our sense of balance. (b) Cross-section of cochlea; sound waves are translated into waves that stimulate hair cells in the organ of Corti. The resulting nerve impulses reach the brain via the auditory nerve. (c) Different waves are created by different sound frequencies. (d) Varying frequencies maximally stimulate different areas of the basilar membrane. High-frequency waves peak quickly and stimulate the membrane close to the oval window.

neurons have higher thresholds than others, so that they will fire only when the hair cells bend considerably in response to an intense sound. What we experience as loudness is coded in terms of both the *rate* of firing in the axons of the auditory nerve and also the *specific hair cells* that are sending messages (Plack, 2013).

The coding of wave frequency that produces our perception of pitch also involves two different processes, one for frequencies below about 1,000 hertz and another for higher frequencies. Historically, as in the case of colour vision, two competing theories were proposed to account for our perception of pitch. According to the **frequency theory of pitch perception**, nerve impulses sent to the brain match the frequency of the sound wave. Thus a 30-hertz (30 cycles per second) sound wave from a piano should send 30 volleys of nerve impulses per second to the brain.

Unfortunately, frequency theory encounters a major problem. Because neurons are limited in their rate of firing, individual impulses or volleys of impulses fired by groups of neurons cannot produce high enough frequencies of firing to match sound-wave frequencies above 1,000 hertz. How then do we perceive higher frequencies, such as a 4,000-hertz note from the same piano? Experiments conducted by Georg von Békésy (1957) uncovered a second mechanism for coding pitch that earned him the 1961 Nobel Prize. His pioneering work in the 1940s famously involved the cochleae of an elephant that died at Budapest Zoo. He heard of the demise of the animal and excitedly dispatched his research

> **frequency theory of pitch perception** nerve impulses sent to the brain match the frequency of the sound wave

assistant to retrieve the cochleae. On his return Békésy was disappointed to find that the cochleae were missing, and that his assistant had removed the outer ears only, slicing through the auditory canal. His mistake was in not realizing that the auditory canal of the elephant is approximately 20 cm in length. All was not lost. He returned to the glue-factory to which the elephant had been sent and returned with the prized cochleae. Békésy discovered that high-frequency sounds produced an abrupt fluid wave (Figure 5.19c) that peaked close to the oval window, whereas lower-frequency vibrations produced a slower fluid wave that peaked farther down the cochlear canal. Békésy's observations supported a **place theory of pitch perception**, suggesting that the specific point in the cochlea where the fluid wave peaks and most strongly bends the hair cells serves as a frequency coding cue (Figure 5.19d). Researchers later found that similar to the manner in which the retina is mapped onto the visual cortex (retinotopic mapping), the auditory cortex has a tonal frequency map (tonotopic mapping) that corresponds to specific areas of the cochlea. By analysing the specific location of the cochlea from which auditory nerve impulses are being received, the brain can code individual pitches, like those produced by tuning forks and the individual strings of a piano.

Thus, like trichromatic and opponent-process theories of colour vision, which were once thought to contradict one another, frequency and place theories of pitch perception both proved applicable in their own ways. At low frequencies, frequency theory holds true; at higher frequencies, place theory provides the mechanism for coding the frequency of a sound wave.

Sound Localization

Have you ever wondered why you have two ears, one located on each side of your head? As is usually the case in nature's designs, there is a good reason. Our very survival can depend on our ability to locate objects that emit sounds. The nervous system uses information concerning the time and intensity differences of sounds arriving at the two ears to locate the source of sounds in space (Moore, 2013; Plack, 2013).

Sounds arrive first and loudest at the ear closest to the sound. When the source of the sound is directly in front of us, the sound wave reaches both ears at the same time and at the same intensity, so the source is perceived as being straight ahead. Our binaural (two-eared) ability to localize sound is amazingly sensitive. For example, a sound 3 degrees to the right arrives at the right ear only 300 millionths of a second before it arrives at the left ear, and yet we can tell which direction the sound is coming from (Yin & Kuwada, 1984). Our outer ear (pinnae) also provides us with some sense of the height, or the *elevation* of an object. The folds of your ears are unique to you. Sounds arriving from a particular elevation are given a 'shape' by these folds that your brain recognizes. It is the folds in your ears that code the elevation of the sound.

Other animals have even more exotic sound-localization systems. For example, the barn owl comes equipped with ears that are exquisitely tailored for pinpoint localization of its prey during night hunting. Its right ear is directed slightly upward, its left ear slightly downward. This allows it to localize sounds precisely both vertically and horizontally, thereby allowing it to zero in on its prey with deadly accuracy.

Hearing Loss

If you had to make the unwelcome choice of being blind or being deaf, which impairment would you choose? When asked this question, most people say that they would rather be deaf. Yet hearing loss can have more devastating social consequences than blindness does. Helen Keller, who was both blind and deaf, considered deafness to be more socially debilitating. She wrote, 'Blindness cuts people off from things. Deafness cuts people off from people'.

The vast majority of people who suffer from hearing loss were born with normal hearing. These individuals suffer from two major types of hearing loss. **Conduction deafness** (also known as **conductive hearing loss**) involves problems with the mechanical system that transmits sound waves to the cochlea. For example, a punctured eardrum or a loss of function in the tiny bones of the middle ear can reduce the ear's capacity to transmit

place theory of pitch perception the specific point in the cochlea where the fluid wave peaks and most strongly bends the hair cells serves as a frequency coding cue

Focus 5.11 Describe the frequency and place theories of pitch perception. In what sense are both theories correct?

conduction deafness (also known as **conductive hearing loss**) involves problems with the mechanical system that transmits sound waves to the cochlea

vibrations. Use of a hearing aid, which amplifies the sounds entering the ear, may correct many cases of conduction deafness.

An entirely different matter is **nerve deafness** (also known as **sensorineural hearing loss**), caused by damaged receptors within the inner ear or damage to the auditory nerve itself. Although an amplifying hearing aid is often of limited or no use in these circumstances a combination approach may be applied. Where the listener still has some low frequency sensitivity, but has significant higher frequency loss a hearing aid and a cochlea implant may both be used to provide some additional stimulation in the same ear. Although ageing and disease can produce sensorineural hearing loss, exposure to loud sounds is one of its leading causes. Repeated exposure to loud sounds of a particular frequency (as might be produced by a machine in a factory) can eventually cause the loss of hair cells at a particular point on the basilar membrane, thereby causing hearing loss for that frequency.

Extremely loud music can also take a serious toll on hearing (West & Evans, 1990). Figure 5.20 shows the devastating results of a guinea pig's exposure to a sound level approximating that of loud rock music heard through earphones. As shown in Table 5.3, even brief exposure to sounds exceeding 140 decibels can cause irreversible damage to the receptors in the inner ear, as can more continuous sounds at lower decibel levels. Other activities, such as motorcycling, can also produce relatively high level and constant noises, not, as you might expect, from the sound of the engine or from distortion from the bike itself as it cuts through the air. This noise is generated as wind passes over the motorcyclist's helmet just as wind might pass over an aircraft wing. The noise inside the helmet at 100 kph is actually above that considered legal in the workplace (Kennedy, Adetifa, Carley, Holt, & Walker, 2011).

TASTE AND SMELL: THE CHEMICAL SENSES

Gustation, the sense of taste, and **olfaction**, the sense of smell, are chemical senses; their receptors are sensitive to chemical molecules rather than to some form of energy. These senses are so intertwined that some scientists consider them a 'common chemical sense' (Halpern, 2002). Enjoying a good meal usually depends on the simultaneous activity of taste and odour receptors, as becomes apparent when we have a stuffy nose and our food tastes bland. People who lose their sense of smell typically believe they have lost their sense of taste as well (Beauchamp & Bartoshuk, 1997). It seems then that 'holding your nose' when forced to take an unpleasant tasting medicine really does have something to be said for it.

Gustation: The Sense of Taste

You may be surprised to learn that your sense of taste responds to only four qualities: sweet, sour, salty and bitter. Every taste experience combines these qualities and those of other senses, such as smell, temperature and touch. For example, part of the taste of popcorn

---

nerve deafness (also known as **sensorineural hearing loss**) caused by damaged receptors within the inner ear or damage to the auditory nerve itself

Focus 5.12 What are the two kinds of deafness, and how can they be treated?

gustation sense of taste
olfaction sense of smell

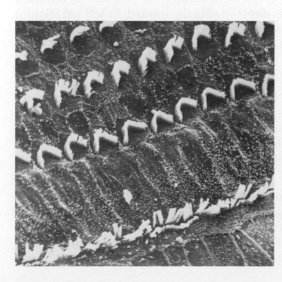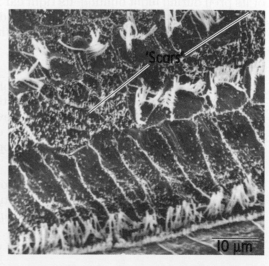

FIGURE 5.20 Danger! Hearing loss.

Exposure to loud sounds can destroy auditory receptors in the inner ear. These pictures, taken through an electron microscope, show the hair cells of a guinea pig before (*left*) and after (*right*) exposure to 24 hours of noise comparable to that of a loud rock concert.

Source: Reproduced with the permission of Dr Jochen Schacht, Kresge Research Instituite, University of Michigan

includes its complex texture, its crunchiness and its odour. In addition to its chemical receptors, the tongue is richly endowed with tactile (touch) and temperature receptors.

Taste buds are chemical receptors concentrated along the tip, edges and back surface of the tongue (Figure 5.21). Each taste bud is most responsive to one or two of the basic taste qualities but responds weakly to the others as well. An additional mysterious taste sensation, called *umami*, increases the intensity of other taste qualities. This sensory response is activated by certain proteins, as well as by monosodium glutamate, a substance used by some restaurants to enhance the flavour of their food.

Humans have about 9,000 taste buds, each consisting of several receptor cells arranged like the segments of an orange. A small number of receptors are also found in the roof and back of the mouth, so that even people without a tongue can taste substances. Hair-like structures project from the top of each cell into the taste pore, an opening to the outside surface of the tongue. When a substance is taken into the mouth, it interacts with saliva to form a chemical solution that flows into the taste pore and stimulates the receptor cells. A taste results from complex patterns of neural activity produced by the four types of taste receptors (Halpern, 2002).

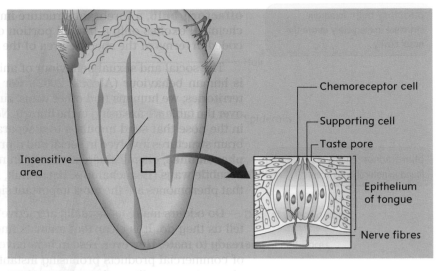

FIGURE 5.21 Taste organs.

The receptors for taste are specialized cells located in the tongue's 9000 taste buds, found on the tip, back and sides of the tongue. Certain areas of the tongue are especially sensitive to chemical stimuli that produce particular taste sensations but these different sensitivities are really just a matter of degree, as all kind of taste buds are found in most areas of the tongue.

> **taste buds** chemical receptors concentrated along the tip, edges and back surface of the tongue

The sense of taste not only provides us with pleasure but also has evolutionary, adaptive significance in discriminating between nutrients and toxins (Scott, 1992). Our response to some taste qualities is innate. For example, newborn infants respond positively to sugar water placed on the tongue and negatively to bitter substances such as quinine (Davidson & Fox, 1988). Many poisonous substances in nature have bitter tastes, so this emotional response seems to be hardwired into our physiology. In nature, sweet substances are more likely to occur in high-calorie (sugar-rich) foods. Many humans now live in an environment that is different from the food-scarce environment in which preferences for sweet substances evolved (Scott & Giza, 1993). As a result, people in affluent countries tend to consume sweet foods in relatively large quantities.

Olfaction: The Sense of Smell

The sense of smell (olfaction) is of great importance for many species. Humans are more orientated to sound and vision. Bloodhounds, for example, have relatively poor eyesight but a highly developed olfactory sense that is about 2 million times more sensitive than ours (Shier, Butler, & Lewis, 2004; Thomas, 1974). A bloodhound can detect a person's scent in a footprint that is four days old, something no human could do. Recent research has shown that dogs need the olfactory trace of only five human steps to determine the direction the person has walked (Porter et al., 2007). People who are deprived of other senses often develop a highly sensitive olfactory sense. Helen Keller, though blind and deaf, exhibited a remarkable ability to smell her environment. With uncanny accuracy, she could tell when a storm was brewing by detecting subtle odour changes in the air. She could also identify people (even those who bathed regularly and did not wear scents of any kind) by their distinctive odours (Keller, 1955).

The receptors for smell are long cells that project through the lining of the upper part of the nasal cavity and into the mucous membrane. Humans have about 40 million olfactory receptors, and 350 different types of them; bloodhounds about 4 billion (Shier et al., 2004). Unfortunately, our ability to discriminate among different odours is not well understood. Olfactory receptors have structures that resemble neurotransmitter binding sites on neurons. Any of the thousands of potential odour molecules can lock into sites that are tailored to fit them (Buck & Axel, 1991). The receptors that fire send their input to the

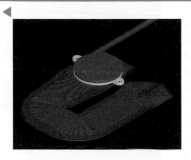

FIGURE 5.25 A camera mounted on glasses sends signals to a small device surgically implanted in the retina, such as the one above. Electrodes on this device stimulate the retina, sending signals to the optic nerve and the vision-processing centre of the brain.

Source: Reprinted with permission of Bionic Vision Australia.

Researchers have built a prototype of this device. The current stimulator, shown in Figure 5.26a, receives digital data from a camera and provides patterns of stimulation to the tongue through a 144-electrode array. The array can transmit shapes that correspond to the main features of the visual stimulus. Initial trials with blindfolded sighted people and blind people show that with about nine hours of training, users can 'read' the letters of a Snellen eye chart with an acuity of 20/430, a modest but noteworthy beginning (Simpaio, Maris, & Bach-y-Rita, 2001).

CORTICAL IMPLANTS

A different approach to a visual prosthesis is being investigated. Researchers have developed a device to stimulate the visual cortex directly (Normann, Maynard, Rousche, & Warren, 1999). When cells in the visual cortex are stimulated electrically, discrete flashes of light called *phosphenes* are experienced by both sighted and blind people. Because sensory neurons in the visual cortex are arranged in a manner that corresponds to the organization of the retina, a specific pattern of stimulation applied to individual neurons in the cortex can form a phosphene pattern that conforms to the shapes of letters or objects. The acuity of the pattern depends on the area of the visual cortex that is stimulated (the portion receiving input from the densely packed fovea produces greatest acuity) and on the number of stimulating electrodes in the array.

Researchers have developed the device shown in Figure 5.26b. The Utah Intracortical Electrode Array consists of a silicon strip containing thousands of tiny stimulating electrodes that penetrate directly into individual neurons in the visual cortex, where they can stimulate phosphene patterns. Eventually, a spectacle-mounted television camera will provide visual information to a microcomputer that will analyse the scene and then send the appropriate patterns of electrical stimulation through the implanted electrodes to produce corresponding phosphene patterns in the visual cortex. The researchers have shown that sighted participants who wear darkened goggles that produce phosphene-like patterns of light flashes like those provided by cortical stimulation can quickly learn to navigate through complex environments and are able to read text at about two-thirds their normal rate (Normann, Maynard, Guillory, & Warren, 1996; Normann et al., 1999). Blind people who have had the stimulating electrodes implanted in their visual cortex have also been able to learn a kind of cortical Braille for reading purposes.

COCHLEAR IMPLANTS

People with hearing impairments have also been assisted by the development of prosthetic devices. The cochlear implant, a device that can restore hearing in people suffering from nerve deafness (sensorineural hearing loss) has helped many. Instead of amplifying sound like a conventional hearing aid (people with nerve deafness cannot be helped by mere sound amplification), the cochlear implant sorts out useful sounds and converts them into electrical impulses, bypassing the disabled hair cells in the cochlea and stimulating the auditory nerve directly (Figure 5.27). With a cochlear implant, patients can hear everyday sounds such as sirens, and many wearers can understand speech (Meyer, Svirsky, Kirk, & Miyamoto, 1998; Parkinson, Parkinson, Tyler, Lowder, & Gantz, 1998). Sounds heard with currently developed implants tend to be a little muffled, so patients should not expect their hearing to be restored to 'normal'. Training and practice with the implant are required to get used to the sound and to make the most of the additional stimulation it provides. Electrical recording of cortical responses to sounds revealed that hearing-impaired people provided with a cochlear implant show a more widespread pattern of neural activity in the auditory cortex than do people with normal hearing, perhaps helping to account for their poorer sound discrimination (Ito et al., 2004).

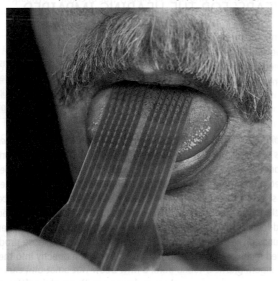

(a)

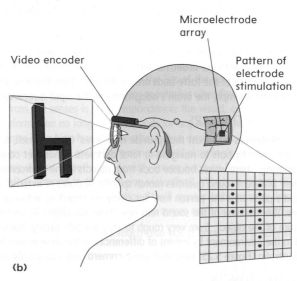

Video encoder

Microelectrode array

Pattern of electrode stimulation

(b)

FIGURE 5.26 Two approaches to providing artificial vision for the blind.

(a) Bach-y-Rita's device converts digitized stimuli from a camera to a matrix of electrodes, which stimulate tactile receptors in the tongue to communicate spatial information to the brain. (b) Tiny electrodes implanted into individual neurons in the visual cortex produce patterns of phosphenes that correspond to the visual scene observed through the video camera and encoder. Note how the cortical image is reversed as in normal visual input.

Source: Jeff Miller/University of Wisconsin-Madison

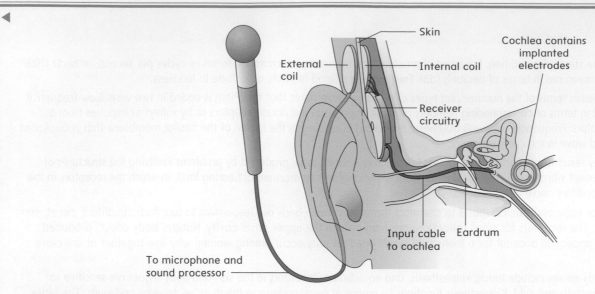

FIGURE 5.27 Cochlear implants.

Cochlear implants provide direct stimulation of the auditory nerve in people whose hair cells are too damaged to respond to fluid waves in the cochlea. Sound enters a microphone and is sent to a processor that breaks the sound down into its principal frequencies and sends electrical signals to external and internal coils. The receiver circuitry stimulates electrodes implanted in cochlear areas associated with particular frequencies.

THE BIONIC HAND THAT RESTORES TACTILE SENSATIONS

In 2009, researchers in Sweden and Italy announced the development of the SmartHand, a prosthetic device that restores the sense of touch in people who have lost their hands (*ScienceDaily*, 11 November 2009). The SmartHand contains sensors that are connected to the sensory nerves in the arm of an amputee (Figure 5.28). Four motors, also linked to the brain through their attachment to motor nerves in the arm, allow patients to move the fingers in very precise ways. This prosthetic hand allows a level of control of movement that comes only through tactile feedback. With it, an amputee can actually experience the feeling of stroking a loved one's cheek and can handle delicate objects with just the right amount of pressure. Among the first to receive the device when it is available commercially will be returning soldiers who have lost their hands in battle.

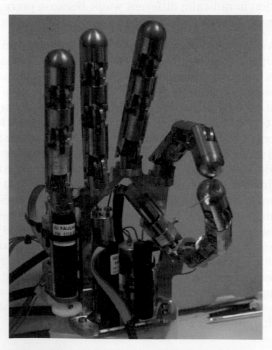

FIGURE 5.28 Shown here without its skin-like covering; the SmartHand's leads connect to both sensory and motor nerves in the arm. The resulting motor control, combined with sensory feedback from the bionic hand's movements, allows an amputee to perform this precision act without dropping or crushing the soft plastic bottle.

Source: SmartHand. Due to copyright reasons the patient's face has been blurred.

In review

- Sound waves, the stimuli for audition, have two characteristics: frequency, measured in terms of cycles per second, or hertz (Hz); and amplitude, measured in terms of decibels (dB). Frequency is related to pitch, amplitude to loudness.

- Loudness is coded in terms of the number and types of auditory nerve fibres that fire. Pitch is coded in two ways. Low frequency tones are coded in terms of corresponding numbers of nerve impulses in individual receptors or by volleys of impulses from a number of receptors. Frequencies above 4,000 hertz are coded according to the region of the basilar membrane that is displaced most by the fluid wave in the cochlear canal.

- Hearing loss may result from conduction deafness (conductive hearing loss), produced by problems involving the structures of the ear that transmit vibrations to the cochlea, or from nerve deafness (sensorineural hearing loss), in which the receptors in the cochlea or the auditory nerve are damaged.

- The receptors for taste and smell respond to chemical molecules. Taste buds are responsive to four basic qualities: sweet, sour, salty and bitter. The receptors for smell (olfaction) are long cells in the upper nasal cavity. Natural body odours produced by pheromones appear to account for a menstrual synchrony that may occur among women who live together or are close friends.

- The skin and body senses include touch, kinaesthesis, and equilibrium. Receptors in the skin and body tissues are sensitive to pressure, pain, warmth and cold. Kinaesthesis functions by means of nerve endings in the muscles, tendons and joints. The sense organs for equilibrium are in the vestibular apparatus of the inner ear.

- Principles derived from the study of sensory processes have been applied in developing sensory prosthetics for the blind and the hearing impaired and those with missing limbs.

PERCEPTION: THE CREATION OF EXPERIENCE

Sensory systems provide the raw materials from which experiences are formed. Our sense organs do not select what we will be aware of or how we will experience it; they merely transmit information through our nervous system. Yet our experiences are not simply a one-to one reflection of what is external to our senses. Different people may experience the same sensory information in radically different ways, because perception is an active, creative process in which raw sensory data are organized and given meaning.

To create our perceptions, the brain carries out two different kinds of processing functions (Figure 5.29). In **bottom-up processing**, the system takes in individual elements of the stimulus and then combines them into a unified perception. Your visual system operates in a bottom-up fashion as you begin to 'read' letter shapes on a page. Its feature detectors analyse the elements in each letter of every word and then recombine them into your visual perception of the letters and words. In **top-down processing**, sensory information is interpreted in light of existing knowledge, concepts, ideas and expectations. Top-down processing is occurring as you interpret the words and sentences constructed by the bottom-up process. Here you make use of higher-order knowledge, including what you have learned about the meaning of words and sentence construction. Indeed, a given sentence may convey a different personal meaning to you than to another person if you relate its content to some unique personal experiences. Top-down processing accounts for many psychological influences on perception, such as the roles played by our motives, expectations, previous experiences and cultural learning. My personal favourite example of top-down processing is the alleged demonic or occult messages that rock bands like Led Zeppelin allegedly 'hid' in their songs. These are examples of supposed subliminal messages. The problem is the 'alternative' lyrics are not really there at all. You will find these examples easily on the Internet; they are described as 'back masking'. It is only when you know what you are looking for, when you have an expectation of what you should be perceiving, that the lyrics reveal themselves to you.

bottom-up processing system takes in individual elements of the stimulus and then combines them into a unified perception

top-down processing sensory information is interpreted in light of existing knowledge, concepts, ideas and expectations

Focus 5.17 Compare bottom-up and top-down processing of sensory information.

PERCEPTIONS HAVE ORGANIZATION AND STRUCTURE

Have you ever stopped to wonder why we perceive the visual world as being composed of distinct objects? After all, the information sent by the retina reflects nothing but an array

of varying intensities and frequencies of light energy. The light rays reflected from different parts of a single object have no more natural 'belongingness' to one another than those coming from two different objects. Yet we perceive scenes as involving separate objects, such as trees, buildings and people. These perceptions must be a product of an organization imposed by our nervous system (Jenkin & Harris, 2005; Tarr & Vuong, 2002). This top-down process of perceptual organization occurs so automatically that we take it for granted. But Dr Richard, a prominent psychologist who suffered brain damage in an accident, no longer does. His story makes fascinating reading and is reported here by Oliver Sacks.

There was nothing wrong with his eyes, yet the input he received from them was not put together correctly. Dr Richard reported that if he saw a person, he sometimes would perceive the separate parts of the person as not belonging together in a single body. But if all the parts moved in the same direction, Dr Richard then saw them as one complete person. At other times, he would perceive people in crowds wearing the same colour clothes as 'going together' rather than as separate people. He also had difficulty putting sights and sounds together. Sometimes, the movement of the lips did not correspond to the sounds he heard, as if he were watching a badly dubbed foreign movie. Dr Richard's experience of his environment was thus disjointed and fragmented. (Sacks, 1985, p. 76)

Goodale, Milner, Jakobson and Carey (1991) report a similar example known as an apperceptive agnosia. DF, a 35-year-old woman, suffered carbon monoxide poisoning from a heater in her house. Her visual system was damaged as a result and she lost the ability to recognize both real and drawn objects. She was also unable to identify the size and orientation of objects. She was, however, able to draw objects from memory quite successfully, but was unable to identify the objects once drawn. Copying an object from real life was impossible for her, resulting in seemingly random lines and curves on the page. When reaching to pick up an object DF could not orientate her hand correctly or open her hand to the correct size to accommodate the object for which she was reaching. It is clear from this example that she was able, at least from memory, to access some perceptual aspects of the world. It seems we are more *conscious* of some aspect of perception than others. We pick up on DF at the beginning of the next chapter.

Gestalt Principles of Perceptual Organization

Early in the twentieth century, Gestalt psychologists set out to discover how we organize the separate parts of our perceptual field into a unified and meaningful whole. *Gestalt* is the German term for 'pattern', 'whole', or 'form'. Gestalt theorists were early champions of top-down processing, arguing that the wholes we perceive are often more than (and frequently different from) the sum of their parts. Thus your perception of the photograph in Figure 5.30 is likely to be more than a collection of small islands.

The Gestalt theorists emphasized the importance of **figure–ground relations**, our tendency to organize stimuli into a central or foreground figure and a background. In vision, the central figure is usually in front of or on top of what we perceive as background. It has a distinct shape and is more striking in our perceptions and memory than the background. We perceive borders or contours wherever there is a distinct change in the colour or lightness (illumination level) of a visual scene, but we interpret these contours as part of the figure rather than background. Likewise, we tend to hear instrumental music as a melody (figure) surrounded by other chords or harmonies (ground).

Separating figure from ground or background can be challenging (Figure 5.31), yet our perceptual systems are usually equal to the task. Sometimes, however, what is figure and what is ground is not completely obvious, and the same stimulus can give rise to two different perceptions. Consider Figure 5.32, for example. If you examine it for a while, two alternating but equally plausible perceptions will emerge, one based on the inner portion

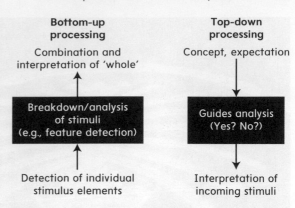

FIGURE 5.29 Perceptual processing.

Bottom-up perceptual processing builds up from an analysis of individual stimulus features to a unified perception. Top-down processing begins with a perceptual whole, such as an expectation or an image of an object, and then determines the degree of fit with the stimulus features.

figure–ground relations our tendency to organize stimuli into a central or foreground figure and a background

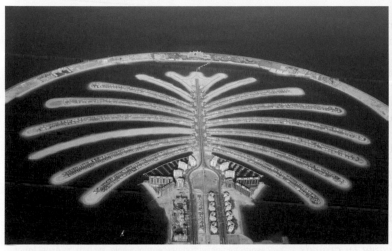

FIGURE 5.30 As Gestalt psychologists emphasize, what we perceive (in this case, the famous Palm development in Dubai) is more than simply the sum of its individual parts; much more than a collection of islands.

Source: Konstantin Stepanenko/Shutterstock

FIGURE 5.31 What do you see?

Source © Renee Keith.

FIGURE 5.32 One stimulus, two perceptions.

This reversible figure illustrates alternating figure–ground relations. It can be seen as a candlestick/vase or as two people facing one another. Whichever percept exists at the moment is seen as figure against background.

and the other formed by the two outer portions. When the alternative perception occurs, what was previously the figure becomes the background.

In addition to figure–ground relations, the Gestalt psychologists were interested in how separate stimuli come to be perceived as parts of larger wholes. They suggested that people group and interpret stimuli in accordance with four **Gestalt laws of perceptual organization**: similarity, proximity, closure and continuity. These organizing principles are illustrated in Figure 5.33. What is your perception of Figure 5.33a? Do you perceive 16 unrelated dots or two triangles formed by different-sized dots? If you see triangles, your perception obeys the Gestalt *law of similarity*, which says that when parts of a configuration are perceived as similar, they will be perceived as belonging together. The *law of proximity* says that elements that are near each other are likely to be perceived as part of the same configuration. Thus most people perceive Figure 5.33b as three sets of two lines rather than six separate lines. Illustrated in Figure 5.33c is the *law of closure*, which states that people tend to close the open edges of a figure or fill in gaps in an incomplete figure, so that their identification of the form (in this case, a circle) is more complete than what is actually there. Finally, the *law of continuity* holds that people link individual elements together so they form a continuous line or pattern that makes sense. Thus Figure 5.33d is far more likely to be seen as combining components a–b and c–d rather than a–d and c–b, which have poor continuity. Or consider Fraser's spiral, shown in Figure 5.34, which is not really a spiral at all! (To demonstrate, trace one of the circles with a pencil.) We perceive the concentric circles as a spiral because, to our nervous system, a spiral gives better continuity between individual elements than does a set of circles. The spiral is created by us, not by the stimulus.

> **Gestalt laws of perceptual organization** similarity, proximity, closure and continuity

> **Focus 5.18** Which Gestalt psychology principles and laws underlie perceptual organization?

   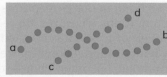

(a) Similarity   (b) Proximity   (c) Closure   (d) Continuity

FIGURE 5.33 Gestalt perceptual laws.

Among the Gestalt principles of perceptual organization are the laws of (a) similarity, (b) proximity, (c) closure, and (d) continuity. Each principle causes us to organize stimuli into wholes that are greater than the sums of their parts.

FIGURE 5.34 A spiral that is not.

Fraser's spiral illustrates the Gestalt law of continuity. If you follow any part of the 'spiral' with a pencil, you will find that it is not a spiral at all but a series of concentric circles. The 'spiral' is created by your perceptual system because that perception is more consistent with continuity of the individual elements.

PERCEPTION INVOLVES HYPOTHESIS TESTING

Recognizing a stimulus implies that we have a **perceptual schema** – a mental representation or image containing the critical and distinctive features of a person, object event or other perceptual phenomenon. Schemas provide mental templates that allow us to classify and identify sensory input in a top-down fashion.

> **perceptual schema** a mental representation or image containing the critical and distinctive features of a person, object, event or other perceptual phenomenon

Imagine, for example, that a person approaches you and calls out your name. Who is this person? If the stimuli match your internal schemas of your best friend's appearance and voice closely enough, you identify the person as your friend (McAdams & Drake, 2002). Many political cartoonists have an uncanny ability to capture the most noteworthy facial features of famous people so that we can easily recognize the person represented by even the simplest line sketch.

Perception is, in this sense, an attempt to make sense of stimulus input, to search for the best interpretation of sensory information we can arrive at based on our knowledge and experience. Gregory (1966, 2005) suggested that each of our perceptions is essentially a hypothesis about the nature of the object or, more generally, the meaning of the sensory information. The perceptual system actively searches its gigantic library of internal schemata for the interpretation that best fits the sensory data.

An example of how effortlessly our perceptual systems build up descriptions or hypotheses that best fit the available evidence is found in the comic strips created by Gustave Verbeek in the early 1900s. The Sunday *New York Herald* told Verbeek that his comic strip had to be restricted to six panels. Verbeek wanted 12 panels, so he ingeniously created 12-panel cartoons in only six panels by drawing. The reader viewed the first six panels, and then turned the newspaper upside down to read the last six and finish the story. Try this yourself on the panel shown in the figure, and you will find that a bird story becomes a story about a fish. The point is that you do not see an upside-down bird; you see an entirely different picture because the stimuli created by the new orientation match other perceptual schemas.

In some instances, sensory information fits two different internal representations, and there is not enough information to permanently rule out one of them in favour of the other. For example, examine the Necker cube, shown in Figure 5.35b. If you stare at the cube for a while, you will find that it changes before your very eyes as your nervous system tries out a new perceptual hypothesis.

Gregory (1996) points out that there is one big difference between experimental hypotheses and perpetual hypotheses – *qualia*. Perceptions have sensations, feelings of

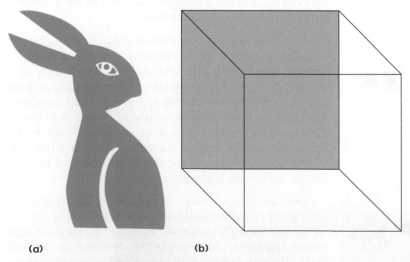

(a)   (b)

FIGURE 5.35 Reversible perceptions.

"Here are two examples of how the same stimulus can give rise to different perceptions. (a) Stare at this reversable image, you will see it switch between a rabbit and a bird. (b) Stare at this Necker cube for a while; the front of the cube will suddenly become the back, and it will appear as if you are viewing the cube from a different angle."

Focus 5.19 What roles do perceptual schemas and perceptual sets play in our sensory interpretations?

things like blue and green, hot and cold and pain. Gregory says that the perceptual system does indeed test hypotheses and store up the results for later use, for when we may experience a similar situation – but the qualia are flags, issues about the present that identify stimuli and experiences in the here and now, the present, and so prepare us for immediate present action. Ramachandran and Hirstein (1997) agree with Gregory in many ways and indicate that qualia are a way of helping the organism, or signalling to the organism to pay attention to certain things in their very busy environment. You can think of qualia as a perceptual highlighting pen – components of an otherwise sea of black and white ink can be highlighted, just as parts of the busy perceptual world can be identified with aspects of qualia.

PERCEPTION IS INFLUENCED BY EXPECTATIONS: PERCEPTUAL SET

There are occasions where your expectation of a scene may significantly influence your perception of it. In times of war, for instance, tragic mistakes have been made. The modern parlance is 'friendly fire' where death is caused by fire from allied forces. The press is often full of such cases. In 1988, the USS *Vincennes* shot down an airliner containing 290 passengers, which it had mistaken for an F-14 fighter-plane. Why might these terrible events have happened? Psychologists have identified a phenomenon known as perceptual set. Just as the central unit in each line in Figure 5.2 depends on the context in which it is presented – on the identity of the flanking items, so too can our perception of a scene be influenced by the context in which the scene is viewed. We might describe those who pulled the triggers, or released the bombs and missiles, in the many friendly fire incidents that have occurred as having had a **perceptual set** – a readiness to perceive stimuli in a particular way. Sometimes, believing is seeing.

perceptual set a readiness to perceive stimuli in a particular way

STIMULI ARE RECOGNIZABLE UNDER CHANGING CONDITIONS: PERCEPTUAL CONSTANCIES

perceptual constancies allow us to recognize familiar stimuli under varying conditions

When a closed door suddenly swings open, it casts a different image on our retina, but we still perceive it as a door. Our perceptual hypothesis remains the same. Were it not for **perceptual constancies**, which allow us to recognize familiar stimuli under varying conditions, we would have to literally rediscover what something is each time it appeared under different conditions. Thus you can recognize a tune even if it is played in a different octave or register, or even by another instrument, as long as the relations among its notes are maintained.

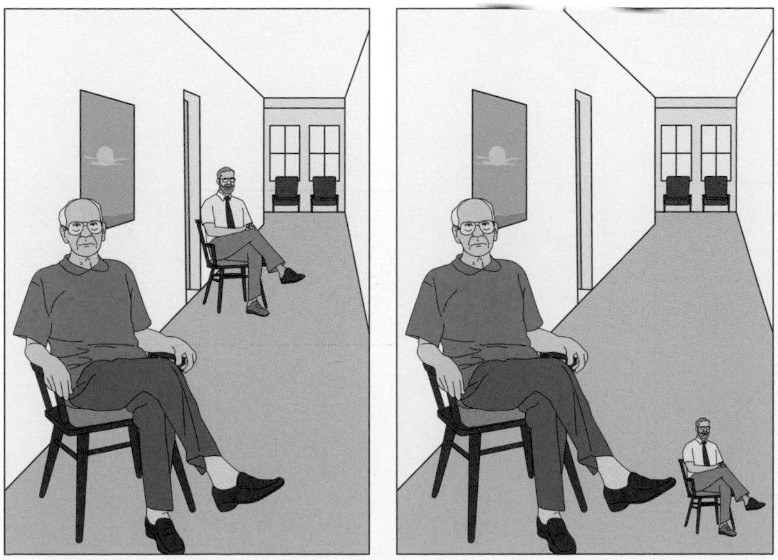

In vision, several constancies are important. *Shape constancy* allows us to recognize people and other objects from many different angles. Take a look at a nearby door, as it is opened the image arriving at your perceptual systems changes, but you still perceive the door as door-shaped, nearly always a rectangle! Sitting close to the screen in a cinema can make it appear at first a little distorted. After a while the visual system corrects for the distortion and objects on the screen look normal again.

Because of *lightness constancy*, the relative lightness of objects remains the same under different conditions of illumination (brightness), such as full sunlight and shade. Lightness constancy occurs because the ratio of light intensity between an object and its surroundings is usually constant. The actual brightness of the light that illuminates an object does not matter, as long as the same light intensity illuminates both the object and its surroundings.

FIGURE 5.36 Who's bigger?

Size constancy based on distance cues causes us to perceive the person in the background as being of normal size. When the same stimulus is seen in the absence of the distance cues, size constancy breaks down.

When we take off in an aeroplane, we know that the cars and buildings below are not shrinking as we climb away from them. *Size constancy* is the perception that the perceived size of objects remains relatively constant even though images on our retina change in size with variations in distance. Thus a man who is judged to be 6 feet (1.83 m) tall when standing 5 feet (1.5 m) away is not perceived to be 3 feet (0.9 m) tall at a distance of 10 feet (3 m), even though the size of his image on the retina is reduced to half its original size (Figure 5.36).

> **Focus 5.20** What factors account for shape, lightness and size constancy in vision?

 In review

- Perception involves both bottom-up processing, in which individual stimulus fragments are combined into a perception, and top-down processing, in which existing knowledge and perceptual schemas are applied to interpret stimuli.

- Gestalt psychologists identified a number of principles of perceptual organization, including figure-ground relations and the laws of similarity, proximity, closure and continuity. Gregory suggested that perception is essentially a hypothesis about what a stimulus is, based on previous experience and the nature of the stimulus.

- Perceptual set involves a readiness to perceive stimuli in certain ways, based on our expectations, assumptions, motivations and current emotional state.

- Perceptual constancies allow us to recognize familiar stimuli under changing conditions. In the visual realm, there are three constancies: shape, lightness and size.

PERCEPTION OF DEPTH, DISTANCE AND MOVEMENT

The ability to adapt to a spatial world requires that we make fine distinctions involving distances and the movement of objects within the environment. Humans are capable of great precision in making such judgements. Consider, for example, the perceptual task faced by a tennis player (Figure 5.37). A service in tennis can reach in excess of 190 kph. This gives the receiver a split second to react. A slower service of, say, 170 km/h will reach the receiver a little later. To adequately return the service and stand a good chance of winning the point the receiver must judge speed and point of arrival moments after the ball has been struck. If any of the judgements are wrong, the ball may well be mis-hit or the point lost through a poor return. The perceptual demands of such a task are imposing indeed – as are the salaries earned by those who can perform this task consistently. How does the visual perception system make such judgements?

DEPTH AND DISTANCE PERCEPTION

One of the more intriguing aspects of visual perception is our ability to perceive depth. The retina receives information in only two dimensions (length and width), but the brain translates these cues into three-dimensional perceptions. It does this by using both monocular (*one eye*) *depth cues* and binocular (*both eyes*) *depth cues*.

Monocular Depth Cues

This last, it is recorded, entered into a competition with Zeuxis, who produced a picture of grapes so successfully represented that birds flew to the stage-buildings; whereupon Parrhasius himself produced such a realistic picture of a curtain that Zeuxis, proud of the verdict of the birds, requested that the curtain should now be drawn and the picture displayed; and when he realized his mistake, with a modesty that did him honour he yielded up the prize, saying that whereas he had deceived birds Parrhasius had deceived him, an artist.   (Rackham's translation of Pliny, 1952, pp. 309–311)

FIGURE 5.37 The demands faced by a world-class tennis player in judging the speed, distance and movements of a service within thousandths of a second underscore the capabilities of the visual perceptual system.

Source: © PCN Photography/Alamy

FIGURE 5.38 In this mural the artist has skilfully used depth cues to create a striking three-dimensional depth effect.

Source: Chris Jackson/Getty Images

Judging the relative distances of objects is one important key to perceiving depth. When artists paint on a flat canvas, they depend on a variety of monocular cues to create perceptions of depth in their pictures. One such cue is *patterns of light and shadow*. Twentieth-century artist M.C. Escher skilfully used light and shadow to create the three-dimensional effect. The depth effect is as powerful if you close one eye as it is when you use both.

Another cue, *linear perspective*, refers to the perception that parallel lines converge, or angle towards one another, as they recede into the distance. Thus if you look down rail tracks, they appear to angle towards one another with increased distance, and we use this as a depth cue as in Figure 5.38. The same occurs with the edges of a highway or the sides of an elevator shaft. *Interposition*, in which objects closer to us may cut off part of our view of more distant objects, provides another cue for distance and depth.

An object's *height in the horizontal plane* provides another source of information. For example, a ship 10 km offshore appears in a higher plane and closer to the horizon than does one that is only 2 km from shore. *Texture* is a fifth cue, because the texture or grain of an object appears finer as distance increases. Likewise, *clarity* can be an important cue for judging distance; we can see nearby hills more clearly than ones that are far away, especially on hazy days.

Relative size is yet another basis for distance judgements. If we see two objects that we know to be of similar size, then the one that looks smaller will be judged to be farther away. For example, this cue may figure prominently in the illusion (Figure 5.39). If you have experienced the moon illusion you will know quite how striking it can be. As the moon sneaks up over the horizon it seems absolutely enormous. Even though we know that the size of the moon does not change so dramatically, we experience the overwhelming feeling that something odd has happened, something unusual and more often than not people call you over to take a look at the HUGE moon. Imagine for a moment how our ancestors must have felt when they experienced the same illusion without any understanding of why the moon appears so large. The moon is NOT any larger when it is nearer the horizon than it normally is, follow the instructions in the caption for Figure 5.39 and you will see that this is the case. This means that the moon is the very same size on your retina when near the horizon than it is when it is directly above you in the dark night sky. We can conclude then that the moon illusion comes about, is caused by, our perceptual system. It is worth noting here a very important point, that sensation (the stimulation of the perceptual organs – in this case the retina) and perception (what we actually experience) are two different things, and that this difference is shown up clearly by this type of illusion. 'Relative size' is a powerful cue to perception, and is one possible reason we see the moon illusion. In normal experience we use items we are familiar with – trees, buildings etc. – to judge the relative size of things behind them, further away from them. When we view items in the distance through a busy perceptual scene, with trees, houses, other buildings, hills etc., they appear to be further away than they actually are. Our perceptual system knows that the moon does not actually change in size, so when it appears further away, when viewed against the horizon, perhaps with familiar buildings and objects in the scene, we 'scale' the moon up, make it bigger, to compensate for the perception that it is further away. The result is that the physically unchanged moon is 'scaled up' and made to seem much larger than it should be. This is an example then, of 'inappropriate size scaling' in order to maintain the size of objects we know to remain constant. Ordinarily we do this size scaling quite appropriately. Take your first finger and thumb of one hand and look across the room at someone you know. Use your finger and thumb to see how big their heads are – pinch their heads between finger and thumb. Their head is actually tiny on your retina, no more than a few centimetres, it fits between your finger and thumb easily, but you know from considerable experience how big heads are, and so

you scale up the tiny head so that it appears perceptually the normal size. This is appropriate scaling to maintain size constancy. In the example of the moon illusion the scaling is done inappropriately and the result is the perception of a much larger moon than it should be. We discuss the idea of constancy a little more later in the chapter.

None of these monocular cues involve movement of the object(s), but a final monocular cue, *motion parallax*, tells us that if we are moving, nearby objects appear to move faster in the opposite direction than do those further away. Like the other monocular cues, motion provides us with information that we can use to make judgements about distance and therefore about depth.

Figure 5.39 illustrates the cues just described, with the exception of motion parallax. Linear perspective is produced by the converging lines within the mural and in the environment in which it sits. The components of the mural in the background are smaller than those in the foreground (relative size). The background is in a higher horizontal plane than in the foreground. The objects in the background are less detailed than the 'closer' ones (texture and clarity). The parts of the mural in the foreground cut off parts of those 'behind' them in the background (interposition). Light and shadow are also used to create a depth effect.

FIGURE 5.39 The moon illusion.

When you see it, hold your arm out at full length to the moon holding a familiar object in your hand, a key perhaps. As the moon rises and appears to get smaller repeat the action and you will see that the relative size of the key to that of the moon does not change, showing that the moon's apparently huge size when near the horizon is illusory.

Source: © Marcos Molina/Alamy

Binocular Depth Cues

The most dramatic perceptions of depth arise with binocular depth cues, which require the use of both eyes. For an interesting binocular effect, hold your two index fingers about 6 inches (15 cm) in front of your eyes with their tips about 1 inch (2.5 cm) apart. Focus on your fingers first, and then focus beyond them across the room. Doing so will produce the image of a third finger between the other two. This third finger will disappear if you close either eye.

Most of us will be familiar with looking at images, and indeed movies that appear to be in 3D. These devices originate from the stereoscopes of the late nineteenth century (Figure 5.40). The stereoscope makes use of the principle of **binocular disparity**, in which each eye sees a slightly different image. Within the brain, the visual input from the two eyes is analysed by feature detectors that are attuned to depth (Howard, 2002; Livingstone & Hubel, 1994b). Some of the feature detectors respond only to stimuli that are either in front of or behind the point on which we are fixing our gaze. The responses of these depth-sensitive neurons are integrated to produce our perception of depth (Goldstein, 2008).

binocular disparity each eye sees a slightly different image
convergence produced by feedback from the muscles that turn your eyes inward to view a close object

Recent developments in movie technology are making the 3D image a common experience to those of us who love movies. Many of us will have experienced 3D with green and red glasses where the red image seen on screen is perceived by one eye, the green by the other. The principle is the same as the stereoscope – the two separate images are combined to give a 3D percept. There are different methods of developing the 3D percept, however, the most common of which these days is through polarization. Two separate images are projected onto the screen at the same time. Each lens in the glasses worn by the moviegoer only allows light through from one of the projections. In this way different images are passed to each eye. Surprisingly, using polarized images as a way of producing 3D films has been known since the 1930s, but is now more popular than ever.

A second binocular distance cue, **convergence**, is produced by feedback from the muscles that turn your eyes inward to view a close object. You can experience this cue by holding a finger about 1 foot (30 cm) in front of your face and then moving it slowly towards you. Messages sent to your brain by the eye muscles provide it with a depth cue.

FIGURE 5.40 A stereoscope from the early twentieth century.

Two slightly different images are printed on a card at the end of the rod. The right-hand image can only be seen by the right eye and the left-hand image by the left eye. When combined to a single image by the perceptual system the result is a three-dimensional image.

Source: © Danny Smythe.

Research close-up

SPACE – PERCEPTUAL MALFUNCTION

INTRODUCTION

Spaceflight is known to cause some physical difficulties in those that are fortunate, talented and fit enough to be chosen to take part. These problems include issues relating to bone density and visual acuity, but perceptual problems have not been widely researched. Clément and Reschke (2008) report some issues of motion sickness, and there have also been reports of face-processing problems associated with sustained space flight and the corresponding weightlessness (Léone, 1998) and also problems with tasks requiring objects to be mentally rotated (Matsakis, Lipshits, Gurfinkel, & Berthoz, 1993). In this paper the authors look at whether there is any alteration of how astronauts perceive distance and size during a lengthy flight. As we have described, the relative size of known objects can serve as a powerful cue to their perceived distance from one another. When an object's distance is underestimated, we attribute to it a smaller size. Earlier in the chapter we learned of the case of DF (Goodale et al., 1991), and how perception of

FIGURE 5.41 The International Space Station.
Source: ©iStock.com/t.light

objects from memory was possible. The authors here applied similar thinking with their astronaut participants – the thinking here being that drawings of objects perceived in space, from memory, after the person had been subject to a long space flight, will include the same perceptual distortions as will be found in visual tests. This is because there is a constancy between perceptions of 3D objects and our drawings of them – we draw things from memory as we have perceived them. Astronauts were tested on four tasks at varying times leading up to their flights and then after their flights and the results compared.

Task 1: Cube-size perception

Astronauts were asked to perceive cubes, presented stereoscopically with apparatus similar, but more technologically advanced of course, to that shown in Figure 5.44. In each trial, one dimension of the cube, its height, width or depth was clearly different (shorter) than it should be. Astronauts had to adjust the line in the stereoscopic image so that they felt it was correct.

Task 2: Cube Hand drawing

Here astronauts were shown a line by line video of a 'necker cube' (Figure 5.39b). After the short video of the production of the cube each astronaut was required to reproduce it six times using on a tablet.

Task 3: Distance perception with cubes

In this task astronauts viewed three cubes presented stereoscopically. They were asked to adjust, using a trackball, the perceived relative distance of the cubes so that the apparent distance between the cubes was equal.

Task 4: Distance perception in natural scenes

Astronauts viewed stereoscopic views of natural scenes on earth, of a range of things including buildings, cities, mountains and bridges. Superimposed were yellow targets. The task was to estimate the distance between themselves and the targets.

RESULTS

In *task 1* there was a notable difference in measurements taken inflight, than pre-flight for the 'height' dimension of the cube to appear smaller, and its depth to appear larger (deeper).

In *task 2* similar, although not as marked, differences in the height and depth dimensions to those shown in task 1 – cube-size perception – were found.

In *task 3* astronauts consistently, although not statistically significantly, underestimated the amount of adjustment required to 'position' the cubes equidistantly from one another.

In *task 4* no significant differences were found between pre-flight judgements of distance and post-flight judgements.

DISCUSSION AND CONCLUSIONS

The authors conclude that there are indeed errors in the perceived distance and size of objects and also in the mental representations of spatial cues in prolonged low-gravity situations. Even thought the number of participants was relatively low (eight astronauts, one woman and seven men), the findings do suggest that the role of perceptual psychology is an important one in identifying issues which may well have significant

▶

implications for future space exploration. The reasons for and mechanisms behind the observed changes in the astronauts' perceptions are unclear, but it may be that the cues we use for distance and height judgements on the ground are not as relevant, or not as salient in a zero or low gravity situation. Our eye height on the ground, for instance, is relatively constant, whereas in zero gravity it most certainly is not. As such, size-scaling of objects that are also not necessarily attached to the ground, or not behaving in a way that is commensurate with earth-bound gravity is difficult, and the result is an altered perception of height and distance. Before going boldly into space, these are the types of things The Federation is likely to need to know...

PERCEPTION OF MOVEMENT

The perception of movement is a complex process, sometimes requiring the brain to integrate information from several different senses. To demonstrate, hold a pen in front of your face. Now, while holding your head still, move the pen back and forth. You will perceive the pen as moving. Now hold the pen still and move your head back and forth at the same rate of speed. In both cases, the image of the pen moved across your retina in about the same way. But when you moved your head, your brain took into account input from your proprioceptive and vestibular systems and concluded that you were moving but the pen was not.

The primary cue for perceiving motion is the movement of the stimulus across the retina (Sekuler, Watamaniuk, & Blake, 2002). Under optimal conditions, a retinal image need move only about one-fifth the diameter of a single cone for us to detect movement (Nakayama & Tyler, 1981). The relative movement of an object against a structured background is also a movement cue (Gibson, 1979). For example, if you fixate on a bird in flight, the relative motion of the bird against its background is a strong cue for perceived speed of movement.

The illusion of smooth motion can be produced if we arrange for the sequential appearance of two or more stimuli. Gestalt psychologist Max Wertheimer (1912) demonstrated this in his studies of **stroboscopic movement**, illusory movement produced when a light is briefly flashed in darkness and then, a few milliseconds later, another light is flashed nearby. If the timing is just right, the first light seems to move from one place to the other in a manner indistinguishable from real movement.

Stroboscopic movement (termed the 'phi phenomenon' by Wertheimer) has been used commercially in numerous ways. For example, think of the strings of successively illuminated lights on railway platforms or electronic notice-boards that seem to move endlessly around the border or that spell out messages in a moving script. Stroboscopic movement is also the principle behind motion pictures, which consist of a series of still photographs, or frames, that are projected on a screen in rapid succession with dark intervals in between (Figure 5.42). The rate at which the frames are projected is critical to our perception of smooth movement. Early films, such as the silent films of the 1920s, projected the stills at only 16 frames per second, and the movements appeared fast and jerky. Today the usual speed is 24 frames per second, which more perfectly produces an illusion of smooth movement. Television presents at 30 images per second.

Focus 5.21 Describe the major monocular and binocular depth/distance cues, as well as the basis for movement perception.

stroboscopic movement illusory movement produced when a light is briefly flashed in darkness and then, a few milliseconds later, another light is flashed nearby

FIGURE 5.42 Stroboscopic movement is produced in moving pictures as a series of still photographs projected at a rate of 24 per second.

Source: ©iStock.com/proxyminder

ILLUSIONS: FALSE PERCEPTUAL HYPOTHESES

Our analysis of perceptual schemas, hypotheses, sets and constancies allows us to understand some interesting perceptual experiences known as **illusions**, compelling but incorrect perceptions. Such perceptions can be understood as erroneous perceptual hypotheses about the nature of a stimulus. Illusions are not only intriguing and sometimes delightful visual experiences, but also provide important information about how our perceptual processes work under normal conditions (Gregory, 2005; Harris, 2014). Magicians are terribly good at encouraging us to make false perceptual hypotheses about what we are seeing, only to dash our understanding of what we are experiencing as the trick is completed. We expect the coin to be in the magician's hand, since we did not see her slip it carefully into her sleeve so as the hand is opened to reveal a magically vanished coin … our perceptual hypothesis, built upon past experiences that tell us that solid objects remain solid objects even though they are briefly removed from our sight by a closed fist, is dashed and we experience surprise, and often wonderment.

Ironically, most visual illusions can be attributed to perceptual constancies that ordinarily help us perceive more accurately (Frisby, 1980). For example, size constancy results in part from our ability to use distance cues to judge the size of objects. But as we saw in the discussion of the moon illusion, distance cues can sometimes fool us. In the Ponzo illusion, shown in Figure 5.43a, the depth cues of linear perspective (the tracks converging) and height of the horizontal plane provide distance cues that make the upper bar appear farther away than the lower bar. Because it seems farther away, the perceptual system concludes that the bar in the background must be larger than the bar in the foreground, despite the fact that the two bars cast retinal images of the same size. The same occurs in the vertical arrangement seen in Figure 5.43b.

Distance cues can be manipulated to create other size illusions. To illustrate this, Adelbert Ames constructed a special room. Viewed through a peephole with one eye, the room's scene presents a startling size reversal (Figure 5.44a). Our perceptual system assumes that the room has a normal rectangular shape because, in fact, most rooms do. Monocular depth cues do not allow us to see that, in reality, the left corner of the room is twice as far away as the right corner (Figure 5.44b). As a result, size constancy breaks down, and we base our judgement of size on the sizes of the retinal images cast by the two people.

The study of perceptual constancies shows that our perceptual hypotheses are strongly influenced by the context, or surroundings, in which a stimulus occurs. Figure 5.45 shows some examples of how context can produce illusory perceptions.

Some of the most intriguing perceptual distortions are produced when monocular depth cues are manipulated to produce a figure or scene whose individual parts make sense but whose overall organization is 'impossible' in terms of our existing perceptual schemas. Figure 5.46 shows three impossible figures. In each case, our brain extracts information about depth from the individual features of the objects, but when this information is put together and matched with our existing schemas, the percept that results simply does not make sense. The 'devil's tuning fork', for example, could not exist in our universe. It is a two-dimensional image containing

(a)

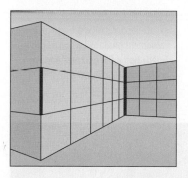

(b)

FIGURE 5.43 Two examples of the Ponzo illusion.

Which lines in (a) and (b) are longer? The distance cues provided by the converging rail tracks and the walls affect size perception and disrupt size constancy. You may also notice that the bars and 'fins' at their ends, formed by the walls and panels in the picture resemble the different parts of the Müller-Lyer illusion shown in Figure 5.45.

FIGURE 5.44 A size illusion.

(a) The Ames Room produces a striking size illusion because it is designed to appear rectangular. (b) The room, however, is actually a trapezoid, and the figure on the left is actually much farther away from the viewer than the one on the right and thus appears smaller.

(a)

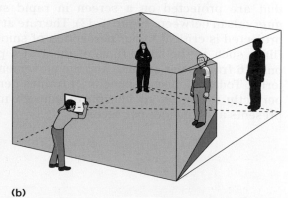

(b)

paradoxical depth cues. Our brain, however, automatically interprets it as a three-dimensional object and matches it with its internal schema of a fork – which turns out to be a bad fit. The never-ending staircase provides another compelling example of an impossible scene that seems perfectly reasonable when we focus only on its individual elements.

Illusions are not only personally and scientifically interesting, but they can have important real-life implications. Our 'Research close-up' describes one scientist's search for an illusion having life-and-death implications.

Focus 5.22 What is an illusion? How are constancies and context involved in visual illusions?

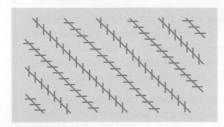

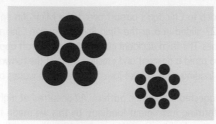

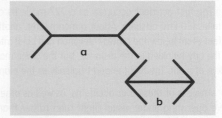

The long lines are actually parallel, but the small lines make them appear crooked.

Which inner circle is larger? Check and see.

The Müller-Lyer illusion. Which line, a or b, is longer? Compare them with a ruler.

FIGURE 5.45 Context-produced geometric illusions.

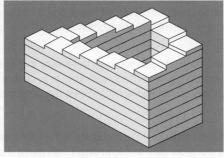

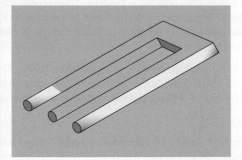

FIGURE 5.46 Things that could not be.

Monocular depth cues are cleverly manipulated to produce an impossible triangle, a never-ending staircase, and the 'devil's tuning fork'.

FACE PERCEPTION

Faces are a particularly important and salient stimulus. We know both from experience and research that infants find the face extremely compelling. The face can provide the infant and mother, or caregiver a means of communicating before language can be shared. Pascalis and de Haan (2002) have shown that infants are in fact more sensitive to changes in faces than older humans, and in Chapter 12 we explore the development of face processing in the first year of life in more depth. Their research indicates that infants can even tell the difference in faces from different species, an ability that becomes dulled or is lost entirely in older humans, who become focused on or tuned to the type of face most important to them, the human face. Face processing is thought of as a special process, different from our perceptions of other items and objects.

THE IMPORTANCE OF 'FEATURES'

Bruce and Young (1986) say that basic information about the person is perceived, including gender and age. Facial expression features are then processed. The model of the face that is produced is consigned to memory where personal identity is coded along with these features. This is the *feature theory* of face perception. When the person experiences a

Research close-up

STALKING A DEADLY ILLUSION

Source: C. L. Kraft (1978). A psychophysical contribution to air safety: Simulator studies of illusions in night visual approaches. In H. L. Pick, Jr, H. W. Leibowitz, J. E. Singer, A. Steinschneider, & H. W. Stevenson (Eds.), *Psychology: From research to practice*. New York: Plenum.

INTRODUCTION

When the Boeing Company introduced the 727 jet airliner in the mid-1960s, it was the height of technology and design in aviation technology. The plane performed well in test flights, but four fatal crashes soon after it was placed in service raised fears that there might be a serious flaw in its design.

The first accident occurred as a 727 made its approach to Chicago's airport over Lake Michigan on a clear night. The plane plunged into the lake 19 miles (30 km) offshore. About a month later, another 727 glided in over the Ohio River to land in Cincinnati. Unaccountably, it struck the ground about 12 feet (4 m) below the runway elevation and burst into flames. The third accident occurred as an aircraft approached Salt Lake City over dark land. The lights of the city twinkled in the distance, but the plane made too rapid a descent and crashed short of the runway. Months later, a Japanese airliner approached Tokyo at night. The flight ended tragically as the plane, its landing gear not yet lowered, struck the waters of Tokyo Bay, 6 miles (9.5 km) from the runway.

Analysis of these four accidents, as well as others, suggested a common pattern. All occurred at night under clear weather conditions, so the pilots were operating under visual flight rules rather than performing instrument landings; by this we mean that the pilots were watching the real horizon, monitoring the aero plane's performance by visually checking flight orientation and position through the windows, not only by using the dials. In each instance, the plane was approaching city lights over dark areas of water or land. In all cases, the lights in the background terrain sloped upward to varying degrees. Finally, all the planes crashed short of the runway. These observations led a Boeing industrial psychologist, Conrad L. Kraft, to suspect that the cause of the crashes might be pilot error based on some sort of visual illusion.

To test this possibility, Boeing engineers constructed an apparatus to simulate night landings. It consisted of a cockpit and a miniature lighted city named Nightertown. The city moved towards the cockpit on computer-controlled rollers, and it could be tilted to simulate various terrain slopes. The pilot could control simulated air speed and rate of climb and descent, and the Nightertown scene was controlled by the pilot's responses just as a true visual scene would be.

The participants were 12 experienced Boeing flight instructors who made virtual-reality landings at Nightertown under systematically varied conditions created by the computerized simulator. All their landings were visual landings so as to be able to test whether a visual illusion was occurring. Every aspect of their approach and the manner in which they controlled the aircraft were measured precisely.

RESULTS

The flight instructors' landings were nearly flawless until Kraft duplicated the conditions of the fatal crashes by having the pilots approach an upward-sloping distant city over a dark area. When this occurred, the pilots were unable to detect the upward slope, assumed that the background city was flat, and consistently overestimated their approach altitude. On a normal landing, the preferred altitude at 4.5 miles (7 km) from the runway is about 1240 feet (377 m). As Figure 5.48 shows, the pilots approached at about this altitude when the simulated city was in a flat position. But when it was sloped upward, 11 of the 12 experienced pilot instructors crashed about 4.5 miles (7 km) short of the runway.

CRITICAL DISCUSSION

This study shows the value of studying behaviour under highly controlled conditions and with precise measurements. By simulating the conditions under which the fatal crashes had occurred, Kraft identified the visual illusion that was the source of pilot error. He showed that the perceptual hypotheses of the flight instructors, like those of the pilots involved in the real crashes, were tragically incorrect. It would have been ironic if one of the finest jetliners ever built had been removed from service because of presumed mechanical defects while other aircraft remained aloft and at risk of tragedy.

Kraft's research not only saved the 727 from months – or perhaps years – of needless mechanical analysis but, more important, it also identified a potentially deadly illusion and the precise conditions under which it occurred. On the basis of Kraft's findings, Boeing recommended that pilots attend carefully to their instruments when landing at night, even under perfect weather conditions. Today, commercial airline pilots are required to make instrument landings not only at night but also during the day.

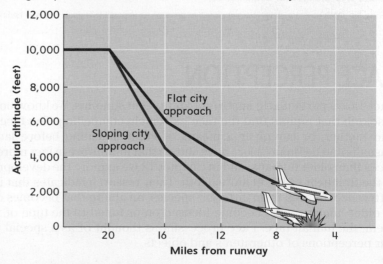

FIGURE 5.48 Misperceptions of experienced pilots.

The illusion created by upward-sloping city lights caused even highly experienced pilots to overestimate their altitude, and 11 of the 12 flight instructors crashed short of the runway. When the lights were flat, all the pilots made perfect approaches.

Source: Based on Kraft, 1978.

face again, the appropriate 'face-recognition unit' is activated, and we realize that we have seen the face before, we have recognition. Some features may be more important than others though. Sadr, Jarudi and Sinha (2003) have suggested that the eyebrows are extremely important. They had participants identify celebrity faces with various features removed. The pictures with the eyebrows missing were significantly harder to identify than those with the eyes removed. However, different features are more reliable in different situations. If features are presented in isolation (without the rest of the face) then the eyes are the most reliable indicator of gender (Burton, Bruce, & Dench, 1993). It seems then that features distinguish faces from one another, but there are general rules that help us identify more global differences, such as gender. Bruce, Valentine and Baddeley (1987) for instance, showed that gender is very quickly identified, quicker even than familiarity. The features of a face that distinguish gender include the shape and length of the nose, and how the brows and eyes are set (males have deeper set eyes, and more prominent brows, altering a relatively large portion of the visual array). In 1980, Peter Thompson identified a phenomenon that has become known as the Thatcher illusion, because it was first shown, by Thompson, with an image of the late politician (see Figure 5.49 for an example of the illusion).

While upside down the images look reasonably normal, when turned the right way up something dramatic happens in our perceptual system as we experience the illusion. The eyes and mouth have been turned upside down in the image on the left. This suggests that we process the components of the face separately. If we did not, if we saw only the face as a whole, we would immediately see that the images were very different. The illusion also shows that face perception, where we combine the features into a single 'face' happens only when faces are the right way up.

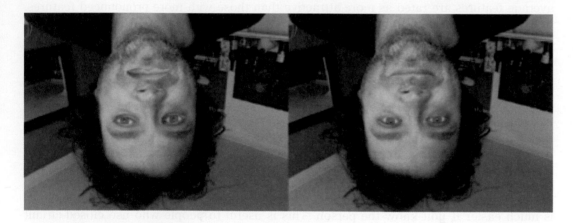

FIGURE 5.49 An example of the Thatcher illusion (Thompson, 1980). Turn the book upside down for the illusory effect.

Source: Photography and image manipulation by Nigel Holt.

EMOTION

Bruce and Young (1986) show that extremely important information is available from faces, not least our perception of others' emotions. Women, it seems, are better at identifying emotions from facial expressions than men. The gender difference extends through childhood into adulthood, with all females showing better performance than males of their own age group (McClure, 2000). There are other interesting factors associated with gender in face perception. During the menstrual cycle, women change their preference for male faces, preferring a more masculine face when in the follicular stage (Penton-Voak & Perrett, 2000). It is at this stage that conception is most likely following sexual intercourse. In terms of evolutionary psychology, we might describe this as a desire to choose a father who shows certain attributes that the woman sees as beneficial. These attributes might be the stereotypical masculine traits described in a face as a strong jaw, deep set eyes, etc. Other research, however, has indicated that the behaviour of the male can also significantly influence his attractiveness to the female at different times in her menstrual cycle (Gangestad, Thornhill, & Garver-Apgar, 2005).

ATTRACTIVENESS

The concept of attractiveness is very subjective. It is widely regarded that what we find attractive may depend on our culture, but research suggests that it may not. Our treatment of people we regard as attractive is, it seems, independent of culture, according to Langlois et al. (2000), who showed startling cross-cultural agreement on attractiveness ratings of pictures of individuals. They also showed that attractive people were treated better than unattractive people in the cultures they tested. The youthfulness of the face has been identified as a factor in attractiveness (Ji, Kamachi, & Akamatsu, 2004). Researchers used a technique to blend faces into one another, and change, or morph, the faces they used to look more youthful. Their results showed that the younger faces, and those that had been made to look more feminine (feminized) were judged as more attractive than the older or more masculine faces. Evolution suggests that the perceived attractiveness of a face is related to the pressure to produce young of optimal genetic make-up. The perceived healthiness of the face is also a factor in attractiveness ratings, and healthiness has obvious evolutionary advantages. Rhodes (2006) has shown that more attractive faces were rated as healthier. But what about the features that people find attractive? People are constantly engaged in complex, costly and painful plastic surgery in pursuit of the ideal face, but what is it that makes a face ideal? Perrett, May and Yoshikawa (1994) show that faces are consistently rated as more attractive if they have larger eyes and higher cheeks relative to the size and shape of the face. In their experiment, Perrett and colleagues morphed faces together and had them rated in attractiveness by a panel. They then produced the average of the most attractively rated faces and enhanced them, to make them 'highly attractive'. Their participants rated this 'highly attractive' composite face higher in attractiveness than a similarly produced 'average' composite face, suggesting that enhancing some features does indeed produce a more attractive face. In contrast to this, Bruce, Burton and Dench (1994) showed that faces with average features are rated as more attractive than those with more pronounced features. In evolutionary terms this makes sense. An average face means a mate that is of familiar genetic construction. This means less risk to the genetic make-up of the offspring.

RECOGNIZING FACES

Sometimes people lose the ability to recognize faces. In these cases we say that the person has a form of *prospagnosia*. This is usually caused by a traumatic brain injury of some kind. Imagine not being able to process faces, not knowing who you have met previously and whether you should recognize someone you see. Face perception is indeed an extremely important part of our social world. You can find more on this in **Chapter 6**. Recognition is extremely important, and there is evidence (Bruce, Henderson, Newman, & Burton, 2001; Burton, Bruce, & Hancock, 1999) that matching clear faces to even very degraded images is much easier if you know the person. This is useful to people who use closed-circuit television (CCTV). When a witness identifies someone on an often very degraded CCTV image as someone they know, then the likelihood of this being a correct identification is much higher than if the person in the image is not known to the witness.

Chapter 6, Page 212

In review

- Monocular cues to judge distance and depth include linear perspective, relative size, height in the horizontal plane, texture and clarity. Depth perception also occurs through the monocular cues of light and shadow patterns, interposition and motion parallax.
- Binocular disparity occurs as slightly different images are viewed by each eye and acted on by feature detectors for depth. Convergence of the eyes provides a second binocular cue.
- The basis for perception of movement is absolute movement of a stimulus across the retina or relative movement of an object in relation to its background. Stroboscopic movement is illusory.
- Illusions are erroneous perceptions. They may be regarded as incorrect perceptual hypotheses. Perceptual constancies help produce many illusions, including the moon illusion and a variety of other context-produced illusions.

EXPERIENCE, CRITICAL PERIODS AND PERCEPTUAL DEVELOPMENT

Development of sensory and perceptual systems results from the interplay of biological and experiential factors. Genes play a very significant role in biological development, but this development is also influenced by environmental experiences. For example, if you were to be blinded in an accident and later learned to read Braille, the area of the somatosensory cortex that is devoted to the fingertips would enlarge over time as it borrowed other neurons to increase its sensitivity (Pool, 1994). By the time they are old enough to crawl, children placed on a 'visual cliff' formed by a glass-covered table that suddenly drops off beneath the glass will not ordinarily venture over the edge (Figure 5.50). This aversion may result from the interaction of innate depth-perception abilities and previous experience (Gibson & Walk, 1960).

FIGURE 5.50 Eleanor Gibson and Richard Walk constructed this 'visual cliff' with a glass-covered drop-off to determine whether crawling infants and newborn animals can perceive depth. Even when coaxed by their mothers, young children refuse to venture onto the glass over the cliff. Newborn animals also avoid the cliff.

Source: Baby Center, Berkley University/Reprinted with kind permission of Professor Joseph J. Campos

Studies of feral children such as Victor of Averyron (**Chapter 12**) and others (Curtiss, 1977, **Chapter 9**) show delayed acquisition of language where their experience of it is limited or restricted at a young age. This has led to the development of the critical or sensitive period hypothesis – also known as the Lennenberg hypothesis after his work in 1967 on the biological foundations of language. It is clear from these and other studies that delayed access to language can significantly influence language acquisition, but what might a lifetime of experience in a limited environment do to perceptual abilities that seem innate? Sometimes, conditions under which people live, or are forced to live as in the case of feral children, create natural experiments that help provide answers. For example, the Ba Mbuti pygmies, who live in the rainforests of Central Africa, spend their lives in a closed-in green world of densely packed trees without open spaces. Turnbull (1961) once brought a man named Kenge out of the forest to the edge of a vast plain. A herd of buffalo grazed in the distance. To Turnbull's surprise, Kenge remarked that he had never seen insects of that kind. When told that they were buffalo, not insects, Kenge was deeply offended and felt that Turnbull was insulting his intelligence. To prove his point, Turnbull drove Kenge in his jeep towards the animals. Kenge stared in amazement as the 'insects' grew into buffalo before his eyes. To explain his perceptual experience to himself, he concluded that witchcraft was being used to fool him. Kenge's misperception occurred as a failure in size constancy. Having lived in an environment without open spaces, he had no experience in judging the size of objects at great distances.

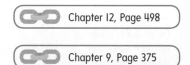

Chapter 12, Page 498

Chapter 9, Page 375

As noted earlier, when light passes through the lens of the eye, the image projected on the retina is reversed, so that right is left and up is down. What would happen if you were to wear a special set of glasses that undid this natural reversal of the visual image and created a world like that in Figure 5.51?

> *Only after a set of relations and perceptions had become organized into a norm could something enter which was in unusual relation to this organized whole and be (for instance) upside down.*   (Stratton, 1896)

In 1896, perception researcher George Stratton became the first human ever to have a right-side up image on his retina while standing upright. Reversing how nature and a lifetime of experience had fashioned his perceptual system disoriented Stratton at first. The ground and his feet were now up, and he had to put on his hat from the bottom up. He had to reach to his left to touch something he saw on his right. Stratton suffered from nausea and could not eat or get around for several days. Gradually, however, he adapted to his inverted world, and by the end of eight days he was able to successfully reach for objects and even cycle successfully. Years later, people who wore inverting lenses for longer periods of time did the same. Some were

FIGURE 5.51 A challenging world.

Inverted vision would create a world that looks like this. How would you make your way around in this upside-down environment where right is left and left is right? Adaptation to such a world is possible but challenging.

Source: © ZUMA Press, Inc./Alamy

able to ski down mountain slopes or ride motorcycles while wearing the lenses, even though their visual world remained upside down and never became normal for them. When they removed the inverting lenses, they had some initial problems but soon readapted to the normal visual world (Dolezal, 1982).

CROSS-CULTURAL RESEARCH IN PERCEPTION

As far as we know, humans come into the world with the same perceptual abilities, regardless of where they are born. From that point on, however, the cultures they grow up in helps determine the kinds of perceptual learning experiences they have. Cross-cultural research can help identify which aspects of perception occur in all people, regardless of their culture, as well as perceptual differences that result from cultural experiences (Deregowski, 1989; Posner & Rothbart, 2007b). Although there are far more perceptual similarities than differences among the peoples of the world, the differences that do exist show us that perception can indeed be influenced by experience.

Consider the perception of a picture that depends on both the nature of the picture and characteristics of the perceiver. In Figure 5.52a, what is the object above the woman's head? In one study, most Europeans instantly identified it as a window. They also tended to see the family sitting inside a dwelling. But when the same picture was shown to East Africans, nearly all perceived the object as a basket or box that the woman was balancing on her head. To them, the family was sitting outside under a tree (Gregory & Gombrich, 1973). These interpretations were more consistent with their own cultural experiences.

In our earlier discussion of monocular depth cues, we used paintings such as that in Figure 5.38 to illustrate monocular depth perception. In Western culture, we have constant exposure to two-dimensional pictures that our perceptual system effortlessly turns into three-dimensional perceptions. Do people who grow up in cultures where they are not exposed to pictures have the same perceptions? When presented with the picture in Figure 5.52b and asked which animal the hunter was about to shoot, tribal African people answered that he was about to kill the 'baby elephant'. They did not use the monocular cues that cause Westerners to perceive the man as hunting the antelope and to view the elephant as an adult animal in the distance (Hudson, 1960).

Illusions occur when one of our common perceptual hypotheses is in error. Previously we showed you the Müller-Lyer illusion (see Figure 5.45), in which a line appears longer when the V-shaped lines at its ends radiate outward rather than inward. Westerners are

Focus 5.23 What evidence shows that cultural factors can influence perceptual interpretations, constancies and susceptibility to illusions?

(a)

(b)

FIGURE 5.52 Does culture influence perception?

(a) What is the object above the woman's head? East Africans had a far different answer than did North Americans and Europeans. (b) Cultural differences also occurred when people were asked which animal the archer was about to shoot.

Sources: (a) adapted from Gregory and Gombrich, 1973; (b) adapted from Hudson, 1960.

very susceptible to this illusion. They have learned that in their 'carpentered' environment, which has many corners and square shapes, inward-facing lines occur when corners are closer and outward-facing lines occur when they are farther away (Figure 5.53). But when people from other cultures who live in more rounded environments are shown the Müller-Lyer stimuli, they are more likely to correctly perceive the lines as equal in length (Segall, Campbell, & Herskowitz, 1966). They are less likely to fall prey to a perceptual hypothesis that normally is correct in an environment like ours that is filled with sharp corners but wrong when applied to the lines in the Müller-Lyer illusion (Deregowski, 1989).

Cultural learning affects perceptions in other modalities as well. Our perceptions of tastes, odours and textures are strongly influenced by our cultural experiences. A taste that might produce nausea in one culture may be considered delicious in another. The taste and gritty texture experienced when chewing a large raw insect or the rubbery texture of a fish eye may appeal far less to you than it would to a person from a culture in which that food is common or considered a delicacy.

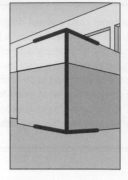
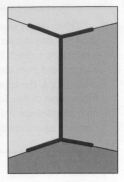

FIGURE 5.53 Which vertical line is longer?
Perceptual experiences within our 'carpentered' environment make us susceptible to the Müller-Lyer illusion (see Figure 5.45), which appears here in vertical form. Again, the vertical lines are the same physical length.

💬 Current topic

CROSS-CULTURAL DIFFERENCES IN MULTI-SENSORY PERCEPTIONS

The 'Bouba-Kiki effect' is a relatively well-known effect in research carried out with Westerners (see Spence, 2011 for a review). It is called a 'sound-shape' symbolism effect where shapes with rounded edges are associated with the word 'Bouba' and shapes with sharper pointed edges are associated with the word Kiki. Examples of such shapes can be seen in Figure 5.54, and are redrawn from Bremner, Caparos, Davidoff, de Fockert, Linnell and Spence (2013).

This is a cross-modal effect or interaction, that is to say our perceptual experience of something in one modality or perceptual property, in this case 'shape', can relate to, and possibly give rise to, experience in another modality or perceptual property, in this case sound. Up until the work of Bremner et al. (2013) relatively little empirical work had been done on such interactions cross-culturally although there had

FIGURE 5.54 On the left a softer rounded shape, on the right a more angular shape.

been less-formal reports that suggested that cultural differences in such cross-modal effects may be present. The researchers travelled to Namibia to work with the Himba people who had very little interaction with, and so influence from, Western cultures, and who did not use any written form of language. Here was an excellent opportunity to investigate how different cultures experienced the Bouba-Kiki Effect. Research (Deroy & Valentin, 2011; Gallace et al., 2011) had also suggested cross-modal effects between shapes and tastes and flavours, and so the project was expanded to include these concepts.

Each person was tested on their own, but in the presence of a researcher and a translator to ensure that the person fully understood what was being asked of them. One at a time, different sounds were presented or different drinks or foods, and on each presentation participants were asked to match the stimulus (the sound, food or drink) to one of the two shapes shown in Figure 5.54. All in all there were three categories of task: a shape-sound matching task where Bouba and Kiki were matched to the shapes; a shape-bitterness matching task, where different types of chocolate of differing levels of bitterness, as denoted by their coco-content were matched to the shapes; and a carbonation task where sparkling or still water was matched to the shapes.

The results were very interesting indeed. In the shape-sound task, the Himba showed similar results to Westerners, that is, they overwhelmingly matched the rounded shape to the sound 'Bouba' and the sharper shape to the sound 'Kiki'. This is at first unsurprising, but a little thought shows quite how exciting this finding is. The Himba have developed in relative isolation from any Western influences which would otherwise have included television, film, radio and written language. Their perceptual world lacked any links between shapes that may denote language and sounds as our Western cultures do. This result showed that the sound-shape correspondence can indeed arise independent of sound-shape links readily available in the immediate culture. It follows that such sound-shape correspondences are part of our being human.

▶

◄　Other results show some cross-cultural differences, however. There was no consistency within the participant group, for instance, in matching sparkling and still water to the shapes, although in the West the majority match sparkling to the sharper shape and still to the smoother shape. The researchers suggest that this may be because of a lack of advertising imagery relating to water in the Himba environment – in the West sharper imagery and more angular branding are often associated with sparkling water, for instance. In the bitterness test the Himba matched bitterness to the softer shape, the opposite of what had been seen in the West. The researchers looked into the language used by the Himba, Otjiherero, as a possible explanation of this. In Otjiherero no word exists for bitter, but the word denoting sour had more vowels than the word for sweet and so would equate on a sound-shape link to the softer, more rounded shape. There are then, some cross-cultural similarities in cross-modal perception of this kind, but there are also some differences that this very rich and new vein of psychology is beginning to reveal.

CRITICAL PERIODS: THE ROLE OF EARLY EXPERIENCE

critical periods during which certain kinds of experiences must occur if perceptual abilities and the brain mechanisms that underlie them are to develop normally

The examples in the preceding section suggest that experience is essential for the development of perceptual abilities. For some aspects of perception, there are also **critical periods** during which certain kinds of experiences must occur if perceptual abilities and the brain mechanisms that underlie them are to develop normally. If a critical period passes without the experience occurring, it is too late to undo the deficit that results.

Earlier we saw that the visual cortex has feature detectors composed of neurons that respond only to lines at particular angles. What would happen if newborn animals grew up in a world in which they saw some angles but not others? In a classic experiment, Blakemore and Cooper (1970) created such a world for newborn kittens. The animals were raised in the dark except for a five-hour period each day, during which they were placed in round chambers that had either vertical or horizontal stripes on the walls. Figure 5.55a shows one of the kittens in a vertically striped chamber. A special collar prevented the kittens from seeing their own bodies while they were in the chamber, guaranteeing that they saw nothing but stripes.

When the kittens were five months old, Blakemore and Cooper presented them with bars of light at differing angles and used microelectrodes to test the electrical responses of individual feature-detector cells in their visual cortex. The results for the kittens raised in the vertically striped environment are shown in Figure 5.55b. As you can see, the kittens had no cells that fired in response to horizontal stimuli, resulting in visual impairments. They also acted as if they could not see a pencil when it was held in a horizontal position and moved up and down in front of them. However, as soon as the pencil was rotated to a vertical position, the animals began to follow it with their eyes as it was moved back and forth.

As you might expect, the animals raised in the horizontally striped environment showed the opposite effect. They had no feature detectors for vertical stimuli and did not seem to see them. Thus the cortical neurons of both groups of kittens developed in accordance with the stimulus features of their environments.

Other visual abilities also require early exposure to the relevant stimuli. Sugita (2004) raised infant monkeys in rooms illuminated with only monochromatic light. As adults, these monkeys were clearly deficient in colour perception. They had particular difficulty with colour constancy, being unable to recognize the same colours under changing levels of brightness.

Some perceptual abilities are influenced more than others by restricted stimulation. In other research, monkeys, chimpanzees and kittens were raised in an environment devoid of shapes. The animals distinguished differences in size, lightness

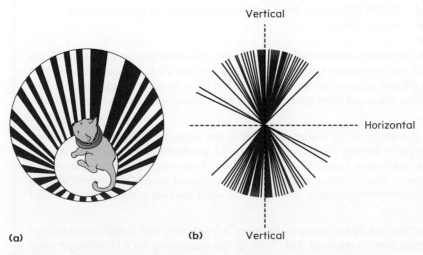

(a)　　　　**(b)**

FIGURE 5.55 Effects of visual deprivation.

(a) Kittens raised in a vertically striped chamber such as the one shown here lacked cortical cells that fired in response to horizontal stimuli. (b) The kittens' perceptual 'holes' are easily seen in this diagram, which shows the orientation angles that triggered nerve impulses from feature detectors.

and colour almost as well as normally reared animals do, but for the rest of their lives they performed poorly on more complex tasks, such as distinguishing different types of objects and geometric shapes (Riesen, 1965).

RESTORED SENSORY CAPACITY

Suppose it had been possible to restore Helen Keller's vision when she reached adulthood, what would she have seen? Could she have perceived visually the things that she had learned to identify through her other senses?

Unfortunately, it was not possible to provide Helen Keller with the miracle of restored vision. However, scientists have studied the experiences of other visually impaired people who acquired the ability to see later in life. For example, people born with cataracts grow up in a visual world without form. The clouded lenses of their eyes permit them to perceive light but not patterns or shapes. One such person was Virgil, who had been almost totally blind since childhood. He read Braille, enjoyed listening to sports on the radio and conversing with other people, and had adjusted quite well to his disability. At the urging of his fiancée, Virgil agreed to undergo surgery to remove his thick cataracts. The day after the surgery, his bandages were removed. Neurologist Oliver Sacks (1999) recounts what happened next.

> *There was light, there was colour, all mixed up, meaningless, a blur. Then out of the blur came a voice that said, 'Well?' Then, and only then . . . did he finally realize that this chaos of light and shadow was a face – and, indeed, the face of his surgeon . . . His retina and optic nerve were active, transmitting impulses, but his brain could make no sense of them.*   *(p. 132)*

Virgil was never able to adjust to his new visual world. He had to touch objects in order to identify them. He had to be led through his own house and would quickly become disoriented if he deviated from his path. Eventually, Virgil lost his sight once again. This time, however, he regarded his blindness as a gift, a release from a sighted world that was bewildering to him.

Virgil's experiences are characteristic of people who have their vision restored later in life. Marius von Senden (1960), compiled data on patients born with cataracts who were tested soon after their cataracts were surgically removed in adulthood. These people were immediately able to perceive figure–ground relations, to scan objects visually and to follow moving targets with their eyes, which suggests that such abilities are innate. However, they could not visually identify objects, such as eating utensils, that they were familiar with through touch; nor were they able to distinguish simple geometric figures without counting the corners or tracing the figures with their fingers.

After several weeks of training, the patients were able to identify simple objects by sight, but their perceptual constancies were very poor. Often they were unable to recognize the same shape in another colour, even though they could discriminate between colours. Years later, some patients could identify only a few of the faces of people they knew well. Many also had great difficulty judging distances. Apparently, no amount of subsequent experience could make up for their lack of visual experience during the critical period of childhood.

Gregory and Wallace (1963) had the extraordinary opportunity to study a man they referred to only as SB but who we now know as Sydney Bradford who had lost effective sight in both eyes at 10 months of age. Medical advances had been made since his birth in 1906, and two corneal grafts restored his vision. Gregory and Wallace ran a long series of tests with Bradford, and showed him illusions he would never had seen. Their findings were extremely interesting. For instance, he could not experience the reversal of the Necker cube (Figure 5.39). He amazed the researchers by successfully naming a magazine they had with them. The name of the magazine was:

Everybody's

The image on the magazine was of two musicians wearing striped pullovers but Bradford could not understand the image. Wallace and Gregory were interested to know how he could read the name of the magazine, and he said he had guessed. He had learned to understand the shapes of uppercase letters from wooden blocks when in school, but

had no understanding of lowercase letters. From the first two letters E and V he guessed the magazine was 'Everybody's', a popular publication at that time. Bradford had other interesting anomalies, for instance, he was unable to understand depth presented in two-dimensional art but he could judge the relative distances between items in his room as he had experienced this through touch. Tragically, he died only two years after his operation.

All of these – cross-cultural perceptual differences, animal studies involving visual deprivation and observations of congenitally impaired people whose vision has been restored – suggest that biological and experiential factors interact in complex ways. Some of our perceptual abilities are at least partially present at birth, but experience plays an important role in their normal development. How innate and experiential factors interact promises to be a continued focus of perception research. Perception is very much a biopsychological process whose mysteries are best explored by examining them from biological, psychological and environmental levels of analysis.

Focus 5.24 How do studies of restricted stimulation and restored vision illustrate the role of critical periods in perceptual development?

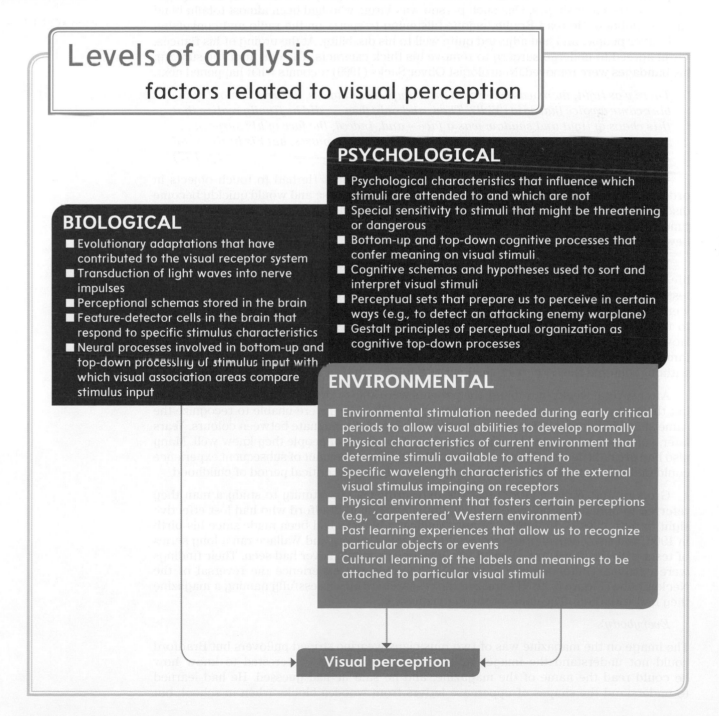

Levels of analysis
factors related to visual perception

PSYCHOLOGICAL

- Psychological characteristics that influence which stimuli are attended to and which are not
- Special sensitivity to stimuli that might be threatening or dangerous
- Bottom-up and top-down cognitive processes that confer meaning on visual stimuli
- Cognitive schemas and hypotheses used to sort and interpret visual stimuli
- Perceptual sets that prepare us to perceive in certain ways (e.g., to detect an attacking enemy warplane)
- Gestalt principles of perceptual organization as cognitive top-down processes

BIOLOGICAL

- Evolutionary adaptations that have contributed to the visual receptor system
- Transduction of light waves into nerve impulses
- Perceptional schemas stored in the brain
- Feature-detector cells in the brain that respond to specific stimulus characteristics
- Neural processes involved in bottom-up and top-down processing of stimulus input with which visual association areas compare stimulus input

ENVIRONMENTAL

- Environmental stimulation needed during early critical periods to allow visual abilities to develop normally
- Physical characteristics of current environment that determine stimuli available to attend to
- Specific wavelength characteristics of the external visual stimulus impinging on receptors
- Physical environment that fosters certain perceptions (e.g., 'carpentered' Western environment)
- Past learning experiences that allow us to recognize particular objects or events
- Cultural learning of the labels and meanings to be attached to particular visual stimuli

Visual perception

In review

■ Perceptual development involves both physical maturation and learning. Some perceptual abilities are innate or develop shortly after birth, whereas others require particular experiences early in life in order to develop.

■ Cultural factors can influence certain aspects of perception, including picture perception and susceptibility to illusions. However, many aspects of perception seem constant across cultures.

■ Visual-deprivation studies, manipulation of visual input and studies of restored vision have shown that the normal biological development of the perceptual system depends on certain sensory experiences at early periods of development.

Recommended Reading

CLASSIC

Gregory R. L (1970) *The intelligent eye*. London: Weidenfeld & Nicolson.

Gregory, R. L. (Ed.) (1987). *Oxford companion to the mind: 'Perception as hypotheses'*. Oxford: Oxford University Press.

Gescheider, G. (1997). *Psychophysics: The fundamentals* (3rd ed.). Mahwah, NJ: Lawrence Erlbaum.

CONTEMPORARY

Delavaux, C. (2013). *The museum of illusions: Optical tricks in art*. Munich: Prestel.

Harris, J. (2014). *Sensation and perception*. London: Sage Publications.

Moore, B. C. J. (2013). *An introduction to the psychology of hearing* (6th rev. ed.). Leiden: Brill.

Experience is never limited, and it is never complete; it is an immense sensibility, a kind of huge spider-web of the finest silken threads suspended in the chamber of consciousness, and catching every air-borne particle in its tissue.

Henry James

Consciousness

6

Chapter Outline

FIGURE 6.1 Perception without conscious awareness.

A rectangular slot was rotated to different angles on a series of trials. When asked simply to hold and tilt a rectangular card to match the slot's angle, DF performed poorly. She could not consciously recognize the orientation of the slot. Despite this, when asked to rapidly insert the card into the slot, as illustrated here, she performed well.

Source: Kosslyn, Stephen M., and Daniel N. Osherson, eds., *An Invitation to Cognitive Science, second edition, Volume 2: Visual Cognition*, figure: "Perception without conscious awareness", © 1995 Massachusetts Institute of Technology, by permission of The MIT Press.

> **visual agnosia** an inability to visually recognize objects

Three unrelated people, whom we will call Sondra, Katrien and Jason, sought treatment for an unusual problem: eating while asleep. They would rise from bed several times each night and sleepwalk to the kitchen. Sondra would

> *consume cat food or salt sandwiches, buttered cigarettes and odd concoctions prepared in a blender. . . . She frequently binged on large quantities of peanut butter, butter, salt and sugar. . . . Once she awakened while struggling to open a bottle of ammonia cleaning fluid, which she was prepared to drink on account of being thirsty.* (Schenck, Hurwitz, Bundlie, & Mahowald, 1991, p. 430)

While sleepwalking, Jason and Katrien also consumed odd foods (such as raw bacon), and sometimes Jason spoke coherently with his wife. Upon awakening, they could not remember their experiences, but empty packages and half-eaten food indicated that something was amiss.

After evaluation by sleep specialists, Sondra was treated with medication and Jason was referred to his primary physician. Neither drugs nor psychotherapy helped Katrien, so a new plan was tried: locking the kitchen door before turning in, putting the key in a hard-to-find location, and placing crackers and a pitcher of water by the bed. Usually, when Katrien wakes in the morning, the crackers and water are gone, and she has no memory of having consumed them (cf. Whyte & Kavey, 1990).

At age 34, DF lost consciousness and suffered brain damage from carbon monoxide exposure. As psychologist Melvin Goodale (2000) describes, when DF regained consciousness,

> *she was unable to recognize the faces of her relatives and friends or identify the visual form of common objects. In fact, she could not even tell the difference between simple geometric shapes such as a square and a triangle. At the same time, she had no difficulty recognizing people from their voices or identifying objects placed in her hands; her perceptual problems appeared to be exclusively visual.* (p. 367)

DF's condition is called **visual agnosia**, an inability to visually recognize objects. Visual agnosia is not blindness. DF can see, and brain imaging has revealed that her primary visual cortex is largely undamaged. Regions that are damaged have left her, according to Goodale (2000), without the ability to perceive the size, shape and orientation of objects.

But how, then, is DF able to walk across a room while easily avoiding obstacles? And if she cannot consciously perceive the difference in shape and size between, say, a spoon and a glass, how does she know to open her hand to the proper width to grasp objects? On a laboratory task, how is DF able to insert an object into a tilted rectangular slot when, just moments before, she could not consciously recognize the slot's orientation (see Figure 6.1)?

Sondra, Jason and Katrien's sleep-eating and DF's visual agnosia are clear departures from our normal state of conscious awareness. Yet their experiences contain features that are not as far removed from our daily existence as we might think.

How can someone be asleep yet find the kitchen and prepare food? Well, consider this: why don't you fall out of bed at night? You are not consciously aware of your many postural shifts when you are sound asleep, yet a part of you somehow knows where the edge of the bed is. And what of DF's ability, while awake, to avoid obstacles and grasp objects without conscious awareness of their shape or size? Again, consider this: have you ever lost concentration while driving? Suddenly you snap out of it, with no memory of the miles you have just driven. While you were consciously focused inward, some part of you – without conscious awareness – kept track of the road and controlled your hand movements at the wheel. The mysteries of consciousness range from normal waking states to sleep and dreams, drug-induced experiences, and beyond (Figure 6.2).

THE PUZZLE OF CONSCIOUSNESS

When psychology was founded in the late 1800s, its 'great project' was to unravel some of the puzzles of consciousness (Natsoulas, 1999). A resurgence of the cognitive and biological perspectives has led us to rethink long-standing conceptions about the 'mind' – which can

(a)

(b)

FIGURE 6.2 (a) During a Sufi religious ceremony in Istanbul, Turkey, whirling dervishes perform a spinning dance – a prayer in motion – that induces an altered state of consciousness. (b) Buddhists believe that meditation produces inner peace, facilitates insight and enlightenment, and opens the path to different dimensions of consciousness.

Source: (a) mehmetcan/Shutterstock; (b) ©iStock.com/Vicky_bennett

be defined as the part of a person that enables them to show an awareness of the world and their experiences, and as the faculty of consciousness. Rethinking these conceptions has led psychologists to address the puzzle of consciousness in a number of different ways.

CHARACTERISTICS OF CONSCIOUSNESS

Consciousness is often defined as our moment-to-moment awareness of ourselves and our environment. Among its characteristics, consciousness is:

- *subjective and private.* Other people cannot directly know what reality is for you, nor can you enter directly into their experience.

- *dynamic (ever changing).* We drift in and out of various states throughout each day. Moreover, though the stimuli of which we are aware constantly change, we typically experience consciousness as a continuously flowing stream of mental activity, rather than as disjointed perceptions and thoughts (James, 1950).

- *self-reflective and central to our sense of self.* The mind is aware of its own consciousness. Thus no matter what your awareness is focused on – a lovely sunset or an itch on your back – you can reflect on the fact that you are the one who is conscious of it.

- *intimately connected with the process of selective attention*, discussed in the next section. William James noted that 'the mind is at every stage a theatre of simultaneous possibilities. Consciousness consists in . . . the selection of some, and the suppression of the rest by the . . . agency of Attention' (1879, p. 13). **Selective attention** is the process that focuses awareness on some stimuli to the exclusion of others. If the mind is a theatre of mental activity, then consciousness reflects whatever is illuminated at the moment – the bright spot on the stage – and selective attention is the spotlight or mechanism behind it (Baars, 1997).

> **consciousness** our moment-to-moment awareness of ourselves and our environment

> **selective attention** the process that focuses awareness on some stimuli to the exclusion of others

MEASURING STATES OF CONSCIOUSNESS

Scientists who study consciousness must operationally define private inner states in terms of measurable responses. *Self-report measures* ask people to describe their inner experiences. They offer the most direct insight into a person's subjective experiences but are not always verifiable or possible to obtain. While asleep, most of us do not speak; nor can we fill out self-report questionnaires.

Behavioural measures record, among other things, performance on special tasks. By examining DF's performance on the card-slot task under different conditions (see Figure 6.1), researchers concluded that despite being unable to consciously perceive the slot's orientation, her brain nonetheless processed this information. Behavioural measures are objective, but they require us to infer the person's state of mind. Figure 6.3 illustrates another behavioural measure, where selfawareness is investigated. Plotnik de Waal and Reiss (2006) have shown this behaviour in the elephant, like humans and chimpanzee (Gallupp 1970), and other animals that live in complex and extended social groups. 'Happy' the elephant, marked on the head with a white cross, moved immediately to a mirror

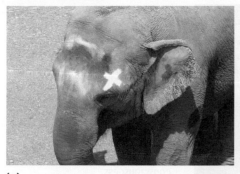

(a)   (b)

FIGURE 6.3 Touching a cross, or mark on the face as reflected in a mirror indicates that the person (or indeed elephant, as in the case of 'Happy' here) realises that the reflection is an image of themselves, suggesting self-awareness.

Source: (a) Plotnik, J.M., de Waal, F.B.M., and Reiss, D. Self-recognition in an Asian elephant, *Proceedings of the National Academy of Sciences USA*, volume 103, no.43, 7 November. Copyright (2006) National Academy of Sciences, U.S.A; (b) THIERRY BERROD, MONA LISA PRODUCTION/SCIENCE PHOTO LIBRARY

placed in her exercise yard and spent a significant amount of time touching the mark on her head with her trunk. Such self-recognition is also shown by pigeons (Toda & Watanabe, 2008) and magpies (Prior, Schwarz, & Güntürkün, 2008), showing that it is not restricted to mammals.

Physiological measures establish the correspondence between bodily processes and mental states. Through electrodes attached to the scalp, the electroencephalograph (EEG) measures brainwave patterns that reflect the ongoing electrical activity of large groups of neurons. Different patterns correspond to different states of consciousness, such as whether you are alert, relaxed or in light or deep sleep. Brain-imaging techniques allow scientists to more specifically examine brain regions and activity that underlie various mental states. Physiological measures cannot tell us what a person is experiencing subjectively, but they have been invaluable for probing the inner workings of the mind. The problem with consciousness is that it cannot be seen, it is difficult to describe, and quite how one thought leads to another, and how an opinion, image or a stimulus of some other kind can influence our behaviour is not easily described at all. Consider the issue of brain imaging, for instance. A researcher presenting a picture of a politician to a person in an MRI scanner will be rewarded with a brain scan. Interpreting what it was about the image that generated the activation seen in the scan is neither simple nor possible. Yes, portions of the brain that deal with visual images, perhaps familiar or famous faces may have responded, but the person's political opinion, memories of past experiences as a once politically active student, or the fact that the politician looks a little like the person's great aunt who is expected for dinner at the weekend will not be coded in the scan. In short, our consciousness cannot be 'read'. As Papanicolaou (1998) points out, no one currently would be likely to insist that statements such as 'the subject just saw this red nose, then he felt an itch on his forehead and, while raising his hand to scratch, a fleeting image of another red nose went through his mind's eye' (p. 129), could possibly be correct. Functional imaging techniques cannot presently accomplish feats such as these, although whether this may be possible in the future is open to debate.

> **Focus 6.1** Describe the basic characteristics of consciousness. How are states of consciousness measured?

LEVELS OF CONSCIOUSNESS

Much of what occurs within your brain is beyond conscious access. You do not consciously perceive the brain processes that lull you to sleep, wake you or regulate your body temperature. You are aware of your thoughts but not of how your brain creates them. What else lies outside of conscious awareness?

The Freudian Viewpoint

In 1900 Sigmund Freud (1953) proposed that the human mind consists of three levels of awareness. The *conscious* mind contains thoughts and perceptions of which we are currently aware. *Preconscious* mental events are outside current awareness but can

easily be recalled under certain conditions. For instance, you may not have thought about a friend for years, but when someone mentions your friend's name, you become aware of pleasant memories. *Unconscious* events cannot be brought into conscious awareness under ordinary circumstances. Freud proposed that some unconscious content – such as unacceptable sexual and aggressive urges, traumatic memories and threatening emotional conflicts – is *repressed*; that is, it is kept out of conscious awareness because it would arouse anxiety, guilt or other negative emotions.

Behaviourists roundly criticized Freud's ideas. After all, they sought to explain behaviour without invoking conscious mental processes, much less unconscious ones. Cognitive psychologists and many contemporary psychodynamic psychologists also take issue with specific aspects of Freud's theory. As psychodynamic psychologist Drew Westen (1998b) notes, 'Many aspects of Freudian theory are indeed out of date, and they should be. Freud died in 1939, and he has been slow to undertake further revisions' (p. 333), although the non-scientific nature of Freud's work has been defended by some, including Grünbaum (1986), who said that strong statements and claims made by Freud for the power of psychoanalysis lend themselves strongly to testing, and attempts at disproving them. If a more suitable form of therapy is available, then the proposal that psychotherapy is the most appropriate form of therapy has been disproved. In this way Freud's theory can be seen as following a 'scientific' method of sorts. In addition to this, research supports Freud's general premise that unconscious processes can affect behaviour. Silverman has used a method called SPA (subliminal psychodynamic activation) to investigate psychoanalytic theory. A phrase is presented subliminally to a participant and their performance on a task is measured. Silverman found that presenting male dart throwers with the sentence 'Beating dad is OK' drew better performance than the sentence 'Beating dad is wrong' leading him to conclude that the oedipal wish to compete with and beat the father figure is activated and sanctioned by the 'Beating dad is OK' sentence. Additional work has led Silverman and Weinberger (1985) to conclude that the sentence 'Mommy and I are one' is extremely important as it taps an unconscious desire for a state where the person finds him or herself at one with their mother figure. Silverman and Weinberger say that fulfilling this wish can influence the person in some way. The researchers reported a reduction in the symptoms experienced by a range of clinical groups, including schizophrenics and neurotics – evidence, say the researchers, for the role of the subconscious in modifying our behaviour.

The Cognitive Viewpoint

Cognitive psychologists reject the notion of an unconscious mind driven by instinctive urges and repressed conflicts. Rather, they view conscious and unconscious mental life as complementary forms of information processing that work in harmony (Reisberg, 2001). To illustrate, consider how we perform everyday tasks.

Many activities, such as studying, require **controlled (conscious or explicit) processing**, the conscious use of attention and effort. Other activities involve **automatic (unconscious or implicit) processing** and can be performed without conscious awareness or effort.

Automatic processing occurs most often when we carry out routine actions or very well-learned tasks, particularly under familiar circumstances (Ouellette & Wood, 1998). Learning to ride a bicycle and type both involve controlled processing; at first, a lot of conscious attention to what you are doing is needed as you learn. With practice, performance becomes more automatic and certain brain areas involved in conscious thought become less active (Jansma, Ramsey, Slagter, & Kahn, 2001). Through years of practice, athletes and musicians are able to execute highly complex skills with a minimum of conscious thought.

Automatic processing, however, has a key disadvantage because it can reduce our chances of finding new ways to approach problems (Langer, 1989). Controlled processing is slower than automatic processing, but it is more flexible and open to change. Still, many well-learned behaviours seem to be performed faster and better when our mind is on autopilot, with controlled processing taking a back seat. Tasks ranging from putting a golf ball to playing video games, in experiments suggest that too much self-focused thinking

controlled (conscious, or explicit) processing the conscious use of attention and effort

automatic (unconscious, or implicit) processing can be performed without conscious awareness or effort

Focus 6.2 Contrast the psychodynamic and cognitive views of the mind, and controlled versus automatic processing.

can damage task performance and cause people to make a mistake under pressure (Beilcock & Carr, 2001).

Automatic processing also facilitates **divided attention**, the capacity to attend to and perform more than one activity at the same time. We can talk while we walk, type as we read, and so on. Yet divided attention has limits and is more difficult when two tasks require similar mental resources. For example, we cannot fully attend to separate messages delivered simultaneously through two earphones, something we will discuss in more detail in the section that follows.

divided attention the capacity to attend to and perform more than one activity at the same time

UNCONSCIOUS PERCEPTION AND INFLUENCE

The concept of unconscious information processing is widely accepted among psychologists today, but this was not always the case. It has taken painstaking research to demonstrate that stimuli can be perceived without conscious awareness and in turn can influence how we behave or feel. Let us look at some examples.

Visual Agnosia

Studies of people with brain damage can provide scientists with important insights into how the mind works. Recall that DF, the woman with visual agnosia, could not consciously perceive the shape, size or orientation of objects, yet she had little difficulty performing a card-insertion task and avoiding obstacles when she walked across a room. In order to perform these tasks so easily, her brain must have been processing accurate information about the shape, size and angles of objects. And if she professed no conscious awareness of these properties, then this information processing must have occurred at an unconscious level (Goodale, 2000).

There are many types of visual agnosia. For example, people with *prosopagnosia* can visually recognize objects but not faces. When some of these patients look in the mirror, they do not recognize their own faces. Despite this lack of conscious awareness, in laboratory tests the patients display different patterns of brain activity, autonomic arousal and eye movements when they look at familiar rather than unfamiliar faces (Bauer & Verfaellie, 1988). In other words, their brain is recognizing and responding to the difference between familiar and unfamiliar stimuli, but this recognition does not reach the level of conscious awareness.

In 1987, Glyn Humphreys and Jane Ridoch, two researchers from London, published an important case study of their patient 'John', or HJA as he was also known in the many papers that preceded their book, and followed it. HJA's visual agnosia began with a stroke. Objects with which he was previously very familiar seemed strange to him. His wife Iris was unrecognizable to him and even his own image in a mirror appeared as a stranger. The map of HJA's world was also confused because of this inability to recognize his environment, and he got lost very easily, often within very familiar surroundings such as his own house. What makes the case all the more interesting is that HJA was able to recognize objects by touch, and by sound. It seemed that removing the visual component of an object's identity removed, or helped with, his problem. Even though he did not recognize things, when Humphreys and his co-workers asked him to copy the item, HJA could do so very well. His memory for objects was, then, undamaged, and he had a very good knowledge of how objects should appear and behave. Both of these skills are very important to us when perceiving items. HJA was unable to recognize objects, but he was able to see them. There are, however, situations where some processing of objects is available even though they cannot be seen at all. This is true in the case of blindsight.

Blindsight

People with agnosia are not blind, but those with a rare condition called **blindsight** are blind in part of their visual field yet in special tests respond to stimuli in that field despite reporting that they cannot see those stimuli (Kentridge, Heywood, & Weiskrantz, 2004). For example, owing to left-hemisphere damage from an accident or disease, a blindsight patient may be blind in the right half of the visual field. A stimulus (e.g., a horizontal line)

blindsight blind in part of their visual field yet in special tests respond to stimuli in that field despite reporting that they cannot see those stimuli

is flashed on a screen so that it appears in one of several locations within the patient's blind visual field. On trial after trial, the patient reports seeing nothing, but when asked to point to where the stimulus was, she or he guesses at rates much higher than chance. On other tasks, different colours or photographs of facial expressions are projected to the blind visual field. Again, despite saying that they cannot see anything, patients guess the colour or facial expression at rates well above chance. On some tasks, guessing accuracy may reach 80–100% (Lau & Passingham, 2007).

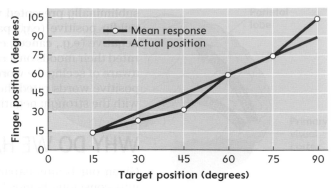

FIGURE 6.4 Blindsight.

This graph shows the results of an experiment whereby an item was presented in the damaged visual field of DB, a blindsight sufferer.

Source: Data redrawn from Weiskrantz et al., 1974.

The first study was a patient identified by Weiskrantz as DB, who had had his occipital cortex removed because of a tumour. Amazingly, DB showed very strong performance in discriminating things in his visual field. He could tell different orientations of things from one another, and if something was moving or not. All this without being able to 'see' the items (Figure 6.4; Weiskrantz, Warrington, Sanders, & Marshall, 1974). DB was the focus of many studies in the following years, providing Weiskrantz and his UK-based teams with much invaluable insight into the condition. Blindsight was further differentiated into Type 1 blindsight and Type 2 blindsight (Weiskrantz, 2002). With Type 1 blindsight, discriminations are possible in the 'blind' area but the person feels nothing at all. With Type 2 blindsight, rapid motion or changes in orientation are experienced as some kind of 'feeling'. DB continues to work with researchers looking into his condition, and work from Trevethan, Sahraie and Weiskrantz (2004) is continuing this by asking whether the properties of blindsight are different, or in some way superior to 'normal' sight. Their research has shown that DB is actually better at discriminating between different objects and images in his blind field than in his sighted field. This rich vein of research has produced many important and fascinating results and it looks set to continue.

Priming

Here is a simple task. Starting with the two letters *ho* _____ (this is called a *word stem*), what is the first word that comes to your mind? Was it *hot, how, home, house, hope, hole* or *honest*? Clearly, you had these and many other words to choose from.

Now imagine that just before completing this word stem you had looked at a screen on which the word *hose* (or perhaps a picture of a hose) was presented *subliminally* (it was displayed so rapidly or weakly that it was below your threshold for conscious perception).

Suppose we conduct an experiment with many participants and many word stems (e.g., *ho* _____, *gr* _____, *ma* _____, etc.). We find that compared to people who are not exposed to subliminal words such as *hose, gripe* and *manage*, people who are subliminally exposed are more likely to complete the word stems with those particular words. This provides evidence of a process called **priming**: exposure to a stimulus influences (i.e., primes) how you subsequently respond to that same or another stimulus. Thus even without consciously seeing *hose*, the subliminal word or image primes people's response to *ho* _____.

Subliminal stimuli can prime more than our responses to word stems. For example, when people are shown photographs of a person, the degree to which they evaluate that person positively or negatively is influenced by whether they have first been subliminally exposed to pleasant images (e.g., smiling babies) or unpleasant images (e.g., a face on fire; Krosnick, Betz, Jussim, & Lynn, 1992). Likewise, being subliminally exposed to words with an aggressive theme causes people to judge another person's ambiguous behaviour as being more aggressive (Todorov & Bargh, 2002).

priming exposure to a stimulus influences (i.e., primes) how you subsequently respond to that same or another stimulus

Focus 6.3 How do visual agnosia, blindsight and priming illustrate unconscious processing?

The Emotional Unconscious

Psychodynamic psychologists writing now tell us that emotional and motivational processes also operate unconsciously and influence behaviour (Westen, 1998a). To illustrate this consider the following possibility. Have you ever wondered why you may be in a good or bad mood? It might be because of immediate and very recent experiences of your environment of which you are not consciously aware. In one study, college students were

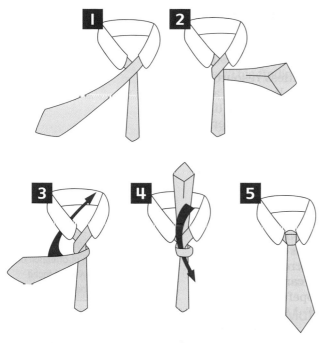

FIGURE 6.10 Learning to tie the perfect knot can be an annoying and time-consuming process. Diagrams like these are supposed to make it a little easier. Practice makes perfect.

Source: Reprinted with permission of mens-ties.com

slower for letters falling away from the letter to which they were attending, suggesting that the spotlight could indeed be narrowed or widened.

Objects or Locations?

The spotlight model and the zoom-lens modification suggest that attention focuses on locations rather than objects. Posner (1980) had participants hold their attention on a spot in a screen, a fixation point. Targets then appeared to the left or the right, and participants indicated left or right accordingly. Arrows could precede the targets either correctly or incorrectly indicating the position in which the target would appear. Responses were faster if preceded by correct arrows, indicating the ability to attend to locations as the participants managed to shift their attention to the left or right as indicated by the arrow. However, other work suggests that we may attend to objects rather than regions. O'Craven, Downing, & Kanwisher (1999) presented participants with two overlaid, transparent images of a face and a house. One of the objects moved slightly. Participants were asked either to attend to the stationary object, or maintain attention on the slightly moving object. Both were in the same place, but one moved slightly. It follows that if attention was location based both stimuli would need to be attended to, as they shared the same spatial location. If object based, attention could be directed to either of the stimuli. The level of attention applied was 'measured' with fMRI. Participants were scanned while attending in different conditions and showed more activity on the object condition rather than the location condition, leading the researchers to conclude that attention was object based.

Automaticity - practice makes perfect

The more we do a task, the less conscious attention we need to apply to it.

There are lots of examples of how this is the case. Tying a complicated tie-knot (Figure 6.10), juggling and riding a bicycle, not necessarily all at the same time, are all good examples. Both require skills that feel entirely unnatural and hopelessly out of our reach until perseverance allows us to finally manage to stumble through them. Before we know it we are cycling, or juggling, as if we had always done it. We no longer need to pay quite as much attention to which end goes where to tie the perfect knot. You may well have the experience of travelling a familiar route, perhaps to university, or from home to the local shops. The familiarity with the task makes it automatic, and you may well have experienced arriving at your destination having navigated busy and dangerous roads but with no memory at all of how you did it. This is partly a memory issue, but **automaticity** explains a good deal of it as far as the allocation of attention is concerned.

automaticity reached when a task no longer requires conscious control

 Chapter 8, Page 352

Shiffrin and Sneider (1977) describe an automatic process as related to memory. They say that our memory processes (see **Chapter 8**) are capacity limited. Shiffrin and Sneider said that automatic tasks are capacity free. They are not limited by memory or attention limitations and as such, a number of them can go on in parallel, in the background if you like, while we carry out other tasks. Controlled processes on the other hand are capacity limited, and take place in series. That is to say, one at a time. Controlled processing is carefully under our conscious control and as such is flexible, dynamic and changeable.

Automatic processing, by its very nature, will always happen automatically. When the correct incidence of stimulus is present the processing will begin automatically. Similarly, with every well-practised and automatic task, changes are very hard to make. They become second nature. Those of us who have been driving for many years know that we have habits that are hard to change, but they are part of a now very automatic process and, as such, breaking them will mean relearning the process of which they are part. This

is extremely difficult. A well-used, but extremely good example of this is the process of reading. The most famous example here is the Stroop test (Stroop, 1935). Consider the stimuli in Figure 6.11. Calling out the colours of the panels in the left-hand section from top to bottom as fast as possible is very simple. Calling out the colours of words in the right-hand panel from top to bottom is much trickier. This is because reading is an automatic process. You cannot help reading the words. The reason you find this difficult is because you can read the words and so you must.

DIVIDED ATTENTION

Up until now we have described selective attention. **Divided attention**, on the other hand, describes how we can do more than one thing at once, often quite successfully. It may be that both, or one, of the tasks have become automatic, such as driving and talking at the same time. How successful we are at completing tasks simultaneously depends on a number of things, including how practised we are at them, and the nature of the tasks themselves. The dual-task paradigm can be used to investigate divided attention, in which participants carry out two tasks simultaneously and performance on one or both is recorded.

> **divided attention** the ability to respond, seemingly simultaneously, to multiple tasks or demands

Rehearsal, Practice and Difficulty

The more we rehearse the better we get. Repeating tasks over and over encourages a move from controlled to automatic processing. Developing skills through practice reduces the errors on that task. Dual-task performance improves as skills develop with practice. The difficulty of the tasks also influences performance, of course. Two easy tasks combined will result in fewer errors than two difficult tasks. Difficulty is, of course, entirely subjective. Replacing the tiny hands on a wristwatch is not terribly difficult to a trained horologist but to mere mortals it is very difficult indeed. Navon and Gopher (1979) said that the difficulty of a task will depend on two things. Those tasks that are 'data-limited' are difficult because of the lack of information supplied. For instance, predicting what the weather will be like tomorrow armed only with some seaweed will be tricky. The way to do it would be to note how the seaweed behaved every hour or so and to make a note of the weather. You could then see if there was any pattern in the appearance of the seaweed at times before it rained perhaps. Data-driven tasks are largely free of the demands of cognitive resources. Performance on them is limited by the amount of information we have to complete the task, not necessarily how clever or skilled we are. The seaweed on my windowsill does not, for instance, get in the way of my writing this paragraph. I can go on with the task in hand as I wait for more data to become available. Those tasks that are resource limited are hard because they require considerable cognitive demands. For instance, completing a book chapter while listening to a play on the radio is difficult because both take up a certain amount of cognitive capacity. Where resources are limited we can improve performance by shifting them from one task to another. Removing the demands required to follow the narrative of a play by turning off the radio makes writing a tricky passage much easier.

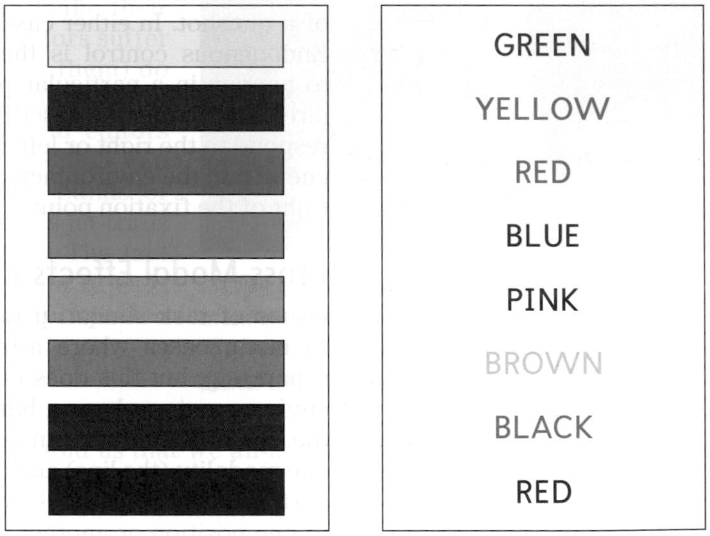

| GREEN |
| YELLOW |
| RED |
| BLUE |
| PINK |
| BROWN |
| BLACK |
| RED |

FIGURE 6.11 After Stroop (1935). Read the colours of the boxes in the left-hand panel from top to bottom as fast as you can. Now read the colours in which the words in the right-hand panel are written from top to bottom as fast as you can – this is harder because you cannot help automatically reading the words.

Similarity

Another thing that influences performance on dual tasks is the similarity of the tasks involved. This is related to the idea of modality in perception and attention. Tasks requiring auditory attention arrive at the auditory modality and are dealt with accordingly. Those requiring visual attention are similarly dealt with within the visual

FIGURE 6.13 Circadian rhythms.

(a) Changes in our core body temperature, (b) levels of melatonin in our blood, and (c) degrees of alertness are a few of the bodily functions that follow a cyclical 24 hour pattern called a *circadian rhythm*. Humans also have longer and shorter biological cycles, such as the 28-day female menstrual cycle and a roughly 90-minute brain activity cycle during sleep.

Source: Adapted from Monk, Folkard and Wedderburn, 1996.

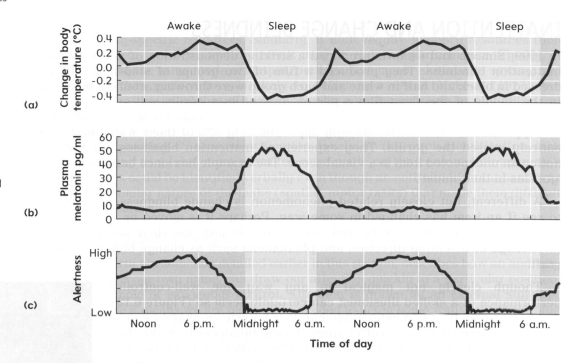

KEEPING TIME: BRAIN AND ENVIRONMENT

As Figure 6.14 shows, most circadian rhythms are regulated by the brain's **suprachiasmatic nuclei (SCN)**, located in the hypothalamus. These SCN neurons have a genetically programmed cycle of activity and inactivity, functioning like a biological clock. They link to the tiny pineal gland, which secretes **melatonin**, a hormone that has a relaxing effect on the body. The SCN neurons become active during the daytime and reduce the pineal gland's secretion of melatonin, raising body temperature and heightening alertness. At night SCN neurons are inactive, allowing melatonin levels to increase and promoting relaxation and sleepiness (Zhdanova & Wurtman, 1997).

Our circadian clock is biological, but environmental cues such as the day–night cycle help keep SCN neurons on a 24-hour schedule. Your eyes have neural connections to the SCN, and after a night's sleep, the light of day increases SCN activity and helps reset your 24-hour biological clock. What would happen, then, if you lived in a laboratory or an underground cave without clocks and could not tell whether it was day or night outside? In experiments in which people did just that, most participants drifted into a natural wake–sleep cycle, called a *free-running circadian rhythm*, which is longer than 24 hours (Mills, Minors, & Waterhouse, 1974).

For decades, research suggested that our free-running rhythm was about 25 hours long. In these studies, however, the bright room lights that participants kept on artificially lengthened their circadian rhythms. Under more controlled conditions, the free-running rhythm averages around 24.2 hours (Lavie, 2000). Yet even this small deviation from the 24-hour day is significant. If you were to follow your free-running rhythm, two months from now you would be going to bed at noon and waking at midnight.

Early Birds and Night Owls

Circadian rhythms also influence our tendency to be a morning person or a night person (Duffy, Rimmer, & Czeisler, 2001). Compared to night people ('night owls'), morning people ('early birds') go to bed and rise earlier, and their body temperature, blood pressure and alertness peak earlier in the day. As Figure 6.15 shows, a study of university students found that early birds are more likely than night owls to enrol in and perform better in early (8 a.m.) classes.

---

suprachiasmatic nuclei (SCN) regulate most circadian rhythms

melatonin hormone that has a relaxing effect on the body

Focus 6.8 How do the brain and environment regulate circadian rhythms? What are free-running circadian rhythms?

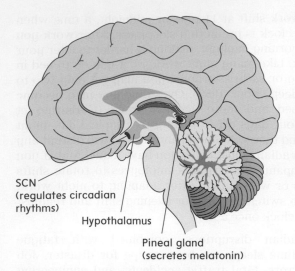

FIGURE 6.14 The master circadian clock.

The suprachiasmatic nuclei (SCN) are the brain's master circadian clock. Neurons in the SCN have a genetically programmed cycle of activity and inactivity, but daylight and darkness help regulate this cycle. The optic nerve links our eyes to the SCN, and SCN activity affects the pineal gland's secretion of melatonin. In turn, melatonin influences other brain systems governing alertness and sleepiness.

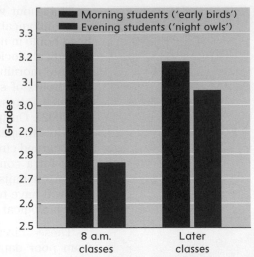

FIGURE 6.15 Course grades of early birds and night owls.

In a study of 454 university students, 'night owls' struggled in their 8 a.m. classes, as compared with 'early birds'. In later classes the two groups performed more similarly. Stated differently, early birds did slightly better in their earliest class than in later classes, whereas night owls did better in their later classes rather than their earliest class.

Source: Based on Guthrie, Ash and Bendapudi, 1995.

Cultures may differ in their overall tendency towards 'morningness'. Carlla Smith and her co-workers (2002) used questionnaires to measure the degree of morningness among college students from six countries. They predicted and found that students from Colombia, India and Spain – regions with warmer annual climates – exhibited greater morningness than students from England, the USA and the Netherlands (Table 6.1). In addition to this, a person may inherit the tendency and may be influenced by their physiology to be a morning or evening person (Vink, Groot, Derkhof, & Boomsma, 2001). As with many things, both nature and nurture are likely to play a role in this aspect of a person's behaviour.

ENVIRONMENTAL DISRUPTIONS OF CIRCADIAN RHYTHMS

Our circadian rhythms are vulnerable to disruption by both sudden and gradual environmental changes. Jet lag is a sudden circadian disruption caused by flying across several time zones in one day. Flying east, you lose hours from your day; flying west extends your day to more than 24 hours. Jet lag, which often causes insomnia and decreased alertness, is a significant concern for business people, athletes, airline crews and others who frequently travel across many time zones (Ariznavarreta et al., 2002). The body naturally adjusts about one hour or less per day to time-zone changes. Typically, people adjust faster when flying west, presumably because lengthening the travel day is more compatible with our natural free-running circadian cycle.

Night-shift work, affecting millions of full-time workers around the globe, is the most problematic circadian disruption for society. Imagine having to begin

TABLE 6.1 Morningness among college students from six countries

Country	Morningness score
Colombia	42.4
India	39.4
Spain	33.9
England	31.6
USA	31.4
Netherlands	30.1

Note: Scores can range from 13 ('extreme evening type') to 55 ('extreme morning type'). Source: Smith et al., 2002.

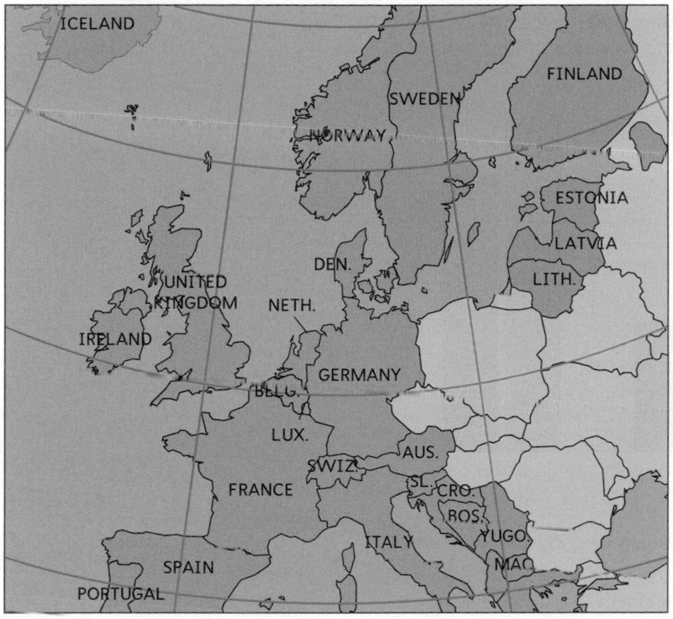

FIGURE 6.16 The latitude at which you live may influence levels of SAD, but other factors need to be considered, including a possible genetic influence, climate and your sociocultural environment.

Focus 6.9 Describe environmental disruptions of circadian rhythms.

seasonal affective disorder (SAD) a cyclic tendency to become psychologically depressed during certain seasons of the year

Focus 6.10 Describe ways to minimize circadian disruptions involved in jet lag, night-shift work and SAD.

an eight-hour work shift at 11 p.m. or midnight, a time when your biological clock is promoting sleepiness. After work you head home in morning daylight, making it harder to alter your biological clock. Like many night workers, if you go to bed in the late morning or early afternoon, you may get only two to four hours of sleep (Kogi, 1985). Over time you may become fatigued, stressed and more accident-prone (Garbarino et al., 2002). On your days off, reverting to a typical day–night schedule to spend time with family and friends will disrupt any hard-earned circadian adjustments you have made. And, if you work for a company that requires employees to rotate shifts every few days or weeks, then after adapting to night work, you will have to switch to a day or evening shift and readjust your biological clock once again.

These circadian disruptions, combined with fatigue from poor daytime sleep, can be a recipe for disaster. Job performance errors, fatal traffic accidents, and engineering and industrial disasters peak between midnight and 6 a.m. (cf. Folkard & Tucker, 2003). In some cases, night operators at nuclear power plants have been found asleep at the controls. On-the-job sleepiness is also a major concern among long-distance truck drivers, airline crews, doctors and nurses, and others who work at night.

Seasonal affective disorder (SAD) is a cyclic tendency to become psychologically depressed during certain seasons of the year. Some people become depressed in spring and summer; however, in the vast majority of cases, SAD begins in autumn or winter, when there is less daylight, and then lifts in spring (Rosenthal & Wehr, 1992). The circadian rhythms of SAD sufferers may be particularly sensitive to light, so as sunrises occur later in winter, the daily onset time of their circadian clocks may be *delayed* to an unusual degree, altering the beginning time of the person's 'biological' morning. On late-autumn and winter mornings, when many people must rise for work and school in darkness, SAD sufferers remain in sleepiness mode long after the morning alarm clock sounds.

Where you live may influence SAD. Mersch, Middendorp, Bouhuys, Beersma and van den Hoofdakker (1999) suggested that the prevalence of seasonal affective disorder increases in the USA, with latitude. The higher the latitude (Figure 6.16), the fewer hours of daylight. This relationship was not seen in Europe, although there is some disagreement in the literature (Eagles, 2003). It seems that climate, genetics and sociocultural context all influence SAD.

⊚ Applying psychological science

OUTSMARTING JET LAG, NIGHT-WORK DISRUPTIONS AND WINTER DEPRESSION

Circadian research provides important insights on the nature of consciousness. It also offers several treatments for circadian disruptions affecting millions of people.

CONTROLLING EXPOSURE TO LIGHT

Reducing jet lag

When you fly east across time zones, your body's internal clock falls behind the time at your destination. This alters the onset time of your 'biological' morning. Exposure to outdoor light in the morning – and avoiding light late in the day – moves the circadian clock forward and helps it catch up to local time. (Think of morning light as jump-starting your circadian clock at a time when you would be asleep back home.) Flying west, your body clock moves ahead of local time. So, to reduce jet lag, you want to delay your circadian cycle by avoiding bright light in the morning and exposing yourself

to light in the afternoon or early evening. These are general rules, but the specific timing and length of exposure to light depend on the number of time zones crossed (Houpt, Boulos, Moore, & Martin, 1996). For jet travellers, spending time outside (even on cloudy days) is the easiest way to get the needed exposure to light.

Adjusting to night work

When night employees go home after work, their circadian adjustment can be increased by (1) keeping the bedroom dark and quiet to foster daytime sleep and (2) maintaining a schedule of daytime sleep even during days off (Boulos, 1998). Day sleepers are advised to install light-blocking window shades, unplug the phone and use earplugs. Wearing sunglasses is also recommended when the night-worker travels home in the morning. Smith and Eastman (2008) used a carefully designed procedure where dark glasses and lighter glasses were worn by participants to control light received, help simulate the shift patterns, and also to help generate a carefully controlled sleep pattern. Carefully controlling the delivery of bright light meant that even though participants were on shifts, sleep on days off, and performance on cognitive tasks could be helped to become relatively normal. With careful light interventions shift workers were able to maintain their daytime interactions with family and friends on their days off.

Treating SAD

Many experts believe that phototherapy can be useful in treating the effects of winter depression and winter SAD. This involves properly timed exposure to specially prescribed bright artificial lights (Rosenthal and Benton, 2013). Several hours of daily phototherapy, especially in the early morning, can shift circadian rhythms by as much as two to three hours per day (Neumeister, 2004). The fact that phototherapy effectively treats SAD is the strongest evidence that SAD is triggered by winter's lack of sunlight rather than by its colder temperatures (Figure 6.17).

FIGURE 6.17 For many people, the depression from SAD can be reduced by daily exposure to bright fluorescent lights.

Source: © iStock.com/Rocky89.

MELATONIN TREATMENT: USES AND CAUTIONS

The hormone melatonin is a key player in the brain's circadian clock. Melatonin also exists in pill or capsule form; it is a prescription drug in some countries and is unavailable to the public in others. In the USA it is a non-prescription dietary supplement. Depending on when it is taken, oral melatonin can shift some circadian cycles forward or backward by as much as 30 to 60 minutes per day of use. Melatonin treatment has been used with some success to decrease jet lag, help employees adapt to night-shift work and alleviate SAD (Arendt, Skene, Middleton, Lockley, & Deacon, 1997). For shiftworkers, it may indeed be beneficial to take melatonin just before going to bed after a night shift. However, if the worker is working shifts, that is, three night shifts followed by two day shifts, then delaying the phase of the circadian rhythm in this way may cause additional problems for the worker when moving from night to day shift.

But there is reason for caution. Doses of 0.1 to 0.5 milligrams are often sufficient to produce circadian shifts, but tablet doses are often 3 to 5 milligrams, producing melatonin levels in the blood that are over 10 times the normal concentration (Sack, Hughes, Edgar, & Lewy, 1997). Melatonin use is supervised during research, but individuals who self-administer it may do themselves more harm than good. Taking melatonin at the wrong time can backfire and make circadian adjustments more difficult. Daytime use may decrease alertness (Graw, Werth, Kraeuchi, Gutzwiller, Cajochen, & Wirz-Justice, 2001; Chellappa, Steiner, Blattner, Oelhafen, Götz, & Cajochen, 2011). Some experts are also concerned that millions of people are using melatonin tablets as a nightly sleeping aid even though possible side effects of long-term use have not been adequately studied.

It is not only melatonin that needs to be administered at the correct time to optimize the wanted effects, and limit the unwanted ones. Both light and melatonin follow similar *phase-responses*. Their actions are to advance or delay the phase of the rhythm depending on when they are administered. If melatonin is taken in the person's 'biological' morning, the circadian rhythm is delayed. If it is taken in the person's 'biological' evening, the phase of the circadian rhythm is advanced. The effects of bright light are the opposite. If bright light is administered in the 'biological' morning, the phase of the circadian rhythm is advanced, if administered in the 'biological' evening the phase is delayed.

REGULATING ACTIVITY SCHEDULES

Properly timed physical exercise may help shift the circadian clock (Mistlberger, Antle, Glass, & Miller, 2000). For example, compared with merely staying up later than normal, exercising when you normally go to bed may help push back your circadian clock, as you would want to do when flying west (Baehr, 2001). To reduce jet lag, you can also begin synchronizing your biological clock to the new time zone in advance. To do so, adjust your sleep and eating schedules by 30 minutes to 1 hour per day, starting several days before you leave. Schedule management can also apply to night-shift work. For workers on rotating shifts, circadian disruptions can be reduced by a forward-rotating shift schedule – moving from day to evening to night shifts – rather than a schedule that rotates backward from day to night to evening shifts (Knauth, 1996). The forward schedule takes advantage of our free-running circadian rhythms. When work shifts change, it is easier to extend the waking day than to compress it.

FIGURE 6.20 Cycling through a
night's sleep.

This graph shows a record of a night's
sleep. The REM stages are shown in blue.
People typically average four to five REM
periods during the night, and these tend
to become longer as the night wears on.
On this night, the REM 5 period has been
cut short because the person awakened.

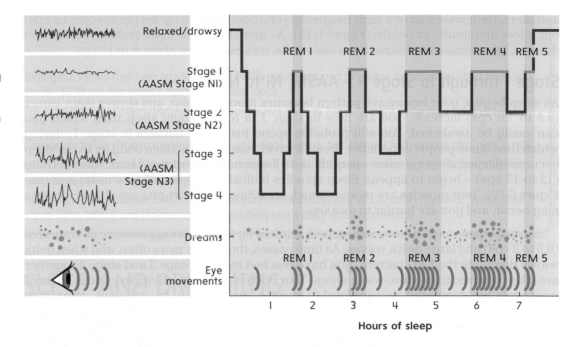

Moreover, falling asleep is not just a matter of turning off brain systems that keep us awake. There are separate systems that turn on and actively promote sleep.

Certain areas at the base of the forebrain (called the *basal forebrain*) and within the brain stem regulate our falling asleep. Other brain stem areas – including where the reticular formation passes through the pons (called the *pontine reticular formation*) – play a key role in regulating REM sleep (Hobson, Pace-Schott, & Stickgold, 2000). This region contains neurons that periodically activate other brain systems, each of which controls a different aspect of REM sleep, such as eye movement and muscular paralysis.

Brain images taken during REM sleep reveal intense activity in limbic system structures, such as the amygdala that regulate emotions – a pattern that may reflect the emotional nature of many REM sleep dreams (Figure 6.21). The primary motor cortex is active, but its signals for movement are blocked and do not reach our limbs. Association areas near

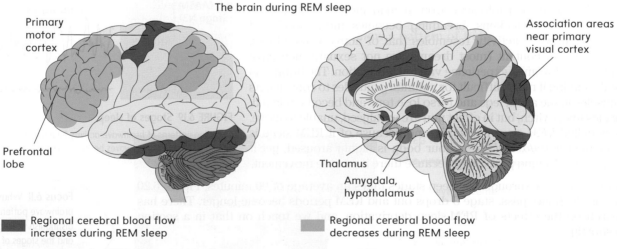

FIGURE 6.21 Brain activity during REM sleep.

As compared to the waking brain, during REM sleep several brain regions display markedly decreased (blue) and increased (red) activity. Note the decreased activation in certain prefrontal lobe regions and increased activity in parts of the amygdala and hypothalamus, thalamus, primary motor cortex, and association areas near the primary visual cortex in the occipital lobe.

Source: Adapted from Schwartz and Maquet, 2002.

the primary visual cortex are active, which may reflect the processing of visual dream images. In contrast, decreased activity occurs in regions of the prefrontal cortex involved in high-level mental functions, such as planning and logical analysis. This may indicate that our sleeping mind does not monitor and organize its mental activity as carefully as when awake, enabling dreams to be illogical and bizarre (Hobson et al., 2000).

Environmental factors, such as changes in season, also affect sleep. In autumn and winter, most people sleep about 15 to 60 minutes longer per night. Shift work, stress at work and school, and night-time noise can decrease sleep quality (Bronzaft, Ahern, McGinn, O'Connor, & Savino, 1998), Routine can significantly influence our sleeping too – doing the same things at the same time has been shown to be beneficial (Dautovich, Shoji, & McCrae, 2013).

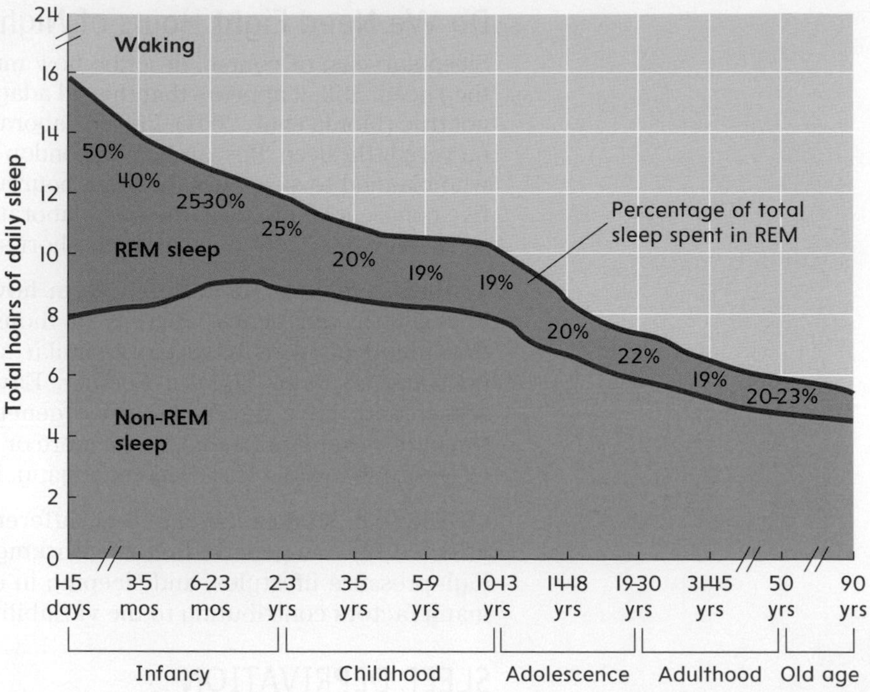

Several aspects of sleep, such as its timing and length, vary across cultures (Short et al., 2013). One study of 818 Japanese and Slovak adolescents found that, on average, the Japanese teenagers went to sleep later at night and slept for a shorter time than their Slovak peers (Iwawaki & Sarmany-Schuller, 2001). Many people, particularly those living in cultures in tropical climates, enjoy the traditional ritual of a one- to two-hour midday nap and reduce the length of night-time sleep (Kribbs, 1993).

Cultural norms also influence several behaviours related to sleep. Do you sleep on a cushioned bed? In some cultures people sleep on floors or suspended in hammocks. *Co-sleeping*, in which children sleep with their parents in the same bed or room, is not common in Europe, as children's sleeping alone is seen as a way to foster independence (Raeff, 2010). But in many cultures, co-sleeping is the norm.

FIGURE 6.22 Ageing and sleep.

Daily total sleep time and the percentage of sleep time in REM and non-REM sleep change with age.

Source: Adapted from Roffwarg, Muzioand Dement, 1966.

HOW MUCH DO WE SLEEP?

The question seems simple enough, as does the answer for many of us: not enough! In reality, the issue is complex. First there are substantial differences in how much people sleep at various ages (Figure 6.22). Newborn infants average 16 hours of sleep a day, and almost half of their sleep time is in REM (De Weerd & van den Bossche, 2003). But as we age, three important changes occur:

1. We sleep less: 19- to 30-year-olds average around seven to eight hours of sleep a night, and elderly adults average just less than six hours.
2. REM sleep decreases dramatically during infancy and early childhood but remains relatively stable thereafter.
3. Time spent in stages 3 and 4 declines. By old age we get relatively little slow-wave sleep.

Second, individual differences in the amount of sleep occur at every age. Sleep surveys indicate that about two-thirds of young adults sleep between 6.5 and 8.5 hours a night (Webb, 1992). About 1% sleep more than 10 hours a night and 1% less than five hours. Similarly, our sleep habits change with age, with some teenagers, for instance, falling asleep later, and waking later if allowed to remain in their beds (De Weerd, van den Bossche, & Peeters, 2003).

Focus 6.12 What factors regulate nightly sleep and differences in people's sleep behaviour? How does sleep change with age?

Do We Need Eight Hours of Nightly Sleep?

Sleep surveys, of course, describe how much sleep people believe they get, not how much they need. Still, it appears that the old adage, 'everyone needs eight hours of sleep a night', is not true (Monk, et al., 2001). Indeed, laboratory studies reveal that a few people function well on very little sleep. Researchers in London examined a healthy, energetic 70-year-old woman who claimed to sleep less than one hour a night (Meddis, Pearson, & Langford, 1973). Over five consecutive nights at the sleep laboratory, she averaged 67 minutes of sleep a night and showed no ill effects. Such extreme short-sleepers, however, are rare.

What accounts for differences in how much we sleep? Part of the answer appears to reside in our genes. Surveys of thousands of twins in Finland and Australia reveal that identical twins have more similar sleep lengths, bedtimes and sleep patterns than do fraternal twins (Heath, Kendler, Eaves, & Martin, 1990). Using selective breeding, researchers have developed some genetic strains of mice that are long- versus short-sleepers, other strains that spend more or less time in REM and still others that spend more or less time in slow-wave sleep (Ouyang, Hellman, Abel, & Thomas, 2004).

The twin studies indicate that differences in sleep length and sleep patterns are also affected by non-genetic factors. Working day versus night jobs, having low-key versus high-pressure lifestyles, and sleeping in quiet versus noisy environments are among the many factors contributing to the variability in people's sleep.

SLEEP DEPRIVATION

Sleep deprivation is a way of life for many students and other adults. Pilcher and Huffcutt (1996) meta-analysed 19 studies in which participants underwent either 'short-term total sleep deprivation' (up to 45 hours without sleep), 'long-term total sleep deprivation' (more than 45 hours without sleep), or 'partial deprivation' (being allowed to sleep no more than five hours a night for one or more consecutive nights). The researchers measured participants' mood (e.g., irritability) and responses on mental tasks (e.g., logical reasoning, word memory) and physical tasks (e.g., manual dexterity, treadmill walking).

What would you predict? Would all types of deprivation affect behaviour, and which behaviours would be affected the most? In fact, all three types of sleep deprivation impaired functioning. Combined across all studies, the typical sleep-deprived person functioned only as well as someone in the bottom 9% of non-deprived participants. Overall, mood suffered most, followed by cognitive and then physical performance, although sleep loss significantly impaired *all three* behaviours.

But what about students who pull all-nighters or cut back their sleep, claiming they still perform as well as ever? June Pilcher and Amy Walters (1997) found that university students deprived of one night's sleep performed more poorly on a critical-thinking task than students allowed to sleep – yet they incorrectly perceived that they had performed better. The authors concluded that students underestimate the negative effects of sleep loss on performance.

Most total-sleep-deprivation studies with humans last less than five days, but 17-year-old Randy Gardner set a world record (since broken) of staying awake for 11 days for his 1964 high school science-fair project in San Diego. Grateful sleep researchers received permission to study him (Figure 6.23; Gulevich, Dement, & Johnson, 1966). Contrary to a popular myth that Gardner suffered few negative effects, at times during the first few days he became irritable, forgetful and nauseated. By the fifth day he had periods of disorientation and mild hallucinations. Over the last four days he developed finger tremors and slurred speech. Still, in his final day without sleep he beat sleep researcher William Dement 100 consecutive times at a pinball-type game.

FIGURE 6.23 Student Randy Gardner (left) and researcher William Dement.

Source: Don Cravens/The LIFE Images Collection/Getty Images

When Gardner finally went to bed, he slept almost 15 hours the first night and returned to his normal amount of sleep within a week. In general, it takes several nights to recover from extended

sleep deprivation, and we do not make up all the sleep time that we have lost. Dinges and Kribbs (1991) say that those deprived of sleep and those that are rested function similarly at baseline level. However, sleep-deprived people have the occasional lapses of attention where their functioning suffers. This has become known as the 'lapse hypothesis'. However, research from Dinges et al. (1997) has suggested that the more hours of sleep that are lost the more variable people's reactions become on a typical task that measures the participants' ability to watch out for a target on a screen and respond to it quickly. This variation would not be predicted by the lapse hypothesis.

So what happens when a person is sleep deprived? There is some evidence that sleep deprivation can alter people's confidence of how well they have performed a task that requires them to think critically and be vigilant. The effects of the sleep loss can depend on the type of task being performed, for example, whether it is complex or simple, whether the person is familiar with it, or whether it is novel, and whether the person is motivated or not. For instance, a complex, novel task with little or no motivation will not be performed well under conditions of sleep deprivation. Leproult, Van Reeth, Byrne, Sturis and Van Cauter (1997) indicate that speed of processing information reduces with the amount of time spent awake. Attention also suffers similarly. Chee and Choo (2004) indicate that memory, and in particular working memory, tasks are harder as we begin to lose sleep.

Fatal familial insomnia is a condition related to sleep deprivation. It is a rare condition that runs in families. Those who suffer with it have relatively normal sleep patterns until they reach middle age where they begin to suffer with chronic and persistent insomnia. After a few years the person dies. The causes are unknown, and the rarity of the condition makes its investigation very difficult.

Other relevant research is conducted in sleep laboratories where volunteers are monitored as they experience sleep deprivation. Horne (1988) conducted a meta-analysis of over 50 sleep deprivation studies carried out in this way, concluding that deprivation results in relatively little cognitive impairment even after two or three days, but maintenance of performance requires greater motivation than non-sleep-deprived participants. For instance, Horne and Pettitt (1985) showed that greater financial incentives were required to maintain performance on a task where tones were to be detected. Lim and Dinges (2010) carried out a meta-analysis of the effects of short-term (less than 48 hours) sleep deprivation and showed some agreement with the earlier review of Horne (1988) and Durmer and Dinges (2005), notably that relatively little impairment in cognitive performance is reported across the body of the work, but speed and accuracy in performance does suffer.

> **Focus 6.13** How do different types of sleep deprivation affect mood and behaviour?

WHY DO WE SLEEP?

Given that we spend almost a third of our lives sleeping, it must serve an important purpose. But what might that purpose be?

Sleep and Bodily Restoration

According to the **restoration model**, sleep recharges our run-down bodies and allows us to recover from physical and mental fatigue (Hess, 1965). Sleep-deprivation research strongly supports this view, indicating that we need sleep to function at our best.

> **restoration model** sleep recharges our run-down bodies and allows us to recover from physical and mental fatigue

If the restoration model is correct, activities that increase daily wear on the body should increase sleep. Evidence is mildly supportive. A study of 18- to 26-year-old ultra-marathon runners found that they slept much longer and spent a greater percentage of time in slow-wave sleep on the two nights following their 57-mile run (Shapiro, Bortz, Mitchell, Bartel, & Jooste, 1981). For the rest of us mere mortals, a meta-analysis of 38 studies found that we tend to sleep longer by about 10 minutes on days we have exercised (Youngstedt, O'Connor, & Dishman, 1997).

What is it that gets restored in our bodies while we sleep? Are vital chemicals depleted during the day and replenished at night? Does waking activity produce toxins that are purged during sleep? We don't have precise answers, but many researchers believe that

a cellular waste product called *adenosine* plays a role (Alanko, Laitinen, Stenberg, & Porkka-Heiskanen, 2004). Like a car's exhaust emissions, adenosine is produced as cells consume fuel. As adenosine accumulates, it inhibits brain circuits responsible for keeping us awake, thereby signalling the body to slow down because too much cellular fuel has been burned. During sleep, however, our adenosine levels decrease.

Sleep as an Evolved Adaptation

> **evolutionary/circadian sleep models** sleep's main purpose is to increase a species' chances of survival in relation to its environmental demands

Evolutionary/circadian sleep models emphasize that sleep's main purpose is to increase a species' chances of survival in relation to its environmental demands (Webb, 1974). Our prehistoric ancestors had little to gain – and much to lose – by being active at night. Hunting, food gathering and travelling were accomplished more easily and safely during daylight. Leaving the protection of one's shelter at night would have served little purpose other than to become dinner for night-time predators.

Over the course of evolution, each species developed a circadian sleep–wake pattern that was adaptive in terms of its status as predator or prey, its food requirements and its methods of defence from attack. For small prey animals such as mice and squirrels, which reside in burrows or trees safely away from predators, spending a lot of time asleep is adaptive. For large prey animals such as horse, deer and zebra, which sleep in relatively exposed environments and whose safety from predators depends on running away, spending a lot of time asleep would be hazardous (Figure 6.24). Sleep may also have evolved as a mechanism for conserving energy. Our body's overall metabolic rate during sleep is about 10 to 25% slower than during waking rest (Zhang et al., 2002). The restoration and evolutionary theories highlight complementary functions of sleep, and both contribute to a two-factor model of why we sleep (Webb, 1994).

Sleep and Memory Consolidation

When a person is deprived of REM sleep, by regularly waking them when REM is detected their sleep patterns following the period of disruption are altered. Lavie, Pratt, Scharf, Peled and Brown (1984) indicate that even though it may seem counterintuitive, the consequences of REM disruption are not terribly significant. Patients who have suffered brain injury that results in reduced periods of REM or no REM at all have gone on to perform extremely well both academically and professionally.

So, do specific sleep stages have special functions? To answer this question, imagine volunteering for a sleep-deprivation study in which we will awaken you only when you

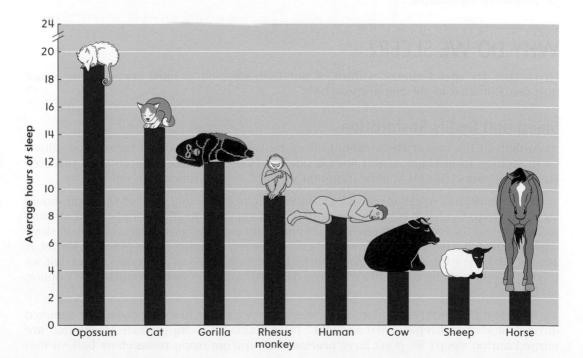

FIGURE 6.24 Daily hours of sleep.
The average daily hours of sleep vary across species.

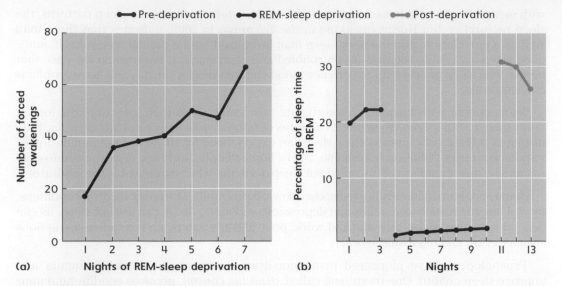

● Pre-deprivation   ● REM-sleep deprivation   ● Post-deprivation

(a)   **Nights of REM-sleep deprivation**

(b)   **Nights**

FIGURE 6.25 REM-sleep deprivation.

(a) In REM-sleep-deprivation studies, participants start to go into REM periods more times with each passing night, as the brain tries to get REM sleep.
(b) After REM deprivation ends, the sleeper spends more time than usual in REM sleep for a few nights. This is the REM-rebound effect.

Source: Adapted from Agnew, Webb and Williams, 1967.

enter REM sleep; you will be undisturbed through the other sleep stages. How will your body respond? First, on successive nights, we will have to wake you more often, because your brain will fight back to get REM sleep (Figure 6.25a). Second, when the study ends, for the first few nights you probably will experience a *REM-rebound effect*, a tendency to increase the amount of REM sleep after being deprived of it (Figure 6.25b).

This suggests that the body needs REM sleep (similar effects are found for slow-wave sleep). But for what purpose? It is widely considered the high level of brain activity in REM sleep helps us remember important events by enhancing **memory consolidation**, a gradual process by which the brain transfers information into long-term memory (C. T. Smith, Nixon, & Nader, 2004; Stickgold, 2006). Morgenthaler et al. (2014) while agreeing that sleep itself does indeed help us consolidate memory (cf. Rasch & Born, 2013), concluded the amount of REM sleep experienced during sleep makes no difference whatsoever on consolidation. In their research participants were divided into two groups – one was REM sleep deprived, and one was not. Each group had previously worked on a memory task and results showed that there was no difference in performance as a function of the amount of REM sleep experienced. The memory task included emotional pictures (ones that may cause some kind of arousal – this may be a funny image, or one that is shocking in some way) and non-emotional – neutral images. Previous research (Walker & van der Helm, 2009) had suggested that relative to neutral types of memory, emotional memory was enhanced during sleep. Morgenthaler et al. (2014) found nothing to support these theories, but did show that sleep itself was very useful in memory consolidation.

Some researchers argue that the function of REM sleep is biological. The periodic high activation of REM sleep keeps the brain healthy during sleep and offsets the periods of low brain arousal during restful slow-wave sleep (Vertes & Eastman, 2003).

memory consolidation a gradual process by which the brain transfers information into long-term memory

Focus 6.14 Explain the restoration, evolutionary/circadian and memory-consolidation models of sleep.

SLEEP DISORDERS

As the sleep–eating cases of Sondra, Jason and Katrien illustrate, the processes that regulate sleep are complex and can go wrong in many ways. Almost 75% of American adults feel that they have some type of sleep problem (National Sleep Foundation, 2002).

Insomnia

True or false: someone who falls asleep easily can still have insomnia. The statement is true because **insomnia** refers to chronic difficulty in falling asleep, staying asleep or experiencing restful sleep. If you occasionally have trouble getting a good night's sleep, do not worry. Almost everyone does. People with true insomnia have frequent and persistent sleep troubles. There is evidence (Young, 2009) that suggests that insomnia and poor sleep may result in psychological problems. Whereas it is the case that many people

insomnia chronic difficulty in falling asleep, staying asleep or experiencing restful sleep

with mental health problems do indeed suffer with interrupted or poor sleep patterns, the sleep researcher Jim Horne, speaking in the *Telegraph* in 2009, indicates that there may well be a correlation, and the poor sleep may be caused by the mental illness itself, since good sleep invariably requires an untroubled and clear mind. It is certainly the case that people who sleep poorly may experience mood changes during the day and have problems concentrating.

Many people with insomnia overestimate how much sleep they lose and how long it takes them to fall asleep. To some, 20 minutes of lying awake may seem like an hour. Still, insomnia is the most common sleep disorder, experienced by 10–40% of the population of various countries (Ohayon & Lemoine, 2004). Some people, however, display *paradoxical insomnia*; they complain of insomnia but sleep normally when examined in the laboratory.

Some people are genetically predisposed towards insomnia. Moreover, medical conditions, mental disorders such as anxiety and depression, and many drugs can disrupt sleep, as can general worrying, stress at home and work, poor lifestyle habits, and circadian disruptions such as jet lag and night-shift work.

Psychologists have pioneered many non-drug treatments to reduce insomnia and improve sleep quality. One treatment, called *stimulus control*, involves conditioning your body to associate stimuli in your sleep environment (such as your bed) with sleep, rather than with waking activities and sleeplessness (Bootzin, 2002). For example, if you are having sleep difficulties do not study, watch television or snack in your bedroom. Use your bed only for sleeping. If you cannot fall asleep within 10 minutes, get up and leave the bedroom. Do something relaxing until you feel sleepy, and then return to bed. Other methods of helping with insomnia include the application of relaxation techniques, and the careful control of your sleep habits (known as sleep hygiene). Poor sleep hygiene can result in poor sleep, and includes the habit of taking naps during the day, and drinking alcohol or caffeine before bed. Table 6.2 contains more guidelines from sleep experts regarding good sleep hygiene for reducing insomnia and achieving better sleep. In some cases, sleep restriction therapy has been found to be useful. Essentially this means staying awake even if you feel sleepy. This can help the person suffering from insomnia reduce the amount of time they spend awake in their bed trying to fall asleep. By restricting sleep, the insomniac can become tired and fall asleep naturally, at the correct time.

Alcohol and Sleep – A Gender Difference

Alcohol seems to be a bigger problem for woman than men when it comes to sleep. Arendt et al. (2011) indicate that whereas alcohol disrupts sleep in both men and women, the effects on men are less pronounced. Alcohol has the effect of deepening sleep at the start

---

TABLE 6.2 How to improve the quality of your sleep

Sleep experts recommend a variety of procedures to reduce insomnia and improve the general quality of sleep:
Maintain a regular sleep-wake pattern to establish a stable circadian rhythm.
Get the amount of sleep you need during the week, and avoid sleeping in on weekends, as doing so will disrupt your sleep rhythm. Even if you sleep poorly or not at all one night, try to maintain your regular schedule the next.
If you have trouble falling asleep at night, avoid napping if possible. Evening naps should be especially avoided because they will make you less sleepy when you go to bed.
Avoid stimulants. This includes not just tobacco products and coffee but also caffeinated soft drinks and chocolate (sorry), which contains caffeine. It can take the body four to five hours to reduce the amount of caffeine in the bloodstream by 50%.
Avoid alcohol and sleeping pills. As a depressant, alcohol may make it easier to go to sleep, but it disrupts the sleep cycle and interferes with REM sleep. Sleeping pills also impair REM sleep, and their constant use can lead to dependence and insomnia.
Try to go to bed in a relaxed state. Muscle-relaxation techniques and meditation can reduce tension, remove worrisome thoughts and help induce sleep.
Avoid physical exercise before bedtime because it is too stimulating. If you are unable to fall asleep, do not use exercise to try and wear yourself out.
If you are having sleep difficulties, avoid performing non-sleep activities in your bedroom.

Sources: Bootzin, 2002; King, Dudley, Melvin, Pallant and Morawetz, 2001.

of the night but disrupting it later on in the night (Carskadon, Acebo, & Jenni, 2006), but family history and gender moderate the effect. The differences between men and women are to be expected as women and men metabolize alcohol differently. Arendt et al. (2011) showed that after drinking, women reported greater feelings of sleepiness than men, slept for less time and that time was more broken than in men. In the study, breath alcohol content was measured throughout the night and showed no differences between male and female participants. They also showed that women tended to show a faster decline in breath alcohol content than men – a reflection of the differences in the way alcohol is metabolized. Since there were very few physiological differences, and since experience and drinking history were controlled, the differences – maybe due to the way alcohol is metabolized – should be considered when investigating the effect alcohol has on sleep.

Narcolepsy

About one out of every 2,000 people suffers not from an inability to sleep but from an inability to stay awake (Ohayon & Lemoine, 2004). **Narcolepsy** involves extreme daytime sleepiness and sudden, uncontrollable sleep attacks that may last from less than a minute to an hour. No matter how much they rest at night, individuals with narcolepsy may experience sleep attacks at any time, with hypnagogic (dream-like) hallucinations and sleep paralysis being common among sufferers.

> **narcolepsy** extreme daytime sleepiness and sudden, uncontrollable sleep attacks that may last from less than a minute to an hour

When a sleep attacks occurs, they may go right into a REM stage. People with narcolepsy also may experience attacks of *cataplexy*, a sudden loss of muscle tone often triggered by excitement and other strong emotions. In severe cases, the knees buckle and the person collapses, conscious but unable to move for a few seconds to a few minutes. Cataplexy is an abnormal version of the normal muscular paralysis that takes place during night-time REM sleep, and some expert's view narcolepsy as a disorder in which REM sleep intrudes into waking consciousness.

Narcolepsy can be devastating. People with narcolepsy are more prone to accidents, feel that their quality of life is impaired and may be misdiagnosed by doctors as having a mental disorder rather than a sleep disorder (Kryger, Walid, & Manfreda, 2002). Some people may be genetically predisposed towards developing narcolepsy. It can be selectively bred in dogs (Figure 6.26). In humans, if one identical twin has narcolepsy, the other has a 30% chance of developing it (Mignot, 1998). Narcolepsy is today perceived as an auto-immune disorder – as it has been linked to some specific human antigen variants. An area in the hypothalamus which produces a neurotransmitter called 'hypocretine' seems to be specifically affected. Thus, patients suffering from narcolepsy typically have very low levels of hypocretine in their cerebrospinal fluid.

At present there is no cure for narcolepsy, but stimulant drugs and daytime naps often reduce daytime sleepiness, and antidepressant drugs (which suppress REM sleep) can decrease attacks of cataplexy. The H1N1 virus, better known perhaps as Swine Flu, caused great concern, particularly in Europe where many were vaccinated against it. Unfortunately a relatively small number of children and young adults who had been vaccinated developed narcolepsy (Persson, Granath, Askling, Ludvigsson, Olsson, & Feltelius, 2014) as did a number of sufferers of the virus in China (Han et al., 2013). The link between the virus and narcolepsy suggests that there may well have been a predisposition to the sleep disorder that was triggered by the vaccination.

FIGURE 6.26 This dog lapses suddenly from alert wakefulness into a limp sleep while being held by sleep researcher William Dement. Using selective breeding, researchers at Stanford's Sleep Disorders Center have established a colony of narcoleptic canines.

Source:© Louie Psihoyos/Corbis

REM-Sleep Behaviour Disorder

Kaku Kimura and his colleagues in Japan (Kimura, Tachibana, Aso, Kimura, & Shibasaki, 1997) reported the case of a 72-year-old woman who, during a night in

a sleep laboratory, repeatedly sang and waved her hands during REM sleep. One episode lasted three minutes. She was experiencing **REM-sleep behaviour disorder (RBD)**, in which the loss of muscle tone that causes normal REM-sleep paralysis is absent. If awakened, RBD patients often report dream content that matches their behaviour, as if they were acting out their dreams: 'A 67-year-old man . . . was awakened one night by his wife's yelling as he was choking her. He was dreaming of breaking the neck of a deer he had just knocked down' (Schenck, Milner, Hurwitz, & Bundlie, 1989, p. 1169).

REM-sleep behaviour disorder sleepers may kick violently, throw punches or get out of bed and move about wildly, leaving the bedroom in shambles. Many RBD patients have injured themselves or their sleeping partners. Research suggests that brain abnormalities may interfere with signals from the brain stem that normally inhibit movement during REM sleep, but in many cases the causes of RBD are unknown (Zambelis, Paparrigopoulos, & Soldatos, 2002). REM-sleep behaviour disorder has also been associated with other degenerative diseases such as Parkinson's disease. One possible treatment is to give melatonin. Boeve, Solber and Ferman (2003) showed that it is often, but not always, effecting even a year after treatment is over.

Sleepwalking

Unlike RBD, sleepwalking, or somnambulism, typically occurs during a stage-3 or stage-4 (AASM, N3) period of slow-wave sleep (Guilleminault, Poyares, Abat, & Palombini, 2001). Sleepwalkers (Figure 6.27) often stare blankly and are unresponsive to other people. Many seem vaguely conscious of the environment as they navigate around furniture, yet they can injure themselves accidentally, such as by falling down stairs. Some go to the bathroom or – like Sondra, Jason and Katrien – find something to eat. The pattern, however, is variable. Recall that Jason, while eating during his sleepwalking episodes, could have intelligible conversations with his wife. People who sleepwalk often return to bed and wake in the morning with no memory of the event.

About 10–30% of children sleepwalk at least once, but less than 5% of adults do. If you did not sleepwalk as a child, the odds are less than 1% that you will do so as an adult (Hublin, Kaprio, Partinen, Heikkilä, & Koskenvuo, 1997).

A tendency to sleepwalk may be inherited, and daytime stress, alcohol, and certain illnesses and medications can increase sleepwalking (Hublin, Kaprio, Partinen, & Koskenvuo, 2001), with the most likely thing to bring on a bout of sleepwalking in those that suffer from it being a period of sleep deprivation. Treatments may include psychotherapy, hypnosis and waking children before the time they typically sleepwalk (Frank, Spirito, Stark, & Owens-Stively, 1997). But for children, the most common approach is simply to wait for the child to outgrow it while creating a safe sleep environment to prevent injury. Contrary to common belief, waking people who sleepwalk is generally not harmful, the most common experience is that they may be confused for a few minutes and the disorientation may cause them to fall or harm themselves, so it should be done very carefully.

FIGURE 6.27 John Everett Millais (1829–1896): *The Somnambulist* (1871) **The inspiration for Wilkie Collins' story** *The Woman in White.*

Source: Private Collection, courtesy of the Delaware Art Museum, Wilmington Delaware USA/Sir John Everett Millais, PRA (British, 1829-1896) A Somnambulist

Nightmares and Night Terrors

Nightmares are bad dreams, and virtually everyone has them. Like all dreams, they occur more often during REM sleep. Arousal during nightmares typically is similar to levels experienced during pleasant dreams.

Night terrors are frightening dreams that arouse the sleeper to a near-panic state. In contrast to nightmares, night terrors are most common during slow-wave sleep (stages 3 and 4), are more intense and involve greatly elevated physiological arousal; the heart rate may double or triple. In some cases the terrified sleeper may suddenly sit up, let out a scream or flee the room – as if trying to escape from something. Come morning the sleeper usually has no memory of the episode. If brought to full consciousness during an episode – which is hard to do – the person may report a sense of having been choked, crushed or attacked (Fisher, Kahn, Edwards, Davis, & Fine, 1974).

Up to 6% of children, but only 1–2% of adults, experience night terrors (Ohayon, Guilleminault, & Priest, 1999). In most childhood cases, treatment is simply to wait for the night terrors to diminish with age.

Sleep Apnoea

An *apnoea* is a period of 10 seconds or more when a person stops breathing. People with **sleep apnoea** repeatedly stop and restart breathing during sleep. Stoppages usually last 20 to 40 seconds but can continue for 1 to 2 minutes. In severe cases they occur 400 to 500 times a night. Obstructive sleep apnoea is most commonly caused by an obstruction in the upper airways, such as sagging tissue as muscles lose tone during sleep. The chest and abdomen keep moving, but no air gets through to the lungs in obstructive apnoea. Finally, reflexes kick in and the person gasps or produces a loud, startling snore, followed by a several-second awakening. The person typically falls asleep again without remembering having been awake. In *central apnoea* the chest and abdomen do not continue to move.

About 1–5% of people have some form of sleep apnoea, and the obstructive type is most common among overweight, middle-aged males. Surgery may be performed to remove the obstruction, and sleep apnoea sometimes is treated by having the sleeper wear a mask that continuously pumps air to keep the air passages open, a CPAP – continuous positive airway pressure device (Sage, Southcott, & Brown, 2001). It is often the partner of a person with sleep apnoea – repeatedly woken by the gasps, loud snores and jerking body movements – who encourage the person to seek treatment.

> **sleep apnoea** repeatedly stop and restart breathing during sleep

> **Focus 6.15** Describe the symptoms, causes and treatment of major sleep disorders.

THE NATURE OF DREAMS

Dreams play a key role in the social fabric of many traditional cultures, such as the Timiar (Senoi) of Malaysia (Greenleaf, 1973). To the Timiar, dreams provide a link to the spirit world, and dream interpretation, particularly when performed by shamans, is highly valued. Although western societies attach less importance to dreams than do many cultures, dreams remain a source of endless curiosity in everyday life.

When Do We Dream?

Mental activity occurs throughout the sleep cycle. Some of our students say they experience vivid images soon after going to bed and ask if this is unusual. It is not. When Jason Rowley and his colleagues (Rowley, Stickgold, & Hobson, 1998) woke college students merely 45 seconds after sleep onset, about 25% of the students reported that they had been experiencing visual hallucinations (visual images that seemed real). As this *hypnagogic state* – the transitional state from wakefulness through early stage-2 sleep – continued, mental activity became less 'thoughtlike' and more 'dreamlike'. By five minutes after sleep onset, visual hallucinations were reported after 40% of awakenings.

Throughout the night we dream most often during REM sleep, when activity in many brain areas is highest. Awaken a REM sleeper and you have about an 80–85% chance of catching a dream. Stoerig (2007) woke sleepers during REM and 80% reported dreaming at that time. In contrast, people awakened from non-REM (NREM) sleep report dreams about 15–50% (Stoerig, 2007) of the time. Also, our REM dreams are more likely to be vivid, bizarre and storylike than NREM dreams. Some researchers attribute this to the fact that REM dreams typically are longer, allowing more time for vivid content to unfold (Domhoff, 1999). But like the proverbial chicken and the egg, other researchers argue that it is the greater richness of REM dreams that causes them to be longer (Hobson et al., 2000).

Despite these REM–NREM differences, do not believe the fallacy (often reinforced by the popular media) that dreaming only happens during REM sleep. Figure 6.28 (on the next page) shows an analysis of 1,576 reports collected from 16 college students woken from various sleep stages (Fosse, Stickgold, & Hobson, 2001). Even during NREM sleep, hallucinatory images were more common than non-dreamlike thoughts. By some estimates, about 25% of the vivid dreams we have each night actually occur during NREM periods (Solms, 2002),

What Do We Dream About?

Much of our knowledge about dream content derives from 40 years of research using a coding system developed by Calvin Hall and Robert Van de Castle (1966). Analysing 1,000 dream reports (mostly from college students), they found that although some dreams certainly are bizarre, dreams overall are not nearly as strange as they are stereotyped to be.

> **Focus 6.16** When do dreams occur, and what are common characteristics of dream content? How can science explain 'psychic' dreams?

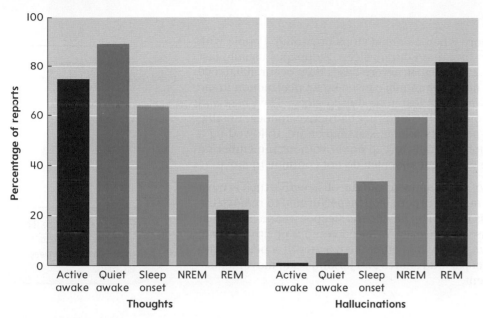

FIGURE 6.28 Mental activity during sleep.

This graph shows the percentage of verbal reports that reflected thoughts and visual hallucinations recorded during active and quiet wakefulness and when awakened during sleep onset, REM sleep and NREM sleep.

Source: Adapted from Fosse et al., 2001

Most take place in familiar settings and often involve people we know.

Given the stereotype of 'blissful dreaming', it may surprise you that most dreams contain negative content. In their research, Hall and Van de Castle (1966) found that 80% of dream reports involved negative emotions, almost half contained aggressive acts and a third involved some type of misfortune. They also found that women dreamt almost equally about male and female characters, whereas about two-thirds of men's dream characters were male. Although the reason for this gender difference is not clear, a similar pattern has been found across several cultures and among teenagers and pre-adolescents.

Our cultural background, life experiences, and current concerns can shape dream content (Domhoff, 2001). Pregnant women, for example, have dreams with many pregnancy themes, and Palestinian children living in violent regions of the Gaza Strip dream about persecution and aggression more often than do their peers living in non-violent areas (Punamäki & Joustie, 1998). In the weeks following the 11 September 2001 terrorist attacks, a study of 1,000 residents of Manhattan found that one in 10 experienced distressing dreams about the attacks (Galea et al., 2002). Overall, it appears that up to half of our dreams contain some content reflecting our recent experiences (Harlow & Roll, 1992).

Why Do We Dream?

Questions about the purpose and meaning of dreams have intrigued humankind for ages. Let us examine a few viewpoints. It is during REM sleep that the majority of dreaming occurs, and we have already described the role of REM in memory consolidation. According to *evolutionary theory*, for instance, the function of dreams might be to prepare us for a hostile environment. Revonsuo (2000) indicates that most dreams have a negative emotional content. It could be that this allows us to experience a dangerous environment in the safety of our dreams.

Freud's psychoanalytic theory

Sigmund Freud (1953) believed that the main purpose of dreaming is **wish fulfilment**, the gratification of our unconscious desires and needs. These desires include sexual and aggressive urges that are too unacceptable to be consciously acknowledged and fulfilled in real life. Freud distinguished between (1) a dream's *manifest content*, the surface story that the dreamer reports and (2) its *latent content*, which is its disguised psychological meaning. Thus a dream about being with a stranger on a train that goes through a tunnel (manifest content) might represent a hidden desire for sexual intercourse with a forbidden partner (latent content).

Dream work was Freud's term for the process by which a dream's latent content is transformed into the manifest content. It occurs through symbols (e.g., train = penis; tunnel = vagina) and by creating individual dream characters who combine features of several people in real life. This way, unconscious needs can be fulfilled and, because they are disguised within the dream, the sleeper does not become anxious and can sleep peacefully.

wish fulfilment the gratification of our unconscious desires and needs

Although dreams often reflect ongoing emotional concerns, many researchers reject the specific postulates of Freud's theory. They find little evidence that dreams have disguised meaning or that their general purpose is to satisfy forbidden, unconscious needs and conflicts (Domhoff, 1999). Critics of dream analysis say that it is highly subjective; the same dream can be interpreted differently to fit the particular analyst's point of view.

Modern psychodynamic psychologists emphasize that beyond the types of unconscious processing discussed earlier, emotional and motivational processes also operate unconsciously and influence behaviour (Westen, 1998b). At times these hidden processes can cause us to feel and act in ways that mystify us. Consider the case of a 47-year-old amnesia patient who could not remember new personal experiences. One day, as Swiss psychologist Edouard Claparède (1911) shook this woman's hand, he intentionally pricked her hand with a pin hidden between his fingers. Later, Claparède extended his hand to shake hers again. The woman could not consciously recall the pinprick or even having met Claparède, but despite her amnesia, she suddenly withdrew her hand. Apparently, an unconscious memory of the painful experience influenced her behaviour.

Numerous experiments support the view that unconscious processes can have an emotional and motivational flavour (LeDoux, 2000). For example, have you ever been in a bad or a good mood and wondered why you were feeling that way? Perhaps it is because you were influenced by events in your environment of which you were not consciously aware.

In one study, Tanya Chartrand and her colleagues (2002) subliminally presented college students with nouns that were either strongly negative (e.g., *cancer, cockroach*), mildly negative (e.g., *Monday, worm*), mildly positive (e.g., *parade, clown*), or strongly positive (e.g., *friends, music*). Later, students rated their mood on psychological tests. Although not consciously aware of seeing the nouns, students shown the strongly negative words reported the saddest mood, whereas those who had seen the strongly positive words reported the happiest mood.

Activation-synthesis theory

Is it possible that dreams serve no special purpose? In 1977, J. Allan Hobson and Robert McCarley proposed a physiological theory of dreaming.

According to the activation-synthesis theory, dreams do not serve any particular function – they are merely a by-product of REM neural activity. When we are awake, neural circuits in our brain are activated by sensory input – sights, sounds, tastes, and so on. The cerebral cortex interprets these patterns of neural activation, producing meaningful perceptions. During REM sleep the brain stem bombards our higher brain centres with random neural activity (the activation component). Because we are asleep, this neural activity does not match any external sensory events, but our cerebral cortex continues to perform its job of interpretation. It does this by creating a dream – a perception – that provides the best fit to the particular pattern of neural activity that exists at any moment (the synthesis component).

This helps to explain the bizarreness of many dreams, as the brain is trying to make sense of random neural activity. Our memories, experiences, desires and needs can influence the stories that our brain develops, and therefore dream content may reflect themes pertaining to our lives. In this sense, dreams can have meaning, but they serve no special function (McCarley, 1998).

Critics claim that activation-synthesis theory overestimates the bizarreness of dreams and pays too little attention to NREM dreaming (Solms, 2002). Nevertheless, this theory revolutionized dream research by calling attention to a physiological basis for dreaming, and it remains a dominant dream theory (Hobson et al., 2000).

Cognitive theories

According to problem-solving dream models, because dreams are not constrained by reality, they can help us find creative solutions to our problems and ongoing concerns

activation-synthesis theory dreams do not serve any particular function – they are merely a by-product of REM neural activity

problem-solving dream models because dreams are not constrained by reality, they can help us find creative solutions to our problems and ongoing concerns

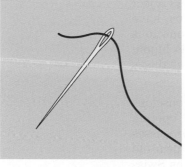
Hand-held needle

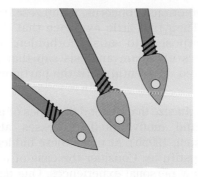
Spears in Howe's dream

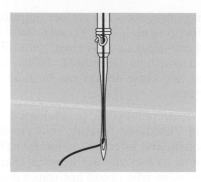
Sewing machine needle

FIGURE 6.29 Dreams and problem-solving.

In 1846 American inventor Elias Howe patented a sewing machine. He had struggled unsuccessfully for years to figure out how to get a machine to stitch using a needle with the threading hole in the back (blunt) end – as in a traditional hand-held needle. Allegedly, one night he had a dream that he was being pursued by spear-throwing tribesmen. In the dream he saw that each spearhead had a hole in it. When Howe woke, he recognized that for a sewing machine to work, the threading hole needed to be at the front (sharp) end of the needle, as it had been on the spears. This is not evidence for the theory and is used only to illustrate the principle. To be clear, there is no literature or evidence of any kind to support any of Howe's story and so it should be used as illustrative only, and referenced as such.

(Cartwright, 1977). Self-help books and numerous websites promote this idea, and history offers some intriguing examples of inventors, scientists and authors who allegedly came upon creative ideas or solutions to problems in a dream (Figure 6.29). But critics argue that because so many of our dreams do not focus on personal problems, it is difficult to see how problem-solving can be the broad underlying reason for *why* we dream. They also note that just because a problem shows up in a dream does not mean that the dream involved an attempt to solve it. Moreover, we may think consciously about our dreams after waking and obtain important new insights; in this sense dreams may indeed help us work through ongoing concerns. However, this is not the same as solving problems *while* dreaming (Squier & Domhoff, 1998).

Cognitive-process dream theories focus on the process of how we dream and propose that dreaming and waking thought are produced by the same mental systems in the brain (Foulkes, 1982). For example, research indicates that there is more similarity between dreaming and waking mental processes than was traditionally believed (Domhoff, 2001). Consider that one reason many dreams appear bizarre is because their content shifts rapidly. 'I was dreaming about an examination and all of a sudden, the next thing I knew, I was in Hawaii on the beach.' (Don't we wish!) Yet if you reflect on the contents of your waking thoughts – your stream of consciousness – you will realize they also shift suddenly. About half of REM dream reports involve rapid content shifts, but when people are awake and placed in the same environmental conditions as sleepers (a dark, quiet room), about 90% of their reports involve rapid content shifts (Antrobus, 1991). Thus rapid shifting of attention is a process common to dreaming and waking mental activity.

> **cognitive-process dream theories** propose that dreaming and waking thought are produced by the same mental systems in the brain

> **Focus 6.17** Contrast the psychoanalytic, activation-synthesis and cognitive dream theories.

Towards integration

Although there is no agreed-on model of why or even of how we dream, theorists are developing models that integrate several perspectives. In general, these models propose that dreaming involves an integration of perceptual, emotional, motivational and cognitive processes performed by various brain modules. For example, *neurocognitive models* (such as the activation-synthesis model) bridge the cognitive and biological perspectives by attempting to explain how various subjective aspects of dreaming correspond to the physiological changes that occur during sleep (Hobson et al., 2000). And, as noted previously, these models allow for the possibility that motivational factors – our needs and desires – can influence how the brain goes about its business of attaching meaning to the neural activity that underlies our dreams.

DAYDREAMS AND WAKING FANTASIES

Our dreams and fantasy lives are not restricted to the nocturnal realm. Daydreams are a significant part of waking consciousness, providing stimulation during periods of boredom and letting us experience a range of emotions (Hartmann, Kunzendorf, Rosen, & Grace, 2001). In *The Secret Life of Walter Mitty*, author James Thurber (1942) portrayed the fictional Mitty as a person who transformed his humdrum existence into an exhilarating fantasy world of adventure. Like Mitty, people who have a **fantasy-prone personality** often live in a vivid, rich fantasy world that they control, and most are female. In one study, about three-quarters of fantasy-prone people were able to achieve sexual orgasm merely by fantasizing about sex, and all could experience fantasies 'as real as real' in each of the five senses (Wilson & Barber, 1982).

Daydreams typically involve greater visual imagery than other forms of waking mental activity but tend to be less vivid, emotional and bizarre than night-time dreams (Kunzendorf, Hartmann, Cohen, & Cutler, 1997). There also is surprising similarity in the themes of daydreams and night-time dreams, suggesting once again that nocturnal dreams may be an extension of daytime mental activity (Beck, 2002). Figure 6.22 summarizes some of the biological, psychological and environmental factors that contribute to our understanding of sleep and dreaming.

> **fantasy-prone personality**
> often live in a vivid, rich fantasy world that they control

> **Focus 6.18** What functions do daydreams serve? How are they different from and similar to night-time dreams?

 Current topic

LUCID DREAMING

We spend about 30% of our lives asleep, so the fact that the vast majority of research is based on wakeful cognition seems to be an imbalance. Lucid dreaming offers a fascinating insight into sleep. Lucid dreaming is a state where those that experience it become aware, or 'conscious' of their dreaming (Hearne, 1980). Hobson (1988), for instance, is of the mind that our cognition while dreaming is deficient in some way when related to wakeful cognition. This is a widely held view; perhaps because of our ability to reflect on our own thinking, to experience metacognition (the monitoring and awareness of one's own thoughts) when awake. Kahan and LaBerge (1994) describe lucid dreaming as metacognitive also, however. They say that to achieve this state, dreamers must practise a kind of reflective commentary within their dream, an evaluative commentary if you like that provides a metacognitive dialogue. They go on to indicate that as with waking, once this state has been achieved the 'dreamer' is able to 'consciously' alter the course of events within their dream. Research in lucid dreaming typically requires the dreamer to report their dream once awake, and the dialogues reported are, typically, very rational indeed and very much like wakeful experiences. LaBerge has conducted a number of experiments in different paradigms in the investigation of lucid dreaming. He has shown, for instance, that lucid dreamers are able to perform actions that indicate the onset of their lucid dream from within their dream. These actions may be simple fist clenches or eye movements, both of which can be recorded and observed outside the dream by the researchers in the laboratory. Similarly, strategic points within the dreams, perhaps when they began certain actions such as singing, could be indicated and so marked on recording devices with eye movements.

LaBerge (1983) indicates that there appear to be three different variations in the initiation of lucid dreams. The first is known as Dream Initiated Lucid Dreams (DILD). These are lucid dreams that begin from within a non-lucid dream and are most common. The second type is called Wake Initiated Lucid Dreams (WILD). In these cases the wakeful experience is transferred into the dream itself. Finally, LaBerge describes ambiguities in lucidity induction – with experience those able to achieve lucidity do so habitually, thus resulting in the hard categorization of dreams as WILD or DILD.

The implications of lucid dreaming to our understanding of cognition are potentially quite significant. The view of dreaming as a deficient state is questioned when we can show, as LaBerge and colleague's research is describing, that sleepful cognition is a lot more like wakefulness than we once thought. Other, perhaps more philosophical and phenomenological questions are raised (Waggoner, 2008). The process of lucid dreaming allows us an interesting perspective on 'the self' and elevates the 'self' into the study of cognition – not typically a place we may find it discussed. In lucid dreaming different aspects of self are experienced. We monitor our own actions metacognitively as if watching ourselves behave. We then influence our actions to alter this behaviour within the dream, while remaining distant and able to reflect on our behaviour. In wakeful cognition this reflection is not experienced or described and in many cases, such as in the working memory model (Chapter 8), actions are subconscious, and automatic; decisions are taken executively without conscious control. Lucid dreaming provides an extremely interesting insight and viewpoint into both consciousness and cognition, and it is likely to be a feature of the study of psychology for some time.

Levels of analysis
factors related to sleep and dreaming

PSYCHOLOGICAL

- Learned sleep habits that facilitate or impair a sound night's sleep
- Worries and stress that may hinder falling asleep
- Cognitive activity during sleep (e.g., dreams, thoughts, images)
- Ongoing problems or concerns that may show up in dream content

BIOLOGICAL

- Circadian rhythms that affect sleepiness and alertness
- Evolution of sleep–wake cycle that is adaptive for each species
- Brain regions and neural activity that regulate sleep and dreaming
- Genetic and age-related processes that influence sleep length and patterns
- Genetic factors that predispose some people towards developing sleep disorders

ENVIRONMENTAL

- Day–night cycle and time cues that help regulate circadian rhythms and sleep readiness
- Events that disrupt circadian rhythms and impair sleep
- Night-time stimuli that affect sleep quality (e.g., quiet or noisy room)
- Events and experiences from waking life that show up in dream content
- Cultural norms that influence sleep-related behaviour (e.g., co-sleeping) and the meaning attached to dreams

Sleep and dreaming

In review

- Sleep has five main stages. Stages I and 2 are lighter sleep, and stages 3 and 4 are deeper, slow-wave sleep. These are also known as AASM NI-3. High physiological arousal and periods of rapid eye movement characterize the fifth stage, REM sleep.

- Several brain regions regulate sleep, and the amount we sleep changes as we age. Genetic, psychological and environmental factors affect sleep duration and quality.

- Sleep deprivation negatively affects mood and performance. The restoration model proposes that we sleep to recover from physical and mental fatigue. Evolutionary/circadian models state that each species developed a sleep–wake cycle that maximized its chance of survival.

- Insomnia is the most common sleep disorder, but less common disorders such as narcolepsy, REM sleep behaviour disorder and sleep apnoea can have serious consequences. Sleepwalking typically occurs during slow-wave sleep, whereas nightmares most often occur during REM sleep. Night terrors create a near-panic state of arousal and typically occur in slow-wave sleep.

- Dreams occur throughout sleep but are most common during REM periods. Unpleasant dreams are common. Our cultural background, current concerns and recent events influence what we dream about.

- Freud proposed that dreams fulfil unconscious wishes that show up in disguised form within our dreams. Activation-synthesis theory regards dreaming as the brain's attempt to fit a story to random neural activity. Cognitive-process dream theories emphasize that dreaming and waking thought are produced by the same mental systems.

- Daydreams and nocturnal dreams often share similar themes. People with fantasy-prone personalities have especially vivid daydreams.

DRUG-INDUCED STATES

Like sleep and dreaming, drug-induced states have mystified humans for ages. Three thousand years ago, the Aztecs considered hallucinogenic mushrooms to be a sacred substance for communicating with the spirit world. Today drugs are a cornerstone of medical practice and, as Figure 6.28 shows, a pervasive part of social life. They alter consciousness by modifying brain chemistry, but drug effects are also influenced by psychological, environmental and cultural factors (Julien, 2007). Drugs are used socially by a huge number of people. Unfortunately, we should be careful not to forget a darker side to the social use of drugs such as GHB (sodium gamma-hydroxybutyrate), used as a means of assault. These designer drugs are often known as 'date-rape' drugs and have an anaesthetic effect, rendering the person that takes them immobile. In larger doses they can induce coma. Tiny amounts need to be ingested for the desired effects that begin to manifest themselves about 20 minutes after the dose is taken. Worryingly, much GHB is 'homemade' by amateurs in uncontrolled conditions and so the purity and corresponding effect of the drug are often impossible to determine before it is used, making it even more dangerous to the unsuspecting victim.

DRUGS AND THE BRAIN

Like any cell, a neuron is essentially a fragile bag of chemicals, and it takes a delicate chemical balancing act for neurons to function properly. Drugs work their way into the bloodstream and are carried throughout the brain by an extensive network of small blood vessels called capillaries. These capillaries contain a **blood-brain barrier**, a special lining of tightly packed cells that lets vital nutrients pass through so neurons can function. The blood-brain barrier screens out many foreign substances, but some, including various drugs, can pass through. Once inside they alter consciousness by facilitating or inhibiting synaptic transmission (Julien, 2007).

> **blood-brain barrier** a special lining of tightly packed cells that lets vital nutrients pass through so neurons can function

Neuromodulators

Just as a reminder (you will find much more on this in **Chapter 4**), a neurotransmitter is a chemical substance that carries information across the synaptic space to other neurons, muscles or glands. Examples of neurotransmitters are dopamine and serotonin, and each has excitatory or inhibitory effects on specific sets of neurons, as do most neurotransmitters. They have their own 'systems' in which they operate. A **neuromodulator** is a special kind of neurotransmitter that knows no such boundary. Its influence on the transmission of information across the synapse is widespread. Endorphins are a good example of these, having a generalized pain relief and pleasure generating action right across the brain and an antagonist action which we describe in the next section.

 Chapter 4, Page 125

> **neuromodulator** a specific group of neurotransmitters that have a widespread and generalized influence on synaptic transmission

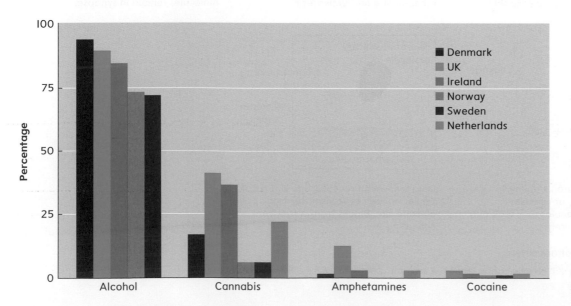

FIGURE 6.30 Drug use among students.

This graph illustrates non-medical drug use among students from a number of different countries. The percentage of those using each drug is shown. (The figure for alcohol consumption in the Netherlands is not available.)

Source: Reprinted from *Drug and Alcohol Dependence*, Vol 60, No. 3, Smart and Ogborne 'Drinking and heavy drinking by students in 18 countries.' (2001). With permission of Elsevier.

How Drugs Facilitate Synaptic Transmission

Chapter 4, Page 125

Chapter 4 provides much more information about synaptic transmission than we present here. The chemical movement of information across the synaptic space is called synaptic transmission and it involves several steps. First, neurotransmitters are synthesized inside the presynaptic (sending) neuron and stored in vesicles. Next, neurotransmitters are released into the synaptic space, where they bind with and stimulate receptor sites on the postsynaptic (receiving) neuron. Finally, neurotransmitter molecules are deactivated by enzymes or by re-uptake.

Certain drugs are designed to interfere in some way with this process. Many of the drugs are entirely legal and carefully controlled, some are illegal. Those that take these drugs aim to alter the synaptic flow, and so interfere with chemical information transmission in the brain. Drugs can have several actions, including those of agonist and antagonist.

An agonist is a drug that increases the activity of a neurotransmitter. Figure 6.31 shows that agonists may:

- enhance a neuron's ability to synthesize, store, or release neurotransmitters
- bind with and stimulate postsynaptic receptor sites (or make it easier for neurotransmitters to stimulate these sites)
- make it more difficult for neurotransmitters to be deactivated, such as by inhibiting re-uptake.

Consider two examples. First, *opiates* (such as morphine and codeine) are effective pain relievers. Recall that the brain contains its own chemicals, endorphins, which play a major role in pain relief. Opiates have a molecular structure similar to that of endorphins

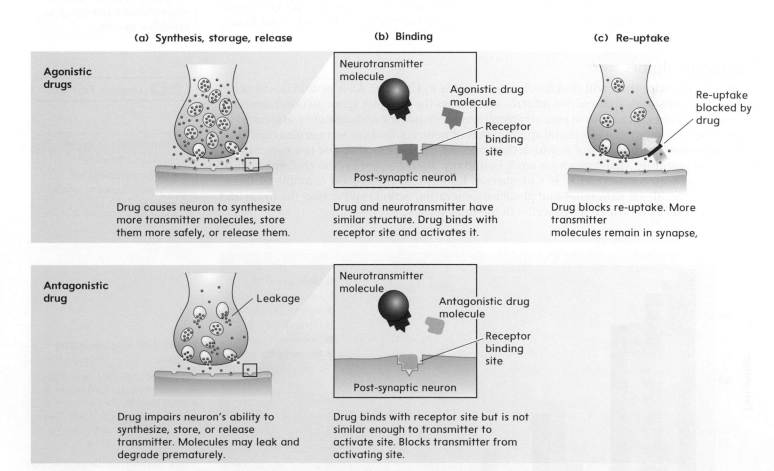

(a) Synthesis, storage, release

Agonistic drugs

Drug causes neuron to synthesize more transmitter molecules, store them more safely, or release them.

(b) Binding

Neurotransmitter molecule

Agonistic drug molecule

Receptor binding site

Post-synaptic neuron

Drug and neurotransmitter have similar structure. Drug binds with receptor site and activates it.

(c) Re-uptake

Re-uptake blocked by drug

Drug blocks re-uptake. More transmitter molecules remain in synapse,

Antagonistic drug

Leakage

Drug impairs neuron's ability to synthesize, store, or release transmitter. Molecules may leak and degrade prematurely.

Neurotransmitter molecule

Antagonistic drug molecule

Receptor binding site

Post-synaptic neuron

Drug binds with receptor site but is not similar enough to transmitter to activate site. Blocks transmitter from activating site.

FIGURE 6.31 How drugs affect neurotransmitters.

(*Top*) Agonistic drugs increase the activity of a neurotransmitter. (*Bottom*) Antagonistic drugs decrease the activity of a neurotransmitter.

They bind to and activate receptor sites that receive endorphins. To draw an analogy, think of trying to open a lock with a key. Normally an endorphin molecule acts as the key, but owing to its very similar shape, an opiate molecule can fit into the lock and open it. As far as the brain is concerned, an endorphin has opened the 'lock', and so taking an opiate, such as morphine, or heroin has the same effect.

Second, *amphetamines* boost arousal and mood by causing neurons to release greater amounts of dopamine and norepinephrine and by inhibiting re-uptake. During re-uptake, neurotransmitters in the synapse are absorbed back into presynaptic neurons through special channels. Because the channels back into the presynaptic neuron are filled by the amphetamine, this means that the drugs in the synapse (the gap between the presynaptic neuron and the postsynaptic neuron) can only remain where they are or travel to the postsynaptic receptor sites. As shown in Figure 6.31c, amphetamine molecules block this re-uptake process. Therefore, dopamine and norepinephrine remain in the synaptic space longer and keep stimulating postsynaptic neurons.

How Drugs Inhibit Synaptic Transmission

Just like an agonist, an antagonist interferes with synaptic transmission, but has exactly the opposite effect. An antagonist is a drug that inhibits or decreases the action of a neurotransmitter. As Figure 6.31 shows, an antagonist may:

- reduce a neuron's ability to synthesize, store or release neurotransmitters, or
- prevent a neurotransmitter from binding with the postsynaptic neuron, such as by fitting into and blocking the receptor sites on the postsynaptic neuron, or degradation in the synapse.

Consider the action of drugs called *antipsychotics* used to treat *schizophrenia*, a severe psychological disorder whose symptoms may include hallucinations (e.g., hearing voices) and delusions (clearly false beliefs, such as believing you are Napoleon). Dopamine is a hugely important neurotransmitter and these psychotic symptoms are often associated with over activity within the dopamine system. To restore dopamine activity to more normal levels, pharmaceutical companies have developed drugs with a molecular structure similar, but importantly not identical, to dopamine. Returning to the lock-and-key analogy, imagine finding a key that fits into a lock but will not turn. The key's shape is close enough to the real key to get in but not to open the lock. Antipsychotic drugs fit into dopamine receptor sites but not well enough to stimulate them. In effect, they block up the keyhole, which means that the lock cannot be opened by the dopamine in the system. Dopamine released by presynaptic neurons is blocked and cannot get in, and the schizophrenic symptoms usually decrease.

Knowledge of how drugs affect the brain is terribly important to those engaged in the development of drugs to help those suffering with pain or mental illness. Unfortunately, drugs are also produced by those aiming to alter consciousness for recreational purposes. The danger here is that the drugs are not as carefully designed as we might hope. **Chapter 4** provides more information of how agonists and antagonists are used in society, with both legal and illegal examples.

 Chapter 4, Page 128

DRUG TOLERANCE AND DEPENDENCE

When a drug is used repeatedly, the intensity of effects produced by the same dosage level may decrease over time. This decreasing responsivity to a drug is called **tolerance**. As it develops, the person must take increasingly larger doses to achieve the same physical and psychological effects. Tolerance stems from the body's attempt to maintain a state of optimal physiological balance, called *homeostasis*. If a drug changes bodily functioning in a certain way, by, say, increasing heart rate, the brain tries to restore balance by producing **compensatory responses**, which are reactions opposite to that of the drug (e.g., reactions that decrease heart rate).

What happens when drug tolerance develops and the person suddenly stops using the drug? The body's compensatory responses may continue and, no longer balanced out by the drug's effects, the person can experience strong reactions opposite to those

tolerance decreasing responsivity to a drug

compensatory responses reactions opposite to that of the drug

produced by the drug. This occurrence of compensatory responses after discontinued drug use is known as withdrawal. For example, in the absence of alcohol's sedating and relaxing effects, a chronic drinker may experience anxiety and hypertension. One of the consequences of abrupt drug withdrawal is called 'rebound insomnia'. This happens with a class of drugs called 'hypnotics' that are designed to help a patient sleep. Stopping these drugs abruptly can cause the patient to suffer with insomnia, which was why they were taking the hypnotic in the first place. The result is that the 'rebound insomnia' is seen by the patient as a reoccurrence of their original insomnia. They believe that they still need the drug, and the habit persists, as the patient lapses and begins taking the drug once more. The person is now showing the symptoms of drug dependency.

withdrawal occurrence of compensatory responses after discontinued drug use

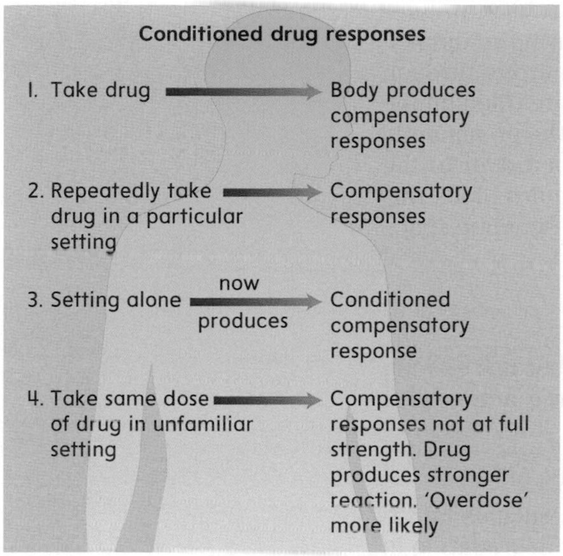

FIGURE 6.32 Conditioned drug responses and overdose.
Environmental stimuli that are repeatedly paired with the use of a drug can eventually trigger compensatory responses on their own. If the same drug dose is now taken in a new setting, compensatory responses will not be at full strength, thereby increasing the risk of an 'overdose' reaction.

Focus 6.19 How are tolerance, compensatory responses, withdrawal and dependence related? How does learning affect tolerance?

substance dependence maladaptive pattern of substance use that causes a person significant distress or substantially impairs that person's life

Learning, Drug Tolerance and Overdose

Tolerance for various drugs depends partly on the familiarity of the drug setting. Figure 6.32 illustrates how environmental stimuli associated with repeated drug use begin to elicit compensatory responses through a learning process called *classical conditioning*. As drug use continues, the physical setting triggers progressively stronger compensatory responses, increasing the user's tolerance. This helps explain why drug addicts often experience increased cravings when they enter a setting associated with drug use. The environmental stimuli trigger compensatory responses that, without drugs to mask their effect, cause the user to feel withdrawal symptoms (Duncan, Alici, & Woodward, 2000).

There is a hidden danger in this process, particularly for experienced drug users. Compensatory responses serve a protective function by physiologically countering part of the drug's effects. If a user takes his or her usual high dose in a familiar environment, the body's compensatory responses are at full strength – a combination of compensatory reactions to the drug itself and also to the familiar, conditioned environmental stimuli. But in an *unfamiliar* environment, the conditioned compensatory responses are weaker, and the drug has a stronger physiological net effect than usual (Siegel, Baptista, Kim, McDonald, & Weise-Kelly, 2000).

Shepard Siegel (1984) interviewed people addicted to heroin who experienced near-fatal overdoses. He found that in most cases they had not taken a dose larger than their customary one. Rather, they had injected a normal dose in an unfamiliar environment. Siegel concluded that the addicts were not protected by their usual compensatory responses, resulting in an 'overdose' reaction.

Drug Addiction and Dependence

Drug addiction, which is formally called substance dependence, is a maladaptive pattern of substance use that causes a person significant distress or substantially impairs that person's life. Substance dependence is diagnosed as occurring with *physiological dependence* if drug tolerance or withdrawal symptoms have developed. The term *psychological dependence* is often used to describe situations in which people strongly crave a drug because of its pleasurable effects, even if they are not physiologically dependent. However, this is not a diagnostic term, and some drug experts feel it is misleading. Drug cravings do have a physical basis; they are rooted in patterns of brain activity (Sun & Rebec, 2005).

Misconceptions about substance dependence

Many people mistakenly believe that if a drug does not produce tolerance or withdrawal, one cannot become dependent on it. In reality, neither tolerance nor withdrawal is needed for a diagnosis of substance dependence.

The popular media image of a shaking alcoholic desperately searching for a drink or a heroin junkie looking for a fix reinforces another misconception, namely, that the motivation to avoid or end withdrawal symptoms is the primary cause of addiction.

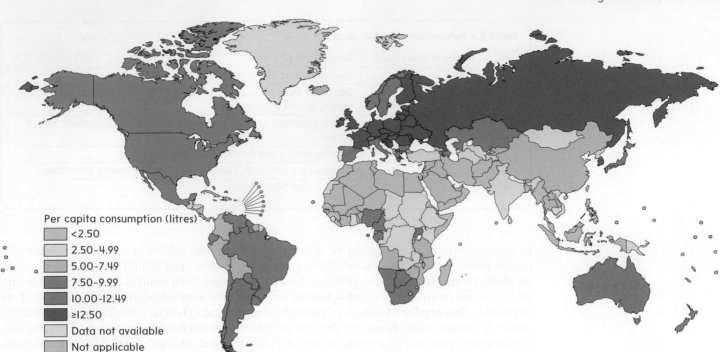

FIGURE 6.33 Adult per capita alcohol consumption in the world measured in pure alcohol consumption per person per year.

Alcohol consumption across the world varies. The level in Europe is almost twice that of the world average.

Source: Reproduced, with the permission of the publisher, from Global Status report on Alcohol and Health, 2011 (http://www.who.int/substance_abuse/publications/global_alcohol_report/msb_gsr_2014_l.pdf. Accessed 25 Sept 2014)/WHO

Such physiological dependence contributes powerfully to drug dependence, but consider these points:

- People can become dependent on drugs, such as cocaine, that produce only mild withdrawal (Kampmann et al., 2002). The drug's pleasurable effects – often produced by boosting dopamine activity – play a key role in causing dependence.

- Many drug users who quit and make it through withdrawal eventually start using again, even though they are no longer physiologically dependent.

- Many factors influence drug dependence, including genetic predispositions, personality traits, religious beliefs, family and peer influences, and cultural norms.

> **depressants** decrease nervous system activity

DEPRESSANTS

Depressants decrease nervous system activity. In moderate doses, they reduce feelings of tension and anxiety, and produce a state of relaxed euphoria. In extremely high doses, depressants can slow down vital life processes to the point of death.

Alcohol

Alcohol is the most widely used recreational drug in many cultures. The World Health Authority indicates that the European region has the highest alcohol consumption of all its regions, with consumption levels twice those of the world average (Figure 6.33). Alcohol is a major cause of death in Europe (Figure 6.34). In addition to death, continued consumption of alcohol can cause other problems. Tolerance develops gradually and can lead to physiological dependence. Alcohol dampens the nervous system by increasing the activity of GABA, the brain's main inhibitory neurotransmitter, and by decreasing the activity of glutamate, a major excitatory neurotransmitter (Anton, 2001). Why, then, if alcohol

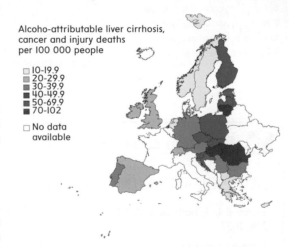

FIGURE 6.34 Alcohol related standardized death (rates per 100,000 people).

Source: Reproduced, with the permission of the publisher, from Status report on alcohol and health in 35 European countries, 2013 (http://www.euro.who.int/en/publications/abstracts/status-report-on-alcohol-and-health-in-35-european-countries-2013. Accessed 25 Sept 2014)/WHO

TABLE 6.3 Behavioural effects of alcohol

BAL	Hours to leave body	Behavioural effects
.03	1	Decreased alertness, impaired reaction time in some people
.05	2	Decreased alertness, impaired judgement and reaction time, good feeling, release of inhibitions
.10	4	Severely impaired reaction time, motor function and judgement; lack of caution
.25	?	Extreme sensory and motor impairment, staggering
.30	?	Stuporous but conscious, cannot comprehend immediate environment
.40	?	Lethal in over 50% of cases

is a depressant drug, do many people initially seem less inhibited when they drink and report getting a high from alcohol? In part, the weakening of inhibitions occurs because alcohol's neural slowdown depresses the action of inhibitory control centres in the brain. As for the subjective high, alcohol boosts the activity of several neurotransmitters, such as dopamine, that produce feelings of pleasure and euphoria (Lewis, 1996; Tupala & Tiihonen, 2004). At higher doses, however, the brain's control centres become increasingly disrupted, thinking and physical coordination become disorganized, and fatigue may occur as blood-alcohol level (BAL) rises (Table 6.3). For reference, the BAL deemed legal for driving in Europe ranges between 0.2mg/ml to 0.8mg/ml. In Turkey, it is illegal to have consumed any alcohol at all, when taking passengers in your car. In South Africa the limit is 0.2mg/ml if you are a professional driver, or if you are carrying paying customers, such as a taxi driver might be; otherwise the limit is 0.5mg/ml.

Alcohol consumption can significantly influence judgement and performance. *Blood-alcohol level* is a measure of alcohol concentration in the body. Elevated BALs impair reaction time, coordination and decision-making, and increase risky behaviours. The problem is very serious, so much so that the European Union has set itself a target to halve deaths in road traffic; 40,000 people were killed and over 1.7 million people injured in accidents where alcohol was involved (Eurocare, 2003).

Why do intoxicated people often act in risky ways that they would not when sober? It is not simply a matter of lowered inhibitions. Alcohol also produces what Steele and Josephs (1990) call **alcohol myopia**, short-sighted thinking caused by the inability to pay attention to as much information as when sober. People who drink start to focus only on aspects of the situation (cues) that stand out. In the absence of strong cautionary cues (such as warnings) to inhibit risky behaviour, they do not think about long-term consequences of their actions as carefully as when they are sober. Our 'Research close-up' illustrates this effect.

Focus 6.20 How do depressants affect the brain? How does alcohol intoxication affect decisions about drinking and driving?

alcohol myopia short-sighted thinking caused by the inability to pay attention to as much information as when sober

---

 Research close-up

ALCOHOL + DRIVING: AN ACCIDENT WAITING TO HAPPEN

Source: E. L. R. Harrison & M. T. Fillmore (2011). 'Alcohol and distraction interact to impair driving performance. *Drug and Alcohol Dependence, 117*(1), 2011, 31–37.

INTRODUCTION

Here we have the opportunity to draw together two different, but equally important, aspects of psychology covered in this chapter: the effects of alcohol and the psychology of attention. Most people have negative attitudes about drunk driving and say they would not do it. They realize that the cons (e.g., risk of accident, injury, death and police arrest) far outweigh the pros (e.g., not having to ask someone for a lift). Why, then, do so many people decide to drive after becoming intoxicated?

▶

Based on the lapse of attention that comes with alcohol-myopia principles, Harrison and Fillmore (2011) looked at how drinking and driving means that we are more distracted and so less focused on the task in hand.

The authors looked closely at the driving task and recognized that in everyday situations, many distractions are present that do not impair performance. They went on to look at how these distractions became a problem when the driver was intoxicated. In short, they looked at how a relatively straightforward task, requiring a certain amount of attention and concentration, took on a very different perspective when alcohol was thrown into the mix. The work tests the hypothesis that divided attention (see page 221) has no impairing effect on driving performance in sober drivers but, under the influence of alcohol, divided attention exacerbates the impairing effects of alcohol on driving precision.

METHOD

Laboratory experiment

Forty participants (20 male and 20 female) took part. The mean age of the group was 24 years with a standard deviation of 3.8 years. The sample was screened, using a questionnaire that provided information on numerous variables, including the participants' drinking habits as well as their physical and mental health. As part of the screening procedure, each participant provided data for the Michigan alcoholism screening test (Selzer, Vinokur, & van Rooijen, 1975). Those scoring 5 or higher were excluded from the study. In addition to these measures, urine tests were assessed for recent drug use, and those testing positive were excluded. Pregnant or breast-feeding volunteers were also excluded. All volunteers held a full driving licence and all were paid for their contribution to the research.

The simulated driving task

A simulated driving task was developed. Participants were presented with a view of a road on a computer screen. They could also see a simulated dashboard at the bottom of the display. A steering wheel, accelerator and brake controlled the 'vehicle'. The task required participants to drive in daytime conditions along a 9.5-kilometre route obeying the traffic laws at all times. The route included traffic lights and intersections, junctions and straight roads, each requiring different skills. Traffic lights may have been red or green and participants were required to respond appropriately to each. Any crashes into other vehicles resulted in a crashing sound and a restart of the participant vehicle in the middle of the road to continue the given route. It took participants up to 10 minutes to complete the task, depending on their speed.

The divided attention condition

When in the divided attention condition, participants were required to complete a secondary task while navigating the simulated vehicle along its virtual route. The task was extremely simple. Arrows appeared either at the top right or top left of the screen during the driving task and participants were required to respond to them using two buttons, relating to each of the two arrows, on their steering wheel as quickly and as accurately as possible. This task resembled the simple distraction we might expect in an everyday driving task.

In addition, all participants were questioned to assess their personal driving habits. After each driving session participants were required to report their perception of their own driving impairment (on a scale of 0 for 'not impaired at all' to 100 for 'very impaired'). Finally, a measure of blood-alcohol level was determined from breath samples.

The experiment

All volunteers arrived at the laboratory and were fully assessed. Each was briefed and the appropriate notifications of informed consent signed. Volunteers were randomly assigned to one of four groups.

Group 1: Alcohol

Group 2: Alcohol + divided attention

Group 3: Placebo

Group 4: Placebo + divided attention

All completed a simulated driving test before any 'treatments' with alcohol or placebo to provide a sober, baseline measurement of their performance. Each was then given their 'treatment'. A fizzy lime drink was the base for both placebo and alcohol treatments. The alcohol dose gave an average level of 80mg/100ml 60 minutes after consumption. The placebo solution was of the same volume as the alcoholic drinks. A tiny quantity of alcohol was placed on the top of the placebo drink, providing an alcoholic scent identical to that in the alcoholic drink.

Drivers were encouraged to break the speed limit through the test with monetary rewards. The faster the task was completed the more money they were to be given.

Performance criteria

Driver precision (assessment of lateral road position), driver speed (time taken to complete the course), reckless driving (number of failures to stop at red lights) and secondary task performance were all measured.

RESULTS

There were no differences between the groups in the drinking habits they reported, and the blood-alcohol levels of the groups that were given alcohol were not significantly different. The blood-alcohol levels of the placebo groups were both negligible. The number of collisions was negligible

in all groups. The driving performance, however, measured in terms of a deviation from lateral position on the road, was interesting and is plotted in Figure 6.35.

These results show that alcohol impairs driving performance when measured in terms of deviation from driving in the correct road position, irrespective of whether attention was divided or not. However, where attention is divided the driving performance is further affected.

In addition to this very clear finding, the results also showed that driver speed was also influenced by alcohol and divided attention. Sober drivers would slow their speed when faced with distractions whereas those who had drunk alcohol would not. Similarly, those in the placebo group would slow their speed when faced with distractions.

DISCUSSION

The busy roads we travel on today are peppered with distractions. Keeping within the white lines as we navigate, avoiding traffic at junctions and remaining within the speed limit are often hard enough, but with the many signs and additional distractions that appear in and around our towns we are constantly in danger of dividing our attention. This situation is dangerous enough, but when alcohol is introduced into the system the problem is dramatically increased. Alcohol myopia means that the problems of divided attention are increased. The original hypothesis, that divided attention has no impairing effect on driving performance in sober drivers but, under the influence of alcohol, divided attention exacerbates the impairing effects of alcohol on driving precision, is upheld and, in addition to this, drivers did not compensate for the effects of alcohol by reducing their speed.

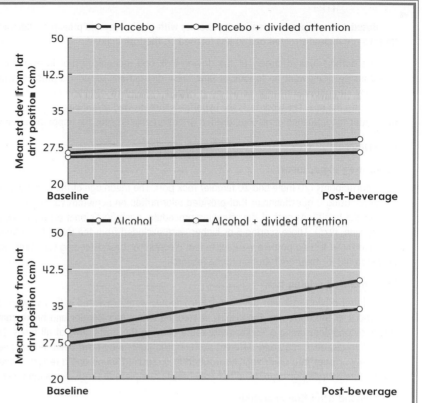

FIGURE 6.35 Mean standard deviation from lateral driving position, in centimetres.

Source: Reprinted from *Alcohol and Drug Dependence* 60 (3) "Drinking and heavy drinking by students in 18 countries" by Reginald G Smart, Alan Ogborne. Reprinted with permission of Elsevier (2000).

Barbiturates and Tranquillizers

Physicians sometimes prescribe barbiturates (sleeping pills) and tranquillizers (anti-anxiety drugs, such as Valium) as sedatives and relaxants. Like alcohol, they depress the nervous system by increasing the activity of the inhibitory neurotransmitter GABA (Nishino, Mignot, & Dement, 2001).

Mild doses of drugs belonging to the benzodiazepine group are effective as sleeping pills but are highly addictive. As tolerance builds, addicted people may take up to 50 sleeping pills a day. At high doses, barbiturates trigger initial excitation, followed by slurred speech, loss of coordination, depression and memory impairment. Overdoses, particularly when taken with alcohol, may cause unconsciousness, coma and even death. Barbiturates and tranquillizers are widely overused, and tolerance and physiological dependence can occur. Users often do not recognize that they have become dependent until they try to stop and experience serious withdrawal symptoms, such as anxiety, insomnia and, possibly, seizures. It must be said, though, that more modern hypnotics (drugs that help people sleep) do not cause people to suffer quite so badly with these side effects. Some doctors prescribe other drugs for insomnia, such as antidepressants and antihistamines, as these have a sedative effect, but avoid the problem of tolerance.

STIMULANTS

> **stimulants** increase neural firing and arouse the nervous system

Stimulants increase neural firing and arouse the nervous system. They increase blood pressure, respiration, heart rate and overall alertness. While they can elevate mood to the point of euphoria, they also can heighten irritability.

Amphetamines

Amphetamines are powerful stimulants prescribed to reduce appetite and fatigue, decrease the need for sleep and reduce depression. Unfortunately, they are widely overused to boost energy and mood (Anthony, Warner, & Kessler, 1997).

Amphetamines increase dopamine and noradrenaline (aka norepinephrine) activity. Tolerance develops, and users may crave their pleasurable effects. Eventually, many heavy users start injecting large quantities, producing a sudden surge of energy and rush of intense pleasure. With frequent injections, they may remain awake for a week, their bodily systems racing at breakneck speed. Injecting amphetamines greatly increases blood pressure and can lead to heart failure and cerebral haemorrhage (stroke); repeated high doses may cause brain damage (Diaz, 1997).

There is an inevitable crash when heavy users stop taking the drug. They may sleep for one to two days, waking up depressed, exhausted and irritable. This crash occurs because the neurons' noradrenaline (norepinephrine) and dopamine supplies have become depleted. Amphetamines tax the body heavily.

Cocaine

Cocaine is a powder derived from the coca plant, which grows mainly in western South America. Usually inhaled or injected, it produces excitation, a sense of increased muscular strength and euphoria. Cocaine increases the activity of noradrenaline (norepinephrine) and dopamine by blocking their re-uptake.

At various times in history, cocaine has been hailed as a wonder drug and branded as a menace. It was once widely used as a local anaesthetic in eye, nose and throat surgery. Novocain, a synthetic form of cocaine, is still used in dentistry as an anaesthetic. Owing to its stimulating effects, cocaine found its way into potions sold to the public to enhance health (Figure 6.36). In 1885 John Pemberton developed Coca-Cola by mixing cocaine with the kola nut and syrup. When Coca-Cola was first produced it was advertised that it 'relieved fatigue', there was a clear reason why: it contained cocaine.

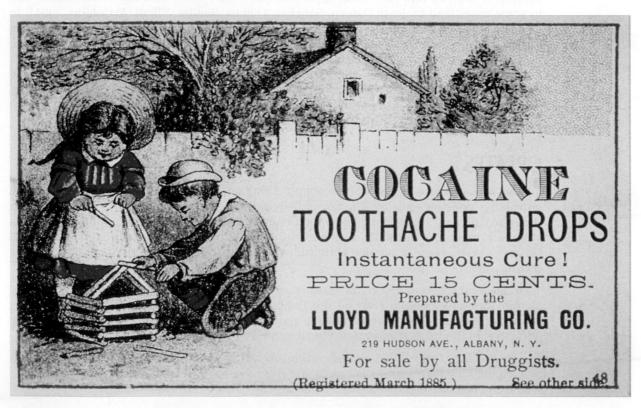

FIGURE 6.36 Before it was made illegal, cocaine was found in a variety of medicinal products.

Source: © CORBIS

FIGURE 6.37 Frequent ecstasy use and the brain.

(*Left*) This PET-scan image shows the brain of a person who never used ecstasy. (*Right*) This image shows the brain of a person who used ecstasy 70 times or more over a period of at least 1.5 years but who stopped using the drug for several weeks before these images were taken. Areas of lighter colour indicate a higher density of special proteins (called *transporters*) necessary for normal serotonin re-uptake. The darker image of the brain on the right suggests that there is damage to the serotonin re-uptake system.

Source: Reprinted from *The Lancet*, Vol. 352, McCann et al 'Positron emission tomographic evidence of toxic effect of MDMA ("Ecstasy") on brain serotonin neurons in human beings.' (1998). With permission from Elsevier.

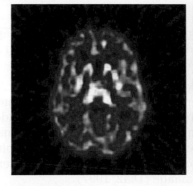
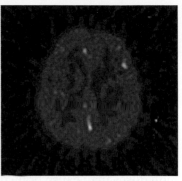

In large doses, cocaine can produce vomiting, convulsions and paranoid delusions (Boutros et al., 2002). A depressive crash may occur after a cocaine high. Tolerance develops too many of cocaine's effects, and chronic use has been associated with an increased risk of cognitive impairments and brain damage (Franklin et al., 2002). Crack is a chemically converted form of cocaine that can be smoked, and its effects are faster and more dangerous. Overdoses can cause sudden death from cardiorespiratory arrest.

Ecstasy (MDMA)

Ecstasy, also known as MDMA (methylenedioxymethamphetamine), is artificially synthesized and has a chemical structure that partly resembles both methamphetamine (a stimulant) and mescaline (a hallucinogen). Ecstasy produces feelings of pleasure, elation, empathy and warmth. In the brain, it primarily increases serotonin functioning, which boosts one's mood but may cause agitation. After the drug wears off, users often feel sluggish and depressed – a rebound effect partly due to serotonin depletion (Travers & Lyvers, 2005). They may have to take increasingly stronger doses to overcome tolerance to ecstasy.

Ecstasy is called a *rave drug* because it is used at nightclubs and rave parties. It causes locomotor activity and can cause hyperthermia, which when used in hot nightclubs can in some cases lead to death (Green, Sanchez, O'Shea, Saadat, Elliott, & Colado, 2004). In experiments with laboratory rats, ecstasy has produced long-lasting damage to the axon terminals of neurons that release serotonin (Mechan, Moran, Elliot, Young, Joseph, & Green, 2002). Human studies of habitual ecstasy users suggest a similar possibility (Figure 6.37), but it is not clear whether such damage is permanent. In the long run, ecstasy may produce consequences that are anything but pleasurable. Continued use has been associated with impaired memory, sleep difficulties and a diminished capacity to experience sexual pleasure (Parrott, 2001).

> **Focus 6.21** How do amphetamines, cocaine and ecstasy affect the brain? Why can their use lead to a 'crash'?

OPIATES

> **opiates** opium and drugs derived from it, such as morphine, codeine and heroin

Opium is a product of the opium poppy. Opium and drugs derived from it, such as morphine, codeine and heroin, are called **opiates**. Opiates have two major effects: they provide pain relief and cause mood changes which may include euphoria. Opiates stimulate receptors normally activated by endorphins, thereby producing pain relief. Opiates also increase dopamine activity, which may be one reason they induce euphoria (Bardo, 1998).

In medical use, opiates are the most effective agents known for relieving intense pain. Heroin was developed in 1889 by the Bayer company (which today produces aspirin). Initially thought to be a non-addictive painkiller, heroin is, like other opiates, highly addictive. In the 1920s it was made illegal in the USA.

Heroin users feel an intense rush within several minutes of an injection, but they often pay a high price for this transient pleasure. High doses may lead to respiratory depression, which can be fatal, and coma, and overdoses can cause death (Julien, 2007).

HALLUCINOGENS

Hallucinogens are powerful mind-altering drugs that produce hallucinations. Many are derived from natural sources; mescaline, for example, comes from the peyote cactus. Natural hallucinogens have been considered sacred in many tribal cultures because of their ability to produce unearthly states of consciousness and contact with spiritual forces (Figure 6.38). Other hallucinogens, such as LSD (lysergic acid diethylamide, or 'acid') and phencyclidine ('angel dust') are synthetic.

Hallucinogens distort sensory experience and can blur the boundaries between reality and fantasy. Users, such as Timothy Leary, who publicly advocated and encouraged the use of the drug, speak of having mystical experiences and of feeling exhilarated. They may also experience violent outbursts, paranoia and panic, and have flashbacks after the trip has ended. The mental effects of hallucinogens are always unpredictable, even if they are taken repeatedly.

LSD is a powerful hallucinogen that causes a flooding of excitation in the nervous system. Tolerance develops rapidly but decreases quickly. It increases the activity of serotonin and dopamine at certain receptor sites, but scientists still do not know precisely how LSD produces its effects (Nichols & Sanders-Bush, 2002).

MARIJUANA

Marijuana, a product of the hemp plant (*Cannabis sativa*), is the most widely used and controversial illegal drug which has found a prominent role in popular culture over the years (Figure 6.39). **THC (tetrahydrocannabinol)** is marijuana's major active ingredient, and it binds to receptors on neurons throughout the brain. But why does the brain have receptor sites for a foreign substance such as marijuana? The answer is that the brain produces its own THC-like substances called *cannabinoids* (Kirkham, 2004). With chronic use, THC may increase GABA activity, which slows down neural activity and produces relaxing effects (Diaz, 1997). THC also increases dopamine activity, which may account for some of its pleasurable subjective effects (Maldonado & Rodriguez de Fonseca, 2002). THC has been shown to have some therapeutic potential, for example in cases of chemotherapy-induced nausea, in some pain conditions and as a drug that may alleviate some symptoms of multiple sclerosis (Carlini, 2004). However, there is research linking the use of cannabis with clinical manifestations of psychological disorders such as schizophrenia and certainly schizotypal personality symptoms (Compton, Goulding, & Walker, 2007). We will discuss schizophrenia further in **Chapter 17**.

Misconceptions about Marijuana

One misconception about marijuana is that chronic use causes people to become unmotivated and apathetic towards everything, a condition called *amotivational syndrome*. Another misconception is that marijuana causes people to start using more dangerous drugs. Neither statement is supported by scientific evidence (Diaz, 1997; Rao, 2001). A third misconception is that using marijuana has no significant dangers. In fact, marijuana smoke contains more cancer-causing substances than does tobacco smoke. At high doses, users may experience negative changes in mood, sensory distortions, and feelings of panic and anxiety. While users are high, marijuana can impair their reaction time, thinking, memory, learning and driving skills (Lane, Cherek, Lieving, & Tcheremissine, 2005).

FIGURE 6.39 Marijuana has featured prominently in popular culture for a very long time.

Films like *Reefer Madness* (1936) were clearly propaganda focused on those considering the use of the drug. Other media used popular myths about marijuana to sensational effect. Books such as *The Marijuana Mob* by James Hadley Chase (1950), and *Reefer Girl* by Jane Manning (1956) were just two of many.

Source: © Bettmann/CORBIS

hallucinogens powerful mind-altering drugs that produce hallucinations

FIGURE 6.38 Hallucinogenic drugs are thought by some to 'open doors of perception'. Famously Aldous Huxley was rumoured to have been introduced to peyote by the occultist Aleister Crowley.

Source: © Pictorial Press Ltd/Alamy

THC (tetrahydrocannabinol) marijuana's major active ingredient

Chapter 17, Page 753

Focus 6.22 Describe the major effects and dangers of opiates, hallucinogens and marijuana.

Another misconception is that users cannot become dependent on marijuana. Actually, repeated marijuana use produces tolerance and, at typical doses, some chronic users may experience mild withdrawal symptoms, such as restlessness. People who use chronically high doses and suddenly stop may experience vomiting, disrupted sleep and irritability. About 5–10% of people who use marijuana develop dependence (Coffey, Carlin, Degenhardt, Lynskey, Sanci, & Patton, 2002).

FROM GENES TO CULTURE: DETERMINANTS OF DRUG EFFECTS

Table 6.4 summarizes some typical drug effects, but a user's reaction depends on more than the drug's chemical structure.

Biological Factors

Animal research indicates that genetic factors influence sensitivity and tolerance to drugs' effects (Boehm, Reed, McKinnon, & Phillips, 2002). The most extensive research has focused on alcohol. Rats and mice can be genetically bred to inherit a strong preference for drinking alcohol instead of water. Even in their first exposure to alcohol, these rats show greater tolerance than normal rats.

Among humans, identical twins have a higher concordance rate for alcoholism than do fraternal twins (Heath et al., 1997). Scientists have also identified a gene that is found more often among alcoholics and their children than among non-alcoholics and their offspring (Noble, 1998). No one claims that this is an 'alcoholism gene'; rather, it may influence how the brain responds to alcohol.

People who grow up with alcoholic versus non-alcoholic parents respond differently to drinking alcohol under laboratory conditions. Adults who had alcoholic parents typically display faster hormonal and psychological reactions as blood-alcohol levels rise, but these responses drop off more quickly as blood-alcohol levels decrease (Newlin & Thomson, 1997). Compared with other people, they must drink more alcohol over the course of a few hours to maintain their feeling of intoxication. Overall, many scientists see evidence for a genetic role in determining responsiveness and addiction to alcohol (Knopik et al., 2004).

Psychological Factors

At the psychological level, people's beliefs and expectancies can influence drug reactions (George, Stoner, Norris, Lopez, & Lehman, 2000). Experiments show that people may behave as if drunk if they simply think they have consumed alcohol but actually have not. If a person's fellow drinkers are happy and gregarious, he or she may feel it is expected

TABLE 6.4 Effects of some major drugs

Class	Typical effects	Risks of high doses and/or chronic use
Depressants		
Alcohol	Relaxation, lowered inhibition, impaired physical and psychological functioning	Disorientation, unconsciousness, possible death at extreme doses
Barbiturates, tranquillizers	Reduced tension, impaired reflexes and motor functioning, drowsiness	Shallow breathing, clammy skin, weak and rapid pulse, coma, possible death
Stimulants		
Amphetamines, cocaine, ecstasy	Increased alertness, pulse and blood pressure; elevated mood, suppressed appetite, agitation, sleeplessness	Hallucinations, paranoid delusions, convulsions, long-term cognitive impairments, brain damage, possible death
Opiates		
Opium, morphine, codeine, heroin	Euphoria, pain relief, drowsiness, impaired motor and psychological functioning	Shallow breathing, convulsions, coma, possible death
Hallucinogens		
LSD, mescaline, Phencyclidine	Hallucinations and visions, distorted time perception, loss of contact with reality, nausea	Psychotic reactions (delusions, paranoia), panic, possible death
Marijuana	Mild euphoria, relaxation, enhanced sensory experiences, increased appetite, impaired memory and reaction time	Fatigue, anxiety, disorientation, sensory distortions, possible psychotic reactions, exposure to carcinogens

that he or she responds the same way. Personality factors also influence drug reactions and usage. People who have difficulty adjusting to life's demands or whose contact with reality is marginal may be particularly vulnerable to severe and negative drug reactions and to drug addiction (Ray & Ksir, 2004).

Environmental Factors

The physical and social setting in which a drug is taken can strongly influence a user's reactions. As noted earlier, merely being in a familiar drug-use setting can trigger compensatory physiological responses and cravings. Moreover, the behaviour of other people who are sharing the drug experience provides important cues for how to respond, and a hostile environment may increase the chances of a bad trip with drugs such as LSD (Palfai & Jankiewicz, 1991).

Cultural learning also affects how people respond to a drug (Bloomfield, Greenfield, Kraus, & Augustin, 2002). In many western cultures, increased aggressiveness and sexual promiscuity are commonly associated with drunken excess. In contrast, members of the Camba culture of Bolivia customarily drink large quantities of an almost pure alcohol, remaining cordial and non-aggressive between episodes of passing out. In the 1700s, Tahitians introduced to alcohol by European sailors reacted at first with pleasant relaxation when intoxicated, but after witnessing the violent aggressiveness exhibited by drunken sailors, they too began behaving aggressively (MacAndrew & Edgerton, 1969).

Focus 6.23 Explain how drug reactions depend on biological, psychological and environmental factors.

Cultural Factors also Affect Drug Consumption

Traditionally, members of the Navajo tribe do not consider drinking any amount of alcohol to be normal, whereas drinking wine or beer is central to social life in some European countries (Tanaka-Matsumi & Draguns, 1997). In some cultures, hallucinogenic drugs are feared and outlawed, whereas in others they are used in medicinal or religious contexts

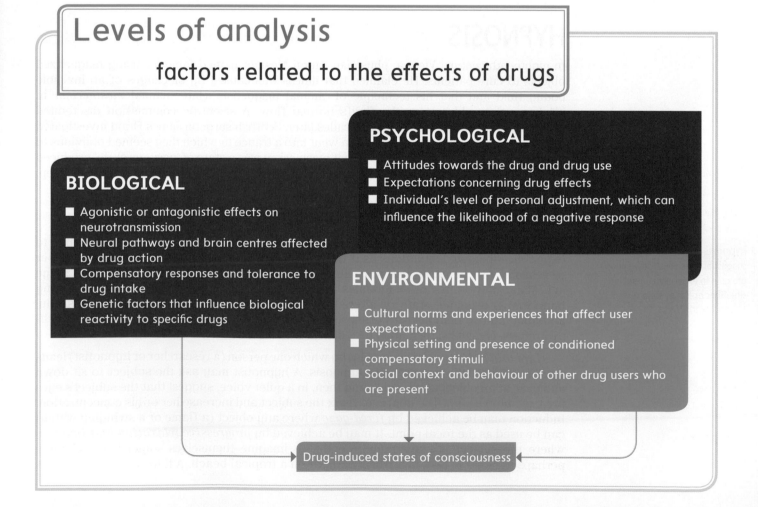

Levels of analysis
factors related to the effects of drugs

PSYCHOLOGICAL
- Attitudes towards the drug and drug use
- Expectations concerning drug effects
- Individual's level of personal adjustment, which can influence the likelihood of a negative response

BIOLOGICAL
- Agonistic or antagonistic effects on neurotransmission
- Neural pathways and brain centres affected by drug action
- Compensatory responses and tolerance to drug intake
- Genetic factors that influence biological reactivity to specific drugs

ENVIRONMENTAL
- Cultural norms and experiences that affect user expectations
- Physical setting and presence of conditioned compensatory stimuli
- Social context and behaviour of other drug users who are present

Drug-induced states of consciousness

In review

- Drugs alter consciousness by modifying neurotransmitter activity. Agonists increase the activity of a neurotransmitter, whereas antagonists decrease it.
- Tolerance develops when the body produces compensatory responses to counteract a drug's effects. When drug use is stopped, compensatory responses continue and produce withdrawal symptoms.
- Substance dependence is a maladaptive pattern of drug use. It can occur with or without physiological dependence.
- Depressants, such as alcohol, barbiturates and tranquillizers, decrease neural activity. The weakened inhibitions often associated with low alcohol doses partly occur because alcohol depresses inhibitory brain centres.
- Amphetamines and cocaine are stimulants that increase arousal and boost mood. Ecstasy produces elation but can also cause agitation. A depressive crash can occur after these drugs wear off. Repeated use may produce serious negative psychological effects and bodily damage.
- Opiates increase endorphin activity, producing pain relief and mood changes that may include euphoria. Opiates are important in medicine but are highly addictive.
- Hallucinogens, such as LSD, powerfully distort sensory experience and can blur the line between reality and fantasy.
- Marijuana produces relaxation at low doses but can cause anxiety and sensory distortions at higher doses. It can impair thinking and reflexes.
- A drug's effect depends on its chemical actions, the physical and social setting, cultural norms and learning, as well as the user's genetic predispositions, expectations and personality.

to seek advice from spirits. The 'levels of analysis' summarizes some of the biological, environmental and psychological factors that may influence drug experiences.

HYPNOSIS

In eighteenth-century Vienna, physician Anton Mesmer gained fame for using magnetized objects to cure patients. He claimed that illness was caused by blockages of an invisible bodily fluid and that his technique of 'animal magnetism' (later named *mesmerism* in his honour) would restore the fluid's normal flow. A scientific commission discredited mesmerism, but its use continued. Decades later, Scottish surgeon James Braid investigated the fact that mesmerized patients often went into a trance in which they seemed oblivious to their surroundings. Braid concluded that mesmerism was a state of 'nervous sleep' produced by concentrated attention, and he renamed it *hypnosis*, after Hypnos, the Greek god of sleep.

THE SCIENTIFIC STUDY OF HYPNOSIS

hypnosis a state of heightened suggestibility in which some people are able to experience imagined situations as if they were real

Hypnosis is a state of heightened suggestibility in which some people are able to experience imagined situations as if they were real. Hypnosis is interesting for a number of reasons, one being its use in treating mental disorders. Hypnosis is not just a stage act. Many universities offer modules and courses in hypnosis with scientists exploring hypnosis as a unique state of altered consciousness. Those hypnotized act decisively, and ably, and so demonstrate primary consciousness, but they do not demonstrate self-awareness. Hypnosis, then, may be a different kind of consciousness.

Hypnotic induction is the process by which one person (a researcher or hypnotist) leads another person (the subject) into hypnosis. A hypnotist may ask the subject to sit down and gaze at an object on the wall, and then, in a quiet voice, suggest that the subject's eyes are becoming heavy. The goal is to relax the subject and increase her or his concentration. Induction may be achieved by *fixed-gaze* where any object (a flame or a swinging watch) can be used as the focal point. It may be achieved by *progressive relaxation and imagery* where the subject is encouraged, gently, to imagine themselves somewhere relaxing, perhaps at home in bed, in a warm bath, or on a tropical beach. A third induction route is

TABLE 6.5 Sample test items from the Stanford Hypnotic Susceptibility Scale, Form C

Item	Suggested behaviour	Criterion for passing
Lowering arm	Right arm is held out; subject is told arm will become heavy and drop	Arm is lowered by 6 inches (15 cm) in 10 seconds
Moving hands apart	With hands extended and close together, subject is asked to imagine a force pushing them apart	Hands are 6 or more inches (15 cm or more) apart in 10 seconds

Source: Based on Weitzenhoffer and Hilgard, 1962.

rapid induction where the hypnotist speaks forcefully, and convincingly. The idea here is that the nervous subject is confused in some way, with their conscious mind overloaded suddenly resulting in a hypnotic state.

Contrary to popular belief, people cannot be hypnotized against their will. Even when people want to be hypnotized, they differ in how susceptible (i.e., responsive) they are to hypnotic suggestions. **Hypnotic susceptibility scales** contain a standard series of pass–fail suggestions that are read to a subject after a hypnotic induction (Table 6.5). The subject's score is based on the number of passes. About 10% of subjects are completely non-responsive, 10% pass all or nearly all of the items, and the rest fall in between (Sanchez-Armass & Barabasz, 2005). There is also evidence that susceptibility to hypnosis may have a genetic element. Morgan (1973) reported that monozygotic (identical) twins showed very similar scores on the Stanford Hypnotic Susceptibility Scale (SHSS) (Hilgard, 1965) than did dyzygotic twins. Additionally, Lichtenberg, Bachner-Melman, Gritsenko and Ebstein (2000) reports that men with certain sub-types of the COMT gene may be more susceptible than others; data for women is not yet available.

> **hypnotic susceptibility scales** a standard series of pass-fail suggestions that are read to a subject after a hypnotic induction

HYPNOTIC BEHAVIOURS AND EXPERIENCES

Does hypnosis alter people's psychological functioning and behaviour? Let us examine some claims.

Involuntary Control and Behaving against One's Will

Hypnotized people *subjectively experience* their actions to be involuntary (Kirsch, 2001). For example, look at the second item in Table 6.5. To hypnotized subjects, it really feels like their hands are being pushed apart by a mysterious force, rather than by their conscious control.

If behaviour seems involuntary under hypnosis, then can a hypnotist make people perform acts that are harmful to themselves or others? Martin Orne and Frederick Evans (1965) found that hypnotized subjects could be induced to dip their hands briefly in a foaming solution they were told was acid and then to throw the 'acid' in another person's face. This might appear to be a striking example of the power of hypnosis to get people to act against their will. However, Orne and Evans tested a control group of subjects who were asked to simply pretend that they were hypnotized. These subjects were just as likely as hypnotized subjects to put their hands in the 'acid' and throw it at someone.

In **Chapter 14** you will learn about experiments in which researchers induced hundreds of 'normal' adults to keep giving what they believed were extremely painful electric shocks to an innocent man with a heart condition who begged them to stop (Milgram, 1974). Not one participant was hypnotized; they were simply following the researcher's orders. Hypnosis does not involve a unique power to get people to behave against their will (Kirsch & Braffman, 2001; Wagstaff, 2008). A legitimate authority figure can induce people to commit out-of-character and dangerous acts whether they are hypnotized or not.

 Chapter 14, Page 589

Amazing Feats

You will have heard of stage hypnotists who have audience members perform amazing physical feats. One such example is the 'human plank'. A subject, usually male, is hypnotized and lies outstretched between two chairs. He is told that his body is rigid

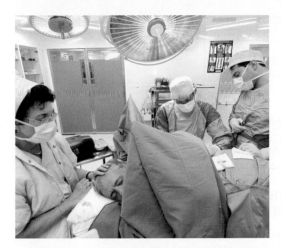

FIGURE 6.40 This patient is undergoing surgery with hypnosis as the sole anaesthetic.

Source: BSIP, RAGUET H/SCIENCE PHOTO LIBRARY

and then, amazingly, another person successfully stands on the subject's legs and chest.

Similarly, hypnosis can have striking physiological effects. Consider a classic experiment involving 13 people who were strongly allergic to the toxic leaves of a certain tree (Ikemi & Nakagawa, 1962). Five of them were hypnotized, blindfolded and told that a leaf from a harmless tree to which they were not allergic was touching one of their arms. In fact, the leaf really was toxic, but four out of the five hypnotized people had no allergic reaction. Next, the other arm of each hypnotized person was rubbed with a leaf from a harmless tree, but he or she was falsely told that the leaf was toxic. All five people responded to the harmless leaf with allergic reactions.

Should we attribute the human-plank feat and the unusual responses of the allergic people to unique powers of hypnosis? Here is where a healthy dose of critical thinking is important.

Pain Tolerance

Scottish surgeon James Esdaile performed more than 300 major operations in the mid-1800s using hypnosis as the sole anaesthetic (Figure 6.40). Experiments confirm that hypnosis often increases pain tolerance and that this is not due to a placebo effect (Milling, 2008; Montgomery, DuHamel, & Redd, 2000). For patients who experience chronic pain, hypnosis can produce relief that lasts for months or even years (Patterson, 2004). Brain-imaging research reveals that hypnosis modifies neural activity in brain areas that process painful stimuli, but non hypnotic techniques, such as mental imagery and performing distracting cognitive tasks, also alter neural functioning and reduce pain (Petrovic & Ingvar, 2002).

Spanos and Katsanis (1989) used the cold-pressor task to investigate pain tolerance under hypnosis. Those under hypnosis plunge their arm into iced-water until they can no longer stand the discomfort. Results showed that those under hypnosis could indeed stand the discomfort better than when not hypnotized (cf. Hilgard, Morgan, & Macdonald, 1975; see also Figure 6.41), but they also showed that highly motivated participants could perform just as well as those under hypnosis. In Hilgard's neodissociation theory of hypnosis he posits that the hypnotized person has deliberately, under their own volition, divided their consciousness. One part listens and responds to the hypnotist, following instructions given and the other part remains as an observer, aware of what is actually going on. In this way the person may be aware of their experience (in Figure 6.41 their pain) but they are still able to listen to the suggestions of the hypnotist. You will find more on this under Theories of Hypnosis below.

We do not know exactly how hypnosis produces its pain-killing effects. It may influence the release of endorphins, decrease patients' fear of pain, distract patients from their pain or somehow help them separate the pain from conscious experience (Barber, 1998). It may also be that those who have experienced hypnosis may experience an expectation

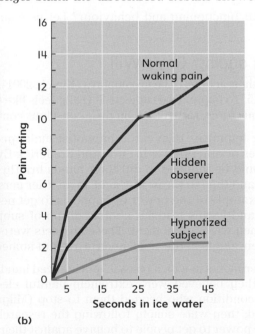

(a)   (b)

FIGURE 6.41 Hypnosis and the hidden observer.

(a) This hypnotized woman's hand is immersed in painfully cold ice water, in the cold-pressor test. Placing his hand on her shoulder, Ernest Hilgard contacts her dissociated hidden observer. (b) This graph shows pain intensity ratings given by a woman when she is not hypnotized, when she is under hypnosis and by her hidden observer in the same hypnotic state. The hidden observer reports more pain than the hypnotized woman but less than the subject when she is not hypnotized.

Source: (a) Jose Mercado/Stanford News Service/Stanford University

of positive or pain-killing effects which may themselves influence the resulting experience of pain (Milling, 2008).

Hypnotic Amnesia

You may have seen television shows or films in which hypnotized people are given a suggestion that they will not remember something (such as a familiar person's name), either during the session itself (*hypnotic amnesia*) or after coming out of hypnosis (*post-hypnotic amnesia*). A reversal cue also is given, such as a phrase ('You will now remember everything') that ends the amnesia once the person hears it. Is this Hollywood fiction?

Research indicates that about 25% of hypnotized college students can be led to experience amnesia (Kirsch, 2001). Although researchers agree that hypnotic and posthypnotic amnesias occur, they debate the causes. Some feel it results from voluntary attempts to avoid thinking about certain information; others believe it is caused by an altered state of consciousness that weakens normal memory systems (Kihlstrom, 1998, 2007; Spanos, 1986).

Hypnosis, Memory Enhancement and Eyewitness Testimony

In contrast to producing forgetting, can hypnosis enhance memory? Law enforcement agencies sometimes use hypnosis to aid the memory of eyewitnesses to crimes. In a famous 1977 case in California, a bus carrying 26 children and its driver disappeared without a trace. The victims, buried underground in an abandoned trailer truck by three kidnappers, were later found alive. After the rescue, a police expert hypnotized the bus driver and asked him to recall the ordeal. The driver formed a vivid image of the kidnappers' white van and could 'read' all but one digit on the van's licence plate. This information allowed the police to track down the kidnappers.

Despite occasional success stories like this one, controlled experiments find that hypnosis does not reliably improve memory. In some experiments, participants watch videotapes of simulated bank robberies or other crimes. Next, while hypnotized or not, they are questioned by police investigators or criminal lawyers. Hypnotized people display better recall than non-hypnotized people in some studies but no better recall in others (Lynn, Neuschatz, Fite, & Kirsch, 2001). In still other experiments, hypnotized participants perform more poorly than non-hypnotized controls; they recall more information, but much of that extra recall is inaccurate (Burgess & Kirsch, 1999).

Another concern is that some memories recalled under hypnosis may be *pseudomemories*, false memories *created* during hypnosis by statements or leading suggestions made by the examiner. In some experiments, hypnotized and non-hypnotized subjects are intentionally exposed to false information about an event (e.g., about a bank robbery). Later, after the hypnotized subjects have been brought out of hypnosis, all participants are questioned. Highly suggestible people who have been hypnotized are most likely to report the false information as being a true memory, and often are confident that their false memories are accurate (Sheehan, Green, & Truesdale, 1992).

Although some psychologists are exploring ways to minimize hypnosis-induced memory errors, at present, many courts have banned or limited testimony obtained under hypnosis (Wagstaff, Brunas-Wagstaff, Cole, & Wheatcroft, 2004). The increased suggestibility of hypnotized people makes them particularly susceptible to memory distortion caused by leading questions, and they may honestly come to believe facts that never occurred (Scoboria, Mazzoni, Kirsch, & Milling, 2002). Similarly, if a therapist uses hypnosis to help patients recall long-forgotten memories of sexual abuse, what shall we conclude? Are the horrible memories real, or are they pseudomemories created during therapy? We explore this issue in **Chapter 8**.

> **Focus 6.24** Evaluate claims that hypnosis can produce involuntary behaviour, amazing feats, pain relief and altered memory.

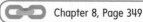 Chapter 8, Page 349

THEORIES OF HYPNOSIS

Hypnos may have been the Greek god of sleep, but studies of brain physiology reveal that hypnosis definitely *is not* sleep. What is hypnosis, and how does it produce its effects?

Dissociation Theories

Several researchers propose **dissociation theories** that view hypnosis as an altered state involving a division (dissociation) of consciousness (Kihlstrom, 2007). Hilgard (1977, 1991) proposed that hypnosis creates a division of awareness in which the person simultaneously experiences two streams of consciousness that are cut off from one another. One stream responds to the hypnotist's suggestions, while the second stream – the part of consciousness that monitors behaviour – remains in the background but is aware of everything that goes on. Hilgard refers to this second part of consciousness as the *hidden observer*.

Suppose a hypnotized subject is given a suggestion that she will not feel pain. Her arm is lowered into a tub of ice-cold water for 45 seconds, and every few seconds she reports the amount of pain. In contrast to non-hypnotized subjects, who find this experience moderately painful, she probably will report feeling little pain. But suppose the procedure is done differently. Before lowering the subject's arm, the hypnotist says, 'Perhaps there is another part of you that is more aware than your hypnotized part. If so, would that part of you report the amount of pain.' In this case, the subject's other stream of consciousness, the hidden observer, will report a higher level of pain (Figure 6.41).

For Hilgard, this dissociation explained why behaviours that occur under hypnosis seem involuntary or automatic. Given the suggestion that 'your arm will start to feel lighter and will begin to rise', the subject intentionally raises his or her arm, but only the hidden observer is aware of this. The main stream of consciousness that responds to the command is blocked from this awareness and perceives that the arm is rising all by itself.

Social Cognitive Theories

To other theorists, hypnosis does not represent a special state of dissociated consciousness. Instead, **social cognitive theories** propose that hypnotic experiences result from expectations of people who are motivated to take on the role of being hypnotized (Kirsch, 2001; Spanos, 1991). Most people believe that hypnosis involves a trance-like state and responsiveness to suggestions. People motivated to conform to this role develop a readiness to respond to the hypnotist's suggestions and to perceive hypnotic experiences as real and involuntary.

In a classic study, Martin Orne (1959) illustrated the importance of expectations about hypnosis. During a classroom demonstration, college students were told that hypnotized people frequently exhibit spontaneous stiffening of the muscles in the dominant hand. (Actually, this rarely occurs.) An accomplice of the lecturer pretended to be hypnotized and, sure enough, he 'spontaneously' exhibited hand stiffness. When students who had seen the demonstration were later hypnotized, 55% of them exhibited stiffening of the hand without any suggestion from the hypnotist. Control-group participants saw a demonstration that did not mention or display hand stiffening. Not one of these students exhibited hand stiffening when they were hypnotized.

Does social cognitive theory imply that hypnotized people are faking or play-acting? Not at all. Role theorists emphasize that when people immerse themselves in the hypnotic role, their responses are completely real and may indeed represent altered experiences (Kirsch, 2001). Our expectations strongly influence how the brain organizes sensory information. Often, we literally see what we expect to see. According to social cognitive theory, many effects of hypnosis represent an extension of this principle. The hypnotized subject whose arm automatically rises in response to a suggestion genuinely perceives the behaviour to be involuntary because this is what the subject expects and because attention is focused externally on the hypnotist and the hypnotic suggestion.

THE HYPNOTIZED BRAIN

Can peering inside the brain help us determine the nature of hypnosis? To find out, take a look at the coloured drawing and the grey-scale drawing in Figure 6.42. Now, do two simple tasks:

FIGURE 6.42 Colour perception and the hypnotized brain.

These colour and grey-scale drawings are similar to those used by Kosslyn and his colleagues (Kosslyn, Thompson, Costantini-Ferrando, Alpert, & Spiegel, 2000).

Source: based on S.M. Kosslyn, W.L. Thompson, M.F. Constantini-Fernando, N.M. Alpert & D. Spieel, 2000, "Hypnotic Visial Ilusion Alters Color Processing in the Brain,"American Journal of Psychiatry, 157, 1279-1284, Fig I.

1. Look at the coloured drawing again, form a mental image of it, and try to drain the colour out of it. In other words, try to visualize it as if it were a grey-scale figure.
2. Next, look at the grey-scale drawing, form a mental picture of it, and try to add colour to it. In other words, visualize it as if it were a coloured figure.

Kosslyn et al. (2000) identified eight people who scored high in hypnotic susceptibility and who reported they could successfully drain away or add colour to their mental images of such drawings. Subjects then performed these tasks (in varying order) while inside a PET scanner. On some trials they were hypnotized, and on other trials they were not hypnotized.

The PET scans revealed that whether subjects were hypnotized or not, an area in the right hemisphere that processes information about colour was more active when subjects visualized the grey drawing as having colour (Task 2) than when they visualized the colour drawing as grey (Task 1). In other words, this right-hemisphere region actually responded to mental images involving colour, and subjects did not need to be hypnotized for this brain activity to occur. In the left hemisphere, however, visualizing the grey drawing as having colour increased brain activation in one particular region only when the subjects were hypnotized. As the researchers noted, 'The right hemisphere appeared to respond to imagery per se, whereas the left required the additional boost provided by hypnosis' (Kosslyn et al., 2000, p. 1283).

The results of brain-imaging studies converge with other physiological findings in leading to an important conclusion: hypnotized people are not faking it but rather are experiencing an altered state of brain activation that matches their verbal reports (Raz & Shapiro, 2002). In this study, when hypnotized subjects mentally added colour to the drawing and drained colour from it, their brain activity changed in ways beyond those brought about by mental imagery in a non-hypnotized state. Likewise, other studies reveal that giving hypnotized subjects pain-reducing suggestions not only decreases their subjective report of pain but also decreases activity in several brain regions that process pain signals (Petrovic & Ingvar, 2002). But do these findings indicate that hypnosis is an altered state of dissociation?

Cojan et al. (2009) looked at brain activity during a simple task, testing the suggestion from Oakley and Halligan (2009) that hypnosis may be the result of some kind of inhibition or disconnection of part of the brain process responsible for central control. They tested three groups. In group 1, participants were hypnotized and convinced that their left hand was paralysed. In group 2, participants were left unhypnotized, but told to imagine or pretend that their left hand was paralysed. In the third control group participants were not hypnotized and were given no instructions at all. The task that followed was in two stages. In stage 1 an instruction was given as a cue on a screen, to *prepare to push a button* with the left or right hand. Directly following this an image appeared on the screen. If it was green participants would go ahead and push the button; if red, they should not push the button. Results were very interesting. The hypnotized group (group 1) showed similar brain responses to the unhypnotized group during the preparation stage of the task. However, when the hypnotized group was told to follow through on the action for their 'paralysed' hand the cortex did not send the appropriate signal to the part of the brain responsible for this movement, and the hand would not move. Instead, the information was sent to an area

Focus 6.25 Contrast dissociation and social cognitive theories of hypnosis. What does research on the hypnotized brain reveal?

of the brain responsible for visualizing movements and actions called the precunius. The desire to act was there, but the ability to do so was short-circuited or redirected and the action could not take place.

Social cognitive theorists would argue that these findings do not resolve the issue (Kirsch, 2001). They note that hypnotic experiences are subjectively real, and the fact that brain activity patterns under hypnosis differ from those of simple mental imagery does not contradict their position that people's expectations are what lead them to become hypnotized in the first place. In sum, cognitive neuroscience is providing us with fascinating insights into the hypnotized brain, but it will take more research to resolve the debate about hypnosis.

 In review

- Hypnosis involves an increased receptiveness to suggestions. Hypnotized people experience their actions as involuntary, but hypnosis has no unique power to make people behave against their will, alter their physiological reactions or perform amazing feats. Hypnosis increases pain tolerance, as do other psychological techniques.

- Some people can be led to experience hypnotic amnesia and post-hypnotic amnesia. The use of hypnosis to improve memory is controversial. Hypnosis increases the danger that people will develop distorted memories about events in response to leading questions asked by a hypnotist or examiner.

- Dissociation theories view hypnosis as an altered state of divided consciousness. Social cognitive theories state that hypnotic experiences occur because people have strong expectations about hypnosis and are highly motivated to enter a hypnotized role.

- Brain imaging reveals that hypnotized people display changes in neural activity consistent with their subjectively reported experiences. This supports the view that hypnosis involves an altered state, but whether it is a dissociated state and the extent to which people's expectations bring about this state are still unclear.

 Recommended reading

CLASSIC

Dennet, D. (1993). *Consciousness explained* (new ed.). London: Penguin.

CONTEMPORARY

Blackmore, S. (2010). *Consciousness - An introduction*. Abingdon: Routledge.

Green, S. (2011). *Biological rhythms, sleep and hypnosis*. Basingstoke: Palgrave Macmillan.

Horne, J. (2007). *Sleepfaring: A journey through the science of sleep*. Oxford: Oxford University Press.

Zelato, P. D., Moscovitch, M. & Thompson, E. (Eds.) (2007). *The Cambridge handbook of consciousness*. New York: Cambridge University Press.

A man who carries a cat by the tail learns something he can learn in no other way.

Mark Twain

Learning: the role of experience

7

Chapter Outline

ADAPTING TO THE ENVIRONMENT

HABITUATION AND SENSITIZATION

CLASSICAL CONDITIONING: ASSOCIATING ONE STIMULUS WITH ANOTHER

- Pavlov's pioneering research
- Basic principles
- Applications of classical conditioning

OPERANT CONDITIONING: LEARNING THROUGH CONSEQUENCES

- Thorndike's law of effect
- Skinner's analysis of operant conditioning
- Antecedent conditions and consequences
- Shaping and chaining: taking one step at a time
- Generalization and discrimination
- Schedules of reinforcement

- Escape and avoidance conditioning
- Applications of operant conditioning
- Applying psychological science *Using operant principles to modify your behaviour*

CHALLENGES TO BEHAVIOURISM

- Biological constraints: evolution and preparedness
- Cognition and conditioning
- Cognitive and behavioural learning in psychological therapies

OBSERVATIONAL LEARNING: WHEN OTHERS SHOW THE WAY

- Bandura's social-cognitive theory
- Current topic *Imitation: babies' brains respond to watching others' actions*
- Applications of observational learning
- Research close-up *Using social-cognitive theory to help us better understand eating behaviour*

THE ADAPTIVE BRAIN

- Learning through connections
- Where does learning happen in the brain?

Thanks to six sessions with a clinical psychologist, Michelle's life is normal again. She is now free from the intense fear of something many of us do without a qualm every day: riding in a car. Michelle was severely injured in a car crash and hospitalized for months. A year later, she described to a clinician how the fear began when her husband came to take her home from the hospital.

> *As we walked towards the new car he had bought, I began to feel uneasy. I felt nervous all the way home. It started to get worse after that. I found myself avoiding riding in the car, and couldn't drive it at all. I stopped visiting friends and tried to get them to come to our house. . . . After a while, even the sight of a car started to make me nervous. . . . You know, this is the first time I've left the house in about four months.*

To help Michelle, the clinical psychologist used a highly successful procedure based, in part, on century-old principles of learning discovered in laboratory investigations of salivating dogs.

On a high street in a suburb of London, a woman volunteers her time soliciting donations for a local charity. Though cold, wet and tired, she remains upbeat and thanks each person who drops money in her collection tin. Inside an amusement arcade on the same street, a man has been playing the slot machines all day. He is exhausted and down to his last few pounds, having fed the machine coins all day long for the past six days. The till attendant mutters under his breath, 'I'll never understand what keeps these guys going'.

Wendy, a mother of two young boys has noticed a change in their behaviour, and she is concerned that this is due to the television programmes they are watching. The brothers spend several hours a day watching professional wrestling, and have recently become more violent towards each other and towards their friends. One of the brothers came very close to being expelled from school for applying a 'choke hold' on another boy in class. Wendy is pretty sure that this is all down to the television her boys are watching, but she is becoming afraid of what they might do should she attempt to ban them from watching it.

Although quite different, the behaviours in these examples share an important characteristic: they are all learned to some extent. Our genetic endowment creates the potential for these behaviours to occur, but we are not biologically programmed to fear cars, solicit donations or bet on horses. As we shall see, beyond an almost endless list of skills, learning also affects our emotional reactions, physiological responses and even our perception. Through experience, we learn to think, act and feel in ways that contribute richly to our individual identities, and we use this experience to help us make sense of the world around us.

Learning is a *process by which experience produces a relatively enduring and adaptive change in an organism's capacity for behaviour*. Importantly, this definition specifies that learning is a change in the *capacity* for behaviour. This highlights a distinction made by psychologists: that between 'learning' and 'performance'. The distinction is especially important, as it tells us that changes in behaviour do not always mean that we have learned something. For example, an increase in our searching for food is usually due to our physiological hunger, rather than our having learned something. The challenge for psychologists researching learning is to disentangle when measured changes in behaviour (performance) are actually due to learning. For example, when we observe two boys applying choke holds to each other (a change in performance), this could be due to their having watched a wrestling match on television earlier in the day (learning), but other factors could be involved: maybe they have aggressive personalities or maybe the fact that they could not agree what to watch next on television was an important stimulus.

> **learning** process by which experience produces a relatively enduring and adaptive change in an organism's capacity for behaviour

> **Focus 7.1** What is learning?

ADAPTING TO THE ENVIRONMENT

> Chapter 3, Page 77

The concept of learning calls attention to the importance of adapting to the environment. In this way it is similar to evolution (see **Chapter 3**). However, whereas evolution focuses on species' adaptations passed down biologically across generations, learning represents a process of personal adaptation. That is, learning focuses on how an organism's behaviour changes in response to environmental stimuli encountered during its lifetime. Although

specific behaviours that each organism learns may be unique to its species – we have yet to encounter a deer that has learned to order takeaway food – all animal species face some common adaptive challenges, such as finding food. Because environments contain many events, each organism must learn: (1) which events are, or are not, important to its survival and well-being, (2) which stimuli signal that an important event is about to occur, and (3) whether its responses will produce positive or negative consequences. The learning processes examined in this chapter enable humans and other species to respond to one or more of these adaptive challenges.

In this chapter we explore five basic learning processes. The first two, *habituation* and *sensitization* are the simplest, involving changes in behaviour that result merely from repeated exposure to a stimulus. Next, we look in depth at two types of *associative learning* or *conditioning*, which involve learning associations between events. *Classical conditioning* occurs when two stimuli become associated with each other (for example, being inside a car and being severely burned) such that one stimulus (being in a car) now triggers a response (intense fear) that previously was triggered by the other stimulus (being burned). In *operant conditioning*, organisms learn to associate their behavioural responses with specific consequences; for example, asking for a charitable donation leads to a monetary gift. Finally, we consider *observational learning*, in which observers imitate the behaviour of a model; for example, children imitate choke holds performed by wrestlers on television.

This chapter focuses on how environmental experiences modify behaviour and knowledge, but you will see that biological and cognitive factors also play important roles in learning. You will also find some key examples of how psychologists have creatively applied learning principles to enhance human welfare.

HABITUATION AND SENSITIZATION

First, we consider the simplest forms of learning in which we change our responses to just one stimulus over time: *habituation* and *sensitization*. Imagine that you are a participant in an experiment. You are sitting alone in a quiet laboratory when suddenly (as part of the experiment) a loud sound startles you. Your body jerks slightly, you become aroused, and you look towards the source of the sound. Over time, as you hear it again and again, your startle response diminishes until eventually you ignore the sound. You have habituated to the noise.

Habituation is a decrease in the strength of response to a repeated stimulus. It occurs across species ranging from humans to dragonflies to sea snails. Touch the skin of a sea snail in a certain location, and it will reflexively contract its gill. With repeated touches, this response habituates. This is a simple form of learning in that it occurs in response to only a single stimulus (in contrast to more complex forms of learning, discussed later in the chapter, in which two or more stimuli are associated in some way).

Imagine that you are taking an examination. Five minutes in, an examination invigilator walks down the aisle to provide someone with some paper. The examination invigilator is wearing high heels and her shoes make a quite audible sound as she walks through the examination hall. Initially you think nothing of the sound and get under way with your first essay. However, people keep raising their hands for extra paper, and one hour into the examination you are so aggravated by the repeated noise that you can no longer concentrate on writing. You have sensitized to the sound of the invigilator's shoes,

Sensitization is an increase in the strength of response to a repeated stimulus. Like habituation, sensitization is also classified as a simple learning mechanism as it occurs in response to only a single stimulus. Also like habituation, sensitization serves an adaptive function. In fact, you may see sensitization referred to as dishabituation in some places, highlighting the relationship between the two concepts. There are some aspects of the environment to which it is important for us to attend. Often, these stimuli are harmful to us in some way, and so sensitization provides humans with a way of responding appropriately to potentially dangerous or threatening stimuli. When a stronger tactile stimulus is applied to sea snails, on repeated presentation they will respond by withdrawing more parts of their body than they did initially (Kandel, 2004; Figure 7.1). The strength of their response increases on repeated presentation of the stimulus.

> **habituation** a decrease in the strength of response to a repeated stimulus
>
> **sensitization** an increase in the strength of response to a repeated stimulus. Like habituation, sensitization is also classified as a simple learning mechanism as it occurs in response to only a single stimulus

FIGURE 7.1 Eric Kandel (born 1929) – awarded Nobel Prize for Physiology in 2000 for his work on the physiological basis of memory storage in neurons.

Source: courtesy of Dr Eric Kandel.
© Eve Vagg

instance, a Cubist and similar in some ways to Picasso, could be successfully discriminated from the work of Cezanne, an impressionist like Monet. The authors concluded that the results suggested that there was something in the scenes that was controlling their categorization behaviour. When the paintings were turned upside down, the pigeons could no longer categorize the Monets, but they could still respond appropriately to the Picasso paintings. This suggests that there was something in the paintings that the birds were using for the task, something they could discern, perhaps identifiable objects or shapes in the Cubist representations that were not significantly altered by the inversion.

Higher-Order Conditioning

> **higher-order conditioning**
> a neutral stimulus becomes a CS after being paired with an already established CS

Imagine that we expose a dog to repeated tone–food pairings and the tone becomes a CS that elicits a strong salivation response. Next, suppose that we present a neutral stimulus, such as a black square, and the dog does not salivate. Now, we present the black square just prior to the tone, but we do not present any food. After repeated pairings of the square and the tone, the square will become a CS and elicit salivation by itself (Figure 7.10). This process is called **higher-order conditioning** (sometimes referred to as second-order conditioning); a neutral stimulus becomes a CS after being paired with an already established CS.

> **Focus 7.4** Explain stimulus generalization, discrimination, higher order conditioning and their adaptive significance.

Higher-order conditioning greatly expands the influence of conditioned stimuli and can affect what we come to value, fear, like or dislike (Gewirtz & Davis, 2000). For example, political candidates frequently try to gain a favourable response from voters by associating themselves with the latest trends. As we could argue that voters have recently learned their favourable response to the newest trend, the attempt to associate with that learned favourable response can be conceptualized as higher-order conditioning. Unfortunately, for politicians using these strategies, a higher-order CS typically produces a CR that is weaker and extinguishes more rapidly than the original CR. In our Pavlovian example above, the dog will salivate less to the black square than to the tone, and its response to the square will extinguish sooner. Voters are often similarly as sceptical.

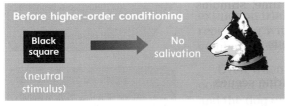

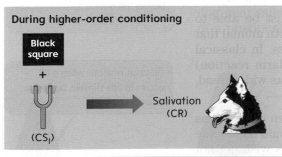

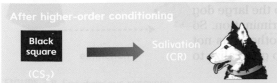

FIGURE 7.10 Higher-order conditioning.
Once a tone has become a conditioned stimulus that triggers salivation, we can now use it to condition a salivation response to a new neutral stimulus: a black square. The tone is the CS1. The black square becomes the CS2.

APPLICATIONS OF CLASSICAL CONDITIONING

Pavlov's belief that salivation was merely the tip of the classical conditioning iceberg has proven correct. Conditioning principles discovered in laboratory research – much of it with non-human species – help us understand diverse human behaviours and problems.

Acquiring and Overcoming Fear

Building on Pavlov's discoveries, pioneering behaviourist John B. Watson challenged Freud's view of the causes of mental disorders, such as phobias. To explain Michelle's car phobia, no assumptions about hidden unconscious conflicts or repressed traumas are needed. Instead, from the behaviourist viewpoint, cars have become a fear-triggering CS due to a one-trial pairing with the UCS (crash) and stimulus generalization.

Does this explanation seem reasonable? It may, but almost any explanation can seem plausible with hindsight. Therefore, Watson and Rayner (1920) set out to obtain stronger evidence that fear could be conditioned. They studied an 11-month-old infant named Albert. One day, as little Albert played in a hospital room, Watson and Rayner showed him a white rat. Albert displayed no sign of fear. Later, knowing that Albert was afraid of loud noises, they hit a steel bar with a hammer, making a loud noise as they showed Albert the rat. The noise scared Albert and made him cry. After several rat–noise pairings, the sight of the white rat alone made Albert cry.

To examine stimulus discrimination and generalization, Watson and Rayner exposed Albert to other test stimuli several days later.

Albert displayed no fear when shown coloured blocks, but a rabbit and a bearded Santa Claus mask made him cry (Figure 7.11). Watson and Rayner concluded that fear can be conditioned, but unfortunately their results were not very clear cut. After several attempts to condition fear in Albert to several animals (including the rat again, but also a rabbit and a dog), Albert showed little reaction to all of these animals in a different room (Harris, 1979). Records do not tell us whether Albert went on to experience phobias in later life.

Applying today's ethical standards to the 'little Albert' study; we believe it clearly would have been rejected (see **Chapter 2** for a discussion of research ethics). Even with informed consent and a secure system in place to guarantee that an infant would receive treatment afterward, the risks would have been considered too high (especially given the poor controls used in Watson and Rayner's study; see Harris, 1979).

 Chapter 2, Page 47

Two other sources of evidence suggest that at least some fears are conditioned. First, laboratory experiments convincingly show that animals become afraid of neutral stimuli that are paired with electric shock (Ayres, 1998). Second, in humans, behavioural treatments partially based on classical conditioning principles are among the most effective psychotherapies for phobias (Wolpe & Plaud, 1997). The key assumption is that if phobias are learned, they can be unlearned.

An early example of a therapy for unlearning a phobia comes from the work of Jones (1924) who successfully treated a boy named Peter who had a strong fear of rabbits. Jones's approach was a forerunner of current **exposure therapies**, in which a patient is exposed to a stimulus (CS) that arouses an anxiety response (such as fear) without the presence of the UCS, allowing extinction to occur. These are discussed in more detail in **Chapter 18**. In this particular case Jones gradually increased Peter's proximity progressively over a number of steps such that he became gradually more and more tolerant (see Table 7.1). The origin of a patient's phobia is often unknown, and psychologists debate whether all phobias are learned. But, even so, in many cases, exposure treatments are effective.

> **exposure therapies** a patient is exposed to a stimulus (CS) that arouses an anxiety response (such as fear) without the presence of the UCS, allowing extinction to occur

 Chapter 18, Page 786

Mental imagery, real-life situations, or both can be used to present the phobic stimulus. In one approach called *systematic desensitization*, the patient learns muscle-relaxation techniques and then is gradually exposed to the fear-provoking stimulus (Wolpe, 1958). Another approach, sometimes called *flooding*, immediately exposes the person to the phobic stimulus (Nesbitt, 1973). In Michelle's case, her therapist extinguished the car phobia in six sessions of flooding. He asked her to imagine vivid scenes in which she drove in motorway traffic and travelled at high speeds on narrow mountain roads. As Michelle's initially strong anxiety decreased, she was able to sit in her car and eventually drive it. Exposure therapies are highly effective and represent one of behaviourism's

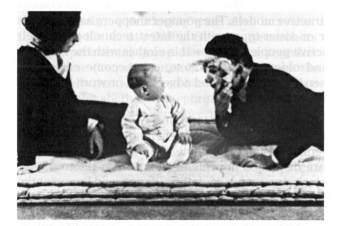

FIGURE 7.11 Watson and Rayner examine how little Albert reacts to a furry mask.

Source: Reprinted with the permission of Professor Ben Harris

TABLE 7.1 Reduction of fear by exposure training

This table lists 10 of the 17 steps in Jones's (1924) pioneering exposure training procedure.

Step	Peter's progress
1.	Rabbit anywhere in room triggers fear
2.	Rabbit 12 feet (3.7 m) away tolerated
4.	Rabbit 3 feet (0.9 m) away tolerated
5.	Rabbit close in cage tolerated
6.	Rabbit free in room tolerated
8.	Rabbit touched when free in room
10.	Rabbit allowed on tray of high chair
12.	Holds rabbit on lap
16.	Fondles rabbit affectionately
17.	Let's rabbit nibble his fingers

Source: adapted from Jones, 1924.

In review

- Thorndike's law of effect states that responses followed by satisfying consequences will be strengthened, whereas those followed by annoying consequences will be weakened.
- Skinner analysed operant conditioning in terms of relations between antecedents, behaviours and consequences. Discriminative stimuli are antecedents that signal the likely consequences of particular behaviours in a given situation.
- Reinforcement occurs when a response is strengthened by an outcome (a reinforcer) that follows it. With positive reinforcement, a response is strengthened by the presentation of a stimulus that follows it. With negative reinforcement, a response is strengthened by the removal of an aversive stimulus.
- Operant extinction is the weakening and eventual disappearance of a response because it no longer is reinforced.
- Punishment occurs when a behaviour is weakened by an outcome (a punisher) that follows it. With aversive punishment, the behaviour becomes weaker when it is followed by the presentation of an aversive stimulus. With response cost, the behaviour becomes weaker when it is followed by the removal of a stimulus.
- The use of corporal punishment with children is controversial and is correlated with several negative outcomes for children's development.
- Shaping, which uses the method of successive approximations, involves reinforcing behaviours that increasingly resemble the final desired behaviour. Chaining is used to develop a sequence of responses by reinforcing each response with the opportunity to perform the next response.
- Operant generalization occurs when behaviour changes in one situation due to reinforcement or punishment, and the new response then carries over to similar situations. In contrast, operant discrimination occurs when an operant response is made to one discriminative stimulus but not to another.
- On a continuous reinforcement schedule, every response is reinforced. Partial reinforcement may occur on a ratio schedule, in which a certain percentage of responses are reinforced, or on an interval schedule, in which a certain amount of time must pass before a response gets reinforced. In general, ratio schedules produce higher rates of performance than interval schedules.
- On a fixed-ratio schedule, reinforcement occurs after a fixed number of responses; on a fixed interval schedule, it occurs after a fixed time interval. On variable schedules, the required number of responses or interval of time between them varies around some average.
- Escape conditioning and avoidance conditioning result from negative reinforcement. According to the two-factor theory, fear is created through classical conditioning. This fear motivates escape and avoidance, which are then negatively reinforced by fear reduction.
- Operant conditioning principles can enhance human performance in educational and work settings, reduce a wide array of behaviour problems, and help people self-regulate their behaviour. Animals can be operantly trained to perform many specialized tasks.

CHALLENGES TO BEHAVIOURISM

Behaviourists built much of the foundation on which our knowledge of learning principles rests, and behaviourism remains influential today (Leslie, 2002). Over the years, however, psychologists who viewed behaviour from biological and cognitive perspectives enriched our understanding of learning by challenging some of behaviourism's key assumptions.

BIOLOGICAL CONSTRAINTS: EVOLUTION AND PREPAREDNESS

 Chapter 3, Page 110

preparedness through evolution, animals are biologically predisposed (pre-wired) to learn some associations more easily than others

Behaviourists never suggested that a rat could learn to fly, but for decades they assumed that they could condition virtually any behaviour an organism was physically capable of performing. Yet evidence mounted that 'conditioned' animals did not always respond as they were supposed to. The behaviourist assumption was wrong because it ignored a key principle discussed both at the outset of this chapter and in **Chapter 3**: behaviour is influenced by an organism's evolutionary history, and this places biological constraints on learning.

Martin Seligman's (1970) concept of *preparedness* captures this idea. **Preparedness** means that through evolution, animals are biologically predisposed (pre-wired) to learn

some associations more easily than others. In general, behaviours related to a species' survival are learned more easily than behaviours contrary to an organism's natural tendencies. Let us consider some examples.

Constraints on Classical Conditioning: Learned Taste Aversions

Imagine eating or drinking something, then becoming sick and vomiting. Perhaps it is a case of the flu, or it could be food poisoning. When a food is associated with nausea or vomiting, that particular food can become a CS that triggers a **conditioned taste aversion**, a conditioned response in which the taste (and sometimes the sight and smell) of a particular food becomes disgusting and repulsive (Garcia, Lasiter, Bermudez, & Deems, 1985). The very thought of it may even make us feel queasy, and we learn to avoid it. For instance, during pregnancy many women experience nausea and vomiting, a response commonly associated with food, and they may develop aversions to foods that they associate with these symptoms (Bayley, Dye, Jones, DeBono, & Hill, 2002).

> **conditioned taste aversion** a conditioned response in which the taste (and sometimes the sight and smell) of a particular food becomes disgusting and repulsive

John Garcia pioneered numerous taste-aversion experiments that challenged two basic assumptions of classical conditioning. First, behaviourists had assumed that the CS–UCS time interval had to be relatively short: usually a few seconds. Garcia showed that animals learned taste aversions even though the food (CS) was consumed up to several hours – or even a day – before they became ill (in this case, the UCS).

Second, in a classic experiment, Garcia illustrated how biological preparedness influences learned aversions (Garcia & Koelling, 1966). Whenever rats licked a drinking tube, they were simultaneously exposed to three neutral stimuli: sweet-tasting water, a bright light and a buzzer (Figure 7.28). The rats were then divided into two conditions. In one condition, the rats were exposed to X-rays upon drinking the water, which later made them ill (UCS). Would the rats develop an aversion to all three neutral stimuli? No, they avoided the sweet water but not the light or buzzer. Why did only the sweet taste become a CS? Because rats are biologically primed to form taste–illness associations, which means that in nature they most easily identify poisonous or bad food by its taste (or smell). In nature, sounds and lights do not make rats sick.

When rats in the second condition licked the tube, the light, buzzer and sweet taste were all paired with an electric shock. Would these rats learn to fear all three neutral stimuli? No, they avoided the light and buzzer but kept drinking the sweet water. This also makes adaptive sense. In nature, sights and sounds – but not how food and drink taste – signal fear-provoking situations (e.g., a cat about to pounce).

The same principle applies to humans. When a food makes us violently sick, we may develop an aversion to it but not to the friends we ate with.

Psychologists have applied knowledge about conditioned aversions to save animals' lives. To prevent coyotes from killing farmers' sheep, scientists (Gustavson, Garcia, Hankins, & Rusiniak, 1974) laced pieces of meat with lithium chloride, a nausea-inducing drug. They wrapped the meat

Stage I: All Rats
When rats touch the drinking tube, sweet water is delivered and a light and buzzer turn on.

Stage 2

Illness condition	Fear condition

Group 1 rats get nauseating X-rays when they drink.

Group 2 rats get electric shocks when they drink.

Stage 3

Group 1 rats avoid the sweet water and prefer the plain water with the light and buzzer.

Group 2 rats still drink the sweet water, but avoid the plain water with the light and buzzer.

FIGURE 7.28 Biological preparedness in classical conditioning.
This figure illustrates the design and main results of Garcia and Koelling's (1966) aversion experiment.

Focus 7.16 How does research on learned taste aversions and fear conditioning support the concept of biological preparedness?

in sheep hide and left it out for coyotes to eat. The coyotes ate it, became ill, and developed an aversion to the meat, thereby becoming less likely to kill sheep. This saved the livelihoods of the farmers, saved the lives of sheep – and of the coyotes, who otherwise would have been shot by the farmers. Figure 7.29 illustrates nature's own wildlife management based on learned taste aversions.

Are We Biologically Prepared to Fear Certain Things?

Seligman (1971) proposes that like other animals, humans are biologically prepared to acquire certain fears more readily than others. In one anecdotal but illustrative case, a 4-year-old girl saw a snake in a park but was not frightened by it (Marks, 1977). Soon thereafter she returned to the family car and accidentally trapped her hand in the car door. She subsequently developed a phobia not of car doors or cars, but of snakes.

FIGURE 7.29 A conditioned aversion in nature.

This blue jay has never eaten a monarch butterfly but does not pass up an easy meal. Soon, toxins in the butterfly poison the jay. The jay feels discomfort, vomits and develops a conditioned aversion triggered by the sight of the monarch's brightly patterned wings. From now on, it will leave monarchs alone.

Source: Reprinted with the permission of Professor Lincoln Brower, Sweet Briar College

In the laboratory, Swedish psychologists showed people pictures of various stimuli, flashing each picture on a screen and pairing it with electric shock (the UCS). Next, they measured people's physiological responses when those stimuli were presented alone (Öhman & Soares, 1998). When the pictures showed snakes, spiders or angry faces, people quickly acquired conditioned fear responses to these stimuli, even when the pictures were flashed too briefly to be consciously perceived. But participants who received shocks while looking at slides of flowers, houses or happy faces displayed much weaker fear conditioning.

Humans develop phobias to many stimuli, but most often we fear things that seem to have greater evolutionary significance: snakes, spiders and potentially dangerous animals and places (Hofmann, Moscovitch, & Heinrichs, 2004). Is this the result of evolution-based biological preparedness, or might it be due to learning experiences that teach us to expect that some stimuli can be dangerous? Multiple factors may affect human fear conditioning, but one thing is clear: as with taste aversions, fear can be conditioned much more easily to some stimuli than to others.

Later in this chapter, in the 'Current topic', we discuss some of the ways in which psychologists have argued that we, as humans, are evolutionarily prepared to learn by observing others.

COGNITION AND CONDITIONING

Early behaviourists believed that learning involves the relatively automatic formation of bonds between stimuli and responses. This viewpoint came to be known as *S-R (stimulus-response) psychology*. Behaviourists opposed explanations of learning that went beyond observable stimuli and responses. They did not deny that people had thoughts and feelings, but argued that behaviour could be explained without referring to such mentalistic concepts (Skinner, 1953, 1990).

Even in psychology's early years, some learning theorists challenged the S-R model, arguing that in between stimulus and response there is something else: the organism's (O) cognitive representation of the world. This came to be known as the *S-O-R*, or *cognitive, model of learning*. Today the cognitive perspective represents an important force in learning theory.

Early Challenges to Behaviourism: Insight and Cognitive Maps

In the 1920s, German psychologist Wolfgang Köhler (1925) challenged Thorndike's behaviourist assumption that animals learn to perform tasks only by trial and error. Köhler exposed chimpanzees to novel learning tasks and concluded that they were able to learn by **insight**, the sudden perception of a useful relationship that helps to solve a problem. Figure 7.30 shows how one of his apes solved the problem of how to retrieve bananas that were dangling beyond reach. Köhler emphasized that the apes often spent time staring at the bananas and available tools, as if they were contemplating the problem, after which the solution suddenly appeared.

Behaviourists argued that insight actually represents the combining of previously learned responses (Epstein, Kirshnit, Lanza, & Rubin, 1984). Imagine a pigeon placed inside a chamber where a miniature model of a banana dangles from the ceiling, out of reach. A small box sits in the corner of the chamber. Similar to Köhler's apes, the pigeon looks around, goes to the box, moves it under the banana by pushing it with its beak, then stands on the box and pecks the banana. Without knowing the pigeon's behavioural history (just as we do not know the entire behavioural history of Köhler's apes), we might conclude that this is a novel behaviour reflecting remarkable insight. But instead, the pigeon has simply combined several independent behaviours (e.g., pushing a box, stepping onto a box) that researchers had operantly conditioned using reinforcement.

Research with New Caledonian crows, is reigniting the argument for the existence of unreinforced insightful behaviour in animals. Weir, Chappell and Kacelnik (2002) report the observation that a female Caledonian crow ('Betty') spontaneously manufactured a hook by bending a straight piece of wire. Betty then used the manufactured hook to successfully retrieve food by lifting a bucket from the bottom of a vertical pipe (Figure 7.31). Importantly Weir and colleagues state that the animals had very little prior experience with pliant (bendable) material before the observation, and this experience had been with pipe-cleaners and not the wire used in the experiment.

The debate about insight rages, and Weir and colleagues' work with crows and other reports of spontaneous tool use by Taylor, Hunt, Holzhaider and Gray (2007) have reinvigorated Köhler's ideas and the argument for cognitive learning. Research from Oxford's Behavioral Ecology Research group suggests clearly that the crows can not only learn to solve discreet problems, but their experiences with one task can be used to help them solve another task, and kills learned through experience can be transferred (von Bayern, Heathcote, Rutz, & Kacelnik, 2009).

Another cognitive pioneer, American learning theorist Edward Tolman, studied spatial learning in rats. Consider the maze in Figure 7.32a. A rat runs to an open circular table, continues across and follows the only path available to a goal box containing food. After 12 trials, the rat easily negotiates the maze. Next, the maze is changed. The rat runs its usual route and reaches a dead end (Figure 7.32b). Tolman found that at this point in the procedure rats returned to the table, briefly explored most of the 18 new paths for just a few inches, and then chose one. By far, the largest number – 36% – chose the fourth path to the right of their original route, which took them closest to where the goal box had been. In short, the rats behaved as you would, given your advantage of seeing the maps.

It is difficult for reinforcement theory to explain this behaviour. Tolman (1948) suggested that the rats had developed a **cognitive map**, a mental representation of the spatial layout. The concept of cognitive maps supported Tolman's belief that learning does not merely represent stimulus response associations. Rather, he argued that learning provides knowledge, and based on their knowledge, organisms develop an expectancy, a cognitive representation, of 'what leads to what'.

Behaviourists disagreed with Tolman's interpretations and, as with insight, the debate over cognitive maps continues (Lew, 2011). Nevertheless, Tolman's concept of expectancy remains a cornerstone of today's cognitive approaches to classical and operant conditioning.

insight the sudden perception of a useful relationship that helps to solve a problem

FIGURE 7.30 Wlofgang Kohler's partner in research, Sultan.

Source: Photo by Lilo Hess/The LIFE Images Collection/Getty Images

FIGURE 7.31 Betty using the hook tool she has manufactured in order to pull up food in a bucket from the bottom of a vertical pipe.

Source: Behavioural Ecology Research Group, Oxford

cognitive map a mental representation of the spatial layout

> **latent learning** learning that occurs but is not demonstrated until later, when there is an incentive to perform.

Latent learning

Tolman's research illustrated in Figure 7.32 suggested that the rats developed cognitive maps when they were reinforced with food for running a maze. Tolman also believed that cognitive maps could be learned without reinforcement, posing an even greater challenge to the behaviourist viewpoint. In one experiment, three groups of rats learned the correct path through a complex maze (Tolman & Honzik, 1930). Rats in the first group found food each time they reached the goal box. Rats in the second group found the goal box empty each time they reached it. Rats in the third group found no food at the end of the maze for the first 10 days but did find food in the goal box starting on the eleventh day.

FIGURE 7.32 Cognitive maps in rats.

(a) Rats first learned to run the simple maze. (b) When the maze was switched, many rats chose the fourth path to the right of the original route. Tolman proposed that the rats had developed a cognitive map of the maze.

Source: Adapted from Tolman, 1948.

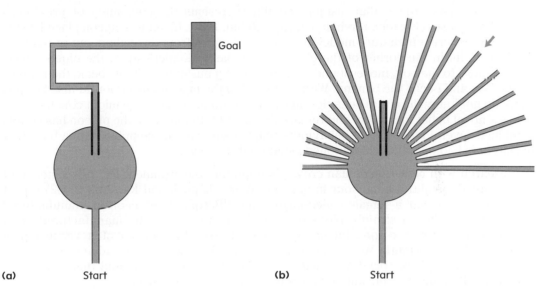

(a) Start

(b) Start

> **Focus 7.17** Discuss how research on insight and cognitive maps challenged behaviourist views of learning.

The results are shown in Figure 7.33, and the key finding is this: on day 11, the rats in the third group discovered food in the goal box for the first time. By the very next day, they were performing just as well as the first group, which had been reinforced all along. What could explain this significant, sudden performance improvement? According to Tolman, during days 1 to 10, rats in the third group were learning the spatial layout of the maze as they wandered about. They were not being reinforced by food, but they gained knowledge and developed their cognitive maps. This learning remained *latent* (hidden) until the rats discovered a good reason on day 11 to get to the goal box quickly; it was then immediately displayed in performance the next day. Tolman's experiments support the concept of **latent learning**, which refers to learning that occurs but is not demonstrated until later, when there is an incentive to perform (Blodgett, 1929). In other words, we may learn how to do something at one time but not display that knowledge until we perform a task at a future time.

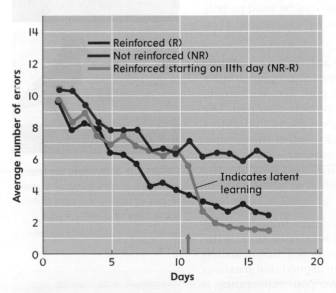

FIGURE 7.33 Tolman's demonstration of latent learning.

Rats had one trial in the maze per day. Group R was reinforced with food every time they reached the end of the maze. Group NR never received reinforcement. The critical group, NR-R, received food reinforcement on day 11. Their immediate performance improvement suggested that they had learned the maze prior to the introduction of reinforcement.

Source: Tolman and Honzik, 1930.

Cognition in Classical Conditioning

Expectancy in classical conditioning

Early American behaviourists such as Hull (1943) believed that classical conditioning created a direct reflex like connection between the CS (e.g., tone) and CR (e.g., salivation). Interestingly, Pavlov held a different view, proposing that a neural bond is formed between the CS and the UCS. Thus for Pavlov's dogs, the tone triggered an association with food, which then triggered salivation.

Cognitive learning theorists also believe that classical conditioning forms a CS–UCS link. In cognitive terminology, the link is an expectancy that the CS will be followed by the UCS (Hollis,

1997). *Expectancy models* states that the most important factor in classical conditioning is not how often the CS and the UCS are paired, but how well the CS predicts (i.e., signals) the appearance of the UCS (Pearce & Hall, 1980; Rescorla & Wagner, 1972).

Expectancy models came to the fore owing to the necessity of having to explain some phenomena which had been observed in adaptations of traditional Pavlovian conditioning experiments. One important finding made by Robert Rescorla (1968), was that the number of times a CS and US are paired together does not determine whether learning occurs. Rescorla (1968) conducted a fear conditioning experiment in which rats were divided into one of two learning conditions. Rats in one condition received electric shocks (UCS), and each shock was preceded by a tone. As usual, the tone soon became a CS that elicited a fear response when presented alone. In the second condition, rats received the same number of tone–shock pairings as the first group, but they also received as many shocks that were not preceded by the tone. Would the tone become a CS for fear? According to traditional learning theory, the answer should be yes, because the number of tone–shock pairings was the same as in the first group. But the expectancy model predicts no, because the tone does not reliably predict when the shock will occur. Rescorla's (1968) results supported the expectancy model: the tone did not elicit a fear response for the second group.

Other evidence supports the expectancy model. For example, recall that forward pairing (e.g., a tone followed by food) typically produces the strongest learning, whereas backward pairing (e.g., food followed by a tone) produces the weakest learning. This makes sense based on the expectancy model. In forward pairing, the tone predicts the imminent arrival of the food; it is a signal that something meaningful is about to happen. In backward pairing, the tone has no predictive value because the food has already arrived. In sum, the expectancy model has been highly influential and provides good evidence that cognition plays a role in classical conditioning (Siegel & Allan, 1996; Boddez, Baeyens, Luyten, Vansteenwegen, Hermans, & Beckers, 2013).

> **Focus 7.18** Describe the role of cognition in classical and operant conditioning. How did Tolman illustrate latent learning?

Blocking

Another important phenomenon which emerged at about the same time as Rescorla's findings was the '**blocking** effect'. This was first documented in experiments conducted by Leon Kamin (1968, 1969). Like Rescorla, Kamin used a fear conditioning procedure. Rats were divided into two experimental groups (Figure 7.34). In the experimental condition the rat is first given trials in which CS A (e.g., light) is presented before the UCS (shock). Then, in phase two, the experimental group of rats are given trials in which both CS A (e.g., light) and CS B (e.g., a noise) are presented before the shock. In the control group the rats only receive phase 2 training in which both light and sound are presented with the shock. Kamin found that only the control group showed evidence of having learned the association between CSB and the shock (by demonstrating the fear response to the noise). Kamin proposed that the previous pairing of the light with the shock 'blocked' the rats' acquisition of an association between the sound and the shock.

> **blocking** obstruction of conditioning of a CR, because that response has already been conditioned to a different stimulus

The phenomenon of blocking again demonstrates how associative learning is not simply due to the number of times which a CS and a UCS have been presented together. Rather, animals and indeed humans (e.g., Oades, Roepcke, & Schepker, 1996) appear to examine how well the CS predicts the UCS.

Here is an example to make it clearer how blocking works in an everyday situation. Imagine you have just been introduced to a new social group, a group of friends who always drink in the same pub. As a newcomer you are trying to ascertain what relationships the group comprises. You have seen Amy arrive at the pub closely followed by Lawrence several times, and have formed the association that they are a couple. However, a few weeks later you see Amy arrive with Jane and then Lawrence. Do you then start to think that Jane and Lawrence may be an item? This seems an irrational conclusion, as you already have strong evidence that it is Amy who is seeing Lawrence.

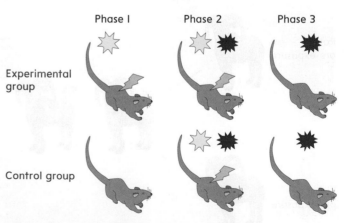

FIGURE 7.34 The blocking procedure.

The rats in the experimental condition did not show learning of the relationship between the sound (the red symbol) and the shock, because learning had been blocked by the prior pairing of the light (the yellow symbol) and the shock.

The Rescorla-Wagner theory of classical conditioning

The blocking effect led researchers to argue that the strength of the association formed in classical conditioning was determined by how surprising the UCS was, or how unexpected it was. To go back to Kamin's blocking experiment, by the time the rat in the experimental condition reaches phase 2 it has already learned to expect the light following the shock so it will no longer be surprised when the shock is administered – it will expect the shock. Rescorla and Wagner (1972) argue that no association is formed between the sound and the shock, because the shock is already expected – thus there is no surprise. The take-home message of **Rescorla and Wagner's theory** was that if the UCS (e.g., a shock) is surprising or unexpected, then it will be more strongly associated with a CS (e.g. a noise). If the shock is unsurprising or expected, for instance when it has already been predicted by a prior event, then it will not form so strong an association. Rescorla and Wagner's (1972) model was very influential because it was the first formalized model of conditioning which went beyond a simple associative explanation, like that used by the S-R theorists, by considering the mediating role of cognitive processes in learning; in this case the expectancy of the UCS.

> **Rescorla–Wagner theory** a theory of classical conditioning which states that the strength of conditioning is determined by how surprising the UCS is

Latent inhibition and attentional theories of conditioning

However, as is the process in scientific method, researchers set out to test the Rescorla–Wagner model, and identified a number of learning phenomena which were difficult for it to explain. **Latent inhibition**, described by Lubow and Moore (1959), is probably the most notable of these phenomena. Latent inhibition is the weakening of classical conditioning due to the prior presentation of the CS on its own.

> **latent inhibition** the weakening of classical conditioning due to the prior presentation of the CS on its own

In the original work, Lubow and Moore (1959) showed sheep and goats either a light flash *or* a spinning rotor. They then trained them to expect a shock after seeing both of these (Figure 7.35). They found that the animals were slower to learn an association between the shock (UCS) and the stimulus to which they had already been exposed. So just the fact of having seen a particular CS (a light or a rotor) before slowed their learning down.

One simple way to think of latent inhibition is in terms of humans. If you look up 'latent' in the dictionary you will find that it means 'dormant' or 'hidden'. So latent inhibition means an inhibition response that is just waiting to happen, lying dormant for now, but which may appear at any moment.

It might be that a person experiences a stimulus and does not learn anything from it. The stimulus is perceived, but is regarded as insignificant, as unimportant and so the person does not make any learning links to it. This 'decision' not to learn from the stimulus may be because the person is busy doing something else at the time and so in order to carry out that task properly they need all their focus. Later, the person may actually respond as if classically conditioned to the stimulus. That is to say, they did indeed learn from the earlier experience of the stimulus and only now does the inhibition show itself.

Latent inhibition makes a lot of adaptive sense. There are lots of different stimuli in our environment all the time and it would make little sense to associate these with novel unconditioned stimuli. For example, imagine a plate of food in front of you. The plate contains vegetables you are used to, some bread and some unidentified seafood which you have never sampled before. After eating your meal, you are violently sick. Do you develop a taste aversion to vegetables and bread, items of food that you are used to or that have never made you ill before? No. Sensibly, you develop an aversion to the novel unidentified seafood which you have eaten. The process of latent inhibition has prevented you from forming an aversion to bread and vegetables. Latent inhibition helps us to filter out spurious associations from our learning. However, it is clearly difficult for the

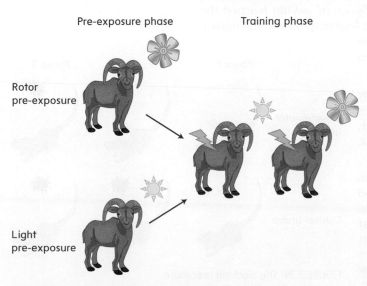

Pre-exposure phase   Training phase

Rotor pre-exposure

Light pre-exposure

FIGURE 7.35 Lubow and Moore's (1959) latent inhibition experiment.
Pre-exposure to a stimulus on its own prevents later learning of an association between that stimulus and new UCS (in this case an electric shock).

Rescorla–Wagner model to explain. The UCS (shock) is only introduced after the pre-exposure phase. It is just as surprising to the goat whether it has been pre-exposed to CS or not. Rescorla–Wagner would therefore predict that latent inhibition should not occur, but it does.

The most influential current accounts of why latent inhibition occurs are those which suggest that the amount of attention which is paid to a CS determines how well we learn a new stimulus pairing. British psychologists, Neil Mackintosh (1975) and, later, John Pearce and Geoffrey Hall (1980) developed models of classical conditioning which suggest that the strength of the learned associations is determined by how much attention is paid to the CS during the learning episode. The amount of attention paid to the CS is said to be determined by factors such as how novel it is, and how well it predicts the UCS.

These **attentional theories of classical conditioning** explain latent inhibition by suggesting that the effect of presenting the CS (e.g., a light) in the absence of the UCS (e.g., a shock) is to habituate the animal to the CS. As we learned at the beginning of the chapter, habituation is a simple process whereby repeated presentation of a single stimulus reduces our response towards it. If we consider attention to be an orienting response to a stimulus, then we can see that the effect of presenting the CS on its own can habituate our attention towards the CS. Thus, attentional theories of classical conditioning suggest that the decreased attention towards the CS caused by habituation during pre-exposure reduces the strength of the association formed once the UCS is presented. To go back to Lubow and Moore's (1959) demonstration (see Figure 7.35), the goats were pre-exposed to either a rotor or a light, having the effect of habituating these groups to these particular stimuli. The attentional models of conditioning by Mackintosh (1975) and Pearce and Hall (1980) propose that because the animals are now paying less attention to one CS (e.g., the rotor), they will be more likely to attend to the other CS (e.g., the light) when it is presented during the training phase, and thus more likely to learn an association between it and the UCS (the shock).

In addition to *latent inhibition*, attentional theories can explain a wide variety of other phenomena in classical conditioning. For example, they explain blocking (see Figure 7.35) by suggesting that attention is paid to a CS when it is a good predictor of the UCS; thus because a CS (e.g., a light) is already a good predictor of the UCS following phase 1 of a blocking experiment, more attention is paid to it at phase 2, at the expense of the newly introduced CS (e.g., a sound), and thus little association is formed between the sound and the UCS.

> **attentional theories of classical conditioning** state that the strength of conditioning is determined by how much attention is paid to the CS during the learning episode

COGNITIVE AND BEHAVIOURAL LEARNING IN PSYCHOLOGICAL THERAPIES

As we have seen earlier in the chapter, psychologists have made good use of theories of behavioural learning in attempting to explain and alleviate psychological disorders. For example, the use of exposure therapies (such as 'systematic desensitization') to treat phobias (like Michelle's fear of cars) is based on the knowledge that extinction of learned fear can occur when we are placed in situations (e.g., in and around cars) where our fear is no longer associated with the stimulus which initially caused the phobia (e.g., a car crash). The 'two-process' theory of avoidance learning (Mowrer, 1947; Rescorla & Solomon, 1967) was also very important in informing understanding of why anxiety disorders persist, and how it is possible to challenge them (by preventing avoidance).

But given the more recent acknowledgement that cognitive processes are important in learning, should we not also conclude that cognitive processes also have an important role in psychological disorders? The answer, of course, is yes. Just as cognitive approaches to learning have gradually risen to the fore, so have cognitive therapies in which irrational thoughts and expectations are challenged (Beck, Freeman, & Davis, 2004; Clark, 2004). Indeed, as we shall see in **Chapter 18**, currently the most widely used – and many argue the most effective – therapies are cognitive behavioural therapies (CBT) which combine

Chapter 18, Page 782

both elements for modifying both maladaptive cognitions and behaviours. The success of cognitive approaches to learned psychological disorders is another argument for the role of cognition in learning. CBT has also been successfully used as part of the rehabilitation process with criminals (Andrews & Bonta 2010) – the role of cognition in learning and the benefit of such work seem clear.

In review

- An organism's evolutionary history prepares it to learn certain associations more easily than others, and this places biological constraints on learning. Thus organisms show faster classical conditioning when a CS has evolutionary significance.

- It is difficult to operantly condition animals to perform behaviours that are contrary to their evolved natural tendencies. Instinctive drift occurs when a conditioned behaviour is abandoned in favour of a more natural response.

- Studies of animal insight (such as Köhler's work with chimpanzees) and Tolman's research on cognitive maps suggested that cognition plays a role in learning. Tolman emphasized that learning is based on knowledge and an expectation of 'what leads to what'.

- Cognitive learning theorists view operant conditioning as the development of expectancy that certain behaviours will produce certain consequences under certain conditions. Research on latent learning indicates that learning can occur without reinforcement.

- Cognitive interpretations of classical conditioning propose that organisms learn an expectancy that the CS will be followed by the UCS.

- There has been much debate concerning what determines how well an association, or expectancy, is learned in classical conditioning. Rescorla and Wagner (1972) argue that the strength of the association is determined by how surprising the UCS is. This theory can explain the phenomenon of 'blocking'. On the other hand, Mackintosh (1975) and Pearce and Hall (1980) argue that the strength of the association is determined by how much attention is paid to the CS during the learning episode. These theories can explain both 'blocking' and 'latent inhibition'.

- The success of cognitive therapies for learned psychological disorders is another reason why almost all psychologists today acknowledge the importance of cognitive processes in learning.

OBSERVATIONAL LEARNING: WHEN OTHERS SHOW THE WAY

> **observational learning**
> learning that occurs by observing the behaviour of a model

How did you learn to write, dance and drive a car, or spread peanut butter evenly across a piece of bread? Reinforcement was certainly involved, but so was **observational learning**, the learning that occurs by observing the behaviour of a model. Teachers, parents and trainers often help us learn by intentionally demonstrating skills. But observational learning extends beyond such contexts. We also learn fears, prejudices, likes and dislikes, and social behaviours by watching others (Olsson & Phelps, 2004). Through observation we may learn desirable responses, or like the two boys in our opening vignette who overenthusiastically emulated their television wrestling heroes, we may acquire undesirable behaviours. If parents who swear in front of their children complain to one another, 'Why do our kids use that **** language?' observational learning can help us answer their question.

Observational learning can be highly adaptive. By observing others, an organism can learn which events are important, which stimuli signal that such events are about to occur, and which responses are likely to produce positive or negative consequences. For example, hens may learn which other hens they can safely pick a fight with, and which ones they should avoid, by observing the hens that emerge as victors and losers in battles (Hogue, Beaugrand, & Lauguee, 1996). And monkeys may learn adaptive fears – such as a fear of snakes – by observing other monkeys react with fear (Öhman & Mineka, 2001).

Humans' capacity to learn by observation, which is also called *modelling*, far outstrips that of other creatures. It helps us bypass the potentially time-consuming and dangerous

learning process of trial and error. For example, we would not want each new generation of brain surgeons or airline pilots to learn their craft only through trial and error!

BANDURA'S SOCIAL-COGNITIVE THEORY

As you have seen, research on biological preparedness and cognitive factors in conditioning challenged behaviourism's S-R view of learning. Psychologist Albert Bandura's pioneering research and theorizing on observational learning also helped carry forward the S-O-R challenge to behaviourism. Bandura's **social-cognitive theory**, also known by its former name **social-learning theory**, emphasizes that people learn by observing the behaviour of models and acquiring the belief that they can produce behaviours to influence events in their lives (Bandura, 1969, 2004).

The Modelling Process and Self-Efficacy

Bandura views modelling as a four-step process that includes several cognitive factors:

1. *Attention:* we must pay attention to the model's behaviour.
2. *Retention:* we must retain that information in memory so that it can be recalled when needed.
3. *Reproduction:* we must be physically capable of reproducing the model's behaviour or something similar to it.
4. *Motivation:* we must be motivated to display the behaviour.

According to Bandura, **self-efficacy**, which represents people's belief that they have the capability to perform behaviours that will produce a desired outcome, is a key motivational factor in observational learning. Recall that at the beginning of the chapter we defined learning as a change in an organism's behaviour or capabilities based on experience. According to Bandura, the knowledge or capability to perform a behaviour may be acquired at one time but not displayed until a later time when the motivational conditions are favourable.

Tolman's research on latent learning in rats demonstrated this point, and a classic experiment by Bandura (1965) on modelling demonstrated the learning-versus-performance distinction in humans. In this experiment, children watched a film in which a model acted aggressively towards a 'Bobo doll' (an inflatable plastic clown), punching, kicking and hitting it with a mallet. One group saw the model rewarded with praise and candy, a second group saw the model reprimanded for aggression and a third group saw no consequences for the model. After the film, each child was placed in a room with various toys, including a Bobo doll (Figure 7.36).

Children who saw the model punished performed fewer aggressive actions towards the Bobo doll than did children in the other two groups. Does this mean that this group failed to learn how to respond aggressively? To find out, the experimenter later offered the children attractive prizes if they could do what the model had done. All of the children quickly reproduced the model's aggressive responses. Note that just as Tolman showed that rats apparently learned the layout of a maze while they were not receiving reinforcement, Bandura demonstrated that regardless of whether the model was reinforced or punished, children had indeed learned the model's behaviour.

Imitation of Aggression and Pro-Social Behaviour

Bandura's work helped stir a societal controversy that was brewing in the 1960s and continues to this day: what effect does viewing aggressive models on television or in films have on our attitudes and behaviour? We discuss this issue, and violent video games, more fully in **Chapter 14**. In brief, research strongly suggests that viewing media violence:

- decreases viewers' concerns about the suffering of victims
- habituates us to the sight of violence
- provides aggressive models that increase viewers' tendency to act aggressively (Eron, 2000; Huesmann et al., 2003).

> **social-cognitive theory** (also known by its former name **social-learning theory**) emphasizes that people learn by observing the behaviour of models and acquiring the belief that they can produce behaviours to influence events in their lives
>
> **self-efficacy** people's belief that they have the capability to perform behaviours that will produce a desired outcome

> **Focus 7.19** What is the adaptive significance of observational learning? Describe Bandura's theory and the four steps in the modelling process.

 Chapter 14, Page 621

If watching media violence can enhance our tendency to act aggressively, might watching pro-social models (models who do good deeds) increase our tendency to help others? Indeed, many studies similarly indicate that exposure to pro-social models enhances people's helping behaviour (Hearold, 1986).

FIGURE 7.36 In Bandura's (1965) experiment, most children who watched an aggressive model attack a Bobo doll later imitated that behaviour.

Source: Reprinted with the permission of Professor Albert Bandura

---

● **Current topic**

IMITATION: BABIES' BRAINS RESPOND TO WATCHING OTHERS' ACTIONS

As discussed in this chapter, we know from a great deal of research that humans and animals are able to learn by observation. However, the kinds of observational learning that various species employ are quite varied. Some authors have argued that humans have evolved to be able to learn from observation in a special way – through imitation – and research from Saby, Meltzoff and Marshall (2013) shows how that evolution may manifest itself neurologically.

If you get a chance, spend a little time watching a baby behaving. You will see that just like you and I in a coffee shop, babies just love to watch people and unlike us they are not just being nosey. This observation serves a terribly important purpose – they are learning, their brains are developing and responding to the actions and activities they see. They themselves may not yet be able to carry out some of the actions they are watching, but their brains are certainly responding to them.

▶

Saby et al. (2013) looked at how a baby's brain responded to watching an actor carrying out simple activities that were similar but quantifiably different. Scalp electroencephalograms (EEG) of 14-month-old infants were taken as they observed a woman reaching to touch an object either with her foot or with her hand. The results were very interesting and showed quite clearly that activity in the sensorimotor cortex, a brain region responsible for combining perceived and motor actions, was dependent on the activity being observed. Readings relating to the hand region of the sensorimotor cortex became desynchronized when viewing the image of the woman reaching for the object with her hand was observed by the baby, and similarly, the region related to the foot showed desynchronized activity when the image of the woman touching the object with her foot was shown.

This observation links up two very important things. We know that babies learn through observation and we know that their brains are developing. Here the authors are able to show that there are components of their young brains that respond to body parts carrying out activities that they are simply watching. This neurological organization, the authors claim, could well be evidence for how infants learn through observation.

APPLICATIONS OF OBSERVATIONAL LEARNING

In everyday life we learn many skills from observing models. Elementary school teachers model how to write, pronounce and use words. In college, foreign-language instructors do the same. Parents, teachers, business managers and athletic coaches model how to solve problems and perform tasks. If you play sports or video games, you may have picked up strategies or moves by watching other players.

Psychologists have also used observational learning to enhance pro-social behaviour. For example, researchers showed secondary school students an audio-visual programme that featured models (other students) who donated blood. Subsequently, donations to a blood bank increased by 17% (Sarason et al., 1991).

More ambitiously, observational learning has been used to address global social problems. In 1975, Miguel Sabido, a vice-president in charge of research at one of Mexico's largest media companies, used Bandura's theory to help develop the first project to tackle an important social problem (in this case high levels of illiteracy) with social-cognitive theory (D. Smith, 2002). When a national literacy programme in Mexico failed to draw a good turnout, Sabido created a television soap opera to give the literacy programme a boost. The popular soap opera aired for a year and featured a literate female character who, as part of the national programme, organized a self-study group for teenagers and adults who struggled with illiteracy.

Sabido hoped that by showing soap-opera characters learning to read, this would provide viewers with positive role models, increase viewers' self-efficacy that they could learn to read, and motivate viewers to enrol in the literacy programme. His hope bore fruit. After one episode in which viewers were directly asked to enrol, 'about 25,000 people descended on the distribution centre in Mexico City to get their reading materials' (Bandura, 2002a, p. 224). New annual enrolments in the literacy programme jumped from 100,000 in the previous year to over 900,000 in the year the soap opera aired and decreased to about 400,000 the year after the soap opera ended.

Mass media programmes incorporating social-cognitive learning principles have since tackled social problems all over the world. Our 'Research close-up' describes an experiment that implemented and evaluated one of these programmes.

Focus 7.20 Describe applications of social cognitive theory to solve large-scale societal problems.

Research close-up

USING SOCIAL-COGNITIVE THEORY TO HELP US BETTER UNDERSTAND EATING BEHAVIOUR

Source: K. Ball, A. MacFarlane, D. Crawford, G. Savige, N. Andrianopoulos & A. Worsley (2009). Can social-cognitive theory constructs explain socioeconomic variations in eating behaviours? A mediation analysis. *Health Education Research, 24*(3), 496–506.

INTRODUCTION

Eating properly is very important to maintain health, and to avoid drifting into the problems associated with unhealthy eating, including obesity – something we see our governments working to avoid more and more now. Importantly, eating habits are often secured at earlier, more formative years where children form habits and a palate associated with their early food-learning experiences. Bad habits learned at a younger age can follow a person into late life. Adolescents' diets are not always consistent with advice to eat the requisite portions of vegetables, and to cut down on sugar, for instance. Ball et al. (2009) identify that those in lower socioeconomic groups are at particular risk in these respects. This difference in diet between the different socioeconomic groups runs in parallel with patterns of chronic health problems. The motivation for this research was to look further into the diet of adolescents in different socioeconomic groups as relatively little was known about it. This would not only add to our knowledge in this area, but would better inform those targeting and shaping healthy eating campaigns. The pressures on dietary choice include social support for healthy eating and other environmental and social pressures. The research had three goals; to analyse the diets of adolescents in different socioeconomic groups, to see whether key components of socio cognitive theory (SCT) – (including self-efficacy, perceived importance of healthy eating, observation of others – modelling) are also part of the pattern of differences between different socioeconomic groups; and whether any variations in the SCT factors investigated could explain dietary behaviour. It is the relationship between what we experience at home, what we experience significant others doing and our own behaviour that is important here. We take our lead from significant others in many cases, learning through experience and feedback, and through how we see ourselves as in control of our choices is vital for us to understand. Randomly making choices to various stimuli does not sufficiently link a stimulus with a response and so careful pairing of stimulus (healthy food) and response (praise, and support from mothers or family) is an important way to train our eating habits.

METHOD

A total of 2,529 (a subset of a much larger sample) of students aged between 12 and 15 were identified and parental consent was given for their inclusion in the study. Questionnaires were administered to the parents/caregivers and data about diet was gathered. In addition to this, parents were asked to include information about their socioeconomic status. Students were instructed by teachers to complete an online questionnaire of eating habits in class in the days that followed. Three categories of data were collected. *Outcome measures (food intake)* – as you might expect, the types, quantities and frequency of eating different foods – were measured here. *Predictor measures* – it was here the socioeconomic status was measured as an assessment of maternal education level. This was chosen because previous work (Winkleby, Jatulis, Frank, & Fortman, 1992) had shown that it was the strongest predictor of health behaviours. Finally, *Mediators* were assessed. Here were included cognitive, social and environmental constructs, such as self-efficacy, perceived importance of advertising, social learning in terms of observation of others' eating behaviour, and the availability of foods.

RESULTS

The results showed clearly that compared with other students with highly educated mothers, those with less well-educated mothers had lower perceived importance of eating healthily, and less healthy eating habits of their mothers. They also reported lower support in their families for healthy eating, and more unhealthy food available in their homes. They also reported lower levels of self-efficacy (under their own control) for increasing healthier eating in terms of fruit intake and reducing unhealthier eating in terms of volumes of junkfood consumed. The results further showed that by far the strongest predictor of junk food intake was its presence in the home. Put bluntly, the easier it is to pick it up and eat it at home, the more likely the adolescents were to do so.

DISCUSSION

The results supported previous research, showing that those with lower socioeconomic status did indeed have diets that were generally less in line with guidelines for healthier eating than those from higher socioeconomic groups. The results also showed the great importance of many of the constructs of social-cognitive theory measured. Those with poorly educated mothers scored poorly (relative to those with better educated mothers) on social constructs (support for healthier eating), cognitive constructs (self-efficacy for own eating behaviour) and environmental constructs (availability of healthy food). The authors concluded that the SCT constructs were very important mediators of socioeconomic factors, and as such both should be carefully considered where the desire is to moderate eating behaviour in society – although the long-term relationships between SCT factors and socioeconomic status are unclear at present, the research does indicate that a better knowledge of the influences of both will be helpful in generating any campaign for healthier eating. The strong influence of cognitive factors, particularly perceived self-efficacy in food choices, indicates clearly that any campaign must work carefully to develop this factor and the perceived reward for choosing healthier food. Where there is agency in food choice and the perceived rewards, both socially as well as in terms of health of choosing the healthier option is higher, then learning will be enhanced and longer-term food choices can be better influenced.

In review

- Observational learning occurs by watching the behaviour of a model.
- Bandura's social-cognitive theory proposes that modelling involves four steps: attention, retention, reproduction and motivation. Observing successful models can increase people's self-efficacy and thus motivate them to perform the modelled behaviour.
- Children can learn aggressive and pro-social behaviours by watching models. Even when viewing an aggressive model that is punished, children may learn the behaviour and display it at a later time.
- Modelling is often a key instructional technique in everyday skill-learning situations. Psychologists have applied modelling concepts to increase people's pro-social behaviour.
- Social-cognitive theory can help direct and stimulate intervention programmes to address social problems, such as healthy eating behaviours.

THE ADAPTIVE BRAIN

We began this chapter by noting that learning represents your personal adaptation to the circumstances you encounter throughout your life. To close the chapter, we would like to emphasize that your ability to learn and adapt depends not only on networks of brain structures and circuits, but also on the brain's own ability to adapt – to modify its structure and functioning – in response to experience.

LEARNING THROUGH CONNECTIONS

How do these modifications take place? In the 1800s, the prevalent view was that new memories are formed through the growth of new cells in the brain. However, Spanish physiologist, Santiago Ramon y Cajal (see Figure 7.37a), proposed that learning might

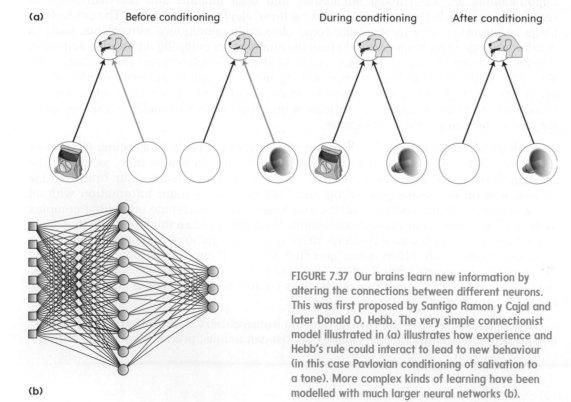

(a)

Before conditioning   During conditioning   After conditioning

(b)

FIGURE 7.37 Our brains learn new information by altering the connections between different neurons. This was first proposed by Santigo Ramon y Cajal and later Donald O. Hebb. The very simple connectionist model illustrated in (a) illustrates how experience and Hebb's rule could interact to lead to new behaviour (in this case Pavlovian conditioning of salivation to a tone). More complex kinds of learning have been modelled with much larger neural networks (b).

occur through changes in the strengths of connection between nerve cells. In the mid-twentieth century, Donald Hebb (1949) took this idea a step further by proposing that these changes in connection strength may be caused by concurrent activity across a connection or synapse in the brain. This mechanism has become known as the Hebb rule. Can simple mechanisms like this explain how learning happens in the brain? Modern-day 'neural network modellers' attempt to understand how learning and memory can be instantiated in the neurons and synapses in our central nervous systems. They construct **neural network** (or **connectionist**) **models** which learn new information through changes in the connections between mathematically simulated neurons (or 'nodes').

neural network (or **connectionist**) **models** learn new information through changes in the connections between mathematically simulated neurons

Figure 7.37c shows a very simple neural network which illustrates how the Hebb rule could lead to the kind of learning which occurs in classical conditioning. Strong connections are indicated by solid black arrows, and weaker connections by grey connections. Important here is that the node responding to the CS and the cell controlling salivation are *active* at the same time during conditioning, meaning that the connection between them is strengthened (the red arrow indicates where learning is happening). Later the tone node will activate the salivation node on its own. Similar processes could be happening in the neurons and synapses of a dog's brain while it takes part in a Pavlovian conditioning experiment.

Neural network and connectionist modellers usually focus on more complex forms of learning such as the ability to learn to read words (Rumelhart & McClelland, 1986). These kinds of learning require more complicated neural networks containing more nodes and more connections (Figure 7.37d). We return to the role of connections when we discuss the neural basis of memories in the next chapter (**Chapter 8**, 'Memory').

Chapter 8, Page 327

WHERE DOES LEARNING HAPPEN IN THE BRAIN?

No single part of the brain controls learning. For example, the hypothalamus and neural pathways involving dopamine play a key role in regulating our ability to experience reward (Olds, 1958; Rolls, 2000). Humans report pleasure when specific areas of the hypothalamus are electrically stimulated, and both humans and rats will learn to repeatedly press a button or lever to receive these electrical reinforcers. The cerebellum plays an important role in acquiring some classically conditioned movements, such as conditioned eye blink responses, whereas the amygdala is centrally involved in acquiring conditioned fears (Schafe & LeDoux, 2002). Gottfried, O'Doherty and Dolan (2003) also showed that the relationship between activity in the amygdala and another part of the brain, the orbitofrontal cortex, helps us make predictions of how rewarding certain stimuli will be to us. We take a closer look at brain processes that underlie learning when we discuss memory in the next chapter.

Biology affects learning, but learning also influences brain functioning (Fanselow & Poulos, 2005). As we noted in the previous chapter, in a new task, as you make the transition from inexperienced novice to experienced master, your brain is able to rely less on conscious processing and instead process more information without consciousness. Highly trained athletes and musicians can execute incredibly complex skills with a minimum of conscious thought. No doubt you can think of skills that seem almost automatic to you now (perhaps driving a car or typing on a keyboard) but which required considerable effort when you first learned them. As we gain experience at novel tasks, the brain's frontal lobes – the seat of executive functions such as decision-making and planning – tend to exercise less control and become less active (Eliassen, Souza, & Sanes, 2003).

Learning also etches its imprints on the brain's physical structure. During countless hours of practice and performance, a violinist makes continuous, precise movements with the

fingers of his or her left hand while the right hand moves the bow. This constant fingering of the strings provides a great deal of sensory stimulation to the somatosensory cortex of the right hemisphere. By using brain imaging, researchers found that the area in this brain region that is devoted to representing the fingers was larger among string-instrument musicians (who averaged almost 12 years of experience) than among non-musicians. Moreover, the earlier in life that the musicians had started to play their instruments, the greater the size of this brain area. In contrast, the left-hemisphere somatosensory area representing the right-hand fingers of the musicians and non-musicians did not differ (Elbert et al., 1995).

Because these findings are correlational, they cannot clearly establish cause and effect. Perhaps it was not playing music that caused the brain differences. Maybe it was the other way around: pre-existing brain differences helped these individuals become musicians. Yet controlled experiments with animals do indeed show that learning leaves its mark not only on the somatosensory cortex but on other parts of the brain as well. For example, when monkeys and rats learn skilled movements that require them to use their fingers or paws, the representations of these body parts in their motor cortex change (Kleim et al., 2002).

A recent topic of interest in learning research is our ability to improve our skills while we are not actually practising them – *offline learning* or *consolidation*. A number of laboratories are now uncovering evidence that some large improvements in ability at certain learned skills such as perceptual discriminations and sequential finger movements (as when learning a new piece on the violin) are observable after we have been asleep (Robertson, Pascual-Leone, & Miall, 2004). In addition, these improvements have been found to be linked to the amount of time we spend in particular stages of sleep. In particular, increased time spent in sleep stage 2 (see **Chapter 6**) is implicated in improvements in motor skill (Walker, Brakefield, Morgan, Hobson, & Stickgold, 2002). It seems that active processes in our brain consolidate what we have learned while we sleep.

 Chapter 6, Page 228

Learning's effects on the brain occur throughout the life cycle. Compared with newborn rats that grow up in standard cages, litter mates that grow up in enriched environments – with toys and greater opportunities to learn – develop heavier brains whose neurons have more dendrites and synapses and greater concentrations of various neurotransmitters (Rosenzweig, 1984). In turn, this increased brain development enables animals to perform better on subsequent learning tasks (Meaney, Mitchell, Aitken, & Bhatnagar, 1991). And in humans, exposure to stimulating environments and new learning opportunities during late adulthood seems to slow declines in brain functioning, as measured by better performance on intellectual and perceptual tasks (Goldstein, Cajko, Oosterbroek, Van Houten, & Salverda, 1997; Schaie, 2005). In a sense, then, every day you are alive your brain adapts and continues its own personal evolution; its neural networks and patterns of activity are affected not only by your genetic endowment but by your learning experiences as well.

In closing, the 'Levels of analysis' summarizes some of the environmental, psychological, and biological factors that play key roles in learning. As you study the learning concepts we have covered, try to apply them to your own behaviour. Think about the roles that classical conditioning, operant conditioning and observational learning play in developing and maintaining important behaviours in your life.

Levels of analysis
factors related to learning

BIOLOGICAL

- Adaptive significance of behaviour
- Evolution-based preparedness to learn certain associations
- Brain regions and neurotransmitters that regulate learning
- Changes in brain activity and neural circuits as a result of experience

PSYCHOLOGICAL

- Knowledge: insight, cognitive maps and latent learning
- Expectancies concerning CS–UCS associations
- Awareness of reinforcement contingencies
- Self-evaluative standards and reinforcers (e.g., pride, shame)

ENVIRONMENTAL

- Classical conditioning experiences
- Operant conditioning experiences
- Live and media models who demonstrate behaviour
- Cultural norms and socialization processes that affect what we learn

Learning

 In review

- The brain's ability to adapt and modify itself in response to experience underlies our ability to learn.
- No single part of the brain regulates all learning. The hypothalamus and dopamine pathways play a role in enabling us to experience reward. The cerebellum and the amygdala are involved in acquiring different types of classically conditioned responses.
- Studies examining the brains of people and animals who have learned specific skills, as well as environmental-enrichment experiments with animals, support the conclusion that learning alters the brain.

Recommended reading

CLASSIC

Rescorla, R. A. & A. R. Wagner (1972). A theory of Pavlovan conditioning: Variations in the effectiveness of reinforcement and nonreinforcement. In *Classical Conditioning II*: Current Theory and Research Black & Prokasy (eds), p. 64-99. New York: Appleton-Century.

Todes, D. (2000). Ivan Pavlov (Oxford Portraits in Science). Oxford: Oxford University Press.

CONTEMPORARY

Buss, D. (2013) Evolutionary Psychology: The New Science of The Mind Pearson, 4th Edition

Buzan, Deborah Skinner (12 March 2004). "I was not a lab rat". 29 May 2012

Pearce, J (2008) Animal Learning and Cognition, 3rd Edition: An Introduction, Psychology Press, 3rd edition

Slater, L. (2004) Opening Skinner's Box: Great Psychological Experiments of the Twentieth Century, London, Bloomsbury

The charm, one might say the genius of memory, is that it is choosy, chancy, and temperamental.

Elizabeth Bowen

Memory

8

Chapter Outline

Some people are famous for their extraordinary remembering; others for their extraordinary forgetting. Consider Rajan Mahadevan, who at age 5 sauntered outside his home in India one day while his parents entertained about 40 to 50 guests at a party. Rajan studied the guests' parked cars, returned to the party and then recited all the licence plate numbers from memory, matching each to the proper guest in the order they had parked. While in college, Rajan set a world record by flawlessly recalling the first 31,811 digits of pi. He averaged 3.5 digits per second!

How does Rajan perform such amazing feats? When memory researchers at Kansas State University (where Rajan was a student) asked him this very question, he said 'that being asked to describe how he learned numbers was like being asked to describe how he rode a bicycle. He knew how to do both tasks, but he found it difficult to describe either process' (Thompson, Cowan, & Frieman, 1993, p. 13).

In most other ways, Rajan's memory is ordinary. Indeed, he uses a shopping list to remember what to buy at the supermarket. As he notes, 'Unless I put my glasses, wallet and keys together near the door before I leave to start my day, I will surely forget them' (Harris, 2002).

Consider the case of patient HM, who at age 27 had most of his hippocampus and surrounding brain tissue surgically removed to reduce his severe epileptic seizures. The operation succeeded, but it unexpectedly left HM with *amnesia*, or memory loss.

When you talked with HM, he could discuss his childhood, teens and early twenties, for those memories were intact. Indeed, for the most part, at age 27 HM's amnesia did not rob him of his past. Rather, it robbed him of his future.

HM lost the ability to form new memories that he could consciously recall. Typically, once an experience or fact left his immediate train of thought, he could not remember it. If you spent a day with HM, departed and returned just minutes later, he would not recall having met you. He read magazines over and over as if he had never seen them before. A favourite uncle had died, but HM could not remember. Thus every time HM asked how his uncle was, he experienced shock and grief as though it were the first time he learned of his uncle's death.

HM's surgery took place in 1953, and researchers studied him for over 50 years (Skotko et al., 2004) until his death in 2008. No matter how many years passed HM's memory for events contained little after 1953. Even his sense of identity was frozen in time. HM recalled himself looking like a young man but could not remember the ageing image of himself that he saw in the mirror.

memory the processes that allow us to record, store and later retrieve experiences and information

Memory refers to the processes that allow us to record, store and later retrieve experiences and information. Memory adds richness and context to our lives, but even more fundamentally, it allows us to learn from experience and thus adapt to changing environments. From an evolutionary standpoint, without the capacity to remember we would not have survived as a species.

As the cases of Rajan and HM illustrate, memory is complex. How did Rajan remember over 31,000 digits of pi? Why is it, as Figure 8.1 shows, that HM can remember the skilled

FIGURE 8.1 Learning without consciously remembering.

(a) On this complex task, a participant traces a pattern while looking at its mirror image, which also shows the writing hand moving in the direction opposite to its actual movement. (b) HM's performance on this task rapidly improved over time – he made fewer and fewer errors – indicating that he had retained a memory of how to perform the task. Yet each time he performed it, he stated that he had never seen the task before and had to have the instructions explained again.

Source: Adapted from Milner, 1965.

(a)

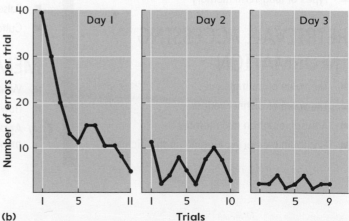

(b)

movements needed to perform a new task yet swear each time he encounters the task that he has never even seen it before (Milner, 1965)? In this chapter we explore the fascinating nature of memory. Initially we consider memory from an information-processing point of view, that is, memory consists of processes that encode, store and retrieve mental representations that stand for something in the world. Later in the chapter we consider memory as a constructive process whereby memories are *constructed* from various sources of stored information and that they may not be as accurate as we might like to think, or indeed feel, that they are.

MEMORY AS INFORMATION PROCESSING

Psychological research on memory has a rich tradition, dating back to late nineteenth-century Europe. By the 1960s, computer advances and the cognitive revolution in psychology led to a new metaphor that continues to guide memory research: the mind as a processing system that encodes, stores and retrieves information. **Encoding** refers to getting information into the system by translating it into a neural code that your brain processes. This is a little like what happens when you type on a computer keyboard; your keystrokes are translated into an electrical code that the computer can understand and process. **Storage** involves retaining information over time. Once in the system, information must be filed away and saved, as happens when a computer stores information temporarily in RAM (random access memory) and more permanently on a hard drive. Finally, **retrieval** refers to processes that access stored information. On a computer, retrieval occurs when you give a software command (e.g., 'open file') that transfers information from the hard drive back to RAM and the screen, where you can scroll through it. Keep in mind, however, that this analogy between human and computer is crude. For one thing, people routinely forget and distort information, and sometimes 'remember' events that never occurred (Loftus & Bernstein, 2005). Human memory is highly dynamic, and its complexity cannot be fully captured by any existing information-processing model.

Encoding, storage and retrieval represent what our memory system does with information. Before exploring these processes more fully, let us examine some basic components of memory.

> **encoding** getting information into the system by translating it into a neural code that your brain processes
>
> **storage** retaining information over time
>
> **retrieval** processes that access stored information

> **Focus 8.1** What is memory, and how is it like an information-processing system?

A THREE-STAGE MODEL

The model in Figure 8.2, developed by Atkinson and Shiffrin (1968) and subsequently modified, depicts memory as having three major components: sensory memory, working (short-term) memory and long-term memory. Other models have been proposed, but this three-stage framework has been the most influential.

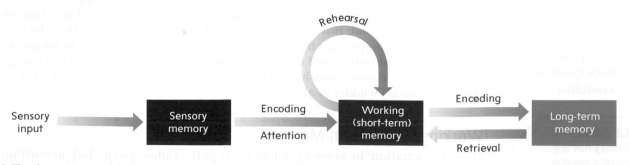

FIGURE 8.2 The three-stage model of memory.

In this model, memory has three major components: (1) sensory memory, which briefly holds incoming sensory information; (2) working (short-term) memory, which processes certain information received from sensory memory and information retrieved from long-term memory; and (3) long-term memory, which stores information for longer periods of time.

Source: Adapted from Atkinson and Shiffrin, 1968.

serial position effect the ability to recall an item is influenced by the item's position in a series

hearing the last word, you are to recall as many words as you can, in any order you wish. As Figure 8.7 illustrates, most experiments find that words at the end and beginning of a list are the easiest to recall. This U-shaped pattern is called the **serial position effect**, meaning that the ability to recall an item is influenced by the item's position in a series.

The serial position effect has two components: a *primacy effect*, reflecting the superior recall of the earliest items, and a *recency effect*, representing the superior recall of the most recent items. Findings such as these and other research that will be covered in this chapter do suggest that short-term and long-term memory are indeed distinct.

What causes the primacy effect? According to the three-stage model, as the first few words enter short-term memory, we can quickly rehearse them and transfer them into long-term memory. However, as the list gets longer, short-term memory rapidly fills up and there are too many words to keep repeating before the next word arrives. Therefore, beyond the first few words, it is harder to rehearse the items and they are less likely to get transferred into long-term memory. Glanzer and Cunitz examined this idea in some detail in a seminal article. In their first experiment they manipulated factors that were likely to influence the primacy effect by increasing the likelihood that items would enter the long-term store. They did this by manipulating the interval between the presentation of items. They used intervals of 3, 6 and 9 seconds and predicted that the longer the interval, the more likely it was that the item would be recalled. The results can be seen in Figure 8.8. The findings supported their prediction and show that as the inter-item interval increases so does the likelihood of the item being recalled. This suggests that the longer interval increases the likelihood of the item entering the long-term store and thus it is more likely to be recalled. Note that there is no effect of interval for the last four items on the list.

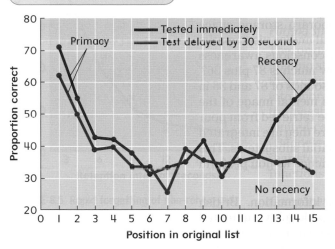

FIGURE 8.7 The serial position effect.

Immediate recall of a word list produces a serial position curve, where primacy and recency effects are both evident. However, even a delay of 15 to 30 seconds in recall (during which rehearsal is prevented) eliminates the recency effect, indicating that the later items in the word list have disappeared from short-term memory.

Source: Adapted from Glanzer and Cunitz, 1966.

Focus 8.4 Describe long-term memory and its limits. Based on the three-stage model, why does the serial position effect occur?

Alternatively, the primacy effect should decrease if we are prevented from rehearsing the early words, say, by being presented the list at a faster rate. Indeed, this is what happens (Glanzer, 1972).

As for the recency effect, the last few words still linger in short-term memory and have the benefit of not being bumped out by new information. Thus, if we try to recall the list immediately, all we have to do is recite the last words from short-term memory before they decay (i.e., fade away). In sum, according to the three-stage model, the primacy effect is due to the transfer of early words into long-term memory, whereas the recency effect is due to the continued presence of information in short-term memory.

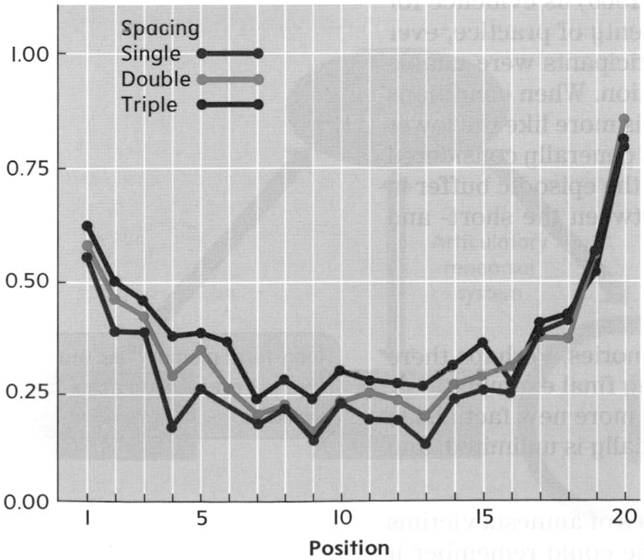

If this explanation is correct, then it must be possible to wipe out the recency effect – but not the primacy effect – by eliminating the last words from short-term memory. This happens when the recall test is delayed, even for as little as 15 to 30 seconds, *and* we are prevented from rehearsing the last words. To prevent rehearsal, we might be asked to briefly count a series of numbers immediately after the last word is presented (Glanzer & Cunitz, 1966; Postman & Phillips, 1965). Now by the time we try to recall the last words, they will have faded from short-term memory or been bumped out by the numbers task (6 . . . 7 . . . 8 . . . 9 . . .). Figure 8.7 shows that under delayed conditions, the recency effect disappears while the primacy effect remains.

Having examined some basic components of memory, let us now explore more fully how information is encoded, stored and retrieved.

FIGURE 8.8 Two storage mechanisms in free recall.

Source: From Glanzer and Cunitz, 1966. Reprinted with permission from Elsevier.

In review

- Memory involves three main processes (encoding, storage and retrieval) and three components (sensory memory, working/short-term memory and long-term memory).
- Sensory memory briefly holds incoming sensory information. Some information reaches working memory and long-term memory, where it is mentally represented by visual, phonological, semantic or motor codes.
- Working memory actively processes a limited amount of information and supports other cognitive functions. It has phonological, visuospatial, episodic and executive (coordinating) components.
- Long-term memory stores large amounts of information for up to a lifetime. Research on amnesia and on the serial position effect support the distinction between working- and long-term memory.

ENCODING: ENTERING INFORMATION

The holdings of your long-term memory, like those of a library, must be organized if they are to be available when you wish to retrieve them. The more effectively we encode material into long-term memory, the greater the likelihood of retrieving it. Let us explore two basic types of encoding and then examine some ways to optimize encoding quality.

EFFORTFUL AND AUTOMATIC PROCESSING

Think of the parade of information that you have to remember every day: names, meeting times and mountains of university work. Remembering it all involves *effortful processing*, encoding that is initiated intentionally and requires conscious attention (Hasher & Zacks, 1979). When you rehearse information, make lists and take notes, you are engaging in effortful processing.

In contrast, have you ever been unable to answer an examination question and thought, 'I should know this! I can even picture the diagram on the upper corner of the page!' In this case, you have apparently transferred information about the diagram's location on the page (which you were not trying to learn) into your long-term memory through *automatic processing*, encoding that occurs without intention and requires minimal attention. Information about the frequency, spatial location and sequence of events is often encoded automatically (Jimenez & Mendez, 2001).

LEVELS OF PROCESSING: WHEN DEEPER IS BETTER

Imagine that you are participating in a laboratory experiment and are about to be shown a list of words, one at a time. Each word will be followed by a question, and all you have to do is answer yes or no. Here are three examples:

1. POTATO 'Is the word in capital letters?'
2. HORSE 'Does the word rhyme with *course*?'
3. TABLE 'Does the word fit in the sentence, "The man peeled the _____"?'

Each question requires effort but differs from the others in an important way. Question 1 requires superficial *structural encoding*, as you only have to notice how the word looks. Question 2 requires a little more effort. You must engage in *phonological* (also called *phonemic*) *encoding* by sounding out the word to yourself and then judging whether it matches the sound of another word. Question 3 requires *semantic encoding* because you must pay attention to what the word means.

Like the three examples above, the words you are about to be presented with in this experiment will be followed by a question that requires either structural, phonological or semantic encoding. Unexpectedly, you will then be given a memory test in which you

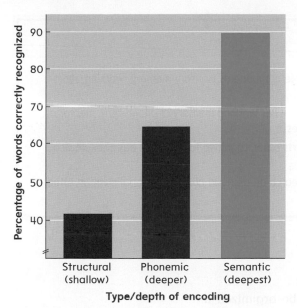

FIGURE 8.9 Depth of processing and memory.

Participants were shown words and asked questions that required (1) superficial structural processing, (2) somewhat deeper phonemic processing, or (3) deeper semantic processing of each word. Depth of processing increased later recognition of the words in a larger list.

Source: Based on Craik and Tulving, 1975.

Focus 8.5 Contrast effortful and automatic processing, and discuss the levels-of-processing model.

levels of processing the more deeply we process information, the better we will remember it

maintenance rehearsal simple, rote repetition

elaborative rehearsal focusing on the meaning of information or expanding (i.e., elaborating) on it in some way

will be shown a list of words and asked to identify which words were presented earlier. Which group of words will you recognize most easily? Those processed structurally, phonologically or semantically?

According to the concept of **levels of processing**, the more deeply we process information, the better we will remember it (Craik & Lockhart, 1972). Thus you should best remember those words that you processed semantically, as shown in Figure 8.9. Merely perceiving the structural properties of the words (e.g., uppercase versus lowercase) involves shallow processing, and phonemically encoding words is intermediate. Semantic encoding, however, involves the deepest processing because it requires us to focus on the meaning of information.

Although many experiments have replicated this finding, at times depth of processing can be difficult to measure. If some students prepare for an examination by creating hierarchical outlines while others create detailed flashcards, which method involves deeper processing? If the first group performs better, should we assume that they processed the information more deeply? To do so, warns Baddeley (1990), is to fall into a trap of circular reasoning. Still, the levels-of-processing model has stimulated much research (Clifford, 2004). There are situations where few would argue with at least a broad distinction between shallow and deep processing. Here is one of them.

EXPOSURE AND REHEARSAL

Years ago one of our students sought advice after failing an examination. He said that he had been to all the lectures and read each chapter three times. Yet not a word in his textbook had been underlined or highlighted. When asked whether he took notes as he read the text or paused to reflect on the information, he said no. Instead, he read and reread each chapter quickly, much like a novel, and assumed that the information would somehow sink in.

Unfortunately, mere exposure to a stimulus without focusing on it represents shallow processing. To demonstrate, try drawing from memory a picture of the smallest-value coin in your country (e.g., a UK penny), accurately locating all the markings. Few people can do this. Even thousands of shallow exposures to a stimulus do not guarantee long-term retention.

Rehearsal goes beyond mere exposure. When we rehearse information, we are thinking about it. But not all rehearsals are created equal. For example, actors may learn the lines of a play through **maintenance rehearsal** or simple rote repetition, and some students rely on this to learn their course material. While maintenance rehearsal keeps information active in working memory, it is not usually an optimal method to transfer information into long-term memory.

What, then, is a better method? Professional actors begin not by memorizing but by studying the script in great depth, trying to get into the mindset of their characters. Based on detailed research, Noice and Noice (2002a) note that actors, 'before they gave any thought to memorization, stressed the notion of understanding the ideas behind the utterances, and the reasons the characters used those words to express those ideas' (p. 9). The techniques actors use are examples of **elaborative rehearsal**, which involves focusing on the meaning of information or expanding (i.e., elaborating) on it in some way.

If your study habits include (1) organizing and trying to understand the material rather than just memorizing it, (2) thinking about how it applies to your own life and (3) relating it to concepts or examples you already know, then you are using elaboration. According to Craik and Lockhart (1972), elaborative rehearsal involves deeper processing than maintenance rehearsal, and experiments show that it is more effective in transferring information into long-term memory (Benjamin & Bjork, 2000).

ORGANIZATION AND IMAGERY

JC is an awe-inspiring restaurant waiter. Perhaps you would like a filet mignon, medium-rare, a baked potato, and Thousand Island dressing on your salad? Whatever you order, it represents only one of over 500 options (7 entrees × 5 serving temperatures × 3 side dishes × 5 salad dressings) available at the restaurant where JC works. Yet you and 20 of your friends can place your selections with JC, and he will remember them perfectly without writing them down.

Ericsson and Polson (1988) studied JC and found that he invented an organizational scheme to aid his memory. He divided customers' orders into four categories (entree, temperature, side dish, dressing) and used a different system to encode the orders in each category. For example, he encoded dressings by their initial letter, so orders of Thousand Island, oil and vinegar, blue cheese, and oil and vinegar would become TOBO. Organizational schemes are an excellent way to enhance memory.

> **Focus 8.6** Contrast maintenance and elaborative rehearsal. Describe ways to use organization and imagery to enhance encoding.

Hierarchies and Chunking

Organizing material in a *hierarchy* takes advantage of the principle that memory is enhanced by associations between concepts (Bower, Clark, Lesgold, & Winzenz, 1969). A logical hierarchy enhances our understanding of how individual items are related; as we proceed from top to bottom, each category serves as a cue that triggers our memory for the items below it. Because hierarchies have a visual organization, imagery can be used as a supplemental memory code. The hierarchy in Figure 8.10, for example, may help you remember some concepts about encoding.

As noted earlier, chunking refers to combining individual items into larger units of meaning. To refresh your memory, read the letters below (one per second), then try to recall as many as you can in the same sequence.

I R S Y M C A I B M C I A F B I

If you recalled five to nine letters in order, you did well. Now let us reorganize these 16 letters into five larger, more meaningful chunks: IRS, YMCA, IBM, CIA and FBI.

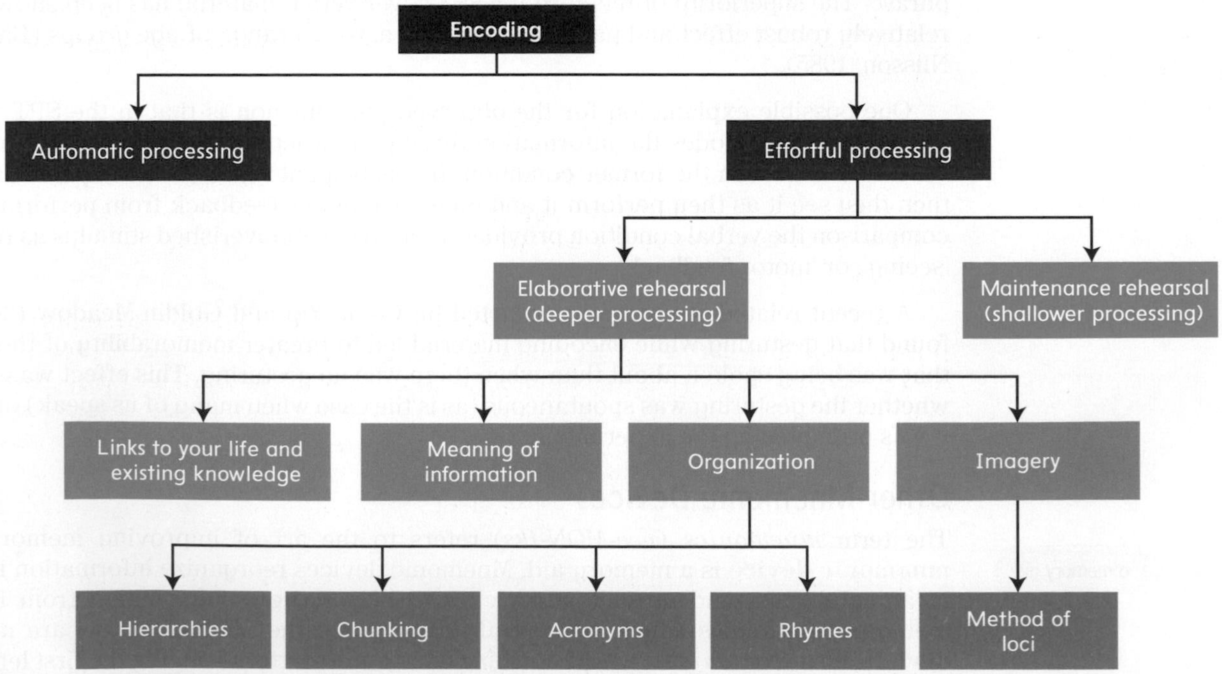

FIGURE 8.10 Meaningful hierarchical organization enhances memory. Placing information into a meaningful hierarchy enhances encoding and memory.

These chunks are easier to rehearse, keep active in working memory, and transfer into long-term memory. When learning a new telephone number (e.g., 123-456-7890), you probably encode it in chunks.

Visual Imagery

What did your Year 6 classmates look like? To answer this question, you might construct mental images in your working memory, based on information that you draw out of long-term memory.

Allan Paivio (1969) proposes that information is stored in long-term memory in two forms: verbal codes and visual codes. According to his **dual coding theory**, encoding information using both verbal and visual codes enhances memory because the odds improve so that at least one of the codes will be available later to support recall. Dual coding, however, is harder to use with some types of stimuli than it is with others. Try to construct a mental image of (1) a fire truck and (2) jealousy. You probably found the second task more difficult because jealousy represents an abstract concept rather than a concrete object (Paivio, Khan, & Begg, 2000).

A memory technique based on the effectiveness of visual imagery is the **method of loci** (*loci* is Latin for 'places'), a memory aid that associates information with mental images of physical locations. To use this technique, imagine a place that has distinct locations, such as your campus. Next, link each location with an item you are trying to remember. For example, to remember the components of working memory, imagine walking to the administration building (central executive), an art studio (visuospatial sketchpad), a music room (phonological loop) and the campus newspaper room (episodic buffer). It may take some practice to use this imagery technique effectively, but many studies support its effectiveness (Wang & Thomas, 2000).

The Enactment Effect

There is a large body of research that has shown that memory for a subject performed task (SPT) is far better than memory for the same information when presented verbally (Bäckman & Nilsson, 1985; Cohen, 1981). With an SPT the participant is required to act out the command that they have been given by the experimenter, for example, 'comb your hair' or 'scratch your head'. In a verbal condition the participant only reads or hears the phrase. The superiority of memory for SPTs over verbal material has been shown to be a relatively robust effect and has been observed across a range of age groups (Bäckman & Nilsson, 1985).

One possible explanation for the observed phenomenon is that in the SPT condition the participant encodes the information through a variety of modalities compared to the verbal condition. In the former condition the participant reads (or hears) the instruction, then they see it as they perform it and they have motor feedback from performing it. By comparison the verbal condition provides a relatively impoverished stimulus as there is no 'seeing', or 'motor feedback'.

A recent related study was conducted by Cook, Yip and Goldin-Meadow (2010) who found that gesturing while encoding material led to greater memorability of the material that was being spoken about than when there was no gesturing. This effect was observed whether the gesturing was spontaneous (as is the case when many of us speak) or whether it was prompted by the experimenter.

Other Mnemonic Devices

The term *mnemonics* (*nee-MON-iks*) refers to the art of improving memory, and a **mnemonic device** is a memory aid. Mnemonic devices reorganize information into more meaningful units and provide extra cues to help retrieve information from long-term memory. Hierarchies, chunking, visual imagery and the method of loci are mnemonic devices. So are *acronyms*, which combine one or more letters (usually the first letter) from each piece of information you wish to remember. For example, many students learn the acronym ROY G. BIV to help remember the hues in the visible spectrum (the colours of the rainbow: red, orange, yellow, green, blue, indigo, violet).

---

dual coding theory encoding information using both verbal and visual codes enhances memory because the odds improve that at least one of the codes will be available later to support recall

method of loci a memory aid that associates information with mental images of physical locations

mnemonic device a memory aid

Even putting information in a rhyme may enhance memory. In one experiment, adults listened to a 10-minute radio programme into which researchers had inserted an advertisement for a fictitious mouth rinse (Cavoloss). The advertisement either contained a rhyme ('Toss the floss, use Cavoloss') or presented the same information without a rhyme. Tested one week later, participants exposed to the rhyme remembered more product information and showed better brand-name recall (Smith & Phillips, 2001).

HOW PRIOR KNOWLEDGE SHAPES ENCODING

Can you recall the paragraph you just read word for word? Typically, when we read, listen to someone speak or experience some event, we do not precisely encode every word, sentence or moment. Rather, we usually encode the *gist* – the general theme (e.g., 'rhymes can enhance memory') – of that information or event.

Schemas: Our Mental Organizers

The themes that we extract from events and encode into memory are often organized around *schemas*. A schema is a mental framework – an organized pattern of thought – about some aspect of the world (Bartlett, 1932; Koriat, Goldsmith, & Pansky, 2000). For example, the concepts 'dog', 'shopping' and 'love' serve as schemas that help you organize your world. To see more clearly what a schema is and how it can influence encoding, read the following paragraph.

> *The procedure is actually quite simple. First you arrange things into different groups. Of course, one pile may be sufficient depending on how much there is to do. If you have to go somewhere else due to lack of facilities, that is the next step; otherwise you are pretty well set . . . it is better to do too few things at once than too many. In the short run this might not seem important, but complications can easily arise. A mistake can be expensive as well. . . . After the procedure is completed, one arranges the materials into different groups again. Then they can be put into their appropriate places. Eventually they will be used once more, and the whole cycle will have to be repeated.   (Bransford & Johnson, 1972, p. 722)*

Asked to recall the details of the preceding paragraph, you would probably have trouble. However, suppose we tell you that the paragraph is about a common activity: washing clothes. Now if you read the paragraph again, you will find that the abstract and seemingly unrelated details suddenly make sense. Thus, your schema for 'washing clothes' helps you organize and encode these details as a meaningful pattern and thus remember more of them.

Schemas, Encoding and Expertise

When most people look at a musical score, they see sheets of uninterpretable information. In contrast, musicians see organized patterns that they can easily encode. In music, as in other fields, acquiring *expertise* is a process of developing schemas that help encode information into meaningful patterns (Boschker, Baker, & Michaels, 2002).

Chase and Simon (1973) demonstrated this point in an intriguing study. Three chess players – an expert ('master'), an intermediate player and a beginner – were allowed 5 seconds to look at a chessboard containing about 25 pieces. Then they looked away and, on an empty board, attempted to reconstruct the placement of the pieces from memory. This was repeated over several trials, each with a different arrangement of pieces. On some trials, the chess pieces were arranged in *meaningful positions* that actually might occur in game situations. With only a five-second glance, the expert typically recalled 16 pieces, the intermediate player eight, and the novice only four. But when the pieces were in *random positions*, each player did poorly, accurately recalling only two or three pieces.

How would you explain these results? We have to reject the conclusion that the expert had better overall memory than the other players, because he performed no better than they did with the random arrangements. But the concepts of schemas and chunking do explain the findings (Gobet & Simon, 2000). When the chess pieces were arranged in meaningful positions, the expert could apply well-developed schemas to recognize patterns

schema is a mental framework – an organized pattern of thought – about some aspect of the world

FIGURE 8.11 Schemas, expertise and memory.

When chess players of varying ability are required to recall mid-game positions after just five seconds exposure it is clear that masters (M) are at an advantage over class A (A) players and beginners (B). However, when the pieces are placed randomly then there is no difference in recall between players of different ability.

Sources: wavebreakmedia/Shutterstock.

mnemonist (or memorist) a person who displays extraordinary memory skills

and group pieces together. For example, he would treat as a unit all pieces that were positioned to attack the king. The intermediate player and especially the novice, who did not have well-developed chess schemas, could not construct the chunks and had to try to memorize the position of each piece.

However, when the pieces were not in positions that would occur in a real game, they were no more meaningful to the expert than to the other players. When that happened, the expert lost the advantage of schemas and had to approach the task on a piece-by-piece basis just as the other players did (Figure 8.11).

ENCODING AND EXCEPTIONAL MEMORY

Ericsson and colleagues (Ericsson & Chase, 1982, Ericsson, Delaney, Weaver, & Mahadevan, 2004) argue that exceptional memory is a highly learned skill that involves prior knowledge, meaningful associations, efficient storage and retrieval, and extensive practice rather than an innate ability.

Mnemonists take advantage of basic memory principles using many of the ideas discussed above such as creating visual images or stories to help them encode information, chunking information into larger units, combining smaller chunks into larger ones, and elaborating material by associating chunks with other meaningful information (Ericsson, Chase, & Faloon, 1980).

Charles Thompson and co-workers (1993) studied Rajan and his memory for pi. They found that Rajan used chunking; but surprisingly, Rajan did not associate the chunks with meaningful material. Rather, he relied primarily on the brute force of rote memorization and extensive practice. How much practice? Thompson and co-workers estimated that it took Rajan over a year to learn the digits of pi.

Realize that just because rote memorization *can* transfer information into long-term memory, it is not necessarily the best way. Mnemonists often use elaborative rehearsal. Moreover, rote memorization is better suited to learning a string of numbers than to learning material that has meaning. When Rajan applied his rote strategy to memory tasks that involved meaningful stimuli (e.g., written stories), he performed more poorly or no better than college students in a control group.

Focus 8.7 How do schemas affect encoding? What role do schemas and mnemonic devices play in expertise and exceptional memory?

So, is exceptional memory a learned skill? After a year of practice, could the average person really remember 32,000 digits of pi? Thompson and co-workers (1993) believe that in memory, as in sports and music, endless skilled practice will not enable most people to rise to the top unless they also have the requisite innate ability. Yet Ericsson and co-workers (1993, 2004) disagree, arguing that 'many characteristics once believed to reflect innate talent are actually the result of intense practice' (Ericsson, Krampe, & Tesch, 1993, p. 363).

 In review

- Effortful processing involves intentional encoding and conscious attention. Automatic processing occurs without intention and requires minimal effort.
- Deep processing enhances memory. Elaborative rehearsal provides deeper processing than maintenance rehearsal. Hierarchies, chunking, dual coding that includes visual imagery, and other mnemonic devices facilitate deeper encoding.
- Schemas are mental frameworks that shape how we encode information. As we become experts in any given field, we develop schemas that allow us to encode information into memory more efficiently.
- People who display exceptional memory take advantage of sound memory principles and mnemonic devices.

STORAGE: RETAINING INFORMATION

At a moment's notice you can recall an incredible wealth of information, from the name of Russia's capital to how you spent your most recent holiday. This ability to rapidly access diverse facts, concepts and experiences has influenced many cognitive models of how information is stored and organized in memory.

MEMORY AS A NETWORK

We noted that memory is enhanced by forming associations between new information and other items already in memory. The general principle that memory involves associations goes to the heart of the *network* approach.

Associative Networks

One group of theories proposes that long-term memory can be represented as an **associative network**, particularly semantic knowledge like concepts (Collins & Loftus, 1975). Figure 8.12 shows what a tiny portion of such a network might be like. In this network, each concept or unit of information – 'fire engine', 'red', and so on – is represented by a *node* somewhat akin to each knot in a huge fishing net. The lines in this network represent associations between concepts, with shorter lines indicating stronger associations. For simplicity, Figure 8.12 shows only a few connections extending from each node, but there could be hundreds or more. Notice that items within the same category – types of flowers, types of fruit, colours, and so on – generally have the strongest associations and therefore tend to be clustered closer together. In essence, an associative network is a type of schema; it is a mental framework that represents how we have organized information and how we understand the world (Roediger & McDermott, 2000).

Collins and Loftus (1975) theorize that when people think about a concept, such as 'fire engine', there is a *spreading activation* of related concepts throughout the network. For example, when you think about a 'fire engine', related concepts such as 'truck', 'fire' and 'red' should be partially activated as well. The term **priming** refers to the activation of one concept (or one unit of information) by another. Thus 'fire engine' primes the node for 'red', making it more likely that our memory for this colour will be accessed (Chwilla & Kolk, 2002).

The notion that memory stores information in an associative network helps explain how hints and mnemonic devices stimulate recall (Reisberg, 1997). For example, when you hear 'Name the colours of the rainbow', the nodes for 'colour' and 'rainbow' jointly activate the node for 'ROY G. BIV', which in turn primes your recall for 'red', 'orange', 'yellow', and so forth.

> **associative network** a massive network of associated ideas and concepts
>
> **priming** the activation of one concept (or one unit of information) by another

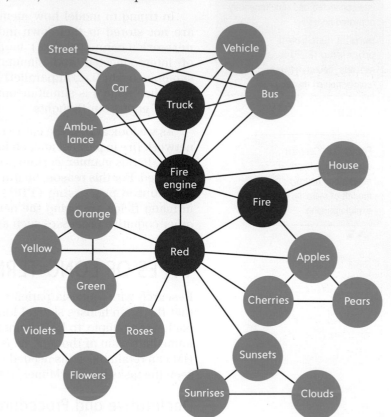

FIGURE 8.12 Semantic networks.

Each node in this semantic network represents a concept. The lines represent associations between concepts, with shorter lines indicating stronger associations.

Source: Adapted from Collins and Loftus, 1975.

Neural Networks

Neural network models take a different approach to explain why spreading activation and priming occur (Chappell & Humphreys, 1994). Neural network models are computer models whose programming incorporates principles taken from the operation of the nervous system. A neural network has nodes (often called *units*) that are linked to each other, but unlike the nodes in associative network models, each node in a neural

network model does not contain an individual unit of information. There is no single node for 'red', no single node for 'fire engine', and so on. Instead, each node in a neural network is more like a small information-processing unit. As an analogy, think of each neuron in your brain as a node. A neuron processes inputs and sends outputs to other neurons, but as far as we know, the concepts of 'red' and 'fire engine' are not stored within any single neuron.

Recall that in the brain, neurons have synaptic connections with many other neurons, receive and send signals that can be excitatory (increasing the likelihood that a neuron will fire) or inhibitory (decreasing the likelihood of firing), and will fire if the overall input they receive moves their electrical potential to a certain threshold point (see **Chapter 4**). Similarly, nodes in neural network models have connections with many other nodes, are programmed to receive and transmit excitatory or inhibitory signals, and become activated when the input they receive reaches a certain threshold strength. Just as learning experiences modify the brain's neural circuitry, in computer simulations neural networks 'gain experience' by processing different bits of information, such as sounds or visual patterns. As they do, connections among various nodes become stronger or weaker (reflected by changes in the mathematical weight assigned to each connection) and the network learns to recognize and distinguish between different types of stimuli (e.g., images of faces, spoken words, and so on).

In trying to model how memory operates, if concepts such as 'red' and 'fire engine' are not stored in their own individual nodes, then where are they stored? In **neural network (connectionist) models**, each memory is represented by a unique pattern of interconnected and simultaneously activated nodes. When node 4 is activated simultaneously (i.e., in parallel) with nodes 95 and 423, the concept 'red' comes to mind. But when node 4 is simultaneously activated with nodes 78 and 901, the concept of 'fire engine' enters our thoughts.

As we look across the entire neural network, various nodes *distributed* throughout the network fire in parallel at each instant and simultaneously spread their activation to other nodes. In this manner, certain nodes prime other nodes, and concepts and information are retrieved. For this reason, neural network (connectionist) models are often called **parallel distributed processing (PDP) models** (Rumelhart et al., 1986). Increasingly, scientists in many fields are using the neural network approach to model learning, memory, and other cognitive processes such as perception and decision making (Vogel, 2005).

TYPES OF LONG-TERM MEMORY

Research with amnesia patients, brain-imaging studies, and animal experiments indicate that the brain houses several long-term memory systems (Park & Gutchess, 2005). Think back, for example, to HM's amnesia. Once new facts or new personal experiences leave his immediate train of thought, he is unable to consciously remember them. Yet with practice, HM can retain the skills needed to perform new tasks even though he cannot recall having seen the tasks before (Milner, 1965).

Declarative and Procedural Memory

Declarative memory involves factual knowledge and includes two subcategories (Figure 8.13). **Episodic memory** is our store of knowledge concerning personal experiences: when, where, and what happened in the episodes of our lives. Your recollections of childhood friends, a favourite film, and what you ate this morning represent episodic memories. **Semantic memory** represents general factual knowledge about the world and language, including memory for words and concepts. You know that Mount Everest is the world's tallest peak and that $e = mc^2$. Episodic and semantic memories are called *declarative* because to demonstrate our knowledge, we typically have to declare it: we tell other people what we know.

HM's brain damage impaired both components of his declarative memory. He could not remember new personal experiences, nor could he remember new general facts.

Chapter 4, Page 121

neural network (connectionist) models each memory is represented by a unique pattern of interconnected and simultaneously activated nodes

parallel distributed processing (PDP) models neural network (connectionist) models

Focus 8.8 Contrast associative network models and neural network models of memory, and explain priming.

declarative memory factual knowledge

episodic memory knowledge concerning personal experiences: when, where, and what happened in the episodes of our lives

semantic memory general factual knowledge about the world and language, including memory for words and concepts

For example, HM retained good memory for words that he had learned growing up (Kensinger, Ullman, & Corkin, 2001). Yet no matter how many times he was told their definition, he could not remember the meaning of new words (e.g., *Xerox*, *biodegradable*) that entered the English language in the years after his operation. In contrast, some brain-injured children cannot remember their daily personal experiences but can remember new factual knowledge, enabling them to learn language and attend mainstream schools (Vargha-Khadem, Gadian, Watkins, Connelly, Van Paesschen, & Mishkin, 1997).

Procedural (non-declarative) memory is reflected in skills and actions (Gupta & Cohen, 2002). One component of procedural memory consists of skills that are expressed by doing things in particular situations, such as typing or riding a bicycle. HM formed a new procedural memory when he learned how to perform the mirror-tracing task.

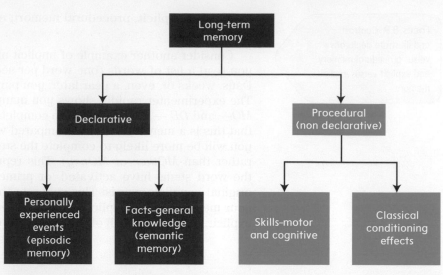

FIGURE 8.13 **Multiple long-term memory systems.**
Some theorists propose that we have separate but interacting declarative and procedural memory systems. Episodic and semantic memories are declarative; their contents can be verbalized. Procedural memory is non-declarative; its contents cannot readily be verbalized.

Classically conditioned responses also reflect procedural memory. After a tone was repeatedly paired with a puff of air blown towards HM's eye, he began to blink involuntarily to the tone alone (Woodruff-Pak, 1993). Although HM could not consciously remember undergoing this procedure (i.e., he did not form a declarative memory), his brain stored a memory for the tone–air puff association, and thus he blinked when subsequently exposed to the tone alone (i.e., he formed a procedural memory).

Explicit and Implicit Memory

Many researchers distinguish between *explicit* and *implicit memory*. **Explicit memory** involves conscious or intentional memory retrieval, as when you consciously recognize or recall something. *Recognition* requires us to decide whether a stimulus is familiar, as when an eyewitness is asked to pick out a suspect from a police line-up or when students take multiple-choice tests. In recognition tasks, the target stimuli (possible suspects or answers) are provided to you. *Recall* involves spontaneous memory retrieval, in the sense that you must retrieve the target stimuli or information on your own. This occurs when you are briefly shown a list of words and then asked to recall them. With *cued recall*, hints are given to stimulate memory. If you cannot recall the word *hat* from the list, we might say, 'It rhymes with *bat*'. As a student, you are no doubt familiar with test items that involve recall or cued recall, such as essay, short-answer and fill-in-the-blank questions.

Implicit memory occurs when memory influences our behaviour without conscious awareness (May, Hasher, & Foong, 2005). HM was able to form a procedural memory for performing the mirror-tracing task, although he had no conscious awareness of having learned it. His memory for the task (in this case, procedural memory) was implicit. In **Chapter 6** we encountered another amnesia patient, whose hand Edouard Claparède (1911) intentionally pricked with a pin during a handshake. Shortly thereafter the patient could not consciously recall this incident, but despite her amnesia, she showed implicit memory of their encounter by withdrawing her hand when Claparède offered to shake it again.

In less dramatic ways, each of us demonstrates memory without conscious awareness. Riding a bicycle, driving or performing any well-learned skill are common examples. Cycling to class, you may be consciously thinking about an upcoming examination

procedural (non-declarative) memory reflected in skills and actions

explicit memory conscious or intentional memory retrieval, as when you consciously recognize or recall something

implicit memory when memory influences our behaviour without conscious awareness

 Chapter 6, Page 241

Focus 8.9 Contrast and illustrate declarative versus procedural memory and explicit versus implicit memory.

while your implicit, procedural memory enables you to keep pedalling and to maintain your balance.

Consider another example of implicit memory. Suppose that as part of an experiment you read a list of words (one word per second) that includes *kitchen, moon* and *defend*. Days, weeks or, even, a year later, you participate in another, seemingly unrelated study. The experimenter rapidly shows you many word stems, some of which might be *KIT—*, *MO—* and *DE —*, and asks you to complete each stem to form a word. You are not aware that this is a memory test, but compared with people not given the original list of words, you will be more likely to complete the stems with words on the original list (e.g., *MOon*, rather than *MOther* or *MOney*). This represents one of many types of *priming tasks*: the word stems have activated, or primed, your stored mental representations of the original complete words. This suggests that information from the original list is still in your memory and is implicitly influencing your behaviour even though you may have no explicit, conscious recall of the original words (Schacter, 1992).

In review

- Associative network models view long-term memory as a network of associated nodes, with each node representing a concept or unit of information.
- Neural network models propose that each piece of information in memory is represented not by a single node but by multiple nodes distributed throughout the brain. Each memory is represented by a unique pattern of simultaneously activated nodes.
- Declarative long-term memories involve factual knowledge and include episodic memories (knowledge concerning personal experiences) and semantic memories (facts about the world and language). In contrast, procedural memory is reflected in skills and actions.
- Explicit memory involves conscious or intentional memory retrieval, whereas implicit memory influences our behaviour without conscious awareness.

RETRIEVAL: ACCESSING INFORMATION

retrieval cue a stimulus, whether internal or external, that activates information stored in long-term memory

Storing information is useless without the ability to retrieve it. A **retrieval cue** is a stimulus, whether internal or external, that activates information stored in long-term memory. If I ask you, 'Have you seen Sonia today?' the word *Sonia* is intended to serve as a retrieval cue. Likewise, a yearbook picture can act as a retrieval cue that triggers memories of a class-mate. Priming is another example of how a retrieval cue (*MO—*) can trigger associated elements (*MOon*) in memory, presumably via a process of spreading activation (Chwilla & Kolk, 2002).

THE VALUE OF MULTIPLE CUES

Experiments by Mäntylä (1986) vividly show the value of having multiple retrieval cues. In one, Swedish college students were presented with a list of 504 words. Some students were asked to think of and write down one association for each word, while others produced three associations per word. To illustrate, what three words come to your mind when I say *banana*? Perhaps you might think of *peel, fruit* and *ice cream*.

The students had no idea that their memory would be tested, and after finishing the association task they were given an unexpected recall test for 252 of the original words. For some words, students were first shown the one or three associations they had just generated. As a control, for other words they were first shown one or three associations another participant had generated. Then they tried to recall the original word.

The results were remarkable. When the associations (i.e., retrieval cues) were self-generated, students shown one cue recalled 61% of the words and those shown three cues recalled 91%. In contrast, when students were shown cues that someone else had generated, recall with one cue dropped to 11% and with three cues to 55%. Further, when given another surprise recall test one week later on the remaining 252 words, students still remembered 65% of the words when they were first provided with three self-generated retrieval cues.

Why does having multiple, self-generated retrieval cues maximize recall? On the encoding side, generating your own associations involves deeper processing than does being presented with associations generated by someone else. Similarly, generating three associations involves different and deeper processing than generating only one, and provides multiple cues to gain access to the material. On the retrieval side, these self-generated associations become cues that have personal meaning. And with multiple cues, if one fails, another may activate the memory. The implication for studying academic material is clear. Think about the material you are studying, and draw one or (preferably) more links to ideas, knowledge, or experiences that have meaning for you.

THE VALUE OF DISTINCTIVENESS

To demonstrate a simple point, here is a brief self-test. A list of words appears below. Say each word to yourself (one per second); then when you see the word *WRITE*, look away and write down as many words as you can recall, in any order. Here's the list:

sparrow, eagle, nest, owl, feather, goose, crow, artichoke, rooster, fly, robin, parrot, chirp, hawk, pigeon, WRITE.

If you are like most of our own students, you probably recalled *artichoke* even though it appeared in the middle of the list. The other words all relate to birds, but *artichoke* is a food: it is distinctive. In general, distinctive stimuli are better remembered than non-distinctive ones (Ghetti, Qin, & Goodman, 2002).

In school, when all the material starts looking the same, you can make it more distinctive by associating it with other information that is personally meaningful to you. According to Mäntylä (1986), this is one reason why students who generated their own three-word associations remembered almost all of the original 504 words. The associations formed a distinctive set of cues.

Distinctive events stand a greater chance of etching long-term memories that seem vivid and clear. In one study, college students listed their three clearest memories (Rubin & Kozin, 1984). Distinctive events such as weddings, romantic encounters, births and deaths, holidays and accidents were among the most frequently recalled. In another study, university students watched a videotape of a guest lecturer who engaged in some distinctive, atypical behaviours (e.g., ate crisps, burped) and some typical ones (e.g., sat down, took off jacket). On a memory test a week later, students correctly remembered about 80% of all the lecturer's behaviours, but they were more likely to report having a clear image of the distinctive ones (Neuschatz, Lampinen, Preston, Hawkins, & Toglia, 2002).

AROUSAL, EMOTION AND MEMORY

Many experiences in our lives, such as romantic encounters, deaths, graduations, accidents, and local or world events, may be better remembered not only because they were distinctive, but also because they stirred up our emotions and aroused us (Figure 8.14). In experiments, people shown arousing and neutral stimuli (e.g., pictures of happy, fearful, or neutral faces; violent or neutral film scenes) typically remember the arousing stimuli best, even when tested several weeks later (Matlin & Stang, 1978; Putman,

> **Focus 8.10** How do retrieval cues assist memory? What is the benefit of having multiple, self-generated cues and distinctive cues?

FIGURE 8.14 A memory of an emotionally arousing, distinctive event can seem so vivid and clear that we feel we can picture it as if it were a snapshot of a moment in time. Researchers call this a flashbulb memory.

Source: Dan Howell/Shutterstock.com

van Honk, Kessels, Mulder, & Koppeschaar, 2004) or even up to one year later (Bywaters, Andrade, & Turpin, 2004).

Why do emotionally arousing stimuli wind their way more deeply into memory? By physiologically monitoring people during these tasks, researchers have found that arousing stimuli trigger the release of stress hormones. This causes neurotransmitters to increase activation of the amygdala, a brain structure that helps encode the emotional aspects of experiences into longer-term memories (McGaugh & Roozendaal, 2002). Injecting rats with drugs that stimulate or inhibit stress hormone activity will, respectively, boost or impair the rats' ability to remember responses that they are learning or have recently learned.

Outside the laboratory, researchers have found that emotional arousal enhances **autobiographical memories**, memory for the events of one's life (Conway & Rubin, 1993). When people are asked to record their unique daily experiences in a diary and rate the emotional pleasantness and intensity of each event (e.g., say, on a seven-point scale ranging from 'extremely unpleasant' to 'extremely pleasant'), it typically is the more intense events that they recall most vividly when tested days, months or years later. Over time, however, the emotionality of most pleasant and unpleasant memories may fade a bit, as Richard Walker and his colleagues (Walker, Vogl, & Thompson, 1997) found when they asked college students to (1) remember diary events that were experienced during the prior month or year and (2) rate how pleasant or unpleasant each event 'feels to you now'.

Interestingly, even though the students originally rated their pleasant and unpleasant events as equally arousing when the events happened, the intensity of memories for the pleasant events faded a little less rapidly over time. This slower emotional fading of positive memories, combined with cross-cultural findings that most people express positive life satisfaction, led Walker, Skowronski and Thompson (2003a) to proclaim that 'life is pleasant – and memory helps to keep it that way!' (p. 203). Of course, as they emphasize, life surely is not pleasant for everyone, and some people do not exhibit these memory effects. They found, for example, that among mildly depressed students, the intensity of pleasant and unpleasant memories faded at the same rate (Walker, Skowronski, Gibbons, Vogl, & Thompson, 2003b). Moreover, some people's memories of traumatic experiences may remain emotionally intense for years.

Overall, then, distinctive and emotionally arousing events are recalled most easily or vividly over time. But just because a memory seems vivid does not guarantee its accuracy. In the experiment where a guest lecturer ate chips, burped and performed other odd behaviours, some students vividly remembered events (e.g., the lecturer zipped up his pants) that actually never occurred. Do similar errors occur when we retrieve memories of even more distinctive, dramatic real-world events – events that we seemingly remember like it was just yesterday?

FLASHBULB MEMORIES: FOGGING UP THE PICTURE?

Because **flashbulb memories** seem vivid and are easily recalled, we often feel confident of their accuracy. But are they accurate? Hornstein, Brown and Mulligan, (2003) reported a study of long-term memory for the death of Diana Princess of Wales and found that at testing periods of both 3 months and 18 months after the event recollection of the reception event was still highly accurate, suggesting that memories for such shocking events are robust and immune to the forgetting seen in normal everyday memories. However, in 1986 the space shuttle *Challenger* exploded shortly after takeoff, killing all on board. The next day, Ulric Neisser and Nicole Harsch (1993) asked college students to describe how they learned of the disaster, where they were, who they were with, and so on. Re-interviewed three years later, about half of the students remembered some details correctly but recalled other details inaccurately. One-quarter of the students completely mis-remembered all the major details and were astonished at how inaccurate their memories were after reading their original descriptions.

autobiographical memories memory for the events of one's life

flashbulb memories recollections that seem so vivid, so clear, that we can picture them as if they were snapshots of moments in time

Conway et al. (1994) noted that in order for flashbulb memories to be formed the original event must be both surprising and consequential for the individual, something that may not have been the case for those recalling the *Challenger* disaster. In order to study the importance of these factors they investigated the formation of flashbulb memories for the resignation of the British Prime Minister Margaret Thatcher, comparing the recall of UK and non-UK participants. Conway et al. reported that over 86% of the UK participants had flashbulb memories 11 months after the event and these participants were able to produce detailed and accurate accounts of the reception event. However, only 29% of non-UK participants had flashbulb memories and their accounts typically contained errors and there was a significant amount of forgetting. Here is how one student's recollection of the event altered over time:

> [Initial test] I was taking my study break in my dorm and was switching the TV channels. It was on the news and I almost turned right past it. I finally figured out what was being said and realised what was going on.
>
> [Retest – 11 months later] I was walking to class with my boyfriend and he brought it up. I couldn't believe that I hadn't heard; how cut off from the news had I been. I was surprised but when I thought about how many other countries were having a change in government I didn't find it that strange.
>
> *(Conway et al., 1994, p. 342)*

It seems to be important that both surprise and consequences must be present for the formation of flashbulb memories. This is why Conway et al. found higher incidence of flashbulb memory in their UK participants – the event had greater consequences for this group than it did for the non-UK participants.

CONFIDENCE AND MEMORY ACCURACY

If people are highly confident in their memory, is it likely to be accurate? After the car crash that killed Princess Diana in 1997, a study in England found that 44% of participants said that they had seen a videotape on the television news showing the crash take place. No such tape was ever shown, yet they were as confident in their memory as people who said they never saw such a tape (Ost, Vrij, Costall, & Bull, 2002), raising questions about the relationship between accuracy and confidence. Similarly, a few weeks after the 9/11 terrorist attacks, Kathy Pezdek (2003) asked students attending college in New York City (Manhattan), Southern California, and Hawaii: 'On September 11, did you see the videotape on television of the first plane striking the first tower?' Overall, 73% of the students said yes. Yet this was impossible, because a videotape of the first plane crashing was not broadcast until after 11 September. Moreover, students who incorrectly responded yes were more confident in their memory than the students who correctly said no!

Indeed, one day after 9/11, Jennifer Talarico and David Rubin (2003) asked Duke University students to report the personal details (e.g., where were you, who were you with) for two events: (1) the moment they learned about the 9/11 terrorist attacks and (2) a typical college event of their choice that they had recently experienced (e.g., a party, sports event, studying). A week, 6 weeks and 32 weeks later, the students did not display any more accurate autobiographical memory for 9/11 than for the everyday personal event, even though they rated 9/11 as a more emotionally intense event. As Figure 8.15a shows, students' recall for both events, though still good, became less accurate (i.e., less consistent with their original reports) over time. The key difference: for the everyday event, over time students said that they were less confident in their memory and that it was less vivid, but not so for 9/11. After 32 weeks, students were as confident in their memory and said it was as vivid (e.g., 'I feel as though I am reliving the experience') as the day after the attacks happened (Figure 8.15b). Similarly, another study asked people to report personal details surrounding 9/11 within two days after the attacks; over the next year, respondents remained highly confident of their memories despite the fact that those memories actually became less accurate (Weaver & Krug, 2004).

A more recent study of flashbulb memories around the 9/11 attacks looked at flashbulb memories for the event of a far longer time period than these earlier studies. Kvavilashvili,

Focus 8.12 Describe and illustrate encoding specificity, context- and state-dependent memory, and mood-congruent recall.

or events that are congruent with our current mood (Fiedler, Nickel, Muehlfriedel, & Unkelbach, 2001). When happy we are more likely to remember positive events, and when sad we tend to remember negative events.

Thus far we have focused on how information is remembered, and the 'Levels of analysis' summarizes some of the factors involved. We have more to say about the brain's role later, but first, in the next two sections we examine why we forget and why we sometimes remember events that never occurred.

Levels of analysis
factors related to remembering

PSYCHOLOGICAL

- Memory codes (visual, phonological, semantic, motor)
- Working memory, maintenance and elaborative rehearsal
- Schemas and expertise
- Memory as a network of associations
- Emotional arousal at time of event; mood at time of retrieval

BIOLOGICAL

- Evolutionary adaptiveness of memory
- Brain regions involved in sensory, working and long-term memory
- Changes in brain activity during encoding and retrieval
- Stress hormones and biological states (e.g., emotion- or drug-induced) that affect memory

ENVIRONMENTAL

- Amount and rate of information
- Order of information (serial position effect)
- Stimulus characteristics (e.g., distinctiveness, hierarchical structure, pleasant/unpleasant events)
- Retrieval cues and context-dependent memory

Remembering

In review

- Retrieval cues activate information stored in long-term memory. Memory retrieval is more likely to occur when we have multiple cues, self-generated cues and distinctive cues.
- We experience flashbulb memories as vivid and clear snapshots of an event and are confident of their accuracy. However, over time many flashbulb memories become inaccurate. Overall, memory accuracy and memory confidence are only weakly related.
- The encoding specificity principle states that memory is enhanced when cues present during retrieval match cues that were present during encoding. Typically it is easier to remember a stimulus when we are in the same environment (context-dependent memory) or same internal state (state-dependent memory) as when the stimulus was originally encoded.
- Mood states provide an exception to encoding specificity. In general, we tend to recall stimuli that are congruent with our current mood.

FORGETTING

Some very bright people are legendary for their memory failures. The eminent French writer, Voltaire, began a passionate letter, 'My Dear Hortense', and ended it, 'Farewell, my dear Adele'. The splendid absentmindedness of English nobleman Canon Sawyer once led him, while welcoming a visitor at a railway station, to board the departing train and disappear (Bryan, 1986). Indeed, how we forget is as interesting a scientific question as how we remember.

THE COURSE OF FORGETTING

German psychologist Hermann Ebbinghaus (1964) pioneered the study of forgetting by testing only one person – himself. He created over 2,000 *nonsense syllables*, meaningless letter combinations (e.g., *biv, zaj, xew*), to study memory with minimal influence from prior learning, as would happen if he used actual words. In one study, Ebbinghaus performed over 14,000 practice repetitions trying to memorize 420 lists of nonsense syllables.

Ebbinghaus typically measured memory by using a method called *relearning* and then computing a savings percentage. For example, if it initially took him 20 trials to learn a list but only half as many trials to relearn it a week later, then the savings percentage was 50%. In one series of studies, he retested his memory at various time intervals after mastering several lists of nonsense syllables. As Figure 8.17a shows, forgetting occurred rapidly at first and slowed noticeably thereafter.

Do we indeed forget most of what we learn so quickly? Ebbinghaus studied so many lists of nonsense syllables that his ability to distinguish among them undoubtedly suffered. If you learned just a few lists, the shape of your forgetting curve might resemble Ebbinghaus's, but the amount you forgot would likely be less. Moreover, when material is meaningful (unlike nonsense syllables), we are likely to retain more of it over time (Bahrick, 2005).

Consider the forgetting curve in Figure 8.17b, based on a study examining the vocabulary retention of people who had studied Spanish in school anywhere from 3 to 50 years earlier and then rarely used it (Bahrick, 1984). Once again, forgetting occurred more rapidly at first, but notice that the Spanish retention study employed a time frame of years rather than hours and days as in Ebbinghaus's studies.

> **Focus 8.13** Describe Ebbinghaus's research, its value and its limitations.

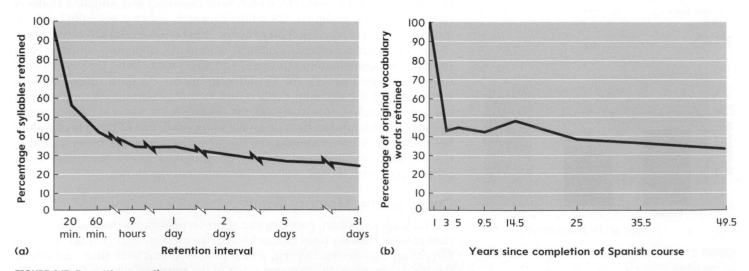

(a) **Retention interval**

(b) **Years since completion of Spanish course**

FIGURE 8.17 Forgetting over time.

(a) Hermann Ebbinghaus's forgetting curve shows a rapid loss of memory for nonsense syllables at first and then a more gradual decline. The rapid decline is probably due to the meaningless nature of the nonsense syllables. (b) The forgetting of vocabulary from high school Spanish language classes follows a similar curve, except that the time frame is in years, not days.

Sources: Based on (a) Ebbinghaus, 1964, and (b) Bahrick, 1984.

(a)   (b)   (c)   (d)

FIGURE 8.18 Which coin portrays a real pound?

If you want to try your skill at picking it out, do it before reading further. Most people have difficulty choosing the correct one because they have never bothered to encode all of the features of a real pound coin.

The correct coin is (d). The 'T' in Elizabeth is bigger in (a). The 'G' of D.G is stretched in (b). Part of the top of the crown is missing on (c).

WHY DO WE FORGET?

If some memories last a lifetime, why do we forget so much? Explanations for normal memory loss emphasize difficulties in encoding, storage and retrieval.

Encoding Failure

Many memory failures result not from forgetting information that we once knew, but from failing to encode the information into long-term memory in the first place. Perhaps you had the radio or television on this morning while eating breakfast, but chances are you can recall only those songs or stories that you found especially interesting. Much of what we sense simply is not processed deeply enough to commit to memory.

> **decay theory** with time and disuse the long-term physical memory trace in the nervous system fades away

We noted earlier that few people can accurately draw a coin from memory. Even when the task is made easier by requiring only recognition, as in Figure 8.18, most people cannot identify the correct coin (Nickerson & Adams, 1979). Can you? The details of a coin's appearance are not meaningful to most of us, and we may not notice them, no matter how often we see coins.

We may notice information but fail to encode it deeply because we turn our attention to something else. Brad Bushman and Angelica Bonacci (2002) randomly assigned 328 adults to watch either a sexually explicit, violent or neutral television programme. Nine commercial advertisements (e.g., for snacks, cereal, laundry detergent) appeared during each programme. Immediately afterward and again a day later, the researchers tested viewers' memory for the advertisements. At both times, viewers who watched the sexually explicit and violent programmes remembered the fewest number of advertisements (Figure 8.19). Several factors might account for this, and as the researchers proposed, one of them is encoding failure: all the viewers clearly saw the advertisements, but those watching the sexually explicit and violent programmes likely were the most preoccupied with thoughts about the content of the shows.

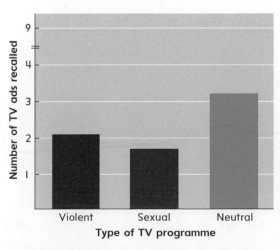

FIGURE 8.19 Violence, sex and memory for television commercials.

In one study, television viewers who watched programmes with violent or sexual content recalled fewer commercials than viewers who watched a neutral programme.

Source: Based on Bushman and Bonacci, 2002.

Decay of the Memory Trace

Information in sensory memory and short-term memory decays quickly as time passes. Do long-term memories also decay? One early explanation for forgetting was **decay theory**, which proposed that with time and disuse the long-term physical memory trace in the nervous system fades away. Decay theory soon fell into disfavour because scientists could not locate physical memory traces nor measure physical decay. In recent decades, however, scientists have begun to unravel how neural circuits change when a long-term memory is formed. This has sparked new interest in

examining how these changes might decay over time (Villarreal, Do, Haddad, & Derrick, 2002).

Unfortunately, decay theory's prediction – the longer the time interval of disuse between learning and recall, the less should be recalled – is problematic. Some professional actors display perfect memory for words they had last spoken on stage two years earlier – this despite having moved on to new acting roles and scripts (Noice & Noice, 2002b). Moreover, when research participants learn a list of words or a set of visual patterns and are retested at two different times, they sometimes recall material during the second testing that they could not remember during the first. This phenomenon, called *reminiscence*, seems inconsistent with the concept that a memory trace decays over time (Greene, 1992). In sum, scientists still debate the validity of decay theory.

Interference

According to *interference theory*, we forget information because other items in long-term memory impair our ability to retrieve it (Postman & Underwood, 1973). Figure 8.20 illustrates two major types of interference. **Proactive interference** occurs when material learned in the past interferes with recall of newer material. Suppose that Kim changes residences, gets a new phone number, and memorizes it. That night, when a friend asks Kim for her new number, she can recall only three digits and instead keeps remembering her old phone number. Memory of her old phone number is interfering with her ability to retrieve the new one.

Retroactive interference occurs when newly acquired information interferes with the ability to recall information learned at an earlier time. Suppose Kim has now had her new phone number for two months and recalls it perfectly. If we ask her 'What was your old number?', Kim may have trouble recalling it, perhaps mixing up the digits with her new number. In general, the more similar two sets of information are, the more likely it is that interference will occur. Kim (or you) would probably experience little interference in recalling highly dissimilar material, such as her new phone number and French vocabulary.

Why does interference occur? It takes time for the brain to convert short-term memories into long-term memories, and some researchers propose that when new information is entered into the system, it can disrupt (i.e., retroactively interfere with) the conversion of older information into long-term memories (Wixted, 2005). Others believe that once long-term memories are formed, retroactive and proactive interference are caused by competition among retrieval cues (Anderson & Neely, 1996). When different memories become associated with similar or identical retrieval cues, confusion can result and accessing a cue may call up the wrong memory. Retrieval failure also can occur because we have too few retrieval cues or the cues may be too weak.

Almost all of us have experienced a retrieval problem called the **tip-of-the-tongue (TOT) state**, in which we cannot recall something but feel that we are on the verge of remembering it. When Bennett Schwartz (2002) asked 56 college students to record a diary for four weeks, he found that they averaged just over one TOT experience per week. Most often, TOT states aroused emotion and were triggered by the inability to remember the name of an acquaintance, a famous person or an object. Sooner or later, the answer often popped into the mind spontaneously, but in many cases students had to consult a book or another person.

Motivated Forgetting

Psychodynamic and other psychologists propose that, at times, people are consciously or unconsciously motivated to forget. Sigmund Freud often observed that during therapy, his patients remembered long-forgotten traumatic or anxiety-arousing events. One of his patients suddenly remembered with great shame that while standing beside her sister's coffin she had thought, 'Now my brother-in-law is free to marry me'. Freud concluded that the thought had been so shocking and anxiety arousing that the woman had *repressed* it – pushed it down into her unconscious mind, there to remain until it was uncovered years

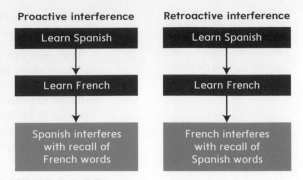

FIGURE 8.20 Interference and forgetting.

Interference is a major cause of forgetting. With proactive interference, older memories interfere with the retrieval of newer ones. With retroactive interference, newer memories interfere with the retrieval of older ones.

proactive interference occurs when material learned in the past interferes with recall of newer material

retroactive interference occurs when newly acquired information interferes with the ability to recall information learned at an earlier time

tip-of-the-tongue (TOT) state we cannot recall something but feel that we are on the verge of remembering it

Focus 8.14 Explain why we forget based on concepts of encoding failure, decay and interference.

repression a motivational process that protects us by blocking the conscious recall of anxiety-arousing memories

later during therapy. Repression is a motivational process that protects us by blocking the conscious recall of anxiety-arousing memories.

The concept of repression is controversial. Some evidence supports it, and other evidence does not (Karon, 2002). People certainly do forget unpleasant events – even traumatic ones – yet they also forget very pleasant events. If a person cannot remember a negative experience, is this due to repression or to normal information-processing failures (Epstein & Bottoms, 2002)? Overall, it has been difficult to demonstrate experimentally that a special process akin to repression is the cause of memory loss for anxiety-arousing events (Holmes, 1990). We will return to this topic shortly.

FORGETTING TO DO THINGS: PROSPECTIVE MEMORY

prospective memory remembering to perform an activity in the future

Have you ever forgotten to mail a letter, turn off the oven, keep an appointment or purchase something at the market? In contrast to *retrospective memory*, which refers to memory for past events, prospective memory concerns remembering to perform an activity in the future. That people forget to do things as often as they do is interesting, because prospective memories typically involve little content. Often we need only recall that we must perform some event-based task ('Remember, on your way out, mail the letter.') or time-based task ('Remember, take your medication at 4 p.m.'). Successful prospective memory, however, draws on other cognitive abilities, such as planning and allocating attention while performing other tasks. Li, Loft, Weinborn and Maybery (2014) examined the effect of different levels of depression on prospective memory, finding that under some conditions high depressive symptom patients performed less well on prospective memory tasks than those with low depressive symptoms. The authors argued that this was due to the inefficient use of attentional resources, possibly as a result of problems with executive function associated with depression.

During adulthood, do we become increasingly absentminded about remembering to do things, as a common stereotype suggests? Numerous laboratory experiments support this view (Vogels, Dekker, Brouwer, & deJong, 2002). Typically, participants perform a task that requires their ongoing attention while trying to remember to signal the experimenter at certain time intervals or whenever specific events take place. Older adults generally display poorer prospective memory, especially when signalling is time based. However, when prospective memory is tested outside the laboratory using tasks such as simulated pill-taking, healthy adults in their sixties to eighties often perform as well as or better than adults in their twenties (Rendell & Thomson, 1999). Perhaps older adults are more motivated to remember in such situations, or they rely more on habit and setting up a standard routine (Anderson & Craik, 2000).

AMNESIA

As HM's case illustrates, the most dramatic instances of forgetting occur in amnesia. The term *amnesia* commonly refers to memory loss due to special conditions, such as brain injury, illness or psychological trauma. However, as we will see shortly, there is one type of amnesia that all of us experience.

Retrograde and Anterograde Amnesia

retrograde amnesia memory loss for events that took place sometime in life before the onset of amnesia

anterograde amnesia memory loss for events that occur after the initial onset of amnesia

Amnesia takes several forms. Retrograde amnesia represents memory loss for events that took place sometime in life before the onset of amnesia. For example, HM's brain operation, which took place at age 27, caused him to experience mild memory loss for events in his life that had occurred during the preceding year or two (i.e., when he was 25 to 26 years old). Rugby players experience retrograde amnesia when they are knocked out by a concussion, regain consciousness and cannot remember the events just before being hit (Hinton-Bayre, Geffen, & Friis, 2004).

Anterograde amnesia refers to memory loss for events that occur after the initial onset of amnesia. HM's brain operation, and particularly the removal of much of his

hippocampus, produced severe anterograde amnesia and robbed him of the ability to consciously remember new experiences and facts. Similarly, the woman whose hand was pinpricked by Swiss psychologist Edouard Claparède during a handshake also suffered from anterograde amnesia; moments later she could not consciously remember the episode. Unlike HM's anterograde amnesia, hers was caused by *Korsakoff's syndrome*, which can result from chronic alcoholism and may also cause severe retrograde amnesia.

A famous and interesting case of severe amnesia, reported by Wilson, Baddeley and Kapur (1995), was that of musician Clive Wearing. Clive's amnesia was caused by herpes simplex virus encephalitis, resulting in inflammation of the brain and almost total destruction of the hippocampus. Like HM, Clive suffered retrograde and anterograde amnesia, although even more severely. Clive could recall very few events from before his illness. When shown pictures from Cambridge, where he lived and studied, he could recognize only one building and struggled to state whether very famous people were alive or dead, claiming never to have heard of John Lennon or John F. Kennedy. Clive also struggled to acquire new memories, and constantly felt like he had just woken up and that it was 'like being dead'. Wilson et al. stated that Clive's active record of information was certainly no more than a few minutes, evidenced by the way he would greet people who had momentarily left the room as if they had been away for weeks.

Despite his profound amnesia, Clive's musical knowledge and skill remained intact. While perhaps not at pre-illness levels, he retained the ability to play, sight read and transpose pieces with relative ease, although when watching recordings of himself play he was unable to explain his ability. Thus while there was extensive damage to declarative knowledge, including episodic and semantic memory there was relatively little, if any, damage to procedural memory.

Dementia and Alzheimer's Disease

Dementia refers to impaired memory and other cognitive deficits that accompany brain degeneration and interfere with normal functioning. There are more than a dozen types and causes of dementia, and although it can occur at any point in life, dementia is most prevalent among elderly adults.

Alzheimer's disease (AD) is a progressive brain disorder that is the most common cause of dementia among adults over the age of 65, accounting for about 50–60% of such cases. Overall, 2–4% of elderly adults are estimated to have AD.

The early symptoms of AD, which worsen gradually over a period of years, include forgetfulness, poor judgement, confusion and disorientation. Often, memory for recent events and new information is especially impaired. By itself, forgetfulness is not necessarily a sign that a person is developing AD. However, memory is the first psychological function affected, as AD initially attacks subcortical temporal lobe regions – areas near the hippocampus and then the hippocampus itself – that help convert short-term memories into long-term memories.

Alzheimer's disease spreads across the temporal lobes and to the frontal lobes and other cortical regions (Figure 8.22). As German physician, Alois Alzheimer, first noticed a century ago, patients with this disease have an abnormal amount of plaques and tangles in their brain. *Plaques* are clumps of protein fragments that build up on the outside of neurons, whereas *tangles* are fibres that get twisted and wound together within neurons (Cattabeni, Colciaghi, & Di Luca, 2004). Neurons become damaged and die, brain tissue shrinks and communication between neurons is impaired as AD disrupts several neurotransmitter systems, especially the acetylcholine system. Acetylcholine plays a key role in synaptic transmission in several brain areas involved in memory, and drugs that help maintain acetylcholine functioning have had some temporary success in improving AD patients' cognitive functioning (Ritchie, Ames, Clayton, & Lai, 2004).

Working memory and long-term memory worsen as AD progresses. If you read a list of just three words to healthy 80-year-old adults and then test their recall after a

Focus 8.15 Why is motivated forgetting a controversial concept? Describe some types and causes of amnesia and the nature of prospective memory.

dementia impaired memory and other cognitive deficits that accompany brain degeneration and interfere with normal functioning

Alzheimer's disease (AD) a progressive brain disorder that is the most common cause of dementia among adults over the age of 65

The progression of Alzheimer's disease

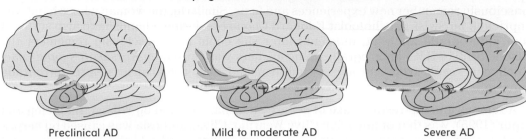

Preclinical AD   Mild to moderate AD   Severe AD

Blue indicates areas affected at various stages of AD

FIGURE 8.22 The progression of Alzheimer's disease.

Source: based on National Institute of Health, 2002.

brief time delay, they will typically remember two or all three words. Patients with AD, however, typically recall either no words or one word (Chandler et al., 2004). Anterograde and retrograde amnesia become more severe, and procedural, semantic, episodic and prospective memory can all be affected. Patients may lose the ability to learn new tasks or remember new information or experiences, forget how to perform familiar tasks and have trouble recognizing even close family members.

What causes AD and its characteristic plaques and tangles? Scientists have identified several genes that contribute to early-onset AD, an inherited form of the disease that develops before the age of 65 (and as early as age 30) but accounts for only 5–10% of Alzheimer's cases (Cattabeni et al., 2004). The precise causes of the more typical, late-onset AD remain elusive, but researchers have identified one genetic risk factor. This gene helps direct the production of proteins that carry cholesterol in the blood plasma, and high cholesterol and other risk factors for cardiovascular disease may likewise increase the risk of developing AD. Indeed, a recent study found that even healthy elderly adults who carried this particular gene, as compared to peers who did not, performed more poorly on a prospective memory task (Driscoll, McDaniel, & Guynn, 2005).

If you know someone who has AD, then you are aware that it involves much more than memory loss. Patients experience language problems, disorganized thinking, and mood and personality changes. Ultimately, they may lose the ability to speak, walk, and control bladder and bowel functions. We have more to say about the psychological, physical and social aspects of dementia and ageing in **Chapter 12**.

⊂⊃ Chapter 12, Page 527

Infantile (Childhood) Amnesia

There is one type of amnesia that almost all of us encounter: an inability to remember personal experiences from the first few years of our lives. Even though infants and preschoolers can form long-term memories of events in their lives (Peterson & Whalen, 2001), as adults we typically are unable to recall these events consciously. This memory loss for early experiences is called **infantile amnesia** (also known as *childhood amnesia*). Our memories of childhood typically do not include events that occurred before the age of 3 or 4, although some adults can partially recall major events (e.g., the birth of a sibling, hospitalization or a death in the family) that happened before the age of 2 (Eacott & Crawley, 1998).

 infantile amnesia memory loss for early experiences

What causes infantile amnesia? One hypothesis is that brain regions that encode long-term episodic memories are still immature in the first years after birth. Another is that we do not encode our earliest experiences deeply and fail to form rich retrieval cues for them. Additionally, because infants lack a clear self-concept, they do not have a personal frame of reference around which to organize rich memories (Harley & Reese, 1999).

MEMORY AS A CONSTRUCTIVE PROCESS

Retrieving information from long-term memory is not like viewing a digital replay. Our memories are often incomplete or sketchy. We may literally *construct* (or, as some say, *reconstruct*) a memory by piecing together bits of stored information in a way that seems

Research close-up

METAMEMORY: CAN CHILDREN PREDICT HOW GOOD THEIR MEMORY WILL BE?

Source: Kvavilashvili, L. & Ford, R.M. (2014). Metamemory prediction accuracy for simple prospective and retrospective memory tasks in 5-year-old children. *Journal of Experimental Child Psychology*, 127, Special issue 65–81.

INTRODUCTION

Metamemory involves the understanding of your own memory capacity, your ability to predict your future memory performance (both likelihood of forgetting and remembering) and your ability to use strategies to maximize your memory. Our understanding of our own memory capacity and how best to use it has important implications for everyday life – just think about how you judge whether or not you will remember everything you need for a weekend away or whether you need to make a list. Psychologists still have much to understand about how and when metamemory develops. Understanding this development in children is important as it has implications for issues like early years education, where effective practice is that which is aligned with children's memory capacity.

This research close-up examines a three-part study on children's metamemory by Kvavilashvili and Ford. They investigated the relationship between memory predictions and performance in 5-year-olds on two types of memory task: a retrospective memory task (trying to remember items from a list of pictures previously shown) and a prospective memory task (remembering to do something in the future).

Study 1: Children's Prospective Memory

In Study 1, 51 children were introduced to a toy mole, Morris. As Morris is frightened of tractors, children were told to reassure him at any point in the research task when a picture of a tractor is seen. The children were asked whether they thought they were likely to remember or to forget to deliver the message to Morris, and to rate their confidence in this prediction.

Following this, half of the sample listened to a neutral story ('The Clumsy Alligator') and the other half listened to a priming story ('The Forgetful Spider') in which the spider forgets to pass on a message four times. Of interest was whether the priming story would affect children's memory to reassure Morris. Finally, the children were asked to name 10 pictures. One of these (image 6) was of a tractor. At this point, children should have reassured Morris.

Children's prediction of their ability to remember to tell Morris was generally quite accurate: 78% of children predicted their performance correctly and most children were very confident. However, only 52% of the sample actually remembered to reassure Morris, meaning that 26% of the sample thought they would remember, but failed to do so. Accuracy of predictions was better than chance only in those children who remembered the task, whereas those who forgot the task had predictions of their memory capacity that were close to chance level. Thus, children more likely to complete the task also had better metamemory for prospective memory, suggesting that similar processes may underlie both prospective memory and predictions about it.

The priming story was found to have an effect on prospective memory performance only in those children who had predicted that they would be successful (88% of those predicting success were successful in the reminder story compared to only 58% in the neutral story; Figure 8.21). The authors argue that successful prospective memory may involve imagining yourself doing the thing you are required to remember. If you have done this, then a story about remembering is likely to appear more salient than to those who predicted they would forget the task – as these do not, presumably, think into the future and imagine themselves not doing the thing that they are supposed to remember to do!

Study 2: Children's Prospective and Retrospective Memory

In Study 2, eighty 5-year-olds took part in an experiment very similar to Study 1 except that there was no manipulation of story type and the memory task was slightly manipulated. Half of the sample were told that Morris was frightened of animals and that they should reassure him if a picture of an animal appeared during the task. The other half were told that Morris was frightened of horses and they should reassure him if they see a picture of a horse. As with Study 1, children were asked to give a prediction of their performance on the task and to rate their confidence in their prospective memory. They then listened to neutral story before undergoing the picture naming task. A picture of a horse or animal was shown in position 7 of 10.

To test children's retrospective memory, they were asked to recall the 10 pictures from the picture naming task. The children were shown the pictures again and asked to predict the likelihood of remembering each picture, as well as their confidence in this. They were then asked to name the 10 pictures for Morris.

In Study 2, 66% of children remembered to deliver the message to Morris and 69% correctly predicted their performance, suggesting

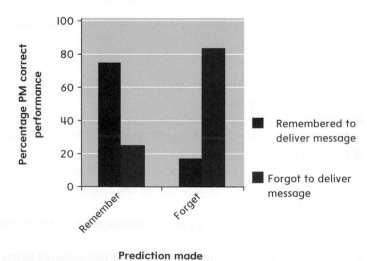

FIGURE 8.23 PM success by PM prediction based on Kvavilashvili and Ford (2014).

▶

reasonable insight into their prospective memory ability. Receiving a specific instruction (i.e., that Morris was afraid of horses) seemed to enable them to remember the task better than a general cue (afraid of animals): 31 of 40 in the specific condition remembering the task compared to 22 receiving the general cue, although there was no difference in the predictions made by these two groups. As with the first study, prediction accuracy was far better in those who successfully performed the task than in those who did not, supporting the idea that the remembering, and judging what you will remember, may rely on similar processes.

Of particular interest in Study 2, was the outcome of the retrospective memory task. Taking all 80 children together, they predicted a 96% accuracy level on naming the pictures they were shown, with high levels of confidence in their predictions. Actual performance was 46% accuracy. Thus, the children had far superior understanding of their prospective memory abilities than their retrospective abilities. However, the task is very different – apart from anything else children were trying to remember 10 things not just 1 (as in the prospective memory task). To address this, Study 3 required recall of just one item.

Study 3: Children's Retrospective Memory

In this study, 80 children undertook a single retrospective memory task – to remember the mole's surname. Half of the sample was told that his name was 'Mr. Rainbow' and the other half were told it was 'Mr. Tainbow'. Children gave predictions of their ability to do this, and rated their confidence in their predictions. As in Study 2, children listened to a story and underwent the picture naming task. At the sixth picture, the children were asked to remember the mole's surname.

The results from Study 3 are very clear. All children predicted that they would remember the mole's surname, with high levels of confidence. In the 'Mr. Rainbow' condition, 94% correctly recalled his name, while in the 'Mr. Tainbow' condition none did. With the unfamiliar surname all of the children overestimated their ability to recall. Thus, at least in relation to unfamiliar material, there is evidence that retrospective memory prediction is poor in children at this age.

DISCUSSION

Across the three studies, with some variability depending on task type and manipulations used, there was evidence of good prospective memory accuracy, with about 70% of children correctly predicting their ability to remember to do something. By contrast, none of the children were able to accurately predict that they would forget the mole's unfamiliar surname. Based on these studies, the authors argue that prospective and retrospective memory may be distinct types of memory. This is in keeping with earlier findings as well (Kvavilashvili, Messer, & Ebdon, 2001). Kvavilashvili and Ford suggest that prospective memory may develop earlier alongside developing awareness of their prospective memory abilities. One possible explanation for this is that the processes involved in predicting performance on prospective memory tasks may actually be integral to the process of prospective memory itself. For example, future thinking of oneself in the time and place where the to-be-remembered act should be carried out increases the likelihood that memory will be cued when that context is encountered. The ability to future think appears to develop between 3 and 6 years of age (Ford, Driscoll, Shum, & Macaulay, 2012). Retrospective memory cannot employ future thinking in the same way and hence may rely on different processes. Applying this knowledge to the classroom, teachers may need to consider how best to scaffold children's prospective memory, but in particular, their retrospective memory.

 In review

- Forgetting tends to occur most rapidly soon after initial learning, but the time frame and degree of forgetting can vary widely depending on many factors.
- We often cannot recall information because we never encoded it into long-term memory in the first place. Decay theory proposes that physical memory traces in long-term memory deteriorate with disuse over time.
- Proactive interference occurs when material learned in the past impairs recall of newer material. Retroactive interference occurs when newly acquired material impairs the ability to recall information learned at an earlier time.
- Psychodynamic theorists propose that we may forget anxiety-arousing material through repression, an unconscious process of motivated forgetting.
- Whereas retrospective memory refers to memory for past events, prospective memory refers to our ability to remember to perform some activity in the future.
- Retrograde amnesia is memory loss for events that occurred before the onset of amnesia. Anterograde amnesia refers to memory loss for events that occur after the initial onset of amnesia. Alzheimer's disease produces both types of amnesia and is the leading cause of dementia among elderly adults. Infantile amnesia is our inability to remember experiences from the first few years of our lives.

real and accurate. Yet, as our discussion of flashbulb memories illustrated, we may be highly confident of memories that in fact are inaccurate.

Memory construction can be amusing at times. Many of us have a tendency to recall the world through slightly rose-tinted glasses, which helps us feel good about ourselves. For example, when college students in one study recalled their high-school grades, the worse the grade was, the less often students remembered it accurately. Students correctly recalled almost all of their As, but only a third of their Ds (Figure 8.23). Most important, errors were positively biased; students usually mis-remembered their Bs as having been As, their Cs as Bs, and their Ds as Cs (Bahrick, Hall, & Berger, 1996). As we will see, however, memory construction also can have serious personal and societal consequences.

MEMORY DISTORTION AND SCHEMAS

Decades ago, Sir Frederick Bartlett (1932) asked residents of Cambridge, England, to read stories and then retell them days or months later. One story, a Pacific Northwest Indian tale called 'The War of the Ghosts', describes two young men who go down to a river to hunt seals. While there, warriors in canoes come up the river, and one of the young men agrees to join them for a raid on a town. During the raid, the man discovers that his companions are ghosts, and later he dies a mysterious death.

Bartlett's participants were twentieth-century residents of England, not eighteenth-century Native Americans. When they retold the story, they partly reconstructed it in a way that made sense to them. A day after reading the story, one participant shortened it by almost half, described the hero as fishing rather than as hunting seals, and substituted the word *boat* for *canoe*. Bartlett found that the longer the time interval between the reading and retelling of the story, the more the story changed to fit English culture.

Bartlett, who coined the term *schema*, believed that people have generalized ideas (schemas) about how events happen, which they use to organize information and construct their memories. Recall, for example, the laundry-washing description. Schemas, however, often distort our memories by leading us to encode or retrieve information in ways that make sense and fit in with our pre-existing assumptions about the world.

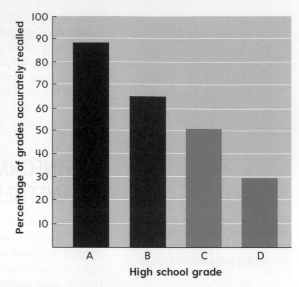

FIGURE 8.23 Rosy recall of high school grades.

The lower the grade, the less likely students were to recall it accurately. When students incorrectly recalled a grade, they almost always overestimated how well they did.

Source: Adapted from Bahrick et al., 1996.

> **Focus 8.16** Discuss examples of memory construction, and explain how schemas influence this process.

(a)

(b)

FIGURE 8.24 Boundary extension: What you see . . . what you remember.

Helene Intraub and her colleagues (1996) have found that when people (a) briefly look at close-up pictures, such as this one of a teddy bear, and then (b) draw the pictures from memory, they unknowingly convert the image into a wide-angle scene in which the size of the main object shrinks. This effect is less likely to occur if the original picture is already a wide-angle scene.

Source: Professor Intraub/From Figure 1 in Intraub, Gottesman, Willey & Zuk (1996).

Quite literally, memory construction extends to how we visualize the world (Intraub, 2002). As Figure 8.24 illustrates, when college students in one study looked at photographs that had a main object within a scene and then drew what they saw from memory, they consistently displayed *boundary extension*; they remembered the scene as more expansive (in this case, wider angled) than it really was (Intraub, Gottesman, Willey, & Zuk, 1996). In real life, objects usually occur against an expansive background, creating a schema for how we expect scenes to look. Thus when we remember close-up images, our schemas lead us to recall a broader scene than the one we saw.

MISINFORMATION EFFECTS AND EYEWITNESS TESTIMONY

If memories are constructed, then information that occurs *after* an event may shape that construction process. This **misinformation effect**, the distortion of a memory by misleading post-event information, has frequently been investigated in relation to mistaken eyewitness testimony. In one celebrated case, Father Bernard Pagano, a Roman Catholic priest, was positively identified by seven eyewitnesses as the perpetrator of a series of armed robberies in the Wilmington, Delaware, area. He was saved from almost certain conviction when the true robber, dubbed the 'gentleman bandit' because of his politeness and concern for his victims, confessed to the crimes.

Two key factors may have distorted the witnesses' memory. First, the polite manner of the robber is consistent with the schema many people have of priests. Second, before presenting pictures of suspects to the eyewitnesses, the police let it be known that the suspect might be a priest. Father Pagano was the only suspect wearing a clerical collar (Tversky & Tuchin, 1989).

Even one or two words can produce a misinformation effect while questioning an eyewitness. Imagine that after witnessing a two-car crash, a police officer takes your statement and asks you, 'About how fast were the cars going when they *contacted* each other?' In one experiment, college students viewed films of car accidents and then judged how fast the cars were going. As Figure 8.25 shows, the judged speed increased by up to 33% when the word *contacted* was changed to *hit, bumped into, collided with* or *smashed into* (Loftus & Palmer, 1974).

Source Confusion

Misinformation effects also occur because of **source confusion** (also called source monitoring error), our tendency to recall something or recognize it as familiar but to forget where we encountered it. Suppose an eyewitness to a crime looks through a series of photographs and reports that none of the individuals in the photographs is the perpetrator. Several days later, the eyewitness is brought back to view a live line-up and is asked to identify the person who committed the crime. In reality, none of the people in the line-up

misinformation effect the distortion of a memory by misleading post-event information

source contusion our tendency to recall something or recognize it as familiar but to forget where we encountered it

How fast were the two cars going when they _____ each other?	
Words	**Perceived speed**
Smashed into	41 mph
Collided with	39 mph
Bumped into	38 mph
Hit	34 mph
Contacted	31 mph

FIGURE 8.25 A misinformation effect.

College students' memory of how fast two cars were moving just before an accident varied significantly depending on how the question was phrased.

Source: Adapted from Loftus and Palmer, 1974.

did, but one suspect was pictured in a photograph that the eyewitness had seen days earlier. 'That's the person', says the eyewitness. Source confusion occurs because the eyewitness recognizes the individual's face but fails to remember that this recognition stems from the photograph. Instead, the witness mistakenly assumes that he or she saw the familiar-looking suspect committing the crime.

In an experimental analogue to this situation, 29% of participants who witnessed a staged event and later viewed photographs misidentified *innocent* suspects as having been involved in the event because of source confusion (Brown, Deffenbacher, & Sturgill, 1977). Source confusion also occurs when people witness an event (e.g., a video of an unarmed home burglar) and then are exposed to misleading, suggestive statements about it (e.g., that the burglar had a gun). They may forget that the source of the misinformation was a question or statement made by someone else and then come to believe it was part of the event they had witnessed (Mitchell & Zaragoza, 2001).

Researchers have begun to use brain-imaging techniques to study the neural activity that occurs when false memories are created by misinformation (Okado & Stark, 2005), but the debate over whether misinformation permanently alters a witness's original memory is far from resolved. Still, researchers overwhelmingly agree that misinformation can distort eyewitness reports. Results like these have raised concerns about the reliability of eyewitness testimony not only from adults but also from children in cases of alleged physical and sexual abuse.

THE CHILD AS EYEWITNESS

In cases of alleged child sexual abuse, there is often no conclusive corroborating medical evidence and the child is usually the only witness (Bruck, Ceci, & Hembrooke, 1998). If the charges are true, failing to convict the abuser and returning the child to an abusive environment is unthinkable. Conversely, if the charges are false, the consequences of convicting an innocent person are equally distressing.

Accuracy and Suggestibility

A single instance of suggestive questioning can distort some children's memory, but suggestive questioning most often leads to false memories when it is repeated. Young children are typically more susceptible to misleading suggestions than older children (Ceci, Bruck, & Battin, 2000).

In one experiment by Michelle Leichtman and Stephen Ceci (1995), 3- to 6-year-old children were told about a man named Sam Stone. Over several weeks, some children were repeatedly told stories that portrayed Sam as clumsy. Later Sam visited their classroom, was introduced, and behaved innocuously. The next day, the children were shown a ripped book and soiled teddy bear, things for which Sam was not responsible. Over the next 10 weeks they were interviewed several times, and some were asked suggestive questions about Sam (e.g., 'When Sam Stone tore the book, did he do it on purpose, or was he being silly?'). Two weeks later a new interviewer asked all the children to describe Sam's visit to the classroom.

Children who had heard suggestive information about Sam – whether before, after, or especially before *and* after Sam's appearance – made more false reports about Sam's behaviour than a control group that had never heard suggestive information. One child stated that after soaking the teddy bear in the bath, Sam smeared it with a crayon. These findings are troubling, because during many sexual-abuse investigations, the child initially denies being abused, but then after repeated suggestive questioning during therapy or police interviewing, the child acknowledges the abuse (Bruck et al., 1998). Was the child understandably reluctant to open up at first, or did suggestive questions produce a false allegation?

Recall of traumatic events

How well do children remember traumatic events? Elaine Burgwyn-Bailes and co-workers (Burgwyn-Bailes, Baker-Ward, Gordon, & Ornstein, 2001) interviewed 3- to 7-year-olds a few days, six weeks, and one year after the children underwent emergency plastic surgery for facial lacerations. At each interview, children accurately remembered most of the

Focus 8.18 Describe the misinformation effect, why it occurs, and how it affects memory accuracy in children and adults.

details of their operations, but they also mistakenly agreed with about 15% of leading questions ('Did the doctor's helper use any needles?') and suggestive questions ('The lady took off your watch, didn't she?') about events that never occurred. Compared to older children, younger children remembered fewer true details and agreed more often to leading and suggestive questions.

Given the susceptibility of children to misleading information, the use of effective and appropriate questioning techniques is essential, as during investigations around child sexual abuse it is important that the information gained is as accurate as possible. Along with the findings that children are highly susceptible to suggestive questioning, research has also shown that the most accurate information is generally gained through the use of free recall, with the child describing an event in their own words (e.g. Lamb, Hershkowitz, Orbach, & Esplin, 2008; Poole & Lamb, 1998). Approaches that are less successful include the use of closed questions, such as forced choice yes/no questions, which lead to lower levels of accuracy (Peterson, Dowden, & Tobin, 1999). Waterman, Blades and Spencer (2004) found that children were more likely to guess answers to 'unanswerable' questions when they were of the yes/no type than to wh-type (what, who, where-etc.), rather than to correctly state that they did not know the answer. Such 'wh' questions are useful in forensic settings to follow up information that the children have mentioned in their free recall, but it is important to note that they should only be used to follow up information already mentioned, otherwise there is the possibility of suggestibility, to which children are particularly susceptible as has already been discussed (Leichtman & Ceci, 1995).

Michael Lamb and his colleagues have conducted a large amount of research into the effective methods of questioning and also into how frequently these techniques are put into practice by the police when questioning children as witnesses. In a recent study of police practices in Scotland, La Rooy, Lamb and Memon (2011) found that a significant proportion of police interviewers, 20%, rarely or never used open-ended prompts when interviewing children and fewer than half, 43%, said that they always or nearly always did. Psychological research has much to say about the best way to interview children; however, constraints on police time and the need for swift action do not always allow for these guidelines to be followed as closely as might be the case.

True Versus False Reports: Can Professionals Tell Them Apart?

Can professionals reliably distinguish between children's accurate and false reports? The answer appears to be no, at least when false reports are caused by repeated, suggestive questioning. Mental health workers, social workers, prosecutors and judges shown videotapes of children's reports in the Sam Stone experiment often rated false reports as highly credible. Perhaps many children who make false reports are credible because they are not intentionally lying; rather, they believe their memories are accurate. After suggestive questioning, children are as confident of their false memories as they are of their accurate ones (Roebers, 2002).

What should society do? Like adults, young children accurately remember a lot, but they also misremember and are susceptible to repeated suggestive questioning. Thanks to psychological research, law enforcement officials, mental health workers and legal professionals are now paying more attention to how children's admissions of abuse are elicited, and training programmes are helping practitioners minimize suggestive interviewing techniques (Sternberg, Lamb, Esplin, Orbach, & Hershkowitz, 2002). The goal is not to discredit children's allegations of abuse. On the contrary, the hope is that by minimizing the risk of false allegations, non-suggestive interviewing will elicit allegations judged as even more compelling, thereby helping to ensure that justice is done.

In 1997 a woman from Illinois settled a lawsuit against two psychiatrists and their hospital for $10.6 million. She alleged that her psychiatrists used hypnosis, drugs and other treatments that led her to develop false memories of having been a high priestess in a sexually abusive satanic cult (*APA Monitor*, 1997). Yet only years earlier, there had been a wave of cases in which adults – usually in the course of psychotherapy – began to remember long-forgotten childhood sexual abuse and sued their parents, other family members and former teachers for the alleged trauma.

Current topic

THE RECOVERED OR FALSE MEMORY CONTROVERSY

The scientific controversy over the validity of recovered memories involves two issues. First, is a recovered memory of sexual abuse accurate? Second, if the abuse happened, what caused the memory to be forgotten – repression or another psychological process?

What about the first question? Can someone forget childhood sexual abuse, and then recover that memory as an adult? Survivors of disasters, victims of rape, sexual abuse and combat veterans have shown limited or no memory of their traumas (Epstein & Bottoms, 2002; Williams, 1994). Some victims of child sexual abuse do not recall their trauma when they are adults, with accurate memories of abuse returning years post-trauma (Kluft, 1999). However, memory loss after trauma is usually short, with memory returning over weeks, months or a few years. In many cases the victim's problem is not memory loss but an *inability* to forget, which may involve involuntary nightmares or flashbacks (Berntsen, 2001).

When exposed to suggestive questioning, students developed false memories of non-existent childhood events (e.g., being hospitalized) and residents of Moscow developed false memories for fictitious details of a terrorist bombing (Nourkova, Bernstein, & Loftus, 2004). Such studies may not tap the intense trauma of abuse, but added to what we know about forgetting and constructive memory, the conclusion is that we should not take the accuracy of recovered memories at face value (Pickrell, Bernstein, & Loftus, 2003).

With regard to the second issue, many researchers such as Loftus and Ketcham (1994) question Freud's concept of repression. Repression implies a psychological mechanism that pushes traumatic memories into the unconscious, and researchers have had difficulty demonstrating this experimentally (Holmes, 1995), whereas false memories are relatively easy to recreate (e.g. Roediger & McDermott, 1995).

Recovered memories of sexual abuse cannot be taken as automatic evidence of repression. Memory loss may have occurred because of 'ordinary' forgetting, because the victim avoided thinking about the abuse or reinterpreted the trauma to make it less upsetting (Epstein & Bottoms, 2002). However, Williams (1994) reported that years after identification as survivors of abuse, nearly 40% of women had no memory for the event. While this does not necessarily equate to evidence for repression it adds to the debate. This controversy will not be resolved soon.

The difficulties for attempts to resolve the controversy are compounded because memories are hard to validate and experimental work is ethically sensitive. Experimental studies have tried to recreate repression; however, due to ethical constraints they cannot recreate the trauma associated with abuse and hence they are not a suitable comparison (Holmes, 1970).

Loftus and Davis (2006) expressed concern that in recovered-memory therapy, therapists suggest the possibility of abuse to people who are emotionally vulnerable. However, many therapists argue such 'suggestion' is necessary to access memories that have been repressed over time. Poole, Lindsay, Memon and Bull (1995) found that over 70% of therapists indicated that they used techniques such as hypnosis or dream interpretation to recover memories. Others have argued that these 'suggestive' techniques result in false memories (Lindsay & Read, 1994; Loftus, 1993).

Recent research has examined what the underlying causes of recovered memories might be. For example, Jelinek, Peters and Moritz (2009) investigated whether individuals suffering from post-traumatic stress disorder are more open to suggestibility than others, reporting that trauma sufferers, with or without PTSD, were no more open to suggestibility than controls. In addition, Raymaekers, Smeets, Maarten and Merckelbach (2010) found that participants who had reported recovered memories of sexual abuse did not have greater difficulty retrieving autobiographical memories than controls. Alternatively, Rubin and Boals (2010) reported that people who consider themselves likely to undergo therapy are also more likely to believe that they have been involved in some form of traumatic childhood event for which they had no memory.

The message from science is that not all claims of recovered traumatic memories should be dismissed. This is summarized clearly by Geraerts et al. (2009) who noted 'recovered memories may at times be fictitious and may at other times be authentic' (p. 92).

FALSE CONFESSIONS

A topic related to false memory that is particularly intriguing is that of false confession. While it is hard to believe in many ways that anybody would confess to committing a crime of which they were innocent there is considerable evidence to suggest that such confessions do indeed take place. There are examples throughout the history of psychological research that clearly support the idea that behaviour can be influenced quite dramatically in response to the requests of authority figures, for example the groundbreaking works of Milgram (1974) and Zimbardo (1982) which are covered in some detail in **Chapter 14**. The idea of false confessions is of interest to psychologists and, of course, it has important practical implications. For example, the US public policy organization, The Innocence Project, claims that of 317 convictions that have been overturned on the basis of DNA evidence about 30% involved some form of false confession. In a European study Gudjonsson and Sigurdsson (1994) questioned prisoners in Iceland and found that 12% of them claim to have made a false confession at some point.

Focus 8.19 Discuss the recovered memory controversy, the two key issues involved and relevant evidence.

 Chapter 14,
Pages 589 & 599

The American psychologist Saul Kassin has conducted much of the research in this area and it is his work which will be the focus of this section. Kassin (e.g., 2008) divided false confessions into three main types:

1. Voluntary false confession – this is most likely to take place in high profile cases and such confessions are usually made to gain attention or for some pathological reason. Perhaps the most famous example of this was in relation to the murder of actress Elizabeth Short to which approximately 50 people confessed.

2. Compliant false confessions – confessions such as this are made in order for the ordeal of being interrogated to end, or in order to get something that the interviewee requires, such as sleep, food or in some cases an end to physical punishment. It has been proposed that the British case of the Birmingham Six, six Irish men found guilty of bombing a public house in Birmingham who later had their conviction overturned, was based on confessions of this kind. However, it should be noted that although members of the police were charged in relation to this case they were never prosecuted. Drizin and Leo (2004) looked at a number of false confessions and found that 34% came from interrogations that lasted 6–12 hours, while 39% came from interrogations of between 12 and 24 hours with the mean time of interrogations that resulted in false confessions being in excess of 16 hours.

3. Internalized false confessions – these are of the greatest interest to psychologists. These are cases where the person confesses to a crime that they did not commit and truly believe that they have committed the crime.

Drizin and Colgan (2004) cite the case of 14-year-old Michael Crowe who confessed to murdering his sister, having been led to believe that there was a great deal of evidence against him. He admitted committing the crime, although he had no idea how he had done it, eventually he came to believe that he was suffering from a split personality and the bad side had killed his sister while the good side was suppressing the truth. All charges were subsequently dropped when the true perpetrator of the crime was subsequently arrested. Another famous case of false confession is that of the Norfolk four, convicted for the rape and murder of a young woman in Virginia. False confessions were given, and although these were frequently inconsistent and there was no DNA evidence linking them to the crime, they were convicted, spending between 6 and 10 years in prison before their release when the true perpetrator was found and convicted on the basis of DNA evidence. Such cases show that although it is hard to believe that people would confess to crimes that they have not committed, there is evidence to suggest that this can happen from controlled psychological experiments as well as from examples such as those above.

A recent study found evidence to support the idea of internalized false confessions through the use of manipulated video evidence. It is important to note here that in the USA it is acceptable for the police to suggest that incriminating evidence exists, whether it does or not, as this is believed to encourage suspects to confess. Nash and Wade (2009) had participants complete a computerized gambling task and later accused them of having cheated on the task, which none of them had. Participants were also told that there was footage of them cheating on the task. Half of the participants were only told about the video evidence whereas the other half actually saw the manipulated footage. Nash and Wade reported that those participants who actually saw the video evidence were more likely to confess to the crime and to internalize this confession – that is, to actually believe that they had cheated – than participants who were only told about the 'incriminating' evidence. Among those participants who saw the manipulated footage there was a mean of over 95% compliance rate and a mean of 70% 'full internalization' rate across their two experiments. This study clearly shows that it is possible to induce internalized false confessions even in the relatively innocuous setting of the psychology laboratory.

CULTURE AND MEMORY CONSTRUCTION

Culture and memory have a reciprocal relation. On the one hand, cultural survival depends on transmitting knowledge and customs from one generation to the next. Without our capacity to remember events and information, culture simply could not exist (nor could we, as a species).

At the same time, culture and environment influences memory. One clear example of the environment influencing memory was reported by Kearins (1981) who found that Australian Aborigines had better visou-spatial memory skills than non-Aborigines, due to the need to survive and navigate in a desert environment. Our cultural upbringing shapes the schemas that we acquire and use to perceive ourselves and the world. For example, as we discussed in **Chapter 1**, most people living in northern Europe and North America learn to view the world through a relatively *individualistic* lens in which self-identity is based primarily on one's own attributes and achievements. People living in many Asian, African and South American cultures tend to see the world through a more *collectivistic* framework in which personal identity is defined largely by ties to the extended family and other social groups. If cultural socialization influences our schemas and our schemas influence how we encode and reconstruct events, then people from different cultures may recall events in somewhat distinct ways. In keeping with this suggestion, Wang and Conway (2004) reported that Chinese adults considered their autobiographical memories as less central to their self-image than their Western counterparts. Wang (2008) reported that bicultural Asian Americans asked to focus on their American identity responded with more self-relevant memories, whereas those who focused on their Asian identity reported more collectivist-type memories. A cultural difference has also been noted in the type of memory reported in terms of whether memories are specific or general. Specific memories tend to be more personally relevant and general memories more socially based, and Wang (2009) reported that Western participants reported more specific memories than their Eastern counterparts did.

Let us consider an example: our earliest memories. In one study, Wang (2001) asked over 200 college students from Harvard University and Beijing University to describe their earliest memories (Figure 8.26). He predicted and found that the Americans were more likely than their Chinese counterparts to recall events that focused on individual experiences and self-determination (e.g., 'I was sorting baseball cards when I dropped them. As I reached down to get them, I knocked over a jug of iced tea.'). In contrast, Chinese students were more likely than American students to recall memories that involved family or neighbourhood activities (e.g., 'Dad taught me ancient poems. It was always when he was washing vegetables that he would explain a poem to me.').

Wang also found that American college students dated their earliest personal memory back to the time when they were, on average, three years old. Students in China, however, reported memories that, on average, dated to the time they were almost four years old.

Chapter 1, Page 19

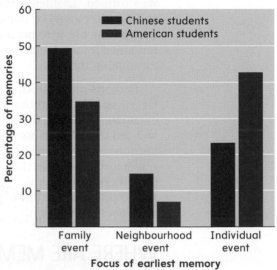

FIGURE 8.26 Culture and our earliest memories.

What is your earliest memory? In one study, Chinese students recalled events that, overall, were more family and neighbourhood oriented than events recalled by American students. How else might our cultural upbringing and worldview influence memory?

Source: (Left) XiXinXing/Shutterstock. (Right) based on Wang, 2001.

Focus 8.20 Illustrate how culture influences memory construction.

Although the reason is not clear, it may relate to American students' greater tendency to report earliest memories of single, distinctive events that involved greater emotionality, whereas Chinese students were more likely than Americans to report more routine events that involved collective activity and, as we have seen earlier, distinctive, emotional memories are more likely to be recalled. An individualistic society is also more likely to lead to individuals to attend to, encode, rehearse and discuss individual personal self-important memories. Other researchers also have found cross-cultural differences in age of earliest memories. When Shelley MacDonald and co-workers (2000) studied New Zealand European, New Zealand Asian, New Zealand Maori, and Chinese adults, they found that Maori adults – whose traditional culture strongly values the past – recalled the earliest personal memories.

 In review

- Our schemas may cause us to misremember events in ways that fit with our pre-existing concepts about the world; they also may lead us to recall events that never occurred.

- Misinformation effects occur when our memory is distorted by misleading post-event information, and they often occur because of source confusion – our tendency to recall something or recognize it as familiar but to forget where we encountered it.

- Like adults, children experience misinformation effects. Vulnerability is greatest among younger children and when suggestive questions are asked repeatedly. Experts cannot reliably tell when children are reporting accurate memories versus sincerely believed false memories.

- Psychologists debate whether recovered memories of child abuse are accurate and whether they are forgotten through repression or other psychological processes. Concern about the possibility of false memory has led many experts to urge caution in unconditionally accepting the validity of recovered memories.

MEMORY AND THE BRAIN

Where in your brain are memories located? How were they formed? The quest for answers has taken some remarkable twists. Psychologist Karl Lashley spent decades searching for the *engram* – the physical trace that presumably was stored in the brain when a memory was formed. Lashley (1950) trained animals to perform tasks, such as running mazes, and later removed or damaged (lesioned) specific regions of their cortexes to see if they would forget how to perform the task. No matter what small area was lesioned, memories remained intact. Lashley never found the engram and concluded that a memory is stored throughout the brain.

Perhaps most striking was James McConnell's (1962) discovery of 'memory transfer'. He classically conditioned flatworms to a light that was paired with electric shock, eventually causing the worms to contract to the light alone. Next he chopped them up and fed the RNA (ribonucleic acid) from their cells to untrained worms. Amazingly, the untrained worms showed some conditioning to the light, suggesting that RNA might be a memory molecule that stores experiences. Some scientists replicated these findings, but others were unable to, and McConnell eventually gave up on the idea (Rilling, 1996). Yet despite the inevitable dead ends, scientists have learned a great deal about memory processes in the brain.

WHERE ARE MEMORIES FORMED AND STORED?

To answer this question, scientists examine how damage to different brain regions affects the memory of human patients and laboratory animals; they also peer into the healthy human brain as research participants perform various memory tasks. These lines of research reveal that memory involves many interacting brain regions. Figure 8.27 shows a few of the major regions.

Sensory and Working Memory

Sensory memory depends on our visual, auditory, and other sensory systems to detect stimulus information (e.g., the sounds of 'Hi, my name is Carlos'), transform it into neural codes, and send it to the brain, where sensory areas of the cerebral cortex initially process it. As working memory becomes involved in different types of tasks – remembering a person's name and face, recalling a list of numbers or learning and rehearsing a concept in your textbook – a network of cortical areas located across different lobes of the brain becomes more active (Zhang et al., 2004). For example, using visuospatial working memory to form a mental image of an object will activate some of the same areas of the visual cortex and other brain regions that become more active when looking at the actual object (Ganis, Thompson, & Kosslyn, 2004).

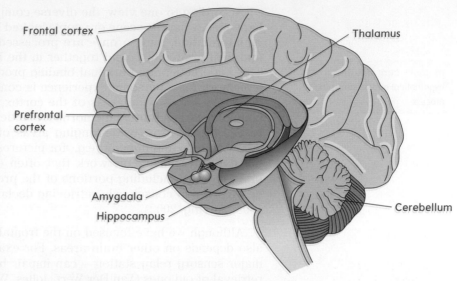

FIGURE 8.27 Some brain regions involved in memory.

Many areas of the brain, such as the regions shown here, play key roles in memory.

The frontal lobes – especially the prefrontal cortex – play key roles in working memory. The frontal lobes generally become more active during tasks that place greater demands on working memory. In one brain-imaging experiment, students had to pay attention to the meaning of words (i.e., deep, semantic encoding) or to whether the words were in capital or lowercase letters (i.e., shallow, perceptual encoding). Deeper encoding produced better memory for the words and, as Figure 8.28 shows, also produced greater activity in specific areas of the left prefrontal cortex (Gabrieli, Desmond, Demb, & Wagner, 1996). Other imaging studies have found that spatial working-memory tasks produce somewhat greater activation in the right prefrontal cortex than verbal tasks do (Walter et al., 2003).

The frontal lobes seem to be particularly important in supporting central-executive functions, such as allocating attention to the other components of working memory. This does not mean, however, that the central executive resides exclusively within the frontal lobes. Frontal-lobe damage often – but not always – impairs central-executive functions of working memory. Moreover, patients with intact frontal lobes but damage in other brain areas may exhibit central-executive impairments (Adrés, 2003). Thus even the 'master control' executive functions of working memory depend on a network of neural activity that connects regions across the brain.

Long-Term Memory

Where are long-term memories formed and stored? Once again, multiple brain areas are involved, but the hippocampus and its adjacent areas appear to play important roles in encoding certain types of long-term memories (Squire, Stark, & Clark, 2004).

Declarative memory

Like HM, many patients with extensive hippocampal damage retain the use of their short-term memory but cannot form new, explicit long-term declarative memories – memories for new personal experiences and facts. For example, one patient could recall the names of presidents elected before his brain injury occurred but not the names of presidents elected after his injury (Squire, 1987). The hippocampus does not seem to be the site where long-term declarative memories are permanently stored, which explains why HM retained his long-term memories acquired earlier in life. Rather, it helps to gradually convert short-term memories into permanent ones.

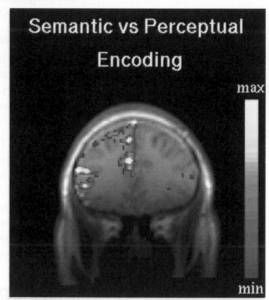

FIGURE 8.28 Depth of processing and the prefrontal lobes.

Four participants in one experiment performed shallow perceptual (i.e., structural) encoding and deep (semantic) encoding tasks while undergoing functional magnetic resonance imaging (fMRI). The results, shown here for one participant, revealed that semantic encoding was accompanied by greater neural activity in specific regions of the left prefrontal cortex.

Source: Reprinted with permission of John Gabrieli.

According to one view, the diverse components of an experience – where something happened, what the scene or people looked like, sounds we heard, the meaning of events or information, and so on – are processed initially in different regions of the cortex and then gradually bound together in the hippocampus (Squire & Zola-Morgan, 1991). This hypothetical and gradual binding process is called **memory consolidation**. Once a memory for a personal experience is consolidated, its various components appear to be stored across wide areas of the cortex, although we retrieve and reintegrate these components as a unified memory. Semantic memories (factual information) also appear to be stored across wide-ranging areas of the brain. As John Gabrieli (1998) notes, 'knowledge in any domain [e.g., for pictures or words] . . . is distributed over a specific, but extensive, neural network that often extends over several lobes' (p. 94). Several brain regions, including portions of the prefrontal cortex and hippocampus, appear to be involved in consciously retrieving declarative memories (LePage, Habib, & Tulving, 1998; Tulving, 2002).

> **memory consolidation**
> hypothetical and gradual binding process

Although we have focused on the frontal lobes and hippocampus, memory formation also depends on other brain areas. For example, damage to the thalamus – the brain's major sensory relay station – can impair both the encoding of new memories and the retrieval of old ones (Van Der Werf, Jolles, Witter, & Uylings, 2003). In one famous case, a young US Air Force technician named NA was injured in a freak accident (Squire, 1987). While his room-mate was practising thrusts with a miniature fencing foil, NA suddenly turned around in his seat and was stabbed through the right nostril, piercing his brain and damaging a portion of his thalamus. The damage permanently limited his ability to form new declarative memories. In many cases, thalamic damage also can cause permanent retrograde amnesia.

The amygdala encodes emotionally arousing aspects of stimuli and plays an important role in helping us form long-term memories for events that stir our emotions (McGaugh, 2004). As we discussed earlier, in laboratory experiments, most people remember emotionally arousing stimuli (e.g., film clips, slides) better than neutral ones. Damage to the amygdala eliminates much of this 'memory advantage' from arousing stimuli (LaBar & Phelps, 1998).

Procedural memory

Along with other parts of the brain, the cerebellum plays an important role in forming procedural memories. This helps explain why HM, whose cerebellum was not damaged by the operation, showed improved performance at various hand–eye coordination tasks (e.g., mirror tracing) even though he was unable to consciously remember having performed the tasks.

Richard Thompson (1985) and co-workers have examined another type of procedural memory. Studying rabbits, they repeatedly paired a tone (CS) with a puff of air to the eyes (UCS), and soon the tone alone caused the rabbits to blink. As the rabbits learned this conditioned response, electrical recordings revealed increased activity in the cerebellum. Later, Thompson found that removing a tiny portion of the cerebellum completely abolished the memory for the *conditioned* eye-blink but did not affect the rabbits' general (unconditioned) eye-blink response. Similarly, eye-blink conditioning fails to work with human patients who have a damaged cerebellum (Green & Woodruff-Pak, 2000).

HOW ARE MEMORIES FORMED?

How does the nervous system form a memory? The answer appears to lie in chemical and physical changes that take place in the brain's neural circuitry.

Synaptic Change and Memory

Eric Kandel (2001) and his co-workers have studied a marine snail, *Aplysia californica*, for over 25 years – work for which Kandel received a Nobel Prize in 2000. *Aplysia* is no mental giant, but it can learn, form memories, and has only about 20,000 neurons (compared with our 100 billion) that are larger and easier to study than ours. For

example, *Aplysia* retracts its gill slightly in self-defence when a breathing organ on top of the gill is gently squirted with water. But if a squirt is paired with electric shock to its tail, *Aplysia* covers up its gill with a protective flap of skin. After repeated pairings, *Aplysia* acquires a classically conditioned response and will cover its gill with the protective flap when the water is squirted alone. In other words, *Aplysia* forms a simple procedural memory.

Kandel and his co-workers have traced the formation of this procedural memory to a series of biochemical events that occur between and within various sensory neurons and motor neurons. How long these events last seems to be one key in determining whether short-term memories become long-term memories. If a single shock is paired with the squirt of water, certain chemical reactions shut off after a brief period and no permanent memory is formed. But with repeated pairings, these chemical reactions persist and a long-term memory forms. Days later, a squirt of water will still trigger a conditioned response.

During the conditioning procedure, various sensory neurons become densely packed with neurotransmitter release points, and postsynaptic motor neurons (which cause the protective flap to cover the gill) develop more receptor sites. These structural changes result in a greater ease of synaptic transmission that may be the basis for memory consolidation (Abel & Kandel, 1998). Some researchers have argued that the large amounts of activity that take place during REM sleep are due to the process of memory consolidation (Smith, Nixon, & Nader, 2004).

Long-Term Potentiation

A different line of research, involving rats and other species with more complex nervous systems, supports the hypothesis that synaptic changes may be the basis for memory consolidation. Here, researchers try to mimic (albeit very crudely) a process of long-term memory formation by stimulating specific neural pathways with rapid bursts of electricity (say, 100 impulses per second for several seconds). They find that once this rapid stimulation ends, the neural pathway becomes stronger – synaptic connections are activated more easily – for days or even weeks (Martinez, Barea-Rodriguez, & Derrick, 1998). This enduring increase in synaptic strength is called **long-term potentiation (LTP)**. Long-term potentiation has been studied most extensively in regions of the hippocampus where neurons send and receive using glutamate, the most abundant neurotransmitter in the brain.

long-term potentiation (LTP) enduring increase in synaptic strength

For LTP to occur, complex biochemical events must take place inside and between these neurons. Administering drugs that inhibit these events will block LTP. Moreover, mice can be genetically bred to be deficient in certain proteins required for LTP. These mice not only have impaired long-term potentiation but also display memory deficits on a variety of learning tasks (Schimanski & Nguyen, 2005).

Focus 8.21 Describe brain structures involved in memory and how changes in neural circuitry may underlie memory formation.

How, then, does LTP occur? At least in some cases, it appears that when neural pathways are sufficiently stimulated, the postsynaptic neurons alter their structure so that they become more responsive to glutamate. For example, post-synaptic neurons may change the shape of some receptor sites, or they may increase the number of receptor sites by developing additional tiny branches (spines) on their dendrites. This means that in the future, presynaptic neurons will not need to release as much glutamate in order to stimulate presynaptic neurons to fire. In sum, the formation of a long-term memory seems to involve long-lasting changes in synaptic efficiency that result from new or enhanced connections between presynaptic and postsynaptic neurons (Kandel, 2001).

In closing, we hope that this chapter has piqued your interest in understanding why we remember, forget and sometimes misremember. 'Levels of analysis' summarizes some factors involved in forgetting and memory distortion. We also hope that the chapter has applied value for you. Following the 'In review' summary, our 'Applying psychological science' feature describes some ways to enhance your own memory and academic learning.

Focus 8.22 Identify practical principles for enhancing memory.

Levels of analysis

factors related to forgetting and memory distortion

PSYCHOLOGICAL

- Failure to encode information (e.g., inadequate rehearsal)
- Weak retrieval cues and interference
- Mental schemas distort information
- Motivated forgetting of anxiety-arousing information

BIOLOGICAL

- Evolutionary adaptiveness of forgetting
- Inadequate brain chemical activity
- Memory not consolidated in hippocampus
- Brain damage that produces amnesia

ENVIRONMENTAL

- Stimulus overload
- Information lacks distinctiveness, meaning or organization
- Mismatch between learning and recall environments
- Misinformation effects: post-event stimuli distort information

Forgetting and memory distortion

In review

- Memory involves numerous interacting brain regions. Sensory memory depends on input from our sensory systems and sensory areas of the cortex that initially process this information.
- Working memory involves a network of brain regions. The frontal lobes play a key role in performing the executive functions of working memory.
- The hippocampus helps consolidate long-term declarative memories. The cerebral cortex stores declarative memories across distributed sites.
- The amygdala encodes emotionally arousing aspects of events, and the cerebellum helps form procedural memories. Damage to the thalamus can produce severe amnesia.
- Research with sea snails and studies of long-term potentiation in other species indicate that as memories form, complex chemical and structural changes that enhance synaptic efficiency occur in neurons.

Applying psychological science

IMPROVING MEMORY AND ACADEMIC LEARNING

There are no magical or effortless ways to enhance memory, but psychological research offers many principles that you can put to your advantage. Memory-enhancement strategies fall into three broad categories:

- *external aids*, such as shopping lists, notes and appointment calendars
- *general memory strategies*, such as organizing and rehearsing information
- *formal mnemonic techniques*, such as acronyms, the method of loci and other systems that take practice to be used effectively.

Memory researchers strongly recommend using external aids and general strategies to enhance memory (Park, Smith, & Cavanaugh, 1990). Of course, during closed-book university examinations, external aids may land you in the dean's office! The following principles can enhance memory.

USE ELABORATIVE REHEARSAL TO PROCESS INFORMATION DEEPLY

Elaborative rehearsal – focusing on the meaning of information – enhances deep processing and memory (Benjamin & Bjork, 2000). Put simply, if you are trying to commit information to memory, make sure that you understand what it means. You may think we are daft for stating such an obvious point, but many students try to learn material by rote memorization rather than by making an effort to understand it. Students who find material confusing sometimes try to bypass their confusion with rote memorization – an approach that often fails – whereas they should be seeking assistance to have the material explained. The learning objectives and practice tests that appear in the Online Learning Centre (OLC) can help you process the course material more deeply by helping you focus on and think about key points.

LINK NEW INFORMATION TO EXAMPLES AND ITEMS ALREADY IN MEMORY

Once you understand the material, process it more deeply by associating it with information you already know. This creates memory 'hooks' onto which you can hang new information. Because you already have many memorable life experiences, make new information personally meaningful by relating it to your life.

Pay attention to examples, even if they are unrelated to your own experiences. In one study, participants read a 32-paragraph essay about a fictitious African nation. Each paragraph contained a topic sentence stating a main theme, along with zero, one, two or three examples illustrating that theme. The greater the number of examples, the better the participants recalled the themes (Palmere, Benton, Glover, & Ronning, 1983).

ORGANIZE INFORMATION

Organizing information keeps you actively thinking about the material and makes it more meaningful. Before reading a chapter, look at its outline or headings to determine how the material is logically developed. When studying, take notes from a chapter and use outlining to organize the information. This hierarchical structure forces you to arrange main ideas above subordinate ones, and it becomes an additional retrieval cue that facilitates recall (Bower et al., 1969).

USE IMAGERY

As dual coding theory predicts, images provide a splendid additional 'cognitive hook' on which to hang and retrieve information (Paivio et al., 2000). Instead of writing down customers' orders, some restaurant waiters and waitresses form images, such as visualizing a man who has ordered a margarita as turning light green.

As one waitress remarked, 'After a while, customers start looking like drinks' (Bennett, 1983, p. 165). Be creative. For example, to help you remember that flashbulb memories often are less accurate than people think, imagine a camera flashbulb with a big red X through it.

OVERLEARN THE MATERIAL

Overlearning refers to continued rehearsal past the point of initial learning, and it significantly improves performance on memory tasks (Driskell, Willis, & Copper, 1992). Moreover, much of this memory boost persists for a long time after overlearning ends. In short, just as elite athletes keep practising their already honed skills and professional actors continue to rehearse scripts they already know, keep studying material after you have first learned it (Noice & Noice, 2002a).

> **overlearning** continued rehearsal past the point of initial learning, and it significantly improves performance on memory tasks

DISTRIBUTE LEARNING OVER TIME AND TEST YOURSELF

You have finished the readings and organized your notes for an upcoming test. Now it is time to study and review. Are you better off with *massed practice*, a marathon session of highly concentrated learning, or with *distributed practice*, several shorter sessions spread out over a few days? Research indicates that you will retain more information with distributed practice and that periodically testing yourself on the material before an examination can further enhance learning (Cull, 2000). Distributed practice can reduce fatigue and anxiety, both of which impair learning. Testing yourself ahead of time (e.g., using practice items, if available, or questions such as those in the margins of this textbook) helps you to further rehearse the material and to identify content that you do not understand.

▶

◄
MINIMIZE INTERFERENCE

Distributed practice is effective because rest periods between study sessions reduce interference from competing material. However, when you need to study for several examinations on the same or consecutive days, there really are few rest periods. There is no simple solution to this problem. Suppose you have a psychology examination on Thursday and a sociology examination on Friday. Try to arrange several sessions of distributed practice for each examination over the preceding week. On Wednesday, limit your studying to psychology if possible. Once your psychology examination is over, return your attention to studying sociology. This way, the final study period for each course will occur as close as possible to test time and minimize interference from other cognitive activities.

Studying before you go to sleep may enhance retention by temporarily minimizing interference, but if you are carrying a typical college course load, you will likely have to contend with interference much of the time. This is why you are advised to study the material beyond the point where you feel you have learned it.

 ## Recommended Reading

CLASSIC

Tulving, E. & Craik, F.I.M. (2000). *The Oxford handbook of memory.* New York: Oxford University Press.

CONTEMPORARY

Baddeley, A. (2012). Working Memory: Theories, Models, and Controversies. *Annual Review of Psychology 63,* 1-29.

Baddeley, A., Eysenck, M.W. & Anderson, M.C. (2009). *Memory.* Hove: Psychology Press.

Best, D.L. & Intons-Peterson (2014). *Memory Distortions and Their Prevention.* Hove: Psychology Press.

Byrne, J.H. (2008). Concise learning and memory: the editor's selection. London: Academic.

Eysenck, M.W. & Keane, M.T. (2010). *Cognitive Psychology: A Student's Handbook* (6th ed.). Hove: Psychology Press.

*Let language be the
divining rod that finds
the sources of thought.*
Karl Krauss

Language and thinking

9

Chapter Outline

LANGUAGE

- Adaptive functions of language
- Properties of language
- The structure of language
- Understanding and producing language
- 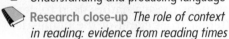 Research close-up *The role of context in reading: evidence from reading times*
- Acquiring a first language
- Bilingualism
- Linguistic influences on thinking

THINKING

- Thought, brain and mind
- Concepts and propositions
- Reasoning

- Current topic *What does it mean to be rational?*
- Problem-solving and decision-making
- Applying psychological science *Guidelines for creative problem-solving*
- Knowledge, expertise and wisdom
- Mental imagery
- Metacognition: knowing your own cognitive abilities
- Research close-up *Why did I get that wrong?' improving college students' awareness of whether they understand text material*

For the crew and passengers of United Airlines Flight 118, the skies over Hawaii were about to become the scene of a terrifying test of human resourcefulness, with survival at stake. On a routine flight, 20,000 feet above the Pacific Ocean, the unthinkable happened. With an explosive popping of rivets and a shriek of tearing metal, part of the surface at the front of the plane suddenly ripped away from the rest of the aircraft, exposing the flight deck and forward passenger compartments to the air. Inside, terrified passengers and flight attendants quite literally hung on for dear life as gale-force winds swirled through the cabin and the plane threatened to spin out of control.

The sudden change in the aerodynamics of the plane meant that it could not be flown normally. The captain, an experienced pilot, needed to develop a mental model of the plane in its altered form to keep it from plunging into the ocean. Thanks to his flight experience and his knowledge of the principles under which the aircraft normally responded to its controls, the captain quickly recognized what needed to be done and formulated a plan for doing it.

Yet formulating the plan was not enough. The captain needed his co-pilot's help to execute the appropriate actions. Under normal circumstances this would pose no problem: the captain would simply use spoken language to describe his thoughts, convey the plan and tell the co-pilot what to do. But in a torn-open jetliner flying at several hundred miles per hour, the noise of the engines and the roar of the wind rendered speech useless, so the captain and the co-pilot switched to hand signals to communicate their thoughts and coordinate their activities. Through perfect teamwork, they landed the aircraft safely at an auxiliary airfield, a feat described by one aeronautical engineer as 'astonishing'.

Incidents like this illustrate the power of human communication, reasoning and problem-solving – cognitive skills that underlie adaptive behaviour. Yet as we shall see, the basic communication procedures and mental operations these aviators used to deal with this life-and-death challenge were really no different from many of the linguistic, reasoning and problem-solving activities that we engage in each day.

We humans are physically puny and relatively defenceless in comparison to some other species, but we dominate our world because we communicate more effectively and think better than do other animals. Humans have a remarkable ability to create *mental representations* of the world and to manipulate them in the forms of language, thinking, reasoning and problem-solving (Simon, 1990). **Mental representations** include images, ideas, concepts and principles. At this very moment, through the printed words you are reading, mental representations are being transferred from our minds to yours. Indeed, the process of education is all about transferring ideas and skills from one mind to another.

mental representations images, ideas, concepts and principles

LANGUAGE

Language has been called 'the jewel in the crown of cognition' (Pinker, 2000) and 'the human essence' (Chomsky, 1972). Much of our thinking, reasoning, and problem-solving involves the use of language. In turn, these advanced cognitive processes build on the large store of knowledge that resides in memory, and they provide a foundation for intelligent behaviour.

Language consists of a system of symbols and rules for combining these symbols in ways that can generate an infinite number of possible messages and meanings. To most of us, using our native language comes as naturally as breathing, and we give it about as much thought. Yet using language actually involves a host of complex skills. **Psycholinguistics** is the scientific study of the psychological aspects of language, such as how people understand, produce and acquire language. Before delving into some of these topics, let us consider some adaptive functions and characteristics of language.

language a system of symbols and rules for combining these symbols in ways that can generate an infinite number of possible messages and meanings

psycholinguistics the scientific study of the psychological aspects of language

ADAPTIVE FUNCTIONS OF LANGUAGE

According to anthropologists who have studied the skulls of prehistoric humans, the brain probably achieved its present form some 50,000 years ago (Pilbeam, 1984). Yet it took another 35,000 years before lifelike paintings began to appear on cave walls and another 12,000 years after that before humans developed a way to store knowledge outside the brain in the form of writing (Kottak, 2000). These time lags tell us that human thought and behaviour depend on more than the physical structure of the brain; although the structure of the brain may not have evolved much over the past 50,000 years, human cognitive and linguistic skills clearly have.

Over the course of evolution, humans adopted a more socially oriented lifestyle that helped them survive and reproduce (Flinn, 1997). Some evolutionary theorists believe that the use of language evolved as people gathered to form larger social units. As the social environment became more complex, new survival problems emerged: the need to create divisions of labour and cooperative social systems, to develop social customs and communicate thoughts, and to pass on knowledge and wisdom. The development of language made it easier for humans to adapt to these environmental demands (Bjorklund & Pellegrini, 2002).

It is no coincidence, then, that every human culture, no matter how isolated or geographically remote, has developed one or more languages. Nor is it a coincidence that the human brain seems to have an inborn capacity to acquire any of the roughly 5,000 to 6,000 languages spoken across the globe. Humans have evolved into highly social creatures who need to communicate with one another and have the physical characteristics (e.g., a highly developed brain, a vocal tract) that allow them to do so in the most flexible way known: through language.

Language underlies so much of what we do that it is almost impossible to imagine functioning without it. Our conscious thinking usually takes the form of self-talk, or inner speech. Through language, we are also able to share our thoughts, feelings, goals, intentions, desires, needs and memories with other people, and thus interact socially in rich and diverse ways that would not otherwise be possible.

In ways small and big, language also is an extremely powerful learning mechanism. To get to a friend's house for the first time, you do not have to drive or walk all over the area (trial-and-error learning) or wait until someone shows up to lead the way (observational learning). Instead, you simply ask for directions or read a map. More broadly, in oral and written form – through storytelling, books, instruction, mass media and the Internet – language puts the customs and knowledge accrued over generations at your fingertips.

> **Focus 9.1** What are some adaptive functions of language?

PROPERTIES OF LANGUAGE

What is it that first captures your attention when someone uses a foreign language that you do not speak? Perhaps it is how different that language sounds or looks when written, or simply how incomprehensible it seems to you. Yet what is truly striking about the world's languages is not their differences but the underlying features that they share.

As we noted earlier, language is a system of symbols and rules for combining these symbols in ways that can generate an infinite number of messages and meanings. This definition encompasses four properties that are essential to any language: symbols, structure, meaning and generativity. We also describe a fifth property: displacement.

Language Is Symbolic and Structured

Language uses sounds, written characters or some other system of symbols (e.g., hand signs) to represent objects, events, ideas, feelings and actions. Moreover, the symbols used in any given language are arbitrary. For example, list the words used to represent 'dog' in

several languages. None of these written words looks like a dog and, when spoken, there is nothing about how any one of these words sounds that makes it an intrinsically correct choice for representing the concept of 'dog'. In English, *gerk*, *kreg*, *woof*, *zog*, *professor* or countless other words could be used to represent what we call a *dog*. But they are not (even though 'No Professors Allowed on the Lawn' has a certain ring). Regardless of how the word *dog* came into being, it has an agreed-upon meaning to people who speak English. The same holds true for all the other words we use, although there are some rare exceptions in the form of onomatopoeic words like crash and smash. Formally this is known as *arbitrariness* as outlined in Hockett's (1960) design features of spoken language.

> **grammar** the set of rules that dictate how symbols can be combined to create meaningful units of communication
>
> **syntax** the rules that govern the order of words
>
> **semantics** the meaning of words and sentences
>
> **generativity** he symbols of language can be combined to generate an infinite number of messages that have novel meaning
>
> **displacement** language allows us to communicate about events and objects that are not physically present

Language also has a rule-governed structure. A language's **grammar** is the set of rules that dictate how symbols can be combined to create meaningful units of communication. Thus if we ask you whether *zpflrovc* is an English word, you will almost certainly say that it is not. Why? Because it violates the rules of the English language; *z* is not to be followed by *pf*, and five consonants (*z*, *p*, *f*, *l*, *r*) cannot be put in an unbroken sequence. Likewise, if we ask you whether 'Bananas have sale for I' is an appropriate English sentence, you will shake your head and say 'No. It should read: "I have bananas for sale".' In this case, 'Bananas have sale for I' violates a portion of English grammar called **syntax,** the rules that govern the order of words.

You may not be able to verbalize the formal rules of English that are violated in these examples, but you know them implicitly because they are part of the language you speak. The grammars of all languages share common functions, such as providing rules for how to change present tense ('I am walking the dog') into the past tense ('I walked the dog') or a negative ('I didn't walk the dog'). Yet just as symbols (e.g., words) vary across languages, so do grammatical rules. In English, for example, we say 'green salad' and 'big river', which follow the rule that adjectives almost always come before the noun they modify. In French and Spanish, however, adjectives often follow nouns ('salade verte', 'rio grande'). Although language changes over time, with new words appearing regularly, new words and new phrases need to conform to the basic rules of that language.

Language Conveys Meaning

No matter the arbitrary symbols or grammatical rules used, once people learn those symbols and rules, they are able to form and then transfer mental representations to the mind of another person. Thus you can talk with a friend about your courses, your favourite foods, how you feel, and so on. Based in part on the words you use and how they are organized, both you and your friend will extract meaning – and, it is hoped, the correct or intended meaning – from what is being said. But understanding **semantics,** the meaning of words and sentences, actually is a tricky business. For example, when you ask a friend 'How did you do on the test?' and the reply is 'I nailed it', you know that your friend is not saying 'I hammered the test to the desk with a nail'. Someone who is familiar with English knows from experience not to interpret this expression literally; someone just beginning to learn English might find this expression perplexing.

Language Is Generative and Permits Displacement

Generativity means that the symbols of language can be combined to generate an infinite number of messages that have novel meaning. The English language, for example, has only 26 letters, but they can be combined into over half a million words, which in turn can be combined to create a virtually limitless number of sentences. Thus you can create and understand a sentence like 'Why is that sparrow standing underneath my pancake?' even though you are unlikely to have heard anything like it before.

> **Focus 9.2** Describe key properties of language.

Displacement refers to the fact that language allows us to communicate about events and objects that are not physically present. In other words, language frees us from being restricted to focusing on events and objects that are right before us in the present. You can discuss the past and the future, as well as people, objects and events that currently exist or are taking place elsewhere. You can even discuss completely imaginary situations, such as a sparrow standing underneath a pancake.

THE STRUCTURE OF LANGUAGE

Psycholinguists describe language as having a *surface structure* and a *deep structure*. They also examine the hierarchical structure of language, in which smaller elements are combined into larger ones. Let us look at both of these issues.

Surface Structure and Deep Structure

When you read, listen to, or produce a sentence, its **surface structure** consists of the symbols that are used and their order. As noted earlier, the syntax of a language provides the rules for ordering words properly. In contrast, a sentence's **deep structure** refers to the underlying meaning of the combined symbols, which brings us back to the issue of semantics.

Sentences can have different surface structures but the same deep structure. Consider these examples:

1. Sam ate the cake.
2. The cake was eaten by Sam.
3. Eaten by Sam the cake was.

Each sentence conveys the underlying meaning: that the cake ended up in Sam's stomach. Notice that the syntax of the third sentence is incorrect. English is not spoken this way, except, perhaps, by the fictional *Star Wars* character Yoda. Still, in this case its meaning is clear enough.

Sometimes, a single surface structure can give rise to two deep structures, as happens when people speak or write ambiguous sentences. Consider this example:

The police must stop drinking after midnight.

On the one hand, this sentence could mean that police officers need to enforce a curfew designed to prevent citizens from drinking alcohol after midnight. On the other hand, it could mean that if police officers go out for a few drinks after work, they need to cease drinking by midnight.

In everyday life, when you read or hear speech, you are moving from the surface structure to deep structure: from the way a sentence looks or sounds to its deeper level of meaning. After time you may forget the precise words used in the sentence, but you are likely to recall its essential meaning. In contrast, when you express your thoughts to other people, you must transform deep structure (the meaning that you want to communicate) into a surface structure that others can understand. Eloquent speakers and writers have the ability to convert their deep-structure meanings into clear and pleasing surface-structure expressions.

The Hierarchical Structure of Language

Human language has a hierarchical structure, and its most elementary building block is the **phoneme,** the smallest unit of sound that is recognized as separate in a given language. Linguists have identified about 100 phonemes that humans can produce, including the clicking sounds used in some African languages, but no language uses all of these sounds. The world's languages vary considerably in phonemes, some employing as few as 15 and others more than 80. English uses about 40 phonemes, consisting of the various vowel and consonant sounds, as well as certain letter combinations such as *th* and *sh*. Thus sounds associated with *th*, *a* and *t* can be combined to form the three-phoneme word *that*.

Phonemes have no inherent meaning, but they alter meaning when combined with other elements. For example, the phoneme *d* creates a different meaning from the phoneme *l* when it precedes *og* (i.e., *dog* versus *log*). At the next level of the hierarchy, phonemes are combined into **morphemes,** the smallest units of meaning in a language. Thus *dog*, *log* and *ball* are all morphemes, as are prefixes and suffixes such as *pre-*, *un-*, *-ed* and *-ous*. Notice in Figure 9.1 that morphemes are not always syllables. For example, in English *s* is not a syllable, but the final *s* on a noun is a morpheme that means 'plural'. Thus the word *fans*

Research close-up

THE ROLE OF CONTEXT IN READING: EVIDENCE FROM READING TIMES

Source: R. K. Morris (1994). Lexical and message-level sentence context effects on fixation times in reading, *Journal of Experimental Psychology: Learning, Memory and Cognition,* 20 (1), 92–103.

INTRODUCTION

In a series of experiments Robin Morris examined whether the meaning of a sentence speeded up the reading of a target word when sentence meaning was congruent with the target word compared to when it was incongruent. We have already seen that there are top-down influences in language and this experiment was designed to look in detail at these top-down influences.

If the meaning of a sentence speeds up, or facilitates, the reading time of a particular word then it would suggest that there is a top-down influence of sentence meaning on word recognition. When Morris conducted the experiment there was already a body of evidence to suggest that context could influence the naming of a word (reading it aloud) but Morris investigated whether this facilitation would also happen when participants were reading silently by examining their eye movements and specifically the length of time participants spent looking at the target word.

METHOD

Morris's experiment was designed to examine whether the meaning of a sentence would influence the reading time of a word embedded in that sentence when participants were reading silently. In order to do this it was necessary to measure where the participants were looking during reading and for how long using eye movement equipment like that shown in Figure 9.5.

Morris used sentences like:

1. The friend talked as the barber trimmed the *moustache* after lunch.

2. The friend talked to the barber and trimmed the *moustache* after lunch.

3. The friend talked to the person and trimmed the *moustache* after lunch.

FIGURE 9.5 The use of eye movement recording is common in research on reading.
Source: Morris (1994)

The dependent variable was the time taken to read the target word 'moustache' in each sentence. Sentence 1 is a congruent-related sentence because it has meaning that relates to the target word 'barber'. Sentence 2 on the other hand is congruent-altered. This is because it contains the words 'barber' and 'trimmed', hence congruent and yet the meaning of the sentence is altered because it is not the barber that is doing the trimming. Thus for these two sentences the lexical (word-based) information related to moustache is the same in both cases. Finally sentence 3 is a neutral sentence because it does not contain the word 'barber'.

RESULTS

Morris found that there was an effect such that the meaning of the sentence did speed up the processing of the target word. It was found that there was a reduction of reading time in sentences where the message was congruent with the target word compared to similar sentences, in terms of lexical content but where the message was incongruent with the target word. This suggests that the representation of the sentence that the reader is constructing has an influence on the processing of words even while that representation is being constructed.

DISCUSSION

Morris's findings showed that the *meaning* of a sentence is an important influence on the time taken to read a target word embedded in a sentence. When the meaning of the sentence was consistent with the target word then there was a facilitation effect (reading time was faster). When the meaning of the sentence was inconsistent with the target word this facilitation effect disappeared. This was observed even when the lexical content of the two sentence types was almost identical. This suggests that there are influences on lexical access other than just the surrounding words. Findings such as this help to discriminate between competing models of lexical access, some of which suggest that there should not be an influence of the sentence meaning.

The experiment also shows that the use of eye movement data is important in the study of language processing. The recording of eye movement data is now quite common in cognitive psychology (for example, see Ball et al., 2003; Reilly & Radach, 2006; Wilkie & Wann, 2006).

---

pragmatics knowledge of the practical aspects of using language

These examples illustrate that it takes more than having a vocabulary and arranging words grammatically to understand language and communicate effectively with others. It also involves **pragmatics**, a knowledge of the practical aspects of using language (Cummings, 2005). Language occurs in a social context, and pragmatic knowledge not only helps you understand what other people are really saying, it helps you make sure that

other people get the point of what you are communicating. In essence, pragmatics is another example of how top-down processing influences language use.

Psycholinguists have identified social rules that guide communication between people (Grice, 1975). One rule states that messages should be as clear as possible. Thus, depending on whether you are speaking with an adult who is proficient in your language, a 5-year-old child, or a foreign visitor who speaks little English, you usually adjust your rate of speech, choice of words and the complexity of your sentences.

Pragmatics also depend on other aspects of the social context. For example, when you write a term paper or go for a job interview, you normally would use a more formal tone than when writing an email or speaking to friends. Thus when a university student sent an email to her lecturer (it was not to one of us) that read 'I cnt find assmnt 4 2moz cud u plz send 2 me? thx m8' the lecturer sternly let the student know about her violation of pragmatics, namely, that the style of the message was completely inappropriate for the context.

Language Functions, the Brain and Sex Differences

Language functions are distributed in many areas of the brain, but the regions shown in Figure 9.6 are especially significant. As discussed in **Chapter 4**, Broca's area, located in the left hemisphere's frontal lobe, is most centrally involved in word production and articulation (lower-right brain scan). Wernicke's area, in the rear portion of the temporal lobe, is more centrally involved in speech comprehension (upper-left scan). People with damage in one or both areas typically suffer from **aphasia,** an impairment in speech comprehension and/or production that can be permanent or temporary (LaPointe, 2005). The visual area of the cortex is also involved in recognizing written words.

Aphasia can be the result of various forms of damage such as a stroke, head injury or a brain tumour. The range of symptoms and pattern of deficits associated with various aphasias is dependent on the location of the damage that has occurred. For example, Corsten, Mende, Cholewa, & Huber (2007) reported the case of patient 'PS' a 52-year-old German male who suffered a left-hemisphere stroke that resulted in a range of difficulties in language, including speech that included errors such as substituting letters and/ or syllables and word finding difficulties. PS also showed difficulty naming pictures of three-syllable items (e.g., 'banana') compared with one-syllable items (e.g., 'cat'). Due to the highly individual and specific pattern of damage associated with aphasia, individually tailored treatment programmes may be required, such as that outlined by Kiran, Roches, Balachandran and Ascenso (2014).

Years ago scientists noted that men who suffer left-hemisphere strokes are more likely than women to show severe aphasic symptoms. In female stroke victims with left-hemisphere damage, language functions are more likely to be spared, suggesting that more of their language function is shared with the right hemisphere. Many studies in the past have reported gender effects in language such that females tend to outperform males in various areas of language processing (e.g. Halpern, 2000; Hiscock, Inch, Jacek, Hiscock-Kalil, & Kalil, 1994). The development of various brain imaging techniques now allows researchers to examine what patterns of activation may underlie these observed differences in performance.

Brain-imaging research by Susan Rossell and co-workers (2002) supports this hypothesis. In their study, men and women engaged in a language task in which words and non-words were presented on each side of a computer screen. Participants had to identify which was the real word as quickly as possible by pressing one of two computer keys. Functional MRIs (fMRIs) were recorded during the task and during a non-language control task. As the image in Figure 9.7 shows, men exhibited greater left-hemisphere activation

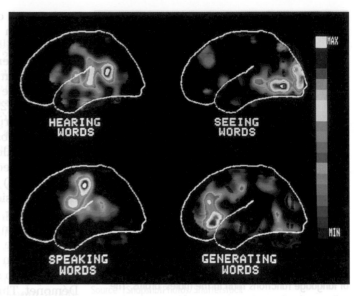

FIGURE 9.6 Brain areas involved in various aspects of language.

In these PET scans, regions of white, red and yellow show the greatest activity. Notice in the upper-left image that Wernicke's area (in the temporal lobe) is especially active when we hear words, and in the lower-right image that Broca's area (located in the frontal lobe) is especially active when we generate words.

Source: Marcus E. Raichle, Washington University

⊂⊃ Chapter 4, Page 131

aphasia an impairment in speech comprehension and/or production

Focus 9.5 What sex differences exist in the brain's language processing?

TABLE 9.1 Course of normal language development in children

Age	Biological
1–3 months	Infant can distinguish speech from non-speech sounds and prefers speech sounds (phonemes). Undifferentiated crying gives way to cooing when happy.
4–6 months	Babbling sounds begin to occur. These contain sounds from virtually every language. Child vocalizes in response to verbalizations of others.
7–11 months	Babbling sounds narrow to include only the phonemes heard in the language spoken by others in the environment. Child moves tongue with vocalizations ('lalling'). Child discriminates between some words without understanding their meaning and begins to imitate word sounds heard from others.
12 months	First recognizable words typically spoken as one-word utterances to name familiar people and objects (e.g., da-da or block).
12–18 months	Child increases knowledge of word meanings and begins to use single words to express whole phrases or requests (e.g., 'out' to express a desire to get out of the cot); primarily uses nouns.
18–24 months	Vocabulary expands to between 50 and 100 words. First rudimentary sentences appear, usually consisting of two words (e.g., more milk) with little or no use of articles (the, a), conjunctions (and) or auxiliary verbs (can, will). This condensed, or telegraphic, speech is characteristic of first sentences throughout the world.
2–4 years	Vocabulary expands rapidly at the rate of several hundred words every 6 months. Two-word sentences give way to longer sentences that, though often grammatically incorrect, exhibit basic language syntax. Child begins to express concepts with words and to use language to describe imaginary objects and ideas. Sentences become more correct syntactically.
4–5 years	Child has learned the basic grammatical rules for combining nouns, adjectives, articles, conjunctions and verbs into meaningful sentences.

The importance of early language exposure applies to any language, not just spoken language. Because sign languages share the deep-structure characteristics of spoken languages, deaf children who learn sign language before puberty develop normal linguistic and cognitive abilities even though they never hear a spoken word (Marschark & Mayer, 1998). In contrast, deaf people who are not exposed to sign language before age 12 show language-learning deficits later in life (Morford, 2003).

Can Animals Acquire Human Language?

 Chapter 7, Page 297

In **Chapter 7** there were examples of animal 'intelligence' including examples of primates like Sultan (Köhler, 1925) and birds like Betty (Weir et al., 2002), problem-solving. In addition to this behaviour it is clear that non-human species communicate in diverse ways. Chimpanzees grunt, bark, scream and make gestures to other chimps. Dolphins make clicking sounds and high-pitched vocalizations (Figure 9.9). Many species use special calls to warn of predators and to attract mates (Alcock, 2002).

Communication also abounds in the insect world. Honeybees use a repertoire of body movements – so-called dances – to communicate. When a honeybee discovers nectar, it returns to the hive and performs a turning 'waggle dance' (von Frisch, 1974). The dance's pattern and duration convey information about the nectar's location, which other bees receive by sensing vibrations as they stay in contact behind the dancer. Using this information and odour cues, they can zero in on the food source. Honeybees also vibrate their bodies from side to side in a 'grooming invitation dance' that signals other bees to come by and help clean them (Land & Seeley, 2004).

FIGURE 9.9 Human scientists debate whether dolphins and other animals use language. Could the opposite also be occurring?

Source: Elena Larina/Shutterstock

In some species, communication shows interesting parallels to human language. Just as humans have different languages, each songbird species has its own songs. Remarkably, some songbirds also have local dialects, as humans do (Catchpole & Rowell, 1993). Slater (1981) conducted research on chaffinches on one of the Orkney Islands and found that birds in different areas of the island sang slightly different songs, with the song altering slightly from one area to the next until eventually being quite different. Thus it should be possible for an expert to be able to say which part of the island a bird is from just by hearing the song that it produces. And just as

humans have a sensitive period in childhood for language acquisition, some songbirds will not sing normally in adulthood unless they hear the songs of their species while growing up (Wilbrecht & Nottebohm, 2003).

Although other species can communicate in intriguing and sophisticated ways, the capacity to use full-fledged language has long been regarded as the sole province of humans. Several decades ago, some scientists attempted to challenge this assumption by teaching apes to use human language.

Washoe: early signs of success

At first, investigators tried to teach chimpanzees to speak verbally, but chimps lack a vocal system that would permit humanlike speech. A breakthrough came in 1966 when Allen Gardner and Beatrice Gardner (1969) took advantage of chimps' hand and finger dexterity and began teaching American Sign Language to a 10-month-old chimp named Washoe. They *cross-fostered* Washoe: they raised her at home and treated her like a human child. By age 5, Washoe had learned 160 signs. More important, at times she combined signs (e.g., 'more fruit', 'you tickle Washoe') in novel ways. For example, when a researcher showed Washoe a baby doll inside a cup and signed 'What that?' Washoe signed back 'Baby in my drink'. Other researchers also had success. A gorilla named Koko learned over 600 signs (Bonvillian & Patterson, 1997), and a chimp named Lana learned to communicate via visual symbols on a specially designed keyboard (Rumbaugh, 1990).

Project Nim: dissent from within

At Columbia University, behaviourist Herbert Terrace (1979) taught sign language to a chimp he named Nim Chimpsky – a play on the name of linguist Noam Chomsky. But after years of work and videotape analysis of Nim's 'conversations', Terrace concluded that when Nim combined symbols into longer sequences, he was either imitating his trainer's previous signs or 'running on' with his hands until he got what he wanted. Moreover, Nim spontaneously signed only when he wanted something, which is not how humans use language. Terrace concluded that Nim had not learned language.

Not surprisingly, some ape-language researchers disputed Terrace's conclusions. They agreed that although apes signed mainly to request things, other types of communication also occurred. For example, Chantek, an orang-utan who had been taught a symbol for 'dirty' in regard to faeces and urine, spontaneously began applying the symbol to spilled food, soiled objects and toilets (Miles, Mitchell, & Harper, 1996). At Central Washington University, Roger Fouts and Deborah Fouts continued working with Washoe and other cross-fostered chimps. They intentionally refrained from signing in front of Loulis, Washoe's adopted son, and found that Loulis acquired over 50 signs by observing other chimps communicate (Fouts, Fouts, & Van Cantfort, 1989). The chimps also signed with each other when humans were not present, and signing occurred across various contexts, such as when they were playing, feeding and fighting (Cianelli & Fouts, 1998).

Kanzi: chimp versus child

Sue Savage-Rumbaugh of Georgia State University has worked extensively with a chimpanzee species called the *bonobo* (Figure 9.10). At age 1½, a bonobo named Kanzi spontaneously showed an interest in using plastic geometric symbols that were associated with words. By age 4, with only informal training during social interactions, Kanzi had learned more than 80 symbols and produced a number of two- and three-word communications. Kanzi typically combined gestures and symbols that he pointed to on a laminated board or typed on a specially designed keyboard. For example, Kanzi created the combinations 'Person chase Kanzi', 'Kanzi chase person' and 'Person chase person' to designate who should chase whom during play. Kanzi also responded readily to spoken English commands.

Savage-Rumbaugh and her co-workers (1993; Segerdahl, Fields, & Savage-Rumbaugh, 2006) also tested Kanzi's ability to understand unfamiliar spoken sentences under controlled conditions. For example, when told 'Give the doggie a shot', Kanzi picked up a toy dog, grabbed a toy hypodermic needle, and gave the dog a shot. Kanzi also

example, the ability of sexist language to evoke gender stereotypes. In one study, college students read one of the following statements about psychology:

The psychologist believes in the dignity and worth of the individual human being. He is committed to increasing man's understanding of himself and others.

Psychologists believe in the dignity and worth of the individual human being. They are committed to increasing people's understanding of themselves and others.

The students then were asked to rate the attractiveness of a career in psychology for men and women. Those who had read the first statement rated psychology as a less attractive profession for women than did the students who read the second statement, written in gender-neutral language (Briere & Lanktree, 1983). Apparently, the first statement implied that psychology is a male profession (when, actually, the majority of psychology doctorates awarded over the past decade went to women). In such ways, language can help create and maintain stereotypes.

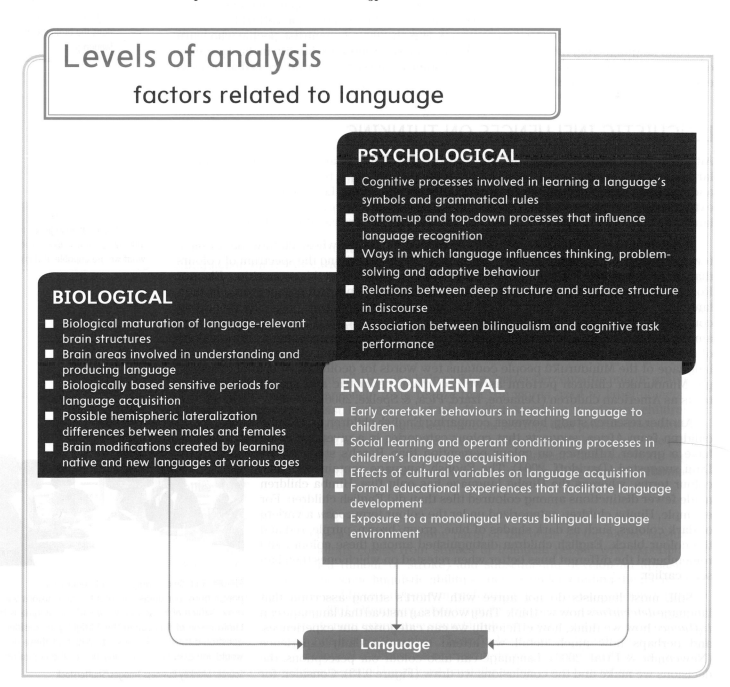

Levels of analysis
factors related to language

PSYCHOLOGICAL
- Cognitive processes involved in learning a language's symbols and grammatical rules
- Bottom-up and top-down processes that influence language recognition
- Ways in which language influences thinking, problem-solving and adaptive behaviour
- Relations between deep structure and surface structure in discourse
- Association between bilingualism and cognitive task performance

BIOLOGICAL
- Biological maturation of language-relevant brain structures
- Brain areas involved in understanding and producing language
- Biologically based sensitive periods for language acquisition
- Possible hemispheric lateralization differences between males and females
- Brain modifications created by learning native and new languages at various ages

ENVIRONMENTAL
- Early caretaker behaviours in teaching language to children
- Social learning and operant conditioning processes in children's language acquisition
- Effects of cultural variables on language acquisition
- Formal educational experiences that facilitate language development
- Exposure to a monolingual versus bilingual language environment

Language

Language not only influences *how* we think, but also may influence *how well* we think in certain domains. For example, English-speaking children consistently score lower than children from Asian countries in mathematical skills such as counting, addition and subtraction (Zhou, Peverly, & Lin, 2005). One reason may be the words and symbols the languages use to represent numbers. Asian languages make it far easier to learn the base-10 number system, particularly the numbers between 10 and 100. For example, in Chinese, the number 11 is 'ten-one', 12 is 'ten-two' and 13 is 'ten-three'. In contrast, English speakers struggle with such words as *eleven*, *twelve* and *thirteen*, which bear little conceptual relation to a base-10 mode of thinking. Regardless of their counting proficiency, American and British children fail to grasp the base-10 system by age 5; in contrast, by age 5 many Chinese children understand this concept, enabling them to do addition and subtraction with greater ease (Miller & Stigler, 1987). In this manner, the English language appears to hamper the development of skills in using numbers, whereas Asian languages seem to facilitate the development of mathematical skills. However, more recently Laski and Yu (2014) argued that the general approach to education itself has a greater influence on development of understanding of numbers than the number system itself.

In sum, language provides the foundation of many human behaviours and capabilities, and in this section we have touched on only a few of its complexities. As a central topic of psychological research, it continues to be studied vigorously at the biological, psychological and environmental levels of analysis.

Focus 9.10 How does language influence thinking?

In review

- Human languages across the globe share the same underlying features. Language is symbolic and structured, conveys meaning, is generative and permits displacement. Language has many adaptive functions, such as facilitating cooperative social systems and allowing people to transmit knowledge to one another. Scientists believe that humans have evolved an innate capacity for acquiring language.

- The surface structure of a language refers to how symbols are combined; the deep structure refers to the underlying meaning of the symbols. Language elements are hierarchically arranged: from phoneme to morpheme to words, phrases and sentences. Discourse involves higher-level combinations of sentences.

- Understanding and producing language – including pattern recognition of words and the hierarchical structure of language – involve bottom-up and top-down processing.

- In infancy, babies can perceive all the phonemes that exist in all the languages of the world. Between 6 to 12 months of age, their speech discrimination narrows to include only the sounds specific to their native tongue. By ages 4 to 5, most children have learned the basic grammatical rules for combining words into meaningful sentences.

- Language development seems to depend heavily on innate mechanisms that permit the learning and production of language, provided that the child is exposed to an appropriate linguistic environment during a sensitive period that extends from early childhood to puberty.

- Researchers have attempted to teach animals, primarily apes, but also parrots to use hand signs or keyboard symbols to communicate in language-like fashion. At best, these animals are capable of learning, combining and communicating with symbols at a level similar to that of a human toddler. Sceptics question, however, whether they can learn syntax and generate novel ideas.

- Although research findings are not entirely consistent, it appears that a second language is most easily mastered and fluently spoken if it is learned during a sensitive period that ranges from early childhood possibly through mid-adolescence. Bilingual children tend to perform better than monolingual children on a variety of cognitive tasks.

- In general, it appears that when people acquire a second language early in life or learn it to a high degree of proficiency later in life, both languages share a common neural network.

- Language influences what people think and how effectively they think. Expansion of vocabulary allows people to encode and process information in more sophisticated ways.

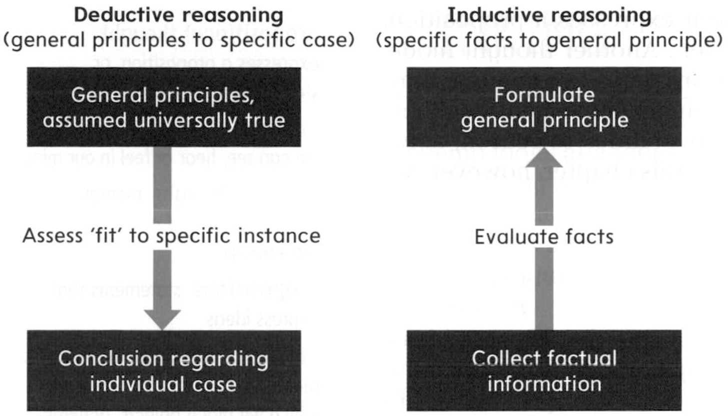

Deductive reasoning
(general principles to specific case)

| General principles, assumed universally true |

Assess 'fit' to specific instance

| Conclusion regarding individual case |

Inductive reasoning
(specific facts to general principle)

| Formulate general principle |

Evaluate facts

| Collect factual information |

FIGURE 9.16 A comparison of deductive and inductive reasoning.

unlikely to nail or screw boards together at random in the hope that the finished product will serve your purposes. Instead, you will develop mental representations to guide your efforts, such as a visual image of the finished product and general principles for its successful construction (e.g., 'build from the bottom up').

Deductive Reasoning

Two types of reasoning underlie many of our attempts to make decisions and solve problems (Figure 9.16). In **deductive reasoning**, we reason from the top down, that is, from general principles to a conclusion about a specific case. When people reason deductively, they begin with a set of *premises* (propositions assumed to be true) and determine what the premises imply about a specific situation. Deductive reasoning is the basis of formal mathematics and logic. Logicians regard it as the strongest and most valid form of reasoning because the conclusion *cannot be false* if the premises (factual statements) are true. More formally, the underlying deductive principle may be stated: Given the general proposition 'if X then Y', if X occurs, then you can infer Y. Thus, to use a classic deductive argument, or *syllogism*,

> *If* all humans are mortal (first premise), and
>
> *if* Socrates is a human (second premise),
>
> *then* Socrates must be mortal (conclusion).

One form of deductive reasoning – *conditional reasoning* (reasoning about if . . . then statements) has been extensively studied over the past 40 years using the Wason four-card selection task (Wason, 1966). A form of the original abstract task can be seen in Figure 9.17.

Participants are told that the cards have a letter on one side and a number on the other and they are given the conditional statement 'if there is an A on one side of the card then there is a 2 on the other side' or more formally, in logical terms, *if p then q*. They are then asked which of the four cards representing an example of each possible case they would need to turn over to assess whether the rule is true or false. Figure 9.17 shows the four cards used in the task along with the logical values assigned to them; *p, not-p, q, not-q, or A, D, 2 and 7* for the rule if there is an A on one side then there is a 2 on the other side.

Although the task appears to be relatively straightforward, performance is generally poor with typically only 10% of participants correctly solving the task. The correct solution is to turn over the A card and the 7 card or the *p* and *not-q* cards. This is because these are the only two cards that can show the potentially falsifying combination of an A with a number other than 2. If we think of this in purely logical terms it is clear to see that if the claimed rule is *if p then q* then the occurrence of *p* with *not-q* means that the rule is false. The most common response is to select the A and the 2 cards. Evans and Lynch (1973) demonstrated that participants tend to select the cards that have been mentioned in the rule itself, hence the selection of A and 2 in the example above.

Although this finding would suggest that participants do not reason in accordance with formal logic it appears that the picture is not this straightforward. There are numerous versions of the task that lead to improved performance and hence cloud the issue of whether we reason in accordance with logic or not.

For example, consider the version used by Cheng and Holyoak (1985) in which a scenario was used which involved participants checking the forms of passengers which stated whether passengers were in transit or entering the country on one side and listed the inoculations that a passenger had had on the other side. Participants were told that if the form says 'entering' on one side, then the other side includes cholera among the list of diseases. Participants were required to indicate which

deductive reasoning reason from the top down, that is, from general principles to a conclusion about a specific case

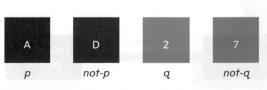

| A | D | 2 | 7 |
| *p* | *not-p* | *q* | *not-q* |

FIGURE 9.17 The Wason four-card selection task.

If there is an A on one side of the card then there is a 2 on the other (*if p then q*).

of the forms in Figure 9.18 they would need to turn over to check that the rule was not violated.

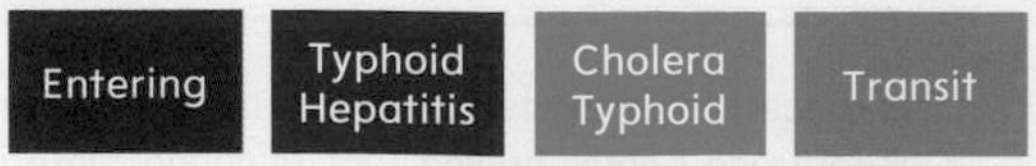

This version of the task has a correct solution rate of about 90% and yet, it could be argued, is logically isomorphic to the abstract task above. It seems that the role of content of a task can have a dramatic effect on how effectively we reason and is one of the aspects of reasoning that any proposed theory must be able to account for. What seems to be crucial here is that this version of the task requires participants to identify what represents a violation of the rule (entering the country when not vaccinated against cholera) rather than testing whether a rule is true or false, which is what is required in the original abstract version of the task. This form of reasoning, reasoning about actions rather than matters of fact, is known as deontic reasoning.

Although there is still some debate as to whether the task is purely one of logic or not (Evans & Lynch, 1973; Evans, Over, & Manktelow, 1993; Oaksford & Chater, 1994) it is clear that the task is central to the psychological study of reasoning and is as widely used now as ever (for example, see, Lucas & Ball, 2005; Manktelow, Sutherland, & Over, 1995; Manktelow & Over, 1991).

| Entering | Typhoid Hepatitis | Cholera Typhoid | Transit |

FIGURE 9.18 Cheng and Holyoak's (1985) immigration version of the four-card selection task.

 Current topic

WHAT DOES IT MEAN TO BE RATIONAL?

Traditionally the Wason (1966) selection task has been considered a test of conditional reasoning with participants required to apply rules of logic to successfully solve the task, and generally failing to do so.

Consider Figure 9.17: the logically 'correct' solution is to select the A and 7 cards (or *p* and *not-q*), yet this is rarely the selection made by participants. Does this mean that humans are poor at logical tasks? Do people behave in an irrational manner? There has been much debate about the selection task phenomena and how they should be explained and interpreted (Evans et al., 1993).

Traditional theories such as inference rule theories (Braine & O'Brien, 1991, 1998; Rips, 1994) and mental models theory (Johnson-Laird, 1983, 2008; Johnson-Laird & Byrne, 1991) have accepted this interpretation of the task and attempted to offer accounts for poor performance according to the dictates of formal logic.

More recently there has been a radical new approach applied to the selection task and it has met with considerable success. Rather than conceiving of the task as a test of logical reasoning, Oaksford and Chater (1994) proposed that participants may not be engaging in any reasoning at all, but rather trying to decide between two competing hypotheses. They apply the rules of probability theory rather than the rules of logic to the task.

According to Oaksford and Chater's account a participant must try to discover whether the rule 'if there is an A on one side of the card then there is a 2 on the other side' (*if p then q*) is true or false. Essentially this means that participants must decide between two competing hypotheses:

That *if p then q* is true – the dependence hypothesis, that when p occurs q will also occur or

That *if p then q* is false – the independence hypothesis, that p and q occur independently of each other.

To begin with both hypotheses are equally likely; the participant has no reason to believe otherwise, and is at the point of greatest uncertainty needing to decide what information to consider, or which cards to turn, in order to choose between the two hypotheses. Oaksford and Chater equate information gain with a reduction in uncertainty, so the best information gives the greatest reduction in uncertainty. This means that the most useful cards to select are the ones that move the participant as far away from this point of maximum uncertainty as possible.

A crucial aspect of the theory is the *rarity assumption*, the idea that things in the world are rare compared to things that are not those things. For example, fish are rare in respect to things that are not fish; birds are rare in respect to things that are not birds. Or, more crucially here, 'A' is rare compared to letters that are not 'A'.

Using probability theory and complex mathematics, which will not be described here, Oaksford and Chater calculated the expected information gain of the four cards. Information gain is *expected* rather than actual because participants do not physically turn the card, so they have to speculate as to how valuable the turning of a card will be in terms of information gain. The higher the expected information gain value of a card the more likely it is that it will be selected by a participant.

When these calculations are performed the following expected information gain for each card is found:

p>q>not-q>not-p

▶

This suggests that the two most *informative* cards in the array are the p and q cards (A and the 2), and this is a very common selection pattern. Oaksford and Chater argued that selecting these cards is rational if the goal is to reduce uncertainty between the two competing hypotheses. Consequently, Oaksford and Chater see the task in a fundamentally different way to other theorists and their approach suggests that the behaviour of participants is rational. Oaksford and Chater's theory has been very influential and has been extended to other areas of reasoning.

The development of this probabilistic approach is one of the most exciting advances in reasoning in recent years and there is no doubt that the argument between probability based accounts and more traditional theoretical accounts will continue for some time.

Inductive Reasoning

In **inductive reasoning**, we reason from the bottom up, starting with specific facts and trying to develop a general principle. Scientists use induction when they discover general principles, or laws, as a result of observing a number of specific instances of a phenomenon. After Ivan Pavlov observed repeatedly that the dogs in his laboratory began to salivate when approached by the experimenter who fed them, he began to think in terms of a general principle that eventually became the foundation of classical conditioning (repeated CS–UCS pairings produce a CR). A college student who experiences repeated negative consequences when she gets drunk may eventually conclude that binge drinking is a high-risk behaviour to be avoided.

> inductive reasoning reason from the bottom up, starting with specific facts and trying to develop a general principle

An important difference between deductive and inductive reasoning lies in the certainty of the results. Deductive conclusions are certain to be true *if* the premises are true, but inductive reasoning leads to likelihood rather than certainty. Even if we reason inductively in a flawless manner, the possibility of error always remains because some new observation may disprove our conclusion. Thus you may observe that every person named Jordan you have ever met has blue eyes, but it would obviously be inaccurate to reason that, therefore, all people named Jordan have blue eyes.

In daily life and in science, inductive and deductive reasoning may be used at different points in problem-solving and decision-making. For example, psychologists often make informal observations (e.g., hearing about crime victims like Kitty Genovese who do not receive help when many bystanders are present). These specific observations may prompt them to construct an initial explanation (e.g., diffusion of responsibility) for the observed phenomenon. This is inductive reasoning, so the explanation could be wrong even if it is consistent with all the known facts. Therefore scientists move to a deductive process in which they design experiments to formally test specific *if–then* hypotheses, moving now from a general explanatory principle to a specific observation (the experiment's results). If the results of these experimental tests do *not* support their hypotheses, they conclude that their explanation or theory cannot be correct and needs to be revised or discarded.

Stumbling Blocks in Reasoning

The ability to reason effectively is a key factor in critical thinking, in making sound decisions, and in solving problems. Unfortunately, several factors may prevent us from selecting the information needed to draw sound conclusions.

Distraction by irrelevant information

Distinguishing relevant from irrelevant information can be challenging. Consider the following problem. As you solve it, analyse the mental steps you take, and do not read on until you have decided on an answer.

> *Your drawer contains 19 black socks and 13 blue socks. Without turning on the light, how many socks do you have to pull out of the drawer to have a matching pair?*

As you solved the problem, what information entered into your reasoning? Did you take into account the fact that there were 19 black socks and 13 blue ones? If so, you are like many of Robert Sternberg's Yale University students who did the same thing, thereby making the problem much more difficult than it should be (Davidson and Sternberg, 1984). In this case, all that matters is how many *colours* of socks there are. It would not

matter if there were 1,000 socks of each colour; once you have selected any three of them, you are bound to have at least two of the same colour. People often fail to solve problems because they simply do not focus on the *relevant* information. Instead, they take into account irrelevant information that leads them astray.

Belief bias

Belief bias is the tendency to abandon logical rules in favour of our own personal beliefs. To illustrate, let us consider an experiment in which college students were asked to judge whether conclusions followed logically from syllogisms like the following:

All things that are smoked are good for one's health.

Cigarettes are smoked.

Therefore cigarettes are good for one's health.

What do you think? Is the logic correct? Actually, it is. If we accept (for the moment) that the premises are true, then the conclusion *does* follow logically from the premises. Yet students in one study frequently claimed that the conclusion was not logically correct because they disagreed with the first premise that all things smoked are good for one's health. In this case, their beliefs about the harmful effects of smoking got in the way of their logic. When the same syllogism was presented with a nonsense word such as *ramadians* substituted for *cigarettes*, the errors in logic were markedly reduced (Markovits & Nantel, 1989). Incidentally, we agree that the conclusion that cigarettes are good for one's health is factually false. However, it is false because the first premise is false, not because the logic is faulty. Unfortunately, many people confuse factual correctness with logical correctness. The two are not at all the same.

Emotions and framing

When we evaluate problems or make decisions, at times we may abandon logical reasoning in favour of relying on our emotions – 'trusting one's gut' – to guide us (Slovic & Peters, 2006). And even when we try to reason logically, emotions may still creep into the picture.

Reasoning also can be affected by the particular way that information is presented to us, or 'framed'. **Framing** refers to the idea that the same information, problem or options can be structured and presented in different ways. For example, in one classic study, college students who were told that a cancer treatment had a 50% success rate judged the treatment to be significantly more effective and expressed a greater willingness to have it administered to a family member than did participants who were told that the treatment had a 50% failure rate (Kahneman & Tverksy, 1979). Representing outcomes in terms of positives or negatives has this effect because people tend to assign greater costs to negative outcomes (such as losing £100) than they assign value to an equivalent positive outcome (finding £100). The proposition that 'there is a 50 per cent chance of failure' evokes thoughts about the patient's dying and causes the 50–50 treatment to appear riskier (Slovic, Fischhoff, & Lichtenstein, 1988). Similarly, graphs or other visual displays can be designed to make identical information 'look different' and thus influence people's judgements and decisions (Diacon & Hasseldine, 2007).

Framing influences how we perceive information and can interfere with logical reasoning. This may be especially so when choices are framed to highlight potential positive or negative outcomes, thereby triggering emotions – such as, fear, anger or sadness – that may alter our perceptions of the risks associated with various choice options (Slovic & Peters, 2006). Framing also can enhance reasoning, however, as you will see next in our closer look at problem-solving and decision-making.

PROBLEM-SOLVING AND DECISION-MAKING

Humans have an unmatched ability to solve problems and adapt to the challenges of their world. As illustrated in our chapter-opening vignette, the remarkable problem-solving abilities of the pilot and co-pilot of Flight 118 enabled them to rapidly implement and execute a plan for successfully flying their badly mangled jetliner and saving the lives of the terrified passengers.

belief bias the tendency to abandon logical rules in favour of our own personal beliefs

Focus 9.12 Distinguish between deductive reasoning and inductive reasoning. How does irrelevant information and belief bias affect reasoning?

framing the idea that the same information, problem or options can be structured and presented in different ways

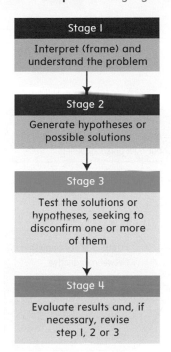

| Stage 1 |
| Interpret (frame) and understand the problem |

↓

| Stage 2 |
| Generate hypotheses or possible solutions |

↓

| Stage 3 |
| Test the solutions or hypotheses, seeking to disconfirm one or more of them |

↓

| Stage 4 |
| Evaluate results and, if necessary, revise step 1, 2 or 3 |

FIGURE 9.19 The stages of problem-solving.

Focus 9.13 Summarize the four major stages of problem-solving. Why are problem framing and mental sets important?

Steps in Problem-Solving

In accomplishing their astonishing feat, the pilot and co-pilot had to rapidly gain an understanding of the problem they were facing, generate a solution, test that solution, and then evaluate the results. Problem-solving typically proceeds through four stages (Figure 9.19). How well we carry out each of these stages determines our success in solving the problem.

Understanding, or framing, the problem

Most of us have had the experience of feeling totally frustrated in our attempts to solve a problem. We may even think that the problem is unsolvable. Then someone suggests a new way of looking at the problem, and the solution suddenly becomes obvious. How we mentally represent, or *frame*, a problem can make a huge difference. Consider the following problem (illustrated in Figure 9.20):

> *Train A leaves Manchester for its 50-mile trip to Leeds, at a constant speed of 25 mph. At the same time, train B leaves Leeds, bound for Manchester at the same speed of 25 mph. The world's fastest crow leaves Manchester at the same time as train A, flying above the tracks towards Leeds at a speed of 60 mph. When the crow encounters train B, it turns and flies back to train A, then instantly reverses its direction and flies back to train B. The supercharged bird continues this sequence until trains A and B meet midway between Manchester and Leeds. Try to solve this problem before reading on: what is the total distance the bird will have travelled in its excursions between trains A and B?*

Many people approach the problem as a distance problem, which is quite natural because the question is stated in terms of distance. They try to compute how far the bird will fly during each segment of its flight between trains A and B, sometimes filling up several pages with increasingly frenzied computations in the process. But suppose you approach the problem by asking not how far the bird will fly but *how long* it will take the trains to meet. The crow will have flown the same period of time at 60 mph. Now that you have reframed it as a time problem, the problem becomes much easier to solve. (Check your solution against the answer given on page 405.)

As you can see, our initial understanding of a problem is a key step towards a successful solution. If we frame a problem poorly, we can easily be led into a maze of blind alleys and ineffective solutions. If we frame it optimally, we at least have a chance to generate an effective solution. A knack for framing problems in effective ways that differ from conventional expectations has been called *outside-the-box thinking*, a prized ability in many academic and work environments.

Generating potential solutions

Once we have interpreted the problem, we can begin to formulate potential solutions or explanations. Ideally, we might proceed in the following fashion:

1. Determine which procedures and explanations will be considered.
2. Determine which solutions are consistent with the evidence that has so far been observed.
3. Rule out any solutions that do not fit the evidence.

Testing the solutions

Consider the possible solutions that remain. If a solution requires you to choose between specific explanations, ask if there is any test that should give one result if one explanation is true and another result if a different explanation is true. If so, evaluate the explanations again in light of the evidence from that test. In essence, this is what scientists do when they design experiments.

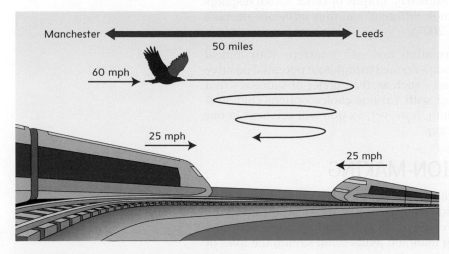

Manchester ←————————————————→ Leeds
50 miles
60 mph →
25 mph →
25 mph ←

FIGURE 9.20 The crow-and-trains problem.

Let us consider a common difficulty in the process of discovering and applying solutions to problems. Consider problem 1 in Figure 9.21:

You have a 21-cup jug, a 127-cup jug, and a 3-cup jug. Drawing and discarding as much water as you like, how will you measure out exactly 100 cups of water?

Try to solve all seven problems in Figure 9.21 in order, and write down your calculations for each one before reading on. Does a common solution emerge? If so, can you specify what it is?

As you worked the problems, you probably discovered that they are all solvable by the same formula, namely $B - A - (2 \times C)$ = desired amount. In problem 1, for example, $127 - 21 - (2 \times 3) = 100$. If you discovered this, it gave you a logical formula that you could apply to the rest of the problems. And it worked, did it not? However, by applying this successful formula to problems 6 and 7, you may have missed even easier solutions for these last two problems, namely $A - C$ for problem 6 and $A + C$ for problem 7.

Abraham Luchins (1942) developed the water jugs problems to demonstrate the manner in which a **mental set** – the tendency to stick to solutions that have worked in the past – can result in less effective problem-solving. Luchins found that most people who worked on problems 6 and 7 were blinded by the mental set they had developed by working the first five problems. In contrast, people who had not worked on problems 1 to 5 almost always applied the simple solutions to problems 6 and 7. Studies of mental set show how easy it is to become rigidly fixated on one particular approach that has been successful in the past.

Problem	Given jugs of these sizes A	B	C	Measure out this much water
1	21	127	3	100
2	14	46	5	22
3	18	43	10	5
4	7	42	6	23
5	20	57	4	29
6	23	49	3	20
7	15	39	3	18

FIGURE 9.21 Luchins's water jugs problems.

Using containers A, B and C with the capacities shown in the table, how would you measure out the volumes indicated in the right-hand column? You may discover a general problem-solving schema that fits all seven problems.

> **mental set** the tendency to stick to solutions that have worked in the past
>
> **problem-solving schemas** mental blueprints or step-by-step scripts for selecting information and solving specialized classes of problems
>
> **algorithms** formulas or procedures that automatically generate correct solutions

Evaluating results

The final stage of problem-solving is to evaluate the solutions. As we saw in the water jugs problems, even solutions that prove successful may not be the easiest or the best. Thus, after solving a problem, we should ask ourselves, 'Would there have been an easier or more effective way to accomplish the same objective?' This can lead to the development of additional problem-solving principles that may be applicable to future problems.

The Role of Problem-Solving Schemas

In solving problems, people often learn to employ short-cut methods that apply to specific situations (Rips, 1997). **Problem-solving schemas** are like mental blueprints or step-by-step scripts for selecting information and solving specialized classes of problems. We have all learned a great many of them, from schemas for cooking dinner to schemas for studying and mastering academic course content (Figure 9.22). Once we master them, we seem to know what to do without having to engage in step-by-step formal problem-solving procedures.

Algorithms and heuristics

Algorithms and *heuristics* are two important strategies for problem-solving. **Algorithms** are formulas or procedures that automatically generate correct solutions. Mathematical and chemical formulas are algorithms; if you use them correctly, you will always get the correct answer. Consider another example of an algorithm. If the letters of a word are scrambled in random order to produce an anagram like teralbay, we can identify the word by using a process in which we rearrange the eight letters in all possible combinations – all 40,320 combinations, that is. As you can see, using algorithms can be very time-consuming. You might therefore decide to use some rule-of-thumb strategy, such as trying out only consonants in the first and last positions, because you know that more words begin and end in consonants than in vowels. When we adopt rule-of-thumb approaches like this, we are using heuristics.

FIGURE 9.22 Experienced snowboarders and skiers learn schemas for various types of snow, which can affect planning and decision-making.

This boarder might approach a slope covered with 'powder' differently than one covered with 'corn' or 'hardpack' because of their different effects on the board and potentially on the boarder's safety.

Source: ©iStock.com/evilknevil

heuristics general problem-solving strategies that we apply to certain classes of situations

means–ends analysis identify differences between the present situation and the desired state, or goal, and then make changes that will reduce these differences

subgoal analysis formulating subgoals, or intermediate steps, towards a solution

Heuristics are general problem-solving strategies that we apply to certain classes of situations. *Means–ends analysis* is one example of a heuristic (Newell & Simon, 1972). In **means–ends analysis**, we identify differences between the present situation and the desired state, or goal, and then make changes that will reduce these differences. Assume, for example, that you have a 30-page paper due at the end of the term and have not begun working on it yet. The present situation is no pages written; the desired end state is a 30-page paper. What, specifically, needs to be done to reduce that discrepancy, and how are you going to do it?

You would be foolish to decide, 'There are 30 days until the paper is due, so all I have to do is write 1 page a day'. This approach is likely to result in a 30-page paper, but it is unlikely to result in one that will earn a passing grade. Instead, you would be wise to use another heuristic known as **subgoal analysis**, formulating subgoals, or intermediate steps, towards a solution. In this case, your expertise as a student will likely lead you to break down the task of writing a paper into subgoals, such as (1) choosing a topic, (2) doing library and Internet research on the topic to get the facts you need, (3) organizing the facts within a general outline of the paper, (4) writing a first draft or specific sections of the paper, (5) reorganizing and refining the first draft, and so on. In so doing, a huge task becomes a series of smaller and more manageable tasks, each with a subgoal that leads you towards the ultimate goal of a quality 30-page paper.

The value of setting subgoals can be seen in the Tower-of-Hanoi problem, which is explained in Figure 9.23. Breaking this task into subgoals helps us solve the problem. The first subgoal is to get ring C to the bottom of peg 3. The second subgoal is to get ring B over to peg 3. With these two subgoals accomplished, the final subgoal of getting ring A to peg 3 is quite easy. The solution requires planning (hypothesis formation), checking, and revising hypotheses. The correct seven-step sequence of moves appears on page 405.

Heuristics enter not only into problem-solving strategies but also into a wide range of decisions and judgements, from judgements about other people to judgements about our own health to decisions about buying products (Katapodi, Facione, Humphreys, & Dodd, 2005). As we shall see, heuristics can also contribute to errors in judgement.

Focus 9.14 What are problem-solving schemas? Distinguish between algorithms and heuristics. Describe the means–ends and subgoal analysis heuristics.

Uncertainty, Heuristics and Decision-Making

Few decisions in everyday life can be made with the absolute certainty that comes from applying some mathematical formula or other algorithm. Typically, the best we can hope for is a decision that has a high probability of a positive outcome. Because we seldom know what the exact probabilities are (for example, how likely it is that the stock market will be up or down when you need your money in the future, or how probable it is that a new dating relationship will become permanent), we tend to apply certain heuristics to form judgements of likelihood.

In daily life, we routinely make decisions about what other people are like. Suppose, for example, you are given the following description of a young woman:

Linda is 31 years old, single, outspoken, and very bright. She majored in philosophy. As a student, she was deeply concerned with issues of discrimination and social justice, and she also participated in anti-nuclear demonstrations.

Now rate the likelihood that each of the following hypotheses is true. Use 1 to indicate the most likely statement, 8 to indicate the least likely statement, and any number between 2 and 7 to indicate the likelihood of the second most likely statement.

_____ Hypothesis A: Linda is active in the feminist movement.

_____ Hypothesis B: Linda is a bank clerk.

_____ Hypothesis C: Linda is active in the feminist movement and is a bank clerk.

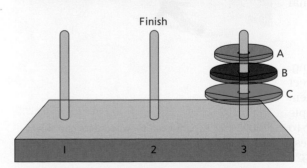

Start

Finish

FIGURE 9.23 The Tower-of-Hanoi problem.

The object is to move the rings one at a time from peg 1 to peg 3 in no more than seven moves. Only the top ring on a peg can be moved, and a larger ring can never be placed on top of a smaller one. (The answer appears on page 405.)

Cognitive psychologists Daniel Kahneman and Amos Tversky (1982) used this problem in a series of experiments that studied the role of heuristics in judgement and decision-making. They showed that certain heuristics underlie much of our inductive decision-making (drawing conclusions from facts) and that their misuse results in many of our thinking errors. Let us examine how that occurs.

The representativeness heuristic

'What does it look (or seem) like?' This is probably the first decision faced by our perceptual system when it processes incoming stimuli. Earlier, we discussed the importance of prototypes in concept formation. We use the **representativeness heuristic** to infer how closely something or someone fits our prototype for a particular concept, or class, and therefore how likely it is to be a member of that class. In essence, we are asking, 'How likely is it that this [person, object, event] *represents* that class?' In this case, does Linda seem like a feminist? This is a perfectly logical question to ask ourselves. Sometimes, however, our use of representativeness can cause us to make decisions that fly in the face of logic.

For example, what was your order of likelihood judgements concerning Linda? Figure 9.24 shows the mean likelihood estimates that college students attached to each statement (a low number indicating greater likelihood). First, there is a clear tendency to favour hypothesis A (Linda is a feminist). This is not surprising; the description does make her sound like a feminist. However, the significant finding is that hypothesis C (Linda is a feminist bank clerk) was favoured over hypothesis B (Linda is a bank clerk). But this cannot possibly be correct. Why not? Because everyone who is both a feminist and a bank clerk is also *simply* a bank clerk. Furthermore, there are many bank clerks who are not feminists, and Linda could be one of them. Stated differently, any person is more likely to be simply a bank clerk than to be a bank clerk *and* a feminist – or, for that matter, a bank clerk and anything else. People who say that hypothesis C is more likely than hypothesis B (and about 85% of people given this problem do so) violate the logical principle that the combination of two events cannot be more likely than either event alone.

Tversky and Kahneman believe that the reason people make this sort of error is that they confuse representativeness with probability. Linda represents our prototype for a feminist bank clerk better than she fits our prototype for a bank clerk. Therefore, we erroneously think the former is more likely than the latter. Notice how this argument fits with the ideas about memory discussed in **Chapter 8**. The description of Linda as 'outspoken' and 'concerned with issues of discrimination and social justice' serves a *priming* function, activating the elements in memory that are associated with the concept of 'feminist', so it is hard to think of Linda without thinking of a feminist. On the other hand, there is nothing in Linda's description that would activate the concept of 'bank clerk'. Thus if Linda is to be a bank clerk at all, we think she must be a feminist bank clerk.

However, although Tversky and Kahneman have argued that this is an error, it has been suggested that their findings are a result of the way that the task has been presented. Gigerenzer (1991) cites the version of the problem that was presented to participants by Fielder (1988). In this version of the task, participants are given the same description of Linda as used by Tversky and Kahneman, and then asked the following:

There are 100 persons who fit the description above. How many of them are:

a. bank clerks?

b. bank clerks and active in the feminist movement?

When the task was presented in this form the 'conjunction fallacy' outlined by Tversky and Kahneman almost disappears with only 17% of participants committing the fallacy. Gigerenzer's claims led to a heated debate with Kahneman and Tversky in *Psychological Review* (Gigerenzer, 1996; Kahneman & Tversky, 1996).

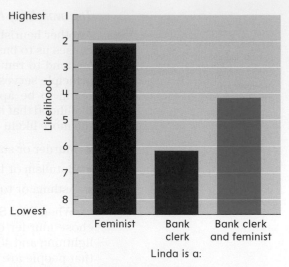

FIGURE 9.24 Illogical judgements.

This graph shows the mean likelihood judgements made by participants on the basis of the description of Linda (top-left column). Overall, people judge it to be more likely that Linda is a bank clerk and a feminist rather than just a bank clerk. Logically, this is impossible.

Source: Based on Tversky and Kahneman, 1982.

> **representativeness heuristic** how closely something or someone fits our prototype for a particular concept, or class, and therefore how likely it is to be a member of that class

 Chapter 8, Page 327

The availability heuristic

Another heuristic that can sometimes lead us astray is the **availability heuristic**, which causes us to base judgements and decisions on the availability of information in memory. We tend to remember events that are most important and significant to us. Usually that principle serves us well, keeping important information at the forefront in our memories, ready to be applied. But if something easily comes to mind, we may exaggerate the likelihood that it could occur. For example, consider each of the following pairs and choose the more likely cause of death:

- Murder or suicide?

- Botulism or lightning?

- Asthma or tornadoes?

When Paul Slovic and co-workers (1988) asked people to make these judgements, 80% chose murder over suicide as the more likely cause of death, 63% chose botulism over lightning and 43% chose tornadoes over asthma. In actuality, public health statistics show that people are 25% less likely to be murdered than to kill themselves, that lightning kills 53 times more people than botulism does, and that death by asthma is 21 times more likely than death as a result of a tornado. Yet murder, botulism and tornadoes are more highly and dramatically publicized when they do occur and thus are more likely to come to mind.

A recent memorable event can increase people's belief that they may suffer a similar fate. After the terrorist hijackings of 11 September 2001, airline bookings and tourism declined dramatically within the USA for a significant period. Demand for office space in landmark high-rise buildings also declined and many businesses sought space in less conspicuous suburban settings. Similarly, in the summer of 1975, when Steven Spielberg's film *Jaws* burned into people's memories graphic images of a great white shark devouring swimmers at a New England seaside town, beach attendance all over the country decreased. In fact, *Jaws* was blamed for a drop in tourism on the New England coast so dramatic that in the summer of 1976 many beachfront resorts nearly went bankrupt. The images available in memory – even though the film was clearly fiction – increased people's perceived likelihood that they, too, could become shark bait.

Thus at times the representativeness and availability heuristics can lead us astray by distorting our estimates of how likely an event really is. In other words, they can blind us to the *base rates*, or actual frequencies, at which things occur. In general, it is always best to find out what the actual probabilities are and make judgements on that basis; that is the strategy that allows insurance companies to flourish.

Confirmation Bias and Overconfidence

Sometimes one of the most challenging tasks is obtaining new evidence to test a hypothesis or solution. But what's the best type of evidence? Here is a principle that may seem puzzling to you: The best thing we can do to test our ideas is to seek evidence that will *disconfirm* them, rather than look for evidence that supports them. Why? Because the most informative piece of evidence we can obtain is one that rules out a hypothesis or idea. Disconfirming evidence proves conclusively that our idea *cannot* be true in its current form. In contrast, confirming evidence only supports our idea. It does not prove it with certainty, for it is possible that some future observation will disconfirm it or that another explanation fits the facts even better. Especially in the area of causal beliefs, you can be absolutely sure when you are wrong about something, but you cannot be absolutely sure when you're right because there might be a better explanation or an impending observation that calls your belief into question.

Following this disconfirmation principle is easier said than done, because people are often unwilling to challenge their cherished beliefs. Instead, they are prone to fall into a trap called **confirmation bias**, tending to look for evidence that will confirm what they currently believe rather than looking for evidence that could disconfirm their beliefs. Often, when people have strong beliefs about something – including beliefs about themselves – they are very selective in the kinds of information they expose

---

availability heuristic causes us to base judgements and decisions on the availability of information in memory

Focus 9.15 What role do uncertainty and heuristics play in decision-making? How do the representativeness and availability of heuristics distort probability judgements?

confirmation bias tending to look for evidence that will confirm what they currently believe rather than looking for evidence that could disconfirm their beliefs

overconfidence the tendency to overestimate one's correctness in factual knowledge, beliefs and decisions

themselves to (Chen, English, & Peng, 2006). They seek out like-minded people, compatible mass-media sources and Internet sites, and recall feedback from others that confirms their beliefs about themselves. The fact that people find it difficult or even upsetting to test and challenge their ideas, particularly those to which they are strongly committed, can be a major obstacle to getting the evidence needed to make a correct decision.

Confirmation bias often contributes to a distorted sense of how correct our opinions and beliefs are. **Overconfidence**, the tendency to overestimate one's correctness in factual knowledge, beliefs and decisions, is another reason people do not challenge their beliefs. This tendency, like confirmation bias, is widespread. In one study, college students were asked at the beginning of the academic year to make predictions about how likely it was (from 0% to 100%) that they would experience any of a long list of personal events, such as dropping a course, breaking up with a romantic partner, or joining a fraternity or sorority. They also indicated how confident they were in their probability estimates (i.e., how likely it was that they would be correct). At the end of the following semester and at the end of the academic year, they indicated which events had in fact occurred. As shown in Figure 9.25, confidence exceeded accuracy overall, and the difference between the two was equally great when the students were originally 100% confident in their predictions (Vallone, Griffin, Lin, & Ross, 1990). Similar overconfidence effects have been found in studies involving investment professionals, military strategists, weather forecasters and other populations. It apparently stems from people's need to see themselves as knowledgeable and competent (Blanton, Pelham, DeHart, & Carvallo, 2001).

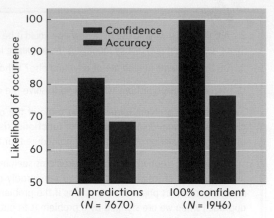

FIGURE 9.25 Displaying overconfidence.

Overconfidence is illustrated in the discrepancy between the accuracy with which students predicted that specific events would occur to them during the coming academic year and the degree of confidence that they had in their predictions. Overall, accuracy was considerably lower than confidence level, even for those events for which the students expressed complete certainty.

Source: Based on Vallone et al., 1990.

Focus 9.16 When making decisions, why is disconfirming evidence important? How does overconfidence contribute to confirmation bias?

 Applying psychological science

GUIDELINES FOR CREATIVE PROBLEM-SOLVING

creativity the ability to produce something that is both new and valuable

divergent thinking the generation of novel ideas that depart from the norm

Creativity is the ability to produce something that is both new and valuable (Sternberg, 2006). The product may be virtually anything, from a creative painting to a novel approach to solving a problem. In this case, we will be concerned with creative problem-solving.

Research on reasoning offers insights into how effective and creative problem solvers think and how they approach problems. In some ways, as experts so often demonstrate, there is no substitute for experience, for it teaches us useful heuristics and problem-solving schemas. Yet one of the marks of creativity is the ability to break out of conventional schemas when the occasion demands it and to engage in **divergent thinking**, the generation of novel ideas that depart from the norm (Guilford, 1959). In part, this means being able to apply concepts or propositions from one domain to another unrelated domain in a manner that produces a new insight. It also means refusing to be constrained by traditional approaches to a problem (Sternberg, 2006). Creative people are, in this respect, intellectual rebels. The constraints created by the tried and true can be difficult to overcome.

Consider, for example, the nine-dot problem in Figure 9.26. Many people have difficulty solving this problem. Did you? If so, it is probably because you imposed a traditional but unnecessary constraint on yourself and tried to stay within the boundary formed by the dots. But nothing in the statement of the problem forced you to do so. To solve the problem, you have to think outside the box.

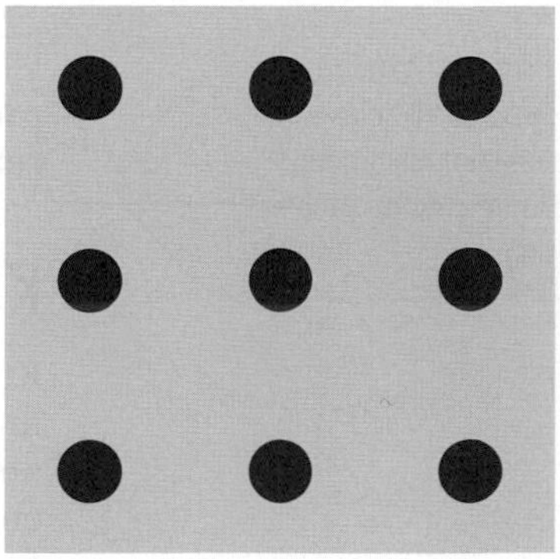

Creative problem solvers are often able to ask themselves questions such as the following to stimulate divergent thinking (Simonton, 1999):

I. What would work instead?

FIGURE 9.26 The nine-dot problem.

Without lifting your pencil from the paper, draw no more than four straight lines that will pass through all nine dots. (The answer appears on page 405.)

2. Are there new ways to use this? How else could it be used if I modified it in some way? By adding, subtracting, or rearranging parts, or by modifying the sequence in which things are done, could I make it more useful?

3. Do the elements remind me of anything else? What else is like this?

Use some of these questions when trying to solve the candlestick problem illustrated in Figure 9.27.

Solving the problem requires using some of the objects in unconventional ways. Many people, however, are prevented from doing so because of **functional fixedness**, the tendency to be so fixed in their perception of the proper function of an object or procedure that they are blinded to new ways of using it.

Sometimes creative solutions to problems seemingly appear out of the blue, suddenly popping into our mind in a flash of insight after we have temporarily given up and put the problem aside. **Incubation** is the name given to this phenomenon; it is as if the problem is incubating and being worked on at a subconscious level (Cattell, 1971). Sometimes the best approach when we are stymied by a problem is to put it aside for a while and gain a bit of psychological distance from it. Perhaps this causes mental sets and other biases to dissipate somewhat, allowing a new idea to emerge (Anderson, 1985). In addition, as time passes, new internal or external stimuli may activate a different perspective on the problem, aiding its solution.

As you can see, creative problem-solving involves many of the principles discussed earlier in the chapter. We see the operation of means–ends reasoning, the testing of hypotheses and the need to overcome biases that may cause us to overestimate or underestimate the likelihood of certain outcomes. Here are some other general problem-solving guidelines:

1. When you encounter a new problem you have not solved before, ask yourself if it is similar to other problems you have solved. Maybe the schema for solving a problem with similar features can be modified to solve this one. Take advantage of the store of knowledge in long-term memory.

2. Make a true effort to test your ideas. Try to find evidence that would disconfirm your ideas, not evidence that would confirm what you already believe. For example, if you are asked to accept statement X as true, see if you can imagine situations in which X would be false. Beware of the human tendency towards confirmation bias.

3. Be careful not to confuse representativeness with probability. The bird you see that looks too big to be a sparrow but just the right size to be a rare Patagonian warbler is probably . . . a big sparrow; the odds are overwhelmingly in favour of it being a sparrow because there are so many more sparrows (even big ones) than Patagonian warblers.

4. Make use of the means–ends problem-solving heuristic. Ask yourself what you are trying to accomplish, what the present state of affairs is, and what means you have for reducing the discrepancy.

5. Do not be afraid to use pencil and paper. Orderly notes and schematics can substitute for our rather limited working memory and allow us to have more information at hand to work with.

> **functional fixedness** the tendency to be so fixed in their perception of the proper function of an object or procedure that they are blinded to new ways of using it
>
> **incubation** problem is incubating and being worked on at a subconscious level

FIGURE 9.27 The candlestick problem.

Using these objects, find a way to mount the candle on a wall so it functions like a lamp. (The answer appears on page 405.)

Focus 9.17 Discuss some factors that inhibit and facilitate creative problem solving.

Overconfidence and confirmation bias can be potent adversaries in our search for correct predictions and decisions. When we are confident in the correctness of our views and reluctant to seek evidence that could prove them wrong, we can easily be blinded to the truth.

KNOWLEDGE, EXPERTISE AND WISDOM

Knowledge forms a foundation for expertise and wisdom. Each culture passes down its knowledge and world view from one generation to the next through language, instruction and socialization. This vast library of knowledge, shaped by cultural learning and by other environmental experiences (including trial-and-error learning), also supports the reasoning, decision-making and problem-solving skills that we have been discussing in this chapter.

Acquiring Knowledge: Schemas and Scripts

> **schema** a mental framework, an organized pattern of thought about some aspect of the world

One way to think about knowledge acquisition is as a process of building schemas. Most broadly, a **schema** is a mental framework, an organized pattern of thought about some aspect of the world. Concepts and categories represent types of schemas, and together they help you build a mental framework of your world, such as 'interesting versus dull people' or 'easy versus hard examinations'. Algorithms and heuristics also are types of

schemas – problem-solving schemas – that provide you with mental frameworks for solving certain types of problems.

Another type of schema, called a script, is a mental framework concerning a sequence of events that usually unfolds in a regular, almost standardized order. For example, if we tell you that 'John and Linda went to the cinema', these mere seven words convey a lot of information because 'going to the cinema' is a fairly standardized (i.e., scripted) activity. You can reasonably assume that John and Linda got to the cinema, waited in the ticket line and bought tickets (or bought them online), entered the cinema where someone checked their tickets, then they bought a snack, found seats, and so on. The scripts that you learn – 'attending class', 'shopping', 'driving', and so on – provide knowledge to guide and interpret actions. In sum, your knowledge grows as you acquire new scripts, concepts and other types of schemas; as your existing schemas become more complex; and as you form connections between schemas.

script a mental framework concerning a sequence of events that usually unfolds in a regular, almost standardized order

The Nature of Expertise

Schemas help explain what it means to be an expert. Masters and grand masters in chess can glance at a chessboard and quickly plan strategies and make adjustments in the heat of competition. The world's best players can store in memory as many as 50,000 board configurations, together with the locations of the individual pieces (Chase & Simon, 1973). As was discussed in **Chapter 8** this apparently exceptional memory performance is the result of both schemas and chunking. Certain chess-piece configurations have a name and the experts may use this information to recall the position of the pieces. For years, world chess champion Garry Kasparov's sophisticated schemas enabled him to regularly defeat chess-playing computers that used logical rules, even those capable of logically analysing up to 100,000 moves per second. It took Deep Blue, a 1.4-ton behemoth capable of calculating at a rate of 200 million positions and 200,000 moves per second, to finally defeat the schemas within Kasparov's 3-lb brain.

 Chapter 8, Page 325

Whether in medicine, science, sports, politics or other fields, experts have developed many schemas to guide problem-solving in their field, and just as critically, they are much better than novices at recognizing when each schema should be applied (Montgomery, Lipshitz, & Brehmer, 2005). Applying the correct mental blueprint provides a proven route to solving a problem quickly and effectively.

Chapter 8, Page 325

Focus 9.18 What roles do schemas play in knowledge acquisition and expertise?

Williams and Hodges (2005) presented a review of the literature relating to expertise and the development of football skills through training and practice (Figure 9.28). Although they show that there are benefits to be gained by considering the nature of the practice in which footballers engage, one factor is clearly crucial. No matter how great the innate talent of a player, it is practice that will lead to true expertise, with professional players having done nearly 10,000 hours of practice by their mid-twenties (Helsen, Starkes, & Hodges, 1998).

Expert Schemas and Memory

Consider what the ability to flexibly apply schemas means in terms of what we know about human memory and pattern recognition. As you learned in **Chapter 8**, schemas reside in long-term memory. Because they rely on learned schemas, experts take advantage of their spacious long-term memory. They can quickly analyse a problem deductively, select the retrieval cues needed to pull the appropriate schema from memory, and apply the schema to solve the problem at hand (Horn & Masunaga, 2000). In contrast, novices who have not yet learned specialized schemas must use general problem-solving methods in working memory, the space-limited blackboard of the mind (Newell & Simon, 1972). In so doing, they tax their working memory – the weakest link in the human mind.

When people develop expertise, their brain functioning changes in ways that increase processing efficiency. This occurs even in animals. Thus, as macaque monkeys in one study became experts in categorizing objects, brain recordings revealed quicker and stronger activity in the specific neurons that responded to the stimulus features of importance in categorizing the stimuli (Sigala & Logothetis, 2002).

What Is Wisdom?

The British journalist Miles Kington suggested that knowledge tells you that a tomato is a fruit, and that wisdom tells you not to put it in a fruit salad. However, defining a concept

FIGURE 9.28 Professional footballers like Cristiano Ronaldo engage in upwards of 10,000 hours of practice to achieve their levels of expertise.

Source: © kolvenbach/Alamy

FIGURE 9.29 Among the Inuit of the Canadian Arctic, wisdom involves extensive cultural knowledge, involvement in community life and teaching young people about cultural values.

Source: © H. Mark Weidman Photography/Alamy

> **wisdom** a system of knowledge about the meaning and conduct of life

> **Focus 9.19** What are some components of wisdom? How do wisdom and expertise differ?

> **mental image** a representation of a stimulus that originates inside your brain, rather than from external sensory input

like wisdom is not always straightforward. The anthropologist Peter Collings (2001) notes that, as in many cultures, the Inuit living in the Arctic of Western Canada accord their elders special status and great respect (Figure 9.29). Young and old Inuit alike regard wisdom as a key component of ageing successfully. To them, wisdom reflects 'the individual's function as a repository of cultural knowledge and his or her involvement in community life by interacting with younger people and talking to them, teaching them about "traditional" cultural values' (Collings, 2001, p. 146).

Does the Inuit conception of wisdom coincide with yours? If not, how would you define wisdom? Until the past 20 years, relatively few psychologists explored this issue, but their interest in studying wisdom has grown considerably since then (Sternberg, 1998). To German psychologist Paul Baltes and his colleagues, **wisdom** represents a system of knowledge about the meaning and conduct of life (Baltes & Kunzmann, 2004). What, then, are the components – the types of schemas – that make up this system of knowledge? One way to answer this question would be to study the characteristics of people who are widely esteemed for their wisdom. Yet, say Baltes and Kunzmann, this approach is not ideal, because 'Wise persons are approximations to wisdom, but they are not wisdom' (2004, p. 290). Instead, Baltes and his colleagues took another approach, pouring over numerous cultural, historical, philosophical, religious and psychological views of wisdom (Baltes & Staudinger, 2000). They concluded that wisdom has five major components:

1. *Rich factual knowledge about life.* This includes knowledge about human nature and human development, social norms and social relationships, major life events and how one's own well-being is interrelated with the well-being of other people.

2. *Rich procedural knowledge about life.* Such procedural knowledge includes strategies for making decisions, handling conflict, giving advice and weighing the importance of life goals.

3. *An understanding of lifespan contexts.* This understanding includes an awareness that life involves many contexts, such as family, friends, work and leisure. It also involves an awareness that these contexts need to be viewed from a broad temporal perspective that includes the past, present and future.

4. *An awareness of the relativism of values and priorities.* This includes recognizing that values and priorities differ across people and societies.

5. *The ability to recognize and manage uncertainty.* This ability stems from an awareness that the future cannot be fully known and that there are inherent limitations in the ways humans gather and process information.

You can readily see from this discussion that expertise and wisdom, though they may partly intersect, are not the same. For example, being an expert does not guarantee the breadth of qualities and knowledge that comprise wisdom. True wisdom, say Baltes and Staudinger, is hard to achieve, for it combines extraordinary scope with 'a truly superior level of knowledge, judgement, and advice . . . used for the good or well-being of oneself and that of others' (2000, p. 123).

MENTAL IMAGERY

Having spent most of this chapter discussing language and the types of thought that primarily involve what we subjectively experience as inner speech, let us turn to another mode of thought: *mental imagery*. A **mental image** is a representation of a stimulus that originates inside your brain, rather than from external sensory input. Night-time dreams are among the most common forms of mental imagery. During daydreaming, people may intentionally create and manipulate mental images to get a break from reality or relieve boredom. Many elite athletes receive psychological training in how to effectively use mental imagery to rehearse skills, and people from all walks of life may use mental imagery to help solve problems. By using mental imagery to conduct experiments in their minds, Sir Isaac Newton and Albert Einstein gained insights that led to the discovery of several laws of physics. In a daydream at age 16:

Einstein imagined himself running alongside a light beam and asked himself the fateful question: what would the light beam look like. Like Newton visualizing throwing a rock until it orbited the earth like the moon, Einstein's attempt to imagine such a light beam would yield deep and surprising results.

(Kaku, 2004, p. 43)

Although people have mental images that subjectively involve sounds, tastes, smells, and so on, visual mental images are the most common and most thoroughly researched. Thus, we focus on them here.

Mental Rotation

Take a look at the objects shown in Figure 9.30. In each pair, are the two objects different, or are they the same object that has simply been rotated to a different orientation? This activity is called a *mental rotation task*. Typically, people rotate one object in their mind's eye until it lines up sufficiently with the other object to permit a same–different judgement. By the way, in pairs (a) and (b) the objects are the same. In pair (c) they are different.

In 1971 the journal *Science* published an experiment by psychologists Roger Shepard and Jacqueline Metzler that helped place the study of mental imagery on the scientific map. At a time when cognitive psychology was still in its infancy and emerging from under the shadow of behaviourism's half-century-long dominance, this elegant experiment demonstrated that mental images could be studied by gathering objective data, rather than by relying exclusively on people's subjective self-reports.

Shepard and Metzler presented each participant in their study with 1,600 pairs of rotated objects, including the objects shown in Figure 9.30. Upon seeing each pair, participants pulled one of two levers to signal whether the two objects were the same or different, and their speed of response was measured. In 800 of the pairs, the objects within the pair were identical and were rotated from each other at an angle of either 0, 20, 40, 60, 80, 100, 120, 140, 160 or 180 degrees. The two objects in pair (a) and pair (b) in Figure 9.30, for example, are rotated 80 degrees from one another. Because the two objects in pair (c) differ from one another, the concept of angle of rotation does not apply.

Subjectively, the participants reported that they were able to mentally rotate the objects as if the objects existed physically in three-dimensional space (i.e., they could rotate the objects vertically, horizontally and from front to back) but that the speed of this mental rotation process was limited. Shepard and Metzler's key finding concerned the pairs in which the two objects were the same. On these trials, the greater the difference in rotation between the two pictured objects, the longer it took participants to reach their decision. Moreover, as Figure 9.30d shows, this relation was linear. Shepard and Metzler (1971) concluded that 'If we can describe this process as some sort of "mental rotation in three-dimensional space,"

Focus 9.20 Why was Shepard and Metzler's mental rotation study important? What did they find?

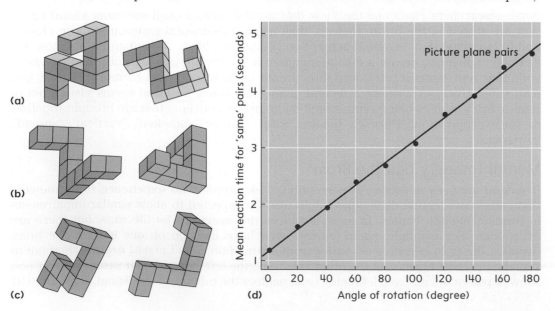

(a)

(b)

(c)

(d)

FIGURE 9.30 Mental rotation.
(a, b, c) These are three of the many pairs of objects used in Shepard and Metzler's (1971) mental rotation study. (d) This graph shows the average number of seconds it took participants to decide that the two objects in each pair were similar, as a function of the initial angle of rotation. Factoring in the time that it took to make a physical response, participants' speed of mental rotation was approximately 60 degrees per second.

then . . . the average rate at which these particular objects can be thus "rotated" is roughly 60° per second' (p. 703).

Are Mental Images Pictures in the Mind?

Many researchers believe that mental images, while not literally pictures in the mind, function in ways analogous to actual visual images and are represented in the brain as a type of perceptual code (Kosslyn, Thompson, & Ganis, 2006). If this is the case, then mental images should have qualities similar to those that occur when we perceive objects and scenes in the real world. For example, if the objects portrayed in Figure 9.30 were real objects, you would be able to physically rotate them in three-dimensional space. Shepard and Metzler's (1971) experiment revealed that mental images likewise can be rotated within mental space.

Mental imagery as perception

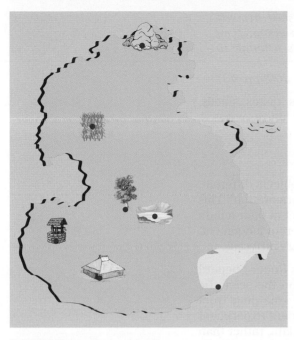

FIGURE 9.31 **Imagine an island.**
This island is similar to one used in Kosslyn, Ball and Reiser's (1978) mental imagery scanning study.

Based on studies by Stephen Kosslyn, a leading researcher in the field of mental imagery, let us consider two other examples that illustrate the perceptual nature of mental imagery. For the first example, take a look at the island shown in Figure 9.31, and notice that it contains seven landmarks (e.g., a hut, lake, hill, beach), each of which is marked by a red dot. Suppose that after giving you time to memorize this map, we ask you to close your eyes and focus on a mental image of the map. Next, we ask you to (1) focus on a particular landmark (say, the beach), (2) scan the map until you come to the hill and (3) press a button (which measures your response time) when you find the hill. In another trial, we might ask you to start at the tree and scan the map until you come to the lake. In total, you will end up taking 21 of these mental trips as you scan once between every possible pair of locations.

In the real world, visually scanning between two objects takes longer when they are farther apart. When Stephen Kosslyn and his colleagues (1978) conducted the actual experiment, they found that the greater the distance between the two locations on the mental image of the map, the longer it took participants to scan and find the second location. This supports the view that mental images involve a spatial representation. Kosslyn also conducted experiments (involving mental images of animals rather than walls) that indicated that the size and level of detail of mental images can be changed in ways that correspond to perceiving actual objects.

Mental imagery as language

Some researchers challenge the view that mental images originate from visual codes that are stored in the brain. Instead, they argue that mental imagery is more closely tied to language than to visual perception (Pylyshyn, 2003). According to this view, for example, when you create a mental image of a brick wall, you are not pulling a visual code that represents a brick wall directly out of your long-term memory. Rather, you may subjectively experience a mental image of a brick wall that seems visual, but in reality 'brick wall' is being represented by linguistic concepts that are brought together to form propositions ('brick', 'bonded with', 'mortar', 'stacked', 'vertical', 'spread', 'horizontal').

Mental Imagery and the Brain

If mental imagery is rooted in perception, then people who experience brain damage that causes perceptual difficulties might also be expected to show similar impairments in forming mental images. In most instances this seems to be the case, but there are exceptions. For example, some patients who have damage on one side of the brain (usually, the right hemisphere) suffer from a condition called *visual neglect*: they fail to visually perceive objects on the other side (e.g., the left side) of their visual field. If you showed patients who have left-side visual neglect the picture of the island in Figure 9.31

Focus 9.21 Does research, including brain research, support the view that mental images are perceptual in nature? Explain.

and asked them to draw a copy, they would draw the right side of the island but fail to copy the left side. However, in some cases, if you were to ask the patients to draw the picture from memory (by calling up a mental image of the picture of the island) rather than to copy it (which relies on direct visual perception), they would be able to draw the entire island (Halligan, Fink, Marshall, & Vallar, 2003). Most often, however, damage to brain regions involved in perception also disrupts people's ability to form mental images.

Brain-imaging studies of healthy people reveal that many brain regions that become more active when people perceive actual objects also become more active when people form mental images of those objects (Ganis et al., 2004). Moreover, research found evidence of neurons, which they called *imagery neurons*, that fired in response to a particular stimulus regardless of whether it was visual (a photograph of a fish) or imagined (a mental image of a fish). Altogether, studies of brain functioning suggest that while mental imagery and visual perception do not map onto all of the same neural components, there is a lot of overlap between these two processes (Slotnick, Thompson, & Kosslyn, 2005).

Recent research into the brain areas involved in mental imagery has revealed some interesting findings. For instance, Sack, Camprodon, Pascual-Leone and Goebel (2005) asked participants to imagine two clock faces showing different times and they were required to state which time formed the larger angle between the two hands on the clock faces. Sack et al. used transcranial magnetic stimulation which is used to disrupt cortical activity during the completion of a task, thereby helping to investigate the contribution of each hemisphere to the completion of this task. Sack et al. reported that the left parietal lobe was primarily involved in the generation of the image whereas the right parietal lobe was involved in the comparison of the images. They also reported that the right hemisphere was able to compensate and complete the tasks usually performed by the left hemisphere.

METACOGNITION: KNOWING YOUR OWN COGNITIVE ABILITIES

Have you ever had a friend or classmate say to you after an examination, 'I don't understand why I got this question wrong?' or 'I don't understand how I got such a low grade? I thought I really knew this stuff'. Have you ever felt that way?

Recognizing What You Do and Do Not Know

To cognitive psychologists, the term **metacognition** refers to your awareness and understanding of your own cognitive abilities. For example, *comprehension* has to do with understanding something, such as a concept that you just read about. You may *think* you understand the concept, but in actuality you may or may not understand it. Metacognition has to do with truly knowing whether you do or do not understand the concept. The particular component of metacognition that we are discussing in this case is *metacomprehension*. In other words, people who display good metacomprehension are accurate in judging what they do or do not know, whereas people with poor metacomprehension have difficulty judging what they actually do and do not understand. They may typically think they understand things that, in fact, they do not, or they may often think they do not understand things that they actually do.

Metacomprehension is only one aspect of metacognition. Another component, called *metamemory*, represents your awareness and knowledge of your memory capabilities. For example, suppose that you try to memorize a list of definitions or facts. Your ability to accurately judge how well you will be able to remember those items for an upcoming test reflects one aspect of metamemory. (Note that being able to remember material, as in the case of rote memorization, does not necessarily mean that you understand it.) Your awareness of how to use various memory strategies (e.g., mnemonic devices) to improve your memory also constitutes part of your metamemory. In this discussion, however, we focus on metacomprehension.

metacognition your awareness and understanding of your own cognitive abilities

Focus 9.22 What is metacognition? Identify two types of metacognition, and provide examples.

As a student, your ability to effectively monitor what you do and do not know is an important ingredient in studying efficiently (Koriat & Bjork, 2005; Son & Metcalfe, 2000). Some students excel at this. Unfortunately, many studies have found that when it comes to reading text material, students, overall, are only mildly to moderately accurate in judging how well they understand what they are reading. Dunlosky and Rawson (2012) clearly demonstrated a link between the accuracy of students' judgements about what they do and do not know and retention accuracy. They argued that overconfidence, feeling that you know something that you do not, leads to a termination of practice and hence less retention. You should be particularly interested in this study as they used definitions of psychological terms as the test material for this study! Our 'Research close-up' examines one technique for improving students' metacomprehension.

 ## Research close-up

'WHY DID I GET THAT WRONG?' IMPROVING COLLEGE STUDENTS' AWARENESS OF WHETHER THEY UNDERSTAND TEXT MATERIAL

Source: K. W. Thiede and M. C. M. Anderson (2003). Summarizing can improve metacomprehension accuracy. *Contemporary Educational Psychology*, *28*, 129–60.

INTRODUCTION

According to psychologists Keith Thiede and Mary Anderson, this study is the first to examine whether students' metacomprehension for text material can be enhanced by requiring them to write summaries of that material. Based on other metacognition research, Thiede and Anderson hypothesized that students who write delayed summaries of passages of text material will show better metacomprehension than students who write immediate summaries or no summaries. Presumably, the task of writing delayed rather than immediate summaries taps more powerfully into students' long-term memory and provides them with a better opportunity to assess whether they truly understand what they have read.

METHOD

Ethnically diverse samples of 75 and 90 college students taking introductory psychology participated, respectively, in Experiment 1 and Experiment 2. The students in each experiment read six passages of text material, with each passage focusing on a different topic (e.g., black holes, global warming, genetics, intelligence, Norse settlements). In Experiment 1 the passages were each about 220 words long, whereas in Experiment 2 they were much longer (1,100 to 1,600 words) and more similar in style to material presented in textbooks.

Research design (Experiments 1 and 2)		
Question: Will writing summaries of text material that they have read improve college students' accuracy in judging how well they understand that material?		
Type of study: Experiment		

Independent variable	**Dependent variables**
Writing summaries of text material (random assignment to no-summary, immediate-summary or delayed-summary groups)	• Actual comprehension of material • Students' perceptions of how well they comprehend the material • Metacomprehension accuracy (degree of association between actual and perceived comprehension)

Students in each experiment were randomly assigned to one of three groups. In the no-summary group (control group), they read all six passages and then rated their comprehension of each passage ('How well do you think you understood the passage') on a scale ranging from 1 ('very poorly') to 7 ('very well'). In the immediate-summary group, students summarized each passage immediately after they read it and then, after finishing all six summaries, rated their comprehension of each one. In the delayed-summary group, students read all six passages before summarizing each one and then rating their comprehension of each passage.

All students, after rating their comprehension, took a multiple-choice comprehension test for each passage that included both factual and conceptual questions. These tests enabled Thiede and Anderson to measure how well students' *beliefs* about their comprehension (measured by the rating scales) correlated with their actual comprehension (measured by their test scores).

RESULTS

In all three conditions, there was a positive correlation between students' comprehension ratings and comprehension scores, but in the no-summary and immediate-summary groups, this correlation was only weak to moderate. The critical finding was that in both experiments, students in the

delayed-summary group were much more accurate than the other students in judging whether they knew or did not know the material. In other words, the correlation between their comprehension ratings and their comprehension test scores was much stronger (Figure 9.32).

The data also revealed that, overall, the three groups did not differ in their comprehension ratings or in their test performance. In other words, students in the delayed-summary group did not feel that they knew the material better, and in fact they did not. Rather, summarizing the passages after a time delay helped them become more accurate in distinguishing the material they did know from the material they did not.

DISCUSSION

Both experiments supported the researchers' hypothesis: students' ability to accurately determine how well they understood passages of text improved greatly when they summarized that material after a time delay. Because the delayed-summary group did not rate their comprehension higher or perform better on the comprehension tests than the other groups, we want to take special care in making sure that you do *not* reach the wrong conclusion of 'So what if metacomprehension improved; the students didn't do better on the test'.

Realize that the students in this experiment were not allowed to go back and study the text passages again before taking the comprehension tests. Therefore, students in the delayed-summary group did not have the opportunity to act on their superior metacognitive knowledge (i.e., to revise the material that they accurately felt they did not know). But in real-world test situations, students who are better at recognizing what they know and do not know can indeed put that information to efficient use in the days and hours before a test. They can allocate more time to studying the material they have found difficult and less time to the material that they already understand. Students with poor metacomprehension may end up allocating their study time less efficiently, ignoring material that they think they know but truly do not. Indeed, Thiede and Anderson found in Experiment 2 that when all the students were asked to identify which passages of text, hypothetically, they would select to restudy for an examination, students in the delayed-summary group were the most likely to accurately select the passages that they had learned least well.

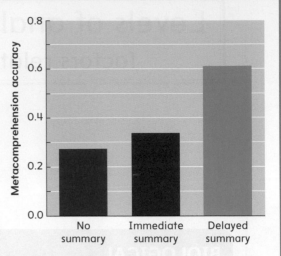

FIGURE 9.32 Writing summaries helps us recognize what we do and do not know.

Students who wrote delayed summaries of text material showed far better metacomprehension than did students who wrote immediate summaries or no summaries.

Further Advice on Improving Metacomprehension

In **Chapter 1**'s 'Applying psychological science' feature we discussed several study strategies that can enhance your academic performance. As a student, you also want to be able to accurately assess your understanding of how well you know the material *before* it is time to take a test. One way to do this is to take advantage of practice tests, such as those found in study guides. Trying to memorize specific questions and answers from practice tests – as some students do – will do little to help you assess your broader understanding of the material. Instead, seriously study the material first and then try to answer the questions. For each question, rate how confident you are that your answer is right; this may help you develop a better sense of whether your metacomprehension is good.

The 'Research close-up' study found that writing delayed summaries improved students' metacomprehension, and other research finds that writing summaries boosts actual comprehension of text material (Winne & Hadwin, 1998). Many college textbooks provide preview questions or review questions in each chapter. In this textbook there are focus questions in the margins of each chapter. Use these focus, preview or review questions as the basis for writing brief summaries of the text. It is not magic. It takes time and effort. But in writing these summaries, if you find yourself struggling to remember the material or if you have a hard time articulating the main concepts, then you have gained the knowledge that you need to restudy this material or seek assistance in trying to understand it.

In closing this chapter, the 'Levels of analysis' provides a summary of some of the aspects of thinking that we have discussed.

Focus 9.23 Based on the 'Research close-up' and other research, describe some ways to enhance metacomprehension.

 Chapter I, Page 31

Levels of analysis
factors related to human thought

PSYCHOLOGICAL
- Concepts and propositions that underlie propositional thought
- Deductive/inductive reasoning and factors such as belief bias that impair reasoning
- Framing a problem and the use of problem-solving schemas
- Heuristics, confirmation bias and overconfidence, which can influence decision making and problem-solving
- Schemas that underlie the acquisition of knowledge, expertise and wisdom
- Use of mental imagery to plan and to solve problems
- Metacognitive abilities, such as metacomprehension and metamemory

BIOLOGICAL
- Patterns of neural activity, integrated across brain areas, that underlie our conscious thoughts at any particular moment
- Development of expertise, which alters brain functioning in ways that improve processing efficiency
- Brain damage that disrupts visual perception and, often, visual imagery
- General correspondence of brain activation during imagery and visual perception

ENVIRONMENTAL
- Problems requiring solution presented by the environment
- Cultural and educational experiences that teach problem-solving and foster expertise and wisdom
- Presence of irrelevant stimuli that can impair reasoning
- Resemblance of stimuli to prototypes, prompting use or misuse of representativeness heuristic
- Dramatic and vivid events that can increase likelihood of future similar events through availability heuristic

Thinking

In review

- At the level of the brain, thoughts are patterns of neural activity. At the level of the mind, thoughts are propositional, imaginal or motoric mental representations.

- Concepts are mental categories, or classes, that share certain characteristics. Many concepts are based on prototypes, the most typical and familiar members of a class. How much something resembles the prototype determines whether the concept is applied to it. Propositional thought involves the use of concepts in the form of statements.

- In deductive reasoning, we reason from general principles to a conclusion about a specific case. Inductive reasoning involves reasoning from a set of specific facts or observations to a general principle. Deduction is the strongest and most valid form of reasoning because the conclusion cannot be false if the premises are true. Inductive reasoning cannot yield certainty.

- Unsuccessful deductive reasoning can result from (1) failure to select relevant information, (2) failure to apply the appropriate deductive reasoning rules, particularly in novel situations, (3) belief bias, the tendency to abandon logical rules in favour of personal beliefs, and (4) emotional reactions and framing effects.

- Problem-solving proceeds through several steps: (1) understanding the nature of the problem, (2) establishing initial hypotheses or potential solutions, (3) testing the solutions against existing evidence, and (4) evaluating the results of these tests.

- People use several types of problem-solving schemas. Algorithms are formulas or procedures that guarantee correct solutions. Heuristics are general strategies that may or may not provide correct solutions. Means–ends analysis is a common heuristic. The representativeness heuristic is the tendency to judge evidence according to whether it is consistent with an existing concept or schema. The availability heuristic is the tendency to base conclusions and probability judgements on what is readily available in memory.

- Humans exhibit confirmation bias, a tendency to look for facts to support hypotheses rather than to disprove them. They also suffer from overconfidence, a tendency to overestimate their knowledge, beliefs and decisions.

- In some situations, divergent thinking is needed for generating novel ideas or variations on ideas. Functional fixedness can blind us to new ways of using an object or procedure, thereby interfering with creative problem-solving. Sometimes, a period of incubation permits problem-solving to proceed on a subconscious level while giving the problem solver psychological distance from the problem.

- Knowledge acquisition can be viewed as a process of building schemas, which are mental frameworks. Scripts, which are one type of schema, provide a framework for understanding sequences of events that usually unfold in a regular, almost standardized order.

- Experts rely heavily on schemas that they have developed from experience. Compared to novices, experts have more schemas to guide problem-solving in their field and are much better at recognizing when each schema should be applied. Schemas also enable experts to take greater advantage of long-term memory.

- Wisdom represents a system of knowledge about the meaning and conduct of life. According to one model, wisdom has five major components: rich factual knowledge, rich procedural knowledge, an understanding of lifespan contexts, an awareness of the relativism of values and priorities, and the ability to recognize and manage uncertainty.

- A mental image is a representation of a stimulus that originates inside the brain, rather than from external sensory input. The objective, quantifiable study of mental imagery received a huge boost from research examining people's ability to mentally rotate objects.

- Mental images of objects seem to have properties that are analogous to the properties of actual objects (e.g., you can rotate them, visually scan them). Thus one viewpoint holds that mental images are basically perceptual in nature. A second viewpoint proposes that mental images actually are based on language. Overall, brain research offers more support to the imagery-as-perception view.

Answers to Problems in the Text

Figure 9.20

Manchester and Leeds are 50 miles apart. The trains are travelling at the same speed (25 mph). Hence they will meet at the halfway point, which is 25 miles, after 1 hour of travel time. Since the crow is flying at 60 mph, it will have flown a total of 60 miles when the trains meet.

Figure 9.23

Sequence of moves: A to 3, B to 2, A to 2, C to 3, A to 1, B to 3, A to 3.

Figure 9.26

Here are two solutions to the nine-dot problem. Both require you to think outside the box, literally.

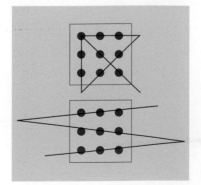

Figure 9.27

Solution to the candlestick problem:

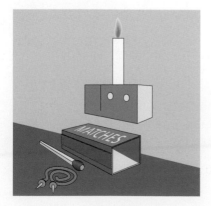

Recommended Reading

CLASSIC

Pinker, S. (1994). *The Language Instinct*. New York: Morrow.

CONTEMPORARY

Harley, T.A. (2012). *The Psychology of Language* (4th ed.). Hove: Psychology Press.

Holyoak, K.J. & Morrison, R.G. (2012). *The Oxford handbook of Thinking and Reasoning*. Oxford: Oxford University Press.

Johnson-Laird, P.N. (2006). *How we Reason*. Oxford University Press.

Kahneman, D. (2012). *Thinking fast and slow*. London: Penguin.

Manktelow, K.I. (2012) *Thinking and Reasoning: Psychological Perspectives on Reason, Judgment and Decision Making*. Hove: Psychology Press.

Many highly intelligent people are poor thinkers. Many people of average intelligence are skilled thinkers. The power of a car is separate from the way the car is driven.

Edward De Bono

Intelligence

10

Chapter Outline

INTELLIGENCE IN HISTORICAL PERSPECTIVE

- Sir Francis Galton: quantifying mental ability
- Alfred Binet's mental tests
- Binet's legacy: an intelligence-testing industry emerges

THE NATURE OF INTELLIGENCE

- The psychometric approach: the structure of intellect
- Cognitive process approaches: the nature of intelligent thinking
- Broader conceptions of intelligence: beyond mental competencies

THE MEASUREMENT OF INTELLIGENCE

- Increasing the informational yield from intelligence tests
- Theory-based intelligence tests

- Should we test for aptitude or achievement?
- Psychometric standards for intelligence tests
- Assessing intelligence in non-western cultures

HEREDITY, ENVIRONMENT AND INTELLIGENCE

- Current Topic *Genetics, the environment and intelligence*
- Applying Psychological Science *Early-childhood interventions: a means of boosting intelligence?*

GROUP DIFFERENCES IN INTELLIGENCE

- Sex differences in cognitive abilities
- Beliefs, expectations and cognitive performance
-  Research close-up *Stereotype threat and cognitive performance*

EXTREMES OF INTELLIGENCE

- The intellectually gifted
- A concluding thought

FIGURE 10.1 The skills required to adapt successfully to environmental demands may differ from culture to culture, suggesting to some theorists that what constitutes intelligence may be somewhat culture-specific.

Source: ©iStock.com/ Morgan Lane Studios; ©iStock.com/ Bartosz Hadyniak

> **intelligence** the ability to acquire knowledge, to think and reason effectively, and to deal adaptively with the environment

We know that you highly esteem the kind of learning taught in those colleges. . . . But you, who are wise, must know that different nations have different conceptions of things: and you will not therefore take it amiss, if our ideas of this kind of education happen not to be the same with yours. We have had some experience of it; several of our young people were formerly brought up at the colleges of the Northern provinces; they were instructed in all your sciences; but, when they came back to us, they were bad runners, ignorant of every means of living in the woods, unable to bear either cold or hunger, knew neither how to build a cabin, take a deer, nor kill an enemy, spoke our language imperfectly, were therefore neither fit for hunters, warriors, nor counsellors; they were totally good for nothing. . . .

> *We are, however not the less obligated by your kind offer, though we decline accepting it; and to show our grateful sense of it, if the gentlemen of Virginia will send us a dozen of their sons, we will take care of their education, instruct them in all we know, and make men of them.*
>
> *(A Native American leader quoted in Franklin, 1784)*

This response to a well-intentioned offer by American colonists to provide Native American boys with access to European educational opportunities reminds us that people have different conceptions of what it means to be clever. In Western cultures, being clever is typically thought of as having good mental skills that are instrumental to succeeding in school and in higher-level jobs and occupations. As we shall see, people with good mental skills do indeed do better in school and in jobs in our culture. But if we view intelligence in broader perspective as the ability to respond adaptively to the demands of a particular environment, we can understand why the Native American leader was less impressed with the products of Anglo-Saxon education than were the colonists. It is important to remember, then, that intelligence is not something that has concrete existence; it is, instead, a socially constructed concept (Sternberg, 2004; Figure 10.1).

In previous chapters, we have explored general principles of human learning, memory, thinking, reasoning and problem-solving. In all these areas we have seen that people differ widely in how effectively they learn, remember, think and behave. Is it therefore the case that some people are generally more intelligent than others? If so, can we measure these differences and use the measures to predict success and failure in real-life settings? What is the nature of intelligence, and what factors account for the differences we observe in people's cognitive, emotional and behavioural skills? Attempts to answer these questions have influenced our culture enormously. Today, there exists a multi-billion-dollar intelligence-testing industry. Increasing levels of testing in schools demand that we assess the aptitudes and learning outcomes of children in a search for educational accountability. You yourself have undoubtedly taken mental ability tests for educational or occupational reasons. In fact, your results in one or more examinations may have played an important role in your admission to university.

As we shall see, however, even after more than a century of research and theory development, there are still sharp disagreements about what intelligence is. In our discussion, we use the following definition, which accommodates most viewpoints: **intelligence** is the ability to acquire knowledge, to think and reason effectively, and to deal adaptively with the environment.

INTELLIGENCE IN HISTORICAL PERSPECTIVE

Historically, two scientists with entirely different agendas played seminal roles in the study and measurement of mental skills. The contributions of Sir Francis Galton and Alfred Binet set the stage for later attempts to measure intelligence and discover its causes.

SIR FRANCIS GALTON: QUANTIFYING MENTAL ABILITY

Sir Francis Galton was a cousin of Charles Darwin and was strongly influenced by Darwin's theory of evolution. In his book, *Hereditary Genius* (1869), Galton showed through the

study of family trees that eminence and genius seemed to occur within certain families. No intellectual slouch himself, young Francis wrote a childhood letter to his sister that contained the following: 'My dear Adele, I am 4 years old, and I can read any English book. I can say all of the Latin substantives and adjectives and active verbs besides 52 lines of Latin poetry.'

Galton's research convinced him that eminent people had 'inherited mental constitutions' that made them more fit for thinking than their less successful counterparts. Exhibiting his own belief bias, Galton dismissed the fact that the more successful people he studied almost invariably came from privileged environments.

Galton then attempted to demonstrate a biological basis for eminence by showing that people who were more socially and occupationally successful would also perform better on a variety of laboratory tasks thought to measure the 'efficiency of the nervous system'. He developed measures of reaction speed, hand strength and sensory acuity. He even measured the size of people's skulls, believing that skull size reflected brain volume and hence intelligence.

In time, Galton's approach to mental skills measurement fell into disfavour because his measures of nervous-system efficiency proved unrelated to socially relevant measures of mental ability, such as academic and occupational success. Nonetheless, Galton's work created an interest in the measurement of mental abilities, setting the stage for the pioneering work of Alfred Binet.

FIGURE 10.2 Alfred Binet developed the first intelligence test to assess the mental skills of French schoolchildren. His test launched the modern intelligence-testing movement.

Source: © Everett Collection Historical/Alamy

ALFRED BINET'S MENTAL TESTS

The modern intelligence-testing movement began at the turn of the twentieth century, when the French psychologist Alfred Binet was commissioned by France's Ministry of Public Education to develop the test that was to become the forerunner of all modern intelligence tests (Figure 10.2). Unlike Galton, with whom he had trained, Binet was interested in solving a practical problem rather than supporting a theory. Certain children seemed unable to benefit from normal public schooling. Educators wanted an objective way to identify these children as early as possible so that some form of special education could be arranged for them.

In developing his tests, Binet made two assumptions about intelligence: first, mental abilities develop with age; second, the rate at which people gain mental competence is a characteristic of the person and is fairly constant over time. In other words, a child who is less competent than expected at age 5 should also be lagging at age 10.

To develop a measure of mental skills, Binet asked experienced teachers what sorts of problems children could solve at ages 3, 4, 5, and so on, up through the school years. He then used their answers to develop a standardized interview in which an adult examiner posed a series of questions to a child to determine whether the child was performing at the correct mental level for his or her age (Table 10.1). The result of the testing was a score called the *mental age*. For instance, if an 8-year-old child could solve problems at the level of the average 10-year-old, the child would be said to have a mental age of 10. For the French school system, the practical implication was that educational attainment could be enhanced if placement in school were based at least in part on the child's mental age. An 8-year-old child with a mental age of 6 could hardly be expected to cope with the academic demands of a normal classroom for 8-year-olds.

The concept of mental age was subsequently expanded by the German psychologist William Stern to provide a relative score – a common yardstick of intellectual attainment – for people of different chronological ages. Stern's **intelligence quotient (IQ)** was the ratio of mental age to chronological age, multiplied by 100: IQ = (mental age/chronological age) × 100. Thus a child who was performing at exactly his or her age level would have an IQ of 100. In our previous example, the child with a mental age of 10 and a chronological age of 8 would have an IQ of (10/8 × 100 =125). A 16-year-old with a mental age of 20 would also have an IQ of 125, so the two would be comparable in intelligence even though their ages differed.

intelligence quotient (IQ) the ratio of mental age to chronological age, multiplied by 100: IQ = (mental age/chronological age) × 100

Focus 10.1 How did Galton and Binet differ in their approaches to measuring mental abilities?

TABLE 10.1 Sample problems from the stanford–binet intelligence test that should be answered correctly at particular ages

Age 3 – Child should be able to:	Point to objects that serve various functions such as 'goes on your feet'
	Name pictures of objects such as *chair, flag*
	Repeat a list of two words or digits such as *car, dog*
Age 4 – Child should be able to:	Discriminate visual forms such as squares, circles and triangles
	Define words such as *ball* and *bat*
	Repeat 10-word sentences
	Count up to four objects
	Solve problems such as 'In daytime it is light; at night it is . . .'
Age 6 – Child should be able to:	State the differences between similar items such as *bird* and *dog*
	Count up to nine blocks
	Solve analogies such as 'An inch is short; a mile is . . .'
Age 9 – Child should be able to:	Solve verbal problems such as 'Tell me a number that rhymes with tree'
	Solve simple arithmetic problems such as 'If I buy 4 cents' worth of candy and give the storekeeper 10 cents, how much money will I get back?'
	Repeat four digits in reverse order
Age 12 – Child should be able to:	Define words such as *muzzle*
	Repeat five digits in reverse order
	Solve verbal absurdities such as 'Bill's feet are so big he has to pull his trousers over his head. What is foolish about that?'

Source: Terman and Merrill, 1972.

FIGURE 10.3 Lewis Terman imported the intelligence test developed by Binet to the USA and revised it as the Stanford–Binet Scale. The Stanford–Binet became the standard for future individually administered intelligence tests and is still used today.

Source: Courtesy of the Stanford University Archives/Stanford University

Focus 10.2 Why do today's intelligence tests no longer use the concept of mental age? How is IQ now defined?

Today's tests no longer use the concept of mental age. Although the concept works pretty well for children, many of the basic skills measured by intelligence tests are acquired by about age 16 through normal life experiences and schooling, so that Stern's quotient is less useful for adults. Moreover, some intellectual skills show an actual decline at advanced ages. If we applied Stern's definition of IQ to a 20-year-old who performed at the typical level of an 80-year-old, we would have to say that the 20-year-old's IQ was 400! To deal with these problems, today's intelligence tests provide an 'IQ' score that is not a quotient at all. Instead, it is based on a person's performance relative to the scores of other people the same age, with a score of 100 corresponding to the average performance of that age group.

BINET'S LEGACY: AN INTELLIGENCE-TESTING INDUSTRY EMERGES

Lewis Terman (Figure 10.3), a professor at Stanford University, was intrigued by Binet's work. He revised Binet's test for use in the USA, translating it into English and rewriting some of its items to improve their relevance to American culture. Terman's revised test became known as the *Stanford–Binet*. By the mid-1920s, it had become widely accepted in North America as the gold standard for measuring mental aptitude. The Stanford–Binet contained mostly verbal items, and it yielded a single IQ score.

At about the time that the Stanford–Binet test was introduced in 1916, the USA entered the First World War. One of Terman's students at Stanford, Arthur Otis, had been working on a group-administered test of intellectual ability. This test became the prototype for the *Army Alpha*, a verbally oriented test that was used to screen large numbers of US Army recruits for intellectual fitness. Because some recruits were unable to read, a non-verbal instrument using mazes, picture completion problems and digit-symbol tasks was also developed and given the name *Army Beta*. Before the war's end, more than 1.7 million men had been screened for intelligence using these tests.

Inspired by the success of the Army Alpha and Army Beta for measuring the intelligence of large numbers of people in a group setting, educators clamoured for similar instruments to test groups of children. New group tests of intelligence, such as the Lorge–Thorndike

Intelligence Test and the Otis–Lennon School Ability Test, soon appeared and became an important part of educational reform and policy. Many schools use these or similar tests (e.g., Cognitive Abilities Test, Thorndike, Hagen, & France, 1986) routinely, and you are likely to have taken one or more of them during your earlier school years.

Two decades after Terman introduced the American version of Binet's test, psychologist David Wechsler developed a major competitor to the Stanford–Binet. Wechsler believed that the Stanford–Binet relied too much on verbal skills. He thought that intelligence should be measured as a group of distinct but related verbal *and* non-verbal abilities. He therefore developed intelligence tests for adults and for children that measured both verbal and non-verbal intellectual skills. In 1939 the Wechsler-Bellevue Scale appeared, followed by the Wechsler Adult Intelligence Scale (WAIS) in 1955 along with a children's version of the scale (WISC) and the Wechsler Pre-school and Primary Scale of Intelligence (WPPSI) in 1967. The Wechsler scales have undergone several revisions. Today, the Wechsler tests (WAIS-III and WISC-IV) are the most popular individually administered intelligence tests (Mackintosh, 1998). The latest version of the Wechsler test, the WAIS-IV, was released in 2008 and has updated normative data and revised measures of working memory and fluid reasoning designed to reflect developments in our understanding of intelligence. Following Wechsler's lead, the Stanford–Binet has also been revised to measure a wider range of mental abilities. Later in the chapter, we take a closer look at the Wechsler tests, as well as other measures that assess various classes of mental skills.

Intelligence has long been a major focus of psychological research, much of which has been inspired by questions that, even after a century of research, continue to evoke disagreement and controversy (Bartholomew, 2005). Should we regard intelligence as a single aptitude or as many specific abilities? Is intelligence an innate mental capacity, or is it a product of our upbringing? What kinds of brain processes underlie mental skills? Are there actually multiple intelligences, including some that may have little to do with mental skills? These and other questions have inspired a fascinating odyssey of scientific discovery. We begin with the most basic question of all: just what is this attribute we call *intelligence*?

Focus 10.3 What was Wechsler's concept of intelligence? How do the Wechsler scales reflect this concept?

 In review

- Intelligence is the ability to acquire knowledge, to think and reason effectively, and to deal adaptively with the environment. Because cultural environments differ in the skills most important for adaptation, different cultures may consider intelligence in different ways. This is an important issue in the assessment and definition of intelligence.

- Galton's studies of hereditary genius and Binet's methods for measuring differences in children's mental abilities were important historical milestones in the study of intelligence.

THE NATURE OF INTELLIGENCE

Psychologists have used two major approaches in the study of intelligence (Sternberg, Lautrey, Lubart, 2003). The *psychometric approach* attempts to map the structure of intellect and to discover the kinds of mental competencies that underlie test performance. The *cognitive processes approach* studies the specific thought processes that underlie those mental competencies.

THE PSYCHOMETRIC APPROACH: THE STRUCTURE OF INTELLECT

Psychometrics is the statistical study of psychological tests. The psychometric approach to intelligence tries to identify and measure the abilities that underlie individual differences in performance; in essence, it tries to provide a measurement-based map of the mind.

psychometrics the statistical study of psychological tests

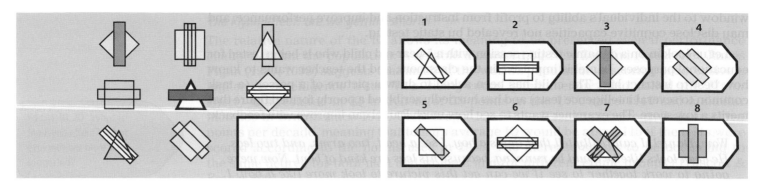

FIGURE 10.13 Culture-fair measurement?

This non-verbal measure tests fluid-intelligence ability, requiring subjects to perceive relationships and decipher the rules underlying the pattern of drawings in the rows and columns of the upper figure and then to select the figure that is the missing entry from the eight alternatives below. (The answer appears on page 442.)

Source: Carpenter, Just and Shell, 1990.

Focus 10.22 How is intelligence assessed in non-Western cultures?

matrices, which are, somewhat obviously, printed on coloured paper and designed to be more stimulating for younger children of ages 5–11, along with those who may have limited academic ability for some reason. Finally, the advanced progressive matrices are particularly challenging versions of the tests and are used by some of the high-IQ societies around the world as part of their admissions process!

A second and more challenging approach is to create measures that are tailored to the kinds of knowledge and skills that are valued in the particular culture. Such tests may measure how smart an individual is in terms of the practical skills and adaptive behaviours within that culture. Of course this requires the acceptance of the idea that there is such a concept as intelligence that exists independent of training of any kind, which is an idea not necessarily accepted by all. Scores may be unrelated or even negatively correlated with other measures of intelligence, yet they may predict successful functioning within that culture (Sternberg, 2004). If intelligence is defined as the ability to engage in culture-specific adaptive behaviour, then who is to say that the culture-specific measure is not a valid measure of intelligence in that context?

In review

- Most modern intelligence tests, such as the Wechsler scales, measure an array of different mental abilities. In addition to a global, or full-scale, IQ, they provide scores for each subtest and summary scores for broader abilities, such as verbal and performance IQs. Some recent tests are derived directly from theories of intelligence. The Kaufman scale provides separate scores for crystallized and fluid intelligence, and Sternberg's STAT measures analytical, practical and creative intelligence.

- Achievement tests measure what has already been learned, whereas aptitude tests are assumed to measure potential for future learning and performance. Most intelligence tests measure combinations of achievement and aptitude, for it is difficult to separate past learning and future learning potential.

- Three important standards for psychological tests are reliability (consistency of measurement over time, within tests, and across scorers), validity (successful measurement of the construct and acceptable relations with relevant criterion measures) and standardization (development of norms and standard testing conditions).

- IQ scores successfully predict a range of academic, occupational and life outcomes, including how long people live. Such findings indicate that intelligence tests are measuring important adaptational skills.

- The Flynn effect refers to the notable rise in intelligence test scores over the past century, possibly due to better living conditions, more schooling or more complex environments.

- In dynamic testing, standard test administration is followed by feedback and suggestions from the examiner and a retaking of the test, thus allowing an assessment of how well the person profits from feedback and how intellectual skills might be coached in the future. Dynamic testing provides information that static testing does not, and retest scores sometimes relate more strongly to criterion measures.

- Intelligence testing in non-Western cultures is a challenge. One approach is to use tests that are not tied to any culture's knowledge base. Another approach is to devise tests of the abilities that are important to adaptation in that culture. These culture-specific abilities may bear little relation to the mental skills assessed by Western intelligence tests.

HEREDITY, ENVIRONMENT AND INTELLIGENCE

Genes and environment both influence intelligence, but they rarely operate independently of one another. The environment can influence how genes express themselves, as when prenatal factors or malnutrition retard gene-directed brain development. Likewise, genetic factors can influence the effects produced by the environment. For example, genetic factors influence which environments people select for themselves, how they respond to the environment and how the environment responds to the person (Plomin & Spinath, 2004; Scarr & McCartney, 1983).

As we saw in **Chapter 3**, intelligence clearly has a strong genetic component, with heritability coefficients ranging between .50 and .70 being reported consistently in both twin and adoption studies (Plomin et al., 2007). This indicates that more than half, and perhaps more than two-thirds, of the within-group variation in IQ is attributable to genetic factors. Overall, the pattern is quite clear: the more genes people have in common, the more similar they tend to be in IQ. In identical twins, the IQ correlation remains at about .80 from age 4 through adulthood. In adulthood, correlations for fraternal twins drop to around .40. Doubling this difference in correlations yields a heritability coefficient of .80 in adulthood, indicating that genetic factors become even more important as we age (Plomin & Spinath, 2004). One reason may be that new genes come on line to affect intelligence as more-advanced cognitive processes emerge during development. Another is that genetic influences snowball during development as people create and select environments that are compatible with their genetic characteristics.

Chapter 3, Page 95

Although genes are important foundations of the *g* factor (Plomin et al., 2007), there clearly is not a single 'intelligence gene'. The diverse abilities measured by intelligence tests are undoubtedly influenced by large numbers of interacting genes, and different combinations seem to underlie specific abilities (Lykken, 2006; Plomin & Spinath, 2004). The ability now to measure the genome directly has led to a search for specific genes and gene combinations that underlie intelligence. This brings us ever closer to an understanding of the neurological basis for human cognition, and a handful of candidate genes associated with intelligence have already been identified (Posthuma & de Geus, 2006).

Focus 10.23 What evidence supports a genetic contribution to intelligence, and how much IQ group variation is accounted for?

Genes are not the whole story, however. As we noted in **Chapter 3** (Table 3.2 on p. 000), IQ correlations for identical twins raised together are slightly higher than those for identical twins raised apart. The same is true for other types of siblings raised together and raised apart. This rules out an entirely genetic explanation. Although one's genotype is an important factor in determining intelligence test scores, environment seems to account for 30–50% of the IQ variation among people. Both shared and unshared environmental factors are involved. Behaviour-genetic studies indicate that between a quarter and a third of the population variability in intelligence can be attributed to shared environmental factors, particularly the family environment (Figure 10.14). The importance of the home environment is also shown in studies of children who are removed from deprived environments and placed in middle- or upper-class adoptive homes. Typically, such children show a gradual increase in IQ, typically in the order of 10 to 12 points (Scarr & Weinberg, 1977; Schiff & Lewontin, 1986). Conversely, when deprived children remain in their impoverished environments, they either show no improvement in IQ, or they actually deteriorate intellectually over time (Serpell, 2000). Scores on general intelligence correlate around .40 with the socio-economic status of the family in which a child is reared (Lubinski, 2004).

Chapter 3, Page 96

Recall also the Flynn effect – the notable IQ increases that have occurred in Western countries during the last century. It is highly unlikely that genetic changes can explain such gains. More likely, they are due to better and longer schooling during the past century, more complex and stimulating environments provided by better-educated parents and by technological advances (even television and video games), and better nutrition (Greenfield, 1998). Although the environment we live in may be more complex, fast-paced and stressful than it was a century ago, it is also more conducive to learning the mental skills that are assessed on measures of intelligence.

FIGURE 10.14 Shared family environment has a significant influence on intelligence, accounting for between a quarter and a third of IQ variation in children.

Source: © Joshua Hodge Photography.

Focus 10.24 How much do family and school environments contribute to intelligence?

As we might expect, educational experiences can have a significant positive impact on intelligence. Many studies have shown that school attendance can raise IQ and lack of attendance can lower scores (Ceci & Williams, 1997). It appears that the opportunity to practise mental skills like those assessed on cognitive tests is important in solidifying mental skills. Research on intelligence has had a strong impact on educational curricula, and much has been learned about what, when, and how to teach. Mayer (2000) claimed that school-related gains in intelligence are most likely to be observed when children are taught specific cognitive skills and problem-solving approaches that underlie success with instruction in *how* to learn. However, Finn et al. (2014) noted that improved test performance is not always related to such improved cognitive skills, and highlighted aspects such as class size and teacher effectiveness. With regard to specific cognitive abilities Gathercole and her colleagues reported relationships between working-memory capacity and attainment in national curriculum test scores (Gathercole, Pickering, Knight & Stegmann, 2004; St. Clair-Thompson & Gathercole, 2006), noting that children with poor working-memory function would benefit from classroom activities that do not overload working memory and being encouraged to develop their use of external memory aids.

Current topic

GENETICS, THE ENVIRONMENT AND INTELLIGENCE

Psychologists have long established that aspects of both our environment *and* our genes influence our intelligence. However, that does not mean that we have understood all there is to know about what influences intelligence. Issues still perplexing psychologists include whether genes and environment play equal roles consistently across one's life. Starting at the very beginning of life, both genes and environment impact on intellectual abilities. For example, a mother's health and lifestyle can adversely influence the development of the foetus (see foetal alcohol syndrome in Chapter 12) and genetic abnormalities can impair mental functioning (e.g., Down's syndrome). Environmental impacts, such as parenting and schooling, continue to influence the

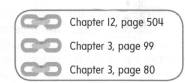

Chapter I2, page 504
Chapter 3, page 99
Chapter 3, page 80

development of intelligence across childhood and into adulthood (see gene–environment interactions in Chapter 3). To discern the continued influence of genetics on intelligence, we turn to studies with twin and biological versus adoptive families (before this, you may wish to briefly refresh your understanding of behavioural genetics covered in Chapter 3).

Across a number of twin studies, the average *g* correlation for monozygotic twins (MZ or identical twins) is .86 (Jensen, 1998), but falls to .60 for dizygotic (DZ or non-identical twins). To put this into perspective, re-administering intelligence tests to the same person yields a correlation for *g* of .90. Thus, compared to DZ twins, MZ twins are considerably closer in *g*, underlining the strong role that genetics play. But does this strong effect remain across the lifespan? Intuitively, we might think that, as we age, the environment would have a greater influence on intelligence compared to genetics as we become exposed to more and more environmental factors. A considerable number of studies have addressed this issue, and results show an intriguing pattern. It is important to note here that although some have presented twin studies as the 'perfect natural experiment' (Martin, Boomsma, & Machin, 1997) this is clearly not the case. Some have argued that twins are not representative of the population as the 'experience' of being a twin is different from that of singletons. However, as Bouchard and McGue (2003) note this is a weak argument at best. Such twin studies have also been criticized on the basis of their methodology, but this too has been addressed recently through the use of more sophisticated designs (Keller, Medland, & Duncan, 2010).

In Plomin et al.'s (1997) study, they conducted intelligence tests on adopted children and both their adoptive and biological parents as well as with non-adopted children and their parents. Findings indicated that, initially, the intelligence of adopted children was most like that of their adoptive parents but that reasonably quickly they come to more closely resemble their biological parents, suggesting an overall stronger genetic influence than an environmental one. A more recent study by Haworth et al. (2010) found similar results, reporting that the influence of genetics on intelligence *increases* rather than decreases over time. Their data indicated that, while genetics made a 41% contribution at age 9, this increased to 66% by the age of 17.

Thus, although substantial evidence indicates that both genes and environmental factors interact to influence intellectual development, it appears that the influence of genetics becomes more prominent over the lifespan. Why might this be? Haworth et al. (2010) proposed an interesting hypothesis. They suggest that genetics and the environment interact in a way that leads individuals to seek out, adapt and even create environments that match and heighten their genetic predispositions for intelligence. So, we can see how psychologists have moved from thinking about the traditional nature–nurture debate to exploring the amount of intellectual development that can be accounted for by each factor and when these factors exert their influence. What remains clear is that the relative contribution of genes and environment and the timing of their influence will remain of interest to psychologists for some considerable time to come. Much of the recent research in this area has attempted to identify the genes that play a prominent role in the development of intelligence. We have seen that this is a complex topic, but nonetheless progress is being made and genetic variants of dopamine receptors have been found to play an important role in cognitive functioning including IQ (Schwartz & Beaver, 2013; Tsai, Yu, Lin, Chen, Chen, & Hong, 2002).

Many children begin their lives in conditions that are not conducive to developing intellectual skills. An important outgrowth of intelligence research is the attempt to intervene early in the lives of such children. Let us examine several of these programmes and what they have accomplished.

> **Focus 10.25** What effects have been shown in early-intervention programmes for disadvantaged children?

 Applying psychological science

EARLY-CHILDHOOD INTERVENTIONS: A MEANS OF BOOSTING INTELLIGENCE?

The belief that early-childhood education can influence the life success of poor children can be found in the eighteenth-century writings of the French social philosopher Jean-Jacques Rousseau. In the USA today, that belief translates into the annual expenditure of more than $10 billion on early-intervention programmes designed to reverse the downward course of cognitive and social development, school dropout rate and joblessness that is so often seen in children from low-income families (Ramey, Ramey, & Lanzi, 1998).

In the 1960s, researchers and educators began to design early-childhood intervention programmes such as Head Start in an attempt to compensate for the limited learning environments of disadvantaged children. Head Start began as a summer programme and gradually increased in scope. But even when it was extended to a full school year, Head Start was only a half-day programme that did not begin until age 4. The results were disappointing. Within two years, Head Start children were performing in school no better than children who had not attended Head Start (McKey et al., 1985).

What had gone wrong? Was the Head Start programme too little, too late? How much might a more intensive programme begun earlier in life help disadvantaged children? These questions inspired several notable intervention programmes, namely, the Abecedarian Program and the High/Scope Perry Pre-school Program.

Participants in the Abecedarian Program were healthy infants born to impoverished families in a southern US community. Many were African-American. The children were randomly assigned to an experimental pre-school programme or to a control group whose families received normal social services. The pre-school group was given an intensive early-childhood educational programme beginning when they were 6 months old and continuing until they began kindergarten at 5 years of age. Within an educational childcare setting, highly trained pre-school personnel exposed the children to many stimulating learning experiences designed to foster the growth of cognitive skills (Figure 10.15). At age 5, the pre-school programme ended, but half of the pre-school children and half of the control children were enrolled in a special home-and-school educational programme during the first three years of school. This experimental design allowed the researchers to test the effects of early versus later intervention.

The long-term effects of the programme have now been evaluated. By the time the children had been in the programme for a year, they tested 18 IQ points higher than the control group. By age 15, the IQ advantage of the children in the pre-school condition had decreased to about five points, but they also had higher scores on standardized tests of reading and mathematics than did the control-group children. Only about half as many had been held back a grade or placed in special education.

A particularly notable IQ effect was found for children in the pre-school condition whose mothers were classed as having a learning disability, having IQs below 70. In this sample, every one of the children who had the early intervention attained an IQ at least 20 points higher than their mother's, with an average difference of 32 IQ points. No such effect was found in the control group (Landesman & Ramey, 1989). A difference of this magnitude is truly remarkable for children of learning disabled parents, one reason being that such parents are unable to provide much in the way of intellectual stimulation for their children. Apparently, the pre-school programme provided the environmental stimulation needed for normal intellectual development to occur.

What of the control-group children who did not attend the pre-school programme but were exposed to the special programme from 5 to 8 years of age? This delayed training had little effect on any of the outcome measures. Also, the later training had almost no added effects on the children who had been in the pre-school programme. It thus appears that early intervention has a much stronger effect than does later training. By the time disadvantaged children are in school, it may be too late to influence their future cognitive development to any great degree (Ramey & Ramey, 1998).

The Abecedarian Program showed positive intervention effects that were still apparent in adolescence. What effect does early intervention have on later adult functioning? Here, we turn to another programme, the High/Scope Perry Preschool Program, carried out with African-American children who lived in an impoverished area of Ypsilanti, Michigan. The participants were considered at high risk for educational and social problems. They

FIGURE 10.15 The Abecedarian Program provided intensive pre-school learning experiences for low-income, high-risk children. Here a trainer in an early-intervention programme teaches number concepts to a pre-school child.

Source: ©iStock.com/ jo unruh

◀ were 2 or 3 years old when they were matched on IQ and family variables and randomly assigned to either an intensive pre-school programme or to a control group that did not receive the programme. The intervention continued for three years.

The two groups of children have been followed up at age 27, and the results are encouraging. Figure 10.16 compares what happened to the two groups in the 22 years after the programme ended. The early-education group had lower crime rates, required less welfare assistance, exhibited better academic performance and progress, and had higher income and home ownership. A cost–benefit analysis showed that the early-intervention programme provided taxpayers with a return of $7.16 for every dollar invested in the programme (Schweinhart & Weikart, 1998).

Does early intervention work? The Abecedarian and High/Scope Perry programmes prove it can provide social, intellectual, educational and psychological dividends if the programme is intensive enough and administered very early in life (Masten & Coatsworth, 1998; Reppucci, Wollard, & Fried, 1999). A more recent early-intervention programme conducted with low-birthweight children, also considered at risk for later cognitive impairment and academic failure, showed significant IQ gains of 7 to 10 points, but only for those children who had attended the programme for at least 400 days between the ages of 2 and 3 (Hill, Brooks-Gunn, & Waldfogel, 2003). We should also note that the positive effects of early-intervention programmes seem to occur only for disadvantaged children, for whom quality programmes offer learning opportunities and support that the children would not experience at home. Such programmes do little for middle- and upper-class children who already have those resources in their homes (Hetherington, 1998).

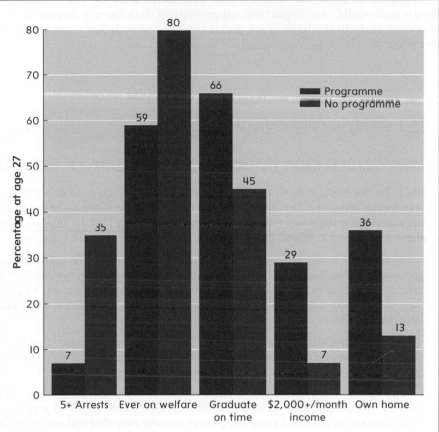

FIGURE 10.16 Effects of early intervention.
This graph shows the differences by age 27 between disadvantaged children who received the High/Scope Perry Pre-school Program and matched control children.

Source: Based on Schweinhart and Weikart, 1998.

Such early-intervention programmes are not limited to the USA. In 1999 the UK government established the Sure Start programme which was established to tackle poverty and disadvantage in 0–3-year-olds. The Sure Start programme has expanded rapidly, from 210 Sure Start Local Programmes (SSLP) in 2001 to 524 in 2004, and by October 2009 there were over 3,100. Sure Start is an area-based programme and is run in targeted areas rather than being targeted at individual families. The aim of this is to reduce the stigma sometimes associated with such early-intervention programmes.

Although the programme is still in the process of expanding there is some evidence to suggest that it is having a positive effect in the communities where it is being implemented that may not be directly related to intelligence. The National Evaluation of Sure Start (NESS, 2004, 2005) reported that in areas where there was an SSLP there was less household chaos reported by mothers of 9-month-old children, and mothers of 36-month-old children were observed as being more accepting of their children. In addition to this the majority of mothers reported that they showed less negative parenting, that there were fewer behavioural problems with their children and that their children showed greater social confidence.

In an evaluation of the effectiveness of SSLPs, Melhuish et al. (2007) reported that those programmes that were assessed as being more effective produced the greatest improvements on child and parenting outcomes, and although the effects were modest they do have implications for the design of future SSLPs. The study found that there were positive benefits associated with an increased sense of empowerment among users and staff as well as better identification of users and strong ethos in the SSLP.

GROUP DIFFERENCES IN INTELLIGENCE

Some of the most controversial issues in the study of intelligence revolve around group differences. There are differences based on social class and differences between males and females. The meaning of these differences – and their political, social and educational implications – has often sparked bitter debate and, at times, discriminatory policies. It has also inspired stereotypes about certain groups and influenced the self-image of group members.

SEX DIFFERENCES IN COGNITIVE ABILITIES

Men and women differ in physical attributes and reproductive function. They also differ in their performance on certain types of intellectual tasks. The gender differences lie not in levels of general intelligence but rather in the patterns of cognitive skills that men and women exhibit. Men, on average, tend to outperform women slightly on certain spatial tasks, such as those shown in Figure 10.17. Men are more accurate in target-directed skills, such as throwing and catching objects, and they tend to perform slightly better on tests of mathematical reasoning. Women, on average, perform better on tests of perceptual speed, verbal fluency and mathematical calculation, and on precise manual tasks requiring fine motor coordination (Collins & Kimura, 1997; Lippa, 2005). Although typically small, these ability differences have been reported quite consistently by researchers (Halpern, 2004; Hines, 2005). Keep in mind, however, that men and women also vary considerably among themselves in all of these skills, and the performance distributions of males and females overlap considerably.

Deary, Thorpe, Wilson, Starr and Whalley (2003) reported a large study as part of the Scottish Mental Health survey of 1932. However, despite nearly 90,000 participants being in the study, they found no difference in mean IQ scores, although they did report that there was greater variability of the scores for males with them being over-represented in both the high and low extremes of the cohort.

Problem-solving tasks favouring women

Women tend to perform better than men on tests of perceptual speed, in which people must rapidly identify matching items – for example, pairing the house on the far left with its twin.

On some tests of ideational fluency, for example those in which people must list objects that are the same colour, and on tests of verbal fluency, for example those in which participants must list words that begin with the same letter, women also outperform men.

L _ _ _	Limp, Livery, Love, Laser, Liquid, Low, Like, Lag, Live, Lug, Light, Lift, Liver, Lime, Leg, Load, Lap, Lucid . . .

Problem-solving tasks favouring men

Men tend to perform better than women on certain spatial tasks. They do well on tests that involve mentally rotating an object or manipulating it in some fashion, such as choosing which of the three objects at the right is the same as the one on the left.

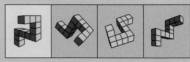

Men are also more accurate than women in target-directed motor skills, such as guiding or intercepting projectiles.

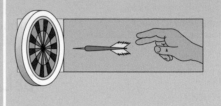

FIGURE 10.17 Male–female cognitive differences.
Among the most consistent gender differences in cognitive abilities reported in the scientific literature are tasks like these.

A more recent English study (Strand, Deary, & Smith, 2006) reported that there was very little difference between males and females on the Cognitive Abilities Test, although there was a small difference on verbal reasoning, but no difference on qualitative tests or on non-verbal reasoning. Again though, they reported that there was greater variability in the males' scores compared with females' scores.

This lack of any large difference in ability is particularly interesting given that in UK public examinations taken at age 16, girls consistently outperform boys. The findings of Strand et al. would suggest that this difference is not simply due to ability. It is also worthy of note here that Strand et al. (2006) stressed the notion that, despite the typical differences in examination performance, the fact that there was little, if any, difference in terms of 'ability' shows it is important that boys are not stereotyped as 'low achievers' (see 'Research close-up' on stereotype threat on page 436).

Psychologists have proposed explanations for these gender differences, citing both biological and environmental factors. The environmental explanations typically focus on the socialization experiences that males and females have as they grow up, especially the kinds of sex-typed activities that boys and girls are steered into (Crawford & Chaffin, 1997). Prior to the early 1980s, for example, boys were far more likely than girls to play sports that involve throwing and catching balls, which might help account for their general superiority in this ability. Evolutionary theorists have also weighed in on the differences, suggesting that sex-role specialization developed in ancestral environments. Men's roles, such as navigating and hunting, favoured the development of the visuospatial abilities that show up in sex-difference research. Women's roles, such as child-rearing and tool-making activities, favoured the development of verbal and manual-precision abilities (Joseph, 2000).

Biological explanations have increasingly focused on the effects of hormones on the developing brain (Halpern & Tan, 2001; Hines, 2005). These influences begin during a critical period shortly after conception, when the sex hormones establish sexual differentiation. The hormonal effects go far beyond reproductive characteristics, however. They also alter brain organization and appear to extend to a variety of behavioural differences between men and women, including aggression and problem-solving approaches (Hines, 2005; Lippa, 2005).

Do hormonal factors also influence cognitive performance later in life? Several studies have shown that fluctuations in women's hormonal levels during the menstrual cycle are related to fluctuations in task performance. When women have high levels of the female hormone oestrogen, they perform better on some of the 'feminine-ability' measures while showing declines in performance on some of the 'male-ability' measures (Kimura, 1992; Moody, 1997). However, a more recent study measured a wide range of sex hormones in men and women before they performed a variety of cognitive tasks. Men and women showed the typically reported differences in cognitive skills, but no relations were found between any of the measured hormones and cognitive performance (Halari et al., 2005). Thus the role of sex hormones in adulthood remains unclear.

> **Focus 10.26** What sex differences exist in cognitive skills? What biological and environmental factors might be involved?

A study conducted by Ostatnikova et al. (2007) of pre-pubescent children between the ages of 6 and 9 measured the levels of testosterone in saliva of three different groups separated by their IQ scores (gifted, average and mentally challenged). They found that there were significantly lower levels of testosterone in boys in both the gifted and intellectually challenged groups compared with those of average intelligence. They found no difference in testosterone levels in girls in the different IQ groups. It appear then that hormone levels are important in terms of IQ but the role of hormonal factors still needs to be fully explored.

BELIEFS, EXPECTATIONS AND COGNITIVE PERFORMANCE

Cognitive abilities are not the only mental determinants of how well people perform on intellectual and academic measures. Beliefs are also very important. Our beliefs about others' capabilities can affect how we respond to them. For example, many studies have shown that if teachers are told that a particular child has hidden potential or, alternatively, intellectual limitations, they increase or decrease the amount of attention and effort expended on that child, thereby influencing the child's development of cognitive skills (Rosenthal, 1985).

> **stereotype threat** they believe that certain behaviours on their part would confirm a negative stereotype in the minds of others

Even more important at times are our own self-beliefs, which tell us who we are and what we can and cannot do. Can self-beliefs and widely held social beliefs about the groups we identify with affect our performance on cognitive tasks? An important line of research, described in the following 'Research close-up', suggests that stereotypes about the capabilities of minorities and women may indeed affect their performance.

 Research close-up

STEREOTYPE THREAT AND COGNITIVE PERFORMANCE

Source: C. M. Steele (1997). A threat in the air: How stereotypes shape intellectual identity and performance. *American Psychologist, 52,* 613–629.

INTRODUCTION

Our self-concept is based on numerous experiences that convey to us who we are, how valued we are and what we are capable of achieving in our lives. Some of this information comes from observing the consequences of our own behaviour. But our self-concept can also be influenced by our membership of racial and gender groups. If certain stereotypes are widely associated with these groups, we may incorporate them into our self-concept. Once accepted, these self-beliefs may push us to behave in a way that is consistent with our self-concept. But even if not incorporated into the self, group members can experience **stereotype threat** if they believe that certain behaviours on their part would confirm a negative stereotype

▶

in the minds of others. Claude Steele believes that stereotype threat evokes anxiety and undermines performance. To test this hypothesis, Steele and his co-workers assessed the academic-performance effects of evoking two widely held stereotypes: (1) that women have less mathematical ability than do men, and (2) that African-Americans have less intellectual ability than do white Americans.

METHOD

Two studies were conducted with students at Stanford University (Spencer, Steele, & Quinn, 1999; Steele & Aronson, 1995). In the first, men and women who were good at mathematics were given a difficult examination whose items were taken from the advanced mathematics test of the Graduate Record Examination (GRE). Participants were randomly assigned to one of two experimental conditions designed to either activate the gender stereotype or not. Participants in the stereotype-relevant condition were told that the test generally showed sex differences (expected to activate the stereotype of women as being inferior to men in mathematics). In the other condition, the students were told that scores on the test showed no sex differences. The dependent variable was the students' scores on the mathematics problems.

In the second study, African-American and white American students were tested on the most difficult items from the GRE verbal test. Again, there were two experimental conditions, this time varying the racial relevance of the test. In one condition, the students were told that the test was a measure of intelligence (expected to activate the stereotype of African-Americans as being less intelligent than white Americans). In the other condition, the students were told that the items were part of a laboratory task that was unrelated to general intellectual ability.

Research design

Question: Can stereotype threat impair cognitive performance?
Type of study: Experiment

Independent variables	**Dependent variables**
Experimental manipulation: Experimenter's description of the maths and verbal tasks → Participant groups: Males and females African-American, Whites	Measures of task performance by males vs females and African-Americans vs Whites in the threat vs non-threat experimental conditions

RESULTS

The results of the two experiments, shown in Figure 10.18, were strikingly similar. In the first (Figure 10.18a), women and men performed at an equivalent level on the mathematics problems when they were told there were no sex differences on the test. However, the picture changed dramatically when the task was made relevant to the gender stereotype. Women's performance dropped, and men's performance increased, producing a marked performance difference between the two sexes. In Figure 10.18b, we see a similar pattern of results when the racial stereotype was activated. When the researchers controlled statistically for pre-existing ethnic-group differences in verbal ability by using students' college-entrance SAT scores, the black–white performance difference on the experimental task was far greater if students thought that the task measured intelligence.

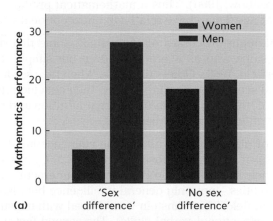

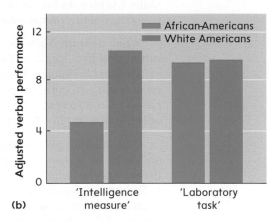

FIGURE 10.18 Effects of stereotype threat on cognitive performance.

(a) The activation of the stereotype that women do less well than men in mathematics was associated with poorer performance by women and enhanced performance by men compared with the control condition, where men and women performed at the same level. (b) Reference to the task as involving intelligence resulted in reduced performance by African-American students.

Source: American Psychological Association/A threat in the air: How stereotypes shape intellectual identity and performance. Steele, Claude M. *American Psychologist,* Vol 52(6), Jun 1997, 613-629

DISCUSSION

This research illustrates how stereotype-based aspects of the self-concept can affect behaviour, in this case, cognitive performance. Steele (1997) believes that in the stereotype-relevant conditions, the threat of doing poorly on the test and being branded as a 'math-deficient woman' or an 'intellectually inferior African-American' aroused anxiety that lowered performance. Other studies have supported this interpretation and also suggest that stereotype threat creates distracting thoughts that impair performance (Bosson, Haymovitz, & Pinel, 2004; Croizet, Despres, Gauzins, Huguet, Leyens, & Meot, 2004).

◄

The results have broad societal implications and might help explain the fact that, over the course of their academic careers, women exhibit less inclination to pursue mathematics, even though, on average, they are slightly superior to men in mathematical calculation skills (Kimura, 1992; Lee, 1998). Later research has shown that the more strongly women are identified with their female sex role, the more susceptible they are to stereotype threat (Schmader, Johns, & Barquissau, 2004). Perhaps stereotype threat also helps account for the fact that African-American children become progressively less identified with, and invested in, academics as they progress through school and that many drop out altogether (Major, Spencer, Schmader, Wolfe, & Crocker, 1998). In both cases, the fact that females and minorities confront, and perhaps internalize, the stereotypes about their mental abilities may be an important environmental determinant of their performance.

You should also note that while stereotype threat is frequently cited as an explanation for attainment gaps not all researchers agree. For example, Stoet and Geary (2012) examined a number of articles that reported stereotype threats and found that only around 30% of them replicated the original findings. Consequently, they concluded that while there may be some influence of stereotype threat on performance, its impact was likely to be smaller than is currently believed and that researchers should look elsewhere for other explanations of, and solutions to, the issue of performance gaps.

EXTREMES OF INTELLIGENCE

> **Focus 10.27** How can teachers' expectations and stereotype threat influence academic performance?

Because of the many genetic and environmental influences on intelligence, there are individuals at both ends of the intelligence distribution who have unusual mental abilities. At the upper end are the 'intellectually gifted'; at the low end are those labelled as having 'learning difficulties'.

THE INTELLECTUALLY GIFTED

At the top end of the intelligence bell curve are the intellectually gifted, whose IQs of 130 or higher place them in the top 1% of the population. However, as we might expect from the theories of multiple intelligences, many of these 'gifted' individuals are enormously talented in one area of mental competence but quite average in other domains. Even with IQs over 150, large discrepancies are often found between verbal and spatial-mathematical skills (Achter, Lubinski, & Benbow, 1996). Thus a mathematical prodigy who figures out rules of algebra on his own at age 3 may have relatively unexceptional verbal skills.

What distinguishes the thought processes of the gifted? Some theorists believe that gifted children think in the same way as average children but simply do it much more efficiently (Jackson & Butterfield, 1986). Others disagree. When they see a child capable of memorizing an entire musical score after hearing it once, they conclude that this ability is based on a different quality of thinking that involves great intuition and a passion for the specific domain in which the child excels (Winner, 2000).

Only a small percentage of gifted children attain true eminence in later life. Eminence seems to be a special variety of giftedness. Joseph Renzulli (2002) has studied this rare group, and he believes that their success is a product of three interacting factors. The first is highly developed mental abilities – not only general intelligence but also specific mental abilities related to one's chosen field. Thus Einstein was blessed with unusual mathematical and spatial abilities (but not exceptional verbal skills). The second factor is the ability to engage in creative problem-solving, that is, to come up with novel and unconventional ideas, to judge their potential value, and to apply them to challenging problems (Sternberg & Davidson, 2005). The third factor is motivation and dedication. Eminence involves a great deal of hard work and a determination to attain the highest levels of performance. Studies of eminent scientists, artists, musicians, writers and athletes reveal that they tend to work much harder and to dedicate themselves more strongly to excellence than do their less eminent counterparts (Simonton, 2001). Given that the person has the requisite level of intelligence, these non-intellectual factors become especially important. Many eminent figures, including Sigmund Freud and Charles Darwin, showed no signs of being exceptionally gifted as children, but their motivation and dedication helped them achieve greatness in their professions.

Like children at the low end of the competence continuum, intellectually gifted children often need special educational opportunities. They may become bored in regular classrooms and even drop out of school if they are not sufficiently challenged (Fetterman, 1988). The UK

educational system incorporates a 'Gifted and Talented' programme whereby those children who are identified as gifted (frequently defined as the top 10%) may receive additional support and challenge outside regular classroom sessions.

However, many school systems have de-emphasized programmes for the gifted in the same spirit of egalitarianism that places cognitively challenged children in regular classrooms. Increasingly, parents of gifted children are enrolling their children in special camps and extracurricular programmes to provide the needed intellectual stimulation and exposure to peer groups with common interests and abilities (Winner, 2000).

Focus 10.28 What factors allow gifted people to become eminent?

Learning Disability

A term such as 'learning disability' can, as we will see, cover a range of issues and can be mild or profound; consequently, it can be difficult to agree on a definition. In the UK the Department of Health (DoH) defines 'learning disability' as: *a significantly reduced ability to understand new or complex information, to learn new skills and a reduced ability to cope independently which starts before adulthood with lasting effects on development.*

Although it is difficult to give precise figures on the number of people with learning disabilities the DoH in the UK estimates that there are about 210,000 people with severe and profound learning disabilities. However, the DoH estimates that the occurrence of moderate and mild learning disabilities is around 2.5% or about 1.2 million people in England. The American Psychiatric Association used the criteria outlined in the *Diagnostic and Statistical Manual of Mental Disorders* (2000) to devise a four-level system that classifies learning disabilities as mild, moderate, severe or profound on the basis of IQ scores. Table 10.5 describes these classifications. As you can see, the vast majority are

TABLE 10.5 Adaptive capabilities of cognitively challenged people over the lifespan

Category	Percentage of learning disability population	Characteristics from birth to adulthood		
		Birth through age 5	**Age 6 through age 20**	**Age 21 and older**
Mild: 50–70 IQ	85	Often not noticed as delayed by casual observer but is slower to walk, feed himself or herself and talk than most children	Can acquire practical skills and master reading and arithmetic to a third- to sixth-grade level with special education. Can be guided towards social conformity	Can usually achieve adequate social, vocational, and self-maintenance skills. May need occasional guidance and support when under unusual social or economic stress
Moderate: 35–50 IQ	10	Noticeable delays in motor development, especially in speech. Responds to training in various self-help activities	Can learn simple communication, elementary health and safety habits, and simple manual skills. Does not progress in functional reading or arithmetic	Can perform simple tasks under sheltered conditions, participate in simple recreation, and travel alone in familiar places. Usually incapable of self-maintenance
Severe: 20–35 IQ	4	Marked delay in motor development. Little or no communication skill. May respond to training in elementary self-help, such as self-feeding	Usually walks, barring specific disability. Has some understanding of speech and some response. Can profit from systematic habit training	Can conform to daily routines and repetitive activities. Needs continuing direction and supervision in protective environment
Profound: below 20 IQ	1	Gross disability. Minimal capacity for functioning in sensorimotor areas. Needs nursing care	Obvious delays in all areas of development. Shows basic emotional responses. May respond to skilful training in use of legs, hands and jaws. Needs close supervision	May walk, need nursing care, have primitive speech. Usually benefits from regular physical activity. Incapable of self-maintenance

mildly disabled, obtaining IQs between about 50 and 70. Most members of this largest group, given appropriate social and educational support, are capable of functioning adequately in mainstream society, holding jobs and raising families. Progressively greater environmental support is needed as we move towards the profoundly disabled range, where institutional care is usually required.

Mildly disabled children can attend school but they have difficulties in reading, writing, memory, and mathematical computation. Many of these difficulties result from poorly developed problem-solving strategies. They often have deficiencies in the executive functions discussed in **Chapter 4**: reasoning, planning and evaluating feedback from their efforts (Molfese & Molfese, 2002).

Chapter 4, Page 144

Learning disability has a variety of causes: some genetic, some owing to other biological factors, and some owing to environmental causes. Genetic abnormalities account for about 28% of all cases (Winnepenninckx, Rooms, & Kooy, 2003). More than 100 different genetic causes of such learning disability have been identified (Brown & Percy, 2007). For example, *Down's Syndrome*, which is characterized by mild to severe mental disability, is caused by an abnormal division of the twenty-first chromosome pair.

Heritability plays a different role in mild learning disability than it does in profound cases (Plomin & Spinath, 2004). Cases of profound disability are more likely to be caused by genetic accidents instead of an inherited genotype (Zechner, Wilda, Kehrer-Sawatzki, Vogel, Fundele, & Hameister, 2001). Therefore, profound learning disability does not run in families. In one study of 17,000 children, about 0.5% had profound disability. None of these children's siblings had an IQ below 85, and their mean IQ was 103. In contrast, the siblings of the 1.2% who had mild learning disability had mean IQs of 85, and a third of the siblings had IQs below 75 (Nichols, 1984).

Focus 10.29 How do causal factors differ in mild and profound learning disability?

Such disabilities can also be caused by accidents at birth, such as severe oxygen deprivation (anoxia); and by diseases experienced by the mother during pregnancy, such as rubella or syphilis. Likewise, drugs and alcohol taken by the mother – especially in the first weeks of pregnancy when a woman is often unaware she is pregnant – can cause neural damage and learning disability. Despite this range of potential causes, in a significant majority (75–80%) of those with learning disabilities, no clear biological cause can be found. Experts theorize that these cases may be due to undetectable brain damage, extreme environmental deprivation, or a combination of the two.

FIGURE 10.19 To an increasing extent, children with low IQ scores have been included in normal classrooms rather than being confined to special education programmes.

Source: © E.D. Torial / Alamy

In the UK the government has clearly outlined educational policy that is designed to cater specifically for those with learning disabilities. Part of this programme is to ensure that children with learning difficulties have the right to be educated in the mainstream education system. There is a similar situation in the USA where federal law requires that children with learning disabilities, who were formerly segregated into special education classes, be given individualized instruction in the 'least restrictive environment'. This has resulted in the practice of *mainstreaming*, or *inclusion programmes*, which allows many cognitively challenged children to attend school in regular classrooms and experience a more normal peer environment (Figure 10.19). Many schools also provide for individualized instruction for such children so that they can receive the special attention they may require.

A CONCLUDING THOUGHT

In the preceding chapters, we have seen how humans learn, how they remember what they have learned and how they think and solve problems. Language, thinking and intelligent behaviour are intimately related to one another and to the processes of learning and memory. As we have also seen, intelligent behaviour has many causal factors. Some of these factors are summarized in 'Levels of analysis'.

In today's world, intellectual skills have become increasingly important for successful adaptation. General intelligence, or the *g* factor, captures the kinds of general mental

flexibility needed to cope with novelty, read the environment, draw conclusions and choose how and when to act (Lubinski, 2004). In addition to the importance of general mental ability, more specific skills, such as those at the first and second levels of Carroll's three-stratum model (see page 417), may be needed to cope successfully with more narrowly defined situations and task demands. To an increasing degree, the study of intelligence is focusing on these real-life adaptations and on ways to help people develop and apply their intellectual abilities.

Levels of analysis
factors related to intellectual functioning

PSYCHOLOGICAL

- Contribution of a general mental capacity (*g* factor)
- Specific cognitive and perceptual skills that also underlie intellectual ability
- Adaptive skills that may constitute different types of intelligence
- Beliefs, anxieties and expectations that affect cognitive performance in specific situations (e.g., stereotype threat)
- Motivation to achieve

BIOLOGICAL

- Genetic factors, which account for significant variation in intelligence
- Biological reaction range, which sets broad limits for potential intellectual development
- Neural efficiency that may underlie intellectual differences
- Possible role of sex hormones in certain types of mental abilities

ENVIRONMENTAL

- Learning environments that interact with biological reaction range
- Cultural factors that influence which behaviours are prized and defined as intelligent
- Sex roles, which may influence the abilities that men and women master
- Intelligence measures, which may place culturally different people at a disadvantage

Intellectual functioning

 In review

- Intelligence is determined by interacting hereditary and environmental factors. Genes account for between 50% and 70% of population variation in IQ. Shared family environment accounts for perhaps one-quarter to one-third of the variance during childhood, but its effects seem to dissipate as people age. Educational experiences also influence mental skills. Heredity establishes a reaction range with upper and lower limits for intellectual potential. Environment affects the point within that range that will be reached.

- Intervention programmes for disadvantaged children have positive effects on later achievement and life outcomes if they begin early in life and are applied intensively. They have little effect when applied after school begins or with middle- or upper-class children.

◀

- Heritability estimates of intelligence can vary, depending on sample characteristics. In impoverished families, shared environment was more important than genes, whereas the opposite was found in affluent families. Twin studies also show that heritability effects on intelligence increase in adulthood.

- Evidence exists for both genetic and environmental determinants.

- Although the differences are not large, there is some evidence to suggest that men tend, as a group, to score higher than women on certain spatial and mathematical reasoning tasks. Women perform slightly better than men on tests of perceptual speed, verbal fluency, mathematical calculation and fine motor coordination. Both environmental and biological bases of sex differences have been suggested. Stereotype threat is one potential psychological factor for gender-based performance differences.

- Even people with IQs in the 150s often show discrepancies in specific skills. Those who achieve eminence tend to have, in addition to high IQs, high levels of interest and motivation in their chosen activities.

- Cognitive disability can be caused by a number of factors. Biological causes are identified in only about 28% of cases. Cognitive disability can range from mild to profound. The vast majority of disabled individuals are able to function in the mainstream of society, given appropriate support. Genetic factors seem relatively unimportant in profound learning difficulties, but they seem to play an important role in mild learning difficulties, which is more likely to run in families.

Answer to the Problem in Figure 10.15

The correct choice is geometric form number 5. Can you specify why?

Recommended Reading

CLASSIC

Bouchard, T.J. & McGue, M. (1981). Familial studies of intelligence: A review. *Science* , *212*, 1055–1059.

Carroll, J.B. (1993). *Human cognitive abilities: a survey of factor-analytic studies.* Cambridge: Cambridge University Press.

Sternberg, R.J. (2000). *Handbook of intelligence.* Cambridge: Cambridge University Press.

CONTEMPORARY

Gardner, H. (2006). Multiple intelligences: new horizons. NY: Basic Books

Flynn, J.R. (2009). *What is intelligence?* Cambridge: Cambridge University Press.

Maltby, J. Day, L. & Macaskill, A. (2010). *Personality, Individual Differences, and intelligence* (2nd ed.). Harlow: Pearson.

One can never consent
to creep when one feels
an impulse to soar.
Helen Keller

© Kemal Taner/ Shutterstock.com

Motivation and emotion

11

Chapter Outline

Lal Bahadur Shastri was invested as the Prime Minister of India in 1964. The two years he served as Prime Minister represented the culmination of a long career as an academic, a political activist and a politician. But if we look at how Lal Bahadur started out in life it would be very hard to imagine, let alone predict, his lifetime of achievement.

Lal Bahadur was born at the beginning of the twentieth century, to poor parents living in a town by the river Ganges. His father died when he was very young, and he was brought up by his mother and her family. It is a testament to Lal Bahadur's personal motivations that he was able to overcome these disadvantages to excel in his education, and later become one of the leading politicians of his age.

However, the barriers placed before Lal Bahadur went beyond his simple origins. At the time of his birth, India was ruled by the British Raj, and much of his life was dedicated to the political movement for an independent India. These political efforts were not without their setbacks. Like other prominent activists such as Mahatma Ghandi, Lal Bahadur spent a number of years in prison as a consequence of his outspoken political views. Nonetheless, in the long run it was through the efforts of activists such as Lal Bahadur that the people of India were eventually able to govern themselves in an independent republic (Srivastava, 1995).

Sara gained 6.8 kg (15 lbs) during her first year of university thanks to late-night pizza-and-beer parties. She dieted and returned to her normal weight of 52 kg (8 st 3 lb). Proud of her success, Sara (just over 5 feet [1.52 m] tall) continued dieting and lost 11 more kilogrammes (25 lbs). Her menstrual period stopped, but she was so afraid of gaining weight that she could not bring herself to eat normally. Finally, weighing a mere 36 kg (5 st 9 lb), she was hospitalized and began psychotherapy.

Lisa also gained weight during her first year at university. Her greater weight made her feel 'like a failure'. She gradually fell into a pattern of eating lightly during the day but bingeing at night on crisps and biscuits. She later began to take laxatives to ward off the effects of the bingeing, such that she was eventually consuming 50 laxatives, along with 10 diet pills, each morning with breakfast. After a laxative-consuming friend suffered a heart attack at age 20, Lisa became scared. Worried about her own eating patterns, Lisa sought professional help (Hubbard, O'Neill, & Cheakalos, 1999).

Motivation and emotion, two central concepts in psychology, are closely linked. When our motives and goals are gratified, threatened or thwarted, we often experience emotions. Lal Bahadur worked hard in the struggle to free India and felt tremendous pride when he succeeded. Sara also took pride in her success at losing weight. Emotions, in turn, can motivate us to act. Lisa's fear upon seeing a friend nearly die from bingeing and purging prompted her to seek treatment. As we will now see, both our motives and our emotions stem from a confluence of biological, psychological and environmental factors.

MOTIVATION

Motivation is the force which prompts us to take action, whether it be to eat, work hard or seek company. It can be defined as a process that influences the direction, persistence and vigour of goal-directed behaviour. The task for investigators of motivation is to identify major patterns of behaviour and link them to underlying psychological processes, which can be biological, social, emotional and/or cognitive.

THEORIES OF MOTIVATION

> **motivation** a process that influences the direction, persistence and vigour of goal-directed behaviour

Different theories of **motivation** have been proposed, each attending to the varying contribution of these factors to behaviour, and can be broadly categorized as either biological, social, cognitive or humanistic theories. As you will see, more recent theories attempt to explain the interrelationship between factors underpinning motivation, rather than focusing on just one domain.

Biological Theories of Motivation

Instincts

Darwin's theory of evolution inspired early psychological views that instincts motivate much of our behaviour. An **instinct** (also called a *fixed action pattern*) is an inherited characteristic, common to all members of a species, that automatically produces a particular response when the organism is exposed to a particular stimulus. By the 1920s, researchers had proposed thousands of human instincts (Atkinson, 1964).

Human instinct theories faded because little evidence supported them and they often relied on circular reasoning: why are people greedy? Because greed is an instinct. How do we know that greed is an instinct? Because people are greedy. As we have seen in earlier discussions of scientific thinking, circular reasoning explains nothing.

Scientists now study genetic contributions to motivation more productively. In gene knockout experiments with animals (see **Chapter 3**), they disable specific genes and examine the resulting effects on motivation. Researchers also conduct twin and adoption studies to examine how strongly heredity accounts for differences among people in many aspects of motivated behaviour. Modern evolutionary psychologists also propose that many human motives have evolutionary underpinnings expressed through the actions of genes (Palmer & Palmer, 2002).

Drive theory

The drive theory of motivation draws upon the concept of homeostasis. Walter Cannon, in 1932, proposed that **homeostasis** is a state of internal physiological equilibrium that the body strives to maintain for survival purposes (e.g. shivering when cold or sweating when hot).

Maintaining homeostasis requires a sensory mechanism for detecting changes in the internal environment, a response system that can restore equilibrium, and a control centre that receives information from the sensors and activates the response system (Figure 11.1). The control centre functions somewhat like the thermostat in a furnace or air-conditioning unit. Once the thermostat is set at a fixed temperature, or *set point* (page 452), sensors detect temperature changes in either direction. The control unit responds by turning on the furnace or air conditioner until the sensor indicates that the set point has been restored, and then turns it off.

Applied to the study of motivation, Clark Hull's (1943) influential *drive theory of motivation* proposed that physiological disruptions to homeostasis produce **drives**, defined as states of internal tension that motivate an organism to reduce that tension. Drives such as hunger and thirst arise from tissue deficits (e.g., lack of food and water) and push an organism into action. Hull extended this proposal by drawing upon learning theory, and argued that any behaviour that resulted in a reduction in these drives would be reinforced. Consequently, if after feeling hunger an animal engages in a behaviour that results in the reduction of hunger, then that behaviour is reinforced and more likely to be repeated (see **Chapter 7** on learning). Over time, the animal learns which behaviours result in the best reduction of certain drives (hunger, thirst, desire for a mate, etc.). Hull later extended his theory to include external incentives as well as those resulting from internal drives.

The role of drive reduction and subsequent learning is an interesting one. For example, if we are hungry and we eat then we learn that eating removes the drive of hunger and thus the behaviour is reinforced. But what happens when there is no relationship between the behaviour and the outcome? Seligman (1975) suggested that this is the basis of learned helplessness. His early work explored how animals responded to the drive to escape a fearful context.

Seligman and Maier (1967) used three experimental conditions: in the first, dogs were given a shock which they had no control over; no matter

---

> **instinct** an inherited characteristic, common to all members of a species, that automatically produces a particular response when the organism is exposed to a particular stimulus

 Chapter 3, Page 102

 Chapter 7, Page 280

> **homeostasis** a state of internal physiological equilibrium that the body strives to maintain
>
> **drives** states of internal tension that motivate an organism to behave in ways that reduce this tension

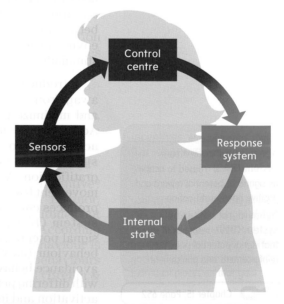

FIGURE 11.1 Homeostatic adaptation.

Your body's internal environment is regulated by homeostatic mechanisms. Sensors detect bodily changes and send this information to a control centre, which in turn regulates a response system that restores bodily equilibrium.

Work with humans has produced similar findings. Montague et al. (1997) reported the case of cousins who were both obese and who both displayed a congenital deficiency in the production of leptin, suggesting that it plays an important role in the regulation of appetite. Both children were both born at normal weights but rapidly gained weight, regularly complained of feeling hungry and consumed more than their siblings. Farooqi et al. (1999) reported that the elder of two children underwent leptin treatment and that this resulted in a decrease in both hunger and food intake and, consequently, a drop in body weight.

Do these specific *ob* and *db* gene mutations underpin human obesity? Probably not, for these genetic conditions seem to be rare among humans. However, when these gene mutations do occur, they are associated with extreme obesity, suggesting the importance of normal leptin functioning in human weight regulation.

Brain mechanisms

 Chapter 4, Page 136

Many brain regions regulate hunger and eating (Berthoud, 2002). But is there a master control centre? Early experiments pointed to two regions in the hypothalamus. The *lateral hypothalamus (LH)* was originally thought of as a 'hunger-on' centre (Figure 11.6). Electrically stimulating a rat's LH would cause it to start eating, and lesioning (damaging or destroying) the LH would cause it to refuse to eat, even to the point of starvation (Anand & Brobeck, 1951).

Similarly, the *ventromedial hypothalamus* (*VMH*), seems to comprise a 'hunger-off' centre. Electrically stimulating the VMH would cause even a hungry rat to stop eating, whereas lesioning the VMH would cause doubling or tripling of body weight.

As scientists explored further, they learned that although the LH and VMH play a role in hunger regulation, they are not really hunger-on and hunger-off centres. For example, rats with LH damage stop eating and lose weight in part because they develop trouble swallowing and digesting, and they become generally unresponsive to external stimuli, not just to food. Moreover, axons from many brain areas funnel into the hypothalamus and then fan out again upon leaving it. Cutting these nerve tracts anywhere along their paths – not just within the hypothalamus – duplicates some of the effects of the LH and VMH lesions (Schwartz, 1984). Damage to the VMH and the surrounding areas can cause dramatic weight gain but this is not caused by overeating. Rather the effect of the lesions is to cause the overproduction of insulin which leads to more of the food consumed being stored as fat. This has the twin effect of causing weight gain and the requirement that more food be consumed in order to maintain the current energy needs of the animal (Friedman & Stricker, 1976). The rats also show increased rates of secretion which means that they have a tendency to have a shorter gap between meals than was previously the case, resulting in the consumption of more meals per day (Duggan & Booth, 1986).

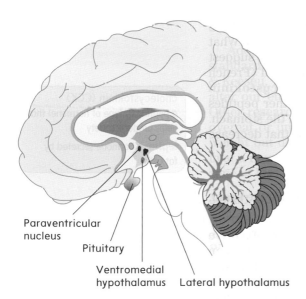

Paraventricular
nucleus

Pituitary

Ventromedial
hypothalamus   Lateral hypothalamus

FIGURE 11.6 Motivation and the hypothalamus.

Various structures within the hypothalamus play a role in regulating hunger, thirst, sexual arousal and body temperature. The lateral hypothalamus (LH), ventromedial hypothalamus (VMH) and paraventricular nucleus (PVN) are involved in hunger regulation.

Source: American Journal of Psychiatry

Researchers are continually examining other explanations for the drive to stop and start eating. Through brain imaging techniques we know that many brain areas are involved in food consumption. The hypothalamus plays a central role, and areas beyond the LH and VMH are involved. There is evidence of leptin receptors in the VMH and this appears crucial in meal termination. However, there are similar receptors located in other brain areas such as the thalamus, cerebellum and substantia nigra as well as non-brain areas such as the liver and gastrointestinal tract (Elmquist, Bjorbaek, Ahima, Flier, & Saper, 1998) and these areas too may impact on meal termination.

paraventricular nucleus (PVN) a cluster of neurons packed with receptor sites for various transmitters that stimulate or reduce appetite

Also involved is the **paraventricular nucleus (PVN)**, a cluster of hypothalamic neurons packed with receptor sites for various transmitters that stimulate or reduce appetite (Berthoud, 2002). Benzon et al. (2014) found that the PVN contained receptors specifically associated with regulating intake of high-fat foods, reporting that rats unable to detect certain neuropeptides in the PVN would eat considerably more high-fat food compared to control rats. However, this overeating was not observed with standard laboratory food, suggesting that certain receptors are sensitive only to those foods high in

fat. Of course, research like this may help in the treatment of obesity. Rolls, Murzi, Yaxley, Thorpe and Simpson (1986) reported that when a food has been consumed to satiety, neurons in the lateral hypothalamus stop responding to both the sight and taste of that same food, but continue to fire to other types of food, perhaps designed to ensure that a variety of foods are consumed.

The hypothalamus receives a lot of information about energy balance in the body, but our eating behaviour is dependent on much more than simply maintaining the correct balance of intake and expenditure, and we have seen that there is little evidence for something as simple as a hunger-on–hunger-off centre in the brain.

As well as receiving a great deal of information about the body's energy status the hypothalamus also has connections to other areas of the brain. Specific areas that are now the subject of increased investigation include the hippocampus – a structure crucial in memory development and the amygdala, often referred to as the 'emotion centre' of the brain.

As we saw in **Chapter 8** the hippocampus is directly involved in memory, but it also seems that it may play a role in feeding behaviour too, Clifton, Vickers and Sommerville (1998) reported that lesions to rats' brain in the hippocampus resulted in the same level of food intake, but more frequent and smaller meals, while Parent, Darling and Henderson (2014) suggested that the hippocampus inhibits eating during the period between meals and that overeating damages hippocampal functioning and hence leads to greater overeating.

Chapter 8, Page 314

The amygdala is associated with emotional responses (LeDoux, 1998) and establishing emotional memories, but it also has a role to play in eating and hunger. Not all eating behaviour is governed by homeostasis and we sometimes eat when full and do not eat when hungry, so these physiological systems can be overridden. The process of integrating physiological and psychological motivations to eat remains unclear (Stellar & Stellar, 1985) but there is increasing information to suggest that the amygdala may play an important role (Petrovich, 2013).

What this entire body of research shows is that the regulation of food intake and appetite is complex. British psychologist John Blundell has offered an impressive attempt to combine all known factors influencing appetite and has argued that appetite centres on the complex interaction between a number of levels including the psychological (food cravings, sensation of hunger) and associated behavioural aspects (eating, snacking), the physiological and metabolic level and finally, neurotransmitter and metabolic events in the brain (Blundell, 1991). Obviously attempting to combine and make predictions from such a complex set of factors is a mammoth task for science to explain.

Focus 11.2 What physiological factors help regulate hunger, satiety, general appetite, and weight?

Psychological Aspects of Hunger

Attitudes, habits and psychological needs also regulate food intake. Have you ever felt stuffed during a meal, yet finished it and even had dessert? Beliefs such as 'don't leave food on your plate' and conditioned habits (e.g., eating crisps while watching television) may lead us to eat in the absence of hunger. Conversely, countless dieters intentionally restrict their food intake even though they *are* hungry.

Food restriction often stems from social pressures to conform to cultural standards of beauty (Figure 11.7). Studies of *Playboy* centrefolds, Miss America contestants and fashion models indicate a clear trend towards a thinner and increasingly unrealistic ideal female body shape from the 1950s into the 1990s (Owen & Laurel-Seller, 2000). Given the prevalence of thin models in advertising and cultural media in many parts of the globe, it seems unsurprising that national surveys in these areas have revealed that:

- although most young Australian women are of average, healthy weight, only a fifth are happy with their weight (Kenardy, Brown, & Vogt, 2001)
- among 12- to 19-year-old female Chinese students, 80% are concerned about their weight and feel fat at least some of the time (Huon, Mingyi, Oliver, & Xiao, 2002)
- compared with male American high school students, female students are less likely to be overweight but much more likely to diet and think of themselves as overweight (Centers for Disease Control and Prevention [CDC], 2002b).

FIGURE II.7 Throughout much of Western history, a full-bodied woman's figure was esteemed, as illustrated by (*left*) Peter Paul Rubens's seventeenth-century painting *The Three Graces* and by (*centre*) actress Lillian Russell, who represented the American ideal of feminine beauty a century ago. In recent decades, the norm of 'thin = beautiful' is illustrated (*right*) by these men and women in swimsuits.

Source: (left) The Three Graces by Rubens, Pieter Paul (1577-1640), Museo del Prado, Madrid, c.1635/Superstock; (right) © iStock. com/GlobalStock.

The cultural cause of body dissatisfaction is underlined by findings indicating that relative to men, women have become increasingly dissatisfied with their body image throughout the second half of the twentieth century (Feingold & Mazzella, 1998). Also, that discrepancies between actual weight and ideal weight are smaller in cultures which have less exposure to Western positive values of thinness. For example, Toriola, Dolan, Evans and Adetimole (1996) found that Nigerian women in Britain had a greater dissatisfaction with their weight than Nigerian women in Nigeria. Finally, Tucci and Peters (2008) reported that their female participants reported lower body satisfaction scores following exposure to images of models with thin physiques and higher body satisfaction scores following exposure to models with larger physiques.

A classic study by April Fallon and Paul Rozin (1985) suggests an additional reason why this is so. This study showed that women at university overestimated how thin they needed to be to conform to men's preferences, whereas men overestimated how bulky they should be to conform to women's preferences (Figure 11.8). Women also perceived their body shape as heavier than ideal, whereas men viewed their body shape as close to ideal (see also Carlson & McAndrew, 2004). As Fallon and Rozin noted, 'Overall, men's perceptions serve to keep them satisfied with their figures, whereas women's perceptions place pressure on them to lose weight' (1985, p. 102). It is argued that men's greater propensity to adopt more positive perceptions about their body shape occurs across various cultures (Demarest & Allen, 2000). However, recent research (Mikolajczyk, Maxwell, El Ansari, Stock, Petkeviciene, & Guillen-Grima, 2010) reported the findings of

FIGURE II.8 Preferred body shapes.

When making judgements while viewing body-size drawings, college women overestimated how thin they needed to be to conform to men's preferences, and they viewed their own body shape as heavier than ideal. Men overestimated how bulky or 'buff' they needed to be to conform to women's preferences, but they viewed their body shape as close to ideal.

Source: Based on Fallon and Rozin, 1985.

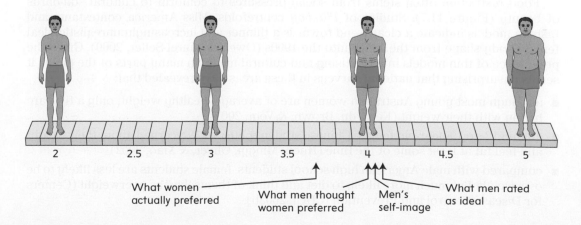

a large-scale European study in which nearly 6,000 students were used as participants. It was found that weight ideals are broadly similar across European countries and that females within the normal BMI range were more likely to consider themselves 'too fat' and males within the same range more likely to consider themselves 'too thin', challenging the notion that males maintain a more positive body image than females.

Men too, however, may be influenced by cultural ideals. Men's satisfaction with their bodies decreases when they are exposed to a series of advertisements showing muscular males, but not when the advertisements contain men with average builds (Lorenzen, Grieve, & Thomas, 2004). Male athletes, who value muscle function, believe that women prefer a more muscular body type than their own, and most would prefer to be more muscular than they are (Raudenbush & Meyer, 2003). In general it appears that women typically want to be thin; males who are overweight also want to be thinner, but those who are thin want to be heavier and more 'buff' (Kostanski, Fisher, & Gullone, 2004).

Environmental and Cultural Factors

Food availability is the most obvious environmental regulator of eating. For millions of people who live in poverty or famine-ravaged regions, food scarcity limits consumption. In contrast, abundant high-fat food in many countries contributes to a high rate of obesity (Wadden, Brownell, & Foster, 2002).

Food taste and variety also regulate eating. Good-tasting food increases food consumption, but during a meal and from meal to meal we can become tired of eating the same thing, causing us to terminate a meal more quickly (Rolls, Rolls, Rowe, & Sweeney, 1981). In contrast, food variety increases consumption, which you may have observed when you eat at a buffet.

Through classical conditioning, we learn to associate the smell and sight of food with its taste, and these food cues can trigger hunger. Eating may be the last thing on your mind until your nose detects the sensuous aroma wafting from a bakery or popcorn machine. Similarly, rats who have recently eaten and do not appear to be hungry (e.g., they ignore available food) will eat again when presented with classically conditioned sounds and lights that they have learned to associate with food (Weingarten, 1983).

Many other environmental stimuli affect food intake. For example, we typically eat more when dining with other people than when we eat alone (deCastro, 2002). Cultural norms influence when, how and what we eat. In Mediterranean countries such as Spain and Greece, people often begin dinner in the late evening (say, around 9 p.m.), by which time most people in the UK have finished supper. And although we like variety, we usually feel most comfortable selecting familiar foods and often have difficulty overcoming our squeamish thoughts about unfamiliar dishes (Figure 11.9). The 'Levels of analysis' summarizes several factors that help regulate hunger and eating.

Obesity

The heaviest known man and woman in recorded history, both Americans, weighed 635 and 544 kg (100 st and 85 st 7 lb), respectively (*Guinness Book of Records*, 2000). The *body mass index (BMI)*, which takes height and weight into account, demonstrates that obesity varies substantially between countries. In Europe obesity prevalence varies between 5% and 23% for men and 7% and 36% for women. Percentages of the population who are defined as overweight (but not obese) vary between 27% and 57% for men, and 18% and 43% for women. Uzbekistan and Kazakhstan are among the countries demonstrating the lowest levels of obesity, while the UK and Bosnia and Herzegovina have some of the highest (WHO Summary, 2007).

Obesity places people at greater risk not only for many medical problems but also for being the target of stereotypes and prejudice (Teachman, Gapinski, Brownell, Rawlins, & Jeyaram, 2003). Obesity is often blamed on a lack of willpower, a dysfunctional way of coping with stress, heightened sensitivity to external food cues (e.g., the sight and aroma of food) and emotional disturbances. Research, however, does not consistently find such psychological differences between obese and non-obese people (Faith, Matz, & Jorge, 2002; Leon & Roth, 1977).

FIGURE 11.9 Cultural upbringing strongly affects food preferences.

Would you like to eat these fried spiders? Many Europeans and Americans would be squeamish at the thought of eating them. Other foods whose consumption is strongly affected by cultural preferences include reptiles, camel eyes, dog meat and rotten fish.

Source: ©iStock.com/c850I089

Focus 11.3 Describe how psychological, environmental and cultural factors influence hunger and eating.

Levels of analysis

factors related to hunger and eating

PSYCHOLOGICAL

- Thinking about food, anticipation of tasty food
- Learned food preferences and eating habits
- Memory of when and how much we have recently eaten
- Beliefs and feelings concerning body image

BIOLOGICAL

- Genetic factors that influence energy metabolism
- Bodily sensations, such as stomach distention
- Chemical signals (e.g., glucose utilization, CCK, leptin)
- Neural circuits within and passing through the hypothalamus

ENVIRONMENTAL

- The abundance or scarcity of food
- Food appearance, aroma, taste and variety
- Other stimuli (e.g., time of day, people) associated with eating
- Norms that affect what, when, where and how much we eat

Hunger and eating

Genes and environment

Do you know people who seem to gain weight easily and others who seem to eat as much as they want without adding pounds? Heredity influences one's basal metabolic rate and the tendency to store energy as either fat or lean tissue. Indeed, identical twins raised apart are about as similar in body mass as identical twins reared together. Overall, genetic factors appear to account for about 40–70% of the variation in BMI among women and among men (Maes, Neale, & Eaves, 1997).

More than 200 genes have been identified as possible contributors to human obesity (Comuzzie & Allison, 1998). However, although heredity affects our susceptibility to obesity, so does the environment. Genes have not changed much in recent decades, but obesity rates have increased significantly. According to some experts, the culprits are:

- an abundance of inexpensive, tasty foods that are high in fat and/or carbohydrates
- a cultural emphasis on getting the best value, which contributes to supersizing menu items
- technological advances that decrease the need for daily physical activity (Wadden et al., 2002)
- high levels of dopamine in the brain's 'reward pathways' may make some people especially sensitive to the reinforcing properties of foods (Davis, Patte, Levitan, Reid, Tweed, & Curtis, 2007).

The Pima Indians of Arizona in the USA provide a striking example of how genes and environment interact to produce obesity. The Pimas are genetically predisposed to obesity and diabetes, but both conditions were rare among tribe members before the twentieth century. Their native diet and physically active lifestyle prevented their genetic predisposition from expressing itself. But particularly among Pimas born after the Second World War, obesity rates increased dramatically as they adopted a Westernized diet and sedentary lifestyle. Today Pimas living in Arizona have one of the highest rates of obesity (and diabetes) in the world. In contrast, Pimas living in north-west Mexico eat a more traditional diet and perform more physical labour, and their obesity rate is much lower than that of their Arizonan counterparts (Esparza et al., 2000). The findings of this study were replicated by Schulz et al. (2006) supporting the notion that the prevalence of both obesity and type 2 diabetes is a result of environmental factors and are therefore largely preventable.

> **Focus 11.4** Describe biological and environmental factors in obesity and how their interaction affects obesity among the Pima.

Dieting and weight loss

Unfortunately for millions of overweight people, being fat primes them to stay fat, in part by altering body chemistry and energy expenditure (Logue, 1991). For example, obese people generally have higher levels of *insulin* (a hormone secreted by the pancreas that helps convert glucose into fat) than do people of normal weight. Substantial weight gain also makes it harder to exercise vigorously, and dieting slows basal metabolism because the body responds to food deprivation with decreased energy expenditure.

Does this mean that diets are doomed to fail? The common adage that '95 per cent of people who lose weight regain it within a few years' evolved from just one study decades ago. According to Albert Stunkard, one of the researchers, 100 obesity patients were 'just given a diet and sent on their way. That was state of the art in 1959' (quoted in Fritsch, 1999). In truth, we do not have good long-term estimates of weight-loss success rates, partly because we rarely hear from people who succeed (or fail) on their own without going to clinics or treatment programmes.

The number of books and advertisements which describe dieting procedures that we can observe day to day is testament to the fact that many people are trying to lose weight. A question of interest concerns whether there are any differences in the number of people engaging in dieting behaviour between gender and ethnic groups. Figure 11.10 shows the results of a study in the USA which demonstrated that there are significant sex and ethnic differences in dieting that emerge even in adolescence (CDC, 2002b). Health concerns motivate some dieters, but psychological concerns and social pressures to be thin are the primary motivators for many others. Especially among women, what begins as a diet may unfortunately evolve into a health-threatening eating disorder.

Sara and Lisa, the first-year university students described at the beginning of the chapter, suffered from eating disorders. Victims of **anorexia nervosa**, like Sara, have an intense fear of being fat and severely restrict their food intake to the point of self-starvation (Figure 11.11). Despite looking emaciated and weighing less than 85% of what would be expected for their age and height, people with anorexia continue to view themselves as fat. Anorexia causes menstruation to stop, produces bone loss, stresses the heart and increases the risk of death (Neumäker, 2000; Treasure, 2005).

People like Lisa who suffer from **bulimia nervosa** are also afraid of becoming fat, and they binge-eat and then purge the food, usually by inducing vomiting or using laxatives. People with bulimia often consume 2,000 to 4,000 calories during binges, and in some cases may consume 20,000 calories per day (Geracioti, Loosen, Ebert, & Schmidt, 1995). Although most bulimia sufferers are of normal body weight, repeated purging can

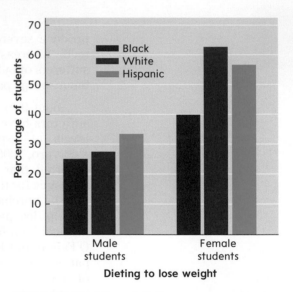

FIGURE 11.10 Ethnicity and dieting.

Whether Hispanic, black or white, female high school students in America are less likely than male students to actually be overweight or at risk for overweight but, as this graph shows, they are more likely to be dieting to lose weight. Especially among female students, Hispanics and whites are most likely to diet.

Source: Based on CDC, 2002b.

> **anorexia nervosa** an intense fear of being fat so that victims severely restrict their food intake to the point of self-starvation
>
> **bulimia nervosa** a fear of becoming fat, which causes victims to binge-eat and then purge the food

FIGURE II.II Anorexia nervosa is a potentially life-threatening disorder in which people virtually starve themselves to be thin. This anorexia patient returned to normal weight after therapy.

Source: © Ed Quinn/Corbis

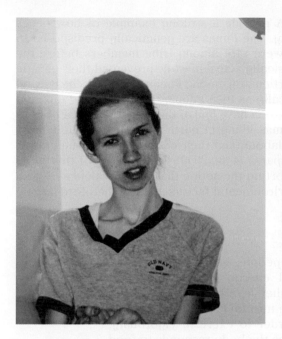

produce severe physical consequences, including gastric problems and badly eroded teeth. Whereas most people with anorexia do not see their food restriction as problematic, sufferers of bulimia typically do. Nonetheless, they find it extremely difficult to alter their binge–purge pattern.

About 90% of people with anorexia and bulimia are women. About 7% of anorexia sufferers have a previous diagnosis of bulimia, and this group tends to exhibit higher levels of psychological disturbance (Santonastaso, Scicluna, Colombo, Zanetti, &·Favaro, 2006). Although estimates of prevalence vary, Hoek and van Hoeken (2003) reported that approximately 0.3% of young women suffer from anorexia nervosa. Statistics for the prevalence of this eating disorder in males are difficult to come by and may be unreliable for a variety of reasons, such as many of the diagnostic tools being largely designed for females and the possibility that males may be reluctant to seek medical help for what they consider to be a 'female disorder'. However, Lucas, Beard, O'Fallon and Kurland (1991) reported that males account for between 5% and 10% of patients with anorexia nervosa and Braun, Sunday, Huang and Halmi (1999) found that of nearly 800 cases of various eating disorders males accounted for only 6.7%. Rates for bulimia nervosa are a little higher at around 1% for young women and 0.1% for young men (Hoek & van Hoeken, 2003). One recent, and rare, study that compared eating disorders in males and females reported that males tend to have better outcomes than females in that they have shorter times between onset and remission and higher rates of remission for anorexia and other non-specified eating disorders (Stóving, Andries, Brixen, Flyvbjerg, Hòrder, & Frystyk, 2009).

Causes of anorexia and bulimia

What motivates such abnormal eating patterns? Researchers obviously cannot do experiments to manipulate possible causes and see if people will develop anorexia or bulimia, but they can examine factors associated with the disorders and changes that occur in people when they are successfully treated. Such research suggests that a combination of environmental, psychological and biological factors may be involved.

Anorexia and bulimia are more common in industrialized cultures where thinness is equated with beauty. However, cultural norms alone cannot account for eating disorders, because only a small percentage of women within a particular culture suffer from anorexia or bulimia. Personality factors are another piece of the puzzle. People with anorexia often are perfectionists and high achievers who strive to live up to lofty self-standards, including strict ideals of an acceptably thin body (Soares et al., 2009; Tyrka, Waldron, Graber, & Brooks-Gunn, 2002). For them, losing weight becomes a battle for

success and control: 'It's me versus food, and I'm going to win.' As Espíndola and Blay (2009) observed, an understanding of this battle for control is essential if treatment is to be appropriate and successful. Their perfectionism and need for control may partly stem from their upbringing. They often describe their parents as disapproving and as setting abnormally high achievement standards. For some children and teenagers with anorexia, food refusal may be reinforced by the distress they cause their parents to feel. In essence, self-starvation becomes a way to punish parents and gain some control (Chan & Ma, 2002), as illustrated by the following quotation taken from one young teenager with anorexia in a therapy session,

> It was, like, a power thing. I was like, look mum, I don't have to eat. I can piss you off . . . That's the last thing your parents want is for you to die. . . . You can get back at anybody. And I guess . . . I need to find a way to forgive her . . . because . . . I'm killing myself.
>
> (Dying to Be Thin, 2000)

A different pattern emerges for people with bulimia, who tend to be depressed and anxious, exhibit low impulse control and seem to lack a stable sense of personal identity (McElroy, Kotwal, & Keck, 2006). Their food cravings are often triggered by stress and negative mood, and bingeing temporarily reduces their negative emotional state (Waters, Hill, & Waller, 2001). But guilt, self-contempt and anxiety follow the binge, and purging may be a means of reducing these negative feelings.

On the biological side, genetic factors appear to predispose some people towards eating disorders. Concordance rates for eating disorders are higher among identical twins, than fraternal twins, and higher among first-degree relatives (parents and siblings) than second- or third-degree relatives (Kortegaard, Hoerder, Joergensen, Gillberg, & Kyvik, 2001). Researchers are now searching for specific genes and combinations of genes that contribute to eating disorders.

People with anorexia and bulimia also exhibit abnormal activity of serotonin, leptin and other body chemicals (Kaye, Strober, & Klump, 2002). Some researchers believe that neurotransmitter and hormonal imbalances help cause eating disorders. Others propose that such chemical changes initially are a *response* to abnormal eating patterns but that once started they *perpetuate* eating and digestive irregularities (Walsh & Devlin, 1998). Other bodily changes also help perpetuate eating disorders. For example, stomach acids expelled into the mouth during vomiting cause those with bulimia to lose taste sensitivity, making the normally unpleasant taste of vomit more tolerable (Rodin et al., 1990).

Focus 11.5 What are the major symptoms, health consequences and causes of anorexia and bulimia?

Treating eating disorders is difficult and may take years, but with professional help, about half of all patients with anorexia and bulimia fully recover (Russell, 2006; Westen, Novotny, & Thompson-Brenner, 2004). Others are able to eat more normally but maintain their preoccupation with food and weight.

 Current topic

WHAT CAUSES ANOREXIA?

Anorexia nervosa, which has the highest mortality rate of any psychiatric disorder (Papadopoulos, Ekbom, Brandt, & Ekselius, 2009), continues to perplex researchers and clinicians, both in terms of understanding what causes it, and how best to treat it, with conflicting evidence as to whether an explanation of causes is even necessary for effective treatment (Berens, Witteman, & Van de Ven, 2011). Considerable evidence now exists about some factors likely to contribute to the onset of anorexia, although the debate still rages about which factors are most important, and how they might interact, to render someone highly vulnerable to developing the disorder.

Historically, anorexia was thought to be largely a result of sociocultural factors which, at least in the developed world, associate thinness with beauty, success and self-control. Haines and Neumark-Sztainer (2006) reported that factors such as media exposure and weight-related teasing could also play an important role in the development of eating disorders; thus, environmental cues, and people's differential sensitivity and response to them, can play an important role in the development of anorexia. However, in addition to such sociocultural influences, psychological research has identified further complex and inter-related factors which seem to establish a vulnerability to developing anorexia (Attia, 2010). Such risk factors include being ▶

◄

female, having a history of childhood eating and gastrointestinal problems, early adverse experiences (including sexual abuse), prematurity or being small for gestational age (Bulik, Slof-Op't Landt, van Furth, & Sullivan, 2007), negative affect and negative self-evaluation (Pike et al., 2008).

Anorexia also often runs in families, and while evidence for a genetic component is compelling, genetic studies remain in the early stages and face a number of difficulties, including recruiting adequate sample sizes and those that include adoptive families. However, a purely genetic explanation is difficult to accept because as Campbell, Mill, Uher and Schmidt (2011) note, any genetic variation associated with a loss in fertility, as is the case in advanced anorexia, would be removed from the gene pool in a relatively short space of time as it is simply not supportable in evolutionary terms.

Disentangling the influence of environment and genes is also challenging (Bulik et al., 2007). For example, anxiety, obsessionality and perfectionism, which are risk factors for the onset of anorexia, also tend to be present in family members unaffected by anorexia so cannot be necessarily considered as definitive pre-onset indicators of anorexia. Biological studies also face challenges as it is often difficult to discern whether biological disturbances are stable features of those at risk of developing anorexia, or whether they result from malnutrition (Attia, 2010).

Thus, as is the case with many serious mental illnesses, the likely causes of anorexia nervosa appear complex, variable and difficult to define. Nonetheless, current research is focused on pursuing the contribution of individual factors, environmental influences and their interaction with genes to illuminate how they might place someone at risk for developing an eating disorder. Although at an early stage, the understanding of the gene-environment interaction is the most likely candidate to provide insight into understanding this condition. Consequently, such studies will probably have the greatest influence on the development of effective therapeutic interventions. However, at the current time it is unclear whether such treatment is likely to be based on dietary or pharmacological interventions or therapies, or indeed a combination of the two.

In review

■ Physiological processes attempt to keep the body in energy homeostasis. Changes in the supply of glucose available to cells provide one signal that helps initiate hunger. During meals, hormones such as CCK are released into the bloodstream and help signal the brain to stop eating. Fat cells release leptin, which acts as a long-term signal that helps regulate appetite. The hypothalamus plays an important role in hunger regulation.

■ The expected good taste of food motivates eating, and the thought of food can trigger hunger. Our memory, habits and psychological needs affect our food intake.

■ The availability, taste, and variety of food powerfully regulate eating. Through classical conditioning, neutral stimuli can acquire the capacity to trigger hunger. Cultural norms affect our food preferences and eating habits.

■ Heredity and the environment affect our susceptibility to becoming obese.

■ Anorexia and bulimia occur more often in cultures that value thinness and are associated with somewhat different psychological profiles. Heredity predisposes some people towards developing these eating disorders.

SEXUAL MOTIVATION

Why do people have sex? If you are thinking, 'Isn't it obvious?' let us take a look. Sex often is described as a biological reproductive motive, yet people usually do not have sex to conceive children. A drive to reproduce does not explain why people masturbate or why couples in their seventies and eighties have sex. Pleasure, then, must be the key. Evolution shaped our physiology so that sex feels good; periodically, having sex for pleasure leads to childbirth, through which our genes are passed on. But consider this:

■ in a study asking adolescents why they have sex, both genders cited peer pressure more often than sexual gratification (Stark, 1989)

■ in the 1920s, British sex researcher Helena Wright found that most women she surveyed viewed sex as an unenjoyable marital duty (Kelly, 2001)

■ in America about 10% of men and 20% of women report that sex is not pleasurable (Laumann et al., 1994)

■ Basson (2001) notes a number of factors that influence female sexual arousal beyond mere pleasure. These include aspects such as emotional closeness, sharing and letting a partner know that they have been missed.

In reality, people engage in sex to reproduce, obtain and give sensual pleasure, as well as less obvious reasons, such as to express love, foster intimacy, fulfil one's 'duty' and to conform to peer pressure.

The Physiology of Sex

In 1953 Masters and Johnson began a landmark study in which they examined the sexual responses of 694 men and women under laboratory conditions. In total, they physiologically monitored about 10,000 sexual episodes.

The sexual response cycle

Masters and Johnson (1966) concluded that most people, when sexually aroused, go through a four-stage **sexual response cycle** of excitement, plateau, orgasm and resolution (Figure 11.12). During the excitement phase, arousal builds rapidly. Blood flow increases to arteries in and around the genital organs, nipples and women's breasts, where it pools and causes these body areas to swell. The penis and clitoris begin to become erect, the vagina becomes lubricated and muscle tension increases throughout the body. In the *plateau phase*, arousal continues to build until there is enough muscle tension to trigger orgasm.

> **sexual response cycle**
> excitement, plateau, orgasm and resolution

During the *orgasm phase* in males, rhythmic contractions of internal organs and muscle tissue surrounding the urethra project semen out of the penis. In females, orgasm involves rhythmic contractions of the outer third of the vagina, surrounding muscles and the uterus. In males, orgasm is ordinarily followed by a *resolution phase*, during which physiological arousal decreases rapidly and the genital organs return to their normal condition. During the resolution phase, males enter a *refractory period*, during which they are temporarily incapable of another orgasm. Females may have two or more successive orgasms before the onset of the resolution phase, but Masters and Johnson reported that most women experience only one. Of course, people may experience orgasm on some occasions but not others, and orgasm is not the only goal of all human sexual activity.

Hormonal influences

As with hunger, the hypothalamus plays a key role in sexual motivation. It controls the pituitary gland, which regulates the secretion of hormones called gonadotropins into the bloodstream. In turn, these hormones affect the rate at which the *gonads* (testes in the male and ovaries in the female) secrete *androgens*, the so-called masculine sex hormones such as *testosterone*, and *oestrogens*, the so-called feminine sex hormones such as *oestradiol*. Realize that despite these labels, both men and women produce androgens and oestrogens.

Sex hormones have *organizational effects* that direct the development of male and female sex characteristics (Byer, Shainberg, & Galliano, 2002). In the womb, male and

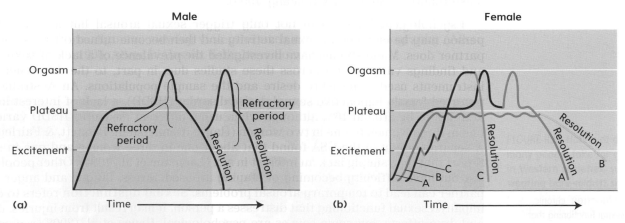

FIGURE 11.12 The human sexual response.

Masters and Johnson discovered a four-stage pattern of sexual response. (a) In males, there is a refractory period after orgasm during which no further response is possible. (b) In females, pattern A represents one or more orgasms followed by resolution, pattern B shows a plateau stage with no orgasm and pattern C shows an orgasm with no preceding plateau stage.

Source: Based on Masters and Johnson, 1966.

Controlled experiments paint a clearer causal picture. In some studies, male university students were randomly assigned to view material whose content was either neutral (i.e., non-sexual), sexually explicit but non-violent (e.g., a couple having consensual sex) or sexually aggressive (e.g., a rape-myth depiction showing a woman who initially resists sexual assault but then becomes a willing participant). Later, the students interacted with another person (a female or male accomplice of the experimenter), who made errors on a learning task. Participants were instructed to punish the person with an electric shock for each error, but they were free to choose the shock intensity and thus the aggression by giving stronger shocks. (The accomplice did not really receive any shock.)

The strongest experimental effects emerged when participants viewed violent pornography (Malamuth, Addison, & Koss, 2000). At least temporarily, this increased men's tendency to aggression towards women but not towards other men. However, certain types of people, such as those who reported the greatest attraction to sexual violence, were most strongly affected by viewing it. In addition to its connection with aggression, pornography also promotes a belief that sex is impersonal. An unwelcome side effect is that exposure to pornography decreases viewers' satisfaction with their own sexual partners (Donnerstein & Malamuth, 1997).

Sexual Orientation

Sexual orientation refers to one's emotional and erotic preference for partners of a particular sex. Determining one's sexual orientation seems simple: heterosexuals prefer opposite-sex partners, homosexuals prefer same-sex partners, and bisexuals are sexually attracted to members of both sexes. So how would you classify the sexual orientation of these two 25-year-olds?

- Susan feels sexually attracted to men and women, but she has had sex only with men and thinks of herself as heterosexual.

- Keith has had sex with other men twice since puberty, yet he is not attracted to men and views himself as heterosexual.

Some researchers view sexual orientation as a single dimension ranging from 'exclusively heterosexual' to 'exclusively homosexual', with 'equally heterosexual and homosexual' at the midway point. But others argue that sexual orientation has three dimensions: *self-identity*, *sexual attraction* and *actual sexual behaviour* (Kelly, 2001).

Determinants of sexual orientation

Theories about the origins of sexual orientation abound. An early and unsupported biological view proposed that homosexual and heterosexual males differ in their adult levels of sex hormones. Other early theories hypothesized that male homosexuality develops when boys grow up with a weak, ineffectual father and identify with a domineering mother, or that being sexually seduced by an adult homosexual causes children to divert their sex drive towards members of their own sex.

All of these theories have taken a scientific beating. In one study, Alan Bell and co-workers (Bell, Weinberg, & Hammersmith, 1981) interviewed nearly 1,000 homosexual and over 500 heterosexual men and women. They searched extensively for childhood or adolescent experiences that might predict adult sexual orientation, but only one consistent pattern emerged: even in childhood, homosexual men and women felt that they were somehow different from their same-sex peers and were more likely to engage in *gender-nonconforming behaviours*. Similarly, compared with heterosexual women, homosexual women in Brazil, Peru, the Philippines and the USA were about twice as likely during childhood to be considered tomboys and to be interested in boys' clothes and toys (Whitam & Mathy, 1991). Study after study has obtained similar results (Cohen, 2002).

So why do such patterns arise? Highly publicized studies appeared in the early 1990s reporting anatomical differences in the brains of heterosexual versus homosexual men and identifying a genetic marker shared by some homosexual men. Subsequent research, however, has not consistently replicated these findings (Lasco, Jordan, Edgar, Petito, & Byne, 2002). Nonetheless, there is growing evidence that heredity influences human sexual orientation. In one study, among gay men who had a brother, the concordance rates for sexual orientation (i.e., the brother was gay also) were 52% among identical twins, 22% among fraternal twins and 11%

Focus II.8 Describe what is known about the effects of watching violent pornography.

sexual orientation one's emotional and erotic preference for partners of a particular sex

among adoptive brothers (Bailey & Pillard, 1991). A later study of homosexual women yielded similar results (Bailey, Pillard, Neale, & Agyei, 1993). Thus the closer the genetic relatedness, the higher the concordance rates for sexual orientation (Kirk, Bailey, & Martin, 2000).

Another perspective suggests that the brain develops a neural pattern that predisposes an individual to prefer either female or male sex partners, depending on whether prenatal sex hormone activity follows a masculine or feminine path (Rahman, 2005). Experimentally altering animals' prenatal exposure to sex hormones can influence their sexual orientation. Moreover, in rare cases among humans, some genetically male foetuses are insensitive to their own androgen secretions and some female foetuses experience an atypical build-up of androgens. Studies of these individuals suggest a relation between prenatal sex-hormone exposure and adulthood sexual orientation (Williams et al., 2000). Of course, the human research is correlational and must be interpreted cautiously. For example, male foetuses who have androgen insensitivity develop the external anatomy of females and are typically raised as girls; socialization could account for their sexual orientation.

What about environmental influences? Even among identical twins, when one is homosexual, often the other is heterosexual. Thus a biological predisposition and socialization experiences may combine to determine sexual orientation. At present, scientists simply do not know what all the factors are. It is also possible, argues Bem (1996, 2001), that heredity affects sexual orientation only indirectly, by influencing children's basic personality style. He proposes that different personality styles then steer children towards gender-conforming or gender-nonconforming activities, causing them to feel similar to or different from same-sex peers. Ultimately, this affects their attraction to same-sex and opposite-sex peers. Bem's theory has mixed support and needs further testing (Bailey, Dunne, & Martin, 2000; Peplau, Garnets, Spalding, Conley, & Veniegas, 1998).

Finally, there may be multiple paths towards developing a sexual orientation, and the paths for men and women may differ. Consider the intriguing finding shown in Figure 11.14: the greater the number of older brothers (but not older sisters) a newborn boy has, the greater the probability that he will develop a homosexual orientation. In contrast, a woman's sexual orientation is not related to the number of older sisters or brothers in the family. Ray Blanchard (2001), the leading researcher of this *fraternal birth order effect*, has found it in 14 studies, involving over 7,000 total participants.

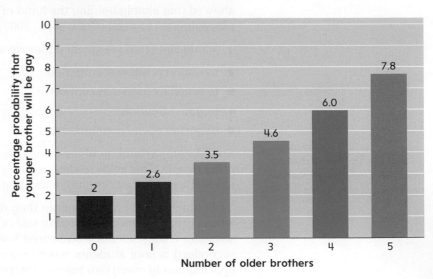

FIGURE 11.14 Homosexuality: the fraternal birth order effect.

The presence of each older brother increases by about one-third the relative probability that a later-born male child will be gay. Thus if there is a 2% probability that a man with no older brothers is gay, then the probability for a man with one older brother is about 2.6–2.7%, roughly a one-third relative increase.

Source: Adapted from Blanchard and Bogaert, 1996.

 In review

■ During sexual intercourse, people often experience a four-stage physiological response pattern consisting of excitement, plateau, orgasm and resolution.

■ Sex hormones have organizational effects that guide prenatal organ development along either a male or female pattern. Sex hormones also have activational effects that influence sexual desire.

■ Sexual fantasy can trigger arousal, whereas psychological difficulties can interfere with sexual arousal. Cultural norms help determine the sexual practices and beliefs that are considered proper.

■ Environmental stimuli affect sexual desire. Viewing sexual violence reinforces men's belief in rape myths and generally increases men's aggression towards women, at least temporarily.

■ Sexual orientation involves dimensions of self-identity, sexual attraction and actual sexual behaviour. Scientists still do not know conclusively what determines an individual's sexual orientation.

SOCIAL MOTIVATION

What makes your life most meaningful? To many people, close relationships are one key. Abraham Maslow (1954) viewed belongingness as a basic psychological need, and considerable research indicates that, indeed, 'the need to belong is a powerful, fundamental, and extremely pervasive motivation' (Baumeister & Leary, 1995, p. 497).

Why Do We Affiliate?

Humans are social beings who affiliate in many ways, in peer groups, in families, with work colleagues and, even, in the bus queue with strangers. Some theorists propose that over the course of evolution, individuals whose biological make-up predisposed them to affiliate were more likely to survive and reproduce than those who were reclusive. By affording greater access to sexual mates, more protection from predators, an efficient division of labour and the passing of knowledge across generations, a socially oriented lifestyle had considerable adaptive value (Kottak, 2000).

In today's world, research has shown that positive social relationships are important contributors to life satisfaction (Diener, Tamir, & Scollon, 2006; Haller & Hadler, 2006). Social relationships also help insulate us from stressors in our lives. One recent study showed that simply holding the hand of another person during a stressful event can lower physiological arousal (Coan et al., 2006).

Craig Hill (1987) suggested that we affiliate for four basic psychological reasons:

- to obtain positive stimulation
- to receive emotional support
- to gain attention
- to permit social comparison.

social comparison comparing our beliefs, feelings and behaviours with those of other people

Social comparison involves comparing our beliefs, feelings and behaviours with those of other people. This helps us determine whether our responses are 'normal' and enables us to judge the level of our cognitive and physical abilities (Festinger, 1954).

People differ in how strongly they desire friendship. In one study, university students who scored high on a personality test of 'need for affiliation' made more friends during the semester than students who scored low (Byrne & Greendlinger, 1989). In another study, secondary school students wore beepers over a one-week period. They were signalled approximately every two hours, at which time they recorded their thoughts and activities. Participants with a high need for affiliation were more likely than their peers to report that they were thinking about friends and wishing that they could be with people (Wong & Csikszentmihalyi, 1991). Still, even people with strong affiliation needs, however, usually desire some time alone. Conversely, people with lower affiliation needs still seek periodic social contact. Some theorists, therefore, view affiliation needs within a homeostatic model (O'Connor & Rosenblood, 1996). They propose that each of us has our own optimal range of social contact. After periods when contact exceeds that range, we compensate by temporarily seeking more solitude. After periods when social contact falls below the optimal range, we increase our effort to be with others. Although some human and animal findings are consistent with this model, it needs much more testing.

Many studies have shown, however, that situational factors influence our tendency to affiliate. For example, fear-inducing situations increase our desire to be with others. During emergencies, as in the aftermath of earthquakes, floods and hurricanes, many people find themselves bonding with strangers. When afraid, we may prefer to be with others who face the same situation we do, which helps us gauge the normalcy of our reactions (Schachter, 1959).

When possible, we seem to desire most strongly to be with others who have already been through the same or similar situations (Kulik & Mahler, 2000). Doing so can provide us with information about what to expect. In one study, hospital patients awaiting open-heart surgery expressed a stronger desire to have room-mates who already had been through surgery than pre-operative room-mates like themselves. In a later study, when

patients were actually assigned post-operative rather than pre-operative room-mates, they became less anxious and later recovered from surgery more quickly (Kulik, Mahler, & Moore, 1996).

Being rejected or excluded from social relationships is a painful event for most people, and exclusion evokes a desire for social reconnection. In one set of experiments, threat of social exclusion caused university students to express greater interest in working with others and making new friends, and to provide more rewards to their new interaction and partners (Maner, DeWall, Baumeister, & Schaller, 2007).

More recently it has been found that this exclusion and its effects need not even be in the real world. Abrams, Weick, Thomas, Colbe and Franklin (2011) reported that something as simple as being ostracized from an online game can have negative effects on a number of measures: self-esteem, a sense of belonging, a sense of a meaningful existence, and had a detrimental effect on mood state. However, it is worth noting that Abrams et al. found that ostracism had different effects on different age groups – with younger participants feeling that their self-esteem was more threatened than other groups, whereas for adolescents there was a greater effect of ostracism on sense of belonging. These effects may reflect different groups' goals and aims at the time of ostracism, of course. For example, a sense of belonging may be more important to adolescents than to younger children, hence the stronger effect in this group.

> **Focus 11.9** Discuss evolutionary and psychological views of affiliation and factors that influence the desire to affiliate.

 In review

- Humans seek to affiliate in many ways. Affiliation has adaptive advantages and allows people to obtain positive stimulation, receive emotional support, gain attention and engage in social comparison.
- People differ in how strongly they need to affiliate, and some theorists view affiliative behaviour as governed by homeostatic principles.
- Situations that induce fear often increase people's tendency to affiliate. When afraid, people often seek the company of others who have been through or are currently experiencing the same or a similar situation.
- Some reliable sex differences occur in people's mating strategies and preferences, such as men's tendency to seek younger women and women's tendency to seek older men.
- Social exclusion is a painful experience for most people, and it often leads to attempts to reconnect socially in new relationships.

ACHIEVEMENT MOTIVATION

In striving to create an independent republic of India, Lal Bahadur exemplified the desire to achieve. As a university student, you are keenly aware of society's emphasis on achievement, and you know that whether in school, sports, music or other fields, some people seek out and thrive on challenges and others do not. In the 1950s, David McClelland, John Atkinson, and their co-workers (McClelland, Atkinson, Clark, & Lowell, 1953) began to explore individual differences in **need for achievement**, a positive desire to accomplish tasks and compete successfully with standards of excellence.

> **need for achievement**
> a positive desire to accomplish tasks and compete successfully with standards of excellence

Motive for Success and Fear of Failure

McClelland and Atkinson proposed that achievement behaviour can stem from a positively oriented *motive for success* and a negatively oriented motivation to avoid failure, more commonly called *fear of failure*. Need for achievement is the positive orientation towards success. In terms of the behavioural activation and behavioural inhibition systems discussed earlier, motive for success is the part of the BAS that relates to the achievement domain. Fear of failure is a BIS function.

McClelland and Atkinson measured the motive for success with a psychological test that asked participants to write stories in response to a number of pictures, such as the

FIGURE II.15 Pictures like this are used to elicit stories that are scored for the motive to succeed.

Which of the following two stories, written by different people, reflects a stronger motive to succeed? (I) This young man is sitting in school, but he is dreaming about the day when he will become a doctor. He will study and work harder than anyone else. He goes on to become one of the top medical researchers in the world. (2) The boy is daydreaming about how much he hates being in school. . . . He would like to run away from home and just take it easy on a tropical island. However, he is doomed to be in the rat race the rest of his life.

Source: ©iStock.com/ Juanmonino

one in Figure 11.15. The stories were then analysed for achievement-relevant themes using a standardized coding system. The avoidance motive, fear of failure, was measured by psychological tests that asked people to report how much anxiety they experienced in achievement situations. McClelland and Atkinson found that their measures of need for achievement and fear of failure were independent (uncorrelated) dimensions, so that people could be high in both motives, low in both, or high in one and low in the other.

People who have a strong motive for success seek the thrill of victory, whereas those motivated by fear of failure seek to avoid the agony of defeat. Common sense suggests that a strong motive for success combined with a strong fear of failure might lead a person to perform better than someone who is motivated only by a desire for success. But this is not so. The anxiety associated with fear of failure can negate the impact of the need for achievement and can impair performance. In sports, the athlete with a high fear of failure is the one who tends to succumb to pressure (R. E. Smith, 1996).

People high in achievement and low in fear of failure, called *high-need achievers*, do not necessarily outperform low-need achievers when conditions are relaxed and tasks are easy. However, when tasks are challenging or the importance of doing well is stressed, high-need achievers outshine low-need achievers. They perform at a higher level, and they are more persistent when they encounter barriers to achievement (McClelland, 1989). In general, high-need achievers are most likely to strive hard for success when they perceive themselves as personally responsible for the outcome, when they perceive some risk of not succeeding, and when there is an opportunity to receive performance feedback (Koestner & McClelland, 1990).

When given a choice of performing a task that is very easy (a high probability of success), moderately difficult (a 40–60% probability of success) or very difficult (a low probability of success), which do you predict that high-need achievers will choose? Contrary to what you might expect, they prefer intermediate risks to extremely high or low risks because the outcome – success versus failure – *is most uncertain* (Atkinson & Birch, 1978). In contrast, low-need achievers are more likely to choose tasks that are easy (where success is almost assured) or very difficult (where success is not expected, so that nothing is on the line).

To understand this pattern, realize that it is the individual's *perception* of outcome uncertainty that counts. For most of us, the probability of successfully climbing Mount Everest is virtually zero. But to highly trained mountaineers, the task is neither impossible nor easy. Decades ago, sociologist and mountain climber Dick Emerson (1966) joined a Mount Everest expedition. As he predicted, the team members' communications with one another throughout the long climb struck a balance between optimistic and pessimistic comments about the chances of reaching their goal. This kept the climbers' perceived chance of success or failure close to 50:50 and maintained maximum motivation.

Achievement Goal Theory

Another way to understand achievement motivation is to examine the success goals that people seek to attain in task situations. **Achievement goal theory** focuses on the manner in which success is defined both by the individual and within the achievement situation itself. At the individual level, achievement goal theorists are interested in the achievement goal orientation that people have (Dweck, 1999). They differentiate between a **mastery orientation**, in which the focus is on personal improvement, giving maximum effort and perfecting new skills, and an **ego orientation**, in which the goal is to outperform others (hopefully, with as little effort as possible). At the situational level, the theory focuses on the **motivational climate** that encourages or rewards either a mastery approach or an ego approach to defining success (Figure 11.16).

Achievement Goal Orientations

Another way to understand achievement motivation is to examine the goals that people seek to attain in task situations. Think for a moment of a class you are taking. On a scale of 1 ('not at all true of me') to 7 ('very true of me'), rate statements:

1. I want to learn as much as possible from this class.
2. I am motivated by the thought of outperforming the other students in this class.

achievement goal theory focuses on the manner in which success is defined both by the individual and within the achievement situation itself

mastery orientation focus is on personal improvement, giving maximum effort and perfecting new skills

ego orientation the goal is to outperform others (hopefully, with as little effort as possible)

motivational climate situation which encourages or rewards either a mastery approach or an ego approach to defining success

3. My goal is to avoid learning less than I possibly could in this class.

4. The main thing is to avoid doing more poorly than the others in this class.

These statements represent four different achievement goals, two of which are approach goals and two of which are avoidance or fear of failure goals (Curry, Elliot, Fonseca, & Moller, 2006; Elliot & McGregor, 2001). **Mastery-approach goals** (statement 1) focus on the desire to master a task and learn new knowledge or skills, whereas **ego-approach goals** (statement 2) reflect a competitive orientation that focuses on being judged favourably relative to other people. On the avoidance side, **master-avoidance goals** (statement 3) reflect a fear of not performing up to one's own standards, whereas **ego-avoidance goals** (statement 4) centre on avoiding being outperformed by others. These four goals are embodied in a 2 (definitions of success) × 2 (approach versus avoidance) framework as different motivational approaches (Figure 11.16). According to the **2 × 2 achievement goal theory**, each of us can be described in terms of an 'achievement motivation profile' using statements such as the four above. In one sample of university students, Van Yperen (2006) found that 34.4% were highest in mastery-approach, 13.7% in ego-approach, 33.6% in mastery-avoidance and 18.3% in ego-avoidance. Men were twice as likely as women to report ego avoidance goals and women were more likely than men to report mastery-avoidance goals. No sex differences were apparent in the two approach-goal orientations.

The 2 × 2 achievement goal framework is relatively new, but already preliminary results indicate that the four motives have different relations to other variables (Schunk, Pintrich, & Meese, 2007). University students' achievement goals for a particular class, measured early in the academic term, help predict their psychological responses to the course as well as their course performance. Students with dominant mastery-approach motivation have higher intrinsic motivation to learn the material, perceive examinations as a positive challenge, and rate the course as more interesting and enjoyable. Students with ego avoidance motivation show exactly the opposite pattern. They lack intrinsic motivation, perceive examinations as anxiety-provoking threats, report low levels of interest and enjoyment, and perform more poorly than any other motivational group. Interestingly, ego-approach motivation is most strongly associated with high performance, but with less intrinsic motivation and enjoyment than mastery-approach motivation. Finally, in relation to intrinsic motivation, enjoyment, and feelings of competence, mastery-avoidance motivation seems more positive than ego-avoidance motivation and less positive than mastery-approach motivation, but it bears little relation to quality of performance (Curry et al., 2006; Van Yperen, 2006).

By incorporating both desire for success and fear of failure into one theory, the 2 × 2 framework represents a promising approach to understanding the various forms that achievement-related motives can take. Where performance in academic settings is concerned, the optimal motivational pattern may be a combination of mastery-approach and ego-approach goals. The mastery-approach goal enhances enjoyment and interest in the activity, and the ego-approach goal fosters higher performance within the competitive college environment, where grades are often determined by one's performance relative to others (Harackiewicz, Barron, Tauer, & Elliot, 2002; McGregor & Elliot, 2002). The same may be true within competitive sports settings (McArdle & Duda, 2002).

FIGURE 11.16 Achievement goal theory.

Achievement goal theory focuses on the ways in which success is defined, both by individuals and within achievement environments. Individuals may have mastery or ego goal orientations, and the motivational climate created in achievement situations by significant others may emphasize and support mastery goals, such as effort and skill improvement, or ego definitions of success, such as outperforming others.

mastery-approach goals the desire to master a task and learn new knowledge or skills

ego-approach goals a competitive orientation that focuses on being judged favourably relative to other people

mastery-avoidance goals a fear of not performing up to one's own standards

ego-avoidance goals avoiding being outperformed by others

2 × 2 achievement goal theory each of us can be described in terms of an 'achievement motivation profile'

Not all people are high on both mastery and ego orientations, however. If you are going to be high on one or the other, which would be preferable? Although both goal orientations contribute to success, in achievement contexts ranging from academic to work and sport settings, research indicates that a mastery goal orientation has several psychological advantages over an ego orientation (Dweck, 1999; McArdle & Duda, 2002). When success is defined as 'being one's best' rather than 'competing with others', people can focus on and enjoy their own improvement and accomplishments. They are more likely to experience intrinsic motivation and enjoyment of the activity, persist in the face of difficulties, select challenging goals and exert maximum effort.

For an ego-oriented person, experiencing personal improvement or knowing that one did one's best would not in itself occasion feelings of success or competence. Indeed, knowing that one tried hard and failed to outperform others would cause an ego-oriented person to feel especially incompetent. If ego-oriented people begin to question their ability to meet performance demands or to compete successfully with others, they are more likely to reduce persistence and avoid the challenge at hand (Nicholls, 1989). This would be especially likely in those high in the avoidance variant of ego orientation (Elliott & Church, 1997). If you turn winning and losing at everyday tasks into life-or-death situations, it seems likely that problems will arise. For one thing, you will be dead a lot.

Motivational climate

Besides individual differences in goal orientations, situational factors influence how success is defined. The motivational climate of an achievement setting is influenced by significant others, such as parents, teachers, coaches and supervisors (Ames, 1992; Chi, 2004). In an ego-involving climate, performers are compared with one another, urged to compete to be the best, and those who perform best get special attention. In a mastery-involving climate, effort, enjoyment of the activity and personal improvement are emphasized and rewarded. The assumption is that if people work to achieve their potential and give maximum effort, winning will take care of itself. These differing conceptions of success can have strong effects on participants. In children, they help shape the achievement goal orientation(s) that are internalized.

Mastery-involving achievement environments have been linked to a variety of positive effects in school and sport settings. They foster higher intrinsic motivation and enjoyment of the setting, enhance perceptions of learning and mastery, and bolster self-esteem. Performance anxiety is also lower in such settings because the emphasis is on doing one's best (which is personally controllable) rather than on a win outcome that is dependent in part on how others perform. An ego-involving climate fosters the belief that ability, rather than hard work, leads to success, and satisfaction is gained by outperforming others rather than through skill improvement. At the level of task performance, mastery climates result in better skill development and higher performance levels, due in part to increased effort, greater enjoyment, and lowered anxiety (Dweck, 1999; McArdle & Duda, 2002).

Attempts to influence motivational climate have yielded encouraging results. When youth sport coaches were trained to create a mastery environment, their young athletes showed increased mastery-approach motivation and reduced fear of failure over the course of the sport season (Smith, Smoll, & Cumming, 2007; Smoll, Smith, & Cumming, 2007).

Family, Culture and Achievement Needs

How does achievement motivation develop? Providing a cognitively stimulating home environment fosters children's intrinsic motivation to perform academic tasks (Gottfried, Fleming, & Gottfried, 1998). And when parents or other key caregivers encourage and reward achievement but do not punish failure, they foster a strong motive for success (Koestner & McClelland, 1990). Conversely, fear of failure seems to develop when caregivers take successful achievement for granted but punish failure, thereby teaching the child to dread the possibility of failing (Weiner, 1992). Providing a mastery motivational climate in the home, the school, and the athletic setting also encourages the development of a mastery achievement orientation (Dweck, 1999; McArdle & Duda, 2002).

Cultural norms also shape achievement motivation. Individualistic cultures, such as those in Europe and North America, tend to stress personal achievement. In cultures that nurture collectivism, such as those in China and Japan, achievement motivation more strongly reflects

Focus II.I0 How do the motives and task behaviours of high- versus low-need achievers differ? Describe the achievement goal orientations and motivational climates in achievement goal theory.

a desire to fit into the family and social group, meet its expectations and work for its goals (Markus & Kitayama, 1991). Chinese secondary school students, for example, typically care more about meeting their parents' expectations for academic success than do American students (Chen & Lan, 1998). In collectivistic Japan, business organizations have traditionally adopted the concept of *kaizen* (continuous improvement), encouraging workers to develop skills and increase productivity (Elsey & Fujiwara, 2000). Such companies assume responsibility for their employees' welfare, promote them gradually and are willing to retain them for life. In turn, the workers are more strongly motivated by loyalty to their managers and to the organization as the company becomes integral to their identities.

At the same time, the human desire to achieve transcends culture and can manifest itself in intriguing ways. Throughout history, some people have left their homelands to seek adventure or better lives elsewhere. Might achievement motivation relate to the desire to emigrate? To answer this question, researchers measured the achievement motivation of university students in Albania, the Czech Republic and Slovenia, and asked students where they would like to live for most of their adult lives. In each sample, students who expressed a desire to emigrate had higher average achievement motivation scores than students who said they wanted to remain in their homeland (Boneva, Frieze, Ferligoj, Pauknerová, & Orgocka, 1998).

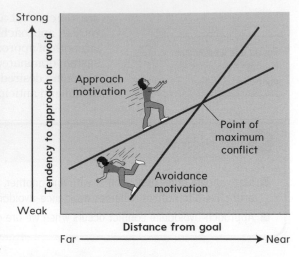

FIGURE 11.17 Approach–avoidance conflict.

According to Neal Miller (1944), the tendency to approach and the tendency to avoid grow stronger as one moves closer to the goal. However, the tendency to avoid increases faster than the tendency to approach. Maximum conflict is experienced where the two gradients cross, because at this point the opposing motives are equal in strength.

 In review

- High-need achievers have a strong motive for success and relatively low fear of failure. They tend to seek moderately difficult tasks that are challenging but attainable. Low-need achievers are more likely to choose easy tasks, where success is assured, or very difficult tasks where success is not expected.

- Mastery, ego-approach, and ego-avoidance goals are four basic achievement goals. Mastery goals are associated with viewing achievement tasks as a positive challenge, whereas ego-avoidance goals are linked to viewing such tasks as threatening. Ego-approach goals are most strongly linked to eventual course grades for college students, mastery goals to course enjoyment.

- Compared with ego-involving environments, mastery-involving motivational climates foster higher enjoyment and intrinsic motivation, greater feelings of self-determination, lower levels of performance anxiety, and better learning of skills, greater effort and higher performance.

- Child-rearing and cultural factors influence the nature and expression of achievement motivation.

MOTIVATIONAL CONFLICT

Motivational goals sometimes conflict with one another. Our desires to achieve success and to have fun may clash, for example, when we must choose between studying for an examination and attending a party. When something attracts us, we tend to approach it; when something repels us, we tend to avoid it. Different combinations of these tendencies can produce three basic types of conflict.

Approach–approach conflict occurs when we face two attractive alternatives and selecting one means losing the other. Conflict is greatest when both alternatives, such as a choice between two desirable careers, are equally attractive. In contrast, **avoidance–avoidance conflict** occurs when we must choose between two undesirable alternatives. Do I study boring material for an examination, or do I skip studying and fail? **Approach–avoidance conflict** involves being attracted to and repelled by the same goal. A squirrel being offered food by a person on a park bench is motivated by hunger to approach and by fear to keep its distance. A man desires an intimate relationship with a woman but fears the possibility of future rejection.

Approach and avoidance tendencies grow stronger as we get nearer to a desired goal (Miller, 1944). Usually, the avoidance tendency increases in strength faster than the approach (Figure 11.17). Thus at first we may be attracted to a goal and only slightly repelled by its

Focus 11.11 How do family and cultural factors influence achievement motivation?

approach–approach conflict when we face two attractive alternatives and selecting one means losing the other

avoidance–avoidance conflict when we must choose between two undesirable alternatives

approach–avoidance conflict being attracted to and repelled by the same goal

Focus II.I2 Explain and illustrate three types of motivational conflict.

drawbacks, but as we get closer to it the negative aspects become dominant. We may stop, retreat, approach again and continue to vacillate in a state of conflict. However, the general strength of approach and avoidance tendencies differs across people. Behavioural activation system-dominated individuals are more attuned to positive stimuli and the possibility of obtaining desired outcomes, whereas those with strong BIS tendencies are more sensitive to actual and anticipated negative outcomes (Elliot & Thrash, 2002; Sutton, 2002).

In review

■ Motivational goals may conflict with one another. Approach–approach conflict occurs when a person has to select between two attractive alternatives, whereas avoidance–avoidance conflict involves choosing between two undesirable alternatives.

■ Approach–avoidance conflict occurs when we are attracted to and repelled by the same goal.

EMOTION

emotions feeling (or affect) states that involve a pattern of cognitive, physiological and behavioural reactions to events

Life without emotion would be bland and empty. Our experiences of love, anger, joy, fear and other emotions energize and add colour to our lives. **Emotions** are feeling (or affect) states that involve a pattern of cognitive, physiological and behavioural reactions to events. Emotion theorist Richard Lazarus (2001) believes that motivation and emotions are always linked, because we react emotionally only when our motives and goals are gratified, threatened, or frustrated (Figure 11.18).

(a)   (b)

FIGURE II.18 The intimate relations between motivation and emotion are seen in the strong emotional responses that occur when important goals are either attained or lost.

Source: (a) © Leo Mason sports photos/Alamy; (b) DAMIEN MEYER/AFP/Getty Images

The intimate relations between motivation and emotion are seen in the strong emotional responses that occur when important goals are either attained or lost.

Emotions have important adaptive functions. Some emotions, such as fear and alarm, are part of an emergency arousal system that increases our chances of survival, as when we fight or flee when confronted by threat or danger. But positive emotions, such as interest, joy, excitement, contentment and love, also have important adaptive functions. They help us form intimate relationships and broaden our thinking and behaviour so that we explore, consider new ideas, try out new ways to achieve goals, play and savour what we have (Fredrickson, 1998).

Emotions are also an important form of social communication. By providing clues about our internal states and intentions, emotions influence how other people behave towards us (Isaacs, 1998). Consider, for example, the effects of a baby's crying on adults, who generally respond with caretaking behaviours that have obvious survival value for the infant. Adults' expressions of sadness and distress also evoke concern, empathy and helping behaviour from others.

Positive emotional expressions also pay off. A smiling infant is likely to increase parents' feelings of affection and caring, thereby increasing the likelihood that the child's biological and emotional needs will be satisfied. Happy adults also tend to attract others and to have richer and more supportive relationships (Diener et al., 2006).

Focus II.I3 In what ways are negative and positive emotions adaptive?

Positive emotions are an important part of life satisfaction, and negative emotions foster unhappiness (Diener et al., 2006). Negative emotions also are typically involved in normal stress reactions (Evans-Martin, 2007) and in many psychological disorders (Rottenberg & Johnson, 2007). The ability to self-regulate one's emotions is one mark of psychological adjustment (Denollet, Nyklicek, & Vingerhoets, 2007; Garber & Dodge, 2007).

THINKING ABOUT EMOTION

The study of emotion is a difficult one for psychologists for a variety of reasons. The nature of emotions has been very difficult to pin down and there is often little agreement about

the definition of emotion. This has led to many psychologists avoiding the topic altogether, despite it being a fascinating area in many ways. This avoidance was clearly shown in Gardner's 25-year-old claim that emotion 'may be important for cognitive functioning but whose inclusion at this point would unnecessarily complicate the cognitive-scientific enterprise' (Gardner, 1985, p. 6).

Nonetheless, emotion has been extensively studied by psychologists and we now have some understanding of the area. One important issue is that of terminology. In everyday usage we may not differentiate a great deal between terms like 'mood' and 'emotion' but this is not the case in the scientific study of emotion. When psychologists use the term 'emotion' they are referring to relatively short, stimulus-elicited responses that are often quite intense (joy, anger, sadness) whereas the term 'mood' is used to refer to rather less intense, more stable, trait-like states.

Further debate arises through the consideration of how best to conceive of emotion. The first notion to be considered here is that of the basic emotion model. This is the idea that all emotions are derived from a set of innate and universal emotions – sadness, anger, fear, happiness, for example (Darwin, 1965 [first published in 1872], and more recently, Ekman, 1992, 1999). However, even under this conception there has been relatively little consensus on how many and what these basic emotions are. Ekman has argued for six or seven basic emotions whereas others have argued for more with Plutchik (1980) suggesting eight and Izard (1992) up to 10.

However, the alternative view is that of the dimensional approach (Osgood, 1969; Schlosberg, 1954) in which emotions are not considered to be discrete and do not result from unique, independent neural systems but rather from activity on two different dimensions: arousal and valence. This notion is expressed in the circumplex model (e.g. Colibazzi et al., 2010; Posner, Russell, & Peterson, 2005; Russell, 1980). Valence ranges from pleasure to displeasure and arousal from activated to deactivated and the notion is that all emotions can be interpreted as being at some point of activation across these dimensions. For example, as can be seen in Figure 11.19 excitement can be conceptualized as reflecting relatively high levels of both arousal and positive valence.

There has been considerable debate over these categorical and dimensional models and there has been little agreement among researchers and there are arguments for and against both positions. Ultimately, both conceptualizations of emotion are likely to have some validity and are useful in extending our understanding of emotion.

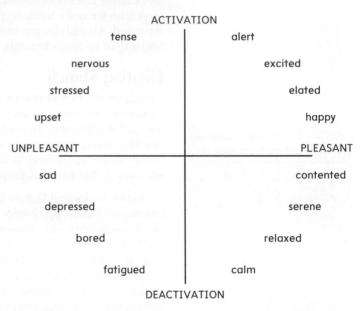

FIGURE 11.19 The circumplex model of affect showing valence on the horizontal axis (ranging from pleasant to unpleasant) and arousal on the vertical axis (ranging from activation to deactivation).

THE NATURE OF EMOTIONS

Our emotional states share four common features:

1. Emotions are triggered by external or internal *eliciting stimuli*.

2. Emotional responses result from our *appraisals* of these stimuli, which give the situation its perceived meaning and significance.

3. Our *bodies respond physiologically* to our appraisals. We may become physically aroused, as when we feel fear, joy or anger; or we may experience decreased arousal, as when we feel contentment or depression.

4. Emotions include *behaviour tendencies*. Some are *expressive behaviours* (e.g., smiling with joy, crying). Others are *instrumental behaviours*, ways of doing something about the stimulus that evoked the emotion (e.g., studying for an anxiety-arousing test, fighting back in self-defence).

Focus 11.14 Describe the four major components of emotion and how they influence one another.

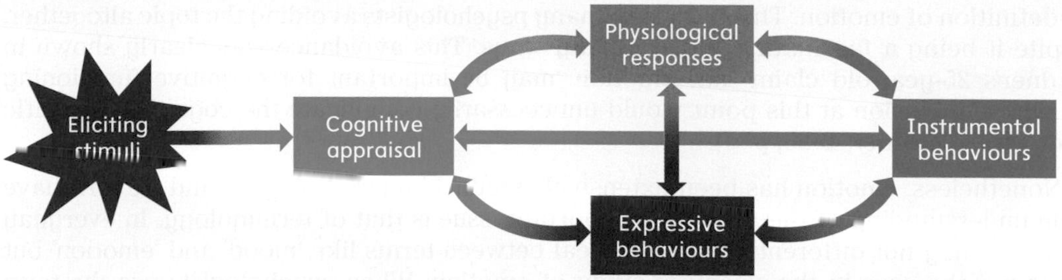

FIGURE 11.20 Components of emotion.

Emotion involves relations between eliciting stimuli, cognitive appraisal processes, physiological arousal, expressive behaviours and instrumental behaviours. Note the reciprocal (two-way) causal relations that exist among the appraisal, physiological arousal and behavioural components. Appraisal influences arousal and expressive behaviours, and the latter affect ongoing appraisals.

Eliciting stimuli → Cognitive appraisal → Physiological responses / Expressive behaviours → Instrumental behaviours

Figure 11.20 illustrates the general relations among these four emotional components. For example, an insulting remark from another person (eliciting stimulus) may evoke a cognitive appraisal that we have been unfairly demeaned, an increase in physiological arousal, a clenching of jaws and fists (expressive behaviour), and a verbal attack on the other person (instrumental behaviour). As the two-way arrows indicate, these emotional components can affect one another, so that our thoughts influence our feelings and our feelings influence our appraisals (Frijda, Manstead, & Bem, 2005). They exist in a larger associative network that also includes links to motives, memories, ideas and action tendencies. Stimulation of any of the network's components can trigger other elements, depending on the strengths of the associative links (Berkowitz & Harmon-Jones, 2004). For example, some people can generate strong anger and a tendency towards aggression just by recalling an event in which they were wronged. We will discuss other linkages as well. Thus emotion is a dynamic, ongoing *process*, and any of its four elements can change rapidly in the course of an emotional episode.

Eliciting Stimuli

Emotions do not occur in a vacuum. They are responses to situations, people, objects or events. We become angry *at* something or someone; fearful or proud *of* something; in love *with* someone. Moreover, the **eliciting stimuli** that trigger cognitive appraisals and emotional responses are not always external; they can be internal stimuli, such as a mental image of an upcoming holiday that makes us feel happy or a memory of an unpleasant encounter that arouses anger in us.

Innate biological factors help determine which stimuli have the greatest potential to arouse emotions (Panksepp, 2005). Newborn infants come equipped with the capacity to respond emotionally with either interest or distress to events in their environment (Galati & Lavelli, 1997). Adults, too, may be biologically primed to experience emotions in response to certain stimuli that have evolutionary significance. As we saw in **Chapter 7**, this may help explain why the majority of human phobias involve 'primal' stimuli such as heights, water, sharks, snakes or spiders, rather than modern threats such as guns, electrical transformers and automobiles (Öhman & Wiens, 2005). A wide variety of aversive stimuli – pain, heat and cold, foul odours – can evoke anger and aggressive tendencies towards people who had nothing to do with creating the discomfort (Berkowitz & Harmon-Jones, 2004).

Learning also influences our emotions. Previous experiences can turn certain people or situations into eliciting stimuli. The mere sight of one's lover can evoke feelings of passion; the sight of a disliked person can trigger instantaneous revulsion that seems almost reflexive. On the broadest level, cultures have different standards for defining the good, the bad and the ugly that affect how we appraise and respond to stimuli. Physical features that provoke sexual arousal and feelings of infatuation in one culture, such as ornamental facial scars, may elicit quite different feelings in another.

The Cognitive Component

Cognitions (thoughts, images, memories, interpretations) are involved in virtually every aspect of emotion. Mental processes can evoke emotional responses. They are part of our inner experience of the emotion, and they influence how we express our emotions and act on them. A situation may evoke pleasure or distress, depending on how we appraise it (Scherer, 2001). For example, a sexual advance may elicit anger, fear or disgust instead of pleasure if it is unwanted or deemed inappropriate. **Cognitive appraisals** are the interpretations and meanings that we attach to sensory stimuli. In his component process model Scherer

eliciting stimuli trigger cognitive appraisals and emotional responses

 Chapter 7, Page 296

cognitive appraisals the interpretations and meanings that we attach to sensory stimuli

(2001, 2004) argued that the results of appraisal yield a unique response for any given emotional event. He argues that emotion is designed to be adaptive and that appraisal will equip the individual to respond appropriately in an emotional situation. This response will include aspects such as behavioural intentions and facial expressions. Interestingly, some of Scherer's work has found support for models of emotion that are dimensional in nature rather than categorical (e.g., Scherer & Ellgring, 2007). The issue of appraisal is an important one in emotion and we will return to it later in the chapter in terms of whether it comes before or after the experience of emotion.

FIGURE 11.21 Differences in appraisal can trigger entirely different emotional reactions, as in this instance. What kinds of appraisals are likely occurring in these people?

Source: ©iStock.com/© LifesizeImages

Both conscious and unconscious processes are involved in appraisals (Feldman-Barrett, Niedenthal, & Winkielman, 2007). Often we are not consciously aware of the appraisals that underlie emotional responses. Some appraisals seem to involve little more than an almost automatic interpretation of sensory input based on previous conditioning (Smith & Kirby, 2004). Indeed, most strong emotions are probably triggered initially in this automatic fashion, after which we may appraise the situation in a more reasoning manner. Even at this more 'cognitive' level, however, our habitual ways of thinking can run off in a subconscious shorthand with little or no awareness on our part (Clore & Centerbar, 2004; Phelps, 2005). We often fail to appreciate how arbitrarily we interpret 'the way things are'.

The idea that emotional reactions are triggered by cognitive appraisals rather than external situations helps account for the fact that different people (or even the same person at different times) can have different emotional reactions to the same object, situation, or person (Figure 11.21).

Culture and appraisal

Cross-cultural researchers have asked people in various countries to recall events that triggered certain emotions and to answer questions about how they appraised or interpreted the situations. In one study conducted in 27 different countries, people exhibited strong cross-cultural similarities in the types of appraisals that evoked joy, fear, anger, sadness, disgust, shame and guilt (Wallbott & Scherer, 1988). Whenever any of these emotions occurred, similar appraisals were involved, regardless of the culture.

Despite these cross-cultural commonalities in appraisal, particular situations can evoke different appraisals and emotional reactions, depending on one's culture (Mesquita & Markus, 2005). Consider, for example, the circumstance of being alone. Tahitians often appraise being alone as an opportunity for bad spirits to bother a person, and fear is the most common emotional response. In the close-knit Utku Inuit, an Eskimo culture, being alone signifies social rejection and isolation, triggering sadness and loneliness. In Western cultures, being alone may at times represent a welcome respite from the frantic pace of daily life, evoking contentment and happiness (Mesquita, Frijda, & Scherer, 1997). Thus, where appraisals are concerned, there seem to be certain universals but also some degree of cultural diversity in the more subtle aspects of interpreting situations.

 In review

- An emotion is a positive or negative feeling (or affective) state consisting of a pattern of cognitive, physiological and behavioural reactions to events that have relevance to important goals or motives. Emotions further our well-being in several ways: by rousing us to action, by helping us communicate with others, and by eliciting empathy and help.

- The primary components of emotion are the eliciting stimuli, cognitive appraisals, physiological arousal, and expressive and instrumental behaviours. Innate factors and learning play important roles in determining the arousal properties of stimuli.

- The cognitive component of emotional experience involves the evaluative and personal appraisal of the eliciting stimuli. Initial appraisals often occur in an automatic fashion that involves little thinking. The ability of thoughts to elicit emotional arousal has been demonstrated clinically and in experimental research. Cross-cultural research indicates considerable agreement across cultures in the appraisals that evoke basic emotions but also some degree of variation in more complex appraisals.

Physiological Component

When our feelings are stirred up, one of the first things we notice is bodily changes. Many parts of the body are involved in emotional arousal, but certain brain regions, the autonomic nervous system and the endocrine system play especially significant roles.

Brain structures and neurotransmitters

Emotions involve important interactions between several brain areas, including the limbic system and cerebral cortex (Berridge, 2004; Damasio, 2005). If animals are electrically stimulated in specific areas of the limbic system, especially the amygdala, they will growl at and attack anything that approaches. Destroying the same sites produces an absence of aggression, even if the animal is provoked or attacked. Other limbic areas show the opposite pattern: lack of emotion when they are stimulated and unrestrained emotion when they are removed.

The cerebral cortex has many connections with the hypothalamus, amygdala and other limbic system structures. Cognitive appraisal processes surely involve the cortex, where the mechanisms for language and complex thought reside. Moreover, the ability to regulate emotion depends heavily on the executive functions of the prefrontal cortex, a region of the brain which lies immediately behind the forehead (Denollet et al., 2007; LeDoux & Phelps, 2000).

Ground-breaking research by psychologist Joseph LeDoux (2000) has revealed that when the thalamus (the brain's sensory switchboard) receives input from the senses, it can send messages along two independent neural pathways, a 'high road' travelling up to the cortex and a 'low road' going directly to the nearby amygdala (Figure 11.22). The low road enables the amygdala to receive direct input from the senses and generate emotional reactions before the cerebral cortex has had time to fully interpret what is causing the reaction. LeDoux suggests that this primitive mechanism (which is the only emotional mechanism in species such as birds and reptiles) has survival value because it enables the organism to react with great speed before the cerebral cortex responds with a more carefully processed cognitive interpretation of the situation. This may be what occurs when a hiker sees what looks like a snake and jumps out of the way, only to realize an instant later that the object is actually a piece of rope.

The amygdala also seems to function as an early-warning system for threatening social stimuli. Consider a study by Winston et al. (2002) of the amygdala's response to different

Focus II.I5 According to LeDoux, which brain structures allow emotional responses to occur at two levels of processing?

FIGURE II.22 Dual emotional pathways.

Parallel neural processes may produce conscious and unconscious emotional responses at about the same time. LeDoux's research suggests that sensory input to the thalamus can be routed directly to the amygdala in the limbic system, producing an 'unconscious' emotional response before cognitive responses evoked by the other pathway to the cortex can occur.

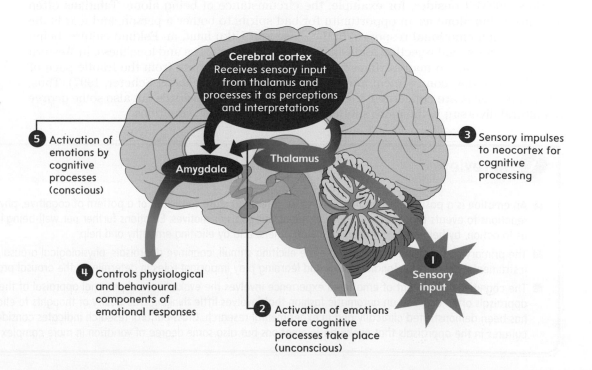

Cerebral cortex
Receives sensory input from thalamus and processes it as perceptions and interpretations

5 Activation of emotions by cognitive processes (conscious)

Amygdala

Thalamus

3 Sensory impulses to neocortex for cognitive processing

4 Controls physiological and behavioural components of emotional responses

I Sensory input

2 Activation of emotions before cognitive processes take place (unconscious)

kinds of faces. Brain scans using fMRI indicated a burst of activity in the amygdala when people viewed faces they rated as particularly untrustworthy, but showed a much smaller response to faces they judged as particularly trustworthy (Winston, Strange, O'Doherty, & Dolan, 2002). Another fMRI study showed that the amygdala also reacts to stimuli that evoke strong positive emotions (Hamann & Mao, 2002).

The existence of a dual system for emotional processing may help explain some puzzling aspects of our emotional lives. For example, most of us have had the experience of suddenly feeling a strong emotion without understanding why. LeDoux (2000) suggests that not all emotional responses register at the level of the cortex. He also suggests that people can have two simultaneous but different emotional reactions to the same event, a conscious one occurring as a result of cortical activity and an unconscious one triggered by the amygdala. This might help explain instances in which people are puzzled by behavioural reactions that seem to be at odds with the emotion they are consciously experiencing: 'I don't know why I came across as being angry. I felt very warm and friendly.' Some psychodynamic theorists are hailing these discoveries as support for the existence of conscious emotional processes (Westen, 1998b). Indeed, there is now little doubt that important aspects of emotional life can occur outside of conscious awareness (Bargh & Chartrand, 1999).

Neuroscientist Candace Pert (1997) argues that because all of the neural structures involved in emotion operate biochemically, it is the ebb and flow of various neurotransmitter substances that activate the emotional programmes residing in the brain. For example, dopamine and endorphin activity appears to underlie some pleasurable emotions, whereas serotonin and norepinephrine play a role in anger and in fear (Damasio, 2005; Depue & Collins, 1999). When the final story of the brain and emotion can at last be told, it will undoubtedly involve complex interactions between brain chemicals and neural structures (Frijda, 2006).

Hemispheric activation and emotion

Decades ago in Italy, psychiatrists who were treating clinically depressed patients with electric shock treatments to either the right or the left hemisphere observed a striking phenomenon. The electric current temporarily disrupted neural activity in the targeted hemisphere. With the left hemisphere knocked out (forcing the right hemisphere to take charge), patients had what physicians termed a 'catastrophic' reaction, wailing and crying until the shock effects wore off. But when they applied shock to the right hemisphere, allowing the left hemisphere to dominate, the patients reacted much differently; they seemed unconcerned, happy and sometimes even euphoric. Researchers noted a similar pattern of emotions in patients in whom one hemisphere had been damaged by lesions or strokes (Gainotti, 1972).

These findings suggest that left-hemisphere activation may underlie certain positive emotions and right-hemisphere functioning negative ones (Sutton, 2002). To test this proposition, Richard Davidson and Nathan Fox (1988) obtained EEG measures of frontal lobe activity as people experienced positive and negative emotions. They found that when people felt positive emotions by recalling pleasurable experiences or watching a happy film, the left hemisphere was relatively more active than the right. But when sadness or other negative emotions were evoked by memories or watching a disgusting film, the right hemisphere became relatively more active. Moreover, this hemispheric pattern seems to be innate. Infants as young as 3 to 4 days old showed a similar pattern of hemispheric activation: left-hemisphere activation when given a sweet sucrose solution, which infants like, and right-hemisphere dominance in response to a citric acid solution, which apparently disgusts them.

Davidson and Fox also found individual differences in typical, or *resting*, hemispheric activation when they recorded people's EEG responses under emotionally neutral conditions. These resting differences predicted the tendency to experience positive or negative emotions. For example, human infants with resting right-hemisphere dominance were more likely to become upset and cry if their mothers later left the room than were those with resting left-hemisphere dominance. In adults, a higher resting level of right-hemisphere EEG activity may be a risk factor for the later development of adult depressive disorders (Tomarken & Keener, 1998).

Focus 11.16 What evidence exists that positive and negative emotions involve different patterns of brain activation?

Autonomic and hormonal processes

You are afraid. Your heart starts to beat faster. Your body draws blood from your stomach to your muscles, and digestion slows to a crawl. You breathe harder and faster to get more energy-sustaining oxygen. Your blood-sugar level increases, producing more nutrients for your muscles. The pupils of your eyes dilate, admitting more light to increase your visual acuity. Your skin perspires to keep you cool and to flush out waste products created by extra exertion. Your muscles tense, ready for action.

Some theorists call this state of arousal the *fight-or-flight response*. It is produced by the sympathetic branch of the autonomic nervous system and by hormones from the endocrine system. The sympathetic nervous system produces arousal within a few seconds by directly stimulating the organs and muscles of the body. Meanwhile, the endocrine system pumps epinephrine, cortisol and other stress hormones into the bloodstream. These hormones produce physiological effects like those triggered by the sympathetic nervous system, but their effects are longer lasting and can keep the body aroused for a considerable length of time.

Do different emotions produce different patterns of arousal? Only subtle autonomic differences occur among basic emotions as different as anger and fear (Cacioppo, Berntson, Poehlmann, & Ito, 2000). Moreover, people differ from one another in their patterns of general arousal, so that we do not all show the same pattern of bodily arousal even when we are experiencing the same emotion. For example, when afraid, some of us might show marked changes in heart rate or blood pressure but only minor changes in muscle tension and respiration. Others would show different patterns. Thus there are no distinctive and universal physiological signatures for the basic emotions.

The Behavioural Component

Although we can never directly experience another person's feelings, we can often infer that someone is angry, sad, fearful or happy on the basis of **expressive behaviours**, the person's observable emotional displays. Indeed, others' emotional displays can even evoke similar responses in us, a process known as *empathy*. While watching a film, have you ever experienced the same emotion as the central character? Professional actors sometimes become so immersed in the expressive behaviours of their characters that the boundaries between self and role begin to fade. A particularly challenging role is that of Woyzeck, in Georg Büchner's play of the same name. Woyzeck is a soldier who is gradually driven insane through the immoral actions of those around him. Klaus Kinski, a famous German actor, had refused to play the role of Woyzeck on stage for fear that the experience would have a negative psychological effect upon him. Finally, he agreed to play the part in Werner Herzog's 1979 film. Kinski 'found himself much like the character he portrayed – pushed to the edge of insanity in a way which very nearly destroyed him. Some say he never fully recovered' (Knipfel, 2004). In a similar anecdote by Kirk Douglas, an American actor who played Vincent Van Gogh, the disturbed Dutch painter (who reportedly once cut off his ear and offered it to a prostitute):

> *I was close to getting lost in the character of Van Gogh. . . . I felt myself going over the line, into the skin of Van Gogh. . . . Sometimes I had to stop myself from reaching my hand up and touching my ear to find out if it was actually there. It was a frightening experience. That way lies madness. . . . I could never play him again.*
> (Lehmann-Haupt, 1988, p. 2)

Evolution and emotional expression

Where do emotional expressions come from? In his classic work *The Expression of Emotions in Man and Animals* (1965), Charles Darwin argued that emotional displays are products of evolution because they contributed to species survival. Darwin emphasized the basic similarity of emotional expression among animals and humans. For example, both wolves and humans bare their teeth when they are angry (Figure 11.23). As Darwin explained it, this behaviour makes the animal look more ferocious and thus decreases its chances of being attacked and perhaps killed in a fight. Darwin did not maintain that all forms of emotional expression are innate, but he believed that many of them are.

expressive behaviours the person's observable emotional displays

FIGURE II.23 Similarities among species in the expression of certain basic emotions convinced Darwin and other theorists that certain expressive behaviours have an evolutionary origin.

Source: (left) © twildlife ; (right) © DRB Images, LLC

Like Darwin, modern evolutionary theorists stress the adaptive value of emotional expression (Izard, 1989; Plutchik, 1994). They believe that a set of **fundamental emotional patterns**, or innate emotional reactions, are wired into the nervous system (Panksepp, 2005). Their research shows that certain emotional expressions (e.g., rage and terror) are similar across all cultures, suggesting a universal biological basis for them. The fundamental emotional patterns proposed by three evolutionary theorists are shown in Table 11.1. They argue that other emotions are based on some combination of these innate emotions. The evolutionary view does *not* assume that all emotional expressions are innate, nor does it deny that innate emotional expressions can be modified or inhibited as a result of social learning.

> **fundamental emotional patterns** innate emotional reactions

Facial expression of emotion

Most of us are fairly confident in our ability to read the emotions of others. Although many parts of the body can communicate feelings, we tend to concentrate on what the face tells us. Most other species have relatively few facial muscles, so their facial expressions are limited. Only monkeys, apes and humans have the well-developed facial muscles needed to produce a large number of expressions.

The development of sophisticated measuring procedures, such as Ekman and Friesen's (1987) Facial Action Coding System (FACS), have permitted the precise study of facial expressions. The FACS requires a trained observer to dissect an observed expression in terms of all the muscular actions that produced it. It takes about 100 minutes to score each minute of observed facial expression.

TABLE II.I Fundamental or primary innate emotions proposed by three leading evolutionary theorists

Carroll Izard	Silvan Tomkins	Robert Plutchik
Anger	Anger	Anger
Fear	Fear	Fear
Joy	Joy	Enjoyment
Disgust	Disgust	Disgust
Interest	Interest	Anticipation
Surprise	Surprise	Surprise
Contempt	Contempt	
Shame	Shame	
	Sadness	Sadness
	Distress	
Guilt		
		Acceptance

Sources: Based on Izard, 1982; Tomkins, 1991; Plutchik, 1994.

Although facial expressions can be valuable cues for judging emotion, even people within the same culture may learn to express the same emotions differently. For example, some people can appear very calm when they are angry or fearful, whereas others express even mild forms of those same emotions in a highly expressive manner. Fortunately, we usually know something about the situation to which people are reacting, and this often helps us judge their emotions. Researchers have found that people's accuracy and agreement in labelling emotions from pictures are considerably higher when the pictures reveal situational cues (Keltner & Ekman, 2000). If a woman is crying, is she weeping because of sadness or because of happiness? A background showing her being declared the winner of a lottery will result in a different emotional judgement than one showing her standing at a graveside.

Across many different cultures, women have proven to be more accurate judges of emotional expressions than men (Zuckerman, Hall, DeFrank, & Rosenthal, 1976). Perhaps the ability to read emotions accurately has greater adaptive significance for women, whose traditional role within many cultures has been to care for others and attend to their needs (Buss, 1991). This ability may also result from cultural encouragement for women to be sensitive to others' emotions and to express their feelings openly (Taylor, Klein, Lewis,

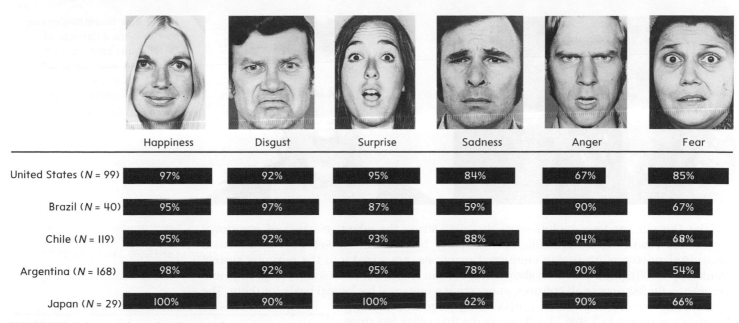

	Happiness	Disgust	Surprise	Sadness	Anger	Fear
United States (N = 99)	97%	92%	95%	84%	67%	85%
Brazil (N = 40)	95%	97%	87%	59%	90%	67%
Chile (N = 119)	95%	92%	93%	88%	94%	68%
Argentina (N = 168)	98%	92%	95%	78%	90%	54%
Japan (N = 29)	100%	90%	100%	62%	90%	66%

FIGURE II.24 Culture and emotional expression.

Percentages of people from five different cultures who judged each face as expressing the emotions listed beneath the pictures.

Source: *Darwin and Facial Expressions* by P. Ekman, Malor Books/Paul Ekman Group

Gruenewald. Gurung, & Updegraff, 2000b). However, it is worth noting that men who work in professions that emphasize these skills (such as psychotherapy, drama and art) are as accurate as women in judging others' emotional expressions (Rosenthal, Archer, DiMatteo, Koivumaki, & Rogers, 1974).

What of Darwin's claim that certain facial expressions universally indicate specific emotions? Do people in different cultures agree on the emotions being expressed in facial photographs? Figure 11.24 shows the results of one study. You can see that there is generally high agreement on these photos of basic emotions, but there are also some cultural variations. Other researchers have found levels of agreement ranging from 40% to 70% across a variety of cultures, well above chance but still far from perfect (Russell, 1994).

An experiment by Ekman, Friesen and Ellsworth (1972) nicely illustrates cultural commonalities and differences in emotional expression. Japanese and American students viewed a gory, stressful film in private. Unbeknown to them, their facial expressions were being videotaped by a hidden camera. The FACS codings of the students' facial displays showed no differences between the Japanese and American students; they expressed negative emotions of disgust and anxiety in the same way and with similar intensity as they watched the film. Afterwards, the students were individually interviewed by a person of their ethnic group concerning their reactions to the film. The Japanese masked their earlier feelings of anxiety and disgust and presented a happy face throughout the interview, whereas the Americans' negative facial expressions closely mirrored those photographed while they watched the stressful movie. Based on such findings, many emotion theorists conclude that innate biological factors and cultural display rules *combine* to shape emotional expression across different cultures.

> **Focus II.I7** How do evolutionary and cultural factors influence emotionally expressive behaviour?

Instrumental behaviours

Emotional responses are often calls to action, requiring a response to the situation that aroused the emotion. A highly anxious student must find some way to cope with an impending test. A mother angered by her child's behaviour must find a non-destructive way to get her point across. A person in love searches for ways to evoke affection from his or her partner. These are **instrumental behaviours**, directed at achieving some emotion-relevant goal and they clearly show the link between emotion and motivation as discussed earlier.

> **instrumental behaviours**
> directed at achieving some emotion-relevant goal

People often assume that high emotional arousal enhances task performance, as when athletes try to 'psych' themselves up for competition. Yet as students who have experienced extreme anxiety during examinations could testify, high emotional arousal can also interfere with performance. In many situations, the relation between emotional arousal and performance seems to take the shape of an upside-down, or inverted, U. As physiological arousal increases up to some optimal level, performance improves. But beyond that optimal level, further increases in arousal impair performance. It is thus possible to be either too 'flat' or too 'high' to perform well.

The relation between arousal and performance depends not only on arousal level but also on how complicated the task is and how much precision it requires (Yerkes & Dodson, 1908). Generally speaking, the more complex the task, the lower the optimal arousal level. Thus even a moderate level of arousal can disrupt performance on a highly complex mental or motor task.

Figure 11.25 illustrates this principle and shows that performance drops off less at high levels of arousal for the simplest task than for the others. In fact, even extreme arousal can enhance performance of very simple motor tasks, such as running or lifting something.

In contrast, high emotionality can interfere with performance on complex mental and physical tasks. People may underachieve on intelligence tests if they are too anxious, and muscle tension can interfere with the skilful execution of complex physical movements (Landers & Arent, 2001). For example, the sport of golf requires precise and complex movements, so the optimal level of arousal is relatively low. Champion golfers often exhibit peak performance in high-pressure competition because they can control their level of arousal and keep it within the optimal range, whereas their opponents succumb to the pressure of a putt worth hundreds of thousands of euros.

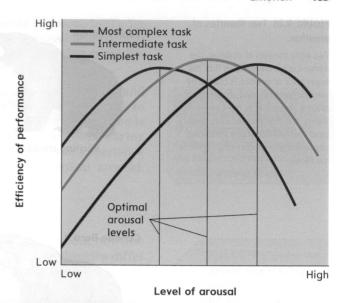

FIGURE 11.25 Arousal and performance.

The relation between arousal and performance takes the form of an inverted U, with performance declining above and below an optimal arousal level. However, the more complex a task is, the lower the optimal level of arousal for performing it. For which of these figures should the optimal level be lower?

> **Focus 11.18** How do level of arousal and task complexity interact to affect task performance?

 In review

- Our physiological responses in emotion are produced by the hypothalamus, the limbic system, the cortex and the autonomic and endocrine systems. There appear to be two systems for emotional behaviour, one involving conscious processing by the cortex, and the other unconscious processing by the amygdala.

- Negative emotions seem to reflect greater relative activation of the right hemisphere, whereas positive emotions are related to relatively greater activation in the left hemisphere.

- The validity of the polygraph as a lie detector has been questioned largely because of the difficulty of establishing the meaning of recorded physiological responses.

- The behavioural component of emotion includes expressive and instrumental behaviours. Different parts of the face are important in the expression of various emotions. The accuracy of people's interpretation of these expressions is enhanced when situational cues are also available. Evolutionary theorists propose that certain fundamental emotional patterns are innate but agree that cultural learning can influence emotional expression.

- There is an optimal level of arousal for the performance of any task. This optimal level varies with the complexity of the task; complex tasks have lower optimal levels.

THEORIES OF EMOTION

Physiological Theories of Emotion

Where do emotional experiences come from? For more than 100 years, scientists have explored this question. We begin our consideration of theories of emotion by looking at two classic theories of emotion which influenced much of the early thinking about emotional responses.

facial feedback hypothesis
feedback from the facial muscles to the brain plays a key role in determining the nature and intensity of emotions that we experience

messages to the brain, and these muscles are active even in patients with spinal injuries who receive no sensory input from below the neck. According to the **facial feedback hypothesis**, feedback from the facial muscles to the brain plays a key role in determining the nature and intensity of emotions that we experience, as the James–Lange theory would suggest (Adelmann & Zajonc, 1989).

According to the theory, sensory input is first routed to the subcortical areas of the brain that control facial movements. These centres immediately send signals that activate the facial muscles. Sensory feedback from movement of facial muscles is then routed to the cerebral cortex, which produces our conscious experience of the emotion. To return to James's example of the bear, the facial feedback hypothesis says that we are frightened when the bear approaches partly because an automatic expression of terror appears on our face and sends signals from our facial muscles to the cortex, where the subjective feelings of fear are produced.

The theory can be thought of in two separate, though related, forms – a strong and a weak version. In the strong version of the theory it is argued that the facial expression actually *causes* the emotional response as outlined above. However, in its weaker form it is proposed that the function of emotional expression is to *intensify* the emotional response – so if you smile when you feel happy then you will experience that happiness more intensely.

In support of the facial feedback hypothesis, research shows that feedback from facial muscle patterns can arouse specific emotional reactions and certainly intensify them (Soussignan, 2002). In one study, Fritz Strack, Martin and Stepper (1988) found that when participants held pens in their teeth, activating muscles used in smiling (Figure 11.27a), they rated themselves as feeling more pleasant than when they held the pens with their lips, activating the muscles involved in frowning (Figure 11.27b). Participants also rated cartoons as funnier while holding pens in their teeth and activating the 'happy muscles' than while holding pens with their lips (Figure 11.27c). In another study, researchers compared the subjective experiences of people who pronounced different sounds, such as *eee* and *ooh*. Saying *eee*, which activates muscles used in smiling, was associated with more pleasant feelings than saying *ooh*, which activates muscles involved in negative facial expressions (Zajonc, Murphy, & Inglehart, 1989).

More recently research on the notion of embodiment has added to our understanding of the importance of facial expressions in processing emotions. The idea of embodiment in terms of emotional processing is that when we think about an emotional concept we re-experience that emotion in some way, perhaps not even consciously. It is argued that this happens because thinking about an emotional concept involves a partial reactivation of the neural state associated with that emotional experience (e.g. Niedenthal, 2007). Niedenthal, et al. (2009) required participants to classify words as being related to emotion

FIGURE II.27 Facial feedback and emotional experience.

(a) Holding a pencil in the teeth, which activates the muscles used in smiling, evokes more pleasant feelings than (b) holding the pencil in one's lips, which activates muscles associated with negative emotions. (c) The findings shown in this graph provide support for the facial feedback hypothesis.

Source: (c) ©Based on Strack et al., 1988.

(a)

(b)

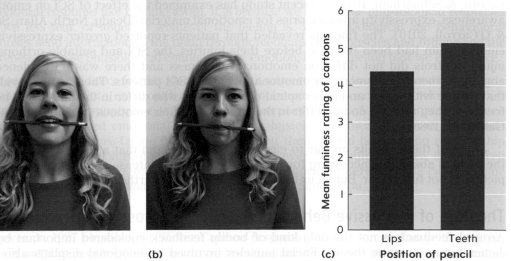
(c)   Position of pencil

or not. They reported that when participants were blocked from being able to make facial expressions for the emotions joy and disgust there was a drop in the accuracy of processing of words related to these emotions but not for other words whether neutral or anger related. Niedenthal et al. argued that facial expressions have a causal role to play in the accurate processing of emotional concepts.

The Role of Appraisal

Later theories of emotion have combined the physiological approach of the James–Lange theory with some input from cognition. The 'Research close-up' box which follows outlines an experiment by Schachter and Wheeler (1962) that demonstrates that the appraisal of an emotional event can be influenced by the level of arousal.

Another famous study that examines this principle is the bridge or abyss study reported by Dutton and Aron (1974). In this study participants were stopped on a bridge and asked to complete a number of questions and tasks – the crucial task being to write a short story based on a picture with which they were presented (from the Thematic Apperception Test). The crucial manipulations in the experiment were whether the participants were approached by a male or female experimenter and whether the experiment was conducted on a fear-inducing bridge or a non-fear-inducing bridge.

Results showed that the participants approached by a female on the fear-inducing bridge were far more likely to include sexual content in the stories they produced and to try to make post-test contact with the experimenter. They argued that this was consistent with previous work by Schachter and his colleagues that environmental cues are used to provide an explanation for unexplained levels of arousal. Consequently, in this study it appears that the arousal induced by the bridge was misattributed to the attractiveness of the female.

According to Schachter's two-factor theory of emotion, the intensity of physiological arousal tells us *how strongly* we are feeling something, but situational cues give us the information we need to label the arousal and tell ourselves *what* we are feeling – fear, anger, love or some other emotion (Schachter, 1966). If appraisal and arousal affect one another in the ways these theories suggest, then by manipulating appraisals we should be able to influence physiological arousal. Moreover, if we can manipulate arousal, we should be able to influence cognitive appraisals of the situation. Let us examine some research that tests these propositions before turning attention to cognitive theories of emotion.

 ### Research close-up

COGNITION-AROUSAL RELATIONS: TWO CLASSIC EXPERIMENTS

Sources: J. Speisman, R. S. Lazarus, A. Mordkoff and L. Davison (1964). Experimental reduction of stress based on ego-defence theory. *Journal of Abnormal and Social Psychology*, 68, 367–380; S. Schachter and L. Wheeler (1962). Epinephrine, chlorpromazine, and amusement. *Journal of Abnormal and Social Psychology*, 65, 121–128.

Two researchers who were at the forefront as appraisal arousal theories of emotion were being developed in the 1960s were Richard Lazarus and Stanley Schachter. These two experiments are still considered classics in the field of emotion, and they gave impetus to the idea that appraisal and arousal influence one another.

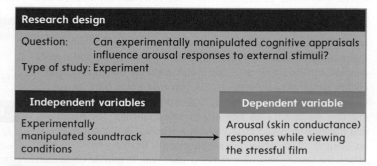

Research design

Question: Can experimentally manipulated cognitive appraisals influence arousal responses to external stimuli?

Type of study: Experiment

Independent variables	Dependent variable
Experimentally manipulated soundtrack conditions	Arousal (skin conductance) responses while viewing the stressful film

LAZARUS: MANIPULATING APPRAISAL TO INFLUENCE AROUSAL

INTRODUCTION

Lazarus and his colleagues at the University of California in the USA examined how differences in cognitive appraisal can influence physiological arousal. To do so, they needed to measure physiological arousal in response to eliciting stimuli, which were held constant for all participants, while

▶

influencing the manner in which the eliciting stimuli were appraised. If people in different appraisal conditions showed different arousal responses to the same eliciting stimuli, it would support the notion that arousal is influenced by appraisal.

METHOD

The researchers monitored college students' physiological responses while they watched an anthropology film, *Subincision in the Arunta*, which depicts in graphic detail an aboriginal puberty rite during which the penises of adolescent boys are cut with a jagged flint knife. The film typically elicits a high level of physiological arousal in viewers (and, according to the researchers, many leg-crossing responses in males). The dependent variable, measured by recording electrodes attached to the participants' palms, was changes in electrical skin conductance caused by sweat gland activity.

To study the effects of participants' appraisal of the filmed visual stimuli on arousal, the researchers experimentally varied the film's sound track. Four different sound track conditions were used to manipulate the independent variable:

■ A *trauma* soundtrack emphasized the pain suffered by the boys, the danger of infection, the jaggedness of the flint knife, and other unpleasant aspects of the operation.

■ A *denial* soundtrack was just the opposite; it denied that the operation was excessively painful or traumatic and emphasized that the boys looked forward to entering adulthood by undergoing the rite and demonstrating their bravery.

■ The *intellectualization* soundtrack, also designed to produce a more benign appraisal, ignored the emotional elements of the scenes altogether and focused on the traditions and history of the tribe.

■ In a *silent* control condition, the film was shown without any soundtrack at all, leaving viewers to make their own appraisals.

RESULTS

As shown in Figure II.28, the soundtracks produced markedly different levels of arousal. As predicted, the trauma soundtrack resulted in the highest arousal, followed by the silent film condition, which likely evoked dire appraisals as well. The denial and intellectualization soundtracks, designed to create more benign appraisals, resulted in much lower levels of arousal. This classic study supported Lazarus's contention that appraisal can influence arousal.

SCHACHTER: MANIPULATING AROUSAL TO INFLUENCE APPRAISAL

INTRODUCTION

Is the reverse also true? Can level of arousal influence people's appraisal of an eliciting stimulus? To test this hypothesis, one must cause people to experience different levels of arousal without knowing the true reason. The level of arousal should then be attributed to whatever eliciting cues are present in the situation.

METHOD

In Schachter's laboratory at Columbia University in the USA, participants were told they were in a study involving the effects of a new vitamin called suproxin on visual perception. The researchers directly manipulated level of physiological arousal by injecting participants with one of three difference 'suproxin' substances. In one condition, participants received adrenaline (sometimes called epinephrine), a hormonal drug that increases arousal. In a second experimental condition, participants received a tranquillizer drug that would decrease arousal. A placebo control group received a saline injection that would have no effects on arousal. The experimenters told all participants that the suproxin injection would have no side effects (when, in fact, the adrenaline and tranquillizer would begin to have immediate and opposite effects on arousal). Then, while presumably waiting for the vitamin to take effect, the participants were shown a short film 'to provide continuous black and white stimulation to the eyes'. The film was a comedy that included a slapstick chase scene. The experimenters hypothesized that the participants in the two drug conditions would attribute their heightened or lowered level of arousal to the funniness (or lack thereof) of the film, because they would know of no other reason why they should feel as they did.

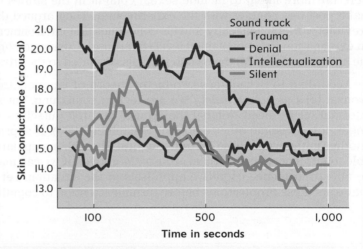

FIGURE II.28 Does appraisal influence arousal?

Participants who viewed a film showing a painful tribal rite in vivid detail exhibited different levels of physiological arousal, depending on the soundtrack that accompanied the film.

Source: Speisman et al., 1964.

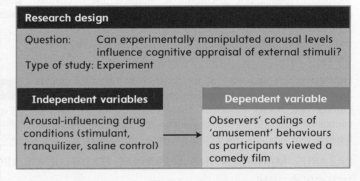

Research design

Question: Can experimentally manipulated arousal levels influence cognitive appraisal of external stimuli?

Type of study: Experiment

Independent variables	Dependent variable
Arousal-influencing drug conditions (stimulant, tranquilizer, saline control)	Observers' codings of 'amusement' behaviours as participants viewed a comedy film

RESULTS

Participants were observed from behind a one-way mirror while they watched the movie. The observers, who were unaware of which participants had received which injections, recorded how frequently the participants smiled, grinned, laughed, threw up their hands, slapped their legs or doubled over with laughter. These behaviours were combined into an 'amusement score' that served as the dependent variable measure of how funny the participants found the film to be.

It appears that arousal cues can indeed influence their appraisal of the situation. As Figure II.29 shows, the results supported the hypothesis that level of arousal would influence participants' appraisal of the film. The aroused participants in the epinephrine group found the film funnier than the tranquillized participants did, and the placebo control group fell in the middle. Thus, a person injected with adrenaline might think, 'Here I am watching this film and getting all excited. This film's really funny!'

CRITICAL DISCUSSION

These two studies were among the first to experimentally manipulate appraisal and arousal so as to study their effects upon one another. In the first study, even though it was not possible to completely control for participants' own tendencies to appraise situations in certain ways, the four soundtrack conditions did have effects on the arousal responses of participants as they watched the subincision film. When Schachter and Wheeler turned Lazarus's procedure around and manipulated arousal levels with the stimulant and tranquillizing drugs, they found the expected differences in appraisal of the funniness of the films, and they were able to measure these differences in terms of observable behaviour rather than self-report. Thus, these two studies show that appraisal influences arousal and that arousal can influence appraisals, demonstrating the two-way causal relation between cognition and arousal shown in the model of emotion originally presented in Figure II.20.

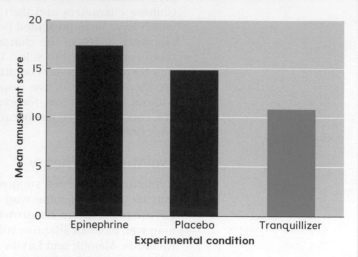

FIGURE II.29 Does arousal influence appraisal?

Participants were injected with either epinephrine, a tranquillizer, or a placebo to affect arousal and then were shown a humorous film. The amount of amusement they displayed varied with their state of arousal.

Source: Schachter and Wheeler, 1962.

COGNITIVE THEORIES OF EMOTION

Lazarus's Approach

The 'Research close-up' box outlines a fine example of the evidence that has been cited to support Lazarus's approach to emotion. The basis of Lazarus's model is that arousal can be influenced by the appraisal of an emotional situation, although it goes further than that with Lazarus claiming that appraisal must precede an emotional response. This means that there can be no emotion without cognition. Lazarus (1982) claims there are two forms of appraisal, with primary appraisal assessing the very basic situation – is it positive, negative or neutral? Following this initial assessment, secondary appraisal evaluates what resources are at hand to deal with the current situation. There can be subsequent reappraisal where the situation and resources are monitored and the earlier forms of appraisal can be adjusted if appropriate. Smith and Lazarus (1993) developed the notion of appraisal to cover six elements, two of which are primary appraisal, motivational relevance and motivational incongruence. This allows individuals to assess a situation in relation to their own goals and this may result in an emotional response, such as anger, if goals are blocked. Secondary appraisal goes further than the primary assessment and involves appraisal which addresses issues such as who is accountable for the situation? Can the situation be rectified? Is the emotional response manageable? And finally, will the situation change in the future? While there is undoubtedly research that has been used to support Lazarus's approach, it was considered to be quite contentious and there was much debate over how important the role of appraisal was in emotional response.

The primary objector to Lazarus's view was Robert Zajonc (1980, 1984) who argued that emotions do not need to be preceded by cognition. Zajonc claimed that emotional responses are too quick for cognition and that this means that emotion must come before cognition and not following it. The major piece of evidence cited by Zajonc, though, is the *mere exposure effect*. This effect is robust and replicated across a range of stimuli and

presentations. A typical example would be to show a group of participants a number of Chinese characters and then sometime later to show more Chinese characters some of which have been presented before and some of which have not. Despite not being able to recognize which of the characters they have seen before, when asked which they prefer there is a tendency to select the ones that were initially presented. The argument here is that there has been no cognitive processing of the stimuli – they are not recognized – and yet there is an affective response towards the familiar items. This interpretation is not without its difficulties, for example, cognitive processing (or appraisal) need not happen at a conscious level; just because there is no recognition does not mean that there has been no cognition.

Evolutionary Theory

Evolutionary theories suggest that there must be some adaptive purpose for emotions, that they have in some way been shaped to enable us to survive in, and adapt to, our environment. There is a growing body of evidence in psychology to suggest that emotions may well have an adaptive role in survival, with Chang and Wilson (2004) and Blanchette, Richards, Melnyk and Lavda (2007) both finding evidence that emotion, when congruent with the material to be reasoned about, can facilitate reasoning and thinking processes.

The eminent Dutch psychologist Nico Frijda proposed an evolutionary theory of emotion (e.g. 1986, 1988) that attempts to outline what the adaptive function of emotion might be. Like some of the theories that we have already seen, Frijda argues that there is some appraisal of the environment and whether there is the need for any response. This is the crucial aspect of the theory. Frijda argues that what distinguishes felt emotions from mere sensations of pleasantness and unpleasantness are 'action tendencies' or readiness to act. Thus for Frijda, different action tendencies *are* different emotions. Different appraisals result in different action tendencies. Any situation is considered as emotional if it is likely to harm or benefit the individual or (as we have already seen in Lazarus's approach) their goals or motives. Various action tendencies may then become available including different facial expressions or the option of flight or fight.

These appraisals of our environment, regardless of the theoretical nature behind them, all suggest that we are looking, to a greater or lesser extent, to maximize our survival, or to examine the environment for potentially harmful factors that we will need to manage in some way, presumably because, ultimately, we all want to be happy. However, the study of happiness and what makes people happy is not as straightforward as you might initially think.

HAPPINESS

For many years, psychologists have tried to understand what life experiences contributed to poor mental health and how they might then treat or alleviate it. Hence, we know a great deal about psychological disorders such as anxiety and depression. However, people want more from life than just being free of depression or worry – they want to feel content and happy. Thus, researchers have begun exploring the role of positive emotions and psychological assets (such as resilience) in shaping later outcomes (Aspinwall & Staudinger, 2003; Seligman, 2002). Termed 'positive psychology', research in this field indicates that positive emotions are associated with numerous benefits related to health, work, family and economic status (Kobau et al., 2011).

subjective well-being (SWB)
people's emotional responses and their degree of satisfaction with various aspects of their life

Happiness, or its more technical term **subjective well-being (SWB)**, can be defined as people's emotional responses and their degree of satisfaction with various aspects of their life (Diener & Seligman, 2002). Some researchers, though, suggest that SWB is more than just being satisfied with life, or with feeling pleasant emotions. Instead, they suggest it is a positive and sustainable condition characterized by vitality, fulfilment, interest, engagement, affection and a sense of flourishing (Huppert, 2009). Whatever the precise definition, there is agreement that SWB does not mean the complete absence of negative emotions or difficult times. As psychologists have engaged with the study of SWB, it has become apparent that it is a highly complex, but extremely important concept, as research findings on SWB may play a vital role in helping both individuals and societies to thrive.

How Happy Are People?

Given the importance of well-being to both individuals and societies, governments and international organizations (like the World Health Organization) have become increasingly attentive to national well-being. For example, the UK Prime Minister, David Cameron, has argued that a country's progress can be indicated by levels of well-being as well as its gross domestic product, and in 2010, he launched work on a UK well-being index. Drawing upon data from national surveys and from happiness apps (e.g. www.mappiness.org.uk), the UK's well-being can be established and compared with other European countries. In addition, particular domains of well-being can be tracked for different sub-groups in the population.

Subjective well-being is typically assessed by self-report ratings of contentment, happiness and satisfaction. Before reading on, please see Table 11.2.

Well-being has been of interest to psychologists well before politicians took notice. Diener and Diener (1996) reviewed findings from nearly 1,000 representative samples in 43 Westernized and developing nations. Across all countries, the mean rating of personal happiness on the 0-to-10 scale was 6.33, indicating mild happiness. Indeed, most of the 43 countries examined demonstrated a level of happiness above neutral, and this general happiness appeared to cut across both Westernized (e.g., European states and the USA) and less Westernized nations (e.g., Japan, Brazil, Mexico, South Korea and Thailand). In only two economically poor nations, India and the Dominican Republic, did average SWB fall into the unhappy range of the scale. In the USA, all ethnic groups scored well above the neutral point on the happiness scale (Andrews, 1991).

More recent comparisons of happiness across Europe (Office for National Statistics, 2014) indicates that SWB can depend on what question you ask people. When asked 'How satisfied are you with your life these days?' Danish people appeared the most satisfied, and Bulgarians the least satisfied, from 22 European countries. When asked whether they agree with the statement that 'I generally feel that what I do in life is worthwhile', both Danish and Dutch people scored highest, with Greek respondents scoring the lowest. However, when asked 'Taking all things together, how happy would you say you are?', Finnish people were the happiest, and Bulgarians the least happy.

What Makes People Happy?

A core challenge in research on well-being is unravelling the direction of relationship and causality between positive emotions and positive behaviour. Do people feel happy because of good experiences or do good experiences happen to happy people? Thus, researchers have examined the *resources or contexts* that might contribute to happiness, such as attractiveness, intelligence, wealth and relationships as well as the internal *psychological processes* that seem to underlie our experiences of happiness (Huppert, 2009).

Personal resources

Is health required for happiness? Not necessarily. On average, individuals with severe and disabling medical conditions such as paralyses do report lower levels of life satisfaction than non-disabled people, yet about two-thirds of disabled people rate their lives as somewhat or very satisfying (Mehnert, Krauss, Nadler, & Boyd, 1990).

TABLE 11.2 How happy are you?

Here are two measures of subjective well-being. Answer the following questions, then see the text to compare yourself with others.
1. How would you rate your own general life satisfaction on the following scale? 0   1   2   3   4   5   6   7   8   9   10 *Most unhappy*   *Most happy*
2. Answer the following questions: What percentage of the time are you happy? _____ What percentage of the time are you neutral? _____ What percentage of the time are you unhappy? _____ (Make sure your percentages add up to 100).

If you had more money, you would be happier? Correct? Well, perhaps not. Although people in affluent countries are happier on average than people who live in abject poverty, such countries differ in many ways besides wealth (e.g., in terms of social and political turmoil) that could also affect SWB. When wealth and SWB are correlated within the same country, whether the country is poor or affluent, wealth is only weakly related to happiness (Diener, Suh, Lucas, & Smith, 1999). Even extreme changes in wealth, such as a big inheritance or winning a lottery, have only a temporary positive impact on SWB (Brickman, Contes, & Janoff-Bulman, 1978). Thus where health and wealth are concerned, not having enough of these resources may create unhappiness because important basic needs cannot be met, but once adequate levels are attained, further increases seem to do little to promote lasting happiness.

How about being wise? Overall, intelligence bears little relation to happiness (Seligman, 2002). Educational level does have a weak positive relation to SWB, probably because it helps people avoid poverty and compete for satisfying jobs. Unemployment is one of the strongest predictors of life dissatisfaction, and an adequate educational level can help people avoid this fate (Clark, 1998).

If being healthy, wealthy, and wise will not guarantee happiness, perhaps intimate relationships will. Here researchers consistently find that happy people have more satisfying social relationships (Diener & Seligman, 2002). Additionally, married men and women are significantly happier on average than are single and divorced people. Still, the meaning of these correlational results is not clear. Do social relationships promote greater life satisfaction, or are happier, better-adjusted people more able to establish and sustain good social relationships and stable marriages? Or is there some third variable, such as a personality factor like being more extraverted (i.e., more outgoing), that promotes both happiness and the ability to develop satisfying social relations?

Who are happier, men or women? Research shows that the sexes are about equal in global happiness, but there is an important qualifier: women on average experience *both* positive and negative emotions more intensely than do men (Wood, Rhodes, & Whelan, 1989). The more extreme emotional responses of women balance out, resulting in an average level of happiness similar to that produced by men's less extreme highs and lows. Furthermore, married people are consistently happier than co-habiting or single people (see review by Dolan, Peasgood, & White, 2008), although the direction of causality is unclear. Nes, Roysamb, Harris, Czajkowski and Tambs (2010) explored whether the genetic underpinnings of happiness, which are strong, were influenced by environmental context. Twin studies showed that the genetic influence on SWB is contingent on environmental factors, particularly whether one is married or not.

Having a sense of meaning in life also is correlated with happiness. Many people report that their spiritual or religious beliefs contribute to a sense of meaning, and some – though not all – studies find a positive correlation between religiosity and happiness (Diener & Seligman, 2002; Diener et al., 1999). Giving of oneself, such as helping others as a volunteer, contributes to a sense of meaning and life satisfaction (Snyder, Clary, & Stukas, 2000). But again, causality is difficult to infer. Does a greater sense of meaning promote happiness? Does happiness lead people to feel that their life is more meaningful? Or does some third factor cause both?

Psychological processes

Overall, personal resources and external circumstances account for only about 15–20% of the total variability among people in happiness ratings (Argyle, 1999). Perhaps psychological processes, rather than resources, are the keys to happiness, and studies have explored a range of influences including biological, psychological and social processes.

Biological factors may predispose some people to be happier than others. A study of 2,310 identical and fraternal twins revealed that the identical twins were far more similar in SWB, regardless of their life circumstances (Lykken & Tellegen, 1996). The short allele variant of the serotonin transporter (5-HTT) gene has been identified as conferring vulnerability to depression, but this vulnerability needs to be triggered by environmental factors. The long allele variant of 5-HTT acts as a resilience or protective factor (Kendler, Kuhn, Vittum, Prescott, & Riley, 2005). Perhaps genetic factors contribute in some way to the individual differences in right- and left-hemisphere activation, discussed previously, or perhaps they

influence neurotransmitter systems that underlie positive and negative emotions (Hamer & Copeland, 1998). There is also indication of influences on brain activation linked to happiness in childhood. Davidson and Rickman (1999) examined prefrontal activation asymmetry in 65 children, 3 to 11 years of age and over a period of 8 years. They found considerable plasticity in the brain's emotional and cognitive circuitry and argued that parenting, life experiences and other influences from the environment are highly likely to play a crucial role during this formative period in establishing or shifting patterns of prefrontal activation.

Personality factors clearly predispose some people to be happier than others. Individuals who are sociable, optimistic, altruistic, curious and open to new experiences report higher levels of happiness and are rated by others as happier than are those who have the opposite traits (Larsen & Buss, 2002). Underlying traits in relation to emotional processing are also important. In **Chapter 15** on personality, you will learn about *traits* and *states* in relation to personality and individual differences. These concepts have been applied to the study of SWB and, in this context, *traits* denote someone's underlying emotional temperament, sometimes referred to as their affective style. *State*, in comparison, refers to current mood or feeling and may be momentary or longer term. Of course, the two are related, since positive or negative affective styles imply more positive moods or negative moods. What is interesting here is that, in relation to happiness, individuals have a *set point* which can be understood as a baseline from which a person responds to their environment and appears linked to the *trait* concept (Huppert, 2005).

 Chapter 15, Page 645

Focus 11.21 What factors predict and fail to predict happiness?

Social processes also play a part. For example, research reveals that feelings of life satisfaction are based on how we compare ourselves and our circumstances with other people and their circumstances and with past conditions we have experienced (Bruunk & Gibbons, 1997). When we engage in **downward comparison**, seeing ourselves as better off than the standard for comparison, we experience increased satisfaction. In contrast, **upward comparison**, when we view ourselves as worse off than the standard for comparison, produces dissatisfaction. In one study, students kept a written record of every time they compared their appearance, grades, abilities, possessions or personality with someone else's over a two-week period. At the same time, they recorded their current mood. Downward comparisons with less fortunate or less talented people were consistently associated with positive moods, and upward comparisons were associated with negative emotional reactions (Wheeler & Miyake, 1992).

downward comparison seeing ourselves as better off than the standard for comparison

upward comparison when we view ourselves as worse off than the standard for comparison

One's culture may also influence the factors that contribute to happiness. Suh, Diener, Oishi and Triandis (1998) found that in the individualistic 'me' societies of North America and Europe, successes that people can attribute to their own skill and effort contribute to happiness. In collectivistic cultures of Southeast Asia, however, the well-being of the group seems to be a more important factor in personal happiness than one's own emotional life, and people derive more pleasure from accomplishments achieved as part of a group effort (Kitayama, Markus, & Kurokawa, 2000).

Thus, happiness is a complex phenomenon having biological, psychological and environmental determinants. Much attention is now being given to intervention that might improve the well-being of individuals and of populations or entire countries. Work in the area of mindfulness is proving particularly exciting. Mindfulness is a psycho-educational intervention that enhances people's internal resources and coping skills relevant to daily life (Semple, Reid, & Miller, 2005). It reduces stress and discourages preoccupying negative self-evaluations by improving one's capacity to monitor and regulate cognitive and emotional states but without trying to alter, antagonize or dismiss them (Bishop et al., 2004). In this way, mindfulness differs from dominant cognitive-behavioural approaches which focus on restructuring cognitive formulations (and their associated affect). Instead, mindfulness promotes benevolent acceptance of one's thoughts and feelings for what they are, and disengages people from habitual, maladaptive ways of responding to them as definitive ways of understanding the world. In addition, with its attention to present-moment thinking, mindfulness prohibits rumination on the past (and negative effects such as guilt, self-blame and depression) and chronic worry about the future (and negative effects such as anticipatory failure and anxiety) (Baer et al., 2008; Brown, Ryan, & Cresswell, 2007). Studies show that practising mindfulness can have a significant effect in improving depression and anxiety, as well as promoting well-being, in children, adolescents and adults.

Levels of analysis

factors related to happiness

PSYCHOLOGICAL

- Internalized cultural standards for being happy (e.g., individual vs group well-being)
- Upward and downward comparison processes
- Personality traits, such as optimism, extraversion
- Meaning-of-life values, spiritual beliefs, desire to be of service to others

BIOLOGICAL

- Possible genetic predisposition for positive emotions
- Relatively greater left hemisphere activation
- Neurotransmitters in positive emotion systems (e.g., dopamine)

ENVIRONMENTAL

- Recent positive life events
- Presence of positive relationships
- External cultural standards for being happy
- Individual or group successes, depending on culture

Happiness

 Applying psychological science

BEING HAPPY: GUIDELINES FROM PSYCHOLOGICAL RESEARCH

As research has accumulated on factors that relate to happiness, psychologists have been able to offer advice based on data rather than intuition (Seligman, 2002; Snyder & Lopez, 2007). Most psychologists believe that happiness, like a good marriage, is something that one must work at (Seligman & Peterson, 2004). Here, then, are some suggestions that may help you maintain and enhance personal happiness.

- *Spend time with other people, and work to develop close relationships.* Research consistently suggests that good relationships provide the strongest basis for life satisfaction. Even if you tend to be introverted, form at least a few close relationships and nurture them. Make time for social interactions.

- *Look for ways to be helpful to others, and reach out to the less fortunate.* Try to make a positive difference in the lives of others. Doing so will increase your sense of self-worth, add meaning to your life, and deepen relationships with those whose lives you touch. It will also help put your own problems in perspective and direct your energies away from self-absorption. There is a lot to be said for the proposition that we receive by giving.

- *Seek meaning and challenge in work.* Enjoying one's work is a prime ingredient of happiness. If you feel stuck doing something that provides little gratification, be it your job or your major, consider looking for something more satisfying. Everyone has to make a living, but many people spend their lives doing things they do not derive satisfaction or meaning from – hardly a recipe for a happy life. Even if you love your work, strive for balance between work and personal pursuits. People on their death beds rarely, if ever, express the wish that they had spent more time at the office.

- *Set meaningful personal goals for yourself, and make progress towards them.* Whether in work, school or relationships, engaging in goal-directed activity and seeing yourself moving towards your goals will provide a basis for life satisfaction and foster feelings of being in greater control of your life. Many people find that spiritual development (religiously based or not) confers meaning in their life.

- *Make time for enjoyable activities.* One of the benefits of time-management skills is the ability to schedule everyday activities that provide pleasure around school, work and other obligations. Make time for a hobby, reading, and recreational activities.

▶

◀

- *Nurture physical well-being.* Many studies show that even moderate physical exercise contributes to emotional well-being (Morgan, 1997). Such activities provide a temporary respite from life stressors. When done in a social context, they add the benefits of social interaction as well. People who exercise, get sufficient sleep and practise good dietary habits tend to be more stress resistant and satisfied with themselves and their lives (Taylor, 2006a).

- *Be open to new experiences.* Some of our most pleasurable experiences can occur when we try new things. It is easy to fall into a rut, so whether it is travelling, developing a new hobby or taking a college course on a new subject, be open to doing something you have not done before.

- *Cultivate optimism, and count your blessings.* As we have seen, cognitive appraisals influence emotions, and an upbeat, optimistic approach to life is linked with subjective well-being. Try to look on the positive side of things, to see demanding events as challenges and opportunities rather than threats. Learn to appreciate and be grateful for even the mundane, average day in which nothing bad happens to you. There is a Buddhist saying: 'Happiness is a day without a toothache.' All of us are gifted in ways that we may take for granted. Perhaps we should focus more often on these typically ignored aspects of good fortune.

A CONCLUDING THOUGHT

As you have seen in this chapter, motivation and emotion lie at the crossroads of cognition, physiology and behaviour. The diversity of human motives, factors that influence their development and strength, and methods for satisfying them help account for important differences both within and across cultures.

Emotion plays a central role in many aspects of normal and abnormal behaviour. Emotion also illustrates the many fascinating interfaces between evolutionary processes and social learning. It is little wonder, then, that the study of emotion is a major thrust in contemporary psychological research. We still have much to learn about the basic mechanisms that underlie our emotional experiences and about what we can do to self-regulate them in order to amplify pleasurable emotions and dampen those that create distress.

Focus II.22 Summarize research-based guidelines for increasing your happiness.

 ## In review

- There are several theories of emotion. The James–Lange theory maintains that we first become aroused and then judge what we are feeling. The Cannon-Bard theory proposes that arousal and cognition are independent and simultaneously triggered by the thalamus. According to Lazarus's cognitive-affective theory, appraisals trigger emotional arousal; in contrast, according to Schachter's two-factor theory of emotion, arousal tells us how strongly we are feeling while cognitions derived from situational cues help us label the specific emotion.

- As the James–Lange theory maintained, expressive behaviours may trigger other aspects of emotions. The facial feedback hypothesis states that feedback from facial muscle patterns associated with innate emotional displays influences cognitive and physiological processes.

- There is a two-way relation between the cognitive and physiological components. It is possible to manipulate appraisals and thereby influence level of arousal, but arousal changes can also influence appraisal of the eliciting stimuli.

- In most countries, the average person is mildly happy. Psychological processes, such as downward comparison and a sense of personal meaning, are more consistently related to subjective well-being than are resources such as wealth, physical attractiveness and high intelligence. Cultural differences may exist in the bases for happiness.

 ## Recommended Reading

CLASSIC

LeDoux, J. (1996). *The Emotional Brain.* Englewood Cliffs, NJ: Simon & Schuster.

CONTEMPORARY

Carlson, N.R. (2013). *The physiology of behavior (11th ed.).* Boston: Pearson.

Deckers, C. (2010). *Motivation: Biology, Psychology and Environment* (3rd ed.). Boston, MA: Allyn & Bacon.

Forgas, J.P. & Harmon-Jones, E. (2014). *Motivation and its Regulation: The Control Within.* Hove: Psychology Press.

Lewis, M., Haviland-Jones, J., & Barrett, L. (2008). *Handbook of Emotions,* (3rd ed.). New York: Guilford Press.

Strongman, K.T. (2003). *The Psychology of emotion: From everyday life to theory* (5th ed.). Chichester: John Wiley and Sons.

My friend has a baby. I'm recording all the noises he makes so later I can ask what he meant.

Steven Wright

Lifespan development I: physical and cognitive development

12

Chapter Outline

THE SCOPE OF DEVELOPMENTAL PSYCHOLOGY

- Linking social and cognitive development

MAJOR ISSUES AND METHODS IN DEVELOPMENTAL PSYCHOLOGY PRENATAL DEVELOPMENT

- Genetics and epigenetics
- Threats to prenatal development

INFANCY AND CHILDHOOD

- The amazing newborn
- **Research Close-ups** *The development of face discrimination in the first year of life*

- Physical development
- ⌕ **Current topic** *What is the role of the brain in development?*
- Cognitive development
- ◉ **Applying psychological science** *Applying principles from cognitive development to produce better educational techniques*

ADOLESCENCE, ADULTHOOD AND OLD AGE

- Physical development
- Cognitive development

In 1799 three hunters discovered a remarkable child living in the forests of Aveyron, France. Most likely abandoned at a young age, he grew up isolated from human contact, foraging for food and surviving naked in the wild. About 12 years old, he easily climbed trees, ate nuts and roots, scratched and bit people who interfered with him, and made few sounds. He could walk upright yet ran quickly on all fours. Some regarded him as half-human, half-beast, and they called him the 'Wild Boy of Aveyron' (Itard, 1962).

Several medical experts concluded that the boy was incurably 'mentally deficient', but others disagreed, noting that it took intelligence to survive in the wild. They argued that special education and care would enable the child to flower into a normal, civilized adult. In Paris, the boy was placed under the care of a prominent young physician, Jean-Marc Itard, who named him Victor and diligently supervised his training.

At first, Victor was unresponsive to stimuli that most people find aversive. Unfazed, he would stick his hand into boiling kitchen water to grab food or eagerly roll around half-naked on the cold winter ground. Eventually he learned to sense temperature differences, dress himself and perform other self-care behaviours. Victor's emotional responses, which at first fluctuated without reason, began to fit the situation: he laughed in playful situations, shed tears over someone's death and displayed some signs of affection towards Itard. Victor learned to read and write some words, communicate basic needs and perform simple tasks.

Although Victor changed in important ways, as he grew older his progress slowed considerably. He never learned to speak, and after five years of education his cognitive, emotional and social development remained limited. Pessimism over further progress grew, and Itard's 'project' ended. Victor was moved to a nearby home, where a woman cared for him for the rest of his life.

In the early 1800s, people expected Victor's case to resolve an intense debate about a key question in developmental psychology, that which asks whether nature or nurture is more important in shaping who we are. But it raised more questions than it answered. For a start, it is very difficult to determine whether Victor was born 'mentally deficient', or whether he had become irreparably harmed by his childhood isolation. If the latter, then why was Itard unable to fully repair the damage done?

Some children exposed to extreme adversity are highly resilient and thrive later in life (Ryff & Singer, 2003). We cannot pinpoint why Victor failed to recover, but his famous historical case begs a fundamental question: just how does the miracle of human development unfold, and what conditions are required for typical (normal) development?

THE SCOPE OF DEVELOPMENTAL PSYCHOLOGY

In this chapter and the next (Chapter 13, 'Lifespan development II: social and emotional development') we explore what developmental psychologists have discovered about the changes which take place across the whole of human development, starting with the newly fertilized ovum and ending in old age. We also identify where researchers have tried to unfold the more difficult question of what factors and processes drive psychological development – the question of how nature interacts with nurture.

We were all young once. It follows that every psychological phenomenon which you can read about in this book has a developmental history. For this simple reason, developmental psychology comprises one of the largest subdivisions within psychology, with huge numbers of scientific papers dedicated to attempting to answer the questions it poses. The journal *Developmental Psychology* receives the second highest number of submitted articles out of all of the American Psychological Association (APA) journals. Because of the sheer volume of research in developmental psychology we have decided to dedicate two chapters to its coverage. In addition to the volume of work which goes on in developmental psychology, the questions which it poses and the methods which it uses to answer these questions are very varied. On the one hand, questions about the development of cognitive abilities are

usually addressed with experimental methods in which stimuli and conditions are precisely controlled. On the other hand, questions about social development, by their nature, are often best answered with more observational methods in which the scientist attempts to analyse a portion of social behaviour which they have had relatively little influence upon – social behaviour which is ecologically valid. Because of the differences in approach to cognitive and social questions we have divided the two chapters, such that physical and cognitive development is addressed in this chapter (Chapter 12), and social and emotional development, and the development of personality is discussed in Chapter 13.

LINKING SOCIAL AND COGNITIVE DEVELOPMENT

It is, of course, somewhat artificial to separate cognitive and social questions about development, as emerging cognitive abilities and social interactions can have important influences on each other (social abilities can influence cognitive development, and cognitive abilities can influence social development). It would be very odd to argue, for example, that all cognitive abilities can develop in the absence of social interaction! Likewise, the cognitive 'information-processing' abilities we possess at different stages in development have an important bearing on how we understand and can interact in social situations. After all, our social environment is just another, perhaps more complex, form of 'information'. Because of the importance of social cognitive links in human development, we have highlighted within each chapter where such links have been studied.

For the moment, though, let us consider an example of how social development can influence cognitive development. In Chapter 13, we will describe research conducted into types of attachment between infants and their caregivers. The striking message from this research is that different infants can demonstrate quite different kinds of relationships with parental caregivers. Mary Ainsworth developed a test which we will describe in detail in **Chapter 13** called the 'Strange Situation'. In this test, infants were observed in a relatively unconstrained way with their parents. Ainsworth showed that infants who demonstrated what she called 'secure' attachments with their parents were better able to use their parent as a secure base from which to explore their environment (e.g., to crawl away and explore toys in the far corner of the room). Insecurely attached children (especially those classified by Ainsworth as 'anxious resistant') were less likely to explore their environment in a productive way. So here we can see how social-emotional factors (the attachment relationship between parent and child) can have important influences on the kinds of behaviours which are likely to foster good cognitive development (in this case, exploring and playing).

Chapter 13, Page 545

MAJOR ISSUES AND METHODS IN DEVELOPMENTAL PSYCHOLOGY

Whether we are interested in cognitive abilities or social interaction, *developmental psychology* has two main goals. The first is to examine and describe biological, physical, psychological, social and behavioural changes that occur as we age. The second, and as some have argued the more important, question is to ask what it is that causes or drives these changes. We now describe four broad issues which arise in most developmental research. The first two issues are concerned with describing developmental changes. Issues three and four are concerned with identifying the factors which cause or drive developmental change.

1. *Stability versus change*: do our characteristics remain consistent as we age? This is per-haps the simplest question we can ask in developmental psychology: Is there any devel-opment? While both this chapter and the next attempt to describe development across the lifespan, there is a tendency to consider most developmental *changes* to happen in the first years of life, with long periods of *stability* in adulthood. However, as we shall see there are a great number of developmental changes that continue into adulthood and old age.

PRENATAL DEVELOPMENT

zygote fertilized egg

embryo develops from the end of week 2 through to week 8 after conception

foetus develops from week 9 after conception until birth

Chapter 3, Page 89

Prenatal development consists of three stages spanning approximately 38 weeks or nine months (Figure 12.2). The *germinal stage* comprises approximately the first two weeks of development, beginning when a sperm fertilizes a female egg (*ovum*). This fertilized egg is called a **zygote**, and through repeated cell division it becomes a mass of cells that attaches to the mother's uterus about 10 to 14 days after conception. The fertilization of the egg is the point at which a new person's genetic make-up is determined. Genes are contributed by both the sperm cell and the ovum, to make a new combination which will determine to a great extent how the new person will appear, behave and think. In **Chapter 3** we discuss the effects of genetic inheritance in more detail.

The *embryonic stage* is next. The cell mass, now called an **embryo**, develops from the end of week 2 through to week 8 after conception. Two life-support structures, the placenta and umbilical cord, develop at the start of this stage. Located on the uterine wall, the *placenta* contains membranes that allow nutrients to pass from the mother's blood to the umbilical cord. In turn, the *umbilical cord* contains blood vessels that carry these nutrients and oxygen to the embryo and transport waste products back from the embryo to the mother. Supplied with nutrients, embryonic cells rapidly divide and become specialized. Bodily organs and systems begin to form, and by week 8 the heart of the inch-long (2.5 cm-long) embryo is beating, the brain is forming and facial features such as eyes can be recognized.

FIGURE 12.2 These remarkable photos show (a) the moment of conception, as one of many sperm cells fertilizes the ovum, (b) the embryo at 6 to 7 weeks, and (c) the foetus at 3 months of age.

Source: (a) Francis Leroy, Biocosmos/ Science Photo Library; (b) Edelmann/ Science Photo Library; (c) Bernard Benoit/Science Photo Library.

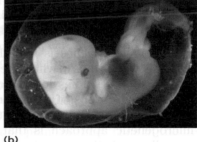
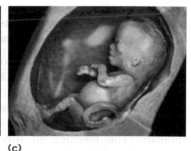

(a)   (b)   (c)

Finally, during the *foetal stage*, the **foetus** develops from week 9 after conception until birth. Muscles strengthen and other bodily systems develop. At about 24 weeks the eyes open, and by 27 weeks (or, more recently with advances in medical care, several weeks younger) the foetus attains the *age of viability*: it is likely to survive outside the womb in case of premature birth (Subramanian, Yoon, & Toral, 2002).

Perhaps most importantly for developmental psychology, the brain and nervous system undergo a great deal of development prenatally. All of the major subdivisions of the brain and nervous system are present by the end of the embryonic stage. Prenatal growth of neurons is very rapid, such that by the time of birth the newborn's brain contains the majority of the neurons which will be eventually present in adulthood (Johnson & de Haan, 2011). Later in this chapter we will discuss the important changes in the brain which occur postnatally and into adulthood.

GENETICS AND EPIGENETICS

It is impossible to overplay the importance of genes in development. Genes provide the foundations for development – they make us human and determine the many characteristics which make us individual humans, different from one another. The ways in which our genetic inheritance works is covered in detail in **Chapter 3**. However, let's consider an example here.

Chapter 3, Page 89

Throughout history, many women have been blamed for failing to give birth to a male heir. But, in fact, it is the genetic contribution of one of the father's sperm cells that determines the sex of a baby. A female's egg cells and a male's sperm cells both have half

the normal number of chromosomes; each with 23. At conception, an egg and sperm unite to form the zygote, which now contains the full set of 23 *pairs* (46 chromosomes in total) found in other human cells. The twenty-third pair of chromosomes determines the baby's sex. A genetic female's twenty-third pair contains two X chromosomes (XX), so called because of their shape (Figure 12.3). Because women carry only X chromosomes, the twenty-third chromosome in the egg is always an X. A genetic male's twenty-third pair contains an X and a Y chromosome (XY). Thus the twenty-third chromosome in the sperm is an X in about half of the cases and a Y in the other half. The Y chromosome contains a specific gene, the *TDF (testis determining factor) gene* that triggers male sexual development. The union of an egg with a sperm cell having a Y chromosome results in an XY combination and therefore a boy. A sperm containing an X chromosome produces an XX combination and therefore a girl.

But how is it that genes provide us with particular characteristics? We can ask, for instance, how the Y chromosome determines male sex characteristics? This kind of question is covered in more detail in **Chapter 3.** However, in brief, genes in our DNA mean that particular kinds of chemicals called proteins are created. Proteins are the building blocks of human tissue. In the case of sex determination, at roughly 6–8 weeks after conception, the TDF gene causes the production of proteins which make up testes. Once formed, the testes secrete sex hormones called *androgens* that continue to direct a male pattern of organ development. If the TDF gene is not present, as happens when there is an XX combination in the twenty-third chromosome pair, testes do not form and – in the absence of sufficient androgen activity during this *prenatal critical period* – an inherent female pattern of organ development ensues.

Perhaps one of the most striking aspects of genetic inheritance is the means by which different parts of our bodies and nervous systems become specialized for particular tasks or functions. All of the cells in our body have the same DNA and genes. How is it that some cells go into making the bones in the big toes, but others become neurons specialized for particular functions in a specific part of the brain? The answer to this question lies in what we know of as **epigenetics** or the study of how genes are *expressed*. Whether or not genetic code in our DNA is expressed in a particular way depends on a large array of factors. The chemical environment in which a cell exists determines which genes are expressed and which lie dormant. This means that cells which have the same DNA can produce very different kinds of protein, and undertake very different tasks depending on where they develop in the body. The environment of a cell is influenced not only by other genes, but other environmental factors such as temperature, and even electrical activity in the case of neurons. So we can see how environmental stimulation can influence even the earliest stages of biological development. Our environments and experiences even influence how the building blocks of our bodies and brains are assembled. In the next section we will see how environmental factors can threaten early development.

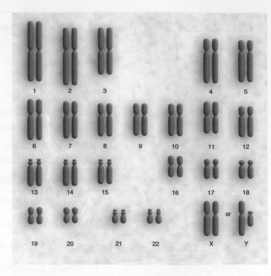

FIGURE 12.3 Most human cells contain 23 pairs of chromosomes.

Each pair consists of one chromosome from each parent. The twenty-third pair determines a person's sex. In males, this pair consists of an X chromosome and a Y chromosome. In females, this pair contains two X chromosomes.

Source: ©iStock.com/somersault 18:24

 Chapter 3, Page 86

epigenetics study of changes in gene expression due to environmental factors and independent of the DNA

teratogens agents that cause abnormal prenatal development

THREATS TO PRENATAL DEVELOPMENT

Our genetic blueprint provides the foundations of prenatal development, but as we have just seen, environmental factors exert an influence from the earliest stages of cellular development. This is the case both before and after we are born. Table 12.1 displays some of the most important risk factors to pre- and postnatal development. **Teratogens** are agents from the environment and from the mother that can cause abnormal prenatal development. Teratogens can be chemicals from the environment, ingested by the mother either accidentally or otherwise (e.g., in the case of legal and illegal drugs), but they can also be diseases passed to the infant either during gestation or during birth, and they can also be chemicals produced naturally by the mother. The placenta prevents many dangerous substances from reaching the embryo and foetus, but some harmful chemicals and diseases can pass through.

TABLE 12.1 Examples of teratogens and other prenatal risk factors*

Chemicals	
Alcohol	Foetal alcohol syndrome (FAS) (growth defects, mental retardation); risk of sudden infant death syndrome (SIDS)
Tobacco smoke	Both active and passive smoking are risk factors for SIDS; low birthweight; higher susceptibility to illness
Illegal drugs	Exposure to various drugs (including cocaine, heroin, morphine, methamphetamine, LSD [lysergic acid diethylamide] and marijuana) can lead to a variety of different behavioural and physical problems
Environmental toxins	Radiation, heavy metals (lead, mercury), herbicides, pesticides and even household cleaners can lead to a variety of different behavioural and physical problems
Maternal diseases (can be passed to the infant during gestation or at the time of delivery)	
Rubella (German measles)	Infant may be born deaf or mentally retarded or have cardiac disorders or cataracts
Herpes Type I or II	Infected infant may be blind, mentally retarded, or have motor abnormalities or a wide range of neurological disorders
Toxoplasmosis	Eye and brain damage in the developing baby
Cytomegalovirus	Early delivery, susceptibility to illness, delayed development
Other viruses	Mumps, hepatitis are all known to present a risk to the foetus and newborn; STDs (including HIV, syphilis) can also cause major complications
Characteristics of the mother	
Age	Teenage mothers tend to live in risky environments, to neglect their health and diets, and to use drugs, thus raising their risk of delivering premature and low-birthweight babies; older mothers risk bearing a Down's syndrome child as well as problems posed by illnesses that are more common as people age
Diet	Malnourishment can lead to miscarriage, stillbirths, prematurity, low birthweight, physical and neural defects, smaller size in newborns and, sometimes, cognitive difficulties
Emotional state	Mothers who are stressed (and are producing stress hormones) may have troubled pregnancies, miscarriages, long labour and delivery complications, and more need for childbirth anesthesia; their infants may be hyperactive and irritable and have feeding and sleep problems

Note: *It is important to note that this table is for illustrative purposes and does not represent an exhaustive list of prenatal risk factors and teratogens.
Source: Adapted from Parke and Gauvain (2009).

foetal alcohol syndrome a disorder of the developing foetus caused by the ingestion of alcohol by the foetus's mother during gestation. It is characterized by stunted growth, a number of physical and physiological abnormalities, and often, mental retardation

foetal alcohol spectrum disorders (FASD) a group of abnormalities that results from varying kinds of prenatal exposure to alcohol

Mercury, lead, radiation and many other environmental toxins can produce birth defects, as can many drugs. **Foetal alcohol syndrome (FAS)** is a severe group of abnormalities that results from prenatal exposure to alcohol (Streissguth, 1977, 2001). Foetal alcohol syndrome children have facial abnormalities and small, malformed brains (Figure 12.4). Psychological symptoms include mental retardation, attentional and perceptual deficits, irritability and impulsivity. Other children exposed to alcohol in the womb may display milder forms of these deficits. Given the wide distribution of severity of such problems, researchers have defined a continuum of maternal alcohol consumption related problems in the child as **foetal alcohol spectrum disorders (FASD)** (Streissguth, 2007).

The threshold level of alcohol exposure needed to produce FAS is not known. About one-third to one-half of infants born to alcoholic mothers have FAS, but even social drinking or a single episode of binge drinking can increase the risk of prenatal damage and long-term cognitive impairment (Larroque & Kaminski, 1998). Because no amount of prenatal alcohol exposure has been confirmed to be absolutely safe, pregnant women and those trying to become pregnant are best advised to completely avoid drinking alcohol (Floyd, O'Connor, Sokol, Bertrand, & Cordero, 2005).

Nicotine is also a teratogen. Maternal smoking increases the risk of miscarriage, premature birth and low birthweight (Kirchengast & Hartmann, 2003). Owing to second-hand smoke ('passive smoking'), regular tobacco use by fathers also has been linked to low infant birthweight and increased risk of respiratory infections (Wakefield, Reid, Roberts, Mullins, & Gillies, 1998). Babies of pregnant mothers who regularly use heroin or cocaine are often born addicted and experience withdrawal symptoms after birth. Their cognitive functioning and ability to regulate their arousal and attention may also be impaired (Lewis, Misra, Johnson, & Rosen, 2004).

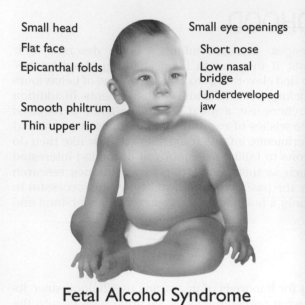

Small head
Flat face
Epicanthal folds

Smooth philtrum
Thin upper lip

Small eye openings
Short nose
Low nasal bridge
Underdeveloped jaw

Fetal Alcohol Syndrome

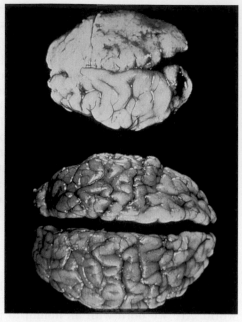

FIGURE 12.4 Children who suffer from foetal alcohol syndrome (FAS) not only look different but also have brains that are underdeveloped and smaller than those of normal children.

Source: Left, Gwen Shockey/Science Photo Library. Right, © Reproduced with the kind permission of Jean Kinney, Project Cork, Dartmouth Medical School..

One set of teratogens which are produced naturally by the mother are stress hormones from the mother. Prolonged maternal stress is associated with increased risk of premature birth (Austin & Leader, 2000). An example of a disease which is a particular risk factor for the developing infant is rubella (German measles). If the mother contracts rubella it can cause blindness, deafness, heart defects and mental retardation in the infant (Plotkin, 2006), especially when the embryo's eyes, ears, heart and central nervous system are beginning to form early in pregnancy. Sexually transmitted diseases can pass from mother to foetus and produce brain damage, blindness and deafness, depending on the disease. Among pregnant women with untreated syphilis, about 25% of foetuses are born dead. Likewise, without treatment during pregnancy or delivery by Caesarean section at birth, about 25% of foetuses born to mothers with the human immunodeficiency virus (HIV) are also infected (Meleski & Damato, 2003).

It is important to remember that teratogens do not exert the same effects throughout development. For instance, the developing child is especially vulnerable to the effects of teratogens during the embryonic stage as it is a period in which there is a great deal of change and growth. Where changes are occurring there is a greater likelihood that external influences can give rise to atypical development. In fact, different organs or groups of organs in the body vary with regard to the periods of development in which they are vulnerable to teratogenic influence. For instance, whereas the heart is most vulnerable during the embryonic stage, the genitals are more vulnerable during the latter part of the embryonic stage, and the foetal stage. The nervous system and brain have probably the most extended period of vulnerability to teratogens, spanning both the embryonic and foetal periods.

> **Focus 12.2** Describe the stages of prenatal development, how sex is determined and the effects of various teratogens.

 In review

- Prenatal development involves the germinal, embryonic and foetal stages.
- Genetics play a very important role in development, but interact with environmental factors from the word go in a process called gene expression.
- The twenty-third chromosome in a mother's egg cell is always an X chromosome. If the twenty-third chromosome in the father's sperm cell is an X, the child will be genetically female (XX); if it is a Y, the child will be genetically male (XY).
- Teratogens (which can include maternal stress hormones, diseases, drug use and environmental toxins) can cause abnormal prenatal development.

INFANCY AND CHILDHOOD

Studying infancy poses unique challenges. Because infants cannot describe their experiences, developmental psychologists, if they are to learn anything about infants' perceptual and cognitive abilities, have to find clever ways to take advantage of behaviours which infants produce readily, such as sucking behaviour and eye movements. In addition to the special techniques infancy researchers use, a great deal of patience is required as infants do not always comply with the wishes of experimenters in the same way that adults and even children do. During experiments, infants frequently cry, just like they do outside the laboratory. They are also prone to falling asleep or just becoming interested in something completely extraneous, such as their new stripy socks. Infancy research is not easy, but methods developed over the past 50 years have been very successful in demonstrating how well babies of even only a few days old can perceive, understand and interact with their environment.

THE AMAZING NEWBORN

A question that has occupied philosophy for hundreds of years, and psychology since its inception as a scientific field, concerns what perceptual skills we bring with us into the world. Are we born with an ability to perceive the environment around us, or is this a skill which we must learn? William James (1950) took the view shared by the empiricist philosophers of the seventeenth century such as John Locke (see **Chapter 1**); like them, he argued that we bring relatively little with us and that we need to learn how to perceive even simple stimuli. Thus, he famously suggested that after emerging from the womb, the newborn's world is a 'blooming, buzzing confusion'! However, contrary to this long-held view of newborns as helpless and passive, research reveals that they may be surprisingly sophisticated at processing information.

Chapter 1, Pages 10 & 13

Reflexes and Learning

Neonates require some ways of acting on their environment. Luckily, they are equipped with a number of **reflexes,** automatic, inborn behaviours that occur in response to specific stimuli. Some have obvious adaptive significance. Stroke a baby's cheek, and he will turn his head towards the location in which he was touched and open his mouth – the *rooting reflex*. When something is placed in an infant's mouth, she will suck on it – the *sucking reflex*. Together, these reflexes increase the infant's ability to feed. Breathing is another example of a reflex which helps the infant to survive.

reflexes automatic, inborn behaviours that occur in response to specific stimuli

However, we cannot have an innate reflex for every action we need in order to interact successfully with our environment. We need learning mechanisms in order to change and adapt our behaviours to new stimuli in the environment. In Chapter 7 we described several ways in which humans and animals learn. Newborns also learn in several ways. One important way in which they learn is through habituation; they decrease their responses to repetitive, non-threatening stimuli. As we shall see shortly, developmental psychologists have used newborns' habituation to gain knowledge about how they perceive their environment. As we described in **Chapter 7**, habituation is useful as it helps us orient away from the old and towards new information. Newborns can also acquire classically conditioned responses. After a tone (CS) is repeatedly paired with a gentle puff of air to the eye (UCS), they will develop a conditioned eye-blink response to the tone alone (Lipsitt, 1990). Through operant conditioning, newborns learn that they can make things happen. For example, 3-day-old infants can learn to suck a plastic nipple with a certain pattern of bursts to activate a tape-recording of their mother's voice (Moon & Fifer, 1990).

Chapter 7, Page 269

Sensory Capabilities and Perceptual Preferences

The visual preference technique

Just after birth, newborns' eye movements are not well coordinated, and this fact among others led early developmental psychologists to assume that we are blind in the first weeks of life. However, in 1961, Robert Fantz conducted a pioneering study which demonstrated

that this assumption was wrong. Fantz developed a *preferential looking procedure* to study infants' visual preferences. He placed infants on their backs, showed them two or more stimuli at the same time, and observed their eyes to record how long they looked at each stimulus. Infants preferred complex patterns, such as realistic or scrambled drawings of a human face, to simple patterns and solid colours (Figure 12.5). The mere fact that very young babies preferred some stimuli over others indicates that they are able to make perceptual discriminations between such stimuli.

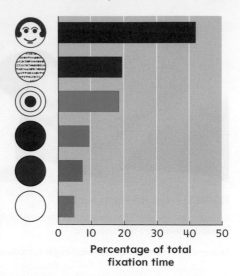

The visual habituation technique

But there is a problem with the visual preference procedure, in that if babies have no preference for one stimulus over the other then we will not be able to tell whether they can discriminate between them or not. In order to get around this problem Fantz (1964) also pioneered another method for examining infants' perceptual abilities – the *visual habituation* technique. This technique makes use of the fact that after a period of exposure to visual stimuli, infants begin to habituate to them – they look at them less than they did initially. Correspondingly, when we present infants with stimuli to which they have been habituated and stimuli which are novel, they demonstrate a strong visual preference for the novel stimulus (a 'novelty preference'). Thus, we can use habituation to determine whether infants can discriminate between visual stimuli. If they show a novelty preference when presented with pairs of novel and familiar stimuli (stimuli to which they have been habituated) then we can conclude that they are able to discriminate between those stimuli. Using this technique, Alan Slater at the University of Exeter has shown that newborn infants are able to make a wide variety of perceptual discriminations between different visual stimuli. Figure 12.6 shows some of the visual form discriminations which newborns can make.

FIGURE I2.5 Infants' visual preferences.

Whether 2 days old or 2 to 3 months old (the data shown here), infants prefer to look at complex patterns more than simple patterns or solid colours.

Source: Based on Fantz, 1961.

Despite the success of the visual preference and visual habituation techniques for investigating visual perceptual abilities in very young infants, they are not completely without their complications. One particular problem lies in what we can conclude from a perceptual discrimination. Take, for instance, Slater et al.'s (1983) demonstration of form discrimination (see Figure 12.6). Do newborn infants discriminate between these stimuli in the same way we might – by comparing the configural shapes of the stimuli? From this evidence alone we cannot be sure. It is possible that the infants are focusing on some much more basic perceptual cues, such as the orientation of component lines. For example, they might discriminate the triangle from the other shapes by simply registering that it contains a diagonally oriented line.

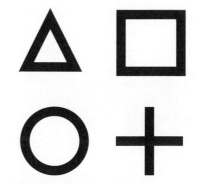

Taste, smell, touch and hearing at birth

Newborns' other senses function well at birth also. Just as you would make different facial expressions after tasting sweet, sour or bitter substances, newborns' facial responses tell us that they have a reasonably well-developed sense of taste. Newborns also orient to touch, and can discriminate between different parts of their bodies being touched (Kisilevsky & Muir, 1984). They also distinguish different odours – if exposed to pads taken from inside the bras of several nursing mothers, week-old infants will orient towards the scent of their own mother's pad. Newborns can hear fairly well. They prefer human voices to other sounds and can distinguish their mother's voice from that of a female stranger (DeRegnier, Wewerka, Georgieff, Mattia, & Nelson, 2002). Indeed, newborns seem to prefer sounds that become familiar to them in their last weeks of foetal development. DeCasper and Spence (1986) describe a now famous experiment (see Figure 12.7) in which they demonstrated that prenatal infants can learn about speech sounds from the outside world, which they can hear through the wall of the uterus in the womb. DeCasper and Spence asked a group of mothers to read out loud the same passage from Dr Seuss's *The Cat in the Hat*. Two or three days after birth, their newborns were able to turn on a recording of their mother reading either *The Cat in the Hat* rhyme or an unfamiliar rhyme by sucking on a sensor-equipped nipple at different rates. Compared with infants in a control condition, these newborns changed their sucking rate in order to select the familiar rhyme. This particular kind of method is called operant conditioning. The experiment is set up so

FIGURE I2.6 Visual habituation in newborns

If habituated to any one of the four shapes shown here, infants only a few days old will demonstrate a novelty preference for any of the other three stimuli.

Source: Based on Slater, Morison and Rose, 1983.

that the familiar rhyme is switched on by one pattern of sucking and the novel rhyme by another pattern. The newborns showed a conditioned response to suck in the way which switched on the familiar rhyme; they learned in the experimental session to switch on the preferred soundtrack. This kind of learning (operant conditioning) is covered in detail in **Chapter 7**.

FIGURE 12.7 Can the foetus learn?

DeCasper and Spence (1986) showed that newborn infants can recognize speech which their mother had spoken to them before they were born.

Source: (left) © KatarzynaBialasiewicz; (right) Reproduced with permission of Professor Melanie Spence

Chapter 7, Page 269

Chapter 13, Page 539

Face Perception in Newborn Infants

As we shall discuss more in **Chapter 13**, the newborn infant is able to identify and respond to a range of aspects of their social environment. Perhaps the most important thing for a newborn infant to be able to do is identify people who are likely to be a parent or caregiver. One obvious aspect of this is being able to single out faces in the visual environment. Despite Fantz's (1961) demonstration of a face preference in young infants (between 2 days to 3 months of age), controversy remained concerning whether this visual preference represented an ability to discriminate faces from other stimuli in the environment. One interpretation is that the infants looked longer at schematic faces because of the symmetry of the features. Another interpretation was that the infants preferred the faces as they were more complex than other patterns. Of course, they could also prefer these figures for *both* reasons!

Furthermore, it is difficult to know what these abilities mean in terms of early development. Do the infants have an innate ability to recognize faces over other stimuli or are they simply attending to a stimulus which they have learned about in the first days and weeks of life? After all, Fantz had tested a group of infants ranging between 2 days and 3 months. It was difficult to determine whether the youngest infants were able to make the discrimination at all. There followed several failures to replicate Fantz's findings with infants who were younger than 2 months of age (Koopman & Ames, 1968; Maurer & Barrera, 1981).

In order to resolve these issues, Mark Johnson of the University of London and his colleagues made use of a straightforward adaptation of the visual preference technique – preferential tracking, in which is measured infants' preferential tendencies to follow a stimulus with their eyes as it is moved through their visual field (see Figure 12.8). In order to examine whether preferences were innate, they tested infants who were only an hour old at the most. Three stimuli were presented to the infants (a face-like pattern, a pattern in which facial features were symmetrical but scrambled, and a blank pattern).

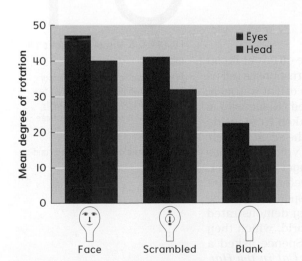

FIGURE 12.8 The stimuli shown to newborn infants.

This graph shows the mean number of degrees through which the newborn infants rotated their eyes and heads when following the stimuli.

Source: Reprinted from *Cognition*, Vol.40, No.1-2, Johnson et al 'Newborns' preferential tracking of face-like stimuli and its subsequent decline (1991). With permission from Elsevier.

The number of degrees through which the infants followed each of the stimuli was compared. They found that the infants tracked (with their eyes and head) the face-configured stimuli further into the periphery than both the scrambled stimuli and the blank stimuli. In addition they tracked the scrambled face stimulus further than the blank stimulus. The fact that the infants preferred the face stimulus over the scrambled face stimulus is quite convincing evidence of a preference for faces over other stimuli as both the face stimulus and the scrambled face stimulus contain exactly the same features, and both are symmetrical in their configuration. The only difference is the configural layout of the features.

These results demonstrate convincingly that only a few minutes after birth newborn infants can discriminate between faces and other stimuli in their environment, and that they prefer to orient towards faces over other stimuli, even when the other stimuli are of equal complexity. This study is also impressive in demonstrating face preference only a few minutes after birth, providing compelling evidence that early infant face preferences are innate and not learned in the first days of life.

Perceptual Development in Early Infancy

Even though newborns show surprising competence, some very important developments in perceptual abilities take place in the first year of life across all sensory modalities. In the domain of vision, developments are particularly striking in the way infants make shape discriminations. Cohen and Younger (1984) conducted an elegant habituation-novelty study which demonstrates that infants start off by making shape discriminations on the basis of orientation rather than the relationships between parts of a visual pattern (what we can call 'configural' shape; see Figure 12.9). They examined whether infants could discriminate between obtuse and acute angles. Obtuse and acute angles are different by virtue of their component lines being differently related to one another (see Figure 12.9), Cohen and Younger (1984) habituated infants to an acute angle (labelled 'habituation' in Figure 12.10), and then examined whether they would show a novelty preference for each of the test figures A–D (see Figure 12.10). At 1½ months old, infants showed a novelty preference for the figures composed of lines which differed in orientation from the habituation stimulus (B and D in Figure 12.9), but they showed no increase in looking towards a figure which was composed of the same orientations of lines even though it was a different configural shape – an obtuse angle. Thus, 1½-month-olds discriminate between objects on the basis of the orientations of their component lines and not their configural shape. On the other hand, 3½-month-olds discriminated on the basis of configural shape rather than orientation (they only showed a novelty preference for C and D in Figure 12.9).

In the auditory domain some of the most significant developments are in infants' abilities to discriminate between phonemes, the sounds of which speech is composed. Werker and Tees (1984) investigated this ability in infants ranging from 6 to 12 months of age with English-speaking parents. They found that the youngest infants were just as competent as the older infants at discriminating speech sounds in English. They also tested the young and older infants on their ability to make speech sound discriminations which are not made in English, but are discriminated in different languages to which they had not been exposed (Hindi, and also Thompson, a language spoken by Salish Native Indians in Canada). When tested on these non-native speech sounds, the youngest 6- to 8-month-old infants performed better than the older 10- to 12-month-olds. This indicates that perceptual development can sometimes follow a process known as perceptual narrowing, in which infants lose the ability to make discriminations which they do not need across the first year of life.

Bremner, Mareschal, Lloyd-Fox and Spence (2008) have investigated developments in the ability to localize touch sensations across the first year of life (see Figure 12.10). They tested two age groups of infants (6½-month-olds and 10-month-olds), and examined the ability to localize touch stimuli presented to their hands. Both age groups responded in the correct direction when their hands were in a familiar place (when they were adopting an uncrossed hands posture), but when their hands were crossed over the 6½-month-olds often responded in the wrong direction (they looked at and moved the hand which had not been 'buzzed'). The 10-month-olds were equally good at responding wherever their hands were placed. This research indicates that infants get better at keeping track of tactile locations as they get older – they get better at keeping track of where their limbs are. Interestingly, movement of the limbs across the midline increases between 6 and 10 months also. Perhaps it is this experience which enables the infants to respond correctly across both arm postures (Rigato, Begum Ali, van Velzen, & Bremner, 2014).

Habituation   A   B   C   D

FIGURE 12.9 Can young infants discriminate between acute and obtuse angles?

A study conducted by Cohen and Younger (1984). After habituation 1½-month-old infants preferred patterns containing lines which were oriented differently to the habituation stimulus (B and D); 3½-month-old infants preferred patterns which comprised different configural shapes to the habituation stimulus (C and D). Thus the younger infants discriminate angles on the basis of orientation, whereas the older infants discriminate angles on the basis of configural shape.

Source: adapted from Cohen and Younger, 1984.

Uncrossed hands   Crossed hands

FIGURE 12.10 Do infants know where touch stimuli come from even when their hands are crossed?

Bremner and colleagues tested this ability by presenting mild tactile 'buzzes' to infants' hands using vibrating 'tactors' – one placed in the palm of each hand.

Source: Bremner et al., 2008.

Focus 12.3 Describe the newborn's sensory capabilities, perceptual preferences, reflexes and ability to learn.

And so human infants arrive in the world with a range of perceptual skills already available to them across several sensory modalities (sight, hearing, touch, taste and smell). This suggests a significant role for genetic factors in our perceptual abilities. Nonetheless, there are a number of ways in which perceptual skills are honed across the first months of life. Infants have to learn to adapt the structure of their perceptual environment (for example, by homing in on the speech sound discriminations which are important in the language which they hear, and by learning to ignore the distinctions which are only made in other languages). They also have to cope with challenges presented by their increasing motor abilities (for example, they have to learn to track tactile locations around when they become able to move their hands into new positions).

Research close-up

THE DEVELOPMENT OF FACE DISCRIMINATION IN THE FIRST YEAR OF LIFE

Source: O. Pascalis, M. de Haan, & C. A. Nelson (2003). Is face processing species-specific during the first year of life? Science, 296, 1321–1323.

INTRODUCTION

A number of researchers have suggested that we get better at discriminating between faces of different people over the first years of life (e.g., Morton & Johnson, 1991). Pascalis, de Haan and Nelson (2003) thus examined changes in the ability to discriminate between different faces in 6- and 10-month-old infants. Specifically, they examined whether these age groups could discriminate between different human faces, and between different monkey faces. Pascalis et al. (2003) used a visual habituation method in which they exposed infants to a single face and, after a few seconds' exposure, examined whether they would show a preference when presented with the familiar and a novel face paired together. A novelty preference would indicate recognition and discrimination of the familiar from the novel face.

METHOD

Two age groups of 30 healthy full-term infants were tested (younger group were an average 6 months of age, and the older group were an average of 9 months of age). Half of the infants in each group were tested on human face recognition, the other half were tested on monkey face recognition.

Infants were seated facing a screen on which pictures of faces were presented (seated on a parent's lap). A single face was presented on the screen in a learning phase. This face was taken away once the infant had looked at it for a total of 20 seconds. The total fixation duration was recorded by an experimenter with a stopwatch. After the learning phase a retention test was given in which the familiar face (the one already seen in the learning phase) was presented side by side with a novel face (both faces were either human or monkey faces), not seen before (Figure 12.11). These were presented for 10 seconds, during which the infants' fixations were measured. The extent to which participants preferred to look at the novel of the two faces was used as a measure of recognition. The question which Pascalis et al. (2003) were asking was whether the infants in each age group were able to discriminate between two different human faces and also whether they were able to discriminate between two monkey faces.

FIGURE 12.11 The stimuli shown to the infants.

Half of the infants in each age group were tested on the monkey face discrimination. The other half were tested on the human face discrimination.

Source: From *Science*, Vol. 296, Pascalis et al 'Is face processing species-specific during the first year of life?' (2002). Reprinted with permission from AAAS.

RESULTS

Pascalis et al. found that the younger age group showed a preference for both novel human faces and novel monkey faces (they looked at the novel face for longer than the familiar face). In Table 12.2 you can see that a statistically reliable preference was shown by that age group for both human and monkey faces. The older age group, however, only showed a reliable preference for novel human faces. Pascalis et al. concluded that the 9-month-olds had lost the ability to discriminate between individual monkey faces. It seems that face discrimination undergoes perceptual narrowing in the first year of life. Infants are initially able to discriminate between both monkey faces and human faces. However, by 9 months they lose the ability to discriminate between monkey faces.

▶

DISCUSSION

In a sense these findings are rather surprising. We might have expected that infants would increase in the kinds of face discrimination which they can make as they get older. These findings demonstrate something quite different. While 6-month-olds were able to make discriminations of both human and monkey faces, 9-month-olds could only manage human faces. But on closer consideration this result makes more sense. When infants emerge into the world it seems sensible that they should be able to make as many discriminations of individual people as possible, so that they can home in on the differences which are of most importance (i.e. the differences between human faces). It seems that face discrimination undergoes perceptual narrowing in the first year of life. Infants are initially able to discriminate between faces, whatever species of primate they belong to. However, by 10 months they lose the ability to discriminate between faces of a species they do not usually see in their everyday environment; they undergo perceptual narrowing, homing in on and discriminating only the important information in their environment. Interestingly, this perceptual narrowing phenomenon demonstrates a parallel with speech sound discrimination (as discussed earlier). Recent research which has exposed young human infants to monkey faces (Pascalis et al., 2005) and, in another study, to speech sounds in a different language (Kuhl, Tsao, & Liu, 2003), has found that narrowing can be avoided if infants are exposed to a particular perceptual difference (e.g. different monkey faces, or speech sounds not usually differentiated in one's own language).

TABLE 12.2 The percentage preference infants showed for the novel face in pascalis et al.'s task

Age group	Discrimination	
	Human faces	Monkey faces
6 months	56%*	64%*
9 months	55%*	51%

Greater than 50% is a novelty preference, anything around 50% is no preference, and less than 50% is a familiarity preference. The asterisks indicate which novelty preferences were statistically reliable.

QUESTION

Do infants change in their ability to discriminate between faces? Does it matter whether the faces are of their own species (human) or of another species (monkey)? Type of study: *Experimental*

Independent variables	Dependent variables
Age group (6-month-olds/9-month-olds)	Recognition of a familiar face (indicated by percentage visual preference for a novel face over a familiar face)
Face recognition test given (human faces/monkey faces)	

PHYSICAL DEVELOPMENT

Our bodies and movement (motor) skills develop rapidly during infancy and childhood. On average, by our first birthday our body weight triples and our height increases by 50%. Developmental researchers have focused a great deal on how infants and children master certain motor skills. The ages at which babies achieve certain 'motor milestones' (like grasping an object, or walking for the first time) have been used to measure their developmental progress and identify children who are developmentally delayed. As Figure 12.12 shows, infants vary in the age at which they acquire particular skills. The figure also suggests that sequence in which skills appear is broadly the same across children. However, it is important to bear in mind that these kinds of charts of developmental progress vastly oversimplify what is actually going on in development. It is not just that different children reach milestones at different ages. The ways in which they reach those milestones differ dramatically (Adolph & Berger, 2011). Crawling is often described as a precursor to walking, but in reality there are a huge range of ways in which children move around before they can walk. They can roll, bum-shuffle, crawl like an army commando with their body against the ground, or like a bear on hands and feet. Individual babies use idiosyncratic mixtures of these techniques, and so it is clear that there is not one particular developmental road to walking (Adolph, Berger, & Leo, 2011; Adolph & Robinson, 2013).

Physical and motor development have been characterized as following two direction trajectories. The **cephalocaudal trajectory** is the tendency for development to proceed in a head-to-foot direction. Thus, as you can see in Figure 12.3, the head of a foetus (and infant) is disproportionately large because physical growth concentrates first on the head. In terms of motor skill development, an infant will master the ability to maintain postural balance of the head on the neck, before he or she can sit or stand up. The **proximodistal trajectory** states that development begins along the innermost parts of the body and continues towards the outermost parts. Thus a foetus's arms develop before the hands

cephalocaudal trajectory the tendency for development to proceed in a head-to-foot direction

proximodistal trajectory development begins along the innermost parts of the body and continues towards the outermost parts

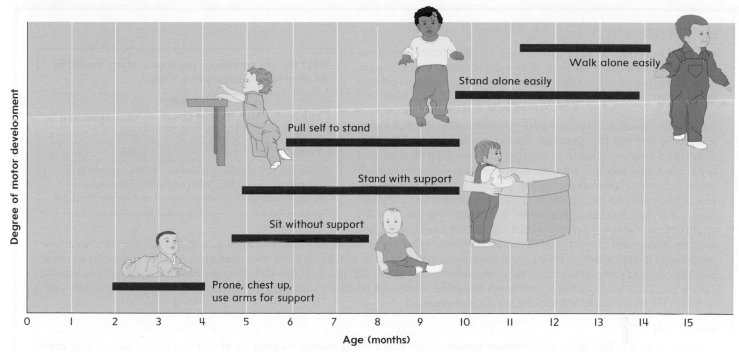

FIGURE 12.12 Infant motor development.

Infant motor development occurs in an orderly sequence, but the age at which abilities emerge varies greatly across children. The left end of each bar represents the age by which 25% of children exhibit the skill; the right end represents the age by which 90% have mastered it.

and fingers. Likewise, infants' arm movements develop before their ability to manipulate objects with their fingers.

Motor development is not just important for its own sake. Newly acquired motor abilities play important roles in development in other domains. The ability to crawl, for instance, brings new and more varied experiences with the environment. There are now numerous observations demonstrating how emerging abilities to move around the environment, such as the onset of crawling and walking lead to changes in infants' perceptions and understanding of the world and their emotional reactions to it (Adolph & Berger, 2006; Campos, Anderson, Barbu-Roth, Hubbard, Hertenstein, & Witherington, 2000).

The Young Brain

The most important part of the body for psychological functioning is the brain and central nervous system (see **Chapter 4**). No organ develops more dramatically than the brain. At birth the newborn's brain is far from mature and has reached only about 25% of its eventual adult weight. By age 6 months, however, the brain reaches 50% of its adult weight. As Figure 12.13 shows, neural networks that form the basis for psychological functioning develop rapidly. It is interesting to note that the main changes in the brain following birth are not in the growth of new neurons (most neuronal cell birth has taken place by the time the baby is born; Johnson & de Haan, 2011). However, new connections between cells (synapses) continue to form well into postnatal life, and unnecessary synapses are also pruned back and lost. Further changes include myelination, a process in which the neurons become more efficient conductors because of greater insulation by fatty myelin sheaths (see **Chapter 4**).

The first brain areas to mature fully lie deep within the brain and regulate basic survival functions such as heartbeat and breathing. Among the last areas to mature is the frontal lobe which is vital to our highest-level cognitive functions.

Rapid brain growth during infancy and early childhood slows in later childhood (Sowell, Thompson, Tessner, & Toga, 2001). Yet, although 5-year-olds' brains have reached almost 90% of their adult size, brain maturation continues. Again, myelination, synaptic proliferation and pruning all continue well into adolescence.

Chapter 4, Page 115

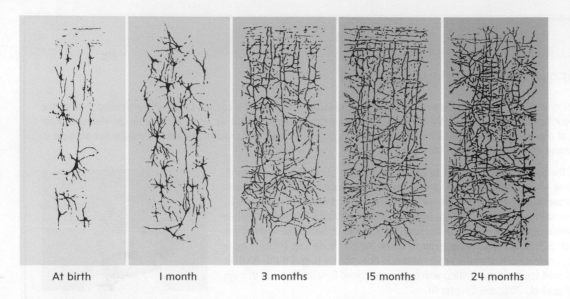

At birth   1 month   3 months   15 months   24 months

FIGURE 12.13 The brain matures and adapts.

Increases in the density of neural networks during early development are apparent in these drawings of tissue from the human cerebral cortex.

Source: The postnatal development of the human cerebral cortex, Vols. I–VIII, Harvard University Press.

Environmental and Cultural Influences

Although guided by genetics, physical development is also strongly influenced by experience. Diet is an obvious example. Chronic, severe malnutrition not only stunts general growth and brain development but also is a major source of infant death worldwide (Pelletier & Frongillo, 2003).

Babies thrive in an enriched environment – one in which the infant has the opportunity to interact with others and to manipulate suitable toys and other objects (Needham, Barrett, & Peterman, 2002). Newborn rats (i.e., pups) raised in an enriched environment develop heavier brains, larger neurons, more synaptic connections and greater amounts of brain neurotransmitters that enhance learning (Rosenzweig & Bennett, 1996; Simpson & Kelly, 2011).

Physical touch, too, affects growth in infancy. Depriving well-nourished rat pups of normal physical contact with their mothers stunts their development, whereas vigorously stroking the pups with a brush helps restore normal growth (Schanberg, Ingledue, Lee, Hannun, & Bartolome, 2003). Similarly, massaging premature and full-term human infants accelerates their weight gain and neurological development (Field, Diego, Hernandez-Reif, Deeds, & Figuereido, 2006).

Experience also can influence basic motor skill development. Infants of the South American Ache tribe typically do not begin to walk until they are almost 2, about a year later than the average Western infant (Kaplan & Dove, 1987). The Ache people roam the dense rain forests of eastern Paraguay foraging for food. For safety, mothers keep their children in direct physical contact almost constantly until the age of 3, providing them little opportunity to move about. Experience also affects various types of complex movement skills that toddlers and children acquire (Figure 12.14).

Our discussion of physical growth reinforces three points that apply across the realm of human development:

1. *Biology sets limits on environmental influences.* For example, because the frontal areas of the brain (which subserve abilities like behavioural inhibition and planning) are particularly late to mature, self-control has a particularly slow development across childhood.

2. *Environmental influences can be powerful.* Nurturing environments foster physical and psychological growth, and impoverished environments can stunt growth.

3. *Biological and environmental factors interact.* Enriched environments enhance brain development. In turn, brain development facilitates our ability to learn and benefit from environmental experiences.

Focus 12.4 Explain how nature and nurture jointly influence infants' physical growth and motor development.

FIGURE 12.14 At the Parker Ranch in Hawaii, USA, this 2-year-old is learning to ride a horse and use a lasso.

Source: National Geographic/Steve Raymer/National Geographic Creative

Current topic

WHAT IS THE ROLE OF THE BRAIN IN DEVELOPMENT?

In recent years, developmental psychologists have begun turning their attention towards methods which can tell us about the development of the neural processes which underlie our psychological abilities. Whereas previously we learned much of what we know about brain development from studying animals, the refinement of non-invasive techniques for studying neural responses in infants and children has led to a substantial increase in what we know about the development of human brain function.

The younger the age group, the more challenging it is to gather information about brain functioning. Functional MRI makes a lot of noise which unsettles infants, and so most studies have been conducted with children older than 5 or 6 years, or sedated or sleeping infants (although some researchers have managed this; Dehaene-Lambertz, Dehaene, & Hertz-Pannier, 2002). Perhaps the most widely used brain imaging technique with young infants has been to measure electrical activity on the scalp (EEG; Figure 12.15a). Some might argue that the most important advances in this technique have been to make the electrode cap (or net) more comfortable so that the infant stays contented during the experiment and does not try to pull it off! Another new method is functional near infrared spectroscopy (fNIRS) which measures blood flow in the brain through patterns of reflected light (Lloyd-Fox et al., 2010; see Chapter 4).

These methods have revealed some exciting differences concerning how infants' and children's brains respond while they are looking at displays or undertaking cognitive tasks at difference ages. The key debate, though, is how these changes in neural function arise. Mark Johnson at the Centre for Brain and Cognitive Development (Birkbeck, University of London) proposes some alternative ways of envisaging changes in brain function over development (Johnson & de Haan, 2011). One approach, the 'Maturational' account of brain development, suggests that the development of perceptual and cognitive abilities is held up by the maturation of relevant parts of the brain; for example, children may take a long time to master tasks where they have to inhibit a behaviour because their frontal cortex (responsible for inhibition) takes longer to grow than some other parts of the brain. Researchers who take the view that many of our cognitive abilities are provided by our inheritance (e.g., Diamond, 1990; Leslie, 2004; Spelke, 1998) generally adhere to a maturational position. This view thus implies that brain areas specialized for particular tasks (e.g., face perception) mature without the need for a major input from the environment.

FIGURE 12.15 Infant participants taking part in EEG and NIRS studies.

Source: (a) Jon Wilson/Science Photo Library; (b) courtesy of Sarah Lloyd-Fox, Birkbeck, University of London.

Another approach, favoured by Johnson and de Haan (2011), is the 'interactive specialization' account. Unlike the maturational account, interactive specialization suggests that particular parts of the brain are not pre-designed for specific tasks, but rather that the brain becomes gradually differentiated into a range of areas and networks which specialize at different tasks. Importantly, interactive specialization also argues that the environment which infants and children are exposed to plays an important role in shaping brain specialization.

But which approach is the correct one? It is certainly early days in answering this question, and it is important to acknowledge that maturation and interactive specialization could both be going on at once. However, evidence showing that the regions involved in particular tasks (e.g., in face perception; Cohen Kadosh, Cohen Kadosh, Dick, & Johnson, 2011; Halit, de Haan, & Johnson, 2003) change substantially over development is certainly strong support for Johnson's interactive specialization account.

Another, perhaps more fundamental, debate about the role of the brain in development concerns whether we even need to pay attention to neural processes in order to understand psychological development. Historically a number of developmental psychologists have suggested that cognitive development is best understood by observing changes in behaviour. However, the discovery that both brain structure and function change dramatically across development implies that changes in the brain may have an important bearing on emerging cognitive abilities. It is therefore becoming more important to understand cognitive development at the level of neural processes (Johnson & de Haan, 2011).

COGNITIVE DEVELOPMENT

How do the thought processes of a child develop? Swiss psychologist Jean Piaget (e.g., 1926, 1977) spent over 50 years exploring this question. The body of work which he published as a result of his research led him to become probably the most influential developmental psychologist of the twentieth century.

Piaget's Stage Model

Early in his career, Piaget worked for French psychologist Alfred Binet, a pioneer of intelligence testing. Piaget became intrigued when he noticed that children of the same

age often made similar errors on test questions. The key to understanding how children think, Piaget believed, was not whether they got the right answers but *how* they arrived at their answers.

Piaget observed children and listened to them reason as they tried to solve problems. He proposed that children's thinking changes *qualitatively* with age and that it differs from the way adults think. Piaget believed that cognitive development results from an interaction of the brain's biological maturation and personal experiences. He viewed children as natural-born scientists who seek to understand their world.

To achieve this understanding, the brain builds **schemas** (or *schemata*), which are organized patterns of thought and action. Think of a schema as a mental framework that guides our interaction with the world. For example, infants are born with a sucking reflex that provides a primitive schema for interacting with physical objects. In other words, sucking is a basic way in which the infant 'knows' the world. When a child says 'doggie' to describe a family pet, this word reflects a schema – a concept that the child is using to understand this particular experience.

Cognitive development occurs as we acquire new schemas and as our existing schemas become more complex. According to Piaget, two key processes are involved. **Assimilation** is the process by which new experiences are incorporated into existing schemas. When a young infant encounters a new object – a small plastic toy, a blanket, a doll – he or she will try to suck it. The infant tries to fit this new experience into a schema that he or she already has: objects are suckable. Similarly, a child who sees a squirrel for the first time may exclaim 'cat!' After all, a squirrel is nearly as big as a cat, is furry, and has four legs and a tail. The child tries to make sense of this new experience by applying his or her familiar schema: 'cat'.

Accommodation is the process by which new experiences cause existing schemas to change. As the infant tries to suck different objects, he or she will eventually encounter some that are too big or that taste bad. Similarly, the child who calls a squirrel a 'cat' may discover that this 'cat' exhibits some behaviours not found in cats (like eating nuts). This imbalance, or *disequilibrium*, between existing schemas and new experiences ultimately forces those schemas to change. Thus the infant's 'suckability' schema will become more complex: some objects are suckable, some are not. The child's 'cat' schema

> **schemas** organized patterns of thought and action
>
> **assimilation** the process by which new experiences are incorporated into existing schemas
>
> **accommodation** the process by which new experiences cause existing schemas to change

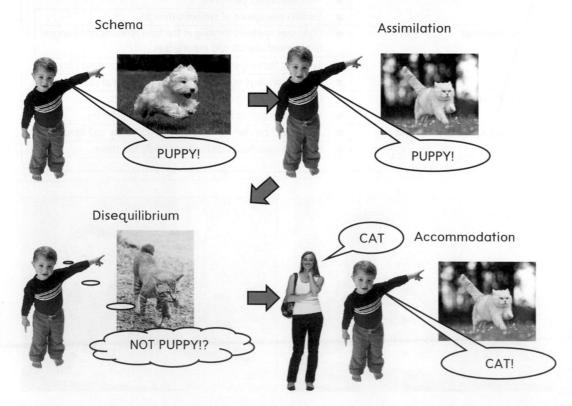

FIGURE 12.16 Assimilation and accommodation in action

Here a child uses a pre-existing naming schema for puppy, and assimilates a novel instance (a cat) to it. Because the cat displays non-puppy behaviours (eating a mouse), disequilibrium occurs, and the naming schema accommodates this novel instance with a new name provided by a parent (cat!).

Source: ©iStock.com/HKPNC; ©iStock.com/ 4x6; ©iStock.com/Wavetop; Rita Kochmarjova/Shutterstock; © Khlongwangchao

also will change, and he or she will begin to develop new schemas for 'dog', 'squirrel', and so on. To the infant and child, this is a fundamental change in their understanding of the world.

Importantly, this change in structure (accommodation) is something which infants and children bring about themselves, by actively assimilating the environment into their schemas (see Figure 12.16). When Piaget introduced these ideas, psychology was under considerable influence from the behaviourist tradition, which considered skills and knowledge as being passively shaped by the environment. Piaget's assertion that infants and children actively change the structure of their own knowledge was a challenge to the existing behaviourist view, and helped bring about a qualitative change in the development of psychology as a field – from behaviourism to cognitivism (see **Chapter 1**).

Cognitive growth thus involves a give and take between trying to understand new experiences in terms of what we already know (assimilation) and having to modify our thinking when new experiences do not fit into our current schemas (accommodation). As we have just indicated, qualitative changes in thought processes can continue well into adulthood. However, the biggest changes occur in infancy and childhood. As Table 12.3 shows, Piaget charted four major stages of cognitive growth from birth through to adolescence.

Sensorimotor stage

From birth to about age 2, infants in the **sensorimotor stage** understand their world primarily through sensory experiences and physical (motor) interactions with objects. Reflexes are infants' earliest schemas, and as infants mature, they begin to explore their surroundings and realize that they can bang spoons, take objects apart and make things happen.

Piaget argued that once objects are 'out of sight' young infants do not understand their continued existence. If you hide 3-month-old Emily's favourite toy from view, she will

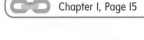
Chapter 1, Page 15

sensorimotor stage
Infants understand their world primarily through sensory experiences and physical (motor) interactions with objects

TABLE 12.3 Piaget's stages of cognitive development

Stage	Age (years)	Major characteristics
Sensorimotor	Birth to 2	■ Infant understands world through sensory and motor experiences
		■ Achieves object permanence
		■ Exhibits emergence of symbolic thought
Pre-operational	2 to 7	■ Child uses symbolic thinking in the form of words and images to represent objects and experiences
		■ Symbolic thinking enables child to engage in pretend play
		■ Thinking displays egocentrism, irreversibility and centration
Concrete operational	7 to 12	■ Child can think logically about concrete events
		■ Grasps concepts of conservation and serial ordering
Formal operational	12 on	■ Adolescent can think more logically, abstractly and flexibly
		■ Can form hypotheses and systematically test them

FIGURE 12.17 During the early sensorimotor period, a baby will reach for a visible toy (*left*) but not for one that has been hidden from view while the infant watches (*right*). According to Piaget, the child lacks the concept of object permanence; when something is out of sight, the infant does not understand that it still exists in a place from which the infant can retrieve it.

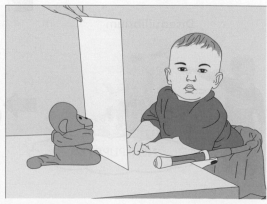

not search for it, as if the toy no longer exists (Figure 12.17). But around age 8 months, Emily will search for and retrieve the hidden toy. She now grasps the concept of **object permanence**, the understanding that an object continues to exist in a particular place even when it is no longer visible.

Infants begin to acquire language after age 1, and towards the end of the sensorimotor period they increasingly use words to represent objects, needs and actions. Thus in the space of two years, infants grow into independent thinkers who form simple concepts, solve some problems and communicate their thoughts.

Pre-operational stage

At about age 2, children enter a **pre-operational stage**, in which they represent the world symbolically through words and mental images but do not yet understand basic mental operations or rules. Rapid language development helps children label objects and represent simple concepts, such as that two objects can be the 'same' or 'different'. Children can think about the past ('yesterday') and future ('soon') and can better anticipate the consequences of their actions. Symbolic thinking enables them to engage in make-believe, or pretend, play.

Despite these advances, children's cognitive abilities have major limitations. According to Piaget, the pre-operational child does not understand **conservation**, the principle that basic properties of objects, such as their volume, mass, or quantity, stay the same (are 'conserved') even though their outward appearance may change (Figure 12.18). For example, 4-year-olds often say that the taller beaker in Figure 12.18c has more liquid than the shorter one. You understand that the liquid can be poured back into the short beaker to return to the original, equal state of affairs, but children's thinking at this age displays *irreversibility*: it is difficult for them to reverse an action mentally. You also pay attention to height and width, recognizing that the liquid is 'taller' because the beaker is narrower. But pre-operational children exhibit *centration*, focusing (centring) on only one aspect of the situation, such as the height of the liquid.

> **object permanence** an object continues to exist in a particular place even when it is no longer visible
>
> **pre-operational stage** the stage in which children represent the world symbolically through words and mental images but do not yet understand basic mental operations or rules
>
> **conservation** the principle that basic properties of objects, such as their volume, mass, or quantity, stay the same (are 'conserved') even though their outward appearance may change

(a)   Initial equality

(b)   Transformation

(c)   Which glass has more juice?

Conservation of number

Initial equality   Now, which row has more objects?

(d)

Conservation of mass

Initial equality   Now, which piece has more clay?

(e)

FIGURE I2.I8 Conservation tasks.

(a, b, c) Conservation of volume: at the end of this sequence (*from left to right*), when the pre-operational child is asked which beaker contains more liquid, he points to the taller one. (d) Conservation of number: two rows with an equal number of objects are aligned. After one row is spread out, pre-operational children will say that it has more objects than the other row. (e) Conservation of mass: pre-operational children watch as one of two identically sized clay balls is rolled into a new shape. They typically will say that the new shape now has more clay.

FIGURE 12.19 The three-mountain problem.

Piaget used the three-mountain problem to illustrate the egocentrism of young children. Suppose that a pre-operational child named Luke is looking at the mountains just as you are. Another child, Beth, is standing at the opposite (far) side of the table. Luke is asked what Beth sees. Because Luke is able to see the road, he will mistakenly say that Beth also can see it, indicating that he has failed to recognize Beth's perspective as different from his own.

egocentrism difficulty in viewing the world from someone else's perspective

concrete operational stage can perform basic mental operations concerning problems that involve tangible (i.e., 'concrete') objects and situations

formal operational stage individuals are able to think logically and systematically about both concrete and abstract problems, form hypotheses, and test them in a thoughtful way

Pre-operational children often display *animism*, attributing lifelike qualities to physical objects and natural events. When it rains, 'the sky is crying', and stars twinkle at night 'because they're winking at you'. Their thinking also reflects **egocentrism**, difficulty in viewing the world from someone else's perspective. By *egocentrism* Piaget did not mean 'selfishness' but rather that children at this stage believe that other people perceive things in the same way they do (Figure 12.19).

Concrete operational stage

From about ages 7 to 12, said Piaget, children in the **concrete operational stage** can perform basic mental operations concerning problems that involve tangible (i.e., 'concrete') objects and situations. They now grasp the concept of reversibility, display less centration and easily solve conservation problems that baffled them as pre-schoolers.

When concrete operational children confront problems that are hypothetical or require abstract reasoning, however, they often have difficulty or show rigid types of thinking. To demonstrate this, ask a few 9-year-olds, 'If you could have a third eye, where on your body would you put it? Draw a picture'. Then ask them to explain their reasons. David Shaffer (1989) reports that 9-year-olds typically draw a face with a row of three eyes across it. Their thinking is concrete, bound by the reality that eyes appear on the face, and their justifications often are unsophisticated (e.g., 'so I could see you better'). Many find the task silly because 'Nobody has three eyes' (Shaffer, 1989, p. 324).

Formal operational stage

Piaget's model ends with the **formal operational stage**, in which individuals are able to think logically and systematically not just about both concrete problems as they could in concrete operations, but also concerning more abstract problems. Piaget's view was that the final stage of cognitive attainment was an ability to think hypothetically about events or instances which had not actually been observed in the world. According to Piaget, formal thinking begins around ages 11 to 12 and increases through adolescence (Ward & Overton, 1990).

It is certainly the case that children entering the stage of formal operations begin to think more flexibly when tackling hypothetical problems, such as brain-teasers, and may actually enjoy these kinds of challenges. For instance, Shaffer (1989) reports that 11- to 12-year-olds provide more creative answers and justifications in the third-eye problem than do 9-year-old concrete thinkers. One child placed the eye on the palm of his hands so that he could use it to 'see around corners'. Another placed it on top of his head, so that he could 'revolve the eye to look in all directions'. Formal operational children enjoy these hypothetical tasks and often ask for more.

More recently Piaget's argument that there is a qualitative shift into formal operational thinking has been challenged. Although most researchers are happy to accept that hypothetical thinking increases at this age, but most would not like to support the idea that there is a sudden shift after which children and adolescents suddenly think in a formal operational way (Kuhn & Franklin, 2006). In fact, some now argue that the origins of hypothetical reasoning occur much earlier in life, and perhaps even in infancy (Onishi & Baillargeon, 2005).

Assessing Piaget's Theory: Stages, Ages and Culture

Tests of Piaget's theory conducted around the world yield several general findings. First, it appears that *the general cognitive abilities associated with Piaget's four stages occur in the same order across cultures* (Berry, Poortinga, Segall, & Dasen, 1992). For example, children understand object permanence before symbolic thinking blooms, and concrete reasoning emerges before abstract reasoning.

Second, *children acquire many cognitive skills and concepts at an earlier age than Piaget believed* (Bryant, 1974; Donaldson, 1978). In the next section we describe research which demonstrates that even 3½- to 4½-month-olds appear to have a basic grasp of

objective permanence when they are tested on special tasks that only require them to look at events rather than physically search for a hidden object. In addition, simple modifications of Piaget's tests of older children's ability appear to reveal logical abilities beyond the stage of development attributed to them by Piaget's theory (see the section on 'the social context of cognitive development', page 520).

Third, *cognitive development within each stage seems to proceed inconsistently*. A child may perform at the pre-operational level on most tasks yet solve some tasks at a concrete operational level (Siegler, 1986). This challenges the idea that stage-wise development is domain general (i.e., that the advances which children make between stages affect their performance on a wide range of tasks). According to Piaget, development is domain general so a child at a given stage should not show large inconsistencies in solving conceptually similar tasks. Researchers such as Siegler (1986) and Karmiloff-Smith (1992) have argued that rather than being domain general, cognitive development is 'domain specific'. They argue that stage-wise shifts in ability occur independently in a range of different domains.

Fourth, *culture influences cognitive development*. Later in the chapter we introduce the work of Vygotsky. Vygotsky maintained that the culture in which we live has a profound effect on the way in which we solve cognitive problems. Piaget's Western perspective equated cognitive development with scientific-logical thinking, but 'Many cultures ... consider cognitive development to be more relational, involving the thinking skills and processes to engage in successful interpersonal contexts' (Matsumoto & Hull, 1994, p. 105). In Africa's Côte d'Ivoire, the Baoulé people most strongly value a type of social intelligence that reflects the skills to get along with others and to be respectful, helpful and responsible (Dasen et al., 1985).

Fifth, and most broadly, *cognitive development is more complex and variable than Piaget proposed* (Larivée, Normandeau, & Parent, 2000). Although all children progress from simpler to more sophisticated thinking, they do not all necessarily follow the same developmental path (Siegler, 1998).

In sum, newer research challenges many of Piaget's ideas. Nevertheless, he revolutionized thinking about children's cognitive development, and his work still guides many researchers, often referred to as *neo-Piagetians*, who have modified his theory to account for the issues discussed above (Becker, 2004).

> **Focus 12.5** Discuss Piaget's concepts of assimilation and accommodation, his four-stage model, and findings that help us evaluate his theory.

Young Infants' Understanding of the Physical World

We noted above that infants and children acquire many concepts at an earlier age than Piaget proposed. Because infants cannot express their knowledge in words, developmental psychologists have created some ingenious approaches – such as the *violation-of-expectation experiment* – to examine infants' understanding of basic concepts (Baillargeon, 2004). This approach assesses infants' cognitive abilities by taking measures of their attention, in this case, the time they spend looking at a stimulus.

In violation-of-expectation experiments, researchers begin with the hypothesis that young infants possess a certain concept – an expectation – about how the world works. For example, let us make the radical assumption that young infants have an expectation about the addition of very small numbers of objects, such as 'one of a thing' plus 'another one of the thing' equals 'two of the things'. Then researchers expose the infants to an 'impossible event' that violates this expectation and a 'possible event' that does not violate this expectation, as shown in Figure 12.20. If the infants stare longer at the impossible event, then the researchers take this as evidence that the infants understand the concept being tested. In other words, just as you would stare longer at a dropped pencil that suddenly stopped in mid-air than you would at one that fell to the ground, infants pay more attention to events that violate their understanding of the world.

These experiments suggest that infants possess basic concepts about the physical properties of objects, such that they continue to exist when out of sight (Baillargeon, Spelke, & Wasserman, 1985), much earlier than is claimed by Piaget. Other knowledge infants seem to demonstrate is that two solid objects cannot occupy the same space at the same time (Baillargeon, 1987), and about the addition and subtraction of small numbers of objects, such as $1 + 1 = 2$, $2 + 1 = 3$, and $2 - 1 = 1$ (Spelke, 1994; Wynn, 1998). This

> **Focus 12.6** Explain violation-of-expectation research. Does this approach represent a valid challenge to Piaget's views?

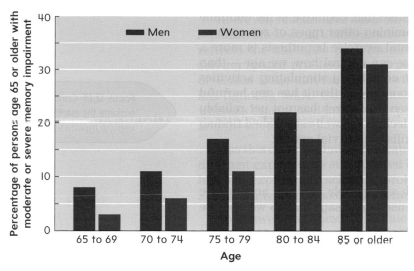

FIGURE 12.30 Impaired memory on a word-recall task.

Participants in this US sample were read a list of 20 words and asked to recall as many as they could. Most healthy adults were able to recall between five and nine words. This graph shows that the percentage of people who recalled four or fewer words increased steadily during late adulthood.

Source: Federal Interagency Forum on Aging-Related Statistics, 2006.

(Pinquart & Sörensen, 2003). More than half of the people diagnosed with senile dementia show combinations of depression, anxiety, agitation, paranoid reactions and disordered thinking that may resemble schizophrenia. Ultimately, they may not even be able to walk, talk or recognize close friends or family members

In-depth studies in Finland, Germany and the USA find that among adults over the age of 65 who do not suffer from dementia, 20–25% do have mild cognitive impairment (Unverzagt et al., 2001). Combining cases of mild impairment and dementia, some experts estimate that 79% of 65- to 74-year-olds and 45% of people age 85 and older remain 'cognitively normal' (Unverzagt et al., 2001). These are not pleasant statistics, but they also make clear that even well into old age, cognitive impairment is not inevitable. 'Levels of analysis' summarizes some of the diverse factors that affect cognitive development.

Levels of analysis
factors related to lifespan development

PSYCHOLOGICAL

- Changes in schemas, information-processing and intellectual capacities
- Development of an understanding of objects in the physical world (including an understanding of numbers and permanence)
- Development of an understanding of the mental states of the self and others
- Developing use of logical operations, and hypothesis-testing procedures (e.g., in the pendulum task)

BIOLOGICAL

- Sex determination and genetic contribution to temperament
- Brain maturation underlying cognitive growth in childhood
- Pubertal changes, including early and late maturation
- Biologically based physical and cognitive changes in adulthood

ENVIRONMENTAL

- Teratogens that affect prenatal development
- Exercise and lifestyle norms that affect biological functions at all ages
- Collaboration of others in cognitive development
- Physical exercise can improve cognitive ability in later life

Lifespan development

In review

■ Adolescence is a transition period between childhood and adulthood. Puberty is a major component of adolescence. Generally, early maturation is a more positive experience for boys than it is for girls.

■ Young adults are at the peak of their physical capabilities, but brain functioning undergoes a general decline later in adulthood.

■ Adolescents may show egocentrism in their social thinking. Their abstract thinking blossoms and information-processing abilities (social and non-social) continue to improve.

■ Information-processing speed slows beginning in early adulthood, but many intellectual abilities do not begin to decline reliably until late adulthood. Wisdom appears to increase steadily from early adolescence through the mid-twenties and then levels off through the mid-seventies.

Recommended Reading

CLASSIC

Gold, R. (1987). *The description of cognitive development: Three Piagetian themes.* Oxford: Clarendon Press/Oxford University Press.

Siegler, R. S. (1998). *Emerging minds: The process of change in children's thinking.* Oxford: Oxford University Press.

Vygotsky, L. S. (1980). *Mind in society: The development of higher psychological processes.* Cambridge, MA: Harvard University Press.

CONTEMPORARY

Goswami, U. (2008). *Cognitive development: The learning brain.* Hove, UK: Psychology Press.

Johnson, M. H. & De Haan, M. (2011). *Developmental Cognitive Neuroscience* (3rd edn.) Oxford: Wiley-Blackwell.

Babies don't need a vacation but I still see them at the beach. I'll go over to them and say, 'What are you doing here? You've never worked a day in your life!'
Stephen Wright

Lifespan development II: social and emotional development

13

Chapter Outline

INFANCY AND EARLY CHILDHOOD

- Newborn emotions and emotional development
- Personality development
- Social development and attachment

💬 Current Topic *The childcare controversy*

🌀 Applying psychological science *Understanding how divorce and remarriage affect children*

- Moral development

ADOLESCENCE, ADULTHOOD AND OLD AGE

- Social-emotional development in adolescence
- Social-emotional development in adulthood

📖 Research close-up *What does it take to become an adult?*

- Social-emotional development in old age

In 1944 John Bowlby, the famous psychoanalyst, published an article entitled, 'Forty-four juvenile thieves: their characters and home-life'. In this article he reported his observations concerning the psychopathology of 44 juvenile delinquent thieves, and examined the links between their delinquency, their psychopathology and the environment in which they had grown up. In 1940s Britain, theft accounted for nine out of ten criminal cases. Over half of those concerned individuals under the age of 21, and one-sixth concerned children under the age of 14. Bowlby's aim was to discover the causes of this apparent epidemic of criminal behaviour in young people.

The 'forty-four juvenile thieves' ranged from 5 to 17 years of age. All had engaged in some form of theft, be that a single incident or persistent and serious stealing. Their IQ and socio-economic status were normal if not slightly above average for the population. Bowlby identified a variety of mental health problems among them, including depression, mania, impairments in affection, and schizophrenia. But unsatisfied with mental health as an explanation for the thieves' criminal activity, Bowlby wanted to examine the root causes of both their mental health problems and their antisocial behaviour. He focused specifically on the quality of parental care which the children had received in early life, and found that 17 of the thieves had suffered complete and prolonged separation from their mothers or foster mothers during the first five years of life. Of the other 27 thieves, 17 had mothers who he considered to be hostile towards them, and five had extremely hostile fathers. Perhaps most strikingly he found that prolonged separation from the mother was a strong predictor of the more chronic thieving behaviours among the 44.

The 44 thieves study, among other observations which Bowlby made, led him to propose the 'maternal deprivation hypothesis': the hypothesis that attachment bonds between infant and parent in the first years of life are vital to ensure well-adjusted socio-emotional development. He thus proposed that *maternal deprivation* led to the maladjusted behaviours of the 44 thieves. While researchers have argued over some of the details of Bowlby's hypothesis, it is quite intuitive to all of us that, on some level, the social bonds we form must have a role in shaping who we are, both in terms of the ways in which we think about the world and in the social bonds we in turn form with others.

For Bowlby these ideas may have had more than an academic resonance. Born in 1907, to an upper-middle class family, he grew up in rather a reserved and distant family arrangement. He, and his brother, did not see much of their parents; their mother for perhaps an hour a day, and their father only on Sundays. The children were cared for and educated mainly by a household nanny and nursemaids. Bowlby's favourite nursemaid left when he was four years old, and it seems that he was very hurt by this, describing such separations, which were quite usual in that period, as being like the loss of a mother (Van der Horst, 2011).

Chapter 12,
Pages 511 & 514

As with physical and cognitive development (see **Chapter 12**), researchers examining social and emotional development tend to consider two main questions. First, how can we describe the changes in emotional and social behaviour which individuals undergo as they progress from newborn to adult and old age? Second, what factors cause these changes? Bowlby's maternal deprivation hypothesis made a strong statement that normal, or well-adjusted, social development was determined by the social bonds infants form with their mother in the first years of life. As we shall see, researchers have questioned whether such a large role can be placed on the family environment, and whether in fact, the temperament or personality that an individual's genes bestow upon them, or indeed the social environment outside the home, may play just as important roles in our social development. In this chapter we describe what research has shown us so far.

INFANCY AND EARLY CHILDHOOD

Children grow not only physically and mentally but also emotionally and socially. They form attachments and relationships, and each child displays a unique personality – a distinctive yet somewhat consistent pattern of thinking, feeling and behaving.

(joy)　　　　　　(sadness)　　　　　　(disgust)

(anger)　　　　　　(interest)　　　　　　(fear)

FIGURE 13.1 (*Left*) Emotional responses communicate our internal states, and they can influence how others respond to us, providing us with the aid and comfort we need. (*Right*) Young infants display a variety of emotions.

Source: (left) © istock.com; (right) © Sheryl Griffin.

NEWBORN EMOTIONS AND EMOTIONAL DEVELOPMENT

Emotional responses communicate our inner states to other people and influence how others respond to us (Figure 13.1). Although infants cannot describe their feelings, Figure 13.1 illustrates that their facial expressions, vocalizations and other behaviours provide a window into their emotional life (Izard, 1982). If you have heard a newborn cry (and cry and cry) or watched a newborn's face after it has been fed, then you know that they can experience distress and contentment. We can also perceive a number of other emotions in young infants. For example, when we see a baby focusing their gaze and staring at objects, this gives a palpable sense that they are interested in the focus of their attention. As infants get older and turn into children, these more basic emotions branch out and divide into more fine-grained distinctions. About six months after birth, infants begin to show joy and surprise ('peekaboo . . . I see you!'), and distress branches out into the separate emotions of disgust, anger, fear and sadness (Lewis, 2000). For example, Izard, Hembree and Huebner (1987), observed infants between the ages of 2 and 8 months, while they received routine vaccination injections. The younger infants showed a more general distressed response to this unpleasant event, whereas the older infants began to demonstrate expressions of anger.

A sense of self emerges early but develops gradually over the first years of life, beginning with infants' ability to perceive their own bodies and limbs (Cowie et al., 2013; Rigato et al., 2014; Rochat, 2010). One important milestone in understanding the self occurs at around 18 months of age, when infants start to respond appropriately to seeing themselves in a mirror (Lewis & Brooks-Gunn, 1979). This growing self-awareness sets the stage for envy, embarrassment and empathy to emerge. After age 2, as toddlers learn about performance standards and rules that they are supposed to follow, they begin to display pride and shame. Around the same age, they also display guilt – as evidenced by avoiding eye contact, shrugging shoulders and making facial expressions (Kochanska, Casey, & Fukumoto, 1995).

Just as emotional reactions become more diverse with age, so does **emotion regulation**, the processes by which we evaluate and modify our emotional reactions. Young infants may suck their thumb or pacifier, turn their head away from something unpleasant or cling to a parent or other caregiver to soothe themselves. To reduce distress, toddlers may seek out a caretaker, cling to a doll or teddy bear, fling unpleasant objects away, and learn to

> **emotion regulation** the processes by which we evaluate and modify our emotional reactions

species, offspring must be exposed to parents within hours or days after entering the world to attach to them.

John Bowlby was influenced by ethological observations of imprinting to propose that a similar biologically programmed process occurs in humans. He argued that infants seek proximity with a caregiver, and that this develops into an **attachment** relationship. Attachment refers to the strong emotional bond that develops between children and their primary caregivers (see Figure 13.5). There are some differences with imprinting in geese, however, as human infants do not automatically imprint on a caregiver, and there is not an immediate post-birth critical period during which contact is required for infant–caregiver bonding. Instead, the first few years of life seem to be a sensitive period when we can most easily form a secure bond with caregivers that enhances our adjustment later in life (Sroufe, 2002; for a discussion of critical and sensitive periods, see **Chapter 12**). Although it may be more difficult to form strong first attachments to caregivers later in childhood or later still in adulthood, it is still possible.

> **attachment** the strong emotional bond that develops between children and their primary caregivers

> Chapter 12, Page 500

> **Focus 13.5** Discuss imprinting, Harlow's attachment research, and attachment in humans.

The attachment process

For decades, people assumed that infant–caregiver bonding resulted primarily from the mother's role in satisfying the infant's need for nourishment. Harry Harlow (1958) tested this notion by separating infant rhesus monkeys from their biological mothers shortly after birth. Each infant was raised in a cage with two artificial 'surrogate mothers'. One was a bare-wire cylinder with a feeding bottle attached to its 'chest'. The other was a wire cylinder covered with soft terry cloth without a feeding bottle.

Faced with this choice, the infant monkeys became attached to the cloth mother. When exposed to frightening situations, the infants ran to the cloth figure and clung tightly to it. They even maintained contact with the cloth mother while feeding from the wire mother's bottle (Figure 13.6). Thus Harlow showed that *contact comfort* – body contact with a comforting object – is more important in fostering attachment than the provision of nourishment.

Based on Harlow's work, and his own observations concerning maternal deprivation (like those in the study of the 44 thieves) John Bowlby (1969) proposed that attachment in infancy emerges not in response to a need for nourishment, but rather as a biologically programmed need for a secure base from which to explore and learn about the environment, and yet return to for protection should something frightening occur. Bowlby proposed that attachment develops in five phases:

1. *Indiscriminate attachment behaviour*: newborns cry, vocalize and smile towards everyone, and these behaviours evoke care-giving from adults.

2. *Discriminating attachment behaviour*: around 3 months of age, infants direct their attachment behaviours more towards familiar caregivers than towards strangers.

3. *Specific attachment behaviour*: by 7 or 8 months of age, infants develop a meaningful attachment to specific caregivers. The caregiver becomes a secure base from which the infant can explore his or her environment.

4. *Goal-corrected attachment behaviour*: by 3 years of age the child can now take account of the caregiver's needs when expressing attachment. For example, they begin to be able to wait alone until the return of the caregiver to allow the mother to achieve something independently. In this sense the attachment relationship becomes more of a 'partnership'.

5. *Lessening of attachment*: at school age, children become happy to spend significant amounts of time further away from the caregiver. At this point Bowlby suggested that the relationship becomes more based upon abstract conceptions of attachment, including trust and affection.

FIGURE 13.5 (Left) Ducks and geese follow and 'imprint' upon the great Konrad Lorenz who has become to represent their mother; (right) in humans, infant–caretaker attachment is more complex and forms over a much longer period.

Source: (left) Thomas D. Mcavoy/The LIFE Picture Collection/Getty Images; (right) ©iStock.com/Blend_Images

According to Bowlby, as an infant's attachment becomes more focused, two types of anxiety occur. **Stranger anxiety**, distress over contact with unfamiliar people, often emerges around age 6 or 7 months and ends by age 18 months. When approached by, touched by or handed over to a stranger, the infant becomes afraid, cries and reaches for the caregiver. **Separation anxiety**, distress over being separated from a primary caregiver, typically begins a little later, peaks around age 12 to 16 months and disappears between 2 and 3 years of age. Here the infant becomes anxious and cries when the caregiver is out of sight. Both forms of anxiety show a similar pattern across many cultures (Figure 13.7).

These responses, which coincide with infants' increasing cognitive and physical abilities, may be adaptive reactions shaped through evolution (Bowlby, 1973). At an age when infants master crawling and then learn to walk, fear of strangers and of separation may help prevent them from wandering beyond the sight of caretakers, especially in unfamiliar situations.

Around age 3 to 4 years, as children's cognitive and verbal skills grow, they develop a better understanding of their attachment relationships. According to Bowlby (1969), a stage of *goal-corrected partnership* emerges, in which children and caregivers can describe their feelings to each other and maintain their relationship whether they are together or apart.

The strange situation

As interest in Bowlby's theory grew, there became a need for a method with which to measure the attachment relationship. In order to achieve this, Mary Ainsworth and co-workers (Ainsworth, Blehar, Waters, & Wall, 1978) developed the **strange situation**, a standardized procedure for examining infant attachment. Ainsworth focused on the forms of anxiety which Bowlby described in attachment: *stranger anxiety* and *separation anxiety*. The strange situation was thus specifically a method for examining infants' reactions to strangers and to separation from their attachment figure. In the strange situation, a series of events (see Table 13.2) occur while an infant is being covertly observed. The infant's reactions to the various events are used to classify them into one of several different attachment types.

Types of attachment

Ainsworth defined three types of attachment (see Table 13.3). 'Securely attached' show the best use of the mother as a secure base for learning – they explore the playroom and react positively to the stranger (Ainsworth et al., 1978). They are distressed when the mother leaves and happily greet her when she returns. In contrast, there are three types of 'insecurely attached' infants, whose relationships with their parent allow for less optimal exploration of the environment. 'Anxious-resistant' infants are fearful when the mother is present, demand her attention and are distressed when she leaves. They are not soothed when she returns and may angrily resist her attempts at contact. 'Anxious-avoidant' infants show few signs of attachment, seldom cry when the mother leaves and do not seek contact when she returns. Later researchers (Main & Solomon, 1986) added a further type of insecure attachment which they labelled 'Disorganized attachment'. Infants demonstrating disorganized attachment seem disoriented and uncertain of what to do in the strange situation, especially when the caregiver figure returns. Attachment types are also apparent later in childhood (see Table 13.3).

Across most cultures studied, about one-half to three-quarters of infants are securely attached. But what is the cause of these differences in attachment? Is it the nature of the relationships which the child is exposed to or is it more to do with the temperament of the child him or herself? Mothers who are more sensitive to their babies' needs at home

FIGURE 13.6 Infant monkeys, reared with a cloth-covered surrogate and a bare-wire surrogate from birth, preferred contact with the cloth 'mother' even though the wire 'mother' satisfied nutritional needs.

Source: Science Source/Science Photo Library.

> **stranger anxiety** distress over contact with unfamiliar people
>
> **separation anxiety** distress over being separated from a primary caregiver
>
> **strange situation** a standardized procedure for examining infant attachment

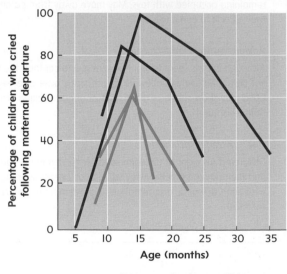

- ▬ Botswana bushmen, Africa
- ▬ Urban Antiguans, Guatemala
- ▬ Israeli kibbutzniks
- ▬ Rural Indians, Guatemala

FIGURE 13.7 Separation anxiety across cultures.
The rise and fall of separation anxiety in infancy shows a similar pattern across cultures.

Source: Based on Kagan, Kearsley and Zelazo, 1978.

TABLE 13.2 The strange situation scenario

Episode number	Persons present	Duration	Brief description of actions
1	Mother, baby, and observer	30 seconds	Observer introduces mother and baby to experimental room, then leaves. (Room contains many appealing toys scattered about)
2	Mother and baby	3 minutes	Mother is non participant while baby explores; if necessary, play is stimulated after 2 minutes
3	Stranger, mother, and baby	3 minutes	Stranger enters. First minute: stranger silent. Second minute: stranger converses with mother. Third minute: stranger approaches baby. After 3 minutes: mother leaves unobtrusively
4	Stranger and baby	3 minutes or less	First separation episode. Stranger's behaviour is geared to that of baby
5	Mother and baby	3 minutes or more	First reunion episode. Mother greets and/or comforts baby, then tries to settle the baby again in play. Mother then leaves, saying 'bye-bye'
6	Baby alone	3 minutes or less	Second separation episode
7	Stranger and baby	3 minutes or less	Continuation of second separation. Stranger enters and gears behaviour to that of baby
8	Mother and baby	3 minutes	Second reunion episode. Mother enters, greets baby, then picks baby up. Meanwhile, stranger leaves unobtrusively

Source: Parke and Gauvain, 2009.

TABLE 13.3 Children's attachment behaviour in the strange situation: a typology

1 year old	6 years old
Secure attachment	
On reunion after brief separation from parents, children seek physical contact, proximity, interaction; often try to maintain physical contact. Readily soothed by parents and return to exploration and play	On reunion, children initiate conversation and pleasant interaction with parents or are highly responsive to parents' overtures. May subtly move close to or into physical contact with parents, usually with rationale such as seeking a toy. Remain calm throughout
Anxious-avoidant attachment	
Children actively avoid and ignore parents on reunion, looking away and remaining occupied with toys. May move away from parents and ignore their efforts to communicate	Children minimize and restrict opportunities for interaction with parents on reunion, looking and speaking only as necessary and remaining occupied with toys or activities. May subtly move away with rationale such as retrieving a toy
Anxious-resistant attachment	
Although infants seem to want closeness and contact, their parents are not able effectively to alleviate their distress after brief separation. Child may show subtle or overt signs of anger, seeking proximity and then resisting it	In movements, posture, and tones of voice, children seem to try to exaggerate both intimacy and dependence on parents. They may seek closeness but appear uncomfortable (e.g., lying in parent's lap but wriggling and squirming). These children sometimes show subtle signs of hostility
Disorganized attachment	
Children show signs of disorganization (e.g., crying for parents at door and then running quickly away when door opens; approaching parent with head down) or disorientation (e.g., seeming to 'freeze' for a few seconds)	Children seem almost to adopt parental role with parents, trying to control and direct parents' behaviour either by embarrassing or humiliating parents or by showing extreme enthusiasm for reunion or overly solicitous behaviour toward parents

Source: Parke and Gauvain 2009.

tend to have infants who are more securely attached in the strange situation (Posada et al., 2002). Are the babies more securely attached because of maternal sensitivity, or are the mothers more sensitive to their infants' needs because they are influenced by the secure nature of their attachment to the child? This question illustrates an important point which was at the heart of Bowlby's ideas. When we talk about attachment we are not just considering the child's behaviour in the relationship, but rather a bidirectional attachment

relationship as a whole, including the mother's attachment to the child. Nonetheless behavioural genetics studies (see **Chapter 3**) indicate only a modest genetic heretability of attachment type (van IJzendoorn, Moran, Belsky, Pederson, Bakermans-Kranenburg, & Kneppers, 2000), suggesting that environmental influences are more important in the formation of attachment relationships.

 Chapter 3, Page 97

How do these environmental influences come about? One thing we can say quite confidently now is that the precursors of attachment styles are present in early infancy. A number of studies have shown that certain behaviours observed in infants as young as 3 months of age predicting attachment type at 1 year of age. The behaviours observed at 3 months of age were infants' responses to what is known as the **still face paradigm** (Tronick, Als, Adamson, Wise, & Brazelton, 1978). In the still face paradigm, the infant is presented with another 'strange' situation in which a parent becomes unresponsive and maintains a neutral facial expression. Studies have shown that the more an infant tries to elicit responses from the parent and shows positive emotions during the still face episode, the more likely they will have a secure attachment at 12 months (Mesman, van IJzendoorn, & Bakermans-Kranenburg, 2009).

> **still face paradigm** an infant is presented with a situation in which their parent looks at them without moving their face

But what are the environmental influences which give rise to attachment types and the different kinds of responses young infants make in the still face paradigm? While parental sensitivity (i.e., the parent's responsiveness) was put forward as a candidate by Ainsworth and colleagues (1978), and has been found to be related to both attachment style (Belsky, 1999; Isabella, 1993) and infants' still face responses (Tarabulsy et al., 2003; Mesman et al., 2009) researchers have more recently suggested that parents' ability to consider their children's internal emotional state is as important as their responsiveness to the infants' behaviour (Meins, Fernyhough, Fradley, & Tuckey, 2001).

What are the consequences of attachment? It turns out that whether raised by their biological parents or by adoptive parents, securely attached infants seem to be better adjusted socially during childhood. Establishing a secure attachment early in life also may help foster a capacity for compassion and altruism that carries forward into adulthood (Mikulincer & Shaver, 2005). This lends credence to Erikson's view that entering a stable, trusting relationship with a caregiver is an important component of early social development. As we will see later in the chapter attachment types are aspects of our social-emotional behaviour which stay with us to an extent through our lives influencing how we form and maintain relationships with other people.

Attachment Deprivation

If infants and young children are deprived of a stable attachment with a caregiver, how do they fare in the long run? Bowlby's (1944) study of the 44 thieves was influential in making the argument that such early deprivation is harmful to social development. Harry Harlow studied attachment deprivation under controlled conditions with monkeys. After rearing 'isolate' monkeys either alone or with artificial surrogate mothers, Harlow returned them to the monkey colony at 6 months of age. Exposed to other monkeys, the isolates were indifferent, terrified or aggressive. When they became adults, some female isolates were artificially inseminated and gave birth, and they were highly abusive towards their firstborns (Harlow & Suomi, 1970). Harlow concluded that being raised without a secure attachment to a real, interactive caregiver produced long-term social impairment.

One important factor to consider is the stage at which attachment is deprived. Studies of adopted children, who are thought to experience attachment deprivation to a greater extent than children growing up with their biological parents, are one source of information about this. In one relatively recent study van den Dries, Juffer, van IJzendoorn and Bakermans-Kranenburg (2009) found in a meta-analytic review that groups of adopted and non-adopted children were as securely attached as each other, so long as they had

Chapter 12, Page 498

been adopted before 12 months of age. The sensitive period for attachment seems to be from one year onwards.

A number of cases of extreme deprivation in human infants have been documented. Victor, the Wild Boy of Aveyron (see **Chapter 12**), was severely impaired after his isolation and showed only limited recovery after intensive remedial training. In the 1960s, twin boys in Czechoslovakia were forced by their father and stepmother to live in extreme isolation beginning at 18 months of age. The twins were discovered at age 7, emotionally and socially retarded, with the cognitive development of a 3-year-old and speech skills of a 2-year-old. Jarmila Koluchova (1972, 1991) studied the boys for over 20 years and found that they went on to become happy, sociable and firmly attached to their foster family. Their IQs increased to normal levels, and they became well-adjusted adolescents and young adults.

Why the difference? One reason may be that Victor had some kind of brain damage which was present from birth. However, other explanations for the difference are also plausible. Unlike Victor, the twins had each other's company. Could that have helped prevent long-term harm? Nonetheless, in other cases even 'lone' isolate children have recovered. Perhaps more important, the twins' isolation ended and their rehabilitation began at a younger age than that of Victor, when their brains' neural plasticity was greater. They were 7; Victor was about 12.

In the 1980s, 100,000 Romanian infants and children were warehoused in orphanages under the most neglectful and squalid conditions imaginable (Figure 13.8). Despite this horrific neglect, after being adopted about a third of the Romanian infants studied had become securely attached to their adoptive parents (Wilson, 2003).

However, there are a number of problems in drawing strong conclusions about the effects of parental deprivations from all of the studies mentioned so far. As well as being deprived of parental care, all the children and monkeys mentioned above were being deprived of a number of other important stimuli. Harlow and Suomi's monkeys were placed in situations of general social and sensory deprivation. Although many of the Romanian orphans grew up in the proximity of other children, their malnutrition may have prevented them from benefiting from this social input. We can often get better information by examining less extreme circumstances. For example, Tizard and Hodges (1978) studied children raised in orphanages where the nurses were attentive but high staff turnover prevented the children from forming a stable bond with any caretaker. Those adopted between ages 2 and 8 years typically formed healthy attachments with their adoptive parents, although in adolescence many had difficulty forming peer relationships because they were viewed as needing 'too much attention' (Hodges & Tizard, 1989). However, Bowlby's ideas, and research like that of Tizard and Hodges (1978) have had an important beneficial effect on the standard of institutional care, such that the vast majority of adopted children are nowadays normally adjusted and differ little from children raised by their biological parents (Miller, Fan, Christensen, Grotevant, & van Dulmen, 2000).

In sum, infancy appears to be a sensitive, though not critical, period during which an initial attachment to caregivers forms most easily and facilitates subsequent development. Prolonged attachment deprivation creates developmental risks, but when deprived children are placed into a nurturing environment at a young enough age, many if not most become attached to their caretakers and grow into well-adjusted adults. Bowlby's ethological theory of attachment has been particularly influential in our understanding of how the attachment process arises, arguing that attachment relationships are mutual in nature in that both caregiver and child become attached to one another. Perhaps the most controversial of his claims concern the idea that attachment behaviours are pre-programmed into the infant. It seems reasonable to consider the possibility that at least some of the ways in which we try to form attachments could be learned from our social environments (Leman, Bremner, Parke, & Gauvain, 2012).

FIGURE 13.8 In the 1980s, about 100,000 Romanian infants and children were warehoused in filthy, disease-ridden orphanages where they were often left unattended for days and had no opportunity to bond with caretakers.

Studies of Romanian infants who were adopted into American homes before age 2 showed that about a third formed secure attachments, in contrast to the more typical 60% figure found in attachment studies.

Source: © Mike Abrahams/Alamy

Focus 13.6 Describe types of attachment, how they are measured and how attachment deprivation affects development.

Current topic

THE CHILDCARE CONTROVERSY

The work of Bowlby, Harlow and Ainsworth has implications that need careful consideration. If deprivation of primary caregivers has negative effects on development, we have to ask how much parental presence should we provide. Over the past decades, the traditional model of maternal care in the home has gradually given way to a more liberal view of parenting and care in which the mother and father may spend the day at work while the child is cared for at home by a nanny, or in a day-care centre with other children. Day care is pervasive in Europe and the USA. However, there is fierce debate about this issue. Many researchers have argued that large amounts of care provided by people other than a child's parents, early in life, can have negative effects on social-emotional adjustment (e.g., Belsky, 1988). On the other hand, some researchers and many educators view early childcare as an important means of supplementing early education before school begins (e.g., Lamb & Ahnert, 2006). This debate, of course, courts significant controversy outside the realm of science, not least because the provision of early childcare has important implications for the social mobility of the parents, and particularly women parents.

The most comprehensive investigation of the effects of day care to date has been carried out by psychologists working with the National Institute of Child Health and Human Development (NICHD) Early Child Care Research Network in the USA. These researchers have studied approximately 1,400 American children from birth to 12 years of age. Interestingly, this study seems to support both sides of the debate. It has confirmed that extensive early non-parental childcare can have some negative social-emotional effects, but it has also shown that high-quality childcare can enhance cognitive (and sometimes social) development, particularly in economically deprived areas. High-quality childcare is defined as that which provides a stimulating environment with well-trained caretakers who are responsive to children's needs, few children per caretaker and low staff turnover. Poor quality childcare, on the other hand, does not provide these (Marshall, 2004).

Here are some major findings from the NICHD study:

1. *Attachment*: overall, as measured by the strange-situation procedure, high-quality day care did not seem to disrupt infants' or very young children's attachment to their parents, even when they attended for several hours a week. However, when the parents were not sensitive to the child in the home, an increased amount of and poorer quality day care increased the risk of insecure attachment (NICHD, 2001a).

2. *Social behaviour*: compared to children with less day-care experience, by age 3, children with more experience exhibited better social skills when interacting with peers at day care, although this did not generalize to play situations with friends outside day care (NICHD, 2001b). By age 4, however, children who averaged 30 or more hours a week in day care displayed more behaviour problems (e.g., arguing) than children who spent less than 10 hours a week in childcare (NICHD, 2002). The number of months that children spent in day care before starting school also predicted aggressive and impulsive behaviour in the class right up to 12 and 15 years of age (Belsky et al., 2007; Vandell et al., 2010).

3. *Cognitive performance*: regardless of their sex or ethnicity or their parents' socio-economic status or parenting quality, 4-year-olds who spent a lot of time in day-care centres performed better on several cognitive and linguistic tasks than did peers who spent less time in day-care centres (NICHD, 2002). Exposure to high-quality day care was associated with even better cognitive performance. These benefits seemed to persist at least through to 9 years (Vandell, Burchinal, & Belsky, 2005), and higher quality of day care predicted higher vocabulary scores at age 12 (Belsky et al., 2007; Vandell et al., 2010).

Styles of Parenting

How do different child-rearing practices affect children's development? After studying how parents interacted with their pre-school children, Diana Baumrind (1967) identified two key dimensions of parental behaviour. The first is *warmth versus hostility*. Warm parents communicate love and care for the child. Hostile parents express rejection and behave as if they do not care about the child. The second dimension is *restrictiveness versus permissiveness*. Parents differ in the extent to which they make and enforce rules. As Figure 13.9 shows, combining these dimensions yields four parenting styles that are associated with different patterns of child development (Linver, Brooks-Gunn, & Kohen, 2002).

Authoritative parents are controlling but warm. They establish clear rules, consistently enforce them, and reward children's compliance with warmth and affection. They communicate high expectations, caring and support. This style is thought to be associated with the most positive childhood outcomes. Children with authoritative parents tend to have higher self-esteem, are higher achievers in school and have fewer conduct problems.

Authoritarian parents also exert control but do so within a cold, unresponsive or rejecting relationship. Their children are thought to have lower self-esteem, be less

authoritative parents controlling but warm

authoritarian parents exert control but do so within a cold, unresponsive or rejecting relationship

indulgent parents have warm, caring relationships with their children but do not provide the guidance and discipline that help children learn responsibility and concern for others

neglectful parents provide neither warmth nor rules nor guidance

Focus 13.7 Identify parenting styles and their associated child outcomes. How do parenting and children's heredity interact?

popular with peers and perform more poorly in school than children with authoritative parents.

Indulgent parents have warm, caring relationships with their children but do not provide the guidance and discipline that help children learn responsibility and concern for others. Their children are thought to be more immature and self-centred.

Neglectful parents provide neither warmth nor rules nor guidance. Their children are most likely to be insecurely attached, to have low achievement motivation and disturbed peer relationships, and to be impulsive and aggressive. Neglectful parenting is thought to be associated with the most negative developmental outcomes.

Do parenting styles influence development in adolescence? Steinberg, Lamborn, Darling and Mounts (1994) found that overall, authoritative parenting and neglectful parenting were, respectively, associated with the most positive and negative developmental outcomes. Lamborn, Mounts, Steinberg and Dornbusch (1991) have shown that this holds true across a wide variety of ethnicities.

Parenting–Heredity Interactions

Keep in mind that parent–child influences are bidirectional, illustrating once again the interaction of biology and environment in shaping behaviour. For example, children whose biologically based temperament is irritable tend to elicit harsher and less warm parenting behaviours, which in turn can further promote the child's difficult behaviour. Also, realize that parents do not mould their children's personality and behaviour like lumps of clay. Parenting makes a difference, but the way children turn out also depends on their heredity, peer and community influences, other experiences, and interactions among these factors (Mezulis, Hyde, & Abramson, 2006).

Antisocial behaviour provides another example of how the family environment and heredity interact. Children of a highly antisocial parent (i.e., a parent with high aggression, irritability and a history of illegal activities) are at increased genetic risk for displaying antisocial behaviour (e.g., lying, fighting, having a hot temper). This genetic risk is present, of course, even if the highly antisocial parent (usually the father) is completely absent from the home and the child is raised by the other parent. However, as Sara Jaffee and co-workers found (Jaffee, Moffitt, Caspi, & Taylor, 2003), when high-antisocial fathers live at home and are involved in caretaking, this further increases children's antisocial behaviour and risk of developing a conduct disorder. In contrast, when low-antisocial fathers live at home and participate in caretaking, this tends to decrease children's antisocial behaviour. Jaffee and co-workers concluded that children of high-antisocial fathers who are involved in caretaking receive what they call a 'double-whammy' of genetic and environmental contributions to their own antisocial behaviour.

FIGURE 13.9 Four styles of child rearing.

Combining two basic dimensions of parental behaviour (warmth-hostility and restrictiveness-permissiveness) yields four different styles of child rearing.

Source: Adapted from Maccoby and Martin, 1983.

Gender Identity and Socialization

gender identity a sense of 'femaleness' or 'maleness' that becomes a central aspect of one's personal identity

gender constancy the understanding that being male or female is a permanent part of a person

Parenting also influences children's development in other ways, such as helping children develop a **gender identity**, a sense of 'femaleness' or 'maleness' that becomes a central aspect of one's personal identity. Most children develop a basic gender identity between the ages of 2 and 3 and can label themselves (and others) as being either a boy or a girl, but their understanding of gender is still fragile. They may believe that a boy wearing a dress is a girl and that a girl can grow up to become a man. **Gender constancy**, which is the understanding that being male or female is a permanent part of a person, develops around age 6 to 7 (Szkrybalo & Ruble, 1999).

As gender identity develops, children also acquire *gender role stereotypes*, which are beliefs about the characteristics and behaviours that are appropriate for boys and girls to

possess. Every group, including family and cultural groups, has norms for expected and accepted gender behaviour. Parents, siblings, friends, the mass media and other socializing agents convey these norms to us as we grow up. Ultimately, as we internalize these norms, they become part of our identity (Martin & Ruble, 2004).

Gender typing involves treating others differently based on whether they are female or male. From infancy onwards, girls and boys are viewed and treated differently. Fathers use more physical and verbal prohibition with their 12-month-old sons than with their daughters, and they steer their sons away from activities that are considered stereotypically feminine (Snow, Jacklin, & Maccoby, 1983). Even when their sons and daughters display equal interest and aptitude in science, fathers and mothers are more likely to believe that sons have the greater interest and will find science easier (Tenenbaum & Leaper, 2003). Indeed, as Figure 13.10 shows, when parents interact with their 1- to 8-year-olds at science exhibits in a children's museum, they are much more likely to explain the exhibits to their sons than to their daughters – even though the children rarely ask for such explanations (Crowley, Callanan, Tenenbaum, & Allen, 2001).

Gender role stereotypes are also transmitted through observational learning and operant conditioning (Figure 13.11). Children observe and often attempt to emulate parents, other adults, peers, and television and movie characters (Bandura, 1965). In ways obvious and subtle, others approve of us and reinforce our behaviour when we meet their expectations and disapprove of us when we do not. In turn, this influences the way children think about gender. Some children as young as 2 to 3 years of age display gender role stereotypes in their ability to identify objects (such as hammers and brooms) and behaviours as 'belonging with' one gender or the other (Campbell, Shirley, & Candy, 2004). By age 7 or 8, stereotyped thinking is firmly in place; children believe that boys and girls possess different personality traits and should hold different occupations as adults.

As children enter secondary school, they often display more flexible thinking about gender. Some come to believe that traditionally masculine and feminine traits can be blended within a single person – what is called an *androgynous gender identity* – as when a person is both assertive and compassionate. During secondary school, some adolescents maintain this view, but overall, gender stereotypes seem to become a little more rigid at this age, so that by early adulthood most people continue to adhere to relatively traditional beliefs (Alfieri, Ruble, & Higgins, 1996).

The Influence of Peers

As well as parents, the peer group has an important effect on children's social development. If you are a child, your 'peers' are children who you know who are of about the same age as yourself, and would often be in the same class as you at school or live in the same neighbourhood. The influence of peers may begin from an early age. Lewis, Young, Brooks and Michalson (1975) show that 12- to 18-month-old infants, while they maintain closer proximity to their caregiver, will spend the most time looking at a peer (see Figure 13.12).

> **Focus 13.8** How does socialization influence children's beliefs about gender?

> **gender typing** treating others differently based on whether they are female or male

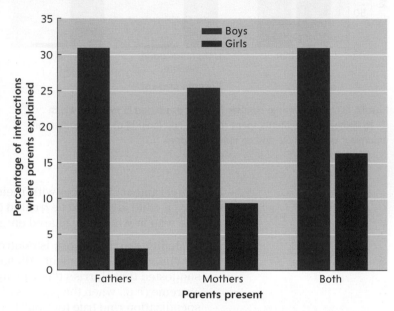

FIGURE 13.10 Do parents provide more scientific explanations to sons than daughters?

Fathers and mothers provided more explanations to their 1- to 8-year-old sons than to their daughters while engaged with science exhibits at a children's museum. Similar results were obtained regardless of the children's age.

Source: Adapted from Crowley et al., 2001.

FIGURE 13.11 In subtle and not so subtle ways, cultures socialize most female and male children in gender-stereotypic ways.

Source: ©iStock.com/bowdenimages; ©iStock.com/PhotoInc

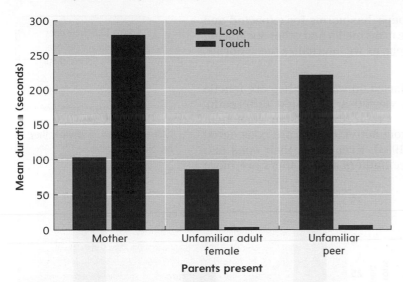

FIGURE 13.12 The average number of seconds (during 15 minutes) which 12- to 18-month-olds infants spent touching and looking at their mother, an unfamiliar adult female and an unfamiliar peer.

Judith Harris is a developmental researcher who has argued that the peer group may have as important, if not more important, a role as parents (or home environment) in shaping our social development. This view has become known as the 'group socialization' theory of development (Harris, 1995). Evidence in favour of Harris's theory comes from behavioural genetics research, including twin and adoption studies. These studies demonstrate that the shared environment of siblings (i.e., the home environment provided by their parents) may have a less substantial effect on development than the 'non-shared environment'. Plomin and Daniels (1987; see also Plomin, Defries, McClearn, & McGuffin, 2001) demonstrated that children who are born or adopted into the same family show very little similarity in their personalities, and thus environmental influences are concluded to come from environment outside the family. Harris thus suggests that peers may be much more important in shaping our personality. Harris's theory is still under scrutiny, however, as non-shared environment can result not just from influences outside the home environment, but also from differences in the way children's genetic inheritance (e.g., their temperament) interacts with their home environment. As has already been discussed, a happy child is likely to be treated differently by their parents than an irritable child. This is one way in which non-shared environmental differences can arise in the home.

Judith Harris's theory is controversial as it suggests that parents can have little effect on children's development. Michael Rutter, an eminent developmental psychologist, has suggested that Harris's theory may apply less in situations where the parental influence is extreme (e.g., when the parents abuse their children). Does Judith Harris's theory of group socialization ring true for you? Do you feel your personality has been shaped more by your parents or your peers?

The Influence of Media

Other important influences on the development of social identity come from books, television, radio, the internet and online social media. All of these media often emphasize culturally held stereotypes. On television, for instance, males are more likely than females to be portrayed as aggressive, professional, powerful and decisive. Females more often than males are portrayed as warmer, more emotional and social, and happier. But do these kinds of gender role stereotypes have an influence on children? The answer to this is yes. Children who watch more television are more likely to conform to cultural norms about gender role typing (Ward & Friedman, 2006). In a particularly striking study, Kimball (1986) found that when television was introduced for the first time in a small town in Canada, children's attitudes towards gender roles became much more conservative.

 Applying psychological science

UNDERSTANDING HOW DIVORCE AND REMARRIAGE AFFECT CHILDREN

Divorce creates a stressful life transition for parents and their children. Because most divorced parents remarry, they and their children also experience a second major transition: becoming part of a step-family. Decades ago, there was little scientific information on children of divorce and remarriage, but research now provides us with a better understanding of how these major transitions affect children. With this knowledge, we can attempt to take measures to alleviate some of the negative consequences of divorce on children.

◄

HOW DOES DIVORCE AFFECT CHILDREN?

Many children report that parental divorce is one of the most painful experiences of their lives. In the short term, they may experience anxiety, fear, anger, confusion, depression and behaviour problems at school. In the long term, children of divorce remain at greater risk for various difficulties, including academic problems, troubled relationships with family members and peers, low self-esteem and depression (Dawson-McClure, Sandler, Wolchik, & Millsap, 2004). When they become adolescents, children of divorced parents are more likely to drop out of school, be unemployed, use drugs and become unmarried teenage parents. In adulthood, they experience more marital conflict and have a higher divorce rate (Huurre, Junkkari, & Aro, 2006; Wauterickx, Gouwy, & Bracke, 2006).

Most of these problems, however, tend to cluster together into an overall pattern of maladjustment. Hetherington, Bridges and Insabella, (1998) estimate that about 20–25% of children in divorced families, versus 10% of children in non-divorced families, experience this cluster of problems. This is a significantly elevated risk for maladjustment, but still, most children of divorced parents grow up to be normally adjusted adults.

SHOULD WE STAY TOGETHER FOR THE SAKE OF THE CHILD?

Many parents considering divorce wonder whether they should stay together for the child's sake. Reviewing 92 studies, Amato and Keith (1991) found that when divorce ends a highly conflictual marriage, children's psychological adjustment typically benefits in the long run. High marital conflict can cause the children to feel 'caught in the middle' in the battle between their parents, and decrease the children's feelings of well-being (Amato & Afifi, 2006). Children living with married but contentious parents have poorer school achievement, lower self-esteem and more behaviour problems than children from divorced families. But many unhappy marriages do not involve extensive conflict, and in those cases divorce usually puts children at greater risk of maladjustment (Booth & Amato, 2001).

HOW CAN DIVORCED PARENTS HELP THEIR CHILDREN?

The major factor affecting a child's adjustment to divorce is the quality of life within the post-divorce family. The period during and after divorce can intensify parents' anger and conflicts. By fighting over their children or trying to enlist them in loyalty battles, parents can damage their children's well-being. In contrast, cooperative and amicable parental behaviours can cushion the negative effects of divorce during this rocky transition (Hetherington & Stanley-Hagan, 2002). By remaining emotionally close to his or her children, the parent who does not have custody (usually the father) can help them adjust to living with the custodial parent (Marsiglio, Amato, Day, & Lamb, 2000). For children, the lasting problems of divorce often lie in lingering parental conflicts, economic hardships that parents (especially mothers) often experience after divorce, and other factors that destabilize the parents' own lives.

HOW DO CHILDREN RESPOND TO REMARRIAGE AND STEP-FAMILIES?

Forming a step-family temporarily disrupts children's relationships with the remarried custodial parent and typically increases children's problem behaviours in the short term. In turn, such behaviour can increase the risk of marital conflict between the step-parents (Jenkins, Simpson, Dunn, Rasbash, & O'Connor, 2005). It can take several years for parents and children to adjust to their new roles within the step-family. In general, young adolescents seem to have the most difficulty coping with the transition into a step-family.

In remarriages, children may be hostile and reject the step-parent, especially when the step-parent attempts to be a strong disciplinarian. Children usually adjust better to living in a step-family when the custodial parent is warm but firm and has primary responsibility for discipline, and when the step-parent is warm but supports the custodial parent's authority (Bray & Berger, 1993).

MORAL DEVELOPMENT

We all have a sense of the difference between right and wrong. At school we can often observe teachers attempting to instil the moral views of society into their students. How does children's moral thinking change as they grow older? What factors cause moral development?

Moral Thinking

Drawing on Piaget's cognitive stage model, and some of Piaget's observations on early morality in children, Lawrence Kohlberg (1963, 1984), a Canadian psychologist, developed an influential theory of moral development across the lifespan. He presented children, adolescents and adults with hypothetical moral dilemmas such as the following:

Heinz's wife was dying from cancer. There was a rare drug that might save her, but the druggist who made the drug for $200 would not sell it for less than $2,000. Heinz tried hard, but he could only raise $1,000. The druggist refused to give Heinz the drug for that price even though Heinz promised to pay the rest later. So Heinz broke into the store to steal the drug. What do you think? Should Heinz have stolen the drug? Why or why not?

TABLE 13.4 Kohlberg's stages of moral reasoning

Level of moral reasoning	Basis for judging what is moral
Level I: Pre-conventional morality	*Actual or anticipated punishments or rewards, rather than internalized values*
Stage I: Punishment-obedience orientation	Obeying rules and avoiding punishment
Stage 2: Instrumental-hedonistic orientation	Self-interest and gaining rewards
Level 2: Conventional morality	*Conformity to the expectations of social groups; person adopts other people's values*
Stage 3: Good-child orientation	Gaining approval and maintaining good relationships with others
Stage 4: Law-and-order orientation	Doing one's duty, showing respect for authority and maintaining social order
Level 3: Post-conventional morality	*Moral principles that have been internalized as part of one's belief and value system*
Stage 5: Social-contract orientation	General principles agreed on by society that foster community welfare and individual rights; recognition that society can decide to modify laws that lose their social utility
Stage 6: Universal ethical principles	Abstract ethical principles based on justice and equality; following one's conscience

Source: Adapted from Kohlberg, 1984.

Kohlberg was interested not in whether people agreed or disagreed with Heinz's behaviour but rather in the *reasons for their judgement*. He analysed responses to various moral dilemmas and identified three main levels of moral reasoning, with two substages within each level (Table 13.4).

Pre-conventional moral reasoning is based on anticipated punishments or rewards. Consider reasons given for stealing the drug. In stage 1, children focus on punishment: 'Heinz should steal the drug because if he lets his wife die he'll get into trouble.' In stage 2, morality is judged by anticipated rewards and doing what is in the person's own interest: 'Heinz should steal the drug because that way he'll still have his wife with him.'

Conventional moral reasoning is based on conformity to social expectations, laws, and duties. In stage 3, conformity stems from the desire to gain people's approval: 'People will think that Heinz is bad if he doesn't steal the drug to save his wife.' In stage 4, children believe that laws and duties must be obeyed simply because rules are meant to be followed. Thus: 'Heinz should steal the drug because it's his duty to take care of his wife.'

Post-conventional moral reasoning is based on well-thought-out, general moral principles. Stage 5 involves recognizing the importance of societal laws but also taking individual rights into account: 'Stealing breaks the law, but what Heinz did was reasonable because he saved a life.' In stage 6, morality is based on abstract, ethical principles of justice that are viewed as universal: 'Saving life comes before financial gain, even if the person is a stranger.'

Kohlberg believed that progress in moral reasoning depends on the development of cognitive ability. Thus, like Piaget (see **Chapter 12**), he believed that powers of logic underlay children's competence in a wide variety of domains – including their moral behaviours. Piaget and Kohlberg suggested that cognitive (and moral) development was driven by opportunities to confront moral issues, particularly when such issues can be discussed with someone who is at a higher stage of development.

pre-conventional moral reasoning based on anticipated punishments or rewards

conventional moral reasoning based on conformity to social expectations, laws and duties

post-conventional moral reasoning based on well-thought-out, general moral principles

Chapter 12, Page 514

Culture, Gender and Moral Reasoning

From Europe, Asia, and Africa to North, Central and South America, studies of moral reasoning indicate that, overall:

- from childhood through adolescence, moral reasoning changes from pre-conventional to conventional levels
- in adolescence and even in adulthood, post-conventional reasoning is relatively uncommon
- a person's moral judgements do not always reflect the same level or stage within levels (Eckensberger & Zimba, 1997).

Critics claim that Kohlberg's theory has a Western cultural bias. Fairness and justice are Kohlberg's post-conventional ideals, but in many cultures the highest moral values focus on principles that do not fit easily into Kohlberg's model, such as respect for all animal life, collective harmony and respect for the elderly (Iwasa, 2001).

Carol Gilligan (1982) argues that Kohlberg's emphasis on justice also reflects a male bias. She claims that highly moral women place greater value than do men on caring and responsibility for others' welfare. Overall, however, evidence of gender bias is mixed. Women use justice reasoning when the situation calls for it, and men use reasoning based on caring and relationships when appropriate. Nevertheless, Gilligan's analysis reinforces the key point that the identification of 'high-level' moral reasoning can be based on values other than justice (Gump, Baker, & Roll, 2000).

Moral and Prosocial Behaviour

Moral reasoning does not necessarily translate into moral behaviour. The ways in which children make moral judgements are often unrelated to their actual behaviour and this is especially the case for young children (Blasi, 1983). B.F. Skinner (1971) proposed that we learn which behaviours are 'good' and 'bad' through their association with reinforcement and punishment (see **Chapter 7**). Other researchers propose that for children to conform to their culture's moral standards, they must understand that there are moral rules, be able to control their impulses to engage in forbidden behaviour, and experience some negative emotion when they violate these rules.

Chapter 7, Page 281

By the age of 2, children come to understand that there are rules for behaviour, and their emotional expressions suggest that they experience guilt when they break a known rule. Children's ability to stop themselves from engaging in forbidden behaviour develops slowly, but even toddlers can do so at times. This internal regulatory mechanism, often referred to as *conscience*, tends to restrain individuals from acting in destructive or antisocial ways when they are not being monitored by parents or other adults (Kochanska, Forman, Aksan, & Dunbar, 2005).

Sigmund Freud (1935) believed that children develop a conscience by identifying with their parents. Few developmental psychologists adhere to Freud's theory of how identification occurs (which we discuss in **Chapter 15**), but they acknowledge that internalizing the societal values transmitted by parents or other caretakers provides the basis of a moral conscience. Children are most likely to internalize parents' values when they have a positive relationship with them, when parents establish clear rules and provide explanations that facilitate children's awareness of parental values, and when discipline is firm but not harsh (Laible & Thompson, 2000).

Chapter 15, Page 632

Children's temperament also enters into the picture. Fearful, inhibited children tend to internalize parental values more easily and at an earlier age than less fearful children, particularly when their parents provide gentle discipline. For relatively fearless, uninhibited children, however, whether discipline is gentle or harsh is less important. A secure attachment with warm parents, rather than fear of punishment, appears to motivate fearless children to internalize their parents' standards. Thus the development of moral behaviour is linked not only to children's moral thinking but also to their emotional development, attachment and temperament (Kochanska, Aksan, Knaack, & Rhines, 2004).

In the context of these developmental changes in moral behaviour, a number of researchers are now arguing that moral development is underpinned in early life by an early predisposition to prosocial behaviour. Warneken and Tomasello (2006, 2007) found that both human infants (as young as 14 months of age) and young chimpanzees will intervene in various situations to help adults (e.g., reaching to pass an out-of-reach object, or helping to complete a task which has failed a few times). Because these behaviours were not praised or rewarded in other ways, and could not be learned from imitation, Warneken and Tomasello (2009) argue that there is a natural (innate) bias to prosocial behaviour in humans and also chimpanzees. It is possible that these biases are crucial for setting children on the right path to moral development in early life.

Focus 13.9 Describe Kohlberg's model of moral thinking and factors that influence the development of moral behaviour.

In review

- Children display more types and greater complexity of emotions as they age. The strategies they use to regulate their emotions also become more varied.

- Temperament reflects a biologically based pattern of reacting emotionally and behaviourally to the environment. Extreme temperamental styles in infancy and childhood can predict some aspects of functioning years later.

- Erikson believed that personality development proceeds through eight major psychosocial stages. Each stage involves a major crisis, and how we resolve it affects our ability to meet the challenges of the next stage.

- Infants demonstrate a variety of social behaviours in the first days of life. They prefer to orient towards faces, and direct eye contact. 'Periodicity' in their movements and vocalizations may represent the first conversations between infant and child. Newborns also imitate their parent's facial expressions.

- Infant–caretaker attachment develops in three phases, and infants experience periods of stranger and separation anxiety. Secure attachment is associated with better developmental outcomes than is insecure attachment. For most children, day care does not disrupt attachment. Divorce typically disrupts children's short-term psychological adjustment; for some, it is associated with a long-term pattern of maladjustment.

- Parenting styles vary along dimensions of warmth–hostility and restrictiveness–permissiveness. The children of authoritative parents generally display the best developmental outcomes. Gender identity begins to form early in childhood, and socialization influences children's acquisition of gender role stereotypes.

- Kohlberg proposed that moral reasoning proceeds through pre-conventional, conventional and post-conventional levels. The development of moral behaviour is linked to children's cognitive, emotional and social development. Recently researchers have argued that there is an innate bias for human infants to engage in prosocial behaviours.

ADOLESCENCE, ADULTHOOD AND OLD AGE

FIGURE 13.13 A White Mountain Apache girl participates in the Sunrise Dance, a four-day ceremony that initiates her into womanhood.

Source: © Anders Ryman/Alamy

We call it Sunrise Dance. It's the biggest ceremony of the White Mountain Apache – when a girl passes from childhood to womanhood. . . . On Friday evening Godmother dressed me . . . Saturday is like an endurance test. Men begin prayer chants at dawn. Godmother tells me to dance. . . . When the time comes for running, I go fast around a sacred cane. . . . Next, my father pours candies and corn kernels over me to protect me from famine. My Godfather directs my dancing on Sunday. . . . Godfather paints me. . . . On Monday there is more visiting and blessing.   (Quintero, 1980, pp. 262–71)

In some cultures, ceremonies like the Sunrise Dance represent *rites of passage* that mark a transition from childhood into adulthood status (Figure 13.13). But what of **adolescence**, the period of development and gradual transition between childhood and adulthood? Alice Schlegel and Herbert Barry (1991) found that among almost 200 non-industrial societies worldwide, nearly all recognize some type of transition period between childhood and adulthood. Yet in many societies this period is brief and is not marked by a special term analogous to *adolescence*.

As we know it, the lengthy period called *adolescence* is largely an invention of eighteenth- to twentieth-century Western culture (Valsiner & Lawrence, 1997). In pre-industrial times, biological maturity was a major criterion for adult status. In many cultures, for example, girls were expected to marry once they became capable of bearing children. But as the Industrial Revolution brought new technology and a need for more schooling, recognition of adult status was delayed and the long transition period of adolescence evolved.

Adolescence differs from **puberty**, the period of rapid maturation in which the person becomes capable of sexual reproduction (see **Chapter 12**). These developmental periods overlap, but puberty is a biologically defined period, whereas adolescence is a broader social construction (Spear, 2000). Puberty is an important aspect of adolescence, but adolescence is also ushered in and out by changes in thinking, interests, social circumstances, and parental and societal expectations. In research studies, 12- to 18-year-olds – give or take a year at

adolescence the period of development and gradual transition between childhood and adulthood

puberty the period of rapid maturation in which the person becomes capable of sexual reproduction

Chapter 12, Page 527

each end – are typically considered to be adolescents, but it is essential to keep in mind that the transition into, through and out of adolescence is not always sudden (Arnett, 2001).

SOCIAL-EMOTIONAL DEVELOPMENT IN ADOLESCENCE

G. Stanley Hall (1904), the first psychologist to study adolescence, viewed it as a time of 'storm and stress'. Indeed, adolescents may grapple with difficult issues and experience substantial conflict, yet many find it to be a positive period of life. Thus, Jeffrey Arnett proposes a modified view, noting that 'not all adolescents experience storm and stress, but storm and stress is more likely during adolescence than at other ages' (Arnett, 1999, p. 317).

Adolescents' Search for Identity

'Who am I?' 'What do I believe in?' Erik Erikson (1968) proposed that such questions reflect the pivotal crisis of adolescent personality development: *identity versus role confusion* (see Table 13.1, page 542). Erikson believed that an adolescent's 'identity crisis' (a term he coined) can be resolved positively, leading to a stable sense of identity, or it can end negatively, leading to confusion about one's identity and values.

Building on Erikson's work, Marcia (1966, 2002) studied adolescents' and young adults' search for identity. Marcia classified the 'identity status' of each person as follows:

1. *Identity diffusion*: these teens and adults had not yet gone through an identity crisis. They seemed unconcerned or even cynical about identity issues and were not committed to a coherent set of values.

2. *Foreclosure*: these individuals had not yet gone through an identity crisis either, but for a different reason: they committed to an identity and set of values before experiencing a crisis. For example, some automatically adopted peer-group or parental values without giving these values much thought.

3. *Moratorium*: these people wanted to establish a clear identity, were currently experiencing a crisis, but had not yet resolved it.

4. *Identity achievement*: these individuals had gone through an identity crisis, successfully resolved it and emerged with a coherent set of values.

Marcia found that most young adolescents are in identity diffusion or foreclosure; they have not experienced an identity crisis. But during the teen years, people typically begin to think more deeply about who they are, or they reconsider values they had adopted previously. This often leads to an identity crisis, and more than half successfully resolve it by early adulthood.

Identity, of course, is not a simple concept, and our sense of identity has multiple components (Camilleri & Malewska-Peyre, 1997). These include (1) our gender, ethnicity, and other attributes by which we define ourselves as members of social groups ('daughter', 'student', 'athlete'); (2) how we view our personal characteristics ('shy', 'friendly'); and (3) our goals and values. Typically, we achieve a stable identity regarding some components before others, and changing situations may trigger new crises and cause us to re-evaluate prior goals and values.

Culture plays a key role in identity formation, one that goes beyond the simple idea that we view ourselves as belonging to certain cultural groups. Our cultural upbringing influences the very way we view concepts such as 'self' and 'identity'. Having grown up in an individualistic culture, my sense of identity assumes that I am an autonomous individual with clear boundaries separating me from other people. But in collectivistic cultures, the concept of 'self' is traditionally based more strongly on the connectedness between people (Kagitçibasi, 1997). Thus, the question 'Who am I?' is more likely to be answered in ways that reflect a person's relationships with family members, friends and others. Still, keep in mind that we are talking about relative differences. Across cultures, people's sense of identity incorporates elements that involve autonomy from – and interdependence with – other people (Mascolo & Li, 2004).

Relationships with Parents and Peers

When it comes to teenagers' relationships with their parents, is 'storm and stress' the rule or the exception? A number of studies have suggested that this may be an exaggeration. For example,

FIGURE 13.14 In one study, 229 students attending a public high school were asked how often they lied to their parents about six issues. For each issue, this graph shows the percentage of students who reported lying to their parents at least once during the past year.

Source: Jensen et al., 2004.

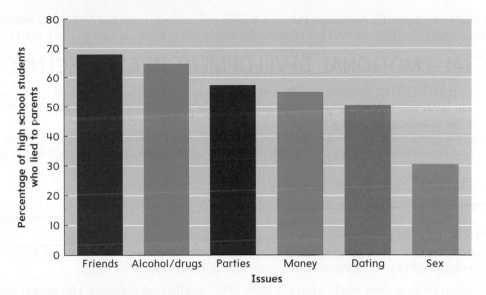

Moore, Guzman, Hair, Lippman and Garrett (2004) report a national survey in the USA, in which about 80% of American teenagers reported thinking highly of, and enjoying spending time with, the parents with whom they lived at home. About two-thirds of the teens reported an overall positive relationship with their parents. In a longitudinal study, Galambos and Almeida (1992) found that conflict over chores, appearance and politeness actually decrease as children enter adolescence. However, they did also note an increase in conflict over money.

Likewise, research in China and the Netherlands, and with various American ethnic groups, suggests that teenager–parent conflict is not as severe as often assumed (Chen, Greenberger, Lester, Dong, & Guo, 1998). And despite the differences between the family-centred 'collectivistic' cultures of China and the more individualistic style of European and US families, the kinds of conflicts which adolescents have with their parents have a lot in common. For example, Yau and Smetana (1996) found that the children of Chinese families in Hong Kong argue with their parents about choice of activities (e.g., phone conversations, television watching), household chores and homework.

The USA's National Center on Addiction and Substance Abuse (2005) reports, however, that most adolescents state that if they face a serious problem, they can confide in one or both parents. Yet many adolescents also feel that for various reasons, including the right to preserve their independence, it is acceptable to lie to their parents at times. As Figure 13.14 shows, in one study most secondary school students said that they had lied to their parents on several issues in the past year (Jensen, Arnett, Feldman, & Cauffman, 2004).

Some parents and teenagers do struggle a lot, and parent–teenager conflict is correlated with other signs of distress. For example, among American, Chinese and Taiwanese teens, those who report more conflict with parents also display higher levels of school misconduct (e.g., skipping school), more antisocial behaviour (e.g., getting into fights), lower self-esteem, more drug use and less life satisfaction (Caughlin & Malis, 2004; Chen et al., 1998). Recalling the principle that correlation does not equal causation, we must consider that although parent–teenager conflict may be a cause of teenagers' psychological problems, it also is likely to be caused *by* such problems.

A typical stereotype of a teenager is someone who likes to spend time hanging out with friends. Peer relationships increase in importance during adolescence, and some studies find that teenagers spend more time with peers than doing almost anything else. But this pattern may be stronger in Europe and North America than in Asia, where people of all ages, teenagers included, generally place a relatively strong emphasis on family relationships (Chen et al., 1998).

Adolescent friendships are typically more intimate than those at previous ages and involve a greater sharing of problems. Peers can strongly influence a teenager's values and behaviours, thereby facilitating the process of separating from parents and establishing one's own identity. For some adolescents, however, experiences with peers increase the

Focus 13.10 Discuss adolescents' search for identity and their relationships with parents and peers.

risk of misconduct, such as skipping school, damaging property or using drugs (Larson, Hansen, & Moneta, 2006). Fortunately, peer pressure *against* misconduct typically has an even stronger effect, and closeness to parents is an added buffer that helps many teenagers resist peer pressure to do misdeeds (Chen et al., 1998). Despite increased peer influence during adolescence, parental influence remains high on political, religious, moral and career issues. In many ways, the so-called generation gap is narrower than is often assumed.

Emotional Changes in Adolescence

As you progressed from childhood through your teenage years, did you generally become a more or less happy person? Larson, Moneta, Richards and Wilson (2002) examined changes in teenage emotionality in a creative and powerful way. They randomly selected 328 10- to 14-year-olds from working- and middle-class suburban families. Students carried electronic pagers and paper booklets with them for one week, and the time of year that each student did this was randomly determined. From morning to evening each student was beeped at random times. On a questionnaire, the students rated how happy or unhappy, cheerful or irritable, and friendly or angry they felt at that moment. The researchers also measured students' self-esteem, depression and the number of major stressful events experienced during the previous six months. This procedure was repeated with the same students four years later, when the students were 14 to 18 years old.

Overall, girls' and boys' daily emotional experiences were more positive than negative. Still, teenagers' daily emotionality became less positive as they moved into and through early adolescence, with changes levelling off and emotions becoming more stable during late adolescence. As they aged, 34% of the teenagers showed a major downward change (less-positive emotions), and 16% showed a major upward change (more-positive emotions). The remaining half of the students showed a smaller amount of change in emotions, although once again, downward changes were twice as common as upward changes (Figure 13.15).

The study also revealed that students who reported less-positive emotions tended to have lower self-esteem and more frequent major stressful events during the preceding six months.

FIGURE 13.15 Research suggests that emotionality changes during adolescence, with an overall decrease in positive emotions being more likely to occur than an overall increase. By late adolescence, these changes tend to level off.

Source: ©iStock.com/cjp

> **Focus 13.11** How do emotions change during adolescence?

SOCIAL-EMOTIONAL DEVELOPMENT IN ADULTHOOD

The Transition to Adulthood

In traditional cultures, marriage typically is the key transitional event into adulthood (Arnett, 2001). Through socialization, males develop skills that will enable them to protect and provide for a family of their own, and females learn skills needed eventually to care for children and run a household. Marriage signifies that, in the eyes of the culture, each partner has acquired these skills and is deemed capable of raising a family.

In industrialized societies, how do we know when someone has become an adult? Our 'Research close-up' examines this question.

> **Focus 13.12** How do people judge whether someone has reached adulthood?

 Research close-up

WHAT DOES IT TAKE TO BECOME AN ADULT?

Source: J. J. Arnett (2001). Conceptions of the transition to adulthood: Perspectives from adolescence through midlife. *Journal of Adult Development, 8,* 133–143.

INTRODUCTION

If we asked you, 'Have you reached adulthood?', how would you answer? And in your view, just what does it take to be considered an adult? Jeffrey Arnett examined how American adults in various age groups viewed the transition to adulthood. Whereas previous research focused on the viewpoints of adolescents and people in their twenties, this study also examined the viewpoints of older adults.

▶

METHOD

Men and women from a mid-sized community were recruited to participate. There were 519 participants, representing three age groups: 13- to 19-year-olds, 20- to 29-year-olds and 30- to 55-year-olds. Participants rated ('yes' or 'no') whether each of 38 specific characteristics 'must be achieved before a person can be considered an adult'. These characteristics were presented in random order and represented six general categories of criteria for judging adult status. These categories and some sample items appear below.

General category	Sample of specific characteristics
Individualism	Be responsible for one's actions; determine own values/beliefs; attain financial freedom
Family capacities	Be capable of caring for and financially supporting a family
Norm compliance	Refrain from crime, irresponsible sex, drunk driving, illegal drug use
Biological transitions	Be capable of fathering/bearing children
Legal/chronological transitions	Reach age 18; reach age 21; obtain driver's licence
Role transitions	Full-time employment; establish career, finish education, get married

Each participant also was asked, 'Do you think that you have reached adulthood?' The answer options were 'yes', 'no', and 'in some respects yes, in some respects no'.

RESULTS

What qualities were judged as necessary to be considered an adult? Regardless of age group, about 90% of participants endorsed the importance of accepting responsibility for one's actions. Establishing one's own values and beliefs, seeing oneself as an equal with one's parents, and attaining financial independence were the next most frequently chosen qualities among all age groups. Items such as 'reaching age 18', 'employed full-time' and 'marriage', were endorsed by only 47%, 32% and 13% of participants, respectively. In fact, if you look at the six general categories shown in the 'Methods' section, they are listed in the overall order of importance, as determined by the average ratings of all the items in each category. Overall, there was strong consistency in how the various age groups viewed the importance of these characteristics.

In contrast, substantial age differences emerged in whether participants viewed themselves as having reached adulthood. As Figure 13.16 shows, among adolescents (average age 16 years), fewer than a fifth said that they had reached adulthood. Among people in their twenties (average age 24 years), almost half said that they had reached adulthood. Still, in both these age groups, the transitional 'yes and no' response was most common. Only among people in mid-life (average age 42 years) did most view themselves as having fully attained adulthood.

DISCUSSION

This study suggests that on the psychological road to adulthood, biological, legal, chronological, and role transitions take a back seat. *Individualism* – becoming a responsible, independent person – was judged to be the single most important general criterion. Still, in making the transition from adolescence to adulthood, multiple factors appear to come into play for most people.

This study had several strengths. It addressed an interesting question, one likely to assume great personal relevance for many people at some point in their lives. The 38 characteristics for judging adulthood status were carefully chosen on the basis of prior research, and the participants represented a broader age range than in previous studies. All studies have limitations, however, and as a critical thinker you should recognize that this study employed a cross-sectional design. The findings tell us, at a given point in time, how various age groups view the transition to adulthood. It would be interesting to study the same participants using a longitudinal design and thus examine more precisely how people's views of 'becoming an adult' change as they grow older. In addition, most participants in this study (84%) were white Americans. As Arnett notes, although the overall findings were consistent with those of studies conducted elsewhere in the world (see Bynner, 2005), the question of whether the transition to adulthood is viewed differently in different parts of the world, and in different ethnic groups, needs careful consideration. What do you think? Do Arnett's findings match up with your evaluation of 'adulthood'. Do they match up with the views of other people you know?

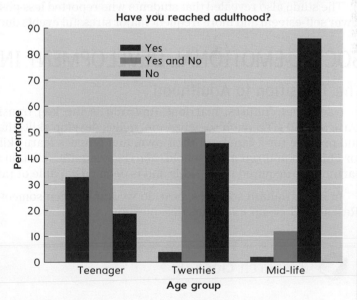

Research design

Question: How do people of various ages view the transition to adulthood?

Type of study: Correlational

Independent variables	Dependent variable
Age (Three age groups 13 to 19, 20 to 29 and 30 to 55 years)	View of transition to adulthood, (e.g., is this characteristic necessary to be considered an adult/ are you an adult?)

FIGURE 13.16 Have you reached adulthood?

This graph shows the percentage of people in their teens, twenties and thirties to mid-fifties who felt that they had not, partially had or fully had reached adulthood.

Source: Based on Arnett, 2001.

Social and Emotional Developmental Changes in Adulthood

Perhaps one of the things which people find most surprising about research into adult development is the fact that we do not become less happy as we get older. In one study of adolescents and people in early, middle and late adulthood from eight West European countries, about 80% of each age group reported they were 'satisfied' or 'very satisfied' with their lives (Ingelhart & Rabier, 1986). More recently studies seem to indicate that on average adults show increasing happiness as they get older (Mroczek & Kolarz, 1998). Why might this be? It can seem odd that young adults, who are likely at the peak of their physical fitness, are less happy than later points in their life. One likely explanation of lower levels of happiness in early adulthood is that the many transitions that we go through at this stage in life can cause stress and unhappiness. Early adulthood is the time when many people attempt to form lasting relationships, establish a career, and enter into the considerable task of bringing up young children. This idea of early adulthood as being a qualitatively different part of life, prompts us to think about adulthood as being comprised of distinct stages.

Many researchers view adult social development as a progression through age-related stages (Levinson, 1990). According to Erik Erikson's psychosocial stage theory (1980; see also Table 13.1), *intimacy versus isolation* is the major developmental challenge of early adulthood (ages 20 to 40). Intimacy is the ability to open oneself to another person and to form close relationships. This is the period of adulthood when many people form close adult friendships, fall in love and marry.

Middle adulthood (ages 40 to 65) brings with it the issue of *generativity versus stagnation*. Through their careers, raising children or involvement in other activities, people achieve generativity by doing things for others and making the world a better place. Certainly, many young adults make such contributions, but generativity typically becomes a more central issue later in adulthood (Slater, 2003).

Late adulthood (age 65 and older) accentuates the final crisis, *integrity versus despair*. Older adults review their life and evaluate its meaning. If the major crises of earlier stages have been successfully resolved, the person experiences integrity: a sense of completeness and fulfilment. Older adults who have not achieved positive outcomes at earlier stages may experience despair, regretting that they had not lived their lives in a more fulfilling way. Findings that happiness increases with age (Mroczek & Kolarz, 1998) suggest that most people manage to avoid this route in later life.

Consistent with Erikson's model, many goals increase in importance as people age, and successfully resolving certain life tasks contributes to mastering others (McAdams & de St Aubin, 1998). But critics caution that we should avoid viewing early, middle and late adulthood as strict stages in which one life task takes over while others fade away. Although older adults are more concerned about generativity and integrity than are younger adults, they remain highly concerned about intimacy (Sheldon & Kasser, 2001).

Focus 13.13 According to Erikson, what are three major developmental challenges of adulthood?

Attachment in Adulthood

Given intimacy is such an important theme in adulthood, how should we understand the relationship between attachment in early life and the relationships we form later? One of Bowlby's ideas concerning attachment was that the nature of early attachment relationships had a profound effect on the ways in which adolescents and adults formed relationships with friends and partners in later life. As children's attachment behaviours become less based on proximity and more on conceptions of love, affection and trust, Bowlby suggests that they develop an 'internal working model' of attachment. Researchers have in fact developed an Adult Attachment Interview (AAI) to examine different kinds of conceptions of attachments in adults. Main, Kaplan and Cassidy (1985) describe four styles of thinking about attachment in adults:

1. *Autonomous*: adults who are able to reflect objectively and openly on their previous attachment relationships, even if these were not always positive experiences.

2. *Dismissive*: adults who dismiss the importance of attachment relationships.

3. *Enmeshed*: adults who think a lot about their dependency on their parents and worry about pleasing them.

4. *Unresolved*: adults who have experienced a traumatic attachment, or loss of an attachment figure, and are still resolving their thoughts on this.

It turns out that there are some relationships between early attachment styles (as measured in the strange situation and described earlier in this chapter) and adult attachment classifications as measured by the AAI. Smith, Cowie and Blades (2003) summarize the data as indicating that there is continuity between: (a) secure attachment in infancy and autonomous attachment in adulthood, (b) anxious-avoidant attachment in infancy and dismissive attachment in adulthood, and (c) anxious-resistant attachment in infancy and enmeshed attachment in adulthood.

Theorists such as Belsky (Belsky, Steinberg, & Draper, 1991) have attempted to explain why patterns of attachment should affect the nature of relationships in later life. Belsky et al.'s (1991) point is that our attachment styles are an attempt to make the best of the situation in which we find ourselves. They argue that attachment types are likely to be a product of the environment: an insecure attachment is likely to result from the stressful environment in which infant and child find themselves, whereas a secure attachment is likely to result from a less stressful environment for both. Belsky et al. argue that the evolutionarily adaptive response in the context of a stressful environment is to orient towards maturing and mating at an earlier age and simply passing on one's genes to as many others as is possible (the 'quantity' approach). On the other hand, they argue that the most evolutionarily adaptive response to an unstressful environment is to focus more on personal skills, and the acquisition of resources prior to childbirth so as to better serve child-rearing (the 'quality' approach). Thus, Belsky and colleagues explain the continuity of attachment styles between infancy and adulthood in terms of two different evolutionary strategies. Their approach has some support from evidence indicating that stressful parent–child relationships lead to faster physical development and earlier menarche in young women (Steinberg, 1988), but it suffers from the problems which all evolutionary accounts have. Their explanation is made after the fact (it is '*post hoc*'), and we have no way of testing it. What do you think? Is their explanation simple and intuitive, or do you feel it has been forced to explain the data?

Marriage and Family

Around the world, most people marry or form another type of family union at some point in their lives, and family structures can vary widely both across and within different cultures (Figure 13.17). The 'average' family in many countries across the world has changed in several ways over recent generations. For example, Baby Boomers were born a few years after the end of the Second World War, and their children (born in the 1960s through to the early 1980s) became known as Generation X. As Figure 13.18 shows, compared with the families that Baby Boomers grew up in, members of Generation X are more likely to have experienced parental divorce, had two working parents, had a smaller number of siblings and yet maintained a similar level of closeness to their parents (Bengtson, 2001).

Adults typically expect much from marriage, but a high divorce rate in many countries indicates that marital happiness is by no means automatic. Successful marriages are characterized by emotional closeness, positive communication and problem-solving, agreement on basic values and expectations, and a willingness to accept and support changes in the partner (Cordova, Gee, & Warren, 2005). On average, marital satisfaction declines over the first few years of the marriage (McNulty & Karney, 2004). This does not mean, however, that most couples are unhappy. They are still satisfied, just less so than they were. In a sense, the honeymoon is over.

FIGURE 13.17 These herders in the Republic of Mongolia, are living in an extended family unit that includes children, parents, grandparents, great-grandparents and other relatives. In more Western cultures it is much more common to grow up in a single-parent environment.

Source: Thierry Falise/Gamma-Rapho via Getty Images.

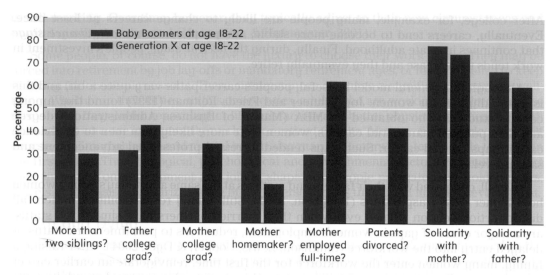

FIGURE 13.18 Growing up in different generations.

Baby Boomers were surveyed when they were 18 to 22 years old and asked to identify various characteristics of the families in which they had grown up. A generation later, when the Baby Boomers' children (Generation X) had turned 18 to 22 years old, they answered the same survey questions as their parents had.

Source: Bengtson, 2001.

The birth of a first baby dramatically alters the way couples spend their time. For many couples, marital satisfaction decreases in the year or two after their first child is born (Cowan & Cowan, 2000). Compared with husbands, wives are more likely to leave their outside jobs, spend more time parenting, and feel that their spouses are not helping enough. Disagreements over the division of labour and parenting are a major contributor to the drop in marital satisfaction (Frisco & Williams, 2003).

Over a broader age period, cross-sectional studies suggest a U-shaped relation between marital satisfaction and progression through major life events. The percentage of couples reporting that they are 'very satisfied' in their marriage typically is highest before or just as the first child is born, drops during child-rearing years and increases after all the children have left home (Orbuch, House, Mero, & Webster, 1996). Contrary to the popular 'empty nest' stereotype, most middle-aged couples do not become significantly depressed or suffer a crisis when their children leave home (Chiriboga, 1989). Couples maintain meaningful relationships with their children but have more time to spend with each other and to pursue leisure activities.

Despite the stresses that accompany marriage and parenthood, studies around the globe find that married people experience greater subjective well-being than unmarried adults (Keyes & Waterman, 2003). They tend to be happier and live longer. Although raising children is demanding, parents often report that having children is one of the best things that has happened in their lives.

Some couples in committed relationships *cohabit* – that is, live together without being married. Some couples cohabit as a permanent alternative to marriage, but many do so as a 'trial marriage' to determine if they are compatible before marrying. In Sweden, premarital cohabitation appears to be the norm (Duvander, 1999).

> **Focus 13.14** Describe research findings on family structure, cohabitation and the course of marital satisfaction.

Establishing a Career

In the adult world, one of the first questions a new acquaintance typically asks is 'So, what do you do?' A career helps us earn a living and defines part of our identity. Work provides an outlet for achievement, gives us structure and is a significant source of social interactions. Having satisfying relationships at work is especially important in collectivistic countries (Siu, 2003).

According to Donald Super (1957), a pioneer in the field of vocational psychology, from childhood through to our mid-twenties, we first enter a *growth stage* of career interests in which we form initial impressions about the types of jobs we like or dislike, followed by a more earnest *exploration stage* in which we form tentative ideas about a preferred career and pursue the necessary education or training.

From the mid-twenties to mid-forties, people often enter an *establishment phase* during which they begin to make their mark. Initially, they may experience some job instability.

Without the human community, one single human being cannot survive.
The Dalai Lama

Social thinking and behaviour

14

Chapter Outline

SOCIAL THINKING

- Forming and maintaining impressions
- Self-concept
- Attribution: perceiving the causes of behaviour
- Attitudes and attitude change
- Concluding remarks

SOCIAL INFLUENCE AND BEHAVIOUR IN GROUPS

- The mere presence of others
- Compliance
- Research close-ups *The dilemma of obedience: when conscience confronts malevolent authority*
- Social influence in groups
- Behaviour in groups

SOCIAL RELATIONS: INTERGROUP DYNAMICS

- Understanding intergroup relations
- Prejudice and discrimination

SOCIAL RELATIONS: INTERPERSONAL DYNAMICS

- Attraction: liking and loving others
- Applying psychological science *Making close relationships work: lessons from psychological research*
- Pro-social behaviour: helping others
- Current topic *Does pure altruism exist?*
- Aggression: harming others

In the previous chapter we saw that parent–child influences are bidirectional, illustrating once again the interaction of biology and environment in shaping behaviour. In trying to understand a person's behaviour, we can similarly ask ourselves whether the *person* or the *situation* is more influential in determining behaviour – the so-called person–situation debate. For example, is there anything about the personality of a terrorist that can explain why they commit such atrocious acts? Or are factors outside of the individual, such as the norms of *others* in the surrounding, better at explaining why a specific individual commits the act terrorism? In this chapter and the next we will explore this question. As both chapters will illustrate, human behaviour can best be understood in terms of the *interaction* between personality and situational variables. The current chapter focuses more generally on how situational variables influence behaviour, whereas the next chapter focuses more generally on how personality influences behaviour. In both chapters we will illustrate this with reference to the act of terrorism, and ask ourselves to what extent such extreme acts are influenced by situational and personality variables.

The term 'terrorism' is defined as premeditated violence, perpetrated against non-combatant targets by subnational groups or clandestine agents, usually intended to influence an audience for the purpose of furthering some ideological, religious or political objective (Atran, 2003; Borum, 2007). What makes terrorist attacks horrific and shocking, is the brutal, indiscriminate violence for maximum impact and terror on those witnessing the event either directly or indirectly (through stories, the media, or any other verbal communication). Indeed, 'the primary target is not those actually killed or injured in the attack, but those made to witness it' (Atran, 2003, p. 1534).

All too often we are reminded of the devastating effects of terrorism. Recent examples include bomb attacks in public transport in the city Volgograd, Russia (October and December 2013), the Mogadishu restaurant attack (September 2013), the shootings at the Westgate Shopping Mall in Nairobi, Kenya (September 2013), and the Toulouse and Montauban shootings in France (2012). Unfortunately the list goes on and on. Over 10,000 terrorist attacks occurred in 2011, resulting in over 12,500 deaths (NCTC, 2012), most of which occurred in the Middle East and South Asia (75% of the attacks in 2011).

The effects of terrorism do not stop with the physical damage inflicted on the targets. Social scientists have examined the psychological and societal implications of such attacks (for a review, see Woods, 2011). For example, after an attack, people (a) experience psychological effects such as post-traumatic stress disorders, (b) overestimate the chance of being personally victimized by terrorists, (c) show a greater adherence to conventional values, (d) derogate and reject outsiders, (e) show an increased trust in the government, (f) experience enhanced feelings of patriotism, as evidenced in voter receptiveness to leaders who emphasized the 'greatness' of the nation. Indeed, some research even suggests that such attacks can change a country's culture and values quite dramatically in response. For example, Perrin (2005) analysed the content of 'letters to the editor' of newspapers, and found an increase in authoritarianism, showing a higher willingness to punish those who violated existing norms and conventional values.

These effects, and the brutality of terrorists in the face of death, beg our understanding. Who in their 'right mind' would do such a thing? Popular Western belief deems terrorists 'crazed cowards bent on senseless destruction who thrive in poverty and ignorance' (Atran, 2003, p. 1534). However, nothing indicates that the attackers are indeed impoverished, ignorant, poorly educated or psychologically disturbed. In contrast, many of them are highly educated and no worse off than most in similar situations. In other words, researchers have struggled to identify specific personal variables that could describe a coherent motivational account for the act of terror. Some psychologists therefore suggest that, in order to understand terrorism, it is necessary to investigate how individual behaviour is determined by extreme, but quite easily manipulated, *situational demands*. This brings the study of terrorism straight into the domain of social psychology, which tends to focus on situational variables for understanding human behaviour.

Social psychology has a long history showing the influence of the social context (the behaviour, norms, attitudes and emotions of *other people* in our environment) on our own feelings, thoughts and behaviour, over and above individual differences that may exist. Social psychology took shape in the 1940s and 1950s, when governments were trying to

understand the processes behind the atrocities of the First and Second World War. With specific laboratory techniques, most prominently that of deception (Nicks, Korn, & Mainieri, 1997), social psychology has provided some convincing examples of the actual strength of the situation to motivate behaviour. In this chapter we will discuss some of the more extreme examples of studies conducted by social psychologists, showing how behaviour can be elicited by situational demands even when strong moral convictions exist (e.g., torturing or killing another person; Milgram, 1974; Zimbardo, Haney, Banks, & Jaffe, 1973).

The current chapter explores the field of social psychology, which is particularly interested with the question of how people view, react to and influence other individuals. Gordon W. Allport gave a particularly influential definition of the discipline of social psychology as:

> an attempt to understand and explain how the thought, feeling and behaviour of individuals is influenced by the actual, imagined or implied presence of others. The term 'implied presence' refers to the many activities the individual carries out because of his position (role) in a complex social structure and because of his membership in a cultural group.   (Allport, 1954, p. 3)

In relation to terrorism, we ask ourselves why people willingly enact such devastating attacks. In other words, we all try to understand why people behave as they do and why they feel what they feel; in this way we are all social psychologists. While watching other people behave on television, at school, on the streets or in parks, we form ideas about their thoughts and their relationships with others around them. Indeed, the ability to understand our own and other people's behaviour is of great importance for making coordinated social life possible. However, are these common-sense interpretations which we derive from our observations always correct? Obviously it is quite difficult to oversee the whole range of influences determining our own and other people's behaviours. Most of the time we can only observe *actual* behaviour, while being completely oblivious as to what others really think. For example, if someone does you a favour, did he do so out of generosity or in an attempt to make you reciprocate in kind? If you like someone, is it because the person is genuinely likeable or is it because this person tries to present him- or herself in a manner which pleases you?

This chapter is divided into three major domains of social psychology. The first question we 'attempt to understand and explain', is that concerning our social thinking; that is, how we see and what we think of ourselves, and others around us. We ask questions such as, 'how accurate are the ideas we form of others and ourselves?' and 'how strong is the link between what we think and how we act?' The second topic covered in this chapter is social influence and within-group behaviour. As you can see from Allport's definition, one of the key themes of social psychology has been to understand the way in which other individuals *influence* the way we think, feel and behave. Indeed, being social *is* to influence and be influenced by others, a process that often occurs within the framework of group membership (Leach and Vliek, 2008). Social influence then can be seen as providing a link between 'social thinking' and the third topic of this chapter, 'social relations'. This topic is divided into two domains of interest to social psychologists: *intergroup relations* and *interpersonal relations*. Here we are interested in the way individuals and groups of individuals behave in relation to each other. What leads us to love, hurt, or even kill another person or group of persons? It is important to understand that these three topics, social thinking, social influence and social relations, do not stand for separate bodies of inquiry. All three domains are intricately related, with perceptions *influencing* behaviour, and behaviour *influencing* perceptions.

SOCIAL THINKING

In your judgement, do you think *you* would act in a similarly brutal manner as terrorists? And if not, why do others? What is your impression of such people who do commit these acts? Do you feel they should be punished? Answers to these questions depend in part on the way you construe reality; that is, individuals do not often respond to so-called

'objective' reality, but respond to their own subjective construction of it. For example, people often differ in who they deem a terrorist, or instead who they see as a 'freedom fighter'. It is interesting to note, for example, that Nelson Mandela was at one point designated a terrorist. For this reason, it is important to understand how individuals think about their surroundings and construe their own reality, or what we call *social thinking*.

The first thing to note when we start discussing *social thinking*, is something that at first might seem quite obvious: *people are not things*. There are a number of ways in which people and things differ in the way they influence our thinking of them (e.g., Fiske & Taylor, 2013). When we are busy forming impressions of others, these others are forming impressions of us. They also behave differently in different contexts, and may have intentions and traits that are hidden from us. In other words, people are intentional causal agents that may affect us in ways inanimate objects do not. As a result of these differences, cognitive processes involved in social perception differ markedly from cognitive processes involved in object perception (e.g., Castelli, Happé, Frith, & Frith, 2000). Social psychology as a field of inquiry is especially interested in this social side of our mental processes, called **social cognition**, wondering how people make sense of themselves and others around them.

> **social cognition** concerns the social side of our mental processes and how people make sense of themselves and others around them

Another important aspect of our social thinking is that we tend to engage in *motivated social cognition*: the way we acquire, process and store (social) information is dependent on specific goals, motives and needs. As we will see in this chapter, our needs and goals colour the way we perceive our social world and how we interact with others. Although there is considerable disagreement among psychologists regarding the existence of a set of basic human needs, at least three needs can be identified (for a discussion see Pittman & Zeigler, 2007). First, people have a strong *need to belong*; feeling accepted by friends, family, or important social groups makes us feel secure, safe and relaxed (Baumeister & Leary, 1995). People are also motivated by a *need for control* over their everyday activities and of the world they live in, even if this control is actually an illusion (Bandura, 2001; Whitson & Galinsky, 2008). Finally, one striking human feature is the extent to which we seem able to view the self positively. Here the *need for self-enhancement* motivates us to seek out and remember information that makes us feel good about ourselves (e.g., Sedikides, 1993).

One last thing to note is that individuals do not live in (cognitive) isolation. That is, the way in which we make sense of our social surrounding is influenced by the historical and cultural context within which we function and interact with others (e.g., Billig, 2008). It is not easy to 'step outside' this cultural and historical frame of reference to see how it influences the way we think about and relate to others. Indeed, social scientists themselves are often criticized for failing to do exactly that, relying heavily on so-called WEIRD participants – WEIRD standing for Western, Educated, Industrialized, Rich and Democratic – for their research (Heinrich, Heine, & Norenzayan, 2010). This WEIRD group of individuals makes up the vast majority of subjects in published articles in top psychology journals (96%), but only a small minority of the world's population (12%; Arnett, 2008). This is an important observation, as different social psychological phenomena could be expected to be more or less culturally dependent. As we will see in this chapter, social psychology has made some significant steps in unravelling the complex social nature of human behaviour, starting with an understanding of how we form impressions of others and ourselves.

FORMING AND MAINTAINING IMPRESSIONS

People have the ability to judge each other within a fraction of a second. Some evolutionary psychologists propose that evaluating stimuli quickly (such as rapidly distinguishing friend from foe) was adaptive for our survival (Krebs & Denton, 1997).

Evidence for our ability of rapid impression formation comes from Willis and Todorov (2006). They asked participants to judge male and female faces on dimensions such as attractiveness, likeability, trustworthiness and aggressiveness. Some participants only saw the pictures for 100 milliseconds, whereas others saw the pictures for 500 ms, 1,000

ms, or for as long as they wanted. The results demonstrated that judgements did not differ markedly as a result of exposure time, suggesting that people rapidly form first impressions of others.

These results also suggest that such initial, snapshot judgements may come to dominate subsequent impression formation. Try this exercise, for example. Tell a few people that you know someone who is 'intelligent, industrious, impulsive, critical, stubborn and envious', and ask them how much they 'like' this person. Repeat the process with a few others, but describe the person as 'envious, stubborn, critical, impulsive, industrious and intelligent'. Solomon Asch (1946) found that the person in the first description is perceived more positively – as more sociable and happier – than the person in the second description, even though both groups received identical information but in reverse order.

As we described in **Chapter 8**, the ability to recall an item from memory is influenced by the item's position in a series, and this serial position effect has two components: a primacy and a **recency effect**. When forming impressions, the **primacy effect** refers to our tendency to attach more importance to the initial information that we learn about a person. New information can change our opinion, but it has to 'work harder' for two reasons. First, we tend to be most alert to information we receive first. Second, initial information may shape how we perceive subsequent information. Imagine an athlete who gets off to a great start in training camp. The coach attributes high ability to the athlete. But as time goes on, the athlete's performance declines. To maintain this positive initial impression, the coach may attribute the performance decline to fatigue or a string of bad breaks. First impressions also carry extra weight because they influence our desire to make further contact with a person (Sunnafrank, Ramirez, & Metts, 2004). It is difficult to overcome someone's negative first impression of you if that person subsequently avoids or ignores you.

Primacy is the rule of thumb in impression formation, especially for people who dislike ambiguity and uncertainty (Kruglanski, 2004). But we are not slaves to primacy. Primacy effects decrease – and *recency effects* (giving greater weight to the most recent information) may occur – when we are in a negative mood, asked to avoid making snap judgements, reminded to consider the evidence carefully and made to feel accountable for our judgements (Forgas, 2011; Webster, Richter, & Kruglanski, 1996).

 Chapter 8, Page 320

> **primacy effect** the tendency to attach more importance to the initial information that we learn about a person
>
> **recency effect** the tendency to attach more importance to the most recent information that we learn about a person

Seeing What We Expect to See

Imagine that we are going to a party and I tell you that the host, George, is a distant, aloof, cold person. You meet him and try to make conversation, but George does not say much and avoids eye contact. A bit later, you say to me, 'You were right, he's really a cold fish'. Now let us rewind this scene. Suppose I describe George as nice but extremely shy. Later when you try to make conversation, he does not say much and avoids eye contact. You say to me, 'You were right, he's really shy'. Same behaviour, different impression. This example reminds us of a basic perceptual principle highlighted in **Chapter 5**. Whether perceiving objects or people, our *mental set*, which is a readiness to perceive the world in a particular way, powerfully shapes how we interpret a stimulus.

 Chapter 5, Page 187

What creates our mental sets? One set of factors that we have discussed throughout the book are *schemas*, mental frameworks that help us organize and interpret information. By telling you that our host is 'cold' or 'shy', I activate, or prime, a set of concepts and expectations (your schema) for how such a person is likely to behave. This activation increases its cognitive accessibility, in turn increasing the likelihood that you will categorize the host's behaviour in terms of the activated schema (Kelly, 1950).

An alternative explanation, however, is that you may have simply conformed to my judgement of George, without your responses necessarily reflecting your personal judgement or recollection of his behaviour. Higgins, Rholes, and Jones (1977) tried to disentangle these competing hypotheses by unobtrusively priming subjects with several trait terms. They asked subjects to memorize several words while identifying different colours as quickly as possible. Some of these memory words included object nouns (e.g., 'furniture', 'corner', etc.) and some included personality trait terms, with one group of subjects memorizing positive trait terms (e.g., 'adventurous') and one

group memorizing negative trait terms (e.g., 'reckless'). Subjects were then led to believe they would participate in a 'second study on reading comprehension'. Here they read an ambiguous story about Donald, who was portrayed as a thrill-seeker. Results indicated that subjects described and evaluated Donald consistent with the trait categories that had been previously activated, not only directly after reading the story, but even 10 to 14 days later during a follow-up study. This set of results seems to corroborate the conclusion that your categorization of George depends in part on the schema that has been activated, or primed, by the description you received prior to meeting him.

A **stereotype**, which is a shared belief about person attributes, usually personality traits, but often also behaviours, of a group or category of people, represents a powerful type of schema (Yzerbyt, Rocher, & Schadron, 1997). In one study, participants watched a videotape of a 9-year-old girl named Hannah and then judged her academic potential (Darley & Gross, 1983). They were told either that Hannah came from an upper middle-class environment and had parents with white-collar careers or that she came from a poor neighbourhood and had parents who were blue-collar workers. On the videotape, Hannah displayed average performance, answering some questions correctly and missing others. All participants saw the same performance, but those who thought Hannah came from a poor background rated her as having less ability. This study illustrates how our stereotypes (e.g., about social class) can bias the way we perceive other people's behaviour. Making judgements based on stereotypes is not inevitable though, and can be avoided through practice (Kawakami, Dovidio, Moll, Hermsen, & Russin, 2000) or by taking the other's perspective (Galinsky & Moscowitz, 2000). In general, such stereotype suppression is most likely to succeed when one is motivated and has the cognitive capacity to do so (for a review, see Fiske, Lin, & Neuberg, 1999).

Creating What We Expect to See

Seeing what we expect to see is only one way we confirm our initial impressions. Usually without conscious awareness, a **self-fulfilling prophecy** occurs when people's erroneous expectations lead them to act towards others in a way that brings about the expected behaviours, thereby confirming their original impression. Returning to our party example, if you expect George to be cold and aloof, then perhaps when you meet him you smile less and stand farther away than you would have if I had told you that George was a great guy. Perhaps when he looks at you, you avert your gaze, leading him to perceive you as less likeable (Mason, Tatkow, & Macrae, 2005). In any case, his reserved response, in part, could be a reaction to *your* behaviour (Figure 14.1).

How self-fulfilling prophecies may influence behaviour is nicely illustrated in a longitudinal study reported by Madon, Guyll, Spoth and Willard (2004). These researchers obtained longitudinal data during the course of one year, from 115 families with children around the age of 12. The first assessment measured parents' beliefs about their child's future alcohol use. The second assessment, one year later, measured the children's *actual* recent alcohol use. The results suggested that parents' overestimation of their children's alcohol use in the future *predicted* the children's actual future alcohol use. Thus, the more the parents thought their children would drink, the more the children drank one year later. Remember, however, that correlational designs do not provide strong evidence of causality, and make it difficult to rule out that both a predictor (parents' overestimation) and a dependent measure (children's alcohol use) is caused by a third, unmeasured variable. In this case, the relationship could stem from the parents' ability to accurately predict their children's alcohol use in the future. Although such influence could never be ruled out completely, follow-up research indicates that the occurrence of self-fulfilling prophecies does seem to play an important role in understanding children's alcohol use in the future (Madon, Willard, Guyll, Trudeau, & Spoth, 2006; Madon, Guyll, Buller, Scherr, Willard, & Spoth, 2008).

stereotype a shared belief about person attributes, usually personality traits, but often also behaviours, of a group or category of people

self-fulfilling prophecy when people's erroneous expectations lead them to act towards others in a way that brings about the expected behaviours, thereby confirming their original impression

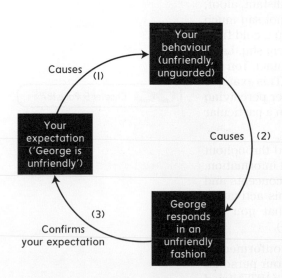

FIGURE 14.1 A self-fulfilling prophecy.

Your expectation concerning George may influence your behaviour (1), which in turn influences his response to you (2), confirming your expectation of him (3).

Self-fulfilling prophecies have been demonstrated in hundreds of studies across different settings, including schools, businesses, sports, close relationships and interactions with strangers (Eden, 2003; Snyder, 2001). When we interact with other people, our initially unfounded expectations can influence how we behave towards them, shaping their behaviour in a way that confirms our expectations. Here then we can also see the importance of impression formation: the impression we form of others can be highly consequential for the person being judged. If you judge someone to be unreliable, you will not be likely to lend this person money. On the other hand, inaccurate judgements can also be highly consequential for ourselves. If you *do* lend money because you think the person is reliable, then you made an expensive mistake if this impression turns out to be wrong, something the victims of financial frauds such as Bernard Madoff know only too well (Figure 14.2). This begs the question how accurate we actually are in forming impressions of other people.

Obviously, we make mistakes in judging others, especially if these others are out to mislead us, such as Bernard Madoff. Nonetheless, people seem quite accurate in judging others under 'normal' situations, or at least accurate enough to navigate the complex social world (see Funder, 2012). Accuracy is higher for people we know for a long time, who are emotionally stable, and who have more visible traits such as extraversion or expressiveness (Human & Biesanz, 2013). Accuracy is also enhanced if we meet people in situations where they can freely express themselves, such as in bars or cafés, as opposed to more highly structured or competitive surroundings (Letzring, Wells, & Funder, 2006). So, if you'd like to have a more accurate impression of your fellow students, it might make sense to socialize with them after class!

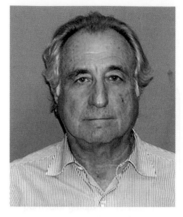

FIGURE 14.2 Bernard Madoff: one of the biggest financial frauds in history.

In 2009 Bernard Madoff, a former stockbroker and investment adviser, was sentenced to 150 years in federal prison for financial fraud. Some sources estimate investors lost approximately €13 billion and consider it the largest financial fraud in US history.

Source: © Mug Shot / Alamy

SELF-CONCEPT

Just as we form impressions of others, we also have a representation of ourselves – the self-concept. As the ancient Greek saying 'know thyself – and thou shall know all the mysteries of the gods and of the universe' already suggests, the knowledge we have of ourselves is quite similar to knowledge we have of other people around us. And, indeed, if we think about the behaviour of others, we often relate it to how we think *we* would behave. Therefore, having some insight into the self-concept (i.e., where it comes from, what form it takes and how we evaluate it) is important for understanding how we also form impressions of others.

> **Focus 14.1** Discuss how the primacy effect, stereotypes and self-fulfilling prophecies influence impression formation.

Sources of Self-Knowledge

The knowledge we have of ourselves is complex and contains multiple views of the self. In one situation you may see yourself as a son or daughter, at other times as leader or follower and yet at other times as a scientist or a student. Thus, the self-concept is made up of many different components, also called **self-schemas** (Markus & Wurf, 1987). Some self-schemas are more important to a person's self-concept than others. Think a moment how you would describe yourself. In your description you probably draw upon those dimensions that have a particular importance to you, like your political beliefs, specific character traits such as extraversion, or the type of music you like. Dimensions that have a specific self-relevance are also called *schematic*. In contrast, dimensions you do *not* use to describe yourself, such as your sporting interests or your religious beliefs, are called *aschematic*.

> **self-schemas** refer to mental templates, derived from memory of past experience, that represent a person's beliefs about the self in a particular domain

The experience of ourselves is highly context and culturally dependent and in part linked to the roles we have in society (Markus & Wurf, 1987). For example, many Asian cultures (e.g., Japan, China) have conceptions of the self that are distinctly different from many Western cultures (e.g., USA, UK). According to Markus and Kitayama (1991) Asian cultures emphasize the fundamental interrelatedness between people and place more importance on harmonious interdependence and the value of 'fitting in'. In contrast, Western cultures emphasize the fundamental independence of the self from others and place more importance on the self as a unique individual and expressing one's unique attributes. One dimension that is likely to be schematic in China, for example, is the

example, jurors' attributions about a defendant's behaviour influence their decisions about guilt versus innocence (e.g., Williams, Bourgeois, & Croyle, 1993).

Personal versus Situational Attributions

Our attempts to understand why people behave as they do and predict their future behaviour, typically involve either personal attributions or situational attributions (Heider, 1958). *Personal (internal) attributions* infer that people's characteristics cause their behaviour: 'Bill insulted Linda because he is rude.' 'My A in the end-of-year examination reflects my high ability.' *Situational (external) attributions* infer that aspects of the situation cause a behaviour: 'Bill was provoked into insulting Linda.' 'I received an A because the test was easy.'

How do we decide whether a behaviour is caused by personal or situational factors? Suppose you ask Kim for advice on whether to take a particular evening class in 'History of Art', and she tells you that the course is terrible. Is the 'History of Art' evening class really poor (a situational attribution), or is it something about Kim (a personal attribution) that led to this response? According to Harold Kelley's covariation model (1973), people tend to make such decisions based on conditions that are present (that co-vary) at the time the behaviour takes place. According to Kelley three types of covariation information determine the attribution we make: *consistency, distinctiveness* and *consensus.* First, is Kim's response consistent over time? If you ask Kim again two weeks later and she still says that the evening class is terrible, then consistency is high. Second, is her response distinctive? If Kim dislikes only the evening class in 'History of Art', then distinctiveness is high; if she thinks that most of her courses are terrible, then distinctiveness is low. Finally, how do other people respond? If other students agree with Kim that the evening class in 'History of Art' is poor, then consensus is high, but if they disagree with her, then consensus is low.

As Figure 14.3 illustrates, when consistency, distinctiveness and consensus are all high, we are likely to make a situational attribution: 'The course is bad.' But when consistency is high and the other two factors are low, we make a personal attribution: 'Perhaps Kim is overly critical.'

Kelley's model of attribution is supported by many studies (e.g., Försterling, 1989; Harris, Todorov, & Fiske, 2005; Sutton & McClure, 2001). Often, however, it is not enough to know that A (the class is boring) caused B (Kim says the class is boring). We also look for plausible explanations of the reasons *why* A caused B, so-called *causal mechanisms.* In this example, the reasons are quite easy to identify: we asked Kim for her opinion, and either the class is boring or Kim is critical. In everyday life such causal explanations are not always evident and sometimes the explanations given are hotly debated.

For example, what if you hear Kim was sexually harassed by Mark? If Mark is the only person who has sexually harassed Kim (consensus is low), if Mark also harasses other

FIGURE 14.3 Forming personal and situational attributions.

Consistency, distinctiveness and consensus information help us determine whether to make personal or situational attributions for someone else's behaviour. Note that in both examples consistency is high. If Kim's behaviour has low consistency (sometimes she says the class 'History of Art' is boring, and other times she says it is interesting), we typically attribute the behaviour to transient conditions (e.g., changes in Kim's mood) rather than to stable personal or situational factors.

Source: Based on Kelley, 1973.

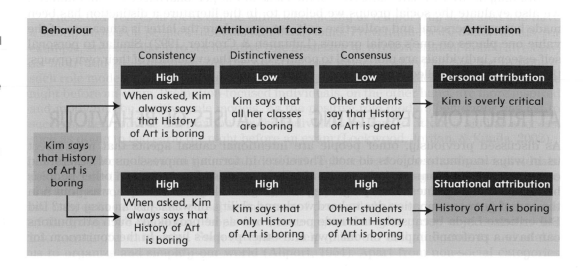

Behaviour	Attributional factors			Attribution
	Consistency	Distinctiveness	Consensus	
	High	**Low**	**Low**	**Personal attribution**
Kim says that History of Art is boring	When asked, Kim always says that History of Art is boring	Kim says that all her classes are boring	Other students say that History of Art is great	Kim is overly critical
	High	**High**	**High**	**Situational attribution**
	When asked, Kim always says that History of Art is boring	Kim says that only History of Art is boring	Other students say that History of Art is boring	History of Art is boring

women (distinctiveness is low) and if Mark harassed Kim before (consistency is high), we are likely to attribute the incident to Mark (Mark is a pervert). However, what if you heard that Kim was drunk at the time the harassment took place? Unfortunately, in such cases Kim's alcohol consumption will be seen as a contributing factor in the incident (part of the reason *why*). Indeed, in 2008, 15 victims of rape had their compensation cut by authorities in the UK due to the fact they had consumed alcohol at the time of the assault. In such cases the perception of the victim's responsibility will lead to less sympathy, thereby reducing the willingness to help the victim (Sperry & Siegel, 2013).

Attributional Biases

The covariation model assumes that we are quite logical when making attributions, weighing consensus, distinctiveness and consistency information carefully before attributing behaviour to either personal or situational factors. Humans, however, are often not so logical. Instead, we often take mental short cuts and make snap judgements that bias our attributions. One such bias is called the **fundamental attribution error**: we underestimate the impact of the situation and overestimate the role of personal factors when explaining other people's behaviour (Ross, 2001). This thinking bias has been found in real-world situations and laboratory experiments (Cowley, 2005).

Imagine that as part of a course assignment you write an essay on whether physicians should be allowed to help terminally ill patients commit suicide. The professor gives you the choice of writing in favour of or against physician-assisted suicide. Your classmates read the essay, and because they know you had a choice, they logically assume that the essay's content reflects your personal views. Thus if the essay opposes physician-assisted suicide, your classmates will conclude that you are against this practice. But suppose instead that the professor assigns you to write a supportive essay or assigns you to write an opposing essay. Your classmates know that you were not given a choice. Logically, the content of the essay reflects the situation to which you were assigned. After all, perhaps you are against physician-assisted suicide but were told to write an essay in favour of it, or vice versa.

Yet experiments indicate that the content of the essay will still influence your classmates' perception of whether you support or oppose the issue (Jones & Harris, 1967). Thus, even when it should be evident that a person's behaviour (the opinion expressed in the essay) is determined by the situation, people still seem to overestimate the role of personal factors (your personal opinion) in this case. Similarly, you would be making the fundamental attribution error if – solely on the basis of their professional roles – you expected television and film stars to have the same personal traits as the characters they played. We also see the fundamental attribution error in people's explanation of terrorist attacks. Instead of attributing terrorism to factors such as uncertainty, perceived injustice or perceived group threat (Doosje, Loseman, & Bos, 2013), terrorism is often personally attributed to 'crazy' or 'deranged' individuals. Obviously, this distinction has serious implications for the way terrorism is combated.

Psychologists debate what causes the fundamental attribution error, but they agree that it is not inevitable (see Sabini, Siepmann, & Stein, 2001). When people have time to reflect on their judgements or are highly motivated to be careful, the fundamental attribution error is reduced. Moreover, keep in mind that the fundamental attribution error applies to how we perceive *other* people's behaviour rather than our own. As comedian George Carlin noted, the slow driver ahead of us is a 'moron', and the fast driver trying to pass us is a 'maniac'. Yet we do not think of ourselves as a moron or a maniac when we do these things, perhaps because we are more aware of situational factors (e.g., an unfamiliar road) impinging on us.

Indeed, when it comes to explaining our own behaviour, we often make attributions that protect or enhance our self-esteem by displaying a **self-serving bias**, the tendency to make personal attributions for successes and situational attributions for failures (Ross & Nisbett, 1991). The strength of this bias, however, depends on many factors. For example, a meta-analysis of 266 studies by Amy Mezulis and her co-workers (Mezulis, Abramson, Hyde, & Hankin, 2004) found that depressed individuals are much less likely than most people to display a self-serving bias. Indeed, depressed people often display the opposite

---

Focus 14.2 What types of information lead us to make situational rather than personal attributions?

fundamental attribution error we underestimate the impact of the situation and overestimate the role of personal factors when explaining other people's behaviour

self-serving bias the tendency to make personal attributions for one's own successes and situational attributions for one's own failures

pattern – taking too little credit for successes and too much credit for failures – which helps keep them depressed. The self-serving bias has also been shown to occur at the group level. Here, people tend to attribute out-group failures and in-group successes to internal properties of the group, whereas in-group failures and out-group successes are attributed to external factors such as luck or chance. This self-serving bias at the group level is called the *ultimate attribution error* (Pettigrew, 1979). As you can see, this is likely to lead to a more positive view of one's own group compared with other groups and helps protect the in-group from negative implications of wrong or immoral actions (Hewstone, 1990).

Culture and Attribution

Culture significantly influences how we think about and perceive our social world. Numerous studies investigating cross-cultural differences suggest that many psychological processes, such as the fundamental attribution error, are not 'universal' but are to a large degree culturally specific (Nisbett, 2003). In general, evidence indicates that many Asian cultures (e.g., China, Japan, Korea) tend to think holistically, and this is reflected in the commonly held belief in these cultures that all events are interconnected. In contrast, Westerners (e.g., UK, USA, Canada) tend to think more analytically (Nisbett, Peng, Choi, & Norenzayan, 2001). Another distinction often made between cultures is that between independence versus interdependence (Markus & Kitayama, 1991) and individualistic versus collectivistic countries (Triandis, 1990, 1995). According to Hofstede (1991), *individualism* characterizes 'societies in which the ties between individuals are loose: everyone is expected to look after himself or herself and his or her immediate family' (p. 51), and *collectivism* characterizes 'societies in which people from birth onwards are integrated into strong, cohesive in-groups, which throughout people's lifetime continue to protect them in exchange for unquestioning loyalty' (p. 51). According to this distinction, the English-speaking countries such as the USA and Australia, and parts of Europe (north European countries) tend to be high on individualism, whereas some parts of Europe and much of Africa, Asia and Latin America tend to be high on collectivism (e.g., Hofstede, 1980; Triandis, 1994).

One consequence of holistic and collectivistic thinking involves an awareness of complexity, leading East Asians, for example, to attend more to the context in processing perceptual stimuli (Kitayama, Duffy, Kawamura, & Larsen, 2003). Given the greater weight attached to the context, it is not surprising that our cultural background also affects how we go about making attributions. In one study, participants of varying ages from India and the USA were asked to attribute the cause of other people's behaviour (Miller, 1984). As Figure 14.4 shows, with increasing age, Indians made more situational attributions, whereas Americans made more personal attributions. Accordingly, Choi and co-workers (Choi, Dalal, Kim Prieto, & Park, 2003) predicted and found that compared with European and American college students, Korean college students scored higher on measures of holistic thinking and took more information into account when making causal attributions for other people's behaviour. The fundamental attribution error, then, seems much less 'fundamental' than previously thought, leading some authors to refer to the phenomenon as the *correspondence bias* instead – a reference to the idea that a person's behaviour *corresponds* to their unique personal disposition instead of situational demands (Smith, Bond, & Kagitcibasi, 2006).

Culture not only influences attributions for other people's behaviour, but also influences attributions for our *own* behaviour. Asians living in their homelands are less likely to display a self-serving attributional bias than are Americans or other Westerners

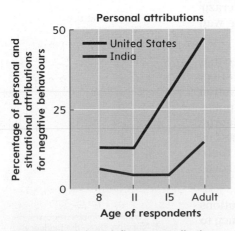

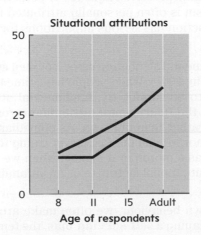

FIGURE 14.4 Culture influences attributions.

With increasing age from childhood to adulthood, Americans show a greater tendency to make personal attributions for other people's behaviours. In contrast, participants from India show an increased tendency to make situational attributions.

Source: Adapted from Miller, 1984.

(Mezulis et al., 2004). Modesty, for example, is highly valued in East Asian collectivistic culture, leading East Asians to take less personal credit for success and accept more responsibility for their failures than do American students. Thus, when asked to reflect on their successes and failures, Muramoto (2003) found that Japanese students attribute their successes to others and their failures to themselves. However, she also found that her Japanese respondents believed their friends and family would blame them less for failure and credit them more for success. This indicates that modesty might well be a tool for self-presentation, as a study by Brown and Kobayashi (2001) suggests. Brown and Kobayashi (2001) compared East Asians' and Westerners' motivations to achieve a positive self-regard. They found that Japanese respondents rated themselves just as highly on traits they valued most, such as modesty and friendliness, as typically Americans do on *their* most highly valued qualities. This suggests that both East Asians and Westerners are motivated to achieve a positive self-regard. This debate regarding the role of modesty and the existence of self-serving biases is important, for it suggests that some universal of human behaviour might exist: behavioural differences between cultures may in part be explained by the norms of behaviour they lay down for their group members to conform to.

> **Focus I4.3** Describe the fundamental attribution error and the self-serving bias, and discuss how they are affected by culture.

ATTITUDES AND ATTITUDE CHANGE

Beyond the question of exactly *how* we think about and perceive of our social world, much of our social thinking also involves the attitudes that we hold towards external stimuli. An **attitude** is a positive or negative evaluative reaction towards a stimulus, such as a person, action, situation, object or concept (Tesser & Shaffer, 1990). Whether agreeing or disagreeing with a political policy or a friend's opinion of a film, you are displaying an evaluative reaction (Figure 14.5). Our attitudes help define our identity, guide our actions, and influence how we judge people (Fazio & Roskos-Ewoldsen, 2005). In the following paragraphs we take a look at the link between attitudes and behaviour, and whether and how attitudes can be changed.

> **attitude** a positive or negative evaluative reaction towards a stimulus, such as a person, action, situation, object or concept

Do Our Attitudes Influence Our Behaviour?

If we tell you that, according to research, people's attitudes strongly guide their behaviour, you might reply, 'So what? That's just common sense'. But consider a classic study by Richard LaPiere (1934). In the 1930s, he toured the USA with a young Chinese couple, stopping at 251 restaurants, hotels and other establishments. At the time, prejudice against Asians was widespread, yet the couple – who often entered the establishment before LaPiere did – were refused service only once. Later LaPiere wrote to all of these establishments, asking if they would provide service to Chinese patrons. More than 90% of those who responded stated that they would not.

We cannot be sure that the people who expressed negative attitudes in the survey were the same ones who, months earlier, had served the Chinese couple. Yet the discrepancy between prejudicial attitudes and non-discriminatory behaviour seemed overwhelming and called the 'common-sense' assumption of attitude–behaviour consistency into question. Decades of better controlled research, however, indicate that attitudes can indeed predict behaviour (Fazio & Roskos-Ewoldsen, 2005). Three factors help explain why the attitude–behaviour relationship is strong in some cases but weak in others.

FIGURE I4.5 Expressing one's attitude.

Attitudes represent an important form of social thinking. They help define who we are, and they affect the way people judge one another. Do the attitudes expressed by these protestors influence your impression of them?

Source: © Janine Wiedel Photolibrary / Alamy

First, *attitudes influence behaviour more strongly when situational factors that contradict our attitudes are weak.* For example, conformity pressures may lead us to behave in ways that are at odds with our inner convictions. According to the theory of planned behaviour (see **Chapter 16**) and similar models (Ajzen, 1991), our intention to engage in a behaviour is strongest when we have a positive attitude towards that behaviour, when subjective norms (our perceptions of what other people think we should do) support our attitudes, and when we believe that the behaviour is under our control. Researchers have used this theory to predict successfully whether people will

 Chapter 16, Page 703

become smokers, exercise regularly, drive safely, donate blood and perform many other behaviours (Victoir, Eertmans, Van den Bergh, & Van den Broucke, 2005).

Second, *attitudes have a greater influence on behaviour when we are aware of them and when they are strongly held*. Sometimes we seem to act without thinking, out of impulse or habit. Attitude–behaviour consistency increases when people consciously think about or are reminded of their attitudes before acting (White, Hogg, & Terry, 2002).

Third, *general attitudes best predict general classes of behaviour, and specific attitudes best predict specific behaviours*. For example, Martin Fishbein and Icek Ajzen (1974) found almost no relation between people's general attitudes towards religion and 70 specific religious behaviours (such as the frequency of attending services). But when they combined the 70 specific behaviours into a single global index of religious behaviour, the relation between general religious attitudes and overall religious behaviour was substantial.

> **Focus 14.4** What is an attitude? Describe three conditions under which people's attitudes best predict their behaviour.

Does Our Behaviour Influence Our Attitudes?

Under the proper conditions, our attitudes guide our behaviour. But attitude–behaviour consistency is not a one-way street: we also come to develop attitudes that are consistent with how we behave (Cooper, Mirabile, & Scher, 2005). After casting a ballot during elections, for example, voters are more convinced that their candidate will win the election than before (Regan & Kilduff, 1988; Mullainathan & Washington, 2009). Similarly, as to-be suicide bombers are immersed in the extremist groups' ideology, they start to see their targets as little more than animals (Moghaddam, 2005). Why should this be?

Cognitive dissonance

Imagine that you volunteer for an experiment, arrive at the laboratory, and repeatedly perform two extremely boring tasks: emptying and filling a tray with spools and turning 48 pegs stuck into holes. After you endure 60 minutes of sheer boredom, the experimenter enters, thanks you for participating and asks for your help: it is important for the next student to begin the study with a positive attitude about the tasks, and all you have to do is tell the student that the boring tasks are interesting. Depending on the condition to which you have been randomly assigned, the experimenter offers to pay you either $1 or $20 for, essentially, lying to the next participant. You agree to do so. Afterwards, you go to the psychology department's main office to collect your money and fill out a 'routine form' that asks how much you enjoyed the tasks in the experiment.

Make a prediction: comparing participants who lied for $1 and who lied for $20 with a control group that simply rated the boring tasks without telling any lie beforehand, which of the three groups rated the task most positively? Why?

Common sense might suggest that participants paid $20 would feel happiest about the experiment and rate the tasks most highly. However, as Leon Festinger and J. Merrill Carlsmith (1959) predicted in a classic experiment, American participants who were paid $1 gave the most positive ratings. Indeed, they actually rated the boring tasks as 'somewhat enjoyable' (Figure 14.6)!

According to Festinger's (1957) **theory of cognitive dissonance**, people strive for consistency in their cognitions. When two or more cognitions contradict one another (such as 'I am a truthful person' and 'I just told another student that those boring tasks were interesting'), the person experiences an uncomfortable state of tension, which Festinger calls *cognitive dissonance*, and becomes motivated to reduce this dissonance. The theory predicts that to reduce dissonance and restore a state of cognitive consistency, people will change one of their cognitions or add new cognitions.

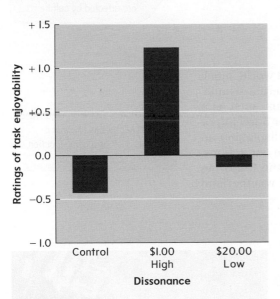

FIGURE 14.6 Cognitive dissonance and external justification.

American participants lied to a fellow student by saying that a boring task was interesting. Those offered $1 to lie, later rated the task most positively. Presumably, they reduced their cognitive dissonance about lying by convincing themselves that the task was interesting after all. Participants offered $20 had an external justification to lie, experienced little dissonance and therefore did not need to convince themselves that the task was enjoyable. They and control participants who had not lied rated the boring task less favourably than the $1 group.

Source: Based on Festinger and Carlsmith, 1959.

> **theory of cognitive dissonance** people strive for consistency in their cognitions

Participants who received $20 could justify their behaviour by adding a new cognition – 'Who wouldn't tell a little lie for $20?' – and there was little reason for them to change their attitude towards the boring tasks. Those who had lied for only $1 could not use this trivial monetary gain to justify their behaviour. But if they could convince themselves that the tasks actually were enjoyable, then they would not have been lying after all. Thus they changed their attitude about the task to bring it more in line with how they had behaved.

Behaviour that is inconsistent with one's attitude is called *counter-attitudinal behaviour*. Many studies now show that counter-attitudinal behaviour creates the experience of dissonance, not only with WEIRD participants (e.g., Elliot & Devine, 1994; Galinsky, Stone, & Cooper, 2000), but also across cultures (Heine & Lehman, 1997), and even in other animals too (Egan, Santos, & Bloom, 2007). However, counter-attitudinal behaviour does not always produce dissonance. Instead, dissonance only occurs if we perceive that our actions were freely chosen rather than coerced. Freely chosen behaviours that produce foreseeable negative consequences or that threaten our sense of self-worth are especially likely to arouse dissonance. Once the behaviour occurs, people start to consider the meaning of what they have done, and this produces dissonance (Cooper et al., 2005).

Dissonance, however, does not always lead to attitude change. People can reduce dissonance by finding external justifications or by making other excuses (Cooper et al., 2005). In Scandinavian surveys, among people who drank alcohol despite having negative attitudes towards drinking, one rationalization seemed to be 'I may not be perfect, but other people are still worse' (Mäkelä, 1997). Despite the many ways to reduce dissonance, the theory helps explain many interesting aspects of human behaviour (Figure 14.7).

Self-perception

If we see someone campaigning for a political candidate, we will likely assume that this person has a positive attitude towards the candidate. If we see someone exerting great effort to achieve a goal, we will logically judge that the goal is important to that person. In short, we infer what other people's attitudes must be by watching how they behave. According to Daryl Bem's (1972) **self-perception theory**, we make inferences about our own attitudes in much the same way: by observing how we behave. Knowing that for very little external justification ($1) you have told a fellow student that the boring experimental tasks are enjoyable, you logically conclude that deep down you must feel that the tasks were at least somewhat enjoyable. In Bem's view, your attitude is not produced by a mysterious concept called *cognitive dissonance*; rather you simply observe how you have acted and infer how you must have felt to have behaved in this fashion.

Self-perception theory and cognitive dissonance theory both predict that counter-attitudinal behaviour produces attitude change. How, then, can we determine which theory more accurately explains the reason behind such attitude change? One key difference is that only dissonance theory assumes that we experience heightened physiological arousal (tension produced by dissonance) when we engage in counter-attitudinal behaviour. Do we? At least in some instances it appears so. In one study, college students consumed an unpleasant-tasting drink and were then asked to write a sentence stating that they liked the taste. Students who were given a high degree of choice whether to write this counter-attitudinal statement showed higher arousal (measured by sweat gland activity) and greater attitude change than participants who were simply told to write the statement (Harmon-Jones, Brehm, Greenberg, Simon, & Nelson, 1996; see also Harmon-Jones & Harmon-Jones, 2007).

These and other findings indicate that dissonance theory best explains why people change their views after behaving in ways that openly contradict their clearly defined attitudes, especially when such behaviours threaten their self-image (Stone & Cooper, 2003). Lying to someone for a minimal sum of money threatens our self-image of honesty, and acting inhumanely towards innocent civilians threatens our self-image of being a good, decent

FIGURE 14.7 Effort justification.
Every year, tennis fans queue for hours in the hope of gaining tickets for the Wimbledon finals. No doubt a major reason for their positive attitude is that they are committed fans. But might cognitive dissonance have played a role? Experiments show that when people invest a lot of time and energy into achieving a goal, finding out that the goal was not all it was supposed to be creates cognitive dissonance. To justify their effort and thus reduce dissonance, people may convince themselves that the goal (e.g., the tennis match) is more attractive or worthwhile than it really is.

Source: Oli Scarff/Getty Images

> **Focus 14.5** Explain the causes of cognitive dissonance and how it produces attitude change

> **self-perception theory** we make inferences about our own attitudes by observing how we behave

Focus 14.6 Evaluate dissonance versus self-perception theory views of why counter-attitudinal behaviour produces attitude change.

person – unless we can somehow justify those actions to ourselves. However, when counter-attitudinal behaviour does not threaten self-worth and we have weak attitudes to begin with, such behaviour is less likely to create significant arousal – yet people may still alter their attitudes to be more consistent with how they have behaved. In this case, self-perception theory may provide the better explanation. Thus both dissonance theory and self-perception theory appear to be correct, but under different circumstances (Tesser & Shaffer, 1990). Both theories, however, agree that *our behaviours can influence our attitudes.*

Persuasion

Persuasion is a fact of everyday life, and it represents the intersection of social thinking and our next topic: social influence. Persuaders try to influence our beliefs and attitudes so that we will vote for them, buy their products, do them favours or otherwise behave as they want us to. Here we examine three aspects of the persuasion process: the audience or 'targets' of persuasion messages, the communicator, and finally the message being communicated.

The audience

Persuasion seems easy: just give people a number of good arguments to change their attitude on a specific subject and they will nod their heads and follow your advice, right? Wrong! If good arguments were so persuasive, why do people smoke, drink alcohol, or eat processed foods even though they know it is bad for their health? Or why do they buy things they don't really need, or vote for political parties without reading their manifest? Indeed, a message loaded with logical arguments and facts may prove highly persuasive to some people yet fall flat on its face with others. Why?

According to the *elaboration likelihood model of persuasion (ELM)* developed by Richard Petty and John Cacioppo, there are two basic routes to persuasion (Petty & Cacioppo, 1986; Petty, Cacioppo, Strathman, & Priester, 2005). The **central route to persuasion** occurs when people think carefully about the message and are influenced because they find the arguments compelling. The **peripheral route to persuasion** occurs when people do not scrutinize the message but are influenced mostly by other factors such as the attractiveness of the person who endorses the product or a message's length or emotional appeal.

Whether a person uses the central or peripheral route, depends on two basic factors: *motivation* and *ability*. Central route persuasion is most likely when individuals are motivated to elaborate on the arguments in a message. Typically this means that the topic or issue is relevant or important to the person. If the topic or issue is not important, he or she will be less inclined to spend the necessary mental effort to process the message via the central route, and instead resort to peripheral processing. However, a person must not only be motivated but also able to engage in central processing. For example, sometimes we do not have the expertise or the knowledge necessary to think carefully about the message and make rational decisions based on the available information. In such cases we also resort to peripheral processing. Finally, a variety of other factors such as lack of time, background noise, or other distractions can also tilt the balance in favour of one of the two routes.

The distinction between central and peripheral route processing has acquired substantial empirical support and has been successfully used to predict people's reactions to persuasive messages. It turns out the type of processing also influences the persistence of persuasion: attitude change that results from the central route tends to last longer and to predict future behaviour more successfully (Petty, Haughtvedt, & Smith, 1995). Central route processing also tends to create attitudes that are more resilient to counterinfluence attempts. So, if you'd like to persuade people, your best bet is to make them think.

The communicator

Communicator credibility – how believable we perceive a communicator to be – is often a key to effective persuasion (O'Keefe, 1990). In fact, audience members who are not highly involved with the issues may pay little attention to the content of a message and simply go along with the opinions of a highly credible source. Credibility has two major components: *expertise* and *trustworthiness* (Hovland, Janis, & Kelley, 1953;

central route to persuasion when people think carefully about the message and are influenced because they find the arguments compelling

peripheral route to persuasion when people do not scrutinize the message but are influenced mostly by other factors such as a speaker's attractiveness or a message's length or emotional appeal

communicator credibility how believable we perceive the communicator to be

Pornpitakpan, 2004). The most effective persuader is one who appears to be an expert and to be presenting the truth in an unbiased manner. Sometimes a title or specific clothing like a white laboratory coat is enough to confer credibility on a source (Cialdini, 2009). We are especially likely to perceive communicators as trustworthy when they advocate a point of view that is contrary to their own self-interest (Petty, Fleming, Priester, & Feinstein, 2001). Communicators who are physically attractive, likeable and similar to us (such as in interests or goals) may also gain a persuasive edge, which is why advertisers spend millions of euros on celebrity endorsements: hiring attractive, likeable stars to promote their products (Reeves, 2012).

The message

In trying to persuade someone, is it more effective to present only your side of the issue or to also present the opposition's arguments and then refute them? Overall, research indicates that the *two-sided refutational approach* is most effective (Allen, 1991). Especially if an audience initially disagrees with the communicator's viewpoint or is aware that there are two sides to the issue, a two-sided message will be perceived as less biased.

Many messages, such as those in Figure 14.8, attempt to persuade by arousing fear. Does it work? Or do people reduce their fear simply by denying the credibility of the message or the communicator? Overall, fear arousal seems to work best when the message evokes moderate levels of fear (Peters, Ruiter, & Kok, 2012). High or extreme levels of fear will lead people to focus only on regulating the fear response, forgetting most of the information that is communicated in the message. The message also needs to provide people with effective, feasible (e.g., low-cost) ways to reduce the threat (Dillard & Anderson, 2004). This is especially important in case of behaviours that are difficult to change, such as habits or addictions.

CONCLUDING REMARKS

As we have seen in this section on social thinking, human behaviour can, at least partly, be understood in terms of intrapersonal, cognitive mechanisms. However, this is a decidedly individualistic approach to understanding how people deal with their social surrounding. Indeed, as mentioned previously, social psychology has been criticized for trying to explain *social* behaviour in terms of *asocial* intrapersonal cognitions and motivations (e.g., Gergen, 1973). For example, a critical approach to social psychology (Potter & Wetherell, 1987) suggests that our understanding of the world does not merely spring from our heads, but is derived from the surrounding social groups, institutions and relations in which we are embedded (Spears, 1997). Therefore, if we want to understand the individual, we will have to understand their social context as well as the way in which their subjective reality is informed through communication with others. In the next section we will therefore turn our focus to the question of how an individual is influenced and informed by their *social* surrounding and the groups to which they belong.

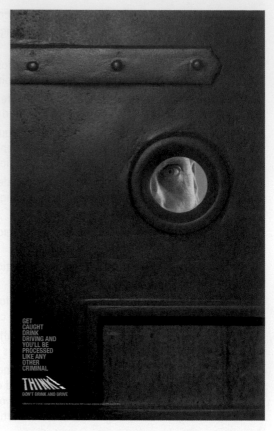

FIGURE 14.8 Think! The UK's road safety awareness campaign.

Fear appeals are a common approach to persuasion. They are most effective when people believe that a feared event could occur ('Driving after drinking can increase my risk of an accident'), that the consequences would be aversive ('I could lose my licence or be killed'), that there is an effective way to reduce the risk ('If I drink, I won't drive') and that they can carry out this behaviour without great cost ('Have a designated driver; call a friend').

Source: The National Archives/ Department for Transport Think! Road Safety Campaign

Focus 14.7 Describe how communicator, message and audience characteristics affect the persuasion process.

 In review

■ Impressions may change over time, but our first impression generally carries extra weight. Stereotypes and schemas create mental sets that shape our impressions.

■ Through self-fulfilling prophecies, our initially false expectations shape the way we act towards someone. In turn, this person responds to our behaviour in a way that confirms our initially false belief.

- Self-knowledge is obtained through observing our own behaviour, through the process of social comparison, and through examining what others think of us.
- An individual's identity is partly based on idiosyncratic characteristics, personality traits and interpersonal relationships (personal identity) as well as on the knowledge of belonging to particular groups (social identity).
- People have a pervasive tendency to evaluate themselves as individuals, captured by the individual's personal self-esteem, as well as the groups to which they belong, captured by the individual's collective self-esteem.
- Attributions, or the judgements about the causes of our own and other people's behaviour, play an important role in forming impressions of ourselves and others. Consistency, distinctiveness, and consensus information jointly influence whether we make a personal or situational attribution for a particular act.
- The fundamental attribution error is the tendency to attribute other people's behaviour to personal factors while underestimating the role of situational factors. The self-serving bias is the tendency to attribute one's successes to personal factors and one's failures to situational factors.
- Cultural differences exist in the extent to which people are likely to attribute the causes of success or failure to either personal or situational factors.
- Attitudes predict behaviour best when situational influences are weak, when the attitude is strong and when we consciously think about our attitude.
- Counter-attitudinal behaviour is most likely to create cognitive dissonance when the behaviour is freely chosen and threatens our self-worth or produces foreseeable negative consequences.
- To reduce dissonance, we may change our attitude to become more consistent with how we have acted. When our attitudes are weak and counter-attitudinal behaviour does not threaten our self-worth, we may change our attitudes through self-perception.
- Communicator, message and audience characteristics influence the effectiveness of persuasion. Communicator credibility is highest when the communicator is perceived as expert and trustworthy. Fear-arousing communications may be effective if they arouse moderate fear and suggest how to avoid the feared result. The central route to persuasion works best with listeners who have a high need for cognition; for those with a low cognition need, the peripheral route works better.

SOCIAL INFLUENCE AND BEHAVIOUR IN GROUPS

In the previous section we talked about persuasion and how persuaders might influence our beliefs and attitudes. However, the way in which others influence us takes many forms, not necessarily leading to a change in attitudes. In some instances our behaviour is influenced merely by the presence of others. Imagine Patricia, a novice piano player, who makes more mistakes after her parents enter the room to listen to her practice. At other times people influence our behaviour because we simply do what people ask us to do. This latter form of influence is called *compliance*, which leads to a change in behaviour but not necessarily a change in beliefs or attitudes. Finally, people influence us in a more indirect manner through our tendency to conform to group norms.

THE MERE PRESENCE OF OTHERS

Norman Triplett (1898) helped launch the field of social psychology by testing a deceptively simple hypothesis: the presence of others energizes performance. Triplett analysed the records from numerous bicycle races. In some races, cyclists performed individually against the clock; in other races of similar distance, they performed together in a pack. As Triplett predicted, cyclists' average speed was much faster in group races than in individual races, but from experience he knew that other factors (e.g., racers riding behind one another to cut wind resistance) could also explain this finding. So in a laboratory experiment, Triplett had children perform a simple physical task, either alone or in the presence of another child (called a *co-actor*) who independently performed the same task. Indeed, the children's performance improved when in each other's presence.

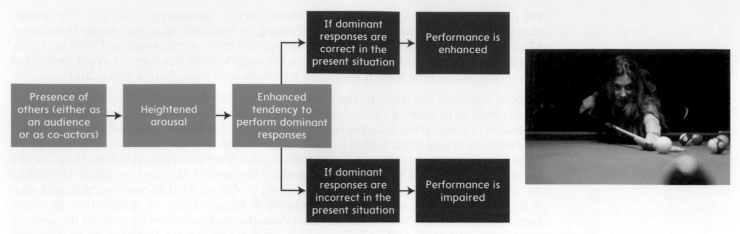

FIGURE 14.9 Social facilitation of dominant responses.

Whether this pool player's performance improves or worsens when other people are watching depends on whether she is highly skilled or a novice (Michaels, Blommel, Brocato, Linkous, & Rowe, 1982).

Source: ©iStock.com/Vladmax

Many early studies revealed that the *mere presence* of co-actors or of a silent audience enhanced performance. Even ants carried more dirt with other ants present (Chen, 1937). Yet some research found that the mere presence of others impaired performance on certain tasks.

In 1965 Robert Zajonc proposed a theory to explain this seeming paradox. First, the mere physical presence of another person (or member of the same species) increases our arousal. Second, as arousal increases, we become more likely to perform whatever behaviours happen to be our *dominant responses* (i.e., most typical responses) to that specific situation. When a task is complex and we are first trying to learn it, our dominant responses are likely to be incorrect ones, so we make errors. Therefore, performing in front of other people will impair performance, even when these others are invisible (e.g., Wühr & Huestegge, 2010). But when a task is either simple or complex but well learned, our dominant responses usually are correct ones. In these situations, performing in the presence of visible or invisible others will enhance performance (Figure 14.9).

This phenomenon is called **social facilitation**, an increased tendency to perform one's dominant responses in the mere presence of others. It may be the most basic form of social influence, occurring in species ranging from fruit flies to hens and humans (Thomas, Skitka, Christen, & Jurgena, 2002; Ward, 2012), and it has an important practical implication: when trying to accomplish a complex task, minimize the presence of other people.

COMPLIANCE

Most of the time, people around us are not strangers 'merely' hanging around. They are important individuals whose opinions of how we should think, feel or behave have a strong influence on us, especially when these others are actively trying to influence us.

Compliance Techniques

From telemarketers and salespeople to television and Internet advertisements, would-be persuaders often come armed with special *compliance techniques*, strategies that may manipulate you into saying yes when you really want to say no. By learning to identify these techniques, you will be in a better position to resist them.

The powerful **norm of reciprocity** involves the expectation that when others treat us well, we should respond in kind. Thus to get you to comply with a request, I can do something nice for you now – such as an unsolicited favour – in the hope that you will feel pressure to reciprocate later when I present you with my request (Cialdini & Sagarin, 2005). Although the norm of reciprocity is universally present, research does suggest that

Focus 14.8 When does the mere presence of others enhance performance or impair performance? Why?

social facilitation an increased tendency to perform one's dominant responses in the mere presence of others

norm of reciprocity the expectation that when others treat us well, we should respond in kind

the pressure to reciprocate is strongest when it occurs between friends or *within* groups that are important to us, but is much less strong, or even absent, *across* group boundaries (Tanis & Postmes, 2005). Especially in more collectivistic cultures such as China or Japan, this pressure can be so strong people often refuse gifts from strangers to avoid feelings of indebtedness that may arise if they cannot reciprocate (Shen, Wan, & Wyer, 2011).

Now consider the **door-in-the-face technique**: a persuader makes a large request, expecting you to reject it (you 'slam the door' in the persuader's face), and then presents a smaller request. Telemarketers feast on this technique. Rather than ask you directly for a modest monetary contribution to some organization or cause, they first ask for a much larger contribution, knowing that you will say no. After you politely refuse, they ask for the smaller contribution. In one experiment, after people declined an initial request to donate $25 to a charity, they were more likely to donate $2 than were participants who were directly asked for $2 (Wang, Brownstein, & Katzev, 1989). To be effective, the same persuader must make both requests. The persuader 'compromises' by making the second, smaller request, so we feel pressure to reciprocate by complying. Refusing the first request also may produce guilt, and complying with the smaller request may help us reduce guilt or feel socially responsible (Tusing & Dillard, 2000).

Using the **foot-in-the-door technique**, a persuader gets you to comply with a small request first (getting the 'foot in the door') and later presents a larger request. Imagine receiving an email from a stranger who asks for simple advice about a word-processing program. It takes less than a minute to reply, and you do – as did all the participants in an actual experiment (Guéguen, 2002). After you comply, the person sends a second email asking you to help with a class project by filling out a 20-minute online questionnaire. In the experiment, 76% of college students complied, compared with only 44% in a control group that received only the class-project request. Although hypotheses abound, researchers are not sure why the foot-in-the-door technique is effective.

With a final technique, **lowballing**, a persuader gets you to commit to some action and then – before you actually perform the behaviour – he or she increases the 'cost' of that same behaviour. Imagine negotiating to buy a used car for €8,000, a 'great price'. The salesperson says, 'I need to confirm this with my manager', comes back shortly, and states, 'I'm afraid my manager says the price is too low. But you can have the car for only €400 more. It's still a great price'. At this point, you are more likely to go through with the deal than you would have been, had the 'real' €8,400 price been set at the outset.

Both lowballing and the foot-in-the-door technique involve moving from a smaller request to a larger, more costly request. But with lowballing, the stakes for the *same behaviour* are raised after you commit to it but *before* you consummate the behaviour. Having made a commitment, you may find it easier to rationalize the added costs or may feel obligated to the person to whom you made the commitment (Cialdini & Sagarin, 2005).

By recognizing when compliance techniques are being used to manipulate your behaviour, you are in a better position to resist them. Consider the norm of reciprocity. Robert Cialdini (2009), an expert on influence techniques, suggests that the key is not to resist the initial gift or favour; instead, accept the unsolicited 'favour', but if the person then asks you for a favour in return, recognize this as a manipulative trick. Similarly, if a telemarketer makes a large initial request and then, after you decline, immediately asks for a smaller commitment, respond by thinking or saying, 'I see. It's the door-in-the-face technique'. Of course, you can still choose to comply if you believe it is the right thing to do. The goal is not to automatically reject every social influence attempt but to avoid feeling coerced into doing something you do not want to do.

Influence of Authority: Obedience

Some people do not need all these compliance techniques to get us to obey their every command: legitimate authority figures. One example, cited by Cohen and Davis in their book *Medication errors: Causes and prevention* (1981), illustrates a remarkable case of blind obedience to an authority figure. A physician ordered eardrops for a patient with a painful infected right ear. Instead of writing 'place in right ear' the physician wrote on the prescription 'place in R ear'. Upon receiving the medicine, the nurse in attendance

door-in-the-face technique a persuader makes a large request, expecting you to reject it and then presents a smaller request

foot-in-the-door technique a persuader gets you to comply with a small request first and later presents a larger request

lowballing a persuader gets you to commit to some action and then – before you actually perform the behaviour – he or she increases the 'cost' of that same behaviour

Focus 14.9 Identify four common compliance techniques and explain how they work.

mistakenly read 'Rear' and subsequently applied the eardrops rectally. However absurd it might seem to apply eardrops rectally, neither the nurse *nor* the patient felt anything like suspicious. It was what the doctor had ordered.

Although rectally applying eardrops might be classified as bad, obedience to an authority figure is inherently neither good nor bad. As an aeroplane passenger, you would not be amused if the co-pilot disregarded the pilot's commands simply because he or she did not feel like obeying, putting the flight and your life at risk. Without obedience, society would face chaos. But obedience can also produce tragic results. After the Second World War, the famous Nuremberg trials were held to judge Nazi war criminals who had slaughtered millions of innocent people in concentration camps. In many instances, the defendants argued that they had only followed orders. No doubt we will continue to hear the cry 'I was just following orders' as accountability is judged for more recent mass atrocities around the globe.

Just as the Nuremberg court did, many of us reject justifications based on obedience to authority as mere rationalizations, secure in our conviction that *we* would behave more humanely in such situations. But would we? Our 'Research close-up' – part of the most famous series of studies ever conducted in social psychology – suggests some provocative answers.

 Research close-up

THE DILEMMA OF OBEDIENCE: WHEN CONSCIENCE CONFRONTS MALEVOLENT AUTHORITY

Source: S. Milgram (1974). *Obedience to authority*. New York: Harper & Row.

INTRODUCTION

Fuelled by a scientific interest in social influence and a desire to understand the horrors of the Holocaust, psychologist Stanley Milgram (1974) asked a disturbing question: would ordinary citizens obey the orders of an authority figure if those orders meant physically harming an innocent person? He conducted 23 studies between 1960 and 1963 to answer this question and to identify factors that increased or decreased obedience to authority. Let us examine one study.

METHOD

Forty men, ranging in age from 20 to 50 and representing a cross-section of occupations and educational backgrounds in the USA, participated in the study. At the laboratory, each participant met a middle-aged man who was introduced as another participant but who was actually a confederate. Participants were told that the experiment examined the effects of punishment on memory. Then through a supposedly random draw (it was rigged), the real participant became the 'teacher' and the confederate became the 'learner'. The teacher presented a series of memory problems to the

(a)

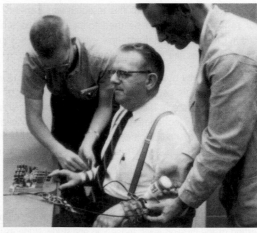

(b)

FIGURE 14.10 (a) Switches on the shock generator ranged from 15 volts ('slight shock') to 450 volts ('XXX').
(b) The participant (teacher) saw the learner being strapped into the chair.

Source: © Reproduced with the permission of Alexandra Milgram.

▶

learner through a two-way intercom system. Each time the learner made an error, the teacher was instructed to administer an electric shock using a machine that had 30 switches, beginning with 15 volts and increasing step-by-step to 450 volts (Figure 14.10a). As the teacher watched, the experimenter strapped the learner into a chair in an adjoining room and hooked him up to wires from the shock generator (Figure 14.10b). The learner expressed concern about the shocks and mentioned that he had a slight heart problem.

Returning to the main room, the experimenter gave the teacher a sample shock (45 volts) and then ordered the experiment to begin. Unbeknown to the teacher, the learner intentionally committed many errors, and he did *not* actually receive any shock. The learner made verbal protests that were standardized on a tape recorder, so that they were the same for all participants.

As the learner's errors mounted, the teacher increased the shock. If the teacher baulked at continuing, the experimenter issued one or more escalating commands, such as 'Please continue', 'You must continue' and 'You have no other choice'. At 75 volts, the learner moaned when the teacher threw the switch. At 150 volts, he moaned again and said, 'Experimenter! That's all. Get me out of here. I told you I had heart trouble. My heart's starting to bother me now. Get me out of here, please. . . . I refuse to go on. Let me out'. Beyond 200 volts, he emitted agonized screams every time a shock was delivered, yelling 'Let me out! Let me out!' At 300 volts, the learner refused to answer and continued screaming to be let out. At 345 volts and beyond, there was only silence. Full obedience was operationally defined as continuing to the maximum shock level of 450 volts.

RESULTS

Participants wrestled with a dilemma. Should they continue to hurt this innocent person, as the experimenter commanded, or should they stop the learner's pain by openly disobeying? Most participants became distressed. Some trembled, sweated, laughed nervously or, in a few cases, experienced convulsions. But would they obey? Make a prediction: what percentage of people do you think obeyed to 450 volts?

Before the study, Milgram had asked psychiatrists, professors, university students and middle-class adults to predict the outcome. They said that virtually no one (1%) would obey fully. Indeed, most participants baulked or protested at one time or another and said they would not continue. But ultimately, 26 of the 40 men (65%) obeyed all the way to the end (Figure 14.11).

A recent meta-analysis on data from 21 of the 23 studies conducted by Milgram, suggests that on average the percentage of participants progressing to maximum voltage is 43.6% (Haslam, Loughnan, & Perry, 2014). The percentage of full obedience differs depending on several factors, such as the proximity of the experimenter to the learner.

DISCUSSION

Milgram's research has generated controversy for decades (Blass, 2002; Miller, 2004; Haslam et al., 2014). Its ethics were harshly criticized because participants were deceived, were exposed to substantial stress and risked long-lasting negative effects to their self-image (Baumrind, 1964). Milgram countered that the research was so socially significant as to warrant the deception, that participants were carefully debriefed afterwards and that psychiatric follow-ups of a sample of obedient participants suggested no long-term ill effects. Indeed, Milgram followed up more than 1,000 participants in his experiments and reported that 83.7% of those who had participated in his studies were in fact glad to have been in the experiment, with only 1.3% indicating they were sorry they participated (Milgram, 1992, p. 186). Weighing the costs and benefits, do you believe that this research was justified? Do you think a similar research design can be used today, given the ethical guidelines described in Chapter 2? And if not, how would you design a study able to answer similar questions like the ones Milgram was interested in?

Researchers also debate why obedience was high, but many agree with Milgram's view that participants psychologically transferred much of the 'responsibility' for the learner's fate to the experimenter. Participants viewed the experimenter as an expert, a legitimate authority figure (Blass & Schmitt, 2001). While administering the shock, some participants stated that they 'were not responsible' for what happened. Others asked, 'Who is responsible if something happens to the learner?' When the experimenter replied, I am responsible', participants felt greater freedom to continue. Yet they were the ones flipping the switch.

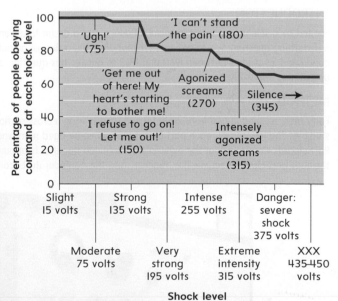

FIGURE 14.11 You must obey.

This graph shows the percentage of male participants who continued to shock the learner through various voltage levels.

Source: Based on Milgram, 1974.

How would you have responded in Milgram's experiment? Almost all of our students say that they would have disobeyed either before or when the victim began protesting at the 150-volt level. Indeed, in one study, students in psychology classes – whether familiar with Milgram's results or not – said that they would stop at around 150 volts (Geher, Bauman, Hubbard, & Legare, 2002). So suppose we conduct an obedience study today but with real electric shocks and with you as the learner. The teacher will be a randomly selected student from your class. Are you confident that this student will disobey the experimenter and stop giving you shocks when you start yelling in protest? Few of our students or other students express such confidence (Geher et al., 2002). In short, virtually all of us are confident that *we* would disobey early on, but we are less sure about *other* people – and they in turn are not so sure about *us*.

Factors that May Influence Obedience

By manipulating the following aspects of the laboratory situation, Milgram and other researchers obtained obedience rates ranging from 0% to over 90%:

1. *Remoteness of the victim*: obedience was greatest when the learner was out of sight. When the teacher and learner were placed in the same room, obedience dropped to 40%. Further, when the teacher had to make physical contact and force the learner's hand onto a 'shock plate', obedience dropped to 30%.

2. *Closeness and legitimacy of the authority figure*: obedience was highest when the authority figure was close by and perceived as legitimate. When the experimenter left the scene and gave orders by phone or when an 'ordinary person' (a confederate) took over and gave the orders, obedience dropped to about 20%.

3. *Diffusion of responsibility*: when another 'participant' (actually a confederate) flipped the shock switch and the real participants only had to perform another aspect of the task, 93% obeyed. In short, *obedience increases when someone else does the dirty work*. In contrast, when Harvey Tilker (1970) made participants feel fully responsible for the learner's welfare, not a single person obeyed to the end.

4. *Personal characteristics*: Milgram compared the political orientations, religious affiliations, occupations, education, length of military service and psychological characteristics of obedient versus disobedient participants. Differences were weak or non-existent.

5. *Gender differences*: Milgram also compared differences between male and female participants but found no difference in obedience – actually obedience was exactly the same for both men and women. Using procedures similar to Milgram's, other researchers also failed to find consistent sex differences in obedience rates (Burger, 2009; Shanab & Yahya, 1977).

Would People Obey Today?

Our students often ask us, 'If Milgram's obedience study were conducted today, would the results be similar?' and for years we have been answering, 'We suspect so'. Here is why. For 40 years after Milgram's research, experiments were conducted in different countries, in 'real-world' settings, TV shows (e.g., *Discovery*, 2011) and laboratories, using a similar 'electric shock' procedure and different obedience procedures, and with children, adolescents and adults as participants. Overall, the findings revealed levels of obedience that were depressingly consistent with Milgram's results (Meeus & Raaijmakers, 1986; Burger, 2009).

Focus 14.10 Describe Milgram's research, factors that increase and decrease obedience, and implications for society.

Lessons Learned

What lessons shall we draw from this research? Certainly, it is *not* that people are apathetic or evil. Participants became stressed precisely because they did care about the learner's welfare. Neither can we conclude that we are sheep. If we were, obedience would be high across all situations, which is not the case. Rather, Milgram sums up a key lesson as follows:

> It would be a mistake . . . to make the simpleminded statement that kindly and good persons disobey while those who are cruel do not . . . often, it is not so much the kind of person a man is as the kind of situation in which he finds himself that determines how he will act.   (Milgram, 1974, p. 205)

Thus, by arranging the situation appropriately, most people – ordinary, decent citizens – can be induced to follow orders from an authority figure they perceive as legitimate, even when doing so contributes to harming an innocent person. The applicability of this principle to the Holocaust and other atrocities seems clear (Blass, 2002). During the Holocaust, obedience was made easier because most of the personnel working at the concentration camps were cogs in a horrendous wheel: they did not pull the switch to flood the chambers with gas but instead performed other tasks. Their victims also were 'remote' at the moment of their murder. Further, to lessen concentration camp workers' feelings of responsibility, Hitler's subordinate, Heinrich Himmler, told them in manipulative speeches that only he and Hitler were personally responsible for what took place (Dawidowicz, 1975).

FIGURE 14.12 Contemporary obedience.

Do you remember how this photograph shocked the world? In 2005, US Army reservist Lynndie England faced a court martial for assaulting prisoners in the 2003 Abu Ghraib Iraqi prisoner scandal. Was this the real Lynndie England? Her family said it could not be the same loving person they knew. Army reservist Charles Graner, the presumed ringleader of the guards involved in the scandal claimed in his own court martial that they were following orders. The military jury rejected the claim. In editorials and news reports, the media turned to the lessons of Milgram's research to try to make sense of the guards' behaviour.

Source: © AP/Press Association Images

> **social norms** shared expectations about how people should think, feel and behave
>
> **social role** a set of norms that characterizes how people in a given social position ought to behave

> **Focus 14.11** What is the difference between compliance and conformity?

Does obedience research suggest that we are not responsible for following orders? This is a moral and legal question, not a scientific one. But if anything, this research should heighten our responsibility for being aware of the pitfalls of blind obedience and prevent us from being so smug or naive as to feel that such events 'could never happen here'. Beyond obedience, Milgram's research provides yet another powerful example of how social contexts can induce people to behave in ways that they never would have imagined possible (Figure 14.12).

SOCIAL INFLUENCE IN GROUPS

We have seen how other people can directly persuade us to comply with a request and obey their orders. Most of these compliance techniques make use of existing social norms, such as the norm to reciprocate, or the norm to obey authority. Such norms can have a powerful influence on behaviour. But exactly how do such norms develop, what is their influence on our beliefs and attitudes, and why are they so influential in guiding our behaviour?

Social norms are shared expectations about how people should think, feel and behave, and they are the glue that binds groups together (Schaller & Crandall, 2004). Some norms are formal laws, but many are implicit and unspoken. Such norms regulate daily behaviour without our conscious awareness; we take them for granted until they are violated. To illustrate this, I recently gave my class an unusual assignment: without doing anything illegal, each student was to violate some unspoken rule of social behaviour and observe how others reacted. One student licked her plate clean at a formal dinner, receiving cold stares from the other guests. Another boarded a nearly empty city bus, sat down next to the only other passenger, and said 'Hi!' The passenger sat up stiffly and stared out the window.

A **social role** consists of a set of norms that characterizes how people in a given social position ought to behave. The social roles of 'college student', 'professor', 'police officer', 'spouse' or 'female' carry different sets of behaviour expectations (e.g., Eagly, 1987). Because we may wear many hats in our daily life, *role conflict* can occur when the norms accompanying different roles clash. College students who hold jobs and have children often experience role conflict as they try to juggle the competing demands of school, work, and parenthood.

Norm Formation

It is difficult to imagine any society, organization or social group functioning well without norms. In a classic experiment, Muzafer Sherif (1935) found that even randomly created groups develop norms. The task involved an optical illusion called the *autokinetic effect*: when people stare at a dot of light projected on a screen in a dark room, they begin to perceive the dot as moving, even though it really is stationary. When Sherif tested college students individually over several trials, each student perceived the light to move a different amount, from an inch or two (2 to 5 cm) to almost a foot (30 cm).

Later the students were randomly placed into groups of three and made further judgements. As group members heard one another's judgements over several sessions, their judgements converged and a group norm evolved. Interestingly, even when Sherif tested his participants the subsequent day while they were alone, they still conformed to this group norm when judging the movement of the light. Sherif's finding has been replicated in other countries and with different tasks. Whether at a cultural level or in small random groups, humans develop common standards for behaviour and judgement (Arrow & Burns, 2004). The participants in such experiments do not say 'Hey, let's develop a group norm'. It just happens. And, just as norms can vary across cultures, the evolved norm for the autokinetic effect varied from group to group (Figure 14.13).

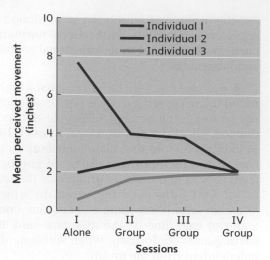

FIGURE 14.13 The evolution of norms across time and cultures.

(*Left*) In 2001, the Netherlands was the first country to allow same-sex marriages. Although still prohibited in most countries, same-sex marriage is increasingly being allowed, totalling 15 countries as of 2013, indicating a shift in social norms regarding same-sex marriages. (*Right*) Even randomly created groups spontaneously form norms. In Sherif's experiments, individuals' autokinetic judgements made alone (session I) began to converge when they were made in the presence of two other participants (sessions II, III and IV). Each mean is based on 100 judgements per session. These data are from one of the three-person groups. Notice that the final norm is not simply the average of the original judgements that the group members made while alone.

Sources: Left, © Martin Purmensky; Right, based on Sherif, 1935.

Conformity

Norms can influence behaviour only if people conform to them. Without *conformity* – the adjustment of individual behaviours, attitudes and beliefs to a group standard – we would have social chaos. Although the experiments on the autokinetic effect show us how group norms develop, it does not tell us exactly why and through what process people conform to these norms. Social psychological research has focused mainly on two varieties of conformity. At times we conform due to **informational social influence**, following the opinions or behaviour of other people because we believe that they have accurate knowledge and that what they are doing is right. In the autokinetic studies this form of influence would have been present. As there was no 'correct' answer, it is not surprising that participants' own judgements were 'informed' by the judgements of others around them.

We may, however, also succumb to **normative social influence**, conforming to obtain the rewards that come from being accepted by other people while at the same time avoiding their rejection (Cialdini & Goldstein, 2004; Deutsch & Gerard, 1955). In a series of landmark conformity experiments, Solomon Asch (1951, 1956) tried to rule out informational influence by using stimuli that *could* be answered correctly. In the experimental condition, groups of college students performed several trials of a simple visual task (Figure 14.14a) in which they were asked – for various sets of lines – which of three comparison lines was the same length as a standard line (line A). Only one member of the group, however, actually was a participant. The rest were accomplices of the experimenter.

Group members sat around a table and were called on in order. The real participant sat next to last. According to plan, every accomplice intentionally gave the same wrong answer on some trials. Imagine yourself hearing the first group member choose line 1. (You think to yourself, 'Huh?') Then the next four members also choose line 1. (You're wondering, 'Can this really be?') Now it is your turn.

Would anybody conform to the group's incorrect judgements? Asch found that overall, participants conformed 37% of the time, compared with a mere 1% error rate in a control condition where people judged the lines by themselves. This finding stunned many scientists because the task was so easy and the confederates did not overtly pressure participants to conform. After the task was over, some participants told the experimenter that they

> **informational social influence** following the opinions or behaviour of other people because we believe that they have accurate knowledge and that what they are doing is right
>
> **normative social influence** conforming to obtain the rewards that come from being accepted by other people while at the same time avoiding their rejection

> **Focus 14.12** Use the concepts of informational and normative social influence to explain how social norms and roles guide behaviour.

FIGURE 14.14 Asch's classic conformity experiment.

In Asch's (1956) conformity experiments, students were asked to judge which of three comparison lines was the same length as the standard line. They performed this task for multiple trials, using a different set of standard and comparison lines each time.

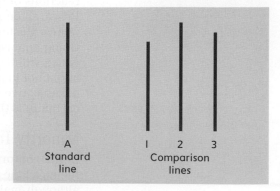

felt the group was wrong but went along to avoid making waves and suffering possible rejection and ridicule. This reflects normative social influence. After several trials, other participants yielded to informational social influence and began to doubt their eyesight and judgement.

It was clear to Asch he had created a highly demanding condition in which participants found it hard to stick to their personal judgements. What struck Asch most was therefore not so much the amount of people that conformed, but actually the amount of people that *did not* (Friend, Rafferty, & Bramel, 1990). In other experiments he therefore sought to identify factors that may contribute to people's independence, or lack of conformity. One of the factors that influenced conformity was *group size*. Conformity decreased from 35% to about 5% as group size decreased from four confederates to one. Another factor that influenced the extent to which participants conformed was the *presence of a dissenter*. According to plan, one confederate disagreed with the others (e.g., the majority said 'line 3'; the dissenter said 'line 2' or even 'line 1'). This greatly reduced participants' conformity. When someone dissents, this serves as a model for remaining independent from the group.

Turner (1991) developed a *third* reason why people might conform to others based on assumptions made in social identity theory (Tajfel & Turner, 1979): **referent informational influence**. Remember that one of the assumptions made by social identity theory is that while the group is external to the self (as the group of confederates in the Asch paradigm) it is also internal to the self (as part of one's self-definition: social identity). So, to the extent that individuals identify with a certain group, they incorporate the group norm as part of the self. This suggests that individuals will be influenced primarily by members of the groups they identify with (i.e., *reference* groups). Indeed, research has demonstrated that individuals are more susceptible to social influence when information is provided by fellow in-group members as compared to out-group members (van Knippenberg & Wilke, 1988).

referent informational influence individuals will be influenced primarily by members of the groups they identify with (i.e., reference groups)

According to Turner's self-categorization theory, there are several reasons why shared social identity is so important for mutual influence between individuals (Turner, 1991). First, the group forms a link between individuals. Subsequently, if people self-categorize as a member of a particular group, they have the tendency to see themselves as similar to fellow in-group members in attitudes and beliefs. This similarity leads to an expectation of agreement with these others when judging reality. If we *are* the same then we should *think* the same, one might say. Second, such agreement with similar others should produce a sense of *subjective validity* of one's own thoughts and behaviour as being correct or appropriate. Indeed, individuals feel more confident about the correctness of their beliefs and attitudes when they are shared with other in-group members (Bar-Tal, 1998; Spears & Manstead, 1990). Third, disagreeing with similar others should produce uncertainty about the validity of one's thoughts and behaviour. Finally, such uncertainty will motivate individuals to engage in a process of mutual influence in order to reach agreement.

One example might clarify this process. Imagine someone entering a mosque wearing shoes (which is not allowed). Who do you think will bring about the most vehement reactions of the people inside the mosque: a fellow Muslim or a non-Muslim, say a tourist? Research on the 'black sheep effect' (Marques, Yzerbyt, & Leyens, 1988) suggests that the fellow Muslim will bring about the strongest reaction. This person should know better. Going against an in-group norm brings about uncertainty about the validity of the norm, which will lead to a strong tendency to engage in mutual influence. The tourist, however, might not know the rules. He or she is also less likely to be a threat for the in-group's sense of subjective validity. Consistent with this, Hogg and Abrams (1993) suggest that subjective certainty is the primary motivation underlying social identification with a group.

Minority Influence

In his conformity studies, Asch was especially interested in the influence of a majority facing a lone participant. When we look around us, everyday live experience shows us that although majority influence is powerful, in politics, in business, and in other real-world contexts, dissenting information presented by the minority can also be very persuasive (see, for example, Figure 14.15).

FIGURE 14.15 Women marching for equal rights.

Although initially an unpopular view, thanks to a small active minority (the suffragette movement) in the late nineteenth and early twentieth centuries women obtained equal voting rights. Women's rights have improved significantly over the past century.

Source: © Bettman/Corbis.

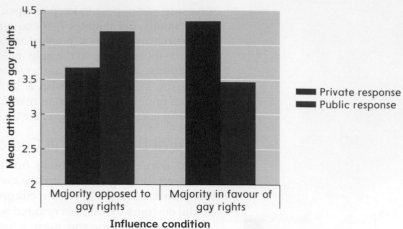

FIGURE 14.16 Majority and minority influence.

Participants' attitudes on gay rights on a seven-point scale after reading the group discussion. Higher scores indicate a stronger *opposition* to gay rights.

Source: Maass and Clark, 1983, study I.

In a first formulation of a theory of minority influence, Moscovici, Lage and Naffrechoux (1969) investigated what happens when a minority tries to influence a majority. Instead of confronting one participant with a majority of confederates, Moscovici and colleagues confronted a majority of naive subjects (six) with a minority of confederates (two). Participants had to judge the colour of a blue slide which varied in intensity. The two confederates responded by saying 'green', either consistently on every trial or on only two-thirds of the trials. Results showed that only 1% of the participants responded with 'green' when the minority was inconsistent in their judgements, whereas 8% of the participants responded with 'green' when the minority consistently gave the answer 'green'.

This line of research culminated in a dual-process theory of social influence (Moscovici, 1976). According to this theory both minorities and majorities can exert strong influence. However, by virtue of its size, majorities are more likely to trigger a need for consensus, with individuals being afraid to publicly disagree with a majority. Majority influence then is more likely to lead to *compliance*, where individuals *publicly* concur to a majority, without necessarily leading to a deeper change of actual attitudes or beliefs. This reflects normative social influence. In contrast, minority influence is more likely to lead to a *private* acceptance and actual attitudinal change or *conversion*, which reflects informational social influence.

One study by Maass and Clark (1983) illustrates this point nicely. In one study, participants were asked to read a summary of a group discussion on gay rights. This discussion had supposedly taken place between five fellow students. In all cases of the discussion, one of the students (minority) had a different opinion regarding gay rights than the four others (majority). In order to avoid possible effects due to the direction of the arguments, half of the participants read a discussion in which the majority was presented as favouring gay rights and the minority as opposing gay rights. For the other half of the participants the roles were reversed, with the minority being presented as favouring gay rights. The participants were subsequently asked to either *publicly* express their attitudes, or express their attitudes in *private*. As can be seen in Figure 14.16, when participants were asked to declare their attitudes in public, they voiced agreement with the majority, regardless of whether or not they favoured or opposed gay rights. In contrast, when asked to express their attitude in private, by writing down their views, participants' attitudes reflected an agreement with the opinion of the minority.

The exact processes underlying minority influence are still being debated by researchers (Stroebe, 2010). Nonetheless, it is clear that dissenting opinions are more likely to sway the majority when they come from several minority members rather than just one (Clark, 2001). Serge Moscovici (1985) proposes that to maximize its influence, the minority must further (1) be highly committed to its point of view, (2) remain independent in the face of majority

pressure, yet appear to keep an open mind, (3) disrupt the majority norm, thereby producing uncertainty and doubt, (4) focus attention on itself, make itself visible, (5) show there is an alternative coherent point of view, and (6) convey the necessity for the majority to shift towards the minority as the only means of restoring social stability. Indeed, reviewing almost 100 studies, Wendy Wood and co-workers (1994) found that minority influence is strongest when the minority maintains a highly consistent position over time. Nonetheless, many studies on minority influence reveal a pattern we might all be familiar with: 'the impact of majority sources is much greater than that of minorities' (Stroebe, 2010, p. 220).

Cultural Differences in Conformity

Social norms lose invisibility not only when they are violated (remember the student boarding a nearly empty city bus and sitting beside the only other passenger) but also when we examine behaviour across cultures and historical periods. In doing so, we see that many social customs we take for granted as 'normal' – from gender roles and child-rearing to views about love, marriage and, even, what constitutes an attractive body shape – are not 'normal' when judged from other cultural perspectives (Tovée, Swami, Furnham, & Mangalparsad, 2006). Norms even regulate such subtle aspects of social behaviour as the amount of *personal space* that we prefer when interacting with people (Li, 2001). For example, Japanese sit farther apart when conversing than do Venezuelans, and Americans prefer an intermediate distance (Sussman & Rosenfeld, 1982). A recent survey among approximately 7,000 individuals across 33 nations also suggests cultures differ in the extent to which they express and adhere to social norms. Some countries are more 'loose', showing a high tolerance for individuals deviating from social norms, and lacking strict formality and discipline (e.g., Estonia, the Netherlands, Israel, Brazil). Other countries are more rigorously formal or 'tight', showing little tolerance for deviant behaviour, and a positive attitude towards discipline and adherence to rules (e.g., Pakistan, Malaysia, Singapore; Gelfand et al., 2011).

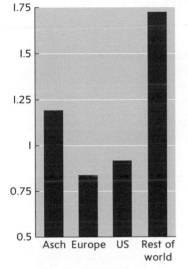

FIGURE 14.17 The amount of conformity found in Asch replication studies around the world.

Source: American Psychological Association/ Psychological Bulletin A

One informative example of how culture influences normative behaviour, comes from a meta-analysis reporting 134 published studies using Asch's line judgement tasks (Bond & Smith, 1996). Of these 134 studies, 97 of the experiments had been conducted in the USA from 1951 to 1990. Rod Bond and Peter Smith (1996) found that the overall level of conformity decreased slightly over a time period from 1951 to 1990. As can be seen in Figure 14.17, the degree of group influence on conformity responses was found to be lowest in Europe, followed by the USA and the 'rest of the world' (e.g., Japan, Brazil, Kuwait). The researchers concluded that individuals from collectivistic countries seem more likely to yield to the majority in the Asch paradigm. This seems to reflect the conceptual difference between individualistic versus collectivistic countries (Triandis, 1990), where individuals in collectivistic countries are assumed to place a higher value on harmony in their interpersonal relationships.

BEHAVIOUR IN GROUPS

No man (or woman) is an island. As social animals, we have a need to affiliate with others. Indeed, Baumeister and Leary (1995) suggest that the most fundamental of all human motives is the *need to belong*. Research on *ostracism* (ignoring or excluding someone) suggests that this might well be the case.

Psychologist Naomi Eisenberger and co-workers (Eisenberger, Lieberman, & Williams, 2003) measured the brain activity of research participants who played an interactive computer game with, presumably, two other unseen players. In reality, there were no other players and the game was computer-controlled. The game, Cyberball, involved tossing a virtual ball back and forth among the three players. After a period during which all three players interacted online, the other two players suddenly ignored the participant by tossing the ball back and forth only to each other. The real participants felt excluded and distressed, and neural activity patterns in their cerebral cortex were 'very similar to those found in studies of physical pain . . . providing evidence that the experience . . . of social and physical pain share a common neuroanatomical basis' (Eisenberger et al., 2003, p. 291). Ostracism, or being ignored and excluded, dampens people's moods, decreases their sense of belonging, and – perhaps by heightening their fear of further rejection – makes them more likely to conform to the clearly incorrect judgements of a group (Williams, 2007).

Focus 14.13 Discuss the psychological effects of ostracism.

Because of our strong need to belong and affiliate, much of human behaviour occurs in groups. People often form groups to share interests and activities (play soccer, climb mountains, have fun), to perform tasks and achieve goals that are too complex or demanding to be accomplished by one person (build offices, develop computers) or to provide comfort and reduce uncertainty (support groups). Apart from forming groups, people are also often born in groups that have their own idiosyncratic system of norms and values (families, ethnic groups, nations). However, although groups come in all sorts of shapes and sizes, with different goals and motivations, they share a number of key features. We discuss some of these features below.

Social Loafing

In 1913 Max Ringelmann, a French agricultural engineer, measured the force that men exerted while pulling on a rope as hard as they could. Individually, the men averaged 63 kilograms (kg) of pull. Thus you might expect that eight men pulling in unison would exert a combined force of about 504 kg (i.e., 8×63 kg). Surprisingly, group performance was 51% below expectations, and one contributing factor was **social loafing**, the tendency for people to expend less individual effort when working in a group than when working alone. In contrast to social facilitation experiments, in which a person performs a task individually (in front of an audience or with a co-actor) and does not pool her or his effort with anyone, social loafing involves collective performance. Why does social loafing occur? Steven Karau and Kipling Williams (1993, 2001) propose a *collective effort model*: on a collective task, people will put forth only as much effort as they expect is needed to attain a valued goal. In support of this model, studies reveal that social loafing is *more* likely to occur when:

- the person believes that individual performance within the group is not being monitored
- the task (goal) or the group has less value or meaning to the person
- the person expects that co-workers will display high effort (Hart, Karau, Stasson, & Kerr, 2004).

Social loafing also depends on gender and culture. It occurs more strongly in all-male groups than in all-female or mixed-sex groups, possibly because women may be more concerned about group outcomes than are men. Participants from individualistic cultures (e.g., Canada, the UK) exhibit more social loafing than people from collectivistic cultures (e.g., China, Japan, Taiwan), in which group goals are especially valued.

Social loafing suggests that in terms of group performance, the whole is less than the sum of its parts. But this is not always the case. Social loafing may disappear when members highly value their group or the task goal. In fact, to achieve a highly desired goal, some people may engage in **social compensation**, working harder in a group than when alone to compensate for other members' lower output (Hart, Bridgett, & Karau, 2001; Todd, Seok, Kerr, & Messé, 2006). To inhibit social loafing it seems important then to both reward (and monitor) individuals for their individual performance, as well as rewarding them for the group's performance (e.g., Pearsall, Christian, & Ellis, 2010).

Group Polarization

Key decisions are often entrusted to groups, such as committees, because groups are assumed to be more conservative than individuals and less likely to be irrational. Is this assumption correct? It is, as long as the group is generally conservative to begin with. In such cases, the group's final opinion or attitude will likely be even *more conservative*. But if the group members lean towards a liberal or risky viewpoint to begin with, the group's decision will tend to become *more liberal or riskier*. This principle is called **group polarization**: when a group of like-minded people discusses an issue, the 'average' opinion of group members tends to become more extreme (Moscovici & Zavalloni, 1969). For example, people who share a sense of injustice and deprivation may join together in isolated groups, such as 'terrorist cells', and through interaction become more extreme over time (Sutton & Douglas, 2013).

Why does group polarization occur? One reason, reflecting normative social influence, is that individuals who are attracted to a group may be motivated to adopt a more extreme position to gain the group's approval. A second reason, reflecting informational

social loafing the tendency for people to expend less individual effort when working in a group than when working alone

Focus 14.14 Compare social loafing and social compensation. What do you think is the main difference?

social compensation working harder in a group than when alone to compensate for other members' lower output

group polarization when a group of like-minded people discusses an issue, the 'average' opinion of group members tends to become more extreme

social influence, is that during group discussions people hear arguments supporting their positions that they had not previously considered (Sia, Tan, & Wei, 2002). A final reason, based on referent informational social influence, is that people will conform to the most prototypical position of the group, where the prototype is often more extreme than the actual average of a group (McGarthy, Turner, Hogg, Davidson, & Wetherell, 1992).

Groupthink

After the US military ignored warning signs of imminent attack by Japan in 1941, the fleet at Pearl Harbor was destroyed in a 'surprise' attack. In 1961 President Kennedy and his advisers launched the hopelessly doomed Bay of Pigs invasion of Cuba. After analysing these and other historical accounts of disastrous group decisions, Irving Janis (1982) concluded that in each case the decision makers fell victim to a process that he named **groupthink**, the tendency of group members to suspend critical thinking because they are striving to seek agreement. As a result, during the build-up to the Bay of Pigs invasion, objections to the plans for invasion were ignored, plans from people close to Kennedy were uncritically accepted, and the inferiority of Cuba's military competence was highly exaggerated.

> **groupthink** the tendency of group members to suspend critical thinking because they are striving to seek agreement

Similar to group polarization, groupthink represents an example of normative influence. Thus, the desire to reach agreement is especially strong in groups that have a high sense of *cohesiveness* (the sense of solidarity and 'oneness' that affectively binds people as group members; Hogg & Vaughan, 2005), are motivated to *maintain a positive view* of their group, and within which a *strong group norm* emerges regarding preferred solutions (Turner & Pratkanis, 1998; Baron, 2005). The members of such highly valued groups can be so committed to reaching consensus, and remaining loyal and agreeable, that they suspend their critical judgement. In the business world, groupthink can contribute to poor management decisions that adversely affect the financial value and public reputation of the company (Eaton, 2001).

Various symptoms signal that groupthink is at work. Group members who express doubt get *direct pressure* to stop rocking the boat. Some members serve as *mind guards* and prevent negative information from reaching the group. Ultimately, members display *self-censorship* and withhold their doubts, creating an *illusion of unanimity* in which each member comes to believe that everyone else seems to agree with the decision. Overall, the group leader and members who favour the leader's position will have their confidence in the decision reinforced, whereas members who have doubts will feel pressure to go along with the group (Henningsen, Henningsen, Eden, & Cruz, 2006).

Groupthink has been thought to occur in many disastrous group decisions. One example concerns the US invasion of Iraq following the 9/11 terrorist attack on the World Trade Center. Here the emergent group norm was based on a 'long shared [...] philosophy regarding the strategic wisdom of using unilateral, pre-emptive military interventions (or their threat) as a key aspect of U.S. foreign policy' (Baron, 2005, p. 242), aka the *Bush Doctrine*. The terrorist attack led to a high sense of group cohesiveness and need to 'defend' the group's positive sense of self. The decision to invade Iraq was partly based on the faulty assumption that 'the US invasion and rebuilding of Iraq would be a relatively painless and rapid affair, with US troops being greeted with cheers and flowers, and the costs of nation building minimized by sales of Iraqi oil and the cooperation of a grateful nation' (Baron, 2005, p. 221).

> **Focus 14.15** Describe social loafing, social compensation, and the causes and consequences of group polarization and groupthink.

Can groupthink be prevented? Janis suggested that it might, if the leader remains impartial during discussions, encourages critical thinking, brings in outsiders to offer their opinions, and divides the larger group into subgroups – to see if each subgroup independently reaches the same decision. Of course, while critical debate may enhance the odds of making a good decision, it does not guarantee a positive outcome and in some cases may cause the group to become deadlocked (Kowert, 2002).

Deindividuation

Years ago in New York City, a man sat perched on the ledge of an upper-story window for an hour while a crowd of nearly 500 people on the street below shouted at him to jump. Fortunately, police rescued the man. New York is not alone. When Leon Mann (1981)

analysed newspaper reports of incidents in which crowds were present when a person threatened to jump off a building, in 10 of 21 cases the crowd had encouraged the person to jump. Why would people in crowds act this way?

In crowds, people may experience **deindividuation**, a loss of individuality that leads to disinhibited behaviour (Festinger, Pepitone, & Newcomb, 1952; Zimbardo, 2004). But what is the primary aspect of deindividuation that disinhibits behaviour? Tom Postmes and Russell Spears (1998) meta-analysed 60 deindividuation studies and determined that *anonymity to outsiders* was the key. Conditions that make an individual less identifiable to people *outside* the group reduce feelings of accountability and, slightly but consistently, increase the risk of antisocial actions (Figure 14.18).

FIGURE 14.18 Deindividuation.

Anonymity to outsiders can lead to a loss of restraint that causes people to engage in uncharacteristic behaviours.

Source: ©iStock.com/erlucho

One of the most striking examples of the effect of deindividuation comes from a famous study conducted by Philip Zimbardo and colleagues, called the *Stanford Prison Experiment* (Zimbardo et al., 1973). In the summer of 1971, Zimbardo and colleagues created a mock prison in the basement of the Stanford University psychology department, containing three prison cells complete with iron bars, dark solitary confinement areas, and offices for guards. They invited students to participate in a study on prison life that would run for two weeks and paid $15 a day. From seventy students they chose two dozen participants who were most normal, average and healthy on a battery of psychological tests and interviews. The participants were randomly assigned to the roles of guards or prisoners. To increase 'mundane realism', and with the help of Californian police, the 'prisoners' were taken into custody during a surprise mass arrest. They were handcuffed, searched, shown their legal rights and taken through a formal booking procedure at police headquarters.

> **deindividuation** a loss of individuality that leads to disinhibited behaviour

When they arrived at the mock prison, the prisoners underwent a degradation ceremony where they were deloused, fitted with ankle chains and nylon stocking caps to simulate their hair being cut off, and dressed in identical prison uniforms, with numbers sewn on front and back and without underwear. The guards met the Saturday before to help in the final stages of constructing the prison and to formulate prison rules. They also received military-style uniforms from a local army surplus store and wore reflecting sunglasses that prevented prisoners from making direct eye contact. No names were used and prisoners had to address guards as 'Mr. Correctional Officer'. All these measures were taken to ensure participants took on their assigned roles and to make them less identifiable as individuals.

Unbeknownst to the participants, the mock prison was fitted with cameras and microphones, and what the researchers observed astonished them. After only a day, the guards asserted their total authority over the prisoners. They made the prisoners ask permission to do virtually anything, including going to the toilet. The guards conducted roll calls in the middle of the night to assert their power and disrupt the prisoners' sleep, and they forced prisoners to do push-ups, sometimes with their foot pushing down on the prisoner's back. For their part, the prisoners became increasingly passive and depressed. They hated the guards but were powerless against them. After a few days, one prisoner cracked emotionally. Soon another broke down. Before long, the demoralized prisoners became nothing more than what the guards expected them to be: piteous objects of scorn and abuse. As one guard recalled, 'I was surprised at myself. I made them . . . clean out the toilets with their bare hands. I practically considered the prisoners cattle' (Zimbardo et al., 1973, p. 42). What began as a two-week simulation of prison life had to be halted after only six days.

Zimbardo and colleagues concluded that deindividuation was a key factor in the cruelty exhibited by the guards and the hatred and emotional reactions by the prisoners. Putting on the uniforms and taking away their individuality enhanced anonymity, thereby weakening the individual's sense of personal responsibility and giving rise to destructive behaviour unregulated by moral and ethical codes normally associated with being individuated. Thus, reducing anonymity – and thereby increasing public accountability – may be one approach to counteracting the negative effects of deindividuation.

Postmes and Spears (1998) take the explanation, and possible solution of the negative effects as a consequence of deindividuation, a step further in their social identity model

of deindividuation effects (Spears, Postmes, Lea, & Watt, 2001). They suggest that being anonymous to outsiders enhances the individual's tendency to focus on his or her *social* identity with the group and makes the person more responsive to emerging group norms. One consequence would be that the antisocial effects of deindividuation actually occur not because of a *lack* of norms, but because of the *existence* of norms that actually approve of antisocial behaviour.

Taking a closer look at Zimbardo's Stanford prison experiment, we can see how a group norm was instilled that might explain the antisocial behaviour of the prison guards. Take the following example of the way in which guards were instructed to behave:

> *You can create in the prisoners feelings of boredom, a sense of fear to some degree, you can create a notion of arbitrariness that their life is totally controlled by us, by the system, you, me – and they'll have no privacy. They'll have no freedom of action, they can do nothing, say nothing that we don't permit. We're going to take away their individuality in various ways. In general what all this leads to is a sense of powerlessness.*   (Zimbardo, 1989, cited in Reicher & Haslam, 2006, p. 4)

If anything, the above instructions are a norm that might easily lead to antisocial behaviour from the guards. Indeed, Reicher and Haslam (2006) conducted an extensive replication of Zimbardo's Stanford prison experiment in cooperation with the BBC, without such instructions to the guards. Interestingly, this replication did not lead to extreme antisocial behaviour, more the opposite. An almost egalitarian system was developed under certain circumstances, with guards giving privileges to prisoners and both prisoners and guards getting along rather well. The results of this replication suggest that the way in which individuals behave in groups is more a matter of the norms and values that are attached to their social identity. These norms can either be antisocial *or* pro-social (Jetten, Spears, & Manstead, 1997). Thus, another way in which antisocial behaviour developing from deindividuation can be counteracted is to make sure that pro-social norms are in place and an integral part of the social group.

Mass Panic

One other instance in which pro-social norms in a group play an important role in guiding behaviour is that of a crowd of strangers faced with an imminent threat. In 1989 a soccer match between FC Liverpool and Nottingham Forest at Hillsborough football stadium ended in tragedy when thousands of soccer fans were directed into already overcrowded pens. Many fans tried desperately to climb over the perimeter fences to get themselves into safety for fear of suffocation or being crushed to death. The unfortunate result of the crush and ensuing panic: 96 people killed and hundreds wounded (Figure 14.19a). More recently in 2010, mass panic at the entrance of the rave party 'Love Parade' in Duisburg, Germany, left 15 people killed and approximately 300 people injured.

In such instances it is difficult to see pro-social norms at work. Indeed, early research on mass panic assumed that injuries and deaths occurring in the process of emergency

Focus 14.16 Describe deindividuation, its main cause, and how conditions in the Stanford prison study may have fostered it.

Focus 14.17 Describe what the role of US Army reservist Lynndie England's superiors might have been (see Figure 14.13). Could they have prevented what happened in the 2003 Abu Ghraib Iraqi prisoner scandal?

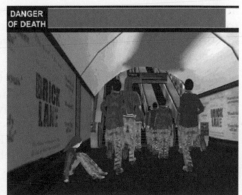

FIGURE 14.19 Mass panic.

(a) Overcrowded pens led to the death of 96 people during a football match between FC Liverpool and Nottingham Forest in Hillsborough football stadium in 1989. (b) A still from a virtual reality simulation depicting an evacuee in need of help (Drury et al., 2009).

Source: (a) Trinity Mirror/Mirrorpics/Alamy; (b) Drury et al., 2009.

(a)   (b)

evacuation were due to contagious outbursts of mass irrationality where the individuals involved had only one concern: 'save me first!' (for a review, see Chertkoff & Kushigian, 1999). These models were quickly disregarded as overly simplistic, given ample evidence that, instead, such mass emergencies were more often characterized by mutual aid, courtesy and orderliness (e.g., Fritz & Williams, 1957). Subsequent investigations suggested that everyday social norms continue to shape the behaviour of individuals even when facing such emergencies (e.g., Johnson, 1988). However, due to practical and ethical restraints, it has been a challenge for social scientists to investigate exactly when and how such norms guide behaviour in emergencies. Indeed, how could you simulate the impending threat of death, necessary to investigate emergency evacuation dynamics, without creating serious stress in your participants and, as a result, breaking ethical guidelines?

Recently, information technology (IT) innovations have made it somewhat easier to investigate crowd dynamics in emergency situations. Using an immersing virtual reality environment, John Drury and colleagues (2009) examined how people react and behave in a crowd of (virtual) strangers (Figure 14.19b). Their results showed that the threat stemming from the emergency made people see the crowd in terms of a collective identity, all sharing a common fate. The more people thought of the crowd in terms of this collective identity, instead of a collection of strangers, the more likely they were to be helpful and the less likely they were to push others aside. In other words seeing the crowd as a collective identity motivated solidarity with strangers in these situations. Group identity then also seems to play an important role in understanding how norms and rules of conduct may guide behaviour in mass emergencies.

 In review

- The mere presence of others can enhance our performance on simple or well-learned tasks but hinder performance on complex or new tasks.
- People often use special techniques to get us to comply with their requests, such as the norm of reciprocity, the door-in-the-face technique, the foot-in-the-door technique and lowballing.
- Milgram's obedience research raised strong ethical concerns and found unexpectedly high percentages of people willing to obey destructive orders. Such obedience is stronger when the victim is remote and when the authority figure is close by, legitimate and assumes responsibility for what happens.
- A social norm is a shared rule or expectation about how group members should think, feel and behave. A social role is a set of norms that defines a particular position in a social system.
- People conform to a group because of informational social influence, normative social influence and informational referent social influence.
- The size of the majority and the presence or absence of dissenters influence the degree of conformity. Minority influence is strongest when the minority maintains a consistent position over time but does not appear too deviant.
- Ostracism produces negative psychological consequences and activates many of the same brain regions that underlie physical pain.
- Social loafing occurs when people exert less individual effort when working as a group than when working alone. Loafing decreases when the goal is valued highly and when performance within the group is individually monitored.
- When the members of a decision-making group share the same conservative or liberal viewpoint, the group's final decision often becomes more extreme than the average initial opinion of the individual members.
- Cohesive decision-making groups that have a high sense of *cohesiveness*, are motivated to *maintain a positive view* of their group, and within which a *strong group norm* emerges regarding preferred solutions, may display groupthink: a suspension of critical thinking to maintain cohesion and reach agreement.
- Deindividuation refers to a temporary loss of individuality that can occur when a person is immersed in a group. Anonymity to outsiders appears to be the key factors in producing deindividuation. Deindividuation enhances the individual's tendency to focus on his or her *social* identity, making them more sensitive to emerging *group* norms.
- Crowd behaviour in emergency situations is often guided by everyday social norms and rules of conduct, especially when the crowd is seen as a collective identity sharing a similar fate.

SOCIAL RELATIONS: INTERGROUP DYNAMICS

As we have seen, individual behaviour often occurs within groups. However, society consists of an enormous number of different groups and these different groups also interact with each other, forming and maintaining relationships. Sometimes these interactions occur at a major scale, with implications far beyond group boundaries. This is the case with the numerous wars between groups and countries, but also with major formalized interactions between countries such as in the European Union. Other interactions occur at a more minor scale, such as work discussions between departments or competitive team sports, but nonetheless can have a big impact on behaviour. Look again at Figure 14.18 for example. Who do you think the flying chair might be aimed at? Fans supporting his team, or fans supporting a rival team?

Relations between groups can be beneficial, but they also have the potential to change dramatically for the worse. One only has to think of the atrocities that occurred during the Second World War, or more recently the conflict between the Hutus and the Tutsis in Rwanda, the apartheid regime in South Africa, the current terrorist threat, and so on. As a result, social psychology has devoted considerable attention to the study of intergroup relations in order to gain an understanding of such problems as prejudice, discrimination and intergroup conflict.

UNDERSTANDING INTERGROUP RELATIONS

What exactly do we mean by intergroup relations? A classic definition of intergroup situations is given by Sherif (1966, p. 12): 'Whenever individuals belonging to one group interact, collectively or individually, with another group or its members in terms of their group identification, we have an instance of intergroup behaviour.' This definition makes clear that intergroup relations do not necessarily imply the presence of two large groups standing face to face. Intergroup relations can also occur at the level of two individuals interacting. Thus, a job interview between a female applicant and a male interviewer can be said to be a dyadic situation with two unique individuals interacting. Where the female is applying for a technical job requiring extensive knowledge of mathematics, the interviewer may let his judgement of the applicant, and subsequently his behaviour, be guided by his stereotype of women being poor in mathematics. To the extent that both applicant and interviewer view each other in terms of their different gender identity, one can also see this as an example of intergroup relations.

Earlier in this chapter we discussed how stereotypes (e.g., about social class) can bias the way we perceive other people's behaviour. Stereotypes are not by definition good or bad, they are rather *mental representations of groups and their members*. Such mental representations can refer to personality traits as well as behaviour, and can include positive and negative attitudes towards a group and its members. For example, the French are seen by some people as rude and snobby, whereas others might view them as having 'joie de vivre', generally enjoying life while sipping wine and eating French bread with smelly cheese (Figure 14.20). Where a derogatory attitude towards people based on their membership in a group exists, we often refer to this as **prejudice** (Allport, 1954). Thus we *prejudge* people – dislike them or hold derogatory beliefs about them – simply because they are female or male, belong to one ethnic group or religion rather than to another, are gay or straight, and so on. This is not to be confused with **discrimination**, which refers to (overt) behaviour that involves treating people unfairly based on the group to which they belong.

For a more thorough understanding of intergroup relations, we need to consider a constellation of factors. These include historical and cultural norms that legitimize differential treatment of various groups and socialization processes through which parents and other adults transmit values and beliefs to their children (e.g., Degner & Dalege, 2013). Let us examine several cognitive and motivational processes that are thought to underlie the development of intergroup relations.

FIGURE 14.20 Stereotypically French.

Stereotypes can include both neutral, positive and negative attitudes towards a group and its members, as in this case of the French, although negative attitudes are often referred to as *prejudice*.

Source: © Izabela Habur.

prejudice a negative attitude towards people based on their membership in a group

discrimination overt behaviour that involves treating people unfairly based on the group to which they belong

Categorization and 'Us–Them' Thinking

In order to organize and simplify our world, we have a tendency to categorize people and objects. At times, this helps us predict other people's behaviour and react quickly to environmental stimuli (Ito & Cacioppo, 2000). But our tendency to categorize people also lays a foundation for intergroup behaviour.

Categorization leads to the perception of in-groups and out-groups, groups to which we do and do not belong, respectively. One important feature of this process of categorization for understanding intergroup relations, is the fact that people have a tendency to exaggerate the difference between categories, called **category accentuation**. This was nicely illustrated in a study by Tajfel and Wilkes (1963). They randomly presented participants with eight lines, varying in length from 16.2 cm to 22.9 cm, and simply asked them to estimate the length of each line. However, for one group of participants these lines were labelled, such that the four smallest lines were labelled 'A' and the four longer lines were labelled 'B'. For the other group no such labelling of lines occurred. Results showed that, in the labelling condition, participants overestimated the difference between the lines labelled 'A' and 'B', such that A essentially meant 'short' where B meant 'long'. This effect was especially marked for the longest line of category A and the shortest line of category B. The perceived differences between these lines (line 1 and 2 in Figure 14.21) was much greater than the actual difference between the lines. No such exaggerations of perceived difference occurred in the 'no label' condition.

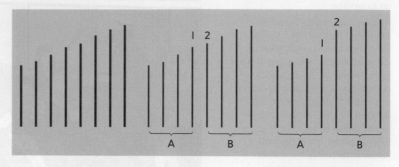

FIGURE 14.21 Category accentuation.
Lines in Tajfel and Wilkes (1963). (*Left*) Lines without labels. (*Middle*) Lines with labels, where participants exaggerated the average height of lines labelled 'B' compared with those labelled 'A', with the biggest perceived difference occurring between lines 1 and 2. (*Right*) An impression of how participants might have perceived the lines in the labelling condition.

Source: Tajfel and Wilkes (1963).

Tajfel and Wilkes (1963) suggested that this accentuation of differences between categories could also explain the exaggeration that occurred between members of different groups. That is, although stereotypes might have some 'kernel of truth', stereotypes are often a simplification of reality and function in a way that exaggerates differences between 'us' and 'them'. This suggests that stereotypes can change depending on the presence or absence of groups that force us to think in terms of 'us' and 'them' (Oakes, Haslam, & Turner, 1994).

Numerous studies have now provided evidence that in-group versus out-group distinctions spawn several common biases. The **out-group homogeneity bias**, for example, refers to the tendency of individuals to generally view members of out-groups as being more similar to one another than are members of in-groups (Brauer, 2001). In other words, we perceive that 'they are all alike' but recognize that 'we are diverse'. This is especially likely to happen for unfamiliar groups that we have never encountered before (e.g., Ostrom & Sedikides, 1992). Although you may recognize this in the way you yourself see other groups too, people often think that it is mostly *other* people who have such biases (e.g., Judd, Park, Yzerbyt, Gordijn, & Muller, 2005). The mere fact that we identify people as 'Asian', 'Hispanic', 'black' and 'white', however, reflects this bias in *all of us*, because each of these ethnic categories contains many subgroups (Huddy & Virtanen, 1995).

Categorization, then, enhances the tendency to judge other people based on their perceived group membership rather than their individual characteristics. Whether at a conscious or unconscious level, category labels pertaining to people's race, gender and other attributes seem to activate stereotypes about them (Wheeler & Fiske, 2005). Figure 14.22 illustrates two ways in which racial categorization and gender categorization activate stereotypes and affect our perceptions.

Not all people easily fit into a group or category; some members seem to be a better representative of a category than others. For example, a sheep seems to be a better representative of the category 'mammals' than a dolphin. Similarly, in the example used in the section on social thinking, if Hannah would be dressed up according to the latest fashion wearing expensive shoes and accessories, she would not fit well with participants' stereotype of people from a poor neighbourhood. Indeed, categories are often 'fuzzy' or 'ill-defined' concepts, where a person is perceived to be a better representative of the category

category accentuation a tendency to exaggerate the difference between categories

out-group homogeneity bias the tendency of individuals to generally view members of out-groups as being more similar to one another than are members of in-groups

FIGURE 14.22 Classic experiments on prejudice.

(a) Who is holding the razor knife? Allport and Postman (1947) showed this picture to one person, who then described it while looking at it. A second person listened to this description and was asked to repeat it 'as exactly as possible' to another person, who repeated this description to another person, and so on (up to six or seven tellings). In over half of the trials following this procedure, at some point the black man was erroneously described as holding the knife. (b) Which person contributes most strongly to this research team? When the drawing shows an all-male group, an all-female group or a mixed-gender group with a man at the head of the table (seat 3), participants say that the person in seat 3 is the strongest member. But in this mixed-gender drawing with a woman in seat 3, most male and female participants pick one of the two men.

Source: Based on Porter and Geis, 1981.

(a)   (b)

the more he or she possesses a number of characteristic features that are 'typical' for the group, the so-called *group prototype* (Rosch & Mervis, 1975; Turner et al., 1987).

What happens when we encounter individual members of out-groups whose behaviour contradicts our stereotypes? When the information is somewhat ambiguous, people are likely to interpret the information such that it confirms their expectations. For example, in one classic study white people were subliminally exposed to stereotypic black terms (e.g., poor, jazz, athletic). When they were subsequently asked to interpret race-unspecific behaviour (e.g., someone refusing to pay the rent until his apartment is repainted) they rated these behaviours as more hostile (Devine, 1989). When the information clearly contradicts our stereotypes, one possibility is that we may change our stereotype; but if we are motivated to hold on to our prejudiced belief, we may explain away discrepant behaviour in several ways. For example, the out-group member may be seen as an exceptional case or as having succeeded at a task not because of high ability but because of tremendous effort, good luck or special advantage (Pettigrew, 1979). Such attributional biases reflect **in-group favouritism**, which represents the tendency to favour in-group members and attribute more positive qualities to 'us' than to 'them', whereas **out-group derogation** reflects a tendency to attribute more negative qualities to 'them' than to 'us'. Although people may display both biases, especially when they feel threatened, in-group favouritism is usually the stronger of the two (Brewer, 1999; Hewstone, Rubin, & Willis, 2002).

Motivational Aspects of Intergroup Relations

People's ingrained ways of perceiving the world – categorizing, forming in-groups and out-groups, and so forth – prepare the wheels of prejudice to go into motion, but motivational factors affect how fast those wheels spin. For example, prejudice and stereotyping increase when social motives squarely focus our attention on the fact that people belong to in-groups or out-groups (Wheeler & Fiske, 2005).

Competition and conflict

According to **realistic conflict theory**, competition for limited resources fosters prejudice. In the USA and Europe, hostility towards minority groups increases when economic conditions worsen (Pettigrew & Meertens, 1995). Originally, it was believed that a threat to one's personal welfare (as in the fear of losing one's job to a minority worker) was the prime motivator of prejudice, but research suggests that prejudice is triggered more strongly by *a perceived threat to one's in-group*. Among whites, prejudice against blacks is not related to personal resource gains and losses but to the belief that white people as a group are in danger of being 'overtaken' (Bobo, 1988). Likewise, as in the Robber's Cave summer camp experiment illustrated in **Chapter 1**, competition between groups can breed intense hostility towards an out-group (Sherif, Harvey, White, Hood, & Sherif, 1961). Indeed, even when people are angry and know that an out-group did not cause that anger, their implicit prejudice still increases towards the out-group. David DeSteno and co-workers (DeSteno,

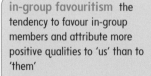

in-group favouritism the tendency to favour in-group members and attribute more positive qualities to 'us' than to 'them'

out-group derogation a tendency to attribute more negative qualities to 'them' than to 'us'

realistic conflict theory competition for limited resources fosters prejudice

Chapter 1, Page 6

Dasgupta, Bartlett, & Cajdric, 2004) suggest that the emotion of anger is so closely linked to conflict and competition between groups that it automatically activates feelings of prejudice towards out-groups. Conflict and competition between groups even enhances the willingness to sacrifice one's *own* interest for the benefit of the group, a pattern of behaviour that is most striking in suicide bombers, offering their life for the interest of the group. Research suggests such sacrifice for the group's interest is most common among (young) men (van Vugt, De Cremer, & Jansen, 2007).

Enhancing self-esteem

According to *social identity theory*, prejudice stems from a need to enhance our self-esteem. Some experiments find that people express more prejudice after their self-esteem is threatened (e.g., receiving negative feedback about their abilities) and that the opportunity to derogate others helps increase self-esteem (Fein & Spencer, 1997). According to social identity theory, however, our self-esteem is based on two components: a personal identity and a group identity (Tajfel & Turner, 1986). We can raise self-esteem not only by acknowledging our own virtues but also by associating ourselves with our in-group's accomplishments (e.g., Cialdini, Borden, Thorne, Walker, Freeman, & Sloan, 1976). Conversely, threats to our in-group threaten our self-esteem and may prompt us to derogate the out-group that constitutes the threat (Perdue, Dovidio, Gurtman, & Tyler, 1990). Indeed, feelings of group deprivation are an important trigger for intergroup aggression, such as terrorism and genocide (Moghaddam, 2005).

If people are motivated to enhance their group-based self-esteem, then membership in high-status groups should be desirable, as this may contribute to a positive social identity. Conversely, it might be suggested that members of low-status groups should be motivated to improve their status position in order to attain a more positive social identity. Social identity theory suggests therefore that people in low-status groups are likely to (1) leave their existing group and join a more positive group, a strategy called *individual mobility*, (2) creatively redefine the positivity of their group (i.e., 'black is beautiful'), a strategy known as *social creativity*, or (3) try to attain a higher status by directly competing with another group, also known as *social competition* (Tajfel & Turner, 1979). Which of these *identity management strategies* is chosen by low-status group members to enhance their social identity, is dependent on a number of group characteristics (e.g., Ellemers, Wilke, & Van Knippenberg, 1993). For example, if group boundaries are *permeable*, low-status group members are more likely to focus on possibilities of individual mobility. In contrast, if it is impossible for individuals to move over to a higher status group, or when the *status inequality* is seen as *insecure* and likely to change, low-status group members are assumed to engage in social competition in order to change the 'status quo' (Ellemers, 1993; Taylor & McKirnan, 1984).

PREJUDICE AND DISCRIMINATION

Even today, overt prejudice and discrimination are in abundant supply. Armed conflicts based on ethnic or religious divisions continue across the globe; hate crimes persist; and people's race, gender, religion and sexual orientation spark unfair treatment (Herek, 2000). Such prejudices are pervasive and often resilient to change, and people expressing prejudice towards one group also tend to do so towards other groups (Akrami, Ekehammar, & Bergh, 2011). Perceived discrimination also has serious psychological consequences for those being discriminated against. A recent meta-analysis involving over 144,000 participants revealed a clear relationship between perceived discrimination and psychological well-being (e.g., self-esteem, depression, anxiety, psychological distress, life satisfaction; Schmitt, Branscombe, Postmes, & Garcia, 2014). As a result, psychologists have been keen on investigating and understanding the causes, consequences and ways to reduce prejudice.

Explicit and Implicit Prejudice

In some ways, the most blatant forms of prejudice and discrimination have decreased in many countries (e.g., Payne, Krosnick, Pasek, Lelkes, Akhtar, & Tompson, 2010). Racial segregation is no longer sanctioned by government policy in the USA or South Africa, and opinion polls indicate that fewer people express prejudiced attitudes towards other (ethnic) groups than was the case decades ago.

explicit prejudice prejudiced attitudes about certain groups that people have some control over

implicit prejudice prejudiced attitudes that are not easily suppressed, but arise more automatically

Although fewer people express prejudiced attitudes, this does not necessarily mean people *are* actually less prejudiced. Instead, many people may intentionally hide their prejudices, expressing them only when they feel it is safe or socially appropriate. As such, modern racism, sexism and other forms of prejudice are more difficult to detect. Interestingly, although people may *control* **explicit prejudices**, or may honestly believe that they are not prejudiced, **implicit prejudices** may still guide their behaviour (De Houwer, Teige-Mocigemba, Spruyt, & Moors, 2009; Fazio, Jackson, Dunton, & Williams, 1995).

We can use questionnaires to measure explicit prejudice, but how can we measure implicit prejudice? Some researchers have found that subtle movements of facial muscles involved in smiling (and in some studies, in frowning) can be used to predict people's biases towards members of another ethnic group (Vanman, Saltz, Nathan, & Warren, 2004). But most often, measures of implicit prejudice assess people's reaction times at special cognitive tasks (Greenwald, McGhee, & Schwartz, 1998; Nosek, Hawkins, & Frazier, 2011).

To give you a general idea of how an implicit prejudice test might work (they are actually more complicated than this), suppose that a series of word pairs, such as 'black–pleasant' and 'white–pleasant' are flashed on a computer screen. As soon as you see each pair, your task is to press a computer key as quickly as you can, and this represents your reaction time. The principle underlying this task is that people react more quickly when they perceive that the concepts (i.e., the two words in each pair) 'fit' together than when the concepts do not. Thus *without conscious control*, a person prejudiced against blacks will react more slowly to the 'black–pleasant' pair than to the 'white–pleasant' pair. Again, this example is simplified. The actual tests measure how quickly people make judgements about concepts and groups.

Psychologists have found that implicit measures, such as the Implicit Association Test (IAT), can reveal many types of unconscious prejudice (Greenwald, Banaji, Rudman, Farnham, Nosek, & Mellott, 2002), even in children as young as 4 years old (Cvencek, Greenwald, & Meltzoff, 2011). These tests also can predict other types of biased responses that explicit measures – which can be easily distorted by people unaware of or trying to hide their prejudice – fail to predict. For example, Kurt Hugenberg and Galen Bodenhausen (2003) used the IAT to measure white college students' implicit prejudice towards blacks; they also used a self-report rating scale to measure explicit prejudice. Finally, they showed the students short, computer-generated movie clips that portrayed the faces of either white or black males making a range of angry, ambiguous and happy expressions. Compared with students who had lower implicit prejudice, those who had higher implicit prejudice were more likely to perceive the ambiguous facial expressions of black males as expressing anger. In contrast, students' reactions to the facial expressions were *not* related to their explicit prejudice scores.

Focus 14.18 How is implicit prejudice measured? Describe cognitive and motivational roots of prejudice.

How Prejudice Confirms Itself

Self-fulfilling prophecies are one of the most invisible yet damaging ways of maintaining prejudiced beliefs. An experiment by Carl Word and his colleagues (Word, Zanna, & Cooper, 1974) illustrates this point. The researchers began with the premise – supported by research at the time – that whites held several negative stereotypes of blacks. In the experiment, white male college students interviewed white and black high-school students who were seeking admission into a special group. The college students used a fixed set of interview questions provided by the experimenter and, unknown to them, each applicant was an accomplice who had been trained to respond in a standard way to the questions. The findings indicated that these white participants sat farther away, conducted shorter interviews, and made more speech errors when the applicants were black. In short, their behaviour was discriminatory.

But this is only half the picture. In a second experiment – a job interview simulation – white male undergraduates served as *job applicants*. Through random assignment, they were treated either as the white applicants had been treated in the first experiment or as the black applicants had been treated. Thus, for half the participants, the interviewer sat farther away, held a shorter interview and made more speech errors. The findings revealed that white participants who were treated more negatively performed worse during the job interview, were less composed, made more speech errors and rated the interviewer as less

friendly. In short, these experiments suggest that an interviewer's negative stereotypes can lead to discriminatory treatment during a job interview, and this discriminatory behaviour can cause the applicant to perform more poorly – ultimately confirming the interviewer's initial stereotype.

Stanford psychologist Claude Steele (1997) has demonstrated another insidious way that prejudice ends up confirming itself. As described in **Chapter 10**, his concept of **stereotype threat** proposes that stereotypes create self-consciousness among stereotyped group members and a fear that they will live up to other people's stereotypes (Shapiro, Williams, & Hambarchyan, 2013). For example, in a study comparing female and male college students who graduate in various fields, women graduating in the traditionally 'male' fields of mathematics, science and engineering reported the highest level of stereotype threat (Steele, James, & Barnett, 2002). They were more likely to feel that they (as well as other women in their field of study) had been targets of sex discrimination and that because of their gender other people (including their professors) expected them to have less ability and do more poorly.

Stereotype threat can occur even if group members do not accept the stereotype themselves (e.g., Shapiro, 2011), and experiments reveal its debilitating consequences. Given the stereotype that 'blacks are not as intelligent as whites', black college students who take a difficult verbal ability test perform more poorly when it is described as an 'intelligence test' than when it is described merely as a 'laboratory task'. In contrast, the intelligence-test description does not decrease white students' performance. Similar results were found for other stereotypes relating to mathematical ability, namely, 'whites are inferior to Asians', 'Latinos are inferior to whites', and 'women are inferior to men'. When a difficult standardized mathematics test is given in situations that activate these stereotypes, whites, Latinos and women perform more poorly than when the test is presented in a more neutral way (Aronson, Lustina, Good, Keough, Steele, & Brown, 1999; Gonzales, Blanton, & Williams, 2002; Maloney, Schaeffer, & Beilock, 2013).

> **stereotype threat** stereotypes create self-consciousness among stereotyped group members and a fear that they will live up to other people's stereotypes

 Chapter 10, Page 436

Reducing Prejudice

Psychologists do more than just study the causes of prejudice; they also develop and examine ways to reduce prejudice and its harmful effects. For example, the negative effects of a stereotype threat on women's mathematics performance can be reduced by allowing them to take mathematics tests without men present and by exposing them to female role models who succeed at such tasks (Marx, Stapel, & Muller, 2005; McIntyre, Paulson, & Lord, 2003). We discuss some of the main approaches identified by psychologists as possible suitable ways to reduce prejudice and discrimination.

Intergroup contact

The best-known approaches to prejudice reduction are based on a principle called *equal status contact*: prejudice between people is most likely to be reduced when they (1) engage in sustained personal, close contact, (2) have equal status, (3) work to achieve a common goal that requires cooperation and (4) are supported by broader social norms (Allport, 1954; Figure 14.23). Interestingly, even *imagined* contact (i.e., imagining that you are talking to someone from a prejudiced group) may reduce prejudice (Miles & Crisp, 2014; Turner & Crisp, 2010).

In 1954 the US Supreme Court handed down a momentous decision in the case of *Brown* v. *Board of Education*, ruling that school segregation based solely on race violates the constitutional rights of racial minorities. Providing key testimony, several psychologists stated that segregation contributed to racial prejudice and hostility. Unfortunately, decades later, when Walter Stephan (1990) reviewed more than 80 evaluation studies of desegregation programmes, he concluded that desegregation did not consistently reduce racial prejudice.

Why were the results not more positive? First, the condition of equal-status contact was often not met, and contact when status is unequal serves only to perpetuate both groups' negative stereotypes of one another. Second, in

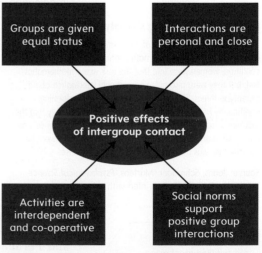

FIGURE 14.23 Reducing prejudice through intergroup contact: equal status contact.

Prejudice between two people or groups is most likely to decrease when contact between them occurs under these four conditions.

many integrated school situations, close and personal contact between group members did not occur. Black students and white students were sometimes placed in different learning tracks that minimized in-class contact, and they tended to associate only with members of their own ethnic group outside class. Third, classroom experiences focused on individual rather than cooperative learning. Finally, intergroup contact was often not supported by broader social norms; in the early years of desegregation, many white politicians, parents, teachers and school officials militantly opposed school integration (for an overview see Pettigrew & Trope, 2013).

 Chapter 1, Page 6

When intergroup contact takes place under proper conditions, however, prejudice can decrease (Pettigrew & Tropp, 2006). In school settings, *cooperative learning programmes* (such as the 'jigsaw classroom' described in **Chapter 1**) place children into multiracial learning groups. Contact is close and sustained, each child is accorded equal status, and each has responsibility for learning and then teaching other group members one piece of the information that is needed for the group to succeed in its assignment (Aronson, Stephan, Sikes, & Snapp, 1978). The children also can forge a common group identity, much as athletes on a team or members of a military unit form a group identity (Gaertner & Dovidio, 2000). Overall, such programmes reduce prejudice and promote appreciation of ethnic group differences (Johnson, 2000).

An educational approach to reducing stereotype threat

Michael Johns and his co-workers (Johns, Schmader, & Martens, 2005) asked male and female college students to take a difficult mathematics test. To minimize stereotype threat, one group of randomly assigned students was told that the test was merely an exercise in problem-solving. To maximize stereotype threat, a second group and a third group were told that the test assessed mathematical aptitude and that women's and men's scores would be compared. The third group, however, also received educational information about stereotype threat, and the women in this group were told that if they felt anxious during the test, stereotype threat might be the cause.

Would teaching women about stereotype threat make them even more anxious and further impair their mathematical performance, or would it improve their performance by letting them know what to expect and allowing them to make an external attribution (i.e., to the societal stereotype) for their anxiety? As Figure 14.24 shows, compared with the 'mathematics test' condition, the teaching intervention boosted women's performance.

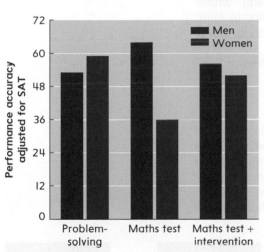

FIGURE 14.24 Reducing stereotype threat.

This graph shows the results of Johns and co-workers' (2005) study of stereotype threat. In the 'mathematics test + intervention' condition, women were told that the task was a mathematics test, but they were also given educational information about stereotype threat. Thus armed, they ended up performing significantly better than the women who were told only that the task was a mathematics test. Moreover, their performance was not significantly poorer than that of the women who were told that the task was merely a problem-solving exercise.

Source: Johns, Schmader, Martens, *Psychological Science*, Vol. 16, No. 3, © 2005. Reprinted with permission of Sage Publications.

Focus 14.19 How do self-fulfilling prophecies and stereotype threat perpetuate prejudice? How can prejudice be reduced?

Using simulations to reduce 'shooter bias'

Finally, let us examine another type of racial bias. In several highly publicized cases over the past decade, police officers investigating a crime have shot and killed unarmed non-white male targets. The officers, faced with a split-second decision about whether to shoot, mistakenly perceived that these men were either reaching for or holding a weapon. Was the victims' race a factor in these shootings? Social psychologists devised experiments in which college students and other adults had to quickly decide whether to shoot armed and unarmed white and non-white suspects who appeared on a computer screen during a video simulation (see Figure 14.25). The results revealed a 'shooter bias' in which participants – both white and non-white participants in some studies – were more likely to shoot unarmed suspects who were non-white (Correll, Park, Judd, & Wittenbrink, 2002; Unkelbach, Forgas, & Denson, 2008).

Subsequently, in separate computer simulation experiments with college students and police officers, Plant and co-workers have been able to reduce this shooter bias (Plant and Peruche, 2005; Plant, Peruche, & Butz, 2005). The shooting simulation programme, like those used in other experiments, was designed so that white and non-white criminal suspects were equally likely to be armed or unarmed. Over time, with repeated exposure to the simulation programme, the shooter bias that students and police officers displayed on the earlier trials disappeared. As the researchers note, these findings are only a promising first step that await further testing in more rigorous police academy training programmes.

FIGURE 14.25 Shooter bias.

Stills from the experiment conducted by Joshua Correll and colleagues (2002) showing unarmed white and non-white suspects.

Source: Corell et al., 2002. © American Psychological Association.

SOCIAL RELATIONS: INTERPERSONAL DYNAMICS

In the previous section we discussed social relations between groups. Because of the tendency to escalate and the implications such relations between groups can have for individuals, social psychology has recently given much attention to this type of relationship. However, as individuals we also form and maintain relationships with other individuals without necessarily having to refer to differing group memberships. Research and theory on *interpersonal* relationships is the focus of the present section.

ATTRACTION: LIKING AND LOVING OTHERS

Commenting on friendship and love, humourist Mason Cooley once quipped, 'Friendship is love minus sex and plus reason. Love is friendship plus sex and minus reason' (Columbia, 1996). Alas, the difference between *liking* and *loving* may not be so simple, but attraction is indeed the first phase of most friendships and romantic relationships. What causes us to connect with some people but not others?

Initial Attraction: Proximity, Mere Exposure and Similarity

People cannot develop a relationship unless they first meet, and proximity (nearness) is the best predictor of who will cross paths with whom. In today's increasingly wired world, friendships and romances sometimes develop after strangers make initial contact through Internet chat rooms or email. Still, *physical proximity* matters. We tend to interact most with people who are physically closer. Residents in student apartments are most likely to form friendships with other residents who live close by, and students assigned specific classroom seats are most likely to become friends with students seated nearby.

Proximity increases the chance of frequent encounters, and over 200 experiments in different countries provide evidence of a mere exposure effect: repeated exposure to a stimulus typically increases our liking for it. No matter the stimuli – college classmates, photographs of faces, random geometric shapes, and so on – as long as they are not unpleasant and we are not oversaturated, exposure generally enhances liking (Peskin & Newell, 2004).

> **mere exposure effect**
> repeated exposure to a stimulus typically increases our liking for it

After two people meet, then what? When it comes to attraction, folk wisdom covers all the bases. On the one hand, 'opposites attract'. On the other hand, 'birds of a feather flock together'. So which is it? Cross-cultural evidence overwhelmingly supports the role of *similarity*: people most often are attracted to others who are similar to themselves. For psychological attributes, similarity of attitudes and values seems to matter the most (Buss, 1985).

In the laboratory, college students' degree of liking for a stranger can be predicted very accurately simply by knowing the proportion of similar attitudes that they share (Byrne, 1997). This is already evident in children as young as three years old: when choosing

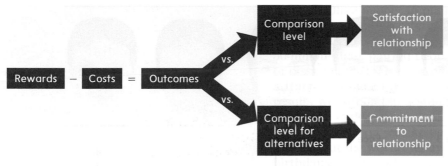

FIGURE 14.28 Social relationships: are you satisfied and committed?
According to Thibaut and Kelley's (1959) social exchange theory, rewards minus costs equal the outcome of a relationship. Comparing our outcomes with two standards, the comparison level and the comparison level for alternatives, determines our satisfaction and commitment to the relationship, respectively.

most attractive people match up, and so on. Another factor is that people may refrain from approaching potential dating partners who are more attractive than they are to lessen the risk of rejection.

As Attraction Deepens: Close Relationships

Budding relationships grow closer as people share more diverse and meaningful experiences (Altman & Taylor, 1973). *Self-disclosure* – the sharing of innermost thoughts and feelings – plays a key role (Dindia, 2002). In friendships, dating relationships and marriages, more extensive and intimate self-disclosure is associated with greater emotional involvement and relationship satisfaction. This relation is reciprocal. Self-disclosure fosters intimacy and trust, and intimacy and trust encourage self-disclosure (Sprecher, Treger, Wondra, Hilaire, & Wallpe, 2013). However, too much self-disclosure may also be counterproductive: it may embarrass our partner, especially if the partner is unwilling or unable to reciprocate in kind (Omarzu, 2000).

social exchange theory the course of a relationship is governed by rewards and costs that the partners experience

Social exchange theory proposes that the course of a relationship is governed by rewards and costs that the partners experience (Thibaut & Kelley, 1959). Rewards include companionship, emotional support and the satisfaction of other needs. Costs may include the effort spent to maintain the relationship, arguments, conflicting goals, and so forth. The overall *outcome* (rewards minus costs) in a relationship can be positive or negative.

Outcomes are evaluated against two standards (Figure 14.28). The first, called the *comparison level*, is the outcome that a person has grown to expect in relationships, and it influences the person's *satisfaction* with the present relationship. Outcomes that meet or exceed the comparison level are satisfying; those that fall below this standard are dissatisfying. The second standard, called the *comparison level for alternatives*, focuses on potential alternatives to the relationship, and it influences the person's degree of *commitment*. Even when a relationship is satisfying, partners may feel low commitment if they perceive that something better is available. In turn, the partners' sense of commitment helps predict whether they will remain together or end their relationship in the future (Sprecher, 2001).

Focus 14.21 According to social exchange theory, what factors determine whether a relationship will be satisfying and will continue?

Sociocultural and Evolutionary Views

According to social exchange theory, a partner's desirable characteristics can be viewed as rewards, whereas undesirable characteristics represent costs. But what specific characteristics do people desire in a partner? In a massive study involving 10,000 men and women from 37 cultures around the world, evolutionary psychologist David Buss and co-workers asked people to identify the qualities they sought in an ideal long-term mate (Buss, 1989; Buss et al., 1990). Overall, for both sexes, mutual attraction/love, dependable character, emotional stability and a pleasing disposition emerged (in that order) as the most highly rated of the 18 characteristics evaluated.

The importance attached to many qualities, however, varied considerably across cultures. For example, whereas American men and women viewed refinement/neatness as having only modest importance, Iranian men and women viewed it as the most important quality they desired in a mate. In many cultures, a mate's chastity (no previous experience in sexual intercourse) was viewed as last or near last in importance, but in China and India, men and women viewed chastity as an important quality in a mate.

There also are remarkably consistent sex differences in mate preferences across cultures. Men tend to place greater value on a potential mate's physical attractiveness and domestic skills, whereas women place greater value on a potential mate's earning potential, status and ambitiousness. Men tend to desire a mate who is a few years younger,

whereas women desire a mate who is a few years older. Men also are more likely to desire and pursue a greater number of short-term romantic encounters than are women (Schmitt, Shackelford, & Buss, 2001).

As we discussed in detail in **Chapter 10**, some evolutionary psychologists argue that these sex differences reflect inherited predispositions, shaped by natural selection in response to different adaptive problems that men and women have faced over the ages (Buss & Schmitt, 1993; Schmitt et al., 2001). According to the *sexual strategies theory*, ancestral men who were predisposed to have sex with more partners increased the likelihood of fathering more children and passing on their genes. Such men may have perceived a woman's youth and attractive appearance as signs that she was fertile and had many years left to bear children (Buss, 1989). Ancestral women, however, maximized their reproductive success by selecting mates who were willing and able to commit time, energy and other resources (e.g., food, shelter, protection) to the family (Buss, 1989).

Do men and women have different biological wiring when it comes to romantic attraction and relationships? *Social structure theory* proposes that most of these sex differences in mating strategies and preferences occur because society directs men into more advantaged social and economic roles (Eagly & Wood, 1999; Johannesen-Schmidt and Eagly, 2002). As this theory predicts, in cultures with more gender equality, many of the sex differences in mate preferences shrink. Women place less emphasis, for example, on a mate's earning power and status, and men and women seek mates more similar in age. Men's tendency to place more emphasis on a mate's physical attractiveness, however, does not decrease in such cultures. But it is still a leap, say critics, to conclude that sex differences in mating preferences reflect a hereditary predisposition rather than some other aspect of gender socialization that may be consistent across cultures.

This issue is far from settled, but perhaps the most important point for you to realize is that the notion that men and women come from 'different planets' when it comes to attraction, romance and close relationships is more pop psychology than reliable science. Sex differences exist, but cross-cultural differences tend to be stronger. That is, men and women within the same culture are typically more similar to one another than are men from different cultures or women from different cultures (Buss et al., 1990).

Indeed, even some evolutionary theorists disagree with the sexual strategies model. Cindy Hazan and Lisa Diamond (2000) argue that evolution has shaped the human psyche towards seeking **attachment**, a deep bond between two individuals. In their view, the same biological hard-wiring that predisposes infants to bond with a caregiver also steers adult humans towards becoming attached to a mate. As they note: 'The (over)emphasis on sex differences has distracted us from the reality that men and women are basically similar in what they seek in a mate, the processes by which they become attached to a mate, and the benefits that accrue to them as a result of being in a stable pair bond' (Hazan & Diamond, 2000, p. 194).

Love

Love must be powerful, for as a common adage says, 'it makes the world go round'. Indeed, Buss and co-workers (1990) found that mutual attraction/love was highly valued in a mate across cultures. But what is love?

When it comes to romantic relationships, many psychologists identify two basic types of love: *passionate* and *companionate* (Hatfield, 1988). **Passionate love** involves intense emotion, arousal, and yearning for the partner. We may ride an emotional roller coaster that ranges from ecstasy when the partner is present to heartsickness when the person is absent. **Companionate love** involves affection and deep caring about the partner's well-being. At least when studied in Westernized countries, both types of love contribute to satisfaction in long-term romantic relationships (Sprecher & Regan, 1998). In general, passionate love is less stable and declines more quickly over time than companionate love, but this does not mean that the flames of passionate love inevitably extinguish.

Psychologist Robert Sternberg (1988, 1997), however, views love as more complex. His **triangular theory of love** proposes that love involves three major components:

 Chapter 10, Page 435

Focus 14.22 Contrast evolutionary and sociocultural explanations for sex differences in mate preferences.

attachment a deep bond between two individuals

passionate love intense emotion, arousal and yearning for the partner

companionate love affection and deep caring about the partner's well-being

triangular theory of love love involves three major components: passion, intimacy and commitment

Focus 14.23 Describe types of love, and discuss research-based principles that may help enhance relationship quality.

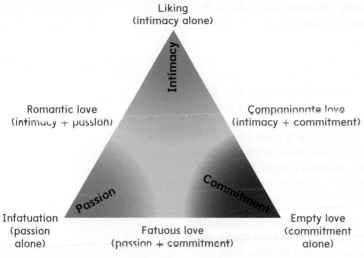

FIGURE 14.29 The complexity of love.

According to Sternberg, different types of love involve varying combinations of intimacy, commitment and passion. Consummate love involves the presence of all three factors, whereas non-love represents the absence of all three.

passion, intimacy and commitment. Passion refers to feelings of physical attraction and sexual desire; *intimacy* involves closeness, sharing and valuing one's partner; and *commitment* represents a decision to remain in the relationship. Research suggests that these three components do a good job of capturing the way people commonly think about love (Aron & Westbay, 1996).

Figure 14.29 shows that different combinations of these components characterize seven types of love (plus *non-love*, which is the absence of all three). Sternberg proposes that the ultimate form of love between people – *consummate love* – occurs when intimacy, passion and commitment are all present. Clearly, for close relationships to develop and endure, they need more than passion alone. Intimacy and commitment provide a basis for the friendship and trust that sustain and increase love (Diamond, 2003, 2004). As our 'Applying psychological science' feature highlights, other behaviours also help make close relationships successful.

● Applying psychological science

MAKING CLOSE RELATIONSHIPS WORK: LESSONS FROM PSYCHOLOGICAL RESEARCH

Close relationships go through good times and bad, persisting or dissolving over time. Consider marriage. Although highly intimate, this union is often fragile, and many marriages end in divorce. How can people make their close relationships more satisfying and stable? Research on marriage suggests several answers that also can be applied to dating relationships and friendships.

For decades, most marital research simply asked people about their marriages. But researchers are now bringing couples into laboratories to videotape their interactions and chart their facial reactions, stress hormones and other physiological responses as they discuss emotionally charged issues (Kiecolt-Glaser, Bane, Glaser, & Malarkey, 2003). Rather than focusing only on unhappy couples to find out what is going wrong in their relationships, researchers are also studying happy couples to discover the secrets of their success.

Using these methods, psychologists have predicted with impressive accuracy whether marriages will last or dissolve. In one laboratory study, John Gottman and co-workers (Gottman, Coan, Carrere, & Swanson, 1998) collected behavioural and physiological data from 130 newly wed couples as they discussed areas of marital conflict (e.g., in-laws, finances, sex) during the first six months of their marriage. Six years later, participants reported whether they were happily married, unhappily married or divorced. Using data collected while the couples were newlyweds, the researchers predicted marital happiness/unhappiness and divorce with 80% accuracy.

Surprisingly, the amount of anger expressed by husbands and wives in their laboratory interactions was not the predictor. Instead, the crucial factor was the manner in which couples dealt with their anger. Four behaviours were particularly important: *criticism, contempt, defensiveness* and *stonewalling* (listener withdrawal and non-responsiveness).

Couples headed for unhappiness or divorce often exhibit these behaviours while discussing conflict, thereby escalating their conflict and negative emotions. When the wife criticizes the husband, he often responds defensively or stonewalls and withdraws from her attempts to reach some resolution. Her resulting frustration leads to stronger emotional displays and criticism, and the interaction degenerates into exchanges of contempt in which the partners tear each other down. Once this negative cycle develops, even positive overtures by one spouse are likely to evoke a negative response from the other.

Happily married couples also experience conflict and anger but keep the spiral of negativity from getting out of control. Instead, they make frequent 'repair attempts' to resolve their differences in a spirit of mutual respect and support. In happy marriages, the wife often introduces the conflict topic gently, rather than with criticism and strong emotion. Next a key factor occurs: the husband responds to the wife's issues with concern and respect, which de-escalates negative emotion. A husband who turns off the television and listens to his wife or who says, 'I can see you're upset, so let us work this out', demonstrates that her concerns are important to him. In happy marriages, after the husband's responsiveness de-escalates the conflict, couples soothe one another with positive comments and humour, resulting in more emotionally positive interchanges and lowered physiological arousal.

▶

◄   Happily married couples maintain a much higher ratio of positive to negative interactions than couples headed for divorce, and this history provides a positive 'emotional bank account' that helps them repair and recover from their immediate anger and conflict (Wilson & Gottman, 2002). They also strive to get to know each other deeply – their fears, dreams, attitudes and values – and they continually update their knowledge. This allows each partner to be more responsive to the other's needs and to navigate around relationship roadblocks (Gottman & DeClaire, 2002). Such behaviour contributes to an essential aspect of happy marriages: an intimate friendship between the partners. The lessons of happy marriages can be applied to other types of close relationships, and affirmative answers to the questions in Table 14.1 suggest that such relationships are on solid psychological ground.

TABLE 14.1 How strong is your relationship?

Answer each question True (T) or False (F):		
I can tell you about some of my partner's dreams	T	F
We just love talking to each other	T	F
My partner is one of my best friends	T	F
My partner listens respectfully, even when we disagree	T	F
We generally mesh well on basic values and goals in life	T	F
I feel that my partner knows me pretty well	T	F
The greater the number of 'True' answers, the stronger your relationship		

Source: courtesy of John Gottman.

PRO-SOCIAL BEHAVIOUR: HELPING OTHERS

Helping, or *pro-social behaviour*, comes in many forms, from performing heroic acts of bravery to tutoring a classmate. Acts of violence often dominate the headlines, but we should not lose sight of the mountains of good deeds performed around the world each day (Figure 14.30).

Why Do People Help?

What motivates pro-social behaviour? Biological, psychological and environmental factors all play a role in motivating pro-social behaviour (Dovidio, Piliavin, Schroeder, & Penner, 2006). Let us examine a few of these factors.

FIGURE 14.30 Like this rescue worker, many people seek careers or join volunteer organizations that allow them to help other people.
Source: ©iStock.com/kbwills

kin selection organisms are most likely to help others with whom they share the most genes, namely, their offspring and genetic relatives

FIGURE 14.31 Kin selection.

Spotting a predator, this female ground squirrel may sound an alarm call that warns other meerkats. Is the call truly a pro-social act, much like a human yelling 'Look out!'? Perhaps it simply indicates the meerkats own sense of alarm, much as we might scream out of fear for our own safety. But if this is the case, why is she more likely to sound this call when her own kin – rather than other squirrels – are nearby?

Source: ©iStock.com/PABimages

Focus 14.24 Discuss evolutionary, social learning and empathy – altruism explanations for helping behaviour.

empathy–altruism hypothesis altruism is produced by empathy – the ability to put oneself in the place of another and to share what that person is experiencing

Chapter 2, Page 38

Evolution and pro-social behaviour

Pro-social behaviour occurs throughout the animal kingdom. Evolutionary psychologists and sociobiologists (biologists who study species' social behaviour) propose that helping has a genetic basis, shaped by evolution (Hamilton, 1964). According to the principle of **kin selection**, organisms are most likely to help others with whom they share the most genes, namely, their offspring and genetic relatives (Figure 14.31). By protecting their kin, pro-social individuals increase the odds that their genes will survive across successive generations, and the gene pool of the species increasingly represents the genes of its pro-social members (West, Pen, & Griffin, 2002). In this manner, over the course of evolution, helping became a biologically predisposed response to certain situations.

But what accounts for the abundant helping that humans display towards friends and strangers, and that some animal species display towards non-kin (Clutton-Brock, 2002)? Sociobiologists propose the concept of *reciprocal altruism*: helping others increases the odds that they will help us or our kin in return, thereby enhancing the survival of our genes (Trivers, 1971).

Critics question sociobiologists' generalizations from non-humans to humans, and in some cases kin selection and reciprocal altruism do not adequately explain why people or animals cooperate (Clutton-Brock, 2002; Nowak, Tarnita, & Wilson, 2010). Sociobiologists counter that genetic factors only predispose us to act in certain ways. Experience also shapes helping behaviour.

Social learning and cultural influences

Beginning in childhood, we are exposed to helpful models and taught pro-social norms. The *norm of reciprocity* states that we should reciprocate when others treat us kindly, and the norm of social responsibility states that people should help others and contribute to the welfare of society (De Cremer & van Lange, 2001). We receive approval for adhering to these norms, receive disapproval for violating them and observe other people receiving praise for following these norms. Eventually, we internalize pro-social norms and values as our own.

Studies in Europe, Asia and North America confirm that socialization matters (Eisenberg, 2004). Children are more likely to act pro-socially when they have been raised by parents who have high moral standards, who are warm and supportive, and who encourage their children to develop empathy and 'put themselves in other people's shoes' (Krevans & Gibbs, 1996). However, there are also cross-cultural differences in beliefs about when and why we should help. For example, Joan Miller and co-workers (Miller, Bersoff, & Harwood, 1990) found that Hindu children and adults in India believe that one has a moral obligation to help friends and strangers, whether their need is serious or mild. In contrast, when a person's need for assistance is mild, American children and adults view helping as more of a choice than an obligation.

Empathy and altruism

C. Daniel Batson (Batson, Ahmad, & Stocks, 2004) proposes that pro-social behaviour can be motivated by altruistic as well as egoistic goals. *Altruism* refers to unselfishness, or helping another for the ultimate purpose of enhancing that person's welfare. In contrast, *egoistic goals* involve helping others to improve our own welfare, such as to increase our self-esteem, avoid feeling guilty for not helping, obtain praise or alleviate the distress we feel when seeing someone suffer. Do humans truly have a capacity to help others without any concern for themselves? Batson believes that true altruism exists, and according to his **empathy–altruism hypothesis**, altruism is produced by empathy – the ability to put oneself in the place of another and to share what that person is experiencing (Batson, 1991).

When Do People Help?

Ordinary citizens often go to great lengths to help strangers yet at times fail to assist people who are clearly in distress (Figure 14.32). Recall the infamous Kitty Genovese murder discussed in **Chapter 2**. Genovese was stabbed and raped by an assailant outside

Current topic

DOES PURE ALTRUISM EXIST?

One long-standing debate in social science has been the question of whether it is possible that humans help others for purely altruistic reasons, without any concern for their own personal interest or well-being.

For some, humans are rational economic organisms driven by self-interest, bent on maximizing their own well-being and enhancing their chances of survival (Ng & Tseng, 2008). This view of human beings as ultimately self-centred and egoistic has a long tradition, and is nicely captured in Dawkins' (1989) book The Selfish Gene: 'We are survival machines – robot vehicles blindly programmed to preserve the selfish molecules known as genes . . . This gene selfishness will usually give rise to selfishness in individual behaviour' (p. vii). This perception of humans as purely egoistic, sees altruism merely as a strategic expression of such egoistic motives. According to this approach, individuals are motivated to help others because of some perceived direct or indirect benefit to the individual. Thus, based on the norm of reciprocity, for example, one might suggest that we are likely to help others because we may expect that others are then more likely to help us in the future. As such, some researchers argue that pure altruism does not exist and that every altruistic act is basically driven by egoistical motives (e.g., D. H. Smith, 2000).

For others, the mere fact that human helping behaviour goes far beyond what is generally observed in the animal world, is evidence that people can and do behave in ways that defy a view of humans as purely egoistic. Human societies, for example, are characterized by large heterogeneous networks in which cooperation between genetically unrelated strangers is a key feature. Indeed, people generally have a strong disposition to cooperate, even if they gain no individual economic benefit from such acts. In addition, people also often reward those who cooperate, and punish those who do not, even if such punishment is costly to the individual. This willingness to punish others to prevent unfair outcomes or prevent unfair behaviour, even at a cost to themselves, is called *altruistic punishment* (Fehr & Fischbacher, 2003). Such acts of altruistic punishment seem to indicate that, in some situations at least, people are willing to forfeit benefits for themselves for the benefit of others.

Batson and many other psychologists believe that, although egoistic motives account for some pro-social behaviour, at times people do help others for *purely* altruistic reasons (Batson, Ahmad, & Lishner, 2002). Yet other psychologists remain unconvinced, arguing that some *negative state relief* is always involved (Cialdini, Brown, Lewis, & Luce, 1997). According to the negative state relief model, high empathy causes us to feel distress when we learn of others' suffering, so by helping them we reduce our own personal distress – a self-focused, egoistic goal, *not* an altruistic one (Cialdini et al., 1997). In addition, they agree that many of our cultural norms, values and practices reward altruistic behaviour and punish selfish behaviours (e.g., Richerson & Boyd, 2005). However, this may then suggest that pro-social tendencies and emotions such as compassion, emerged to benefit from rewards for following cooperative norms (Gintis, 2000; for a review see Goetz, Keltner, & Simon-Thomas, 2010). Interestingly, these arguments in favour of the *absence* of pure altruism, were already voiced by the philosopher and economist Adam Smith (1723–90). He suggested that altruistic behaviour is driven by a feeling of distress when facing another's suffering. According to Smith, the desire to reduce this distress, as well as the desire to attain social approval and prevent social rejection, is the reason behind altruistic behaviours.

Some recent brain-imaging findings add some provocative fuel to this debate. Empathizing with someone else's pain does not produce the same sensations (i.e., somatosensory cortex activation) that we experience when we are in pain, but it does activate many of the brain areas (e.g., other parts of the cortex, brain stem, thalamus and cerebellum) that process emotional aspects of our own pain (Singer, Seymour, O'Doherty, Kaube, Dolan, & Frith, 2004). Moreover, people who feel greater empathy for another's pain experience greater activation in these brain areas. So what do you think? Does this suggest that when helping behaviour stems from empathy, it does indeed involve negative state relief and therefore is not purely altruistic?

her New York City apartment. It was about 3 a.m., the attack lasted for half an hour, and 38 of her neighbours heard her screams and pleas for help. Yet no one even called the police until it was too late, and Genovese died.

What, then, influences whether a bystander will intervene? Many situational and personal factors, such as not being in a hurry, recently observing a pro-social role model, and being in a good mood, increase the odds that we will help someone in need (Eisenberg, 2000).

Bibb Latané and John Darley (1970) view bystander intervention as a five-step process (Figure 14.33). First, a bystander will not help unless he or she notices the situation. So imagine that as you walk along a street, you hear two people yelling and then hear a scream coming from inside a house. Now what? Many social situations are ambiguous, and step 2 involves deciding whether this really is an emergency. This step is important, because people feel they run the risk of embarrassment if the situation turns out not to be an emergency (Latané & Nida, 1981). To answer the question of whether or not a situation is indeed an emergency, we often engage in *social comparison*: we look around to see how other people are responding. You might say to yourself, 'No one else seems concerned, so it mustn't be serious'. In Kitty Genovese's murder, some bystanders mistakenly thought that

FIGURE 14.32 Why do bystanders sometimes fail to assist a person in need?

Source: ©istock.com/art-4-art

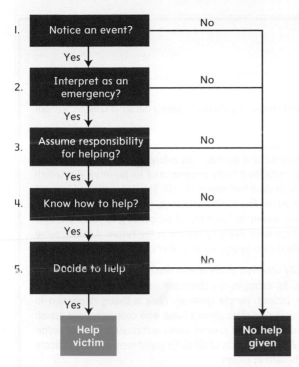

FIGURE 14.33 When will a bystander intervene?

Bystander intervention in an emergency situation can be viewed as a five-step process. If the answer at each step is yes, help is given.

Source: Based on Latané and Darley, 1970.

> **bystander effect** the presence of multiple bystanders inhibits each person's tendency to help, largely due to social comparison or diffusion of responsibility

because nobody else intervened they were merely witnessing a 'lovers' quarrel' (Darley & Latané, 1968).

If you conclude that the situation is an emergency, then you move to step 3: assuming responsibility to intervene. If you are the only person to hear someone screaming, then responsibility for helping falls squarely on you. But if others are present, there may be a *diffusion of responsibility* – 'If I don't help, someone else will' – and if each bystander has this thought, the victim will not receive help. In the Kitty Genovese murder, many bystanders who *did* interpret the incident as an emergency failed to intervene because they were certain that someone must already have called the police (Darley & Latané, 1968).

If you do take responsibility, then in step 4 your self-efficacy (confidence in dealing with the situation) comes into play. Sometimes, we fail to help because we do not know how to or believe our help will be ineffective. But even if self-efficacy is high, in step 5 you still may decide not to intervene. For example, you may perceive that the costs of helping outweigh the benefits (Fritzsche, Finkelstein, & Penner, 2000).

As this model indicates, the common-sense adage 'there is safety in numbers' is not always true when it comes to receiving help. Many experiments find a **bystander effect**: the presence of multiple bystanders inhibits each person's tendency to help, largely due to social comparison (at step 2) or diffusion of responsibility (at step 3). This inhibition is more likely to occur when the bystanders are strangers rather than friends, and when situations are not perceived as dangerous (Fischer et al., 2011). It even occurs when communicating over the Internet. Over a 30-day period, P.M. Markey (2000) sent a general request for help ('Can anyone tell me how to look at someone's profile?') to 200 chat groups. Assistance came more slowly from larger chat groups than from smaller ones.

Whom Do People Help?

Some people are more likely to receive help than others, for the following reasons:

1. *Similarity*: whether in attitudes, nationality or other characteristics, perceiving that a person is similar to us increases our willingness to provide help (Dovidio, 1984).

2. *Gender*: male bystanders are more likely to help a woman than a man in need, whereas female bystanders are equally likely to help women and men (Eagly & Crowley, 1986).

3. *Perceived fairness and responsibility*: beliefs about fairness influence people's willingness to help others (Blader & Tyler, 2002). For example, people are more likely to help someone if they perceive that the person is not responsible for causing his or her own misfortune.

Increasing Pro-Social Behaviour

Can pro-social behaviour be increased? One approach, consistent with social learning theory, is to expose people to pro-social models. Psychologists have used pro-social modelling as part of a nationwide programme to increase blood donations (Sarason, Sarason, Pierce, Shearin, and Sayers, 1991). Students in 66 high schools watched an audiovisual programme showing high-school donors giving blood. Compared with a control condition presented with a standard appeal from the local blood bank, the pro-social video increased blood donations by 17%.

Research suggests that developing feelings of empathy and connectedness with others also may make people more likely to help (Eisenberg, 2000), and simply learning about factors that hinder bystander intervention may increase the tendency to help someone in distress. Arthur Beaman and co-workers (Beaman, Barnes, Klentz, & McQuirk, 1978) exposed some college students to information about the bystander effect. Control participants did not receive this information. Two weeks later, more than half of the

students who had learned about the bystander effect provided aid to the victim of an accident (staged by the researchers), compared with only about one-quarter of the control group participants.

AGGRESSION: HARMING OTHERS

Focus 14.25 When and whom are people most likely to help? How can pro-social behaviour be increased?

We love. We nurture. We help. But as current events and the history of humankind attest, we also harm. In humans, *aggression* represents any form of behaviour that is intended to harm another person. What causes people to be aggressive?

Biological Factors in Aggression

From barnyard bulls to laboratory rats, animals can be selectively bred to be more or less aggressive (Lagerspetz, Tirri, & Lagerspetz, 1968). In some species, certain aggressive behaviours are reflexively triggered by specific environmental stimuli (Figure 14.34). Humans do not display such rigid, inborn aggressive responses, but heredity influences why some people are more aggressive than others. Even when raised in different homes, identical twins display more similar patterns of aggression than do fraternal twins (Beatty, Heisel, Hall, Levine, & La France, 2002).

Some theorists propose that, as in other species, a genetic predisposition towards aggression can be traced to evolutionary adaptation. Aggression at the proper time, they argue, helped our ancestors to compete successfully for mates, food and shelter, and to survive against attack. This increased the odds that individuals who were predisposed to such aggression would pass their genes on to the next generation (Rushton, 1989).

There is no single brain centre for aggression, nor one 'aggression chemical'. Electrically stimulate certain neural pathways in a cat's hypothalamus, and it will arch its back and attack. Surgically destroy areas of the amygdala – an approach that has been used with some violent human criminals – and in many species, defensive aggression will decrease (Aggleton, 1993). Especially in humans, aggression also involves activity in the frontal lobes – the seat of reasoning and impulse control. Deficient frontal-lobe activity makes it more difficult to regulate aggressive impulses generated by deeper brain regions (Raine, 2002).

Atypically low levels of serotonin activity appear to play a role in impulsive aggression, as when people lash out from emotional rage (Moore, Scarpa, & Raine, 2002). In many species of mammals, higher levels of the sex hormone testosterone (found in males and females) contribute to greater *social aggression*, acts that establish a dominance hierarchy among members of a species. But in humans and other primates, the association between testosterone and aggression is weaker (O'Connor, Archer, Hair, & Wu, 2002).

FIGURE 14.34 Sex and the stickleback: triggers for aggression.

During the mating season, the male stickleback fish develops a red belly. The sight of another red-bellied male – a potential rival for a mate – reflexively triggers an attack by the first male. The key releaser stimulus for this fixed action pattern is the red marking. A male stickleback will not attack a realistic-looking male model that has no red belly, but it will attack unrealistic fish models that have this red marking.

Source: Based on Tinbergen, 1951.

Environmental Stimuli and Learning

Our present environment and past learning experiences also influence aggression. *Frustration*, which occurs when some event interferes with our progress towards a goal, increases the risk of verbal and physical aggression, as do aversive events such as extreme heat, provocation, painful stimuli and crowding. But we do not always respond to frustration by acting aggressively. Inhibited by our internal moral standards, we may simply control ourselves and find non-aggressive ways of dealing with conflict (Anderson & Bushman, 2002).

Aggression, like other behaviours, is influenced by learning. Non-aggressive animals can be trained to become vicious aggressors if reinforcement is arranged so that they are consistently victorious in fights with weaker animals. Such operant conditioning also affects human aggression. Pre-school children become increasingly aggressive when their aggressive behaviour produces positive outcomes for them, such as when they successfully force another child to give up a desired toy (Patterson, Littman, & Bricker, 1967).

As Albert Bandura's (1965) classic 'Bobo doll' experiments (see **Chapter 7**) clearly demonstrated, aggression also can be learned by observing others. Children learn how to be aggressive even when they witness an aggressive model being punished. Later, if the

 Chapter 7, Page 303

punishing agent is not present or if rewards are available for being aggressive, children are likely to reproduce the model's actions. Correlational studies, while not establishing cause and effect, find that aggressive and delinquent children tend to have parents who often behave aggressively (Stormshak, Bierman, McMahon, & Lengua, 2000).

Psychological Factors in Aggression

Many psychological factors affect whether we behave aggressively in specific situations. From gang violence to rape, terrorism and war, people may employ several types of *self-justification* to make it psychologically easier to harm other people (Lanier, 2001). Aggressors may blame the victim for imagined wrongs or otherwise convince themselves that the victim 'deserves it'. They may also dehumanize their victims, as often occurs in extreme intergroup aggression where out-group members are seen as vermin, rats or 'cattle'.

Our *attribution of intentionality* and degree of empathy also affect how we respond to provocation (e.g., Malle & Holbrook, 2012). When we believe that someone's negative behaviour towards us was intentional, we are more likely to become angry and retaliate (Graham, Hudley, & Williams, 1992). In this case, the victim may be tempted to take revenge in order to make the offender suffer. However, taking revenge is not enough: taking revenge is only satisfactory when the offender signals that they understand why revenge is taken on them. When offenders signal they do not understand why revenge was taken on them, avengers get even more angry (Gollwitzer & Denzler, 2009). Finally, when someone offends us and then apologizes, whether we forgive the person partly depends on how well we empathize with his or her viewpoint (McCullough, Worthington, & Rachal, 1997).

> **catharsis** performing an act of aggression discharges aggressive energy and temporarily reduces our impulse to be aggressive

Sigmund Freud (1920) believed that impulses from aggressive instincts build up inside us over time, have to be released, and then build up again in a never-ending cycle. His principle of **catharsis** stated that performing an act of aggression discharges aggressive energy and temporarily reduces our impulse to be aggressive. But how does one do this in a world where violence is punished? Freud proposed that we can channel aggressive impulses into socially acceptable behaviours (such as sports) and discharge aggressive impulses *vicariously* by watching and identifying with other people who behave aggressively.

If people cannot express their aggressive impulses, will the pressures build up and explode? Sometimes, meek or unassertive people do commit shocking and brutal crimes. These people, whom Edwin Megargee (1966) describes as having *over-controlled hostility*, show little immediate reaction to provocations. Instead, they bottle up their anger and, after provocations accumulate, suddenly erupt into violence. The final provocation that triggers their outburst is often trivial. One 10-year-old boy with no prior history of aggression stabbed his sister more than 80 times with an ice pick after she changed the channel during his favourite television show. After the aggressive outburst, such people typically revert to their former passive, unassertive state. Female prison inmates who score high on tests measuring over-controlled hostility are more likely to have committed a one-time violent crime than repeated violent crimes or a non-violent crime (Verona & Carbonell, 2000; Figure 14.35).

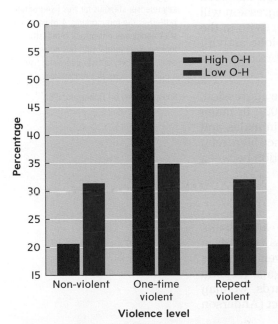

FIGURE 14.35 Over-controlled hostility: behind prison bars.

Female inmates at a state prison completed psychological tests that identified whether they had high over-controlled hostility (High O-H) or low over-controlled hostility (Low O-H). Inmates with high over-controlled hostility – but not inmates with low over-controlled hostility – were much more likely to have committed a one-time violent crime than a non-violent crime or multiple violent crimes.

Source: Adapted from Verona and Carbonell, 2000.

Cases of over-controlled hostility seem to be consistent with the concept of catharsis, but much research is not. For example, hitting a punching bag while thinking about someone who has just angered them increases – not decreases – people's subsequent aggressive behaviour towards that person (Bushman, 2002). New insights are starting to shed some more light on the question *if* and *when* acting out aggressive behaviour might lead to a decrease in subsequent aggressive behaviour (Denzler, Foerster, & Liberman, 2009). This work suggests a decrease *may* occur when people feel they fulfil their goals. For example, hitting a punching bag does not fulfil

the goal of punishing someone who has just angered you. Instead, Denzler and colleagues showed that hitting a doll that symbolically represented a person who had just angered them (a voodoo doll if you will), reduced accessibility of anger-related words, suggesting subsequent aggressive behaviour might be less likely. Future research is needed to determine if such 'functional' catharsis effects hold in real-life settings. For example, what does this say about watching violent films and television programmes? Do these activities help people let off steam, as some stars in the entertainment industry claim?

> **Focus 14.26** Describe how biological factors, environmental stimuli, learning and psychological factors influence aggression.

Media (and Video Game) Violence: Catharsis versus Social Learning

Many films and television programmes are saturated with violence. Indeed, research suggests top-selling films are becoming increasingly more violent (Bushman, Jamieson, Weitz, & Romer, 2013). To psychodynamic theorists, media violence should be a cathartic pot of gold. But social learning theorists argue that by providing numerous aggressive models – including many that are reinforced – media violence is more likely to increase viewers' aggressive behaviour than to reduce it.

Headline-making 'copycat' acts of violence clearly illustrate social learning effects. Still, hundreds of millions of people are entertained by media violence, and few commit copycat crimes. What, then, are the more general effects of media violence on aggression? Over the past 30 years, hundreds of experiments and correlational studies have shed light on the 'catharsis versus social learning' debate.

To most experts, the verdict is clear: the evidence favours the social learning view (Johnson, Cohen, Smailes, Kasen, & Brook, 2002). For example, American children who watch greater amounts of television violence are more likely than their peers to display physical aggression when they become young adults (Eron, 1987; Huesmann & Taylor, 2006). This association is not simply due to the fact that children who watch the most television violence are already more aggressive to begin with. Moreover, boys and girls who perceive television violence to be highly realistic and identify strongly with same-sex aggressive television characters are most likely to act aggressively as adults (Huesmann, Moise-Titus, Podolski, & Eron, 2003). Experiments in laboratory and field settings reveal a clearer causal link between watching media violence and behaving more aggressively (Leyens, Camino, Parke, & Berkowitz, 1975).

FIGURE 14.36 Exposure to violent video games increases aggressive behaviour. The exact mechanism responsible for this is still being hotly debated.

Source: © Rich Seymour/iStock.

Media violence appears to exert its effects through multiple avenues (Huesmann, 1997):

- Viewers learn new aggressive behaviours through modelling.
- Viewers come to believe that aggression usually is rewarded, or at least rarely punished.
- Viewers become desensitized to the sight and thought of violence and to the suffering of victims (Engelhardt, Bartholow, Kerr, & Bushman, 2011).

Beyond films and television, the question of whether violent video games promote aggression also has raised much public and scientific concern (Figure 14.36). In 2005 some Washington State legislators drafted a bill to make it easier for parents to sue violent-video-game manufacturers in cases where playing those games could be linked to the commission of violent crimes (King Broadcasting Company, 2005). Is this a political reaction to a societal problem, or an over-reaction for maximum political effect? A recent meta-analysis involving 136 publications and over 130,000 participants revealed a clear pattern: exposure to violent video games increases aggressive behaviour and cognitions, and decreases empathy and pro-social behaviour (Anderson et al., 2010). However, exactly why this occurs is still hotly debated. For example, research by Andrew Przybylski and colleagues (Przybylski, Deci, Rigby, & Ryan, 2013) shows that video games may increase aggressive behaviour as a result of gamers' failure to master the game and its controls. Thus, aggression may be a side-effect of the frustration felt while playing the game, independent of the actual content of the game.

> **Focus 14.27** Discuss catharsis and social learning views on effects of media violence. How do violent video games promote aggression?

As we close this section on social relations, 'Levels of analysis' highlights some of the biological, psychological and environmental factors that contribute to human aggression.

Levels of analysis
factors related to aggression

PSYCHOLOGICAL

- ■ Perception of potential provocation as intentional versus accidental
- ■ Lack of empathy for the potential target of aggression
- ■ Impaired thinking processes that decrease ability to regulate hostile feelings
- ■ Self-justification of aggressive acts towards a victim
- ■ Overcontrolled hostility

BIOLOGICAL

- ■ Genetic contribution to individual differences in aggressiveness
- ■ Evolutionary adaptiveness of aggressive behaviours that enhanced species' survival
- ■ Brain regions that regulate aggression (e.g., hypothalamus, amygdala, frontal lobes)
- ■ Seratonin, other transmitters and hormones that regulate aggression

ENVIRONMENTAL

- ■ Stimuli that produce frustration, pain, or provocation
- ■ Other averse stimuli, such as crowding and heat
- ■ Past and present reinforcement for aggression
- ■ Exposure to live or mass media aggressive models
- ■ Exposure to violent video games

Aggression

 In review

- ■ Categorization in in-groups and out-groups enhances the tendency to judge other people based on their perceived group membership rather than their individual characteristics.
- ■ Prejudice stems partly from our tendency to perceive in-groups and out-groups. People typically display in-group favouritism and an out-group homogeneity bias. Perceived threats to one's in-group and a need to enhance one's self-esteem can motivate prejudice.
- ■ People display explicit prejudice publicly. When people conceal or are not consciously aware of their prejudice, they are exhibiting implicit prejudice.
- ■ Prejudice often is reduced when in-group and out-group members work closely together, with equal status, on tasks involving common goals, and under conditions of broader institutional support.
- ■ Proximity, mere exposure, similarity of attitudes, and physical attractiveness typically enhance our attraction towards someone. Social exchange theory analyses relationships in terms of the rewards and costs experienced by each partner.
- ■ Evolutionary theorists propose that gender difference in mate preferences reflect inherited biological tendencies, whereas sociocultural theorists believe that these differences result from socialization and gender inequities in economic opportunities.

◄

- Partners are more likely to remain happily married when they understand each other and deal with conflicts by de-escalating their emotions and providing mutual support.

- Some theorists propose that through kin selection and reciprocal altruism, evolution has shaped a genetic predisposition towards pro-social behaviour among humans. Social learning theorists emphasize how norms, modelling and reinforcement shape pro-social behaviour.

- The presence of multiple bystanders may decrease bystander intervention through social comparison processes and a diffusion of responsibility for helping. We are most likely to help others whom we perceive as similar to us and as not responsible for their plight.

- Pro-social behaviour can be increased by enhancing people's feelings of empathy for victims and providing pro-social models.

- Heredity influences an organism's tendency to aggress. The hypothalamus, amygdala and frontal lobes play central roles in aggression.

- Provocation, heat, crowding and stimuli that cause frustration or pain increase the risk of aggression. Learning experiences help shape a tendency to behave more or less aggressively. People are more likely to be aggressive when they find ways to justify and rationalize their aggressive behaviour, perceive provocation as intentional, and have little empathy for others.

- Most research supports the social learning theory prediction that watching film and television violence and playing violent video games increase the risk that children and adults will act aggressively.

 ## Recommended reading

CLASSIC

Allport, G. W. (1954). *The nature of prejudice.* Reading, MA: Addison-Wesley.

Heider, F. (1958). *The psychology of interpersonal relations.* New York: John Wiley & Sons.

Tajfel, H., & Turner, J. C. (1979). An integrative theory of inter-group conflict. In W. G. Austin & S. Worchel (Eds.), *The social psychology of inter-group relations.* Monterey, CA: Brooks/Cole.

CONTEMPORARY

Duck, S. (2007). *Human relationships* (4th ed.). Thousand Oaks, CA: Sage.

Fiske, S. T., & Taylor, S. E. (2013). *Social cognition: From brains to culture* (2nd ed.). London: Sage.

Maio, G., & Haddock, G. (2009). *The psychology of attitudes and attitude change.* London: Sage.

Moghaddam, F. M. & Marsella, A. J. (Eds.) (2003). *Understanding terrorism: Psychosocial roots, consequences and interventions.* Washington, DC: APA.

Stürmer, S., & Snyder, M. (Eds.) (2009). *The psychology of prosocial behaviour: Group processes, intergroup relations, and helping.* Chichester, UK: Wiley-Blackwell.

Much of our lives is spent in trying to understand others and in wishing others understood us better than they do.

Gordon Allport

Personality

15

Chapter Outline

 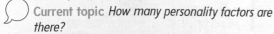

On a hot summer evening in 1966, Charles Whitman, a 25-year-old student at the University of Texas, wrote the following letter:

> I don't really understand myself these days. I am supposed to be an average, reasonable, and intelligent young man. However, lately (I can't recall when it started) I have been the victim of many unusual and irrational thoughts. These thoughts constantly recur, and it requires a tremendous mental effort to concentrate on useful and progressive tasks. In March when my parents made a physical break I noticed a great deal of stress. I consulted a Dr. Cochrum at the University Health Center and asked him to recommend someone that I could consult with about some psychiatric disorders I felt I had. I talked with a doctor once for about two hours and tried to convey to him my fears that I felt overcome by overwhelming violent impulses. After one session I never saw the doctor again, and since then I have been fighting my mental turmoil alone, and seemingly to no avail. After my death I wish that an autopsy would be performed on me to see if there is any visible physical disorder. I have had some tremendous headaches in the past and have consumed two large bottles of Excedrin in the past three months.   (Lavergne, 1997, p. 8)

Later that night, Whitman killed his wife and mother, both of whom were lovingly supportive of him. The next morning he carried a high-powered hunting rifle to the top of a 307-foot tower on the busy University of Texas campus in Austin and opened fire on all those passing by below. Within 90 horrifying minutes, he killed 16 people and wounded 30 others before he himself was killed by police.

On the surface, Whitman (Figure 15.1) seemed as solid and upstanding as the University of Texas tower from which he rained death on unsuspecting strangers. He came from a wealthy, prominent Florida family and was an outstanding student, an accomplished pianist, one of the youngest 'Eagle Scouts' in state history and a former US Marine who had been awarded a Good Conduct Medal and the Marine Corps Expeditionary Medal. He married the woman of his dreams, and the two were seen as an ideal couple. Whitman became a University of Texas student when he was selected by the Marines for a prestigious engineering scholarship. In his spare time, he served as a scoutmaster in Austin.

What could have caused this exemplary citizen to commit such extraordinary acts of violence? In 2001, the Austin History Center opened its records on Charles Whitman to public scrutiny. These records provided important insights into the complexities of Whitman's personality and the turmoil that existed within him. Although the Whitman incident occurred decades ago, it is sadly reminiscent of more recent acts of violence in schools, communities

FIGURE 15.1 (a) Charles Whitman with his wife, whom he later murdered. Few thought this exemplary citizen capable of the heinous acts of violence he committed. (b) Whitman (arrow) fires from the University of Texas tower onto the campus below.

Source: © Bettmann/CORBIS

(a)

(b)

and work places across the world. In this chapter, we consider the factors that triggered Whitman's violence through the lenses of the major personality perspectives. Doing so can help us paint a more complete portrait of Whitman and may further our understanding not only of him but also of others who commit acts of violence and terrorism.

WHAT IS PERSONALITY?

The concept of personality arises from the fascinating spectrum of human individuality. We observe that people differ meaningfully in the ways they customarily think, feel and act. These distinctive behaviour patterns help define one's identity as a person. As one group of theorists noted, each of us is in certain respects like *all other* people, like *some other* people and like *no other* person who has lived in the past or will exist in the future (Kluckhohn & Murray, 1953). Personality researchers attempt to describe these similarities and differences in an informative and predictive way so that we can understand better what it is to be a particular person.

The concept of personality also rests on the observation that a given person seems to behave somewhat consistently over time and across different situations. From this perceived consistency comes the notion of *personality traits* that characterize an individual's customary ways of responding to his or her world. Although only modest stability is found from childhood personality to adult personality (see **Chapter 13** for more information about childhood personality), personality becomes more stable as we enter adulthood (Caspi & Roberts, 2001; Terracciano, Costa, & McCrae, 2006). Nonetheless, even in adulthood, and particularly in old age, a capacity for meaningful personality change remains (Roberts, Helson, & Klohnen, 2002; Specht, Egloff, & Schmukle, 2011).

Chapter 13, Page 540

Combining these notions of individuality and consistency, we can define **personality** as the distinctive and relatively enduring ways of thinking, feeling and acting that characterize a person's responses to life situations. Note that this definition refers not only to personal characteristics, but also to situations. Personality psychologists are therefore interested in studying 'person-by-situation' interactions in their efforts to understand the distinctive behaviours of individuals (Robins, Fraley, & Krueger, 2007).

personality the distinctive and relatively enduring ways of thinking, feeling and acting that characterize a person's responses to life situations

But what are the elements of human behaviour that help us to determine what a person's personality is? Gordon Allport, an important figure in early personality psychology, provides a definition of personality that helps us with this question. Allport defined personality as 'a dynamic organization, inside the person, of psychophysical systems that create the person's characteristic patterns of behaviours, thoughts and feelings' (Allport, 1961, p. 11). There are three facets of this definition which help us here. First, personality behaviours are viewed as being part of the identity which helps distinguish one person from another (Allport states that personality creates 'characteristic patterns of behaviours'). Second, the behaviours are viewed as being caused primarily by *internal rather than environmental factors* (Allport states that personality is 'inside the person'). Third, personality behaviours have *organization and structure*; they seem to fit together in a meaningful fashion, suggesting an inner personality that guides and directs behaviour (Allport states that personality is a 'dynamic organization . . . of . . . systems').

The study of personality has been guided by a number of perspectives; notably, the psychodynamic, humanistic, biological, behavioural, cognitive and sociocultural perspectives. These perspectives often provide quite different conceptions of what personality is and how it functions, and this is summed up in the following quote: 'It seems hard to believe that all the theorists are talking about the same creature, who is now angelic and now depraved, now a black-box robot shaped by reinforcers and now a shaper of its own destiny, now devious . . . and now hardheadedly oriented to solid reality' (Stone & Church, 1968, p. 4). It seems likely that this diversity of viewpoints arises partly from the fact that the theorists are describing personality at different levels of analysis (see **Chapter 1**, 'levels-of-analysis framework). No doubt, you will find some of their theories more in accord with your own life views than you will find others, but bear in mind that the different perspectives are not incompatible. It is possible to make meaningful observations about personality at multiple levels of analysis without contradiction.

Focus 15.1 Identify three characteristics of 'personality behaviours'.

Chapter 1, Page 7

Chapter 2, Page 42

 Focus 15.2 What three standards determine the scientific usefulness of a personality theory?

Importantly, for psychologists, a theory's subjective truth (the degree to which it rings true in your own mind) is less important than its *predictive power*. As discussed in **Chapter 2**, a scientific theory is useful to the extent that it (1) provides a comprehensive framework within which known facts can be incorporated, (2) allows us to predict future events with some precision, and (3) stimulates the discovery of new knowledge. We evaluate each of the theories we describe in terms of these scientific standards. We consider a number of approaches to the study of personality, beginning with the seminal work of Sigmund Freud, whose psychodynamic theory set the stage for a century of progress in the study of personality.

In review

■ The concept of personality arises from observations of individual differences and consistencies in behaviour. Personality refers to the distinctive and relatively enduring ways of thinking, feeling and acting that characterize a person's responses to life situations. Behaviours attributed to personality are viewed as establishing an individual's characteristic identity, having an internal cause, and having a meaningful organization and structure.

■ Personality theories differ considerably in their conceptions of what personality is and how it functions. Scientifically useful personality theories organize existing knowledge, allow the prediction of future events and stimulate the discovery of new knowledge.

THE PSYCHODYNAMIC PERSPECTIVE

The first formal theory of personality was advanced by Sigmund Freud in the early years of the twentieth century, and it is the prototype of the psychodynamic approach. Psychodynamic theorists look for the causes of behaviour in a dynamic interplay of inner motivational forces that often conflict with one another. They also suggest that many of these motivational determinants of behaviour are unconscious. Sigmund Freud's psychoanalytic theory of personality is one of the great intellectual contributions of modern times, and it continues to influence Western thought today, not just in personality and abnormal psychology, but also in cognitive psychology, to which Freud contributed the notion of separate states of consciousness. Though Freud's approach is still taken by modern psychodynamicists, many psychologists from other disciplines now have a strong opposition to Freud's ideas. Indeed, opposition to Freud was a stimulus for the development of most of the other theories discussed in this chapter.

FREUD'S PSYCHODYNAMIC THEORY

Freud (1856–1939) spent most of his life in Vienna, where he attended medical school with the intention of becoming a medical researcher (Figure 15.2). He was particularly interested in brain functioning. A pivotal event in his life occurred when he was awarded a fellowship to study in Paris with the famous French neurologist Jean Charcot. Charcot was treating patients who suffered from a disorder called *conversion hysteria*, in which physical symptoms such as paralysis and blindness appear suddenly and with no apparent physical cause. Freud's experiences in treating these patients convinced him that their symptoms were related to painful memories and feelings that seemed to have been *repressed*, or pushed out of awareness. When his patients were able to re-experience these traumatic memories and unacceptable feelings, which were often sexual or aggressive in nature, their physical symptoms often disappeared or improved markedly.

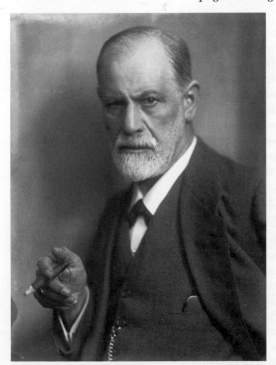

FIGURE 15.2 Sigmund Freud founded psychoanalysis. For more than 50 years, he probed the hidden recesses of the mind.

Source: © GL Archive/Alamy

These observations convinced Freud that an unconscious part of the mind exerts great influence on behaviour. He began to experiment with various techniques to unearth the buried contents of the unconscious mind, including hypnosis, *free association* (saying whatever comes to mind, no matter how

trivial or embarrassing) and dream analysis. In an attempt to relieve his own painful bouts of depression, Freud also conducted an extensive self-analysis based on his own dreams.

In 1900 Freud published 'The interpretation of dreams' (Freud, 1953). The book sold only 600 copies in the first six years after its publication, but his revolutionary ideas began to attract followers. His theory also evoked scathing criticism from a Victorian society that was not ready to regard the human being as a seething cauldron of sexual and aggressive impulses. In the words of one commentator,

> *It is a shattering experience for anyone seriously committed to the Western tradition of morality and rationality to take a steadfast, unflinching look at what Freud has to say. It is humiliating to be compelled to admit the grossly seamy side of so many grand ideals. . . . To experience Freud is to partake a second time of the forbidden fruit.*   (Brown, 1959, p. xi)

Freud based his theory on careful clinical observation and constantly sought to expand it. Over time, psychoanalysis became (1) a theory of personality, (2) an approach to studying the mind, and (3) a method for treating psychological disorders.

Psychic Energy and Mental Events

Inspired by the hydraulic models of nineteenth-century physics, which emphasized exchanges and releases of physical energy, Freud considered personality to be an energy system, somewhat like the steam engines of his day. According to Freud, instinctual drives generate *psychic energy (or* libido*)*, which powers the mind and constantly presses for either direct or indirect release. For example, a build-up of energy from sexual drives might be discharged directly in the form of sexual activity or indirectly through such diverse behaviours as sexual fantasies, farming or painting.

Mental events may be conscious, preconscious or unconscious. The *conscious mind* consists of mental events in current awareness. The *preconscious mind* contains memories, feelings, thoughts and images that we are unaware of at the moment but that can be recalled, such as a friend's telephone number or memories of your sixteenth birthday.

Because we can be aware of their contents, we are likely to see the conscious and preconscious areas of the mind as the most prominent ones. But Freud believed that these areas are dwarfed in both size and importance by the *unconscious mind*, a dynamic realm of wishes, feelings and impulses that lies beyond our awareness. He compared the mind to an iceberg with the unconscious mind represented by the (much larger) part below the surface (see Figure 15.3). Only when impulses from the unconscious are discharged in one way or another, such as in dreams, slips of the tongue or some disguised behaviour, does the unconscious reveal itself, sometimes with unfortunate consequences. Imagine that in the throes of passion, a young man proclaimed his love for his fiancée by saying, 'I love you, Alice'. A problem arises if it turns out that his fiancée's name was Amy, and Alice was a former girlfriend. Freud would probably conclude (as might Amy) that the slip

> **libido** Freud's term for the motivational force or psychic energy which he posited to drive our behaviour and mental lives

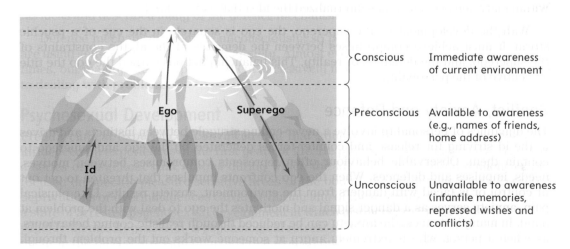

FIGURE 15.3 Freud's model of personality.

Freud's own representation of his three-part conception of personality shows the relation of the id, ego and superego to the unconscious, preconscious and conscious areas of the mind. Note how relatively small the conscious portion of the mind is compared with the unconscious.

Source: Adapted from B. D. Smith, 1998.

Research close-up

ATTACHMENT STYLE AND ABUSIVE ROMANTIC RELATIONSHIPS

Source: V. Zayas and Y. Shoda (2007). Predicting preferences for dating partners from past experiences of psychological abuse: identifying the psychological ingredients of situations, *Personality and Social Psychology Bulletin, 33*, pp. 123–148.

INTRODUCTION

Researchers who study abusive romantic relationships have noted that involvement in such relationships tends to repeat itself over time, and that such experiences are more common in women with an anxious-ambivalent attachment style (Dutton, 2006). Does this occur by chance, or is it possible that people with particular personality patterns somehow seek out one another to re-create destructive relationships marked by psychological abuse? One possibility is that adult attachment styles predispose people to prefer romantic partners who fit their working models of intimate relationships (Figure 15.5). To test this hypothesis, Zayas and Shoda (2007) studied the romantic partner preferences of women with a history of victimization and of men with a history of abusing women in romantic relationships within an Internet-dating procedure.

METHOD

From students in large introductory psychology classes, two groups of women were identified. One group consisted of 32 women who reported being victims of frequent psychological abuse in their most recent long-term romantic relationship. On a 60-item measure of abusive behaviours, these women reported that experiences like the following had often occurred with their romantic partner during a 12-month period: *isolation and emotional control* (e.g., 'My partner tried to keep me from seeing or talking to my family'); undermining self-esteem (e.g., 'My partner treated me like I was stupid'); jealousy (e.g., 'My partner was jealous of my friends'); *verbal abuse* (e.g., 'My partner swore at me'); and *emotional withdrawal* (e.g., 'My partner sulked and refused to talk about a problem'). A comparison group of 33 low-abuse women reported that such experiences occurred seldom or never in their most recent relationship. The women in each group also completed a self-report measure of attachment style, including a scale of attachment anxiety that included items such as 'I worry a lot about my relationships'.

To create a real-life situation to assess romantic partner preference, the women participated in a computer-dating procedure in which they indicated how much they would like to go out with each of 16 different men who provided descriptions of themselves. The self-descriptions of the men comprised statements that had been taken from actual descriptions of themselves given by college men. These statements were rated by a separate sample of women on desirability in a dating partner and potential for being abusive. Statements rated as high in potential for abusiveness reflected a predisposition towards anger (e.g., 'Warning ahead, I do have a very bad temper'), jealousy ('I do admit that I will get jealous if you are always going over to one of your male friends' houses'), themes regarding trust and emotional control (e.g., 'I will treat you like God until you break my trust and then you are just another person'), and possessiveness. The ratings of desirability and abuse potential were used to create potential male dating partners who fell into three categories: (1) potentially abusive (four advertisements); (2) undesirable as a dating partner but not abusive (eight advertisements); and (3) desirable as a dating partner and not abusive (four advertisements).

The high-abuse and low-abuse women viewed each of the sixteen personal advertisements on an experimenter-constructed website, where each male's advertisements had a separate web page with his description of himself but no picture. They made four rounds of forced-choice selections. In the first round, they selected eight of the sixteen advertisements that were most preferable to them. In the second round, they selected four of the eight, in the third round, two of the four, and in the final round they selected the person they were most interested in getting to know better.

In a second part of the study, college men were administered the psychological abuse questionnaire that the women had completed

FIGURE 15.5 Do adult attachment styles lead some women into abusive relationships?

Source: © Mark Bowden.

Research design		
Question:	How is a history of having been psychologically abused or having been the perpetrator of psychological abuse related to preferred characteristics of Future dating?	
Type of study: Correlational		
Variable X		**Variable Y**
Abused vs non-abused women Abusing vs non-abusing men	→	Characteristics of most-preferred dating partner

and were asked how often they had engaged in the abusive behaviours in their previous romantic relationship. The researchers identified 46 men who were abusive and 47 who reported inflicting little or no abuse. These two groups of men engaged in an identical Internet-dating procedure as the women, except that the personal advertisements of the women were designed to express either high or low levels of attachment anxiety. Eight of the descriptions suggested high attachment anxiety and eight did not. The attachment anxiety statements in the personal advertisements were drawn from the measure used to assess attachment anxiety in the women's portion of the study, and an independent sample of men rated the descriptions of these potential dating partners as indicating higher relationship anxiety.

RESULTS

The researchers first examined the relationship between attachment anxiety and past abuse. In agreement with previous research, they found that the high-abuse women were significantly more anxious about their close relationships and fearful of losing them.

Of major interest were the dating preferences of the two groups of women. Table 15.4a shows the percentages of high-abuse and low-abuse women whose top choice from among the 16 was either a desirable, an undesirable or an abusive partner. The low-abuse women overwhelmingly preferred a desirable partner, and very few of them chose one of the potentially abusive men. In striking contrast, the high-abuse women were three times as likely to choose one of the four potentially abusive partners, and nearly as likely to choose an abusive partner as a desirable one.

TABLE 15.4 Percentages of women and men who chose each type of partner

(a) Women's choices

Abuse group	Preferred male partner		
	Desirable	**Undesirable**	**Abusive**
Low-abuse women	66.7	21.2	12.1
High-abuse women	40.6	21.9	37.5

(b) Men's choices

Abuse group	Preferred female partner	
	Low attachment anxiety	**High attachment anxiety**
Non-abusing men	72.3	27.7
Abusing men	39.1	60.9

The men's dating preferences are shown in Table 15.4b. Here again, we see a notable contrast. The vast majority of the non-abusive men preferred a woman who was low in attachment anxiety, whereas a majority of the abusive men chose a potential partner who was high in the characteristic of attachment anxiety, which this and other studies have shown to be common in women who are victimized by abuse.

DISCUSSION

This study illustrates the potential usefulness of concepts derived from object relations theory in understanding human relationships. The notion that early experiences in intimate relationships produce working models of what is to be expected in future relationships has received considerable research support (Rholes & Simpson, 2006). In this study, we see evidence that people may perpetuate self-injurious and destructive relationship patterns. Women with histories of abuse in romantic relationships might be expected to steer clear of future relationships of this kind. Instead, they are as likely to choose a dating partner who has been judged by others to be impulsive, possessive, jealous, aggressive, hostile, degrading and potentially violent as they are to choose a desirable and non-abusive partner.

Men's personality characteristics also influence their choice of potential romantic partners. Men without a history of abusing women show little desire to relate to insecure, relationship-anxious women. In contrast, abusive men are drawn to these women who are more likely to become dependent on them and therefore tolerate their behaviour as they act out their hostile impulses within the relationship. Clearly, the choices of both men and women are based on 'psychological ingredients' of the situation, which includes the stimulus characteristics of the potential partner.

This study also raises several interesting questions that deserve research attention. The focus here was on psychological abuse, which probably occurs more often than physical abuse. Do these findings generalize to physically abusive relationships? Likewise, this investigation addressed relationships in which men abused women. What are the 'active ingredients' of partners in relationships in which men are psychologically abused by women? Answers to questions like these would increase our understanding of how personality and situational factors interact in destructive interpersonal relationships.

environment. His father was a self-made but brutal man who ruled his house with an iron fist and frequently beat his wife. He tolerated no weakness from his sons and viciously belittled them for any perceived failures. Whitman was very close to his mother and deeply resented his father's treatment of her, which, according to Freud, would only enhance any unresolved Oedipal hostility towards the father. In his suicide note, he wrote, 'The intense hatred I feel for my father is beyond description' (Lavergne, 1997, p. 168). Lacking a good paternal model with whom to identify, Whitman seemed to have a poorly developed superego and constantly wrote himself notes about how to behave appropriately, using the notes as a substitute for his tenuous inner controls. A friend describing Whitman said he

was 'like a computer. He would install his values into the machine, then program the things he had to do, and out would come the results' (Lavergne, 1997, p. 79).

Object relations theories also have applicability to Whitman. Despite his hatred for his father, his own family experiences caused him to enter his marriage with an internal working model of 'abusive husband' and 'submissive wife'. To his later regret, he beat his own wife on two occasions in the early years of his marriage. He was determined not to repeat this behaviour and kept a journal in which he constantly wrote self-instructions about how to be a good husband. For the most part, these external constraints were effective in keeping his intense hostility under control – until the accumulation of severe life stressors caused his controls to disintegrate. 'Unusual and irrational thoughts' began to intrude into consciousness as his defences were strained to the breaking point, and he eventually exploded into violence. The psychiatrist at the student health centre who interviewed him several months before the tower incident (referred to in Whitman's letter at the opening of this chapter as 'the doctor') found that he 'had something about him that expressed the all-American boy', but 'seemed to be oozing with hostility'. Whitman told the psychiatrist that he had frequent fantasies about 'going up on the tower with a deer rifle and shooting people', but the psychiatrist did not take them seriously because of his non-violent history (Lavergne, 1997, p. 137).

 In review

- Freud's psychoanalytic theory views personality as an energy system. Personality dynamics involve modifications and exchanges of energy (libido) within this system. Mental events may be conscious, preconscious or unconscious.

- Freud divided the personality into three structures: id, ego and superego. The id is irrational and seeks immediate instinctual gratification on the basis of the pleasure principle. The ego operates on the reality principle, which requires it to test reality and to mediate between the demands of the id, the superego and reality. The superego is the moral arm of the personality.

- The dynamics of personality involve continuous conflict between impulses of the id and counter-forces of the ego and superego. When dangerous id impulses threaten to get out of control or when the environment poses dangers, the result is anxiety. To deal with threat, the ego may develop defence mechanisms to ward off anxiety and permit instinctual gratification in disguised forms.

- Freud's psychosexual theory of personality development held that adult personality traits are moulded by how children deal with instinctual urges and social reality during the oral, anal and phallic stages.

- Neoanalytic theorists modified and extended Freud's ideas in important ways, stressing social and cultural factors in personality development. Today, object relations theorists focus on the mental representations that people form of themselves, others and relationships.

- There has been a great deal of criticism levelled at Freud's approach, and psychodynamic theories more generally. Modern psychologists are particularly concerned about the difficulty of testing psychodynamic theories and the lack of evidence for psychodynamic explanations of personality. Nonetheless, psychodynamics, and particularly the idea of the unconscious, has received some confirmation from cognitive research.

THE PHENOMENOLOGICAL-HUMANISTIC PERSPECTIVE

The approaches we describe next arose in part as a reaction to Freud's conception of people as driven by 'those half-tamed demons that inhabit the human beast' (Freud, 1965, p. 202). In contrast to Freud, these theorists believed that our behaviour is not a reaction to unconscious drives and conflicts but rather a response to our immediate conscious experience of self and environment (Kelly, 1955; Rogers, 1951). This emphasis on the primacy of immediate experience is known as **phenomenology**, and it focuses our attention on the present instead of the past. These theorists also regarded themselves as

phenomenology study of immediate experience

humanists. They embraced a positive view that affirms the inherent dignity and goodness of the human spirit, as well as the individual's creative potential and inborn striving towards personal growth (Figure 15.6).

GEORGE KELLY'S PERSONAL CONSTRUCT THEORY

To the humanist every man is a scientist by disposition as well as by right, every subject is an incipient experimenter, and every person is by daily necessity a fellow psychologist. (Kelly, 1966, quoted in Maher, 1979, p. 205)

A theory developed by George Kelly (1905–67) in the 1950s has had a strong and pervasive influence on many other theorists. According to Kelly, people's primary goal is to make sense out of the world, to find personal meaning in it. When they are unable to do so, they experience uncertainty and anxiety. To achieve understanding, they try to explain and understand the events of their lives, and they test this understanding in the same way scientists do: by attempting to anticipate, to predict.

Kelly's primary interest was how people construct reality. They do so by their individual system of **personal constructs**, cognitive categories into which they sort the persons and events in their lives. In Kelly's theory, the personal construct system was the primary basis for individual differences in personality.

As noted in our discussion of concept formation in **Chapter 9**, all perception involves categorizing. Kelly maintained that, from birth onwards, stimuli are categorized, given meaning and reacted to in terms of the categories, or personal constructs, into which they are placed. Every person has her or his own pattern of preferred personal constructs (such as 'good', 'bad', 'successful', 'powerful' and so on), which vary in personal importance. By understanding these constructs, the rules an individual uses to assign events to categories, and her or his hypotheses about how the categories relate to one another, Kelly believed that we can understand the person's psychological world. If we can understand the individual's internal world, then we can understand and predict that person's behaviour.

Rather than evaluating alternative constructions according to whether or not they are true (which we cannot know), Kelly examined the consequences of construing in particular ways. For example, if one of a couple in a broken relationship interpreted a break-up as 'being rejected', Kelly would try to discover the consequences for the person of construing the situation in that way. If the construction led to bad outcomes, such as feelings of worthlessness or the conclusion that 'No one will ever love me, and I'll never get involved again', then the task would be to find a more useful alternative (for example, 'I am someone who hasn't found the right person yet but who will if I keep trying'). Kelly, a clinical psychologist, saw psychotherapy as a way of demonstrating to clients that their constructions are *hypotheses* rather than facts. Once clients realize this, they can be encouraged to test the hypotheses that govern their lives, just as scientists do, and to replace maladaptive ones with more useful ones.

As people seek to understand events within the world, they develop habitual tendencies related to categorization of people and events. Such tendencies can be measured by tasks that determine the extent to which particular categories are used in making such distinctions (Robinson, Vargas, Tamir, & Solberg, 2004). Kelly developed a measure called the **Role Construct Repertory Test** (or **Rep Test**), to assess individuals' personal construct systems. In taking the Rep Test, you are asked to consider people or events in your life that are important to you. You then consider them in groups of three (for example, father, best friend, romantic partner) and indicate how any two of them are similar to one another and different from the third. In this way, the basic dimensions of similarity and difference that you use to categorize people and events – your personal constructs – will begin to emerge. The Rep Test can also assess other aspects of your construct system, such as the number of different constructs that you use.

FIGURE 15.6 Pablo Picasso poses next to one of his many works of art.

In the view of humanistic theorists like Abraham Maslow and Carl Rogers, creative and artistic accomplishments are an expression of an innate tendency towards self-actualization.

Source: Gamma-Rapho via Getty Images.

 Chapter 9, Page 385

personal constructs cognitive categories into which people sort the persons and events in their lives

Role Construct Repertory Test (or **Rep Test**) assesses individuals' personal construct systems by investigating what dimensions people use to categorize important others

Focus 15.7 What are personal constructs, and how do they account for personality differences?

are less susceptible to social pressure and are more capable of forming satisfying love relationships (Brown, 1998). In contrast, people with poor self-images are less likely to try to make themselves feel better when they experience negative moods in response to perceived failures in their lives (Heimpel, Wood, Marshall, & Brown, 2002). This may be one reason why they are more prone to psychological problems such as anxiety and depression, to physical illness and to poor social relationships and underachievement (Brown, 1998).

People who are low in self-esteem are more reactive to the ups and downs of everyday life. In one study, 15 working couples completed a daily diary and mood ratings during a three-week period. Low self-esteem men and women felt more loved and accepted by their spouses on days when they enjoyed professional successes, but less loved on days when they experienced professional failures. People high in self-esteem were not affected in this manner (Murray, Griffin, Rose, & Bellavia, 2006).

What conditions foster high self-esteem? One important factor appears to be having a well-defined self-concept. Campbell (1990) found a significant relationship between the clarity of one's self-concept (how confident and consistent people were in defining their own identities) and their self-esteem. More recently, Usborne and Taylor (2010) have shown that this also extends to one's national identity.

But what developmental conditions lead to higher self-esteem? Children develop higher self-esteem when their parents communicate unconditional acceptance and love, establish clear guidelines for behaviour, and reinforce compliance while giving the child freedom to make decisions and express opinions within those guidelines (Brown, 1998; Coopersmith, 1967). Beginning in early childhood, success in achieving positive outcomes builds a sense that one is an effective person (Hawley & Little, 2002). Feedback received from other people also has an impact on the child's sense of self. One study showed that when low-self-esteem children were exposed to highly supportive youth sport coaches who gave them large amounts of positive reinforcement and encouragement, the children's self-esteem increased significantly over the course of the sports season (Smoll, Smith, Barnett, & Everett, 1993). Apparently, the positive feedback caused the children to revise their self-concepts in a positive direction.

Self-Verification and Self-Enhancement Motives

Rogers proposed that people are motivated to preserve their self-concepts by maintaining self-consistency and congruence. **Self-verification** refers to this need to confirm the self-concept. In one early study of this phenomenon, researchers asked university students to describe themselves in order to measure their self-concepts. In a later and supposedly unrelated experiment, the students interacted with other participants and received fake feedback from them in the form of adjectives that were either consistent or inconsistent with their self-concepts. Later, when the students were asked to recall and identify the adjectives that had been attributed to them, they showed greater recall for the consistent adjectives, suggesting that people selectively attend to and recall self-consistent information (Suinn, Osborne, & Winfree, 1962).

> **self-verification** the need to confirm the self-concept

Self-verification needs are also expressed in people's tendency to seek out self-confirming relationships. One study found that if people with firmly held negative self-views marry spouses who appraise them favourably, they tend to eventually withdraw from the marriage. Such people are more likely to remain with spouses who agree with the negative image they have of themselves. In contrast, people with positive self-concepts prefer spouses who share their positive views of themselves (Swann, Stein-Seroussi, & Giesler, 1992).

> **self-enhancement** a strong and pervasive tendency to gain and preserve a positive self-image

Rogers (1959) also suggested that people have a need to regard themselves positively, and research confirms the existence of **self-enhancement**, a strong and pervasive tendency to gain and preserve a positive self-image. Self-enhancement needs have been demonstrated across many cultures (Sedikides, Gaertner, & Toguchi, 2003; Sedikides, Gaertner, & Vevea, 2005; Sedikides & Greigg, 2008), and several self-enhancement strategies have been identified. For example, people show a marked tendency to attribute their successes to their own abilities and effort but to attribute their failures to environmental factors. Furthermore, most people rate themselves as

better than average on virtually any socially desirable characteristic that is subjective in nature (Leary, 2004). The vast majority of business people and politicians rate themselves as more ethical than the average. In defiance of mathematical possibility, about 80% of secondary school students rate themselves in the top 10% in their ability to get along with others. Even people who have been hospitalized after causing car accidents rate themselves as more skilful than the average driver (Greenberg, Solomon, & Pyszynski, 1997). People generally view themselves as improving over time, relative to their peers (Ross & Wilson, 2003). Indeed, as evidence on self-serving biases in self-perception continues to accumulate, researchers are concluding that positive illusions of this sort are the rule rather than the exception in well-adjusted people and that these self-enhancement tendencies contribute to people's psychological well-being (Taylor & Brown, 1988; Taylor, Lerner, Sherman, Sage, & McDowell, 2003). We describe this tendency further in **Chapter 14**.

 Chapter 14, Page 572

For people low in self-esteem, self-enhancement needs sometimes override self-verification tendencies (Tesser, 2004). In a series of experimental studies, Bernichon and co-workers (Bernichon, Cook, & Brown, 2003) found that individuals with low self-esteem have a strong tendency to seek out positive feedback about themselves even when it is not self-verifying. The pervasiveness of self-enhancement tendencies makes one wonder why so many people have low self-esteem. One answer is that although they desire positive self-enhancing feedback from others, people with low self-esteem do not provide much internal positive feedback to themselves. One experiment showed that when people low in self-esteem showed the same level of improvement on a laboratory task as did individuals with high self-esteem, they viewed themselves as improving far less. They also judged themselves more harshly when their performance decreased (Josephs, Bosson, & Jacobs, 2003). If one has trouble saying nice things about oneself, the kind of positive input that builds or repairs self-esteem is hard to come by.

Focus 15.9 How does self-esteem develop? Describe the roles of self-verification and self-enhancement as motivational forces.

EVALUATING THE PHENOMENOLOGICAL-HUMANISTIC APPROACH

What matters most in phenomenological-humanistic approaches is how people view themselves and the world. Some critics believe that the humanistic view relies too heavily on individuals' reports of their personal experiences. For example, psychoanalytic critics maintain that accepting what a person says at face value can easily lead to erroneous conclusions because of the always-present influence of unconscious defences.

Self-actualization, the motivational force at the core of humanistic theories, has also come under some criticism for being difficult to examine from a scientific perspective. Some critics believe that it is impossible to define an individual's self-actualizing tendency except in terms of the behaviour that it supposedly produces. This makes it a circular concept: humanists might argue that a person achieved such success because of self-actualization. But how do we know it was self-actualization which produced the success? Unfortunately, because we have no independent measure of self-actualization we can only rely on the fact that the person achieved great success. Unless a construct can be operationally defined in a manner independent of the phenomena it is supposed to cause, it is not scientifically useful. A construct must also be measurable. While it is true that concepts related to the self-actualization motive (such as people's beliefs that they are fulfilling their potential) could potentially be measured, most psychologists suggest that rather than being a scientific construct, self-actualization is better considered a philosophical concept.

Although humanism may indeed seem unscientific to some, Rogers (1959) dedicated himself to developing a theory whose concepts could be measured and whose laws could be tested. One of his most notable contributions was a series of studies on the process of self-growth that can occur in psychotherapy. To assess the effectiveness of psychotherapy, Rogers and his co-workers measured the discrepancy between clients' *ideal selves* (how they would like to be) and their *perceived selves* (their perceptions of what they were actually like). The studies revealed that when clients first entered therapy, the discrepancy

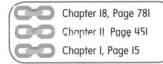

Chapter 18, Page 781

Chapter 11 Page 451

Chapter 1, Page 15

was typically large but that it got smaller as therapy proceeded, suggesting that therapy may help the client become more self-accepting and perhaps also more realistic. Rogers and his co-workers also discovered important therapist characteristics that either aid or impede the process of self-actualization in therapy. We describe this research in **Chapter 18**.

Several recent developments have put humanistic concepts back into the scientific spotlight. Deci and Ryan's self-determination theory, described in **Chapter 11**, has focused new scientific attention on humanistic concepts such as autonomy, competence and relatedness. New methods for measuring brain activation are enabling psychologists to study self-processes as they occur at a biological level (Blakemore, 2008; Heatherton, Macrae, & Kelley, 2004). In addition, the positive psychology movement, described in **Chapter 1**, has redirected many psychologists to the study of human strengths, happiness, virtue and other humanistic concerns (Peterson & Seligman, 2004; Snyder & Lopez, 2007).

Understanding Charles Whitman

What kinds of insights can the phenomenological-humanistic perspective contribute to the Charles Whitman case? The obvious starting point is Whitman's self-concept. Despite the successful façade of achievement and exemplary behaviour erected during his childhood and adolescent years, the abuse and denigration Whitman received from his father took a heavy toll on his self-concept. After years of being belittled, he was eager to prove himself as a man when he enlisted in the Marines. Unfortunately he found military life oppressive. His conduct deteriorated, and he was court-martialled for gambling and for threatening the life of a fellow Marine with a pistol.

Eventually, thanks to his father's political influence, Whitman was honourably discharged and returned to the University of Texas. Academic difficulties there left him riddled with self-doubt, and he struggled desperately to reduce the discrepancy between his ideal self and his perceived self. He frequently studied all night and took amphetamines to stay awake, but the drugs made him even less efficient. After he killed his wife while she slept, Whitman left a letter on her body in which he professed his love for her and his desire to relieve her of the shame she would surely experience as his wife.

 In review

- Humanistic theories emphasize the subjective experiences of the individual and thus deal with perceptual and cognitive processes. Self-actualization is viewed as an innate positive force that leads people to realize their positive potential if not thwarted by the environment.

- Kelly's theory addressed the manner in which people differ in their constructions of reality by the personal constructs they use to categorize their experiences.

- Rogers's theory attaches central importance to the role of the self. Experiences that are incongruous with the established self-concept produce threat and may result in a denial or distortion of reality. Conditional positive regard may result in unrealistic conditions of worth that can conflict with self-actualization. Rogers described a number of characteristics of the fully functioning person.

- Rogers's theory helped stimulate a great deal of research on the self-concept, including studies on the origins and effects of differences in self-esteem, self-enhancement and self-verification motives, and self-concept change. Recent humanistic developments include self-determination theory and the character strengths and virtues identified by Peterson and Seligman.

- Concerns about humanistic theories have centred on the difficulty of measuring self-actualization. Critiques have pointed out that self-actualization is difficult to measure apart from in the behaviour that it supposedly predicts, and so it is difficult to know whether it is a real phenomenon.

MAPPING THE STRUCTURE OF PERSONALITY

What are the ways in which people differ in personality? People have described others' personalities since time immemorial. This is also one of the main goals of personality psychologists: to describe the basic classes of behaviour that define personality, to devise

ways of measuring individual differences in personality, and to use these measures to understand and predict a person's behaviour.

TYPES AND TRAITS OF PERSONALITY

A simple distinction can be drawn between 'type' and 'trait' approaches to describing personality. A type approach attempts to classify people into groups who share the same common personality. An example of this approach can be seen in the earliest documented attempt to define personality. Inspired by the Ancient Greeks, Galen, a second-century physician, proposed four different personality types called: choleric, melancholic, phlegmatic and sanguine (see Figure 15.9). Galen proposed that people belonged to these personality types by virtue of their having an excess of one particular fluid (or humour) in their body. Choleric people had an excess of 'yellow bile', and were said to be bad tempered and aggressive. Melancholic people had an excess of 'black bile', and were said to be of a pessimistic and mournful disposition. Phlegmatic people had an excess of 'phlegm', and were supposed to be slow and easy-going sorts. Sanguine people had more 'blood' and thus were happy-go-lucky and passionate. While this view that personality types are caused by body fluids is now outmoded, remnants of its general approach remain in more recent typological theories such as that of Freud, who defined personality in terms of fixations at particular stages in development (e.g., an anal retentive or an anal expulsive personality type).

FIGURE 15.9 Personality types.
Clockwise from the top-left: phlegmatic, choleric, sanguine and melancholic. This artist clearly thought that facial appearance as well as behaviour was associated with a personality type.

On the other hand, trait theorists attempt to define a person's personality in terms of the *degree to which they possess a particular characteristic*. Rather than the all-or-none (yes or no) classification systems used by type theorists, trait theorists measure where a person sits on a trait *dimension* of personality. An analogy can be used with clothes sizes. Whereas in high-street shops sizes come in small, medium and large (a type system), in an old-fashioned tailor's shop clothes are made to fit a size on a number of different dimensions. The tailor will measure the height, waist size, neck size, and so on. The tailor's system is rather like what trait theorists attempt to do. They try to identify a set of dimensions which can be used to efficiently describe all people.

Personality traits are thus relatively stable cognitive, emotional and behavioural characteristics of people that help establish their individual identities and distinguish them from others. The starting point for the trait researcher is identifying the behaviours that define a particular trait. Years ago, the trait theorist Gordon Allport went through the English dictionary and painstakingly recorded all the words that could be used to describe personal traits. The result: a gigantic list of 17,953 words (Allport & Odbert, 1936). Obviously, it would be impractical, if not impossible, to describe people in terms of where they fall on roughly 18,000 dimensions. The trait theorist's goal is thus to condense all of these behavioural descriptors into a manageable number of basic traits that can capture personal individuality.

> **personality traits** are relatively stable cognitive, emotional and behavioural characteristics of people that help establish their individual identities and distinguish them from others

LEXICAL AND FACTOR ANALYTIC APPROACHES

One of the most influential approaches to uncovering the major personality traits has been to propose traits (e.g., 'dominance', 'friendliness', 'self-esteem') on the basis of words or concepts from everyday discourse or from concepts in existing personality theories. This is referred to as the *lexical approach*. Another very important approach in personality research is to use the statistical tool of *factor analysis*, the approach described in **Chapter 10** that has been used to identify distinct mental abilities. In personality research, **factor analysis** can be used to identify clusters of behaviours that are highly correlated (positively or negatively) with one another, but not with behaviours in other clusters. Such behaviour clusters can be viewed as reflecting a basic dimension, or trait, on which people vary. For example, you might find that most people who are socially reserved also avoid parties, enjoy quiet activities and like being alone. At the other end of the spectrum are people who are very talkative and sociable, like parties and excitement, dislike solitary activities such as reading, and constantly seek out new acquaintances. These behavioural patterns define a general factor, or dimension, that we might label *introversion–extraversion* (or simply *extraversion*). At one end of the dimension are

 Chapter 10, Page 414

> **factor analysis** used to identify clusters of behaviours that are highly correlated (positively or negatively) with one another, but not with behaviours in other clusters

highly introverted behaviours, and at the other end are highly extraverted behaviours. Presumably, each of us could be placed at some point along this dimension in terms of our customary behaviour patterns. In fact, as we will see, factor analytic studies have shown introversion–extraversion to be a major dimension of personality.

The lexical and factor analytic approaches can be brought together in the kinds of self-report questionnaires that people usually associate with 'personality tests'. In these questionnaires people are asked to rate on a scale the extent to which they see themselves as exemplifying a set of adjectives (e.g., 'friendly', 'outgoing', 'honest'). Factor analysis can then be used to determine which adjectives cluster together to form larger traits (Ashton, Lee, & Goldberg, 2004). This was the main method used by Raymond B. Cattell in forming his 16-factor theory which we shall describe next.

Cattell's 16 Personality Factors

If you were asked to describe and compare every person you know, how many different traits would it take to do the job? This is where trait theorists begin to disagree with one another. Because factor analysis can be used and interpreted in different ways, trait theorists have cut up the personality pie into smaller or larger pieces. The question of how many factors are needed to describe personality will be the focus of our 'Current topic' box at the end of this section. For example, the pioneering trait theorist Raymond B. Cattell (1965) asked thousands of participants to rate themselves on numerous adjectives; he also obtained ratings from people who knew the participants well. When he subjected this mass of data to factor analysis, he identified 16 basic behaviour clusters, or factors (Figure 15.10). Using this information, Cattell developed a widely used personality test called the *16 Personality Factor Questionnaire (16PF)* to measure individual differences on each of the dimensions and provide a comprehensive personality description. He was able to develop personality profiles not only for individuals but also for groups of people. For example, Figure 15.10 compares average scores obtained by creative artists and Olympic athletes.

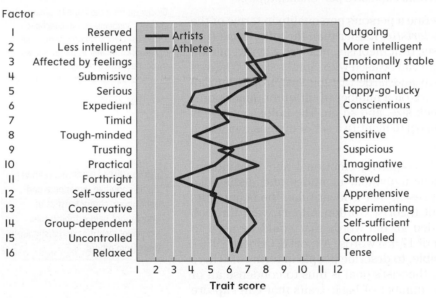

FIGURE 15.10 Cattell's 16 personality factors.

Raymond B. Cattell identified 16 basic personality traits through factor analysis. Here we see personality profiles (mean scores) for Olympic athletes and creative artists on the 16PF, the test developed by Cattell to measure the traits.

Source: Based on The Scientific Analysis of Personality' (1965) by R.B Cattell

Eysenck's Extraversion-Stability Mode

In contrast to Cattell's 16-factor approach, a number of more recent approaches favour a smaller number of personality 'super-traits'. Hans J. Eysenck (1916–97), one of Britain's leading psychologists, suggested that normal personality can be understood in terms of just *two* basic dimensions. These dimensions of introversion–extraversion and stability–instability (sometimes called neuroticism) encompass all of the more specific traits shown in Figure 15.11a. As we shall see, Eysenck's two 'supertraits' are still retained in more recent factor analytic approaches such as 'the Big Five' (see below).

Eysenck's extraversion-stability model is shown in Figure 15.11a. Note that the two basic dimensions intersect at right angles, meaning that they are statistically independent, or uncorrelated. The secondary traits shown in the circle reflect varying combinations, or mixtures, of the two primary dimensions. Thus we can see that the emotionally stable extravert is a carefree, lively person who tends to be well adjusted and to seek out leadership roles. In contrast, unstable extraverts tend to be touchy, aggressive and restless. The stable introvert is calm, reliable and even-tempered, but the unstable introvert tends to be rigid, anxious and moody. Different combinations of the two basic personality

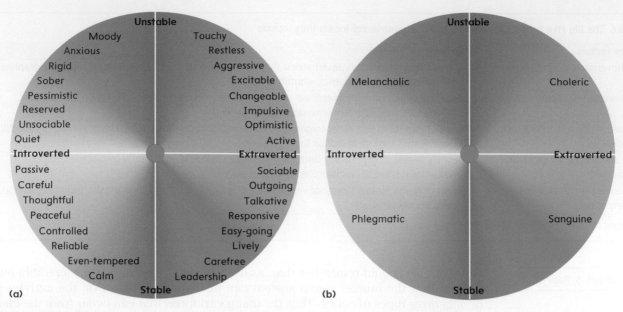

FIGURE 15.11 A two-factor model.

According to Hans Eysenck, (a) various combinations of two major dimensions of personality, introversion–extraversion and stability–instability (or neuroticism), combine to form more specific traits (b).

Source: Based on The biological basis of personality (1967) by H.J Eysenck

dimensions can thus produce very diverse personality patterns. Interestingly, the various combinations of these dimensions can describe the four types identified by Galen. Thus, someone who is unstable and introverted might be typed melancholic, someone who is unstable and extraverted – choleric, someone who is stable and introverted – phlegmatic, and someone who is stable and extraverted – sanguine (see Figure 15.11b).

Think about all the different people you know. Does Eysenck's attempt to describe personality in terms of just two 'super-traits' seem a little oversimplifying? More recently, trait theorists have added a few more 'super-traits', to Eysenck's two. Later in his career Eysenck himself saw the need to add a further trait of 'psychoticism'. Psychoticism was proposed to describe the degree to which someone was *aggressive, cold, egocentric, impersonal, impulsive, antisocial, unempathetic, creative* and *tough-minded*. As some of these traits were formerly considered part of extraversion, this entailed some changes to the conceptualization of that supertrait also. More recently, a number of researchers are converging on the opinion that personality is best described by five factors.

> **Focus 15.10** Describe and compare two models of personality derived from factor analysis.

The Five Factor Model

The five factor model suggests that five higher-order factors (sometimes referred to as the 'Big Five'), each including several of Cattell's more specific factors, are all that we need to capture the basic structure of personality (McCrae & Costa, 2003). These theorists also propose that these 'Big Five' factors may be universal to the human species, for the same five factors have been found consistently in trait ratings within diverse North American, Asian, Hispanic and European cultures (John & Srivastava, 1999; Trull & Geary, 1997).

The five factors from the five factor model are shown in Table 15.6. (The acronym OCEAN –openness, conscientiousness, extraversion, agreeableness and neuroticism – may help you remember them.) Proponents of the *five factor model* believe that when a person is placed at a specific point on each of these five dimensions by means of a psychological test, behaviour ratings or direct observations of behaviour, the essence of her or his personality has been captured (McCrae & Costa, 2003).

What do you think about that conclusion? If you were sceptical about Eysenck's two (or three) trait models you may not feel much happier about the five factor model. Surely there must be more to individuality than can be captured by only five dimensions.

TABLE 15.6 The Big Five personality factors and the behavioural facets they include

Big Five factors	Behaviours (facets)
E Extraversion versus introversion	Gregariousness (sociable), assertiveness (forceful), activity (energetic), excitement-seeking (adventurous), positive emotions (enthusiastic), warmth (outgoing)
A Agreeableness versus antagonism	Trust (forgiving), straightforwardness (not demanding), altruism (warm), compliance (not stubborn), modesty (not show-off), tendermindedness (sympathetic)
C Conscientiousness versus lack of direction	Competence (efficient), order (organized), dutifulness (not careless), achievement striving (thorough), self-discipline (not lazy), deliberation (not impulsive)
N Neuroticism versus emotional stability	Anxiety (tense), angry hostility (irritable), depression (not contented), self-consciousness (shy), impulsiveness (moody), vulnerability (not self-confident)
O Openness versus closedness to experience	Ideas (curious), fantasy (imaginative), aesthetics (artistic), actions (wide interests), feelings (excitable), values (unconventional)

Source: Based on McCrae and Costa, 2003.

Chapter 5, Page 166

However, we should remember that, as discussed in Chapter 5, the incredible number of colours that the human visual system can distinguish is based on the activity patterns of only *three* types of cones. Thus the many variations that can occur from the blending of five personality dimensions could account for enormous variation in personality patterns.

Trait theorists not only try to describe the basic structure of personality but also attempt to predict real-life behaviour on the basis of a person's traits. Even if a few general traits such as the Big Five seem adequate to describe important features of personality, it is entirely possible that a larger number of specific traits such as Cattell's would capture nuances of behaviour within particular situations and would therefore be better for predictive purposes. Measures of the global Big Five factors seldom correlate above .20 to .30 with real-life behavioural outcomes (e.g., Paunonen, 2003). In recognition of this fact, the Big Five model now includes six subcategories, or *facets* (Table 15.6), under each of the five major factors, and the personality test used to measure the Big Five (the *NEO Personality Inventory*, or *NEO-PI*) now provides scores on each of these facets as well as on the corresponding major factor. For example, scores are obtained not only for the main factor of extraversion, but also for facets such as activity and positive emotions. These more specific dimensions permit sharper behavioural predictions (McCrae & Costa, 2003). For example, the positive emotions/cheerfulness facet of extraversion is more highly related to life satisfaction than is the total extraversion score based on all six facets (Schimmack, Oishi, Furr, & Funder, 2004). Nonetheless, the ability of even these more specific traits to predict behaviour across varying situations is limited (Cervone, 1999; Ozer & Benet-Martínez, 2006).

STABILITY OF PERSONALITY TRAITS

One of the central premises of personality research is that personality is a stable thing which can be used to identify a particular individual. Thus, quite a substantial challenge to the view of personality structure arises when we observe that personality traits seem to change over time, and from situation to situation.

Changes in Personality over Time

Because traits are viewed as enduring behavioural predispositions, they should show some degree of stability over time. Yet they should not be unchangeable. As we might expect, the research literature shows evidence for both stability and change (Helson, Jones, & Kwan, 2002; Specht et al., 2011). Some personality dimensions tend to be more stable than others. For example, introversion/extraversion, as well as more basic traits such as emotionality and activity level, tend to be quite stable from childhood into adulthood and across the adult years (Eysenck, 1990; Zuckerman, 1991). Self-esteem also shows strong stability (Trzesniewski et al., 2003). On the other hand, both cross-sectional and longitudinal studies indicate that among the Big Five, neuroticism, openness and extraversion exhibit declines across the population from the late teens to the early thirties, whereas agreeableness and conscientiousness tend to increase (Costa & McCrae, 2002). There are also smaller, but

nonetheless significant changes across the population in middle and old age (Roberts & Mroczek, 2008). On an individual level, individuals can also show developmental changes in many aspects of personality, often given influential life experiences, and even following counselling and psychotherapy.

Certain habits of thought may also be fairly stable. One is our tendency to think optimistically or pessimistically. Burns and Seligman (1991) coded diaries and letters that elderly people had written approximately 50 years earlier for the tendency to respond either optimistically or pessimistically to life events. The elderly people also completed a personality test that measured their current optimistic–pessimistic tendencies. Although little consistency over time was shown for dealing optimistically or pessimistically with positive events, Burns and Seligman found a stable tendency to respond with optimism or pessimism to negative life events. The authors suggested that the tendency to be pessimistic might constitute an enduring risk factor for depression, low achievement and physical illness, and they are now studying such linkages. Table 15.7 contains items from the *Life Orientation Test* (Scheier & Carver, 1985), used by personality researchers to measure the trait of optimism–pessimism.

> **TABLE I5.7 Sample items from a trait measure of optimism–pessimism**
>
> | I. In uncertain times, I usually expect the best |
> | 2. Overall, I expect more good things to happen to me than bad |
> | 3. If something can go wrong for me, it will |
> | 4. I rarely count on good things happening to me |
>
> Note: Items on the Life Orientation Test are answered on a five-point scale ranging from 'strongly disagree' to 'strongly agree'.
> Source: Adapted from Scheier, Carver, & Bridges, 1994.

How Consistent Is Our Behaviour Across Situations?

As noted at the beginning of the chapter, one of the reasons we have a concept of personality is because we view people as behaving consistently across different situations. Is that assumption of consistency warranted by the data? Actually we have known now for quite some time that there is more evidence for inconsistency than for consistency (e.g. Mischel, 1984). Even on a trait so central as honesty, people can show considerable behavioural variability across situations. In a classic study, Hartshorne and May (1928) tested the honesty of thousands of children. The children were given opportunities to lie, steal and cheat in a number of different settings: at home, in school, at a party and in an athletic contest. The rather surprising finding was that 'lying, cheating and stealing as measured by the test situations in this study are only very loosely related . . . Most children will deceive in certain situations but not in others' (Hartshorne & May, 1928, p. 411). Mischel (1984) has reported similar findings for college students on the trait of conscientiousness. A student might be highly conscientious in one situation (e.g., coming to work on time) without being conscientious in another (e.g., turning in class assignments on time). Many other studies revealed similar behavioural inconsistency across situations.

To some, this called the very concept of personality into question. They reasoned that if behaviour is so inconsistent, maybe only the situation is important and we do not need an internal concept called 'personality' to account for behaviour.

Several factors make it difficult to predict on the basis of personality traits how people will behave in particular situations. One of the most important of these is the degree to which people are *self-monitoring*. People differ in their tendency to tailor their behaviour to what is called for by the situation. People who are high in **self-monitoring** are very attentive to situational cues and adapt their behaviour to what they think would be most appropriate. Extreme self-monitors are behavioural chameleons, who act very differently in various situations. Low self-monitors, on the other hand, tend to act primarily in terms of their internal beliefs and attitudes rather than the demands of the situation. The saying 'What you see is what you get' applies well to low self-monitors, and such people show greater consistency across situations than do high self-monitors (Snyder, 1987).

> **self-monitoring** attending to situational cues and adapting behaviour to what would be most appropriate

According to some trait theorists, the stability and distinctiveness that we see in personality does not come from the fact that we behave the same way in every situation. Rather, people exhibit different *average* amounts of extraversion, emotional stability, agreeableness, honesty and other traits across many different situations (Epstein, 1983; Kenrick & Funder, 1988). Nonetheless, if they wish to understand more about these interactions among personality traits, situations and behaviour, personality researchers need to define the relevant characteristics of both the person and the situation (Shoda & Mischel, 2000; Zayas & Shoda, 2007).

> **Focus I5.II** How stable are personality traits across time and situations? What factors decrease consistency across situations?

HOW MANY PERSONALITY FACTORS ARE THERE?

In recent years, McCrae & Costa's (2003) Big Five has been the dominant approach to understanding the structure of personality. However, it has been acknowledged for some time now that there exist significant correlations among the five factors, and not all factors are fully replicable across cultures. This has led some authors to question whether five factors are the most parsimonious way of describing personality (e.g., De Raad et al., 2010, Digman 1997), and such authors have preferred models of personality with fewer factors – like Eysenck's (1992) three factor model, for example. More recently, an even harder line has been taken by researchers like Musek (2007) and Rushton and Irwing (2008), who have suggested that because all five factors are correlated with one another, personality is best described as a single factor.

Musek (2007) found that high openness (O+), conscientiousness (C+), extraversion (E+), agreeableness (A+), and low neuroticism (N−) are correlated with one another and proposed a 'Big One' factor. Rushton and Irwing (2008, 2009) used a meta-analytic approach (see Chapter 2) to demonstrate a similar set of correlations among the Big Five in previous studies. They call the single factor the 'General Factor of Personality' (GFP), and argue that there are good reasons why we should only have one general personality trait. Specifically, they suggest that because certain traits are more desirable than others (e.g., O+, C+, E+, A+, N−), evolution through mate selection (see Chapter 3) will select in favour of people who have correlations among these desirable traits (good people) – leading inexorably towards a situation where one trait exists, and everyone is differentiated along a dimension of 'good person' to 'bad person' (Figueredo & Rushton, 2009; Rushton, Bons, & Hur, 2008).

But debate is fierce. Many personality researchers hold strong reservations about this approach for a number of reasons. Backstrom, Bjorklund and Larson (2009) argue convincingly that correlations among the Big Five traits are due to an experimental artefact – they suggest that the correlations emerge because people answering questionnaires are biased towards rating themselves highly on more socially desirable traits. Others suggest that the evolutionary theory offered by Rushton does not hold up to scrutiny. For instance, Ferguson, Chamorro-Premuzic, Pickering and Weiss (2011) point out that since, according to Rushton et al. (2008) the GFP should correlate with all socially desirable traits, then it should also correlate with intelligence. In fact, intelligence is actually negatively correlated with some of the Big Five factors – conscientiousness for instance (see Chamorro-Premuzic & Furnham, 2006). In addition to this the GFP is also positively correlated with some personality disorders! The debate is in its early stages and it will be interesting to see how long the single factor approaches last.

EVALUATING THE TRAIT APPROACH

Despite differences of opinion concerning the nature and number of basic personality dimensions, trait theorists have made an important contribution by focusing attention on the value of identifying, classifying and measuring stable, enduring personality dispositions. Several challenges confront trait theorists, however. If we are to capture the true complexities of personality, we must pay more attention to how traits combine with one another to affect various behaviours (Hampson, 2012; Smith, Smoll, & Schultz, 1990). All too often, researchers try to make specific predictions on the basis of a single measured personality trait without taking into account other personality factors that might also influence the behaviour in question. This approach sells short the complexity of personality.

In evaluating the trait perspective, we must remember the distinction between description and explanation. To say that someone is outgoing and fun-loving *because* she is high in extraversion is merely to describe the behaviour with a trait name, not to explain the inner disposition and how it operates. Traditionally, the trait perspective has been more concerned with describing the structure of personality, measuring individual differences in personality traits and predicting behaviour than with understanding the psychological or biological processes that underlie the traits. For example, a shortcoming of the five factor model is its lack of explanatory power; it tells us nothing about the causal factors that produce extraverted, neurotic or agreeable people's experiences and actions (Cervone, 1999). However, important exceptions to this are Hans Eysenck and Jeffrey Gray who, as we see later, proposed biological explanations for their trait theories.

Understanding Charles Whitman

What can the trait perspective tell us about Charles Whitman? Personality psychologists with a trait orientation would be interested in where he falls on a number of relevant personality dimensions. On the Big Five, he likely would have scored high on extraversion and agreeableness (with some notable departures from agreeableness when frustrated),

inconsistent on conscientiousness and high on neuroticism. If Whitman had been given a battery of personality tests shortly before the incident, would he have exhibited a profile showing a low level of self-esteem, poor stress-management skills, high hostility and poor impulse control? How would his scores have changed from the period when he was functioning well in adolescence to the period after he was in the Marines? Unfortunately, we will never be able to answer these questions because, to our knowledge, Whitman never took a personality test. It is possible, though, that had Whitman been tested in the days preceding his murderous acts, his test results might have served to warn professionals about his potential for violent behaviour.

 In review

- It is possible to describe personality in terms of types or traits. Type approaches such as those of Galen and Freud classify individuals into specific categories.

- Trait theorists try to identify and measure the basic dimensions of personality. Factor analysis identifies clusters of behaviour that are highly correlated with one another and thus constitute a dimension along which people may vary. Theorists disagree on the number of traits needed to describe personality adequately. Cattell suggested 16 basic traits; other theorists insist that five (or even fewer) may be adequate. Prediction studies indicate that a larger number of more specific traits may be superior for predicting behaviour in specific situations.

- Traits have not proved to be highly consistent across situations, and they also vary in stability over time. Individuals differ in their self-monitoring tendencies, and this variable influences the amount of cross-situational consistency they exhibit in social situations. Traits produce inconsistency by interacting not only with situations but also with one another.

BIOLOGICAL FOUNDATIONS OF PERSONALITY

Both nature and nurture influence the development of personality traits, but their contributions differ according to the trait in question (Caspi, Roberts, & Shiner, 2005). Biological explanations for personality differences focus on three levels. As we saw in **Chapter 3**, one group of theorists uses evolutionary principles to explain why particular traits exist in the human species (e.g., Buss, 1999; Rushton et al., 2008). Others seek the genetic bases for trait inheritance (Plomin, DeFries, McClearn, & McGuffin, 2008). Still others search for differences in the functioning of the nervous system (Heatherton et al., 2004; Pickering & Gray, 1999). Having discussed evolutionary personality theory in Chapter 3, we focus here on genetic and neuroscience approaches.

 Chapter 3, Page 80

GENETICS AND PERSONALITY

Have you ever been told that you share a personality trait with a parent or relative? Could it have been inherited? Twin studies are particularly informative for studying the role of genetic factors because they compare the degree of personality resemblance between monozygotic twins, who have identical genetic make-up, and dizygotic (fraternal) twins, who do not (Lykken, 2006; Rowe, 1999). On a great many psychological characteristics, identical twins are more similar to each other than are fraternal twins, suggesting a role for genetics. However, the issue is clouded by the possibility that identical twins may also have more similar environments than fraternal twins because others are inclined to treat them more similarly.

The ideal solution to this problem would be to compare personality traits in identical and fraternal twins who were raised together and those who were raised apart. If the identical twins who were reared in different families were as similar as those reared together, a more powerful argument could be made for the role of genetic factors. Moreover, this research design would allow us to divide the total variation among individuals on each

TABLE 15.8 Estimates of the percentages of group variance in 14 personality traits attributable to genetic and environmental factors

Trait	Genetic	Familial environment	Unique environment
Well-being	.48	.13	.39
Social potency	.54	.10	.36
Achievement	.39	.11	.50
Social closeness	.40	.19	.41
Stress reaction	.53	.00	.47
Alienation	.45	.11	.54
Aggression	.44	.00	.56
Control	.44	.00	.56
Harm avoidance	.55	.00	.45
Traditionalism	.45	.12	.43
Absorption	.50	.03	.47
Positive emotionality	.40	.22	.38
Negative emotionality	.55	.02	.43
Constraint	.58	.00	.42

Note: The variance estimates are based on a comparison of the degree of personality similarity in identical and fraternal twins who were reared together or apart.
Source: Adapted from Tellegen et al., 1988.

 Chapter 3, Page 93

Focus 15.12 What do twin studies reveal about the roles of heredity and environment in personality development?

personality trait into three components: (1) variation attributable to genetic factors; (2) variation due to a shared family environment in those raised together; and (3) variation attributable to other factors, including unique individual life experiences. The relative influence of these sources of variation can be estimated by comparing personality test correlations in twins raised together and apart.

One of the most famous studies (which included the Jim twins described in **Chapter 3**) was conducted by Tellegen and colleagues (Tellegen, Lykken, Bouchard, Wilcox, Segal, & Rich, 1988). The four groups of twin pairs were administered measures of 14 different personality traits, and the personality variation attributable to genetic, familial environment and unique environment was calculated for each personality characteristic.

As shown in Table 15.8, genetic factors accounted for approximately 40–50% of the variance among people in trait scores. In contrast, the degree of resemblance did not differ much whether the twin pairs were reared together or apart, showing that general features of the family environment, such as its emotional climate and degree of affluence, accounted for little variance in any of the traits. However, this does not mean that experience is not important. Rather than the family environment, it was the individual's unique environmental experiences, such as his or her school experiences and interactions with peers, that accounted for considerable personality variance. Even within the same family, individual children have different experiences while growing up, as parents may treat their children differently. It is these unique experiences that help shape personality development.

PERSONALITY AND THE NERVOUS SYSTEM

One logical place to look for biological underpinnings of personality is in individual differences in brain functioning (Canli, 2006; Zuckerman, 2005). Two examples are Hans Eysenck's research and theorizing on extraversion and emotional stability, and more recent work on temperament.

Eysenck and the Biological Basis of Extraversion and Stability

Eysenck (1967) was one of the first modern theorists to suggest a biological basis for major personality traits. He linked introversion–extraversion and stability–instability to differences in individuals' normal patterns of arousal within the brain. He started with the notion that there is an optimal, or preferred, level of biological arousal in the brain. Eysenck believed that extreme introverts are chronically *over-aroused*; their brains are too electrically active, so they try to minimize stimulation and reduce arousal to get down to their optimal arousal level (or 'comfort zone'). In contrast, the brains of extreme extraverts are chronically *under-aroused*, so they need powerful or frequent stimulation to achieve an optimal level of cortical arousal and excitation. The extravert thus seeks social contact and physical arousal, likes parties, takes chances, is assertive and suffers boredom easily.

Whereas introversion–extraversion reflects a person's *customary* level of arousal, stability–instability represents the suddenness with which *shifts* in arousal occur. Unstable people have nervous systems that show large and sudden shifts in arousal, whereas stable people show smaller and more gradual shifts (Pickering & Gray, 1999). Eysenck also called this stability dimension *neuroticism* because he found that people with extremely unstable nervous systems are more likely to experience emotional problems that require clinical attention.

Eysenck proposed that the arousal patterns that underlie introversion–extraversion and stability–instability have genetic bases. A growing body of evidence from twin studies supports his view. Identical twins are much more alike on these traits than are fraternal twins, and about half of the variance on these traits can be attributed to hereditary factors (Loehlin, Willerman, & Horn, 1988; Plomin, 1997). Eysenck believed that although personality is strongly influenced by life experiences, the ways people respond to those experiences may be at least partly programmed by biological factors. Contemporary research using brain imaging continues to find brain activation patterns related to extraversion and stability (e.g., Smillie, Cooper, & Pickering, 2011). These studies show that the neural bases of these factors go beyond general arousal, involving specific brain structures and functioning (Canli, 2004; Cloninger, 2000).

Genetic bases of personality factors such as extraversion and stability are also beginning to be identified (Smillie, Cooper, Proitsi, Powell, & Pickering, 2010). Research on the genetic bases of personality is, however, still in its infancy. Several recent studies show a complicated picture: attempts to relate differences in personality to specific individual genes have so far been unsuccessful. Instead, the heritability of personality traits seems to be based on the interaction of a very large number of genes (Turkheimer, Pettersson, & Horn, 2014). It will be interesting to see how this research develops and contributes to our understanding of the biological basis of personality.

An alternative to Eysenck's biological explanation of personality was put forward by eminent UK psychologist, Jeffrey Gray. Rather than starting with the factorial structure of personality as Eysenck did, Gray's (1982) reinforcement sensitivity theory takes the biological level of analysis as its starting point (Corr, 2008). Reinforcement sensitivity theory proposes that individual differences in personality originate from variations in the sensitivity of biological systems of reward and punishment (Gray's theory is also discussed in **Chapter 11** in the context of motivation). In **Chapter 7** we described how animals and humans are sensitive to rewards and punishments when they are learning new behaviours (particularly during operant conditioning). Gray's theory is thus influenced by the behaviourist concepts of learning and reinforcement, but also considers these concepts from a biological level of analysis – suggesting that sensitivity to reward and punishment are determined by basic biological factors. From this biological starting point, Gray proposes two supertrait factors in personality – the behavioural approach system (BAS), which describes sensitivity to reward, and the behavioural inhibition system (BIS), which describes sensitivity to punishment. These two neural systems map onto the personality space described by Eysenck but the particular dimensions are positioned at a different orientation to the array of specific traits (see Figure 15.12).

Temperament: Building Blocks of Personality

Temperament refers to individual differences in emotional and behavioural styles that appear so early in life that they are assumed to have a biological basis. Such temperamental factors as emotionality, activity level, sociability and impulsivity are visible even in infancy (Buss & Plomin, 1975, 1984). Temperamental factors are not assumed to be personality traits in their own right, but they are viewed as biological building blocks that influence the subsequent development of personality. The fact that these temperamental factors are more highly correlated in identical than in fraternal twins suggests a genetic link (Buss & Plomin, 1984).

Recent research has focused on biological differences in inhibited and uninhibited people. First identified by Jerome Kagan (1999) on the basis of behavioural observations and biological functioning, inhibited infants and children are shy, restrained in their behaviour, and react to unfamiliar people and situations with distress and avoidance (Figure 15.13a). In contrast, uninhibited children respond positively to new situations and people and seem to enjoy novelty. About 20% of infants are inhibited, and about 40% are uninhibited. Kagan (1999)

Focus 15.13 What biological factors underlie (1) Eysenck's dimensions of extraversion and stability and (2) the behaviours of inhibited children and adults?

 Chapter 11, Page 448

 Chapter 7, Page 280

temperament individual differences in emotional and behavioural styles that appear so early in life that they are assumed to have a biological basis

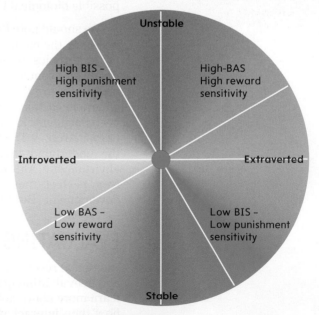

FIGURE 15.12 Gray's reinforcement sensitivity theory of personality.

The behavioural approach system (BAS) and the behavioural inhibition system (BIS) dimensions of personality sit at a 30 degree rotation to Eysenck's extraversion and stability dimensions.

FIGURE 15.13 Does childhood temperament predict adult personality?

(a) Inhibited temperament expresses itself as shyness and negative reactions to novel situations and people (even Santa Claus) early in life and is assumed to have a biological basis. (b) Adults who were identified as inhibited in childhood showed elevated reactions in the amygdala (a brain region known to initiate and organize fear responses) when exposed to faces they had not seen before, suggesting stability of this temperamental factor into adulthood.

Source: (a) ©istock.com/becky rockwood; (b) Data from Schwartz, Wright, Shin, Kagan and Rauch 2003.

(a)

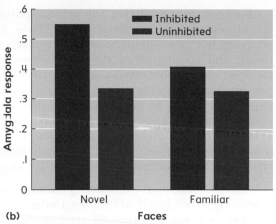

(b)

found that these temperamental patterns can be identified in the first four months of life and that they persist into later childhood in many (but not all) children (Bould, Joinson, Sterne, & Araya, 2013). These two groups of children also differ physiologically, with the inhibited children showing higher levels of physiological arousal and stress-hormone secretion in response to unfamiliar situations and people.

More recent neuroscientific research sheds light on brain regions that contribute to inhibited and uninhibited tendencies. One important region is the amygdala, the structure in the limbic system that organizes fear responses. Kagan suggested that the amygdala was involved in the physiological over-reactivity he measured in inhibited children. In a more recent study, fMRI brain recordings were taken in young adults who had been categorized as either highly inhibited or as uninhibited when they were 2 years old (Schwartz et al., 2003). Of interest was how their amygdala would react to pictures of familiar and unfamiliar human faces. As shown in Figure 15.13b, those adults who had been uninhibited as children showed relatively low amygdala reactivity to both familiar and novel faces, whereas the formerly inhibited participants showed particularly high reactivity to the novel faces. This study thereby demonstrated a negative response to novel stimuli in inhibited people that extended from childhood to adulthood, as well as a possible biological basis for this tendency.

We should note that temperament is not destiny. Although biological factors are clearly involved, the environment also can bring about some degree of change in temperamental characteristics. We should remember that temperamentally based behaviour patterns help create environments that can perpetuate the behaviour patterns. For example, people are unlikely to gravitate towards shy, inhibited individuals, thereby depriving them of positive experiences that might counteract their shyness. Likewise, temperamental traits may need particular kinds of environments to express themselves. Elaine Aron and co-workers (Aron, Aron, & Davies, 2005) found that adult shyness occurred most predictably when the underlying temperamental characteristic was paired with an adverse childhood environment. Although the link between child temperament and adult personality is far from perfect, there is little doubt that temperament is one building block in personality development (Bould et al., 2013).

EVALUATING THE BIOLOGICAL APPROACH

Biological research, spurred by technical advances in measuring nervous system activity and in evaluating genetic influences, is forging new frontiers in personality science. As we learn more about how biological functions are affected by developmental experiences and how they interact with situational factors, new insights about personality development will be achieved.

Behaviour genetics research on personality is moving in some exciting new directions. In the past, twin studies of personality typically have examined degrees of similarity on self-report measures of personality traits. Yet, as we have emphasized,

personality characteristics act in combination with situational factors. In an important study in Germany, Borkenau and co-workers (Borkenau, Riemann, Spinath, & Angleitner, 2006) studied the role of genes and environment on person-by-situation interaction patterns. The behaviours of 168 identical and 132 fraternal twins were carefully observed and coded as each person reacted to 15 different situations, some involving social encounters and others requiring problem-solving. By comparing the degree of similarity in person-by-situation behavioural profiles across the 15 situations in the two types of twin pairs, the researchers established that about 25 per cent of the variation in behavioural profiles could be attributed to genetic factors. As in previous studies, shared-environment effects were negligible. This study shows that genetic factors not only influence what people say about their personality, but how they adjust their behaviour to different situations.

Understanding Charles Whitman

Can the biological perspective offer clues to Charles Whitman's behaviour? In Whitman's letter, we find references to 'tremendous headaches' for which he had been medicating himself and a request that an autopsy be done after his death to see if a 'visible physical disorder' existed. In fact, a postmortem of his brain detected a fast-growing tumour in the hypothalamus, an area that includes some of the aggression circuitry in the brain (Raine, Lencz, Bihrle, LaCasse, & Colletti, 2000). Medical authorities evaluating Whitman's case differed on the importance of the tumour. If the tumour played a role in his violent acts, it seems unlikely that it was the primary causal factor. However, it could have been a predisposing factor that lowered his inhibitions against violent behaviour.

Another possibility arises from information that Whitman's father had a penchant for violent behaviour and frequently beat his wife and children. Thus a second potential biological factor could be the genes Whitman inherited from his father. Aggression can have a genetic basis (Wasserman & Wachbroit, 2001), and it is possible that a genetic predisposition interacted with environmental factors to increase the potential for violent behaviour.

 In review

- Biological perspectives on personality traits focus on differences in the functioning of the nervous system, the contribution of genetic factors, and the possible role of evolution in the development of universal human traits and ways of perceiving behaviour.

- Studies comparing identical and fraternal twins reared together and apart indicate that genetic factors may account for as much as half of the variance in personality test scores, with individual experiences accounting for most of the remainder. Evolutionary theories of personality attribute some personality dispositions to genetically controlled mechanisms based on natural selection.

- Eysenck suggested that normal personality differences can be accounted for by variations on the dimensions of introversion–extraversion and stability–instability, both of which are assumed to have a biological basis. In Eysenck's theory, introversion–extraversion reflects a person's customary level of arousal, whereas stability–instability represents the suddenness with which shifts in arousal occur. A more recent biological explanation of personality has been proposed in Jeffrey Gray's reinforcement sensitivity theory.

- Differences in temperament appear early in life and are assumed to have a biological basis. Temperament is assumed to contribute to the development of personality, and there is evidence for stability of temperamental behaviour tendencies during childhood and into adulthood. Inhibited children and adults appear to have a highly reactive amygdala that triggers fear responses to unfamiliar people and situations.

BEHAVIOURAL AND SOCIAL-COGNITIVE THEORIES

To understand behaviour, psychodynamic, humanistic and trait theorists emphasize internal personal causes of behaviour, such as unconscious conflicts, self-actualization tendencies and personality traits. In a sense, they account for behaviour from the inside

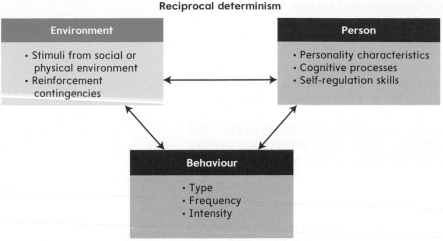

FIGURE 15.14 Reciprocal determinism.

A key concept in social-cognitive theory is reciprocal determinism, in which characteristics of the person, the person's behaviour and the environment all affect one another in reciprocal, or two-way, causal relations.

social-cognitive theories combine the behavioural and cognitive perspectives into an approach to personality that stresses the interaction of a thinking human with a social environment that provides learning experiences

reciprocal determinism the person, the person's behaviour and the environment all influence one another in a pattern of two-way causal links

Focus 15.14 Describe the major features of social-cognitive theories and the importance of reciprocal determinism.

out. In contrast, behaviourists emphasize environmental causes and view humans as reactors to external events (Parker, Bolling, & Kohlenberg, 1998). To them, behaviour is to be explained from the outside in. Behaviourists such as Ivan Pavlov, John Watson and B. F. Skinner were more interested in discovering universal laws of learning than in identifying individual differences in behaviour, and they rejected the notion of an 'internal personality' that directs behaviour. Nonetheless, the laws of learning that they discovered have great relevance for understanding personality. Many behaviours ascribed to personality are acquired through classical and operant conditioning, and the role of life experiences is undeniable.

Despite the power of the environment, however, some behaviourists believed that a purely behavioural account could not fully capture the workings of human personality. They believed that the learner is not simply a passive reactor to environmental forces and that internal processes could not be excluded from an understanding of personality. They viewed the human as perceiver, a thinker and a planner who mentally interprets events, thinks about the past, anticipates the future and decides how to behave. Environmental effects are filtered through these cognitive processes and are influenced – even changed – by them. Social-cognitive theories combine the behavioural and cognitive perspectives into an approach to personality that stresses the interaction of a thinking human with a social environment that provides learning experiences. Social-cognitive theorists believe that the debate on whether behaviour is more strongly influenced by personal factors or by the person's environment is basically a meaningless one (Fleeson, 2004). Instead, according to the social-cognitive principle of **reciprocal determinism**, the person, the person's behaviour and the environment all influence one another in a pattern of two-way causal links (Bandura, 1986; Figure 15.14).

As an example, let us consider how these interactions or linkages might operate in the case of a hostile and disagreeable man we will call Tom. Tom's disagreeableness trait manifests itself in an irritable, cynical and uncooperative behaviour pattern (his personality influences his behaviour). Tom's disagreeable behaviours tend to evoke negative responses from others (his behaviour causes his social environment to respond to him in kind). These negative social consequences reinforce and strengthen still further his personality trait (including his expectations that others will eventually reject him), and they also strengthen his disagreeable behaviour tendencies (his environment influences both his personality trait and his social behaviour). Thus Tom's personality, his behaviour and his environment all influence one another, much to his detriment, the poor fellow.

ROTTER: EXPECTANCY, REINFORCEMENT VALUE AND LOCUS OF CONTROL

In 1954 Julian Rotter laid the foundation for today's social-cognitive approaches. According to Rotter, the likelihood that we will engage in a particular behaviour in a given situation is influenced by two factors: *expectancy* and *reinforcement value*. Expectancy is our perception of how likely it is that certain consequences will occur if we engage in a particular behaviour within a specific situation. Reinforcement value is basically how much we desire or dread the outcome that we expect the behaviour to produce. Thus a student who strongly values academic success and also expects that studying will result in high grades is likely to study (Rotter, 1954). Note that this approach makes use of

TABLE 15.9 Sample items from rotter's internal–external scale

Choose statement (a) or (b) from each numbered choice.
1. (a) Many times I feel that I have little influence over the things that happen to me
(b) It is impossible for me to believe that chance or luck plays an important part in my life
2. (a) The average citizen can have an influence in government decisions
(b) The world is run by the few people in power, and there isn't much the person on the street can do about it
3. (a) In the long run, people get the respect they deserve in this world
(b) Unfortunately, an individual's worth often passes unrecognized no matter how hard one tries

Note: 1b, 2a, and 3a are the internal alternatives.
Source: Adapted from Rotter, 1966.

FIGURE 15.15 Research shows that people with an internal locus of control are more likely to take an active role in social change movements.
Source: Jenny Matthews/Alamy

reinforcement, a central behaviourist concept, but views its effects within a cognitive framework that emphasizes how we think about our behaviour and its expected outcomes.

Locus of Control

One of Rotter's most influential expectancy concepts is **internal–external locus of control**, an expectancy concerning the degree of personal control we have in our lives. People with an *internal* locus of control believe that life outcomes are largely under personal control and depend on their own behaviour (Figure 15.15). In contrast, people with an *external* locus of control believe that their fate has less to do with their own efforts than with the influence of external factors, such as luck, chance, and powerful others. Table 15.9 contains items from Rotter's (1966) *Internal–External (I–E) Scale*, used to measure individual differences in locus of control. Locus of control is called a *generalized expectancy* because it applies across many life domains as a general world view.

Locus of control is a highly researched personality variable (e.g., Cheng, Cheung, Chio, & Chan, 2013). Quite consistently, people with an internal locus of control behave in a more self-determined fashion (Pervin, Cervone, & John, 2005). In the 1960s, African-Americans who actively participated in the civil rights movement were more internal on the I–E Scale than were those who did not (Rotter, 1966). 'Internal' university students achieve better grades than do 'external' students of equal academic ability, probably because they link their studying to degree of success and work harder. Internals are more likely to actively seek out the information needed to succeed in a given situation (Ingold, 1989). Interpersonally, internals are more resistant to social influence, whereas externals tend to give in to high-status people they see as powerful (Eagly, 1981).

Internal locus of control is positively related to self-esteem and feelings of personal effectiveness, and internals tend to cope with stress in a more active and problem-focused manner than do externals (Jennings, 1990). They are also less likely to experience psychological maladjustment in the form of depression or anxiety (Hoffart & Martinson, 1991).

> **internal–external locus of control** an expectancy concerning the degree of personal control we have in our lives

> **Focus 15.15** Describe Rotter's concepts of expectancy, reinforcement value and locus of control.

ALBERT BANDURA: SOCIAL LEARNING AND SELF-EFFICACY

Albert Bandura has made major contributions to the development of the social-cognitive approach. His early studies of observational learning, described in **Chapter 7**, helped combine the psychology of learning with the cognitive perspective. Bandura's social learning analyses of aggression, moral behaviour and behavioural self-control demonstrated the wide applicability of the social-cognitive approach (Bandura, 1986). Perhaps his most influential contribution, however, is his theory and research on self-efficacy.

 Chapter 7, Page 302

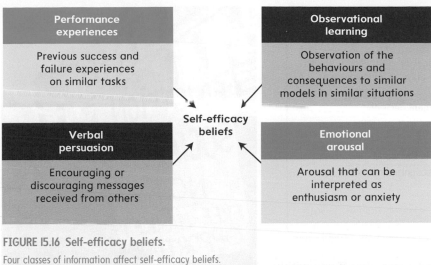

FIGURE 15.16 Self-efficacy beliefs.

Four classes of information affect self-efficacy beliefs.

Source: Based on Bandura, 1997.

---

self-efficacy beliefs concerning an ability to perform the behaviours needed to achieve desired outcomes

---

Focus 15.16 Describe four determinants of self-efficacy.

Self-Efficacy

According to Bandura (1997), a key factor in how people regulate their lives is their sense of **self-efficacy**, their beliefs concerning their ability to perform the behaviours needed to achieve desired outcomes. People whose self-efficacy is high have confidence in their ability to do what it takes to overcome obstacles and achieve their goals.

A good deal of research has been done on the factors that create differences in self-efficacy (Figure 15.16). Four important determinants have been identified (Bandura, 1997). First and most important is our previous *performance experiences* in similar situations. Such experiences shape our beliefs about our capabilities. For example, as shown in Figure 15.17, university women who felt that they had mastered the martial arts and emotional-control skills taught in a physical self-defence training programme showed dramatic increases in their belief that they could escape from or disable a potential assailant or rapist (Weitlauf, Smith, & Cervone, 2000).

Bandura stresses that self-efficacy beliefs are always specific to particular situations. Thus we may have high self-efficacy in some situations and low self-efficacy in others. For example, the women who mastered the physical self-defence skills did not feel more capable in all areas of their lives, despite their enhanced self-defence efficacy.

A second determinant of self-efficacy is *observational learning* – that is, observing others' behaviours and their outcomes. If you observe a person similar to yourself accomplish a particular goal, then you are likely to believe that if you perform those same behaviours you will also succeed. A striking example of how powerful such expectations can be comes from the world of sports. At one time, physiologists insisted that it was physically impossible for a human being to run a mile in less than 4 minutes, and no one in the history of track and field had ever done it. When the Englishman Roger Bannister broke the 4-minute barrier in 1954 (Figure 15.18), that limiting belief was shattered. The impact on other runners' performance was immediate and dramatic. In the year following Bannister's accomplishment, 37 other runners broke the barrier, and in the year after that, nearly 300 runners did the 'impossible'. Apparently, a great many people came to believe that 'if he can do it, so can I', and their new sense of self-efficacy enhanced their performance.

FIGURE 15.17 Effects of self-defence training.

(a) Physical self-defence training has dramatic effects on women's self-efficacy to perform the behaviours needed to defend themselves. (b). The physical defence self-efficacy scores in this study could extend from 6 to 60.

Source: (a) © Chris Schmidt; (b) Based on Weitlauf et al., 2000.

(a)

Third, self-efficacy can be increased or decreased by *verbal persuasion*. The messages we get from other people who affirm our abilities or downgrade them affect our efficacy beliefs. Thus inspirational teachers who convey high standards and a 'you can do it' conviction can inspire their students to great accomplishments.

Fourth, high *emotional arousal* that is interpreted as anxiety or fatigue tends to decrease self-efficacy. However, if we find ourselves able to control such arousal, it may enhance efficacy beliefs and subsequent performance. For example, test-anxious university students who were given training in stress-management relaxation techniques showed increases in their belief that they could remain relaxed and focused during tests, and their test performance and grade point average improved significantly as they controlled anxious arousal (R. E. Smith, 1989).

Efficacy beliefs are strong predictors of future performance and accomplishment (Bandura, 1997). They become a kind of self-fulfilling prophecy. The well-known maxim that if you believe you can do something you will succeed certainly has some truth according to Bandura.

FIGURE 15.18 Roger Bannister breaking the 4-minute mile barrier in Oxford in 1954.

Source: © Pictorial Press Ltd/Alamy.

⊚ Applying psychological science

INCREASING SELF-EFFICACY THROUGH SYSTEMATIC GOAL SETTING

In Chapter 11 we described motivation as the impetus for goal-directed behaviour. Because positive self-efficacy beliefs are consistently related to success in behaving effectively and achieving goals, Bandura and other social-cognitive theorists have been strongly interested in practical measures for enhancing self-efficacy. When people are successful and when they attribute their success to their own competencies (internal locus of control), their self-efficacy increases and assists them in subsequent goal-directed efforts. Moreover, successful people have usually mastered the skills involved in setting challenging and realistic goals, figuring out what they need to do on a day-to-day basis to achieve them, and making the commitment to do what is required. As they achieve each goal they have set, they become more skilful and increase their sense of personal efficacy (Bandura, 1997).

Not all goal-setting procedures are created equal, and it is important to apply the principles that make goal-setting programmes most effective (Locke & Latham, 2002). Here are some research-derived guidelines for effective goal setting.

1. *Set specific, behavioural and measurable goals.* The first step in changing some aspect of your life is to set a goal. The kind of goal you set is very important, because certain kinds of goals encourage us to work harder, enjoy success, and increase self-efficacy. Studies show that specific and fairly narrow goals are far more effective than general 'do your best' goals (Locke & Latham, 2002). A general goal like 'improve my tennis game' is less helpful than 'increase the number of serves I put in play by 20 per cent'. The latter goal refers to a specific behaviour that you can focus on and measure.

   One of the most important aspects of goal setting is systematically measuring progress towards the goal. This was shown in a study by Bandura and Daniel Cervone (1983) in which participants worked on a strenuous bicycle-pedalling task over a number of sessions. Two independent variables were manipulated: (a) whether the participants were given specific improvement goals before each session after the first (one) and (b) whether the participants were given feedback about their performance during the previous session. A control condition got neither goals nor feedback and provided a basis for evaluating the effects of goals and feedback, alone or in combination. The dependent variable was the speed and power with which the participants pedalled.

   As shown in Figure 15.19, simply having goals was not enough, nor was feedback effective by itself. But having both goals and feedback was a powerful combination. This shows how important it is to measure your progress towards the goal so that you get performance feedback and can see your improvement. Visible movement towards realistic goals builds self-efficacy.

2. *Set behavioural, not outcome, goals.* Many of our goals relate to outcomes in the future, such as getting an A in this course. You are more likely to achieve such goals if you use the means–ends heuristic discussed in Chapter 8 and think about the specific things you must *do* to achieve that outcome goal. Behavioural goals (what one has to do) work better than outcome goals because they keep the focus on the necessary behaviours. A behavioural goal might be 'read and outline the textbook and outline the lecture notes for 1 hour each day'. Achieving this behavioural goal can also be measured quickly and repeatedly, giving you constant feedback. Many people focus on outcome goals and forget what has to be done day-to-day to achieve them. In order for goals to actually be achieved it is vital to focus on the steps required to achieve them.

▶

◄

3. *Set difficult but realistic goals.* Moderately difficult goals challenge and motivate us and give us a sense of hope. When reached, they increase self-efficacy. Easy goals do not provide a sense of accomplishment, and extremely difficult or unattainable goals do not provide the success experiences you need to increase your self-efficacy.

4. *Set positive, not negative, goals.* In Chapter 7 we discussed the advantages of positive reinforcement over punishment. Working towards positive goals, such as 'study for 1 hour before dinner' is better than avoiding a negative consequence, as in 'don't waste time'. Again, positive goals keep you focused on the positive steps that you need to take to achieve them.

5. *Set short-range and long-range goals.* Short-range goals are important because they provide the opportunity for immediate mastery experiences, and they keep you working positively. A long-range goal like 'be fit enough to run a marathon in under 4 hours' can easily be divided into a series of subgoals that you can be working towards right now. Short-range goals are like the steps on a staircase leading to the long-range goal. As each step is accomplished, you enjoy mastery experiences that also lead you towards your ultimate goal.

6. *Set definite time spans for achievement.* To keep your goal-setting programme on track, it is important to specify the dates by which you will meet specific performance goals or subgoals, as well as the behaviours needed to attain them in that time span

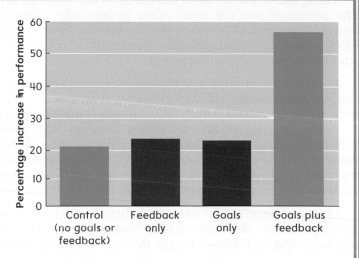

FIGURE 15.19 Goals are not enough.

This graph shows the effects of improvement goals and performance feedback on performance improvement on a gruelling bicycling task. Clearly, the combination of explicit goals *and* performance feedback resulted in greater improvement in performance than did either element by itself.

Source: Based on Bandura and Cervone, 1983.

Most of the preceding guidelines can be summarized in the acronym SMART: specific, measurable, action oriented, realistic and time based. The systematic application of these principles of goal setting is a very good way to work towards goals.

Goal setting is a motivational technique that has resulted in remarkable improvements in productivity in many work, social and academic settings (Locke & Latham, 2002). Moreover, for purposes of increasing self-efficacy, it has the added advantage of providing the repeated mastery experiences that are the most powerful sources of efficacy information.

MISCHEL AND SHODA'S COGNITIVE-AFFECTIVE PERSONALITY SYSTEM

cognitive-affective personality system (CAPS) an organized system of five variables that interact continuously with one another and with the environment, generating the distinctive patterns of behaviour that characterize the person

In the most recent formulation of social-cognitive theory, Mischel and Shoda (1999) describe a **cognitive-affective personality system (CAPS)**, an organized system of five variables that interact continuously with one another and with the environment, generating the distinctive patterns of behaviour that characterize the person (Mischel, 1999). The dynamic interplay among these five variables (encoding strategies, expectancies and beliefs, goals and values, affects, and competencies and self-regulatory processes), together with the characteristics of the situation, account for individual differences among people, as well as differences in people's behaviour across different situations. Let us examine these five personality variables.

Encodings and Personal Constructs

We respond to the world as perceived. As Kelly proposed in his theory of personal constructs, discussed earlier in this chapter, people differ greatly in how they customarily *encode* (mentally represent, categorize, interpret) situations. An unkempt man dressed in a caveman-style loincloth who steps into a lift carrying a large snake might be sorted into the personal construct category 'dangerous' by one fellow passenger and as 'an intriguing person I'd like to get to know' by another. These different encodings, or appraisals, will affect the other elements of the CAPS, including emotions, expectancies and motivation to exit the lift (Mischel, 1999).

Our encodings determine how we respond emotionally and behaviourally to situations. For example, studies of highly aggressive youths reveal that they have a strong tendency to perceive others as having disrespect and hostile intent towards them. Thus they are primed to interpret ambiguous acts by others, such as being unintentionally brushed

against on a stairway at school, as an aggressive act and to react with a violent response (Dodge, 1986). As object relations theorists have suggested, the mental representations or working models we have of relationships influence how we perceive (encode) and respond to others in our later relationships. This is an example of how the social-cognitive approach can incorporate concepts and insights from other theories, including psychodynamic ones.

Expectancies and Beliefs

As Rotter emphasized, what we expect will happen if we behave in a particular way is a strong determinant of our behavioural choices. **Behaviour outcome expectancies** represent the 'if–then' links between alternative behaviours and possible outcomes. *If* I take that course in organic chemistry, *then* what will happen to my marks? How likely is it that I'll be forgiven *if* I apologize? Will I make enough money to support myself *if* I become a teacher? Different people may have very different answers to such questions and therefore vary in their responses to the same situation.

In addition to behaviour–outcome expectancies, beliefs about our competencies and about the degree of personal control we have influence our actions. Thus the CAPS model also includes Bandura's self-efficacy and Rotter's locus of control as important expectancy variables.

> **behaviour outcome expectancies** the 'if–then' links between alternative behaviours and possible outcomes

Goals and Values

Motivation plays a central role in attempts to understand behaviour, and it is represented in the CAPS system as goals and values that guide our behaviour, cause us to persist in the face of barriers, and determine the outcomes and situations we seek and our reactions to them (Higgins, 1996). People differ in the goals that are important to them and the values that guide their lives. These differences can cause people to behave very differently in situations that are relevant to these important personality factors.

Affects (Emotions)

Anything that implies important consequences for us, whether beneficial or harmful, can trigger an emotional response (Lazarus, 2001). Once aroused, emotions colour our perceptions and influence our behaviour. For example, if you are already feeling bad due to an argument with a friend and you then get negative feedback in the form of a poor grade on a test, you may feel demoralized for a time. Emotions also affect other CAPS components. Anxiety, for example, can significantly lower outcome expectancies in performance situations (Shepperd, Grace, Cole, & Kline, 2005).

Research shows that people exhibit stable individual differences in emotionality. For example, people who are high on Eysenck's trait of instability (neuroticism) have a tendency to experience negative *affect*, or emotion, in an intense fashion, a factor that influences many of their perceptions and behaviours. Other people seem predisposed to experience mainly positive affect in their lives (Watson & Clark, 1992).

Competencies and Self-Regulatory Processes

Social-cognitive theorists stress that people extensively control, or regulate, their own behaviour. People's ability to control their own behaviour is a distinguishing aspect of personality, as are the competencies they develop that allow them to adapt to life successfully and pursue important goals. Some of these competencies are cognitive problem-solving methods (such as systematic goal setting) that allow them to plan successful strategies, whereas others involve the ability to exert personal control over thoughts, emotions and behaviours. People who score high on measures of self-esteem tend to have better self-regulation abilities and to enjoy more positive outcomes (Di Paula & Campbell, 2002). These successes undoubtedly contribute to their positive feelings about themselves.

One important way people regulate their own behaviour is through self-administered consequences. (Bandura, 1999; Mischel, 1999). In response to our own behaviours, we generate positive evaluations and emotions such as pride, self-approval and the conviction that we did 'the right thing'. In contrast, we may respond with negative responses such as self-reproach, shame and guilt when we violate our personal standards. **Self-reinforcement processes** often override external consequences, making us more autonomous and self-directed.

> **self-reinforcement processes** refer to internal, self-administered rewards and punishments

Focus 15.17 Describe the five 'person variables' in Mischel and Shoda's cognitive-affective personality system (CAPS).

By considering these five 'person variables', and the way they interact, the CAPS ties together situations, personality, behaviours and their consequences. According to the CAPS model, features of a situation can activate the five 'person variables'. The activation levels of these variables can change depending on previous learning experiences or situational demands. The important contribution of the CAPS model lies in the assumption that there is stability in the way the activation levels change, and thus in the way an individual responds to the specifics of a situation (Shoda, Wilson, Chen, Gilmore, & Smith, 2013).

RECONCILING PERSONALITY COHERENCE WITH BEHAVIOURAL INCONSISTENCY

As noted in our earlier discussion of the trait perspective, people's behaviour often shows a notable lack of consistency across situations, a fact that has caused some to question the traditional concept of personality. How can we have a coherent and stable personality yet show such inconsistency across different situations? Does personality really matter? Recent social-cognitive research and theoretical advances may provide the answer to this paradox of personality coherence and inconsistent behaviour by focusing on person-by-situation interactions.

In CAPS theory, personality is defined in terms of the cognitive-affective person variables and the interactions among them. The CAPS system is assumed to be stable and consistent, although it can surely be modified by significant experiences. Behaviour, however, need not be consistent. How a person behaves depends on many factors, including the features of the situation, how these features are encoded, the expectancies and beliefs that are activated, the goals that are relevant, the emotions that might occur and the plans and self-regulatory processes that help determine the behaviour. Thus it is entirely possible for people to behave inconsistently across situations that seem very similar to an outside observer. People will behave similarly in situations that, *to them*, have important characteristics in common, but they may behave inconsistently in situations that differ in ways that evoke different responses from the CAPS (Shoda & Mischel, 2000).

behavioural signatures
consistent ways of responding in particular classes of situations

As a result of interactions between situations and the personality system, people exhibit distinctive **behavioural signatures**, consistent ways of responding in particular classes of situations. These behavioural signatures are the outward manifestation of personality that establish a person's unique identity (Mischel, Shoda, & Mendoza-Denton, 2002). Research shows that people can have very distinctive behavioural signatures. For example, Figure 15.20 shows the behavioural patterns of two verbally aggressive children in a residential summer camp (Shoda, Mischel, & Wright, 1994). The children's behaviours were systematically observed and coded for more than 150 hours per child. Overall, these two children were quite similar in the overall number of verbally aggressive responses they made. However, inspection of the *situational patterns* of aggression reveals that child A reacted very aggressively towards adults, whether they were behaving towards the child in a warm or a punitive fashion. In contrast, this child consistently showed relatively little aggression towards peers. Child B showed quite a different pattern, consistently reacting with low levels of aggression towards adults or when being

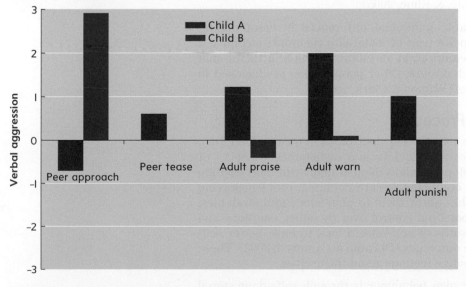

FIGURE 15.20 Stable situation-behaviour patterns.

This chart shows the aggressive responses of two children, A and B, in five different summer camp situations. These data show the children's distinctive behavioural signatures for aggressive responding, even though their aggression scores averaged across the five settings were quite similar. The zero point on the vertical axis represents the average amount of verbal aggression shown in each situation by all the children in the study.

Source: Adapted from Shoda et al., 1994.

teased by peers but showing a consistently high level of aggression when peers approached him in a friendly manner.

The important lesson here is that if we simply averaged the aggressive behaviour counts across the five situations, the two children would look equally aggressive. But in so doing, we would mask the distinctive and consistent behavioural signatures that define each child's individuality. Thus the coherence of personality is shown not at the level of individual behaviours but at the level of behavioural signatures (situation-by-behaviour patterns).

Focus 15.18 How does the concept of behavioural signatures help reconcile the seeming paradox of personality coherence and behavioural inconsistency?

EVALUATING SOCIAL-COGNITIVE THEORIES

A strength of the social-cognitive approach is its strong scientific base. It brings together two perspectives that have strong research traditions: the behavioural and the cognitive. The constructs of social-cognitive theory can be defined, measured and researched with considerable precision. As a result, the social-cognitive approach has advanced our understanding of how processes within the person and characteristics of the situation interact with one another to influence behaviour. Another strength is its ability to translate insights derived from other perspectives into cognitive-behavioural concepts (Mischel et al., 2004).

Social-cognitive theory also helps resolve an apparent contradiction between the central assumption that personality produces stability in behaviour and research findings that people's behaviour is not very consistent across different situations. Mischel and Shoda's CAPS theory suggests that the inconsistency of a person's behaviour across situations is actually a manifestation of a stable underlying cognitive-affective personality structure that reacts to certain features of situations. However, the ability of the CAPS to predict specific behaviour needs further examination, and it will be challenging to measure the numerous interactions among the CAPS components. Much more needs to be learned about how the CAPS operates, but this question is being explored by many current researchers (Cervone & Shoda, 1999; Mischel et al., 2004; Rhadigan & Huprich, 2012). Another major challenge will be to find out what active ingredients of situations cause people to encode them in similar ways, thereby producing the consistencies in behaviour that constitute behavioural signatures (Ten-Berge, Maaike, & De Raad, 2002). The study of abused women and abusive men (Zayas & Shoda, 2007) in this chapter's 'Research close-up' (p. 636) is one attempt to identify the active stimulus ingredients of a situation.

Understanding Charles Whitman

To conclude our analysis of Charles Whitman, let us view him from a social-cognitive perspective. The behavioural aspect of the social-cognitive perspective would focus on past learning experiences that predisposed him to violence. These are not hard to find in his history. First, his father provided an aggressive model during his formative years, controlling his wife and children with physical abuse. His father was also a gun enthusiast, and there were guns hanging in virtually every room of the Whitman home. Family photos show young Charles holding guns when he was only 2 years old, and his father made sure he received plenty of training in using them. Long before he enlisted in the Marines, Whitman was an expert marksman, and the Marines built on this expertise with sniper training that earned him a sharpshooter's badge. As other aspects of his life were crumbling, Whitman's marksmanship was a continuing and positive part of his personal self-identity, and he told several University of Texas acquaintances how easy it would be to pick off people from the tower. His expertise made him a deadly killer as he fired from the tower with stunning accuracy, killing people up to half a mile (800 m) away.

How might Charles Whitman be represented within the CAPS model? At the level of encoding processes, Mischel and Shoda would focus on how he viewed himself and his world. Aggression is fuelled by perceptions that we have been wronged and that the provocation was intentional (Lazarus, 2001). Clearly, Whitman felt victimized both by his father and by the Marines, and he saw the world as so malevolent that he regarded killing his wife and mother as an act of mercy. Moreover, his view of himself became increasingly negative as his life's fortunes declined. His outcome and self-efficacy expectancies became increasingly negative. One source of self-efficacy that remained unchanged was his exceptional marksmanship, and this competency became the medium for the expression of his rage, as well as the means to achieve the death he desired.

Whitman's values involved success in his career, in academics, and as a husband. Success was nowhere in sight, producing feelings of frustration and creating unbearable stress (negative affect) in his life. He felt unworthy of his wife and deeply regretted the two incidents early in their marriage when he had beaten her.

At the level of affect, what also stands out is Whitman's internal rage. In the words of the psychiatrist who saw him shortly before his outburst, he was 'fairly oozing' with generalized hostility. Whitman tried to achieve his goals and exercise self-control with elaborate manuals filled with specific self-instructions about how to act, what to say and how to inhibit his hostility. Eventually, though, in the absence of adequate self-regulation skills, these external controls failed, with tragic consequences.

Having now described the various perspectives on personality, we have seen that each presents us with a different picture of human nature and that each focuses on particular determinants of human individuality. Moreover, each perspective provides us with different pieces of the puzzle that was Charles Whitman.

'Levels of analysis' summarizes the determinants emphasized by the various theories at the biological, psychological and environmental levels.

Levels of analysis
factors related to personality differences

PSYCHOLOGICAL

- Psychodynamic processes involving impulse, defence, unconscious conflicts and psychosexual factors (Freud)
- Differences in object relations and attachment styles
- Differences in personal construct systems (Kelly)
- Processes involving the self-concept and striving for self-actualization (Rogers)
- Personality dispositions to act, think and feel in particular ways (trait theorists)
- Cognitive social learning variables that interact with situational factors (Bandura, Rotter, Mischel)

BIOLOGICAL

- Personality differences shaped by evolutionary factors (evolutionary personality theory)
- Genetic bases for individual differences and temperament (behaviour genetics)
- Individual differences in customary level of cortical arousal and suddenness with which autonomic shifts occur (Eysenck)
- Individual differences in biological bases for temperament

ENVIRONMENTAL

- Early relationship experiences (psychodynamic theories)
- Environmental factors that support or stifle self-actualization (humanistic theorists)
- Past social learning experiences and current environmental factors that interact with social-cognitive person variables (social-cognitive theorists)

Personality differences

In review

- Social-cognitive theories are concerned with how social relationships, learning experiences and cognitive processes jointly contribute to behaviour. A key concept is reciprocal determinism, relating to two-way causal relations between people, their behaviour and the environment.

- Rotter's theory viewed behaviour as influenced by expectancies and the reinforcement value of potential outcomes. His concept of locus of control is a generalized belief in the extent to which we can control the outcomes in our life.

- Bandura's concept of self-efficacy relates to our self-perceived ability to carry out the behaviours necessary to achieve goals in a particular situation. It is influenced by past performance attainments, verbal persuasion, observation of others' attainments and perceived emotional arousal. Self-efficacy can be enhanced through the application of systematic goal-setting procedures.

- According to Mischel and Shoda, situational features activate the person's cognitive-affective personality system (CAPS). The CAPS involves individual differences in encoding strategies, expectancies and beliefs, goals and values, affects, and competencies and self-regulatory processes. The CAPS interacts with features of the environment, helping to explain why people have specific behavioural signatures and do not necessarily behave consistently across situations.

CULTURE, GENDER AND PERSONALITY

As we have seen, personality is a product of interacting biological and environmental influences. Children inherit different biologies that influence how their environment, including culture, affects them (Kagan & Fox, 2006).

Environment exists at many different levels, ranging from the physical surroundings in which we develop to the increasingly global social contexts shown in Figure 15.21. Among the most important environmental influences is the culture in which we develop. We are often unaware of these influences because they serve as an amorphous background against which the specific events of our lives unfold. Culture encompasses unstated assumptions (including assumptions about the very nature of reality), norms, values, sex roles and habitual ways of behaving that are shared by members of a social group. It influences what we perceive, how we perceive, how we relate to ourselves and others, and how we behave.

CULTURE DIFFERENCES

Cultures differ along a number of dimensions that can affect personality development (Triandis & Suh, 2002). One dimension is *complexity*. Consider how much more complex a Western information-age culture is than a hunter-gatherer culture in a remote region of an undeveloped country. Consider also how much more potential for diversity and conflict of values and behavioural norms exists in a highly complex culture.

A second cultural dimension is *interdependence*. Markus and Kitayama (1991) proposed that cultures differ profoundly in the extent to which they weight interdependence. So-called 'Western cultures' including Western Europe and

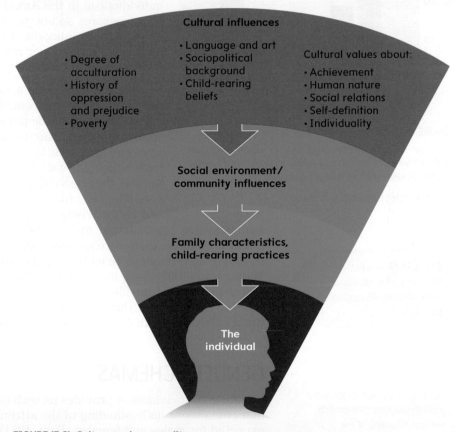

FIGURE 15.21 Culture and personality.

This model shows how cultural elements are transmitted to the individual through the medium of social environment and family influences.

Source: Based on factors cited by Locke, 1992; Sue and Sue, 1990.

the USA, are argued to be rather independent, with an emphasis on individual choice. On the other side of the coin, Markus and Kitayama argue that non-Western cultures such as China and Japan are highly interdependent, and the emphasis is placed on the choices and decisions of groups of people. If we are to consider personality in this light, it seems reasonable to expect that adolescents in 'independent' cultures would show greater diversity and feelings of individuality than those in 'interdependent' cultures. However, adolescents in independent cultures might also experience more conflicts in deciding which values to embrace and what type of person they want to be. These hypothesized cultural differences have found some support in the literature. For example, Markus and Kitayama (1998) describe large differences between Japanese and European-American students' endorsements of descriptions of themselves as 'ordinary'. Whereas only 18% of the European-American students endorsed, this, 84% of the Japanese students did. On the other hand, when asked if they would describe themselves as special, 55% of Japanese students endorsed this, compared with 96% of European-American students.

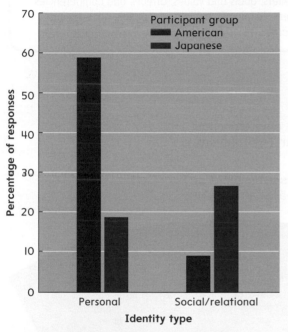

FIGURE 15.22 Cultural differences in the self-concept.

This graph shows the percentages of personal identity and social/relational self-attributes given by Japanese and American college students as key aspects of their self-concepts.

Source: Adapted from Cousins, 1989.

Other researchers have chosen to emphasize the importance of *individualistic* versus *collectivistic* cultures in shaping personality (Triandis & Suh, 2002). In one study, American and Japanese college students were given a self-concept questionnaire on which they listed their five most important attributes. The researchers then classified each statement according to whether it referred to a personal attribute (e.g., 'I am honest', 'I am smart'), a social identity (e.g., 'I am an oldest son', 'I am a student'), or something else, such as a physical trait. As Figure 15.22 shows, the Americans were far more likely than the Japanese to list personal traits, abilities or dispositions, whereas the Japanese more frequently described themselves in social identity terms. Thus Cousins (1989) argued that the social embeddedness of the collectivistic Japanese culture was reflected in their self-perceptions, as was cultural individualism in the Americans' self-concepts. Interestingly, personality trait measures do not predict behaviour as well in collectivistic cultures as they do in individualistic cultures, possibly because environmental factors play a stronger role in the behaviour of collectivistic individuals (Church & Katigbak, 2000).

However, there are a number of criticisms that can be laid against research examining cultural differences in personality. First, it is uncertain whether the personality differences captured in cross-cultural studies are caused by the collectivistic and individualistic nature of their respective cultures. In fact, on average, only about 40% of people within a particular culture strongly embrace individualistic or collectivistic goals. Second, the cross-cultural effects do not seem to be as robust as has often been claimed. In a meta-analysis of studies comparing individualistic and collectivistic values across several cultures, Oyserman, Coon and Kemmelmeier (2002) found that although European-Americans were less collectivistic than the Chinese, they were no less collectivistic than the Japanese or Koreans (cultures traditionally thought to be highly collectivistic in organization). Finally, as pointed out by Matsumoto (1999), very little evidence has examined cultural differences in collectivism and individualism outside of comparisons between European-Americans and East Asians. Can we be sure that these proposed effects of culture on personality will bear out in Europe, Africa, South America and Australasia?

Focus 15.19 In what three ways can cultures differ, thereby influencing personality?

GENDER SCHEMAS

gender schemas organized mental structures that contain our understanding of the attributes and behaviours that are appropriate and expected for males and females

Gender-role socialization provides us with **gender schemas**, organized mental structures that contain our understanding of the attributes and behaviours that are appropriate and expected for males and females (Bem, 1981). Within a given culture, gender schemas tell us what the typical man or woman should be like. In Western cultures, men tend to prize attributes related to achievement, emotional strength, athleticism and self-sufficiency, whereas women prize interpersonal competencies, kindness and helpfulness to others

(Beyer, 1990; Marsh, 1990). In this sense, men in Western cultures tend to develop more of an individualistic self-concept, emphasizing achievement and separateness from others, whereas women's self-concepts tend to be more collectivistic, emphasizing their social connectedness with others (Kashima, Yamaguchi, Kim, Choi, Gelfand, & Yuki, 1995). Nonetheless, as with differences in cultures, we should keep in mind that significant individual differences exist within each gender group, with many women being individualists and many men collectivists (Triandis & Suh, 2002).

 In review

- Cultures differ along several important dimensions, including complexity, interdependence and individualism–collectivism, all of which can affect personality development.

- People in collectivistic cultures tend to see the environment as fixed (i.e., having rigid rules and expectations) and themselves as changeable, with a capacity to fit in. In contrast, members of individualistic cultures are more likely to see themselves and their personalities as relatively stable and the environment as malleable.

- Culture influences self-concept development. People from individualistic cultures tend to describe themselves in terms of personal traits, abilities or dispositions, whereas those from collectivistic cultures are more likely to describe themselves in social identity terms.

- The proposed effects of culture on personality have not been universally accepted. There is widespread variation in the extent to which the cultural values supposed to affect personality are taken up by individuals. Furthermore, most research has been limited to only the USA and East Asia. Can we be sure that culture affects personality in the same way elsewhere in the world?

- Gender schemas are organized mental structures that contain our understanding of the attributes and behaviours that are appropriate and expected for males and females. In Western cultures, men tend to value achievement, emotional strength and self-sufficiency, whereas women prize interpersonal skills, kindness and helpfulness to others.

PERSONALITY ASSESSMENT

If you were to be introduced to Jennifer, a woman you had never met before, and given one week to provide a complete personality description of her, what would you do? The chances are that you would seek information in a variety of ways. You might start by interviewing Jennifer and finding out as much as you could about her. Based on your knowledge of the theories we have discussed, what questions would you ask? Would you ask about early childhood experiences and dreams; about how she sees herself and others? Would you be interested in the kinds of traits embodied in the Big Five model or in Eysenck's dimension of introversion–extraversion? Would you want to know how Jennifer customarily feels and responds in various situations? Your answers to these questions and your other assessment decisions would in some sense reflect your own theory of what is important in describing personality.

You probably would not be content simply to interview Jennifer. You might also decide to interview other people who know her well and get their views of what she is like. You might even ask them to rate her on a variety of traits, and you could ask Jennifer to rate herself on the same measures to see if her self-concept agrees with how others see her.

Finally, you might decide that it would be useful to actually observe how Jennifer behaves in a variety of situations. You would want to observe her in a way that would allow you to get as natural and characteristic a sample of her behaviour as possible. This information, together with that obtained from Jennifer and from those who know her best, might provide a reasonable basis for a personality description.

Figure 15.23 shows the major methods that psychologists use to assess personality characteristics. As you can see, they use some of the same methods you might have chosen: the interview, trait ratings and behaviour reports, as well as behavioural assessment or direct observation and measurement of the subject's behaviour. In addition, psychologists have developed several types of tests, including objective self-report measures and projective tests that ask respondents to interpret ambiguous stimuli, such as inkblots or pictures. Finally, physiological measures can be used to measure various aspects of personality, such as emotional reactivity or levels of cortical arousal.

pressure was monitored before, during and after an earthquake that struck central Italy in 1998, showed a blood pressure increase from 130/85 mmHg (before) to 150/122 mmHg (after). The patient's blood pressure was restored to pre-quake levels only after 1 hour, showing pronounced variability throughout the following 6 hours (Parati, Antonicelli, Guazzarotti, Paciaroni, & Mancia, 2001). Blood pressure levels of 427 hypertensive individuals also significantly increased after the 9/11 attacks in New York (Gerin et al., 2005). The consequences of increased blood pressure levels should not be underestimated. On the day of the 1994 Northridge, California earthquake, the number of sudden deaths due to heart attacks in the greater Los Angeles area nearly tripled from an average of 35.7 per day during the previous seven days to 101 (Leor, Poole, & Kloner, 1996).

Other effects of major stressors on physical well-being are less immediate but no less severe. Within one month following the death of a spouse, bereaved widowers and widows begin to show a higher mortality rate than married people of the same age who have not lost a spouse (Kaprio, Koskenvu, & Rita, 1987), and within one year of spousal death, about two-thirds of bereaved people decline in health (Irwin, Daniels, & Weiner, 1987). A notably increased rate of mortality is found in men, who tend to respond to the death of their spouse with relatively greater distress and health declines than do women (Stroebe, Stroebe, & Schut, 2001). People who experience the chronic stress that attends caring for a spouse with Alzheimer's disease have significantly increased risk of health problems (Vitaliano, Young, & Zhang, 2004). Stressful life events have also been linked to a higher risk of mortality from chronic diseases of ageing such as cancer (Keinan-Boker, Vin-Raviv, Liphshitz, Linn, & Barchana, 2009; Sklar & Anisman, 1981). Studies of children experiencing poverty, abuse, neglect or maltreatment by parents, show heightened vulnerability to cardiovascular disease and autoimmune disorders later in life (Miller, Chen, & Parker, 2011).

Linkages between long-term stress and illness are not surprising, for physiological responses to stressors can directly harm other body systems. For example, the secretion of stress hormones, such as epinephrine, norepinephrine and cortisol, is a major part of the stress response (Miller, Chen, & Cole, 2009). These hormones affect the activity of the heart, and excessive secretions can damage the lining of the arteries. By reducing fat metabolism, the stress hormones can also contribute to the fatty blockages in arteries that cause heart attacks and strokes (Lovallo & Gerin, 2003; Willenberg, Bornstein, & Crousos, 2000).

Stress can also contribute to health breakdowns by causing people to behave in ways that increase the risk of illness. For example, people with diabetes can frequently control their disease through medication, exercise and diet. When under stress, however, diabetics are less likely to regulate their diets and take their medication, resulting in an increased risk of serious medical consequences (Brantley & Garrett, 1993). People are also more likely to quit exercising when under stress, even if the primary reason they began exercising in the first place was to reduce stress (Hamer, 2012; Stetson, Rahn, Dubbert, Wilner, & Mercury, 1997). Stress may also lead to smoking, alcohol and drug use, sleep loss, undereating or overeating, and other health-compromising behaviours. For example, Healey and colleagues (Healey, Kales, Monroe, Bixler, Chamberlin, & Soldatos, 1981) found a positive relationship between the occurrence of major stressful life events and the onset of sleeping disorders (i.e., insomnia; for a discussion of sleep disorders and their consequences see **Chapter 6**). Poor dietary and sleep patterns in students studying for final examinations may increase risk of illness and help ruin the semester break.

> **Focus 16.5** Describe physiological and behavioural mechanisms through which stress can contribute to illness.

 Chapter 6, Page 235

Stress and the Immune System

As early as 430 BC the Greek historian Thucydides, describing the plague of Athens at that time, noted that 'the same man was never attacked twice' (quoted in Ahmed & Gray, 1996). This and later observations suggested the existence of some 'invisible barrier' able to remember previous episodes of illness and protect us from repeated infection. As we now know, every part of our body is protected from infection by a complex immune system made up of many organs and cells. Science has improved on that earlier description and has shown that indeed, a normal, healthy immune system has the exquisite capacity to learn, remember and react to specific challenges (Ahmed & Gray, 1996). Once the immune system has encountered a substance which is foreign to the body, known as antigens (meaning *anti* body *gen*erators), it will recognize the antigen immediately in the future.

Antigens trigger a biological response from the immune system which then starts making the necessary *antibodies* to destroy any bacteria, viruses, abnormal cells or chemical molecules that have antigenic properties (Figure 16.5).

The immune system's memory is the basis for developing vaccines to protect both humans and animals from certain diseases. Unfortunately, although the immune system's memory may be perfect, the body's defences may not be. Considerable evidence suggests, for example, that life stress can weaken immune functioning (Suls & Wallston, 2003; Taylor, 2011). Research by Ronald Glaser, Janet Kiecolt-Glaser and their co-workers has shown that reduced immune system effectiveness is one possible reason for increased risk of illness (Kiecolt-Glaser, McGuire, Robles, & Glaser, 2002; Marsland, Cohen, Rabin, & Manuck, 2001). In one study, researchers closely followed medical students over a one-year period. They collected blood samples from the students during three stressful academic examination periods in order to measure immune cell activity. The researchers found that immune system effectiveness was reduced during the stressful examination periods and that this reduction was linked to the likelihood of becoming ill. Other studies have shown that stress hormones released into the bloodstream by the adrenal glands can suppress the activity of specific immune system cells, increasing the likelihood of illness (Cohen & Herbert, 1996; Maier & Watkins, 1999).

FIGURE 16.5 An electron microscope photograph of an abnormal (cancer) cell (middle) being attacked by immune system cells.

Source: ©iStock.com/selvanegra.

Research has shown that external stressors can 'get into' the immune system in several ways. Fibres extending from the brain into lymph tissues can release a wide variety of chemicals that bind to receptors on white blood cells, thus influencing immune functions. As noted earlier, stress hormones such as cortisol and epinephrine also bind to cells in the immune system and influence their functions. Third, people's attempts to cope with stressors sometimes lead them to behave in ways (e.g., substance use or not sleeping enough) that impair immunity (Lange, Dimitrov, & Born, 2010).

There are two kinds of immune reactions. *Natural immunity* occurs quickly (often within minutes) of an immune challenge and is relatively non-specific in nature. One type of natural immunity is inflammation, in which certain immune cells congregate at the site of an infection and release toxic substances that kill invaders. One class of molecules released by immune cells are **cytokines**, which help produce fever and inflammation, promote healing of injured tissue and activate and direct other immune cells. Natural killer (NK) cells are also part of the natural defence team. These cells attack invaders, as well as tumours, and help keep invaders at bay during the early stages of infection. From an evolutionary perspective, natural immunity is an adaptive feature of the fight-or-flight response to an acute physical stressor that could produce injury and the entry of pathogens into the body through wounds.

cytokines help produce fever and inflammation, promote healing of injured tissue and activate and direct other immune cells

Specific immunity is a much more targeted process and takes longer to occur, sometimes up to several days. One common specific immunity response is the identification of the specific properties of the invader and the development of specific antibodies that can neutralize bacteria, kill cancerous cells or bind to viruses to prevent their entry into healthy cells.

Like immune reactions, stressors can differ in a number of ways, including how they occur and how long they last. Segerstrom and Miller (2004) found that acute, time-limited stressors, such as participating in a stressful job interview, actually enhance natural immunity. The number of natural killer cells in the blood increases and the immune system readies itself for a protective-infection response. Specific immunity does not increase, however, probably because the stressor is very brief. Longer-lasting stressors, such as the days in preparation for an important examination, are associated with a different pattern of immune response, created largely by different types of cytokines. Some cytokines suppress cellular immune responses against viruses, whereas others enhance immune responses against bacteria and parasites. Thus, brief naturalistic stressors of this type might make you more susceptible to a viral infection, but probably not to a bacterial one.

problems (e.g., Solberg Nes & Segerstrom, 2006). Edward Chang (1998), for example, found that people with optimistic beliefs felt less helpless in the face of stress and adjusted better to negative life events than did pessimists. Optimists furthermore feel they have more control over health behaviours, leading them to show lower levels of distress (Lobel, Yali, Zhu, DeVincent, & Meyer, 2002), and more positive health behaviours (Giltay, Geleijnse, Zitman, Buijsse, & Kromhout, 2007).

Finding meaning in stressful life events

Humanistic theorists emphasize the human need to find meaning in one's life and the psychological benefits of doing so (May, 1961; Watson & Greenberg, 1998). Several studies show that finding meaning from traumatic life experiences is related to better physical and mental health (Park, 2010). In other words, those who are able to formulate an answer to the question of 'Why?', adjust better following a stressful life event than those who do not find an answer to the 'Why?' question.

Some people find personal meaning through spiritual beliefs, which can be a great comfort in the face of crises. Daniel McIntosh and co-workers (McIntosh, Silver, & Wortman, 1993) studied 124 parents who had lost their babies to sudden infant death syndrome. They found that grieving parents whose religious beliefs provided some higher meaning to their loss experienced greater well-being and less distress 18 months later. In another study, researchers found that people who were able to find meaning in the death of a family member experienced less distress during the year following the loss. Finding a sense of meaning from their own process of coping with the loss (e.g., the sense that the event helped them grow spiritually) or finding benefit from their loss (e.g., an increased desire to help others) had even longer-term positive effects (Davis, Nolen, & Larson, 1998; Lichtenthal, Currier, Neimeyer, & Keesee, 2010).

Religious beliefs can be a two-edged sword, however: they can either decrease or increase stress, depending on their nature and the type of stressor to which they are applied. In one study of elderly people with medical problems, poorer physical and psychological adjustment occurred in patients who viewed God as punishing them; saw themselves as the victims of demonic forces; expressed anger towards God, clergy or church members; or questioned their faith (Koenig, Pargament, & Nielsen, 1998). Religious beliefs may have positive effects in dealing with some types of stressors but not with others. Such beliefs seem to help people cope more effectively with losses, illnesses and personal setbacks. In contrast, they can increase the negative impact of other stressors such as marital problems and abuse, perhaps by inducing guilt or placing internal pressures on individuals to remain in the stressful relationship (Strawbridge, Shema, Cohen, Roberts, & Kaplan, 1998).

> **Focus 16.10** How do hardiness, coping self-efficacy, optimism/pessimism and spiritual beliefs affect stress outcomes?

Resilient Children: Superkids or Ordinary Magic?

At the beginning of this chapter we described Sarah, a child who grew up in a terrible home environment with a psychotic mother, and a father who abused her and committed suicide in her presence. Somehow, despite these experiences, Sarah grew into a highly successful young woman. Since the 1970s, psychologists such as Emmy Werner have been studying children who show extraordinary resilience, or the ability to tolerate, and even thrive in, highly stressful circumstances (Werner & Smith, 1982).

What factors matter in the lives of resilient children like Sarah, who rise far above what their environments would predict for them? After reviewing many studies of unusually resilient children and adolescents, Ann Masten (2001) concluded that such children are a monument to the ordinary adaptive processes that occur in the lives of most children, factors she termed 'ordinary magic'. Masten and Coatsworth (1998) found that these children have certain characteristics that contribute to a positive outcome even in the face of stressful life events (Table 16.1). These characteristics include adequate intellectual functioning, social skills, self-efficacy and faith (optimism and hope), as well as environmental factors such as a relationship with at least one caring, pro-social adult.

To be resilient, a child need not have all of the characteristics listed in Table 16.1, but he or she must have some of them. Good intellectual functioning and a supportive relationship with a caring adult seem to be the most important (Masten & Coatsworth, 1998). In Sarah's case, this positive adult relationship did not exist with either parent. Instead, the critical

relationship was provided by a loving elementary school teacher who befriended, encouraged and guided her during the critical formative period of middle childhood. This key relationship, combined with Sarah's obvious intelligence, allowed her to develop self-esteem, a belief in her own capabilities and the will to nurture her talents.

However, it is not enough to *hope* that children have enough characteristics that will help them cope with severe adversity. It is also important to *help* them cope. A substantial number of preventive intervention studies have been conducted and such interventions try to promote resilience and reduce problem behaviours (Greenberg, 2006). Waaktaar and colleagues (Waaktaar, Christie, Borge, & Torgersen, 2004) derived important therapeutic principles based on four resilience factors (e.g., self-efficacy). They showed, for example, that clinical intervention programmes focused on creating pro-social, supportive interactions with same-age peers, assisting

TABLE 16.1 Personal and environmental factors that contribute to stress resilience in children

Source	Characteristic
Individual	Good intellectual functioning
	Appealing, sociable, easy-going disposition
	Self-efficacy, self-confidence, high self-esteem
	Talents
	Faith
Family	Close relationship to caring parent figure
	Authoritative parenting: warmth, structure, high expectations
	Socio-economic advantages
	Connections to extended supportive family networks
Extra-familial context	Bonds to pro-social adults outside the family
	Connections to pro-social organizations
	Attending effective schools

Source: Masten and Coatsworth, 1998.

Levels of analysis
factors related to the stress response

PSYCHOLOGICAL

- Cognitive appraisal of environmental demands, resources, potential consequences and personal meaning of consequences

- Personality factors, such as optimism and hardiness, that affect responses to stressors

- Coping strategies and the skill with which they are applied

- Self-efficacy and expectations of available social support

BIOLOGICAL

- Evolutionary mechanisms for responding to stressors

- Physiological responses of autonomic and endocrine systems to situational stressors

- Stress effects on immune system

- Individual differences in physiological reactivity to stressors (e.g., physiological toughness)

ENVIRONMENTAL

- Number, intensity and duration of the stressful events
- Predictability, controllability and chronicity of stressors
- Availability of social support
- Cultural factors that teach one how to respond to stressors

Stress response

Focus 16.11 What factors create stress resilience in children?

them in attaining self-relevant goals and encouraging them to create a meaningful understanding of their past, present and future lives, might prove potent in helping youths to cope with stressful experiences. In Sarah we have an example of what can happen even in the face of great adversity when certain critical protective factors are present. As Masten (2001, p. 235) concluded: 'What began as a quest for the extraordinary has revealed the power of the ordinary. Resilience does not come from rare and special qualities, but from the everyday magic of ordinary, normative human resources in the minds, brains, and bodies of children, in their families and relationships, and in their communities.'

As we have now seen, a variety of biological, cognitive and environmental factors influence stress and its effects on us. 'Levels of analysis' summarizes these important influences.

In review

- Vulnerability and protective factors make people more or less susceptible to stressors. Social support is an important protective factor, having both direct and buffering effects that help people cope with stress.

- Individual differences in physiological reactivity also affect well-being. People who exhibit strong and prolonged arousal responses are more susceptible to negative psychological and health effects. Physiological reactivity can predispose people to health problems, particularly if they respond with high levels of cortisol. The Type A behaviour pattern increases vulnerability to coronary heart disease.

- Hardiness is a protective factor against stress. Hardy individuals are committed, have feelings of personal control and tend to perceive stressful situations as challenges. Other cognitive protective factors are self-efficacy and optimism. Spiritual beliefs often help people cope more effectively with stressful life events, but certain religious beliefs seem capable of increasing stress.

- Studies of highly resilient children reveal important characteristics that contribute to positive outcomes as children mature, such as good intellectual functioning, social skills, self-efficacy and hope, usually nurtured by social support from at least one caring adult in the child's life.

COPING WITH STRESS

My courage sank, and with each succeeding minute it became less possible to resist this horror. My cue came, and on I went to that stage where I knew with grim certainty I would not be capable of remaining more than a few minutes. . . . I took one pace forward and stopped abruptly. My voice had started to fade, my throat closed up and the audience was beginning to go giddily round.   (Aaron, 1986, p. 24)

This account of stage fright was given not by a novice actor in his first play but by Sir Laurence Olivier (1907–89), considered by many the greatest actor of his generation, appearing in more than 120 stage roles, nearly 60 films and more than 15 television productions. Few people were aware that for most of his career, Olivier experienced a private hell before every performance. His audiences saw only what happened once he stepped onto the stage: another flawless performance. Olivier had a remarkable ability to purge the terror from his mind, relax his body and concentrate fully on his role once show-time arrived (Aaron, 1986, p. 24).

People can respond in many different ways to try and cope with stressful life events (Carver & Connor-Smith, 2010). From denying that they are indeed stressed by a specific situation, to indulging in a shopping spree and eating chocolate under a warm blanket watching a favourite feel-good movie – interestingly, some research does indeed suggest that eating dark chocolate reduces emotional stress, stress hormone and other stress-related biochemical changes, although the reason for this effect, if it exists at all, is still unknown (Martin et al., 2009; Semba et al., in press).

problem-focused coping strategies to confront and directly deal with the demands of the situation or to change the situation so that it is no longer stressful

Although there are countless ways people might respond to a stressor, coping strategies can be divided into the three broad classes shown in Figure 16.7. **Problem-focused coping** strategies attempt to confront and directly deal with the demands of the situation

or to change the situation so that it is no longer stressful (Lazarus & Folkman, 1984). Examples of problem-focused strategies might include studying for a test, going directly to another person to work out a misunderstanding, or signing up for a course to improve one's time-management skills.

Rather than dealing directly with the stressful situation, **emotion-focused coping** strategies attempt to manage the emotional responses that result from it. Olivier was obviously able to control his paralysing fear once he stepped on stage. Some forms of emotion-focused coping involve appraising the situation in a manner that minimizes its emotional impact. A person might deal with the stress from an interpersonal conflict by denying that any problem exists. Other forms involve avoidance or acceptance of the stressful situation. Thus a student might decide to deal with anxiety about an upcoming test by going to a party and forgetting about it. Informed that he has a terminal illness, a man might decide that nothing can be done about the situation and simply accept this unwelcome reality – or he might use the avoidance strategy of discontinuing medical treatment and keeping the illness a secret, even from close family members (Lazarus, 2006).

A third class of coping strategies involves **seeking social support**, that is, turning to others for assistance and emotional support in times of stress (Amirkhan, 1990; Carver, Scheier, & Weintraub, 1989). Thus the student might seek the help of a classmate in preparing for the test, and the man with the terminal illness might choose to join a support group for the terminally ill. Sarah accepted and benefited from the social support provided by the teacher who befriended her.

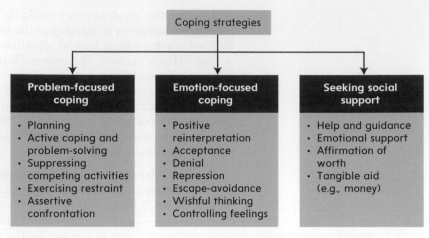

FIGURE 16.7 Ways of coping.
Coping strategies fall into three general categories: (1) problem-focused coping, actively attempting to respond to situational demands; (2) emotion-focused coping, directed at minimizing emotional distress; and (3) seeking or accepting social support.

emotion-focused coping
strategies to manage the emotional responses that result from it

seeking social support
turning to others for assistance and emotional support in times of stress

EFFECTIVENESS OF COPING STRATEGIES

Which of the three general classes of coping strategies would you expect to be most generally effective? Whenever we ask this question in our classes, the majority of our students vote for problem-focused coping. This response is understandable, because many people, particularly in Western cultures, approach problems with the attitude that if something needs fixing, we should fix it.

What does the research literature say? Charles Holahan and Rudolf Moos (1990) studied coping patterns and psychological outcomes in more than 400 American adults over a one-year period. Although people often used several coping methods in dealing with a stressor, problem-focused coping methods and seeking social support were most often associated with favourable adjustment to stressors. In contrast, emotion-focused strategies that involved avoiding feelings or taking things out on other people predicted depression and poorer adjustment. Other studies have yielded similar results. In children and adults and across many different types of stressors, emotion-focused strategies that involve avoidance, denial and wishful thinking seem to be related to less effective adaptation (Aldwin, 2007; Ben-Zur, 2009). On the other hand, there are adaptive emotion-focused strategies, such as identifying and changing irrational negative thinking and learning relaxation skills to control arousal. When you are transgressed against by someone else, for example, people often think negatively about this person, reacting by experiencing unforgiveness (Fehr, Gelfand, & Nag, 2010). One emotion-focused strategy that has been shown to reduce stressful reactions to such transgression is by forgiving the other person, thereby changing negative thinking (Worthington & Scherer, 2004). Such emotion-focused strategies can thus be effective methods for reducing stress responses without avoiding or distorting reality (DeLongis, 2000; Meichenbaum, 1985).

Despite the evidence generally favouring problem-focused coping, attempting to change the situation is not always the most adaptive way to cope with a stressor. Problem-focused coping works best in situations where there is some prospect of controlling the stressor (Park, Armeli, & Tennen, 2004). However, there are situations that we cannot influence or modify, and in those cases problem-focused coping may do more harm than good. Instead, emotion-focused coping may be the most adaptive approach we can take, for while we cannot master the situation, we may be able to prevent or control maladaptive emotional responses to it (Auerbach, 1989). Of course, reliance on emotion-focused coping is likely to be maladaptive if it prevents us from acting to change situations in which we actually *do* have control.

Thomas Strentz and Stephen Auerbach (1988) demonstrated the effectiveness of emotion-focused coping in adapting to a stressful situation with limited personal control. As part of a US Federal Bureau of Investigation (FBI) programme to deal with potential airline hijackings, airline employees volunteered to participate in a training exercise. The employees were randomly assigned to one of two experimental conditions or to a control condition. In one experimental condition, employees were trained in problem-focused techniques that hostages can use to actively deal with their situation. They were shown how to interact with captors and maintain a façade of dignity and composure through appearance and behaviour. They also learned ways of supporting one another non-verbally and communicating with one another by using a prisoner-of-war tap code.

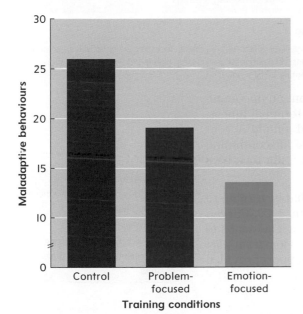

FIGURE 16.8 Coping with captivity.

These data show the behavioural ratings of participants in a mock airline-hostage crisis. Participants who received instruction in emotion-focused coping fared better than did those in the problem-focused and control conditions.

Source: Based on Strentz and Auerbach, 1988.

Training for the second experimental group focused on the emotional reactions the hostages would likely experience and techniques they could use to minimize their stress responses. These emotion-focused techniques included deep breathing, muscle relaxation, stopping unwanted thoughts and generating pleasant fantasies. Employees in the control condition were given no coping-skills training.

Weeks later, the employees were unexpectedly abducted by FBI agents posing as terrorists and held hostage for four days under very realistic and stressful conditions. During their captivity, the hostages completed self-report measures of emotional distress and psychiatric symptoms. In addition, trained observers rated the adaptiveness of their behaviour. Results indicated that the hostage groups trained in either problem-focused or emotion-focused strategies fared better than did the untrained employees on both the self-report and the behavioural measures. However, employees who had received emotion-focused training adapted better to the largely uncontrollable conditions of captivity than did those who had received problem-focused coping instruction (Figure 16.8).

Focus 16.12 Describe the three major classes of coping strategies. How does stressor controllability influence their outcomes?

The important conclusion from this and many other studies is that no coping strategy or technique is equally effective in all situations. Instead, effectiveness depends on the characteristics of the situation, the appropriateness of the technique and the skill with which it is carried out. People are likely to adapt well to the stresses of life if they have mastered a variety of coping techniques and know how and when to apply them most effectively. The importance of controllability in the choice of techniques recalls the wisdom in theologian Reinhold Niebuhr's famous prayer that asks for the courage to change those things that can be changed, the forbearance to accept those that cannot be changed, and the wisdom to discern the difference.

Trauma Disclosure and Emotional Release

Is there any truth to the popular wisdom that when we are stressed out and upset, it is good to talk with someone about it? James Pennebaker (1995, 1997) conducted several studies in which college students talked about past traumas to an experimenter in an adjoining room or they tape-recorded or wrote about the experiences. Many tearfully recounted incidents of personal failure, family tragedies, shattered relationships, sexual or physical abuse and traumatic accidents. Participants in a control group were asked to talk or write about trivial everyday matters. A comparison of blood samples taken from the students before and after

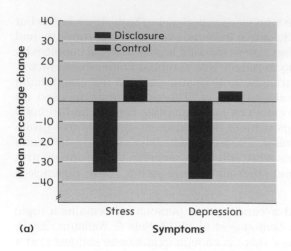

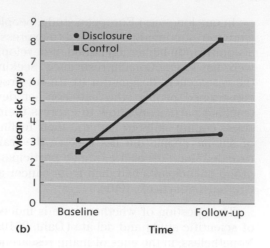

FIGURE 16.9 Does trauma disclosure help?

These data show the effects of written disclosure concerning a previous traumatic life event on (a) subsequent stress symptoms, depression, and (b) number of self-reported sick days.

Source: Based on Sloan and Marx, 2004.

their sessions indicated enhanced immune system functioning in those who had purged themselves of negative emotions but not in those who had not. Moreover, the students who had disclosed the traumatic incidents had 50% fewer visits to the campus health centre over the next six months compared with the control group. A study by Panagopoulou, Maes, Rime and Montgomery (2006) on preoperative psychological distress demonstrates, however, that it is not the *quantity* or number of times individuals have the opportunity to share emotions that leads to the strongest decrease in distress. Instead the perceived *quality* of the disclosure, such as the supportiveness, understanding or appropriateness of the sharing partner, seemed more important for predicting decreased preoperative distress as a function of social sharing.

In another study, Denise Sloan and Brian Marx (2004) used the written-disclosure procedure with college students who had reported experiencing a traumatic event in their lives. The students completed measures of stress symptoms, depression and number of days they had been sick since the beginning of the school term. In an experimental condition, participants were then asked to write about the traumatic event, whereas the control condition did an unrelated task. Physiological arousal was recorded as the participants performed the tasks. One month later, the students again completed the measures of psychological symptoms and sick days. The students had not differed on any of these measures at baseline, but they differed strongly afterwards (Figure 16.9). Those who had written about their traumas showed lowered stress and depression scores. They also reported fewer sick days at the follow-up. The more physiologically aroused the participants in the written-disclosure group became while they wrote about their traumatic events, the healthier they looked physically and psychologically a month later. The researchers concluded that writing or talking about traumatic events affords exposure to the situational cues that accompanied the trauma and now function as conditioned stimuli that trigger distress. Exposure allows extinction to occur, thus reducing the stimuli's emotional impact.

Bottling-up Feelings: The Hidden Costs of Emotional Constraint

You can probably think of several people in your life who differ greatly in how they express their negative emotions in response to stress. While constantly venting strong negative feelings may not be a good way to make friends and influence people, an inability to express negative feelings can also have its costs. Some studies have reported relations between cancer development and the use of denial or repressive coping strategies, but others have not (McKenna, Zevon, Corn, & Rounds, 1999). In order to understand the sometimes equivocal results on the relation between negative health outcomes and the inhibition of expression, it is important to notice that negative effects on health are most likely when individuals *simultaneously* experience high levels of negative affect *and* inhibit their expression of it. This emotional reaction pattern has been linked to, for example, recurrence of cardiac events and higher mortality risk for patients with coronary heart disease (Denollet, 1997). In this sense, denial may also lead to a decrease in experienced negative emotions, thereby undermining the association between inhibition of expression and negative health outcomes.

In one long-term European study, people who were experiencing high stress levels but were too emotionally restrained to express negative feelings, even when appropriate, had a significantly higher likelihood of developing cancer than did highly stressed people who were not so emotionally restrained. Seeking to reduce this potential vulnerability factor, the researchers designed a treatment programme to help stress-ridden but emotionally constrained people who had not yet developed cancer. The programme focused on teaching participants how to express their emotions in an adaptive fashion and to build stress-coping skills to manage their feelings without bottling them up. A control group of similar people did not receive the training. Thirteen years later, a follow-up study revealed that 90% of the trained participants were still alive, whereas 62% of the control group participants had died from cancer and other ailments (Eysenck, 1994; Eysenck & Grossarth-Marticek, 1991).

The question of whether there is indeed a 'cancer-prone personality' remains a topic of scientific study and debate (Dahl, 2010; Lemogne et al., 2013; Suls & Wallston, 2003). Nonetheless, in the eyes of many researchers, there is enough evidence to suggest that a rigid pattern of emotional constraint can have negative effects on health. One impressive example of this comes from two studies by Cole and colleagues (Cole, Kemeny, Taylor, & Visscher, 1996a; Cole, Kemeny, Taylor, Visscher, & Fahey, 1996b). During a five-year period they followed a normal population of gay men and found that participants who concealed the expression of their homosexual identity experienced higher incidence of several infectious diseases like bronchitis and pneumonia, as well as a higher incidence of cancer compared with participants who did not conceal the expression of their homosexual identity. A second study furthermore showed that for HIV-positive gay men who concealed the expression of their homosexuality, the HIV infection advanced more rapidly. These studies provide some strong evidence of the association between bottling up one's feelings and future health outcomes.

> **Focus 16.13** How do trauma disclosure and emotional constraint affect well-being?

The question of whether or not it is better to purge one's feelings or bottle them up, is not that easy, however. As in the earlier discussion of coping strategies, the best outcomes may occur if we have the flexibility to do either, depending on the situation. George Bonanno and co-workers (Bonanno, Papa, Lalande, Westphal, & Coifman, 2004) studied New York City college students shortly after the 11 September terrorist attacks. In a series of laboratory tasks, participants were required to either openly express emotional responses or suppress them. The researchers found that the students who were most able to engage in either expression or suppression reported less distress about the terrorist attacks and less general life distress two years later than did participants who were less flexible in their emotional responses.

Gender, Culture and Coping

Many factors, including gender roles and culture, influence our tendency to favour one coping strategy over another. Although men and women both use problem-focused coping, men are more likely to use it as the first strategy when they confront a stressor (Ptacek, Smith, & Zanas, 1992). Women, who tend to have larger support networks and higher needs for affiliation than men, are more likely than men to seek social support (Billings & Moos, 1984; Schwarzer, 1998). Women are also somewhat more likely than men to use emotion-focused coping (Carver et al., 1989; Pearlin and Schooler, 1978).

This general pattern of coping preferences is consistent with the socialization that boys and girls traditionally experience. In most cultures, boys are pushed to be more independent, assertive and self-sufficient, whereas girls are expected to be more emotionally expressive, supportive and dependent (Eccles, 1991; Lytton & Romney, 1991). In the words of stress researcher Shelley Taylor (2011), the common male response is 'fight or flight', whereas women are more likely than men to 'tend and befriend'. *Tending* involves nurturant activities designed to protect the self, offspring and significant others. These behaviours promote safety and reduce distress. *Befriending* is the creation and maintenance of social networks that may aid in this process. Taylor (2006b) speculates that the tend-and-befriend pattern is a product of biological mechanisms that underlie attachment and care-giving behavioural tendencies in women. The female hormone oxytocin, acting in conjunction with female reproductive hormones and endorphin mechanisms, may be a key player in this biological system.

The importance of support received from a spouse in reducing women's negative emotional responses to threat was assessed in a recent study by Coan, Schaefer and Davidson (2006). In this study women were exposed to threatening stimuli (the possibility of receiving an electric shock), while their brain responses were monitored by a brain scanner (fMRI). Support occurred in the form of having one's hand held during the procedure, a behaviour that is used to express soothing and support in both humans and primates under conditions of threat. In one block of trials, the wife held the hand of her spouse. In a second block of trials, an anonymous and unseen male experimental assistant held the woman's hand. In the third block, no one held the woman's hand. At the end of each trial block, the woman rated how unpleasant the situation was and how much fear and arousal she was experiencing. As expected, the fMRI recordings of brain activation yielded dramatic proof that social support, particularly from a spouse, reduces the brain's response to threat. That is, the spouse's hand-holding was associated with the lowest physiological arousal. One other important finding occurred. Despite the fact that all of the couples were in satisfying marriages, the researchers found that even in this restricted marital-satisfaction group, satisfaction scores were significantly correlated with reduced brain activation on the threat trials when the spouse was holding the woman's hand (Figure 16.10). This relation did not occur when the woman's hand was being held by a stranger. The question of whether the same findings would occur if husbands were being shocked and the wife was doing the hand-holding is as of yet unresolved and awaits further investigation.

Researchers have also found cultural differences in coping (Bardi & Guerra, 2011). North Americans and Europeans show a tendency to use problem-focused coping more than do Asian and Hispanic people, who tend to favour emotion-focused coping and social support (Essau & Trommsdorff, 1996; Jung, 1995). Asians also show a greater tendency to avoid stressful situations involving interpersonal conflict, perhaps reflecting their culture's emphasis on interpersonal harmony (Chang, 1996). In a study of how American married couples deal with marital stress, African-Americans reported a greater tendency than Caucasian-Americans to seek social support (Sistler & Moore, 1996). The manner in which particular coping strategies affect well-being under differing cultural conditions is an important topic for future research.

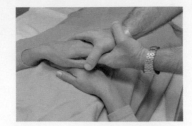

FIGURE 16.10 Support in the form of holding hands significantly reduced the brain's response to threat in women.

Source: © Nancy Louie.

Focus 16.14 How do gender and cultural factors affect the tendency to use particular coping strategies?

STRESS-MANAGEMENT TRAINING

Because stress takes a toll on people's physical and psychological well-being, much effort has gone into developing methods for reducing stress. The model shown in Figure 16.2 suggests that we can reduce stress by modifying any of its major components (Linden, 2005). Thus we can change the situation that constitutes the stressor, modify cognitive appraisals that trigger the rest of the stress response, or learn ways to control the physiological arousal. Finally, we can adopt more effective behaviours for meeting the demands of the situation.

In many coping-skills programmes, people learn to modify habits of thought that trigger inappropriate emotional responses and to control physiological arousal responses through relaxation skills (Barlow, Rapee, & Reisner, 2001; Greenberg, 2005). Figure 16.11 previews the most common stress-management techniques taught by psychologists.

Cognitive Coping Skills

Because cognitive appraisal processes play a central role in generating stress, Richard Lazarus, Albert Ellis and other cognitive theorists maintain that the most powerful means

FIGURE 16.11 Stress-management training.

Many stress-management/coping-skills programmes teach self-modification techniques, such as cognitive restructuring and self-instructional training to alter stress-producing cognitive appraisals. Relaxation techniques such as progressive relaxation and meditation help counter physiological arousal.

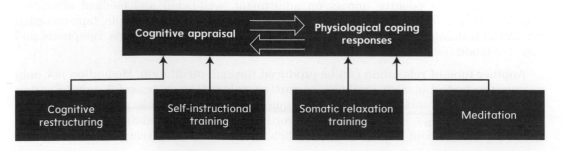

of regulating feelings is by controlling how we think about stressful situations and about ourselves. Ellis (1962) suggests that a relatively small number of irrational core beliefs lie at the root of most maladaptive negative feelings. For example, we tell ourselves that we *must* achieve and be approved of in virtually every respect if we are to consider ourselves worthwhile people; that it is terrible, awful and *catastrophic* when life or other people are not the way that we demand they be; that people who do not behave as we wish are bad and therefore deserving of punishment. In Ellis's terms, these '*must*urbation' and 'catastrophizing' tendencies, together with other irrational ideas, generate unnecessary anxiety, despair and anger. When people use the technique of **cognitive restructuring** to systematically detect, challenge and replace these irrational ideas, their feelings can change dramatically, as in the following case:

> *Whenever I find myself getting guilty or upset, I immediately tell myself that there must be some silly sentence that I am saying to myself to cause this upset; and almost immediately . . . I find this sentence. . . . [It] invariably takes the form of 'Isn't it terrible that . . .' or 'Wouldn't it be awful if . . .' And when I look at and question these sentences and ask myself, 'How is it really terrible that . . . ?' or 'Why would it actually be awful if . . . ?' I always find that it isn't terrible or wouldn't be awful, and I get over being upset very quickly. . . . I can hardly believe it, but I seem to be getting to the point, after so many years of worrying over practically everything and thinking I was a slob no matter what I did, of now finding that nothing is so terrible or awful, and I now seem to be recognizing this in advance rather than after I have seriously upset myself.* (Ellis, 1962, pp. 31–2)

Another approach to changing cognitions does not involve attacking irrational ideas that cause disturbance. In **self-instructional training**, people learn to talk to themselves and guide their behaviour in ways that help them cope more effectively (Meichenbaum, 1985). They prepare different self-instructions to use at four critical stages of the stressful episode: preparing for the stressor, confronting the stressor, dealing with the feeling of being overwhelmed and appraising coping efforts after the stressful situation. For example, when preparing for a stressor a person might tell themselves to 'Stop worrying. Worrying won't help anything' or 'Remember, stick to the issues and don't take it personally'. In a similar way, when confronting the stressor, people can direct their behaviour using self-statements such as 'As long as I keep my cool, I'm in control of the situation'. In order to deal with the feeling of being overwhelmed by a stressor, adaptive self-statements might include statements like 'Let's take the issue point by point'. And finally, when appraising coping efforts after the stressful situation people might tell themselves 'I handled it pretty well!' or 'It didn't work, but that's OK. I'll do better next time'.

Relaxation Techniques

Coping-skills training can also help people control their physiological responses in stressful situations. Because relaxation is incompatible with arousal, **somatic relaxation training** provides a means of voluntarily reducing or preventing high levels of arousal. To learn this skill, people typically tense the various muscle groups of their body and pair tension release with a trigger word (e.g., 'Relax') and the exhalation (relaxing) phase of the breathing cycle. The goal is to condition relaxation to the trigger word and to exhalation so that a state of relaxation can be immediately produced in stressful situations by exhaling and mentally saying the trigger word. Most people can learn this technique with about a week of practice. Somatic relaxation training is a cornerstone of most stress-management training programmes, and evidence suggests that this type of intervention has a positive impact on adjustment, well-being and medical utilization (e.g., Brantley & Jones, 1993). In a study on adult asthmatics for example, tape-recorded relaxation training led to a decrease in the number of reported asthma symptoms and negative mood (Smyth, Soefer, Hurewitz, & Stone, 1999).

Another type of relaxation can be produced through meditation. Meditation not only relaxes the body but also produces **cognitive relaxation**, a peaceful, mind-clearing state. In one approach, the person sits quietly in a comfortable position with eyes closed and mentally concentrates on the word *one* with each exhalation. This procedure is continued for about 20 minutes and, when mastered, quickly relaxes both body and

cognitive restructuring systematically detect, challenge and replace these irrational ideas

self-instructional training people learn to talk to themselves and guide their behaviour in ways that help them cope more effectively

somatic relaxation training a means of voluntarily reducing or preventing high levels of arousal

cognitive relaxation a peaceful, mind-clearing state

Focus 16.15 Which stress-management/coping-skills training procedures are used to control cognitive and physiological stress responses?

mind (Benson & Klipper, 1976). Several studies show both relaxation procedures lead to decreases in distress and increases in positive mood, and don't differ much in terms of effectiveness (Jain et al., 2007). However, one key difference between meditation and somatic relaxation is that the latter can be applied at any time during the stressful situation, whereas meditation is best done in a quiet, private space. Many people who meditate practise their technique daily as a means of counteracting ongoing stressors in their lives and preventing short-term stressors from taking a toll.

 In review

- Three major ways of coping with stressors are problem-focused coping, emotion-focused coping and seeking social support. Problem-focused coping and seeking social support generally relate to better adjustment than emotion-focused coping. However, in situations involving low personal control, emotion-focused coping may be the most appropriate and effective strategy.
- Trauma disclosure has shown positive effects on physical and psychological well-being. Severe emotional constraint may be a risk factor for cancer and perhaps other disorders. Flexibility in emotional expression and suppression seems desirable.
- Stress-management training teaches people adaptive coping skills for handling stressful situations. Cognitive restructuring and self-instructional training can be used to develop adaptive cognitive coping responses; somatic relaxation training and meditation can be used to develop greater control of physiological arousal.

PAIN AND PAIN MANAGEMENT

Physical pain surely is one of the most unpleasant realities of life, and most of us do our best to avoid it. Hundreds of thousands seek relief from unbearable pain, and one-third of all people experience pain that requires medical attention at some time in their lives. Pain is a significant feature of many illnesses, and some form of pain is responsible for 80% of all medical complaints in North America and Europe (Hunter, Goodie, Oordt, & Dobmeyer, 2009).

On the surface, we might think that pain is a purely sensory phenomenon and wonder why it is of interest to psychologists. When we examine it more carefully, however, we see that pain is a complex perceptual phenomenon that involves the operation of numerous psychological processes. For example, it is possible for people to experience excruciating pain in the absence of tissue damage (Melzack, 1998). Conversely, people may suffer severe physical damage and experience no pain, as has occurred in soldiers engaged in combat who were unaware for several hours that they had been wounded (Fordyce, 1988).

BIOLOGICAL MECHANISMS OF PAIN

Pain receptors are found in all body tissues with the exception of the brain, bones, hair, nails and non-living parts of the teeth. Free nerve endings in the skin and internal organs respond to intense mechanical, thermal or chemical stimulation and then send nerve impulses into the spinal cord, where sensory tracts carry pain information to the brain. Once in the brain, the sensory information about pain intensity and location is relayed by the thalamus to the somatosensory and frontal areas of the cerebral cortex (Fields, 2005). Other tracts from the thalamus direct nerve impulses to the limbic system, which is involved in motivation and emotion. These tracts seem to control the emotional component of pain (Melzack, 1998). Thus pain has both a sensory and an emotional component. *Suffering* occurs when both painful sensations and a negative emotional response are present (Fordyce, 1988; Turk, 2001).

Spinal and Brain Mechanisms

Gate control theory, developed by Canadian psychologist Ronald Melzack and physiologist Patrick Wall (1982), was a major advance in the study of pain. **Gate control theory** proposes that the experience of pain results from the opening and closing of gating mechanisms in the nervous system. Events in the spinal cord can open a system of spinal

gate control theory the experience of pain results from the opening and closing of gating mechanisms in the nervous system

cord 'gates' and allow the nerve impulses to travel towards the brain. However, other sensory input can partially or completely close the gates and blunt our experiencing of pain. For example, rubbing a bruise or scratching an itch can produce relief. Gate control theorists also suggest that acupuncture achieves its pain-relieving effects because the acupuncture needles stimulate mostly tactile receptors that close the pain gates.

From a psychological perspective, perhaps the most intriguing feature of gate control theory is that nerve impulses in fibres descending from the brain can also influence the spinal gates, thereby increasing or decreasing the flow of pain stimulation to the brain. This *central control mechanism* allows thoughts, emotions and beliefs to influence the experience of pain and helps explain why pain is a psychological phenomenon as well as a physical phenomenon. Gate control theory has been valuable in suggesting techniques for pain control and in stimulating research on psychological factors in pain (Turk & Melzack, 2001).

Gate control and other theorists have traditionally viewed pain as reflecting solely the action of neurons. However, the immune system also plays a role in pain. Research has shown that glial cells, which structurally support and service neurons within the spinal cord, are involved in the creation and maintenance of pathological pain (Watkins & Maier, 2003). These glial cells become activated by immune challenges (viral or bacterial infection) and by substances released by neurons within the pain pathway. They then amplify pain by releasing cytokines (messenger molecules) that promote inflammation. This may help account for that 'ache all over' sensation that many of us experience when we are ill.

Focus 16.16 How does gate control theory explain pain perception and control? How are glial cells and cytokines involved?

The Endorphins

In 1680 an English physician wrote, 'Among the remedies which it has pleased Almighty God to give man to relieve his suffering, none is so universal and so efficacious as opium' (quoted in Snyder, 1977). Opiates (such as opium, morphine and heroin) have been used for centuries to relieve pain, and they strongly affect the brain's pain and pleasure systems. In the 1970s, scientists discovered that opiates produce their effects by locking into specific receptor sites in brain regions associated with pain perception.

endorphins endogenous, or internally produced, morphines

But why would the brain have built-in receptors for opiates unless there was some natural chemical in the brain for the receptor to receive? Later research disclosed what had to be true: the nervous system has its own built-in analgesics (painkillers) with opiate-like properties. These natural opiates were named **endorphins** (meaning endogenous, or internally produced, morphines). Endorphins exert some of their painkilling effects by inhibiting the release of neurotransmitters involved in the synaptic transmission of pain impulses from the spinal cord to the brain (Fields, 2005). Some endorphins are enormously potent. One of the brain endorphins isolated by scientists is more than 200 times more powerful than morphine (Franklin, 1987). Endorphins are of great interest to psychologists because they may help explain how psychological factors 'in the head' can have such strong effects on pain and suffering.

In 2001 John-Kar Zubieta and co-workers published a landmark study that showed the endorphins in action within the brain. They injected a radioactive form of an endorphin into volunteer participants, then stimulated them with painful injections of salt water into the jaw muscles. Brain scans allowed the researchers to see which areas of the brain lit up from endorphin activity and to relate this activity to pain reports given by the participants every 15 seconds. The scans revealed a surge of endorphin activity within several brain regions, including the thalamus (the sensory switchboard), the amygdala (an emotion centre) and a sensory area of the cortex. As the endorphin surge continued over 20 minutes of pain stimulation, participants reported decreased sensory and emotional ratings of pain.

Two other findings were noteworthy. First, people differed in their pain experiences despite identical pain stimulation. Second, these differences were linked to variations in (1) the number of opioid receptors the participants had for the endorphins to bind to and (2) their own ability to release endorphins. Thus biological factors seem to be an important determinant for understanding differences in people's ability to tolerate pain (Zubieta et

FIGURE 16.12 Pain reduction.

Acupuncture is a proven pain-reduction procedure (e.g., Manheimer, White, Berman, Forys, & Ernst, 2005). Gate control theory attributes its effects to the stimulation of sensory fibres that close sensory gates in the pain system. In addition, there is evidence that acupuncture stimulates endorphin release.

Source: Jessica Rinaldi for The Boston Globe via Getty Images

al., 2001). Acupuncture is a pain-reduction technique that may ultimately be understood in terms of endorphin mechanisms. Injections of naloxone, a drug that counteracts the effects of endorphins, greatly decrease the pain-reducing effects of acupuncture (Oleson, 2002). This suggests that acupuncture normally releases endorphins (Figure 16.12).

Another phenomenon attributable to endorphins is **stress-induced analgesia**, a reduction in – or absence of – perceived pain that occurs under stressful conditions (Butler & Finn, 2009). For example, research has shown that about 65% of soldiers wounded during combat report having felt no pain at the time of their injury (Warga, 1987). Likewise, people involved in accidents are sometimes unaware of serious injuries until the crisis is over. This analgesic response could be highly adaptive. In a life-threatening situation, fight-or-flight defensive behaviour must be given immediate priority over normal responses to pain, which typically involve immobility. By reducing or preventing pain sensations through the mechanism of endorphin release, stress-induced analgesia helps suppress these pain-related behaviours so that the person or animal can perform the actions needed for immediate survival, such as fleeing, fighting or getting help (Fanselow, 1991). As an example, consider the report of a man who was so severely bitten during an attack by a grizzly bear that he required more than 200 stitches:

> *I had read the week before about someone who was killed and eaten by a grizzly bear. So I was thinking that this bear was going to eat me unless I got away. I did not have time for pain. I was fighting for my life. It was not until the next day that I started feeling pain and fear.*   (Kolb & Whishaw, 2001, p. 386)

The release of endorphins seems to be part of the body's natural response to stress, but we may pay a price for this temporary relief from pain. It appears that chronically high levels of endorphin release help block the activity of immune system cells that recognize and selectively kill tumour cells. This may be one way in which stress makes us more susceptible to serious illnesses such as cancer (Shavit, 1990).

> **stress-induced analgesia** a reduction in—or absence of—perceived pain that occurs under stressful conditions

> **Focus 16.17** How do endorphins influence pain perception and physical well-being?

CULTURAL AND PSYCHOLOGICAL INFLUENCES ON PAIN

As a complex perception, pain is influenced by numerous factors. Cultural learning, meanings attributed to pain, beliefs, and personality factors all affect our experiences of pain.

Cultural Factors

Our interpretation of pain impulses sent to the brain depends in part on our experiences and beliefs, and both of these factors are influenced by the culture in which we develop (Rahim-Williams, Riley, Williams, & Fillingim, 2012; Rollman, 1998). Consider, for example, the experience of childbirth. This event is widely perceived as a painful ordeal in Western cultures, and many women express considerable anxiety about going through it (Blechman & Brownell, 1998). Yet in some cultures, women show virtually no distress during childbirth. Indeed, in one culture studied by anthropologists, it was customary for the woman's husband to get into bed and groan as if he were in great pain while the woman calmly gave birth to the child. The husband stayed in bed with the baby to recover from his terrible ordeal while the mother returned to work in the fields almost immediately (Kroeber, 1948).

Certain societies in India practise an unusual hook-hanging ritual. A holy person, chosen to bless children and crops, travels from village to village on a special ceremonial cart. Large steel hooks, attached by ropes to the top of the cart, are shoved under the skin and muscles on each side of the holy person's back. At the climax of the ceremony, he leaps from the cart and swings free, hanging only by the hooks embedded in his back (Figure 16.13). Incredibly, though hanging from the hooks with his entire body weight, the celebrant shows no evidence of pain during the ritual; on the contrary, he appears to be in a state of ecstasy. When the hooks are removed, the wounds heal rapidly and are scarcely visible within two weeks (Kosambi, 1967).

FIGURE 16.13 Cultural beliefs and pain tolerance.
Illustrated here is a hook-swinging ceremony practised in remote villages in India. After blessing all the children and farm fields in a village, the celebrant leaps from the cart and hangs suspended by the hooks embedded in his back in a state of ecstasy, showing no sign of pain.

Source: Adapted from Kosambi, 1967.

Meanings and Beliefs

Although different cultural groups do not appear to differ in their ability to discriminate among pain stimuli, members of different cultural groups may differ greatly in their interpretation of pain and the amount of suffering they experience (Rollman, 1998; Zatzick & Dimsdale, 1990). In the Indian hook-hanging ceremony, for example, the religious meanings attached to the act seem to transform the interpretations and meaning of the sensory input from the hooks. Likewise, child-bearing mothers in cultures where the pain of childbirth is not feared do not attach strong negative emotions to the associated sensations, and they therefore suffer far less.

FIGURE 16.14 The amount of pain a wounded soldier experiences may be influenced by the meaning it has for him. Does the wound represent a ticket home to his loved ones, or does it herald a lifetime of pain and disability?

Source: © DOD Photo/Alamy

Differences exist not only between cultural groups but also within them, as physician Henry Beecher (1959) observed while working at Anzio Beachhead in the Second World War and later at Massachusetts General Hospital. At Anzio, Beecher found that only about 25% of the severely wounded soldiers he observed required pain medication, compared with 80% of civilian men who had received similarly serious 'wounds' from surgeons at Massachusetts General. Why the difference? Beecher concluded that for the soldiers, the wounds had a fundamentally positive meaning: they spelled evacuation from the war zone and a socially acceptable ticket back home to their loved ones. For the civilian surgical patients, on the other hand, the operations meant a major life disruption and possible complications. The different meanings attributed to the pain stimuli resulted in very different levels of suffering and, consequently, different needs for pain relief (Figure 16.14).

placebos physiologically inert substances that have no medicinal value but are thought by the patient to be helpful

Chapter 2, Page 64

Chapter 18, Page 807

Perhaps nowhere is the influence of belief on pain perception more evident than in the effects of **placebos**, *physiologically inert substances that have no medicinal value but are thought by the patient to be helpful* (Shapiro & Shapiro, 1997; for a full description of placebos see **Chapters 2 and 18**). At the beginning of this chapter we described the observations made by German physician Hans Rheder, whose female patients responded with startling improvements in their symptoms to the news that he had invoked the healing powers of a faith healer. Similar observations have been made in pain research. In one classic study by Henry Beecher (1959), either a placebo or a morphine injection was given to 122 surgical patients who were suffering post-operative pain. All were told they were receiving pain medication. Of those who received morphine, 67% reported relief, but 42% of those given placebos reported equal relief. More recent medical studies of placebo effects have yielded even higher rates of pain relief, as high as 100% in some studies (Turner, Deyo, Loeser, Von Korff, & Fordyce, 1994). However, it is also clear that placebos work only if people *believe* they are going to work. Research using PET-scan technology at the Karolinska Institute in Sweden indicates that given a positive belief in the placebo's effectiveness, the brain sends messages that result in the release of endorphins to reduce pain (Petrovic, Kalso, Petersson, & Ingvarm, 2002; Petrovic, Kalso, Petersson, Andersson, Fransson, & Ingvar, 2010).

Where pain is concerned, the statement 'I can control it' may be more than an idle boast or an empty reassurance. In one experiment, patients suffering from the prolonged pain of a bone-marrow transplant were randomly assigned to one of two conditions. One group was allowed to directly control the amount of pain medication that they received intravenously. The other patients were given prescribed amounts of the same medication by the hospital staff (and told they could request additional medication if needed). The patients who had direct control over their medication not only rated their pain as less intense but also gave themselves less pain medication (Zucker et al., 1998). As in the case of placebo effects, beliefs about personal control apparently exert their effects by increasing endorphin release. Naloxone injections, which counteract endorphin activity, sharply reduce the ability of people to endure intensely painful stimuli, no matter how high their confidence in their pain tolerance (Bandura, O'Leary, Taylor, Gauthier, & Gossard, 1987).

Focus 16.18 How do cultural factors influence pain experience and behaviour?

Personality Factors and Social Support

Beginning with Sigmund Freud, personality theorists have suggested that emotional and personality factors can play a role in experiencing and responding to pain. Pain and suffering can be a way of attaining certain goals. For some bitter and deprived people,

pain can be a way of dramatizing their unhappiness; eliciting caring, sympathy or guilt from others, or gaining favours. Pain may also be a way of escaping from or avoiding threatening situations. For example, an athlete who dreads the possibility of failing may avoid the feared competition by experiencing severe pain that prevents participation. This coping process, different from consciously faking being hurt, occurs at an unconscious level (May & Sieb, 1987).

People who have the personality trait of neuroticism, the tendency to experience negative emotions such as anxiety and depression, report higher levels of physical pain, both in relation to medical conditions and in controlled laboratory administrations of painful stimuli such as heat, cold, electrical shock or pressure (Asghari & Nicholas, 2006; Turner & Aaron, 2001). In contrast, personality styles that include optimism and a sense of personal control over one's life are associated with lower pain perception and less suffering (Pellino & Ward, 1998). Moreover, patients with chronic pain conditions who are able to simply accept the pain rather than bemoaning their fate and responding emotionally to it have less disability, better social adjustment and higher work performance (McCracken, 1998). Thus it seems clear that psychological factors play important roles in pain perception and adaptation.

A person does not function in a social vacuum, however. A study by Holtzman and colleagues, for example, showed that rheumatoid arthritis (RA) patients' coping with daily pain was associated with reported satisfaction of social support. That is, social support enabled patients to more effectively use coping strategies such as cognitive reframing in order to cope with the daily pain among patients with RA (Holtzman, Newth, & Delongis, 2004). Further evidence that one's emotional state and social support network are associated with one's experience of pain comes from a study by Carmen Alonso and Christopher Coe (2001). In a sample of 184 young women, the researchers found that self-reported depression and anxiety were strongly associated with ratings of menstrual pain. More significantly, perhaps, the greatest pain and distress occurred in women who had recently lost a significant source of social support.

> **Focus 16.19** How do cognitive and personality factors affect people's responses to pain stimuli?

Does life stress increase pain experiences? Many studies with medical patients have suggested that it does (Fields, 2005). Linda Watkins and Steven Maier (2003) explain how this might occur. Normally, sensory nerves cannot respond to stress hormones because they have no receptors for them. After nerve damage resulting from injury, however, receptors for stress hormones begin to appear on the surface of sensory nerves. These new receptors increase the excitability of damaged nerves when stress hormones are present, therefore allowing life stress to increase pain.

The fact that psychological processes are so central to the experience of pain has stimulated many health psychologists to research methods that can be used to control or reduce pain and suffering. The following 'Applying psychological science' feature highlights this important area of application.

> **Focus 16.20** Describe cognitive, informational and behavioural interventions for pain reduction.

 Applying psychological science

PSYCHOLOGICAL TECHNIQUES FOR CONTROLLING PAIN AND SUFFERING

We all occasionally experience physical pain. Such pain may be a normal and short-lived consequence of injury, illness or surgery. Unfortunately, for many people, pain is a never-ending, chronic nightmare. In such cases pain persists beyond an expected period of healing, and can have severe consequences for a person's well-being. Recent research estimates the global prevalence of chronic pain at 20% (Boris-Karpel, 2010). Because of the prevalence and debilitating effects of pain, in recent years, psychological pain-control strategies have received increasing attention from health psychologists (Gatchel, 2005; Kerns, Sellinger, & Goodin, 2011; Turk, 2001).

COGNITIVE STRATEGIES

Recent attention has focused on two classes of cognitive strategies known as *dissociation* and *association*. A *dissociative strategy* involves dissociating, or distracting, oneself from the painful sensory input. This can be done in a variety of ways: by directing your attention to some other feature of the external situation, by vividly imagining a pleasurable experience or by repeating a word or thought to yourself. Research has shown ▶

that dissociative strategies are most effective when they require a great deal of concentration or mental activity, thereby directing attention away from the painful stimuli.

If you are a recreational jogger or a long-distance runner, you may be familiar with the discomfort of extending yourself. Endurance running seems an ideal real-life task to use in the study of cognitive strategies. William Morgan and co-workers (Morgan, Horstman, Cymerman, & Stokes, 1983) gave this simple dissociative strategy to participants who were running on a treadmill to exhaustion: 'Focus your attention on a spot in front of you on the treadmill and say "Down" each time your right foot comes down on the treadmill.' A control group also ran the treadmill but did not receive the strategy. Although the two groups did not differ physiologically while running the treadmill, the mental-strategy group was able to tolerate the discomfort of treadmill running 32% longer than the control group.

A more dramatic, high-tech dissociative strategy is being tested in the burns centre at the Harborview Medical Center in Seattle, Washington. There children and adults with burns covering up to 60% of their bodies are donning virtual reality (VR) goggles during the often agonizing processes of wound cleansing and physical therapy. The goggles take patients into a visually compelling world of shapes and colours. Pain ratings are significantly lower when these patients are immersed in virtual reality than when they are in a non-distracted condition (Hoffman, Patterson, Canougher, & Sharar, 2001). More controlled laboratory research has also shown that VR is highly effective in reducing pain (Malloy & Milling, 2010).

Associative strategies are the opposite of dissociative strategies. Here you focus your attention on the physical sensations and study them in a detached and unemotional fashion, taking care not to label them as painful or difficult to tolerate. It appears that when pain is intense, associative strategies become more effective than dissociative ones (McCaul & Malott, 1984). There seems to be a point at which pain stimuli become too intense to ignore and dissociative strategies become ineffective. Thus one strategy is to use dissociation as long as possible and then shift to an associative mode.

Combined dissociative and associative strategies can be effective in dealing with acute pain. In one study, participants' pain tolerance was tested by measuring how long they could keep their hand immersed in ice water. One group of participants was then trained and practised a number of dissociative coping strategies (such as attention diversion and the use of distracting imagery) and associative strategies (such as imagining that the hand immersed in the ice water was detached from the body and focusing non-emotionally on the pain sensations). Two control groups equated in initial pain tolerance were given either no strategies or a placebo pain reducer. Then their ice-water pain tolerance was tested a second time. As shown in Figure 16.15, the cognitive-skills training resulted in a large increase in pain tolerance (Bandura et al., 1987).

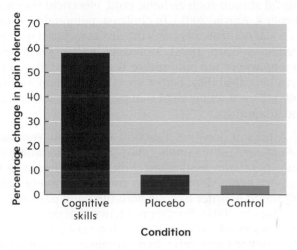

FIGURE 16.15 Coping strategies and pain tolerance.

These data show the increases in pain tolerance in an ice-water/hand-immersion task exhibited by a cognitive-skills training group, a placebo condition and a control group that repeated the task with no intervention.

Source: Based on Bandura et al., 1987.

HOSPITAL INTERVENTIONS: GIVING PATIENTS INFORMATIONAL CONTROL

Having relevant information about a challenging environment and event is also a kind of cognitive control, since it tells us what to expect (Taylor, 2011). In the medical setting of the past, doctors typically gave patients no more information than needed about a specific medical procedure and its aftermath. However, psychological research on how certain types of information reduce anxiety and contribute to positive medical outcomes has ushered in a new era in many medical settings. Imagine that you are in the hospital for major surgery. You know that this surgical procedure entails risk and that your recovery will be painful. What kinds of information would help you cope and recuperate more easily?

You might profit from *sensory information* about what you will feel after the operation. Knowing, for example, that patients often have shooting pains in their stomach after the surgery could prevent surprise or fear if it occurred to you. You would see the pain as a normal consequence of the surgery and the recovery process rather than as a sign of danger.

Second, *procedural information* on the surgery itself would help you understand what exactly is going to be done and why. You might be shown a model of the body part to demonstrate what will be done in the surgery, or you may see a video describing the procedure (Auerbach, Penberthy, & Kiesler, 2004). This kind of information would give you a sense of predictability and control, and reassure you that precautions were being taken to anticipate and reduce possible hazards.

FIGURE 16.16 A key to preventing chronic pain and disability is to begin physical activity again as soon as possible.

Source: © Kali Nine LLC

Third, you could profit from *coping guidance* about handling the pain or other complications from the surgery. For example, you might learn breathing exercises designed to reduce pain by helping you relax (Tollison, Satterswaithe, & Tollison, 2002). You might also be taught some of the cognitive strategies previously described to get through sieges of acute pain during the recovery process.

Informational interventions have proved helpful in many medical settings. Surgical patients show a better course of recovery and require less pain medication than those treated in a traditional fashion (Faust, 1991). Such interventions have proven remarkably successful in decreasing distress in hospitalized children, who are likely to find major medical procedures particularly frightening (Christopherson & Mortweet, 2001).

A KEY BEHAVIOURAL STRATEGY: BECOMING ACTIVE AGAIN

Recovering patients who avoid activity and become overly protective of an injured body part are at risk for developing a chronic pain condition (Turk, 2001). It is important to return to activity after an injury as soon as the healing process will allow (Figure 16.16). A key to successfully treating chronic pain patients who have 'shut themselves down' is to decrease their guarding and resting behaviours and to modify their belief that their pain signals body damage. Such interventions produce significant decreases in patient disability (Jensen, Turner, & Romano, 2001). Wilbert Fordyce (1988), a leader in the behavioural treatment of pain, emphasizes the negative effects that unnecessary rest and disuse of a body part can have on recovery:

> The lavish prescription of rest virtually ensures adverse disuse effects. With disuse in the musculoskeletal system, movement then becomes painful. But pain from disuse risks being interpreted by patient and professional as an indication of lack of healing. The result may become more prescribed rest or practical disuse and yet more pain with movement. . . . Pain problems originating in tissue injury but in which healing has occurred are made better by use. Patients must be helped to understand the dictum 'To make it better, use it.' . . . People who have something better to do don't suffer as much.
>
> *(Fordyce, 1988, p. 282)*

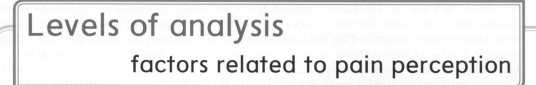

Levels of analysis
factors related to pain perception

PSYCHOLOGICAL

- Cognitive factors, such as beliefs about meaning of pain and personal control
- Placebo effects produced by positive expectations of pain relief
- Cultural beliefs and expectations influence pain perception

BIOLOGICAL

- Stimulation of nerve endings and pressure receptors within the body activates pain centres in the brain
- Action of endorphins reduces pain perception
- Opening, closing of spinal 'gates'
- Downward neural impulses from brain

ENVIRONMENTAL

- Environmental stressors can decrease pain perception through endorphin release
- Cultural learning experiences produce beliefs and expectations regarding pain and its expression
- Painful physical stimuli

Pain perception

In review

■ Pain is a complex perception influenced by biological, psychological and sociocultural factors. At the biological level, the major pain receptors appear to be free nerve endings. Gate control theory attributes pain to the opening and closing of gates in the spinal cord and to influences from the brain. Glial cells and cytokines are also involved in pain. The nervous system contains endorphins, which play a major role in pain reduction.

■ Expectations of relief produced by placebos can markedly reduce medical symptoms and pain. Cultural factors also influence the appraisal and response to painful stimuli, as do control beliefs. Negative emotional states increase suffering and decrease pain tolerance.

■ Psychological techniques for pain control include (1) cognitive strategies, such as dissociative and associative techniques; (2) providing medical patients with sensory and procedural information to increase cognitive control and support; and (3) increasing activity level to counter chronic pain.

HEALTH PROMOTION AND ILLNESS PREVENTION

In 1979 the Surgeon General of the USA issued a landmark report entitled *Healthy People* (US Public Health Service, 1979). The report concluded that improvements in health are more likely to result from efforts to prevent disease and promote health than from new drugs and medical technologies. Considering the leading causes of death provides strong evidence for that assertion. As Figure 16.17 shows, the leading culprits in developed countries such as the UK have changed from influenza, pneumonia, tuberculosis and gastroenteritis to heart disease, cancer and stroke. The major killers of the early 1900s have been largely controlled by medical advances. In contrast, the death rate has almost doubled for heart disease and other circulatory diseases, and is five times higher for cancer since 1900. These diseases and today's other killers are strongly influenced by behavioural factors. Health authorities estimate that half of all cases of early mortality (deaths occurring prior to the life-expectancy age within a culture) from the 10 leading causes of death can be traced to risky behaviours, such as cigarette smoking, excessive alcohol consumption, insufficient exercise, poor dietary habits, use of illicit drugs, failure to adhere to doctors' instructions, unsafe sex practices and failure to wear car seat belts (Mokdad, Marks, Stroup, & Gerberding, 2004).

FIGURE 16.17 Causes of death in the UK (England and Wales), 1900 versus 2009.

Modern causes of death are far more attributable to health-endangering behaviours.

Sources: Based on Murphy, 2000; Sexton, 1979; UK Office for National Statistics (www.statistics.gov.uk).

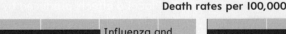
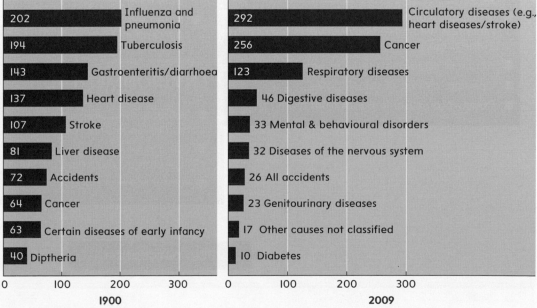

Death rates per 100,000

1900

Rate	Cause
202	Influenza and pneumonia
194	Tuberculosis
143	Gastroenteritis/diarrhoea
137	Heart disease
107	Stroke
81	Liver disease
72	Accidents
64	Cancer
63	Certain diseases of early infancy
40	Diptheria

2009

Rate	Cause
292	Circulatory diseases (e.g., heart diseases/stroke)
256	Cancer
123	Respiratory diseases
46	Digestive diseases
33	Mental & behavioural disorders
32	Diseases of the nervous system
26	All accidents
23	Genitourinary diseases
17	Other causes not classified
10	Diabetes

Recognition of the crucial role that behaviour plays in health maintenance has prompted much research in the field of health psychology. Psychologists have helped identify many of the psychological and social causes for risky health behaviours, and the clear need for lifestyle interventions has spurred attempts around the world to promote positive changes in such behaviours (Suls & Wallston, 2003; Taylor, 2011). Modifying people's health behaviours as a form of illness prevention can reduce medical costs and avert the physical and psychological distress that illness produces.

HOW PEOPLE CHANGE: HEALTH BEHAVIOUR THEORIES

Health-related behaviours fall into two main categories. *Health-enhancing behaviours* serve to maintain or increase health. Such behaviours include exercise, healthy dietary habits, safe sexual practices, regular medical check-ups, and breast and testicular self-examination. *Health-impairing behaviours* promote the development of illness. They include tobacco use, fatty diets, a sedentary lifestyle and unprotected sexual activity. Psychologists have developed programmes that focus on both classes of behaviour (Schneiderman, 2004).

In order to increase health-enhancing behaviours and reduce health-impairing ones, researchers have devoted a great deal of time and effort in understanding the processes that underlie behaviour change in general. This has led to a myriad of health behaviour theories and models which can roughly be subdivided in two categories: cognitive theories and stage theories. Although these theories approach health behaviour change from different perspectives, they all promote a better understanding of the underlying processes of health behaviour. Such theories also provide helpful assistance in the design of interventions to change behaviour.

Cognitive Theories

Most health behaviour theories focus on cognitive variables such as beliefs, attitudes, perceptions of self-efficacy, and intentions in explaining health behaviour. Such theories share the assumption that a person's beliefs, attitudes and expectations of future outcomes are major determinants of health-related behaviours.

The most extensively studied cognitive theory to behaviour change is the theory of planned behaviour (TPB; Ajzen, 1991). According to TPB, the best predictor of behaviour is the person's intention to perform the behaviour. **Intention** can be defined here as *the person's motivation to behave in a particular manner, indicating how much effort a person is willing to invest in order to perform the behaviour*. In turn, intention is determined by three factors (see Figure 16.18). First, the *attitude* towards the specific behaviour is important. Attitudes refer to people's beliefs about the outcomes (e.g., 'not smoking would make me cough less') and the evaluations of the importance of each of these outcomes (e.g., 'coughing less is good/bad'). A second determinant of

intention the person's motivation to behave in a particular manner, indicating how much effort a person is willing to invest in order to perform the behaviour

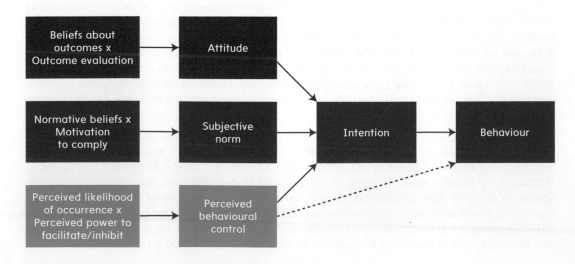

FIGURE 16.18 Model of the theory of planned behaviour.

Source: Adapted from Rutter and Quine, 2002.

intention is the *subjective norm* or perceived social pressure to perform the behaviour (e.g., 'my parents think I should stop smoking'). Finally, people's *perceived behavioural control* also influences their intention. This latter factor involves people's beliefs in their abilities to perform the behaviour (e.g., 'I can stop smoking') as well as the perceptions of obstacles and opportunities that may impede or facilitate performance of the behaviour.

Stage Theories

Stage theories (e.g., Prochaska & DiClemente, 1984; Schwarzer, 1992; Weinstein & Sandman, 1992) suggest that behavioural change is not a continuous process, but something that passes between distinctly different stages. The implication of such theories is that, in order to be effective, interventions should be tailored to the specific stage an individual is currently in. The most widely used stage theory is the **transtheoretical model** (DiClemente, 2003; Prochaska & DiClemente, 1984) which identifies six major stages in the change process.

1. *Precontemplation*: the person does not perceive a health-related problem, denies that it is something that endangers well-being, or feels powerless to change.
2. *Contemplation*: the person perceives a problem or the desirability of a behaviour change but has not yet decided to take action.
3. *Preparation*: the person has decided to change the behaviour, is making preliminary plans to do so, and may be taking preliminary steps such as cutting down on the number of cigarettes per day.
4. *Action*: the person actively begins to engage in behaviour change, perhaps stopping smoking altogether.
5. *Maintenance*: the person has been successful in avoiding relapse and has controlled the target behaviour for at least six months.
6. *Termination:* the change in behaviour is so ingrained and under personal control that the original problem behaviour will never return.

> **Focus 16.21** Describe the six stages of the transtheoretical model.

The transtheoretical model does not assume that people go through the stages in a smooth sequence. For example, it typically takes smokers three to five cycles through the action stage before they finally beat the habit, and New Year's resolutions are typically made for five or more consecutive years before they are finally carried out successfully (Prochaska, Norcross, & DiClemente, 1994; Schachter, 1982).

Theory-Based Interventions

Unfortunately life is not always as easy as a model would suggest. For example, a recent review suggests that there is only limited evidence of the effectiveness of interventions based on the transtheoretical model (Bridle et al., 2005). This might partly be due to the difficulty in accurately classifying the stage an individual is in, as well as methodological weaknesses or lack of details given regarding both methodology and intervention in the studies. The TPB model has received extensive support (e.g., Armitage & Conner, 2000). A review by Godin and Kok (1996) found, for example, that different components of TPB could explain on average 41% of the variance in people's intentions. However, the TPB's predictive value for actual behaviour is far less impressive (Armitage & Conner, 2001), suggesting that other variables might need to be incorporated to enhance the predictive power of TPB.

Although behaviour change theories might be useful frameworks for developing interventions, evidence of their use and effectiveness is still rather scarce (e.g., Hardeman, Johnston, Johnston, Bonetti, Wareham, & Kinmonth, 2002; Prestwich, Sniehotta, Whittington, Dombrowski, Rogers, & Michie, 2014). Nonetheless, the existing evidence seems to suggest that, in general, interventions based on behaviour change models are more effective than those interventions not using a theoretical framework (Glanz & Bishop, 2010). Although interventions are not always explicitly derived by theory, interventions can be successful in changing behaviour, as we will see in the next paragraphs.

HEALTH-ENHANCING BEHAVIOURS

During the 1970s, the role of behaviour in maintaining health and living longer became evident as researchers began to study the effects of lifestyle. Figure 16.19 shows the results of one longitudinal study of nearly 7,000 adults. The researchers studied the relation of seven good health practices to life expectancy. These included sleeping seven to eight hours per day, eating breakfast, not smoking, rarely eating between meals, being at or near one's prescribed body weight, engaging in regular physical activity and drinking only small to moderate amounts of alcohol. For men and women alike, these behaviours predicted a longer life. A higher mortality rate among those with poor health practices began to appear in men between the ages of 45 and 64 and in women between 55 and 64 (Belloc, 1973). Let us examine some of these health-enhancing behaviours and what can be done to encourage them.

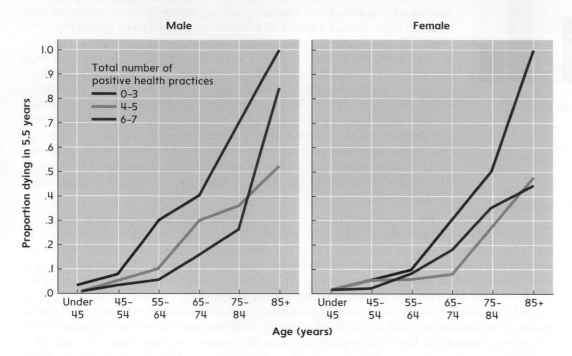

FIGURE 16.19 Healthy habits and longevity.

These data show the relation between the number of positive health practices and longevity in men and women. Those who adhered to few of the health practices experienced earlier mortality, with the pattern appearing earlier in men than in women.

Source: Adapted from Belloc, 1973.

Exercise

The couch potato lives! (But apparently not as long.) A sedentary lifestyle is a significant risk factor for health problems, including coronary heart disease and obesity (Rodin & Salovey, 1989; Taylor, 2011). Despite this widely publicized fact, only about 30% of Americans are sufficiently active to achieve health benefits (Baum, Krantz, & Gatchel, 1997; Ehrman, 2003). In Europe, similar results have been found, with on average 29% of the population performing sufficient physical exercise (ranging from 44% in the Netherlands to 23% in Sweden; Sjöström, Oja, Hagströmer, Smith, & Bauman, 2006). As fewer people now engage in vigorous manual labour, inactivity has helped double the rate of obesity since 1900, despite a 10% decrease in daily caloric intake over the same period (Friedman & DiMatteo, 1989).

Aerobic exercise is sustained activity, such as jogging, swimming and bicycling, that elevates the heart rate and increases the body's need for oxygen. This kind of exercise has many physical benefits. In a body that is well conditioned by regular aerobic exercise, the heart beats more slowly and efficiently, oxygen is better utilized, slow-wave sleep increases, cholesterol levels may be reduced, faster physiological adaptation to stressors occurs and more calories are burned (Baum & Posluszny, 1999; de Geus, 2000).

Exercise is associated with physical health and longevity (Figure 16.20). A study that followed 17,000 Harvard undergraduates into middle age revealed that death rates were one-quarter to one-third lower among moderate exercisers than among those in a less active group of the same age. Surprisingly, perhaps, extremely high levels of exercise were

aerobic exercise sustained activity that elevates the heart rate and increases the body's need for oxygen

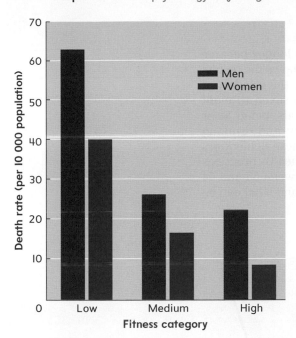

FIGURE 16.20 Aerobic exercise and health.

Aerobic exercise is an important health-enhancing behaviour, contributing to physical well-being. Significantly higher death rates occur for both men and women who are low in physical fitness.

Source: Data from Blair, Kohl, Paffenbarger, Clark, Cooper, and Gibbons, 1989.

Focus 16.22 What is aerobic exercise? What evidence exists that it promotes health and longevity?

Focus 16.23 How large are exercise dropout rates? What factors do and do not predict dropout?

not associated with enhanced health; instead, moderate exercise (burning 2,000 to 3,500 calories per week) on a regular basis produced the best health benefits (Paffenbarger, Hyde, Wing, & Hsieh, 1986). Performing at 70–85% of maximal heart rate non-stop for 15 minutes three times a week significantly reduces risk for coronary heart disease (Dishman, 1982). Interestingly, even simple exercise such as *active transport* (any self-propelled movement for transport such as walking or cycling; Adams, 2010) has been shown to have numerous health-related benefits, ranging from cardiovascular outcome benefits (Hamer & Chida, 2008) to decreased overweight and obesity (Wen, Orr, Millett, & Rissel, 2006). Such exercise also has positive psychological effects, reducing depression and anxiety (Morgan, 1997).

Despite the demonstrated benefits of regular exercise, people in developed countries have a strong tendency either to avoid or discontinue it after a short period. In the UK, for example, only 34% of adults reported achieving government recommendation of moderate physical exercise of 30 minutes for at least 5 days a week (Adams, 2010). In the USA only one-quarter of the adult population exercises at levels high enough to maintain cardio-respiratory fitness and reduce the risk of premature death (Ehrman, 2003). When employers offer exercise programmes to their employees, it is uncommon for more than 30% to participate, and dropout rates of 50% within six months are found in virtually all exercise programmes that have been studied (Chenoweth, 2002; Dishman, 1994). On the other hand, people who are able to persist for three to six months are likely to continue, as exercise becomes a healthy habit (McAuley, 1992).

What factors predict dropout? This is an important research question, for if we can identify the risk factors, we can take measures to counteract them. Research has shown that general attitudes towards physical fitness do *not* predict adherence or dropout; the exercise-related attitudes of dropouts and people who adhere to their exercise programmes are equally favourable (Suls & Wallston, 2003). However, low self-efficacy for success in exercising regularly ('I can't do this'), Type A behaviour pattern ('Sorry, too busy to exercise'), inflated estimates of current physical fitness ('I'm already in great shape from walking from my couch to the refrigerator'), not perceiving oneself as the 'sporty-type' and inactive leisure pursuits (such as watching television or playing computer games) all predict dropout (Martin & Dubbert, 1985; Wilcox & Storandt, 1996; Zunft et al., 1999). The strongest social-environmental factor related to dropout is lack of social support from friends, family or other exercisers (Ehrman, 2003).

Psychologists have been able to increase compliance by helping exercisers identify these impediments and prepare specific strategies to deal with them before they occur (Rosen, 2000; Simkin & Gross, 1994). For example, a person who anticipates feeling too tired to work out at the end of the day might prepare a set of self-statements about how much better he or she will feel after exercising. If the person is not receiving social support and encouragement from others, he or she could also arrange for a pleasurable activity after each workout to positively reinforce his or her exercising (Courneya, 1995).

Weight Control

Obesity (being more than 20% overweight) is becoming an increasingly urgent problem. Since 1960, the incidence of obesity among, for example, American adults has increased from 13% to 34%. In 2005 an estimated 400 million adults and at least 20 million children *under the age of 5* were obese worldwide (World Health Organization, 2008). The World Health Organization (2008) projects that by 2015 more than 700 million people will be clinically obese. Although the incidence of obesity is steadily rising everywhere, Europe now has one of the highest average Body Mass Index (BMI: weight in kilograms divided by the square of a person's height in metres) worldwide (World Health Report, 2002).

Indeed, the prevalence of obesity in many European countries has risen threefold since 1980, with a total of 150 million adults estimated to be obese in 2010. The rise in obesity is especially alarming among children. In the USA, 19% of children 6–11 years of age are overweight, compared with only 7% in 1980, and the corresponding figure among 12- to 19-year-olds has more than tripled, from 5% to 17% (National Center for Health Statistics, 2006). Similarly, in France 16% of children below 15 years of age are overweight compared to 3% in 1960.

Obesity is a risk factor for a variety of chronic diseases, such as cardiovascular disease, kidney disease and diabetes (e.g., Dietz, 1998; Haslam & James, 2005). Some research even suggests that obesity has more detrimental effects on health and health costs than does smoking and drinking alcohol (Sturm, 2002). Indeed, a large number of studies have repeatedly shown a strong relationship between obesity and mortality (e.g., Engeland, Bjørge, Søgaard, & Tverdal, 2003). For example, women who are 30% overweight are more than three times more likely to develop heart disease than normal-weight women (Manson et al., 1990). For reasons yet unknown, fat that is localized in the abdomen is a far greater risk factor for cardiovascular disease, diabetes and cancer than is excessive fat in the hips, thighs or buttocks (Taylor, 2011). Accumulation of abdominal fat is increased by yo-yo dieting that results in big weight fluctuations. Such dieting markedly increases the risk of dying from cardiovascular disease, an excellent reason to avoid this practice (Hafen & Hoeger, 1998; Rodin, Bartoshuk, Peterson, & Schank, 1990).

Were you to enrol in a behavioural intervention programme for weight loss, here is what would happen: the programme would begin with a period of self-monitoring, during which you would keep careful records of what, how much and under what circumstances you eat. This is designed to make you more aware of your eating habits and to identify situational factors (antecedents) that affect your food intake. You would then learn to take control of those antecedents. For example, you would learn to make low-calorie foods such as raw vegetables freely available and to limit high-calorie foods in the house. You would then learn stimulus-control techniques, such as confining your eating to one location in the house and eating only at certain times of the day. Because overeaters tend to wolf down their food and overload their stomachs, you would also learn to slow down your eating by putting down eating utensils until each bite is chewed and swallowed, and you would learn to pause between mouthfuls (Figure 16.21). These behaviours reduce food intake and help you learn to pay attention to how full you are. You would also be told to savour each mouthful of food. The goal is to eat less but enjoy it more. Finally, you would learn to chart the amount of food you eat to provide constant feedback, and you would arrange to positively reinforce yourself for successful performance. These behavioural practices would be combined with nutritional guidelines to help you eat a healthier diet.

FIGURE 16.21 Teaching people to stop wolfing down their food and be more conscious of what they eat, contributes to a healthy diet.
Source: © Ray Roberts/Alamy

Research shows that the addition of an exercise programme increases the positive effects of behavioural eating-control programmes (Avenell et al., 2004; Wadden, Brownell, & Foster, 2002). High levels of physical activity are associated with initial weight loss and its maintenance, and exercise adds to the effectiveness of other weight-loss methods, such as dietary change. Research indicates that many overweight people are able to attain gradual weight loss of about 2 pounds per week for up to 20 weeks and to keep the weight off for two years and beyond (Jackson, Morrow, Hill, & Dishman, 1999; Taylor, 2011).

Lifestyle Changes and Medical Recovery

Teaching people how to control their health-related programmes can have dramatic benefits even for those who are already afflicted with serious illnesses. William Haskell and co-workers (1994) randomly divided a sample of patients suffering from coronary artery disease into two groups. Both groups received the usual high-quality medical care from their physicians at Stanford University Medical School. In addition, the experimental

group received a behavioural self-regulation programme that targeted health factors such as smoking, exercise, weight, nutrition and medication adherence.

A four-year follow-up revealed dramatic results. Those receiving the usual medical care showed either no improvement or a worsening of their condition, and their health habits had not improved. In contrast, those who also received the behavioural self-regulation programme showed significant positive changes in their health habits. They reduced their intake of dietary fat, lowered their bad (LDL) cholesterol and raised their good (HDL) cholesterol, increased their exercise and raised their cardiovascular capacity. The programme also influenced the progression of the disease, as the self-management group had 47% less build-up of blockage material on artery walls. During the four-year follow-up period, 45% of the control patients either died or had non-fatal heart attacks or other cardiac emergencies, compared with only 24% in the behaviour self-regulation group. This study, like the others we have discussed, demonstrates the value of psychologically based health-promotion efforts.

HEALTH-THREATENING BEHAVIOURS

We now turn our attention to several types of health-impairing behaviours. We begin with a class of behaviours that two decades ago was not considered a major health threat. Although a number of serious diseases can be transmitted through sexual contact, the majority of them can be successfully treated. In the early 1980s, however, a mysterious and lethal sexually transmitted disease emerged.

Psychology and the AIDS Crisis

On 5 June 1981, the Centers for Disease Control (CDC) reported the first case of *acquired immune deficiency syndrome (AIDS)*. In the decades that followed, AIDS grew from an unknown disease into a devastating worldwide epidemic for which no medical cure has been found. According to the World Health Organization (2004), about 16,000 new infections occur each day. Worldwide, one in every 100 adults between the ages of 15 and 49 is infected with the HIV virus that causes AIDS, and the disease has so far claimed the lives of nearly 20 million people. Forty-five per cent of the HIV-positive are women. Of the 3.1 million people who died from AIDS in 2004, 37% were women and 20% were children. In some countries of southern Africa, 25–40% of the population is infected, including a third of all pregnant women. Globally, only 5–10% of the cases now occur in homosexual men (the population typically identified with the affliction), and women now make up half of all HIV cases (United Nations, 2002). In the early 2000s, the rates of infection began to rise again among homosexual men in North America, Europe and Australia owing to increases in risky sexual behaviour (CDC, 2006). Worldwide AIDS is among the leading causes of death, ranking 7th in 2010 and killing approximately 650,000 people, mostly in developing countries (see Table 16.2).

AIDS is caused by the *human immunodeficiency virus (HIV)*, which cripples the immune system. The patient then becomes vulnerable to invading viruses, bacteria and tumours, which are the actual killers. Because the HIV virus evolves rapidly, vaccines are at present ineffective in preventing its spread. Moreover, the incubation period between initial HIV infection and the appearance of AIDS symptoms may be as long as 10 years, meaning that an infected person may unknowingly pass the virus on to many other people. The major modes of transmission are direct exposure to infected semen, vaginal fluids and blood through either heterosexual or homosexual contact, the sharing of infected needles in intravenous drug use, and exposure to infected blood through transfusion or in the womb. Breast milk is also a major means of transmission through which many women have unknowingly transmitted the HIV virus to their children.

In the absence of a vaccine or cure, the only existing means of controlling the AIDS epidemic is by changing the high-risk behaviours that transmit the virus. In this respect, AIDS is as much a psychological problem as a medical one. Prevention programmes are

typically designed to: (1) educate people concerning the risks that attend certain behaviours, such as unprotected sex; (2) motivate people to change their behaviour and convince them that they can do so; (3) provide specific guidelines for changing the risky behaviours and teach the skills needed for change; and (4) give support and encouragement for the desired changes (O'Leary et al., 2001).

Early AIDS interventions were directed at homosexual men, who were originally the major at-risk group. In this population, a primary mechanism of HIV transmission is anal intercourse without the use of a condom. In one successful prevention study (Kelly, St. Lawrence, Hood, & Brasfield, 1989), 42 homosexual men went through a programme that instructed them on the risks accompanying unprotected intercourse, helped them develop and rehearse strategies for avoiding high-risk situations (such as sexual relations with strangers) and taught them how to be more assertive in refusing to engage in high-risk behaviours. Another group of 43 homosexual men also completed the programme after initially serving as an untreated control group.

Both groups were assessed before and after the first group went through the programme and then were followed for eight months after completing the programme to assess long-term behaviour changes. As Figure 16.22 shows, the intervention programme resulted in a substantial and lasting increase in the use of condoms during sexual activity. Similar programmes are now being conducted with adolescent populations, where unprotected heterosexual intercourse is resulting in a surge of new infections (Jemmott, Jemmott, & Fong, 1998). Another target for interventions is heterosexual women, who not only are the fastest-growing segment of the HIV population but also have the potential to infect their babies if they become pregnant.

With something as urgent as AIDS prevention, it is important to recognize that research has shown that the success of prevention programmes depends on the extent to which the individual's social system supports the desired changes. Although the principles of health behaviour change are thought to be universal, and can be useful across cultures, the implementations of such principles then need to take into account local cultural contexts (Bell, Bhana, McKay, & Petersen, 2007). Issues such as existing stigmas surrounding the relevant risky behaviours (e.g., Varga, Sherman, & Jones, 2006), population literacy (Carstens, Maes, & Gangla, 2006) and specific substance abuse (Sawyer, Wechsberg, & Meyers, 2006), for example, are important factors in determining the effectiveness of HIV/AIDS prevention interventions. When sexual abstinence or the use of condoms runs contrary to the values of an individual or cultural group, people may continue to engage in high-risk behaviours even though they have been informed of the dangers involved (Herdt & Lindenbaum, 1992; Huff & Kline, 1999). Likewise, within both homosexual and heterosexual populations, and particularly among adolescents and young adults, many individuals continue to have an irrational sense of invulnerability to infection, and this belief contributes to a failure to abstain from sex or to engage in protected sexual practices (Kelly, 2001). Counteracting these barriers to safe sexual behaviour is a major challenge for health psychologists.

Although much of the previous research on HIV/AIDS prevention has been conducted in developed countries, the high prevalence of HIV in developing countries (see Table 16.2), together with the differences in local social and cultural contexts and beliefs about the nature of disease, has directed researchers' attention more and more to the application of intervention programmes in developing countries. Given the high prevalence of AIDS in African countries, the following 'Research close-up' takes a closer look at how cultural beliefs may determine the success of HIV/AIDS intervention programmes.

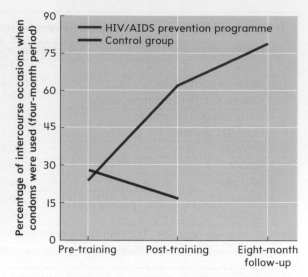

FIGURE 16.22 Effects of an AIDS prevention programme.

An AIDS prevention programme for homosexual men increased their use of condoms during sexual activity. The programme educated the men on the risks involved in sexual behaviours (especially unprotected sex), promoted the use of condoms and taught them coping skills to deal with high-risk situations.

Source: Based on Kelly et al., 1989.

> **Focus 16.24** Describe the nature and effectiveness of behaviour change techniques used in AIDS prevention projects.

TABLE 16.2 Leading causes of death in 2010: Developing versus developed countries

Developing countries	Number of deaths	Developed countries	Number of deaths
1. Stroke	4,164,000	1. Ischaemic heart disease	3,029,000
2. Ischaemic heart disease	4,000,000	2. Stroke	1,710,000
3. Chronic obstructive pulmonary disease	2,410,000	3. Lung cancer	640,000
4. Lower respiratory infections	2,341,000	4. Chronic obstructive pulmonary disease	490,000
5. Diarrhoeal diseases	1,413,000	5. Lower respiratory infections	473,000
6. HIV/AIDS	1,370,000	6. Colorectal cancer	382,000
7. Malaria	1,170,000	7. Alzheimer's disease	373,000
8. Road injury	1,166,000	8. Diabetes	257,000
9. Tuberculosis	1,150,000	9. Cirrhosis	254,000
10. Diabetes	1,024,000	10. Other cardio and circulatory diseases	254,000

Note: Countries grouped by WHO Millennium Development Goal (MDG) regions.

Source: Data based on Institute for Health Metrics and Evaluation (GBD, 2010). http://ihmeuw.org/1zne

 Research close-up

THE INFLUENCE OF INDIGENOUS BELIEFS ON ATTITUDES TO AIDS PRECAUTIONS

Source: C. Liddell, L. Barrett and M. Bydawell (2006). Indigenous beliefs and attitudes to AIDS precautions in a rural South African community: An empirical study, *Annals of Behavioral Medicine*, 32, 218–25.

INTRODUCTION

How do indigenous belief systems influence people's attitudes towards HIV/AIDS prevention? Several studies have suggested that indigenous practices and beliefs with regards to reproduction and sexuality may play an important role in understanding the sustained AIDS epidemic in Africa. However, more general indigenous beliefs about the origin and spreading of illness and diseases may also play a pivotal role in the likelihood of people taking AIDS precautions. Epidemics and sexually transmitted diseases (STDs), for example, are commonly attributed to witchcraft and sorcery in African traditional belief systems. In this sense, STD infection is often associated with supernatural routes, where an infected person may *choose* to infect a lover or spouse when this person behaves unreasonably towards his or her partner, or may infect a lover or spouse through mystical pollutants or sorcery. On the other hand, people's traditional beliefs about the role of ancestral protection against disease and other misfortunes may similarly play an important role in determining the effectiveness of HIV/AIDS prevention programmes.

METHOD

In a remote mountainous area of KwaZulu Natal (KZN), South Africa, an area identified as having the highest prevalence of HIV infection in southern Africa, 407 participants were recruited to participate in the study. The selection of participants was based on their age group, as the researchers suggested that age differences may influence the extent to which indigenous beliefs influenced people's attitudes and behaviours. A total of 206 participants (109 males and 97 females) between 18 and 24 years old, and 201 participants (87 males and 114 females) between the age of 35 and 45 years old, completed questionnaires measuring attitudes to AIDS precautions (e.g., the use of condoms), traditional beliefs about illness (e.g., 'women are able to give men medicines that persuade the men to love them'; TBAI) and ancestral protection (e.g., 'provided that I do not upset them, my ancestors can protect me from harm'; AP), as well as general indigenous knowledge (IK) pertaining to traditional dress, foods, etc.

RESULTS

In general, both old and young individuals in KwaZulu Natal held strong traditional beliefs about illness and disease and strongly endorsed a belief in ancestral protection, as well as being very familiar with indigenous practices and customs. In contrast, all participants were fairly negative about AIDS precautions. More importantly, beliefs in ancestral protection predicted these negative attitudes to AIDS precautions, such that stronger beliefs led to more negative attitudes. This pattern was, however, only significant for the older group of participants. Interestingly, a stronger endorsement of traditional beliefs among the older participants about the causes of illness and disease was also associated with attitudes to AIDS precautions, but in an unexpected direction. That is, the stronger the older people endorsed traditional beliefs, the *less* negative they were about AIDS precautions. An explanation for this unexpected result was given by the researchers who suggested that condom use might 'fit harmoniously with the traditional views of infectious substances, and how these can be avoided' (Liddell, Barrett, and Bydawell, 2006, p. 223). To test this explanation, the researchers extracted five items from the 'attitudes to AIDS precaution' questionnaire that explicitly dealt with condom use and summed them to yield a factor on 'attitudes to condoms'. Results confirmed the idea that condoms fitted with the traditional views of protection from pollutants. Thus, older participants' traditional beliefs about illness were strongly correlated with their attitudes to condoms, but not with the rest of the items of the 'attitudes to AIDS precaution' questionnaire. For the younger participants no such correlation between traditional beliefs and attitudes to condoms was found.

▶

◄ DISCUSSION

The results of this study suggest that, although both younger and older individuals show equally strong endorsements of traditional beliefs about illness and ancestral protection, the attitudes to AIDS protection for younger individuals shows a much weaker association with these beliefs than for older individuals. This suggests that for younger people decision-making around safe sex is less dependent on traditional beliefs. Furthermore, the results indicate that traditional belief systems are not inevitably at odds with Western medicine and HIV/AIDS prevention programmes. Instead, indigenous belief systems are highly complex and can consist of conflicting constructs. It seems important, therefore, to take into account relevant indigenous belief systems and identify the important key aspects that might hinder or benefit the development of effective HIV/AIDS prevention programmes and education campaigns. It may, however, turn out to be a daunting task to acquire in-depth specialist knowledge of a culture, especially as small communities change rapidly in a world with fast-moving changes in public attitude and behaviour.

Combating Substance Abuse

Substance abuse exacts a fearsome toll on society. Tobacco use harms smokers and those who breathe their second-hand smoke. Smoking ranks as the single largest cause of preventable death, currently killing more than 5 million people a year worldwide (World Health Organization, 2008). Because of this, more and more countries worldwide are introducing smoking bans in indoor public places. Interestingly, several recent studies demonstrated a significant short-term reduction in hospital admissions for acute myocardial infarction following these bans (Barone-Adesi, Vizzini, Merletti, & Richiardi, 2006; Sargent, Shepard, & Glantz, 2004). However, although tobacco use has levelled off in West European countries, tobacco products have been aggressively marketed in other countries, and sales have nearly doubled over the past 15 years. The coming decades might therefore witness an appalling increase in the diseases caused by smoking, particularly in developing countries that are ill equipped to provide good medical treatment.

With a global per capita consumption of 6.2 litres of pure alcohol per year (estimated in 2003; Rehm, Mathers, Popova, Thavorncharoensap, Teerawattananon, & Patra, 2009), alcohol abuse also contributes enormously to human suffering. Although in general alcohol consumption has been relatively stable per capita from the 1980s, alcohol intake varies greatly around the world (see Figure 16.23). In general, men drink more than women, and there is a

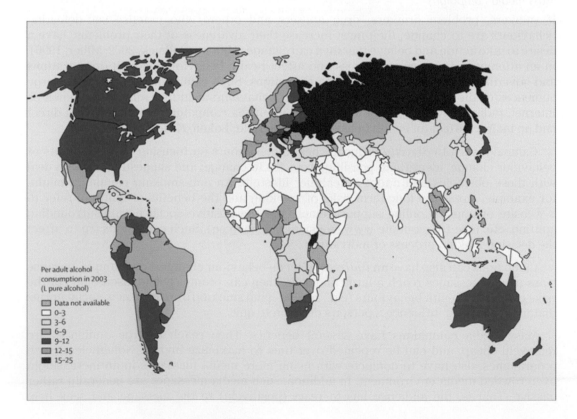

Per adult alcohol
consumption in 2003
(L pure alcohol)

☐ Data not available
☐ 0-3
☐ 3-6
☐ 6-9
■ 9-12
☐ 12-15
■ 15-25

FIGURE 16.23 Exposure to alcohol – recorded and unrecorded adult consumption by country

Source: Reprinted from The Lancet, 373, Rehm et al, Global burden of disease and injury and economic cost attributable to alcohol use and alcohol-use disorders, 2223-2233., (2009), with permission from Elsevier.

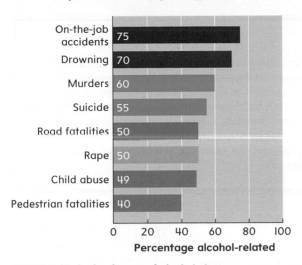

FIGURE 16.24 Societal costs of alcohol abuse.

This graph shows the percentage of common negative events that are alcohol related.

Source: Based on C. R. Carroll, 1993.

trend that young people in Europe are more frequently intoxicated than their elders (Leifman, Österberg, & Ramstedt, 2002). When interpreting these results, it is important to note that most people (45% of men and 66% of women) actually abstain from drinking alcohol worldwide.

The economic costs of alcohol abuse differ greatly per country. In the USA alone, alcohol abuse costs over $100 billion a year in decreased work productivity and treatment costs and $13.8 billion in alcohol-related car accidents (National Center for Health Statistics, 2004). Alcohol is implicated in half of all fatal automobile accidents and is a leading factor in industrial and farm accidents (Figure 16.24). Alcohol abuse is also highly damaging to one's health. Death rates among those who abuse alcohol are two to four times higher for men and three to seven times higher for women, depending on the disease in question. Life expectancy is 10 to 12 years less (CDC, 2002a). The use of alcohol is causally related to over 60 medical conditions (Room, Babor, & Rehm, 2005). Studies show, for example, an increased risk from even moderate alcohol consumption of specific kinds of cancer such as cancer of the stomach, colon, breast, rectum and ovaries (Bagnardi, Blangiardo, LaVecchia, & Corrao, 2001; Single, Robson, Rehm, & Xie, 1999). Alcohol affects the welfare of others as well. Some children are born with foetal alcohol syndrome, and others are subjected to disrupted family relationships, including domestic violence. For every person who has a problem with alcohol, an average of four other people's lives is adversely affected on a daily basis (Levinthal, 1996).

Other varieties of substance abuse also have adverse effects. Many crimes are committed by users of illicit drugs in order to support their habits (Kendall, 1998). Moreover, substance abuse is highly associated with psychological disorders, often being part of a larger pattern of maladjustment in both adolescents and adults (Miller & Brown, 1997).

Psychological principles discussed in earlier chapters have been successfully applied to the treatment of smoking, problem drinking and drug use (Taylor, 2011). Several approaches have proven successful in facilitating positive health behaviour change.

Mass media campaigns

> **mass media campaigns** try to inform large audiences of the risk associated with specific behaviours using existing media such as internet, radio, television and newspapers

If smokers, problem drinkers, drug abusers and others who practise self-defeating behaviours are to change, they must increase their awareness of their problems, have a desire to take action and believe that they can change (Miller & Rollnick, 2002; Miller, 1996). In an attempt to increase awareness and affect health behaviours, health organizations and governments often use mass media campaigns. Such campaigns try to inform large audiences of the risk associated with specific behaviours using existing media, such as Internet, radio, television and newspapers. Mass media campaigns can have both a direct and an indirect effect on health behaviours (Wakefield, Loken, & Hornik, 2010).

Campaigns try to *directly* influence health behaviours by focusing on the benefits of behaviour change, identifying possible obstacles to change, and suggesting ways to deal with these obstacles and adopt a healthier lifestyle. An anti-smoking campaign might, for example, stress the long-term risks of smoking and the benefits of quitting, refer to a website or app for online support, emphasize the positive social norms surrounding quitting, etc. (see for example www.stopsmokingcoach.eu). Such campaigns try to affect the decision-making process of individuals.

Campaigns can also have an *indirect* effect on behaviour change. For example, because mass media messages reach a large audience, they can prompt public discussions of the risks of specific health behaviours (e.g., second-hand smoking), creating new social norms that may indirectly influence a person's decision to quit.

Mass media campaigns have several benefits. They reach a large audience, are relatively cheap, and can be repeated over time to maximize impact. Nonetheless, such programmes also have to compete with many more media messages in an increasingly overcrowded media environment. In addition, such media messages are generally rather passive. That is, the audience has to react (positively) to the message and seek help

themselves. It is not easy, however, to persuade people to change unhealthy behaviour, and it is even more difficult to persuade them to change addictive behaviours merely by providing information through the media. Confronting a person with his or her problem may lead to defensive reactions and driving away people who need help. As a result, the overall effect of mass media campaigns on behaviour is generally small, but significant (Noar, 2006; Wakefield et al., 2010).

Motivational interviewing

Rather than confronting the person with his or her problem through mass media messages, the technique of **motivational interviewing** leads the person to his or her own conclusion by asking questions that focus on discrepancies between the current state of affairs and the individual's ideal self-image, desired behaviours and desired outcomes. Focusing on these discrepancies may help motivate change. Consider the following exchange:

> *Client:* I really don't believe I have a drinking problem.
>
> *Counsellor:* You're the best judge of that. May I ask how many drinks you have a day?
>
> *Client:* Oh, it varies. Probably five or six.
>
> *Counsellor:* Is that about what you'd like to be drinking?
>
> *Client:* Well, I'd probably be better off if I cut down a little – maybe to three or four.
>
> *Counsellor:* How would that be helpful to you?
>
> *Client:* Well, I could study better and reduce the arguments with my room-mate. I can get pretty nasty when I'm buzzed. I hate being nasty. I'm not that kind of person. Our relationship is going downhill, and I'd hate to lose a friend.
>
> *Counsellor:* Well, you know, you don't have to have a big problem in order to want to make a change. I'm sure you could do so if you really want to.
>
> *Client:* I can see that I'd be more the person I want to be if I worked on this.
>
> *Counsellor:* And I'd be happy to help you make your change.

Following a client's decision to pursue behaviour change, the counsellor helps the client set specific goals and select from a menu of behaviour change strategies those he or she would like to employ. Thereafter, the counsellor provides feedback and support for the client's efforts. Motivational interviewing has proven to be an effective and low-cost treatment approach for substance abusers (Miller & Rollnick, 2002). In one large-scale study of alcohol-abuse patients, a four-session motivational interviewing intervention proved to be as effective as a 12-session programme modelled on Alcoholics Anonymous (Project MATCH Research Group, 1997). More than 20 other studies have demonstrated the effectiveness of motivational interviewing with problem drinkers (Vasilaki, Hosier, & Cox, 2006).

Multi-modal treatment approaches

All substance abuse behaviours are resistant to change. Some people may be more vulnerable than others because of genetic factors (Crabbe, 2002). Craving, caused by either psychological need or physical dependence, is a huge barrier to overcome. Negative emotions, such as anxiety, irritability or depression, are temporary results of abstinence that cause many who quit successfully to have relapses. Past conditioning may create stimuli that trigger the behaviour in certain common situations. For example, coffee drinking or social situations are linked with smoking for many individuals, thus encouraging lapses in behavioural control when those stimuli are present. The numerous factors that encourage smoking, drinking or drug abuse make these behaviours very hard to change. Psychologists are therefore willing to combine anything that has proven effective into what they hope will be a more powerful behaviour change package to apply when people are ready to make a change. These **multi-modal treatments** often include biological measures (for example, the use of nicotine patches to help smokers quit), with psychological measures such as the following:

- aversion therapy, in which the undesired behaviour is associated with an aversive stimulus, such as electric shock or a nausea-producing drug, in an attempt to create a negative emotional response to the currently pleasurable substance

motivational interviewing leads the person to his or her own conclusion by asking questions that focus on discrepancies between the current state of affairs and the individual's ideal self-image, desired behaviours and desired outcomes

Focus 16.25 What are the major goals and techniques in motivational interviewing?

multi-modal treatments often include biological measures with psychological measures

- relaxation and stress-management training, which help the person adapt to and deal with stressful situations
- self-monitoring procedures that help the person identify the antecedents and consequences of the abuse behaviours
- coping and social-skills training for dealing with high-risk situations that trigger abuse
- marital and family counselling to reduce conflicts and increase social support for change
- positive-reinforcement procedures to strengthen change.

This broad-based multi-modal approach appears to produce favourable outcomes for many people who have substance addictions. For example, in one of the more successful multi-modal treatment outcome studies, 427 alcoholic patients were followed for 12 to 20 months after completing an in-patient programme that included aversion therapy (using a drug that produces nausea when alcohol is consumed), personal counselling and coping-skills training. Follow-up assessments revealed that 65% were totally abstinent for one year after treatment. The best outcome occurred in cases where the urge to drink had been eliminated (presumably by aversion therapy) and alternate coping skills were increased through the use of cognitive-behavioural techniques such as those just described (Smith & Frawley, 1993).

Despite these encouraging results, typical treatment results are less favourable: long-term maintenance of behaviour changes often occurs in fewer than 30% of treated individuals, whether the target behaviour is smoking, drinking or some other substance abuse (Ockene et al., 2000). Behavioural change programmes can therefore benefit from nationwide programmes and policies. For example, policies regulating alcohol advertising or making alcohol more expensive seem highly cost-effective (Anderson, Chisholm, & Fuhr, 2009). However, most governments seem reluctant to implement effective interventions to curb alcohol intake through national policy (Casswell & Thamarangsi, 2009). The goal of many researchers is therefore to develop more effective treatment packages.

> **Focus 16.26** What kinds of behaviour-change procedures are employed in multi-modal treatments for substance abuse?

Harm-Reduction Approaches to Prevention

Substance abuse not only has negative effects on physical well-being but often results in other severe consequences, such as self-defeating sexual and aggressive behaviours. **Harm reduction** is a prevention strategy that is designed not to eliminate a problem behaviour but, rather, to reduce the harmful effects of that behaviour when it occurs (MacCoun, 1998; Weingardt & Marlatt, 1998). In the area of drug abuse, harm-reduction approaches include needle and syringe exchange programmes to reduce the spread of HIV infections. Another example is methadone maintenance programmes for heroin addicts, which are targeted at reducing addicts' need to engage in criminal activity to feed their heroin habit. The reasoning is that even if an addictive behaviour cannot be eliminated, it is possible to modify how often and under what conditions it occurs and thereby minimize its harmful effects on the person and society. Harm-reduction programmes have enjoyed considerable success in several European countries (Heather, 2006).

> **harm reduction** prevention strategy that is designed not to eliminate a problem behaviour but, rather, to reduce the harmful effects of that behaviour when it occurs

The harm that can befall college students who abuse alcohol has inspired a new generation of intervention programmes focused on helping problem drinkers control how much and under what circumstances they drink. The goal is to reduce harmful consequences to the problem drinkers and others (Marlatt, Blume, & Parks, 2001). In one harm-reduction project carried out at a large western US university, incoming freshmen were screened for alcohol problems before they arrived on campus (Marlatt et al., 1998). Once on campus, those identified as problem drinkers were randomly assigned either to an intervention condition or to a no-treatment control condition. Over the next two years, the students in both conditions regularly reported on their alcohol consumption and alcohol-related problems. People who knew them well also furnished reports, and high agreement between the two sources of data indicated that the students were being truthful and accurate.

The intervention, occurring in the winter of the freshman year, was a brief one based on the motivational-interviewing approach described earlier. The goal was to prevent or reduce harmful consequences of drinking by increasing motivation to make constructive

changes, rather than to stop students drinking. Clinical psychologists met with each student individually for one session. The interviewer reviewed the drinking data submitted by the student over the previous academic term and gave individualized feedback in graphic form. The graph compared his or her drinking rate with college student averages, which were invariably much lower. The interviewers listed the potential risks for heavy college drinkers and discussed environmental risk factors, such as being in a fraternity or sorority or having heavy-drinking friends, if relevant. The interviewers were never confrontational but instead helped students evaluate their situation ('What do you make of this? Are you surprised?'), to think about present and possible future problems ('Would you be worried about something like this happening to you? What impact would it have on your life?'), and to consider the possibility of change. Specific goals of behaviour change were left to the student and not imposed by the interviewer.

At the end of two years, the students in the intervention group were still drinking more than the average college student, and although they continued to have more alcohol-related problems than the average student, they had far fewer alcohol-related problems than did students in the untreated high-risk group (Figure 16.25). Thus, despite the lack of an explicit focus on reducing drinking, the brief one-session intervention had significant positive effects. In particular, students learned to moderate their drinking in potentially hazardous situations, thereby reducing harmful consequences.

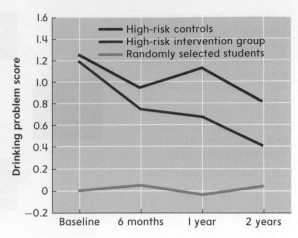

FIGURE 16.25 Effects of a brief intervention on alcohol-related problems.

At one year and two years after the intervention, high-risk drinkers who underwent the harm-reduction programme still reported more alcohol-related problems than the average college student, but fewer than the high-risk drinkers in the control group.

Source: Adapted from Marlatt et al., 1998.

MAINTAINING POSITIVE BEHAVIOUR CHANGE

Despite the availability of effective methods for changing behaviour, high dropout rates and failure to maintain positive behaviour changes are a major problem in every health-relevant behaviour we have discussed, from exercise maintenance to weight control to ending substance abuse. Why do people relapse into their problem behaviours, and what can be done to prevent this? Research on these questions has led to a better understanding of the relapse process and an intervention known as **relapse prevention** that is designed to reduce the risk of relapse (Witkiewitz & Marlatt, 2004). Research with substance abusers shows that most *relapses* (a full-fledged return to the undesirable behaviour pattern) tend to occur after the person has suffered one or more *lapses* (occasional 'slips') in response to high-risk situations. High-risk situations include stressful events, interpersonal conflicts, social pressure to perform the undesirable behaviour, being in the company of other individuals using the substance and experiencing negative emotions (Marlatt, 1996).

The path to relapse is shown in the bottom portion of Figure 16.26. Increased likelihood of relapse occurs when people have not developed strong enough coping skills to deal successfully with the high-risk situations. As a result, they experience low self-efficacy, believing that they are not strong enough to resist the temptation, or they allow expected positive benefits (such as enjoyment of the substance or anticipated stress reduction) to influence their decision to perform the undesirable behaviour. A lapse then occurs, followed by a critically important reaction called the **abstinence violation effect**, in which the person becomes upset and self-blaming over the lapse and views it as proof that he or she will never be strong enough to resist temptation. This sense of hopelessness places people at great risk to abandon all attempts to change, and in many cases a total relapse will occur. In one study of relapses in dieting, the abstinence violation effect was more strongly associated with relapse episodes than were temptations (Carels, Douglass, & Cacciapaglia, 2004).

Relapse resistance is shown in the upper portion of Figure 16.26. When confronting high-risk situations, people who have effective coping skills feel confident in their ability to handle them and are far less likely to relapse, even if they slip once in a while. To develop this adaptive process, relapse prevention specialists tell people that a lapse means only that they have encountered a situation that exceeded their current coping skills. Moreover,

Focus 16.27 What is a harm-reduction approach, and how does it differ from an abstinence-based one?

relapse prevention designed to reduce the risk of relapse

abstinence violation effect the person becomes upset and self-blaming over the lapse and views it as proof that he or she will never be strong enough to resist temptation

FIGURE 16.26 Relapse and relapse prevention.

Relapse is most likely to occur as a result of inadequate coping skills for dealing with high-risk situations, a focus on anticipated positive effects of engaging in the behaviour, and a resulting abstinence violation effect that causes the person to feel incapable of successful change and to abandon attempts at behaviour control.

Source: Based on Marlatt and Gordon, 1985.

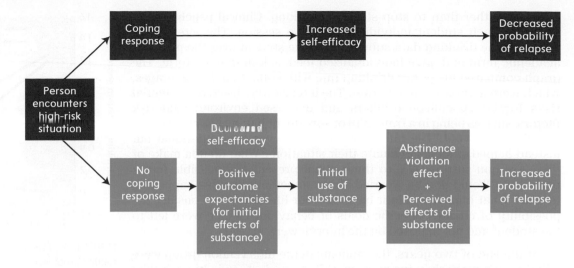

the lapse has given them valuable information about the specific situational, cognitive and emotional antecedents that they must learn to handle more effectively. When they master the needed skills, they will be better able to resist high-risk situations (Quinn, Pascoe, Wood, & Neal, 2010). Attention is then directed at learning and practising the required skills so that self-efficacy improves. The continuing focus is on 'progress, not perfection'.

Relapse prevention training is increasingly being incorporated into many behaviour change programmes. It has proven effective in changing many problematic behaviours, including overeating, smoking, cocaine and marijuana abuse, and sexual offending (Witkiewitz & Marlatt, 2004).

Relapse is one form of **non-adherence**, where a person does not adopt the treatment and behaviours their health-care providers recommend (DiMatteo, 2004). Whereas relapse generally refers to a return to the undesirable behaviour pattern, non-adherence is more general and incorporates the failure to adhere to any kind of treatment recommendation, from taking prescribed medicine to following a restrictive diet. On average, non-adherence to treatment recommendations is around 25% and can vary significantly between treatment regimes. For example, according to one estimate more than 85% of patients are occasionally non-adherent and do not take their medicine exactly as prescribed (O'Connor, 2006). Such non-adherence is very expensive, estimated to cost the EU €125 billion annually, as it generates additional costs for further treatment that would otherwise have been unnecessary (PGEU, 2008). Non-adherence can also have serious health consequences. For example, Ho and colleagues (2006) demonstrated that non-adherence to medicine following myocardial infarction more than tripled the mortality rate in the first year following discharge from the hospital.

Poor patient-provider communication is an important cause for non-adherence. Adherence is highest when the communication is clear and jargon-free, for example explaining the diagnosis, the purpose of the medication, dosing schedule, and the duration of treatment. Unfortunately, critical information is frequently omitted by the health-care professional (Tarn, Heritage, Paterniti, Hays, Kravitz, & Wenger, 2006). For this reason, checklists have been developed for both health-care providers and patients to prevent misunderstanding and omission of relevant information.

Adherence is also higher when patients are satisfied with the patient-provider relationship (Gauchet, Tarquinio, & Fischer, 2007). Providers who seem too busy or impatient, or don't seem to adequately answer a patient's questions, have less adherent patients. In contrast, patients who perceive their providers as warm and genuinely concerned for their welfare, adhere more to the providers' advice and prescribed treatment regime.

Positive Health

As we have seen so far, health-promotion efforts are often oriented towards promoting behaviours that may be beneficial to people's health (such as exercising and eating well)

non-adherence the person does not adopt the treatment and behaviours their health professionals recommend

Focus 16.28 Which factors increase or decrease relapse? How does relapse-prevention training address these factors?

and preventing behaviours that may be detrimental to their health (such as smoking or using alcohol and drugs). Such approaches then are mostly oriented towards preventing or treating physical or mental disease. Inherent in these approaches therefore is the assumption that the mere absence of disease is *equivalent* to health. In contrast, researchers in the field of positive psychology have argued that instead of focusing on trying to alleviate mental or physical suffering, health psychology would be wise to turn its attention to trying to increase and build people's well-being in terms of their engagement, purpose, positive emotions, relations and accomplishments (for a review, see Seligman, 2008).

A growing body of empirical evidence supports this call for a more positive approach to health psychology. For example, several studies have shown a strong positive relationship between people's level of optimism and the occurrence of cardiovascular disease (e.g., Buchanan, 1995; Giltay et al., 2007) as well as improved survival and recovery rates after diagnosis and subsequent medical procedures than pessimists (Allison, Guichard, Fung, & Gilain, 2003; Scheier, Matthews, Owens, & Magovern, 1989). In one study, researchers followed women who came to the National Cancer Institute for breast cancer treatment for five years. On average, women who were optimistic about their recovery lived longer than pessimists, even when the physical severity of the disease was the same at the beginning of the five-year period (Levy, Marrow, Bagley, & Lippman, 1988). In addition, positive affect and a positive style of explaining negative life events have been found to attenuate mortality rates in the elderly (Cohen & Pressman, 2006), delay the progression of HIV (Taylor, Kemeny, Reed, Bower, & Gruenewald, 2000a) and prevent strokes (Ostir, Markides, Peek, & Goodwin, 2001).

Finally, research assessing attitudes towards ageing found similar results. In one study (Levy, Slade, Kunkel, & Kasl, 2002), researchers assessed attitudes towards ageing in a large community sample of men and women who were over 50 years of age and then followed them up over a 23-year period. Statistically controlling for age, physical health and loneliness, the researchers found that attitudes towards ageing predicted even better how long people lived than did their physical health (Figure 16.27)! On average, people with positive attitudes towards their ageing lived an average of 7.6 years longer than did their counterparts with negative attitudes. This survival advantage existed whether the positive-attitude people were in their fifties, sixties, seventies or eighties when the study began. Further research has also shown that more positive attitudes about ageing are related to feelings of self-efficacy and lower subjective age (Teuscher, 2009; Wurm, Tomasik, & Tesch-Römer, 2010).

In other words, making a person *feel* great and confident about their future, may predict longevity, quality of life, mental and physical health, and coping with and recovering from challenges of disease and trauma. Clearly, attitude makes a difference, and perhaps a life-or-death difference.

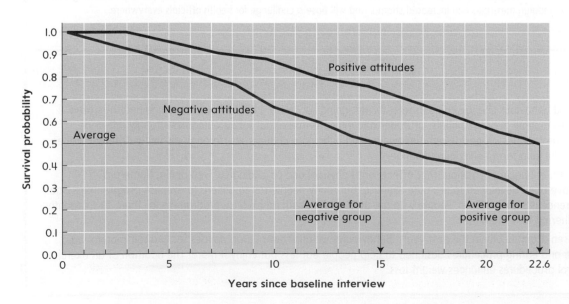

FIGURE 16.27 Ageing attitudes and longevity.

Research has shown a relationship between positive or negative self-perceptions of one's ageing and subsequent longevity. These survival curves show the likelihood that a randomly selected group member will still be alive in a given year after the beginning of the study. The median number of years until death was 15 in the group with negative self-attitudes and 22.6 among positive-attitude participants.

Source: Adapted from Levy et al., 2002.

Current topic

PUBLIC HEALTH MESSAGES AND STIGMA

As discussed earlier in this chapter, health promotion and illness prevention play an important role in the field of health psychology. Interventions aimed at supporting health-enhancing behaviours and preventing health-impairing behaviours may help to reduce not only medical costs, but also the physical and psychological distress that accompanies illness and disease. However, health messages often carry the message that certain behaviours are bad, undesirable and a risk to individual health. By branding certain behaviours and their outcomes as negative in this way, public health messages may have a negative side effect: stigmatizing those individuals exhibiting such behaviours. This current topic highlights one such possible negative side effect: the increase of the so-called 'fat-stigma'.

One important risk factor for a variety of chronic diseases is obesity. Obesity is related to several serious medical problems, such as coronary heart disease, high blood pressure, diabetes mellitus and colorectal cancer among others (Calle, Thun, Petrelli, Rodriguez, & Heath, 1999). As discussed previously, the prevalence of obesity has risen dramatically over the past few decades. It is not surprising, therefore, that health psychologists have recently stepped up efforts to treat and prevent obesity. In order to validate the effectiveness of some of these intervention programmes, Stice and colleagues (Stice, Shaw, & Marti, 2006) evaluated the effectiveness of 61 different obesity prevention programmes. Results showed that 21% of these obesity prevention programmes produced significant intervention effects. Although this may seem somewhat small, the effectiveness of these programmes is similar to that of other prevention programmes oriented towards public health problems such as HIV (Logan, Cole, & Leukefeld, 2002).

Inherent in intervention programmes oriented towards preventing weight gain and promoting weight loss, is the message that obesity is undesirable and a risk to individual health. Partly based on models for behaviour change, such programmes also often refer to the person's sense of control over their own behaviour and body weight. By branding obesity as a health problem and disease as well as stressing the person's responsibility to prevent weight gain, such public health messages may have one major drawback: enhancing the so-called 'fat-stigma'.

Negative stereotypes of obese and overweight individuals as being lazy, lacking in self-discipline, and being unmotivated and incompetent are prevalent throughout Western society (Puhl & Heuer, 2009). These negative stereotypes are rarely challenged in Western society, leaving overweight individuals vulnerable to all forms of prejudice, social injustice and stigma. Consistent with this, obese individuals have less access to education, receive lower pay, are more often denied promotions and are even fired because of their weight, as well as being more likely to be teased, bullied and romantically rejected (e.g., Roehling, Roehling, & Pichler, 2007). In the past decade, prevalence of weight discrimination has increased by 66% in some Western countries such as the USA (Andreyeva, Puhl, & Brownell, 2008). Another recent study by Brewis and colleagues (Brewis, Wutich, Falletta-Cowden, & Rodriguez-Soto, 2011) showed that this increase in negative perceptions of overweight or obese persons is also evident in countries that generally held more positive views of larger bodies, including for example, Puerto Rico and Fiji. This has led researchers to suggest that norms about overweight as being unhealthy and bad are spreading globally and are becoming more and more pervasive.

It is interesting to note that the recent (global) increase in negative perceptions about obesity and being overweight coincides with the global push to mark obesity as a major health threat. Given the serious consequences such negative stereotypes may have for obese persons in domains of health care, education and employment, it is important to discuss how such health messages influence the growing stigma of obesity. It seems likely that a focus on personal responsibility for being overweight, as well as the general message of obesity as a major health threat, may do little to prevent an increase in weight discrimination and beliefs about obese persons being lazy and lacking self-control. The difficulty for health psychologists in future health campaigns will lie therefore in finding the right balance between defining the urgency of decreasing and preventing overweight, while at the same time refraining from health messages that carry strong negative moral judgements about being obese. Unfortunately, research on the relationship between increased negative perceptions of overweight people and increased health campaigns oriented towards preventing weight gain and promoting weight loss, is as of yet non-existent. This topic would benefit from future research oriented to furthering our understanding of the complex relations between health campaign messages and increased stigma, and will pose a challenge for health officials everywhere.

 In review

- Theories about behaviour and behaviour change can be useful for designing successful interventions to change health-related behaviours. Cognitive theories assume people's beliefs, attitudes and expectations about future outcomes strongly influence health-related behaviour. Stage theories suggest health behaviours and behaviour change pass through distinctly different stages during the process of successful long-term behavioural change.

- Exercise is an important health-enhancing behaviour that affects both physical and psychological well-being. Numerous behavioural interventions have been developed to promote exercise, but many people fail to adhere to exercise programmes. One factor that influences adherence is social support. People who are able to stick with an exercise programme for three to six months have a better chance of adhering to it thereafter.

- Prevalence of obesity has risen dramatically in the past years. Behavioural weight-control programmes feature self-monitoring, stimulus-control procedures, and eating procedures designed to help people eat less but enjoy it more. The addition of an exercise programme to weight-control procedures enhances weight loss.

▶

- Because HIV infection is caused by high-risk sexual and drug-abuse behaviours (e.g., sharing needles), a prevention approach is essential. Behavioural changes have been accomplished in homosexual populations, and efforts are centring on high-risk heterosexual populations, such as teenagers. Cultural factors sometimes conflict with safe-sex practices, increasing the challenges of reducing health-endangering behaviours.

- Substance abuse is highly associated with other disorders and is often part of a larger pattern of maladjustment. Multi-modal treatments combine a number of techniques, including aversion training, stress-management and coping-skills training, and positive reinforcement for change. A promising new approach is motivational interviewing, a non-confrontational procedure designed to engage the person's own motivation to change self-defeating behaviours.

- Harm-reduction approaches attempt to reduce the negative consequences that behaviour produces rather than focusing on stopping the behaviour itself. Examples include needle exchange programmes for drug addicts and programmes designed to reduce the destructive consequences of binge drinking among college students.

- Relapse prevention is designed to keep lapses from becoming relapses by building effective coping skills to deal with high-risk situations and countering the abstinence violation effect when lapses occur. This approach enhances the effects of many behaviour-change programmes.

- A positive health approach argues that alleviating mental or physical suffering is not equivalent to increasing health or well-being. Findings from research on optimism suggest building people's well-being in terms of their engagement, purpose and positive emotions, may have beneficial consequences for both mental as well as physical health.

A CONCLUDING THOUGHT

The enterprise of living involves a constant process of adjusting to environmental demands. When those demands exceed our personal and social resources, we experience stress and may attempt to reduce it by changing our environment or our own behaviour. Thus stress can be a catalyst for growth and change, or it can drag us down physically and psychologically, depending on how effectively we respond to it. Psychologists have been at the forefront of stress research and have developed interventions to help people cope more effectively.

We have also seen that people's behaviour contributes strongly to both illness and physical well-being. The field of health psychology focuses on psychological and behavioural processes that affect physical well-being. Health psychologists have made important contributions to helping people reduce health-impairing behaviours and acquire healthier lifestyles, but many challenges remain.

Unfortunately, people do not always have the resources to cope with life's demands. As a result, they may engage in thought processes, emotional responses and behaviours that are hurtful to themselves or to society. In the next chapter, we will consider the behaviour disorders that can result from failures to adapt successfully.

 Recommended Reading

CLASSIC

Lazarus, R. S., & Folkman, S. (1984). *Stress, appraisal, and coping.* New York: Springer.

Lazarus, R. S. (2000). Toward better research on stress and coping. *American Psychologist, 55,* 665–673.

Matarazzo, J. D. (1980). Behavioral health and behavioral medicine: Frontiers for a new health psychology. *American Psychologist, 35,* 807–818.

Pelletier, K. R. (1977). *Mind as healer, mind as slayer.* New York: Delta.

Schofield, W. (1969). The role of psychology in the delivery of health services. *American Psychologist, 24*(6), 565–584.

CONTEMPORARY

Carver, C. S., & Connor-Smith, J. (2010). Personality and coping. *Annual Review of Psychology, 61,* 679–704.

Taylor, S. E. (2011). *Health psychology* (8th ed.). New York: McGraw-Hill.

West, R. (2005). Time for a change: Putting the transtheoretical (stages of change) model to rest. *Addiction, 100,* 1036–1039.

No man has a wholly undiseased mind; in one way or another all men are mad.
Mark Twain

Psychological disorders

17

Chapter Outline

Edward has been at university for just about a year now. At first everything seemed to be going really well. He made a good group of friends in his first week and was really enjoying his psychology. Things changed just before the end of his first year though, things that had before seemed fun an exciting just didn't interest him any more for some reason. His normally happy and easy-going personality appeared to have been replaced by a short-tempered and surly one. The worst thing was things seemed to be getting progressively worse and he found it difficult to control his emotions, crying occasionally when he was on his own. He was having trouble getting on with his daily life, missing lectures and not turning up to meet his friends. The last straw for his friends was that he stopped washing, and just didn't want to leave his room. They thought he should see a doctor, but Edward couldn't see the point, everything seemed pointless to him and he wondered what people would think of him if he admitted to them that he was 'depressed'. He was not sure anyone would really miss him if he just decided to end it all.

Charlotte is not the most confident of women, she is the first to admit that, but the thought of presenting her work to her friends in a seminar was not really something she was bothered about. The morning of her presentation something very strange happened to her. When she entered the student common room she began to shake and sweat profusely. Her heart began to pound uncontrollably and she felt a terrible sense of doom. She felt sure she was about to die there and then. She experienced a number of these events and is now afraid to leave her room in case it happens again.

Michael sleeps under a canal bridge in his hometown in Holland. He has no friends or family and people have become used to seeing him talking to himself and occasionally holding his head in his hands and shouting 'SHUT UP' to try, he says, to get the voices in his head to leave him alone. Whenever he is committed to a mental hospital, as he has been 11 times, he is given drugs that help him greatly and his behaviour returns to resemble those in the community in which he lives. However, as soon as he is released he stops taking his medication and his mental state deteriorates, and he begins shouting at imaginary people and talking gibberish once again.

Edward, Charlotte and Michael are examples of some staggering statistics.

- Between 3% and 5% of people will suffer with a personality disorder (Coid, Yang, Tyrer, Roberts, & Ullrich, 2006)
- It is estimated that 3 in every 100 people will suffer with schizophrenia (Perälä et al., 2007)
- In their lifetime 17% of people in the UK will have had suicidal thoughts (HSCIC, 2009)
- In 2011 it was estimated that approximately 164.8 million people in Europe suffers from a mental disorder in any given year, that is 38.2% of the population (Wittchen et al., 2011)
- 64% of people in care homes have a form of dementia (Mental Health Foundation, 2011)

These statistics are sobering reminders of how prevalent mental illness is in our communities now. Whereas it is true that we are more aware of mental illness, it is also true that the sheer volume of people with problems is such that it is now a huge part of our everyday lives. Perhaps this is one of the reasons why psychology is so very popular. Many people find their way to our subject because they themselves or friends and family have suffered in the past, and studying this component of the topic can often help people come to terms with why this might be.

(a)

(b)

FIGURE 17.1 (a) Abraham Lincoln and (b) Beethoven describes his unhappiness in his letters, speaking of suicide.

Source: (a) ©iStock.com/wynnter; (c) © HultonArchive.

HISTORICAL PERSPECTIVES ON DEVIANT BEHAVIOUR

Madness in great ones must not unwatched go.   *(Shakespeare,* Hamlet*)*

History is filled with accounts of prominent people who suffered from psychological disorders. Tycho Brahe (1546–1601) was an eminent Danish astronomer, designer of astronomical instruments and measurer of the universe. His work allowed Kepler to identify the laws of planetary motion. He was also fond of hosting parties where he employed, full-time, someone suffering from dwarfism to dress as a clown and sit under the table for no apparent reason. Another example would be Mozart, who was convinced he was being poisoned during the time he was composing his *Requiem*.

No great genius has ever existed without some touch of madness.

(Aristotle, 384–322 BC)

Vincent van Gogh suffered from recurring psychotic episodes, and committed suicide at the age of 37. Abraham Lincoln suffered recurrent bouts of depression throughout his life and was, on one occasion, so depressed that he failed to show up for his own wedding (Figure 17.1). Finally, Churchill also periodically suffered from severe depression, referring to it as his 'black dog'.

Throughout history, human societies have explained and responded to dysfunctional or 'abnormal' behaviour in different ways at different times, based on their values and assumptions about human life and behaviour. The belief that abnormal behaviour is caused by supernatural forces was common to Chinese, Egyptian and Hebrew belief, all of whom attributed deviance to the work of the devil. In ancient times a procedure called *trephination*, the earliest of all discovered surgical procedures, was carried out to 'release the evil spirit'. A hole in the skull was made (Figure 17.2). It seems likely that in many cases trephination did indeed successfully eliminate abnormal behaviour by putting an end to the patient's life. Astonishingly trephination is still carried out by some people who claim that the use of the procedure provides the now altered person to concentrate better, listen better, and generally feel better more of the time.

Whom the Gods would destroy, they first make mad.

(Euripides, 484–406 BC)

This quotation, attributed to Euripides, aligns madness with a vengeful god, and so may be thought of in terms of the demonological model. In medieval times, the demonological model of abnormality held that disturbed people either were possessed involuntarily by the devil or had voluntarily made a pact with the forces of darkness. Witch killing was justified on theological grounds and more than 100,000 lost their lives once identified as witches in the sixteenth and seventeenth centuries. Diagnostic 'tests' included binding a woman's hands and feet and throwing her into a lake or pond. Based on the notion that impurities float to the surface, a woman who sank and drowned could be posthumously declared pure. A woman who floated was in *real* trouble.

Anticipating the modern viewpoint in about the fifth century BC, Hippocrates suggested that mental health problems were diseases just like physical disorders and that the site of a mental health problem was the brain. By the 1800s, Western medicine had returned to viewing mental disorders as biologically based and was attempting to extend medical diagnoses to them. The biological emphasis was given impetus by the discovery that *general paresis*, a disorder characterized in its advanced stages by mental deterioration and bizarre behaviour, resulted from massive brain deterioration caused by the sexually

FIGURE 17.2 An early treatment for disordered behaviour was trephination. A hole was drilled through the skull to release the evil spirit thought to be causing the abnormal behaviour.

Source: SSPL/Getty Images

person becomes *hypervigilant* where their sensitivity to physical changes is increased. Next, the person engages in what Clark called *avoidance*, where the person does everything he or she can to avoid these sensations, and stop them getting worse. For instance, if the person feels that being in the sun will cause him or her to develop a skin cancer, then he or she might avoid going out in the sun. This avoidance makes the person more vigilant, and more anxious of the 'stressor', and avoiding it does not provide him or her with any evidence that experiencing sunshine does not (usually) result in a cancer at all. McNally (1994) says that generalizing panic like this is not appropriate. Some clients report that they do not engage in catastrophic misinterpretation at all, whereas others may feel that the physical sensations they experience may indeed lead to death, and they are hard to convince otherwise. Helping those with panic problems replace such mortal-danger appraisals with more benign interpretations of their physical symptoms, for instance regarding a panic attack not as a symptom of a heart attack but only as an indication of raised anxiety or alertness can be beneficial.

It is not surprising then that the first line of therapy for panic disorders is cognitive behavioural therapy (CBT). This now relatively common form of therapy is hugely popular and can provide the sufferer with ways of coping with an anxious situation. These can include exposure therapy, desensitization and also flooding. As part of CBT the person is taught about their disorder in an instructive, educative process. Self-monitoring of their anxiety is carried out between therapy sessions and might include diary keeping. Relaxation techniques might be taught to help the person deal with their anxieties and therapy might include gentle, and sometimes quite vigorous, exposure to the object of their anxiety. The goal is to retrain the person to see their physical sensations as being relatively normal, rather than as heralds of some kind of catastrophe.

> **Focus 17.11** Compare psychodynamic and cognitive explanations of anxiety disorders.

The role of learning

From the behavioural perspective, classical conditioning, observational learning or operant conditioning can contribute to the development of an anxiety disorder. Some fears are acquired as a result of traumatic experiences that produce a classically conditioned fear response (Rachman, 1998). For example, a person who has suffered a traumatic fall from a high place may develop a fear of heights (a conditioned response – CR) because the high place (the conditioned stimulus – CS) was associated with the pain and trauma of the fall (the unconditioned stimulus – UCS).

Classical conditioning cannot be the whole story, however, because many phobic people have never had a traumatic experience with the phobic object or situation that they now fear (Bruce & Sanderson, 1998; Menzies & Clarke, 1995). Most people who are afraid to fly have never been in an aeroplane crash. So how did they learn their fear? Clearly, phobias can also be acquired through observational learning. For example, televised images of aeroplane crashes evoke high levels of fear in some people. Yet most people do not develop phobias under these conditions, so there must be still more going on. It may be that biological dispositions and cognitive factors help determine whether a person develops a phobia from observing or even hearing about a traumatic event. If a person has a biological disposition towards intense fear, experiences traumatic scenes vicariously and comes to believe that 'the same thing could happen to me', the likelihood of developing a phobia on the basis of observational learning may increase.

Once anxiety is learned, either classically or vicariously, it may be triggered either by cues from the environment or by internal cues, such as thoughts and images (Pitman, Shalev, & Orr, 2000). In phobic reactions, the cues tend to be external ones relating to the feared object or situation. In panic disorders, the anxiety-arousing cues tend to be internal ones (Clark, 1986, 1988), such as bodily sensations (e.g., one's heart rate) or mental images (such as the image of collapsing and having a seizure in a public place; Craske, 1999).

In addition to classical conditioning and observational learning, operant conditioning also plays a role. People are highly motivated to avoid or escape anxiety because it is such an unpleasant emotional state. Behaviours that are successful in reducing anxiety, such as compulsions or phobic avoidance responses, become stronger through negative

reinforcement. Thus the obsessive-compulsive mother's scrubbing ritual reduces anxiety about contamination. In the case of agoraphobia, remaining at home also serves as a *safety*, a place where the person is unlikely to experience a panic attack (Khawaja & Oei, 1999). Again, anxiety reduction reinforces the response of staying at home (Figure 17.15). Unfortunately, successful avoidance prolongs the problem because it prevents the learned anxiety response from being extinguished, which would occur eventually if these people exposed themselves to the feared stimuli enough times without experiencing the feared consequence.

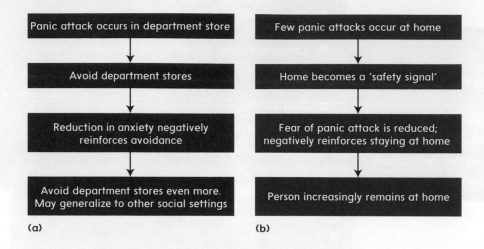

(a)   **(b)**

Focus 17.12 Explain anxiety disorders in terms of classical conditioning, observational learning and operant conditioning.

FIGURE 17.15 Panic and agoraphobia.

Panic disorders contribute to the development of agoraphobia. Negative reinforcement through anxiety reduction fosters avoidance of feared situations (a), as well as an attraction to safety signals, such as one's own home (b), where panic does not occur.

Sociocultural Factors

Social and cultural factors also play a role in the development of anxiety disorders (Lopez & Guarnaccia, 2000). The role of culture is most dramatically shown in **culture-bound disorders** that occur only in certain locales. One such disorder found in Japan is a social phobia called *Taijin Kyofushu* (Tanaka-Matsumi, 1979; Begum & McKenna, 2010). People with this disorder are pathologically fearful of offending others by emitting offensive odours, blushing, staring inappropriately or having a blemish or improper facial expression. Taijin Kyofushu has been attributed to the Japanese cultural value of extreme interpersonal sensitivity and to cultural prohibitions against expressing negative emotions or causing discomfort in others (Kleinknecht, Dinnel, Kleinknecht, Hiruma, & Harada, 1997). Latah, experienced in East Asia is a hypersensitivity, most commonly of middle-aged women, to a sudden fright which can result in the person entering a trance-like state. *Ataque de nervios* is, as it sounds, a nervous disposition found in Latin America that results in crying, and shaking uncontrollably. A heat may be experienced in the chest which may rise to the head and the person may be physically aggressive, or experience seizures and fainting. Another culture-bound disorder is *koro*, a South-East Asian anxiety disorder in which a man fears that his penis is going to retract into his abdomen and kill him. This is also known as *genital retraction syndrome* (GRS) and is an example of a mass hysteria, with outbreaks happening in waves and often large groups, as in Singapore in 1967. Treatment is by removing reminders of the anxiety, by ordering news and media blackouts on reporting of the issue and sometimes by treating with anti-anxiety drugs.

culture-bound disorders occur only in certain locales

Western culture also spawns culture-specific anxiety reactions. Although formally classified as an eating disorder, anorexia nervosa has a strong phobic component, namely the fear of getting fat. It also has obsessive-compulsive elements. This eating disorder is found almost exclusively in developed countries, where being thin has become a cultural obsession (Becker, Grinspoon, Klibanski, & Herzog, 1999).

As we have seen, the causes of anxiety disorders are complex. They often interact with one another and can be viewed at biological, psychological and environmental levels of analysis.

Levels of analysis
factors related to anxiety disorders

BIOLOGICAL

■ Evolutionary preparedness to fear certain stimuli
■ Genetic predisposition
■ Over-reactive autonomic nervous system
■ Low levels of inhibitory transmitter GABA
■ Other possible neurotransmitter dysfunctions
■ Possible sex-linked biological factors

PSYCHOLOGICAL

■ Displacement of neurotic anxiety (e.g., phobia, obsessions)
■ 'Catastrophizing' appraisals of threatening events
■ Exaggerated appraisals of anxiety symptoms (panic disorder)
■ Classically conditioned fear responses
■ Observationally learned fear responses
■ Negatively reinforced avoidance responses

ENVIRONMENTAL

■ Previous exposure to aversive unconditioned stimuli
■ Traumatic experiences (PTSD)
■ Avoidable fear-inducing conditioned stimuli
■ Exposure to fearful models or to others' traumatic experiences
■ Fear-inducing media exposure
■ Cultural learning experiences (culture-bound disorders)

Anxiety disorders

 In review

■ Anxiety involves: (1) subjective-emotional feelings of tension and discomfort; (2) cognitive processes involving worry, perceptions of threat and lack of control; (3) excessive physiological arousal; and (4) behaviours that reflect the anxious state and others that are designed to escape or avoid the feared object or situation.

■ Anxiety disorders include phobic disorder (an irrational fear of a specific object or situation), generalized anxiety disorder (recurrent anxiety reactions that are difficult to link to specific environmental stimuli), panic disorder, obsessive-compulsive disorder (which involves uncontrollable and unwelcome thoughts and repetitive behaviours) and post-traumatic stress disorder.

■ Biological factors in anxiety disorders include both genetic and biochemical processes, possibly involving the action of neurotransmitters, such as GABA, within parts of the brain that control emotional arousal. The greater prevalence of anxiety disorders in women has been explained in both biological and sociocultural terms.

■ Psychoanalytic theorists believe that neurotic anxiety results from the inability of the ego's defences to deal with internal psychological conflicts. The cognitive perspective stresses the role of cognitive distortions, including the tendencies to magnify the degree of threat and danger and, in the case of panic disorder, to misinterpret normal anxiety symptoms in ways that can evoke panic. ▶

- The behavioural perspective views anxiety as a learned response established through classical conditioning or vicarious learning. The avoidance responses in phobias and compulsive disorders are seen as operant responses that are negatively reinforced through anxiety reduction.
- Sociocultural factors are also involved in anxiety disorders, as illustrated by certain culture-bound anxiety disorders.

SOMATOFORM AND DISSOCIATIVE DISORDERS: ANXIETY INFERRED

The anxiety disorders just considered involve anxiety and stress reactions that are vividly experienced by the sufferer and, often, are externally observable. In some other disorders, however, underlying anxiety is largely inferred, or assumed to be present, rather than outwardly expressed. In somatoform and dissociative disorders, for example, the person may not consciously feel any anxiety because the function of the disorders is to protect the person from strong psychological conflict (Comer, 2009). Psychodynamic theorists believe that whatever distress the person may experience in such disorders is less stressful than the underlying anxiety that is being defended against.

SOMATOFORM DISORDERS – SOMATIC SYMPTOM DISORDERS

Somatoform disorders are now described in DSM-V as **Somatic Symptom Disorders**. These involve physical complaints or disabilities that suggest a medical problem but that have no known biological cause and are not produced voluntarily by the person. Elsewhere you will find reference to hypochondriasis and pain disorder, but under the current diagnostic regime those with these disorders will now be diagnosed with Somatic Symptom Disorder (SSD). In the **hypochondriasis** form of the disorder, people become unduly alarmed about any physical symptom they detect and are convinced that they have or are about to have a serious illness. People presenting with these symptoms would receive a diagnosis of Illness-anxiety disorder. People with the **pain disorder** form of SSD experience intense pain that either is out of proportion to whatever medical condition they might have or for which no physical basis can be found. Those diagnosed with SSD will know that the experience of pain, and of the issues of hypochondriasis are extremely real. Those with the disorder are not 'lying' or 'faking' and we should be careful not to make this mistake in their assessment or in our understanding of the problems they may be experiencing. Important in the diagnosis procedure is the need to rule out factitious disorder and malingering. Those expressing factitious disorder will fake or exaggerate symptoms to gain some kind of external gain such as sympathy from others. It may be that they do not know themselves that they are doing this. Those who are malingering exaggerate or fake their symptoms knowingly, possibly to escape work commitments or for financial gain in the form of insurance payouts. Once these have been ruled out the diagnosis of SSD is possible, one of which is Body Dysmorphic Disorder, where people become overly preoccupied with what others would say are minor problems with their bodies – perhaps a small blemish, or a scar. It is possible in these cases that people always cover up the perceived problem, so if there is a minor problem on their hand they will always wear gloves, and if on their arm, they will never be seen in clothing without sleeves.

Perhaps the most fascinating of these disorders is **conversion disorder**, now described as **Functional Neurological Symptom Disorder (FNSD)**, emphasizing the need for

Somatic Symptom Disorder physical complaints or disabilities that suggest a medical problem but that have no known biological cause and are not produced voluntarily by the person

hypochondriasis people become unduly alarmed about any physical symptom they detect and are convinced that they have or are about to have a serious illness. 'Illness Anxiety Disorder' in DSM-V

pain disorder is a form of SSD. People experience intense pain that either is out of proportion to whatever medical condition they might have or for which no physical basis can be found

conversion disorder (now FNSD), serious neurological symptoms, such as paralysis, loss of sensation, or blindness, suddenly occur

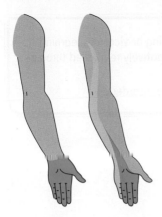

Glove   Actual nerve
anaesthesia   innervation

**FIGURE 17.16 An impossible
conversion symptom.**

In glove anaesthesia all feeling is lost
below the wrist. The skin areas served
by nerves in the arm make this symptom
physiologically impossible.

Focus 17.13 Describe
two kinds of somatoform
disorders. What causal
factors might be involved?

a neurological examination. Serious neurological symptoms, such as paralysis, loss of sensation, or blindness, suddenly occur. In such cases, electrophysiological recordings and brain imaging indicate that sensory and motor pathways in the brain are intact (Black, Seritan, Taber, & Hurley, 2004). People with conversion disorders often exhibit a strange lack of concern about their symptom and its implications, which is often described as *la belle indifference* (Stone, Warlow, & Sharpe, 2010). In some cases, the complaint itself is physiologically impossible. An example is *glove anaesthesia*, in which a person loses all sensation below the wrist. As Figure 17.16 shows, the hand is served by nerves that also provide sensory input to the wrist and arm, making glove anaesthesia anatomically impossible.

Although *psychogenic blindness* is rare in the general population, researchers discovered the largest known civilian group of people in the world with trauma-induced blindness. They were Cambodian refugees who escaped from their country and settled in southern California. These survivors of the 'killing fields' of Cambodia were subjected to unspeakable horror at the hands of the Khmer Rouge in the years following the Vietnam War (Cooke, 1991). More than 150 of them became functionally blind, even though their eyes appeared intact and electrophysiological monitoring showed that visual stimuli registered in their visual cortex. Many of the victims reported that their blindness came on suddenly after they witnessed traumatic scenes of murder. Were the sights from the outer world so painful that the visual system involuntarily shut down? An intriguing but as yet unanswered question is how cultural factors might have affected the development of this response to trauma.

To Freud, conversion symptoms were a symbolic expression of an underlying conflict that aroused so much anxiety that the ego kept the conflict in the unconscious by converting the anxiety into a physical symptom. In one of Freud's cases, a young woman who was forced to take care of her hostile, verbally abusive and unappreciative father suddenly developed paralysis in her arm. According to Freud, this occurred when her repressed hostile impulses threatened to break through and cause her to strike him using that arm (Freud, 1935). Contemporary psychodynamic theorists continue to accept explanations consistent with this approach (Abbass, Sheldon, Gyra, & Kalpin, 2008).

A predisposition to somatoform disorders may involve a combination of biological and psychological vulnerabilities. Somatoform disorders tend to run in families, though it is not clear whether this reflects the role of genetic factors, environmental learning and social reinforcement for bodily symptoms, or both (Cloninger & Dokucu, 2008; Trimble, 2003). Additionally, some people may experience internal sensations more vividly than others, or they may focus more attention on them. People with somatoform disorders are also very suggestible. One study found them to be far more responsive to hypnotic suggestions than were matched controls, and conversion clients' hypnotic susceptibility scores were significantly correlated with the number of conversion symptoms they reported (Roelofs, Hoogduin, Keijsers, Näring, Moene, & Sandijck, 2002), although Brown and colleagues (2007) conducted research that showed that hypnotic susceptibility was not necessarily a feature of somatization disorder (also known as hysteria or Briquet's disorder).

The incidence of these disorders tends to be much higher in cultures that discourage open discussion of emotions or that stigmatize psychological disorders (Matsumoto, 2001; Tanaka-Matsumi & Draguns, 1997). Within Western culture, there are subgroups, such as the police and military, where open discussion of feelings and self-disclosure of psychological problems are frowned on. In such settings, somatic symptoms may be the only acceptable outlet for emotional distress. The same may occur in people who are so emotionally constricted that they cannot acknowledge their emotions or verbally communicate them to others (Trae & Deighton, 2000).

DISSOCIATIVE DISORDERS

Ordinarily, personality has unity and coherence, and the many facets of the self are integrated so that people act, think, and feel with some degree of consistency. Memory plays a critical role in this integration, for it connects past with present and provides a sense of personal identity that extends over time. **Dissociative disorders** involve a breakdown of normal personality integration, resulting in significant alterations in memory or identity. Three forms that such disorders can take are *psychogenic amnesia*, *psychogenic fugue* and *dissociative identity disorder*.

In **psychogenic amnesia**, a person responds to a stressful event with extensive but selective memory loss (Miller, Vandome, & McBrewster, 2011). Some people can remember nothing about their past. Others can no longer recall specific events, people or places, although other contents of memory, such as cognitive, language and motor skills remain intact. These disorders are so extremely unusual and seemingly fantastic that they are the often the stuff of fiction and media depictions.

The Bourne trilogy, starring Matt Damon, is a good example, as is the rather wonderful *Who Am I?* starring Jackie Chan (Figure 17.17), and a similar problem is experienced by Fleming's hero, James Bond at the close of the book *You Only Live Twice*.

Psychogenic fugue is a more profound dissociative disorder in which a person loses all sense of personal identity, gives up his or her customary life, wanders to a new faraway location and establishes a new identity. Usually the fugue (derived from the Latin word *fugere*, 'to flee') is triggered by a highly stressful event or trauma, and it may last from a few hours or days to several years. Some adolescent runaways have been found to be in a fugue state, and married fugue victims may marry someone else and start a new career (Loewenstein, 1991). Typically the fugue ends when the person suddenly recovers his or her original identity and 'wakes up', mystified and distressed at being in a strange place under strange circumstances (Miller, Vandome, & McBrewster, 2011). Related to psychogenic fugue is a kind of psychogenic trance that is said to occur to some after periods of great stress. Famously, the English writer, actor and humorist Stephen Fry disappeared without leaving word to friends and family following a period of great stress, travelling from his home in London to the Belgian city of Bruges.

FIGURE 17.17 Jackie Chan in the film *Who Am I?*
Sources: AF Archive/Alamy.

> **dissociative disorders** a breakdown of normal personality integration, resulting in significant alterations in memory or identity

> **psychogenic amnesia** a person responds to a stressful event with extensive but selective memory loss
>
> **psychogenic fugue** a more profound dissociative disorder in which a person loses all sense of personal identity, gives up his or her customary life, wanders to a new faraway location and establishes a new identity
>
> **dissociative identity disorder (DID)** two or more separate personalities coexist in the same person

Dissociative Identity (Multiple Personality) Disorder

In **dissociative identity disorder (DID)** (formerly called multiple personality disorder), two or more separate personalities coexist in the same person. Dissociative identity disorder is the most striking and widely publicized of the dissociative disorders, and several celebrated cases have been the topic of books and movies, such as *Sybil*, *The Three Faces of Eve*, the case of Chris Sizemore reported in the literature by Thigpen and Cleckley (1954) and *Psycho* (Figure 17.18). In DID, a primary personality, or *host personality*, appears more often than the others (called *alters*), but each personality has its own integrated set of memories and behaviours. The personalities may or may not know about the existence of the others. They can differ in age and gender. The personalities can differ not only mentally and behaviourally but also physiologically. DID is extremely

FIGURE 17.18 In one celebrated depiction of dissociative identity disorder, motel clerk Norman Bates is shocked to discover the body of a woman (Janet Leigh) murdered in her shower by his mother (actually his 'alter' personality) in the movie *Psycho*.

Source: AF Archive/Alamy.

rare, but in 2006 and then again in 2011 the British Press published the story of a woman called Kim Noble, who is reported as having between 20 and 100 different personalities (*Independent* 27 August 2006; *Daily Mail*, 28 September 2011; *Guardian*, 3 September 2011). She uses the pronoun 'us' when she is interviewed, has taken up painting in art therapy and 12 of her different personalities have entirely different styles and exhibit their work publically. She is not dangerous at all, has not been hospitalized for a good while and lives at home in South London where she paints and receives support from case workers occasionally in the week.

Mental health workers and researchers have reported dramatic differences among the 'alter' personalities of those with DID, including physical health differences, voice changes and even changes in right- and left-handedness. Some clients have severe allergies when one personality is present but no allergies when the others are active. One client nearly died of a violent allergic reaction to a bee sting; a week later, when an 'alter' personality was active, another sting produced no reaction. Females with DID frequently have different menstrual cycles for each female personality; one woman had three periods per month. Others need spectacles with different prescriptions for different personalities; one may be far-sighted, another near-sighted (Miller, Vandome, & McBrewster, 2011). Those people with epilepsy and DID often have their seizures in one personality but not another (Drake, Pakalnis, & Denio, 1988).

Focus 17.14 What is the central feature of dissociative disorders? Describe the three major dissociative disorders.

What Causes DID?

According to Frank Putnam's **trauma-dissociation theory**, the development of new personalities occurs in response to severe stress. For the vast majority of clients, this begins in early childhood, frequently in response to physical or sexual abuse. Putnam (1989) studied the life histories of 100 diagnosed DID cases and found that 97 of them reported severe abuse and trauma in early and middle childhood, a time when children's identities are not well established and it is quite easy for them to dissociate. Putnam believes that in response to the trauma and their helplessness to resist it, children may engage in something akin to self-hypnosis and dissociate from reality. They create an alternate identity to detach themselves from the trauma, to transfer what is happening to someone else who can handle it, and to blunt the pain. Over time, it is theorized, the protective functions served by the new personality remain separate in the form of an alternate personality rather than being integrated into the host personality (Meyer & Osborne, 1987; Putnam, 2000).

trauma-dissociation theory the development of new personalities occurs in response to severe stress

Dissociative identity disorder has become a controversial diagnosis. Friedl and Draijer (2000) looked at Dutch psychiatric clients and 2% of the clients they saw over 12 months were identified as having DID, significantly lower than many similarly made US-based estimates. Some critics question how often it actually occurs, and others question its very existence (Beahrs, 1994; Spanos, 1994). Prior to 1970, only about 100 cases had been reported worldwide, and even today DID is virtually unknown in many cultures, including Japan (Takahashi, 1990). But after the disorder was highly publicized in popular books and films, many additional cases appeared, numbering in the tens of thousands by the mid-1990s. The number of alternate personalities also had increased from two or three to an average of about 15 (Spanos, 1994). Could this dramatic increase in the prevalence of DID and number of alters be the result of publicity and client or therapist expectations? People can, such as under hypnosis, become so immersed in an imagined role (such as an 'alter' personality) that it becomes quite real to them, and they act accordingly (Spanos, 1996). The controversy surrounding DID is inspiring research that may advance our understanding of factors that can produce alterations in memory, physiological responses and behaviour.

Focus 17.15 Summarize the trauma-dissociation theory of DID. On what grounds do critics challenge and explain DID?

In review

■ Somatic symptom disorders involve physical complaints that do not have a physiological explanation. They include hypochondriasis, pain disorders and conversion disorders.

■ Familial similarities in somatic symptom disorders may have a biological basis, or they may be the result of environmental shaping through attention and sympathy. Such disorders tend to occur with greater frequency in cultures that discourage open expression of negative emotions.

■ Dissociative disorders involve losses of memory and personal identity. The major dissociative disorders are psychogenic amnesia, psychogenic fugue and dissociative identity disorder (DID).

■ The trauma-dissociation theory holds that DID emerges when children dissociate to defend themselves from severe trauma or sexual abuse. This model has been challenged by other theorists who believe that multiple personalities result from role immersion and therapist expectations.

MOOD DISORDERS

Another set of emotion-based disorders are *mood disorders*, which include depression and mania (excessive excitement). Together with anxiety disorders, mood disorders are the most frequently experienced psychological disorders. There is high *co-morbidity* (co-occurrence) involving anxiety and mood disorders. About half of all depressed people also experience an anxiety disorder. Included in the new DSM-V is a new category within the Mood Disorders section described as 'temper dysregulation with dysphoria (TDD). This will help diagnosticians better differentiate people, in particular children, with this problem from those suffering from other disorders such as bipolar disorder (page 746).

DEPRESSION

Depression is a common feeling. Most of us have experienced it in one form or another. When we lose a loved one or end a relationship we might feel sad and discouraged, apathetic and passive. At times like this the future does not look terribly rosy, and the enjoyment of life seems far away. Such reactions are not unheard of and usually fade after the event has passed or as the person becomes accustomed to the new situation. Time, as they say, is usually a great healer.

In clinical depression, however, the frequency, intensity and duration of depressive symptoms are out of proportion to the person's life situation. Some people may respond to a minor setback or loss with *major depression*, an intense depressed state that leaves them unable to function effectively in their lives. Edward, the young man described at the beginning of the chapter, suffers with a major depression. Other people exhibit **dysthymia**, a less intense form of depression that has less dramatic effects on personal and occupational functioning. Dysthymia, though less intense, is a more chronic and longer-lasting form of misery, occurring for years on end with some intervals of normal mood that never last more than a few weeks or months.

The *negative mood state* is the core feature of depression. When depressed people are asked how they feel, they most commonly report sadness, misery and loneliness. The diagnostic criteria make it clear that whereas people with anxiety disorders retain their capacity to experience pleasure, depressed people lose it (Comer, 2009). Activities that used to bring satisfaction and happiness feel dull and flat. Even biological pleasures, such as eating and sex, lose their appeal.

Although depression is primarily a disorder of emotion or mood, there are three other types of symptoms: cognitive, motivational and somatic (physical) (Figure 17.19). *Cognitive symptoms* are a central part of depression. Depressed people have difficulty

mood disorders include depression and mania (excessive excitement)

major depression an intense depressed state that leaves them unable to function effectively in their lives

dysthymia a less intense form of depression that has less dramatic effects on personal and occupational functioning

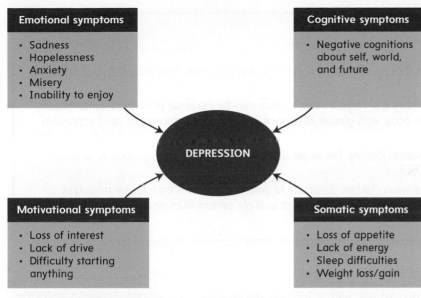

Emotional symptoms		Cognitive symptoms
• Sadness • Hopelessness • Anxiety • Misery • Inability to enjoy		• Negative cognitions about self, world, and future

DEPRESSION

Motivational symptoms		Somatic symptoms
• Loss of interest • Lack of drive • Difficulty starting anything		• Loss of appetite • Lack of energy • Sleep difficulties • Weight loss/gain

FIGURE 17.19 Facets of depression.

---

bipolar disorder depression (which is usually the dominant state) alternates with periods of mania

mania a state of highly excited mood and behaviour that is quite the opposite of depression

FIGURE 17.20 Catherine Zeta Jones, reported in 2011 as suffering with bipolar disorder.

Source: AlamyCelebrity/Alamy.

Focus 17.16 Describe the four classes of symptoms that characterize depression. What is bipolar disorder?

---

concentrating and making decisions. They usually have low self-esteem, believing that they are inferior, inadequate and incompetent. When setbacks occur in their lives, depressed people tend to blame themselves; when failure has not yet occurred, they expect that it will and that it will be caused by their own inadequacies. Depressed people almost always view the future with great pessimism and hopelessness (Clark, Beck, & Alford, 1999).

Motivational symptoms in depression involve an inability to get started and to perform behaviours that might produce pleasure or accomplishment. A depressed student may be unable to get out of bed in the morning, let alone go to class or study. Everything seems too much of an effort. In extreme depressive reactions, the person may have to be prodded out of bed, clothed and fed. In some cases of severe depression, the person's movements slow down and he or she walks or talks slowly and with excruciating effort.

Somatic (bodily) *symptoms* often include loss of appetite and weight loss in moderate and severe depression, whereas in mild depression, weight gain sometimes occurs as a person eats compulsively. Sleep disturbances, particularly insomnia, are common. Sleep disturbance and weight loss lead to fatigue and weakness, which tend to add to the depressed feelings. Depressed people also may lose sexual desire and responsiveness.

BIPOLAR DISORDER

When a person experiences only depression, the disorder is called *unipolar depression*. In a **bipolar disorder**, depression (which is usually the dominant state) alternates with periods of **mania**, a state of highly excited mood and behaviour that is quite the opposite of depression. In a manic state, mood is euphoric and cognitions are grandiose. The person sees no limits to what he or she can accomplish and fails to consider negative consequences that may ensue if grandiose plans are acted on. At a motivational level, manic behaviour is hyperactive. The manic person engages in frenetic activity, be it in work, in sexual relationships or in other areas of life. The nineteenth-century composer Robert Schumann produced 27 works during a one-year manic phase, but his productivity ground to a halt when he sank back into the depressive phase of his bipolar disorder (Jamison, 1995). Jeremy Brett, who for many produced the greatest depiction of Sherlock Holmes, suffered dreadfully with bipolar disorder, as did Kurt Cobain, Edvard Munch and the mathematicians Emil Post and Georg Cantor, and as does the actress Catherine Zeta Jones (Figure 17.20).

Marya Hornbacher (author of *Madness* – 1999) writes clearly and emotionally of her experience with bipolar disorder. This often upsetting and harrowing book provides a brave insight into the problems of those experiencing bipolar disorder.

In a manic state, speech is often rapid or pressured, as if the person must say as many words as possible in the time allotted. With this flurry of activity comes a greatly lessened need for sleep. A person may go for several days without sleeping, until exhaustion inevitably sets in and the mania slows down.

PREVALENCE AND COURSE OF MOOD DISORDERS

Epidemiological studies in Europe estimate that at this moment, 6.5% of people are suffering with major depression, which equates to 30.3 million people. We can add bipolar disorder to this with another 3 million people (Wittchen et al., 2011). No age group is exempt

from depression. It appears in infants as young as 6 months who have been separated from their mothers for prolonged periods. In some studies the rate of depressive symptoms in children and adolescents is as high as the adult rate (cf. Essau & Petermann, 1999). The National Institute for Health and Clinical Excellence (2004) estimates that up to 75% of cases of depression may be undetected, so the incidence in young people is much higher than the numbers that have been diagnosed suggests.

Prevalence of depressive disorders is similar across socio-economic and ethnic groups, but there is a major sex difference in our culture. Although men and women do not differ greatly in prevalence of bipolar disorder, women appear to be about twice as likely as men to suffer unipolar depression (Figure 17.21). Women are most likely to suffer their first episode of depression in their twenties, men in their forties (Keyes & Goodman, 2006).

Many people who suffer depressive episodes never seek treatment. What is likely to happen to such people? Perhaps the one positive thing that can be said about depression is that it usually dissipates over time. After the initial episode, which typically comes on suddenly after a stressful experience (consistent with the diathesis-stress hypothesis depicted in Figure 17.3), depression typically lasts an average of 5–10 months when untreated.

Once a depressive episode has occurred, one of three patterns may follow. In perhaps 40% of all cases, clinical depression will not recur following recovery. Many other cases show a second pattern: recovery with recurrence. On average, these people will remain symptom-free for perhaps three years before experiencing another depressive episode of about the same severity and duration. The interval between subsequent episodes of depression tends to become shorter over the years (Rubin, 2000). Finally, about 10% of people who have a major depressive episode will not recover and will remain chronically depressed (Figure 17.22).

Manic episodes, though less common than depressive reactions, are far more likely to recur. Fewer than 1% of the population experiences mania, but those who do are very likely to experience a recurrence of the reaction. Whether the reaction has occurred before or not is an extremely good indicator here of whether it will again (Di Marzo, Giordano, Pacchiarotti, Colom, Sánchez-Moreno, & Vieta, 2006).

CAUSAL FACTORS IN MOOD DISORDERS

As in the case of anxiety disorders, the mood disorders are a product of interacting biological, psychological and environmental factors.

Biological Factors

Both genetic and neurochemical factors have been linked to depression (Comer, 2009). Genetic factors surface in both twin and adoption studies (McGuffin, Owen, & Gottesman, 2005). Identical twins have a concordance rate of about 67% for experiencing clinical depression, compared with a rate of only 15% for fraternal twins (Gershon, Berrettini, & Golden, 1989). Among adopted people who develop depression, biological relatives are about eight times more likely than adoptive relatives to also suffer from depression. What is likely to be inherited is a predisposition to develop a depressive disorder, given certain kinds

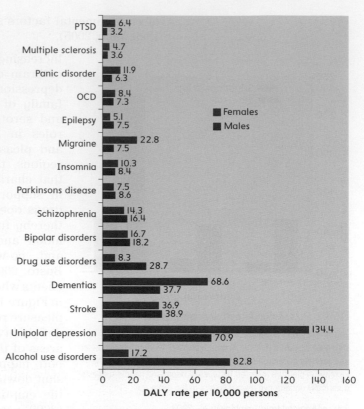

FIGURE 17.21 Sex differences in mental illnesses, including depression.

Source: Adapted from Wittchen et al., 2011. Plotted here are the DALY rates per 10,000. DALY stands for Disability Adjusted Life Years. One DALY can be thought of as 1 year lost due to ill health. So 100 in every 10,000 means that 100 in every 10,000 days are lost due to ill health.

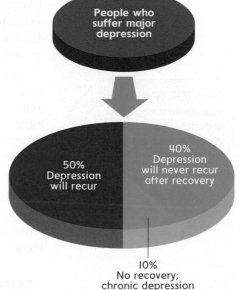

FIGURE 17.22 What follows major depression?

One of three outcomes may follow a major depressive episode. About 40% never have a recurrence, perhaps 50% have a recurrence and about 10% suffer chronic (ever-present) depression.

of environmental factors such as significant losses and low social support (Barondes, 1999; Jang, 2005).

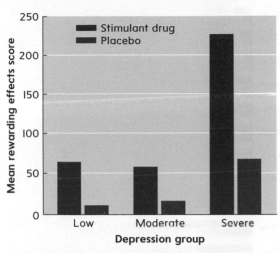

FIGURE 17.23 An underactive reward system?

This graph shows an increase in pleasure ratings produced by a stimulant drug or a placebo in non-depressed, moderately depressed and severely depressed males and females. The magnitude of the increase in pleasure reported by severely depressed people suggests a normally underactive reward system in the brain.

Source: Adapted from Tremblay et al., 2002.

Increasingly, biological research has focused on the possible role of brain chemistry in depression. One influential theory holds that depression is a disorder of motivation caused by underactivity in a family of neurotransmitters that include norepinephrine, dopamine and serotonin (Anisman, 2010). These transmitters play important roles in several brain regions involved in experiencing reward and pleasure. When neural transmission decreases in these brain regions, the result is the lack of pleasure and loss of motivation that characterize depression (Donaldson, 1998; Anisman, 2010) Also in support of this theory, several highly effective antidepressant drugs operate by increasing the activity of these neurotransmitters, thereby further stimulating the neural systems that underlie positive mood and goal-directed behaviour. A study by Lescia Tremblay and co-workers (Tremblay, Naranjo, Cardenas, Hermann, & Busto, 2002) tested the amount of reward experienced by depressed clients when these centres were activated by a stimulant drug. As shown in Figure 17.23, severely depressed individuals showed a much stronger pleasure response to the drug, supporting the hypothesis of a 'pleasure deficit' in the brain. Gotlib et al. (2004a) took fMRI readings of emotion areas of the brain and showed low levels of neuron responsiveness to both happy and sad scenes, as if the emotion response systems had shut down. This may account for the lack of positive emotionality and the 'emptiness' of the depressive emotional experience. Martin-Soelch (2009) provides a review of the research investigating the relationship between depression and the reward system and concludes that although there is good evidence in support of the relationship more research needs to be done. The exact nature of the dysfunction in the reward (dopamine) system is as yet unclear and this exciting area of research continues.

Bipolar disorder, in which depression alternates with less frequent periods of mania, has been studied primarily at the biological level because it appears to have a stronger genetic basis than does unipolar depression (Young & Joffe, 1997). Among both men and women, the lifetime risk of developing a bipolar disorder is just below 1%. Yet about 50% of clients with bipolar disorder have a parent, grandparent or child with the disorder (Barondes, 1999; Rubin, 2000). The concordance rate for bipolar disorder is five times higher in identical twins than in fraternal twins, suggesting a genetic link.

Manic disorders may stem from an overproduction of the same neurotransmitters that are underactive in depression. This might explain the symptom picture that is quite the opposite of that seen in depression. Significantly, lithium chloride, the drug most frequently used to calm manic disorders, works by decreasing the activity of these transmitters in the brain's motivational/pleasure activation system (LeMoal, 1999; Robinson, 1997).

> **Focus 17.17** What evidence exists for genetic and biochemical factors in depression and mania?

Psychological Factors

Biological factors seem to increase vulnerability to certain types of psychological and environmental events that can then trigger the disorders. Other perspectives specify what those events might be.

Personality-based vulnerability

Psychoanalysts Karl Abraham (1911) and Sigmund Freud (1957) believed that early traumatic losses or rejections create vulnerability for later depression by triggering a grieving and rage process that becomes part of the individual's personality.

Subsequent losses and rejection reactivate the original loss and cause a reaction not only to the current event but also to the unresolved loss from the past.

Were he alive today, Freud would surely point to research by sociologists George Brown and Terrill Harris (1978) to support his theory of early loss. Brown and Harris interviewed women in London and found that the rate of depression among women who had lost their mothers before age 11 and who had also experienced a severe recent loss was almost three times higher than that among women who had experienced a similar recent loss but had not lost their mothers before age 11. Experiencing the death of a father during childhood is also associated with increased risk of later depression (Barnes & Prosen, 1985; Bowlby, 2000).

Cognitive processes

According to Aaron Beck (1976), depressed people victimize themselves through their own beliefs that they are defective, worthless and inadequate. They also believe that whatever happens to them is bad and that negative things will continue happening because of their personal defects (Clark, Beck, & Brown, 1989). This **depressive cognitive triad** of negative thoughts concerning (1) the world, (2) oneself and (3) the future seems to pop into consciousness automatically, and many depressed people report that they cannot control or suppress the negative thoughts (Wenzlaff, Wegner, & Roper, 1988). Depressed people also tend to recall most of their failures and few of their successes, and they tend to focus much of their attention on their perceived inadequacies (Clark et al., 1999; Haaga, Dyck, & Ernst, 1991). Depressed people also detect pictures of sad faces at lower exposure times and remember them better than do non-depressed people (Gotlib, Krasnoperova, Yue, & Joormann, 2004b), indicating a perceptual and memory sensitivity to the negative.

Help for those suffering with these problems often comes in the form of cognitive behavioural therapy, where the focus is on refocusing the life-view of the depressed client so that they are able to identify and recall success, and so that their focus is not on their perceived weaknesses or inadequacies.

As noted in the discussion of self-enhancement tendencies in **Chapter 14**, most people tend to take personal credit for the good outcomes in their lives and to blame their misfortunes on factors outside themselves, thereby maintaining and enhancing their self-esteem. According to Beck, depressed people do exactly the opposite: They exhibit a **depressive attributional pattern**, attributing successes or other positive events to factors outside the self while attributing negative outcomes to personal factors (Figure 17.24). Beck believes that taking no credit for successes but blaming themselves for failures helps depressed people maintain low self-esteem and their belief that they are worthless failures. Quite literally, they cannot win, even when they do!

Not surprisingly, low self-esteem operates as a significant risk factor for later depression. This was established in two large-scale longitudinal studies in which over 4,000 adults ranging in age from 18 to 88 years were followed for four to nine years. At all age levels, low self-esteem predicted later depressive episodes (Orth, Robins, Trzesniewski, Maes, & Schmitt, 2009).

Another prominent cognitive account of depression, **learned helplessness theory**, holds that depression occurs when people expect that bad events will occur and that there is nothing they can do to prevent them or cope with them (Seligman & Isaacowitz, 2000). The depressive attributional pattern plays a central role in the learned helplessness model, but learned helplessness theorists take it a step further

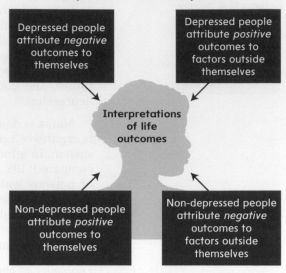

FIGURE 17.24 The depressive attributional pattern.

Cognitive theorists believe that the attributional patterns of depressed people are the opposite of the self-enhancing patterns that characterize non-depressed people. In the depressive attributional pattern, people attribute negative outcomes to themselves and positive outcomes to factors outside themselves.

depressive cognitive triad negative thoughts concerning (1) the world, (2) oneself and (3) the future

 Chapter 14, Page 577

depressive attributional pattern attributing successes or other positive events to factors outside the self while attributing negative outcomes to personal factors

learned helplessness theory depression occurs when people expect that bad events will occur and that there is nothing they can do to prevent them or cope with them

Focus 17.18 Describe the cognitive triad, the depressive attributional pattern and learned helplessness in relation to depression.

by specifying what the negative attributions for failures are like. They suggest that chronic and intense depression occurs as the result of negative attributions for failures that are personal ('It's all *my* fault'), stable ('I'll *always* be this way') and global ('I'm a *total* loser'). Thus people who attribute negative events in their lives to factors such as low intelligence, physical repulsiveness or an unlovable personality tend to believe that their personal defects will render them helpless to avoid negative events in the future, and their sense of hopelessness places them at significantly greater risk for depression.

Mania is dominated by quite another pattern of thinking. The person in a manic state is expansive, optimistic and excited – all emotions linked with the behavioural activation system. In a longitudinal study, Alloy, Abramson, Urosevic, Bender and Wagner (2009) compared 195 people with bipolar disorder with a demographically matched group of persons without bipolar disorder. They found that cognitions involving autonomy (a focus on individualistic achievement and self-sufficiency), high performance standards ('A person should do well at everything') and a tendency towards self-criticism when goals are not obtained predicted not only bipolar group membership but also the occurrence of future hypomanic episodes.

Learning and environmental factors

Lewinsohn et al. (1985) take a behavioural perspective and believe that depression is usually triggered by a loss, by some other punishing event or by a drastic decrease in the amount of positive reinforcement that the person receives from his or her environment. As the depression begins to take hold, people stop performing behaviours that previously provided reinforcement, such as hobbies and socializing. Moreover, depressed people tend to make others feel anxious, depressed and hostile (Joiner & Coyne, 1999). Eventually, these other people begin to lose patience, failing to understand why the person does not snap out of it. This diminishes social support still further and may eventually cause depressed people to be abandoned by those who are most important to them (Nezlek et al., 2000). Longitudinal studies show that reductions in social support are a good predictor of subsequent depression (Burton, Stice, & Seeley, 2004). Figure 17.25 shows the cyclical course of depression.

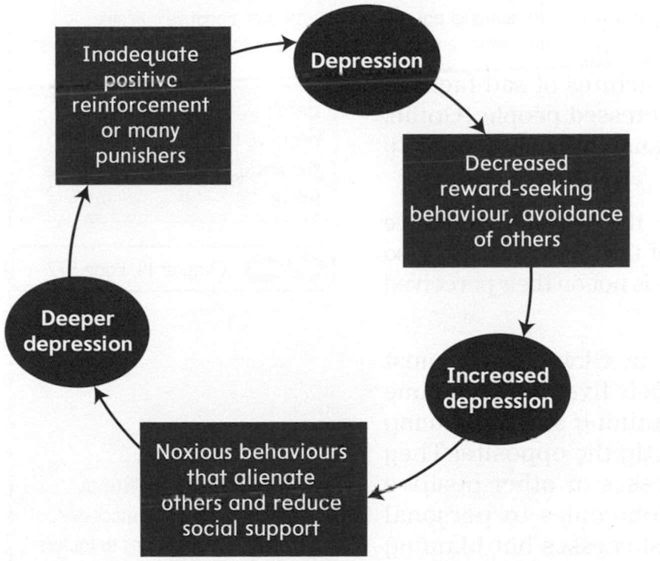

FIGURE 17.25 Lewinsohn's behavioural model of depression.

Behaviourists focus on the environmental causes and effects of depression. Depression results from loss of positive reinforcement and produces further declines in reinforcement and social support in a vicious-cycle fashion.

Behavioural theorists believe that to begin feeling better, depressed people must break this vicious cycle by initially forcing themselves to engage in behaviours that are likely to produce some degree of pleasure. Eventually, positive reinforcement produced by this process of *behavioural activation* will begin to counteract the depressive affect, undermine the sense of hopelessness that characterizes depression, and increase feelings of personal control over the environment (Martell, Addis, & Dimidjian, 2004).

Environmental factors may also help explain why depression tends to run in families. Constance Hammen (1991) studied the family histories of depressed people and concluded that children of depressed parents often experience poor parenting and many stressful experiences as they grow up. As a result, they may fail to develop good coping skills and a positive self-concept, making them more vulnerable later in life to stressful events that can trigger depressive reactions. This conclusion is supported by findings that children of depressed parents exhibit a significantly higher incidence of depression and other disorders as adolescents and young adults (Lieb, Isensee, Hoefier, Pfister, & Wittchen, 2002).

Focus 17.19 How does Lewinsohn's learning theory explain the spiralling-downward course that occurs in depression?

Sociocultural Factors

Although depression exists in virtually all cultures, its prevalence, symptom pattern and causes reflect cultural variation (Lopez & Guarnaccia, 2000). For example, the prevalence

of depressive disorders is far lower in Hong Kong and Taiwan than in Western nations. People in these societies tend to have strong social support from family and other groups, which helps reduce the negative impact of loss and disappointments when they occur (Tseng et al., 1990).

Cultural factors also can affect the ways in which depression is manifested. Feelings of guilt and personal inadequacy seem to predominate in North American and West European countries, whereas somatic symptoms of fatigue, loss of appetite and sleep difficulties are more often reported in Latin, Chinese and African cultures (Manson, 1994).

Finally, cultural factors may influence who develops depression. Women are about twice as likely as men to report feeling depressed in technologically advanced countries. Yet this sex difference is not found in developing countries (Culbertson, 1997; Nolen-Hoeksema, 1990). At present, we do not know why this pattern occurs, but attempts are under way to learn more about how the cultural environment influences the development of depression.

At one time or another, many depressed people consider suicide as a way to escape from the unhappiness of their lives. We now examine suicide, its causes and what can be done to prevent this tragic event.

> **Focus 17.20** What are the major motives and risk factors for suicide? Describe four guidelines for helping a suicidal person.

> **suicide** the wilful taking of one's own life

Applying psychological science

UNDERSTANDING AND PREVENTING SUICIDE

Suicide is the wilful taking of one's own life. The World Health Organization (WHO) estimates that worldwide, nearly 500,000 people commit suicide each year – almost one per minute. Ten times that number engage in non-fatal suicide attempts. Gudjón Magnusson, the director for Europe in charge of mental health with the WHO, told a ministerial summit on mental health that the suicide rate for Europe was 17.5 per every 100,000 (Figure 17.26). This is extremely high and above the world average of 16 per 100,000. Of the 873,000 suicides worldwide, Europe has 163,000.

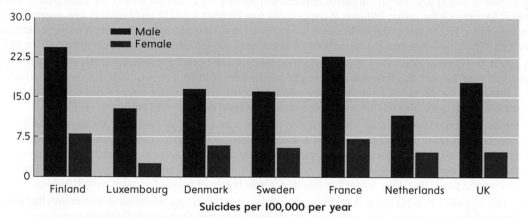

FIGURE 17.26 Suicide rates in countries in Western Europe.
Source: Organization for Economic Cooperation and Development (OECD), 2014.

Women attempt suicide about three times more often than men, but men are, on average, three times more likely to actually kill themselves. These differences may be due to (1) a higher incidence of depression in women and (2) men's choice of more violent and lethal methods, such as shooting themselves or jumping off buildings. The suicide rate for both men and women is higher among those who have been divorced or widowed. Women's suicides are more likely to be triggered, although not certain to be triggered by any means, by failures in love relationships, whereas career failure more often prompts men's suicides (Shneidman, 1976). A history of sexual or physical abuse significantly increases the likelihood of later suicide attempts (Garnefski & Arends, 1998).

Depression is one of the strongest predictors of suicide. About 15% of clinically depressed individuals will eventually kill themselves, a rate that is 22 to 36 times higher than the suicide rate for the general population. An estimated 80% of suicidal people are significantly depressed (Yen et al., 2003). It is worth noting, however, that suicides do not usually occur when depression is deepest. Instead, suicide often occurs unexpectedly as a depressed

person seems to be emerging from depression and feeling better. The lifting of depression may provide the energy needed to complete the suicidal act but not reduce the person's underlying sense of hopelessness and despair.

MOTIVES FOR SUICIDE

There appear to be two fundamental motivations for suicide: the desire to end one's life and the desire to manipulate and coerce other people into doing what the suicidal person wants (Beck, Rush, Shaw, & Emery, 1979; Shneidman, 1998). Those who wish to end their lives have basically given up. They see no other way to deal with intolerable emotional distress, and in death they see an end to their problems. In one study, 56% of suicide attempts were classified as having been motivated by the desire to die (Beck, 1976). These attempts were accompanied by high levels of depression and hopelessness, and they tended to be more lethal than other suicide attempts. In some instances, a suicide decision is based on a desire to stop being a burden to others. High levels of impulsiveness in the individual is also a factor in whether they may engage in a suicide attempt.

The second primary motivation for 'suicide' is manipulation of others. Many *parasuicides* (suicide attempts that do not end in death) are cries for help or attempts to coerce people to meet one's needs. Trying to prevent a lover from ending a relationship, induce guilt in others or dramatize one's suffering are manipulative motives. Manipulative suicide attempters tend to use less lethal means (such as drug overdose or wrist slashing) and to make sure help is available. In the study cited earlier (Beck, 1976), 13% of the suicide attempts were classified as manipulative. The remaining 31% combined the two types of motivation. A small minority of suicides result from altruistic decisions to sacrifice one's life for the survival of others; examples include the soldier who dives on a hand grenade to save his comrades' lives or the mother who elects to give birth rather than aborting her baby, knowing that she will die in the process.

WARNING SIGNS FOR SUICIDE

The best predictor of suicide attempts in both men and women is a verbal or behavioural threat to commit suicide, and such threats should always be taken seriously. One of the most destructive myths about suicide is that people who talk openly about suicide are just seeking attention and do not actually intend to carry out the act. Yet research shows that a high proportion of suicide attempts - perhaps 80% - are preceded by some kind of warning (Bagley & Ramsay, 1997). Sometimes the warning is an explicit statement of intent, such as 'I don't want to go on living' or 'I won't be a burden much longer'. Other times, the warnings are more subtle, as when a person expresses hopelessness about the future, withdraws from others or from favourite activities, gives away treasured possessions, or takes unusual risks. Other important risk factors are a history of previous suicide attempts and a detailed plan that involves a lethal method (Chiles & Strosahl, 1995; Shneidman, 1998). Substance use and abuse also increase suicide risk (Yen et al., 2003).

SUICIDE PREVENTION: WHAT YOU CAN DO

Scientific research has taught us much about the dynamics and prevention of suicide. These findings provide the following guidelines for preventing this tragic answer to life's problems and for helping potentially suicidal people:

1. Another myth about suicide is that broaching the topic with a potentially suicidal person may prompt the person to carry out the act. In truth, the best first step if you suspect that someone may be suicidal is to ask the person directly whether he or she is considering suicide: 'Have you thought about hurting yourself or ending your life?' If the person responds affirmatively, try to find out if he or she has a plan or a time frame in mind. Do not be hesitant to approach the person. Diffusion of responsibility (see Chapters 2 and 11) could result in your assuming that someone else is helping the person when in fact no one is (Goldsmith, 2003). Your ultimate goal should be to help the person receive assistance from a qualified professional as soon as possible, not to treat the person yourself. Nonetheless, you can take some immediate steps that may be helpful.

2. Many suicidal people feel alone in their misery. It is important to provide social support and empathy at this critical juncture. An expression of genuine concern can pave the way for other potentially helpful interventions (Barnett & Porter, 1998). For example, a frank discussion of the problem that is foremost in the person's life can be helpful. Suicidal people often feel totally overwhelmed by life, and focusing on a specific problem may help the person realize that it is not unsolvable and need not cloud his or her total perception of life.

3. When people are distressed and hopeless, their time orientation tends to narrow and they have difficulty seeing beyond their current distress. Try to help the person see his or her present situation within a wider time perspective and to consider positive possibilities that might exist in the future. In particular, discuss reasons for continuing to live, and focus on any doubts the person might have about electing suicide. For example, if the person indicates that his or her family will suffer greatly from the suicide, adopt this as one of your arguments for finding a different solution to the problem. Many suicidal people would like to feel that they do not have to commit suicide. Capitalize on such feelings.

4. If a person is suicidal, stay with him or her and seek professional assistance. Most cities have suicide-prevention centres that offer 24-hour services, including telephone and direct counselling. These centres are usually listed under *suicide* or *crisis* in the phone book.

Helplines:

- Denmark: Livslinien +45 70 201 201
- Netherlands: SOS Telefonische Hulpdiensten Nederland 0900-0767
- Norway: Kirkens SOS i Norge (Landssekretariatet) +47 815 33 300
- Republic of Ireland: Samaritans 116 123
- South Africa: Lifeline Southern Africa 0861 322 322
- Sweden: Nationella Hjälplinjen 020 22 00 60
- UK: Samaritans: 08457 90 90 90

If a local number if not listed here then the Befrienders are an international organization that will be able to help. Information and lots of support numbers for countries all over the world can be found at www.befrienders.org.

⊘ **In review**

- Mood disorders include several depressive disorders and bipolar disorder, in which intermittent periods of mania (intense mood and behaviour activation) occur. Depression has four sets of symptoms: emotional, cognitive, motivational and somatic. The symptoms of negative emotions and thoughts, loss of motivation and behavioural slowness are reversed in mania.

- Both genetic and neurochemical factors have been linked to depression. One prominent biochemical theory links depression to an underactivity of neurotransmitters (norepinephrine, dopamine and serotonin) that activate brain areas involved in pleasure and positive motivation. Drugs that relieve depression increase the activity of these transmitters. Bipolar disorder seems to have an even stronger genetic component than does unipolar depression.

- Psychoanalytic theorists view depression as a long-term consequence of traumatic losses and rejections early in life that create a personality vulnerability pattern.

- Cognitive theorists emphasize the role of negative beliefs about the self, the world and the future (the depressive cognitive triad) and describe a depressive attributional pattern, in which negative outcomes are attributed to personal causes and successes to situational causes. Seligman's theory of learned helplessness suggests that attributing negative outcomes to personal, stable and global causes fosters depression.

- The behavioural approach focuses on the vicious cycle in which depression-induced inactivity and aversive behaviours reduce reinforcement from the environment and thereby increase depression still further.

- Manipulation and a desire to escape distress are the two major motives for suicide. The risk for suicide increases if the person is depressed and has a lethal plan and a past history of parasuicide.

SCHIZOPHRENIA

In many ways, schizophrenia is the most puzzling and often bizarre of the psychological disorders. Effective treatment of schizophrenia is very difficult (Beck, Rector, Stolar, & Grant, 2008), and despite many theories of schizophrenia and related research studies, a detailed and complete understanding of this disorder continues to elude the psychological community. Schizophrenia is characterized by disturbances in thinking, speech, perception, emotion and behaviour (Castle & Buckley, 2008) is one of a family of *psychotic* disorders, all of which involve some loss of contact with reality, as well as bizarre behaviours and experiences.

schizophrenia severe disturbances in thinking, speech, perception, emotion

The term *schizophrenia* was introduced by the Swiss psychiatrist Eugen Bleuler in 1911, but had been identified as a mental illness as early as 1887, by German physician Emile Kraepelin. Literally, schizophrenia means 'split mind'. You should be careful, however, not to make the mistake that many people do, and confuse schizophrenia with dissociative identity disorder ('split personality') or with a Dr Jekyll–Mr Hyde phenomenon. Multiple personalities are not what Bleuler had in mind when he coined the term 'split-mind'. Instead, he intended to suggest that certain psychological functions, such as thought, language and emotion, which are normally integrated with one another, are somehow split apart or disconnected in schizophrenia.

CHARACTERISTICS OF SCHIZOPHRENIA

Schizophrenic disorders are identified generally by the way that the sufferer has problems, or distortions of perception and thinking, and by the way that they show inappropriate or less-clear emotions. The person may hallucinate, both visually and auditorily, but most notably the latter. The person may share their most delicate and personal thoughts with others, where they would ordinarily not do so. Sounds and colours may seem out of the ordinary, appearing more vivid or altered in some way. There is often a belief that everyday situations have a meaning that they do not. These meanings are usually directed towards the sufferer, and may have a sinister quality to them. The mood of the sufferer is also severely affected, with the impression that the person could not care less about what is going on around them sometimes. Other mood variations may be present. The person may sometimes appear to be catatonic. The onset of the problem may be acute, or it may occur gradually over time, the person developing odd thinking and conduct during this

delusions false beliefs that are sustained in the face of evidence that normally would be sufficient to destroy them

hallucinations false perceptions that have a compelling sense of reality

(a)

(b)

FIGURE 17.27 The very famous cat paintings of Louis Wain (1860-1939) changed dramatically as his life progressed – he is thought to have suffered with schizophrenia (a) painted earlier in life (b) painted later in life.

Focus 17.21 What is meant by the term schizophrenia? What are its major cognitive, behavioural, emotional and perceptual features?

process. Sometimes people recover completely with treatment, and sometimes they do not. The gender split is approximately equal for men and women (cf. Wittchen et al., 2011) who go on to indicate that approximately 640,000 days per 10,000 were lost per year (DALY) to schizophrenia in 2011.

The schizophrenic thought disorder sometimes entails **delusions**, false beliefs that are sustained in the face of evidence that normally would be sufficient to destroy them. A schizophrenic person might believe that his brain is being turned to glass by ray guns operated by his enemies from outer space (a *delusion of persecution*) or that Jesus Christ is one of his special agents (a *delusion of grandeur*).

Perceptual disorganization and disordered thought become more pronounced as people progress in schizophrenia (McKenna & Oh, 2003). Unwanted thoughts constantly intrude into consciousness (Silber, 2014). What the world might come to look like from inside the schizophrenic mind is illustrated in art created by schizophrenics during periods of disturbance (Figure 17.27b). Some experience **hallucinations**, false perceptions that have a compelling sense of reality. Auditory hallucinations (typically voices speaking to the person are most common, although visual and tactile hallucinations may also occur.

The language of people with schizophrenia is often disorganized, and it may contain strange words. 'I am here from a foreign university ... and you have to have a "plausity" of all acts of amendment to go through for the children's code ...and it is no mental disturbance or "putenance" ... it is an "amorition" law ... it is like their "privatilinia" ' (Vetter, 1969, p. 189). Language sometimes contains word associations that are based on rhymes or other associations rather than meaning. Consider the following conversation between a psychologist and a hospitalized schizophrenic:

> *After two weeks, the psychologist said to him: 'As you say, you are wired precisely wrong. But why won't you let me see the diagram?' Carl answered: 'Never, ever will you find the lever, the eternalever that will sever me forever with my real, seal, deal, heel. It is not on my shoe, not even on the sole. It walks away.'*
> *(Rosenhan & Seligman, 1989, p. 369)*

Schizophrenia can affect emotions in a number of ways. Many people with schizophrenia have *blunted affect*, manifesting less sadness, joy and anger than most people. Others have *flat affect*, showing almost no emotions at all. Their voices are monotonous, their faces impassive. *Inappropriate affect* can also occur, meaning that the person's emotional responses are often inappropriate to the situation.

In the earlier DSM, various subtypes of schizophrenia were identified. This was done in an attempt to better help the clinician really focus their diagnosis and differentiate between this unusually common problem. In DSM-V the subtypes have been removed making it easier. The older subtypes were characterized by the dominant symptom expressed at the time the person presented. Because it is common for these symptoms to change, the subtype was no longer appropriate and so they were abolished. Aspects of the subtypes such as catatonia do remain, but become identifiers of schizophrenic behaviour, or specifiers rather than defining components of the initial diagnosis.

CAUSAL FACTORS IN SCHIZOPHRENIA

Because of the seriousness of the disorder and the many years of anguish and incapacitation that its victims are likely to experience, schizophrenia has long been a focus of research. There is a growing consensus that schizophrenia results from a biologically based vulnerability factor that is set into motion by psychological and environmental events (Herz & Marder, 2002; McGuffin et al., 2005).

Biological Factors

Genetic and biochemical factors as well as other neurological issues have been investigated. These biological factors are prominent in the incidence of schizophrenia (Abi-Dargham & Guillin, 2007).

Genetic predisposition

Strong evidence exists for a genetic predisposition to schizophrenia, though the specific genes involved and their roles in creating the disposition are still unknown (Hall et al., 2007; Jang, 2005; McGuffin et al., 2005). As Figure 17.28 shows, the more closely one is related to a person diagnosed with schizophrenia, the greater is the likelihood of developing the disorder during one's lifetime. Twin studies show that identical twins have higher concordance rates than fraternal twins, and adoption studies show much higher concordance with biological parents than with adoptive parents (Kety, 1988; Wahlberg et al., 1997). But, again, genetics do not by themselves account for the development of schizophrenia. If they did, the concordance rate in identical twins would be 100%, not 48%.

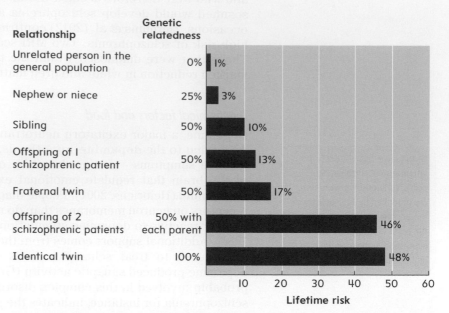

FIGURE 17.28 Genes and schizophrenia.

The degree of risk for developing schizophrenia in one's lifetime correlates highly with the degree of genetic relationship with someone who has that disorder. These data summarize the results of 40 concordance studies conducted in many countries.

Source: Based on Gottesman, 1991.

MacDonald and Shulz (2009) produced a review of the relevant literature and concluded that if one monozygotic twin was schizophrenic this increased the likelihood of the identical other twin being schizophrenic by 99%.

Brain abnormalities

Brain scans have indicated a number of structural abnormalities in the brains of schizophrenics. According to the *neurodegenerative hypothesis*, destruction of neural tissue can cause schizophrenia (Weinberger & McClure, 2002). Magnetic resonance imaging (MRI) studies have shown mild to moderate *brain atrophy*, a general loss or deterioration of neurons in the cerebral cortex and limbic system, together with enlarged ventricles (cavities that contain cerebrospinal fluid; cf. Chan, Di, McAlonan, & Gong, 2011; Figure 17.29). The atrophy is centred in brain regions that influence cognitive processes and emotion, which may help explain the thought disorders and inappropriate emotions that are seen. Likewise, MRI images of the thalamus, which collects and routes sensory input to various parts of the brain, reveal abnormalities (Williamson, 2006). This may help account for the disordered attention and perception reported by those with schizophrenia whose cerebral cortex might be getting garbled or unfiltered information from the thalamus (Andreason et al., 1994). All these structural differences are more common in those who exhibit the negative-symptom pattern (Herz & Marder, 2002). As we have seen, these people have a poorer chance of recovery than those with the positive-symptom pattern. Most recently, Job et al. (2006) have used MRI to show that the density of grey matter and how it changes over time is a useful predictor of whether someone is at risk of schizophrenia. The research, carried out in Edinburgh, looked at people with relatives with schizophrenia,

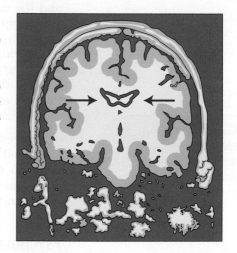

FIGURE 17.29 Schizophrenia and the brain. In the area indicated with arrows, the white butterfly shape illustrates the size of the ventricles in a normal brain, where the outer brown butterfly shape shows how this is enlarged in a schizophrenic brain.

and who were therefore deemed 'at risk'. Job and his team predicted whether the person scanned would develop schizophrenia and they were correct on an amazing 90% of occasions. Ziermans et al. (2012) confirmed this by monitoring younger people at ultra-high risk of schizophrenia. Two MRI scans were carried out, separated by two years. Those that were diagnosed within the two years (some were not of course) showed marked reduction in white and grey matter.

Biochemical factors and food

Dopamine, a major excitatory neurotransmitter, may play a key role in schizophrenia. According to the **dopamine hypothesis**, the symptoms of schizophrenia – particularly positive symptoms – are produced by over-activity of the dopamine system in areas of the brain that regulate emotional expression, motivated behaviour and cognitive functioning (Heinrichs, 2001). People diagnosed with schizophrenia have more dopamine receptors on neuron membranes than do non-schizophrenics, and these receptors seem to be over-reactive to dopamine stimulation (Black, Yates, & Andreason, 1988; Wong et al., 1986). Additional support comes from the finding that the effectiveness of antipsychotic drugs used to treat schizophrenia is positively related to their ability to reduce dopamine-produced synaptic activity (Green, 1997). Other neurotransmitter systems are probably involved in this complex disorder as well. The serotonin (5-HT) hypothesis of schizophrenia for instance, indicates the possible role of this particular neurotransmitter in schizophrenia.

Other neurotransmitter systems are probably involved in this complex disorder as well. But dopamine is not the whole story, and recent research has shown that the dopamine system is part of a much larger and complex network in which a deficiency of neural input from cortical areas also plays a role (Benes, 2010).

The biochemical and brain findings concerning schizophrenia are intriguing. What is not clear is whether they cause the disorder or are caused by it. Work from the Institute of Psychiatry's neurochemical imaging team is showing further links between schizophrenia and the dopamine system, and most recently a deficit in schizophrenics in the NDMA (N-methyl-dasparte) system using a technique called SPET – Single Photon Emission Tomography (Pilowsky et al., 2006). Future research is almost certain to reveal other biological bases for the complex disorders of schizophrenia. The relationship between food and schizophrenia is under investigation. Christensen and Christensen (1988) suggest that diet may be a factor in schizophrenia, particularly fat consumption, and Peleg et al. (2004) have shown a possible relationship between the consumption of gluten and schizophrenia.

Interestingly, the degenerative hypothesis and dopamine hypothesis have been described as one (Walker & Diforio, 1997). Increasing the quantity of dopamine can indeed result in the person developing positive symptoms. However, larger concentrations of dopamine are neurotoxic, and neurons are destroyed, which results in a degeneration of the brain, which in turn results in a reoccurrence of the original symptoms.

Psychological Factors

Freud and other psychoanalytic thinkers viewed schizophrenia as a retreat from unbearable stress and conflict. For Freud, schizophrenia represented an extreme example of the defence mechanism of **regression**, in which a person retreats to an earlier and more secure (even infantile) stage of psychosocial development in the face of overwhelming anxiety. Other psychodynamic thinkers, focusing on the interpersonal withdrawal that is an important feature of schizophrenia, view the disorder as a retreat from an interpersonal world that has become too stressful to deal with. Although Freud's regression explanation has not received much direct research support (Fisher & Greenberg, 1996), the belief that life stress is a causal factor is generally accepted today (Crook & Copolov, 2000).

Some cognitive theorists believe that people with schizophrenias have a defect in the attentional mechanism that filters out irrelevant stimuli, so that they are overwhelmed

---

dopamine hypothesis the symptoms of schizophrenia, particularly positive symptoms, are produced by over-activity of the dopamine system in areas of the brain that regulate emotional expression, motivated behaviour and cognitive functioning

Focus 17.22 Describe the evidence for genetic, neurological, and biochemical factors in schizophrenia.

regression a person retreats to an earlier and more secure (even infantile) stage of psychosocial development in the face of overwhelming anxiety

by both internal and external stimuli. Sensory input thus becomes a chaotic flood, and irrelevant thoughts and images flash into consciousness. The stimulus overload produces distractibility, thought disorganization, and the sense of being overwhelmed by disconnected thoughts and ideas. As one schizophrenic noted, 'Everything seems to come pouring in at once ... I can't seem to keep anything out' (Carson, Butcher, & Coleman, 1988, p. 329). The recent MRI findings of thalamic abnormalities described previously may help explain how this stimulus overload could occur through a malfunction of the brain's switchboard.

Focus I7.23 How do psychoanalytic and cognitive theorists explain the symptoms of schizophrenia?

Environmental Factors

Stressful life events seem to play an important role in the emergence of schizophrenic behaviour (McKenna, 2007). These events tend to cluster in the two or three weeks preceding the 'psychotic break', when the acute signs of the disorder appear (Day et al., 1987). Stressful life events seem to interact with biological or personality vulnerability factors. A highly vulnerable person may require little in the way of life stress to reach the breaking point (van Praag, 2004). In one study, psychotic and non-psychotic people rated their emotional responses as they encountered stressful events in their daily lives. Psychotic individuals reacted to their stressors with more intense negative emotions, suggesting that emotional over-reactivity may be a vulnerability factor (Myin-Germeys, van Os, Schwartz, Stone, & Delespaul, 2001). In a longitudinal study, Docherty, St-Hilaire, Aakre and Seghers (2009) tested schizophrenic patients and matched normal controls for emotional reactivity over nine months. They found that as a group, the schizophrenic patients were more emotionally reactive and that the more reactive the patients were, the more likely they were to respond to stressful life events with an increase in psychotic symptoms.

Family dynamics have long been a prime suspect in the origins of schizophrenia, but the search for parent or family characteristics that might cause the disorder has been largely unsuccessful. Significantly, children of biologically normal parents who are raised by schizophrenic adoptive parents do *not* show an increased risk of developing schizophrenia (Kety, 1988). Although persons with schizophrenia often come from families with problems, the nature and seriousness of those problems are not different from those of families in which non-schizophrenics are raised.

This does not mean that family dynamics are not important; rather, it may mean that an individual must have a biological vulnerability factor in order to be damaged by stressful family events to such a degree. Indeed, there is evidence that this vulnerability factor may appear early in life. In one study, researchers analysed home movies showing pre-schizophrenic children (those who were later to develop schizophrenic behaviours) and their non-schizophrenic brothers and sisters. Even at these early ages – sometimes as young as 2 years old – pre-schizophrenic children tended to show more odd and uncoordinated movements and less emotional expressiveness, especially for positive emotions (Grimes & Walker, 1994). These behavioural oddities may not only reflect a vulnerability factor, but they may also help to create environmental stress by evoking negative reactions from others.

Although researchers have had difficulty pinpointing family factors that contribute to the *initial* appearance of schizophrenia, one consistent finding is that previously hospitalized schizophrenics are more likely to relapse if they return to a home environment that is high in a factor called *expressed emotion* (Vaughn & Leff, 1976). **Expressed emotion** involves high levels of criticism ('All you do is sit in front of that television'), hostility ('We're getting sick and tired of your craziness'), and over-involvement ('You're not going out unless I go with you'). One review of 26 studies showed that within 9 to 12 months of their return home, an average relapse rate of 48% occurred in those whose families were high in expressed emotion, compared with a relapse rate of 21% when families were low in this factor (Kavanagh, 1992).

expressed emotion involves high levels of criticism, hostility and over-involvement

Before we conclude that high expressed emotion causes schizophrenics to relapse, however, we should note a finding from another study in which researchers videotaped actual interactions involving schizophrenics and their families (Rosenfarb, Goldstein,

Mintz, & Nuechterlein, 1995). Analyses of the videotapes revealed that families high in expressed emotion did indeed make more negative comments to schizophrenics when they engaged in strange behaviours, but they also showed that the schizophrenics in these families engaged in about four times as many strange and disruptive behaviours, clouding the issue of what causes what. Thus, high expressed emotion may be either a cause of or a response to schizophrenics' disordered behaviours. Because individuals with schizophrenia may be overly sensitive to stress, even mildly negative family reactions may trigger underlying biological vulnerabilities that could result in relapse (Hooley, 2004).

Sociocultural Factors

social causation hypothesis
attributes the higher prevalence of schizophrenia to the higher levels of stress that low-income people experience

social drift hypothesis
proposes that as people develop schizophrenia, their personal and occupational functioning deteriorates, so that they drift down the socio-economic ladder

Sociocultural factors are undoubtedly linked to schizophrenia (Murray, Jones, Susser, van Os, & Cannon, 2003). Many studies have found that the prevalence of schizophrenia is highest in lower socio-economic populations (Figure 17.30). Why is this? Is poverty a cause of schizophrenia, or is it an effect of the disorder? Two views give opposite answers. The **social causation hypothesis** attributes the higher prevalence of schizophrenia to the higher levels of stress that low-income people experience, particularly within urban environments. In contrast, the **social drift hypothesis** proposes that as people develop schizophrenia, their personal and occupational functioning deteriorates, so that they drift down the socio-economic ladder into poverty and migrate to economically depressed urban environments. Perhaps social causation and social drift are both at work, for the factors that link poverty, social and environmental stressors, and schizophrenia are undoubtedly complex.

In contrast to most of the disorders we have described so far, schizophrenia may be a culture-free disorder. A worldwide epidemiological study sponsored by the World Health Organization indicated that the prevalence of schizophrenia is not dramatically different throughout the world (Jablensky et al., 1992). However, researchers have found that the likelihood of recovery is greater in developing countries than in the developed nations of North America and Western Europe. This may reflect a stronger community orientation and greater social support extended to disturbed people in developing countries (Tanaka-Matsumi & Draguns, 1997).

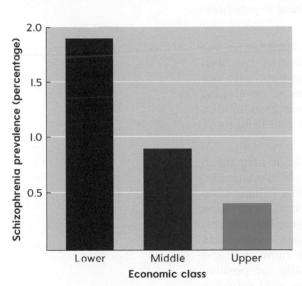

FIGURE 17.30 Social class and schizophrenia.

This graph shows the relation between economic status and prevalence of schizophrenia. Is economic status a cause or an effect of schizophrenia? Or does some other factor cause both?

Source: Based on Keith, Regier and Rae, 1991.

Richard Bentall's work offers a different perspective. Bentall has indicated that there is not, in his opinion, a 'syndrome' of schizophrenia at all. There is no evidence that it has ever in fact, been identified in the way that Kraepelin originally described it. He goes on to indicate that the new diagnostic guidance in DSM-V still does not allow an accurate diagnosis. Regier et al. (2013) agree, showing that the agreement in diagnoses between clinicians conducting diagnostic interviews with schizophrenics was very low indeed. Bentall goes on to indicate a discomfort with the biological model of schizophrenia. There has been little or no improvement in the outcome of those with schizophrenia since its 'identification' but we might have expected some improvements. Medical research in other areas has improved outcomes, but not so in schizophrenia. There is an argument that a medical approach identifies schizophrenia as a tangible, identifiable medical problem that allows society to better understand it and so not to stigmatize those with schizophrenia. However, there is evidence that the stigma is not reduced as proposed (Angermeyer, Holzinger, Carta, & Schomerus, 2011).

What is clear is that schizophrenia reflects complex interactions among biological, psychological, and environmental factors. 'Levels of analysis' presents prominent causal factors identified.

Levels of analysis
factors related to schizophrenia

BIOLOGICAL

- Clear genetic predisposition
- Degenerative brain atrophy
- Abnormalities in thalamus may produce disordered sensory input
- Overactivity of excitatory neurotransmitters, particularly dopamine
- Frontal lobe dysfunction impairs executive functions

PSYCHOLOGICAL

- Regression to early developmental stage under severe stress (psychoanalysis)
- Attentional filtering problem; overwhelmed by stimulation
- Disordered language processes that impair comprehension, communication
- Executive function deficits, resulting in poor self-management
- Deficits in emotional responding
- Thought disorder, including possible delusions

ENVIRONMENTAL

- Stressful life events typically precede breakdown
- Possible but as yet unidentified family dynamics
- Negative responses from others evoked by individual's odd behaviours
- Expressed emotion by family related to relapses
- Low socio-economic settings (may be cause or effect)
- Similar incidence across cultures, but better recovery in developing countries

Schizophrenia

 In review

- Schizophrenia is a psychotic disorder featuring disordered thinking and language; poor contact with reality; flat, blunted or inappropriate emotion; and disordered behaviour. The cognitive portion of the disorder can involve delusions (false beliefs) or hallucinations (false perceptions).

- Psychoanalytic theorists regard schizophrenia as a profound regression to a primitive stage of psychosocial development in response to unbearable stress, particularly within the family. Stressful life events do often precede a schizophrenic episode, but researchers have not been successful in identifying a family pattern related to the onset of schizophrenia. However, expressed emotion is a family variable related to relapse among formerly hospitalized schizophrenic individuals.

- There is strong evidence for a genetic predisposition to schizophrenia that makes some people particularly vulnerable to stressful life events. The dopamine hypothesis states that schizophrenia involves over-activity of the dopamine system, resulting in too much stimulation.

▶

◀

- Cognitive theorists focus on the thought disorder that is central to schizophrenia. One idea is that people with schizophrenia have a defect in their attentional filters, so that they are overwhelmed by internal and external stimuli and become disorganized. Deficiencies may also exist in the executive functions needed to organize behaviour.

- Sociocultural accounts of the higher incidence of schizophrenia at lower socio-economic levels include the social causation hypothesis, which attributes schizophrenia to the higher levels of life stress that poor people experience, and the competing social drift hypothesis, which attributes the relation to the downward drift into poverty as the disorder progresses. Schizophrenia does not appear to differ in prevalence across cultures.

PERSONALITY DISORDERS

> **personality disorders** exhibit stable, ingrained, inflexible and maladaptive ways of thinking, feeling and behaving

People diagnosed with **personality disorders** exhibit stable, ingrained, inflexible and maladaptive ways of thinking, feeling and behaving. In some situations these traits may not only be acceptable but indeed desirable. For instance, stable, ingrained and inflexible thinking might describe a solid, reliable and driven thinker. However, when those suffering with a personality disorder encounter situations in which their typical behaviour patterns do not work, they are likely to intensify their inappropriate ways of coping; their emotional controls may break down and unresolved conflicts tend to re-emerge (Lenzenweger & Clarkin, 2005; Millon, Grossman, Millon, Meagher, & Ramnath, 2004).

Personality disorders are an important part of the DSM system because they increase the likelihood of acquiring particularly anxiety, depression and substance-abuse problems. They are also associated with a poorer course of recovery from these disorders. Ann Massion et al. (2002) followed people suffering from anxiety disorders for five years and found that those also diagnosed with personality disorders were 30–40% less likely to recover from their anxiety disorders.

Table 17.3 briefly describes the 10 personality disorders in DSM-V. The disorders are divided into three clusters that capture important commonalities: dramatic and impulsive behaviours, anxious and fearful behaviours, and odd and eccentric behaviours.

Perhaps reflecting the very complicated nature of personality disorders, the diagnostic criteria associated with them is a course of debate still, and the groups responsible for the development of the current DSM-V had a very difficult job coming to a firm conclusion,

TABLE 17.3 DSM-V personality disorders and their major features

Dramatic/impulsive cluster
Antisocial personality disorder: severe irresponsible and antisocial behaviour beginning in childhood and continuing past age 18; impulsive need gratification and lack of empathy for others; often highly manipulative and seem to lack conscience
Histrionic personality disorder: excessive, dramatic emotional reactions and attention seeking; often sexually provocative; highly impressionable and suggestible; out of touch with negative feelings
Narcissistic personality disorder: grandiose fantasies or behaviour, lack of empathy, and over-sensitivity to evaluation; constant need for admiration from others; proud self-display
Borderline personality disorder: pattern of severe instability of self-image, interpersonal relationships and emotions, often expressing alternating extremes of love and hatred towards the same person; high frequency of manipulative suicidal behaviour
Anxious/fearful cluster
Avoidant personality disorder: extreme social discomfort and timidity; feelings of inadequacy and fearfulness of being negatively evaluated
Dependent personality disorder: extreme submissive and dependent behaviour; fears of separation from those who satisfy dependency needs
Obsessive-compulsive personality disorder: extreme perfectionism, orderliness and inflexibility; preoccupied with mental and interpersonal control
Odd/eccentric cluster
Schizoid personality disorder: indifference to social relationships and a restricted range of experiencing and expressing emotions
Schizotypal personality disorder: odd thoughts, appearance, and behaviour, and extreme discomfort in social situations
Paranoid personality disorder: an unwarranted tendency to interpret the behaviour of other people as threatening, exploiting or harmful

Source: based on DSM-IV-TR, American Psychiatric Association, 2000.

preferring instead to acknowledge that two models of diagnosis were worthy of inclusion. The first of these is similar to the older diagnostic route – a type of personality disorder being allocated to an individual as a function of a major trait in their behaviour, the pathological personality trait approach if you like. So if a person has a dominant personality trait, paranoia for instance, then they will be diagnosed with the appropriate personality disorder. It is this model that is included in the main manual. However, a second 'hybrid' model of diagnosis, where both personality traits and an evaluation of impairments of the person's personality functioning (how they view themselves and others) is included in an appendix as meriting further investigation and so we describe it here as relevant.

A study in Norway found a rate of 13.4%, equally distributed among men and women (Torgersen, Kringlen, & Cramer, 2001). Wittchen et al. (2011) reviewed Torgersen et al. (2001) and Coid et al. (2006) and identified the prevalence of personality disorders conservatively at 1.4% collectively in Europe – 4.3 million people.

ANTISOCIAL PERSONALITY DISORDER

In the past, individuals with antisocial personality disorder were referred to as *psychopaths* or *sociopaths;* those terms are still in use today, though not for formal diagnostic purposes, and they are probably wrong even though clinicians still use them. There is a debate as to whether antisocial personality disorder (also known as sociopathy) and psychopathy are subtly different. Many people use the diagnostic criteria laid out by Hare (1991) described later in this section, even though they disagree with the DSM. The sociopath is characterized as performing antisocial criminal acts, whereas the psychopath is characterized additionally by a lack of empathy and a degree of remorselessness. Hare adds 'thrill seeking' and 'an inability to process emotional information' to these. So, there may also be a different aetiology to the disorder to antisocial disorder (a social/biological versus neurological aetiology). Koch introduced the phrase 'psychopathic inferiority' in 1889 and such people were then sometimes referred to as 'moral imbeciles'. People with antisocial personality disorder are among the most interpersonally destructive and emotionally harmful individuals. Males outnumber females by approximately three to one in this diagnostic group. In a large study carried out in Oslo, Torgersen et al. (2001) estimate prevalence as being approximately 0.7% in the general population.

It is true to say, that people with **antisocial personality disorder** exhibit a lack of emotional attachment to other people. A lack of capacity to care about others can make antisocial individuals a danger to society (Black, 1999). Although antisocial individuals often verbalize feelings and commitments with great sincerity, their behaviours indicate otherwise. They often appear very intelligent and charming, and they have the ability to rationalize their inappropriate behaviour so that it appears reasonable and justifiable. Consequently, they are often virtuosos at manipulating others and talking their way out of trouble.

The characteristics we have discussed can be reflected in psychological test responses as well as in social behaviour. Figure 17.31 shows the Minnesota Multiphasic Personality Inventory (MMPI) profile of notorious serial killer Jeffrey Dahmer. You may not be very familiar with his name, as his terrible crimes were committed in the USA between 1989 and 1991, although other crimes were committed earlier, but his psychology is of relevance here, and the data are interesting. In summary, over the 1989–91 period, he killed and dismembered at least 17 male victims. He slept with the dead bodies, engaged in sex acts with them, stored body parts in jars and cannibalized many of them. He was convicted of the serial murders and sentenced to 1,070 years in prison.

According to Caldwell (1994), several aspects of this MMPI profile help explain Dahmer's bizarre and destructive behaviour. The extraordinarily high score on the psychopathic deviate scale reflects an extreme antisocial impulsiveness coupled with a total lack of capacity for compassion and empathy. His victims were in all likelihood regarded as little more than

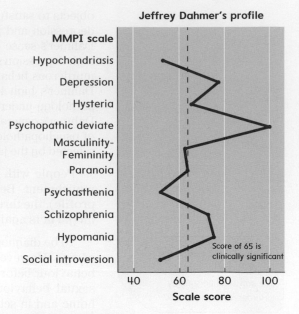

FIGURE 17.31 A serial killer's MMPI.

The Minnesota Multiphasic Personality Inventory (MMPI) profile of serial killer Jeffrey Dahmer reveals severe antisocial tendencies. Scores beyond the dotted line are assumed to reflect pathological tendencies. Dahmer's extraordinarily elevated score on the psychopathic deviate scale reflects a callous disregard for other people and is consistent with his pattern of unrestrained and vicious victimization of others.

Source: based on Caldwell, 1994.

> **antisocial personality disorder** a lack of emotional attachment to other people

objects to satisfy his perverse needs. Caldwell viewed the marked discrepancy between the depression and psychasthenia (anxiety) scales – rarely seen on the MMPI – as reflecting Dahmer's sense of being fated or doomed to repeat his acts until he would be caught (the high depression score), together with an absence of fear that, in normal people, might inhibit murderous behaviour (the low psychasthenia score). Although the profile clearly indicates Dahmer's high level of psychological disturbance, it also reflects an ability to mask his pathology under the normal façade that for years fooled law enforcement officials. Indeed, Dahmer's general demeanour looked so normal that despite the horror of his acts and the level of psychopathology shown in his test results, his plea of not guilty by reason of insanity was rejected by the jury. Instead, he went to prison, where he was murdered by another inmate.

People with antisocial personalities also display a perplexing failure to respond to punishment. Because of their lack of anxiety (seen, for example, in Dahmer's MMPI profile), the threat of punishment does not deter them from engaging in self-defeating or illegal acts again and again. As a result, some of them develop imposing prison records.

To be diagnosed with antisocial personality disorder, a person must be at least 18 years of age. However, the diagnostic criteria also require substantial evidence of antisocial behaviour before the age of 15, including such acts as habitual lying, early and aggressive sexual behaviour, excessive drinking, theft, vandalism and chronic rule violations at home and in school. Thus antisocial personality disorder is the culmination of a deviant behaviour pattern that typically begins in childhood (Kernberg, 2000).

Robert Hare (1991), has identified a number of traits in the psychopath, and has developed the Psychopath Check List (revised) (PCL-R). The PCL-R comes in two parts, an interview, where a clinician uses a 'semi-structured' style to identify ratings on a number of levels, and a review of the person's records and history. The traits that the PCL-R assesses are as follows:

Focus 17.24 Describe the major characteristics of the antisocial personality disorder.

- glib (slick talker) and superficial charm
- grandiose (exaggeratedly high) estimation of self
- need for stimulation
- pathological lying
- cunning and manipulativeness
- lack of remorse or guilt
- shallow affect (superficial emotional responsiveness)
- callousness and lack of empathy
- parasitic lifestyle
- poor behavioural controls
- sexual promiscuity
- early behaviour problems
- lack of realistic long-term goals
- impulsivity
- irresponsibility
- failure to accept responsibility for own actions
- many short-term marital relationships
- juvenile delinquency
- revocation of conditional release
- criminal versatility.

The practitioner gives each of the 20 traits a score out of two. The fully psychopathic individual would, then, score 40.

Causal Factors

Biological factor

Biological research on antisocial personality disorder has focused on both genetic and physiological factors. Evidence for a genetic predisposition is shown in consistently higher rates of concordance for antisocial behaviour among identical twins than among fraternal

twins (Rutter, 1997). Heritability is between .40 and .50 for antisocial behaviour in children, adolescents and adults (Bouchard, 2004). Adoption studies suggest a similar conclusion. When researchers compared the criminal records of men who had been adopted early in life with those of their biological fathers and their adoptive fathers, they found that the criminality rate was nearly twice as high if the biological father had a criminal record and the adoptive father did not, clearly suggesting the operation of genetic factors (Cloninger & Gottesman, 1989).

How might genetic factors predispose individuals to engage in antisocial behaviour? One clue might lie in the relative absence of anxiety and guilt that seems to characterize antisocial personality disorder. Many researchers have suggested that the physiological basis for the disorder might be some dysfunction in brain structures that govern emotional arousal and behavioural self-control (Blair, 2005; Raine, 2008). This results in behavioural impulsiveness and a chronically under-aroused state that impairs avoidance learning, causes boredom and encourages a search for excitement (Arnett, 1997; Ishikawa, Raine, Lencz, Bihrle, & Lacasse, 2001). In support of a physiological basis, both children and adults with antisocial behaviour patterns have lower heart rates, particularly when under stress (Ortiz & Raine, 2004). Magnetic resonance imaging also reveals that antisocial individuals have subtle neurological deficits in the prefrontal lobes – the seat of executive functions such as planning, reasoning and behavioural inhibition; these neurological deficits are associated with reduced autonomic activity (Raine et al., 2000). It thus appears, as long suspected, that severely antisocial individuals may indeed be wired differently at a neurological level, responding with less arousal and greater impulsiveness to both pleasurable and unpleasant stimuli (Verona, Patrick, Curtin, Bradley, & Lang, 2004). Damasio (2000) urges caution in reading too much into these data on neurological differences between those with antisocial personality disorder (APD) and other groups. Raine et al.'s (2000) research on brain volume does indeed show a difference of approximately 11% between the frontal lobes of those with APD and others. However, we should not conclude that this deficit causes the APD. The relationship between the lower capacity of the frontal lobes can be understood only when we take other factors, namely the interaction of the frontal lobes and other areas of the brain, into consideration.

Psychological and environmental factors

Psychodynamic theorists regard antisocial personalities as people without a conscience and who lack anxiety and guilt because they did not develop an adequate superego (Gabbard, 1990). In the absence of a well-developed superego, the restraints on the id are reduced, resulting in impulsive and hedonistic behaviour. The failure to develop a strong superego is thought to result from inadequate identification with appropriate adult figures because these figures were either physically or psychologically unavailable to the child (Kernberg, 2000). In support of this position, the absence of the father from the home is related to a higher incidence of antisocial symptoms in children, even when socio-economic status is equated (Pfiffner, McBurnett, & Rathouz, 2001).

Cognitive theorists believe that an important feature in antisocial individuals is their consistent failure to think about or anticipate the long-term negative consequences of their acts. As a result, they behave impulsively, thinking only of what they want at that moment (Bandura, 1997). From this perspective, a key to preventing these individuals from getting into trouble is to help them develop the cognitive controls (i.e., the executive functions) needed to think before acting.

Learning through modelling may also play an important role. Many antisocial individuals come from homes where parents exhibit a good deal of aggression and are inattentive to their children's needs (Rutter, 1997). Such parents provide role models for both aggressive behaviour and disregard for the needs of others. Another important environmental factor is exposure to deviant peers. Children who become antisocial often learn some of their deviant behaviours from peer groups that both model antisocial behaviour and reinforce it with social approval (Bandura, 1997). It is easy to see how such environmental factors, combined with a possible genetic predisposition for antisocial behaviour, would encourage the development of deviant behaviour patterns (van Goozen, Snoek, Fairchild, & Harold, 2007).

Like some biological theories, learning explanations suggest that persons with antisocial personality disorder lack impulse control. Learning theorists believe that poor impulse control occurs in these individuals because of an impaired ability to develop conditioned

Focus 17.25 How do biological, psychoanalytic and behavioural theorists account for antisocial personality disorder?

fear responses when punished, which would correspond with the lower physiological arousal and amygdala activity identified with brain recordings (Raine, 2008). This results in a deficit in avoidance learning. Hans Eysenck (1964) maintained that developing a conscience depends on the ability to learn fear and inhibitory avoidance responses, and people who fail to do so will be less able to inhibit their behaviour.

In accord with this hypothesis, Raine, Venables and Williams (1996) completed a 14-year follow-up of males who had been subjected at age 15 to a classical conditioning procedure in which a soft tone was used as the CS and a loud, aversive tone as the UCS. Conditioned fear was measured by the participant's skin conductance response when the CS occurred after a number of pairings with the loud UCS. The researchers found that men who accumulated a criminal record by age 29 had shown much poorer fear conditioning at age 15 than had those with no criminal record.

Experimental Psychopathology

Researchers often bring clinical populations into the laboratory to study processes assumed to underlie a particular disorder, under controlled conditions using state-of-the-art science techniques from other areas of psychology, such as cognitive psychology, social psychology and behavioural neuroscience. This kind of research helps identify the mechanisms that contribute to behaviour disorders and allows researchers to test hypotheses derived from existing theories of psychopathology and, sometimes, to directly pit competing theories against one another. In this manner, clinical observation informs science, and science helps inform clinical understanding and, it is hoped, the treatment of behaviour disorders.

A good example of this comes from Schachter and Latané (1964) who looked at the effect punishment has on the destructive behaviour of those with antisocial personality disorder.

Focus 17.26 How does the Schachter-Latané study (below) support the arousal-deficit theory of antisocial personality disorder?

Research close-up

FEAR, AVOIDANCE LEARNING AND PSYCHOPATHY

Source: S. Schachter and B. Latané (1964). Crime, cognition, and the autonomic nervous system, in D. Levine (ed.), *Nebraska Symposium on Motivation - 1964*. Lincoln, NE: University of Nebraska Press.

INTRODUCTION

In antisocial personality disorder, punishment seems to have little effect on future destructive behaviour. As we have seen, one explanation for this is a deficit in fear arousal, which serves to inhibit antisocial behaviour in normal people (Blair, 2005). This lack of fear arousal contributes to poor avoidance learning, so that such people get into trouble repeatedly.

What would happen if it were possible to make people with antisocial personality disorder more physiologically reactive, or fearful? Would their avoidance-learning deficit disappear? Stanley Schachter and Bibb Latané set out to answer this important question.

METHOD

Schachter and Latané selected two groups of inmates at state prisons on the basis of psychologists' diagnoses and life-history data. One group consisted of 'psychopaths'. These prisoners were described by prison psychologists as being free from any symptoms of anxiety, lacking a sense of responsibility or shame, being habitual liars and manipulators, able to commit antisocial acts without guilt or remorse, lacking insight and unable to profit from negative experiences. Most, if not all, of these prisoners would meet current diagnostic criteria for antisocial personality disorder. A normal (non-'psychotic') group consisted of prisoners matched in age and intelligence who did not exhibit this behavioural pattern. Life-history data showed that the psychopaths had been arrested more often (8.3 versus 3.3 arrests) and had spent more of their adult lives in prison (36.2% versus 18.1%).

The two groups of prisoners were recruited as paid participants in an investigation of 'a newly developed hormone thought to enhance learning'. The researchers used an experimental apparatus that required participants to learn a complicated mental maze. It consisted of a metal cabinet on which was mounted a counter, two pilot lights and four switches. The maze consisted of 20 choice points. At each choice point, the participant selected one of the four switches. If it was the correct one, a green light flashed and the learner advanced to the next choice point. If one of the three incorrect switches was selected, a red light flashed and an error was recorded on the counter visible to the participant. When the twentieth choice point was reached, the procedure began again from the start. The learner repeated the maze 21 times, the objective being to learn the correct response at each choice point so as to minimize the total number of errors.

▶

To study avoidance learning, one of the three incorrect switches at each choice point not only activated the red light and recorded an error, but it also resulted in a moderately painful electric shock to the learner. Thus the learner would do well to learn not only the correct switch at each point but also to avoid the one that delivered a shock (i.e., to do good *and* avoid evil).

To manipulate emotional arousal, the prisoners were given an injection of the 'experimental hormone, Suproxin', being tested to see if it enhanced learning ability. They were told that this hormone would have no side effects. The injection was used to manipulate autonomic arousal. It contained either adrenalin, which would increase arousal, or a placebo, which would not. Each participant worked until he learned two different mental mazes, one while under the influence of adrenalin and the other while under the placebo. Half received adrenalin on the first maze and then received the placebo for the second maze; the other half received injections in the reverse order.

RESULTS

The two groups of prisoners did not differ in their overall learning of the two mazes; they made similar numbers of correct responses and errors. Thus the psychopaths did not differ in their ability to learn the positively reinforced 'correct' responses. Of major interest, then, was the avoidance-learning measure, that is, the ability to learn to avoid choosing the switch at each choice point that would result in electric shock. The dependent variable here was the percentage of incorrect responses made by each participant that resulted in electric shock. The lower the percentage of shocked incorrect responses, the better the avoidance learning over trials through each maze.

Figure 17.32a shows avoidance learning under the placebo condition, in which the psychopathic and normal prisoners experienced their normal levels of arousal. As you can see, the normal prisoners made a lower percentage of shocked responses during their later trips through the maze, indicating avoidance learning. In contrast, the psychopaths showed almost no evidence of learning. On their later trials through the maze, they were still as likely to select the shocked switch as they were in their early trials.

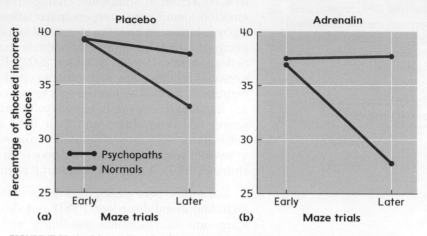

FIGURE 17.32 **Avoidance learning in psychopathic and non-psychopathic prisoners.**
The avoidance ratio is the percentage of errors in which the incorrect choice resulted in electric shock. Performance is shown on early and later trials on each mental maze. Under placebo conditions (a), normal prisoners showed avoidance learning but psychopaths did not. However, increasing arousal with an adrenalin injection (b) resulted in successful avoidance learning in the psychopaths.

If lack of fear underlies the psychopaths' lack of conditioning, what would happen if one artificially increased their level of arousal? In Figure 17.32b, we see the effect of doing so. When injected with adrenalin, the psychopaths showed dramatic evidence of avoidance learning. Indeed, they actually performed better than the normal prisoners, whose performance on this complex task may have been somewhat impaired by increasing their already-existing fear responses.

CRITICAL DISCUSSION

This study, done nearly a half-century ago, is still considered a classic. Schachter and Latané cleverly tested a clinical explanation for a behaviour disorder under controlled laboratory conditions. They not only demonstrated the avoidance-learning deficit presumed to underlie antisocial behaviour, but they also showed that this deficit could be reversed if it were possible to experimentally create the physiological arousal that psychopaths lack. Indeed, the increase in arousal produced by the adrenalin injection had an especially notable effect on the psychopaths, who learned to avoid even better than the normal prisoners did in the placebo condition. This may be because the psychopaths' arousal in this fear-inducing situation was so different from their normal experience.

It is important to rule out other possible explanations for the results. For example, what if the pain experiences of the prisoner groups were affected differently by the injections, thereby affecting motivation to avoid the shock? The researchers were able to rule this out by showing that the two groups of prisoners rated the pain as equally unpleasant under both injection conditions. Therefore, the psychopathic and normal prisoners apparently experienced equal pain when shocked. As in this case, it is important to anticipate factors that could affect results and make sure that they are measured.

This study exemplifies a research area known as *experimental psychopathology*. Researchers bring clinical populations into the laboratory to study processes assumed to underlie a particular disorder under controlled conditions, using state-of-the-art science techniques from other areas of psychology, such as cognitive psychology, social psychology and behavioural neuroscience. This kind of research helps identify the mechanisms that contribute to behaviour disorders. It also allows researchers to test hypotheses derived from existing theories of psychopathology and, sometimes, to directly pit competing theories against one another. In this manner, clinical observation informs science, and science helps inform clinical understanding and, it is hoped, the treatment of behaviour disorders.

BORDERLINE PERSONALITY DISORDER

The borderline personality disorder has become the focus of intense interest among clinical researchers because of its chaotic effects on those who suffer from the disorder, their families and their therapists. The prevalence is disputed in the literature. The disorder may occur in 3–5% of the general population (Clarkin, Marziali, & Munroe-Blum, 1992; Selby & Joiner, 2009), but Torgersen et al. (2001) have it nearer to 0.7% in their sample, and this is the prevalence reported by Wittchen et al. (2011). About two-thirds of those diagnosed are women.

Before 1980 the term *borderline* referred to an intermediate level of disturbance between neurotic and psychotic. Now, however, **borderline personality disorder (BPD)** refers to a collection of symptoms characterized primarily by serious instability in behaviour, emotion, identity and interpersonal relationships. A central feature of borderline is *emotional dysregulation*, an inability to control negative emotions in response to stressful life events, many of which borderline individuals themselves cause (Linehan & Dexter-Mazza, 2008; Selby, Anestis, Bender, & Joiner, 2009). Borderline individuals have intense and unstable personal relationships and experience chronic feelings of extreme anger, loneliness and emptiness, as well as momentary losses of personal identity (Kuo & Linehan, 2009). They are inclined to engage in impulsive behaviour such as running away, promiscuity, binge eating and drug abuse, and their lives are often marked by repetitive self-destructive behaviours, such as self-mutilation and suicide attempts that seem designed to call forth a 'saving' response from other people in their lives (McMurran, Duggan, Christopher, & Huband, 2007). It is safe to say that it is an extremely complex disorder.

Borderline personality disorder is highly associated with a number of other disorders, including mood disorders, PTSD and substance-related disorders. In one study, the BPD symptoms of emotional instability and impulsivity predicted recurrent problems in academic achievement and social relationships two years later (Bagge, Nickell, Stepp, Durrett, Jackson, & Trull, 2004). One intensive study of 57 people diagnosed with BPD revealed a total of 42 suicide threats, 40 drug overdoses, 36 instances of self-mutilation and cutting, 38 episodes of drug abuse, 36 instances of promiscuity with near-strangers, and 14 accidents, mainly caused by reckless driving (Linehan, 1993).

The chaos that marks the lives of those with borderline personality disorder extends to their relationships with their psychotherapists. They are considered to be among the most difficult clients to treat because of their clinging dependency, their irrational anger and their tendency to engage in manipulative suicide threats and gestures as efforts to control the therapist (Linehan, 1993). Many borderline individuals, perhaps 6–9%, eventually do kill themselves, either by miscalculation or by design (Davis, Gunderson, & Myers, 1999; Pompili et al., 2009).

Causal Factors

Borderline clients tend to have chaotic personal histories marked by interpersonal strife, abuse and inconsistent parenting. This history is sometimes reflected in their earliest memories. In one study, borderline and normal participants were asked to describe their earliest memories in life. When the researchers analysed the content of the memory reports, they found that the borderlines reported six times more events in which someone had treated them in a malevolent manner or had injured them emotionally or physically. Borderline individuals also viewed potential helpers as far less helpful to them (Nigg et al., 1992). Parents of many borderline individuals are described as abusive, rejecting and non-affirming, and some theorists suggest that an early lack of acceptance by parents may cripple self-esteem and lead to clinging dependency and an inability to cope with separation (Cardasis, Hochman, & Silk, 1997). As they mature, the behaviours of borderlines tend to evoke negative reactions and rejection from others, affirming their sense of worthlessness and their view of the world as malevolent.

Psychoanalyst Otto Kernberg has focused on the dramatic changes that borderlines exhibit in their relationships with others (Kernberg & Caligor, 2005). Their sudden and vitriolic shifts from extreme love and clinging dependence to intense hatred or feelings of abandonment reflect a cognitive process that he calls **splitting**, the failure to integrate positive and negative aspects of another's behaviour (for example, a parent who is

borderline personality disorder (BPD) a collection of symptoms characterized primarily by serious instability in behaviour, emotion, identity and interpersonal relationships

splitting the failure to integrate positive and negative aspects of another's behaviour

FIGURE 17.33 Susanna Kaysen was committed to hospital in 1967 for two years, following a single visit to a psychiatrist. Her book of her experience of BPD was made into a film starring Wynona Ryder and Angelina Jolie in 1999.

Source: © AF archive/Alamy

usually accepting but sometimes voices disapproval) into a coherent whole. As a result, the borderline may react as if the other person has two separate identities, one deserving of love and the other of hatred. Whichever of these seemingly independent images the borderline individual is reacting to at the moment totally determines how she or he relates or feels. Together with severe problems in emotional control, splitting makes for chaotic and unpredictable relationships. The story of one such woman, Susanna Kaysen, (Kaysen, 1996) was made into the film *Girl Interrupted* in 2008 (Figure 17.33).

Biological factors also seem to be at work (Depue & Lenzenweger, 2005). Close relatives of those with BPD are five times more likely than those in the general population to also have the disorder (Torgersen, 2000). The emotional explosiveness and impulsivity of borderlines may also reflect some biological abnormality in neurotransmitter systems or areas of the brain that contribute to emotional self-regulation (Gurvitz, Koenigsberg, & Siever, 2000). It seems entirely possible that BPD reflects an interaction between biological factors and an early history of trauma, rejection and psychological if not physical abandonment. Finally, sociocultural factors may also contribute. Cases of BPD seem to increase in societies that are unstable and rapidly changing, leaving some of its members with a sense of emptiness, problems of identity and fears of abandonment (Paris, 1993). The complex interplay between all the factors that affect BPD, influences how well a person may show recovery from the problem (Zanarini, Frankenburg, Reich, & Fitzmaurice, 2010).

> **Focus 17.27** Describe the major features of BPD and the hypothesized causes of the disorder.

 In review

- Personality disorders are rigid, maladaptive patterns of behaviour that persist over a long time.
- Antisocial personality disorder is the most studied of the Axis II disorders. It is characterized by an egocentric and manipulative tendency towards immediate self-gratification, a lack of empathy for others, a tendency to act impulsively and a failure to profit from punishment.
- Research on antisocial personality disorder suggests that genetic and physiological factors that result in under-arousal may contribute to the disorder's causes. Psychoanalysts view the disorder as a failure to develop the superego, which might otherwise restrain the individual's impulsive self-gratification.
- Learning explanations focus on the failure of punishment to inhibit maladaptive behaviours and exposure to aggressive, uncaring models.
- Borderline personality disorder is characterized by serious instability in behaviour, emotions, interpersonal relationships, and personal identity, as well as impulsive and self-destructive behaviours.
- It appears that the majority of people with psychological disorders are not a danger to others. Research is identifying the subgroups that are more dangerous, and substance abuse is an important risk factor.

CHILDHOOD DISORDERS

Psychological disorders can occur at any point in the lifespan. Mental health professionals have observed symptoms resembling clinical depression in pre-school infants, and older children exhibit a wide range of problem behaviours (Luby, 2010). In one study of several thousand children between the ages of 2 and 5, researchers diagnosed over 20% of the children with a disorder and considered half of these to be significantly impaired by their symptoms (Lavigne, Gibbons, Christoffel, & Arend, 1996). Similar levels of incidence and impairment exist in children between the ages of 9 and 17 (Satcher, 1999).

Other studies show that only about 40% of children with psychological disorders receive professional attention, and only half of this group is seen by qualified mental health professionals, whereas significantly more children with physical handicaps receive professional help (Satcher, 1999). Failure to treat childhood behaviour disorders not only results in needless distress for children and families, but such disorders tend to continue into adulthood as psychological problems. In one study four in five adults with diagnosed DSM disorders had histories of childhood or adolescent problems that also met DSM criteria (Newman, Moffit, Caspi, Magdol, Silva, & Stanton, 1996). Kim-Cohen, Caspi,

Moffitt, Harrington, Milne, & Poulton (2003) say that among adults diagnosed with a mental disorder 73.9% had a diagnosis before they were 18 and 50.5% had a diagnosis before they were 15 years old.

Although many childhood disorders are the subject of current research, two are receiving particular attention. *Attention deficit / hyperactivity disorder* is of interest because it is the most frequently diagnosed childhood disorder. *Autism* is being scrutinized because it is becoming more common, either because it really is becoming more common or because we are getting very much better at finding it when it occurs.

ATTENTION DEFICIT/HYPERACTIVITY DISORDER

In **attention deficit/hyperactivity disorder (ADHD)**, problems take the form of inattention, hyperactivity/impulsivity, or a combination of the two. Polanczyk, Silva de Lima, Lessa Horta, Biederman and Rohde (2007) carried out an extensive meta-analysis of studies to determine the worldwide incidence of ADHD and identified a figure of approximately 5.29% that was not determined by geographical location. This makes ADHD the most common childhood disorder. Faraone, Sergeant, Gillberg and Biederman (2003) suggest that the diagnosis may depend on the criteria used, with those provided by the DSM, used almost exclusively in the USA, providing the highest number of diagnoses. Estimates of prevalence do differ, but in review Wittchen et al. (2011) puts the best estimate at approximately 5%, calculating that 3.3 million young people – 70% of them male – between the ages of 6 and 17 have the problem. The diagnostic criteria for the new DSM-V have extended the age when symptoms become present from 7 years to 12 years, which will serve to increase the number of diagnoses of ADHD still further in the coming years. They chose to do this because research found no clinical differences between 12 year olds and 7 year olds, and as such the age 7 as a cut off for the initial symptoms to appear was misleading and could lead to mis- and under diagnoses.

> **attention deficit/hyperactivity disorder (ADHD)** problems take the form of inattention, hyperactivity/impulsivity, or a combination of the two

Boys are more likely to exhibit aggressive and impulsive behaviours, whereas girls are more likely to be primarily inattentive. Some professionals believe that the ADHD diagnosis is applied too liberally, since normal children also exhibit the behaviours in question. They worry that some children may be inappropriately labelled and medicated (Colley, 2010).

It may be tempting to assume that children routinely outgrow ADHD, but follow-up studies of individuals diagnosed with the disorder suggest that for many the problems persist into adolescence (Gudjonsson, Sigurdsson, Gudmundsdottir, & Sigurjonsdottir, 2010) and for girls with the disorder the majority continue to experience symptoms in adulthood (Carpenko, Owens, Evangelista, & Doss, 2009). Overall, adults with ADHD have more occupational, family, emotional and interpersonal problems.

Despite many years of research, the precise causes of ADHD are unknown. Genetic factors are probably involved, as concordance rates are higher in identical than fraternal twins. In adoption studies of ADHD children, the children's biological parents are more likely to have ADHD than the adoptive parents (Smalley et al., 2000). Experts have long suspected that the disorder has a biological basis, but EEG studies of electrical brain activity and imaging studies of brain structures and neurotransmitters have failed to reveal consistent differences between people with ADHD and control groups (Green, 1999). This may be due to the fact that ADHD is a multifaceted disorder with several subcategories of biological patterns. Environmental factors, such as inconsistent parenting, are also involved, perhaps in complex combinations with biological factors.

There is a contention that the disorder does not exist at all. Wright (2005) regards ADHD as a 'fad' diagnosis that is currently popular and in fashion but one that will eventually fall from favour. He suggests that these 'diagnoses' are guilty of elevating symptoms to descriptions of symptoms into disorders, and once so described, these result in often serious over-diagnoses and medication. Either way, the diagnosis is there, and is being used. It is useful for the reader to be aware that even though the current status quo is of the mind that a problem is real, and merits treating, there are alternative views that might be considered.

Current topic

THE DRUGS DON'T WORK – OR DO THEY?

The very widespread use of drugs such as Ritalin for ADHD, and Prozac for depression has left some people, particularly science commentators, with a bad taste in their mouths. Ritalin prescriptions in the United Kingdom alone rose by over 400% between 1999 and 2010, and Prozac was prescribed 169 million times in 2009 in the USA. Take a break from your reading and turn to your favourite search engine and you'll see what I mean. Well-established newspapers are carrying passionate opinion pieces about how terrible it is that millions of children are abused with Ritalin. Keep searching and you will find commentary about how Prozac became an everyday word in the 1990s and is now, some would have us believe, handed out like sweeties the minute we show even the slightest signs of being a little grumpy. What we see here, as in other aspects of the press, are expressions of opinion that exist widely in society, and so we are seeing an emotive and passionate reflection of an ongoing debate. It can be summed up simply enough – if something seems to be wrong we should treat it with a pill. Of course in reality the details of such an emotive debate are reliably more complicated than that.

Take antidepressants for the moment. The first thing to make absolutely clear is that depression is not simply 'felling a little grumpy' or 'blue' or 'under the weather'. It is for very many people a serious problem that significantly influences their quality of life and ability to lead a 'normal' existence. One driver of the 'less drugs' side of the debate is that the clinical evidence that the drugs actually work is not terribly clear (Fournier et al., 2010). What is clear is that some people (usually those with more severe depression) do seem to respond to the drugs, some respond a little and some do not respond at all. In a clinical trial it is possible that an average response will be small or minimal because of these individual differences, so we must take these individual responses into consideration. We must also note the very powerful possibility of a placebo effect. The debate, then, depends entirely on your point of view. Many people with depression have tried everything – healthier eating, exercise, re-setting work-life balance, giving up smoking, joining clubs, cutting down on alcohol and just nothing seems to work. For them, the drugs may well be the last resort and I for one hope with all fingers crossed that they can help. The drugs can allow them some clarity to work through whatever problems they may have, possibly with a counsellor, and so a short medical intervention may be all that is required. The other side of the debate is a song of discomfort with a society that is so quick as it sees it, to turn to a 'simple' medical solution. The drugs are costly, the clinical evidence is unclear and people just get better anyway, some of them just don't respond at all, so surely we need to forget about them and move on.

The debate surrounding the medical treatment of ADHD is slightly different. There is no doubt that the psychostimulant methylphenidate hydrochloride (Ritalin) is certainly an active substance. In this case we have to weigh up the pros and cons of the prescription. Some feel that the behavioural problems for which it is prescribed should be better dealt with using other behaviour control and modification techniques. Consider for a moment who the prescription may be for. Clearly, the drug is taken by children, but the benefit is felt throughout the classroom and wider life situations: by other children who are no longer disturbed in their studies by the hyperactive child; by the teacher who can now focus on teaching rather than controlling and managing the child; by the siblings of the child who gain more attention from their parents now that they can direct their time in a more balanced way between their children; and the parents themselves, who being less exhausted, frustrated, scared of having a badly behaved child, are now able to begin to construct the family life of which they may always have dreamt. The medicated child is able to focus in class, perform better academically, and develop in terms of education and socially in ways we would all hope. However, they may not sleep so well after taking the stimulant for some time and may need other medication for that, the side effects of which may be depression which can, of course be further medicated. Here we see the debate opening up. Children do not get a choice whether to take drugs or not, they are made to by parents and guardians who hope that the drug will allow them access to everything other children have, including the opportunities offered by education, and a rich home and social life. So, should we really drug children whose behaviour, some would say, we simply should manage differently? Who are the drugs really for anyway, the children who take them or the rest of society who benefit from having a calmer child among them?

AUTISM SPECTRUM DISORDER (ASD)

One of the most mysterious and perplexing of all disorders is autism spectrum disorder. It is called a spectrum disorder because it encompassed four different disorders identified in the previous DSM. These include Asperger's disorder, childhood degenerative disorder, pervasive developmental disorder and autism itself.

First identified by the American psychiatrist Leo Kanner in 1943, autism spectrum disorder is a long-term disorder characterized by extreme unresponsiveness to others, poor communication skills, and highly repetitive and rigid behaviour patterns. Autism affects about 62 in 10,000 children, about 80% of them boys (Elsabbagh et al., 2012), although there is evidence that girls are underdiagnosed and as such the percentage of boys to girls may in reality be lower (Gould & Ashton-Smith, 2011). Typically appearing in the first three years of life in the form of unresponsiveness and lack of interest in others, autism tends to be a lifelong disorder. Approximately 70% remain severely disabled into adulthood and cannot lead independent lives. It is estimated that 1 in 150 adults will be affected by ASD (Barthélémy, Fuentes, Howlin, & Van der Gaag, 2009), although relatively little is known about how ASD affects older people as the majority of research is carried out with younger people, although work does show that the prevalence, of approximately 1 in 150 people, is constant across ages. More than two-thirds are mentally significantly

> autism spectrum disorder a long-term disorder characterized by extreme unresponsiveness to others, poor communication skills, and highly repetitive and rigid behaviour patterns

below average, having IQs below 70 and frequently below 35. The rest have normal to above-average intelligence. But even the highest functioning adults with autism have problems in communication, restricted interests and activities, and difficulty relating to others (Hillman, Snyder, & Neubrander, 2007).

Simon Baron-Cohen's research in Cambridge is part of the forefront of research in the area and his autism research is a rich and dynamic resource for this fascinating and often perplexing issue. Baron-Cohen has been instrumental in identifying issues and patterns in autism, and developing tests and methods of identifying and measuring it in children. In 1992, Baron-Cohen, Allen and Gillberg published CHAT (the Checklist for Autism in Toddlers) that provides practitioners with a method of identifying autism in young children. The checklist is a series of questions, and observation guidelines used by a family doctor at the 18-month check-up. Parents are asked a number of things, including 'Does your child enjoy playing peek-a-boo/hide and seek?' and 'Does your child ever pretend, for example, to make a cup of tea using a toy cup and teapot, or pretend other things?' Doctors note down whether the child made eye contact during the session, or if they could be encouraged to point to items around them using their index finger (declarative pointing). The completed checklist gives the doctor a guide as to whether further investigation is warranted.

Lack of social responsiveness to others is a central feature of autism. Autistic infants typically do not reach out to or even make eye contact with their parents. They seem not to recognize or care who is around them. Autistic children do not engage in normal play with either adults or peers. They do not include others in their play and often do not even acknowledge their presence.

Language and communication difficulties are also common, with half of autistic people not developing language. The language that does develop is often strange, involving repetition of words or phrases with little recognition of meaning. Many engage in *echolalia*, the exact echoing of phrases spoken by others.

Sameness and routine are very important, and autistic children become extremely upset at even minute changes. The movement of a piece of furniture even slightly or the change of one word in a song may evoke a tantrum. Some theorists believe that sameness is an attempt to avoid over-stimulation, but nobody knows for sure.

FIGURE 17.34 People with autism often engage in odd and repetitive stereotyped behaviours.

For example, an autistic child may manipulate an object for hours at a time, showing no interest in playing with other children or relating to adults.

Source: Reprinted with permission of Nancy Price

Autistic individuals have repetitive and stereotyped behaviour patterns and interests (Figure 17.34). They may spend their time spinning objects, playing with objects like jar tops, flicking their fingers, or rocking their bodies. Some engage in self-injurious behaviours, such as banging their heads against sharp objects or biting chunks of flesh out of their bodies, and these children may have to be physically restrained.

Some autistic people, such as the man portrayed by Dustin Hoffman in *Rain Man*, exhibit extraordinary *savant* (from the French word for 'wise', or 'learned') abilities. A common savant skill is calendar calculation. An autistic person with this ability could tell you in an instant what day of the week your birthday will fall on in 2039. Others can perfectly reproduce any song or commercial after hearing it once. Sometimes, these skills give the impression of superior intelligence, even in people who have learning difficulties. The savant is rather rare though, and only one in 10 autistics exhibit these abilities, so one should be careful not to stereotype autism in this way. Nevertheless, they do exist, and their abilities are often outstanding and beyond belief.

Causal Factors

Leo Kanner (1943), who first described childhood autism, offered a psychodynamic explanation. He speculated that these children had been driven into their own worlds by a cold and ungiving family environment during infancy. Parents (particularly the mother) were described as 'refrigerator parents' who had thawed out just long enough to conceive a child. These were purely theoretical statements, and no evidence for such a family pattern has ever existed, but generations of parents who were exposed to this hypothesis suffered the agony of thinking they had caused their child's autistic disorder.

Today, it is widely accepted that autism has a biological basis (Kabot, Masi, & Segal, 2003; Stokstad, 2001; Sudhof, 2008; Van Spronsen & Hoogenraad, 2010). What that might be remains undetermined, however. Widespread anomalies in the structures and functioning of the brain have been found in autistic children. For example, brain-imaging studies show that the brains of autistic children are larger than average, reflecting abnormal brain growth during the first year of life, and they also reveal abnormal development in the cerebellum, which coordinates movement and is involved in shifting attention (Courchesne, Carper, & Aksboomoff, 2003).

Genetic factors have been linked to autism. Siblings of autistic children are 200 times more likely to have the disorder than are children in the general population, and concordance is highest in identical twins (Piven, Saliba, Bailey, & Arndt, 1997). Yudofsky and Hales (2008) re-examined data from previous twin studies and showed a concordance rate in monozygotic pairs of 36% to 91% for autism. In addition to this, the monozygotic pairs showed a concordance rate of 82% for a wider 'spectrum' of related cognitive and social problems with the dizygotic pairs at 10% concordance. No single gene seems involved; instead, there may be multiple interacting genes. One notable finding is that many relatives of autistic children, though not manifesting the disorder themselves, have unusual personality characteristics that parallel autism, including aloofness and very narrow and specialized interests (Rutter, 2000).

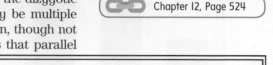

Another line of research is examining autism from the *theory of mind* perspective. As discussed in **Chapter 12**, theory of mind refers to an awareness of what others are thinking and how they may be reacting internally. Children usually become aware of some characteristics of other people's thinking by age 3 or 4 (Ritblatt, 2000). Autistic people seem to have poorly developed skills in this area, making it difficult for them to communicate with others or understand how other people might be internally reacting to them (Heerey, Keltner, & Capps, 2003). Autistic children also show poor comprehension of others' emotional responses, such as expressions of distress (Dawson et al., 2004). Theory of mind deficits could severely impair language and social development, and they are a strong focus of current research on autism.

Baron-Cohen (1995; Baron-Cohen, Leslie, & Frith, 1985) has identified a number of issues of importance that relate to theory of mind in autism. He indicates that the autistic is lacking a mechanism for identifying gaze direction (the Eye Direction Detector – EDD) and also a mechanism for being able to share attention with someone else (the Shared Attention Mechanism – SAM). The SAM is an extremely important issue in those with a theory of mind, where the intentions and perspectives of others can be perceived by the individual. Identifying whether a person has a theory of mind is possible with the 'Sally–Anne task' described in Figure 17.35. However, care must be taken here. Adults with autism can often pass theory of mind tasks that a 6-year-old may fail, but this does not indicate that they are performing in the normal range.

Another test that Baron-Cohen has used to great effect is the 'eyes test' (Baron-Cohen, Wheelwright, & Jolliffe, 1997). The task involves the participant to look at an image of a pair of eyes, and match it to either a simple or complex description of the person's state of mind. A simple state might be 'happy' or 'sad' and a more complex state might be 'reflective' or 'scheming'.

FIGURE 17.35 The Sally–Anne task.

In this task, two dolls, a basket and a box are used. A child watches the scene as it unfolds, acted out with dolls by the researcher, or possibly described in pictures. Sally takes an object (a ball perhaps) and places it in the covered basket, then leaves the scene. Anne then moves the object into the box. On Sally's return, the child is asked 'Where will Sally look for her ball?' Children with a 'theory of mind' will know that Sally was not present when the ball was moved, and as such will return to her covered basket where she left her ball. Those who show less theory of mind will think that Sally has exactly the same information as themselves. They know that the ball is in the box, and so they think Sally will look there.

Source: based on Frith 1989

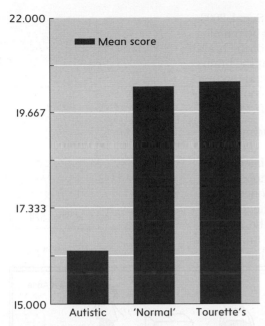

FIGURE 17.36 The eyes test.

In the 'eyes test' participants match a description of a state of mind with an image of a pair of eyes. The graph shows the number of correct responses for each of three groups. Statistics show that the autistic group is reliably and significantly worse at this task than the other two groups.

Source: Data redrawn from Baron-Cohen et al., 1997.

The data are quite striking and can be seen in Figure 17.36. Baron-Cohen et al. used a third participant group as a control, all of whom had Tourette's syndrome. Statistics show that the Tourette's group and the 'normal' groups show the same level of performance, while the autistic group is significantly worse than both. In this 'higher functioning' test of theory of mind, autistics do indeed show a deficit.

In addition to this, Baron-Cohen has identified and extended a theory that relates to the 'maleness' of the autistic brain (Baron-Cohen, 2003; Auyeung, Lombardo, Knickmeyer, & Baron-Cohen, 2011; Baron-Cohen, Auyeung, Knickmeyer, & Ashwin, 2015). Here he indicates that autistic children are extremely male-like in their systematic behaviour, and not female-like in their lack of empathy. This theory was developed in 2005 where Baron-Cohen, Knickmeyer and Belmonte looked at how social development can be significantly influenced by testosterone levels in the amniotic fluid during gestation. These behaviour patterns include the things we know as influenced in autism, including eye contact, language development, empathy and the quality of social relationships. It is clear from this research that there is a biological mechanism that plays a role in the development of autistic spectrum disorders.

Mirror neurons offer another biological perspective that may well be related to 'theory of mind'. Put very briefly, mirror neurons are cells that fire not only when we ourselves perform a particular action or behaviour but when we see and experience others performing the same action or behaviour. This direct neurological link between our actions directed to others and others' actions directed towards us could be interpreted as the neurological basis for 'empathy' or for 'theory of mind'.

If a mirror neuron acts as a neurological marker, or recognition system of the behaviours and emotions of those around us, it could be that theory of mind, and a knowledge of how others react and feel may be related to the mirror neuron. Up until recently, research on mirror neurons has used scanning devices that, although hugely powerful and useful in research, do not provide the type of recording detail that single-cell techniques might.

Oberman et al. (2005) found evidence of different mirror neuron activity when comparing those with and without autistic spectrum disorders using EEG. Dapretto et al. (2006) found a general reduction in the activity of parts of the brain associated with mirror neurons in those with the disorder, but Oberman et al. (2005) described the pattern of activity as different. Those without the disorder show a reduction in mirror neuron activity when watching someone perform the mirrored behaviour compared to when they themselves perform the action. Those with the disorder do not show this reduction or 'suppression' of activity.

Mukamel et al. (2010) have now provided this level of detail, with single-cell and also multi-cell recordings in humans. The research addresses many aspects of the activity of mirror neurons. Of particular interest to us at this point in the book is that the neurons are much more widely spread throughout the brain than had previously been thought. Mukamel et al. (2010) indicate that the cells may well be involved in our understanding of non-verbal communication, imitation and, as previously described, empathy. These are all issues with which those with an autistic spectrum disorder have difficulty.

The mirror neuron is in some circles being hailed as the most important discovery in science in recent times, and that the activity of single cells or groups of cells can explain complex disorders such as autism. A word of caution though, and perhaps scepticism. The mirror neuron is indeed hugely exciting, but beware of the claims of those who now believe that autism is fully explained. As we have seen, autism is a disorder with many facets. Whereas those who have a disorder on the spectrum may share characteristics, they are differentiated by many more. Explaining complex behaviours in terms of the activity of a small number of neurons is clearly reductionist, and where it certainly does form part of the story we as scientists should continue to look at the many other aspects of the disorder from all perspectives open to us.

Finally, the controversial MMR vaccination hypothesis should really be mentioned. The MMR vaccine, sold under a number of trade names by different companies, for measles, mumps and rubella, is a common triple vaccine given to young children. In the UK in 1998 a paper was published in *The Lancet* which strongly suggested a link between the vaccine and autism

(A. J. Wakefield et al., 1998). Following publication of the paper inoculation take-up went down dramatically from over 90% to approximately 80% as nervous parents and guardians feared their actions would cause their children considerable harm. Cases of measles rose by 2696% in 2008 compared with the number of cases in 1998. Andrew Wakefield (the author) was struck off the medical register in 2010 for acting irresponsibly and *The Lancet* fully retracted the article. The claim was made that the triple vaccine stressed the young immune system too much and that single vaccines would be a more appropriate form of action. However, Honda, Shimizu and Rutter (2005) indicate that cases of autism continued to rise when the triple vaccine was discontinued, clearly indicating that it is not linked to autism.

> *The parents should not be apprehensive about the fact that immunization is likely to risk the protection of the child. There is no evidence that autism is caused by any vaccine or any additive or preservative ever used in one. There have been large, well-controlled studies done all over the Western world that have confirmed this finding over and over again. A comparison of the risk factors, such as death or disabilities, as a result of not vaccinating a child is significantly larger than the risk of causing an autism spectrum disorder by immunizing.*   (Paul, 2009, p. 962)

> **Focus 17.28** Describe the major features and causal factors in ADHD and autistic disorder, as well as implications for adult functioning.

 In review

- Psychological disorders can occur at any point in the lifespan, and epidemiological data show that both children and adolescents exhibit a variety of disorders. Moreover, many childhood disorders are precursors for psychological disorders in adulthood.

- Attention deficit/hyperactive disorder (ADHD) and autistic disorder originate in childhood and often persist into adulthood. ADHD can involve inattention, hyperactivity or a combination of the two.

- Autism spectrum disorder is a severe disorder that involves extreme unresponsiveness to others, poor communication skills, and highly repetitive and rigid behaviour. Both disorders appear to have biological underpinnings, but the nature of these causal factors is not fully understood.

- Research into mirror neurons may provide us with evidence of a neurological basis for symptoms of autism and although possibly not the whole answer to all our queries of the disorder, the research does introduce exciting evidence and another rich vein to explore.

A CONCLUDING THOUGHT

All of us do the best we can to adapt to the many demands we face during the course of our lives. In this chapter, we have seen the intense personal and societal suffering that occurs when biologically and experientially produced vulnerabilities combine with stressful demands to create psychological disorders. It is our hope that this discussion has increased your understanding and compassion for those who suffer from these disorders. No one wants to be dysfunctional and miserable, and everyone deserves the opportunity to live a meaningful and fulfilling life. In the next chapter we focus on what can be done through psychological and biological treatments to ease the suffering that results from psychological disorders.

 Recommended Reading

CLASSIC

Kaysen, S. (1996). *Girl, interrupted.* New York: Vintage Books.

CONTEMPORARY

Beck, A. & Bentall, R. (2004). *Madness explained – psychosis and human nature.* Harmondsworth: Penguin.

Hornbacher, M (2009). *Madness: A bipolar life.* New York: Mariner Books.

Perkins-Gilman, C. (2009). *The yellow wallpaper.* Oxford: Oxford Paperbacks.

Szasz, T. (2010). *The myth of mental illness: Foundations of a theory of personal conduct.* New York: Harper Perennial.

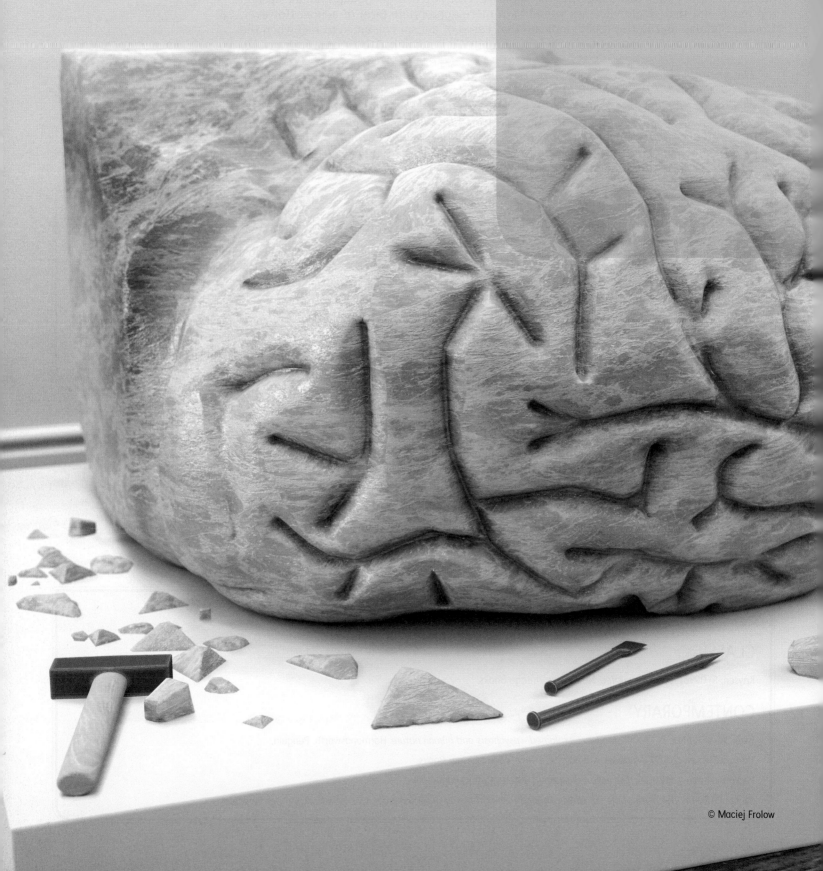

We may define therapy as a search for value.
Abraham Maslow

Treatment of psychological disorders

18

Chapter Outline

FIGURE 18.1 The process of therapy involves a relationship between a client and a therapist, who applies the techniques dictated by his or her approach to treatment.

Source: Izabela Habur.

I often felt at odds with my therapist until I could see that he was a real person and he related to me and I to him, not only as patient and therapist, but as human beings. Eventually I began to feel that I too was a person, not just an outsider looking in on the world. Medication or superficial support is not a substitute for the feeling that one is understood by another human being. For me, the greatest gift came the day I realized that my therapist really had stood by me for years and that he would continue to stand by me and help me achieve what I wanted to achieve. With that realization, my viability as a person began to grow.   ('A recovering patient', 1986, pp. 68–70)

Although first-person reports, like the one above, suggest that many people derive considerable benefit from psychotherapy, psychologists demand much more in the way of evidence. Nearly 65 years of research on psychological treatments has taught us that the question of efficacy, or treatment outcome, is a tremendously complex one that has no simple answers. Yet as we shall see, much has been learned about the effectiveness of these various therapeutic approaches and about the factors that influence treatment outcome.

PSYCHOLOGICAL TREATMENTS

The primary goal of all psychotherapy is to help people change maladaptive thoughts, feelings and behaviour patterns so that they can live happier and more productive lives, and the relationship between the client and the person providing help is a prime ingredient of psychotherapeutic success (Binder & Strupp, 1997; Gabbard, Beck, & Holmes, 2005). Within that helping relationship, therapists use a variety of treatment techniques to promote positive changes in the client. These techniques vary widely, depending on the therapists' own theories of cause and change, and they may range from biomedical approaches (such as administering psychoactive drugs) to a wide variety of psychological treatments. Both of these elements – relationship and techniques – are important to the success of the treatment enterprise (Figures 18.1 and 18.2).

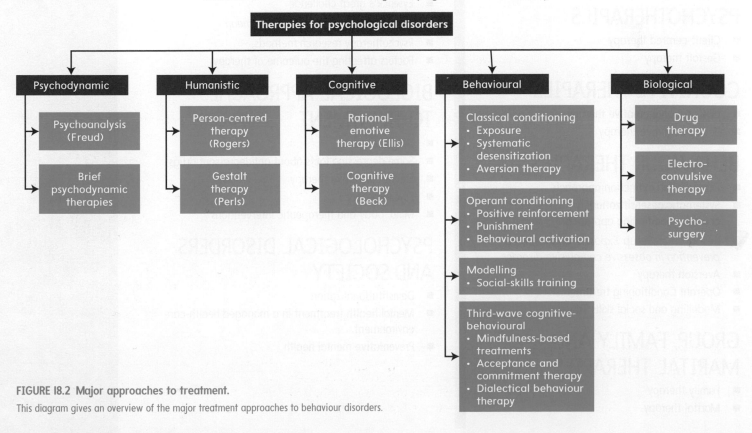

FIGURE 18.2 Major approaches to treatment.

This diagram gives an overview of the major treatment approaches to behaviour disorders.

PROFESSIONAL BODIES AND ORGANIZATIONS

In Chapter 17 we described the professional bodies responsible for overseeing that psychological teaching and research is done ethically, each with their own, but similar, guidelines in this area. These professional bodies also guide and accredit the provision of these therapy and counselling qualifications, and include the British Psychological Association, the Danish Psychologists Association, Suomen Psyckologinen Seura in Finland, the Malta Union of Professional Psychologists, Nederlands Instituut van Psychologen, the Norwegian Psychological Association, the Psychological Society of South Africa and the Swedish Psychological Association.

> **Focus 18.1** How do client, therapist and treatment techniques combine in the process of therapy?

PSYCHODYNAMIC THERAPIES

Of the many psychotherapeutic approaches, psychodynamic treatments have the longest tradition. Their historical roots lie in Sigmund Freud's psychoanalytic theory. Although both the theory and the techniques of therapy were later modified by those that followed, the psychodynamic principles underlying the approach continue be influential (Alexander, 2004).

PSYCHOANALYSIS

The term *psychoanalysis* refers not only to Freud's theory of personality but also to the specific approach to treatment that he developed. The goal of psychoanalysis is to help clients achieve **insight**, the conscious awareness of the psychodynamics that underlie their problems. Such awareness permits clients to adjust their behaviour to their current life situations, rather than repeating the maladaptive routines learned in childhood. Analysts believe that as the client repeatedly encounters and deals with long-buried emotions, motives and conflicts within and outside therapy, the psychic energy that was previously devoted to keeping unconscious conflicts under control can be released and redirected to more adaptive ways of living (Gabbard, 2004).

> **insight** the conscious awareness of the psychodynamics that underlie their problems

Free Association

Freud believed that mental events are meaningfully associated with one another, so that clues to the contents of the unconscious can be found in the ongoing stream of thoughts, memories, images and feelings that we experience. In the technique of **free association**, clients verbally report without censorship any thoughts, feelings or images that enter their awareness. Analysts sit out of sight behind the client so that the client's thought processes will be determined primarily by internal factors (Figure 18.3).

> **free association** clients verbally report without censorship any thoughts, feelings or images that enter their awareness

The analyst does not expect that free association will necessarily lead directly to unconscious material but, rather, that it will provide clues concerning important themes or issues (Hoffer & Youngren, 2004). For example, a client's stream of thoughts may suddenly stop after she mentions her father, suggesting that she was approaching a salient topic that activated repressive defences.

Dream Interpretation

The Freudian approach to psychoanalysis tells us that dreams express impulses, fantasies and wishes that the client's defences keep bottled up in the unconscious during waking hours (Glucksman, 2001). Even in dreams, which Freud termed 'the royal road to the unconscious', defensive processes usually disguise the threatening material to protect the dreamer from the anxiety that the material might evoke. In dream interpretation, the analyst helps the client search for the unconscious material contained in the dreams. One means of doing so is to ask the client to free-associate to each element of the dream. The analyst then helps the client arrive at an understanding of what the symbols in the dream might really represent (Figure 18.4).

FIGURE 18.3 The famous couch from the consulting rooms of Sigmund Freud himself. Note the chair behind the couch where Freud would sit, out of sight to minimize any external stimuli that might influence the person's thought process.

Source: © Bjanka Kadic/Alamy

FIGURE 18.4 Dream analysis is a central technique in psychoanalysis.

Source: Lava 4 images/Shutterstock

resistance defensive manoeuvres that hinder the process of therapy

transference occurs when the client responds irrationally to the analyst as if he or she were an important figure from the client's past

Resistance

Unconsciously, clients have an investment in maintaining the status quo. After all, underlying their problems are unconscious conflicts so threatening and painful that the ego has resorted to maladaptive defensive patterns to deal with them. These avoidance patterns emerge as **resistance**, defensive manoeuvres that hinder the process of therapy. Resistance can appear in many different forms. A client may suddenly experience difficulty in free-associating, arrive late at a therapy session or 'forget' about it altogether, or avoid talking about certain topics. Resistance is a sign that anxiety-arousing material is being approached. An important task of analysis is to explore the reasons for resistance, both to promote insight and to guard against the ultimate resistance: the client's decision to drop out of therapy prematurely.

Transference

During therapy, clients begin to project onto the 'blank screen' of the therapist important perceptions and feelings related to their underlying conflicts. **Transference** occurs when the client responds irrationally to the analyst as if he or she were an important figure from the client's past. Transference is considered a most important process in psychoanalysis, for it brings into the open repressed feelings and maladaptive behaviour patterns that both the therapist and client can discover and explore (Murdin, 2010).

Transference takes two basic forms. *Positive transference* occurs when a client transfers feelings of intense affection, dependency or love to the analyst, whereas *negative transference* involves irrational expressions of anger, hatred or disappointment. Analysts believe that until transference reactions are analysed and resolved, there can be no full resolution of the client's problems. In the following excerpt from a psychoanalytic session, a client traces her transference reaction to its source and then recognizes the operation of similar reactions in other relationships.

Client: *My brother Harry, the one I had the sex experiences with when I was little. He made me do things I didn't want to. . . . I'm afraid of you taking advantage of me. If I tell you I like you, that means you'll make me do what you want.*

Therapist: *Just like Harry made you do what he wanted.*

Client: *Yes. I didn't want to let him do what he did, but I couldn't help myself. I hated myself. That's why. I know it now because there is no reason why I should feel you are the same way. That's why I act that way with other people too. . . . I don't like to have people get too close to me. The whole thing is the same as happens with you. It's all so silly and wrong. You aren't my brother and the other people aren't my brother. I never saw the connection until now.*

(Wolberg, 1967, pp. 660–661)

In this interchange, we see both positive and negative transference reactions based on an important past relationship. The client's feelings about her brother continue to play out in her fear of getting close to others and being exploited once again.

Interpretation

How can analysts help clients detect and understand resistances, the meaning of dream symbols, and transference reactions? The analyst's chief therapeutic technique for these purposes is **interpretation**, any statement by the therapist that is intended to provide the client with insight into his or her behaviour or dynamics. An interpretative statement confronts clients with something that they have not previously admitted into consciousness, for example, 'It's almost as if you're angry with me without realizing it'.

A general rule in psychoanalytic treatment is to interpret what is already near the surface and just beyond the client's current awareness (McWilliams, 2004). Offering 'deep'

interpretation any statement by the therapist that is intended to provide the client with insight into his or her behaviour or dynamics

interpretations of strongly defended unconscious dynamics is considered poor technique because, even if they are correct, such interpretations are so far removed from the client's current awareness that they cannot be informative or helpful. This is one reason that even after the analyst fully understands the causes of the client's problems, psychoanalysis may require several more years of treatment. It is the client who must eventually arrive at the insights, then translate them into behaviour changes within important life domains and relationships.

Focus I8.2 Describe the roles of free association, dream analysis, resistance, transference and interpretation in psychoanalysis.

BRIEF PSYCHODYNAMIC AND INTERPERSONAL THERAPIES

Classical psychoanalysis as practised by Freud (and by a declining number of contemporary analysts) is an expensive and time-consuming process, for the goal is no less than rebuilding the client's personality. In classical psychoanalysis, it is not uncommon for a client to be seen five times a week for five years or more. Today, however, many therapists consider this level of client and therapist commitment both impractical and unnecessary. Their conclusion is supported by psychotherapy studies that measured the degree of improvement that occurred over the course of therapy. One study (Howard, Kopta, Krause, & Orlinsky, 1986) showed that about half of the clients improved markedly within eight sessions, and most therapeutic effects as rated by researchers occurred within 26 sessions. The results of a more recent study, involving 4,676 clients and 204 therapists in a university counselling centre, measured improvement using the Outcome Questionnaire-45, a measure of psychological symptoms and unhappiness. As Figure 18.5 shows, by the tenth session, most of the improvement had occurred. The researchers also found that regardless of the total number of sessions the clients received, the rate of improvement was highest at the beginning and decreased over time (Baldwin, Berkeljon, Atkins, Olsen, & Nielsen, 2009). A study of more than 4,000 clients seen in therapy in the UK also found that clinically significant change did not increase in clients seen beyond 10 sessions (Stiles, Barkham, Mellor-Clark, & Connell, 2008).

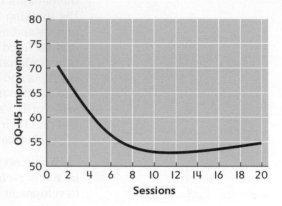

FIGURE I8.5 Decrease in psychological symptoms as a function of number of sessions seen in psychotherapy. The highest rate of improvement is seen early in treatment. Results like these have helped stimulate the development of short-term treatments.

Source: Baldwin et al., 2009.

To an increasing extent, psychodynamic therapists are adopting briefer and more economical approaches (Levenson, 2010). Like psychoanalysis, brief psychodynamic psychotherapies focus on understanding the maladaptive influences of the past and relating them to current patterns of self-defeating behaviour. Many of these brief therapies utilize basic concepts from psychoanalysis, such as the importance of insight and the use of interpretation, but they employ them in a more focused and active fashion (Binder, 2004). The therapist and client are likely to sit facing each other, and conversation typically replaces free association. Clients are seen once or twice a week rather than daily, and the goal is typically limited to helping the client deal with specific life problems rather than attempting a complete rebuilding of the client's personality. Therapy is therefore more likely to focus on the client's current life situations than on past childhood experiences and may involve teaching the client specific interpersonal and emotion-control skills (Benjamin, 2003). One relatively brief therapy, interpersonal therapy, focuses almost exclusively on clients' current relationships with important people in their lives (Weissman, Markowitz, & Klerman, 2007). This therapy, designed in part for research on the treatment of depression, is highly structured and seldom takes longer than 15 to 20 sessions. Therapeutic goals include resolving role disputes such as marital conflict, adjusting to the loss of a relationship or to a changed relationship, and identifying and correcting deficits in social skills that make it difficult for the client to initiate or maintain satisfying relationships. The therapist collaborates very actively with the client in finding solutions to these problems and may invite the client to link issues in current relationships with those in important past relationships, thereby showing that what happened in the past need not be carried into the present. In controlled outcome studies, interpersonal therapy has proven effective for several disorders, particularly depression (Chambless & Hollon, 1998; Coren, 2010).

interpersonal therapy an approach focusing almost exclusively on clients' current relationships with important people in their lives

OBJECT RELATIONS THEORY

It is in object relations theory that we see the development of a psychoanalytic approach that emphasizes the importance of relationships. It is here that we see some great names in the field, such as Kohut, Winnicott, Klein, Fairburn and Winnicott, move away from many of the traditional Freudian views and develop a quite different approach. Object relations theory, put quite simply, focuses on the things that matter to the person, to the things that the person relates themselves to. For instance, I am frightened of flying, I love my parents and I prefer cats to dogs. Flying, parents, cats and dogs are things that concern me, that I hold opinions of and that matter to me. I have a relationship with these objects and so managing these relationships is a way of managing the way I feel.

Melanie Klein, a student of Freud's, provides the link between object relations theory and Freud's more classical approach, indicating that the drives a child experiences are invariably towards objects such as food-giving breasts, and comfort-giving caregivers. Later, Hans Kohut developed a different approach. In his self-psychology, the focus is on the person's issues of identity, meaning and ideals, as well as with their self-expression. His thinking was developed following the Holocaust where he struggled to develop an understanding of how those who experienced such horrors at close hand as well as from afar suffered with their understanding of themselves. For him the self was all important. In a traditional psychodynamic approach, drives, such as sex, aggression and instinct, conflicts and fantasies shape the person's psyche. In Kohut's self psychology, relationships and the dynamics of relationships were all important in our psychological state. For him, self-worth was very important particularly in earlier development where children should feel that their efforts at relationship development with those significant in their early lives are reciprocated.

Winnicott was a British developmental psychologist, interested predominantly in mother–child interactions. He said that this interaction was central to the child's development and was linked closely with how the child interacted with 'objects' other than their mother, as this was how a transition between different stages of development of self progresses. For instance, objects that make the child feel happy, such as blankets, teddy bears and dolls, help the child deal with separation and so are important in the development process as they take on their own self, and begin to experience separation from their caregivers.

William Fairburn and Gordon Guntrip took the view that objects were actively sought out. Freud had previously said that pleasure was the driver of our actions, but Fairburn said that the objects were themselves the focus, with people actively seeking people for their own sake. Guntrip later developed this idea, saying that the focus of therapy should be to develop the shared discussion within a person's important relationships. Guntrip indicated that the person needs a non-erotic relationship with a parent figure that, once developed through careful nurturing, will allow a person to separate themselves from the object of this relationship safely, to become an independent self without feeling cut off.

HUMANISTIC PSYCHOTHERAPIES

In contrast to psychodynamic theorists, who view behaviour as a product of unconscious processes, humanistic theorists view humans as capable of consciously controlling their actions and taking responsibility for their choices and behaviour. These theorists also believe that everyone possesses inner resources for self-healing and personal growth, and that disordered behaviour reflects a blocking of the natural growth process. This blocking is brought about by distorted perceptions, lack of awareness about feelings, or a negative self-image.

When these assumptions about human nature are applied to psychotherapy, they inspire treatments that are radically different from psychoanalysis. Humanistic psychotherapy is seen as a human encounter between equals. The therapist's goal is to create an environment in which clients can engage in self-exploration and remove

the barriers that block their natural tendencies towards personal growth (Greenberg & Rice, 1997). These barriers often result from childhood experiences that fostered unrealistic or maladaptive standards for self-worth. When people try to live their lives according to the expectations of others rather than their own desires and feelings, they often feel unfulfilled and empty and unsure about who they really are. In contrast to classical psychoanalytic therapy, humanistic approaches focus primarily on the present and future instead of the past. Therapy is directed at helping clients to become aware of feelings as they occur rather than to achieve insights into the childhood origins of those feelings.

CLIENT-CENTRED THERAPY

The best-known and most widely used humanistic therapy is the *client-centred* (now sometimes called *person-centred*) *approach* developed by Carl Rogers (1959, 1980; see also **Chapter 1**). In the 1940s, Rogers began to depart from psychoanalytic methods. He became convinced that the important active ingredient in therapy is the relationship that develops between client and therapist, and he began to focus his attention on the kind of therapeutic environment that seemed most effective in fostering self-exploration and personal growth (Bozarth, Zimring, & Tausch, 2002). Rogers's research and experiences as a therapist identified three important and interrelated therapist attributes:

1. **Unconditional positive regard** is communicated when the therapist shows that he or she genuinely cares about and accepts the client, without judgement or evaluation. The therapist also communicates a sense of trust in the client's ability to work through his or her problems. In part, this sense of trust is communicated in the therapist's refusal to offer advice or guidance.

2. **Empathy,** the willingness and ability to view the world through the client's eyes, is a second vital factor (Blackstone, 2007). In a good therapeutic relationship, the therapist comes to sense the feelings and meanings experienced by the client and communicates this understanding to the client. The therapist does this by *reflecting* back to the client what she or he is communicating – perhaps by rephrasing something the client has just said in a way that captures the meaning and emotion involved.

3. **Genuineness** refers to consistency between the way the therapist feels and the way he or she behaves. The therapist must be open enough to express his or her own feelings honestly, whether positive or negative. In the case of negative feelings, this may seem to be contradictory to the attribute of unconditional positive regard, but that is not necessarily the case. Indeed, the most striking demonstrations of both attributes occur when a therapist can express displeasure with a client's behaviour and at the same time communicate acceptance of the client as a person. For example, a therapist might say, 'I feel frustrated with the way you handled that situation because I want things to work out better than that for you'.

Rogers believed that when therapists can express these three key therapeutic attributes, they create a climate in which the client feels accepted, understood, and free to explore basic attitudes and feelings without fear of being judged or rejected. Within such a climate, the client experiences the courage and freedom to grow. These therapeutic attitudes are exhibited in the following excerpt from one of Rogers's therapy sessions:

> Client: *I cannot be the kind of person I want to be. I guess maybe I haven't the guts or the strength to kill myself, and if someone else would relieve me of the responsibility or I would be in an accident, I – just don't want to live.*
>
> Rogers: *At the present time things look so black that you can't see much point in living. (Note the use of empathic reflection and the absence of any criticism.)*
>
> Client: *Yes, I wish I'd never started this therapy. I was happy when I was living in my dream world. There I could be the kind of person I wanted to be. But now there is such a wide, wide gap between my ideal and what I am. . . . (Notice how the client responds to reflection with more information.)*

Focus 18.3 How does the goal of humanistic therapies differ from that of psychodynamic therapies?

 Chapter 1, Page 15

unconditional positive regard communicated when the therapist shows that he or she genuinely cares about and accepts the client, without judgement or evaluation

empathy the willingness and ability to view the world through the client's eyes

genuineness consistency between the way the therapist feels and the way he or she behaves

Rogers: *It's really tough digging into this like you are and at times the shelter of your dream world looks more attractive and comfortable. (Reflection.)*

Client: *My dream world or suicide. . . . So I don't see why I should waste your time coming in twice a week – I'm not worth it – what do you think?*

Rogers: *It's up to you. . . . It isn't wasting my time. I'd be glad to see you whenever you come, but it's how you feel about it. . . . (Note the genuineness in stating an honest desire to see the client and the unconditional positive regard in trusting her capacity and responsibility for choice.)*

Rogers believed that as clients experience a constructive therapeutic relationship, they exhibit increased self-acceptance, greater self-awareness, enhanced self-reliance, increased comfort with other relationships and improved life functioning (Rogers, 1959). Research does indicate that therapists' characteristics have a strong effect on the outcome of psychotherapy. Therapy is most likely to be successful when the therapist is perceived as genuine, warm and empathic (Sachse & Elliott, 2002) and this approach is still influential today (Cain, 2010).

GESTALT THERAPY

Frederick S. (Fritz) Perls, a psychoanalyst who was trained in Gestalt psychology, developed another humanistic approach to treatment. The term *gestalt* ('organized whole') refers to perceptual principles through which people actively organize stimulus elements into meaningful 'whole' patterns. Ordinarily, whatever we perceive, whether external stimuli, ideas, or emotions, we concentrate on only part of our whole experience – the figure – while largely ignoring the background against which the figure appears. For people who have psychological difficulties, that background includes important feelings, wishes, and thoughts that are blocked from ordinary awareness because they would evoke anxiety. Gestalt therapy's goal is to bring them into immediate awareness so that the client can be whole once again.

> **Focus 18.4** What is the goal of Gestalt therapy?

Gestalt therapy, often carried out in groups, entails a variety of imaginative techniques to help clients 'get in touch with their inner selves'. These methods are much more active and dramatic than client-centred approaches and sometimes even confrontational. Therapists often ask clients to role-play different aspects of themselves so that they may directly experience their inner dynamics. In the *empty-chair technique*, a client may be asked to imagine his mother sitting in the chair, then carry on a conversation in which he alternatively role-plays his mother and himself, changing chairs for each role and honestly telling her how he feels about important issues in their relationship. These techniques can evoke powerful feelings and make clients aware of unresolved issues that affect other relationships in their lives as well. Recent research on the empty-chair technique indicates that it does indeed help clients resolve 'unfinished business' with significant others from their pasts (Greenberg & Malcolm, 2002). Although Perls died in 1970, Gestalt therapy remains a vital force, and its principles and techniques are being incorporated into non-humanistic therapies as well (Burley & Freier, 2004; Cain & Seeman, 2002).

COGNITIVE THERAPIES

The greatest discovery of my generation is that human beings can alter their lives by altering their attitudes of mind.   (William James, 1842–1910)

James is not describing any mind-altering states – instead he is saying that by changing the way we think, the way we consider why and how things happen to us and how we influence the things and people around us, we can alter our lives. We here consider two important thought-changing approaches. Although originally labelled as 'cognitive' therapies, they eventually became integral parts of today's 'cognitive-behaviour therapy' movement (Dobson, 2009).

As we saw in the previous chapter, many behaviour disorders, including anxiety, mood and schizophrenic disorders, involve maladaptive ways of thinking about oneself and the world. Cognitive approaches to psychotherapy focus on the role of irrational and self-defeating thought patterns, and therapists who employ this approach try to help clients discover and change the cognitions that underlie their problems.

In contrast to psychoanalysts, cognitive therapists do not emphasize the importance of unconscious psychodynamic processes. They do, however, point out that because our habitual thought patterns are so well-practised and ingrained, they tend to 'start off' almost automatically, so that we may be only minimally aware of them and may simply accept them as reflecting reality (Clark et al., 1999). You can make a link here to cognitive psychology in **Chapter 9** where we talked about heuristics and 'mental set'. Decisions are often made very quickly, based on past experience and rules that we just do not question. Consequently, clients often need help in identifying the beliefs, ideas, and self-statements that trigger maladaptive emotions and behaviours. Once identified, these cognitions can be challenged and, with practice and effort, changed. Albert Ellis and Aaron Beck are the most influential figures in the cognitive approach to therapy, better known now of course as cognitive-behavioural therapies.

Chapter 9, Page 391

ELLIS'S RATIONAL-EMOTIVE THERAPY

The best years of your life are the ones in which you decide your problems are your own. You do not blame them on your mother, the ecology, or the president. You realize that you control your own destiny.   (Albert Ellis)

Albert Ellis originally trained as a psychoanalytic therapist, but became convinced that irrational thoughts, rather than unconscious dynamics, were the most immediate cause of self-defeating emotions. In the 1960s, his new approach of rational emotive therapy helped launch the cognitive revolution in clinical psychology. Ellis's theory of emotional disturbance and his rational-emotive therapy are embodied in his ABCD model (Figure 18.6).

- *A* stands for the *activating event* that seems to trigger the emotion.
- *B* stands for the *belief system* that underlies the way in which a person appraises the event.
- *C* stands for the emotional and behavioural *consequences* of that appraisal.
- *D* is the key to changing maladaptive emotions and behaviours: *disputing*, or challenging, an erroneous belief system.

Ellis points out that people are accustomed to viewing their emotions (C) as being caused directly by events (A). Thus a young man who is turned down for a date may feel rejected and depressed. However, Ellis would insist that the woman's refusal is *not* the true reason for the emotional reaction. Rather, the young man's depression is caused by his irrational belief that 'Because she doesn't want to be with me, I'm worthless, and no one will ever want me'. If the young man does not want to feel depressed and rejected, this belief must be countered and replaced by a more rational interpretation (e.g., 'It would have been nice if she had accepted my invitation, but I don't need to turn it into a catastrophe. It doesn't mean other women will never care about me').

Rational-emotive therapists introduce clients to commonly held irrational beliefs (Table 18.1) and then train them to ferret out the particular ideas that underlie their maladaptive emotional responses (Figure 18.7). Clients are given homework assignments to help them analyse and change self-statements. They may be asked to place themselves in challenging situations and practise control over their emotions by using new self-statements. For example, a shy person might be required to go to a party and practise rational thoughts that counteract social anxiety. Ellis reports that he overcame his own fears of women's rejection by going to Central Park in New York, practising anxiety-reducing self-statements and striking up conversations with more than 100 different women. He reports that he got only one date, but he overcame his anxiety without being either assaulted or arrested. By learning and practising cognitive coping responses, clients can eventually modify underlying belief systems in ways that enhance well-being (Dryden & Branch, 2008).

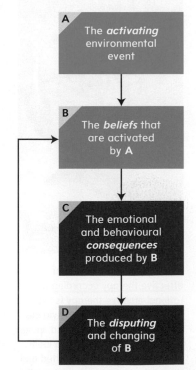

FIGURE 18.6 Ellis's ABCD model.

Albert Ellis's ABCD model describes his theory of the cause – and remediation – of maladaptive emotional responses and behaviours. In rational-emotive therapy, the goal is to discover, dispute, and change the client's maladaptive beliefs.

TABLE 18.1 Irrational ideas that cause disturbance and alternatives that might be offered by a rationale-motive therapist

Irrational belief	Rational alternative
It is a dire necessity that I be loved and approved of by virtually everyone for everything I do	Although we might prefer approval to disapproval, our self-worth need not depend on the love and approval of others. Self-respect is more important than giving up one's individuality to buy the approval of others
I must be thoroughly competent and achieving to be worthwhile. To fail is to be a failure	As imperfect and fallible human beings, we are bound to fail from time to time. We can control only effort; we have incomplete control over outcome. We are better off focusing on the process of doing rather than on demands that we do well
It is terrible, awful and catastrophic when things are not the way I demand that they be	Stop catastrophizing and turning an annoyance or irritation into a major crisis. Who are we to demand that things be different from what they are? When we turn our preferences into dire necessities, we set ourselves up for needless distress. We had best learn to change those things we can control and accept those that we cannot control (and be wise enough to know the difference)
Human misery is externally caused and forced on us by other people and events	Human misery is produced not by external factors but rather by what we tell ourselves about those events. We feel as we think, and most of our misery is needlessly self-inflicted by irrational habits of thinking
Because something deeply affected me in the past, it must continue to do so	We hold ourselves prisoner to the past because we continue to believe philosophies and ideas learned in the past. If they are still troubling us today, it is because we are still propagandizing ourselves with irrational nonsense. We can control how we think in the present and thereby liberate ourselves from the 'scars' of the past

BECK'S COGNITIVE THERAPY

Like Ellis, Aaron Beck's goal is to point out errors of thinking and logic that underlie emotional disturbance and to help clients identify and reprogramme their over-learned automatic thought patterns (Figure 18.8). In Beck's therapy, in treating depressed clients, a first step is to help clients realize that their thoughts, and not the situation, cause their maladaptive emotional reactions. This sets the stage for identifying and changing the self-defeating thoughts:

> *Beck*: So failing a test means a lot to you. But if failing a test could drive people into clinical depression, wouldn't you expect everyone who failed a test to have a depression? Did everyone who failed get depressed enough to require treatment?
>
> *Client*: No, but it depends on how important the test was to the person.
>
> *Beck*: Right, and who decides the importance?
>
> *Client*: I do.
>
> *Beck*: Now what did failing mean?
>
> *Client*: (Tearful) That I couldn't get into law school.
>
> *Beck*: And what does that mean to you?
>
> *Client*: That I'm just not smart enough.
>
> *Beck*: Anything else?
>
> *Client*: That I can never be happy.
>
> *Beck*: And how do those thoughts make you feel?
>
> *Client*: Very unhappy.
>
> *Beck*: So it is the *meaning* of failing a test that makes you very unhappy. In fact, believing that you can never be happy is a powerful factor in producing unhappiness. So you get yourself into a trap – by definition, failure to get into law school equals 'I can never be happy.'
>
> (Beck et al., 1979, pp. 145–146, emphasis added)

Beck's contributions to understanding and treating depression have made his cognitive therapy a psychological treatment of choice for that disorder. In one study, cognitive

FIGURE 18.7 'The essence of effective therapy according to rational-emotive therapy is full tolerance of people as individuals combined with a ruthless campaign against their self-defeating ideas. . . . These can be easily elicited and demolished by any scientist worth his or her salt; and the rational-emotive therapist is exactly that: an exposing and nonsense annihilating scientist' (Albert Ellis).

Source: © Ramin Talaie/Corbis

therapy with booster sessions after depression decreased, resulted in improvement maintenance in 97% of depressed clients, with non-recurrence of depression in 75% of them (Vittengl, Clark, & Jarrett, 2009). Cognitive therapy also has been applied to the treatment of anxiety and personality disorders (Beck et al., 2004; Clark, 2004).

Cognitive behaviour therapies (as they have become known) deserve a little more of the spotlight. The rise in use and acceptance of cognitive behaviour therapy (CBT) of the last few years has been nothing short of extraordinary. In the UK, for instance, it has now risen to be one of the dominant treatments offered by the National Health Service (NHS). Both mental-health policy makers and the politicians who help make the law back its use. The impact of this treatment is very significant. As we have described, the therapies have their roots in cognition and the premise that the problem the client has can be alleviated through carefully helping them modify their thoughts and, importantly, their behaviours. In doing this the clinician influences the client's emotions. It was Arnold Lazarus (1971) who first used the term 'behaviour therapy' in this context, and to some extent he might be regarded as the founding father of this enormously popular style of therapy.

FIGURE 18.8 'The formula for treatment may be stated in simple terms: The therapist helps the patient to identify his warped thinking and to learn more realistic ways to formulate his experience' (Aaron Beck).

Source: Beck Institute for Cognitive Behavior Therapy www.beckinstitute.org.

The focus of CBT is its emphasis on changing our cognitions (the way we think) and the behaviours associated with them. The idea is that altering the way that a person perceives a stressor may alter their physiological and emotional reactions to it (Rodham, 2010). The patterns of thinking that some people slip into might be thought of as 'distortions of reality' and CBT can be engaged in an attempt to remove these distortions.

The therapy can be used for a very wide spectrum of problems, including depression, general anxiety disorders and obsessive compulsive disorder. Cuijpers et al. (2013) compared people on a waiting list for treatment for depression with those given CBT and showed a reliable improvement in the CBT group. It has also been used in helping women suffering with breast cancer. Antoni et al. (2009) noted that women undergoing treatment for breast cancer attempt to adapt to the diagnosis. This adaptation requires considerable coping skills and a positive outlook that CBT can help provide in the form of, for instance, relaxation-technique training that can be useful in terms of helping the woman focus and secure more effective emotional adjustment. CBT is used with adults and with children and adolescents, and can be combined with drug therapy. When combined with drugs, research has shown it to be even more effective in helping those with depression (Leahy & Holland, 2000). It is wide ranging, flexible, relatively cheap and has been shown in very many cases to work. The popularity of cognitive behaviour therapy seems set to rise and rise. A very interesting development in CBT is the development and introduction of computerized sessions. The British National Health Service (Department of Health, 2007) continues to show its support of CBT by backing a project aimed to provide computerized CBT (CCBT) via the NHS. The *Delphi Poll* is a survey carried out every 10 years, begun by Norcross and Prochaska in 1982. The survey asks some of the most prominent psychotherapists around the world to predict the direction psychotherapy might take. When first surveyed in 1982, the *Delphi Poll* correctly predicted that the popularity of CBT would rise over the decade that followed. In fact, the popularity of CBT has continued to rise and rise, in each of the three decades following the first *Delphi Poll*. Merrick and Dattilio (2006) indicate that it is now described as the number one 'theoretical orientation', meaning that, out of all forms of therapy, more therapists regard themselves as cognitive therapists than anything else. Some courses for CBT are even being offered online now, such is the popularity of the therapy and the perceived effectiveness. These are described by the National Health Service in the UK as 'self-help' courses and various courses for problems such as bulimia, panic and phobias are recommended. The ease of access to some forms of this therapy should ensure its popularity for years to come, as is the growing evidence of its effectiveness in improving some psychological difficulties and as part of the equation that goes to improving quality of life in those with some psychological disorders as well as those suffering with some physical problems such as cancer (Kissane et al., 2003; Rodham, 2010).

Focus 18.5 How is the ABCD model used in rational-emotive therapy? Which disorders respond well to Beck's cognitive therapy?

One way to think about CBT and how it progresses is the acronym CHANGE VIEW:

Change thoughts and actions

Homework – Practice the skills you learn

Action and activity – Actually engage with it in real life

Need – Identify what you NEED to change – what the problem is.

Goals – Work towards definable goals

Evidence – trust that it works

View – things can always be looked at from another perspective

I CAN! – know you can do it – have confidence

Experience – Trying things out helps us learn and gives us confidence

Write it down – Keep track of our experiences

(Source: Adapted from Royal College of Psychiatrists)

However, as with all therapies and approaches, the picture for the effectiveness of CBT is not entirely rosy, and although there is evidence for its effectiveness in some areas, there is evidence that it cannot, and should not, be applied to some disorders, notably schizophrenia where a person may have lost connection with reality. A meta-analysis of the evidence from Jauhar et al. (2014) shows only a very small effect of CBT on only some of the symptoms of schizophrenia. This contradicts some of the individual research (Kumari et al., 2011, for instance) that does show some benefit for CBT in reducing symptoms such as hallucinations. We need to do what scientists do best and keep a very close eye on the evidence. At the moment there is a trend, a fashion, based on a wave of interest in CBT, and also some good evidence for the effectiveness of the therapy but it may not be the very best approach in all situations and as new evidence emerges, and new reviews of the literature are carried out, this may change.

BEHAVIOUR THERAPIES

In the 1960s, behavioural approaches emerged as a dramatic departure from the assumptions and methods that characterized psychoanalytic and humanistic therapies. The new practitioners of behaviour therapy denied the importance of inner dynamics. Instead, they insisted that (1) maladaptive behaviours are not merely symptoms of underlying problems but rather *are* the problem; (2) problem behaviours are learned in the same ways normal behaviours are; and (3) maladaptive behaviours can be unlearned by applying principles derived from research on classical conditioning, operant conditioning and modelling. Behaviourists demonstrated that these learning procedures could be applied effectively to change the behaviours of schizophrenia, to treat anxiety disorders, and to modify many child and adult behaviour problems that seemed resistant to traditional therapy approaches (Hersen, 2002).

Classical conditioning procedures have been used in two major ways. First, they have been used to reduce, or decondition, anxiety responses. Second, they have been used in attempts to condition aversive emotional responses to a particular class of stimuli, such as alcohol or inappropriate sexual objects. The most commonly used classical conditioning procedures are *exposure therapies*, *systematic desensitization* and *aversion therapy*.

EXPOSURE: AN EXTINCTION APPROACH

From a behavioural point of view, phobias and other fears result from classically conditioned emotional responses. The conditioning experience is assumed to involve a pairing of the phobic object (the neutral stimulus) with an aversive unconditioned stimulus (UCS). As a result, the phobic stimulus becomes a conditioned stimulus (CS) that elicits the conditioned response (CR) of anxiety. According to the two-factor learning theory discussed in **Chapter 7**, avoidance responses to the phobic situation are then reinforced by

Chapter 7, Page 290

anxiety reduction (operant conditioning based on negative reinforcement). Thus a person who is bitten by a dog may subsequently be afraid of dogs. Moreover, each time he avoids a dog, his avoidance response is strengthened through anxiety reduction.

According to this formulation, the most direct way to reduce the fear is through a process of classical extinction of the anxiety response. This requires **exposure** to the feared CS in the absence of the UCS while using **response prevention** to keep the operant avoidance response from occurring. This is the theoretical basis for the exposure approach (Marks, 1991; Zinbarg, Barlow, Brown, & Hertz, 1992). The client may be exposed to real-life stimuli (Figure 18.9) or asked to imagine scenes involving the stimuli. These stimuli will, of course, evoke considerable anxiety, but the anxiety will extinguish in time if the person remains in the presence of the CS and the UCS does not occur (Rosqvist & Hersen, 2006). The process may need repeating over time.

Some critics of exposure treatment are concerned that the intense anxiety created by the treatment may worsen the problem or cause clients to flee from treatment (Bruce & Sanderson, 1998). In a study of women being treated for post-traumatic stress disorder with exposure created by imaging the traumatic event, 15.4% of the women did indeed show a temporary increase in PTSD symptom intensity when exposure began. However, this increase did not impair treatment effectiveness or increase the likelihood of withdrawal from treatment (Foa, Zoellner, Feeny, Hembree, & Alvarez-Conrad, 2002).

Soldiers returning from the trenches could not sleep, or eat. Sigfried Sassoon puts in very vividly in his poem *Survivors* (1917). Sassoon describes the soldiers as 'stammering' with 'disconnected thought'. He paints a picture of them being only boys, with old and 'scared' faces, of them returning not as men, but as children with 'eyes that hate you, broken and mad'.

Because the condition had not been seen before, the public considered it to be faked by the soldiers so they would not have to return to their regiments at the front. The poor soldiers suffered then doubly, both with their psychological trauma as well as being shunned by the public they had fought to protect (Figure 18.10).

At Seale Hayne, a hospital in the south of England, a pioneering treatment regime was being developed by Major Arthur Hurst. Men with shell shock worked the land, developed a relationship with nature again, and even became comfortable with firearms, shooting as they would normally then in the countryside. One component of the treatment might, though, be considered extraordinary. Hurst reconstructed sections of the trenches on Dartmoor and had his patients relive their experiences. This perhaps could be described as an early form of exposure therapy for shell shock, a condition which has become known now as post-traumatic stress disorder. Hurst had exceptional success with his very careful care regime and exposure therapy has developed since that time.

Exposure has proved effective in extinguishing anxiety responses in both animals and humans (Roth & Fonagy, 2005; Spiegler & Guevremont, 2003). For instance, there is evidence that a one-session exposure treatment can successfully extinguish clinical phobias in children (Ollendick, Davis, & Sirbu, 2009).

Both real life (*in vivo*) and imaginary or virtual exposure are effective. An additional advantage is that clients can administer exposure treatment to themselves under a therapist's direction with high success rates (Anderson et al., 2013). Computer technology has provided a new method for delivering exposure treatments by bringing the external environment into the therapy

FIGURE 18.9 A behaviour therapist guides and supports a client with a dog phobia during an *in vivo* exposure therapy session. As a result of exposure, the man's anxiety will extinguish and he will be able to interact more comfortably with this animal and with other dogs.

Source: Topfoto

exposure to the feared CS in the absence of the UCS

response prevention to keep the operant avoidance response from occurring

Focus 18.6 Which classical and operant conditioning principles underlie exposure therapy? What problems is it applied to?

FIGURE 18.10 Shell-shocked soldiers.

Psychology has a history of exposure therapy, although it was not known as such at the time. In Europe, we are only too aware that the 100th anniversary of the First World War has just passed. The War marked some terrible human experiences we hoped never to see again. Unfortunately human nature being what it is, we have seen similar many times since. The War marked great advances in psychological treatment, born, unfortunately, out of necessity. One example was the treatment of 'shell shock', a condition brought on by the horrors and huge explosions experienced in the trenches in the Great War.

Source: Hulton Archive/Getty Images

FIGURE 18.11 This woman with a spider phobia views a virtual 'spider world' inside the helmet. She also handles a realistic toy spider whose movements inside the virtual environment are linked to her manipulation of the toy. The monitor shows the scene being experienced by the client.

Source: Photo by Stephen Dagadakis, copyright Hunter Hoffman, UW., www.vrpain.com.

virtual reality (VR) the use of computer technology to create highly realistic virtual environments that simulate actual experience so vividly that they evoke many of the same reactions that a comparable real-world environment would

systematic desensitization a learning-based treatment for anxiety disorders

counter-conditioning a new response that is incompatible with anxiety is conditioned to the anxiety arousing CS

stimulus hierarchy 10 to 20 scenes arranged in roughly equal steps from low anxiety to high-anxiety scenes

room. **Virtual reality (VR)** involves the use of computer technology to create highly realistic virtual environments that simulate actual experience so vividly that they evoke many of the same reactions that a comparable real-world environment would. Observers typically wear helmets containing two small video monitors (one for each eye) attached to a high-speed computer. The image to each eye is slightly different, producing binocular depth perception cues that result in a three-dimensional image. With the aid of position-tracking devices, the computer monitors the person's physical movements and adjusts the images and sounds accordingly (Figure 18.11). Observers thus have a vivid sense of being 'present' in a different place when navigating through the virtual world. Virtual reality is increasingly being applied to the treatment of anxiety disorders, particularly phobias (Wiederhold & Wiederhold, 2005; Anderson et al., 2013).

SYSTEMATIC DESENSITIZATION: A COUNTER-CONDITIONING APPROACH

In 1958 Joseph Wolpe introduced **systematic desensitization,** a learning-based treatment for anxiety disorders. Wolpe also presented impressive outcome data for 100 phobic patients he had treated with the technique. Systematic desensitization remains a widely used treatment today. In many controlled studies, its success rate in treating a wide range of phobic disorders, including needle phobia (Jenkins, 2014), has been 80% or better (Rachman, 1998; Spiegler & Guevremont, 2003, 2010; Jenkins, 2014).

Wolpe viewed anxiety as a classically conditioned emotional response. His goal was to eliminate the anxiety by using a procedure called **counter-conditioning,** in which a new response that is incompatible with anxiety is conditioned to the anxiety-arousing CS. The difference between extinction and counter-conditioning is that extinction requires only exposure to the CS; it does not require a substitute response to counter the anxiety response.

The first step in systematic desensitization is to train the client in the skill of voluntary muscle relaxation. Next the client is helped to construct a **stimulus hierarchy** of 10 to 20 scenes arranged in roughly equal steps from low-anxiety to high-anxiety scenes. Table 18.2 (page 790) shows a stimulus hierarchy that was used in treating a college student with high test anxiety.

In the desensitization sessions, the therapist deeply relaxes the client and then asks the client to vividly imagine the first scene in the hierarchy (the least anxiety-arousing one) for several seconds. The client cannot be both relaxed and anxious at the same time, so if the relaxation is strong enough, it replaces anxiety as the CR to that stimulus – the counter-conditioning process. When the client can imagine that scene for increasingly longer periods without experiencing anxiety, the therapist proceeds to the next scene. When low-arousal scenes have been deconditioned, some of the total anxiety has been reduced and the person is now ready to imagine more anxiety-arousing scenes without becoming anxious. Therapists can also accomplish desensitization through carefully controlled exposure to a hierarchy of real-life situations (e.g., having a person with a phobia of heights actually stand on a step stool and, eventually, walk across a suspension bridge while voluntarily relaxing). Both imaginal and real-life desensitization approaches are highly effective in reducing anxiety. Combining different therapies has also been seen to be effective. For instance, McEvoy and Saulsman (2014) combined imagery with cognitive behaviour group therapy and showed a significant improvement in the reduction of social anxiety disorder than when imagery was not used.

Focus 18.7 How does systematic desensitization differ from exposure in terms of its underlying principle and techniques?

Although both exposure therapy based on extinction and systematic desensitization are very effective in reducing fear responses, there are practical trade-offs. Systematic desensitization is sometimes preferred over exposure therapy because it produces far less anxiety for the client during the treatment. Exposure, however, often achieves the desired reduction in anxiety with a briefer course of therapy than does systematic desensitization (Bruce & Sanderson, 1998).

Research close-up

EXPOSURE AND RESPONSE PREVENTION IN OBSESSIVE COMPULSIVE DISORDER

Source: M. B. Himle & M. E. Franklin (2009). The more you do it, the easier it gets: Exposure and response prevention for OCD. *Cognitive and Behavioral Practice, 16*, 29–39.

ERP is a well-known approach dating back to the 1960s. It draws heavily in the learning theory we discussed in Chapter 7, so refresh your memory by reading over those sections before you go on. In 1966, Meyer showed that learned 'fear' responses in dogs and cats could be 'unlearned' by repeatedly exposing them to the stimulus that caused them fear without any fearful or unpleasant consequences, and importantly, without letting the animal engage in any avoidance or safety-seeking behaviours such as running away and hiding. Meyer found that two-thirds of the obsessive compulsive disorder (OCD) patients he treated similarly, with their 'feared' stimulus – not allowing them to engage in their ritualized, obsessive behaviour, showed significant improvement, with reliably reduced habituation to the stimuli. It is a treatment for OCD recommended by the National Institute of Health and Clinical Excellence and the evidence for its effectiveness are clear with 75% reduction in symptoms shown and a greater than 60% recovery (Fisher & Wells, 2005). Here Himle and Franklin report a case study which shows the process and how successful such an approach can be, and how the theory is still used today.

CAROLINE

Caroline has OCD. She expresses a large number of ritualized behaviours all based around her fear that she will do someone harm, perhaps even kill them if she does not carry out the activities. These include washing rituals, to make sure she does not have germs that may be passed to people and so cause them harm; ritualized praying for people not to come to any harm; careful avoidance of saying 'goodbye' to people in case she harms them; chanting, or repeating certain phrases that will protect those dear to her. She forms an imagined circle around the person she would like to avoid harming and she touches that person to prevent their harm. She flicks her fingers to remove dust and bites her tongue to dissolve dust. She blinks her eyes as this, she feels, prevents harm to the person.

The process of treatment takes about 15 sessions with a therapist, in among which Caroline must carry out tasks and homework.

1. *Assessment and review of the symptoms.* Caroline is carefully assessed and her symptoms detailed.

2. *Psychoeducation.* Caroline engages in an educative process designed to help her better understand her OCD. This is a period of *psychoeducation* during which Caroline's feelings of self-blame can be reduced, and so she is able to engage better with her therapist, and clarify for herself the link between stimuli that make her anxious and her ritualistic behaviour.

3. *Providing a cogent rationale for the treatment?* A rationale for the ERP is explained to Jane. It is not important here for the therapist and Caroline to dig to the cause of the ritual; rather, it is important here for Caroline to understand how her ritualistic behaviour is reinforced and maintained through her anxiety to perform the ritualistic behaviour when the opportunity to do so is denied her.

4. *The 'nuts and bolts' of the treatment.* Now that Caroline knows what the treatment is, and the thinking behind it, and she better understands the relevant components of her own OCD, she is able to identify what triggers her anxiety in her everyday life, and carefully monitors her own behaviours and feelings. Later, with her therapist, exposure to these 'triggers' are given a rating of how anxious they make her, enabling her to see that some things make her more anxious than others, and how her anxiety levels can be monitored. For instance, for her fears that shaking hands or saying goodbye to someone may harm them, activities such as shaking her husband's hand are rated relatively low on her anxiety scale, at 20, whereas touching an ill person and deliberately blowing 'dust' onto them rates right at the top, at 100. Imagining these situations causes anxiety and dealing with the anxiety carefully without the ritualized behaviour is the goal. This is exposure therapy, and it can be done in the consulting room with the therapist or as part of the practice that Caroline is able to do at home between sessions. It is this exposure, this thinking about the stimulus, that makes her anxious in a safe, calm environment where she is denied, or denies herself, her ritualistic behaviour. Caroline is slowly able to reduce her habitual response and gain control of her obsessive behaviour. The knowledge and training she has learned will be with her forever now. The skills she now has, and the experience that shows her that they can be applied successfully in future situations she identifies that may cause her anxiety and hence ritualized behaviour to worsen once again, can be applied in new and novel situations from now on.

The effectiveness of the treatment in this, and with other people, will depend on a great number of things. In Caroline's case she has sought, and is engaging actively with treatment, which shows great bravery and motivation on her part. This is a very positive sign. However, those engaging with the treatment are told clearly that they should expect the OCD to flare up in the future, and that when this does happen they should engage with the skills they have learned to help them get through their unwanted experiences.

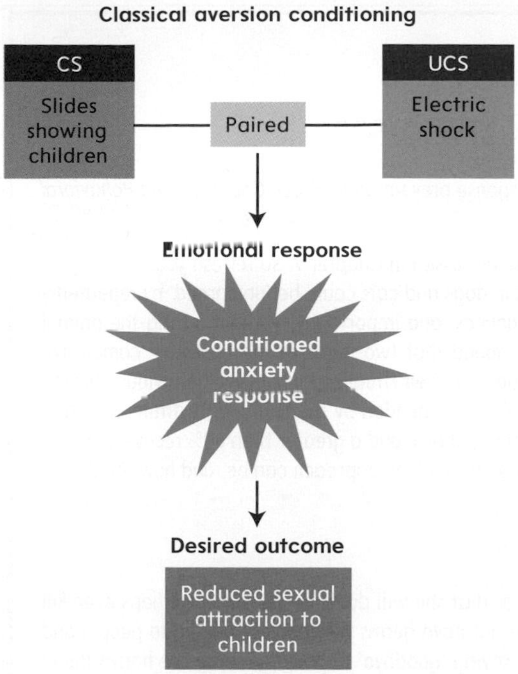

Classical aversion conditioning

FIGURE 18.12 Aversion therapy.

The classical conditioning that occurs in aversion therapy is illustrated in the treatment of paedophiles who receive electric shocks as they view pictures of children. The goal of the treatment is the development of a conditioned aversion in order to reduce sexual attraction to children.

AVERSION THERAPY

For some clients, the therapeutic goal is not to reduce anxiety but actually to condition anxiety to a particular stimulus that triggers deviant behaviour. In **aversion therapy,** the therapist pairs a stimulus that is attractive to the client (the CS) with a noxious UCS in an attempt to condition an aversion to the CS. For example, aversion treatment for alcoholics might involve injecting the client with a nausea-producing drug and then having him or her drink alcohol (the CS) as nausea (the UCS) develops. Electric shock may also be paired with alcohol ingestion. Similarly, paedophiles have undergone treatment in which strong electric shocks are paired with slides showing children similar to those the offenders sexually abused (Figure 18.12). To measure the effects of the treatment for males, therapists can use a physiological recording device that measures penile blood-volume responses to the slides – penile plethysmography; the therapists can then compare the readings before and after aversion therapy sessions (Trottier, Roulear, Renaud, & Goyette, 2013).

Aversion therapies have been applied to a range of disorders, with variable results. In one study of 278 alcoholics who underwent aversion therapy, 190 (63%) were still abstinent a year after treatment had ended. Three years later, a third of the patients were still abstinent, an impressive result given the traditionally high relapse rate in chronic alcoholic individuals (Wiens & Menustik, 1983). Unfortunately, treatment gains from aversion therapies often fail to generalize from the treatment setting to the real world. A recovering alcoholic or drug addict who goes to a party where friends abuse the substance is likely to have difficulty resisting the temptation to relapse. Some experts believe that aversion therapy is most likely to succeed if it is part of a more comprehensive treatment programme in which the client also learns specific coping skills for avoiding relapses (Marlatt & Gordon, 1985).

OPERANT CONDITIONING TREATMENTS

The term **behaviour modification** refers to treatment techniques that apply operant conditioning procedures in an attempt to increase or decrease a specific behaviour. These techniques may use any of the operant procedures for manipulating the

aversion therapy the therapist pairs a stimulus that is attractive to the client (the CS) with a noxious UCS in an attempt to condition an aversion to the CS

behaviour modification treatment techniques that apply operant conditioning procedures in an attempt to increase or decrease a specific behaviour

TABLE 18.2 A stimulus hierarchy used in the systematic desensitization treatment of a test-anxious student

Scene	Hierarchy of anxiety-arousing scenes
1	Hearing about someone else who has a test
2	Instructor announcing that a test will be given in three weeks
3	Instructor reminding class that there will be a test in two weeks
4	Overhearing classmates talk about studying for the test, which will occur in one week
5	Instructor reminding class of what it will be tested on in two days
6	Leaving class the day before the examination
7	Studying the night before the examination
8	Getting up the morning of the examination
9	Walking towards the building where the examination will be given
10	Walking into the testing room
11	Instructor walking into the room with the tests
12	Tests being passed out
13	Reading the test questions
14	Watching others finish the test
15	Seeing a question I cannot answer
16	Instructor waiting for me to finish the test

environment that we discussed in **Chapter 7**: positive reinforcement, extinction, negative reinforcement or punishment.

Chapter 7, Page 280

The focus in behaviour modification is on externally observable behaviours. The behaviours targeted for change are measured throughout the treatment programme, allowing the therapist to track the progress of the treatment programme and to make modifications if behaviour change begins to lag.

Focus 18.8 Which learning principles underlie aversion therapy?

What are its limitations, and how can its effects be enhanced?

Behaviour modification techniques have been successfully applied to many different behaviour disorders. They have yielded particularly impressive results when used in populations that are difficult to treat with more traditional therapies, such as hospitalized schizophrenic patients, profoundly disturbed children and those with learning difficulties. (Ayllon & Azrin, 1968; DeRubeis and Crits-Christoph, 1998; Lovaas, 1977; Mostofsky, 2014). We now consider the use of positive reinforcement and punishment in two of these populations.

Positive Reinforcement Techniques

One of the dangers of long-term psychiatric hospitalization is the gradual loss of social, personal care, and occupational skills needed to survive outside the hospital. Such deterioration is common among chronic schizophrenic patients who have been hospitalized for an extended period. Verbal psychotherapies have very limited success in rebuilding such skills. In the 1960s, Teodoro Ayllon and Nathan Azrin (1968) introduced a revolutionary approach to the treatment of hospitalized schizophrenic patients. The **token economy** is a system for strengthening desired behaviours – such as personal grooming, appropriate social responses, housekeeping behaviours, working on assigned jobs, and participation in vocational training programmes – through the systematic application of positive reinforcement. Rather than being given reinforcers such as food or grounds privileges directly, patients earn a specified number of plastic tokens for the performance of each desired behaviour listed on a kind of menu. Patients can then redeem the tokens for a wide range of tangible reinforcers, such as a private room, exclusive rental of a radio or television set, selection of personal furniture, freedom to leave the ward and walk around the grounds, and recreational activities. The long-term goal of token economy programmes is to jump-start the behaviours that the patient will need to get along in the world outside the hospital. The tangible reinforcers used in these programmes eventually come under the control of social reinforcers and self-reinforcement processes (such as self pride). When this begins to occur, the tokens can be phased out and the desired behaviours will continue (Kazdin, 2012). Using this technique, Ayllon and Azrin reported remarkable increases in adaptive behaviour in patients for whom change seemed hopeless.

token economy a system for strengthening desired behaviours through the systematic application of positive reinforcement

Token-economy programmes have proven highly effective with some of the most challenging populations. In one study, a token-economy programme was carried out over a four-year period with severely disturbed schizophrenic patients who had been hospitalized for an average of more than 17 years. During the course of the programme, 98% of the patients from the behavioural treatment programme were able to be released from the hospital (most to shelter care facilities in the community), compared with only 45% of a control group that received the normal hospital treatments (Paul & Lentz, 1977). Token economies have also been applied successfully within business, school, prison and home environments to increase desirable behaviours (Doll, McLaughlin, & Baretto, 2013; Ayllon & Kazdin, 2013).

A positive-reinforcement programme was used in one study to reduce cocaine and opium use among drug addicts receiving methadone treatment. Patients received weekly urine tests for drug detection. Those who had negative tests were eligible to draw a piece of paper from a bowl. Half of the papers earned them prizes varying in value. Bonus draws were given for extended periods of abstinence (for example, two consecutive weeks of negative urine tests earned six bonus draws). The patients randomly assigned to the positive-reinforcement programme had a significantly higher percentage of negative urine tests over the 12-week period. By abstaining from drugs, the patients had a greater opportunity to build coping responses to avoid relapse following treatment (Petry & Martin, 2002).

Therapeutic Application of Punishment

As we saw previously in this book, punishment is the quickest way to stop a behaviour from occurring, but most psychologists regard it as the least preferred way to control behaviour because of its aversive qualities and potential negative side effects. Therefore, before deciding to use punishment as a therapy technique, therapists ask themselves two important questions. (1) Are there alternative, less painful approaches that might be effective? (2) Is the behaviour to be eliminated sufficiently injurious to the individual or to society to justify the severity of the punishment? Sometimes the answers to these questions lead to a decision to use punishment. For example, some of the most startling self-destructive behaviours occur in certain severely disturbed autistic children. Such children may strike themselves repeatedly, bang their heads on sharp objects, bite or tear pieces of flesh from their bodies, or engage in other self-mutilating behaviours.

Lovaas (1977), a psychologist who pioneered the use of operant conditioning techniques in the treatment of such children, successfully eliminated such behaviours with a limited number of contingent electric shocks. One 7-year old boy had been self-injurious for five years and had to be kept in physical restraints. During one 90-minute period when his restraints were removed, he struck himself more than 3,000 times. With the consent of his parents, shock electrodes were attached to the boy, and he was given a painful electric shock each time he struck himself. Only 12 shocks were needed to virtually eliminate the self-destructive behaviour. In another case, 15 shocks eliminated self-destructive behaviour in a severely disturbed girl with a history of banging her head against objects. Punishment is never employed without the consent of the client or the client's legal guardian in cases when the client is a minor or is mentally incompetent to give consent.

> **Focus 18.9** How are positive reinforcement and punishment used therapeutically? What evidence exists for their effectiveness?

MODELLING AND SOCIAL SKILLS TRAINING

Modelling is one of the most important and effective learning processes in humans, and modelling procedures have been used to treat a variety of behavioural problems. One of the most widely used applications is designed to teach clients social skills that they lack.

> **social skills training** an approach where clients learn new skills by observing and imitating a model performing socially skilful behaviour

In **social skills training**, clients learn new skills by observing and then imitating a model who performs a socially skilful behaviour. In the following example, a therapist served as a model for his client, a socially anxious college student who had great difficulty asking women for dates. The client began by pretending to ask for a date over the telephone:

Client: *By the way (pause), I don't suppose you want to go out Saturday night?*

Therapist: *Up to actually asking for the date you were very good. However, if I were the girl, I might have been offended when you said, 'By the way.' It's like asking her out is pretty casual. Also, the way you posed the question, you are kind of suggesting to her that she doesn't want to go out with you. Pretend for the moment I'm you. Now, how does this sound: 'There's a movie at the Varsity Theater that I want to see. If you don't have other plans, I'd very much like to take you.'*

Client: *That sounded good. Like you were sure of yourself and like the girl, too.*

Therapist: *Why don't you try it?*

(Rimm & Masters, 1979, p. 74).

Social skills training has been used with many populations, including individuals who have minor deficits in social skills, delinquents who need to learn how to resist negative peer pressures and, schizophrenic patients (Rus-Calafell, Gutiérrez-Maldonado, Ortega-Bravoa, Ribas-Sabatéb, & Caqueo-Urízarc, 2013) and those with autism spectrum disorders (Radley, Ford, Battaglia, & McHugh, 2014). It is often used in conjunction with other psychological or biological treatments to jump-start new adaptive behaviours that can then be strengthened by natural reinforcers in the client's everyday environment. Research demonstrates that increased self-efficacy is a key factor in the effectiveness of social skills training. When clients come to believe that they are capable of performing the desired behaviours, they are more likely to be successful in doing so (Bandura, 1997; Maddux, 1999). Observing successful models also increases self-efficacy by encouraging the view, 'If she can do that, so can I'.

> **Focus 18.10** How is modelling used in social skills training? How is self-efficacy involved in its effectiveness?

'Third-Wave' Cognitive-Behavioural Therapies

Since the 1950s, behaviour therapies have developed through three phases. The first phase of treatments was based on animal models of classical and operant conditioning and explicitly excluded cognitive principles. The second wave, beginning in the 1960s, was the emergence of cognitive-behavioural approaches like rational-emotive behaviour therapy (Ellis), and cognitive therapy (Beck). Collectively, these approaches can be called cognitive-behavioural therapies. The past decade has seen the emergence of so-called third-wave cognitive-behavioural approaches (Hayes, Luoma, Bond, Masuda, & Lillis, 2006; Ost, Granhag, Udell, & Roos af Hjelmsäter, 2008). These therapies all incorporate the concept of mindfulness as a central objective of behaviour change, and they represent the addition of humanistic concepts and Eastern methods to behaviour therapy (Koons, 2007). They include a variety of mindfulness-based approaches to various problems, acceptance and commitment therapy and dialectical behaviour therapy.

Mindfulness-Based Treatments

Mindfulness is a mental state of awareness, focus, openness, and acceptance of immediate experience. It also involves a non-judgemental appraisal, so that in a state of mindfulness, difficult thoughts and feelings have much less impact. In some ways, mindfulness is like the *association cognitive techniques* (focusing non-judgementally on the sensations rather than trying to distract oneself) that increase the ability to tolerate painful stimuli. An important tool for learning mindfulness is a meditation technique in which people develop a tranquil state and focus closely on their sensations, thoughts, and feelings, allowing them to come and go without a struggle. It is really a psycho-educational approach in that it provides a training that can be applied to aspects of everyday life (Biegel, Brown, Shapiro, & Schubert, 2009; Rodham, 2010). The meditation technique is being incorporated into a variety of cognitive-behavioural treatments, including mindfulness-based stress reduction (MBSR; Kabat-Zinn et al., 1992; McCown & Reibel, 2010) and mindfulness-based relapse prevention (MBRP; Bowen et al., 2009). Being mindful of our thoughts is a component of metacognition – an understanding or awareness of our own cognitive process. Davey, Dash and Meeten (2014) indicate that metacognitive therapy is a development of the metacognitive model of obsessive compulsive Disorder proposed by Wells (2000). The idea here is not to have the patient think more closely about their actions, but quite the opposite. The intention with obsessive compulsives is to modify the person's belief that the intrusive thoughts they may be experiencing are important, and so require attention and action. During the therapy, the obsessive clients are taught to address any intrusive thoughts with 'detached mindfulness'. They do this with techniques such as thought suppression, and are encouraged to 'notice' the intrusive, obsessive thought, recognize that it is there and let it pass. In short, they are taught to be 'mindful' of their obsessions, and to use this 'mindfulness' as a component in dealing with them.

> **mindfulness** a mental state of awareness, focus, openness and acceptance of immediate experience

As a stress-management approach, mindfulness meditation reduces physiological arousal, and the detached cognitive outlook helps free people from emotion-escalating emotional processes. It is being successfully applied to treat a variety of stress-related medical conditions and psychological disorders, including anxiety and depression (Grossman, Niemann, Schmidt, & Walach, 2004; McCown & Reibel, 2010). Mindfulness meditation can also be used as a relapse-prevention technique. Here, it is used to prevent relapse by increasing awareness of thoughts and emotions that trigger lapses, thereby interrupting the previous cycle of automatic substance-abuse behaviours. It also helps abusers deal with lapses by helping to neutralize self-blame and thoughts of hopelessness, which often turns lapses into complete relapses by producing the abstinence violation effect. In a study by Sarah Bowen and co-workers (2009), MBRP – Mindfulness Based Relapse Prevention – was applied to substance abusers who had completed intensive inpatient or outpatient treatment. As shown in Figure

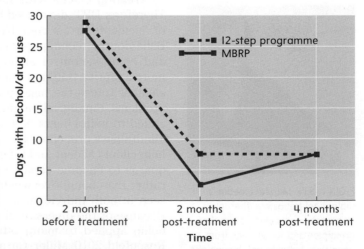

FIGURE 18.13 This graph shows the number of days of alcohol or drug use reported by clients receiving either MBRP treatment or a 12-step programme. Reports were made 2 months before treatment as well as 2 and 4 months after treatment.

Source: Data from Bowen et al., 2009.

18.13, compared with the control group that got traditional community aftercare, the MBRP group had less than half the number of days of alcohol or drug use in the two months following treatment. However, the group difference was no longer evident at four months after treatment, suggesting the need for booster sessions. MBRP, though promising, needs to be compared with relapse-prevention treatment without the mindfulness procedure to see if it adds to the traditional procedures. It has also been used in the treatment of eating disorders and addictions (Wisniewski, Bishop, & Killeen, 2014, Witkiewitz et al., 2014).

Acceptance and Commitment Therapy

> **acceptance and commitment therapy (ACT)** an approach where clients are taught to notice, accept and embrace their thoughts and feelings
>
> **dialectical behaviour therapy (DBT)** developed by Marsha Linehan for the treatment of borderline personality disorder

Developed by Steven Hayes (Hayes et al., 2006), **acceptance and commitment therapy (ACT)** also focuses on the process of mindfulness as a vehicle for change. An important difference in emphasis from traditional cognitive therapy is that instead of teaching people to exert control over their thoughts and feelings, the ACT therapist teaches clients to 'just notice', accept and embrace them, even previously unwanted ones. This matter-of-fact acceptance of a thought (e.g., 'I am thinking that he doesn't like me' by a social phobic) helps reduce the emotional impact of the thought and helps defuse the anxiety it would ordinarily evoke. Even if anxiety were to be aroused, it would simply be examined and accepted as a temporary experience. This helps to strip away its emotional impact. The 'commitment' part of the treatment lies in examining one's life, deciding what is most important to one's true self, and setting life goals in accordance with those values. The therapist then helps the client develop strategies to work towards those goals and to remain committed to them. Although solid randomized clinical trials of ACT are rare, more than 30 efficacy studies have been reported, with moderate therapeutic effect sizes.

Dialectical Behaviour Therapy

Dialectical behaviour therapy (DBT) is a treatment developed specifically for the treatment of borderline personality disorder. As described earlier, this complex disorder is characterized by chaotic interpersonal relationships, poor emotional control, self-destructive behaviours and low self-esteem. As many as 70–80% of borderline individuals attempt suicide, and about 10% eventually kill themselves (Chapman, 2010). Other self-destructive behaviours, such as cutting themselves, also occur when under stress. Borderline clients are among the most challenging to treat because of the severity and diversity of their symptoms, the potential for suicide, and their tendency to have stormy relationships with therapists and to drop out of therapy.

Treating clients with such a diversity of problems requires a variety of techniques. Therefore, DBT, developed by Marsha Linehan (1993) (Figure 18.14), includes a 'package' of elements from cognitive, behavioural, humanistic and psychodynamic therapies. Behavioural techniques are used to help clients learn interpersonal, problem-solving and emotion-control skills. Cognitive approaches are employed to help clients learn more adaptive thinking about the world, relationships and themselves. A psychodynamic element traces the history of early deprivation and rejection that created many of the problems. Finally, a humanistic emphasis on acceptance of thoughts and feelings has been added to help clients better tolerate unhappiness and negative emotions as they occur. Mindfulness procedures are a foundation for the other skills taught in DBT, because they help clients accept and tolerate the powerful emotions they experience in their lives. The goal is to become capable of calmly recognizing situations, thoughts and their impact, rather than being overwhelmed or avoiding them. DBT is intensive in nature, with clients seen in both individual and group sessions by multiple therapists for up to 150 hours. Because of the diversity of skill-building techniques that it contains, DBT is increasingly being applied to many other types of disorders as well (Galietta, Finneran, Fava, & Rosenfeld, 2010; Miller, Carnesale, & Courtney, 2014). A major goal of treatment is to bring self-destructive behaviours, such as suicide attempts and self-mutilation, under control. DBT seems to be uniquely effective in this regard (Barnicot, Savill, Bhatti, & Priebe, 2014). In a comprehensive clinical trial (Linehan et al., 2006), 101 borderline clients were randomly assigned to either DBT or community treatment by non-behavioural therapists identified as experts in treating difficult clients. Clients were treated for one year, and then

FIGURE 18.14 Marsha Linehan's dialectical behaviour therapy approach is an eclectic blend of principles and techniques from cognitive, behavioural, humanistic and short-term psychodynamic treatments.

Source: Reproduced with permission of Marsha Linehan/University of Washington

followed up for one additional year to assess outcomes. As shown in Figure 18.15, DBT was successful in reducing self-destructive behaviour over the two-year period. Although treatment gains were achieved in both treatment conditions, the rate of suicide attempts and psychiatric hospitalizations for suicidal ideation were about twice as high in the non-behavioural condition as in the DBT condition. Borderline clients were also less likely to drop out of DBT (19%, compared with 41% in the community therapy condition). The third-wave therapies have yielded promising results in initial studies, but they do not yet have the extensive research base that older cognitive-behavioural treatments have. Additional well-designed clinical trials are needed to determine their overall effectiveness, the range of disorders that can be treated with them, and the specific contribution of mindfulness procedures (Ost et al., 2008).

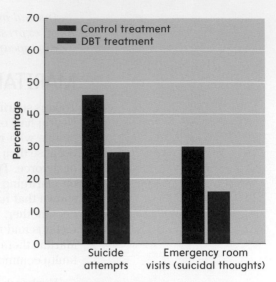

FIGURE 18.15 This graph shows the percentages of borderline personality disorder clients treated with dialectical behaviour therapy or non-behavioural therapy who made suicide attempts on visits to hospital emergency rooms because of suicidal thoughts.

Source: Data from Linehan et al., 2006.

GROUP, FAMILY AND MARITAL THERAPIES

Most of the therapeutic approaches we have discussed so far can be carried out with groups of clients as well as with individuals (Brabender, Fallon, & Smolar, 2004). Therapy groups typically include six to eight clients and a single therapist. Within a group, clients can experience acceptance, support and a sense of belonging. They soon see that other people also struggle with problems, a realization that helps counter feelings of isolation and deviance. Clients can also observe how others approach problems, and the interpersonal relations that develop within the group can be a training ground for learning new interpersonal skills. Furthermore, clients can gain insight into how they are perceived by others (Erford, 2010). The history of group therapy, as with many attempts at therapeutic action, finds its European origins in the Second World War (Harrison & Clarke, 1992). In the UK, Wilfred Bion began treating battle-fatigued soldiers in groups. They realized that other group members, often with very similar experiences, could be extremely influential in helping a person reach a point where transference can occur (described earlier in this chapter). In this respect, each member of the group plays part of the role the therapist does in a traditional, one-on-one therapy situation. Once transference has been reached, the problems expressed can then be worked through within the group.

FAMILY THERAPY

Sometimes the group being treated is a family. Family therapy arose from the clinical observation that many clients who had shown marked improvement in individual therapy – often in institutional settings – suffered relapses when they returned home and began interacting with their families. This observation led to an important concept in the field of psychotherapy, namely, that the disorder shown by the 'identified patient' might reflect dysfunctional relationships within the family system and that permanent change in the client may require that the entire family system be the focus of therapy (Nichols, 2009). Family therapists therefore help the family understand how it functions and how its unique patterns of interaction contribute to conflicts and to the problems of one or more members (Figure 18.16):

> In one family, Jessica, an anorexic 14-year-old girl, was the identified patient. However, as the therapist worked with the family, he saw a competitive struggle for the father's attention and observed that the girl was able to compete and get 'cuddly' affection from her father only when she presented herself to him as a 'sick' person. To bring the hidden dynamics out into the open, the therapist worked at getting the family members to express their desires more directly – in words

FIGURE 18.16 Family therapists focus on the total pattern of family interactions, and they include the entire family in treatment.

Source: © Carmen Martínez Banús.

instead of through hidden behavioural messages. In time, Jessica became capable of expressing her need for affection directly to her father, and her anorexia disappeared. (Based on Aponte & Hoffman, 1973)

MARITAL THERAPY

Today's soaring divorce rate is a stark reflection of the difficulties that exist in many marriages. Nearly half of all first marriages end in divorce, and the divorce rate is even higher among people who remarry (Gurman & Kniskern, 2014). Couples frequently seek marital therapy because they are troubled by their relationship or because they are contemplating separation or divorce. Typically, the therapist works with both partners together, and therapy focuses on clarifying and improving the interactions between them (Harway, 2005). Research has shown that happily married couples differ from distressed couples in that they talk more to one another, keep channels of communication open, show more sensitivity to each other's feelings and needs, and are more skilled at solving problems (Gottman & Levenson, 1992). Marital therapy targets improvement in these areas. Distressed couples frequently have faulty communication patterns, as demonstrated in the following case:

> Husband: *She never comes up to me and kisses me. I am always the one to make the overtures.*
>
> Therapist: *Is this the way you see yourself behaving with your husband?*
>
> Wife: *Yes, I would say he is the demonstrative one. I didn't know he wanted me to make the overtures.*
>
> Therapist: *Have you told your wife you would like this from her – more demonstration of affection?*
>
> Husband: *Well, no. You'd think she'd know.*
>
> Wife: *No, how would I know? You always said you didn't like aggressive women.*
>
> Husband: *I don't, I don't like dominating women.*
>
> Wife: *Well, I thought you meant women who make the overtures. How am I to know what you want?*
>
> Therapist: *You'd have a better idea if he had been able to tell you.*
>
> (Satir, 1967, pp. 72–73)

Focus I8.II What principles underlie family and marital therapy? What is the importance of acceptance in marital therapy?

An important recent addition to marital therapy is a focus on *acceptance* (Jacobson & Christensen, 1996; Gurman & Kniskern, 2014). This addition was based on findings that in well-functioning couples, as well as in those who profit from treatment, partners make a decision to accept those aspects of the partner's behaviour that probably are too ingrained to change. For example, it makes little sense to demand that a person with a highly introverted personality style suddenly become a social gadfly and the life of the party. The therapeutic emphasis is on helping couples work towards change in those areas where change is possible and helping them learn to accept aspects of the partner and the relationship that seem unlikely to change. Doing so reduces frustration, lessens demands on the other spouse, and allows the couple to focus on and enjoy the positive aspects of their relationship. The addition of acceptance training to the other elements of marital therapy has improved treatment outcomes (Christensen, Atkins, Yi, Baucom, & George, 2006; Jacobson, Christensen, Prince, Cordova, & Eldridge, 2000).

CULTURAL AND GENDER ISSUES IN PSYCHOTHERAPY

Psychological treatments reflect the cultural context in which they develop. In Europe personal problems are seen as originating within people in the form of dysfunctional thinking, conflict and stress responses. People are assumed to be capable of expressing their feelings and taking personal responsibility for improving themselves. We can easily see these values and assumptions reflected in the therapies we have discussed. Psychodynamic, humanistic and cognitive treatments all focus on changing these internal factors.

All cultures and ethnic groups do not share these values, however. For example, people from some Asian cultures might view the 'therapeutic' expression of hostility towards one's parents as unthinkable (Hall & Okazaki, 2003). Likewise, the suggestion that assertiveness training would be helpful in competing more successfully with others and standing up for one's rights might be appalling to a person from a more collectivist culture (Cooper & Denner, 1998). Given diverse cultural norms and values, we should not be surprised that some individuals from non-Western cultures view psychotherapy as a totally inappropriate, and even shameful, option for the solution of their problems in living (Foulks, Bland, & Shervington, 1995).

CULTURAL FACTORS IN TREATMENT UTILIZATION

Recent large-scale epidemiological studies suggest that rates of mental health problems differ among ethnic groups. For instance, in the USA, Sue and Chu (2003) concluded that African-Americans appear to have low rates despite a history of prejudice, discrimination and the resulting stress. American Indians and Alaska Natives have high rates, and Mexican-Americans and Asian-American and Pacific Islanders show slightly lower or very similar rates compared with non-Hispanic whites. Even clearer, however, is the fact that members of minority groups use mental health services far less than does the majority white population (Wang, Demler, & Kessler, 2002). Even when minority group members seek out mental health services, they often fail to stay in treatment. As a result, many problems that could benefit from psychological treatment go untreated (Ivey, D'Andrea, Ivey, & Simek-Morgan, 2006; Wang et al., 2002).

These data indicate broad differences between cultures and subcultures in their use of treatment. Other research is more specific and highlights how the frequency of mental illnesses differs between cultures. In a World Health Organization review (1983) symptoms associated with depression across cultures revealed that depressed people across the survey shared many symptoms (sadness, anxiety, tension, etc.) but the presence of some symptoms differed widely. Guilt, for instance, was lowest in Iran and highest in Switzerland, with 22% and 68% (respectively) responding that they did indeed feel guilt. Also, the incidence of mental health differed within cultures, with different cities in the same country suffering different levels of depression. Nagasaki, for instance, had a higher incidence of depression than did Tokyo. Jablensky et al. (1992), on the other hand, looked at the incidence of schizophrenia in ten different countries, including Denmark and the UK, and found comparable levels in each. It is clear, then that there are cultural differences in the diagnoses of different mental illnesses, but the reasons why treatment may not be taken up are still a little unclear. Why might people refuse treatment, or not seek it out?

Sue and Sue (1990) identified several barriers to treatment among minority groups. One of them is a cultural norm against turning to professionals outside one's own culture for help. Instead these individuals turn to family, clergy, acupuncturists, herbalists and folk healers for assistance. Moreover, for many minority group members, a history of frustrating experiences with white bureaucracies makes them unwilling to approach a hospital or mental health centre. There may also be language barriers.

Sometimes access to treatment is a major problem. In certain parts of the world, financial issues and the requirement for health insurance restrict access. Because many minority groups suffer high rates of unemployment and poverty, they may lack the ability to pay for appropriate health insurance – and be unable to afford therapy. Likewise, many community mental health agencies and professional therapists are located outside the areas where the under-served populations live. But even within organized health systems, minorities do not receive equal treatment. In one study of individuals 65 years or older with medical insurance researchers assessed the percentage of members receiving mental health services, rates of follow-up after hospitalization for mental illness, the number of practitioner contacts for antidepressant medication management, and the number of referrals to effective treatments. On all of these measures, elderly members of minority groups received poorer treatment than did whites (Virnig, Huang, Lurie, Musgrave, McBean, & Dowd, 2004).

Applying psychological science

COMPARATIVE PSYCHOLOGY OF DEPRESSION

Understanding complex issues such as depression are hard enough within cultures, let alone between them. In this chapter we have seen how cultural factors play a significant role in how something like depression might be dealt with. In psychology, we often forget that we are part of the animal kingdom and so it may not surprise you to hear that non-human animals also suffer with problems such as depression. The more we learn about depression in our own species, the more we are able to learn about depression in other animals. When humans are depressed they lose the ability to gain pleasure from things that had previously been pleasurable. This behaviour is shown also in animals. Ferdowsian et al. (2011) showed this in primates, relatively close you might think to human, and so not terribly surprising perhaps, but it has also been shown in rodents (Rygula, Abumaria, Flugge, Fuchs, Ruther, & Havemann-Reinecke, 2005). What is more surprising, and very interesting, is how observation of the 'depressed' primates allowed Ferdowsian et al. (2011) to show that they could be diagnosed as depressed using the then current, DSM-IV criteria. The danger here of course is that observing animals and looking for 'human-like' behaviour patterns is dangerous and identifying certain types of antisocial, quiet behaviour as perhaps indicative of unhappiness, or lack of 'joy' is something of a leap but the research does suggest clearly that we are not alone in the way we feel, among our own species and indeed between species. Those of us who suffer with depression may take some comfort in this perhaps, that the way we can sometimes feel, even though it seems very unnatural, is actually more common than we might think. Mammals have similar emotional and motivational responses and urges to humans and as such are extremely useful in our study of depression. This revelation, that animals suffer with depression, will not come as any surprise to the dog owners among you who will know only too well that a dog left alone, a younger dog particularly, can begin to show signs of unhappiness. They may go off their food, stop playing with their toys and become lethargic, just as a human may lose their appetite, or any interest in past-times such as going out to a café they once frequented, preferring instead to remain in bed for longer periods of time. As across cultures, it can be difficult to identify the patterns across species and so managing the depression or unhappiness can be hard. Once we learn how to identify it, how to address it suitably for the culture, or indeed species in question, we can, perhaps begin to make a difference.

One of the biggest problems of all is the shortage of skilled counsellors who can provide culturally responsive forms of treatment (Kohn-Wood & Hooper, 2014; Sue & Zane, 1987). Therapists often have little familiarity with the cultural backgrounds and personal characteristics of ethnic groups other than their own. For example, a therapeutic goal that emphasizes the direct and assertive expression of negative feelings may conflict with the cultural norms of a client from a culture not their own. Sometimes, as well, therapists operate on the basis of inaccurate stereotypes that result in unrealistic and possibly inappropriate goals and expectations, as well as great difficulty in establishing the positive client–therapist relationship that has been shown to be a powerful factor in therapeutic success (Ivey et al., 2006).

cultural congruence a treatment consistent with cultural beliefs and expectations

culturally competent therapists use knowledge about the client's culture to achieve a broad understanding of the client

What can be done to increase access of culturally diverse groups to psychological treatment? One answer is to take therapy to the people. Studies have shown that establishing mental health service agencies in minority population areas increases utilization of mental health services, particularly if agencies are staffed by culturally skilled counsellors (Sue, 1998). Another solution might be to train more therapists from these ethnic groups. Sue and his co-workers (Sue, Fujino, Hu, Takeuchi, & Zane, 1991) found that dropout rates fell and the number of therapy sessions increased when clients saw ethnically similar therapists. However, for clients who elect to remain in therapy, it has *not* been demonstrated that treatment outcomes are better for clients who work with therapists from their own ethnic group. What seems more important than an ethnic match is for the therapist and client to form a good relationship and to share similar viewpoints regarding goals for treatment and preferred means for resolving problems (Figure 18.17). Costantino, Malgady and Primavera (2009) found that **cultural congruence** (a treatment that is consistent with cultural beliefs and expectations) predicted good therapy outcomes for elderly Hispanic clients.

FIGURE 18.17 Research suggests that the outcome of therapy with minority populations is affected more by the cultural sensitivity and competency of the therapist than it is by the ethnic similarity of therapist and client.

Source: © Paula Connelly.

Sue (1998) suggests that **culturally competent therapists** are able to use knowledge about the client's culture to achieve a broad understanding of the client. At the same time, they are attentive to how the client may differ from the cultural stereotype, thereby balancing cultural understanding with the individual characteristics and needs of the client. They are also able to introduce *culture-specific elements* into the therapy. Thus a therapist

might draw on some of the techniques used by folk healers within that culture (e.g., prayer or a specific ritual) to effect changes in the client. Obviously, this would require a good working knowledge of the client's culture, plus a willingness to take advantage of what is therapeutically effective for promoting positive changes in that culture (Mishne, 2002). When therapists receive cultural competence training, they are able to work more effectively with members of other cultures, and clients are more likely to remain in treatment (Wade & Bernstein, 1991; Kelly, Bhagwat, Maynigo, & Moses, 2014). Huey, Tilley, Jones and Smith (2014) point out that all kinds of evidence-based health care, not just (but including therapy) is improved by cultural competency, and so we must look at this when designing systems which are, after all, in place to assist often vulnerable people.

Although the lines between them are blurring, as a broad cross-cultural distinction, the difference between individualist and collectivist cultures can be useful. We can ask, with this categorization in mind, whether the individual sees themselves as a member of society where their own, individual achievements are valued or whether the achievements and goals of the group take precedence. This admittedly broad distinction is important when considering a therapeutic approach. For instance, the decision to engage in therapy in the first instance may well be motivated differently. Those from an individualistic society, where individual choice and individual motivation are prized, may find the motivation to see a therapist alone, whereas a collective decision to comply with help may be the motivation for those from collectivist societies (Smith & Dugan, 1998). Not complying with therapy in the individualistic culture may be done to avoid damage to self-respect and a perception of weakness in not dealing with a problem, but not complying in the collectivist culture may result in a reduction in harmony as a result of going against a group decision that help should be sought. The cultural competence of the therapist (described earlier) is further taxed by this distinction. To engage appropriately with the client, the therapist must be very careful to consider the motivations, both personal and as part of the prevailing society, that the client is experiencing. This understanding of the client's frame of reference is vital in achieving a successful therapeutic relationship and approach. For instance, a person from a collectivist background may have difficulty questioning their society's motivations and approaches, and this may be important in the therapeutic approach. Similarly, they may have difficulty questioning their own desires and aims, and seeing themselves as an individual within the society.

Focus 18.12 What barriers to therapy exist for ethnic minorities?

GENDER ISSUES IN THERAPY

Even within the same culture, the lives of men and women can differ in many ways, as can the life demands they must cope with. As we saw in **Chapter 17**, psychological disorders, particularly those involving anxiety and depression, occur more frequently among women in Western cultures. This may reflect the impact of specific stressors that women face, such as poverty (women are over-represented at the poverty level); lack of opportunity fostered by sexism; strains created by the demanding multiple roles of mother, worker and spouse among married women; and the violence and histories of abuse that many women experience. In many instances, psychological problems arise not so much from internal problems and conflicts but from oppressive elements in the family, social and political worlds. As women strive for more egalitarian relationships with men and for equal opportunity to develop their potential, they often meet external barriers that are deeply embedded in their culture's traditional sex roles and, in some cultures, religious traditions.

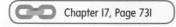 Chapter 17, Page 731

Feminist therapy focuses on women's issues and strives to help women achieve greater personal freedom and self-determination (Brown, 1994; Worell & Remer, 2003). It is not a specific therapeutic technique but rather an orientation that takes into account issues that affect women's lives. In the eyes of many therapists, it may be more important to focus on what can be done to change women's life circumstances than to help them adapt to sex-role expectations that constrain them (Brown, 1994).

It is important for therapists to support people in making choices that meet their needs, whether it be a man who wishes to stay at home and care for children or a woman who wants a career in the military. Whether the therapist is a man or a woman, what seems most important is the therapist's sensitivity to gender issues (Nicolson & Ussher, 2013).

feminist therapy focuses on women's issues and strives to help women achieve greater personal freedom and self-determination What characteristics are found in culturally competent and gender-sensitive therapists?

EVALUATING PSYCHOTHERAPIES

Given the human suffering created by psychological disorders, the effects of psychotherapy have both personal and societal implications. Practising clinicians and clinical researchers want to know which approaches are most effective against which kinds of problems and what the effective active ingredients of each treatment are.

Today the basic question 'Does psychotherapy work?' is viewed as a gross oversimplification of a much more involved question known as the **specificity question**: 'Which types of therapy administered by which kinds of therapists to which kinds of clients having which kinds of problems produce which kinds of effects?' After nearly a half century of psychotherapy research involving many hundreds of studies, this complex question is still not fully answered (Roth & Fonagy, 2005). Nonetheless, for many reasons, this question demands answers. Selecting and administering the most appropriate kind of intervention is vital in human terms. It is also important for economic reasons. A huge amount of money is spent each year on psychological treatments by increasingly stretched health services worldwide. As the need and demand for psychological services increase, the overall costs can only do the same, and those who bear the financial burden, such as taxpayers, and insurance companies who may provide access to private services, increase their demands for accountability and for demonstrations that the treatments they are paying for are useful. Goldfried (2013) points out that whereas there is now strong evidence that in many cases psychotherapeutic approaches do indeed help people, there is also evidence that in some cases patients are actually harmed, and that the patient/practitioner relationship is so very important in the process that when it breaks down, as it sometimes does, the results are unpredictable. A failure in the process may well be the result, as a function of the practitioner/patient bond being so necessary in the first place. The question of whether psychotherapy works is, then, not easy to answer simply.

> **specificity question** 'which types of therapy administered by which kinds of therapists to which kinds of clients having which kinds of problems produce which kinds of effects?'

EYSENCK'S GREAT CHALLENGE

In the 1930s and 1940s, individual case studies provided most of the psychotherapy outcome data. Indeed, Freud and other psychoanalysts opposed the use of experimental methods to evaluate psychoanalysis, insisting that case studies left no doubt regarding its effectiveness (Fisher & Greenberg, 1996). They assumed that without therapy, patients would not improve, and they saw plenty of people who did improve in treatment.

In 1952 Hans Eysenck (Figure 18.18) mounted a frontal assault on this assumption. Using recovery data from insurance companies on people who applied for disability because of psychological problems, Eysenck (1952) concluded that the rate of **spontaneous remission** – symptom reduction in the absence of any treatment – was as high as the success rates reported by psychotherapists. He therefore concluded that troubled people who receive psychotherapy are no more likely to improve than are those who go untreated. He also pointed out, quite correctly, that virtually all of the existing outcome data were based on therapists' evaluations of their clients' improvement, and he suggested that these evaluations could be biased by therapists' needs to see themselves as competent and successful.

FIGURE 18.18 Hans Eysenck (1916–97).
Source: Chris Ware/Keystone/Getty Images

> **spontaneous remission** symptom reduction in the absence of any treatment

> **Focus 18.13** What is the specificity question in psychotherapy research? How did Eysenck challenge beliefs about therapeutic effectiveness?

Eysenck's conclusions sparked intense debate – even outrage – among clinicians, but they provided an important wake-up call that could not be ignored. Eysenck's challenge triggered a vigorous increase in psychotherapy research and stimulated the development of more sophisticated methods for evaluating treatment outcomes. The research goes on as to how to choose the right kind of therapy in each case. A related issue here is 'placebo', discussed a little more on page 807. A placebo is essentially a harmless medical intervention that is given more for the psychological benefit of the client than physiological benefit. It may well be that a therapy acts as a placebo. A person may actively seek out help and in receiving expensive (and so obviously very good indeed) treatment they may well become better. Why they improve though, may be explained in terms of a placebo effect, spontaneous recovery, or in terms of a regression to the mean.

Current topic

REGRESSION TO THE MEAN

Do psychological therapeutic interventions work or might clients get better on their own? Consider this, all too familiar scenario:

Simon is a successful businessman. Just recently he has found himself a little out of sorts. He is angrier than he used to be, shouts at the children more readily, argues with his wife about trivial things. A few months ago his secretary brought him some tea to have for his morning break and he surprised even himself with the ferocity with which he complained to her that it had milk, and he never took milk. She cried as she left the office and he felt just awful. He bought her flowers to apologize, but the event happened nevertheless and he was concerned. The final straw came when he scraped the alloy wheels of his new Audi on the curb outside the bank on the way home. He was so angry with himself that he badly bruised his hand by banging on the steering wheel, just before he unexpectedly burst into tears. This could not go on. He went to the doctor, found a psychotherapist and booked 10 weekly sessions.

After seven sessions Simon felt a whole lot better. After 10 sessions he felt pretty much back to normal – he felt as good as he normally used to. There could be two possible reasons for his improvement. The first is that the therapy worked brilliantly. The second reason is that time has passed and he has just got better all on his own. To work out if the therapy had *caused* the recovery requires a control, an identical Simon, with identical problems and an identical life who remained out of therapy. We could then compare the two and see who was better. This is, of course, impossible. Now consider the second option – that Simon recovered all on his own and returned to his 'usual' state, and it is a good example of something called 'regression to the mean'.

Something more tangible, such as arthritis, provides a useful way to think about it. It can be extraordinarily painful. Those who suffer with it will tell you that very occasionally they have a really good day where the pain is not bad at all. Similarly they may have a really bad day where it seems as if it cannot possibly get any worse. Generally though, they just have days between the two with some pain. This is the average, or 'mean' state of their suffering. Statistically most of their days are better than really bad days, so a really bad day is likely to be followed by a better one. Similarly, most days are worse than really good days, so a really good day is most likely to be followed by a worse one, more like their most common, 'mean' state.

Those who suffer with a problem when feeling terribly low, and low enough and motivated enough to seek the expensive help of a therapist, if left untreated are much more likely to get better than worse. The way they feel 'regresses' (moves back) towards 'the mean' (the most usual state of feeling).

If people get better on their own, should resources that could be better spent elsewhere be 'wasted' on it? In many countries the funds for such treatments are drawn from a form of taxation that would be spent on hospitals, or any number of underfunded projects. On the other hand, if the person gets better, what is the harm in pretending that it is the treatment that has helped them? If they are prepared to pay for it then who is harmed? Are the therapists delivering these treatments aware of this and, if so, are they lying to their clients? Is there, then, an ethical issue to consider? All these questions can form the basis of a debate about the efficacy of treatment, and whether the issue of regression to the mean and placebo play a significant part in the process. The popularity of treatments such as cognitive-behavioural therapy is likely to fuel the debate as we leave recession and expensive treatments such as these, even though more and more popular, become harder to afford.

PSYCHOTHERAPY RESEARCH METHODS

Conducting good psychotherapy research is one of the most challenging tasks in all of psychology because there are so many variables that cannot be completely controlled. In contrast to laboratory studies, in which the experimental conditions can be highly standardized, therapist–client interactions are by their nature infinitely varied. Another difficulty involves measuring the effects of psychotherapy. Figure 18.19 shows some of the typical ways of measuring change. These measures differ in the outcome variable assessed (thoughts, emotions or behaviours) and in the source of the data (the therapist, the client or other informants). Which measures of change are most important or valid? What if one set of measures indicates improvement, another indicates no change and a third suggests that the client is worse off than before treatment? How should we evaluate the effects of the therapy? These are just a few of the vexing issues that can arise in psychotherapy research.

A variety of methods have been used to assess the effects of psychotherapy. The individual case study can provide useful information, particularly if objective data are collected throughout and following therapy. However, it can be difficult to generalize conclusions from the individual case. One remedy to this problem is to present multiple case studies of people who have received similar treatment (Kazdin, 2008).

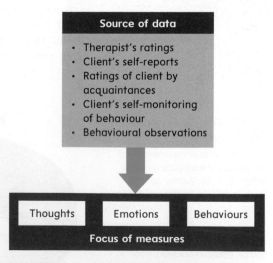

FIGURE 18.19 Psychotherapy outcome measures.
The measures used to assess the outcome of psychotherapy may come from a variety of data sources, and they may measure different aspects of the client's functioning.

A second approach is to survey large numbers of people who have been in therapy and measure their reactions to their experience. This provides us with information about what is in the world of clinical practice. A third method is the experimental approach as embodied in the **randomized clinical trial**, in which clients are randomly assigned to treatment or control conditions, and the treatment and control groups are compared on outcome measures.

Survey Research

A good example of the survey approach is a study carried out by the periodical *Consumer Reports* (*CR*; Seligman, 1995). One form of *CR*'s 1994 annual survey, mailed to 184,000 randomly selected subscribers, contained a section on stress and mental health. Readers were asked to complete the mental health section if they had sought help for emotional problems in the past three years. A total of 22,000 readers responded to the questionnaire – a 13% response rate that is typical of *CR* surveys. Of these, 35% reported that they had a mental health problem, and 40% (approximately 2,900 respondents) of this group reported that they had sought professional help from a psychologist, psychiatrist, social worker or marriage counsellor. The respondents were asked to indicate how much they improved as a result of treatment and how satisfied they were with the treatment they received.

As shown in Figure 18.20, the majority of clients said that they had improved as a result of treatment and that they were satisfied with their therapy. No overall outcome differences were found among mental health professionals, but clients were less satisfied with marriage counsellors than with psychologists, psychiatrists and social workers. The *CR* survey found no effectiveness differences between the various types of psychotherapy the clients said they had received. Seligman concluded that '*CR* has provided empirical validation of the effectiveness of therapy' (1995, p. 974). Further, he concluded that the survey method used in this study might actually have provided data that are more representative of real-life outcomes than data yielded by highly controlled clinical trials.

Meta-Analysis: A Look at the Big Picture

As discussed in **Chapter 2**, the technique of **meta-analysis** allows researchers to combine the statistical results of many studies to arrive at an overall conclusion. In the psychotherapy research literature they can compute an effect size statistic that represents a common measure of treatment effectiveness. The **effect size** tells researchers what percentage of clients who received therapy had a more favourable outcome than that of the average control client who did not receive the treatment.

In 1977 Smith and Glass used meta-analysis to combine the effects of 375 studies of psychotherapy involving 25,000 clients and 25,000 control participants. These studies differed in many ways, but they all compared a treatment condition with a control condition. The results indicated that the average therapy client had a more favourable outcome than 75% of the untreated cases. These results prompted Smith and Glass to dispute

---

randomized clinical trial clients are randomly assigned to treatment or control conditions, and the treatment and control groups are compared on outcome measures

meta-analysis allows researchers to combine the statistical results of many studies to arrive at an overall conclusion

effect size tells researchers what percentage of clients who received therapy had a more favourable outcome than that of the average control client who did not receive the treatment

Focus 18.14 What were the major findings of the *CR* survey? On what bases can Seligman's conclusions be challenged?

 Chapter 2, Page 71

FIGURE 18.20 The *Consumer Report* study.

These graphs show the ratings of (a) self-perceived improvement and (b) satisfaction with therapy outcome made by 2,900 subscribers of *Consumer Reports* who had been in psychotherapy for the treatment of psychological disorders.

Source: Based on Seligman, 1995.

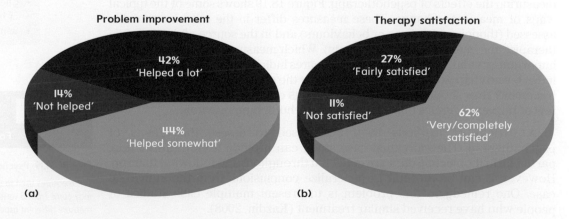

Eysenck's earlier conclusion, maintaining that therapy does indeed have positive effects beyond spontaneous remission. More recent therapy meta-analyses support this conclusion. Glass and Smith also concluded that psychodynamic, client-centred and behavioural approaches were quite similar in their effectiveness. This finding of similar efficacy for widely differing therapies has been termed the **dodo bird verdict**, after the dodo bird's statement in *Alice in Wonderland* that 'Everybody has won and all must have prizes' (Luborsky et al., 2002). Other researchers challenge this conclusion, maintaining that lumping together studies involving different kinds of clinical problems may mask *differential effectiveness*, that is, the fact that specific therapies might be highly effective for treating some clinical disorders but not others (Beutler, 2002; Kazdin, 2008; Westen & Morrison, 2001). Later meta-analyses have tended to focus on specific disorders and the treatments that are most effective for them. Table 18.3 shows the results of some meta-analyses of the application of drugs that have previously been tested and trialled (**empirically supported treatments**) for several disorders (Westen et al., 2004).

In evaluating the results of meta-analyses, we should remember that the studies lumped together in a meta-analysis can differ in many ways, including the nature and severity of the problems that were treated, the outcome measures that were used and the quality of the methodology. Psychotherapy researchers point out that combining good studies with less adequate ones can produce misleading results (Kazdin, 2003). When studies that meet rigorous research standards are compared in meta-analyses with less rigorous studies, the rigorous studies tend to yield more favourable outcomes for therapy conditions (Matt & Navarro, 1997). Apparently, the rigorous methods used in such studies allow effective therapies to show their true effects.

FACTORS AFFECTING THE OUTCOME OF THERAPY

Clearly, not everyone who enters therapy profits from it. There is even evidence that some clients – perhaps 10% – may get worse as a result of treatment (Binder & Strupp, 1997; Lambert, Shapiro, & Bergin, 1986). What, then, are the factors that influence treatment outcome? Research to answer this question has focused on three sets of variables: client variables, therapist variables and technique variables (Castonguay & Beutler, 2005) (Figure 18.21).

Client Variables

Where client variables are concerned, three important factors are the client's openness to therapy, self-relatedness and the nature of the problem (Elkin et al., 2014). **Openness** involves clients' general willingness to invest themselves in therapy and take the risks required to change themselves. **Self-relatedness** refers to clients' ability to experience and understand internal states such as thoughts and emotions, to be attuned to the processes that go on in their relationship with their therapist, and to apply what they learn in therapy to their lives outside of treatment (Howard, Lueger, Maling, & Martinovich, 1993). The third important client factor is the nature of the problem and its degree of fit with the therapy being used. For example, specific problems such as phobias may respond best to a behavioural anxiety-reduction treatment such as systematic desensitization or exposure, whereas a more global problem, such as a search for self-discovery and greater meaning in life, may respond better to a psychodynamic, cognitive or humanistic approach. Patient age, gender, ethnicity and intelligence do not seem to affect outcome (Castonguay & Beutler, 2005).

TABLE 18.3 Meta-analyses of improvement and recovery rates for empirically supported treatments applied to various adult disorders

Disorder	Percentage improved or recovered*
Obsessive-compulsive disorder	66.7
Panic disorder	63.3
Generalized anxiety disorder	52.1
Major depression	50.8
Bulimia	50.0

Note: *Improvement typically means at least a 30–50% reduction in symptoms; recovery means total symptom reduction. The data for bulimia are for recovery only. The number of randomized clinical trials summarized range from 7 to 26 for the various disorders.
Sources: adapted from Thompson-Brenner, Glass and Westen, 2003; Westen et al., 2004; Westen & Morrison, 2001.

dodo bird verdict similar efficacy for widely differing therapies

empirically supported treatments meta-analyses of the application of drugs that have previously been tested and trialled

openness clients' general willingness to invest themselves in therapy and take the risks required to change themselves

self-relatedness clients' ability to experience and understand internal states such as thoughts and emotions, to be attuned to the processes that go on in their relationship with their therapist, and to apply what they learn in therapy to their lives outside of treatment

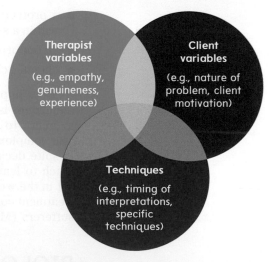

FIGURE 18.21 Determinants of therapy outcome.
Research on factors that influence therapy outcome has focused on three sets of interacting variables: client variables, therapist variables and technique variables.

Focus 18.15 What have meta-analyses shown about the effectiveness of therapies?

Therapist Variables

Among therapist variables, perhaps the most important is the quality of the relationship that the therapist is able to establish with the client (Castonguay & Beutler, 2005). Carl Rogers's emphasis on the importance of therapist qualities such as empathy, unconditional acceptance of the client as a person and genuineness has been borne out in a great many studies. An empathetic, trusting and caring relationship forms the foundation on which the specific techniques employed by the therapist can have their most beneficial effects (Blackstone, 2007). The quality of the therapeutic relationship is so critical, that it is estimated that it accounts for 30% of the variance in treatment outcome (Kazdin, 2008).

When therapists do not manifest these behaviours, the effects of therapy are not simply null; clients can actually get worse. For example, hostile interchanges between therapist and client can contribute to a *deterioration effect* in therapy (Binder & Strupp, 1997).

Assuming the therapy relationship is a positive one, there is still the consideration of technique variables. A therapist needs to be skilled and knowledgeable in selecting and implementing the appropriate techniques for each client and situation. The correctness of the interpretations made by psychoanalytic therapists, as measured by expert ratings, is related to more positive treatment outcome (Crits-Christoph, Cooper, & Luborsky, 1988). Likewise, in a detailed analysis of the audiotaped therapy sessions of 21 psychotherapists, Jones, Cumming and Horowitz (1988) found that the most effective therapists adjusted their techniques to the specific needs of their clients. They concluded that 'general relationship factors, such as therapeutic alliance, are closely bound with the skillful selection and application of psychotherapeutic techniques' (p. 55).

Common Factors

Despite dramatic differences in the techniques they employ, various therapies tend to enjoy similar success rates (Cuijpers, van Straten, Andersson, & van Oppen, 2008), perhaps because people who differ on the client variables are lumped together within studies. This finding has led many experts to search for **common factors**, characteristics shared by these diverse forms of therapy that might contribute to their success. These common factors include:

common factors characteristics shared by these diverse forms of therapy that might contribute to their success

- clients' faith in the therapist and a belief that they are receiving help
- a plausible explanation for clients' problems and an alternative way of helping them look at themselves and their problems
- a protective setting where clients can experience and express their deepest feelings within a supportive relationship
- an opportunity for clients to practise new behaviours
- clients' achieving increased optimism and self-efficacy.

How important these common factors are in comparison with specific therapeutic techniques is currently unknown, and the dodo bird verdict described earlier may reflect a failure to identify specific factors that underlie therapeutic success (Beutler, 2002). The complexities of psychotherapy pose a formidable challenge for clinical researchers. Despite decades of research on the efficacy of psychotherapy techniques, there is still much to learn. We know that some techniques are very effective for certain problems. Yet in the words of the British psychotherapist Isaac Marks, 'Little is known about which treatment components produce improvement, how they do so, and why they do not help all sufferers' (Marks, 2002, p. 200).

BIOLOGICAL APPROACHES TO TREATMENT

In the previous chapter, we found that biological factors play an important role in many psychological disorders. Thus a medical approach designed to alter the brain's functioning is an alternative (or an addition) to psychological treatment.

DRUG THERAPIES

Drug therapies are the most commonly used biological interventions. Discoveries in the field of *psychopharmacology* (the study of how drugs affect cognitions, emotions and behaviour) have revolutionized the treatment of the entire range of disorders. Each year a huge and growing number of prescriptions for drugs that affect mood, thought and behaviour are prescribed around the world. The most commonly prescribed drugs fall into three major categories: antipsychotic drugs, ant-anxiety drugs and antidepressant drugs. Effective drugs (e.g., lithium) also exist for the treatment of mania. Many experts recommend using such drugs in conjunction with psychotherapy to achieve a higher level of long-term success (Hollon, 1996; Thase et al., 1997, Peñate Castro, Roca Sáncheza, Pitti González, Bethencourt, de la Fuente Portero, & Marco, 2014).

Antipsychotic Drugs

Perhaps the most dramatic effects of drug therapy have occurred in the treatment of severely disordered people, permitting many of them to function outside of the hospital setting (Shorter, 1998). This is shown very vividly if we look at the USA as a test case. As shown in Figure 18.22, a sharp decline in the number of inpatients in public mental hospitals has occurred since 1955, when antipsychotic drugs were first introduced to American inpatients on a wide scale.

The revolution in drug therapy for severe psychological disorders began in the early 1950s, when it was accidentally discovered that *reserpine*, a drug derived from the root of the snakeroot plant, calmed psychotic patients. The use of reserpine has been discontinued largely because of some side effects, but is still used to help treat problems of high blood-pressure, because of its action on how the body deals with norepinephrine (noradrenaline). The discovery of reserpine resulted in the development of synthetic *antipsychotic drugs* (also called *major tranquillizers*), used today to treat schizophrenic disorders. The primary effect of the major tranquillizers is to decrease the action of dopamine, the neurotransmitter whose overactivity is thought to be involved in schizophrenia (Schatzberg, Cole, & DeBattista, 2002). These drugs dramatically reduce positive symptoms, such as hallucinations and delusions. However, they have little effect on negative symptoms, such as apathy and withdrawal, and 20–40% of people with schizophrenia get little or no relief from them (Tamminga, 1997). Antipsychotic drugs are now so widely used that nearly all schizophrenic patients living in Western Europe, the USA and Canada have received them at one time or another. It is common practice to continue the medication indefinitely once the individual has returned to the community because patients often relapse very quickly if they stop taking the drugs.

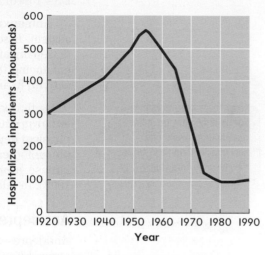

FIGURE 18.22 Effects of antipsychotic drugs.

Antipsychotic drugs have revolutionized the treatment of severely disturbed individuals, allowing many of them to leave mental hospitals. Note the decline that occurred following the introduction of antipsychotic drugs in the mid-1950s.

Source: United States National Institute of Mental Health, 1992.

Antipsychotic drugs have reduced the need for padded cells, straitjackets and other restraints that were formerly used to control the disordered behaviour of hospitalized patients. Although they allow many patients to be released from hospitals, these drugs can produce **tardive dyskinesia**, a severe movement disorder (Kane, 1992). Uncontrollable and grotesque movements of the face and tongue are especially prominent in this disorder, and sometimes the patient's arms and legs flail uncontrollably. Tardive dyskinesia can be more debilitating than the psychotic symptoms that prompted the drug treatment, and it appears to be irreversible once it develops. One study found that within four years of beginning antipsychotic medications, 22% of young adults and 30% of those over 55 developed tardive dyskinesia symptoms (Schatzberg, Cole, & DeBattista, 2010).

tardive dyskinesia a severe movement disorder

Focus 18.16 What is tardive dyskinesia, and what causes it?

Researchers are working to develop new drugs that can control schizophrenic symptoms without producing side effects, such as the devastating symptoms of tardive dyskinesia. A drug called *clozapine* (also called Clozaril, Leponex and Fazalco) reduces not only positive symptoms but negative ones as well, and it appears not to produce tardive dyskinesia (Marangell, 2002). Unfortunately, it produces a fatal blood disease (agranulocytosis) in 1–2% of people who take it, requiring expensive weekly blood tests for patients who use the medication, and for this reason its use was banned soon after it was introduced in the early 1970s. It has now been reintroduced because it really is very effective at helping reduce the risk of suicide in schizophrenic patients.

Antipsychotic drugs can often be used in conjunction with psychotherapy. For example, drugs may be used to bring psychotic symptoms under control so that the patient can benefit from other approaches such as social skills training, family therapy and group therapy. This two-pronged approach is extremely popular and can be extremely effective.

Anti-Anxiety Drugs

The use of anti-anxiety or tranquillizing drugs such as diazepam (marketed as Valium) is widespread. These drugs are designed to reduce anxiety as much as possible without affecting alertness or concentration. Sometimes anti-anxiety drugs are used in combination with psychotherapy to help clients cope successfully with problematic situations (Stahl, 1998). A temporary reduction in anxiety from the use of a drug may allow a client to enter anxiety-arousing situations and learn to cope more effectively with them. The use of these drugs in some cultures is extremely common. Schatzberg et al. (2010) indicate that in the USA 15% of those aged between 18 and 74 use an anti-anxiety drug of some sort.

Anti-anxiety drugs work by slowing down excitatory synaptic activity in the nervous system. *Bisopirone* (marketed as BuSpar or Axoren), for instance, has a simpler effect to diazepam, and functions by blocking receptors of the excitatory transmitter serotonin and by enhancing the postsynaptic activity of GABA, an inhibitory transmitter that reduces neural activity in areas of the brain associated with emotional arousal (Gorman, 2002; Pies, 1998).

Anti-anxiety drugs can have a variety of undesirable side effects, such as drowsiness, lethargy and concentration difficulties. A more serious drawback is psychological and physical dependence that can result from their long-term use. People who have developed physiological dependence can experience characteristic withdrawal symptoms, such as intense anxiety, nausea and restlessness when they stop taking the drug (Lieberman, 1998). In addition, anxiety symptoms often return when people stop taking the drugs.

Focus 18.17 How do anti-anxiety drugs work, and how effective are they? Do they have any drawbacks?

Antidepressant Drugs

Antidepressant drugs fall into three major categories: *tricyclics* (e.g., amitryptyline, brand name *Elavil*, imipramine, brand name *Tofranil*), *monoamine oxidase (MAO) inhibitors* (e.g., phenelzine, brand name *Nardil*, tranylcypromine, brand name *Parnate*), and *selective serotonin re-uptake inhibitors* or *SSRIs* (e.g., fluoxetine, brand name *Prozac*). The first two classes increase the activity of the excitatory neurotransmitters norepinephrine and serotonin, whose lowered level of activity in brain regions involved in positive emotion and motivation is related to depression. The tricyclics work by preventing re-uptake of the excitatory transmitters into the presynaptic neurons, allowing them to continue stimulating postsynaptic neurons. The MAO inhibitors reduce the activity of monoamine oxidase, an enzyme that breaks down the neurotransmitters in the synapse. Other drugs include *serotonin-norepinephrine re-uptake inhibitors (SNRIs)* such as Venlafaxine and Duloxetine.

Monoamine oxidase inhibitors have more severe side effects than the tricyclics. They can cause dangerous elevations in blood pressure when taken with certain foods, such as cheeses and some types of wine. Many patients have abandoned their antidepressant medications because of severe side effects. The SSRIs were designed to decrease side effects by increasing the activity of just one transmitter, serotonin (Marangell, 2002). Like the other antidepressants, however, SSRIs do have side effects, and these are cited as a major cause of non-compliance, where people stop taking their drugs (Balikci, Uzun, Erdem, Doruk, Cansever, & Ates, 2014). For example, about 30% of patients on Prozac report nervousness, insomnia, sweating, joint pain or sexual dysfunction (Hellerstein et al., 1993). Nonetheless, the SSRIs are gradually replacing the tricyclics because, in addition to milder side effects, they reduce depressive symptoms more rapidly and reduce anxiety symptoms that often accompany depression (Lieberman, 1998; Schatzberg et al., 2010). Figure 18.23 shows how the SSRIs produce their effects.

Increasingly, depression researchers are studying the effects of combining drugs and psychotherapy. A meta-analysis of such studies revealed that recovery rates for psychotherapy and the combined treatments did not differ for less severely depressed people. However, the combination of psychotherapy and drug treatment yielded the best recovery rates in more severe cases of depression (Thase et al., 1997).

SOME DEPRESSING FACTS ABOUT ANTIDEPRESSANT DRUGS

Antidepressant drugs have become a treatment of choice for depression in both adults and children. As a less expensive form of treatment than psychotherapy, they are especially attractive to insurers and managed-care providers, and with good reason. Clinicians often observe dramatic improvements in people given SSRIs and other antidepressants. In recent years, however, increasing concerns have been raised about their efficacy and about potential side effects (Schweitzer, McGuire, & Ng, 2009; Balikci et al., 2014).

Placebo Effects

When compared with no-treatment control conditions, antidepressant medication (ADM) effects are quite impressive. But when **placebo control groups** are introduced in randomized clinical trials, the picture can change dramatically. If those taking the placebo simply believe they are receiving an antidepressant, they frequently show improvement that rivals drug effects. By dividing the amount of change shown in the placebo group by the magnitude of change shown by the drug group, one can estimate how much of the drug effect is truly attributable to the pharmacological effects of the drug. For example, in two clinical trials of the SSRI sertraline hydrochloride (sold as *Zoloft* and *Xydep*), in depressed children and adolescents, placebo patients showed 85% as much improvement as those who received sertraline. Both groups showed notable decreases in self-reported depression, but the difference between sertraline and placebo groups was so small as to be of no practical significance (Wagner et al., 2003).

An overview of research where clinicians rated their clients' depression symptoms while unaware of whether the person was taking a drug or a placebo showed interesting results. As shown in Figure 18.24, improvement rates in the placebo conditions ranged from 68% to 89% of those shown in the antidepressant medication conditions, suggesting that expectancies and beliefs account for much of the drugs' effects and that the actual pharmacological effects of the drugs are quite small. Indeed, the data on (brand names) Paxil, Zoloft and Celexa actually underestimate placebo effects because in nine other trials where no significant differences were found between the drugs and placebos, the investigators did not provide depression change scores (Kirsch, Moore, Scoboria, & Nicholls, 2002). In such studies, the placebo effect could account for as much as 100% of patient improvement, so what the placebo effect means for those drugs would be even higher than those shown in Figure 18.24. Even where statistically significant differences were found between drug and placebo conditions on depression ratings, the actual differences were typically too small to be of any clinical significance. Finally, a reanalysis of the data from several major clinical trials revealed that antidepressant drug effects exceeded placebo effects only for the most severely depressed 13% of patients (Fournier et al., 2010). For the vast majority of patients the drugs were no better than a placebo.

The strength of placebo effects may also be underestimated in many studies because of the practice of dropping from clinical trials any

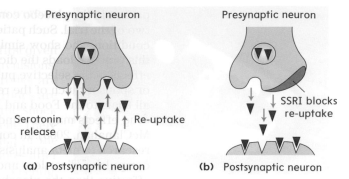

FIGURE 18.23 SSRI mechanisms.

(a) When a presynaptic neuron releases serotonin into the synaptic space, a re-uptake mechanism begins to pull neurotransmitter molecules back into the 'sending' neuron, limiting the stimulation of the postsynaptic neuron. (b) Selective serotonin re-uptake inhibitors (SSRIs) allow serotonin, whose activity is reduced in depressed clients, to continue its stimulation of postsynaptic neurons by inhibiting the re-uptake of serotonin into the presynaptic neuron.

> **placebo control groups** no treatment control conditions

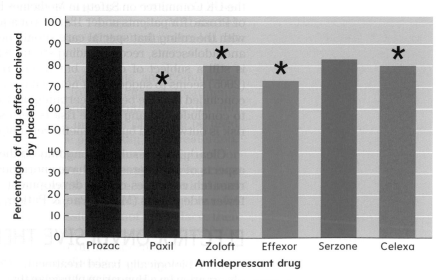

FIGURE 18.24 Placebo effects and antidepressant (SSRI) drugs.

These data were derived by dividing the magnitude of improvement shown by placebo controls by the magnitude of change shown by the drug group. They suggest that, on average, around 79% of the drug effects may be attributable to patient expectations that they will be helped by the drug, rather than to pharmacological effects. The asterisks (*) indicate drugs for which depression improvement scores were not submitted because the drug and placebo groups did not differ significantly, suggesting even stronger placebo effects for those drugs.

Source: Adapted from Kirsch et al., 2002.

PSYCHOSURGERY

> **psychosurgery** surgical procedures that remove or destroy brain tissue in an attempt to change disordered behaviour

Psychosurgery refers to surgical procedures that remove or destroy brain tissue in an attempt to change disordered behaviour. It is the least used of the biomedical procedures, but such was not always the case. In the 1930s, before the advent of antipsychotic drugs, Portuguese surgeon Egas Moniz reported that cutting the nerve tracts that connect the frontal lobes with subcortical areas of the brain involved in emotion resulted in a calming of psychotic and uncontrollably violent patients. The operation eliminated emotional input from the limbic system into the areas of the brain connected with executive functions of planning and reasoning. Walter Freeman developed a 10-minute gruesome sounding *lobotomy* operation called a *spike-lobotomy* performed by inserting an ice pick-like instrument with sharp edges through the eye socket into the brain, then wiggling it back and forth to sever the targeted nerve tracts. During the 1930s and 1940s, tens of thousands of patients underwent the operation. Moniz received a Nobel Prize for his discovery.

Initial enthusiasm for lobotomy was soon replaced by a sober recognition that the massive neural damage it caused had severe side effects on mental and emotional functioning. Seizures, stupor, memory and reasoning impairments, and listlessness occurred frequently. With the development of antipsychotic drugs in the 1950s, the frequency of lobotomies decreased, and they are hardly ever used today. However, more precise and limited psychosurgery procedures are sometimes used in the most extreme cases and when every other avenue has been tried. One procedure called *cingulotomy* involves cutting a small fibre bundle near the corpus callosum that connects the frontal lobes with the limbic system. Cingulotomy has been used successfully in treating severe depressive and obsessive compulsive disorders that have failed to improve with drug treatment or psychotherapy. However, even this more limited procedure can also produce side effects, including seizures (Pressman, 1998). Appropriately, cingulotomy and other forms of psychosurgery are considered to be last-resort procedures, and they are a good deal more precise than they were originally. It was the development and continued research into antipsychotic drugs that changed the way we deal with mental illness, with society and medicine turning its back largely on psychosurgery. But as we have noted, in some cases otherwise unresponsive patients may benefit. For instance, Cumming et al. (1995) and Hay et al. (1993) indicate that those with obsessive compulsive disorder who have not responded to other treatments have benefitted from psychosurgery with relatively few side effects. Others have suggested that severe depression may be treated similarly (Bridges et al., 1994).

> **Focus 18.18** Which disorders do and do not respond favourably to ECT and psychosurgery? What are their drawbacks?

MIND, BODY AND THERAPEUTIC INTERVENTIONS

The impact of drug and electroconvulsive therapies on psychological disorders illustrates once again the important interactions between biological and psychological phenomena. In the final analysis, both psychological and biological treatments affect brain functioning in ways that can change disordered thoughts, emotions, and behaviour. Moreover, they may constitute different routes to the same changes, as illustrated in a study by Tomas Furmark and co-workers (2002) at Uppsala University in Sweden. The researchers randomly assigned patients with social phobia to nine-week treatments that involved either drug therapy with an SSRI or a course of cognitive and behavioural psychotherapy involving exposure to feared social situations and cognitive modification of anxiety-arousing thoughts. Before and after treatment, the participants received PET scans while they gave a hastily prepared speech to a group of six to eight people standing around the scanner bed. They also provided subjective ratings of their anxiety during the procedure. Uniformly high anxiety scores were reported by all participants prior to treatment.

In general, both treatments were effective, although overall, the psychological treatment produced a stronger reduction in fear and social phobia symptoms than did the drug treatment. Nonetheless, when the researchers compared the pre- and post-treatment PET scans of those participants who responded to the two treatments with reduced social anxiety, the psychotherapy and drug groups showed basically the same changes in cerebral blood flow from the first speech situation to the second. These changes involved reduced neural

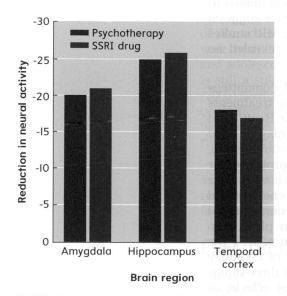

FIGURE 18.26 Drug and therapy effects on the brain.

Clients treated for social phobia received either psychotherapy or drug therapy. Those clients who responded to their respective treatments with reduced anxiety showed nearly identical changes in PET-scan recordings of neural activity in three areas of the brain whose activation is thought to underline anxiety.

Source: Based on Furmark et al., 2002.

activity in an 'anxiety circuit' involving the amygdala, the hippocampus and areas of the temporal cerebral cortex (Figure 18.26). Treatment non-responders did not show these brain changes. Thus different forms of therapy, whether psychological or biological, may result in similar changes at a neurological level and, ultimately, at a behavioural level. One suggestion is that medications can help prime the neural network changes needed for recovery, this allowing psychotherapies to work more effectively (Cozolino, 2010).

An important factor to keep in mind is that drug treatments, however effective they may be in modifying some disordered behaviours in the short term, do not cure the disorder. They suppress symptoms but do not teach the client coping and problem-solving skills to deal with stressful life situations (DeLongis, 2000; Nezu, Nezu, & D'Zurilla, 2000). They may even prevent people from taking steps to confront the real causes of their problems. Many therapists believe that one of the major benefits of psychological treatments is their potential not only to help clients deal with current problems, but also to increase their personal resources so that they might enjoy a higher level of adjustment and life satisfaction in the future (Hollon, 1996).

We have now considered a wide spectrum of approaches to treating abnormal behaviour. 'Levels of analysis' summarizes biological, psychological and environmental mechanisms for therapeutic change.

Levels of analysis

factors related to therapeutic behaviour change

PSYCHOLOGICAL

- Cognitive and emotional changes brought about by cognitive therapies
- Modification of conditioned emotional responses by deconditioning procedures such as exposure desensitization and aversion therapy
- Behavioural changes produced by operant procedures
- Self-concept changes brought about by psychotherapy (e.g. client-centred, Gestalt therapy)
- Insight into unconscious dynamics and development of more mature defences brought about by short- and long-term psychodynamic therapies

BIOLOGICAL

- Changes in neurotransmitter, autonomic, or hormonal activity brought about by drug treatment, psychotherapy or surgical procedures
- Structural changes in brain circuitry and synaptic networks produced by cognitive, emotional and behavioural changes

ENVIRONMENTAL

- Life-situation changes resulting from constructive behaviour changes learned in therapy or produced by biological means
- Exposure to specific therapeutic techniques administered by a mental health expert
- A positive therapeutic relationship that helps promote change and allows therapy techniques to be effective
- Cultural factors that affect access to therapy, type of therapy and exposure to a culturally competent therapist

Therapeutic behaviour change

PSYCHOLOGICAL DISORDERS AND SOCIETY

Since the days of insane asylums, first established in the sixteenth century to segregate the mentally ill from society, severe behaviour disorders have been treated in institutional settings. Many private and government funded institutions were built. The rise in patients being treated in these facilities increased significantly. It became apparent to mental health experts that although there were some high-quality institutions, many mental hospitals were not fulfilling their intended role as treatment facilities. They were overcrowded, understaffed and underfunded. Many of them could provide little more than minimal secure care and a haven from the stresses and demands of the outside world. Moreover, people who were admitted to such hospitals often sank into a chronic 'sick' role in which passive dependence and typically 'insane' behaviour were not only tolerated but also expected (Goffman, 1961; Scheff, 1966). They lost the self-confidence, motivation and skills needed to return and adapt to the outside world, and had little chance of surviving outside the hospital.

DEINSTITUTIONALIZATION

deinstitutionalization to transfer the primary focus of treatment from the hospital to the community

There is a significant movement towards **deinstitutionalization**. The idea is to transfer the primary focus of treatment from the hospital to the community. The World Health Organization indicates that in many of the countries in Europe the number of beds available in mental health institutions, and indeed the number of mental health institutions themselves, have fallen dramatically. With rising costs in health care come difficult and often very unpopular decisions. OECD statistics (2012) indicate a fall in all hospital beds across Europe and those allocated to mental health issues have also fallen. Since the year 2000 the number of beds in total per 1,000 people has fallen by approximately 2% per year. Some countries such as Holland and the UK have deinstitutionalized to a greater extent than other countries, but the trend is certainly there. Traditional psychiatric care is being moved slowly but surely into a more public mental health approach, which is shown, in most cases, to give a better quality of life, and encourage social inclusion rather than exclusion.

MENTAL HEALTH TREATMENT IN A MANAGED HEALTH-CARE ENVIRONMENT

Rising costs and changes in demand have altered the mental health treatment landscape dramatically. Rising populations means rising burdens on health-care systems. The desire to contain health costs very often translates into a strong preference for drug treatments and short-term versus more costly long-term forms of psychotherapy, as well as the use of less expensive counsellors who charge lower fees than psychotherapists. Even then, the demand for mental-health support is often so great that waiting lists to see appropriate practitioners are extremely long. How health care is funded depends on where you live in the world. In some countries, health-care provision is almost entirely private and, as a consequence, often very expensive, so an insurance policy that can be drawn on at times of medical emergency is advised. Of course, insurance policies are, themselves, not inexpensive, so those that cannot afford them find themselves in terrible debt once they fall ill, or worse. If unable to afford mental-health care, a problem may persist and worsen. Health-care organizations and governments are looking at ways to ensure that health financing is in place to ensure that everyone, not just those that can afford it, has access to a decent level of care.

Some countries have an organized system of health care which people pay for through taxation and through some form of national insurance contribution, such as the National Health Service in the UK. Others, as we have heard, rely very heavily on private insurance. In the Netherlands, health care is essentially provided by a number of competing health funds, which all provide funds into a pool, which is spent exclusively on the care of the less affluent in society thus providing for all citizens in one way or another. A similar

situation exists in South Africa, which has recently moved to making access to mental-health facilities easier for those that need it. The South African Mental Health Act that became law in 2004, provided regulations directing private health-care providers in their duty of care to patients requiring both regular medical care and mental-health care. This means that even those without insurance can now gain access to at least some of the services that those wealthy enough to pay for themselves enjoy.

Private health care remains an extremely important part of the health-care system worldwide. Those who eventually pay for the health care are, quite rightly, demanding evidence that the treatments they are paying for are effective. These pressures have had some positive results, including the stimulation of research on treatment outcomes and the development of some effective short-term therapies.

There are, however, some negative effects as well. To many psychologists, the most serious is that many decisions about the type and duration of therapy to be provided are being made by representatives of insurance companies rather than by the client or a trained mental-health professional. In some instances, the number of sessions permitted may be woefully inadequate to treat a serious disorder (Figure 18.27). Although many psychologists concede that some of the more effective treatments are short-term cognitive-behavioural and interpersonal therapies, they do not believe that these treatments are best for every problem and client. It depends on the disorder, and the treatment, but current data suggest that about 12 to 18 sessions are required to achieve a 50% recovery rate for most disorders (Hansen, Lambert, & Forman, 2002). Managed-care plans frequently limit payment to fewer sessions than this, so that many managed-care subscribers do not receive the level of care that they need. Likewise, the preference for drug treatments that require minimal contact between the patient and a professional may provide short-term improvement at the cost of a more satisfactory long-term result that could occur with psychological treatments that allow the development of better coping skills. Moreover, drug therapy has its own negative consequences.

FIGURE 18.27 In environments where private health insurance is required, treatment decisions may be made by untrained representatives of an insurance company instead of a health-care professional.

Source: ©iStock.com/Juanmonino

> **Focus 18.19** What therapeutic issues exist in managed-care environments?

PREVENTATIVE MENTAL HEALTH

Up to now, we have focused entirely on what can be done to help people once they have developed a behaviour disorder. Successful treatment is one way to reduce the toll of human suffering produced by failures to adapt. Another way is to try to *prevent* the development of disorders through psychological intervention. In terms of economic and personal costs, and the costs to society it may be the case that a small amount of time and money spent on prevention will yield much greater benefits. If current efforts to enhance personal well-being and to slow the rise of health-care costs are to be successful, the prevention of behaviour disorders must be a focal point of social policy. In some cases, this may involve treating psychological disorders during childhood in an attempt to prevent their continuation into adult life. Jané-Llopis and Anderson (2006) looked at how mental-health prevention is being tackled by members of the European Union. Sweden, in particular, was praised for a long tradition of preventative work in many areas of health provision. The Swedish attitude and preventative drive to combat alcoholism was singled out as extremely worthy of praise in its influence on more positive mental health. Sweden has a long history of careful supervision of alcohol consumption and instruction of the dangers associated with it, which began at the start of the twentieth century. In addition to this, the Swedish Health Care Act sets out a number of areas which should be targeted by money set aside for preventative measures of health care. Interestingly though, the policy makes it clear that these targeted areas are not, in themselves, the areas we may be concerned with. For instance, 'mental health' does not feature as an item to be targeted. Rather, and interestingly, the items include issues such as 'safe and good conditions in which to grow up' and 'participation and influence in the community'. It is thought that by targeting these areas general health, including mental health, will improve. Elsewhere, more direct action such as school-based intervention programmes have proven effective in

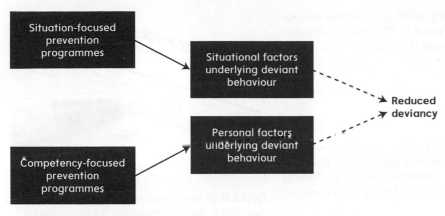

FIGURE 18.28 Preventative mental health.

Two approaches to the prevention of psychological disorders are based on the principle that deviant behaviour represents the interaction of personal and situational factors. Situation-focused approaches increase situational protective factors or reduce vulnerability factors in the environment. Competency-focused approaches reduce personal vulnerability factors or strengthen personal competencies and coping skills.

situation-focused prevention directed at either reducing or eliminating the environmental causes of behaviour disorders or enhancing situational factors that help prevent the development of disorders

competency-focused prevention designed to increase personal resources and coping skills

preventing and reducing antisocial and often aggressive behaviours in children (Wilson, Lipsey, & Derzon, 2003).

People may become vulnerable to psychological disorders as the result of situational factors, personal factors, or both. Thus prevention can be approached from two perspectives (Figure 18.28). **Situation-focused prevention** is directed at either reducing or eliminating the environmental causes of behaviour disorders or enhancing situational factors that help prevent the development of disorders. Programmes designed to enhance the functioning of families, reduce stress within organizations, provide better educational opportunities for children, and develop a sense of connection to other people and the community at large all have the potential to help prevent the development of behaviour disorders (Albee, 1997; Taylor & Wang, 2000). One community intervention programme was designed to prevent the development of antisocial personality disorder in a high-risk inner-city environment. Between the ages of 3 and 5 years, children randomly assigned to the experimental group participated in an intensive nutritional, physical exercise and educational programme. Children exposed to this programme had lower scores on measures of antisocial personality disorder at age 17 and lower criminal records at age 23 compared with a control group (Raine, Mellingen, Liu, Venables, & Mednick, 2003).

The personal side of the equation is addressed by **competency-focused prevention**, designed to increase personal resources and coping skills. Such programmes may focus on strengthening resistance to stress, improving social and vocational competencies, enhancing self-esteem and helping people gain the skills needed to build stronger social support systems. One illustrative programme, developed by Edna Foa, Riggs and Gershuny (1995), focused on preventing post-traumatic stress disorder (PTSD) in women who had recently been raped or assaulted.

The victims were randomly assigned to either a treatment condition or to an untreated control condition. In hourly sessions over a four-week period, the women in the treatment group learned about the common psychological reactions to being raped, helping them to realize that their responses were understandable, given what they had experienced. They relived their trauma through guided imagery to help defuse their lingering fears through exposure. The women also learned stress-management coping skills such as relaxation, and they went through a cognitive therapy procedure to replace stress-producing cognitions with more realistic appraisals.

The results of the prevention programme are shown in Figure 18.29. The women exposed to the prevention treatment had less severe symptoms at both the 2-month and 5.5-month assessments. Moreover, two months after their trauma, diagnostic interviews with the women in the two groups revealed that 70% of the women in the control condition met the DSM-IV criteria for PTSD compared with only 10% of the women who had received the prevention programme. Thus for many of the women, an efficient

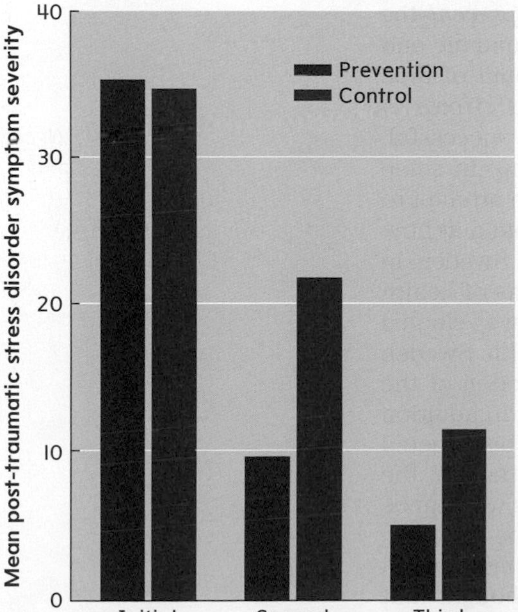

FIGURE 18.29 Preventing PTSD.

A competency-based prevention project was designed to prevent PTSD in women who were victims of rape and assault. The programme, which combined a number of behavioural and cognitive therapy techniques to increase stress-management coping skills, sharply reduced the likelihood of developing PTSD.

Source: based on Foa et al., 1995.

four-week programme prevented what might have been a PTSD disorder that would have created tremendous personal misery and required a far more expensive and time-consuming course of therapy.

To help counter the high incidence of psychological disorders (20–30%) in soldiers who return from combat in Iraq and Afghanistan, an intervention called Battlemind has been developed. It involves a debriefing phase and an emphasis on adapting combat skills soldiers have learned to their home environment. For example, the same skills that helped create close bonds with fellow soldiers can be applied to enhance family cohesion. They also learn how to decrease hypervigilance, startle and irritability. A clinical trial revealed fewer PTSD symptoms, fewer sleep problems, and less depression in those receiving this therapeutic approach (Adler, Bliese, McGurk, Hoge, & Castro, 2009).

Although many mental-health experts believe that more resources need to be focused on the prevention of maladaptive behaviour, they also recognize that prevention presents its own challenges. For example, we cannot develop an intervention programme until we understand the causes of the disorder we want to reduce. Even when causal factors are known, we also need to understand what kinds of interventions will be successful in modifying them. This requires careful research into which types of programmes are most effective in preventing which types of problems in which types of people – our old specificity question.

Another practical problem is that the effects of prevention are usually not immediately obvious. It may take years for their effects to become evident. Moreover, their effects (which usually involve the *absence* of a disorder) can be hard to measure.

For these reasons, prevention programmes can be difficult to justify when funding priorities are being set, even though the programmes may, in the long run, have greater positive impact than programmes that focus on treating disorders that have already developed.

> **Focus 18.20** Describe two major approaches to prevention, and provide an example of each.

 Recommended Reading

CLASSIC

Beck, A. T. (1991). *Cognitive therapy in clinical practice: An illustrative casebook* (new ed.). London: Routledge.

Freud, S. (1920). *A general introduction to psychoanalysis.* New York: Boni and Liveright.-381.

CONTEMPORARY

Barlow, D. H. (Ed.) (2014). *Clinical handbook of psychological disorders: A step-by-step treatment manual* (5h ed.). New York: Guilford Press.

Neenan, M. & Dryden, W. (2005). *Cognitive therapy in a nutshell.* London: Sage Publications.

References

A

'A Recovering Patient' (1986). 'Can we talk?' The schizophrenic patient in psychotherapy. *American Journal of Psychiatry, 143*, 68–70.

Aaron, S. (1986). *Stage fright*. Chicago, IL: University of Chicago Press.

Abbass, A., Sheldon, A., Gyra, J., & Kalpin, A. (2008). Intensive short-term dynamic psychotherapy for DSM-IV personality disorders: A randomized controlled trial. *Journal of Nervous and Mental Diseases, 196* (3), 211–216.

Abel, T., & Kandel, E. (1998). Positive and negative regulatory mechanisms that mediate long-term memory storage. *Brain Research Reviews, 26*, 360–378.

Abi-Dargham, A., & Guillin, O. (2007). *Integrating the neurobiology of schizophrenia*. Amsterdam: Elsevier.

Abraham, K. (1911). Notes on the psychoanalytic investigation and treatment of manic-depressive insanity and allied conditions. In *Selected papers of Karl Abraham*. New York: Basic Books, 1968.

Abramov, I., & Gordon, J. (1994). Color appearance: On seeing red—or yellow, or green, or blue. *Annual Review of Psychology, 45*, 451–485.

Abramowitz, A., & Caron, M. L. (2010). Psychological and neuropsychological testing. In M. K. Dulcan (Ed.), *Dulcan's textbook of child and adolescent psychiatry* (4th ed.). Washington, DC: American Psychiatric Publishing.

Abrams, D., Weick, M., Thomas, D., Colbe, H., & Franklin, K. M. (2011). On-line ostracism affects children differently from adolescents and adults. *British Journal of Developmental Psychology, 29* (1), 110–123.

Achter, J., Lubinski, D., & Benbow, C. P. (1996). Multipotentiality among the intellectually gifted: 'It was never there

and already it's vanishing.' *Journal of Counseling Psychology, 43*, 65–76.

Adams, J. (2010). Prevalence and sociodemographic correlates of 'active transport' in the UK: Analysis of the UK time use survey 2005. *Preventive Medicine, 50*, 199–203.

Adams, P. R., & Cox, K. J. A. (2002). Synaptic Darwinism and neocortical function. *Neurocomputing, 42*, 197–214.

Adelmann, P. K., & Zajonc, R. B. (1989). Facial efference and the experience of emotion. *Annual Review of Psychology, 40*, 249–280.

Ader, R. (2001). Psychoneuroimmunology. *Current Directions in Psychological Science, 10*, 94–98.

Ader, R., & Cohen, N. (1975). Behaviorally conditioned immunosuppression. *Psychosomatic Medicine, 37*, 333–340.

Ader, R., & Cohen, N. (1982). Behaviorally conditioned immunosuppression and murine systemic lupus erythematosus. *Science, 215* (4539), 1534–1536.

Adler, A. B., Bliese, P. D., McGurk, D., Hoge, C. W., & Castro, C. A. (2009). Battlemind debriefing and battlemind training as early interventions with soldiers returning from Iraq: Randomization by platoon. *Journal of Consulting and Clinical Psychology, 77*, 928–940.

Adolph, K. E., & Berger, S. E. (2011). Physical and motor development. In M. H. Bornstein & M. E. Lamb (Eds.), *Developmental science: An advanced textbook* (6th ed., pp. 241–302). New York: Psychology Press.

Adolph, K. E., Berger, S. E., & Leo, A. J. (2011). Developmental continuity? Crawling, cruising, and walking. *Developmental science, 14*(2), 306–318.

Adolph, K. E., & Robinson, S. R. (2013). The road to walking: What learning to walk tells us about development. *Oxford*

handbook of developmental psychology, 1, 403–443.

Adrés, P. (2003). Frontal cortex as the central executive of working memory: Time to revise our view. *Cortex, 39*, 871–895.

Afari, N., Ahumada, S. M., Wright, L. J., Mostoufi, S., Golnari, G., Reis, V., & Cuneo, J. G. (2014). Psychological trauma and functional somatic syndromes: A systematic review and meta-analysis. *Psychosomatic Medicine, 76*, 2–11.

Aggleton, J. P. (1993). The contribution of the amygdala to normal and abnormal emotional states. *Trends in Neurosciences, 16*, 328–333.

Agnew, H. W., Jr., Webb, W. B., & Williams, R. L. (1967). Comparison of stage four and 1-REM sleep deprivation. *Perceptual and Motor Skills, 24*, 851–858.

Ahmed, R., & Gray, D. (1996). Immunological memory and protective immunity: understanding their relation. *Science, 272*, 54–60.

Ahn, H. J. (2005). Child care teachers' strategies in children's socialization of emotion. *Early Child Development & Care, 175*, 49–61.

Ai, A. K., Peterson, C., & Ubelhor, D. (2002). War-related trauma and symptoms of posttraumatic stress disorder among adult Kosovar refugees. *Journal of Traumatic Stress, 15*, 157–160.

Ainsworth, M., Blehar, M. C., Waters, E., & Wall, S. (1978). *Patterns of attachment: A psychological study of the strange situation*. Hillsdale, NJ: Erlbaum.

Aitchison, J. (1998). *The articulate mammal: An introduction to psycholinguistics*. Florence, KY: Taylor & Francis/Routledge.

Ajzen, I. (1991). The theory of planned behavior. *Organizational Behavior and Human Decision Processes, 50*, 179–211.

Akrami, N., Ekehammar, B., & Bergh, R. (2011). Generalized prejudice: Common

and specific components. *Psychological Science, 22,* 57–59.

Alanko, L. O., Laitinen, J. T., Stenberg, D., & Porkka-Heiskanen, T. (2004). Adenosine Al receptor-dependent G-protein activity in the rat brain during prolonged wakefulness. *Neuroreport: For Rapid Communication of Neuroscience Research, 15,* 2133–2137.

Albee, G. W. (1997). Speak no evil? *American Psychologist, 52,* 1143–1144.

Alcock, J. (2002). *Animal behavior: An evolutionary approach.* New York: Sinauer.

Aldridge, S. (1998). *The thread of life: The story of genes and genetic engineering.* New York: Cambridge University Press.

Aldwin, C. M. (2007). *Stress, coping, and development.* New York: Guilford Press.

Alexander, F. (2004). A classic in psychotherapy integration revisited: The dynamics of psychotherapy in the light of learning theory. *Journal of Psychotherapy Integration, 14,* 347–359.

Alfieri, T., Ruble, D. N., & Higgins, E. T. (1996). Gender stereotypes during adolescence: Developmental changes and the transition to junior high school. *Developmental Psychology, 32,* 1129–1137.

Allen Institute for Brain Science (2006, September). *Allen Institute for Brain Science completes brain atlas.* Retrieved from http://www.alleninstitute.org

Allen, M. (1991). Meta-analysis comparing the persuasiveness of one-sided and two-sided messages. *Western Journal of Speech Communication, 55,* 390–404.

Allen, M., D'Alessio, D., & Brezgel, K. (1995). A meta-analysis summarizing the effects of pornography: II. Aggression after exposure. *Human Communication Research, 22,* 258–283.

Allen, M., D'Alessio, D., & Emmers-Sommer, T. M. (2000). Reactions of criminal sexual offenders to pornography: A meta-analytic summary. In M. Roloff (Ed.), *Communication yearbook 22.* Thousand Oaks, CA: Sage.

Allis, D. C. (2009). *Epigenetics.* New York: Cold Spring Harbor Laboratory Press.

Allison, P. J., Guichard, C., Fung, K., & Gilain, L. (2003). Dispositional optimism predicts survival status 1 year after diagnosis in head and neck cancer patients. *Journal of Clinical Oncology, 21,* 543–548.

Alloy, L. B., Abramson, L. Y., Urosevic, S., Bender, R. E. and Wagner, C. A. (2009). Longitudinal predictors of bipolar spectrum disorders: A behavioral approach system (BAS) perspective. *Clinical Psychology: Science and Practice, 16,* 206–226.

Allport, G. W. (1954). *The nature of prejudice.* Oxford and Reading, MA: Addison-Wesley.

Allport, G. W. (1961). *Pattern and growth in personality.* New York: Holt, Rinehart & Wilson.

Allport, G. W., & Odbert, H. S. (1936). Trait names: A psycho-lexical study. *Psychological Monographs, 47* (Whole No. 211).

Allport, G. W., & Postman, L. (1947). *Psychology of rumor.* New York: Russell & Russell.

Alonso, C., & Coe, C. J. (2001). Disruptions of social relationships accentuate the association between emotional distress and menstrual pain in young women. *Health Psychology, 20,* 411–416.

Altman, I., & Taylor, D. A. (1973). *Social penetration: The development of interpersonal relationships.* New York: Holt, Rinehart & Winston.

Altman, J., & Bayer, S. A. (1996). *Development of the cerebellar system: In relation to its evolution, structure and functions.* Boca Raton, FL: CRC-Press.

Amato, P. R., & Afifi, T. D. (2006). Feeling caught between parents: Adult children's relations with parents and subjective wellbeing. *Journal of Marriage and Family, 68,* 222–235.

Amato, P. R., & Keith, B. (1991). Parental divorce and the well-being of children: A meta-analysis. *Psychological Bulletin, 110,* 26–46.

American Psychiatric Association. (2000). *The diagnostic and statistical manual of mental disorders* (4th ed., *text revision*) (*DSM-IV-TR*). Washington, DC: Author.

American Psychiatric Association. (2013). *The diagnostic and statistical manual of mental disorders, fifth edition* (*DSM-V*). Washington, DC: Author.

Ames, C. (1992). Achievement goals and adaptive motivation patterns: The role of the environment. In G. Roberts (Ed.), *Motivation in sport and exercise.* Champaign, IL: Human Kinetics.

Amirkhan, J. H. (1990). A factor analytically derived measure of coping: The Coping Strategy Indicator. *Journal of Personality and Social Psychology, 59,* 1066–1074.

Anand, B. K., & Brobeck, J. R. (1951). Hypothalamic control of food intake in rats and cats. *Yale Journal of Biology and Medicine, 24,* 123–140.

Andersen, B. L., Farrar, W. B., Golden-Kreutz, D. M., Glaser, R., Emery, C. F., Crespin, T. R., Shapiro, C. L., & Carson, W. E., III (2004). Psychological, behavioral, and immune changes after a psychological intervention: a clinical trial. *Journal of Clinical Oncology, 22,* 3570–3580.

Andersen, B. L., Farrar, W. B., Golden-Kreutz, D. M., Emery, C. F., Glaser, R., Crespin, T. R., & Carson, W. E., III (2007). Distress reduction from a psychological intervention contributes to improved health for cancer patients. *Brain, Behavior, and Immunity, 21,* 953–961.

Anderson, C. A., & Bushman, B. J. (2002). Human aggression. *Annual Review of Psychology, 53,* 27–51.

Anderson, C. A., Shibuya, A., Ihori, N., Swing, E. L., Bushman, B. J., Sakamoto, A., ... & Saleem, M. (2010). Violent video game effects on aggression, empathy, and prosocial behavior in eastern and western countries: a meta-analytic review. *Psychological Bulletin, 136*(2), 151.

Anderson, J. R. (1985). *Cognitive psychology and its implications* (2nd ed.). New York: Freeman.

Anderson, M. C., & Neely, J. H. (1996). Interference and inhibition in memory retrieval. In E. L. Bjork & R. A. Bjork (Eds.), *Memory: Handbook of perception and cognition* (2nd ed.). San Diego: Academic Press.

Anderson, N. D., & Craik, F. I. M. (2000). Memory in the aging brain. In E. Tulving & F. I. M. Craik (Eds.), *The Oxford handbook of memory.* New York: Oxford University Press.

Anderson, P., Chisholm, D., & Fuhr, D. C. (2009). Effectiveness and cost-effectiveness of policies and programmes to reduce the harm caused by alcohol. *The Lancet, 373*, 2234–2246.

Anderson, P., Edwards, M., Shannan, M., Obasaju, M. A., Schmertz, S. K., Zimand, E., Calamaras, M. R, (2013) Virtual reality exposure therapy for social anxiety disorder: A randomized controlled trial. *Journal of Consulting and Clinical Psychology, 81*(5), 751–760.

Anderson, V., Spencer-Smith, M., & Wood, A. (2011). Do children really recover better? Neurobehavioural plasticity after early brain insult. *Brain, 134*(8), 2197–2221.

Ando, Y. (2009). *Auditory and visual perception.* New York: Springer.

Andreasen, N.C. (1997) The Role of the Thalamus in Schizophrenia. *Can J Psychiatry, 42*, 1, 27–33.

Andreason, N. C., Arndt, S., Swayze, V., Cizadlo, T., Flaum, M., O'Leary, D., Ehrhardt, J. C., & Yuh, W. T. (1994). Thalamic abnormalities in schizophrenia visualized through magnetic resonance image averaging. *Science, 266*, 294–298.

Andrews, D. A., & Bonta, J. (2010). *The psychology of criminal conduct* (5th ed.). New Providence, NJ: LexisNexis Matthew Bender.

Andrews, F. M. (1991). Stability and change in levels and structure of subjective well-being: USA 1972 and 1988. *Social Indicators Research, 25*, 1–30.

Andrews, G., Stewart, G., Allen, R., & Henderson, A. S. (1990). The genetics of six neurotic disorders: A twin study. *Journal of Affective Disorders, 19* (1), 23–29.

Andreyeva, T., Puhl, R. M., & Brownell, K. D. (2008). Changes in perceived weight discrimination among Americans, 1995–1996 through 2004–2006. *Obesity, 16*, 1129–1134.

Angermeyer, M. C., Holzinger, A., Carta, M. G., & Schomerus, G. (2011). Biogenetic explanations and public acceptance of mental illness: Systematic review of population studies. *British Journal of Psychiatry, 199*, 367–372.

Anisfeld, M. (2005). No compelling evidence to dispute Piaget's timetable of the development of representational imitation in infancy. *Perspectives on imitation: From neuroscience to social science, 2*, 107–131.

Anisfeld, M., Turkewitz, G., Rose, S. A., Rosenberg, F. R., Sheiber, F. J., Couturier-Fagan, D. A., ... & Sommer, I. (2001). No compelling evidence that newborns imitate oral gestures. *Infancy, 2*(1), 111–122,

Anisman, H. (2010). Stress consequences. *Corsini Encyclopedia of Psychology*, 1–3. Published online 30 January, DOI: 10.1002/9780470479216.corpsy0948

Ansseau, M., & Reggers, J. (1999). Epidémiologie des troubles psychiatriques dans la province de Liege et leur prise en charge. Brochure éditée par la plat-forme de concertation de la Provence de Luxembourg. Brochure éditée par la plat-forme psychiatriques Liegeoise.

Anthony, J. C., Warner, L. A., & Kessler, R. C. (1997). Comparative epidemiology of dependence on tobacco, alcohol, controlled substances, and inhalants: Basic findings from the National Comorbidity Survey. In G. A. Marlatt & G. R. VandenBos (Eds.), *Addictive behaviors: Readings on etiology, prevention and treatment.* Washington, DC: American Psychological Association.

Anton, R. F. (2001). Pharmacologic approaches to the management of alcoholism. *Journal of Clinical Psychiatry, 62*, 11–17.

Antoni, M. H., Lechner, S., Diaz, A., Vargas, S., Holley, H., Phillips, K., ... Blomberg, B. (2009). Cognitive behavioral stress management effects on psychosocial and physiological adaptation in women undergoing treatment for breast cancer. *Brain Behaviour Immunology, 23*(5), 580–591.

Antonuccio, D. O., Danton, W. G. & McClanahan, T. M. (2003). Psychology in the prescription era: Building a firewall between marketing and science. *American Psychologist, 58*, 1028–1043.

Antrobus, J. (1991). Dreaming: Cognitive processes during cortical activation and high afferent thresholds. *Psychological Review, 98*, 96–121.

APA Monitor (1997, December). *Author, 28* (12).

Aponte, H., & Hoffman, L. (1973). The open door. A structural approach to a family with an anorectic child. *Family Process, 12*, 1–44.

Apperloo, M., Midden, M., van der Stege, J., Wouda, J., Hoek, A., & Weijmar Schultz, W. (2006). Vaginal application of testosterone: A study on pharmacokinetics and the sexual response in healthy volunteers. *Journal of Sexual Medicine, 3*(3), 541–549.

Archer, T., Beninger, R. J., Palomo T., & Kostrzewa, R. M. (2010). Epigenetics and biomarkers in the staging of neuropsychiatric disorders. *Neurotoxicity Research, 18*(3–4), 347–366.

Arendt, J., Skene, D. J., Middleton, B., Lockley, S. W., & Deacon, S. (1997). Efficacy of melatonin in jet lag, shift work and blindness. *Journal of Biological Rhythms, 12*, 604–617.

Arendt, J. T., Rohsenow, D. J., Almeida, A. B., Hunt, S. K., Gokhale, M., Gottlieb, D. J., & Howland, J. (2011). Sleep following alcohol intoxication in healthy, young adults: effects of sex and family history of alcoholism. *Alcoholism: Clinical and Experimental Research, 35*, 870–878. DOI: 10.1111/j.1530-0277.2010.01417.x

Argyle, M. (1999). Causes and correlates of happiness. In D. Kahneman, E. Diener, & N. Schwarz (Eds.), *Well-being: The foundations of hedonic psychology.* New York: Russell Sage Foundation.

Ariznavarreta, C., Cardinali, D. P., Villanua, M. A., Granados, B., Martín, M,. Chiesa, J. J., & Golombek, D. A., & Tresguerres, J. A. (2002). Circadian rhythms in airline pilots submitted to long-haul transmeridian flights. *Aviation, Space, and Environmental Medicine, 73*, 445–455.

Armitage, C. J., & Conner, M. (2000). Social cognition models and health behaviour: A structured review. *Psychology and Health, 15*, 173–189.

Armitage, C. J., & Conner, M. (2001). Efficacy of the theory of planned behaviour: A meta-analytic review. *British Journal of Social Psychology, 40*, 471–499.

Arnett, J. J. (1999). Adolescent storm and stress, reconsidered. *American Psychologist, 54*, 317–326.

Arnett, J. J. (2001). Conceptions of the transition to adulthood: Perspectives from

adolescence through midlife. *Journal of Adult Development, 8,* 133–143.

Arnett, J. J. (2008). The neglected 95%: Why American psychology needs to become less American. *American Psychologist, 63,* 602–614.

Arnett, P. A. (1997). Autonomic responsivity in psychopaths: A critical review and theoretical proposal. *Clinical Psychology Review, 17,* 903–936.

Aron, A., & Westbay, L. (1996). Dimensions of the prototype of love. *Journal of Personality and Social Psychology, 70,* 535–551.

Aron, E., Aron, A., & Davies, K. M. (2005). Adult shyness: The interaction of temperamental sensitivity and an adverse childhood environment. *Personality and Social Psychology Bulletin, 31,* 181–197.

Aronson, E., Stephan, C., Sikes, J., & Snapp, M. (1978). *The jigsaw classroom.* Beverly Hills, CA: Sage.

Aronson, J., Lustina, M. J., Good, C., Keough, K., Steele, C. M. & Brown, J. (1999). When White men can't do math: Necessary and sufficient factors in stereotype threat. *Journal of Experimental Social Psychology, 35,* 29–46.

Arrow, H., & Burns, K. L. (2004). Self-organizing culture: How norms emerge in small groups. In M. Schaller & C. S. Crandall (Eds.), *The psychological foundations of culture.* Mahwah, NJ: Erlbaum.

Asch, S. E. (1946). Forming impressions of personality. *Journal of Abnormal and Social Psychology, 41,* 258–290.

Asch, S. E. (1951). Effects of group pressure upon the modification and distortion of judgment. In H. Guetzkow (Ed.), *Groups, leadership, and men.* Pittsburgh: Carnegie Press.

Asch, S. E. (1956). Studies of independence and conformity: A minority of one against a unanimous majority. *Psychological Monographs, 70,* 416.

Asghari, A., & Nicholas, M. K. (2006). Personality and pain-related beliefs/coping strategies: a prospective study. *The Clinical Journal of Pain, 22,* 10–18.

Ashton, M. C., Lee, K., & Goldberg, L. R. (2004). A hierarchical analysis of 1,710 English personality-descriptive adjectives. *Journal of Personality and Social Psychology, 87,* 707–721.

Aspinwall, L. G., & Staudinger, U. M. (Eds.) (2003). *A psychology of human strengths: Fundamental questions and future directions for a positive psychology.* Washington, DC: American Psychological Association.

Assanand, S. P., John, P. J., & Lehman, D. R. (1998). Teaching theories of hunger and eating: Overcoming students' misconceptions. *Teaching of Psychology, 25,* 44–46.

Assor, A., Roth, G., & Deci, E. L. (2004). The emotional costs of parents' conditional regard: A self-determination theory analysis. *Journal of Personality, 72,* 47–88.

Atkinson, J. W. (1964). *An introduction to motivation.* Princeton, NJ: Van Nostrand.

Atkinson, J. W. (Ed.). (1958). *Motives in fantasy, action, and society.* Princeton, NJ: Van Nostrand.

Atkinson, J. W., & Birch, D. (1978). *An introduction to motivation.* New York: Van Nostrand.

Atkinson, R. C., & Shiffrin, R. M. (1968). Human memory: A proposed system and its control processes. In K. W. Spence & J. T. Spence (Eds.), *Advances in the psychology of learning and motivation: Research and theory* (Vol. 2). New York: Academic Press.

Atran, S. (2003). Genesis of suicide terrorism. *Science, 299*(5612), 1534–1539.

Attia, E. (2010). Anorexia nervosa: Current status and future directions. *Annual Review of Medicine, 61,* 425–443.

Auerbach, S. M. (1989). Stress management and coping research in the health care setting: An overview and methodological commentary. *Journal of Consulting and Clinical Psychology, 57,* 388–395.

Auerbach, S. M., Penberthy, A. R., & Kiesler, D. J. (2004). Opportunity for control, interpersonal impacts, and adjustment to a long-term invasive health care procedure. *Journal of Behavioral Medicine, 27,* 11–29.

Austin, M., & Leader, L. (2000). Maternal stress and obstetric and infant outcomes: Epidemiological findings and neuroendocrine mechanisms. *Australian and New Zealand Journal of Obstetrics and Gynaecology, 40,* 331–337.

Auyeung, B., Lombardo, M., Knickmeyer, R., & Baron-Cohen, S. (2011). Autism spectrum conditions and 'maleness'. In F. Volkmar & P. Howlin (Eds.), *Encyclopedia of Autism Spectrum Disorders.* New York: Springer.

Avenell, A., Brown, T. J., McGee, M. A., Campbell, M. K., Grant, A. M., Broom, J., Jung, R. T., & Smith, W. C. (2004). What interventions should we add to weight reducing diets in adults with obesity? A systematic review of randomized controlled trials of adding drug therapy, exercise, behaviour therapy or a combination of these interventions. *Journal of Human Nutrition and Dietetics, 17,* 293–316.

Axelsson, E., Ratnakumar, A., Arendt, M.-L., Maqbool, K., Webster, M. T., Perloski, M., … Lindblad-Toh, K. (2013). The genomic signature of dog domestication reveals adaptation to a starch-rich diet. *Nature, 495,* 360–364.

Ayllon, T., & Azrin, N. H. (1968). *The token economy: A motivational system for therapy and rehabilitation.* New York: Appleton-Century-Crofts.

Ayllon, T., & Kazdin, A. (2013). Nathan, H. Arzin (1930–2013), *American Psychologist, 68*(9), 884. doi: 10.1037/a0033763

Ayres, J. J. B. (1998). Fear conditioning and avoidance. In W. T. O'Donohue (Ed.), *Learning and behavior therapy.* Boston: Allyn & Bacon.

Azevedo, F. A., Carvalho, L. R., Grinberg, L. T., Farfel, J. M., Ferretti, R. E., Leite, R. E., Lent, R., & Herculano-Houzel, S. (2009). Equal numbers of neuronal and nonneuronal cells make the human brain an isometrically scaled-up primate brain. *Journal of Comparative Neurology, 513*(5), 532–541.

B

Baars, B. J. (1997). In the theatre of consciousness: Global workspace theory, a rigorous scientific theory of consciousness. *Journal of Consciousness Studies, 4,* 292–309.

Baars, B. J. (2002). The conscious access hypothesis: Origins and recent evidence. *Trends in Cognitive Sciences, 6,* 47–52.

Baayen, R. H., Piepenbrock, R., & Van Rijn, H. (1993). *The CELEX lexical database.* CD-ROM. Philadelphia, PA.

Backhaus, W. G., Kliegl, R., & Werner, J. S. (Eds.) (1998). *Color vision: Perspectives from different disciplines.* New York: Walter de Gruyter.

Bäckman, L., & Nilsson, L. G. (1985). Prerequisites for lack of age differences in memory performance. *Experimental Aging Research, 11,* 67–73.

Backstrom, M., Bjorklund, F., & Larson, M. R. (2009). Five factor inventories have a major general factor related to social desirability which can be reduced by framing items neutrally. *Journal of Research in Personality, 43,* 335–344.

Baddeley, A. D. (1966). Short-term memory for word sequences as a function of acoustic semantic and formal similarity. *Quarterly Journal of Experimental Psychology, 18*(4), 362–365.

Baddeley, A. D. (1990). *Human memory: Theory and practice.* Boston: Allyn & Bacon.

Baddeley, A. D. (2002). Is working memory still working? *European Psychologist, 7,* 85–97.

Baddeley, A. D., & Hitch, G. J. (1974). Working memory. In G. H. Bower (Ed.), *The psychology of learning and motivation* (Vol. 8). New York: Academic Press.

Baddeley, A. D., Thompson, N., & Buchanan, M. (1975). Word length and the structure of short-term memory. *Journal of Verbal Learning and Verbal Behavior, 14,* 575–589.

Baehr, E. K. (2001). Circadian phase-delaying effects of nocturnal exercise in older and young adults. *Dissertation Abstracts International: Section B: The Sciences and Engineering, 62* (4-B), 2105.

Baer, R. A., Smith, G. T., Lykins, E., Button, D., Krietemeyer, J., Sauer, S., … Williams, J. M. (2008). Construct validity of the five facet mindfulness questionnaire in meditating and nonmeditating samples. *Assessment, 15*(3), 329–342.

Bagge, C., Nickell, A., Stepp, S., Durrett, C., Jackson, K., & Trull, T. J. (2004). Borderline personality disorder features predict negative outcomes 2 years later. *Journal of Abnormal Psychology, 113,* 279–288.

Bagley, C., & Ramsay, R. (1997). *Suicidal behaviour in adolescents and adults: Research, taxonomy and prevention.* Aldershot: Ashgate Publishing.

Bagnardi, V., Blangiardo, M., LaVecchia, C., & Corrao, G. (2001). A meta-analysis of alcohol drinking and cancer risk. *British Journal of Cancer, 85,* 1700–1705.

Bahrick, H. P. (1984). Semantic memory content in permastore: Fifty years of memory for Spanish learned in school. *Journal of Experimental Psychology: General, 113,* 1–29.

Bahrick, H. P. (2005). The long-term neglect of long-term memory: Reasons and remedies. In A. F. Healy (Ed.), *Experimental cognitive psychology and its applications: Decade of behavior.* Washington, DC: American Psychological Association.

Bahrick, H. P., Bahrick, P. O., & Wittlinger, R. P. (1975). Fifty years of memory for names and faces: A cross-sectional approach. *Journal of Experimental Psychology: General, 104,* 54–75.

Bahrick, H. P., Hall, L. K., & Berger, S. A. (1996). Accuracy and distortion in memory for high school grades. *Psychological Science, 7,* 265–271.

Bailey, J. M., & Pillard, R. C. (1991). A genetic study of male sexual orientation. *Archives of General Psychiatry, 48,* 1089–1096.

Bailey, J. M., Dunne, M. P., & Martin, N. G. (2000). Genetic and environmental influences on sexual orientation and its correlates in an Australian twin sample. *Journal of Personality and Social Psychology, 78,* 524–536.

Bailey, J. M., Pillard, R. C., Neale, M. C., & Agyei, Y. (1993). Heritable factors influence sexual orientation in women. *Archives of General Psychiatry, 50,* 217–223.

Baillargeon, R. (1987). Object permanence in 3½- and 4½-month-old infants. *Developmental Psychology, 23,* 655–664.

Baillargeon, R. (2004). Infants' physical world. *Current Directions in Psychological Science, 13,* 89–94.

Baillargeon, R., Scott, R. M., & He, Z. (2010). False-belief understanding in infants. *Trends in Cognitive Sciences, 14,* 110–118.

Baillargeon, R., Spelke, E. S., & Wasserman, S. (1985). Object permanence in five-month-old infants. *Cognition, 20,* 191–208.

Baird, L. L. (1985). Do grades and tests predict adult accomplishment? *Readings in Higher Education, 23,* 3–85.

Balconi, M., & Mazza, G. (2010). Lateralisation effect in comprehension of emotional facial expression: A comparison between EEG alpha band power and behavioural inhibition (BIS) and activation (BAS) systems. *Laterality, 15*(3), 361–384.

Baldwin, S. A., Berkeljon, A., Atkins, D. C., Olsen, J. A., & Nielsen, S. L. (2009). Rates of change in naturalistic psychotherapy: Contrasting dose effect and good-enough level models of change. *Journal of Consulting and Clinical Psychology, 77,* 203–211.

Balikci, A., Uzun, O., Erdem, M., Doruk, A., Cansever, A., & Ates, M. A. (2014). Side effects that cause noncompliance to antidepressant medications in the course of outpatient treatment. *Klinik Psikofarmakoloji Bulteni, 24*(1).

Ball, K., MacFarlane, A., Crawford, D., Savige, G., Andrianopoulos, N., & Worsley, A. (2009). Can social cognitive theory constructs explain socioeconomic variations in eating behaviours? A mediation analysis. *Health Education Research, 24*(3), 496–506.

Ball, L. J., Lucas, E. J., Miles, J. N. V., & Gale, A. G. (2003). Inspection times and the selection task: What do eye-movements reveal about relevance effects? *Quarterly Journal of Experimental Psychology, 56A,* 1053–1077.

Baltes, P. B., & Kunzmann, U. (2004). The two faces of wisdom: Wisdom as a general theory of knowledge and judgment about excellence in mind and virtue vs. wisdom as everyday realization in people and products. *Human Development, 47,* 290–299.

Baltes, P. B., & Staudinger, U. M. (2000). Wisdom: A metaheuristic (pragmatic) to orchestrate mind and virtue toward excellence. *American Psychologist, 55,* 122–136.

Bandura, A. (1965). Influence of models' reinforcement contingencies on the acquisition of imitated responses. *Journal*

of Personality and Social Psychology, 1, 589–595.

Bandura, A. (1969). *Principles of behavior modification.* New York: Holt, Rinehart & Winston.

Bandura, A. (1986). *Social foundations of thought and action: A social-cognitive theory.* Englewood Cliffs, NJ: Prentice Hall.

Bandura, A. (1989). Social cognitive theory. *Annals of Child Development, 6,* 3–58.

Bandura, A. (1997). *Self-efficacy: The exercise of control.* New York: W. H. Freeman.

Bandura, A. (1999). Social cognitive theory of personality. In D. Cervone & Y. Shoda (Eds.), *The coherence of personality.* New York: Guilford Press.

Bandura, A. (2000). Health promotion from the perspective of social cognitive theory. In P. Norman, C. Abraham, & M. Conner (Eds.), *Understanding and changing health and behaviour.* Reading, MA: Harwood.

Bandura, A. (2001). Social cognitive theory: An agentic perspective. *Annual Review of Psychology, 52*(1), 1–26.

Bandura, A. (2002a). Environmental sustainability by sociocognitive deceleration of population growth. In P. Schmuck & W. P. Schultz (Eds.), *Psychology of sustainable development.* Dordrecht: Kluwer.

Bandura, A. (2002b). Growing primacy of human agency in adaptation and change in the electronic era. *European Psychologist, 7,* 2–16.

Bandura, A. (2004). Social cognitive theory for personal and social change by enabling media. In A. Singhal, M. J. Cody, E. M. Rogers, & M. Sabido (Eds.), *Entertainment, education and social change: History, research, and practice.* Mahwah, NJ: Erlbaum.

Bandura, A., & Cervone, D. (1983). Self-evaluative and self-efficacy mechanisms governing the motivational effects of goal systems. *Journal of Personality and Social Psychology, 45,* 1017–1028.

Bandura, A., O'Leary, A., Taylor, C., Gauthier, J., & Gossard, D. (1987). Perceived self-efficacy and pain control: Opioid and nonopioid mechanisms.

Journal of Personality and Social Psychology, 53, 563–571.

Banyard, P., & Hunt, N. (2000). Reporting research: Something missing? *Psychologist, 13*(2), 68–71.

Barber, J. (1998). The mysterious persistence of hypnotic analgesia. *International Journal of Clinical and Experimental Hypnosis, 46,* 28–43.

Bardi, A., & Guerra, V. M. (2011). Cultural values predict coping using culture as an individual difference variable in multicultural samples. *Journal of Cross-Cultural Psychology, 42,* 908–927.

Bardo, M. T. (1998). Neuropharmacological mechanisms of drug reward: Beyond dopamine in the nucleus accumbens. *Critical Review of Neurobology, 12,* 37–67.

Bargh, J. A., & Chartrand, T. L. (1999). The unbearable automaticity of being. *American Psychologist, 54,* 462–479.

Barlow, D. H. (2002). *Anxiety and its disorders.* New York: Guilford Press.

Barlow, D. H., Rapee, R. M., & Reisner, L. C. (2001). *Mastering stress 2001: A lifestyle approach.* Dallas, TX: American Health.

Barnes, G. E., & Prosen, H. (1985). Parental death and depression. *Journal of Abnormal Psychology, 94,* 64–69.

Barnett, J. E., & Porter, J. E. (1998). The suicidal patient: Clinical and risk management strategies. In L. VandeCreek & S. Knapp (Eds.), *Innovations in clinical practice: A source book* (Vol. 16). Sarasota, FL: Professional Resource Press.

Barnicot, K., Savill, M., Bhatti, N., & Priebe, S. (2014). A pragmatic randomised controlled trial of dialectical behaviour therapy: Effects on hospitalisation and post-treatment follow-up. *Psychotherapy and Psychosomatics, 83*(3), 192–193.

Baron, R. S. (2005). So right it's wrong: Groupthink and the ubiquitous nature of polarized group decision making. *Advances in Experimental Social Psychology, 37,* 219–253.

Baron, A., & Perone, M. (2001). Explaining avoidance: Two factors are still better than one. *Journal of the Experimental Analysis of Behavior, 75,* 357–361.

Baron, R. S., Cutrona, C. E., Hicklin, D., Russell D. W., & Lubaroff, D. M. (1990).

Social support and immune responses among spouses of cancer patients. *Journal of Personality and Social Psychology, 59,* 344–352.

Baron-Cohen, S. (1995). From attention-goal psychology to belief desire psychology: The development of a theory of mind and its dysfunction. In O. Liverta Sempio & A. Marchetti (Eds.), *Il Pensiero Dell'Altro.* Rafaello Cortina Editore. Reprinted from *Understanding other minds: perspectives from autism.* Oxford: Oxford University Press.

Baron-Cohen, S. (2003). The male and female brain. *Cambridge Medicine, 18,* 20–21.

Baron-Cohen, S., Allen, J., & Gillberg, C. (1992). Can autism be detected at 18 months? The needle, the haystack, and the CHAT. *British Journal of Psychiatry, 161,* 839–843.

Baron-Cohen, S., Auyeung, B., Knickmeyer, R., & Ashwin, E. (2013). The extreme male brain theory of autism: the role of fetal androgens. In D. Amaral, G. Dawson, & D. H. Geschwind (Eds.), *Autism spectrum disorders.* Oxford: Oxford University Press.

Baron-Cohen, S., Knickmeyer, R., & Belmonte, M. (2005). Sex differences in the brain: Implications for explaining autism. *Science, 310,* 819–823.

Baron-Cohen, S., Leslie, A. M., & Frith, U. (1985). Does the autistic child have a 'theory of mind?' *Cognition, 21,* 37–46.

Baron-Cohen, S., Wheelwright, S., & Jolliffe, T. (1997). Is there a 'language of the eyes'? Evidence from normal adults and adults with autism/Asperger's syndrome. *Visual Cognition, 4,* 311–331.

Barondes, S. H. (1999). *Mood genes: Hunting for origins of mania and depression.* New York: Oxford University Press.

Barone-Adesi, F., Vizzini, L., Merletti, F., & Richiardi, L. (2006). Short-term effects of Italian smoking regulation on rates of hospital admission for acute myocardial infarction. *European Heart Journal, 27,* 2468–2472.

Barry, C., Morrison, C. M., & Ellis, A. W. (1997). Naming the Snodgrass and Vanderwart pictures: Effects of age of acquisition, frequency, and name agreement. *Quarterly Journal of Experimental Psychology, 50A,* 560–585.

Bar-Tal, D. (1998). Group beliefs as an expression of social identity. In D. Paez, J-C. Deschamps, S. Worchel & J. F. Morales (Eds.), *Social identity: International perspectives*. Thousand Oakes, CA: Sage Publications.

Barthélémy, C., Fuentes, J., Howlin, P., & Van der Gaag, R. (2009) *Persons with autism spectrum disorders: Identification, understanding, intervention*. Brussels: Autism-Europe.

Bartholomew, D. L. (2005). *Measuring intelligence: Facts and fallacies*. New York: Cambridge University Press.

Bartlett, F. C. (1932). *Remembering: A study in experimental and social psychology*. New York: Cambridge University Press.

Baruffol, E., & Thilmany, M. C. (1993). Anxiety, depression, somatization and alcohol abuse prevalence rates in a general Belgian community sample. *Acta Psychiatrica Belgica, 93*, 136–153.

Basedow, H (1925). *The Australian aboriginal*. Adelaide: F. W. Preece.

Bashinski, H. S., Werner, J. S., & Rudy, J. W. (1985). Determinants of infant visual fixation: Evidence for a two-process theory, *Journal of Experimental Child Psychology, 39*(3), 580–598.

Basson, R. (2001). Female sexual response: The role of drugs in the management of sexual dysfunction. *Obstetrics and Gynecology, 98*(2), 350–353.

Batson, C. D. (1991). *The altruism question: Toward a social-psychological answer*. Hillsdale, NJ: Erlbaum.

Batson, C. D., Ahmad, N., & Lishner, D. A. (2002). Empathy and altruism. In C. R. Snyder & S. J. Lopez (Eds.), *Handbook of positive psychology*. London: Oxford University Press.

Batson, C. D., Ahmad, N., & Stocks, E. L. (2004). Benefits and liabilities of empathy-induced altruism. In A. G. Miller (Ed.), *The social psychology of good and evil*. New York: Guilford Press.

Bauer, R. M., & Verfaellie, M. (1988). Electrodermal discrimination of familiar but not unfamiliar faces in prosopagnosia. *Brain and Cognition, 8*, 240–252.

Baum, A. (1994). Disease processes: Behavioral, biological, and environmental interactions in disease processes. In S. J. Blumenthal, K. Matthews, & S. M. Weiss (Eds.), *New research frontiers in behavioral medicine: Proceedings of the national conference*. Washington, DC: NIH Publications.

Baum, A., & Posluszny, D. M. (1999). Health psychology: Mapping biobehavioral contributions to health and illness. *Annual Review of Psychology, 50*, 137–164.

Baum, A., Krantz, D. S., & Gatchel, R. J. (1997) *An introduction to health psychology* (3rd ed.). Boston: McGraw-Hill.

Baumeister, R. F., & Leary, M. R. (1995) The need to belong: Desire for interpersonal attachments as a fundamental human motivation. *Psychological Bulletin, 117*, 497–529.

Baumeister, R. F., & Tice, D. M. (1990). Anxiety and social exclusion. *Journal of Social and Clinical Psychology, 9*, 165–195.

Baumeister, R. F., Catanese, K. R., & Vohs, K. D. (2001). Is there a gender difference in strength of sex drive? Theoretical views, conceptual distinctions, and a review of relevant evidence. *Personality and Social Psychology Review, 5*, 242–273.

Baumrind, D. (1964). Some thoughts on ethics of research: After reading Milgram's behavioral study of 'obedience.' *American Psychologist, 19*, 421–423.

Baumrind, D. (1967). Child care practices anteceding three patterns of preschool behavior. *Genetic Psychology Monographs, 75*, 43–88.

Baumrind, D., Larzelere, R. E., & Cowan, P. A. (2002). Ordinary physical punishment: Is it harmful? Comment on Gershoff (2002). *Psychological Bulletin, 128*, 580–589.

Bauserman, R. (1996). Sexual aggression and pornography: A review of correlational research. *Basic and Applied Social Psychology, 18*, 405–427.

Bayley, T. M., Dye, L., Jones, S., DeBono, M., & Hill, A. J. (2002). Food cravings and aversions during pregnancy: Relationships with nausea and vomiting. *Appetite, 38*, 45–51.

Beahrs, J. O. (1994). Dissociative identity disorder: Adaptive deception of self and others. *Bulletin of the American Academy of Psychiatric Law, 22*, 223–237.

Beaman, A. L., Barnes, P. J., Klentz, B., & McQuirk, B. (1978). Increasing helping rates through information dissemination: Teaching pays. *Personality and Social Psychology Bulletin, 4*, 406–411.

Beatty, M. J., Heisel, A. D., Hall, A. E., Levine, T. R., & La France, B. H. (2002). What can we learn from the study of twins about genetic and environmental influences on interpersonal affiliation, aggressiveness, and social anxiety? A meta-analytic study. *Communication Monographs, 69*, 1–18.

Beauchamp, G. K., & Bartoshuk L. (Eds.). (1997). *Tasting and smelling*. Philadelphia, PA: Academic Press.

Beck, A. T. (1976). *Cognitive therapy and the emotional disorders*. New York: International Universities Press.

Beck, A. T. (2002). Cognitive patterns in dreams and daydreams. *Journal of Cognitive Psychotherapy, 16*, 23–28.

Beck, A. T., Emery, G., & Greenberg, R. L. (2005). *Anxiety disorders and phobias: A cognitive perspective*. New York: Basic Books.

Beck, A. T., Freeman, A., & Davis, D. D. (2004). *Cognitive therapy of personality disorders* (2nd ed.). New York: Guilford Press.

Beck, A. T., Rector, N., Stolar, N., & Grant, P. (2008). *Schizophrenia: Cognitive theory, research, and therapy*. New York: Guilford Press.

Beck, A. T., Rush, A. J., Shaw, B. F., & Emery, G. (1979). *Cognitive therapy of depression*. New York: Guilford Press.

Becker, A. E., Grinspoon, S. K., Klibanski, A., & Herzog, D. B. (1999). Current concepts: Eating disorders. *New England Journal of Medicine, 340*, 1092–1098.

Becker, J. (2004). Reconsidering the role of overcoming perturbations in cognitive development: Constructivism and consciousness. *Human Development, 47*, 77–93.

Beecher, H. K. (1959). Generalization from pain of various types and diverse origins. *Science, 130*, 267–268.

Begum, M., & McKenna, P. J. (2010). Olfactory reference syndrome: A systematic review of the world literature. *Psychological Medicine, 41*, 453.

Beilcock, S. L., & Carr, T. H. (2001). On the fragility of skilled performance: What

governs choking under pressure? *Journal of Experimental Psychology: General, 130,* 701–725.

Békésy, G. von. (1957). The ear. *Scientific American, 230,* 66–78.

Bell, A. P., Weinberg, M. S., & Hammersmith, S. K. (1981). *Sexual preference: Its development in men and women.* Bloomington, IN: Indiana University Press.

Bell, C. C., Bhana, A., McKay, M., & Petersen, I. (2007). A commentary on the Triadic Theory of Influence as a guide for adapting HIV prevention programs for new contexts and populations: The CHAMP-South Africa story. *Social Work in Mental Health, 5,* 241–267.

Bell, J. H., & Bromnick, R. D. (2003). The social reality of the imaginary audience: A ground theory approach. *Adolescence, 38,* 205–219.

Bellack, J. P., Morjikian, R., Barger, S., Strachota, E., Fitzmaurice, J., Lee, A, … O'Neil, E. H. (2001). Developing BSN leaders for the future: The Fuld Leadership Initiative for Nursing Education (LINE). *Journal of Professional Nursing, 17,* 23–32.

Belloc, N. B. (1973). Relationship of health practices and mortality. *Preventive Medicine, 2,* 67–81.

Belsky, J. (1988). The 'effects' of infant day care reconsidered. *Early Childhood Research Quarterly, 3,* 235–272.

Belsky, J., Steinberg, L., & Draper, P. (1991). Childhood experience, interpersonal development and reproductive strategy: An evolutionary theory of socialization. *Child Development, 62,* 647–670.

Belsky, J. (1999). Interactional and contextual determinants of attachment security. In Cassidy, Jude (Ed); Shaver, Phillip R. (Ed), (1999). Handbook of attachment: Theory, research, and clinical applications (pp. 249–264). New York, NY, US: Guilford Press.

Belsky, J., Vandell, D., Burchinal, M., Clarke-Stewart, K. A., McCartney, K., & Owen, M. T. (2007). Are there long-term effects of early child care? *Child Development, 78,* 681–701.

Bem, D. J. (1972). Self-perception theory. In L. Berkowitz (Ed.), *Advances in Experimental Social Psychology* (Vol. 6). New York: Academic Press.

Bem, D. J. (1996). Exotic becomes erotic: A developmental theory of sexual orientation. *Psychological Review, 103,* 320–335.

Bem, D. J. (2001). Exotic becomes erotic: Integrating biological and experiential antecedents of sexual orientation. In A. R. D'Augelli & C. J. Patterson (Eds.), *Lesbian, gay, and bisexual identities and youth: Psychological perspectives.* London: Oxford University Press.

Bem, D. J., & Honorton, C. (1994). Does psi exist? Replicable evidence for an anomalous process of information transfer. *Psychological Bulletin, 115,* 4–18.

Bem, S. L. (1981). Gender schema theory: A cognitive account of sex typing. *Psychological Review, 88,* 354–364.

Benes, F. M. (2010). Amygdalocortical circuitry in schizophrenia: From circuits to molecules, *Neuropsychopharmacology, 35,* 239–257. doi: 10.1038/npp.2009.116

Bengtson, V. L. (2001). Beyond the nuclear family: The increasing importance of multigenerational bonds. *Journal of Marriage and the Family, 63,* 1–16.

Benjamin, A. S., & Bjork, R. A. (2000). On the relationship between recognition speed and accuracy for words rehearsed via rote versus elaborative rehearsal. *Journal of Experimental Psychology: Learning, Memory, and Cognition, 26,* 638–648.

Benjamin, L. S. (2003). *Interpersonal reconstructive therapy: Promoting change in nonresponders.* New York: Guilford Press.

Bennett, H. L. (1983). Remembering drink orders: The memory skills of cocktail waitresses. *Human Learning, 2,* 157–169.

Benson, H., & Klipper, M. Z. (1976). *The relaxation response.* New York: Morrow.

Benzon, C.R., Johnson, S.B., McCue, D.L., Li, D., Green, T.A. & Hommel, J.D. (2014). Neuromedin U Receptor 2 Knockdown in the paraventricular nucleus modifies behavioural responses to obesogenic high-fat foods and leads to increased body weight. *Neuroscience, 258,* 270–279.

Ben-Zur, H. (2009). Coping styles and affect. *International Journal of Stress Management, 16,* 87–101.

Berens, C., Witteman, C. L. M., & Van de Ven, M. O. M. (2011). Is understanding why necessary for treatment choices? *European Journal of Psychological Assessment, 27,* 81–87.

Berg, C. A. (2000). Intellectual development in adulthood. In R. J. Sternberg (Ed.), *Handbook of intelligence.* New York: Cambridge University Press.

Berkowitz, L., & Harmon-Jones, E. (2004). Toward an understanding of the determinants of anger. *Emotion, 4,* 107–130.

Bermond, B., Nieuwenhuyse, B., Fasotti, L., & Schuerman, J. (1991). Spinal cord lesions, peripheral feedback, and intensities of emotional feelings. *Cognition and Emotion, 5,* 201–220.

Bernichon, T., Cook, K. E., & Brown, J. D. (2003). Seeking self-evaluative feedback: The interactive role of global self-esteem and specific self-views. *Journal of Personality and Social Psychology, 84,* 194–204.

Bernstein, S. E., & Carr, T. H. (1996). Dual-route theories of pronouncing printed words: What can be learned from concurrent task performance? *Journal of Experimental Psychology: Learning, Memory, and Cognition, 22,* 86–116.

Berntsen, D. (2001). Involuntary memories of emotional events: Do memories of traumas and extremely happy events differ? *Applied Cognitive Psychology, 5,* S135–S158.

Berridge, K. C. (2004). Motivation concepts in behavioral neuroscience. *Physiology and Behavior, 81,* 179–209.

Berry, J. W., Poortinga, Y. H., Segall, M. H., & Dasen, P. (1992). *Cross-cultural psychology: Research and application.* New York: Cambridge University Press.

Berscheid, E., & Reis, H. T. (1998). Attraction and close relationships. In D. T. Gilbert, S. T. Fiske, & G. Lindzey (Eds.), *The handbook of social psychology* (4th ed., Vol. 2, pp. 193–281). New York: McGraw-Hill.

Bertelson, P. (1999). Ventriloquism: A case of crossmodal perceptual grouping. In G. Ashersleben, T. Bachmann, & J. Müsseler (Eds.), *Cognitive contributions to the perception of spatial and temporal events.* Amsterdam: Elsevier Science.

Berthoud, H. R. (2002). Multiple neural systems controlling food intake and body

weight. *Neuroscience and Biobehavioral Reviews, 26,* 393–428.

Beutler, L. E. (2002). The dodo bird is extinct. *Clinical Psychology: Science and Practice, 9,* 30–34.

Beyer, S. (1990). Gender differences in the accuracy of self-evaluations of performance. *Journal of Personality and Social Psychology, 59,* 960–970.

Bialystok, E. (2001). *Bilingualism in development: Language, literacy, and cognition.* New York: Cambridge University Press.

Bialystok, E., & Martin, M. M. (2004). Attention and inhibition in bilingual children: Evidence from the dimensional change card sort task. *Developmental Science, 7,* 325–339.

Bialystok, E., Craik, F. I. M., Klein, R., & Viswanathan, M. (2004). Bilingualism, aging, and cognitive control: Evidence from the Simon task. *Psychology and Aging, 19*(2), 290–303.

Biederman, I. (1987). Recognition-by-components: A theory of human image understanding. *Psychological Review, 94,* 115–147.

Biederman, I. (1990). Higher-level vision. In D. N. Osherson, S. M. Kosslyn, & J. M. Hollerbach (Eds.), *Visual cognition and action.* Cambridge, MA: MIT Press.

Biegel, G. M., Brown, K. W., Shapiro, S. L., & Schubert, C. M. (2009). Mindfulness-based stress reduction for the treatment of adolescent psychiatric outpatients: A randomized clinical trial. *Journal of Consulting and Clinical Psychology, 77*(5), 855–866.

Bieling, P. J., Israeli, A. L., & Antony, M. M. (2004). Is perfectionism good, bad, or both? Examining models of the perfectionism construct. *Personality and Individual Differences, 36,* 1373–1385.

Biemiller, A., & Slonim, N. (2001). Estimating root word vocabulary growth in normative and advantaged populations: Evidence for a common sequence of vocabulary acquisition. *Journal of Educational Psychology, 93,* 498–520.

Bijl, R. V., Ravelli, A., & van Zessen, G. (1998). Prevalence of psychiatric disorder in the general population: Results of The Netherlands Mental Health Survey and Incidence Study (NEMESIS).

Social Psychiatry and Psychiatric Epidemiology, 33, 587–595.

Biller, J., Brazis, P., & Masdeu, J. C. (2006). *Localization in clinical neurology.* Philadelphia, PA: Lippincott, Williams, & Wilkins.

Billig, M. (2008). *The hidden roots of critical psychology: Understanding the impact of Locke, Shaftesbury and Reid.* London: Sage.

Billings, A. G., & Moos, R. H. (1984). Coping, stress, and social resources among adults with unipolar depression. *Journal of Personality and Social Psychology, 46,* 877–801.

Binder, J. L. (2004). *Key competencies in brief dynamic psychotherapy.* New York: Guilford Press.

Binder, J. L., & Strupp, H. H. (1997). 'Negative process': A recurrently discovered and underestimated facet of therapeutic process and outcome in the individual psychotherapy of adults. *Clinical Psychology: Science and Practice, 4,* 121–139.

Bishop, S. R., Lau, M., Shapiro, S., Carlson, L., Anderson, N. D., Carmody, J., … Devins, G. (2004). Mindfulness: A proposed operational definition. *Clinical Psychology: Science and Practice, 11* (3), 230–241.

Bjorklund, D. F., & Pellegrini, A. D. (2002). Evolutionary perspectives on social development. In P. K. Smith & C. H. Hart (Eds.), *Blackwell handbook of childhood social development.* Malden, MA: Blackwell.

Black, D. N., Seritan, A. L., Taber, K. H., & Hurley, R. A. (2004). Conversion hysteria: Lessons from functional imaging. *Journal of Neuropsychiatry & Clinical Neurosciences, 16,* 245–251.

Black, D. W. (1999). *Bad boys, bad men: Confronting antisocial personality disorder.* New York: Oxford University Press.

Black, D. W., Yates, W. R., & Andreason, N. C. (1988). Schizophrenia, schizophreniform disorder, and delusional paranoid disorders. In J. A. Talbott, R. E. Hales, & S. C. Yudofsky (Eds.), *Textbook of psychiatry.* Washington, DC: American Psychiatric Press.

Blackstone, J. (2007) *The empathic ground: Intersubjectivity and nonduality in the psychotherapeutic process.* Albany, NY: State University of New York Press.

Blader, S. L., & Tyler, T. R. (2002). Justice and empathy: What motivates people to help others? In M. Ross & D. T. Miller (Eds.), *The justice motive in everyday life.* New York: Cambridge University Press.

Blair, J. (2005). *Development of the psychopath: Emotion and the brain.* St. Louis, MO: Blackwell.

Blair, S. N., Kohl, H. W., III, Paffenbarger, R. S., Clark, D. G., Cooper, K. H., & Gibbons, L. W. (1989). Physical fitness and all-cause mortality: A prospective study of healthy men and women. *Journal of the American Medical Association, 262,* 2395–2401.

Blakemore, C., & Cooper, G. G. (1970). Development of the brain depends on visual environment. *Nature, 228,* 477–478.

Blakemore, S. J. (2008). The social brain in adolescence. *Nature Reviews Neuroscience, 9*(4), 267–277.

Blanchard, R. (2001). Fraternal birth order and the maternal immune hypothesis of male homosexuality. *Hormones and Behavior, 40,* 105–114.

Blanchard, R., & Bogaert, A. F. (1996). Homosexuality in men and number of older brothers. *American Journal of Psychiatry, 153,* 27–31.

Blanchette, I., Richards, A., Melnyk, L., & Lavda, A. (2007). Reasoning about emotional contents following shocking terrorist attacks: A tale of three cities. *Journal of Experimental Psychology Applied, 13*(1), 47–56.

Blanke, O., & Aspell, J. E. (2009). Brain technologies raise unprecedented ethical challenges. *Nature, 458*(7239), 703.

Blanke, O., & Metzinger, T. (2009). Full-body illusions and minimal phenomenal selfhood. *Trends in Cognitive Sciences, 13*(1), 7–13.

Blanke, O., Ortigue, S., Landis, T., & Seeck, M. (2002). Stimulating illusory own-body perceptions. *Nature, 419*(6904), 269–270.

Blanton, H., Pelham, B., DeHart, T., & Carvallo, M. (2001). Overconfidence as dissonance reduction. *Journal of Experimental Social Psychology, 37,* 373–385.

Blascovich, J., & Tomaka, J. (1991). Measures of self-esteem. In L. Wrightsman, J. P. Robinson & P. R. Shaver (Eds.),

Measures of personality and social psychological attitudes. San Diego, CA: Academic Press.

Blasi, A. (1983). Moral cognition and moral action: A theoretical perspective. *Developmental Review, 3*(2), 178–210.

Blass, T. (2002). Perpetrator behavior as destructive obedience: An evaluation of Stanley Milgram's perspective, the most influential social-psychological approach to the Holocaust. In L. S. Newman & R. Erber (Eds.), *Understanding genocide: The social psychology of the Holocaust.* London: Oxford University Press.

Blass, T., & Schmitt, C. (2001). The nature of perceived authority in the Milgram paradigm: Two replications. *Current Psychology: Developmental, Learning, Personality, Social, 20,* 115–121.

Blechman, E., & Brownell, K. D. (1998). *Behavioral medicine and women: A comprehensive handbook.* New York: Guilford Press.

Blessing, W. W. (1997). *The lower brainstem and bodily homeostasis.* New York: Oxford University Press.

Blodgett, H. C. (1929). The effect of the introduction of reward on the maze performance of rats. *University of California Publications in Psychology, 4*(8), 114–126.

Bloomfield, K., Greenfield, T. K., Kraus, L., & Augustin, R. (2002). A comparison of drinking patterns and alcohol-related problems in the United States and Germany, 1995. *Substance Use and Misuse, 37,* 399–428.

Blundell, J. E. (1991). Pharmacological approaches to appetite suppression. *Trends in Pharmacological Science, 12,* 147–157.

Blundell, J. E., Goodson, S., & Halford, J. C. G. (2001). Regulation of appetite: Role of leptin in signalling systems for drive and satiety. *International Journal of Obesity, 25,* S1, S29–S34.

Bobo, L. (1988). Attitudes toward the black political movement: Trends, meaning, and effects of racial policy preferences. *Social Psychology Quarterly, 51,* 287–302.

Boddez, Y., Baeyens, F., Luyten, L., Vansteenwegen, D., Hermans, D., & Beckers, T. (2013). Rating data are underrated: validity of US expectancy in human fear conditioning. *Journal of Behavior Therapy and Experimental Psychiatry, 44*(2), 201–206.

Boehm, S. L., Reed, C. L., McKinnon, C. S., & Phillips, T. J. (2002). Shared genes influence sensitivity to the effects of ethanol on locomotor and anxiety-like behaviors, and the stress axis. *Psychopharmacology, 161,* 54–63.

Boesch, C. (1991). Teaching in wild chimpanzees. *Animal Behaviour, 41*(3), 530–532.

Boeve, B. F., Solber, M. H., & Ferman, T. J. (2003). Melatonin for treatment of REM sleep behavior disorder in neurologic disorders: Results in 14 patients, *Sleep Medicine, 4*(4), 281–284.

Bolling, M. Y., & Kohlenberg, R. J. (2004). Reasons for quitting serotonin reuptake inhibitor therapy: Paradoxical psychological side effects and patient satisfaction. *Psychotherapy and Psychosomatics, 73*(6), 380–385.

Bonanno, G. A., Papa, A., Lalande, K., Westphal, M., & Coifman, K. (2004). The importance of being flexible. *Psychological Science, 15,* 482–487.

Bond, R., & Smith, P. B. (1996). Culture and conformity: A meta-analysis of studies using Asch's (1952b, 1956) line judgment task. *Psychological Bulletin, 119,* 111–137.

Boneva, B., Frieze, I. H., Ferligoj, A., Pauknerová, D., & Orgocka, A. (1998). Achievement, power, and affiliation motives as clues to (e)migration desires: A four countries comparison. *European Psychologist, 3,* 247–254.

Bonvillian, J. D., & Patterson, F. G. P. (1997). Sign language acquisition and the development of meaning in a lowland gorilla. In C. Mandell & A. McCabe (Eds.), *The problem of meaning: Behavioral and cognitive perspectives.* Amsterdam: North-Holland/Elsevier Science.

Boomsma, D., Busjahn, A., & Peltonen, L. (2002). Classical twin studies and beyond. *Nature Reviews Genetics, 3,* 872–882.

Booth, A., & Amato, P. R. (2001). Parental predivorce relations and offspring postdivorce wellbeing. *Journal of Marriage and the Family, 63,* 197–212.

Bootzin, R. R. (2002). Cognitive-behavioral treatment of insomnia: Knitting up the ravell'd sleeve of care. In D. T. Kenny, J. G.

Carlson, F. J. McGuigan, & J. L. Sheppard (Eds.), *Stress and health: Research and clinical applications.* Amsterdam: Harwood.

Boris-Karpel, S. (2010). Policy and practice issues in pain management. In M. Ebert & R. Kerns (Eds.), *Behavioral and Psychopharmacologic Pain Management* (pp. 407–433). New York: Cambridge University Press.

Borkenau, P., Riemann, R., Spinath, F. M., & Angleitner, A. (2006). Genetic and environmental influences on person x situation profiles. *Journal of Personality, 74,* 1451–1480.

Borod, J. C. (2000). *The neuropsychology of emotion.* New York: Oxford University Press.

Borum, R. (2007). *Psychology of terrorism.* Tampa, FL: University of South Florida Tampa, Department of Mental Health Law and Policy.

Boschker, M. S., Baker, F. C., & Michaels, C. F. (2002). Memory for the functional characteristics of climbing walls: Perceiving affordances. *Journal of Motor Behavior, 34,* 25–36.

Bosson, J. K., Haymovitz, E. L., & Pinel, E. C. (2004). When saying and doing diverge: The effects of stereotype threat on self-reported versus non-verbal anxiety. *Journal of Experimental Social Psychology, 40,* 247–255.

Bouchard, G., Guillemette, A., & Landry-Léger, N. (2004). Situational and dispositional coping: An examination of their relation to personality, cognitive appraisals, and psychological distress. *European Journal of Personality, 18,* 221–238.

Bouchard, T. J. (2004). Genetic influence on human psychological traits. *Current Directions in Psychological Science, 13,* 148–151.

Bouchard, T. J., & McGue, M. (1981). Familial studies of intelligence: A review. *Science, 212,* 1055–1059.

Bouchard, T. J., & McGue, M. (2003). Genetic and environmental influences on human psychological differences. *Journal of Neurobiology, 54,* 4–45.

Bouchard, T. J., Lykken, D. T., McGue, M., Segal, N. L., & Tellegen, A. (1990). Sources of human psychological differences: The Minnesota study of twins reared apart. *Science, 250,* 223–228.

Bould, H., Joinson, C., Sterne, J., & Araya, R. (2013). The Emotionality Activity Sociability Temperament Survey: Factor analysis and temporal stability in a longitudinal cohort. *Personality and Individual Differences*, *54*(5), 628–633.

Boulos, Z. (1998). Bright light treatment for jet lag and shift work. In R. Lam & W. Raymond (Eds.), *Seasonal affective disorder and beyond: Light treatment for SAD and non-SAD conditions*. Washington, DC: American Psychiatric Press.

Boutros, N. N., Gelernter, J., Gooding, D. C., Cubells, J., Young, A., Krystal, J. H., & Kosten, T. (2002). Sensory gating and psychosis vulnerability in cocaine-dependent individuals: Preliminary data. *Biological Psychiatry*, *51*, 683–686.

Bowen, S., Chawla, N., Collins, S. E., Witkiewitz, K., Hsu, S., Grow, J., … Marlatt, A. (2009). Mindfulness-based relapse prevention for substance use disorders: A pilot efficacy trial. *Substance Abuse*, *30*, 295–305.

Bower, G. H., Clark, M. C., Lesgold, M. A., & Winzenz, D. (1969). Hierarchical retrieval schemes in recall of categorized word lists. *Journal of Verbal Learning and Verbal Behavior*, *8*, 323–343.

Bowlby, J. (1944). Forty-four juvenile thieves: Their character and home-life. *International Journal of Psychoanalysis*, *25*, 19–52.

Bowlby, J. (1969). *Attachment and loss: Vol. 1. Attachment*. New York: Basic Books.

Bowlby, J. (1973). *Attachment and loss: Vol. 2. Separation: Anxiety and anger*. London: Hogarth.

Bowlby, J. (2000). *Loss: Sadness and depression*. New York: Basic Books.

Bozarth, J. D., Zimring, F. M., & Tausch, R. (2002). Client-centered therapy: The evolution of a revolution. In D. J. Cain (Ed.), *Humanistic psychotherapies: Handbook of research and practice*. Washington, DC: American Psychological Association.

Braams, B.R., van Leijenhorst, L., & Crone, E.A. (2014). Risks, rewards, and the developing brain in childhood and adolescence. In V. F. Reyna & V. Zayas (Eds.), *The neuroscience of risky decision making*. Washington, DC: American Psychological Association.

Brabender, V., Fallon, A. E., & Smolar, A. I. (2004). *Essentials of group therapy*. New York: Wiley.

Bradmetz, J., & Mathy, F. (2006). An estimate of the Flynn effect: Changes in IQ and subtest gains of 10-yr-old French children between 1965 and 1988 *Psychological Reports*, *99*(3), 743–746.

Braine, M. D. S., & O'Brien, D. P. (1991). A theory of If: A lexical entry, reasoning program and pragmatic principles. *Psychological Review*, *98*, 182–203.

Braine, M. D. S., & O'Brien, D. P. (1998). *Mental logic*. Mahwah, NJ: Lawrence Erlbaum Associates.

Bransford, J. D., & Johnson, M. K. (1972). Contextual prerequisites for understanding: Some investigations of comprehension and recall. *Journal of Verbal Learning & Verbal Behavior*, *11*, 717–726.

Brantley, P. J., & Garrett, V. D. (1993). Psychobiological approaches to health and disease. In B. Sutker & H. F. Adams (Eds.), *Comprehensive handbook of psychopathology* (2nd ed.). New York: Plenum.

Brantley, P. J., & Jones, G. N. (1993). Daily stress and stress-related disorders. *Annals of Behavioral Medicine*, *15*, 17–25.

Brauer, M. (2001). Intergroup perception in the social context: The effects of social status and group membership on perceived out-group homogeneity and ethnocentrism. *Journal of Experimental Social Psychology*, *37*, 15–31.

Braun, D. L., Sunday, S. R., Huang, A., & Halmi, K. A. (1999). More males seek treatment for eating disorders. *The International Journal of Eating Disorders*, *25*, 415–424.

Bray, J. H., & Berger, S. H. (1993). Developmental issues in Step Families Research Project: Family relationships and parent–child interactions. *Journal of Family Psychology*, *7*, 76–90.

Brazel, C. Y., & Rao, M. S. (2004). Ageing and neuronal replacement. *Ageing Research Reviews*, *3*, 465–483.

Brehm, J. W., & Self, E. A. (1989). The intensity of motivation. *Annual Review of Psychology*, *40*, 109–131.

Bremner, A. J., Caparos, S., Davidoff, J., de Fockert, J.W., Linnell, K.J., & Spence, C. (2013). 'Bouba' and 'Kiki' in Namibia? A remote culture make similar shape-sound matches, but different shape-taste matches to Westerners. *Cognition*, *126*, 165–172.

Bremner, A. J., & Mareschal, D. (2004). Reasoning ... what reasoning? *Developmental Science*, *7*, 419–421.

Bremner, A. J., Mareschal, D., Lloyd-Fox, S., & Spence, C. (2008). Spatial localization of touch in the first year of life: Early influence of a visual spatial code and the development of remapping across changes in limb position. *Journal of Experimental Psychology: General*, *137*, 149–162.

Bremner, J. D. (2000). Neurobiology of posttraumatic stress disorder. In G. Fink (Ed.), *Encyclopedia of stress*. San Diego, CA: Academic Press.

Breslau, N., Davis, C. G., Peterson, E. L., & Schultz, L. R. (1997). Psychiatric sequelae of posttraumatic stress disorder in women. *Archives of General Psychiatry*, *54*, 81–87.

Brewer, M. B. (1999). The psychology of prejudice: Ingroup love or outgroup hate? *Journal of Social Issues*, *55*, 429–444.

Brewin, C. R., Fuchkan, N., Huntley, Z., Robertson, M., Thompson, M., Scragg, P., d'Ardenne. P., & Ehlers, A. (2010). Outreach and screening following the 2005 London bombings: Usage and outcomes. *Psychological Medicine*, *40*, 2049–2057.

Brewis, A. A., Wutich, A., Falletta-Cowden, A., & Rodriguez-Soto, I. (2011). Body norms and fat stigma in global perspective. *Current Anthropology*, *52*, 269–276.

Brickman, P., Coates, D., & Janoff-Bulman, R. (1978). Lottery winners and accident victims: Is happiness relative? *Journal of Personality and Social Psychology*, *36*, 917–927.

Bridges, P. K., Bartlett, J R., Hale, A. S., Poynton, A. M., Malizia, A. L., & Hodgkiss, A. D. (1994). Psychosurgery: Stereotactic subcaudate tractomy. An indispensable treatment. *British Journal of Psychiatry*, *165*, 599–611; discussion, 612–593.

Bridle, C., Riemsma, R. P., Pattenden, J., Sowden, A. J., Mather, L., Watt, I. S., & Walker, A. (2005). Systematic review of the effectiveness of health behavior interventions based on the transtheoretical model. *Psychology and Health*, *20*, 283–301.

Briere, J., & Lanktree, C. (1983). Sex role-related effects of sex bias in language. *Sex Roles, 9*, 625–632.

Broad, C. D. (1953). The relevance of psychical research to philosophy. In J. Ludwig (Ed.), *Philosophy and parapsychology*. Buffalo, NY: Prometheus.

Broadbent, D. (1958). *Perception and communication*. London: Pergamon Press.

Bronzaft, A. L., Ahern, K. D., McGinn, R., O'Connor, J., & Savino, B. (1998). Aircraft noise: A potential health hazard. *Environment & Behavior, 30*, 101–113.

Brown, E., Deffenbacher, K., & Sturgill, W. (1977). Memory for faces and the circumstances of encounter. *Journal of Applied Psychology, 62*, 311–318.

Brown, G. W., & Harris, T. O. (1978). *Social origins of depression*. London: Tavistock Press.

Brown, I., & Percy, M. (Eds.) (2007). *A comprehensive guide to intellectual and developmental disabilities*. Baltimore, MD: Paul H. Brookes.

Brown, J. A. (1958). Some tests of the decay theory of immediate memory. *Quarterly Journal of Experimental Psychology, 10*, 12–21.

Brown, J. D. (1998). *The self*. Boston, MA: McGraw-Hill.

Brown, J. D., & Kobayashi, C. (2001). Self-enhancement in Japan and America. *Asian Journal of Social Psychology, 5*, 145–167.

Brown, K. W., Ryan, R. M., & Cresswell, J. D. (2007). Mindfulness: Theoretical foundations and evidence for its salutary effects. *Psychological Inquiry, 18*(4), 211–237.

Brown, L. S. (1994). *Subversive dialogues: Theory in feminist therapy*. New York: Basic Books.

Brown, N. O. (1959). *Life against death*. New York: Random House.

Brown, R. (1973). *A first language: The early stages*. Cambridge, MA: Harvard University Press.

Brown, S. L., Nesse, R. M., Vinokur, A. D., & Smith, D. M. (2003). Providing social support may be more beneficial than receiving it: Results from a prospective study of mortality. *Psychological Science, 14*, 320–327.

Brown, T. S., & Wallace, P. (1980). *Physiological psychology*. New York: Academic Press.

Bruce, T. J., & Sanderson, W. C. (1998). *Specific phobias: Clinical applications of evidence-based psychotherapy*. Northvale, NJ: Aronson.

Bruce, V., & Young, A. (1986). Understanding face recognition. *British Journal of Psychology, 77*(3), 305–327.

Bruce, V., Burton, A. M., & Dench, N. (1994). What's distinctive about a distinctive face? *Quarterly Journal of Experimental Psychology, 47A* (1), 119–141.

Bruce, V., Valentine, T., & Baddeley, A. (1987). The basis of the 3/4 view advantage in face recognition. *Applied Cognitive Psychology, 1*, 109–120.

Bruce, V., Henderson, Z., Newman, C., & Burton, A. M. (2001). Matching identities of familiar and unfamiliar faces caught on CCTV images. *Journal of Experimental Psychology: Applied, 7*, 207–218.

Bruck, M., Ceci, S. J., & Hembrooke, H. (1998). Reliability and credibility of young children's reports: From research to policy and practice. *American Psychologist, 53*, 136–151.

Bruner, J. (1983). *Child's talk*. New York: Norton.

Bruner, J. (1986). *Actual minds, possible worlds*. Cambridge, MA: Harvard University Press.

Bruunk, B., & Gibbons, F. X. (Eds.). (1997). *Health, coping, and well-being: Perspectives from social comparison theory*. Mahwah, NJ: Erlbaum.

Bryan, J., III. (1986). *Hodgepodge: A commonplace book*. New York: Ballantine.

Bryant, P. E. (1974). *Perception and understanding in young children: An experimental approach*. London: Methuen.

Buchanan, G. M. (1995). Explanatory style and coronary heart disease. In G. M. Buchanan & M. E. P. Seligman (Eds.), *Explanatory style*. Hillsdale, NJ: Erlbaum.

Buck, L., & Axel, R. (1991). A novel multigene family may encode odorant receptors: A molecular basis for odor recognition. *Cell, 65*, 175–187.

Bulik, C. M., Slof-Op't Landt, M. C. T., van Furth, E. F., & Sullivan, P. F. (2007). The genetics of anorexia nervosa. *Annual Review of Nutrition, 27*, 263–275.

Bullier, J. (2002). Neural basis of vision. In H. Pashler & S. Yantis (Eds.), *Steven's handbook of experimental psychology: Vol. 1. Sensation and perception* (3rd ed.). New York: Wiley.

Burger, J. M. (2009). Replicating Milgram: Would people still obey today? *American Psychologist, 64*, 1–11.

Burgess, A. (1962) *A Clockwork Orange* (Restored edn., 2013). London: Penguin Modern Classics.

Burgess, C. A., & Kirsch, I. (1999). Expectancy information as a moderator of the effects of hypnosis on memory. *Contemporary Hypnosis, 16*, 22–31.

Burgess, N., Maguire, E.A. & O'Keefe, J. (2002) The human hippocampus and spatial and episodic memory, *Neuron, 35*, 4, 625–641.

Burgwyn-Bailes, E., Baker-Ward, L., Gordon, B. N., & Ornstein, P. A. (2001). Children's memory for emergency medical treatment after one year: The impact of individual difference variables on recall and suggestibility. *Applied Cognitive Psychology, 15*, S25–S48.

Burley, T., & Freier, M. C. (2004). Character structure: A gestalt-cognitive theory. *Psychotherapy: Theory, Research, Practice, Training, 41*, 321–331.

Burman, D.D., Bitan, T. & Booth, J.R.(2008). Sex differences in neural processing of language among children. *Neuropsychologia, 46*(5), 1349–1362.

Burns, M. O., & Seligman, M. E. P. (1991). Explanatory style, helplessness, and depression. In C. R. Snyder & D. R. Forsyth (Eds.), *Handbook of social and clinical psychology: The health perspective*. New York: Pergamon Press.

Burton, A. M., Bruce, V., & Dench, N. (1993). What's the difference between men and women? Evidence from facial measurement. *Perception, 22*, 153–176.

Burton, A. M., Bruce, V., & Hancock, P. J. B. (1999). From pixels to people: A model of familiar face recognition. *Cognitive Science, 23*, 1–31.

Burton, E., Stice, E., & Seeley, J. R. (2004). A prospective test of the stress-buffering model of depression in adolescent girls: No

support once again. *Journal of Consulting and Clinical Psychology, 72*, 689–697.

Busey, T. A., Tunnicliff, J. J., Loftus, G. R., & Loftus, E. F. (2000). Accounts of the confidence-accuracy relation in recognition memory. *Psychonomic Bulletin and Review, 7*, 26–48.

Bushman, B. J. (2002). Does venting anger feed or extinguish the flame? Catharsis, rumination, distraction, anger and aggressive responding. *Personality and Social Psychology, 28*, 724–731.

Bushman, B. J., & Bonacci, A. M. (2002). Violence and sex impair memory for television ads. *Journal of Applied Psychology, 87*, 557–564.

Bushman, B. J., Jamieson, P. E., Weitz, I., & Romer, D. (2013). Gun violence trends in movies. *Pediatrics, 132*(6), 1014–1018.

Buske-Kirschbaum, A., Kirschbaum, C., & Hellhammer, D. H. (1994). Conditioned modulation of NK cells in humans: Alteration of cell activity and cell number by conditioning protocols. *Psychologische Beitraege, 36*, 100–111.

Buske-Kirschbaum, A., Kirschbaum, C., Stierle, H., & Lehnert, H. (1992). Conditioned increase of natural killer cell activity (NKCA) in humans. *Psychosomatic Medicine, 54*, 123–132.

Buss, A., & Plomin, R. (1975). *A temperament theory of personality development*. New York: Wiley.

Buss, A., & Plomin, R. (1984). *Temperament: Early developing personality traits*. Hillsdale, NJ: Erlbaum.

Buss, D. M. (1985). Human mate selection. *American Scientist, 73*, 47–51.

Buss, D. M. (1989). Sex differences in human mate preferences: Evolutionary hypotheses tested in 37 cultures. *Behavioral and Brain Sciences, 12*, 1–49.

Buss, D. M. (1991). Evolutionary personality theory. *Annual Review of Psychology, 42*, 459–491.

Buss, D. M. (1995). Evolutionary psychology: A new paradigm for psychological science. *Psychological Inquiry, 6*, 1–30.

Buss, D. M. (1999). Human nature and individual differences: The evolution of

human personality. In L. A. Pervin & O. P. John (Eds.), *Handbook of personality: Theory and research*. New York: Guilford Press.

Buss, D. M. (2007). *Evolutionary psychology. The new science of the mind*. Boston: Allyn & Bacon.

Buss, D. M. (2013). *Evolutionary psychology: The new science of the mind*, New International Edition. London: Pearson.

Buss, D. M., & Schmitt, D. P. (1993). Sexual strategies theory: An evolutionary perspective on human mating. *Psychological Review, 100*, 204–232.

Buss, D. M., Abbott, M., Angleitner, A., Asherian, A., Biaggio, A., Blanco-Villasenor, A. … Yang, K.-S. (1990). International preferences in selecting mates: A study of 37 cultures. *Journal of Cross-Cultural Psychology, 21*, 5–47.

Butler, R. K., & Finn, D. P. (2009). Stress-induced analgesia. *Progress in Neurobiology, 88*, 184–202.

Buunk, B. P., & Verhoeven, K. (1991). Companionship and support at work: A microanalysis of the stress-reducing features of social interaction. *Basic and Applied Social Psychology, 12*, 243–258.

Byer, C. O., Shainberg, L. W., & Galliano, G. (2002). *Dimensions of human sexuality* (6th ed.). Boston, MA: McGraw-Hill.

Bynner, J. (2005). Rethinking the youth phase of the life-course: The case for emerging adulthood? *Journal of Youth Studies, 8*, 367–384.

Byrne, D. (1997). An overview (and underview) of research and theory within the attraction paradigm. *Journal of Social and Personal Relationships, 14*, 417–431.

Byrne, D., & Greendlinger, V. (1989). Need for affiliation as a predictor of classroom friendships. Unpublished manuscript, State University of New York at Albany.

Byrne, D., Ervin, C. R., & Lamberth, J. (1970). Continuity between the experimental study of attraction and real-life computer dating. *Journal of Personality and Social Psychology, 16*, 157–165.

Bywaters, M. J., Andrade, J., & Turpin, G. (2004). Determinants of the vividness

of delayed recall, stimulus affect and individual differences. *Memory, 12*, 479–488.

C

Cabeza, R., Nyberg, L., & Park, D. C. (2005). *Cognitive neuroscience of aging: Linking cognitive and cerebral aging*. New York: Oxford University Press.

Cacioppo, J. T., Berntson, J. T., Poehlmann, K. M., & Ito, T. A. (2000). The psychophysiology of emotion. In M. Lewis & J. M. Haviland-Jones (Eds.), *Handbook of emotions* (2nd ed.). New York: Guilford Press.

Cain, D. J. (2010). *Person-centered psychotherapies*. Washington, DC: American Psychological Association.

Cain, D. J., & Seeman, J. (Eds.) (2002). *Humanistic psychotherapies: Handbook of research and practice*. Washington, DC: American Psychological Association.

Cairns, H. (1952). Disturbances of consciousness in lesions of the mid-brain and diencephalon. *Brain, 75*, 107–114.

Cajal, S. R. (1906). The structure and connections of neurones. Noble Lecture, 12 December.

Caldwell, A. B. (1994). *The profile of Jeffrey Dahmer* [Videotape]. Los Angeles, CA: Caldwell Report.

Calle, E. E., Thun, M. J., Petrelli, J. M., Rodriguez, C., & Heath, C. W. Jr. (1999). Body-Mass Index and mortality in a prospective cohort of U.S. adults. *The New England Journal of Medicine, 341*, 1097–1105.

Cameron, O. G. (2001). Interoception: The inside story – a model for psychosomatic processes. *Psychosomatic Medicine, 63*(5), 697–710.

Camilleri, C., & Malewska-Peyre, H. (1997). Socialization and identity strategies. In J. W. Berry, P. R. Dasen, & T. S. Saraswathi (Eds.), *Handbook of cross-cultural psychology: Basic processes and human development: Vol. 2. Handbook of cross-cultural psychology* (2nd ed.). Boston: Allyn & Bacon.

Campbell, A., Shirley, L., & Candy, J. (2004). A longitudinal study of gender-related cognition and behaviour. *Developmental Science, 7*, 1–9.

Campbell, I. C., Mill, J., Uher, R., & Schmidt, U. (2011). Eating disorders, gene–environment interactions and epigenetics. *Neuroscience and Biobehavioral Reviews, 35,* 784–793.

Campbell, J. D. (1990). Self-esteem and clarity of the self-concept. *Journal of Personal and Social Psychology, 59*(3), 538–549.

Campbell, R., Dworkin, E., & Cabral, G. (2009). An ecological model of the impact of sexual assault on women's mental health. *Trauma, Violence, & Abuse, 10,* 225–246.

Campfield, L. A. (1997). Metabolic and hormonal controls of food intake: Highlights of the last 25 years, 1972–1997. *Appetite, 29,* 135–152.

Campos, J. J., Anderson, D. I., Barbu-Roth, M. A., Hubbard, E. M., Hertenstein, M. J., & Witherington, D. (2000). Travel broadens the mind. *Infancy, 1*(2), 149–219.

Canivez, G. L., & Watkins, M. W. (1998). Long-term stability of the Wechsler Intelligence Scale for Children—Third Edition. *Psychological Assessment, 10,* 285–291.

Canli, T. (2004). Functional brain mapping of extraversion and neuroticism: Learning from individual differences in emotion processing. *Journal of Personality, 72,* 1105–1132.

Canli, T. (Ed.) (2006). *Biology of personality and individual differences.* New York: Guilford Press.

Cannon, W. B. (1927). The James-Lange theory of emotion: A critical examination and an alternative theory. *American Journal of Psychology, 39,* 106–124.

Cannon, W. B. (1929). *Bodily changes in pain, hunger, fear, and rage.* New York: Appleton-Century.

Cannon, W. B. (1932). *Wisdom of the body.* New York: Norton.

Cannon, W. B. (1942). 'Voodoo' death. *American Anthropologist, 44,* 169–181.

Cannon, W. B., & Washburn, A. L. (1912). An explanation of hunger. *American Journal of Physiology, 29,* 441–454.

Cappelletti, M., Barth, H., Fregni, F., Spelke, E. S., & Pascual-Leone, A. (2007). rTMS over the intraparietal sulcus disrupts numerosity processing. *Experimental Brain Research, 179*(4), 631–642.

Cardasis, W., Hochman, J. A., & Silk, K. R. (1997). Transitional objects and borderline personality disorder. *American Journal of Psychiatry, 154,* 250–255.

Cardeña, E., Lynn, S. J., & Krippner, S. (2000). Introduction: Anomalous experiences in perspective. In E. Cardeña, S. J. Lynn, & S. Krippner (Eds.), *Varieties of anomalous experience: Examining the scientific evidence.* Washington, DC: American Psychological Association.

Carels, R. A., Douglass, O. M., & Cacciapaglia, H. M. (2004). An ecological momentary assessment of relapse crises in dieting. *Journal of Consulting and Clinical Psychology, 72,* 341–348.

Carlini, E. A. (2004). The good and bad effects of (-) trans-delta-9-tetrahydrocannabinol (Δ9-THC) on humans. *Toxicon, 44* (4), 461–467.

Carlson, E. A., & McAndrew, F. T. (2004). Body shape ideals and perceptions of body shape in Spanish and American college students. *Perceptual and Motor Skills, 99,* 1071–1074.

Carlson, S. M., Moses, L. J., & Hix, H. R. (1998). The role of inhibitory processes in young children's difficulties with deception and false belief. *Child Development, 69,* 672–691.

Carnicero, J. A. C., Perez-Lopez, J., Salinas, M. D. C. G., & Martinez-Fuentes, M. T. (2000). A longitudinal study of temperament in infancy: Stability and convergence of measures. *European Journal of Personality, 14,* 21–37.

Carpenko, V., Owens, J. S., Evangelista, N. M., & Doss, C. (2009). Clinically significant symptom change in children with ADHD: Does it correspond with reliable improvement in functioning? *Journal of Clinical Psychology, 64,* 76–93.

Carpenter, P. A., Just, M. A., & Shell, P. (1990). What one intelligence test measures: A theoretical account of the processing in the Raven Progressive Matrices Test. *Psychological Review, 97,* 404–431.

Carpenter, R., & Robson, J. (Eds.) (1999). *Vision research: A practical guide to laboratory methods.* New York: Oxford University Press.

Carroll, C. R. (1993). *Drugs in modern society.* Madison, WI: Brown & Benchmark.

Carroll, J. B. (1993). *Human cognitive abilities: A survey of factor-analytic studies.* New York: Cambridge University Press.

Carroll, J. B., & White, M. N. (1973). Word frequency and age of acquisition as determiners of picture naming latency. *Quarterly Journal of Experimental Psychology, 25,* 85–95.

Carskadon, M., Acebo, C., & Jenni, O. (2006 online, originally 2004). Regulation of adolescent sleep: Implications for behavior. *Annals of the New York Academy of Sciences, 1021,* 276–291.

Carson, R. C., Butcher, J. N., & Coleman, J. C. (1988). *Abnormal psychology and modern life* (8th ed.). Glenview, IL: Scott, Foresman.

Carstens, A., Maes, A., & Gangla, B. L. (2006). Understanding visuals in HIV/AIDS education in South Africa: Differences between literate and low-literate audiences. *African Journal of AIDS Research, 5,* 221–232.

Carter G. G., & Wilkinson G. S. (2013). Food sharing in vampire bats: Reciprocal help predicts donations more than relatedness or harassment. *Proc R Soc B 280*: 20122573. Retrieved from http://dx.doi.org/10.1098/rspb.2012.2573

Carter, S. J., & Cassaday, H. J. (1998). State dependent retrieval and chlorpheniramine. *Human Psychopharmacology: Clinical and Experimental, 13,* 513–523.

Cartwright, R. D. (1977). *Night life: Explorations in dreaming.* Englewood Cliffs, NJ: Prentice Hall.

Carver, C. S., & Connor-Smith, J. (2010). Personality and coping. *Annual Review of Psychology, 61,* 679–704.

Carver, C. S., & Scheier, M. F. (2003). *Perspectives on personality* (5th ed.). Boston, MA: Allyn & Bacon.

Carver, C. S., Scheier, M. F., & Weintraub, J. K. (1989). Assessing coping strategies: A theoretically based approach. *Journal of Personality and Social Psychology, 56,* 267–283.

Case, R. (1987). The structure and process of intellectual development. *International Journal of Psychology, 22,* 571–607.

Case, R., Demetriou, A., Platsidou, M., & Kazi, S. (2001). Integrating concepts and tests of intelligence from the differential and developmental traditions. *Intelligence, 29*, 307–336.

Caspi, A., & Roberts, B. W. (2001). Personality development across the life course: The argument for change and continuity. *Psychological Inquiry, 12*(2), 49–66.

Caspi, A., Elder, G. H., & Bem, D. J. (1988). Moving away from the world: Life course patterns of shy children. *Developmental Psychology, 24*, 824–831.

Caspi, A., McClay, J., Moffitt, T. E., Mill, J., Martin, J., Craig, I. W., Taylor, A., & Poulton, R. (2002). Role of genotype in the cycle of violence in maltreated children. *Science, 297*, 851–853.

Caspi, A., Roberts, B. W., & Shiner, R. L. (2005). Personality development: Stability and change. *Annual Review of Psychology, 56*, 453–484.

Casswell, S., & Thamarangsi, T. (2009). Reducing harm from alcohol: Call to action. *The Lancet, 373*, 2247–2257.

Castelli, F., Happé, F., Frith, U., & Frith, C. (2000). Movement and mind: A functional imaging study of perception and interpretation of complex intentional movement patterns. *NeuroImage, 12*, 314–325.

Castle, D. J., & Buckley, P. F. (2008). *Schizophrenia*. New York: Oxford University Press.

Castonguay, L. G., & Beutler, L. E. (2005). *Principles of therapeutic change that work*. New York: Oxford University Press.

Catania, A. C. (1998). *Learning* (4th ed.). Upper Saddle River, NJ: Prentice Hall.

Catania, A. C. (2001). Positive psychology and positive reinforcement. *American Psychologist, 56*, 86–87.

Catchpole, C. K., & Rowell, A. (1993). Song sharing and local dialects in a population of the European wren *Troglodytestroglodytes. Behaviour, 125*, 67–78.

Cattabeni, F., Colciaghi, F., & Di Luca, M. (2004). Platelets provide human tissue to unravel pathogenic mechanisms of Alzheimer disease. *Progress in Neuro-Psychopharmacology & Biological Psychiatry, 28*, 763–770.

Cattell, R. B. (1965). *The scientific analysis of personality*. Chicago, IL: Aldine.

Cattell, R. B. (1971). *Abilities: Their growth, structure, and action*. Boston, MA: Houghton Mifflin.

Cattell, R. B. (1998). Where is intelligence? Some answers from the triadic theory. In J. J. McArdle & R. W. Woodcock (Eds.), *Human cognitive abilities in theory and practice*. Mahwah, NJ: Lawrence Erlbaum.

Caughlin, J. P., & Malis, R. S. (2004). Demand/withdraw communication between parents and adolescents: Connections with self-esteem and substance use. *Journal of Social and Personal Relationships, 21*, 125–148.

Ceci, S. J., & Williams, W. M. (1997). Schooling, intelligence, and income. *American Psychologist, 52*, 1051–1058.

Ceci, S. J., Bruck, M., & Battin, D. B. (2000). The suggestibility of children's testimony. In D. F. Bjorklund (Ed.), *False-memory creation in children and adults: Theory, research, and implications*. Mahwah, NJ: Erlbaum.

Centers for Disease Control and Prevention (CDC) (1988). *Posttraumatic stress disorders*. Atlanta, GA: Author.

Centers for Disease Control and Prevention (CDC) (2002a). *Causes of death in the United States*. Atlanta, GA: Author.

Centers for Disease Control and Prevention (CDC) (2002b). Youth risk behavior surveillance—United States, 2001. *Morbidity and Mortality Weekly Report, 51* (SS04), 1–64. Washington, DC: Author.

Centers for Disease Control and Prevention (CDC) (2006). *Revised recommendations for HIV testing of adults, adolescents, and pregnant women in health-care settings*. MMWR, No. RR-14, 1–17.

Cervone, D. (1999). Bottom-up explanation in personality psychology: The case of cross-situational consistency. In D. Cervone & Y. Shoda (Eds.), *The coherence of personality*. New York: Guilford Press.

Cervone, D., & Shoda, Y. (1999). *The coherence of personality: Social-cognitive bases of consistency, variability, and organization*. New York: Guilford Press.

Chambless, D. L., & Hollon, S. D. (1998). Defining empirically supported therapies. *Journal of Consulting and Clinical Psychology, 66*, 7–18.

Chamorro-Premuzic, T., & Furnham, A. (2006). Intellectual competence and the intelligent personality: A third way in differential psychology. *Review of General Psychology, 10*, 251–267.

Chan, R. C. K., Di, X., McAlonan, G. M. & Gong, Q. (2011). Brain anatomical abnormalities in high-risk individuals, first-episode, and chronic schizophrenia: An activation likelihood estimation meta-analysis of illness progression. *Schizophrenia Bulletin, 37*(1), 177–188. doi:10.1093/schbul/sbp073.

Chan, Z. C. Y., & Ma, J. L. C. (2002). Family themes of food refusal: Disciplining the body and punishing the family. *Health Care for Women International, 23*, 49–58.

Chandler, M. J., Lacritz, L. H., Cicerello, A. R., Chapman, S. B., Honig, L. S., Weiner, M. F., & Cullum, C. M. (2004). Three-word recall in normal aging. *Journal of Clinical and Experimental Neuropsychology, 26*, 1128–1133.

Chang, A., & Wilson, M. (2004). Recalling emotional experiences affects performance on reasoning problems. *Evolution and human behaviour, 25*, 267–276.

Chang, E. C. (1996). Cultural differences in optimism, pessimism, and coping: Predictors of subsequent adjustment in American and Caucasian American college students. *Journal of Counseling Psychology, 43*, 113–123.

Chang, E. C. (1998). Dispositional optimism and primary and secondary appraisal of a stressor: Controlling for confounding influences and relations to coping and psychological and physical adjustment. *Journal of Personality and Social Psychology, 74*, 1109–1120.

Chapman, A. L. (2010). Borderline personality disorder. In D. McKay, J. S. Abramowitz, & S. Taylor (Eds.), *Cognitive-behavioural therapy for refractory cases: Turning failure into success*. Washington, DC: American Psychological Association.

Chappell, M., & Humphreys, M. S. (1994). An auto-associative neural network for sparse representations: Analysis and application to models of recognition and cued recall. *Psychological Review, 101*, 103–128.

Chartrand, T. L., & Bargh, J. A. (2002). Nonconscious motivations: Their activation, operation, and consequences. In A. Tesser, D. A. Stapel, & J. V. Wood (Eds.), *Self and motivation: Emerging psychological perspectives*. Washington, DC: American Psychological Association.

Chartrand, T. L., Bargh, J. A., & van Baaren, R. (2002). Consequences of automatic evaluation for mood. Manuscript submitted for publication.

Chase, J. H. (1950). *The Marijuana Mob*. London: Robert Hale.

Chase, W. G., & Simon, H. A. (1973). Perception in chess. *Cognitive Psychology, 4*, 55–81.

Chee, M. W., & Choo, W. C. (2004). Functional imaging of working memory after 24 hr of total sleep deprivation. *Journal of Neuroscience, 24*, 4560–4567.

Chellappa, S. L., Steiner, R., Blattner, P., Oelhafen, P., Götz, T., & Cajochen, C. (2011). Non-visual effects of light on melatonin, alertness and cognitive performance: Can blue-enriched light keep us alert? *PLoS ONE, 6*(1), e16429. doi:10.1371/journal.pone.0016429

Chen, C., Greenberger, E., Lester, J., Dong, Q., & Guo, M. S. (1998). A cross-cultural study of family and peer correlates of adolescent misconduct. *Developmental Psychology, 34*, 770–781.

Chen, H., & Lan, W. (1998). Adolescents' perceptions of their parents' academic expectations: Comparison of American, Chinese-American, and Chinese high school students. *Adolescence, 33*, 385–390.

Chen, H., Charlat, O., Tartaglia, L. A., Woolf, E. A., Weng, X., Ellis, S. J., … Morgenstern, J. P. (1996). Evidence that the diabetes gene encodes the leptin receptor: Identification of a mutation in the leptin receptor gene in db/db mice. *Cell, 84*, 491–495.

Chen, S. C. (1937). Social modification of the activity of ants in nest-building. *Physiological Zoology, 10*, 420–436.

Chen, S., English, T., & Peng, K. (2006). Self-verification and contextualized self-views. *Personality and Social Psychology Bulletin, 32*, 930–942.

Cheng, C., Cheung, S. F., Chio, J. H. M., & Chan, M. P. S. (2013). Cultural meaning of perceived control: A meta-analysis of locus of control and psychological symptoms across 18 cultural regions. *Psychological bulletin, 139*(1), 152.

Cheng, P. W., & Holyoak, K. J. (1985). Pragmatic reasoning schemas. *Cognitive Psychology, 17*, 391–416.

Chenoweth, D. (2002). *Evaluating worksite health promotion*. Champaign, IL: Human Kinetics.

Cherry, E. C. (1953). Some experiments on the recognition of speech, with one and with two ears. *Journal of the Acoustical Society of America, 25*(5), 975–979.

Chertkoff, J. M., & Kushigian, R. H. (1999). *Don't panic: The psychology of emergency egress and ingress*. Westport, CT: Praeger.

Chesney, M. A., Neilands, T. B., Chambers, D. B., Taylor, J. M., & Folkman, S. (2006). A validity and reliability study of the coping self-efficacy scale. *British Journal of Health Psychology, 11*, 421–437.

Chi, L. (2004). Achievement goal theory. In T. Morris & J. Summers (Eds.), *Sport psychology: Theories, applications, and issues* (2nd ed.). Sydney: Wiley.

Chiappelli, F. (2000). Immune suppression. In G. Fink (Ed.), *Encyclopedia of stress*. San Diego, CA: Academic Press.

Chiles, J. A., & Strossahl, K. D. (1995). *The suicidal patient: Principles of assessment, treatment, and case management*. Washington, DC: American Psychiatric Press.

Chiriboga, D. A. (1989). Mental health at the midpoint: Crisis, challenge, or relief? In S. Hunter & M. Sundel (Eds.), *Midlife myths: Issues, findings, and practice implications*. Newbury Park, CA: Sage.

Chitty, D. (1996). *Do lemmings commit suicide? Beautiful hypothesis and ugly facts*. Oxford: Oxford University Press.

Choi, I., Dalal, R., Kim Prieto, C., & Park, H. (2003). Culture and judgement of causal relevance. *Journal of Personality and Social Psychology, 84*, 46–59.

Chomsky, N. (1965). *Aspects of a theory of syntax*. Cambridge, MA: MIT Press.

Chomsky, N. (1972). *Language and mind*. New York: Harcourt.

Chomsky, N. (1987). Language in a psychological setting. *Sophia Linguistic Working Papers in Linguistics, 22*, Sophia University, Tokyo.

Christensen, A., Atkins, D. C., Yi, J., Baucom, D. H., & George, W. H. (2006). Couple and individual adjustment for 2 years following a randomized clinical trial comparing traditional versus integrative behavioural couple therapy. *Journal of Consulting and Clinical Psychology, 74*, 1180–1191.

Christensen, O., & Christensen, E. (1988). Fat consumption and schizophrenia. *Acta Psychiatrica Scandinavica, 78*, 587–591.

Christianson, S. A., & Nilsson, L. G. (1989). Hysterical amnesia: A case of aversively motivated isolation of memory. In T. Archer & L. G. Nilsson (Eds.), *Aversion, avoidance, and anxiety: Perspectives on aversively motivated behavior*. Hillsdale, NJ: Erlbaum.

Christopherson, E. R., & Mortweet, S. L. (2001). *Treatments that work with children: Empirically supported strategies for managing childhood problems*. Washington, DC: American Psychological Association.

Chrousos, G. P., Kaltsas, G. A., & Mastorakos, G. (2006). *Neuroimmunodulation: Neuroendocrine and immune crosstalk*. London: Blackwell.

Church, A. T., & Katigbak, M. S. (2000). Trait psychology in the Philippines. *American Behavioral Scientist, 44*, 73–94.

Chwalisz, K., Diener, E., & Gallagher, D. (1988). Autonomic arousal feedback and emotional experience: Evidence from the spinal cord injured. *Journal of Personality and Social Psychology, 54*, 820–828.

Chwilla, D. J., & Kolk, H. H. J. (2002). Three step priming in lexical decision. *Memory and Cognition, 30*, 217–225.

Cialdini, R. B. (2009). *Influence: Science and Practice* (5th ed.). Boston: Pearson/ Allyn & Bacon.

Cialdini, R. B., & Goldstein, N. J. (2004). Social influence: Compliance and conformity. *Annual Review of Psychology, 55*, 591–621.

Cialdini, R. B., & Sagarin, B. J. (2005). Principles of interpersonal influence. In T. C. Brock & M. C. Green (Eds.), *Persuasion: Psychological insights and perspectives* (2nd ed.). Thousand Oaks, CA: Sage.

Cialdini, R. B., Borden, R. J., Thorne, A., Walker, M.R., Freeman, S., Sloan, L. R. (1976). Basking in reflected glory: Three (football) field studies. *Journal of Personality and Social Psychology, 34*, 366–375.

Cialdini, R. B., Brown, S. L., Lewis, B. P., & Luce, C. (1997). Reinterpreting the empathy-altruism relationship: When one into one equals oneness. *Journal of Personality and Social Psychology, 73*, 481–494.

Cianelli, S. N., & Fouts, R. S. (1998). Chimpanzee to chimpanzee American Sign Language. *Human Evolution, 13*, 147–159.

Cigales, M., Field, T., Lundy, B., Cuadra, A. & Hart, S. (1997). Massage enhances recovery from habituation in normal infants. *Infant Behavior and Development, 20*, 29–34.

Claparède, E. (1911). Recognition et moïté. *Archives de Psychologies, 11*, 79–90.

Clark, A. E. (1998). The positive externalities of higher unemployment: Evidence from household data. Working paper, Université d'Orléans, Orléans, France.

Clark, D. A. (2004). *Cognitive-behavioral therapy for OCD*. New York: Guilford Press.

Clark, D. A., & Beck, A. T. (2010). *Cognitive therapy for anxiety disorders: Science and practice*. New York: Guilford Press.

Clark, D. A., & O'Connor, K. (2005). Thinking is believing: Ego-dystonic intrusive thoughts in obsessive-compulsive disorder. In D. A. Clark (Ed.), *Intrusive thoughts in clinical disorders: Theory, research, and treatment*. New York: Guilford Press.

Clark, D. A., Beck, A. T., & Alford, B. A. (1999). *Scientific foundations of cognitive theory and therapy of depression*. New York: Wiley.

Clark, D. A., Beck, A. T., & Brown, G. (1989). Cognitive mediation in general psychiatric outpatients: A test of the content-specificity hypothesis. *Journal of Personality and Social Psychology, 56*, 958–964.

Clark, D. M. (1986). A cognitive approach to panic. *Behaviour Research and Therapy, 24*, 461–470.

Clark, D. M. (1988). A cognitive model of panic attacks. In S. Rachman & J. D. Maser (Eds.), *Panic: Psychological perspectives*. Hillsdale, NJ: Erlbaum.

Clark, K. B., & Clark, M. P. (1947). Racial identification and preference in Negro children. In T. N. Newcomb & E. L. Hartley (Eds.), *Readings in social psychology*. New York: Holt.

Clark, R. D., III (1990). The impact of AIDS on gender differences in willingness to engage in casual sex. *Journal of Applied Social Psychology, 20*, 771–782.

Clark, R. D., III (2001). Effects of majority defection and multiple minority sources on minority influence. *Group Dynamics, 5*, 57–62.

Clark, R. D., III, & Hatfield, E. (1989). Gender differences in willingness to engage in casual sex. *Journal of Psychology and Human Sexuality, 2*, 39–55.

Clarke, A. M., & Clarke, A. D. B. (2000). *Early experience and the life path*. London: Kingsley.

Clarkin, J. F., Marziali, E., & Munroe-Blum, H. (1992). *Borderline personality disorder: Clinical and empirical perspectives*. New York: Guilford Press.

Clément, G., & Reschke, M. F. (2008) *Neuroscience in space*. New York: Springer.

Clifford, B. R. (2004). Levels of processing 30 years on: A special issue of memory: Book review. *Applied Cognitive Psychology, 18*, 486–489.

Clifton, P. G., Vickers, S. P. & Somerville, E. M. (1998). Little and often: Ingestive behavior patterns following hippocampal lesions in rats. *Behavioral Neuroscience, 112*(3), 502–511.

Cloninger, C. R. (2000). Biology of personality dimensions. *Current Opinion of Psychiatry, 13*, 611–616.

Cloninger, C. R., & Dokucu, M. E. (2008). Somatoform and dissociative disorders. In P. J. Clayton & S. H. Fatemi (Eds.), *The medical basis of psychiatry*. Totowa, NJ: Humana Press.

Cloninger, C. R., & Gottesman, I. I. (1989). Genetic and environmental factors in antisocial behavior disorders. In S. Mednick, T. Moffitt, & S. Strack (Eds.), *The causes of crime: New biological approaches*. Cambridge: Cambridge University Press.

Clore, G. L., & Centerbar, D. (2004). Analyzing anger: How to make people mad. *Emotion, 4*, 139–144.

Clutton-Brock, T. (2002). Breeding together: Kin selection and mutualism in cooperative vertebrates. *Science, 296*, 69–72.

Coan, J. A., & Allen, J. (2003). Frontal EEG asymmetry and the behavioral activation and inhibition systems. *Psychophysiology, 40*, 106–114.

Coan, J. A., Schaefer, H. S., & Davidson, R. J. (2006). Lending a hand: Social regulation of the neural response to threat. *Psychological Science, 17*, 1032–1039.

Coffey, C., Carlin, J. B., Degenhardt, L., Lynskey, M., Sanci, L., & Patton, G. C. (2002). Cannabis dependence in young adults: An Australian population study. *Addiction, 97*, 187–194.

Coffey, C. E., Weiner, R. D., Djang, W. T., Figiel, G. S., Soady, S. A., Patterson, L. J., … Wilkinson, W. E. (1991). Brain anatomic effects of electroconvulsive therapy: A prospective magnetic resonance imaging study. *Archives of General Psychiatry, 48*, 1013–1020.

Cohen, K. M. (2002). Relationships among childhood sex-atypical behavior, spatial ability, handedness, and sexual orientation in men. *Archives of Sexual Behavior, 31*, 129–143.

Cohen, L. B., & Marks, K. S. (2002). How infants process addition and subtraction events. *Developmental Science, 5*(2), 186–201.

Cohen, L. B., & Younger, B. A. (1984). Infant perception of angular relations. *Infant Behavior and Development, 7*, 37–47.

Cohen, M., & Davis, N. (1981). *Medication errors: Causes and prevention*. Philadelphia, PA: G. F. Stickley.

Cohen, R. L. (1981). On the generality of some memory laws. *Scandinavian Journal of Psychology, 22*, 267–281.

Cohen, S. (1988). Psychosocial models of the role of social support in the etiology of physical disease. *Health Psychology, 7*, 269–297.

Cohen, S., & Herbert, T. B. (1996). Health psychology: Psychological factors and physical disease from the perspective of human psychoneuroimmunology. *Annual Review of Psychology, 47*, 113–142.

Cohen, S., & Pressman, S. D. (2006). Positive affect and health. *Current Directions in Psychological Science, 15*, 122–125.

Cohen, S., Doyle, W. J., Turner, R., Alper, C. M., & Skoner, D. P. (2003). Sociability and susceptibility to the common cold. *Psychological Science, 14*, 389–395.

Cohen, S., Janicki-Deverts, D., & Miller, G. E. (2007). Psychological stress and disease. *JAMA, 298*, 1685–1687.

Cohen Kadosh, K., Cohen Kadosh, R., Dick, F., & Johnson, M. H. (2011). Developmental changes in effective connectivity in the emerging core face network. *Cerebral Cortex, 21*(6), 1389–1394.

Coid, J, Yang, M., Tyrer, P., Roberts, A., & Ullrich, S. (2006). Prevalence and correlates of personality disorder in Great Britain. *British Journal of Psychiatry, 188*, 423–431.

Cojan, Y., Waber, L., Schwartz, S., Rossier, L., Forster, A., & Vuilleumier, P. (2009). The brain under self-control: Modulation of inhibitory and monitoring cortical networks during hypnotic paralysis. *Neuron, 62*(6), 862–875.

Cole, S. W., Kemeny, M. E., Taylor, S. E., & Visscher, B. R. (1996a). Elevated physical health risk among gay men who conceal their homosexual identity. *Health Psychology, 15*, 243–251.

Cole, S. W., Kemeny, M. E., Taylor, S. E., Visscher, B. R., & Fahey, J. L. (1996b). Accelerated course of human immunodeficiency virus infection in gay men who conceal their homosexual identity. *Psychosomatic Medicine, 58*, 219–231.

Colibazzi, T., Posner, J., Wang, Z., Gorman, D., Gerber, A., Yu, S., ... Peterson, B. S. (2010). Neural systems subserving valence and arousal during the experience of induced emotions. *Emotion, 10*(3), 377–389.

Colley, B. (2010). ADHD, science and the common man. *Emotional and Behavioural Difficulties, 15*(2), 83–94.

Collings, P. (2001). If you got everything, it's good enough: Perspectives on successful aging in a Canadian Inuit community. *Journal of Cross-Cultural Gerontology, 16*, 127–155.

Collins, A. M., & Loftus, E. F. (1975). A spreading activation theory of semantic processing. *Psychological Review, 82*, 407–428.

Collins, D. W., & Kimura, D. (1997). A large sex difference on a two-dimensional mental rotation task. *Behavioral Neuroscience, 111*, 845–849.

Colom, R., Abad, F. J., Quiroga, M. A., Shih, P. C., & Flores-Mendoza, C. (2008). Working memory and intelligence are highly related constructs, but why? *Intelligence, 36* (6), 584–606.

Coltheart, M. (1980). Iconic memory and visible persistence. *Perception & Psychophysics, 27*, 183–228.

Columbia (1996). *The Columbia world of quotations*. Retrieved from http://www.bartleby.com

Comer, R. J. (2009). *Abnormal psychology* (7th ed.). New York: Worth.

Compton, M. T., Goulding, S. M., & Walker, E. F. (2007). Cannabis use, first-episode psychosis, and schizotypy: A summary and synthesis of recent literature. *Current Psychiatry Review, 3*, 161–171.

Comuzzie, A. G., & Allison, D. B. (1998). The search for human obesity genes. *Science, 280*, 1374–1377.

Conel, J. L. (1975). *The postnatal development of the human cerebral cortex* (Vols 1 & 8). Cambridge, MA: Harvard University Press. (Original work published 1939.)

Conrad, R. (1964). Acoustic confusions in immediate memory. *British Journal of Psychology, 55*, 75–84.

Conrad, R., & Hull, A. J. (1964). Information, acoustic confusion and memory span. *British Journal of Psychology, 55*(4), 429–432.

Conway, M. A. (1997). Past and present: Recovered memories and false memories. In M. A. Conway (Ed.). *Recovered memories and false memories*. Oxford: Oxford University Press.

Conway, M. A., & Pleydell-Pearce, C. W. (2000). The construction of autobiographical memories in the self-memory system. *Psychological Review, 107*, 261–288.

Conway, M. A., & Rubin, D. C. (1993). The structure of autobiographical memory. In A. F. Collins, S. E. Gathercole, M. A. Conway, & P. E. Morris (Eds.), *Theories of memory*. Hove: Psychology Press.

Conway, M. A., Anderson, S. J., Larsen, S. F., Donnelly, C. M., McDaniel, M. A., McClelland, A. G., Rawles, R. E., & Logie, R. H. (1994). The formation of flashbulb memories. *Memory and Cognition, 22*(3), 326–343.

Cook, S. W., Yip, T. K., & Goldin-Meadow, S. (2010). Gesturing makes memories that last. *Journal of Memory and Language, 63*(4), 465–475.

Cooke, P. (1991, June 23). They cried until they couldn't see. *New York Times Magazine, 25*, 43.

Cooley, C. H. (1902). *Human nature and the social order*. New York: Charles Scribner's.

Cooper, C. R., & Denner, J. (1998). Theories linking culture and psychology: Universal and community-specific processes. *Annual Review of Psychology, 49*, 559–584.

Cooper, J., Mirabile, R., & Scher, S. J. (2005). Actions and attitudes: The theory of cognitive dissonance. In T. C. Brock & M. C. Green (Eds.), *Persuasion: Psychological insights and perspectives* (2nd ed.). Thousand Oaks, CA: Sage.

Coopersmith, S. (1967). *The antecedents of self-esteem*. San Francisco, CA: Freeman.

Corales, T. A. (Ed.). (2005). *Focus on posttraumatic stress disorder research*. Hauppauge, NY: Nova Science.

Cordova, J. V., Gee, C. B., & Warren, L. Z. (2005). Emotional skillfulness in marriage: Intimacy as a mediator of the relationship between emotional skillfulness and marital satisfaction. *Journal of Social and Clinical Psychology, 24*, 218–235.

Coren, A. (2010). *Short-term psychotherapy: A psychodynamic approach* (Chs 1 and 5). Basingstoke: Palgrave Macmillan.

Coren, S. (1999). Do people look like their dogs? *Anthrozoös, 12*, 111–114.

Corr, P. J. (2008). *The reinforcement sensitivity theory of personality*. Cambridge: Cambridge University Press.

Correll, J., Park, B., Judd, C. M., & Wittenbrink, B. (2002). The police officer's

dilemma: Using ethnicity to disambiguate potentially threatening individuals. *Journal of Personality and Social Psychology, 83*, 1314–1329.

Corsten, S., Mende, M., Cholewa, J., & Huber, W. (2007). Treatment of input and output phonology in aphasia: A single case study. *Aphasiology, 21* (6/7/8), 587–603.

Costa, A., Hernandez, M., & Sebastian-Galles, N. (2008). Bilingualism aids conflict resolution: Evidence from the ANT task. *Cognition, 106*(1), 59–86.

Costa, P. T., & McCrae, R. R. (1992). The five-factor model of personality and its relevance to personality disorders. *Journal of Personality Disorders, 6*, 343–359.

Costa, P. T., & McCrae, R. R. (2002). Looking backward: Changes in the mean levels of personality traits from 80 to 12. In D. Cervone & W. Mischel (Eds.), *Advances in personality science*. New York: Guilford Press.

Costantino, G., Malgady, R. G., & Primavera, L. H. (2009). Congruence between culturally competent treatment and cultural needs of older Latinos. *Journal of Consulting and Clinical Psychology, 77*, 941–949.

Couey, J. J., Meredith, R. M., Spijker, S., Poorthuis, R. B., Smit, A. B., Brussaard, A. B., & Mansvelder, H. D. (2007). Distributed network actions by nicotine increase the threshold for spike-timing-dependent plasticity in prefrontal cortex. *Neuron, 54*, 73–87.

Courchesne, E., Carper, R., & Aksboomoff, N. (2003). Evidence of brain overgrowth in the first year of life. *Journal of the American Medical Association, 290*, 337–344.

Courneya, K. S. (1995). Understanding readiness for regular physical activity in older individuals: An application of the theory of planned behavior. *Health Psychology, 14*, 80–87.

Cousins, S. D. (1989). Culture and self-perception in the United States and Japan. *Journal of Personality and Social Psychology, 56*, 124–131.

Cowan, C. P., & Cowan, P. A. (2000). *When partners become parents: The big life change for couples*. Mahwah, NJ: Erlbaum.

Cowan, N. (1999). An embedded-processes model of working memory. In A. Miyake & P. Shah (Eds.), *Models of working memory: Mechanisms of active maintenance and executive control*. Cambridge: Cambridge University Press.

Cowan, N. (2001). The magical number 4 in short-term memory: A reconsideration of mental storage capacity. *Behavioral and Brain Sciences, 24*, 87–185.

Cowie, D., Makin, T., & Bremner, A.J. (2013). Children's responses to the Rubber Hand Illusion reveal dissociable pathways in body representations. *Psychological Science, 24*, 762–769.

Cowley, E. (2005). Views from consumers next in line: The fundamental attribution error in a service setting. *Journal of the Academy of Marketing Science, 33*, 139–152.

Cozolino, L. (2010). *The neuroscience of psychotherapy: Healing the social brain*. New York: Routledge.

Crabbe, J. C. (2002). Genetic contributions to addiction. *Annual Review of Psychology, 53*, 435–462.

Craik, F. I. M., & Lockhart, R. S. (1972). Levels of processing: A framework for memory research. *Journal of Verbal Learning and Verbal Behavior, 11*, 671–684.

Craik, F. I. M., & Tulving, E. (1975). Depth of processing and the retention of words in episodic memory. *Journal of Experimental Psychology: General, 104*, 268–294.

Craske, M. (1999). *Anxiety disorders: Psychological approaches to theory and treatment*. Boulder, CO: Westview Press.

Craske, M. (2003). *Origins of phobias and anxiety disorders: Why more women than men?* New York: Elsevier Science.

Crawford, M., & Chaffin, R. (1997). The meanings of difference: Cognition in social and cultural context. In P. J. Caplan & M. Crawford (Eds.), *Gender differences in human cognition. Counterpoints: Cognition, memory, and language*. New York: Oxford University Press.

Crits-Christoph, P., Cooper, A., & Luborsky, L. (1988). The accuracy of therapists' interpretations and the outcome of dynamic psychotherapy. *Journal of Consulting and Clinical Psychology, 56*, 490–495.

Croizet, J.-C., Despres, G., Gauzins, M.-E., Huguet, P., Leyens, J.-P., & Meot, A. (2004). Stereotype threat undermines intellectual performance by triggering a disruptive mental load. *Personality and Social Psychology Bulletin, 30*, 721–731.

Cronenwett, W. J., & Csernansky, J. (2010). Thalamic pathology in schizophrenia. In *Behavioral Neurobiology of Schizophrenia and its Treatment* (pp. 509–528). Berlin: Springer.

Crook, J. M., & Copolov, D. L. (2000). Schizophrenia. In G. Fink (Ed.), *Encyclopedia of stress*. San Diego, CA: Academic Press.

Crowe, L. C., & George, W. H. (1989). Alcohol and human sexuality: Review and integration. *Psychological Bulletin, 105*, 374–386.

Crowley, K., Callanan, M. A., Tenenbaum, H. R., & Allen, E. (2001). Parents explain more often to boys than to girls during shared scientific thinking. *Psychological Science, 12*, 258–261.

Csibra, G., & Gergely, G. (2006). Social learning and social cognition: The case for pedagogy. In Y. Munakata & M. H. Johnson (Eds.), *Processes of change in brain and cognitive development: Attention and performance XXI*. Oxford: Oxford University Press.

Cuijpers, P., Sijbrandij, M., Koole, S. L., Andersson, G., Beekman, A. T. and Reynolds, C. F. (2013). The efficacy of psychotherapy and pharmacotherapy in treating depressive and anxiety disorders: A meta-analysis of direct comparisons. *World Psychiatry, 12*(2), 137–148.

Cuijpers, P., van Straten, A., Andersson, G., & van Oppen, P. (2008). Psychotherapy for depression in adults: A meta-analysis of comparative outcome studies. *Journal of Consulting and Clinical Psychology, 76*(6), 909.

Culbertson, F. M. (1997). Depression and gender: An international review. *American Psychologist, 52*, 25–31.

Cull, W. L. (2000). Untangling the benefits of multiple study opportunities and repeated testing for cued recall. *Applied Cognitive Psychology, 14*, 215–235.

Cumming, S., Hay, P., Lee, T., et al. (1995) Neuropsychological outcome from psychosurgery for obsessive-compulsive disorder. *Australian and New Zealand Journal of Psychiatry, 29*, 293–298.

Cummings, L. (2005). *Pragmatics: A multidisciplinary perspective*. Mahwah, NJ: Erlbaum.

Cunillera, T., Toro, J. M., Sebastian-Galles, N., & Rodriguez-Fornells, A. (2006). The effects of stress and statistical cues on continuous speech segmentation: An event-related brain potential study. *Brain Research, 1123*, 168–178.

Curry, F., Elliot, A. J., Fonseca, D. D., & Moller, A. C. (2006). The social-cognitive model of achievement motivation and the 2 × 2 achievement goal framework. *Journal of Personality and Social Psychology, 90*, 666–679.

Curtis, G. C., Magee, W. J., Eaton, W. W., Wittchen, H. U., & Kessler, R. C. (1998). Specific fears and phobias: Epidemiology and classification. *British Journal of Psychiatry, 173*, 112–117.

Curtiss, S. (1977). *Genie: A psychological study of a modern day 'wild child'*. New York: Academic Press.

Custers, R. & Aarts, H. (2010).The unconscious will: How the pursuit of goals operates outside of conscious awareness. *Science, 329*, 47–50.

Cvencek, D., Greenwald, A. G., & Meltzoff, A. N. (2011). Measuring implicit attitudes of 4-year-olds: The preschool implicit association test. *Journal of Experimental Child Psychology, 109*, 187–200.

Cytowic, R. E. (2002). *Synesthesia: A union of the senses* (2nd ed.). Boston: MIT Press.

Cytowic, R. E., & Eagleman, D. M. (2009). *Wednesday is indigo blue: Discovering the brain of synesthesia*. Cambridge, MA: MIT Press.

D

Dahl, A. A. (2010). Link between personality and cancer. *Future Oncology, 6*, 691–707.

Dalton, P. (2002). Olfaction. In H. Pashler & S. Yantis (Eds.), *Steven's handbook of experimental psychology: Vol. 1. Sensation and perception* (3rd ed.). New York: Wiley.

Daly, M., & Wilson, M. (1988). *Homicide*. New York: Aldine de Gruyter.

Damasio, A. R. (1994). *Descartes' error: Emotion, reason, and the human brain*. New York: Putnam.

Damasio, A. R. (1999). *The feeling of what happens: Body and emotion in the making of consciousness*. New York: Harcourt Brace.

Damasio, A. R. (2000). A neural basis for sociopathy. *Archives of General Psychiatry, 57*, 128–129.

Damasio, A. R. (2005). Emotions and feelings: a neurobiological perspective. In A. S. R. Manstead, N. H. Frijda, A. H. Fischer, & K. Oatley (Eds.), *Feelings and Emotions: The Amsterdam Symposium*. New York: Cambridge University Press.

Damasio, A. R., Tranel, D., & Damasio, H. (1990). Individuals with sociopathic behavior caused by frontal damage fail to respond autonomically to social stimuli. *Behavioural Brain Research, 41*, 81–94.

Daneman, M., & Carpenter, P. A. (1980). Individual differences in working memory and reading. *Journal of Verbal Learning and Verbal Behavior, 19*(4), 450–466.

Dapretto, M., Davies, M., Pfeifer, J., Scott, A. A., Sigman, M., Bookheimer, S. Y., & Iacoboni, M. (2006). Understanding emotions in others: Mirror neuron dysfunction in children with autism spectrum disorders. *Nature Neuroscience, 9*(1), 28–30.

Darley, J. M., & Gross, P. H. (1983). A hypothesis-confirming bias in labeling effects. *Journal of Personality and Social Psychology, 44*, 20–33.

Darley, J. M., & Latané, B. (1968). Bystander intervention in emergencies: Diffusion of responsibility. *Journal of Personality and Social Psychology, 8*, 377–383.

Darwin, C. (1859). *On the origin of species by means of natural selection*. London: Murray.

Darwin, C. (1965). *The expression of emotion in man and animals*. Chicago, IL: University of Chicago Press. (Original work published 1872.)

Dasen, P. R., Barthélémy, D., Kan, E., Kouame, Â. K., Daouda, K., Adjei, K. K., & Assande, Â. N. (1985). N'glouele, l'intelligence chez les Baoulé [N'glouele, intelligence according to the Baoulé]. *Archives de Psychologie, 53*, 293–324.

Dautovich, N. D., Shoji, K. D., & McCrae, C. S. (2013). Variety is the spice of life: A microlongitudinal study examining age differences in intraindividual variability in daily activities in relation to sleep outcomes. *doi:* 10.1093/geronb/gbt120

Davey, G. (2008). *Clinical psychology*. London: Hodder Education.

Davey, G., Dash, S., & Meeten, F. (2014). *Obsessive compulsive disorder*. Basingstoke: Palgrave Macmillan.

Davidoff, J. (2004). Coloured thinking. *Psychologist, 17*, 570–572.

Davidson, R. J., & Fox, N. A. (1988). Cerebral asymmetry and emotion: Developmental and individual differences. In D. L. Molfese & S. J. Segalowitz (Eds.), *Brain lateralization in children: Developmental implications*. New York: Guilford Press.

Davidson, R. J., & Rickman, M. (1999). Behavioural inhibition and the emotional circuitry of the brain. In L. A. Schmidt & J. Schulkin (Eds.), *Extreme fear, shyness and social phobia: Origins, biological mechanism and clinical outcomes*. New York: Oxford University Press.

Davidson, R. J., Pizzagalli, D., Nitschke, J. B., & Putnam, K. M. (2002). Depression: Perspectives from affective neuroscience. *Annual Review of Psychology, 53*, 545–574.

Davidson, J. E. & Sternberg, R. J. (1984). *The Psychology of Problem Solving*. Cambridge: Cambridge University Press.

Davis, A., & Winstone, N. (2011). Educational implications. In A. Slater & G. Bremner (Eds.) *An introduction to developmental psychology*. Hove: Wiley-Blackwell.

Davis, C., Patte, K., Levitan, R., Reid, C., Tweed, S., & Curtis, C. (2007). From motivation to behaviour: A model of reward sensitivity, overeating, and food preferences in the risk profile for obesity. *Appetite, 48*, 12–19.

Davis, C. G., Nolen, H. S., & Larson, J. (1998). Making sense of loss and benefiting from the experience: Two construals of meaning. *Journal of Personality and Social Psychology, 75*, 561–574.

Davis, T., Gunderson, J. G., & Myers, M. (1999). Borderline personality disorder. In D. G. Jacobs (Ed.), *The Harvard Medical School Guide to suicide assessment and intervention*. San Francisco, CA: Jossey-Bass.

Dawidowicz, L. S. (1975). *The war against the Jews, 1933–1945*. New York: Holt, Rinehart & Winston.

Dawkins, R. (1989). *The selfish gene* (rev. ed.). Oxford: Oxford University Press. (Original work published 1976.)

Dawkins, R. (2006). *The selfish gene* (rev. ed.). New York: Oxford University Press.

Dawson, G., Toth, K., Abbott, R., Osterling, J., Munson, J., Estes, A., & Liaw, J. (2004). Early social attention impairments in autism: Social orienting, joint attention, and attention to distress. *Developmental Psychology, 40*, 271–283.

Dawson-McClure, S. R., Sandler, I. N., Wolchik, S. A., & Millsap, R. E. (2004). Risk as a moderator of the effects of prevention programs for children from divorced families: A six-year longitudinal study. *Journal of Abnormal Child Psychology, 32*, 175–190.

Day, R., Nielsen, J. A., Korten, A., Ernberg, G., Dube, K. C., Gebhart, J., ... Olatawura, M. (1987). Stressful life events preceding the acute onset of schizophrenia. *Culture, Medicine, and Psychiatry, 11*, 123–205.

De Cremer, D., & van Lange, P. A. M. (2001). Why prosocials exhibit greater cooperation than proselfs: The roles of social responsibility and reciprocity. *European Journal of Personality, 15*, 5–18.

De Geus, E. J. C. (2000). Aerobics in stress reduction. In G. Fink (Ed.), *Encyclopedia of stress*. San Diego, CA: Academic Press.

De Houwer, J., Teige-Mocigemba, S., Spruyt, A., & Moors, A. (2009). Implicit measures: A normative analysis and review. *Psychological Bulletin, 135*(3), 347–368.

De Raad, B., Barelds, D. P., Levert, E., Ostendorf, F., Mlačić, B., Blas, L. D., ... Katigbak, M. S. (2010). Only three factors of personality description are fully replicable across languages: a comparison of 14 trait taxonomies. *Journal of Personality and Social Psychology, 98*(1), 160–173.

De Weerd, A. W., & van den Bossche, R. A. S. (2003). The development of sleep during the first months of life. *Sleep Medicine Reviews, 7*, 179–191.

De Weerd, A. W., van den Bossche, R. A. S., & Peeters, E. A. J. (2003). Late in- and out of bed in teenagers. *Sleep, 26* (suppl.), A132–133.

De Zeeuw, C. I., & Cicirata, F. (Eds.) (2005). *Creating coordination in the cerebellum.* St. Louis: Elsevier Sciences/Mosby.

Deady, D. K., North, N. T., Allan, D., Smith, M. J., & O'Carroll, R. E. (2010). Examining the effect of spinal cord injury on emotional awareness, expressivity and memory for emotional material. *Psychology, Health & Medicine, 15*(4), 406–419.

Deary, I. J., Thorpe, G., Wilson, V., Starr, J. M., & Whalley, L. J. (2003). Population sex differences in IQ at age 11: The Scottish mental survey 1932. *Intelligence, 31*, 533–542.

Deary, I. J., Whiteman, M. C., Starr, J. M., Whalley, L. J., & Fox, H. C. (2004). The impact of childhood intelligence on later life: Following up the Scottish Medical Surveys of 1932 and 1947. *Journal of Personality and Social Psychology, 86*, 130–147.

Deary, I. J., Strand, S., Smith, P., & Fernandes, C. (2007). Intelligence and educational achievement. *Intelligence, 35*(1), 13–21.

DeCasper, A. J., & Spence, M. J. (1986). Prenatal maternal speech influences newborns' perceptions of speech sounds. *Infant Behavior and Development, 9*, 133–150.

DeCastro, J. M. (2002). Age-related changes in the social, psychological, and temporal influences on food intake in free-living, healthy, adult humans. *Journals of Gerontology: Series A. Biological Sciences and Medical Sciences, 57A*, 368–377.

Deci, E. L., & Ryan, R. M. (1985). *Intrinsic motivation and self-determination in human behavior*. New York: Plenum Press.

Deci, E. L., & Ryan, R. M. (2002). *Handbook of self-determination theory research*. Rochester, NY: University of Rochester Press.

Degen, L., Matzinger, D., Drewe, J., & Beglinger, C. (2001). The effect of cholecystokinin in controlling appetite and food intake in humans. *Peptides, 22*, 1265–1269.

Degner, J., & Dalege, J. (2013). The apple does not fall far from the tree, or does it? A meta-analysis of parent–child similarity in intergroup attitudes. *Psychological Bulletin, 139*, 1270–1304.

Dehaene, S., & Naccache, L. (2001). Towards a cognitive neuroscience of consciousness: Basic evidence and a workspace framework. *Cognition, 79*, 1–37.

Dehaene, S., Izard, V., Pica, P., & Spelke, E. (2006). Core knowledge of geometry in an Amazonian indigene group. *Science, 311* (5759), 381–384.

Dehaene-Lambertz, G., Dehaene, S., & Hertz-Pannier, L. (2002). Functional neuroimaging of speech perception in infants. *Science, 298*(5600), 2013–2015.

Dekker, E., & Groen, J. (1956). Reproducible psychogenic attacks of asthma. *Journal of Psychosomatic Research, 1*, 56–67.

DeLongis, A. (2000). Coping skills. In G. Fink (Ed.), *Encyclopedia of stress*. San Diego, CA: Academic Press.

Demarest, J., & Allen, R. (2000). Body image: Gender, ethnic, and age differences. *Journal of Social Psychology, 140*, 465–472.

Dement, W. C. (1974). *Some must watch while some must sleep*. San Francisco, CA: W. H. Freeman.

Démonet, J. F. (2005). The dynamics of language-related brain images. *Neurocase, 11*, 148–150.

Démonet, J. F., Thierry, G., & Cardebat, D. (2005). Renewal of the neurophysiology of language: Functional neuroimaging. *Physiological Reviews, 85*, 49–95.

DeMoranville, B. M., Jackson, I., Ader, R., et al. (2000). Endocrine and immune systems. In B. S. Fogel, R. B. Schiffer, & S. M. Rao (Eds.), *Synopsis of neuropsychiatry*. Philadelphia, PA: Lippincott-Raven.

Deng, Y. Q., Li, S., Tang, Y. Y., Zhu, L. H., Ryan, R., & Brown, K. (2012). Psychometric properties of the Chinese translation of the mindful attention awareness scale (MAAS). *Mindfulness, 3*(1), 10–14.

Dennerstein, L., Gotts, G., Brown, J. B., Morse, C. A., Farley, T. M., & Pinol, A. (1994). The relationship between the menstrual cycle and female sexual interest in women with PMS complaints and volunteers. *Psychoneuroendocrinology, 19*(3), 293–304.

Denollet, J. (1997). Personality, emotional distress and coronary heart disease. *European Journal of Personality, 11*, 343–357.

Denollet, J., Nyklicek, I., & Vingerhoets, A. (Eds.) (2007). *Emotional regulation: Conceptual and clinical issues*. New York: Springer.

Denzin, N. K., & Lincoln, Y. S. (Eds.) (2005). *The Sage handbook of qualitative research*. Thousand Oaks, CA: Sage Publications.

Denzler, M., Foerster, J., & Liberman, N. (2009). How goal-fulfillment decreases aggression. *Journal of Experimental Social Psychology, 45*, 90–100.

Department of Health (2007). *Improving access to psychological therapies (IAPT) programme: Computerised cognitive behavioural therapy (cCBT) implementation guidance*. London: DoH.

Depue, R. A., & Collins, P. F. (1999). Neurobiology of the structure of personality: Dopamine, facilitation of incentive motivation, and extraversion. *Behavioral and Brain Sciences, 22*, 491–569.

Depue, R. A., & Lenzenweger, M. F. (2005). A neurobehavioral dimensional model of personality disorders. In M. F. Lenzenweger & J. F. Clarkin (Eds.), *Major theories of personality disorder*. New York: Guilford Press.

DeRegnier, R. A., Wewerka, S., Georgieff, M. K., Mattia, F., & Nelson, C. A. (2002). Influences of postconceptional age and postnatal experience on the development of auditory recognition memory in the newborn infant. *Developmental Psychobiology, 41*, 216–225.

Deregowski, J. B. (1989). Real space and represented space: Cross-cultural perspectives. *Behavior and Brain Sciences, 12*, 51–119.

Deroy, O., & Valentin, D. (2011). Tasting shapes: Investigating cross- modal correspondences. *Chemosensory Perception, 4*, 80–90.

DeRubeis, R. J., & Crits-Christoph, P. (1998). Empirically supported individual and group psychological treatments for adult mental disorders. *Journal of Consulting and Clinical Psychology, 66*, 37–52.

DeStefano, D., & LeFevre, J. (2004). The role of working memory in mental arithmetic. *European Journal of Cognitive Psychology, 16*, 353–386.

DeSteno, D., Dasgupta, N., Bartlett, M. Y., & Cajdric, A. (2004). Prejudice from thin air: The effect of emotion on automatic intergroup attitudes. *Psychological Science, 15*, 319–324.

Deutsch, J. A., & Deutsch, D. (1967). Comments on 'Selective attention: Perception or response?', *Quarterly Journal of Experimental Psychology, 19*, 362–363.

Deutsch, M., & Gerard, H. B. (1955). A study of normative and informational social influence upon individual judgment. *Journal of Abnormal and Social Psychology, 51*, 629–636.

Devine, P. G. (1989). Stereotypes and prejudice: Their automatic and controlled components. *Journal of Personality and Social Psychology, 56*, 5–18.

Dhabhar, F. S., & McEwen, B. S. (2001). Bidirectional effects of stress and glucocorticoid hormones on immune function: Possible explanations for paradoxical observations. In R. Ader, D. L. Feiten, & N. Cohen (Eds.), *Psychoneuroimmunology* (Vol. 1). San Diego, CA: Academic Press.

Di Marzo, S., Giordano, A., Pacchiarotti, I., Colom, F., Sánchez-Moreno, J., & Vieta, E. (2006). The impact of the number of episodes on the outcome of bipolar disorder. *European Journal of Psychiatry, 20*(1), 21–28.

Di Paula, A., & Campbell, J. D. (2002). Self-esteem and persistence in the face of failure. *Journal of Personality and Social Psychology, 83*, 711–724.

Diacon, S., & Hasseldine, J. (2007). Framing effects and risk perception: The effect of prior performance presentation format on investment fund choice. *Journal of Economic Psychology, 28*, 31–52.

Diamond, A. (1990). The development and neural bases of memory functions as indexed by the A B and delayed response tasks in human infants and infant monkeys. In A. Diamond (Ed.), *The development and neural bases of higher cognitive functions*. New York: New York Academy of Science Press.

Diamond, L. M. (2003). What does sexual orientation orient? A biobehavioral model distinguishing romantic love and sexual desire. *Psychological review, 110*(1), 173–192.

Diamond, L. M. (2004). Emerging perspectives on distinctions between romantic love and sexual desire. *Current directions in psychological science, 13*(3), 116–119.

Diaz, J. (1997). *How drugs influence behavior: A neuro-behavioral approach*. Upper Saddle River, NJ: Prentice Hall.

Dickerson, S. S., & Kemeny, M. E. (2004). Acute stressors and cortisol responses: A theoretical integration and synthesis of laboratory research. *Psychological Bulletin, 130*, 355–391.

DiClemente, C. C. (2003). *Addiction and change: How addictions develop and addicted people recover*. New York: Guilford Press.

Diener, E. (2000). Subjective well-being: The science of happiness and a proposal for a national index. *American Psychologist, 55*, 34–43.

Diener, E., & Diener, C. (1996). Most people are happy. *Psychological Science, 7*, 181–185.

Diener, E., & Seligman, M. E. P. (2002). Very happy people. *Psychological Science, 13*, 81–84.

Diener, E., & Seligman, M. (2004). Beyond money: Toward an economy of well-being. *Psychological Science in the Public Interest, 5*, 1–31.

Diener, E., Tamir, M., & Scollon, C. N. (2006). Happiness, life satisfaction, and fulfillment: The social psychology of subjective wellbeing. In P. A. M. Van Lange (Ed.), *Bridging social psychology: Benefits of transdisciplinary approaches*. Mahwah, NJ: Erlbaum.

Diener, E., Suh, E., Lucas, R. E., & Smith, H. L. (1999). Subjective well-being: Three decades of progress. *Psychological Bulletin, 125*, 276–302.

Dietz, W. H. (1998). Health consequences of obesity in youth: Childhood predictors of adult disease, *Pediatrics, 101*, 518–525.

Digman, J. M. (1997). Higher-order factors of the Big Five. *Journal of Personality and Social Psychology, 73*, 1246–1256.

Dilger, W. (1962). The behaviour of lovebirds. *Scientific American, 206*(1), 89–98.

Dillard, J. P., & Anderson, J. W. (2004). The role of fear in persuasion. *Psychology & Marketing, 21*, 909–926.

DiMatteo, M. R. (2004). Social support and patient adherence to medical treatment: A meta-analysis. *Health Psychology, 23*, 207–218.

Dindia, K. (2002). Self-disclosure research: Knowledge through meta-analysis. In M. Allen, R. W. Preiss, B. M. Gayle, & N. A. Burrell (Eds.), *Interpersonal communication research: Advances through meta-analysis*. Mahwah, NJ: Erlbaum.

Dinges, D., & Kribbs, N. (1991). Performing while sleepy: Effects of experimentally-induced sleepiness. In T. Monk (Ed.), *Sleep, sleepiness, and performance*. New York: John Wiley & Sons.

Dinges, D. F., Pack, F., Williams, K., Gillen, K. A., Powell, J. W., Ott, G. E., Aptowicz, C., & Pack, A. I. (1997). Cumulative sleepiness, mood disturbance, and psychomotor vigilance performance decrements during a week of sleep restricted to 4–5 hours per night. *Sleep, 20*, 267–277.

Dishman, R. K. (1982). Compliance/adherence in health-related exercise. *Health Psychology, 1*, 237–267.

Dishman, R. K. (1994). *Advances in exercise adherence*. Champaign, IL: Human Kinetics.

Dobson, K. S. (2009). *Handbook of cognitivebehavioral therapies* (3rd ed.). New York: Guilford Press.

Docherty, N. M., St-Hilaire, A., Aakre, J. M., & Seghers, J. P. (2009). Life events and high-trait reactivity together predict psychotic symptom increases in schizophrenia. *Schizophrenia Bulletin, 35*, 638–645.

Dodge, K. A. (1986). A social information processing model of social competence in children. *Cognitive perspectives on children's social behavioral development. The Minnesota symposium on child psychology, 18*, 77–125.

Dohrenwend, B. P. (2006). Inventorying stressful life events as risk factors for psychopathology: Toward resolution of the problem of intracategory variability. *Psychological Bulletin, 132*, 477–495.

Doise, W., & Mugny, G. (1984). *The social development of the intellect*. Oxford: Pergamon.

Doka, K. J. (1995). Coping with life-threatening illness: A task model. *Omega: Journal of Death and Dying, 32*, 111–122.

Dolan, P., Peasgood, T., & White, M. P. (2008). Do we really know what makes us happy? A review of the economic literature on the factors associated with subjective well-being. *Journal of Economic Psychology, 29*, 94–122.

Dolezal, H. (1982). *Living in a world transformed: Perceptual and performatory adaptation to a visual distortion*. New York: Academic Press.

Doll, C., McLaughlin, T. F. & Baretto, A. (2013) The token economy: A recent review and evaluation. *International Journal of Basic and Applied Science, 2*(1), 131–149.

Domhoff, G. W. (1999). Drawing theoretical implications from descriptive empirical findings on dream content. *Dreaming: Journal of the Association for the Study of Dreams, 9*, 201–210.

Domhoff, G. W. (2001). A new neurocognitive theory of dreams. *Dreaming: Journal of the Association for the Study of Dreams, 11*, 13–33.

Domino, G. (2000). *Psychological testing*. Upper Saddle River, NJ: Prentice Hall.

Domjan, M. (2000a). *The essentials of conditioning and learning* (2nd ed.). Belmont, CA: Wadsworth/Thomson.

Domjan, M. (2000b). General process learning theory: Challenges from response and stimulus factors. *International Journal of Comparative Psychology, 13*, 101–118.

Donaldson, D. (1998). *Psychiatric disorders with a biochemical basis*. New York: Parthenon.

Donaldson, M. (1978). *Children's minds*. New York: Norton.

Donnerstein, E., & Malamuth, N. (1997). Pornography: Its consequences on the observer. In L. B. Schlesinger & E. Revitch (Eds.), *Sexual dynamics of anti-social behavior* (2nd ed.). Springfield, IL: Charles C. Thomas.

Doosje, B., Loseman, A., & Bos, K. (2013). Determinants of radicalization of Islamic youth in the Netherlands: Personal uncertainty, perceived injustice, and perceived group threat. *Journal of Social Issues, 69*, 586–604.

Doppelt, J. E., & Wallace, W. L. (1955). Standardization of the Wechsler Adult Intelligence Scale for older persons. *Journal of Abnormal and Social Psychology, 51*, 312–330.

Dorus, S., Vallender, E. J., Evans, P. D., Anderson, J. R., Gilbert, S. L., Mahowald, M., … Lahn, B. T. (2004). Accelerated evolution of nervous system genes in the origin of Homo sapiens. *Cell 119*(7), 1027–1040.

Dossenbach, M., & Dossenbach H. D. (1998). *All about animal vision*. Chicago, IL: Blackbirch Press.

Dovidio, J. F. (1984). Helping behavior and altruism: An empirical and conceptual overview. In L. Berkowitz (Ed.), *Advances in experimental social psychology* (Vol. 17). New York: Academic Press.

Dovidio, J. F., Piliavin, J. A., Schroeder, D. A., & Penner, L. (2006). *The social psychology of prosocial behavior*. Mahwah, NJ: Erlbaum.

Dowd, H., Zautra, A., & Hogan, M. (2010). Emotion, stress, and cardiovascular response: An experimental test of models of positive and negative affect. *International Journal of Behavioral Medicine, 17*, 189–194.

Drake, M. E., Pakalnis, A., & Denio, L. C. (1988). Differential diagnosis of epilepsy and multiple personality: Clinical and EEG findings in 15 cases. *Neuropsychiatry, Neuropsychology, and Behavioral Neurology, 1*, 131–140.

Driscoll, I., McDaniel, M. A., & Guynn, M. J. (2005). Apolipoprotein E and prospective memory in normally aging adults. *Neuropsychology, 19*, 28–34.

Driskell, J. E., Willis, R. P., & Copper, C. (1992). Effect of over-learning on retention. *Journal of Applied Psychology, 77*, 615–622.

Driver, J., & Spence, C. (2000). Multisensory perception: Beyond modularity and convergence. *Current Biology, 10*, R731–R735.

Drizin, S. A., & Colgan, B. (2004). Tales from the juvenile confession front: a guide to how standard police interrogation tactics can produce coerced and false confessions from juvenile suspects. In G. D. Lassiter (Ed.), *Interrogations, confessions and entrapment*. New York: Kluwer Academic.

Drizin, S. A., & Leo, R. A. (2004). The problem of false confessions in the post-DNA world. *North Carolina Law Review, 82*, 891–1007.

Drury, J., Cocking, C., Reicher, S., Burton, A., Schofield, D., Hardwick, A., Graham, D., & Langston, P. (2009). Cooperation versus competition in a mass emergency evacuation: A new laboratory simulation and a new theoretical model. *Behaviour Research Methods, 41*, 957–970.

Dryden, W., & Branch, R. (2008). *The fundamentals of rational emotive behaviour therapy: A training handbook* (2nd ed.). Chichester: Wiley.

Duffy, J. F., Rimmer, D. W., & Czeisler, C. A. (2001). Association of intrinsic circadian period with morningness-eveningness, usual wake time, and circadian phase. *Behavioral Neuroscience, 115,* 895–899.

Duggan, J. P., & Booth, D. A. (1986). Obesity, overeating and rapid gastric-emptying in rats with ventromedial hypothalamic-lesions. *Science, 231* (4738), 609–611.

Dumontheil, I., Apperly, I. A., & Blakemore, S. J. (2009). Online usage of theory of mind continues to develop in late adolescence. *Developmental Science, 13*(2), 331–338.

Dunbar, M., Ford, G., & Hunt, K. (1998). Why is the receipt of social support associated with increased psychological distress? An examination of three hypotheses. *Psychology & Health, 13,* 527–544.

Duncan, H. J., & Seiden, A. M. (1995). Long-term follow-up of olfactory loss secondary to head trauma and upper respiratory tract infection. *Archives of Otolaryngology – Head and Neck Surgery, 121,* 1183–1187.

Duncan, L. E. (2005). Personal political salience as a self-schema. Consequences for political information processing. *Political Psychology, 26,* 965–976.

Duncan, P. M., Alici, T., & Woodward, J. D. (2000). Conditioned compensatory response to ethanol as indicated by locomotor activity in rats. *Behavioural Pharmacology, 11,* 395–402.

Dunlosky, J. & Rawson, K.A. (2012). Overconfidence produces underachievement: Inaccurate self evaluations undermine students' learning and retention. *Learning and Instruction, 22*(4), 271–280.

Dunn, E.W., Aknin, L.B. & Norton, M.I. (2008) Spending Money on Others Promotes Happiness, *Science, 319,* 5870, 1687–1688.

Dunn, J., & Plomin, R. (1990). *Separate lives: Why siblings are so different.* New York: Basic Books.

Durmer, J. S., Dinges, D. F. (2005) Neurocognitive consequences of sleep deprivation. *Seminars in Neurology, 25*(1), 117–129.

Durrant, J. E. (2000). Trends in youth crime and well-being since the abolition of corporal punishment in Sweden. *Youth and Society, 31,* 437–455.

Dutton, D. G. (2006). *The abusive personality: Violence and control in intimate relationships.* New York: Guilford Press.

Dutton, D. G., & Aron, A. P. (1974). Some evidence for heightened sexual attraction under conditions of high anxiety. *Journal of Personality and Social Psychology, 30*(4), 510–517.

Duvander, A. Z. E. (1999). The transition from cohabitation to marriage: A longitudinal study of the propensity to marry in Sweden in the early 1990s. *Journal of Family Issues, 20,* 698–717.

Dweck, C. (1999). *Self theories: Their role in motivation, personality, and development.* Philadelphia, PA: Psychology Press/Taylor and Francis.

Dying to Be Thin. (2000). *Nova* (Television series). Boston, MA: WGBH.

E

Eacott, M. J., & Crawley, R. A. (1998). The offset of childhood amnesia: Memory for events that occurred before age 3. *Journal of Experimental Psychology: General, 127,* 22–33.

Eagleman, D. M. (2010). Synaesthesia. *British Medical Journal, 340,* b4616. doi: 10.1136/bmj-b4616

Eagles, J. M. (2003). Seasonal affective disorder. *British Journal of Psychiatry, 182,* 174–176.

Eagly, A. H. (1981). Recipient characteristics as determinants of responses to persuasion. In R. E. Petty, T. C. Brock, & T. M. Ostrom (Eds.), *Cognitive responses in persuasion* (pp. 173–196). Hillsdale, NJ: Erlbaum.

Eagly, A. H. (1987). *Sex differences in social behavior: A social-role interpretation.* Hillsdale, NJ: Erlbaum.

Eagly, A. H., & Crowley, M. (1986). Gender and helping behavior: A meta-analytic review of the social psychological literature. *Psychological Bulletin, 100,* 283–308.

Eagly, A. H., & Wood, W. (1999). The origins of sex differences in human behavior: Evolved dispositions versus social roles. *American Psychologist, 54,* 408–423.

Eagly, A. H., & Wood, W. (2006). Three ways that data can misinform: Inappropriate partialling, small samples, and, anyway, they're not playing our song. *Psychological Inquiry, 17,* 131–137.

Eaton, J. (2001). Management communication: The threat of groupthink. *Corporate Communications, 6,* 183–192.

Ebbinghaus, H. (1964). *Über das gedächtnis: untersuchungen zur experimentellen psychologie [Memory: A Contribution to experimental psychology]* (Trans. H. A. Ruger & C. E. Bussenius). New York: Dover. (Original work published 1885.)

Eccles, J. (1991). Gender-role socialization. In R. M. Baron, W. G. Graziano, & C. Stangor (Eds.), *Social psychology.* Fort Worth, TX: Holt, Rinehart & Winston.

Eckensberger, L. H., & Zimba, R. F. (1997). The development of moral judgment. In J. W. Berry, P. R. Dasen, & T. S. Saraswathi (Eds.), *Handbook of cross-cultural psychology* (2nd ed., Vol. 2). Boston, MA: Allyn & Bacon.

Edelman, G. M. (1987). *Neural darwinism.* New York: Basic Books.

Eden, D. (2003). Self-fulfilling prophecies in organizations. In J. Greenberg (Ed.), *Organizational behavior: The state of the science* (2nd ed.). Mahwah, NJ: Erlbaum.

Edser, S. J. (2002). Hypnotically facilitated counter conditioning of anticipatory nausea and vomiting associated with chemotherapy: A case study. *Australian Journal of Clinical Hypnotherapy and Hypnosis, 23,* 18–30.

Edwards, A. E. (1962). A demonstration of the long-term retention of a conditioned galvanic skin response. *Psychosomatic Medicine, 24,* 459–463.

Egan, L. C., Santos, L. R., & Bloom, P. (2007). The origins of cognitive dissonance evidence from children and monkeys. *Psychological Science, 18*(11), 978–983.

Ehlers, A., & Clark, D. M. (2000). A cognitive model of posttraumatic stress disorder. *Behaviour Research and Therapy, 38,* 319–345.

Ehrman, J. (2003). *Clinical exercise psychology.* Champaign, IL: Human Kinetics.

Eisenberg, N. (2000). Emotion, regulation, and moral development. *Annual Review of Psychology, 51,* 665–697.

Eisenberg, N. (2002). Emotion related regulation and its relation to quality of social functioning. In W. Hartup & R. A. Weinberg (Eds.), *Child psychology in retrospect and prospect: In celebration of the 75th anniversary of the Institute of Child Development. The Minnesota symposia on child psychology* (Vol. 32). Mahwah, NJ: Erlbaum.

Eisenberg, N. (2004). Prosocial and moral development in the family. In T. A. Thorkildsen, & H. J. Walberg (Eds.), *Nurturing morality. Issues in children's and families' lives.* New York: Kluwer Academic/Plenum Press.

Eisenberger, N. I., Lieberman, M. D., & Williams, K. D. (2003). Does rejection hurt? An fMRI study of social exclusion. *Science, 302*, 290–292.

Ekman, P. (1973). Cross-cultural studies of facial expression. In P. Ekman (Ed.), *Darwin and facial expression.* San Diego, CA: Academic Press.

Ekman, P. (1992). An argument for basic emotions. *Cognition and Emotion, 6* (3–4), 169–200.

Ekman, P. (1999). Basic emotions. In T. Dalgleish & M. Power (Eds.), *Handbook of Cognition and Emotion*, Hove: John Wiley.

Eckman, P. & Friesen, W. V. (1967). Hand and body cues in the judgement of emotion: A reformulation. *Perceptual and Motor Skills, 24*, 711–724.

Eckman, P. & Friesen, W. V. (1969). The repertoire of nonverbal behaviour: Categories, origins, usage and coding. *Semiotics, 1*, 49–98.

Eckman, P. & Friesen, W. V. (1971). Constants across cultures in the face and emotion. *Journal of Personality and Social Psychology, 17*, 124–129.

Ekman, P., & Friesen, W. V. (1987). *Facial Action Coding System.* Palo Alto, CA: Consulting Psychologists Press.

Ekman, P., Friesen, W. V., & Ellsworth, P. (1972). *Emotion in the human face: Guidelines for research and an integration of findings.* Oxford: Pergamon Press.

Elbert, T., Pantev, C., Wienbruch, C., Rockstroh, B., & Taub, E. (1995). Increased cortical representation of the fingers of the left hand in string players. *Science, 270*, 305–307.

Eliassen, J. C., Souza, T., & Sanes, J. N. (2003). Experience-dependent activation patterns in human brain during visual-motor associative learning. *Journal of Neuroscience, 23*, 10540–10547.

Elkin, I., Falconnier, L., Smith, Y., Canada, K. E., Henderson, E., Brown, F. R., & McKay, D. M. (2014). Therapist responsiveness and patient engagement in therapy. *Psychotherapy Research, 24*(1), 52–66.

Elkind, D. (1967). Egocentrism in adolescence. *Child Development, 38*, 1025–1034.

Ellemers, N. (1993). The influence of sociostructural variables on identity management strategies. In W. Stroebe & M. Hewstone (Eds.), *European review of social psychology* (Vol. 4). Chichester: Wiley.

Ellemers, N., Wilke, H., & Van Knippenberg, A. (1993). Effects of the legitimacy of low group or individual status on individual and collective status-enhancement strategies. *Journal of Personality and Social Psychology, 64*, 766–778.

Elliot, A. J., & Church, M. A. (1997). A hierarchical model of approach and avoidance achievement motivation. *Journal of Personality and Social Psychology, 72*, 218–232.

Elliot, A. J., & Devine, P. G. (1994). On the motivational nature of cognitive dissonance: Dissonance as psychological discomfort. *Journal of Personality and Social Psychology, 67*(3), 382–394.

Elliot, A. J., & McGregor, H. A. (2001). A 2 × 2 achievement goal framework. *Journal of Personality and Social Psychology, 80*, 501–519.

Elliot, A. J., & Thrash, T. M. (2002). Approachavoidance motivation in personality: Approach and avoidance temperaments and goals. *Journal of Personality and Social Psychology, 82*, 804–818.

Ellis, A. (1962). *Reason and emotion in psychotherapy.* New York: Lyle Stuart.

Ellison-Wright, I. & Bullmore, E. (2009) Meta-analysis of diffusion tensor imaging studies in schizophrenia, *Schizophrenia Research, 108*, 1–3, 3–10.

Elmquist, J. K., Bjorbaek, C., Ahima, R. S., Flier, J. S., & Saper, C. B. (1998). Distributions of leptin receptor mRNA

isoforms in the rat brain. *Journal of Comparative Neurology, 395*, 535–547.

Elsabbagh, M., Divan, G., Yun-Joo, Koh, Y. J., Kim, Y. S., Kauchali, S., … Fombonne, E. (2012). Global prevalence of autism and other pervasive developmental disorders. *Autism Research, 5*(3), 160 170.

Elsey, B., & Fujiwara, A. (2000). Kaizen and technology transfer instructors as workbased learning facilitators in overseas transplants: A case study. *Journal of Workplace Learning, 12*, 333–342.

Emerson, R. M. (1966). Mount Everest: A case study of communication feedback and sustained group goalstriving. *Sociometry, 29*, 213–227.

Emlen, S. T. (1975, August). The stellar orientation system of a migratory bird. *Scientific American*, 102–111.

Engel, A. K., Moll, C. K., Fried, I., & Ojemann, G. A. (2005). Invasive recordings from the human brain: Clinical insights and beyond. *Nature Reviews Neuroscience, 6*(1), 35–47.

Engel de Abreu, P. M. J., Conway, A. R. A., & Gathercole, S. E. (2010). Working memory and fluid intelligence in young children. *Intelligence, 38*, 552–561.

Engeland, A., Bjørge, T., Søgaard, A. J., & Tverdal, A. (2003). Body mass index in adolescence in relation to total mortality: 32-year follow-up of 227.000 Norwegian boys and girls. *American Journal of Epidemiology, 157*, 517–523.

Engelhardt, C. R., Bartholow, B. D., Kerr, G. T., & Bushman, B. J. (2011). This is your brain on violent video games: Neural desensitization to violence predicts increased aggression following violent video game exposure. *Journal of Experimental Social Psychology, 47*(5), 1033–1036.

Engle, R. W. (2010). Role of working memory capacity in cognitive control. *Current Anthropology, 51*, S17–S26.

Engle, R. W., Tuholski, S. W., Laughlin, J. E., & Conway, A. R. A. (1999). Working memory, short-term memory, and general fluid intelligence: A latent-variable approach. *Journal of Experimental Psychology: General, 128* (3), 309–331.

Epstein, M. A., & Bottoms, B. L. (2002). Explaining the forgetting and recovery of abuse and trauma memories: Possible

mechanisms. *Child Maltreatment: Journal of the American Professional Society on the Abuse of Children, 7*, 210–225.

Epstein, R., Kirshnit, C. E., Lanza, R. P., & Rubin, L. C. (1984). 'Insight' in the pigeon: Antecedents and determinants of an intelligent performance. *Nature, 308*, 61–62.

Epstein, S. (1983). Aggregation and beyond: Some basic issues on the production of behavior. *Journal of Personality, 51*, 360–392.

Erdberg, P. (2000). Rorschach assessment. In G. Goldstein & M. Hersen (Eds.), *Handbook of psychological assessment* (3rd ed.). New York: Elsevier.

Erford, B. T. (2010). *Group work: Processes and applications.* New York: Prentice Hall.

Ericsson, K. A., & Chase, W. G. (1982). Exceptional memory. *American Scientist, 70*, 607–615.

Ericsson, K. A., & Polson, P. G. (1988). An experimental analysis of the mechanisms of a memory skill. *Journal of Experimental Psychology: Learning, Memory, and Cognition, 14*, 305–316.

Ericsson, K. A., Chase, W. G., & Faloon, S. (1980). Acquisition of a memory skill. *Science, 208*, 1181–1182.

Ericsson, K. A., Krampe, R. T., & Tesch R. C. (1993). The role of deliberate practice in the acquisition of expert performance. *Psychological Review, 100*, 363–406.

Ericsson, K. A., Delaney, P. F., Weaver, G., & Mahadevan, R. (2004). Uncovering the structure of a memorist's superior 'basic' memory capacity. *Cognitive Psychology, 49*, 191–237.

Eriksen, C. W. (1990). Attentional search of the visual field. In D. Brogan (Ed.), *Visual search.* London: Taylor & Francis..

Erikson, E. H. (1968). *Identity, youth and crisis.* New York: Norton.

Erikson, E. H. (1980). *Identity and the life cycle.* New York: Norton. (Original work published 1959.)

Eron, L. D. (1987). The development of aggressive behavior from the perspective of a developing behaviorism. *American Psychologist, 42*, 435–442.

Eron, L. D. (2000). A psychological perspective. In V. B. Van Hasselt &

M. Hersen (Eds.), *Aggression and violence: An introductory text.* Boston, MA: Allyn & Bacon.

Esparza, J., Fox, C., Harper, I. T., Bennett, P. H., Schulz, L. O., Valencia, M. E., & Ravussin, E. (2000). Daily energy expenditure in Mexican and USA Pima Indians: Low physical activity as a possible cause of obesity. *International Journal of Obesity and Related Metabolic Disorders, 24*, 55–59.

Espíndola, C. R., & Blay, S. L. (2009). Anorexia nervosa's meaning to patients: A qualitative synthesis. *Psychopathology, 42*, 69–80.

Essau, C., & Petermann, F. (1999). *Depressive disorders in children and adolescents: Epidemiology, risk factors, and treatment.* Northvale, NJ: Aronson.

Essau, C., & Trommsdorff, G. (1996). Coping with university-related problems: A crosscultural comparison. *Journal of Cross-Cultural Psychology, 27*, 315–328.

Estes, T. H., & Vaughn, J. L. (1985). *Reading and learning in the content classroom: Diagrams and instructional strategies* (3rd ed.). Boston: Allyn & Bacon.

Eurocare (2003). Retrieved from http://ec.europa.eu/health-eu/news_alcoholineurope_en.htm

Evans, J. St. B. T., & Lynch, J. S. (1973). Matching bias in the selection task. *British Journal of Psychology, 64*, 39–397.

Evans, J. St. B. T., Over, D. E., & Manktelow, K. I. (1993). Reasoning, decision-making and rationality. *Cognition, 49*, 165–187.

Evans-Martin, F. F. (2007). *Emotion and stress.* New York: Facts on File.

Exner, J. E. (1991). *The Rorschach – a comprehensive system: Assessment of personality and psychopathology* (Vol. 2). New York: Wiley.

Eysenck, H. J. (1952). The effects of psychotherapy: An evaluation. *Journal of Consulting Psychology, 16*, 319–324.

Eysenck, H. J. (1964). *Crime and personality.* Boston, MA: Houghton Mifflin.

Eysenck, H. J. (1967). *The biological basis of personality.* Springfield, IL: Charles C. Thomas.

Eysenck, H. J. (1990). Biological dimensions of personality. In L. A. Pervin (Ed.), *Handbook of personality: Theory and research.* New York: Guilford Press.

Eysenck, H. J. (1992). Four ways five factors are not basic. *Personality and Individual Differences, 13*, 667–673.

Eysenck, H. J. (1994). Cancer, personality, and stress: Prediction and prevention. *Advances in Behaviour Research and Therapy, 16*, 167–215.

Eysenck, H. J., & Grossarth-Marticek, R. (1991). Creative novation behavior therapy as a prophylactic treatment for cancer and coronary heart disease: II. Effects of treatment. *Behavior Research and Therapy, 29*, 17–31.

F

Fabbro, F. (2001). The bilingual brain: Bilingual aphasia. *Brain & Language, 79*, 201–210.

Fagley, N. S. (1987). Positional response bias in multiple-choice tests of learning: Its relation to testwiseness and guessing strategy. *Journal of Educational Psychology, 79*, 95–97.

Faith, M. S., Matz, P. E., & Jorge, M.A. (2002). Obesity depression associations in the population. *Journal of Psychosomatic Research, 53*, 935–942.

Falcone, B., Coffman, B. A., Clark, V. P., & Parasuraman, R. (2012). Transcranial direct current stimulation augments perceptual sensitivity and 24-hour retention in a complex threat detection task. *PLoS One, 7*(4), e34993.

Fallon, A. E., & Rozin, P. (1985). Sex differences in perceptions of desirable body shape. *Journal of Abnormal Psychology, 94*, 102–105.

Falsetti, S. A., Monnier, J., & Resnick, H. S. (2005). Intrusive thoughts in posttraumatic stress disorder. In D. A. Clark (Ed.), *Intrusive thoughts in clinical disorders: Theory, research, and treatment.* New York: Guilford Press.

Fanselow, M. S. (1991). Analgesia as a response to aversive Pavlovian conditional stimuli: Cognitive and emotional mediators. In M. R. Denny (Ed.), *Fear, avoidance, and phobias: A fundamental analysis.* Hillsdale, NJ: Erlbaum.

Fanselow, M. S., & Poulos, A. M. (2005). The neuroscience of mammalian associative learning. *Annual Review of Psychology, 56*, 207–234.

Fantz, R. L. (1961, May). The origin of form perception. *Scientific American, 204*, 66–72.

Fantz, R. L. (1964). Visual experience in infants: Decreased attention to familiar patterns relative to novel ones. *Science, 146*, 668–670.

Faraone, S. V., Sergeant, J., Gillberg, C., & Biederman, J. (2003). The worldwide prevalence of ADHD: Is it an American condition? *World Psychiatry, 2*, 104–113.

Faravelli, C., Abradi, L., Bartolozzi, D., Cecchi, C., Cosci, F., D'Adamo, D., … Rosi, S. (2004). The Sesto Fiorentino Study: Background, methods and preliminary results. *Psychotherapy Psychosomatics, 73*, 216–225.

Faravelli, C., Guerrini Degl'Innocenti, B., & Giardinelli, L. (1989). Epidemiology of anxiety disorders in Florence. *Acta Psychiatrica Scandinavica, 79*, 308–312.

Farooqi, I. S., Jebb, S. A., Langmack, G., Lawrence, E., Cheetham, C. H., Prentice, A. M., … O'Rahilly, S. (1999). Effects of recombinant leptin therapy in a child with congenital leptin deficiency. *New England Journal of Medicine, 341*, 879–884.

Farroni, T., Csibra, G., Simion, F., & Johnson, M. H. (2002). Eye contact detection in humans from birth. *Proceedings of the National Academy of Sciences of the United States of America, 99*, 9602–9605.

Faust, J. (1991). Same-day surgery preparation: Reduction of pediatric patient arousal and distress through participant modeling. *Journal of Consulting and Clinical Psychology, 59*, 473–478.

Fawcett, C. A., & Markson, L. (2010). Similarity predicts liking in 3-year-old children. *Journal of experimental child psychology, 105*(4), 345–358.

Fazio, R. H., & Roskos-Ewoldsen, D. R. (2005). Acting as we feel: When and how attitudes guide behavior. In T. C. Brock & M. C. Green (Eds.), *Persuasion: Psychological insights and perspectives* (2nd ed.). Thousand Oaks, CA: Sage.

Fazio, R. H., Jackson, J. R., Dunton, B. C., & Williams, C. J. (1995). Variability in automatic activation as an unobstrusive measure of racial attitudes: A bona fide pipeline? *Journal of Personality and Social Psychology, 69*, 1013–1027.

Federal Interagency Forum on Aging-Related Statistics (2006). *Older Americans update 2006: Key indicators of well-being.* Retrieved from http://www.agingstats.gov/update2006/Health_Status.pdf.

Fehr, E., & Fischbacher, U. (2003). The nature of human altruism. *Nature, 425*(23), 785–791.

Fehr, R., Gelfand, M. J., & Nag, M. (2010). The road to forgiveness: a meta-analytic synthesis of its situational and dispositional correlates. *Psychological Bulletin, 136*, 894–914.

Fein, S., & Spencer, S. J. (1997). Prejudice as self-image maintenance: Affirming the self through derogating others. *Journal of Personality and Social Psychology, 73*, 31–44.

Feingold, A. (1988). Matching for attractiveness in romantic partners and same-sex friends: A meta-analysis and theoretical critique. *Psychological Bulletin, 104*, 226–235.

Feingold, A., & Mazzella, R. (1998). Gender differences in body image are increasing. *Psychological Science, 9*, 190–195.

Feldman-Barrett, L., Niedenthal, P. M., & Winkielman, P. (Eds.) (2007). *Emotion and consciousness.* New York: Guilford Press.

Felmlee, D. H. (1998). 'Be careful what you wish for...': A quantitative and qualitative investigation of 'fatal attractions'. *Personal Relationships, 5*, 235–253.

Felton, D. L., & Maida, M. E. (2000). Neuroimmunomodulation. In G. Fink (Ed.), *Encyclopedia of stress.* San Diego, CA: Academic Press.

Fenichel, G. (2006). *Neonatal neurology.* St. Louis: Mosby.

Ferdowsian, H. R., Durham, D. L., Kimwele, C., Kranendonk, G., Otali, E., Akugizibwe, T., Mulcahy, J. B., Ajarova, L. and Johnson, C. M. (2011). Signs of mood and anxiety disorders in chimpanzees. *PLoS ONE, 6*, e19855.

Ferguson, E., Chamorro-Premuzic, T., Pickering, A., & Weiss, A. (2011). Five into one doesn't go: A critique of the general factor of personality. In T. Chamorro-Premuzic, S. von Stumm, & A. Furnham (Eds.), *The handbook of individual differences.* Oxford: Blackwell-Wiley.

Ferguson, E. D. (2000). *Motivation: A biosocial and cognitive integration of motivation and emotion.* New York: Oxford University Press.

Fernald, A., Taeschner, T., Dunn, J., Papousek, M., de Boysson-Bardies, B., & Fukui, I. (1989). A cross cultural study of prosodic modification in mothers' and fathers' speech to preverbal infants. *Journal of Child Language, 16*, 477–501.

Ferster, C. B., & Skinner, B. F. (1957). *Schedules of reinforcement.* Englewood Cliffs, NJ: Prentice Hall.

Festinger, L. (1954). A theory of social comparison processes. *Human Relations, 2*, 117–40.

Festinger, L. (1957). *A theory of cognitive dissonance.* Stanford, CA: Stanford University Press.

Festinger, L., & Carlsmith, J. M. (1959). Cognitive consequences of forced compliance. *Journal of Abnormal and Social Psychology, 58*, 203–210.

Festinger, L., Pepitone, A., & Newcomb, T. (1952). Some consequences of deindividuation in a group. *Journal of Abnormal Psychology, 47*, 382–389.

Fetterman, D. M. (1988). *Excellence and equality: A qualitatively different perspective on gifted and talented education.* Albany, NY: State University of New York Press.

Fiedler, K., Nickel, S., Muehlfriedel, T., & Unkelbach, C. (2001). Is mood congruency an effect of genuine memory or response bias? *Journal of Experimental Social Psychology, 37*, 201–214.

Field, T. M. (2000). Infant massage therapy. In C. H. Zeanah Jr (Ed.), *Handbook of infant mental health* (2nd ed.). New York: Guilford Press.

Field, T. M. (2001). Massage therapy facilitates weight gain in preterm infants. *Current Directions in Psychological Science, 10*, 51–54.

Field, T. M., Diego, M. A., Hernandez-Reif, M., Deeds, O., & Figuereido, B. (2006). Moderate versus light pressure massage therapy leads to greater weight gain in preterm infants. *Infant Behavior & Development, 29*, 574–578.

Field, T. M., Schanberg, S. M., Scafidi, F., Bauer, C. R., Vega-Lahr. N., Garcia, R.,

Nystrom, J., & Kuhn CM. (1986). Tactile/kinesthetic stimulation effects on preterm neonates. *Pediatrics, 77,* 654–658.

Field, T. M., Woodson, R., Greenberg, R., & Cohen, D. (1982). Discrimination and imitation of facial expression by neonates. *Science, 218,* 179–181.

Fielder, K. (1988). The dependence of the conjunction fallacy on subtle linguistic factors. *Psychological Research, 50,* 123–129.

Fields, H. L. (2005). *Pain: Mechanisms and management.* New York: McGraw-Hill.

Figueredo, A. J., & Rushton, P. J. (2009). Evidence for shared genetic dominance between the general factor of personality, mental and physical health, and life history traits. *Twin Research and Human Genetics, 12,* 555–563.

Finn, A. S., Kraft, M. A., West, M. R., Leonard, J. A., Bish, C. E., Martin, R. E., … Gabrieli, J.D.E. (2014). Cognitive skills, student achievement tests, and schools. *Psychological Science, 25*(3), 736–744.

Fischer, P., Krueger, J. I., Greitemeyer, T., Vogrincic, C., Kastenmüller, A., Frey, D., … & Kainbacher, M. (2011). The bystander-effect: a meta-analytic review on bystander intervention in dangerous and non-dangerous emergencies. *Psychological Bulletin, 137*(4), 517.

Fishbein, M., & Ajzen, I. (1974). Attitudes toward objects as predictors of single and multiple behavioral criteria. *Psychological Review, 81,* 59–74.

Fisher, C., Kahn E., Edwards, A., Davis, D. M., & Fine, J. A. (1974). A psychophysiological study of nightmares and night terrors: III. Mental content and recall of stage 4 night terrors. *Journal of Nervous and Mental Disease, 158,* 174–188.

Fisher, P. L. & Wells, A. (2005). Experimental modification of beliefs in obsessive compulsive disorder: A test of the metacognitive model. *Behaviour Research and Therapy, 43,* 821–829.

Fisher, S., & Greenberg, R. P. (1996). *Freud scientifically reappraised: Testing the theories and therapy.* New York: Wiley.

Fiske, S. T., Lin, M., & Neuberg, S. L. (1999). The continuum model: Ten years later. In S. Chaiken & Y. Trope (Eds.), *Dual process theories in social psychology.* New York: Guilford Press.

Fiske, S. T., & Taylor, S. E. (2013). *Social cognition: From brains to culture* (2nd ed.). London: Sage.

Flavell, J. H. (1970). Developmental studies of mediated behavior. In H. W. Reese & L. P. Lipsett (Eds.), *Advances in child development and behavior* (Vol. 5). New York: Academic Press.

Fleeson, W. (2004). Moving personality beyond the person-situation debate. *Current Directions in Psychological Science, 13,* 83–87.

Flinn, M. V. (1997). Culture and the evolution of social learning. *Evolution and Human Behavior, 18,* 23–67.

Flohr, H. (2000). NMDA receptor-mediated computational processes and phenomenal consciousness. In T. Metzinger (Ed.), *Neural correlates of consciousness: Empirical and conceptual questions.* Cambridge, MA: MIT Press.

Floyd, R. L., O'Connor, M. J., Sokol, R. J., Bertrand, J., & Cordero, J. F. (2005). Recognition and prevention of fetal alcohol syndrome. *Obstetrics & Gynecology, 106,* 1059–1064.

Flynn, J. R. (1987). Massive IQ gains in 14 nations: What IQ tests really measure. *Psychological Bulletin, 101,* 171–191.

Flynn, J. R. (1998). IQ gains over time: Toward finding the causes. In U. Neisser et al. (Eds.), *The rising curve: Long-term gains in IQ and related measures.* Washington, DC: American Psychological Association.

Foa, E. B., Riggs, D. S., & Gershuny, B. S. (1995). Arousal, numbing, and intrusion: Symptom structure of posttraumatic stress disorder following assault. *American Journal of Psychology, 152,* 116–120.

Foa, E. B., Zoellner, L. A., Feeny, N. C., Hembree, E. A., & Alvarez-Conrad, J. (2002). Does imaginal exposure exacerbate PTSD symptoms? *Journal of Consulting and Clinical Psychology, 70,* 1022–1028.

Folkard, S., & Tucker, P. (2003). Shift work, safety and productivity. *Occupational Medicine, 53*(2), 95–101.

Følling, A. (1934). Über Ausschiedung von Phenylbrenztraubensaüre in den Harn als Stoffwechselanomalie in *Verbindung mit Imbezillität. Hoppe-Seyler's Z Physiol Chem, 227,* 169–176.

Ford, R. M., Driscoll, T., Shum, D., & Macaulay, C. E. (2012). Executive and

theory-of-mind contributions to event-based prospective memory in children: Exploring the self-projection hypothesis. *Journal of Experimental Child Psychology, 111,* 468–489.

Fordyce, W. E. (1988). Pain and suffering: A reappraisal. *American Psychologist, 43,* 276–283.

Forgas, J. P. (2011). Can negative affect eliminate the power of first impressions? Affective influences on primacy and recency effects in impression formation. *Journal of Experimental Social Psychology, 47*(2), 425–429.

Forster, K. I. (1976). Accessing the mental lexicon. In R. J. Wales & E. C. T. Walker (Eds.), *New approaches to language mechanisms.* Amsterdam: North Holland.

Forster, K. I., & Chambers, S. M. (1973). Lexical access and naming time. *Journal of Verbal Learning and Verbal Behavior, 12,* 627–635.

Fosse, R., Stickgold, R., & Hobson, J. A. (2001). Brain-mind states: Reciprocal variation in thoughts and hallucinations. *Psychological Science, 12,* 30–36.

Försterling, F. (1989). Models of covariation and attribution: How do they relate to the analogy of analysis of variance? *Journal of Personality and Social Psychology, 57,* 615–625.

Foulkes, D. (1982). REM-dream perspectives on the development of affect and cognition. *Psychiatric Journal of the University of Ottawa, 7,* 48–55.

Foulks, F. F., Bland, I. J., & Shervington, D. (1995). Psychotherapy across cultures. *Review of Psychiatry, 14,* 511.

Fournier, J. C., DeRubeis, R. J., Hollon, S. D., Dimidjian, S., Amsterdam, J. D., Shelton, R.C., & Fawcett, J. (2010). Antidepressant drug effects and depression severity: A patient-level meta-analysis. *Journal of the American Medical Association, 303,* 47–53.

Fouts, R. S., Fouts, D. H., & Van Cantfort, T. E. (1989). The infant Loulis learns signs from other cross-fostered chimpanzees. In R. A. Gardner, B. T. Gardner, & T. E. Van Cantfort (Eds.), *Teaching sign language to chimpanzees.* Albany, NY: State University of New York Press.

Fox, N. A., Henderson, H. A., Marshall, P. J., Nichols, K. E., & Ghera, M. M. (2005).

Behavioral inhibition: Linking biology and behavior within a developmental framework. *Annual Review of Psychology, 56*, 235–262.

Frank, J. (1961). *Persuasion & healing: A comparative study of psychotherapy.* Baltimore, MD: Johns Hopkins University Press.

Frank, N. C., Spirito, A., Stark, L., & Owens-Stively, J. (1997). The use of scheduled awakenings to eliminate childhood sleepwalking. *Journal of Pediatric Psychology, 22*, 345–353.

Franklin, B. (1784). *Remarks Concerning the Savage of North America.*

Franklin, J. (1987). *Molecules of the mind: The brave new science of molecular psychology.* New York: Atheneum.

Franklin, T. R., Acton, P. D., Maldjian, J. A., Gray, J. D., Croft, J. R., Dackis, C. A., O'Brien, C. P., & Childress, A. R. (2002). Decreased gray matter concentration in the insular, orbitofrontal, cingulate, and temporal cortices of cocaine patients. *Biological Psychiatry, 51*, 134–142.

Fraser, O. N., Stahl, D., & Aureli, F. (2008). Stress reduction through consolation in chimpanzees. *Proceedings of the National Academy of Sciences, 105*, 8557–8562.

Frayser, S. G. (1985). *Varieties of sexual experience: An anthropological perspective on human sexuality.* New Haven, CT: HRAF.

Fredrickson, B. L. (1998). What good are positive emotions? *Review of General Psychology, 2*, 300–319.

Freedman, A. H., Gronau, I., Schweizer, R. M., Ortega-Del Vecchyo, D., Han, E., Silva, P. M., … Novembre, J. (2014). Genome sequencing highlights the early dynamic history of dogs. *PLOS Genetics.* doi: 10.1371/journal.pgen.1004016.

French, S. J., & Cecil, J. E. (2001). Oral, gastric and intestinal influences on human feeding. *Physiology and Behavior, 74*, 729–734.

Freud, S. (1920). *Jenseits des Lustprinzips [Beyond the pleasure principle].* Leipzig: Internationaler Psychoanalytischer Verlag.

Freud, S. (1923). *The ego and the id.* New York: Norton.

Freud, S. (1935). *A general introduction to psychoanalysis.* New York: Washington Square Press.

Freud, S. (1953). The interpretation of dreams. In J. Strachey (Ed.), *The standard edition of the complete psychological works of Sigmund Freud* (Vols. 4 and 5). London: Hogarth. (Original work published 1900.)

Freud, S. (1957). Mourning and melancholia. In J. Strachey (Ed.), *The standard edition of the complete psychological works of Sigmund Freud* (Vol. 14). London: Hogarth. (Original work published 1917.)

Freud, S. (1965). *The interpretation of dreams.* New York: Avon. (Original work published 1900.)

Freund, P. A., & Kasten, N. (2012). How smart do you think you are? A meta-analysis on the validity of self-estimates of cognitive ability. *Psychological Bulletin, 138*, 296–321.

Friedl, M. C., and Draijer, N. (2000). Dissociative disorders in Dutch psychiatric inpatients. *American Journal of Psychiatry, 157*, 1012–1013.

Friedman, H., & DiMatteo, M. R. (1989). *Health psychology.* New York: Prentice Hall.

Friedman, M. I., & Stricker, E. M. (1976). Physiological-psychology of hunger – physiological perspective. *Psychological Review, 83*(6), 409–431.

Friend, R., Rafferty, Y., & Bramel, D. (1990). A puzzling misinterpretation of the Asch 'conformity' study. *European Journal of Social Psychology, 20*(1), 29–44.

Frijda, N. H. (1986). *The emotions.* Cambridge: Cambridge University Press.

Frijda, N. H. (1988). The laws of emotion. *American Psychologist, 43*, 349–358.

Frijda, N. H. (2006). *The laws of emotion.* Mahwah, NJ: Erlbaum.

Frijda, N. H., Manstead, A. S. R., & Bem, S. (Eds.) (2005). *Emotions and beliefs: How feelings influence thoughts.* New York: Cambridge University Press.

Frisby, J. P. (1980). *Seeing: Illusion, brain and mind.* Oxford: Oxford University Press.

Frisco, M. L., & Williams, K. (2003). Perceived housework equity, marital happiness, and divorce in dual earner households. *Journal of Family Issues, 24*, 51–73.

Frith, U. (1989). *Autism: Explaining the enigma.* Oxford: Blackwell.

Fritsch, J. (1999, May 25). 95% regain lost weight. Or do they? *New York Times*, p. F7.

Fritz, C. E., & Williams, H. B. (1957). The human being in disasters: A research perspective. *Annals of the American Academy of Political and Social Science, 309*, 42–51

Fritzsche, B. A., Finkelstein, M. A., & Penner, L. A. (2000). To help or not to help: Capturing individuals' decision policies. *Social Behavior and Personality, 28*, 561–578.

Frost, J. A., Binder, J. R., Springer, J..A., Hammeke, T. A., Bellgowan, P. S. F., Rao, S. M., & Cox, R. W. (1999). Language processing is strongly left lateralized in both sexes – Evidence from functional MRI. *Brain, 122*, 199–208.

Funder, D. C. (2012). Accurate personality judgments. *Current Directions in Psychological Science, 21*, 177–182.

Funk, S. C. (1992). Hardiness: A review of theory and research. *Health Psychology, 11*, 335–345.

Furmark, T., Tillfors, M., Marteinsdottir, I., Fischer, H., Pissiota, A., Långström, B., & Fredrikson, M. (2002). Common changes in cerebral blood flow in patients with social phobia treated with citalopram or cognitive-behavioral therapy. *Archives of General Psychiatry, 59*, 425–433.

G

Gaab, J., Rohleder, N., Nater, U. M., & Ehlert, U. (2005). Psychological determinants of the cortisol stress response: The role of anticipatory cognitive appraisal. *Psychoneuroendocrinology, 30*, 599–610.

Gabbard, C., & Ammar, D. (2008). The effect of response-delay on estimation reachability. *International Journal of Neuroscience, 118*, 1502–1514.

Gabbard, G. O. (1990). *Psychodynamic psychiatry in clinical practice.* Washington, DC: American Psychiatric Press.

Gabbard, G. O. (2004). *Long-term psychodynamic psychotherapy.* Washington, DC: American Psychiatric Publishing.

Gabbard, G. O., Beck, J., & Holmes, J. (2005). *Oxford textbook of psychotherapy.* New York: Oxford University Press.

Gabrieli, J. D. E. (1998). Cognitive neuroscience of human memory. *Annual Review of Psychology, 49,* 87–115.

Gabrieli, J. D. E., Desmond, J. E., Demb, J. B., & Wagner, A. D. (1996). Functional magnetic resonance imaging of semantic memory processes in the frontal lobes. *Psychological Science, 7,* 278–283.

Gaertner, S. L. and Dovidio, J. F. (2000). *Reducing intergroup bias: The Common Ingroup Identity Model,* Philadelphia, PA: Psychology Press.

Gainotti, G. (1972). Emotional behavior and hemispheric side of lesion. *Cortex, 8,* 41–55.

Galambos, N. L., & Almeida, D. M. (1992). Does parent adolescent conflict increase in early adolescence? *Journal of Marriage and the Family, 54,* 737–748.

Galanter, E. (1962). Contemporary psychophysics. In R. Brown (Ed.), *New directions in psychology.* New York: Holt, Rinehart & Winston.

Galati, D., & Lavelli, M. (1997). Neonate and infant emotion expression perceived by adults. *Journal of Nonverbal Behavior, 21,* 57–83.

Galea, S., Ahern, J., Resnick, H., Kilpatrick, D., Bucuvalas, M., Gold, J., & Vlahov, D. (2002). Psychological sequelae of the September 11 terrorist attacks in New York City. *New England Journal of Medicine, 346,* 982–987.

Galietta, M., Finneran, V., Fava, J., & Rosenfeld, B. (2010). Dialectical behavior therapy for antisocial and psychopathic personalities. In D. McKay, S. Taylor, & J. Abramawitz (Eds.), *The expanded scope of cognitive behavior therapy: Lessons learned from refractory cases.* Washington, DC: American Psychological Association.

Galinsky, A. D., & Moskowitz, G. B. (2000). Perspective-taking: Decreasing stereotype expression, stereotype accessibility, and in-group favoritism. *Journal of Personality and Social Psychology, 78,* 708–724.

Galinsky, A. D., Stone, J., & Cooper, J. (2000). The reinstatement of dissonance and psychological discomfort following failed affirmations. *European Journal of Social Psychology, 30*(1), 123–147.

Gallace, A., Boschin, E., & Spence, C. (2011). On the taste of 'Bouba' and 'Kiki': An exploration of word–food associations in neurologically normal participants. *Cognitive Neuroscience, 2(1),* 34–46.

Gallup, G. G. (1970). Chimpanzees: Self-recognition. *Science, 167*(3914), 86–87.

Galton, F. (1869). *Hereditary genius.* London: Macmillan.

Gangestad, S. W., Haselton, M. G., & Buss, D. M. (2006). Evolutionary foundations of cultural variation: Evoked culture and mate preferences. *Psychological Inquiry, 17,* 75–95.

Gangestad, S. W., Thornhill, R., & Garver-Apgar, C. E. (2005) Adaptations to ovulation: Implications for sexual and social behavior. *Current Directions in Psychological Science, 14,* 312–316.

Ganis, G., Thompson, W. L., & Kosslyn, S. M. (2004). Brain areas underlying visual mental imagery and visual perception: An fMRI study. *Cognitive Brain Research, 20,* 226–241.

Garbarino, S., Beelke, M., Costa, G., Violani, C., & Lucidi, F., Ferrillo, F., & Sannita, W. G. (2002). Brain function and effects of shift work: Implications for clinical neuropharmacology. *Neuro-psychobiology, 45,* 50–56.

Garber, J., & Dodge, K. A. (Eds.) (2007). *The development of emotional regulation and dysregulation.* New York: Cambridge University Press.

Garcia, J., & Koelling, R. A. (1966). The relation of cue to consequence in avoidance learning. *Psychonomic Science, 4,* 123–124.

Garcia, J., Lasiter, P. S., Bermudez, R. F., & Deems, D. A. (1985). A general theory of aversion learning. *Annals of the New York Academy of Sciences, 443,* 8–21.

Gardner, H. (1985). *The mind's new science.* New York: Basic Books.

Gardner, H. (2000). *Multiple intelligences: The theory in practice.* New York: Basic Books.

Gardner, H. (2003). Three distinct meanings of intelligence. In R. J. Sternberg, J. Lautrey, & T. I. Lubart (Eds.), *Models of intelligence: International perspectives.* Washington, DC: American Psychological Association.

Gardner, R. A., & Gardner, B. T. (1969). Teaching language to a chimpanzee. *Science, 165,* 664–672.

Garn, C. L., Allen, M. D., & Larsen, J. D. (2009). An fMRI study of sex differences in brain activation during object naming. *Cortex, 45*(5), 610–618.

Garnefski, N., & Arends, E. (1998). Sexual abuse and adolescent maladjustment: Differences between male and female victims. *Journal of Adolescence, 21,* 99–107.

Gatchel, R. J. (2005). *Clinical essentials of pain management.* Washington, DC: American Psychological Association.

Gathercole, S. E. (1998). The development of memory. *Journal of Child Psychology and Psychiatry and Allied Disciplines, 39,* 3–27.

Gathercole, S. E., Pickering, S. J., Knight, C., & Stegmann, Z. (2004). Working memory skills and educational attainment: Evidence from national curriculum assessments at 7 and 14 years of age. *Applied Cognitive Psychology, 18,* 1–16.

Gauchet, A., Tarquinio, C., & Fischer, G. (2007). Psychosocial predictors of medication adherence among persons living with HIV. *International Journal of Behavioral Medicine, 14,* 141–150.

Gazzaniga, M. S., & Smylie, C. S. (1983). Facial recognition and brain asymmetries: Clues to underlying mechanisms. *Annals of Neurology, 13,* 536–540.

GBD, (2010). *The global burden of disease study.* Retrieved from the institute for Health Metrics and Evaluation database: http://ihmeuw.org/1zne

Geary, D. C. (2005). *The origin of mind: Evolution of brain, cognition, and general intelligence.* Washington, DC: American Psychological Association.

Geher, G., Bauman, K. P., Hubbard, S. E. K., & Legare, J. R. (2002). Self and other obedience estimates: Biases and moderators. *Journal of Social Psychology, 142,* 677–689.

Gelfand, M. J., Raver, J. L., Nishii, L., Leslie, L. M., Lun, J., Lim, B. C., ... & Yamaguchi, S. (2011). Differences between tight and loose cultures: A 33-nation study. *Science, 332*(6033), 1100–1104.

Geller, D. A., Biederman, J., Stewart, S. E., Mullin, B., Martin, A., Spencer, T., & Faraone, S. V. (2003). Which SSRI? A meta-analysis of pharmacotherapy trials in pediatric obsessive-compulsive disorder. *American Journal of Psychiatry, 160*(11), 1919–1928.

George, O., Le Moal, M., & Koob, G. F. (2012). Allostasis and addiction: Role of the dopamine and corticotropin-releasing factor systems. *Physiology & Behavior, 106*(1), 58–64.

George, W. H., Stoner, S. A., Norris, J., Lopez, P. A., & Lehman, G. L. (2000). Alcohol expectancies and sexuality: A self-fulfilling prophecy analysis of dyadic perceptions and behavior. *Journal of Studies on Alcohol*, *61*, 168–176.

Geracioti, T. D., Loosen, P. T., Ebert, M. H., & Schmidt, D. (1995). Fasting and postprandial cerebrospinal fluid glucose concentrations in healthy women and in an obese binge eater. *International Journal of Eating Disorders*, *18*, 365–369.

Geraerts, E., Lindsay, D. S., Merckelbach, H., Jelicic, M., Raymaekers, L., Arnold, M. M., & Schooler, J. W. (2009). Cognitive mechanisms underlying *recovered* memory experiences of childhood sexual abuse. *Psychological Science*, *20*(1), 92–98.

Gergen, K. J. (1973). Social psychology as history. *Journal of Personality and Social Psychology*, *26*, 309–320.

Gergen, K. J. (2000). *An invitation to social constructivism*. Thousand Oaks, CA: Sage.

Gerin, W., Chaplin, W., Schwartz, J. E., Holland, J., Alter, R., Wheeler, R., ... Pickering, T. G. (2005). Sustained blood pressure increase after an acute stressor: The effects of the 11 September 2001 attack on the New York City World Trade Center. *Journal of Hypertension*, *23*, 279–284.

Gershoff, E. T. (2002). Corporal punishment by parents and associated child behaviors and experiences: A meta-analytic and theoretical review. *Psychological Bulletin*, *128*, 539–579.

Gershon, E. S., Berrettini, W. H., & Golden, L. E. (1989). Mood disorders: Genetic aspects. In H. I. Kaplan & B. J. Sadock (Eds.), *Comprehensive textbook of psychiatry/V*. Baltimore, MD: Williams & Wilkins.

Gewirtz, J. C., & Davis, M. (2000). Using Pavlovian higher-order conditioning paradigms to investigate the neural substrates of emotional learning and memory. *Learning and Memory*, *7*, 257–266.

Ghetti, S., Qin, J., & Goodman, G. S. (2002). False memories in children and adults: Age, distinctiveness, and subjective experience. *Developmental Psychology*, *38*, 705–718.

Gibbons, R. D., Hur, K., Bhaumik, D. K., & Mann, J. J. (2005). The relationship between antidepressant medication use and rate of suicide. *Archives of General Psychiatry*, *62*, 165–172.

Gibson, E., & Walk, R. D. (1960). The visual cliff. *Scientific American*, *202*, 80–92.

Gibson, J. J. (1979). *The ecological approach to visual perception*. Boston, MA: Houghton Mifflin.

Gigerenzer, G. (1991). How to make cognitive illusions disappear: Beyond 'heuristics and biases'. In W. Stroebe & M. Hewstone (Eds.), *European Review of Social Psychology* (Vol. 2). Chichester: Wiley.

Gigerenzer, G. (1996). On narrow norms and vague heuristics: A reply to Kahneman and Tversky (1996). *Psychological Review*, *103*, 592–596.

Gilbert, P. (2001). Evolutionary approaches to psychopathology: The role of natural defences. *Australian and New Zealand Journal of Psychiatry*, *35*(1), 17–27.

Gilhooly, K. J., & Logie, R. H. (1981). Word age-of-acquisition, reading latencies and auditory recognition. *Current Psychological Research*, *1*, 269–286.

Gilligan, C. (1982). *In a different voice: Psychological theory and women's development*. Cambridge, MA: Harvard University Press.

Giltay, E. J., Geleijnse, J. M., Zitman, F. G., Buijsse, B., & Kromhout, D. (2007). Lifestyle and dietary correlates of dispositional optimism in men: The Zutphen elderly study. *Journal of Psychosomatic Research*, *63*, 483–490.

Gintis, H. (2000). Strong reciprocity and human sociality. *Journal of Theoretical Biology*, *206*, 169–179.

Glanz, K., & Bishop, D. B. (2010). The role of behavioral science theory in development and implementation of public health interventions. *Annual Review of Public Health*, *31*, 399–418.

Glanzer, M. (1972). Storage mechanisms in recall. In G. H. Bower (Ed.), *The psychology of learning and motivation: Advances in research and theory* (Vol. 5). New York: Academic Press.

Glanzer, M., & Cunitz, A. R. (1966). Two storage mechanisms in free recall. *Journal of Verbal Learning and Verbal Behavior*, *5*, 351–360.

Glucksman, M. L. (2001). The dream: A psychodynamically informative instrument. *Journal of Psychotherapy Practice and Research*, *10*, 223–230.

Gobet, F., & Simon, H. A. (2000). Five seconds or sixty? Presentation time in expert memory. *Cognitive Science*, *24*, 651–682.

Goddard, A. W., Mason, G. F., Almai, A., Rothman, D. L., Behar, K. L., Petroff, O. A., Charney, D. S., & Krystal, J. H. (2001). Reductions in occipital cortex GABA levels in panic disorder detected with sup-1H-magnetic resonance spectroscopy. *Archives of General Psychiatry*, *58*, 556–561.

Godden, D. R., & Baddeley, A. D. (1975). Context-dependent memory in two natural environments: On land and under water. *British Journal of Psychology*, *66*, 325–332.

Godin, G., & Kok, G. (1996). The theory of planned behavior: A review of its applications to health-related behaviors. *American Journal of Health Promotion*, *11*, 87–98.

Goetz, J. L., Keltner, D., & Simon-Thomas, E. (2010). Compassion: An evolutionary analysis and empirical review. *Psychological Bulletin*, *136*, 351–374.

Goffman, E. (1961). *Asylums: Essays on the social situation of mental patients and other inmates*. New York: Doubleday.

Gogtay, N., Giedd, J. N., Lusk, L., Hayashi, K.M., Greenstein, D., Vaituzis, A. C., ... Thompson, P. M. (2004). Dynamic mapping of human cortical development during childhood through early adulthood. *Proceedings of the National Academy of Sciences of the USA*, *101*(21), 8174–8179.

Goldacre, B. (2008). *Bad science* (4th ed.). London: Fourth Estate.

Goldberg, C. (2001). Cognitive processes and panic disorder: An extension of current models. *Psychological Reports*, *88*, 139–159.

Goldberg, L. R. (1981). Unconfounding situational attributions from uncertain, neutral, and ambiguous ones: A psychometric analysis of descriptions of oneself and various types of others. *Journal of Personality and Social Psychology*, *41*, 517–552.

Goldfried, M. R. (2013). What should we expect from psychotherapy? *Clinical Psychology Review*, *33*(7), 862–869.

Goldsmith, S. K. (2003). *Reducing suicide: A national imperative*. Washington, DC: National Academy Press.

Goldstein, B. (2002). *Sensation and perception* (6th ed.). Belmont, CA: Wadsworth.

Goldstein, E. B. (2007). *Sensation and perception* (7th ed.). Belmont, CA: Wadsworth.

Goldstein, E. B. (2008). *Cognitive psychology* (2nd ed.). Belmont, CA: Thomson/Wadworth.

Goldstein, E. B. (2009). *Encyclopedia of perception*. London: Sage.

Goldstein, G. (2000). Comprehensive neuropsychological assessment batteries. In G. Goldstein & M. Hersen (Eds.), *Handbook of psychological assessment* (3rd ed.). New York: Elsevier.

Goldstein, J. H., Cajko, L., Oosterbroek, M., Van Houten, O., & Salverda, F. (1997). Video games and the elderly. *Social Behavior and Personality, 25*, 345–352.

Gollwitzer, M., & Denzler, M. (2009). What makes revenge sweet: Seeing the offender suffer or delivering a message? *Journal of Experimental Social Psychology, 45*, 840–844.

Gonzales, P. M., Blanton, H., & Williams, K. J. (2002). The effects of stereotype threat and double minority status on the test performance of Latino women. *Personality and Social Psychology Bulletin, 28*, 659–670.

Goodale, M. A. (1995). The cortical organization of visual perception and visuomotor control. In S. Kosslyn & D. N. Osheron (Eds.), *Visual cognition: An invitation to cognitive science* (2nd ed.). Cambridge, MA: MIT Press.

Goodale, M. A. (2000). Perception and action in the human visual system. In M. S. Gazzaniga (Ed.), *The new cognitive neurosciences* (2nd ed.). Cambridge, MA: MIT Press.

Goodale, M. A., Milner, A. D., Jakobson, L. S., & Carey, D. P. (1991). A neurological dissociation between perceiving objects and grasping them. *Nature, 349*(6305): 154–156.

Goodall, J. (1986). *The chimpanzees of Gombe: Patterns of behavior*. Cambridge, MA: Harvard University Press.

Goodman, W. (1982, August 9). Of mice, monkeys and men. *Newsweek*, p. 61.

Gopnik, A., & Astington, J. W. (1988). Children's understanding of representational change and its relation to the understanding of false belief and the appearance–reality distinction. *Child Development, 59*, 26–37.

Gordon, H., & Lindkvist, P. (2007). Forensic psychology in Europe. *The Psychiatrist, 31*, 421–424.

Gorman, J. M. (2002). Treatment of generalized anxiety disorder. *Journal of Clinical Psychiatry, 63* (Suppl. 8), 17–23.

Gotlib, I. H., Kasch, K. L., Traill, S., Joormann, J., Arnow, B.A., & Johnson, S. L. (2004a). Coherence and specificity of information-processing biases in depression and social phobia. *Journal of Abnormal Psychology, 113*, 386–398.

Gotlib, I. H., Krasnoperova, E., Yue, D. N., & Joormann, J. (2004b). Attentional biases for negative interpersonal stimuli in clinical depression. *Journal of Abnormal Psychology, 113*, 127–135.

Gottesman, I. I. (1991). *Schizophrenia genesis: The origins of madness*. New York: Freeman.

Gottfried, A. E., Fleming, J. S., & Gottfried, A. W. (1998). Role of cognitively stimulating home environment in children's academic intrinsic motivation: A longitudinal study. *Child Development, 69*, 1448–1460.

Gottfried, J. A., O'Doherty, J., and Dolan, R. J. (2003). Encoding predictive reward value in human amygdala and orbitofrontal cortex. *Science, 301*(5636), 1104–1107.

Gottman, J. M., & DeClaire, J. (2002). *The relationship cure: A five-step guide to strengthening your marriage, family, and friendships*. New York: Three Rivers Press.

Gottman, J. M., & Levenson, R. (1992). Marital processes predictive of later dissolution: Behavior, psychology and health. *Journal of Personality and Social Psychology, 63*, 221–233.

Gottman, J. M., Coan, J., Carrere, S., & Swanson, C. (1998). Predicting marital happiness and stability from newlywed interactions. *Journal of Marriage and the Family, 60*, 5–22.

Gould, J., & Ashton-Smith, J. (2011). Missed diagnosis or misdiagnosis? Girls and women on the autism spectrum. *Good Autism Practice (GAP), 12*(1), 34–41.

Graber, J. A., Seeley, J. R., Brooks-Gunn, J., & Lewinsohn, P. M. (2004). Is pubertal timing associated with psychopathology in young adulthood? *Journal of the American Academy of Child and Adolescent Psychiatry, 43*, 718–726.

Gracely, R. H., Farrell, M. J., & Grant, M. A. B. (2002). Temperature and pain perception. In H. Pashler & S. Yantis (Eds.), *Steven's handbook of experimental psychology: Vol. 1. Sensation and perception* (3rd ed.). New York: Wiley.

Graham, S., Hudley, C., & Williams, E. (1992). Attributional and emotional determinants of aggression among African-American and Latino young adolescents. *Developmental Psychology, 28*, 731–740.

Grammer, K., Schiefenhövel, W., Schleidt, M., Lorenz, B., & Eibl-Eibesfeldt, I. (1988). Patterns on the face: The eyebrow flash in crosscultural comparison. *Ethology, 77*, 279–299.

Grant, H. M., Bredahl, L. C., Clay, J., Ferrie, J., Groves, J. E., McDorman, T. A., & Dar, V. J. (1998). Context-dependent memory for meaningful material: Information for students. *Applied Cognitive Psychology, 12*, 617–623.

Graw, P., Werth, E., Kraeuchi, K., Gutzwiller, F., Cajochen, C., & Wirz-Justice, A. (2001). Early morning melatonin administration impairs psychomotor vigilance. *Behavioural Brain Research, 121*, 167–172.

Gray, J. A. (1982). *The neuropsychology of anxiety: An enquiry into the functions of the septohippocampal system*. Oxford: Oxford University Press.

Gray, J. A. (1991). Neural systems, emotions, and personality. In J. Madden IV (Ed.), *Neurobiology of learning, emotion, and affect*. New York: Raven Press.

Gray, J. R., & Burgess, G. C. (2004). Personality differences in cognitive control? BAS, processing efficiency, and the prefrontal cortex. *Journal of Research in Personality, 38*, 35–36.

Green, A. R., Sanchez, V., O'Shea, E., Saadat, K. S., Elliott, J. M., & Colado, M. I. (2004). Effect of ambient temperature and a prior neurotoxic dose of 3,4-methylenedioxymethamphetamine

(MDMA) on the hyperthermic response of rats to a single or repeated ('binge' ingestion) low dose of MDM A. *Psychopharmacology, 173*, 264–269.

Green, D. M., & Swets, J. A. (1974). *Signal detection theory and psychophysics*. New York: Wiley.

Green, J. D., & Sedikides, C. (2001). When do self-schemas shape social perception? The role of descriptive ambiguity. *Motivation and Emotion, 25*, 67–83.

Green, J. T., & Woodruff-Pak, D. S. (2000). Eyeblink classical conditioning: Hippocampal formation is for neutral stimulus associations as cerebellum is for association-response. *Psychological Bulletin, 126*, 138–158.

Green, M. (1999). Diagnosis of attentiondeficit/hyperactivity disorder. *Technical Review Number 3, Publication No. 99 – 0050*. Rockville, MD: Agency for Health Care Policy and Research.

Green, M. F. (1997). *Schizophrenia from a neurocognitive perspective: Probing the impenetrable darkness*. Boston, MA: Allyn & Bacon.

Greenberg, J. S. (2005). *Comprehensive stress management*. New York: McGraw-Hill.

Greenberg, J., Solomon, S., & Pyszynski, T. (1997). Terror management theory of self-esteem and cultural worldviews: Empirical assessments and conceptual refinements. In M. P. Zanna (Ed.), *Advances in experimental social psychology* (Vol. 29). San Diego, CA: Academic Press.

Greenberg, L. S., & Malcolm, W. (2002). Resolving unfinished business: Relating process to outcome. *Journal of Consulting and Clinical Psychology, 70*, 406–416.

Greenberg, L. S., & Rice, L. N. (1997). Humanistic approaches to psychotherapy. In P. L. Wachtel & S. B. Messer (Eds.), *Theories of psychotherapy: Origins and evolution*. Washington, DC: American Psychological Association.

Greenberg, M. T. (2006). Promoting resilience in children and youth. *Annals of the New York Academy of Sciences, 1094*, 139–150.

Greene, K., Krcmar, M., Walters, L. H., Rubin, D. L., & Jerold, H. L. (2000). Targeting adolescent risk-taking behaviors: The contribution of egocentrism and sensation seeking. *Journal of Adolescence, 23*, 439–461.

Greene, R. L. (1992). *Human memory: Paradigms and paradoxes*. Hillsdale, NJ: Erlbaum.

Greene, R. W., & Ollendick, T. H. (2000). Behavioral assessment of children. In G. Goldstein & M. Hersen (Eds.), *Handbook of psychological assessment* (3rd ed.). New York: Elsevier.

Greenfield, P. M. (1998). The cultural evolution of IQ. In U. Neisser (Ed.), *The rising curve: Long-term gains in IQ and related measures*. Washington, DC: American Psychological Association.

Greenleaf, E. (1973). 'Senoi' dream groups. *Psychotherapy: Theory, Research and Practice, 10*, 218–222.

Greenwald, A. G. (1992). New look 3: Unconscious cognition reclaimed. *American Psychologist, 47*, 766–779.

Greenwald, A. G., Banaji, M. R., Rudman, L. A., Farnham, S. D., Nosek, B. A., & Mellott, D. S. (2002). A unified theory of implicit attitudes, stereotypes, self-esteem, and self-concept. *Psychological Review, 109*, 3–25.

Greenwald, A. G., McGhee, D. E., & Schwartz, J. (1998). Measuring individual differences in implicit cognition: The implicit association test. *Journal of Personality and Social Psychology, 74*, 1464–1480.

Gregory, R. J. (1998). *Foundations of intellectual assessment: The WAIS-III and other tests in clinical practice*. Boston, MA: Allyn & Bacon.

Gregory, R. L. (1996). Editorial: What do qualia do?, *Perception, 25*(4).

Gregory, R. L. (1966). *Eye and brain*. New York: McGraw-Hill.

Gregory, R. L. (2005). *Illusion: The phenomenal brain*. New York: Oxford University Press.

Gregory, R. L., & Gombrich, E. H. (1973). *Illusion in nature and art*. London: Duckworth.

Gregory R. L., & Wallace J. G. (1963). Recovery from blindness: A case study *Experimental Psychology Society Monograph, No. 2*.

Grice, H. P. (1975). Logic and conversation. In P. Cole & J. L. Morgan (Eds.), *Syntax and semantics: Vol. 3. Speech acts*. New York: Seminar.

Griffiths, A. J. F., Miller, J. H., Suzuki, D. T., Lewontin, R. C., & Gelbart, W. M. (2000). *An Introduction to Genetic Analysis* (10th ed.), (Ch. 10). New York: W.H. Freeman and Company.

Grimes, K., & Walker, E. F. (1994). Childhood emotional expressions, educational attainment, and age at onset of illness in schizophrenia. *Journal of Abnormal Psychology, 103*, 784–790.

Grossberg, S., Finkel, L., & Field, D. (Eds.) (2005). *Vision and brain: How the brain sees: New approaches to computer vision*. St. Louis: Elsevier.

Grossman, H., Bergmann, C., & Parker, S. (2006). Dementia: A brief review. *The Mount Sinai Journal of Medicine, 73*, 985–992.

Grossman, P., Niemann, L., Schmidt, S., & Walach, H. (2004). Mindfulness-based stress reduction and health benefits: A meta-analysis. *Journal of Psychosomatic Research, 57*, 35–43.

Groth-Marnat, G. (1999). *Handbook of psychological assessment*. New York: Wiley.

Groves, P. M., & Thompson, R. F. (1970). Habituation: A dual-process theory. *Psychological Review, 77*, 419–450.

Grünbaum, A. (1986). Précis of the foundations of psychoanalysis: A philosophical critique. *Behavioral and Brain Sciences, 9*, 217–284.

Gudjonsson, G. H., & Sigurdsson, J. F. (1994). How frequently do false confessions occur – an empirical study among prison inmates. *Psychology Crime and Law, 1*(1), 21–26.

Gudjonsson, G. H., Sigurdsson, J. F., Gudmundsdottir, H. B., & Sigurjonsdottir, S. (2010). The relationship between ADHD symptoms in college students and core components of maladaptive personality. *Personality and Individual Differences, 48*, 601–606.

Guéguen, N. (2002). Foot in the door technique and computer mediated communication. *Computers in Human Behavior, 18*, 11–15.

Guenther, C. L., & Alicke, M. D. (2010). Deconstructing the better-than-average-effect. *Journal of Personality and Social Psychology, 99*, 755–770.

Guilford, J. P. (1959). Three faces of intellect. *American Psychologist, 14*, 469–479.

Guilford, J. P. (1967). *The nature of human intelligence*. New York: McGraw-Hill.

Guilleminault, C., Poyares, D., Abat, F., & Palombini, L. (2001). Sleep and wakefulness in somnambulism: A spectral analysis study. *Journal of Psychosomatic Research, 51,* 411–416.

Guinness book of records (2000). Stamford, CT: Guinness Media.

Gulevich, G., Dement, W., & Johnson, L. (1966). Psychiatric and EEG observations on a case of prolonged (264 hours) wakefulness. *Archives of General Psychiatry, 15,* 29–35.

Gump, L. S., Baker, R. C., & Roll, S. (2000). Cultural and gender differences in moral judgment: A study of Mexican Americans and Anglo-Americans. *Hispanic Journal of Behavioral Sciences, 22,* 78–93.

Gupta, P., & Cohen, N. J. (2002). Theoretical and computational analysis of skill learning, repetition priming, and procedural memory. *Psychological Review, 109,* 401–448.

Gurman, A. S., & Kniskern, D. P. (Eds.) (2014). *Handbook of family therapy*. Routledge.

Gurvitz, I. G., Koenigsberg, H. W., & Siever, L. J. (2000). Neurotransmitter dysfunction in patients with borderline personality disorder. *Psychiatric Clinics of North America, 23,* 27–40.

Gustavson, C. R., Garcia, J., Hankins, W. G., & Rusiniak, K. W. (1974). Coyote predation control by aversive conditioning. *Science, 184,* 581–583.

Guthrie, J. P., Ash, R. A., & Bendapudi, V. (1995). Additional validity evidence for a measure of morningness. *Journal of Applied Psychology, 80,* 186–190.

Guthrie, R. V. (1976). *Even the rat was white: A historical view of psychology*. New York: Harper & Row.

H

Haaga, D. A. F., Dyck, M. J., & Ernst, D. (1991). Empirical status of cognitive theory of depression. *Psychological Bulletin, 110,* 215–236.

Hafen, B. Q., & Hoeger, W. W. K. (1998). *Wellness: Guidelines for a healthy lifestyle*. Englewood, CO: Morton.

Hailman, J. P. (1967). The ontogeny of an instinct. *Behaviour Supplements, 15,* 1–159.

Hailman, J. P. (1969). How an instinct is learned. *Scientific American, 221,* 98–106.

Haines, J., & Neumark-Sztainer, D. (2006). Prevention of obesity and eating disorders: A consideration of shared risk factors. *Health Education Research, 21*(6), 770–782.

Halari, R., Hines, M., Kumari, V., Mehrotra, R., Wheeler, M., Ng, V., & Sharma, T. (2005). Sex differences and individual differences in cognitive performance and their relationship to endogenous gonadal hormones and gonadotropins. *Behavioral Neuroscience, 119,* 104–117.

Halit, H., de Haan, M., & Johnson, M. H. (2003). Cortical specialisation for face processing: Face-sensitive event-related potential components in 3- and 12-month-old infants. *NeuroImage, 19*(3), 1180–1193.

Hall, C. S., & Van de Castle, R. (1966). *The content analysis of dreams*. New York: Appleton-Century-Crofts.

Hall, G. C. N., & Okazaki, S. (2003). *Asian American psychology: The science of lives in context*. Washington, DC: American Psychological Association.

Hall, G. S. (1904). *Adolescence* (Vols 1 and 2). New York: Appleton-Century-Crofts.

Hall, M. H., Rijsdijk, F., Picchioni, M., Schulze, K., Ettinger, U., Toulopoulou, T., … Sham, P. (2007). Substantial shared genetic influences on schizophrenia and event-related potentials. *The American Journal of Psychiatry, 164,* 804–812.

Hall, W. (2006). How have the SSRI antidepressants affected suicide risk? *The Lancet, 367*(9527), 1959–1962.

Haller, M., & Hadler, M. (2006). How social relations and structures can produce happiness and unhappiness: An international comparative analysis. *Social Indicators Research, 75,* 169–216.

Halligan, P. W., Fink, G. R., Marshall, J. C., & Vallar, G. (2003). Spatial cognition: Evidence from visual neglect. *Trends in Cognitive Sciences, 7,* 125–133.

Halpern, B. (2002). Taste. In H. Pashler & S. Yantis (Eds.), *Steven's handbook of experimental psychology: Vol. 1. Sensation and perception* (3rd ed.). New York: Wiley.

Halpern, D. F. (2000). *Sex differences in cognitive abilities* (3rd ed.). Mahwah, NJ: Erlbaum.

Halpern, D. F. (2004). *Sex differences in cognitive abilities* (3rd ed.). Mahwah, NJ: Erlbaum.

Halpern, D. F., & Tan, U. (2001). Stereotypes and steroids: Using a psychobiosocial model to understand cognitive sex differences. *Brain and Cognition, 45,* 392–414.

Hamann S., & Mao, H. (2002). Positive and negative emotional verbal stimuli elicit activity in the left amygdala. *Neuroreport, 13*(1), 15–19.

Hamer, D. H., & Copeland, P. (1998). *Living with our genes: Why they matter more than you think*. New York: Doubleday.

Hamer, M. (2012). Psychosocial stress and cardiovascular disease risk: The role of physical activity. *Psychosomatic Medicine, 74,* 896–903.

Hamer, M., & Chida, Y. (2008). Active commuting and cardiovascular risk: A meta-analytic review. *Preventive Medicine, 46,* 9–13.

Hamilton, R. J. (1985). A framework for the evaluation of the effectiveness of adjunct questions and objectives. *Review of Educational Research, 55,* 47–85.

Hamilton, W. D. (1963). The evolution of altruistic behaviour. *American Psychologist 97*(869), 354–356.

Hamilton, W. D. (1964). The genetical theory of social behaviour, I, II. *Journal of Theoretical Biology, 12,* 12–45.

Hamlin, J. K., Wynn, K., & Bloom, P. (2007). Social evaluation by preverbal infants. *Nature, 450,* 557–559.

Hamlin, J. K., Wynn, K., & Bloom, P. (2010). Three-month-olds show a negativity bias in their social evaluations. *Developmental science, 13*(6), 923–929.

Hamlin, J. K., & Wynn, K. (2011). Young infants prefer prosocial to antisocial others. *Cognitive development, 26*(1), 30–39.

Hammen, C. (1991). *Depression runs in families: The social context of risk and resilience in children of depressed mothers*. New York: Springer-Verlag.

Hammen, C. (2005). Stress and depression. *Annual Review of Clinical Psychology, 1*, 293–319.

Hampson, S. E. (2012). Personality processes: Mechanisms by which personality traits 'get outside the skin'. *Annual Review of Psychology, 63*, 315–339.

Han, F., Faraco, J., Dong, X. S., Ollila, H. M., Lin, L., Li, J., … Mignot, E. (2013). Genome wide analysis of narcolepsy in China implicates novel immune loci and reveals changes in association prior to versus after the 2009 H1N1 influenza pandemic. *PLoS Genetics, 9*: e1003880.

Handley, R. V., Salkovskis, P. M., & Ehlers, A. (2009). Treating clinically significant avoidance of public transport following the London bombings. *Behavioural and Cognitive Psychotherapy, 37*, 87–93.

Hankin, B. L., Kassel, J. D., & Abela, R. Z. (2005). Adult attachment dimensions and specificity of emotional distress symptoms: Prospective investigations of cognitive risk and interpersonal stress generation as mediating mechanisms. *Personality and Social Psychology Bulletin, 31*, 136–151.

Hansen, N. B., Lambert, M. J., & Forman, E. M. (2002). The psychotherapy dose-response effect and its implications for treatment delivery services. *Clinical Psychology: Science and Practice, 9*, 329–343.

Happé, F. G. E., Winner, E., & Brownell, H. (1998). The getting of wisdom: Theory of mind in old age. *Developmental Psychology, 34*, 358–362.

Harackiewicz, J. M., Barron, K. E., Tauer, J. M., & Elliot, A. J. (2002). Predicting success in college: A longitudinal study of achievement goals and ability measures as predictors of interest and performance from freshman year through graduation. *Journal of Educational Psychology, 94*, 562–575.

Hardeman, W., Johnston, M., Johnston, D. W., Bonetti, D., Wareham, N., & Kinmonth, A. L. (2002). Application of the theory of planned behaviour in behaviour change interventions: A systematic review. *Psychology and Health, 17*, 123–158.

Hare, B., Brown, M., Williamson, C. & Tomasello, M. (2002). The domestication of social cognition in dogs. *Science, 298*, 1634–1636.

Hare, R. D. (1991). *The Hare Psychopathy Checklist*. Toronto: Multi-Health Systems.

Harley, K., & Reese, E. (1999). Origins of autobiographical memory. *Developmental Psychology, 35*, 1338–1348.

Harlow, H. F. (1958). The nature of love. *The American Psychologist, 13*, 673–685.

Harlow, H. F., & Suomi, S. J. (1970). The nature of love simplified. *American Psychologist, 25*, 161–168.

Harlow, J. M. (1868). Recovery from the passage of an iron bar through the head. *Massachusetts Medical Society, 2*, 327.

Harlow, J., & Roll, S. (1992). Frequency of day residue in dreams of young adults. *Perceptual and Motor Skills, 74*, 832–834.

Harmon-Jones, E., Brehm, J. W., Greenberg, J., Simon, L., & Nelson, D. E. (1996). Evidence that the production of aversive consequences is not necessary to create cognitive dissonance. *Journal of Personality and Social Psychology, 70*, 5–16.

Harmon-Jones E., & Harmon-Jones, C. (2007). Cognitive dissonance theory after 50 years of development. *Zeitschrift fur Sozialpsychologie, 38*, 7–16.

Harrell, T. W., & Harrell, M. S. (1945). Army General Classification Test scores for civilian occupations. *Educational and Psychological Measurement, 5*, 229–239.

Harris, B. (1979). Whatever happened to Little Albert? *American Psychologist, 34*, 151–160.

Harris, C. (2002, August 27). Amazing memory for digits still loses track of car keys. *Naples Daily News*.

Harris, J. (2014). *Sensation and perception*. London: Sage.

Harris, J. R. (1995). Where is the child's environment? A group socialization theory of development. *Psychological Review, 102*, 458–489.

Harris, L. T., Todorov, A., & Fiske, S. T. (2005). Attributions on the brain: Neuro-imaging dispositional inferences, beyond theory of mind. *Neuroimage, 28*(4), 763–769.

Harrison, E. L. R., & Fillmore, M. T. (2011). Alcohol and distraction interact to impair driving performance. *Drug and Alcohol Dependence, 117*(1), 31–37.

Harrison, J. E., & Baron-Cohen, S. C. (1997). Synaesthesia: A review of psychological theories. In S. C. Baron et al. (Eds.), *Synaesthesia: Classic and contemporary readings*. Oxford: Blackwell.

Harrison, T. & Clarke, D. (1992). The Northfield experiments. *British Journal of Psychiatry, 160*, 698–708.

Hart, J. W., Bridgett, D. J., & Karau, S. J. (2001). Coworker ability and effort as determinants of individual effort on a collective task. *Group Dynamics, 5*, 181–190.

Hart, J. W., Karau, S. J., Stasson, M. F., & Kerr, N. A. (2004). Achievement motivation, expected coworker performance, and collective task motivation: Working hard or hardly working? *Journal of Applied Social Psychology, 34*, 984–1000.

Hartmann, E., Kunzendorf, R., Rosen, R., & Grace, N. G. (2001). Contextualizing images in dreams and daydreams. *Dreaming: Journal of the Association for the Study of Dreams, 11*, 97–104.

Hartshorne, H., & May, A. (1928). *Studies in the nature of character: Vol. 1. Studies in deceit*. New York: Macmillan.

Hartwell, L., Hood, L., Goldberg, M., Reynolds, A. E., & Silver, L. M. (2010). *Genetics: From genes to genomes*. Maidenhead: McGraw-Hill.

Harway, M. (2005). *Handbook of couples' therapy*. New York: Wiley.

Hasher, L., & Zacks, R. T. (1979). Automatic and effortful processes in memory. *Journal of Experimental Psychology: General, 108*, 356–388.

Haskell, W. L., Alderman, E. L., Fair, J. M., Maron, D. J., Mackey, S. F., Superko, H. R., … Krauss, R. M. (1994). Effects of intensive multiple risk factor reduction on coronary atherosclerosis and clinical cardiac events in men and women with coronary artery disease. *Circulation, 89*, 975–990.

Haslam, D., & James, W. P. (2005). Obesity. *Lancet, 366*, 1197–1209.

Haslam, N., Loughnan, S., & Perry, G. (2014). Meta-Milgram: An empirical synthesis of the obedience experiments. *PloS One, 9*(4), e93927.

Hatfield, E. (1988). Passionate and companionate love. In R. J. Sternberg & M. L. Barnes (Eds.), *The psychology of love*. New Haven, CT: Yale University Press.

Hawley, P., & Little, T. D. (2002). Evolutionary and developmental perspectives on the agentic self. In D. Cervone & W. Mischel (Eds.), *Advances in personality science*. New York: Guilford Press.

Haworth, C. M. A., Wright, M. J., Luciano, M., Martin, N. G., de Geus, E. J., van Beijsterveldt, C. E., ... Plomin, R. (2010). The heritability of general cognitive ability increases linearly from childhood to young adulthood. *Molecular Psychiatry, 15*(11), 1112–1120.

Hay, P., Sachdev, P., Cumming, S., et al. (1993) Treatment of obsessive-compulsive disorder by psychosurgery. *Acta Psychiatrica Scandinavica, 87*, 197–207.

Hayes, R. D., Dennerstein, L., Bennett, C. M., & Fairley, C. K. (2008). What is the 'true' prevalence of female sexual dysfunctions and does the way we assess these conditions have an impact? *Journal of Sexual Medicine, 5*(4), 777–787.

Hayes, S. C., Luoma, J., Bond, F., Masuda, A., & Lillis, J. (2006). Acceptance and commitment therapy: Model, processes, and outcomes. *Behaviour Research and Therapy, 44*, 1–25.

Haynes, S. N. (2000). Behavioral assessment of adults. In G. Goldstein & M. Hersen (Eds.), *Handbook of psychological assessment* (3rd ed.). New York: Elsevier.

Hayslip, B., & Panek, P. E. (1989). *Adult development and aging*. New York: Harper & Row.

Hazan, C., & Diamond, L. M. (2000). The place of attachment in human mating. *Review of General Psychology, 4*, 186–204.

Healy, D. (2004). *Let them eat Prozac: The unhealthy relationship between the pharmaceutical industry and depression*. New York: New York University Press.

Healey, E. S., Kales, A., Monroe, L. J., Bixler, E. O., Chamberlin, K., & Soldatos, C. R. (1981). Onset of insomnia: Role of life-stress events. *Psychosomatic Medicine, 43*, 439–451.

Hearne, K. (1980). Insight into lucid dreams. *Nursing Mirror*, 150(10), 20–22 (March 6).

Hearold, S. (1986). A synthesis of 1043 effects of television on social behavior. In G. Comstock (Ed.), *Public communications and behavior* (Vol. 1). New York: Academic Press.

Heath, A. C., Bucholz, K. K., Madden, P. A. F., Dinwiddie, S. H., Slutske, W. S., Bierut, L. J., ... Martin, N. G. (1997). Genetic and environmental contributions to alcohol dependence risk in a national twin sample: consistency of findings in women and men. *Psychological Medicine, 27*, 1381–1396.

Heath, A. C., Kendler, K. S., Eaves, L. J., & Martin, N. G. (1990). Evidence for genetic influences on sleep disturbance and sleep pattern in twins. *Sleep, 13*, 318–335.

Heath, R. G. (1972). Pleasure and brain activity in man. *Journal of Nervous and Mental Disease, 154*, 3–18.

Heather, N. (2006). Controlled drinking, harm reduction and their roles in the response to alcohol-related problems. *Addiction Research and Theory, 14*, 7–18.

Heatherton, T. F., Macrae, C. N., & Kelley, W. M. (2004). What the social brain sciences can tell us about the self. *Current Directions in Psychological Science, 13*, 190–193.

Hebb, D. O. (1949). *The organization of behavior*. New York: Wiley.

Hebb, D. O. (1955). Drives and the CNS (conceptual nervous system). *Psychological Review, 62*, 243–254.

Heerey, E. A., Keltner, D., & Capps, L. M. (2003). Making sense of self-conscious emotion: Linking theory of mind and emotion in children with autism. *Emotion, 3*, 394–400.

Heider, F. (1958). *The psychology of interpersonal relations*. New York: Wiley.

Heimpel, S. A., Wood, J. V., Marshall, M. A., & Brown, J. D. (2002). Do people with low self-esteem really want to feel better? Self-esteem differences in motivation to repair negative moods. *Journal of Personality and Social Psychology, 82*, 128–147.

Heine, S. J., & Lehman, D. R. (1997). Culture, dissonance, and self-affirmation.

Personality and Social Psychology Bulletin, 23, 389–400.

Heinrich, J., Heine, S. J., & Norenzayan, A. (2010). Most people are not WEIRD. *Nature, 466*, 29.

Heinrichs, R. W. (2001). *In search of madness: Schizophrenia and neuroscience*. New York: Oxford University Press.

Heller, M. A., & Schiff, W. (Eds.) (1991). *The psychology of touch*. Hillsdale, NJ: Erlbaum.

Hellerstein, D., Yankowitch, P., Rosenthal, J., Samstag, L. W., Maurer, M., Kasch, K., ... Winston, A. (1993). A randomized double-blind study of fluoxetine versus placebo in the treatment of dysthymia. *American Journal of Psychiatry, 150*, 1169–1175.

Helsen, W. F., Starkes, J. L., & Hodges, N. J. (1998). Team sports and the theory of deliberate practice. *Journal of Sport and Exercise Psychology, 20*, 12–34.

Helson, R., Jones, C., & Kwan, V. S. Y. (2002). Personality change over 40 years of adulthood: Hierarchical linear modeling analyses of two longitudinal samples. *Journal of Personality and Social Psychology, 83*, 752–766.

Henig, R. M. (2001). *A monk and two peas: The story of Gregor Mendel and the discovery of genetics*. London: Phoenix.

Henningsen, D. D., Henningsen, M. L. M., Eden, J., & Cruz, M. G. (2006). Examining the symptoms of groupthink and retrospective sensemaking. *Small Group Research, 37*, 36–64.

Herdt, G., & Lindenbaum, S. (Eds.) (1992). *Social analysis in the time of AIDS*. Newbury Park, CA: Sage.

Herek, G. M. (2000). The psychology of sexual prejudice. *Current Directions in Psychological Science, 9*, 19–22.

Hernandez, L. M., & Blazer, D. G. (2007). *Genes, behavior, and the social environment: Moving beyond the nature/nurture debate*. Washington, DC: National Academies Press.

Herrington, R., & Lader, M. H. (1996). *Biological treatments in psychiatry* (2nd ed.). New York: Oxford University Press.

Hersen, M. (2002). *Clinical behavior therapy : Adults and children*. New York: Wiley.

Vol. 1. Sensation and perception (3rd ed.). New York: Wiley.

Howard, K. I., Kopta, S. M., Krause, M. S., & Orlinsky, D. E. (1986). The dose–effect relationship in psychotherapy. *American Psychologist, 41,* 159–164.

Howard, K. I., Lueger, R. J., Maling, M. S., & Martinovich, Z. (1993). A phase model of psychotherapy outcome: Causal mediation of change. *Journal of Consulting and Clinical Psychology, 61,* 678–685.

HSCIC (2012) Health Survey for England, available at: http://www.hscic.gov.uk/catalogue/PUB13218

HSCIC (Health and Social Care Information Centre) (2009). Adult psychiatric morbidity in England: Results of a household survey. Retrieved from http://www.hscic.gov.uk/

Hsu, F. L. K. (1985). The self in cross-cultural perspective. In A. J. Marsella, G. De Vos, & F. L. K. Hsu (Eds.), *Culture and self* (pp. 24–55). London: Tavistock.

Huang, J. Y., & Bargh, J. A. (2014). The selfish goal: Autonomously operating motivational structures as the proximate cause of human judgment and behavior. *Behavioral and Brain Sciences, 37,* 121–135.

Hubbard, E. M., & Ramachandran, V. S. (2005). Neurocognitive mechanisms of synesthesia. *Neuron, 48*(3), 509–520.

Hubbard, K., O'Neill, A. M., & Cheakalos, C. (1999, April 12). Out of control. *People, 52,* 72.

Hubel, D. H. & Wiesel, T. N. (1959). Receptive fields of single neurones in the cat's striate cortex. *Journal of Physiology, 148,* 574–591.

Hubel, D. H. & Wiesel, T. N. (1962). Receptive fields, binocular interaction and functional architecture in the cat's visual cortex. *Journal of Physiology, 160,* 106–154.

Hubel, D. H., & Wiesel, T. N. (1979). Brain mechanisms of vision. *Scientific American, 241,* 150–162.

Hubel, D. H., & Wiesel, T. N. (2005). *Brain and visual perception: The story of a 25-year collaboration.* New York: Oxford University Press.

Hublin, C., Kaprio, J., Partinen, M., & Koskenvuo, M. (2001). Parasomnias: Co-occurrence and genetics. *Psychiatric Genetics, 11,* 65–70.

Hublin, C., Kaprio, J., Partinen, M., Heikkilä, K., & Koskenvuo, M. (1997). Prevalence and genetics of sleepwalking: A population based twin study. *Neurology, 48,* 177–181.

Huddy, L., & Virtanen, S. (1995). Subgroup differentiation and subgroup bias among Latinos as a function of familiarity and positive distinctiveness. *Journal of Personality and Social Psychology, 68,* 97–108.

Hudson, W. (1960). Pictorial depth perception in sub-cultural groups in Africa. *Journal of Social Psychology, 52,* 183–208.

Huesmann, L. R. (1997). Observational learning of violent behavior: Social and biosocial processes. In A. Raine, P. A. Brennan, D. P. Farrington, & S. A. Mednick (Eds.), *Biosocial bases of violence.* New York: Plenum Press.

Huesmann, L. R., & Taylor, L. D. (2006). The role of media violence in violent behaviour. *Annual Review of Public Health, 27,* 393–415.

Huesmann, L. R., Moise-Titus, J., Podolski, C. L., & Eron, L. D. (2003). Longitudinal relations between children's exposure to TV violence and their aggressive and violent behavior in young adulthood: 1977–1992. *Developmental Psychology, 39,* 201–221.

Huettel, S. A., Song, A. W., & McCarthy, G. (2005). *Functional magnetic resonance imaging.* New York: Sinauer.

Huey, S. J., Tilley, J. L., Jones, E. O., & Smith, C. (2014). The contribution of cultural competence to evidence-based care for ethnically diverse populations. *Annual Review of Clinical Psychology, 10,* 305–338.

Huff, R. M., & Kline, M. V. (Eds.) (1999). *Promoting health in multicultural populations: A handbook for practitioners.* Thousand Oaks, CA: Sage.

Hugdahl, K., & Davidson, R. A. (Eds.) (2005). *The asymmetrical brain.* Boston: MIT Press.

Hugenberg, K., & Bodenhausen, G. V. (2003). Facing prejudice: Implicit prejudice and the perception of facial threat. *Psychological Science, 14,* 640–643.

Hulbert-Williams, L., Nicholls, W., Joy, J., & Hulbert-Williams, N. (2013). Initial validation of the mindful eating scale. *Mindfulness.* doi 10.1007/s12671-013-0227-5

Hull, C. L. (1943). *Principles of behavior: An introduction to behavior theory.* New York: Appleton-Century.

Human Genome Project (2007). Retrieved from http://www.genome.gov/

Human, L. J., & Biesanz, J. C. (2013). Targeting the good target: An integrative review of characteristics and consequences of being accurately perceived. *Personality and Social Psychology Review, 17,* 248–272.

Humphreys, G. W., & Riddoch, M. J. (1987). *To see but not to see: A case of visual agnosia.* Hove: Erlbaum.

Hunt, E. (1997). The status of the concept of intelligence. *Japanese Psychological Research, 39,* 1–11.

Hunter, C. L., Goodie, J. L., Oordt, M. S., & Dobmeyer, A. C. (2009). *Integrated behavioral health in primary care: Step-by-step guidance for assessment and intervention.* Washington, DC: American Psychological Association.

Hunter, J. E., & Hunter, R. F. (1984). Validity and utility of alternative predictors of job performance. *Psychological Bulletin, 96,* 72–98.

Huon, G. F., Mingyi, Q., Oliver, K., & Xiao, G. (2002). A large-scale survey of eating disorder symptomatology among female adolescents in the people's Republic of China. *International Journal of Eating Disorders, 32,* 192–205.

Huppert, F. A. (2005). Positive mental health in individuals and populations. In F. A. Huppert, N. Baylis, & B. Keverne (Eds.), *The science of wellbeing.* Oxford: Oxford University Press.

Huppert, F. A. (2009). A new approach to reducing disorder and improving well-being. *Perspectives on Psychological Science, 4*(1), 108–111.

Huttenlocher, P. R. (2002). *Neural plasticity.* Cambridge, MA: Harvard University Press.

Huurre, T., Junkkari, H., & Aro, H. (2006). Long-term psychosocial effects of parental divorce: A follow-up study from adolescence to adulthood. *European Archives of Psychiatry and Clinical Neuroscience, 256,* 256–263.

Hyde, J. S., & DeLamater, J. (2003). *Understanding human sexuality* (8th ed.). Boston, MA: McGraw-Hill.

Hyde, M., Ferrie, J., Higgs, P., Mein, G., & Nazroo, J. (2004). The effects of pre-retirement factors and retirement route on circumstances in retirement: Findings from the Whitehall II study. *Ageing & Society, 24*, 279–296.

Hyman, R. (1994). Anomaly or artifact? Comments on Bem and Honorton. *Psychological Bulletin, 115*, 19–24.

I

Ikemi, Y., & Nakagawa, A. (1962). A psychosomatic study of contagious dermatitis. *Kyushu Journal of Medical Science, 13*, 335–350.

Ingelhart, R., & Rabier, J. R. (1986). Aspirations adapt to situations – but why are the Belgians so much happier than the French? A cross-cultural study of the quality of life. In F. M. Andrews (Ed.), *Research on the quality of life*. Ann Arbor, MI: Institute for Social Research, University of Michigan.

Ingold, C. H. (1989). Locus of control and use of public information. *Psychological Reports, 64*, 603–607.

Inhelder, B., & Piaget, J. (1958). *The growth of logical thinking from childhood to adolescence*. New York: Basic Books.

International Genome Sequencing Consortium (2004). Finishing the euchromatic sequence of the human genome. *Nature, 431*, 931–945.

Intraub, H. (2002). Anticipatory spatial representation of natural scenes: Momentum without movement? *Visual Cognition, 9* (1– 2), 93–119.

Intraub, H., Gottesman, C. V., Willey, E. V., & Zuk, I. J. (1996). Boundary extension for briefly glimpsed photographs: Do common perceptual processes result in unexpected memory distortions? *Journal of Memory and Language, 35*, 118–134.

Irie, M., Maeda, M., & Nagata, S. (2001). Can conditioned histamine release occur under urethane anesthesia in guinea pigs? *Physiology and Behavior, 72*, 567–573.

Ironson, G., Kumar, M., Greenwood, D., Schneiderman, N., Cruess, D., Kelsch, C. B., & Baum, A. (2014). Posttraumatic stress symptoms, intrusive thoughts, and disruption are longitudinally related to elevated cortisol and catecholamines following a major hurricane. *Journal of Applied Biobehavioral Research, 19(1),* 24–52.

Irwin, J. R., & McCarthy, D. (1998). Psychophysics: Methods and analyses of signal detection. In K. A. Lattal & M. Perone (Eds.), *Handbook of research methods in human operant behavior: Applied clinical psychology*. New York: Plenum Press.

Irwin, M., Daniels, M., & Weiner, H. (1987). Immune and neuroendocrine changes during bereavement. *Psychiatric Clinics of North America, 10*, 449–465.

Isaacs, K. S. (1998). *Uses of emotion: Nature's vital gift*. New York: Praeger.

Isaacson, R. L. (2002). Unsolved mysteries: The hippocampus. *Behavioral and Cognitive Neuroscience Reviews, 1*, 87–107.

Isabella, R. A. (1993). Origins of attachment: Maternal interactive behavior across the first year. *Child development, 64*(2), 605–621.

Ishikawa, S. L., Raine, A., Lencz, T., Bihrle, S., & Lacasse, L. (2001). Autonomic stress reactivity and executive functions in successful and unsuccessful criminal psychopaths from the community. *Journal of Abnormal Psychology, 110*, 423–432.

Itard, J. M. G. (1962). *The wild boy of Aveyron* (Trans G. Humphrey & M. Humphrey). New York: Appleton-Century-Crofts. (Original work published 1894.)

Ito, K., Momose, T., Oku, S., Ishimoto, S.-I.,·Yamasoba, T.,·Sugasawa, M.·& Kaga, K. (2004). Cortical activation shortly after cochlear implantation. *Audiology & Neurotology, 9*, 282–293.

Ito, T. A., & Cacioppo, J. T. (2000). Electrophysiological evidence of implicit and explicit categorization processes. *Journal of Experimental Social Psychology, 36*, 660–676.

Ivey, A. E., D'Andrea, M. D., Ivey, M. B., & Simek-Morgan, L. (2006). *Theories of counseling and psychotherapy: A multicultural perspective*. Boston, MA: Allyn & Bacon.

Iwasa, N. (2001). Moral reasoning among adults: Japan U.S. comparison. In H. Shimizu & R. A. LeVine (Eds.), *Japanese frames of mind: Cultural perspectives on human development*. New York: Cambridge University Press.

Iwawaki, S., & Sarmany-Schuller, I. (2001). Cross-cultural (Japan-Slovakia) comparison of some aspects of sleeping patterns and anxiety. *Studia Psychologica, 43*, 215–224.

Izard, C. (Ed.) (1982). *Measuring emotions in infants and children*. Cambridge: Cambridge University Press.

Izard, C. E. (1989). The structure and functions of emotions: Implications for cognition, motivation, and personality. In I. S. Cohen (Ed.), *The G. Stanley Hall Lecture Series* (Vol. 9). Washington, DC: American Psychological Association.

Izard, C. E. (1992). Basic emotions, relations among emotions, and emotion–cognition relations. *Psychological Review, 99*, 561–565.

Izard, C. E., Hembree, E. A., & Huebner, R. R. (1987). Infants' emotion expressions to acute pain: Developmental change and stability of individual differences. *Developmental Psychology, 23*, 105–113.

J

Jablensky, A., Sartorius, N., Enberg, C., Anker, M., Korten, A., Cooper, J. E., Day, R., & Bertelsen, A. (1992). Schizophrenia: Manifestation, incidence, and course in different cultures: A World Health Organization ten country study. *Psychological Medicine Monograph Supplement 20*. Cambridge: Cambridge University Press.

Jackson, A., Morrow, J., Hill, D., & Dishman, R. (1999). *Physical activity for health and fitness*. Champaign, IL: Human Kinetics.

Jackson, N., & Butterfield, E. (1986). A conception of giftedness designed to promote research. In R. J. Sternberg & J. E. Davidson (Eds.), *Conceptions of giftedness*. New York: Cambridge University Press.

Jacobs, B. L. (2004). Depression: The brain finally gets into the act. *Current Directions in Psychological Science, 13*, 103–106.

Jacobs, J., & Kahana, M. J. (2010). Direct brain recordings fuel advances in cognitive electrophysiology. *Trends in Cognitive Sciences, 14(4)*, 162–171.

Jacobson, N. S., & Christensen, A. (1996). *Integrative couple therapy: Promoting acceptance and change*. New York: Norton.

Jacobson, N. S., Christensen, A., Prince, S. E., Cordova, J., & Eldridge, K. (2000). Integrative couple behavior therapy: An acceptance-based, promising new treatment for couple discord. *Journal of Consulting and Clinical Psychology, 68*, 351–355.

Jaffee, S. R., Moffitt, T. E., Caspi, A., & Taylor, A. (2003). Life with (or without) father: The benefits of living with two biological parents depend on the father's antisocial behavior. *Child Development, 74*, 109–126.

Jain, S., Shapiro, S. L., Swanick, S., Roesch, S. C., Mills, P. J., Bell, I., & Schwartz, G. E. (2007). A randomized controlled trial of mindfulness meditation versus relaxation training: Effects on distress, positive states of mind, rumination, and distraction. *Annals of Behavioral Medicine, 33*, 11–21.

James, W. (1879). Are we automata? *Mind, 4*, 1–22.

James, W. (1950). *Principles of psychology* (Vol. 2). New York: Dover. (Original work published 1890.)

Jamison, K. (1995, February). Manic-depressive illness and creativity. *Scientific American*, 63–67.

Jané-Llopis, E., & Anderson, P. (Eds.) (2006). *Mental health promotion and mental disorder prevention across european Member States: A collection of country stories.* Luxembourg: European Commission.

Jang, K. (2005). *The behavioral genetics of psychopathology: A clinical guide.* Hillsdale, NJ: Erlbaum.

Janis, I. L. (1982). *Groupthink: Psychological studies of policy decisions and fiascos* (2nd ed.). Boston, MA: Houghton Mifflin.

Jansma, J. M., Ramsey, N. F., Slagter, H. A., & Kahn, R. S. (2001). Functional anatomical correlates of controlled and automatic processing. *Journal of Cognitive Neuroscience, 13*, 730–743.

Janus, S. S., & Janus, C. L. (1993). *The Janus report on sexual behavior.* New York: Wiley.

Jauhar, S., McKenna, P.J., Radua, J., Fung, E., Salvador, R., & Laws. K. R. (2014). Cognitive-behavioural therapy for the symptoms of schizophrenia: Systematic review and meta-analysis with examination of potential bias. *The British Journal of Psychiatry, 1*, 20–29.

Jelinek, L., Hottenrott, B., Randjbar, S., Peters, M. J., & Moritz, S. (2009). Visual false memories in post-traumatic stress disorder (PTSD). *Journal of Behavior Therapy and Experimental Psychiatry, 40*(2), 374–383.

Jemmott, J. B., Jemmott, L. S., & Fong, G. T. (1998). Abstinence and safer sex HIV risk reduction interventions for African American adolescents. *Journal of the American Medical Association, 279*, 1529–1536.

Jenkin, F., (1867, June). Review of 'The origin of species'. *The North British Review, 46*, 277–318.

Jenkin, M., & Harris., L. (2005). *Seeing spatial form.* New York: Oxford University Press.

Jenkins, J., Simpson, A., Dunn, J., Rasbash, J. & O'Connor, T. G. (2005). Mutual influence of marital conflict and children's behavior problems: Shared and nonshared family risks. *Child Development, 76*, 24–39.

Jenkins, K. (2014). Needle phobia: A psychological perspective. *British Journal of Anaesthesia.* doi: 10.1093/bja/aeu013

Jennings, B. M. (1990). Stress, locus of control, social support, and psychological symptoms among head nurses. *Research in Nursing & Health, 13*, 393–401.

Jensen, A. R. (1998). The g factor and the design of education. In R. J. Sternberg & W. M. Williams (Eds.), *Intelligence, instruction, and assessment: Theory into practice.* Mahwah, NJ: Erlbaum.

Jensen, L. A., Arnett, J. J., Feldman, S. S., & Cauffman, E. (2004). The right to do wrong: Lying to parents among adolescents and emerging adults. *Journal of Youth and Adolescence, 33*, 101–112.

Jensen, M. P., Turner, J. A., & Romano, J. M. (2001). Changes in beliefs, catastrophizing, and coping are associated with improvement in multidisciplinary pain treatment. *Journal of Consulting and Clinical Psychology, 69*, 655–662.

Jenson, P. (2009). *The ethology of domestication: An introductory text* (2nd ed.). Wallingford, Oxfordshire: CAB International.

Jéquier, E. (2002). Pathways to obesity. *International Journal of Obesity and Related Metabolic Disorders, 26*, 12–17.

Jetten, J., Spears, R., & Manstead, A. S. R. (1997). Strength of identification and differentiation: The influence of group norms. *European Journal of Social Psychology, 27*, 603–609.

Ji, H. I., Kamachi, M., & Akamatsu, S. (2004). Analyses of facial attractiveness on feminised and juvenilised faces. *Perception, 33*(2), 135–145.

Jimenez, L., & Mendez, C. (2001). Implicit sequence learning with competing explicit cues. *Quarterly Journal of Experimental Psychology: Comparative and Physiological Psychology, 54*, 345–369.

Job, D. E., Whalley, H. C., McIntosh, A. M., Owens, D. G., Johnstone, E. C., Lawrie, S. M. (2006). Grey matter changes can improve the prediction of schizophrenia in subjects at high risk. *BMC Medicine, 4*, 29.

Johannesen-Schmidt, M. C., & Eagly, A. H. (2002). Another look at sex differences in preferred mate characteristics: The effects of endorsing the traditional female gender role. *Psychology of Women Quarterly, 26*, 322–328.

Johannsen, W. (1911). The genotype conception of heredity. *The American Naturalist, 45*(531), 129–159.

John, O. P., & Srivastava, S. (1999). The Big Five trait taxonomy: History, measurement, and theoretical perspectives. In L. A. Pervin & O. P. John (Eds.), *Handbook of personality: Theory and research.* New York: Guilford Press.

Johns, M., Schmader, T., & Martens, A. (2005). Knowing is half the battle: Teaching stereotype threat as a means of improving women's math performance. *Psychological Science, 16*, 175–179.

Johnson, A. M., Wadsworth, J., Wellings, K., & Bradshaw, S. (1992). Sexual lifestyles and HIV risk. *Nature, 360*, 410–412.

Johnson, D. W. (2000). Cooperative learning processes reduce prejudice. In S. Oskamp (Ed.), *Reducing prejudice and discrimination.* Mahwah, NJ: Erlbaum.

Johnson, J. G., Cohen, P., Smailes, E. M., Kasen, S., & Brook, J. S. (2002). Television viewing and aggressive behavior during adolescence and adulthood. *Science, 295*, 2468–2471.

Johnson, M. H., & de Haan, M. (2011). *Developmental cognitive neuroscience* (3rd ed.). Oxford: Wiley-Blackwell.

Johnson, M. H., Dziurawiec, S., Ellis, H., & Morton, J. (1991). Newborns' preferential tracking of face-like stimuli and its subsequent decline. *Cognition, 40,* 1–19.

Johnson, N. R. (1988). Fire in a crowded theatre: A descriptive investigation of the emergence of panic. *International Journal of Mass Emergencies and Disasters, 6,* 7–26.

Johnson-Laird, P. N. (1983). *Mental models.* Cambridge: Cambridge University Press.

Johnson-Laird, P. N. (2008). How we reason: A view from psychology. *The Reasoner, 2,* 4–5.

Johnson-Laird, P. N., & Byrne, R. M. J. (1991). *Deduction.* Hove: Lawrence Erlbaum.

Johnston, M. S., Kelley, C. S., Harris, F. F., & Wolf, M. M. (1966). An application of reinforcement principles to development of motor skills of a young child. *Child Development, 37,* 379–387.

Johnston, V. S., Hagel, R., Franklin, M., Fink, B., & Grammer, K. (2001). Male facial attractiveness: Evidence for hormone-mediated adaptive design. *Evolution and Human Behavior, 22,* 251–267.

Joiner, T. E., & Coyne, J. C. (Eds.) (1999). *The interactional nature of depression: Advances in interpersonal approaches.* Washington, DC: American Psychological Association.

Jones, B. C., Little, A. C., Feinberg, D. R., Penton-Voak, I. S., Tiddeman, B. P., & Perrett, D. I. (2004). The relationship between shape symmetry and perceived skin condition in male facial attractiveness. *Evolution and Human Behavior, 25,* 24–30.

Jones, E., Cumming, J. D., & Horowitz, M. J. (1988). Another look at the nonspecific hypothesis of therapeutic effectiveness. *Journal of Consulting and Clinical Psychology, 56,* 48–55.

Jones, E. E., & Harris, V. A. (1967). The attribution of attitudes. *Journal of Experimental Social Psychology, 3,* 2–24.

Jones, E. G. (2006). *The thalamus.* New York: Cambridge University Press.

Jones, J. T., Pelham, B. W., Carvallo, M., & Mirenberg, M. C. (2004). How do I love thee? Let me count the Js: Implicit egotism and interpersonal attraction. *Journal of Personality and Social Psychology, 87,* 665–683.

Jones, M. C. (1924). A laboratory study of fear: The case of Peter. *Pedagogical Seminary, 31,* 308–315.

Joseph, R. (2000). The evolution of sex differences in language, sexuality, and visualspatial skills. *Archives of Sexual Behavior, 29,* 35–66.

Josephs, R. A., Bosson, J. K., & Jacobs, C. G. (2003). Self-esteem maintenance processes: Why self-esteem may be resistant to change. *Personality and Social Psychology Bulletin, 29,* 920–933.

Judd, C. M., Park, B., Yzerbyt, V., Gordijn, E. H., & Muller, D. (2005). Attributions of intergroup bias and outgroup homogeneity to ingroup and outgroup others. *European Journal of Social Psychology, 35,* 677–704.

Julien, R. M. (2007). *A primer of drug action: A comprehensive guide to the actions, uses, and side effects of psychoactive drugs* (11th ed.). Basingstoke: W. H. Freeman.

Jung, J. (1995). Ethnic group and gender differences in the relationship between personality and coping. *Anxiety, Stress & Coping: An International Journal, 8,* 113–126.

Jureidini, J. N., Doecke, C. J., Mansfield, P. R., Haby, M. M., Menkes, D. B., & Tonkin, A. L. (2004). Efficacy and safety of antidepressants for children and adolescents. *British Medical Journal, 328*(7444), 879–883.

Jurist, E. L., Slade, A., & Bergner, S. (2008). *Reflecting on the future of psychoanalysis: Mentalization, internalization, and representation.* New York: Other Press.

K

Kabat-Zinn, J. (1994). *Wherever you go, there you are: Mindfulness meditation in everyday life.* Hyperion.

Kabat-Zinn, J., Massion, A., Kristeller, J., Peterson, L. G., Fletcher, K. E., Pbert, L., Lenderking, W. R., & Santorelli, S. F. (1992). Effectiveness of a meditation-based stress reduction intervention in the treatment of anxiety disorders. *American Journal of Psychiatry, 149,* 936–943.

Kabot, S., Masi, W., & Segal, M. (2003). Advances in the diagnosis and treatment of autism spectrum disorders. *Professional Psychology: Research and Practice, 34,* 26–33.

Kagan, J. (1989). Temperamental contributions to social behavior. *American Psychologist, 44,* 668–674.

Kagan, J. (1999). The concept of behavioral inhibition. In L. A. Schmidt & J. Schulkin (Eds.), *Extreme fear, shyness, and social phobia: Origins, biological mechanisms, and clinical outcomes.* New York: Oxford University Press.

Kagan, J., & Fox, N. A. (2006). Biology, culture, and individual differences. In N. Eisenberg, Nancy W. Damon, & R. M. Lerner (Eds.), *Handbook of child psychology: Vol. 3, Social, emotional, and personality development* (6th ed.). Hoboken, NJ: Wiley.

Kagan, J., Kearsley, R. B., & Zelazo, P. (1978). *Infancy: Its place in human development.* Cambridge, MA: Harvard University Press.

Kagan, J., Reznick, S., & Snidman, N. (1988). Biological bases of childhood shyness. *Science, 240,* 167–171.

Kagitçibasi, C. (1997). Individualism and collectivism. In J. W. Berry, M. H. Segall, & C. Kagitçibasi (Eds.), *Handbook of crosscultural psychology* (Vol. 3). Boston, MA: Allyn & Bacon.

Kahan, T. L., & LaBerge, S. (1994). Lucid dreaming as metacognition: Implications for cognitive science. *Consciousness and Cognition, 3*(4), 246–264.

Kahneman, D., & Tversky, A. (1979). Prospect theory: An analysis of decisions under risk. *Econometrica, 47,* 263–291.

Kahneman, D., & Tversky, A. (1982). On the study of statistical intuitions. *Cognition, 11,* 123–141.

Kahneman, D., & Tversky, A. (1996). On the reality of cognitive illusions: A reply to Gigerenzer's critique. *Psychological Review, 103,* 582–591.

Kaia, L., Pullmann, H., & Allik, J. (2007). Personality and intelligence as predictors of academic achievement: A cross-sectional study from elementary to secondary school. *Personality and Individual Differences, 42,* 444–451.

Kail, R. (1991). Developmental change in speed of processing during childhood and adolescence. *Psychological Bulletin, 109,* 490–501.

Kaku, M. (2004). *Einstein's cosmos: How Albert Einstein's vision transformed our understanding of space and time*. New York: Norton.

Kalayjian, A., & Eugene, D. (2009). *Handbook of emotional healing around the world: Rituals and practices for resilience and meaning-making. Vol. II: Natural disasters and human made disasters*. New York: Greenwood.

Kaltiala-Heino, R., Marttunen, M., Rantanen, P., & Rimpela, M. (2003). Early puberty is associated with mental health problems in middle adolescence. *Social Science & Medicine, 57*, 1055–1064.

Kamin, L. J. (1968). 'Attention-like' processes in classical conditioning. In M. R. Jones (Ed.), *Miami symposium on the prediction of behavior: Aversive stimulation*. Miami, FL: University of Miami Press.

Kamin, L. J. (1969). Predictability, surprise, attention, and conditioning. In B. A. Campbell, & R. M. Church (Eds.), *Punishment and aversive behavior*. New York: Appleton-Century-Crofts.

Kampmann, K. M., Volpicelli, J. R., Mulvaney, F., Rukstalis, M., Alterman, A. I., Pettinati, H., Weinrieb, R. M., & O'Brien, C. P. (2002). Cocaine withdrawal severity and urine toxicology results from treatment entry predict outcome in medication trials for cocaine dependence. *Addictive Behaviors, 27*, 251–260.

Kandel, E. R. (2001). The molecular biology of memory storage: A dialogue between genes and synapses. *Science, 294*, 1030–1038.

Kandel, E. R. (2004). Nobel Lecture: The molecular biology of memory storage: A dialogue between genes and synapses. *Bioscience Reports, 24*, 477–522.

Kane, J. M. (Ed.) (1992). *Tardive dyskinesia: A task force report of the American Psychiatric Association*. Washington, DC: American Psychiatric Press.

Kaner, A. (1995). Physical attractiveness and women's lives: Findings from a longitudinal study. *Dissertation Abstracts International: Section B. The Sciences and Engineering, 56*, 2942.

Kanfer, F. H., & Goldstein, A. P. (Eds.) (1991). *Helping people change: A textbook of methods* (4th ed.). New York: Pergamon Press.

Kanner, L. (1943). Autistic disturbance of affective contact. *Nervous Child, 12*, 17–50.

Kanwisher, N. (1998). The modular structure of human visual recognition: Evidence from functional imaging. In M. Sabourin et al. (Eds.), *Advances in psychological science: Vol. 2. Biological and cognitive aspects*. Hove: Psychology Press/Erlbaum.

Kaplan, H., & Dove, H. (1987). Infant development among the Ache of eastern Paraguay. *Developmental Psychology, 23*, 190–198.

Kaprio, J., & Silventoinen, K. (2011). Advanced methods in twin studies. *Methods in Molecular Biology, 713*, 143–152.

Kaprio, J., Koskenvu, M., & Rita, H. (1987). Mortality after bereavement: A prospective study of 95,647 widowed persons. *American Journal of Public Health, 77*, 283–287.

Karau, S. J., & Williams, K. D. (1993). Social loafing: A meta-analytic review and theoretical integration. *Journal of Personality and Social Psychology, 65*, 681–706.

Karau, S. J., & Williams, K. D. (2001). Understanding individual motivation in groups: The collective effort model. In M. E. Turner (Ed.), *Groups at work: Theory and research: Applied social research*. Mahwah, NJ: Erlbaum.

Karmiloff-Smith, A. (1992). *Beyond modularity: A developmental perspective on cognitive science*. Cambridge, MA: MIT Press.

Karon, B. P. (2002). Psychoanalysis: Legitimate and illegitimate concerns. *Psychoanalytic Psychology, 19*, 564–571.

Kashima, Y., Yamaguchi, S., Kim, U., Choi, S., Gelfand, M., & Yuki, M. (1995). Culture, gender, and self: A perspective from individualism-collectivism research. *Journal of Personality and Social Psychology, 69*, 925–937.

Kassin, S. M. (2008). The psychology of confessions. *Annual Review of Law and Social Science, 4*, 193–217.

Kastenbaum, R. (2000). *The psychology of death* (3rd ed.). New York: Springer.

Katapodi, M. C., Facione, N. C., Humphreys, J. C., & Dodd, M. J. (2005). Perceived breast cancer risk: Heuristic reasoning and search for a dominance structure. *Social Science & Medicine, 60*, 421–432.

Katz, D. (1925). *Der Aufbau der Taatwelt. Zeitschrift fur psychologie*. Leipzig: Barth.

Katz, J., & Melzack, R. (1990). Pain 'memories' in phantom limbs: Review and clinical observations. *Pain, 43*, 319–336.

Kaufman, A. S., & Kaufman, N. (1997). The Kaufman Adolescent and Adult Intelligence Test. In D. P. Flanagan, J. L. Genshaft, & P. L. Harrison (Eds.), *Contemporary intellectual assessment: Theories, tests, and issues*. New York: Guilford Press.

Kaufmann, G. M., & Beehr, T. A. (1986). Interactions between job stressors and social support: Some counterintuitive results. *Journal of Applied Psychology, 71*, 522–526.

Kavanagh, D. (1992). Schizophrenia. In P. H. Wilson (Ed.), *Principles and practice of relapse prevention*. New York: Guilford Press.

Kawakami, K., Dovidio, J. F., Moll, J. S., Hermsen, S., & Russin, A. (2000). Just say no (to stereotyping): Effects of training in the negation of stereotypic associations on stereotype activation. *Journal of Personality and Social Psychology, 78*, 871–888.

Kaye, W. H., Strober, M., & Klump, K. L. (2002). Serotonin neuronal function in anorexia nervosa and bulimia nervosa. In F. Lewis Hall et al. (Eds.), *Psychiatric illness in women: Emerging treatments and research*. Washington, DC: American Psychiatric Publishing.

Kaysen, S. (1996). *Girl, interrupted*. New York: Vintage Books.

Kazdin, A. E. (Ed.) (2003). *Methodological issues and strategies in clinical research* (3rd ed.). Washington, DC: American Psychological Association.

Kazdin, A. E. (2008). Evidence-based treatment and practice: New opportunities to bridge clinical research and practice, enhance the knowledge base, and improve patient care. *American Psychologist, 63*, 146–159.

Kazdin, A. E. (2012). *The token economy: A review and evaluation.* New York: Springer.

Kearins, J. M. (1981). Visual spatial memory in Australian Aboriginal children of desert regions. *Cognitive Psychology, 13* (3), 434–460.

Keenan, M., Dillenburger, K., Doherty, A., Byrne, T., & Gallagher, S. (2010). The experiences of parents during diagnosis and forward planning for children with autism spectrum disorder. *Journal of Applied Research in Intellectual Disabilities, 23*(4), 390–397.

Keinan-Boker, L., Vin-Raviv, N., Liphshitz, I., Linn, S., & Barchana, M. (2009). Cancer incidence in Israeli Jewish survivors of World War II. *Journal of the National Cancer Institute, 101,* 1489–1500.

Keith, S. J., Regier, D. A., & Rae, D. S. (1991). Schizophrenic disorders. In L. N. Robins & D. A. Regier (Eds.), *Psychiatric disorders in America: The Epidemiological Catchment Area Study.* New York: Free Press.

Keller, H. (1955). *The story of my life.* New York: Doubleday.

Keller, M. C., Medland, S. E., & Duncan, L. E. (2010). Are extended twin family designs worth the trouble? A comparison of the bias, precision, and accuracy of parameters estimated in four twin family models. *Behavior Genetics, 40*(3), 377–393.

Kelley, H. H. (1973). The process of causal attribution. *American Psychologist, 28,* 107–128.

Kellner, C. (2014). Review: maintenance antidepressants reduce risk of relapse in the 6 months following ECT in people with major depression. *Evidence Based Mental Health,* ebmental-2013, doi:10.1136/eb-2013-101663.

Kelly, G. (1955). *The psychology of personal constructs.* New York: Norton.

Kelly, G. F. (2001). *Sexuality today: The human perspective* (6th ed.). Boston, MA: McGraw-Hill.

Kelly, H. H. (1950). The warm-cold variable in first impressions of persons. *Journal of Personality, 18,* 431–439.

Kelly, J. A., St. Lawrence, J. S., Hood, H. V., & Brasfield, T. L. (1989). Behavioral intervention to reduce AIDS risk activities. *Journal of Consulting and Clinical Psychology, 57,* 60–67.

Kelly, S., Bhagwat, R., Maynigo, P., & Moses, E. (2014). Couple and marital therapy: The complement and expansion provided by multicultural approaches. *APA handbook of multicultural psychology, Vol. 2: Applications and training* (pp. 479–497). Washington, DC: American Psychological Association. doi:10.1037/14187-027

Keltner, D., & Ekman, P. (2000). Facial expression of emotion. In M. Lewis & J. M. Haviland-Jones (Eds.), *Handbook of emotions* (2nd ed.). New York: Guilford Press.

Kemeny, M. E. (2004). The psychobiology of stress. *Current Directions in Psychological Science, 12,* 124–129.

Kempermann, G. (2005). *Adult neurogenesis: Stem cells and neuronal development in the adult brain.* New York: Oxford University Press.

Kenardy, J., Brown, W. J., & Vogt, E. (2001). Dieting and health in young Australian women. *European Eating Disorders Review, 9,* 242–254.

Kendall, D. (1998). *Social problems in a diverse society.* Boston, MA: Allyn & Bacon.

Kendler, K. S., Kuhn, J., Vittum, J., Prescott, C. A., & Riley, B. (2005). The interaction of stressful life events and a serotonin transporter polymorphism in the prediction of episodes of major depression: A replication. *Archives of General Psychiatry/American Medical Association, 62,* 529–535.

Kennedy, J., Adetifa, O., Carley, M., Holt, N. J., Walker, I. (2011). Aeroacoustic sources of motorcycle helmet noise. *Journal of the Acoustical Society of America, 130*(3), 1164–1172.

Kenrick, D. T., & Funder, D. C. (1988). Profiting from controversy: Lessons from the person-situation debate. *American Psychologist, 43,* 23–34.

Kensinger, E. A., Ullman, M. T., & Corkin, S. (2001). Bilateral medial temporal lobe damage does not affect lexical or grammatical processing: Evidence from amnesic patient H. M. *Hippocampus, 11,* 347–360.

Kentridge, R. W., Heywood, C. A., & Weiskrantz, L. (2004). Spatial attention speeds discrimination without awareness in blindsight. *Neuropsychologia, 42*(6), 831–835.

Kernberg, O. F. (1984). *Severe personality disorders: Psychotherapeutic strategies.* New Haven, CT: Yale University Press.

Kernberg, O. F. (2000). *Personality disorders in children and adolescents.* Poulsbo, WA: H-R Press.

Kernberg, O. F., & Caligor, E. (2005). A psychoanalytic theory of personality disorders. In M. F. Lenzenweger & J. F. Clarkin (Eds.), *Major theories of personality disorder.* New York: Guilford Press.

Kerns, R. D., Sellinger, J., & Goodin, B. R. (2011). Psychological treatment of chronic pain. *Annual Review of Clinical Psychology, 7,* 411–434.

Kerr, M., Lambert, W. W., & Bem, D. J. (1996). Life course sequelae of childhood shyness in Sweden: Comparison with the United States. *Developmental Psychology, 32,* 1100–1105.

Kessler, R. C., Gilman, S. E., Thornton, L. M., & Kendler, K. S. (2004). Health, well-being, and social responsibility in the MIDUS twin and sibling subsamples. In O. G. Brim, C. D. Ryff, & R. Kessler (Eds.), *How healthy are we? A national study of well-being in midlife.* Chicago, IL: University of Chicago Press.

Kessler, R. C., McGonagle, K. A., Zhao, S., Nelson, C. B., Hughes, M., Eshleman, S., Wittchen, H. U., & Kendler, K. S. (1994). Lifetime and 12-month prevalence of DSM-III-R psychiatric disorder in the United States. *Archives of General Psychiatry, 51,* 8–19.

Ketellar, T. (1995). Emotion as mental representations of fitness affordances: I. Evidence supporting the claim that the negative and positive emotions map onto fitness costs and benefits. Paper presented at the annual meeting of the Human Behavior and Evolution Society, Santa Barbara, CA.

Kety, S. S. (1988). Schizophrenic illness in the families of schizophrenic adoptees: Findings from the Danish national sample. *Schizophrenia Bulletin, 14,* 217–222.

Kety, S. S., Rosenthal, D., Wender, P. H., Schulsinger, F., & Jacobsen, B. (1978). The biological and adoptive families of adopted individuals who become schizophrenic: Prevalence of mental illness and other characteristics. In L. C. Wynne,

R. L. Cromwell, & S. Matthysse (Eds.), *The nature of schizophrenia: New approaches to research and treatment.* New York: Wiley.

Keyes, C. L. M., & Waterman, M. B. (2003). Dimensions of well-being and mental health in adulthood. In. M. H. Bornstein, L. Davidson, C. L. M. Keyes, & K. A. Moore (Eds.), *Well-being: Positive development across the life course: Crosscurrents in contemporary psychology.* Mahwah, NJ: Erlbaum.

Keyes, L. M., & Goodman, S. H. (2006). *Women and depression: A handbook for social, behavioral, and biomedical sciences.* New York: Cambridge University Press.

Khawaja, N. G., & Oei, T. P. S. (1999). The psychobiological correlates of panic attacks during exposure. *Behavioural and Cognitive Psychotherapy, 27*(4), 1352–4658.

Kiecolt-Glaser, J., Bane, C., Glaser, R., & Malarkey, W. B. (2003). Love, marriage, and divorce: Newlyweds' stress hormones foreshadow relationship changes. *Journal of Consulting and Clinical Psychology, 71,* 176–188.

Kiecolt-Glaser, J., McGuire, L., Robles, T. F., & Glaser, R. (2002). Emotions, morbidity, and mortality: New perspectives from psychoneuroimmunology. *Annual Review of Psychology, 53,* 83–107.

Kihlstrom, J. F. (1998). *Exhumed memory, truth in memory.* New York: Guilford Press.

Kihlstrom, J. F. (1999). The psychological unconscious. In L. A. Pervin & O. P. John (Eds.), *Handbook of personality: Theory and research.* New York: Guilford Press.

Kihlstrom, J. F. (2007). The psychological unconscious. In O. John, R. Robins, & L. Pervin (Eds.), *Handbook of personality: Theory and research* (3rd ed.). New York: Guilford Press.

Kimball, M. M. (1986). Television and sex-role attitudes. In T. M. Williams (Ed.), *The impact of television: A natural experiment in three communities* (pp. 265–301). Orlando, FL: Academic Press.

Kim-Cohen, J., Caspi, A., Moffitt, T. E., Harrington, H., Milne, B. J., & Poulton, R.

(2003). Prior juvenile diagnoses in adults with mental disorder: Developmental follow-back of a prospective-longitudinal cohort. *Archives of General Psychiatry, 60*(7), 709–717.

Kimerling, R., Ouimette, P., & Wolfe, J. (2003). *Gender and PTSD.* New York: Guilford Press.

Kimura, D. (1992). Sex differences in the brain. *Scientific American, 267*(3), 119–195.

Kimura, K., Tachibana, N., Aso, T., Kimura, J., & Shibasaki, H. (1997). Subclinical REM sleep behavior disorder in a patient with corticobasal degeneration. *Sleep, 20,* 891–894.

King Broadcasting Company. (2005, March 2). *5 P.M. Evening News.* Seattle, WA.

King, N. J., Dudley, A., Melvin, G., Pallant, J., & Morawetz, D. (2001). Empirically supported treatments for insomnia. *Scandinavian Journal of Behaviour Therapy, 30,* 23–32.

Kiran, S., Roches, C. D., Balachandran, I., & Ascenso, E. (2014). Development of an impairment-based individualized treatment workflow using an iPad-based software platform. *Seminars in Speech and Language, 35*(1), 38–50.

Kirchengast, S., & Hartmann, B. (2003). Nicotine consumption before and during pregnancy affects not only newborn size but also birth modus. *Journal of Biosocial Science, 35,* 175–188.

Kirk, K. M., Bailey, J. M., & Martin, N. G. (2000). Etiology of male sexual orientation in an Australian twin sample. *Psychology, Evolution, and Gender, 2,* 301–311.

Kirkham, T. C. (2004). Cannabinoids and medicine: Eating disorders, nausea and emesis. In V. Di Marzo (Ed.), *Cannabinoids.* New York: Kluwer Academic/Plenum Publishers.

Kirsch, I. (2001). The response set theory of hypnosis: Expectancy and physiology. *American Journal of Clinical Hypnosis, 44,* 69–73.

Kirsch, I., & Braffman, W. (2001). Imaginative suggestibility and hypnotizability. *Current Directions in Psychological Science, 10,* 57–61.

Kirsch, I., Moore, T. J., Scoboria, A., & Nicholls, S. S. (2002). The emperor's new drugs: An analysis of antidepressant medication data submitted to the U. S. Food and Drug Administration. *Prevention & Treatment, 5,* 262–279.

Kisilevsky, B. S., & Muir, D. W. (1984). Neonatal habituation and dishabituation to tactile stimulation during sleep. *Developmental Psychology, 20,* 367–373.

Kissane, D. W. (2009). Beyond the psychotherapy and survival debate: The challenge of social disparity, depression and treatment adherence in psychosocial cancer care. *Psycho-Oncology, 18,* 1–5.

Kissane, D. W., Bloch, S., Smith, G. C., Miach, P., Clarke, D. M., Ikin, J., Love, A., Ranieri, N., & McKenzie, D. (2003). Cognitive-existential group psychotherapy for women with primary breast cancer: a randomised controlled trial. *Psycho-Oncology, 12,* 532–546.

Kissane, D. W., Grabsch, B., Clarke, D. M., Christie, G., Clifton, D., Gold, S., … Smith G. C. (2004). Supportive expressive group therapy: the transformation of existential ambivalence into creative living while enhancing adherence to anti-cancer therapies. *Psycho-Oncology, 13,* 755–768.

Kitayama, S., Markus, H. R., & Kurokawa, M. (2000). Culture, emotion, and well-being: Good feelings in Japan and the United States. *Cognition and Emotion, 14,* 93–124.

Kitayama, S., Duffy, S., Kawamura, T., & Larsen, J. T. (2003). Perceiving an object and its context in different cultures: A cultural look at New Look. *Psychological Science, 14,* 201–206.

Kleim, J. A., Barbay, S., Cooper, N. R., Hogg, T. M., Reidel, C. N., Remple, M. S., & Nudo, R. J. (2002). Motor learning-dependent synaptogenesis is localized to functionally reorganized motor cortex. *Neurobiology of Learning & Memory, 77,* 63–77.

Klein, M. (1975). *The writings of Melanie Klein.* London: Hogarth Press.

Klein, S. B., & Mowrer, R. R. (1989). *Contemporary learning theories: Vol. I. Pavlovian conditioning and the status of tradition.* Hillsdale, NJ: Erlbaum.

Kleinknecht, R. A., Dinnel, D. L., Kleinknecht, E. E., Hiruma, N., & Harada, N.

(1997). Cultural factors in social anxiety: A comparison of social phobia symptoms and Taijin Kyofusho. *Journal of Anxiety Disorders, 11*(2), 157–177.

Kleinman, A. (2004). Culture and depression. *New England Journal of Medicine, 351*, 951–953.

Kleinman, J. E., Law, A. J., Lipska, B. K., Hyde, T. M., Ellis, J. K., Harrison, P. J., Weinberger, D. R. (2011). Genetic neuropathology of schizophrenia: New approaches to an old question and new uses for postmortem human brains. *Biological Psychiatry, 69*(2), 140–145.

Kleitman, N. (1963). *Sleep and wakefulness* (2nd ed.). Chicago, IL: University of Chicago Press.

Kluckhohn, C., & Murray, H. A. (1953). Personality formation: The determinants. In C. Kluckhohn, H. A. Murray, & D. M. Schneider (Eds.), *Personality in nature, society, and culture*. New York: Knopf.

Kluft, R. P. (1999). True lies, false truths, and naturalistic raw data: Applying clinical research findings to the false memory debate. In L. M. Williams & V. L. Banyard (Eds.), *Trauma and memory*. Thousand Oaks, CA: Sage.

Klug, W. S., Cumings, M. R., Spencer, C. A., & Palladino, M. A. (2009). *Essentials of genetics*. Harlow: Pearson.

Knauth, P. (1996). Designing better shift systems. *Applied Ergonomics, 27*, 39–44.

Knipfel, J. (2004). *Herzog Kinski: A film legacy*. Anchor Bay Entertainment.

Knoblauch, K. (2002). Color vision. In H. Pashler & S. Yantis (Eds.), *Steven's handbook of experimental psychology: Vol. 1. Sensation and perception* (3rd ed.). New York: Wiley.

Knopik, V. S., Heath, A. C., Madden, P., Bucholz, K. K., Slutske, W. S., Nelson, E. C., ... Martin, N. G. (2004). Genetic effects on alcohol dependence risk: Re-evaluating the importance of psychiatric and other heritable risk factors. *Psychological Medicine, 34*, 1519–1530.

Kobasa, S. C., Maddi, S. R., Puccetti, M. C., & Zola, M. A. (1985). Effectiveness of hardiness, exercise and social support as resources against illness. *Journal of Psychosomatic Research, 29*, 525–533.

Kobau, R., Seligman, M. E. P., Peterson, C., Diener, E., Zack, M. M., Chapman, D. &

Thompson, W. (2011). Mental health promotion in public health: Perspectives and strategies from positive psychology. *American Journal of Public Health, 101*(8), 1–9.

Koch, C. (2004). *The quest for consciousness: A neurobiological approach*. Denver, CO: Roberts.

Koch, J. L. A. (1889). *Leitfaden der Psychiatrie* (2nd ed.). Ravensburg: Dornschen Buchhandlung.

Kochanska, G., Casey, R. J., & Fukumoto, A. (1995). Toddlers' sensitivity to standard violations. *Child Development, 66*, 643–656.

Kochanska, G., Aksan, N., Knaack, A., & Rhines, H. M. (2004). Maternal parenting and children's conscience: Early security as moderator. *Child Development, 75*, 1229–1242.

Kochanska, G., Forman, D. R., Aksan, N., & Dunbar, S. B. (2005). Pathways to conscience: Early mother–child mutually responsive orientation and children's moral emotion, conduct, and cognition. *Journal of Child Psychology and Psychiatry, 46*, 19–34.

Koenig, H. G., Pargament, K. L., & Nielsen, J. (1998). Religious coping and health status in medically ill hospitalized older adults. *Journal of Nervous and Mental Disease, 186*, 513–521.

Koenig, M. A., Clement, F., & Harris, P. A. (2004). Trust in testimony: Children's use of true and false statements. *Psychological Science, 15*, 694–698.

Koestner, R., & McClelland, D. C. (1990). Perspectives on competence motivation. In L. A. Pervin (Ed.), *Handbook of personality theory and research*. New York: Guilford Press.

Kogi, K. (1985). Introduction to the problems of shift work. In S. Folkard & T. H. Monk (Eds.), *Hours of work*. Chichester: Wiley.

Kohlberg, L. (1963). The development of children's orientations toward a moral order: I. Sequence in the development of moral thought. *Human Development, 6*, 11–33.

Kohlberg, L. (1984). *The psychology of moral development: Essays on moral development* (Vol. 2). New York: Harper & Row.

Köhler, W. (1925). *The mentality of apes* (Trans. from the 2nd rev. ed. by Ella Winter). New York: Harcourt.

Kohn-Wood, L. P., & Hooper, L. M. (2014). Cultural competency, culturally tailored care, and the primary care setting: Possible solutions to reduce racial/ethnic disparities in mental health care. *Journal of Mental Health Counseling, 36*(2), 173–188.

Kohut, H. (1971). *Analysis of the self*. New York: International Universities Press.

Kohut, H. (1977). *The restoration of self*. New York: International Universities Press.

Kolb, B., & Whishaw, I. Q. (2001). *An introduction to brain and behavior*. New York: Worth.

Kolb, B., & Whishaw, I. Q. (2003). *Fundamentals of human neuropsychology* (5th ed.). New York: Worth.

Kolb, B., & Whishaw, I. Q. (2005). *An introduction to brain and behavior* (2nd ed.). New York: Worth.

Koltko-Rivera, M. (2006). Rediscovering the later version of Maslow's hierarchy of needs: Self-transcendence and opportunities for theory, research, and unification. *Review of General Psychology, 10*, 302–317.

Koluchova, J. (1972). Severe deprivation in twins: A case study. *Journal of Child Psychology and Psychiatry, 13*, 107–114.

Koluchova, J. (1991). Severely deprived twins after 22 years of observation. *Studia Psychologica, 33*, 23–28.

Koons, C. R. (2007). The use of mindfulness interventions in cognitive behaviour therapies. In T. Ronen & A. Freeman (Eds.), *Cognitive behaviour therapy in clinical social work practice*. New York: Springer.

Koopman, P. R., & Ames, E. W. (1968). Infants' preferences for facial arrangements: A failure to replicate. *Child Development, 39*, 481–487.

Koriat, A., & Bjork, R. A. (2005). Illusions of competence in monitoring one's knowledge during study. *Journal of Experimental Psychology: Learning, Memory, and Cognition, 31*, 187–194.

Koriat, A., Goldsmith, M., & Pansky, A. (2000). Toward a psychology of memory accuracy. *Annual Review of Psychology, 51*, 481–537.

Kortegaard, L., Hoerder, K., Joergensen, J., Gillberg, C., & Kyvik, K. O. (2001). A preliminary population-based twin study of self-reported eating disorder. *Psychological Medicine, 31*, 361–365.

Kosambi, D. D. (1967). Living prehistory in India. *Scientific American, 216*, 105.

Kosslyn, S. M., Ball, T. M., & Reiser, B. J. (1978). Visual images preserve metric spatial information: Evidence from studies of image scanning. *Journal of Experimental Psychology: Human Perception and Performance, 4*, 47–60.

Kosslyn, S. M., Thompson, W. L., & Ganis, G. (2006). *The case for mental imagery*. New York: Oxford University Press.

Kosslyn, S. M., Thompson, W. L., Costantini-Ferrando, M. F., Alpert, N. M., & Spiegel, D. (2000). Hypnotic visual illusion alters color processing in the brain. *American Journal of Psychiatry, 157*, 1279–1284.

Kostanski, M., Fisher, A., & Gullone, E. (2004). Current conceptualisation of body image dissatisfaction: Have we got it wrong? *Journal of Child Psychology and Psychiatry, 45*, 1317–1325.

Kottak, C. P. (2000). *Cultural anthropology* (8th ed.). Boston, MA: McGraw-Hill.

Kowert, P. A. (Ed.) (2002). *Groupthink or deadlock: When do leaders learn from their advisors? SUNY series on the presidency*. New York: State University of New York Press.

Kraft, C. L. (1978). A psychophysical contribution to air safety: Simulator studies of illusions in night visual approaches. In H. L. Pick, Jr., H. W. Leibowitz, J. E. Singer, et al. (Eds.), *Psychology: From research to practice*. New York: Plenum Press.

Krasnegor, N. A., Lyon, G. R., & Goldman, R. P. S. (1997). *Development of the prefrontal cortex: Evolution, neurobiology, and behavior*. Baltimore, MD: Paul H. Brookes.

Krebs, D. L., & Denton, K. (1997). Social illusions and self-deception: The evolution of biases in person perception. In J. A. Simpson & D. T. Kenrick (Eds.), *Evolutionary social psychology*. Mahwah, NJ: Erlbaum.

Krevans, J., & Gibbs, J. C. (1996). Parents' use of inductive discipline: Relations to children's empathy and prosocial behavior. *Child Development, 67*, 3263–3277.

Kribbs, N. B. (1993). Siesta. In M. A. Carskadon (Ed.), *Encyclopedia of sleep and dreaming*. New York: Macmillan.

Kroeber, A. L. (1948). *Anthropology*. New York: Harcourt Brace Jovanovich.

Krosnick, J. A., Betz, A. L., Jussim, L. J., & Lynn, A. R. (1992). Subliminal conditioning of attitudes. *Personality and Social Psychology Bulletin, 18*, 152–162.

Kruger, J., Wirtz, D., & Miller, D. T. (2005). Counterfactual thinking and the first instinct fallacy. *Journal of Personality and Social Psychology, 88*, 725–735.

Kruglanski, A. W. (2004). *The psychology of closed mindedness*. New York: Psychology Press.

Kryger, M. H., Walid, R., & Manfreda, J. (2002). Diagnoses received by narcolepsy patients in the year prior to diagnosis by a sleep specialist. *Sleep: Journal of Sleep and Sleep Disorders Research, 25*, 36–41.

Ksir, C. J., Hart, C. I., & Ray, O. S. (2008). *Drugs, society, and human behavior*. New York: McGraw-Hill.

Kübler-Ross, E. (1969). *On death and dying*. New York: Macmillan.

Kucera, H., & Francis, W. N. (1967). *Computational analysis of present-day American English*. Providence, RI: Brown University Press.

Kuhl, P. K., Tsao, F. M., & Liu, H. M. (2003). *Proceedings of the National Academy of Sciences, USA, 100*, 9096–9101.

Kuhn, D., & Franklin, S. (2006). The second decade: What develops (and how). In W. Damon & R. M. Lerner (Eds.), *Child and adolescent development: An advanced course*. Chichester: John Wiley & Sons.

Kulik, J. A., & Mahler, H. I. M. (2000). Social comparison, affiliation, and emotional contagion under threat. In J. Suls & L. Wheeler (Eds.), *Handbook of social comparison: Theory and research*. Dordrecht, Netherlands: Kluwer.

Kulik, J. A., Mahler, H. I. M., & Moore, P. J. (1996). Social comparison and affiliation under threat: Effects of recovery from major surgery. *Journal of Personality and Social Psychology, 66*, 301–309.

Kumari, V., Fannon, D., Peters, E. R., Sumich, A. L., Premkumar, P., Anilkumar, A. P., ... & Kuipers, E. (2011). Neural changes following cognitive behaviour therapy for psychosis: a longitudinal study. *Brain, 134*(8), 2396–2407.

Kuncel, N. P., Hezlett, S. A., & Ones, D. S. (2004). Academic performance, career potential, and job performance: Can one construct predict them all? *Journal of Personality and Social Psychology, 86*, 148–161.

Kunzendorf, R. G., Hartmann, E., Cohen, R., & Cutler, J. (1997). Bizarreness of the dreams and daydreams reported by individuals with thin and thick boundaries. *Dreaming: Journal of the Association for the Study of Dreams, 7*, 265–271.

Kunzman, U., & Baltes, P. B. (2003). Beyond the traditional scope of intelligence: Wisdom in action. In R. J. Sternberg, J. Lautrey, & T. I. Lubart (Eds.), *Models of intelligence: International perspectives*. Washington, DC: American Psychological Association.

Kuo, J. R., & Linehan, M. M. (2009). Disentangling emotion processes in borderline personality disorder: physiological and self-reported assessment of biological vulnerability, baseline emotional intensity, and reactivity to emotionally-evocative stimuli. *Journal of Abnormal Psychology, 118*(3), 531–544.

Kurzweil, E. (1989). *The Freudians: A comparative perspective*. New Haven, CT: Yale University Press.

Kvavilashvili, L. & Ford, R. M. (2014) Metamemory prediction accuracy for simple prospective and retrospective memory tasks in 5-year old children. *Journal of Experimental Child Psychology, 127*, Special issue, 65–81.

Kvavilashvili, L., Messer, D.J., & Ebdon, P. (2001). Prospective memory in children: The effects of age and task interruption. *Developmental Psychology, 37*, 418–430.

Kvavilashvili, L., Mirani, J., Schlagman, S., Foley, K., & Kornbrot, D. E. (2009). Consistency of flashbulb memories of September 11 over long delays: Implications for consolidation and wrong time slice hypotheses. *Journal of Memory and Language, 61*, 556–572.

L

La Rooy, D., Lamb, M. E., & Memon, A. (2011). Forensic interviews with children in Scotland: A survey of interview practices among police. *Journal of Police and Criminal Psychology, 26*(1), 26–34.

LaBar, K. S., & Phelps, E. A. (1998). Arousalmediated memory consolidation: Role of the medial temporal lobe in humans. *Psychological Science, 9*, 490–493.

LaBerge, D. (1983). Spatial extent of attention to letters and words. *Journal of Experimental Psychology: Human Perception & Performance, 9*, 371–379.

Lachman, M. E. (2004). Development in midlife. *Annual Review of Psychology, 55*, 305–331.

Lagerspetz, K. Y., Tirri, R., & Lagerspetz, K. M. (1968). Neurochemical and endocrinological studies of mice selectively bred for aggressiveness. *Scandinavian Journal of Psychology, 9*, 157–160.

Lahey, B. B. (2009). Public health significance of neuroticism. *American Psychologist, 64*, 241–256.

Laible, D., & Thompson, R. A. (2000). Mother–child discourse, attachment security, shared positive affect, and early conscience development. *Child Development, 71*, 1424–1440.

Lamb, M. E., & Ahnert, L. (2006). Nonparental child care: Context, concepts, correlates, and consequences. In W. Damon, R. M. Lerner (Series Eds.), K. A. Renninger, I. E. Sigel (Vol. Eds.), *Handbook of child psychology: Vol. 4. Child psychology in practice* (6th ed.). Hoboken, NJ: Wiley.

Lamb, M. E., Hershkowitz, I., Orbach, Y., & Esplin, P. W. (2008). *Tell me what happened: Structured investigative interviews of child victims and witnesses.* Chichester: Wiley.

Lambert, M. J., Shapiro, D. A., & Bergin, A. E. (1986). The effectiveness of psychotherapy. In L. Garfield & A. E. Bergin (Eds.), *Handbook of psychotherapy and behavior change* (3rd ed.). New York: Wiley.

Lambert, W. E., Genesee, F., Holobow, N., & Chartrand, L. (1993). Bilingual education for majority English-speaking children.

European Journal of Psychology of Education, 8, 3–22.

Lamborn, S. D., Mounts, N. S., Steinberg, L., & Dornbusch, S. M. (1991). Patterns of competence and adjustment among adolescents from authoritative, authoritarian, indulgent, and neglectful families. *Child Development, 62*, 1049–1065.

Land, B. B., & Seeley, T. D. (2004). The grooming invitation dance of the honey bee. *Ethology, 110*, 1–10.

Landers, D. M., & Arent, S. (2001). Arousal-performance relations. In J. M. Williams (Ed.), *Applied sport psychology: Personal growth to peak performance* (4th ed.). Boston, MA: McGraw-Hill.

Landesman, S., & Ramey, C. T. (1989). Developmental psychology and mental retardation: Integrating scientific principles with treatment practices. *American Psychologist, 44*, 409–415.

Landman, R., Spekreijse, H. & Lamme, V. A. (2003). Large capacity storage of integrated objects before change blindness. *Vision Research, 43(2)*, 149–164.

Lane, R. D., Reiman, E. M., Ahern, G. L., & Schwartz, G. E. (1997). Neuroanatomical correlates of happiness, sadness, and disgust. *American Journal of Psychiatry, 154*, 926–933.

Lane, S. D., Cherek, D. R., Lieving, L. M., & Tcheremissine, O. V. (2005). Marijuana effects on human forgetting functions. *Journal of the Experimental Analysis of Behavior, 83*, 67–83.

Lang, P. J. (1994). The varieties of emotional experience – a meditation on James-Lange theory. *Psychological Review, 101* (2), 211–221.

Langan-Fox, J., & Grant, S. (2006). The Thematic Apperception Test: Toward a standard measure of the Big Three motives. *Journal of Personality Assessment, 87*, 277–291.

Lange, T., Dimitrov, S., & Born, J. (2010). Effects of sleep and circadian rhythm on the human immune system. *Annals of the New York Academy of Sciences, 1193*, 48–59.

Langer, E. (1989). *Mindlessness.* Reading, MA: Addison-Wesley.

Langlois, J. H., & Roggman, L. A. (1990). Attractive faces are only average. *Psychological Science, 1*, 115–121.

Langlois, J. H., Kalakanis, L., Rubenstein, A. J., Larson, A., Hallam, M., & Smoot, M. (2000). Maxims or myths of beauty? A meta-analytic and theoretical review. *Psychological Bulletin, 126*, 390–423.

Lanier, C. A. (2001). Rape accepting attitudes: Precursors to or consequences of forced sex. *Violence Against Women, 7*, 876–885.

LaPiere, R. T. (1934). Attitudes and actions. *Social Forces, 13*, 230–237.

LaPointe, L. L. (2005). *Aphasia and related neurogenic language disorders* (3rd ed.). New York: Thieme New York.

Larivée, S., Normandeau, S., & Parent, S. (2000). The French connection: Some contributions of French language research in the post Piagetian era. *Child Development, 71*, 823–839.

Larroque, B., & Kaminski, M. (1998). Prenatal alcohol exposure and development at preschool age: Main results of a French study. *Alcoholism: Clinical and Experimental Research, 22*, 295–303.

Larsen, R. J., & Buss, D. M. (2002). *Personality psychology: Domains of knowledge about human nature.* Boston, MA: McGraw-Hill.

Larsen, R. J., & Buss, D. M. (2007). *Personality psychology: Domains of knowledge about human nature* (3rd ed.). Boston, MA: McGraw-Hill.

Larson, R. W., Hansen, D. M., & Moneta, G. (2006). Differing profiles of developmental experiences across types of organized youth activities. *Developmental Psychology, 42*, 849–863.

Larson, R. W., Moneta, G., Richards, M. H., & Wilson, W. (2002). Continuity, stability, and change in daily emotional experience across adolescence. *Child Development, 73*, 1151–1165.

Lasco, M. S., Jordan, T. J., Edgar, M. A., Petito, C. K., & Byne, W. (2002). A lack of dimorphism of sex or sexual orientation in the human anterior commissure. *Brain Research, 936*, 95–98.

Lashley, K. S. (1950). In search of the engram. *Symposia of the Society for Experimental Biology, 4*, 454–482.

Laski, E. V., & Yu, Q. Y. (2014). Number line estimation and mental addition: Examining the potential roles of language and education. *Journal of Experimental Child Psychology, 117*, 29–44.

Latané, B., & Bourgeois, M. J. (2001). Successfully simulating dynamic social impact: Three levels of prediction. In J. P. Forgas & K. D. Williams (Eds.), *Social influence: Direct and indirect processes. The Sydney symposium of social psychology*. Philadelphia, PA: Psychology Press.

Latané, B., & Darley, J. M. (1970). *The unresponsive bystander: Why doesn't he help?* New York: Appleton-Century-Crofts.

Latané, B., & Nida, S. (1981). Ten years of research on group size and helping. *Psychological Bulletin, 89*, 308–324.

Lau, H. C., & Passingham, R. E. (2007). Relative blindsight in normal observers and the neural correlate of visual consciousness. *Proceedings of the National Academy of Sciences of the USA, 103* (49).

Laumann, E. O., Gagnon, J. H., Michael, R. T., & Michaels, S. (1994). *The social organization of sexuality: Sexual practices in the United States*. Chicago, IL: University of Chicago Press.

Lavergne, G. M. (1997). *A sniper in the tower: The Charles Whitman murders*. Denton, TX: University of North Texas Press.

Lavie, P. (2000). Sleep-wake as a biological rhythm. *Annual Review of Psychology, 52*, 277–303.

Lavie, P., Pratt, H., Scharf, B., Peled, R., & Brown, J. (1984). Localized pontine lesion: Nearly total absence of REM sleep. *Neurology, 34*, 118–20.

Lavigne, J. V., Gibbons, R. D., Christoffel, K. K., & Arend, R. (1996). Prevalence rates and correlates of psychiatric disorders among preschool children. *Journal of the American Academy of Child & Adolescent Psychiatry, 35*, 204–214.

Lawler, K. A., & Schmied, L. A. (1992). A prospective study of women's health: The effects of stress, hardiness, locus of control, Type A behavior, and physiological reactivity. *Women and Health, 19*, 27–41.

Lawlor, M. S., Schonert-Reichl, K. A., Gadermann, A. M., & Zumbo, B. D. (2013). A validation study of the mindful attention awareness scale adapted for children. *Mindfulness*, June. doi: 10.1007/s12671-013-0228-4.

Lazarus, A. A. (1971). *Behavior therapy and beyond*. New York: McGraw-Hill.

Lazarus, R. S. (1974). Psychological stress and coping in adaptation and illness. *International Journal of Psychiatry in Medicine, 5*, 321–333.

Lazarus, R. S. (1982). Thoughts on the relations between emotion and cognition. *American Psychologist, 37*, 1019–1024.

Lazarus, R. S. (1991). Progress on a cognitive-motivational- relational theory of emotion. *American Psychologist, 46*, 819–834.

Lazarus, R. S. (1998). *Fifty years of the research and theory of R. S. Lazarus: An analysis of historical and perennial issues*. Mahwah, NJ: Erlbaum.

Lazarus, R. S. (2000). Toward better research on stress and coping. *American Psychologist, 55*, 665–673.

Lazarus, R. S. (2001). Relational meaning and discrete emotions. In B. K. Scherer et al. (Eds.), *Appraisal processes in emotion: Theory, methods, research*. New York: Oxford University Press.

Lazarus, R. S. (2006). Emotions and interpersonal relationships: Toward a person-centered conceptualization of emotions and coping. *Journal of Personality, 74*, 9–46.

Lazarus, R. S., & Folkman, S (1984). *Stress, appraisal, and coping*. New York: Springer.

Leach, C. W., & Vliek, M. L. W. (2008). Group membership as a 'frame of reference' for interpersonal comparison. *Social and Personality Psychology Compass, 2*, 539–554.

Leahy, R. L., & Holland, S. J. (2000). *Treatment plans and interventions for depression and anxiety disorders*. New York: Guilford Press.

Leary, M. R. (2004). The self we know and the self we show: Self-esteem, self-presentation, and the maintenance of interpersonal relationships. In M. B. Brewer & M. Hewstone (Eds.), *Emotion and motivation: Perspectives on social psychology*. Malden, MA: Blackwell.

Leary, M. R., Tambor, E. S., Terdal, S. K., & Downs, D. L. (1995). Self-esteem as an interpersonal monitor: The sociometer hypothesis. *Journal of Personality and Social Psychology, 68*, 518–530.

LeDoux, J. E. (1998). *The emotional brain*. New York: Simon & Schuster.

LeDoux, J. E. (2000). Emotion circuits in the brain. *Annual Review of Neuroscience, 23*, 155–184.

LeDoux, J. E., & Phelps, E. A. (2000). Emotional networks in the brain. In M. Lewis & J. M. Haviland-Jones (Eds.), *Handbook of emotions* (2nd ed.). New York: Guilford Press.

Lee, J. D. (1998). Which kids can 'become' scientists? Effects of gender, self-concepts, and perceptions of scientists. *Social Psychology Quarterly, 61*, 199–219.

Legerstee, M., Markova, G., & Fisher, T. (2007). The role of maternal affect attunement in dyadic and triadic communication. *Infant Behavior and Development, 30*(2), 296–306.

Lehmann-Haupt, C. (1988, August 4). Books of the times: How an actor found success, and himself. *New York Times*, p. 2.

Leichtman, M. D., & Ceci, S. J. (1995). The effects of stereotypes and suggestions on preschoolers' reports. *Developmental Psychology, 31*, 568–578.

Leifman, H., Österberg, E., & Ramstedt, M. (2002). *Alcohol in postwar Europe, ECAS II: A discussion of indicators on alcohol consumption and alcohol-related harm*. Stockholm: National Institute of Public Health.

Leitenberg, H., & Henning, K. (1995). Sexual fantasy. *Psychological Bulletin, 117*(3), 469–496.

Leman, P., Bremner, A. J., Parke, R. D., & Gauvain, M. (2012). *Developmental psychology*. London: McGraw-Hill.

LeMoal, H. (1999). *Dopamine and the brain: From neurons to networks*. New York: Academic Press.

Lemogne, C., Consoli, S. M., Geoffroy-Perez, B., Coeuret-Pellicer, M., Nabi, H., Melchior, M., ... Cordier, S. (2013). Personality and the risk of cancer: A

16-year follow-up study of the GAZEL cohort. *Psychosomatic Medicine, 75,* 262–271.

Lenzenweger, M. F., & Clarkin, J. F. (Eds.) (2005). *Major theories of personality disorder.* New York: Guilford Press.

Leon, G. R., & Roth, L. (1977). Obesity: Psychological causes, correlations, and speculations. *Psychological Bulletin, 84,* 117–139.

Léone, G. (1998). The effect of gravity on human recognition of disoriented objects. *Brain Research Reviews, 28,* 203–214.

Leor, J., Poole, W. K., & Kloner, R. A. (1996). Sudden cardiac death triggered by an earthquake. *New England Journal of Medicine, 334*(7), 413–419.

LePage, M., Habib, R., & Tulving, E. (1998). Hippocampal PET activations of memory encoding and retrieval: The HIPER model. *Hippocampus, 8,* 313–322.

Leproult, R., Van Reeth, O., Byrne, M. M., Sturis, J., & Van Cauter E. (1997). Sleepiness, performance, and neuroendocrine function during sleep deprivation: Effects of exposure to bright light or exercise. *Journal of Biological Rhythms, 12,* 245–258.

Leslie, A. M. (2004). Who's for learning? *Developmental Science, 7,* 417–419.

Leslie, A. M. (2005). Developmental parallels in understanding minds and bodies. *Trends in Cognitive Sciences, 9,* 459–462.

Leslie, J. C. (2002). *Essential behaviour analysis.* London: Arnold.

Letzring, T. D., Wells, S., & Funder, D. C. (2006). Quantity and quality of available information affect the realistic accuracy of personality judgment. *Journal of Personality and Social Psychology, 91,* 111–123.

Levenson, H. (2010). *Brief dynamic therapy.* Washington, DC: American Psychological Association Press.

Levinson, D. J. (1986). A conception of adult development. *American Psychologist, 41,* 3–13.

Levinson, D. J. (1990). A theory of life structure development in adulthood. In C. N. Alexander & E. J. Langer (Eds.), *Higher stages of human development:*

Perspectives on adult growth. New York: Oxford University Press.

Levinson, D. J., Darow, C. N., Klein, E. B., Levinson, M. H., & McKee, B. (1978). *The seasons of a man's life.* New York: Knopf.

Levinthal, C. F. (1996). *Drugs, behavior, and modern society.* Boston, MA: Allyn & Bacon.

Levinthal, C. F. (2007). *Drugs, behavior, and modern society.* New York: McGraw-Hill.

Levitsky, D. A. (2002). Putting behavior back into feeding behavior: A tribute to George Collier. *Appetite, 38,* 143–148.

Levy, B. R., Slade, M. D., Kunkel, S. R., & Kasl, S. V. (2002). Longevity increased by positive self-perceptions of aging. *Journal of Personality and Social Psychology, 83,* 261–270.

Levy, B. S., & Sidel, V. W. (2009). Health effects of combat: A life-course perspective. *Annual Review of Public Health, 30,* 123–136.

Levy, S., Marrow, L., Bagley, C., & Lippman, M. (1988). Survival hazards analysis in first recurrent breast cancer patients: Seven-year follow-up. *Psychosomatic Medicine, 50,* 520–528.

Lew, A. R. (2011). Looking beyond the boundaries: Time to put landmarks back on the cognitive map? *Psychological Bulletin, 137*(3), 484–507.

Lewin, R. (2005). *Human evolution: An illustrated introduction* (5th ed.). Oxford: Blackwell.

Lewinsohn, P. M., Gotlib, I. H., Lewinsohn, M., Seeley, J. R., & Allen, N. B. (1998). Gender differences in anxiety disorders and anxiety symptoms in adolescents. *Journal of Abnormal Psychology, 107,* 109–117.

Lewinsohn, P. M., Rohde, P., & Gau, J. M. (2003). Comparability of self-report checklist and interview data in the assessment of stressful life events in young adults. *Psychological Reports, 93,* 459–471.

Lewinsohn, P. M., Hoberman, H., Teri, L., & Hantzinger, M. (1985). An integrative theory of depression. In S. Reiss & R. Bootzin (Eds.), *Theoretical issues in behavior therapy.* New York: Academic Press.

Lewis, C., & Osborne, A. (1990). Three-year-olds' problems with false belief: Conceptual deficit or linguistic artefact? *Child Development, 61,* 1514–1519.

Lewis, M. (2000). The emergence of human emotions. In M. Lewis & J. M. Haviland-Jones (Eds.), *Handbook of emotions* (2nd ed.). New York: Guilford Press.

Lewis, M., & Brooks-Gunn, J. (1979). *Social cognition and the acquisition of the self.* New York: Plenum Press.

Lewis, M., Young, S., Brooks, J., & Michalson, L. (1975). The beginning of friendship. In M. Lewis & L. A. R. Osenblum (Eds.), *Friendship and peer relations.* New York: Wiley.

Lewis, M. J. (1996). Alcohol reinforcement and neuropharmacological therapeutics. *Alcohol and Alcoholism, 31* (Suppl. 1), 17–25.

Lewis, M. W., Misra, S., Johnson, H. L., & Rosen, T. S. (2004). Neurological and developmental outcomes of prenatally cocaine-exposed offspring from 12 to 36 months. *American Journal of Drug and Alcohol Abuse, 30,* 299–320.

Lewis, S. (2014). Psychiatric disorders: A second chance for ECT? *Nature Reviews Neuroscience, 15*(2), 69.

Lewkowicz, D. J. (2011). The biological implausibility of the nature–nurture dichotomy and what it means for the study of infancy. *Infancy, 16,* 331–367.

Leyens, J. P., Camino, L., Parke, R. D., & Berkowitz, L. (1975). Effects of movie violence on aggression in a field setting as a function of group dominance and cohesion. *Journal of Personality and Social Psychology, 32,* 346–360.

Li, S. (2001). How close is too close? A comparison of proxemic reactions of Singaporean Chinese to male intruders of four ethnicities. *Perceptual and Motor Skills, 93,* 124–126.

Li, Y.R., Loft, S., Weinborn, M. & Maybery, M.T. (2014). Event-based prospective memory deficits in individuals with high depressive symptomatology: Problems controlling attentional resources? *Journal of Clinical and Experimental Neuropsychology, 36*(6), 577–587.

Lichtenberg, P., Bachner-Melman, R., Gritsenko, I., & Ebstein, R. P. (2000).

Exploratory association study between catechol-O-methyltransferase (COMT) high/low enzyme activity polymorphism and hypnotizability. *American Journal of Medical Genetics, 96*, 771–774.

Lichtenthal, W. G., Currier, J. M., Neimeyer, R. A., & Keesee, N. J. (2010). Sense and significance: A mixed methods examination of meaning making after the loss of one's child. *Journal of Clinical Psychology, 66*, 791–812.

Liddell, C., Barrett, L., and Bydawell, M. (2006). Indigenous beliefs and attitudes to AIDS precautions in a rural South African community: An empirical study, *Annals of Behavioral Medicine, 32*, 218–225.

Lidz, C. S. (1997). Dynamic assessment approaches. In D. P. Flanagan, J. L. Genshaft, & P. L. Harrison (Eds.), *Contemporary intellectual assessment: Theories, tests, and issues.* New York: Guilford Press.

Lieb, R., Isensee, B., Hoefier, M., Pfister, H., & Wittchen, H. U. (2002). Parental major depression and the risk of depression and other mental disorders in offspring: A prospective-longitudinal community study. *Archives of General Psychiatry, 59*, 365–374.

Lieberman, J. A. (1998). *Psychiatric drugs.* Philadelphia, PA: Saunders.

Light, P., & Littleton, K. (1999). *Social processes in children's learning* (Vol. 4). Cambridge: Cambridge University Press.

Lilienfeld, S. O., Wood, J. M., & Garb, H. N. (2000). The scientific status of projective techniques. *Psychological Science in the Public Interest, 1*, 25–62.

Lim, J., & Dinges, L. (2010). A meta-analysis of the impact of short-term sleep deprivation on cognitive variables. *Psychological Bulletin, 136*(3), 375–389.

Linden, W. (2005). *Stress management: From basic science to better practice.* Newbury Park, CA: Sage.

Lindsay, D. S., & Read, J. D. (1994). Psychotherapy and memories of childhood sexual abuse: A cognitive perspective. *Applied Cognitive Psychology, 8*, 281–338.

Lindsay, R. of Pitscottie (1814). *The Chronicles of Scotland.* Edinburgh: George Ramsay & Co for Archibald Constable & Co.

Linehan, M. M. (1993). *Cognitive-behavioral treatment of borderline personality disorder.* New York: Guilford Press.

Linehan, M. M., & Dexter-Mazza, E. T. (2008). Dialectical behavior therapy for borderline personality disorder. In D. H. Barlow (Ed.), *Clinical handbook of psychological disorders: A step-by-step treatment manual* (4th ed.). New York: Guilford.

Linehan, M. M., Comtois, K. A., Murray, A. M., Brown, M. Z., Gallop, R. J., Heard, H. L. ... Lindenbom, N. (2006). Two-year randomized controlled trial and follow-up of dialectical behaviour therapy vs. therapy by experts for suicidal behaviors and borderline personality disorder. *Archives of General Psychiatry, 63*, 757–766.

Lingjaerde, O., Bratlid, T., Hansen, T., & Gotestam, K.G. (1986). Seasonal affective disorder and midwinter insomnia in the far north: studies on two related chronobiological disorders in Norway. *Clinical Neuropharmacology, 9*, 187–189.

Linver, M. R., Brooks-Gunn, J., & Kohen, D. E. (2002). Family processes as pathways from income to young children's development. *Developmental Psychology, 38*, 719–734.

Lippa, R. A. (2005). *Gender, nature, and nurture.* Hillsdale, NJ: Erlbaum.

Lipsitt, L. P. (1990). Learning processes in the human newborn: Sensitization, habituation, and classical conditioning. *Annals of the New York Academy of Sciences, 608*, 113–127.

Litz, B. T. (2004). *Early intervention for trauma and traumatic loss.* New York: Guilford Press.

Livingstone, M. S., & Hubel, D. H. (1994a). Stereopsis and positional acuity under dark adaptation. *Vision Research, 34*, 799–802.

Livingstone, M. S., & Hubel, D. (1994b). Segregation of form, color, movement, and depth: Anatomy, physiology, and perception. In H. Gutfreund & G. Toulouse (Eds.), *Biology and computation: A physicist's choice. Advanced series in neuroscience.* Singapore: World Scientific Publishing.

Lloyd-Fox, S., Blasi, A., & Elwell, C. E. (2010). Illuminating the developing brain: the past, present and future of functional near infrared spectroscopy. *Neuroscience & Biobehavioral Reviews, 34*(3), 269–284.

Lobel, M., Yali, A. M., Zhu, W., DeVincent, C. J., & Meyer, B. A. (2002). Beneficial associations between optimistic disposition and emotional distress in high-risk pregnancy. *Psychology and Health, 17*, 77–95.

Lobina, C., Agabio, R., Reali, R., Gessa, G. L., & Colombo, G. (1999). Contribution of GABAA and GABAB receptors to the discriminative stimulus produced by gamma-hydroxybutyric acid. *Pharmacology, Biochemistry and Behavior, 64*(2), 363–365.

Locke, D. C. (1992). *Increasing multicultural understanding: A comprehensive model.* Thousand Oaks, CA: Sage.

Locke, E. A., & Latham, G. P. (2002). Building a practically useful theory of goal setting and task motivation: A 35-year odyssey. *American Psychologist, 57*, 705–717.

Lockwood, P., Jordan, C. H., & Kunda, Z. (2002). Motivation by positive or negative role models: Regulatory focus determines who will best inspire us. *Journal of Personality and Social Psychology, 83*, 854–864.

Loehlin, J. C. (1992). *Genes and environment in personality development.* Newbury Park, CA: Sage.

Loehlin, J. C., Willerman, L., & Horn, J. M. (1988). Genetics and human behavior. *Annual Review of Psychology, 39*, 101–134.

Loewenstein, R. J. (1991). Psychogenic amnesia and psychogenic fugue: A comprehensive review. In A. Tasman & S. M. Goldfinger (Eds.), *American Psychiatric Press review of psychiatry* (Vol. 10). Washington, DC: American Psychiatric Association.

Loftus, E. F. (1993). The reality of repressed memories. *American Psychologist, 48*, 518–537.

Loftus, E. F., & Bernstein, D. M. (2005). Rich false memories: The royal road to success. In A. Healy (Ed.), *Experimental cognitive psychology and its applications.*

Decade of behavior. Washington, DC: American Psychological Association.

Loftus, E. F., & Davis, D. (2006). Recovered memories. *Annual Review of Clinical Psychology, 2,* 469–498.

Loftus, E. F., & Ketcham, K. (1994). *The myth of repressed memory.* New York: St. Martin's Press.

Loftus, E. F., & Palmer, J. C. (1974). Reconstruction of automobile destruction: An example of the interaction between language and memory. *Journal of Verbal Learning and Verbal Behavior, 13,* 585–589.

Logan, T. K., Cole, J., & Leukefeld, C. (2002). Women, sex, and HIV: Social and contextual factors, meta-analysis of published interventions, and implications for practice and research. *Psychological Bulletin, 128,* 851–885.

Logue, A. W. (1991). *The psychology of eating and drinking* (2nd ed.). New York: Freeman.

Lomber, S. J., & Eggermont, J. J. (2006). *Reprogramming the cerebral cortex: Plasticity following central and peripheral lesions.* New York: Oxford University Press.

Lopez, S. R., & Guarnaccia, P. J. (2000). Cultural psychopathology: Uncovering the social world of mental illness. *Annual Review of Psychology, 51,* 571–598.

Lorenz, K. (1937). The companion in the bird's world. *Auk, 54,* 245–273.

Lorenzen, L. A., Grieve, F. G., & Thomas, A. (2004). Exposure to muscular male models decreases men's body satisfaction. *Sex Roles, 51,* 743–748.

Lovaas, O. I. (1977). *The autistic child.* New York: Irvington.

Lovallo, W. R., & Gerin, W. (2003). Psychophysiological reactivity: Mechanisms and path-ways to cardiovascular disease. *Psychosomatic Medicine, 65,* 36–45.

Lowenthal, R., Paula, C. S., Schwartzman, J. S., Brunoni, D. & Mercadante, M. T. (2007). Prevalence of pervasive developmental disorders in Down's syndrome. *Journal of Autism and Developmental Disorders, 37,* 1394–1395.

Luber, B., & Lisanby, S. H. (2014). Enhancement of human cognitive performance using transcranial magnetic stimulation (TMS). *Neuroimage, 85,* 961–970.

Lubinski, D. (2004). Introduction to the special section on cognitive abilities: '100 years after Spearman's (1904) "General intelligence," objectively determined and measured'. *Journal of Personality and Social Psychology, 86,* 96–111.

Luborsky, L., Rosenthal, R., Diguer, L., Andrusyna, T. P., Berman, J. S., Levitt, J. T., Seligman, D. A., & Krause, E. D. (2002). The dodo bird verdict is alive and well – mostly. *Clinical Psychology: Science and Practice, 9,* 2–12.

Lubow, R. E., & Moore, A. U. (1959). Latent inhibition: The effect of non-reinforced preexposure to the conditional stimulus. *Journal of Comparative and Physiological Psychology, 52,* 415–419.

Luby, J. (2010). Preschool depression: The importance of identification of depression early in development. *Current Directions in Psychological Science, 19*(2), 91.

Lucas, A. R., Beard, C. M., O'Fallon, W. M., & Kurland, L. T. (1991). 50-year trends in the incidence of anorexia nervosa in Rochester, Minn.: A population-based study. *The American Journal of Psychiatry, 148,* 917–922.

Lucas, E. J., & Ball, L. J. (2005). Think-aloud protocols and the selection task: Evidence for relevance effects and rationalisation processes. *Thinking and Reasoning, 11,* 35–66.

Lucas, R. E., Clark, A. E., Georgellis, Y., & Diener, E. (2004). Unemployment alters the set point for life satisfaction. *Psychological Science, 15,* 8–13.

Luchins, A. J. (1942). Mechanization in problem solving: The effect of Einstellung. *Psychological Monographs, 54* (6, Whole No. 248).

Luciano, M., Wright, M. J., Smith, G. A., Geffen, G. M., Geffen, L. B., & Martin, N. G. (2001). Genetic covariance among measures of information processing speed, working memory, and IQ. *Behavior Genetics, 31,* 581–592.

Luhtanen, R., & Crocker, J. (1992). A collective self-esteem scale: Self-evaluation of one's social identity. *Personality and Social Psychology Bulletin, 18,* 302–318.

Luna, B., Garver, K. E., Urban, T. A., Lazar, N. A., & Sweeney, J. A. (2004). Maturation of cognitive processes from late childhood to adulthood. *Child Development, 75,* 1357–1372.

Luria, A. R. (1968). *The mind of a mnemonist: A little book about a vast memory.* New York: Basic Books.

Luszczynska, A., Benight, C. C., & Cieslak, R. (2009). Self-efficacy and health-related outcomes of collective trauma: A systematic review. *European Psychologist, 14,* 51–62.

Lykken, D. T. (2006). The mechanism of emergenesis. *Genes, Brain, & Behavior, 5,* 306–310.

Lykken, D. T., & Tellegen, A. (1996). Happiness is a stochastic phenomenon. *Psychological Science, 7,* 186–189.

Lykken, D. T., McGue, M., Tellegen, A., & Bouchard, T. J. (1992). Emergenesis: Genetic traits that may not run in families. *American Psychologist, 47,* 1565–1577.

Lynn, S. J., Neuschatz, J., Fite, R., & Kirsch, I. (2001). Hypnosis in the forensic arena. *Journal of Forensic Psychology Practice, 1,* 113–122.

Lytton, H., & Romney, D. M. (1991). Parents' differential socialization of boys and girls: A meta-analysis. *Psychological Bulletin, 109,* 267–296.

M

Maass, A., & Clark, R. D. (1983). Internalization versus compliance: Differential processes underlying minority influence and conformity. *European Journal of Social Psychology, 13,* 197–215.

MacAndrew, C., & Edgerton, R. B. (1969). *Drunken comportment: A social explanation.* Chicago, IL: Aldine.

Maccoby, E. E., & Maccoby, N. (1954). The interview: A tool of social science. In G. Lindzey (Ed.), *Handbook of social psychology.* Cambridge, MA: Addison-Wesley.

Maccoby, E. E., & Martin, J. A. (1983). Socialization in the context of the family: Parent–child interaction. In E. M. Hetherington (Ed.), *Handbook of child psychology: Socialization, personality, and social development.* New York: Wiley.

Maccoby, E., & Jacklin, C. (1974). *The psychology of sex differences*. Stanford, CA: Stanford University Press.

MacCoun, R. J. (1998). Toward a psychology of harm reduction. *American Psychologist, 53*, 1199–1208.

MacDonald, A. W. & Schulz, S. C. (2009). What we know: Findings that every theory of schizophrenia should explain. *Schizophrenia Bulletin, 35* (3), 493–508. doi:10.1093/schbul/sbp017.

MacDonald, S., Uesiliana, K., & Hayne, H. (2000). Cross-cultural and gender differences in childhood amnesia. *Memory, 8*, 365–376.

Mackintosh, N. J. (1975). A theory of attention. Variations in the associability of stimuli with reinforcement. *Psychological Review, 82*, 276–298.

Mackintosh, N. J. (1998). *IQ and human intelligence*. Oxford: Oxford University Press.

MacLeod, C. M. (1991). Half a century of research on the Stroop effect: An integrative review. *Psychological Bulletin, 109*, 163–203.

MacLeod, C. M. (2005). The Stroop task in cognitive research. In A. Wenzel & D. C. Rubin (Eds.), *Cognitive methods and their application to clinical research*. Washington, DC: American Psychological Association.

Maddux, J. E. (1999). Personal efficacy. In V. J. Derlega, B. A. Winstead, & W. H. Jones (Eds.), *Personality: Contemporary theory and research*. Chicago, IL: Nelson Hall.

Madon, S., Guyll, M., Spoth, R., & Willard, J. (2004). Self-fulfilling prophecies: The synergistic accumulative effect of parent's beliefs on children's drinking behaviour. *Psychological Science, 15*, 837–845.

Madon, S., Willard, J., Guyll, M., Trudeau, L., & Spoth, R. (2006). Self-fulfilling prophecy effects of mothers' beliefs on children's alcohol use: Accumulation, dissipation, and stability over time. *Journal of Personality and Social Psychology, 90*(6), 911–926.

Madon, S., Guyll, M., Buller, A. A., Scherr, K. C., Willard, J., & Spoth, R. (2008). The mediation of mothers' self-fulfilling effects on their children's alcohol use: Self-verification, informational conformity, and modeling processes. *Journal of Personality and Social Psychology, 95*(2), 369–384.

Maes, H. H. M., Neale, M. C., & Eaves, L. J. (1997). Genetic and environmental factors in relative body weight and human adiposity. *Behavior Genetics, 27*, 325–351.

Maguire, E. A., Gadian, D. G., Johnsrude, I. S., Good, C. D., Ashburner, J., Frackowiak, R. S., & Frith, C. D. (2000). Navigation-related structural change in the hippocampi of taxi drivers. *Proceedings of the National Academy of Sciences, 97*(8), 4398–4403.

Maher, B. A. (1979). *Clinical psychology and personality: The collected papers of George Kelly*. Huntington, NY: Wiley.

Mahler, M. (1968). *On human symbiosis and the vicissitudes of individuation: Infantile psychosis*. New York: Basic Books.

Maier, S. F., & Watkins, L. R. (1999). Bidirectional communication between the brain and the immune system: Implications for behaviour. *Animal Behaviour, 57*(4), 741–751.

Main, M., Kaplan, N., & Cassidy, J. (1985). Security in infancy, childhood, and adulthood: A move to the level of representation. *Monographs of the Society for Research in Child Development, 50*, 66–104.

Main, M., & Solomon, J. (1986). Discovery of an insecure-disorganized/disoriented attachment pattern. In T. B. Brazelton and M. W. Yogman (Eds.), *Affective development in infancy* (pp. 95–124). Westport, CT: Ablex Publishing.

Maisel, N. C., & Gable, S. L. (2009). The paradox of received social support: The importance of responsiveness. *Psychological Science, 20*, 928–932.

Major, B., Spencer, S., Schmader, T., Wolfe, C., & Crocker, J. (1998). Coping with negative stereotypes about intellectual performance: The role of psychological disengagement. *Personality and Social Psychology Bulletin, 24*, 34–50.

Mäkelä, K. (1997). Drinking, the majority fallacy, cognitive dissonance and social pressure. *Addiction, 92*, 729–736.

Malamuth, N. M., Addison, T., & Koss, M. (2000). Pornography and sexual aggression: Are there reliable effects and can we understand them? *Annual Review of Sex Research, 11*, 26–91.

Maldonado, R., & Rodriguez de Fonseca, F. (2002). Cannabinoid addiction: Behavioral models and neural correlates. *Journal of Neuroscience, 22*, 3326–3331.

Malina, R. M., Pena Reyes, M. E., Tan, S. K., & Little, B. B. (2004). Secular change in age at menarche in rural Oaxaca, southern Mexico: 1968–2000. *Annals of Human Biology, 31*, 634–646.

Malle, B. F., & Holbrook, J. (2012). Is there a hierarchy of social inferences? The likelihood and speed of inferring intentionality, mind, and personality. *Journal of Personality and Social Psychology, 102*, 661–684.

Malloy, K. M., & Milling, L. S. (2010). The effectiveness of virtual reality distraction for pain reduction: A systematic review. *Clinical Psychology Review, 30*, 1011–1018.

Maloney, E. A., Schaeffer, M. W., & Beilock, S. L. (2013). Mathematics anxiety and stereotype threat: Shared mechanisms, negative consequences and promising interventions. *Research in Mathematics Education, 15*(2), 115–128.

Maner, J. K., DeWall, C. N., Baumeister, R. F., & Schaller, M. (2007). Does social exclusion motivate interpersonal reconnection? Resolving the 'porcupine problem.' *Journal of Personality and Social Psychology, 92*, 42–55.

Manheimer, E., White, A., Berman, B., Forys, K., & Ernst, E. (2005). Meta-analysis: acupuncture for low back pain. *Annals of Internal Medicine, 142*, 651–663.

Manktelow, K. I., & Over, D. E. (1991). Social roles and utilities in reasoning with deontic conditionals. *Cognition, 39*, 85–105.

Manktelow, K. I., Sutherland, E. J., & Over, D. E. (1995). Probabilistic factors in deontic reasoning. *Thinking and Reasoning, 1*, 201–219.

Mann, L. (1981). The baiting crowd in episodes of threatened suicide. *Journal of Personality and Social Psychology, 41*, 703–709.

Manning, J. (1956). *Young Sinners (Reefer Girl)*. London: Venus Books.

Manson, J. E., Colditz, G. A., Stampfer, M. J., Willett, W. C., Rosner, B., Monson, R. R., Speizer, F. E., & Hennekens, C. H. (1990). A prospective study of obesity and risk of coronary heart disease in women. *New England Journal of Medicine, 322,* 882–888.

Manson, S. M. (1994). Culture and depression: Discovering variations in the experience of illness. In W. J. Lonner & R. S. Malpass (Eds.), *Psychology and culture.* Boston, MA: Allyn & Bacon.

Mäntylä, T. (1986). Optimizing cue effectiveness: Recall of 500 and 600 incidentally learned words. *Journal of Experimental Psychology: Learning, Memory, and Cognition, 12,* 66–71.

Marangell, L. B. (2002). *Concise guide to psychopharmacology.* Washington, DC: American Psychiatric Publishing.

Marcia, J. E. (1966). Development and validation of ego identity status. *Journal of Personality and Social Psychology, 3,* 551–558.

Marcia, J. E. (2002). Adolescence, identity, and the Bernardone family. *Identity, 2,* 199–209.

Marian, V., Spivey, M., & Hirsch, J. (2003). Shared and separate systems in bilingual language processing: Converging evidence from eye-tracking and brain imaging. *Brain & Language, 86,* 70–82.

Markey, P. M. (2000). Bystander intervention in computer mediated communication. *Computers in Human Behavior, 16,* 183–188.

Markovits, H., & Nantel, G. (1989). The belief-bias effect in the production and evaluation of logical conclusions. *Memory and Cognition, 17,* 11–17.

Marks, D. M., Pae, C. U., & Patkar, A. A. (2008). Triple reuptake inhibitors: The next generation of antidepressants. *Current Neuropharmacology, 6,* 338–343.

Marks, I. M. (1977). Phobias and obsessions: Clinical phenomena in search of laboratory models. In J. Maser & M. E. P. Seligman (Eds.), *Psychopathology: Experimental models.* San Francisco, CA: Freeman.

Marks, I. M. (1991). Self-administered behavioural treatment. *Behavioural Psychotherapy, 19,* 42–46.

Marks, I. M. (2002). The maturing of therapy: Some brief psychotherapies help anxiety/depressive disorders but mechanisms of action are unclear. *British Journal of Psychiatry, 180,* 200–204.

Markus, H. R., & Kitayama, S. (1991). Culture and the self: Implications for cognition, emotion, and motivation. *Psychological Review, 98,* 224–253.

Markus, H. R., & Kitayama, S. (1998). The cultural psychology of personality. *Journal of Cross-Cultural Psychology, 29,* 63–87.

Markus, H., & Wurf, E. (1987). The dynamic self-concept: A social psychological perspective. In L. W. Porter and M. R. Rosenzweig (Eds.), *Annual Review of Psychology, 38.* Palo Alto, CA: Annual Reviews.

Marlatt, G. A. (1996). Taxonomy of high-risk situations for alcohol relapse: Evolution and development of a cognitive-behavioral model. *Addiction, 91* (Suppl.), S37–S49.

Marlatt, G. A., Baer, J. S., Kivlahan, D. R., Dimeff, L. A., Larimer, M. E., Quigley, L. A., Somers, J. M., & Williams, E. (1998). Screening and brief intervention for high-risk college student drinkers: Results from a 2-year follow-up assessment. *Journal of Consulting and Clinical Psychology, 66,* 604–615.

Marlatt, G. A., Blume, A. W., & Parks, G. A. (2001). Integrating harm reduction therapy and traditional substance abuse treatment. *Journal of Psychoactive Drugs, 33,* 13–21.

Marques, J. M., Yzerbyt, V. Y., & Leyens, J. P. (1988). The 'black sheep effect': Extremity of judgments towards in-group members as a function of identification. *European Journal of Social Psychology, 18,* 1–16.

Marr, D. (1982). *Vision.* New York: W. H. Freeman. (13th printing 1996.)

Marschark, M., & Mayer, T. S. (1998). Interactions of language and memory in deaf children and adults. *Scandinavian Journal of Psychology, 39,* 145–148.

Marsh, H. W. (1990). A multidimensional, hierarchical model of self-concept: Theoretical and empirical justification. *Educational Psychology Review, 2,* 77–172.

Marshall, C. (2001). Make the most of your emotional intelligence. *Chemical Engineering Progress, 97,* 92–95.

Marshall, L. H., & Magoun, H. W. (1997). *Discoveries in the human brain: Neuroscience prehistory, brain structure, and function.* New York: Humana Press.

Marshall, N. L. (2004). The quality of early child care and children's development. *Current Directions in Psychological Science, 13,* 165–168.

Marshall, P. J., & Fox, N. A. (2000). Emotion regulation, depression, and hemispheric asymmetry. In S. L. Johnson & A. M. Hayes (Eds.), *Stress, coping, and depression.* Mahwah, NJ: Erlbaum.

Marsiglio, W., Amato, P., Day, R. D., & Lamb, M. E. (2000). Scholarship on fatherhood in the 1990s and beyond. *Journal of Marriage and the Family, 62,* 1173–1191.

Marsland, A. L., Cohen, S., Rabin, B. S., & Manuck, S. B. (2001). Associations between stress, trait negative affect, acute immune reactivity, and antibody response to Hepatitis B injection in healthy young adults. *Health Psychology, 20,* 4–11.

Martell, C., Addis, M., & Dimidjian, S. (2004). Finding the action in behavioral activation: The search for empirically supported interventions and mechanisms of change. In S. C. Hayes, V. M. Follette, & M. M. Linehan (Eds.), *Mindfulness and acceptance: Expanding the cognitive-behavioral tradition.* New York: Guilford Press.

Martin, C. L., & Ruble, D. (2004). Children's search for gender cues: Cognitive perspectives on gender development. *Current Directions in Psychological Science, 13,* 67–70.

Martin, F. J., Rezzi, S., Peré-Trepat, E., Kamlage, B., Collino, S., Leibold, E., … Kochhar, S. (2009). Metabolic effects of dark chocolate consumption on energy, gut microbiota, and stress-related metabolism in free-living subjects. *Journal of Proteome Research, 8,* 5568–5579.

Martin, J. E., & Dubbert, P. M. (1985). Adherence in exercise. In R. I. Terjung (Ed.), *Exercise and sport sciences review* (Vol. 13). New York: Macmillan.

Martin, N. G., Boomsma, D. I., & Machin, G. (1997). A twin-pronged attack on complex traits. *Nature Genetics, 17,* 387–392.

Martinez, A., Anllo-Vento, L., Sereno, M. I., Frank, L. R., Buxton, R. B., Dubowitz, D. J., ... Hillyard, S. A. (1999). Involvement of striate and extrastriate visual cortical areas in spatial attention. *Nature Neuroscience, 2,* 364–369.

Martinez, J. L., Jr, Barea-Rodriguez, E. J., & Derrick, B. E. (1998). Long-term potentiation, long-term depression, and learning. In J. L. Martinez, Jr, & R. P. Kesner (Eds.), *Neurobiology of learning and memory.* San Diego, CA: Academic Press.

Martinez, M., & Raul, E. (2000). Conducta sexual procesos psicologicos moduladores, en mujeres y hombres [Sexual behavior and modulating psychological processes in women and men]. *Archivos Hispanoamericanos de Sexologia, 6,* 133–152.

Martin-Soelch, C. (2009). Is depression associated with dysfunction of the central reward system? *Biochemical Society Transactions, 37* (Pt 1), 313–317.

Marlatt and Gordon (1985). *Relapse prevention: Maintenance strategies in the treatment of addictive behaviors.* Guildford Publications, Inc.

Marx, D. M., Stapel, D. A., & Muller, D. (2005). We can do it: The interplay of construal orientation and social comparisons under threat. *Journal of Personality and Social Psychology, 88,* 432–446.

Mascolo, M. E., & Li, J. (Eds.) (2004). *Culture and developing selves: Beyond dichotomization.* San Francisco, CA: Jossey-Bass.

Maslow, A. H. (1954). *Motivation and personality.* New York: Harper.

Mason, M. F., Tatkow, E. P., & Macrae, C. N. (2005). The look of love: Gaze shifts and person perception. *Psychological Science, 16,* 236–239.

Massion, A. O., Dyck, I. R., Shea, M. T., Phillips, K. A., Warshaw, M. G., & Keller, M. B. (2002). Personality disorders and time to remission in generalized anxiety disorder, social phobia and panic disorder. *Archives of General Psychiatry, 59,* 434–440.

Masten, A. S. (2001). Ordinary magic: Resilience processes in development. *American Psychologist, 56,* 227–238.

Masten, A. S., & Coatsworth, J. D. (1998). The development of competence in favorable and unfavorable environments: Lessons from research on successful children. *American Psychologist, 53,* 205–220.

Masterpasqua, F. (2009). Psychology and epigenetics. *Review of General Psychology, 13*(3), 194–201.

Masters, W. H., Johnson, V. E., & Kolodny, R. C. (1988). *Human sexuality* (3rd ed.). Boston, MA: Little, Brown.

Masters, W., & Johnson, V. (1966). *Human sexual response.* London: Churchill.

Mather G., & Smith, D. R. R. (2002). Blur discrimination and its relation to blur-mediated depth perception. *Perception, 31,* 1211–1219.

Matlin, M. W., & Stang, D. J. (1978). *The Pollyanna principle: Selectivity in language, memory, and thought.* Cambridge, MA: Schenkman.

Matsakis, Y., Lipshits, M., Gurfinkel, V. S., & Berthoz, A. (1993). Effects of prolonged weightlessness on mental rotation of three-dimensional objects. *Experimental Brain Research, 94,* 152–162.

Matsumoto, D. (1999). Culture and self: An empirical assessment of Markus and Kitayama's theory of independent and interdependent self-construals. *Asian Journal of Social Psychology, 2,* 289–310.

Matsumoto, D. (2001). Emotion in Asia: Linking theories and data around the world. (Introduction to the special section on emotion.) *Asian Journal of Social Psychology, 4* (2), 163–164.

Matsumoto, D., & Hull, P. (1994). Cognitive development and intelligence. In D. Matsumoto (Ed.), *People: Psychology from a cultural perspective.* Pacific Grove, CA: Brooks/Cole.

Matt, G. E., & Navarro, A. M. (1997). What meta-analyses have and have not taught us about psychotherapy effects: A review and future directions. *Clinical Psychology Review, 17,* 1–32.

Matthews, G., Roberts, R. D., & Zeidner, M. (2004). Seven myths about emotional intelligence. *Psychological Inquiry, 15,* 179–196.

Mattys, S. L. (2000). The perception of primary and secondary stress in English. *Perception & Psychophysics, 62,* 253–265.

Maurer, D., & Barrera, M. (1981). Infants' perception of natural and distorted arrangements of a schematic face. *Child Development, 52,* 196–202.

May, C. P., Hasher, L., & Foong, N. (2005). Implicit memory, age, and time of day: Paradoxical priming effects. *Psychological Science, 16,* 96–100.

May, J. R., & Sieb, G. E. (1987). Athletic injuries: Psychosocial factors in the onset, sequellae, rehabilitation, and prevention. In J. R. May & M. J. Asken (Eds.), *Sport psychology: The psychological health of the athlete.* New York: PMA Publishing.

May, R. (1961). The emergence of existential psychology. In R. May (Ed.), *Existential psychology.* New York: Random House.

Mayer, J. D., Salovey, P., & Caruso, D. R. (2004). Emotional intelligence: Theory, findings, and implications. *Psychological Inquiry, 15,* 197–215.

Mayer, R. E. (2000). Intelligence and education. In R. J. Sternberg (Ed.), *Handbook of intelligence.* New York: Cambridge University Press.

McAdams, D. P., & de St. Aubin, E. (Eds.) (1998). *Generativity and adult development: How and why we care for the next generation.* Washington, DC: American Psychological Association.

McAdams, S., & Drake, C. (2002). Auditory perception and cognition. In H. Pashler & S. Yantis (Eds.), *Steven's handbook of experimental psychology: Vol. 1. Sensation and perception* (3rd ed.). New York: Wiley.

McArdle, S., & Duda, J. K. (2002). Implications of the motivational climate in youth sports. In F. L. Smoll & R. E. Smith (Eds.), *Children and youth in sport: A biopsychosocial perspective.* Dubuque, IA: Kendall/Hunt.

McAuley, E. (1992). The role of efficacy cognitions in the prediction of exercise behavior in middle-aged adults. *Journal of Behavioral Medicine, 15,* 65–88.

McCann, U. D., Szabo, Z., Scheffel, U., Dannals, R. F., & Ricaurte, G. A. (1998). Positron emission tomographic evidence of toxic effect of MDMA ('Ecstasy') on brain serotonin neurons in human beings. *Lancet, 352*(9138), 1433–1437.

McCarley, R. W. (1998). Dreams: Disguise of forbidden wishes or transparent reflections of a distinct brastate? In R. M.

Bilder & F. F. LeFever (Eds.), *Neuroscience of the mind on the centennial of Freud's Project for a Scientific Psychology: Annals of the New York Academy of Sciences* (Vol. 843). New York: New York Academy of Sciences.

McCaul, K. D., & Malott, J. J. (1984). Distraction and coping with pain. *Psychological Bulletin, 95,* 516–533.

McClelland, D. C. (1989). *Human motivation.* New York: Cambridge University Press.

McClelland, D. C., Atkinson, J. W., Clark, R. A., & Lowell, E. L. (1953). *The achievement motive.* New York: Appleton-Century-Crofts.

McClure, E. B. (2000). A meta-analytic review of sex differences in facial expression processing and their development in infants, children, and adolescents. *Psychological Bulletin, 126,* 424–453.

McConnell, J. V. (1962). Memory transfer through cannibalism in planarians. *Journal of Neuropsychiatry, 3* (Suppl. 1), 542–548.

McCown, D., & Reibel, D. (2010) Mindfulness and mindfulness-based stress reduction. In D. A. Monti & B. D. Beitman (Eds.), *Integrative psychiatry.* New York: Oxford University Press.

McCracken, L. M. (1998). Learning to live with pain: Acceptance of pain predicts adjustment in persons with chronic pain. *Pain, 74,* 21–27.

McCrae, R. R., & Costa, P. T. (1990). *Personality in adulthood.* New York: Guilford Press.

McCrae, R. R., & Costa, P. T. (2003). *Personality in adulthood: A Five-Factor Theory perspective.* New York: Guilford Press.

McCrae, R. R., Kurtz, J. E., Yamagata, S., & Terracciano, A. (2011). Internal consistency, retest reliability, and their implications for personality scale validity. *Personality and Social Psychology Review, 15*(1), 28–50.

McCullough, M. E., Worthington, E. L., Jr, & Rachal, K. C. (1997). Interpersonal forgiving in close relationships. *Journal of Personality and Social Psychology, 73,* 321–336.

McDaniel, M. A., Einstein, G. O., Stout, A. C., & Morgan, Z. (2003). Aging and maintaining intentions over delays: Do it or lose it. *Psychology and Aging, 18,* 823–835.

McElroy, S. L., Kotwal, R., & Keck, P. E. (2006). Comorbidity of eating disorders with bipolar disorder and treatment implications. *Bipolar Disorders, 8,* 686–695.

McEvoy, P.M. & Saulsman, L.M. (2014). Imagery-enhanced cognitive behavioural group therapy for social anxiety disorder: A Pilot Study. *Behaviour research and trerapy, 55,* 1-6.

McEwen, B. S. (2001). *Coping with the environment: Neural and endocrine mechanisms.* New York: Oxford University Press.

McFarlane, A. C. (2010). The long-term costs of traumatic stress: Intertwined physical and psychological consequences. *World Psychiatry, 9,* 3–10.

McFarlane, J. (1975). Olfaction in the development of social preferences in the human neonate. In M. Hofer (Ed.), *Parent–infant interaction.* Amsterdam: Elsevier.

McGarrigle, J., & Donaldson, M. (1975). Conservation accidents. *Cognition, 3,* 341–350.

McGarthy, C., Turner, J. C., Hogg, M. A., Davidson, B., & Wetherell, M. S. (1992). Group polarization as conformity to the most prototypical group member. *British Journal of Social Psychology, 31,* 1–20.

McGaugh, J. L. (2004). The amygdala modulates the consolidation of memories of emotionally arousing experiences. *Annual Review of Neuroscience, 27,* 1–28.

McGaugh, J. L., & Roozendaal, B. (2002). Role of adrenal stress hormones in forming lasting memories in the brain. *Current Opinion in Neurobiology, 12* (2), 205–210.

McGregor, H. A., & Elliot, A. J. (2002). Achievement goals as predictors of achievement-relevant processes prior to task engagement. *Journal of Educational Psychology, 94,* 381–395.

McGuffin, P., Owen, M. J., & Gottesman, I. I. (Eds.) (2005). *Psychiatric genetics and genomics.* New York: Oxford University Press.

McIntosh, D. N., Silver, R. C., & Wortman, C. B. (1993). Religion's role in adjustment to a negative life event: Coping with the loss of a child. *Journal of Personality and Social Psychology, 65,* 812–821.

McIntyre, R. B., Paulson, R. M., & Lord, C. G. (2003). Alleviating women's mathematics stereotype threat through salience of group achievements. *Journal of Experimental Social Psychology, 39,* 83–90.

McKenna, M. C., Zevon, M. A., Corn, B., & Rounds, J. (1999). Psychological factors and the development of breast cancer: A metaanalysis. *Health Psychology, 18,* 520–531.

McKenna, P., & Oh, T. (2003). *Formal thought disorder in schizophrenia.* New York: Cambridge University Press.

McKenna, P. J. (2007). *Schizophrenia and related syndromes* (2nd ed.). London: Routledge.

McKey, R., Conndelli, L., Gansin, H., et al. (1985). *The impact of Head Start on children, families and communities (Final report of the Head Start Evaluation, Synthesis and Utilization Project).* Washington, DC: CSR, Inc.

McLeod, P. (1977). A dual task response modality effect: Support for multiprocessor models of attention. *Quarterly Journal of Experimental Psychology, 29,* 651–667.

McMillan, T. M., Robertson, I. H., & Wilson, B. A. (1999). Neurogenesis after brain injury: Implications for neurorehabilitation. *Neuropsychological Rehabilitation, 9,* 129–133.

McMurran, M., Duggan, C., Christopher, G., & Huband, N. (2007). The relationships between personality disorders and social problem solving in adults. *Personality and Individual Differences, 42*(1), 145–155.

McNally R. J. (1994). *Panic disorder: A critical analysis.* New York: Guilford Press.

McNulty, J. K., & Karney, B. R. (2004). Positive expectations in the early years of marriage: Should couples expect the best or brace for the worst? *Journal of Personality and Social Psychology, 86,* 729–743.

McWilliams, N. (2004). *Psychoanalytic psychotherapy: A practitioner's guide.* New York: Guilford Press.

Mead, G. H. (1934). *Mind, self, and society from the standpoint of a social behaviorist.* Oxford: Chicago Press.

Meaney, M. J., Mitchell, J. B., Aitken, D. H., & Bhatnagar, S. (Eds.) (1991). The effects of neonatal handling on the development of the adrenocortical response to stress: Implications for neuropathology and cognitive deficits in later life. *Psychoneuroendocrinology, 16*, 85–103.

Meehan, A. O., Moran, P. M., Elliot, J. M., Young, A. M. J., Joseph, M. H., & Green, R. A. (2002). A study of the effect of a single neurotoxic dose of 3,4-methylenedioxymethamphetamine (MDMA; 'ecstasy') on the subsequent long-term behaviour of rats in the plus maze and open field. *Psychopharmacology, 159*, 167–175.

Meddis, R., Pearson, A. J., & Langford, G. (1973). An extreme case of healthy insomnia. *Electroencephalography and Clinical Neurophysiology, 35*, 213–214.

Meehl, P. E. (1995). 'Is psychoanalysis one science, two sciences, or no science at all? A discourse among friendly antagonists': Comment. *Journal of the American Psychoanalytic Association, 43*, 1015–1023.

Meeus, W. H. J., & Raaijmakers, Q. A. W. (1986). Administrative obedience: Carrying out orders to use psychological-administrative violence. *European Journal of Social Psychology, 16*, 311–324.

Megargee, E. I. (1966). Undercontrolled and overcontrolled personality types in extreme antisocial aggression. *Psychological Monographs, 80* (Whole No. 611).

Mehnert, T., Krauss, H. H., Nadler, R., & Boyd, M. (1990). Correlates of life satisfaction in those with disabling conditions. *Rehabilitation Psychology, 35*, 3–17.

Meichenbaum, D. (1985). *Stress inoculation training.* New York: Pergamon Press.

Meins, E., Fernyhough, C., Fradley, E., & Tuckey, M. (2001). Rethinking maternal sensitivity: Mothers' comments on infants' mental processes predict security of attachment at 12 months. *Journal of Child Psychology and Psychiatry and Allied Disciplines, 42*, 637–648.

Meiser-Stedman, R., Shepperd, A., Glucksman, E., Dalgleish, T., Yule, W., & Smith., P. (2014). Thought control strategies and rumination in youth with acute stress disorder and posttraumatic stress disorder following single-event trauma. *Journal of Child and Adolescent Psychopharmacology, 24*(1), 47–51.

Meleski, M. E., & Damato, E. G. (2003). HIV exposure: Neonatal considerations. *Journal of Obstetric, Gynecologic, and Neonatal Nursing, 32*, 109–116.

Melhuish, E., Belsky, J., Anning, A., Ball, M., Barnes, J., Romaniuk, H., & Leyland, A. (2007). Variation in community intervention programmes and consequences for children and families: The example of Sure Start Local Programmes. *Journal of Child Psychology and Psychiatry, 48*(6), 543–551.

Meltzoff, A. N. (2002). Elements of a developmental theory of imitation. In A. N. Meltzoff, N. Andrew, & W. Prinz (Eds.), *The imitative mind: Development, evolution, and brain bases. Cambridge studies in cognitive perceptual development.* New York: Cambridge University Press.

Meltzoff, A. N., & Moore, M. K. (1977). Imitation of facial and manual gestures by human neonates. *Science, 198*, 75–78.

Meltzoff, A. N., & Moore, M. K. (1983). Newborn infants imitate adult facial gestures. *Child Development, 54*, 702–709.

Melzack, R. (1998). Pain and stress. Clues toward understanding chronic pain. In M. Sabourin et al. (Eds.), *Advances in psychological science.* Hove: Psychology Press/Erlbaum.

Melzack, R., & Wall, P. D. (1982). *The challenge of pain.* New York: Basic Books.

Mental Health Foundation Annual Review. (2011).

Menzies, R. G., & Clarke, J. C. (1995). The etiology of acrophobia and its relationship to severity and individual response patterns. *Behaviour Research and Therapy, 33*, 795–803.

Merrick, P. L., and Dattilio, F. M. (2006). Contemporary appeal of cognitive behaviour therapy. *New Zealand Journal of Psychology, 35*(3), 117–119.

Merrill, E. C., & Lookadoo, R. (2004). Selective search for conjunctively defined targets by – children and young adults. *Journal of Experimental Child Psychology, 89*, 72–90.

Mersch, P. P. A., Middendorp, H. M., Bouhuys, A. L., Beersma, D. G. M., & van den Hoofdakker, R. H. (1999). Seasonal affective disorder and latitude: A review of the literature. *Journal of Affective Disorders, 53*, 35–48.

Mesman, J., van IJzendoorn, M. H., & Bakermans-Kranenburg, M. J. (2009). The many faces of the Still-Face Paradigm: A review and meta-analysis. *Developmental Review, 29*(2), 120–162.

Mesquita, B., & Markus, H. R. (2005). Culture and emotion: Models of agency as sources of cultural variation in emotion. In A. S. R. Manstead, N. H. Frijda, A. H. Fischer, & K. Oatley (Eds.), *Feelings and Emotions: The Amsterdam Symposium.* New York: Cambridge University Press.

Mesquita, B., Frijda, N. H., & Scherer, K. R. (1997). Culture and emotion. In J. W. Berry et al. (Eds.), *Handbook of cross-cultural psychology: Vol. 2. Basic processes and human development* (2nd ed.). Boston, MA: Allyn & Bacon.

Methot, L. L., & Huitema, B. E. (1998). Effects of signal probability on individual differences in vigilance. *Human Factors, 40*, 78–90.

Meunier, D., Stamatakis, E. A., & Tyler, L. K. (2014). Age-related functional reorganization, structural changes, and preserved cognition. *Neurobiology of aging, 35*(1), 42–54.

Meyer, C. B., & Taylor, S. E. (1986). Adjustment to rape. *Journal of Personality and Social Psychology, 50*, 1226–1234.

Meyer, D. E., & Schvaneveldt, R. W. (1971). Facilitation in recognizing pairs of words: Evidence of a dependence between retrieval operations. *Journal of Experimental Psychology, 90*, 227–235.

Meyer, G. J., Finn, S. E., Eyde, L. D., Kay, G. G., Moreland, K. L., Dies, R. R., … Reed, G. M. (2001). Psychological testing and psychological assessment: A review of evidence and issues. *American Psychologist, 56*, 128–165.

Meyer, G. J., Hsiao, W. C., Viglione, D. J., Mihura, J. L., & Abraham, L. M. (2013). Rorschach scores in applied clinical practice: A survey of perceived validity by experienced clinicians. *Journal of Personality Assessment, 95*(4), 351–365.

Meyer, R. G. & Osborne, Y. H. (1987). *Case studies in abnormal behavior* (2nd ed.). Boston, MA: Allyn & Bacon.

Meyer, T. A., Svirsky, M. A., Kirk, K. I., & Miyamoto, R. T. (1998). Improvements in speech perception by children with profound prelingual hearing loss: Effects of device, communication mode, and chronological age. *Journal of Speech, Language, and Hearing Research, 41*, 846–858.

Mezulis, A. H., Abramson, L. Y., Hyde, J. S., & Hankin, B. L. (2004). Is there a universal positivity bias in attributions? A metaanalytic review of individual, developmental, and cultural differences in the self-serving attributional bias. *Psychological Bulletin, 130*, 711–747.

Mezulis, A. H., Hyde, J. S., & Abramson, L. Y. (2006). The developmental origins of cognitive vulnerability to depression: Temperament, parenting, and negative life events in childhood as contributors to negative cognitive style. *Developmental Psychology, 42*, 1012–1025.

Michaels, J. W., Blommel, J. M., Brocato, R. M., Linkous, R. A., & Rowe, J. S. (1982). Social facilitation and inhibition in a natural setting. *Replications in Social Psychology, 2*, 21–24.

Mickey, B. J., Zhou, Z., Heitzeg, M. M., Heinz, E., Hodgkinson, C. A., Hsu, D. T., …, Zubieta, J. K. (2011). Emotion processing, major depression and functional genetic variation of neuropeptide. *Archives of General Psychiatry, 82* (2), 158–166.

Middlemist, R., Knowles, E., & Matter, C. (1976). Personal space invasions in the lavatory: Suggestive evidence for arousal. *Journal of Personality and Social Psychology, 33*, 541–546.

Mignot, E. (1998). Genetic and familial aspects of narcolepsy. *Neurology, 50*, S16–S22.

Mihura, J. L., Meyer, G. J., Dumitrascu, N., & Bombel, G. (2013). The validity of individual Rorschach variables: Systematic reviews and meta-analyses of the comprehensive system. *Psychological bulletin, 139*(3), 548.

Miklosi, A., Kubinyi, E., Topal, J., Viranyi, Z. & Csanyi, V. (2003). A simple reason for a big difference: Wolves do not look back

at humans, but dogs do. *Current Biology, 13*, 763–766.

Mikolajczyk, R. T., Maxwell, A. E., El Ansari, W., Stock,C., Petkeviciene, J., & Guillen-Grima, F. (2010). Relationship between perceived body weight and body mass index based on self-reported height and weight among university students: a cross-sectional study in seven European countries. *BMC Public Health, 10*, 40.

Mikulincer, M., & Shaver, P. R. (2005). Attachment security, compassion, and altruism. *Current Directions in Psychological Science, 14*, 34–38.

Mikulincer, M., & Shaver, P. R. (2010). *Attachment in adulthood: Structure, dynamics and change.* New York: Guildford Press.

Miles, C., & Hardman, E. (1998). State-dependent memory produced by aerobic exercise. *Ergonomics, 41*, 20–28.

Miles, E., & Crisp, R. J. (2014). A meta-analytic test of the imagined contact hypothesis. *Group Processes & Intergroup Relations, 17*(1), 3–26.

Miles, H. L., Mitchell, R. W., & Harper, S. E. (1996). Simon says: The development of imitation in an enculturated orangutan. In A. E. Russon & K. A. Bard (Eds.), *Reaching into thought: The minds of the great apes.* Cambridge: Cambridge University Press.

Miles, J. H. (2011). Autism spectrum disorders: A genetics review. *Genetics in Medicine, 13*(4), 278–294.

Milgram, S. (1974). *Obedience to authority: An experimental view.* New York: Harper & Row.

Milgram, S. (1992). *The individual in a social world: Essays and experiments* (2nd ed.). New York: McGraw-Hill.

Miller, A. G. (2004). What can the Milgram obedience experiments tell us about the Holocaust? Generalizing from the social psychology laboratory. In A. G. Miller (Ed.), *The social psychology of good and evil.* New York: Guilford Press.

Miller, A. L., Carnesale, M. T., & Courtney, E. A. (2014). Dialectical behavior therapy. In *Handbook of borderline personality disorder in children and adolescents* (pp. 385–401). New York: Springer.

Miller, B. C., Fan, X., Christensen, M., Grotevant, H. D., & van Dulmen, M. (2000).

Comparisons of adopted and nonadopted adolescents in a large, nationally representative sample. *Child Development, 71*, 1458–1473.

Miller, F. P., Vandome, A. F., & McBrewster, J. (2011). *Post-traumatic amnesia.* Mauritius: Betascript Publishing.

Miller, G., Chen, E., & Cole, S. W. (2009). Health psychology: Developing biologically plausible models linking the social world and physical health. *Annual Review of Psychology, 60*, 501–524.

Miller, G. A. (1956). The magical number seven, plus or minus two: Some limits on our capacity for processing information. *Psychological Review, 63*, 81–97.

Miller, G. E., Chen, E., & Parker, K. J. (2011). Psychological stress in childhood and susceptibility to the chronic diseases of aging: Moving toward a model of behavioral and biological mechanisms. *Psychological Bulletin, 137*, 959–997.

Miller, J. G. (1984). Culture and the development of everyday social explanation. *Journal of Personality and Social Psychology, 46*, 961–978.

Miller, J. G., Bersoff, D. M., & Harwood, R. L. (1990). Perceptions of social responsibility in India and in the United States: Moral imperatives or personal decisions? *Journal of Personality and Social Psychology, 58*, 33–47.

Miller, K. F., & Stigler, J. F. (1987). Counting in Chinese: Cultural variation in a basic cognitive skill. *Cognitive Development, 2*, 279–305.

Miller, N. E. (1944). Experimental studies of conflict. In J. McV. Hunt (Ed.), *Personality and the behavior disorders* (Vol. 1). New York: Ronald Press.

Miller, N. E., & Dollard, J. (1941). *Social learning and imitation.* New Haven, CT: Yale University Press.

Miller, W. R. (1996). Motivational interviewing: Research, practice, and puzzles. *Addictive Behaviors, 21*, 835–842.

Miller, W. R., & Brown, S. A. (1997). Why psychologists should treat alcohol and drug problems. *American Psychologist, 52*, 1269–1279.

Miller, W. R., & Rollnick, S. (2002). *Motivational interviewing* (2nd ed.). New York: Guilford Press.

Milling, L. S. (2008). Recent developments in the study of hypnotic pain reduction: A new golden era of research? *Contemporary Hypnosis, 25* (3–4), 165–177.

Millon, T., Grossman, S., Millon, C., Meagher, S., & Ramnath, R. (2004). *Personality disorders in modern life* (2nd ed.). New York: Wiley.

Mills, J. N., Minors, D. S., & Waterhouse, J. M. (1974). The circadian rhythms of human subjects without timepieces or indication of the alternation of day and night. *Journal of Physiology, 240*(3), 567–594.

Milner, A. D., & Dijkerman, H. C. (2001). Direct and indirect visuals routes to action. In B. De Gelder, E. H. F. De Haan, & C. A. Heywood (Eds.), *Out of mind: Varieties of unconscious processes*. London: Oxford University Press.

Milner, B. (1965). Memory disturbances after bilateral hippocampal lesions. In P. Milner & S. Glickman (Eds.), *Cognitive processes and the brain*. Princeton, NJ: Van Nostrand.

Milton, J., & Wiseman, R. (1999). Does psi exist? Lack of replication of an anomalous process of information transfer. *Psychological Bulletin, 125*(4), 387–391.

Mineka, S., Watson, D., & Clark, L. A. (1998). Comorbidity of anxiety and unipolar mood disorder. *Annual Review of Psychology, 49*, 377–412.

Miniussi, C., Paulus, W., & Rossini, P. M. (Eds.) (2012). *Transcranial brain stimulation*. CRC Press.

Mischel, W. (1984). Convergences and challenges in the search for consistency. *American Psychologist, 39*, 351–364.

Mischel, W. (1999). Personality coherence and dispositions in a cognitive-affective personality system (CAPS) approach. In D. Cervone & Y. Shoda (Eds.), *The coherence of personality*. New York: Guilford Press.

Mischel, W., & Shoda, Y. (1999). Integrating dispositions and personality dynamics within a unified theory of personality: The cognitive-affective personality system (CAPS). In L. Pervin & O. John (Eds.), *Handbook of personality: Theory and research* (2nd ed.). New York: Guilford.

Mischel, W., Shoda, Y., & Mendoza-Denton, R. (2002). Situation-behavior profiles as a locus of consistency in personality. *Current Directions in Psychological Science, 11*, 50–54.

Mischel, W., Shoda, Y., & Smith, R. E. (2004). *Introduction to personality: Toward an integration* (7th ed.). New York: Wiley.

Mishne, J. (2002). *Multiculturalism and the therapeutic process*. New York: Guilford Press.

Mistlberger, R. E., Antle, M. C., Glass, J. D., & Miller, J. D. (2000). Behavioral and serotonergic regulation of circadian rhythms. *Biological Rhythm Research, 31*, 240–283.

Mitchell, K. J., & Zaragoza, M. S. (2001). Contextual overlap and eyewitness suggestibility. *Memory and Cognition, 29*, 616–626.

Miyamoto, S. F., & Dornbusch, S. M. (1956). A test of interactionist hypotheses of self-conception. *American Journal of Sociology, 61*, 399–403.

Moen, P., Kim, J. E., & Hofmeister, H. (2001). Couples' work/retirement transitions, gender, and marital quality. *Social Psychology Quarterly, 64*, 55–71.

Moghaddam, F. M. (2005). The Staircase to Terrorism: A psychological exploration. *American Psychologist, 60*(2), 161–169.

Mokdad, A. H., Marks, J. S., Stroup, D. F., & Gerberding, J. L. (2004). Actual causes of death in the United States, 2000. *Journal of American Medical Association, 291*, 1238–1245.

Molfese, D. L., & Molfese, V. J. (2002). *Developmental variations in learning: Applications to social, executive function, language, and reading skills*. Mahwah, NJ: Erlbaum.

Monk, T. H., Buysse, D. J., Welsh, D. K., Kennedy, K. S., & Rose, L. R. (2001). A sleep diary and questionnaire study of naturally short sleepers. *Journal of Sleep Research, 10*, 173–179.

Monk, T. H., Folkard, S., & Wedderburn, A. I. (1996). Maintaining safety and high performance on shiftwork. *Applied Ergonomics, 27*, 17–23.

Monroe, S. M., & Peterman, A. M. (1988). Life stress and psychopathology. In L. H. Cohen (Ed.), *Life events and psychological functioning: Theoretical and methodological issues*. Newbury Park, CA: Sage.

Monroe, S. M., & Simons, A. D. (1991). Diathesis-stress theories in the context of life stress research: Implications for the depressive disorders. *Psychological Bulletin, 110*, 406–425.

Montague, C. T., Farooqi, I. S., & Whitehead, J. P., Soos, M. A., Rau, H., Wareham, N. J., … O'Rahilly, S. (1997). Congenital leptin deficiency is associated with severe early-onset obesity in humans. *Nature, 387*, 903–908.

Montgomery, G. H., DuHamel, K. N., & Redd, W. H. (2000). A meta-analysis of hypnotically induced analgesia: How effective is hypnosis? *International Journal of Clinical and Experimental Hypnosis, 48*, 138–153.

Montgomery, H., Lipshitz, R., & Brehmer, B. (Eds.) (2005). *How professionals make decisions*. Mahwah, NJ: Erlbaum.

Moody, M. S. (1997). Changes in scores on the Mental Rotations Test during the menstrual cycle. *Perceptual and Motor Skills, 84*, 955–961.

Moon, C., & Fifer, W. P. (1990). Syllables as signals for 2-day-old infants. *Infant Behavior and Development, 13*, 377–390.

Moore, B. C. J. (2013). *An introduction to the psychology of hearing* (6th ed.). Oxford: Academic Press.

Moore, C., & Frye, D. (1986). The effect of the experimenter's intention on the child's understanding of conservation. *Cognition, 22*, 283–298.

Moore, K. A., Guzman, L., Hair, E., Lippman, L., & Garrett, S. (2004). Parent-teen relationships and interactions: Far more positive than not. *Childs Trends Research Brief*, publication no. 2004-25. Retrieved from http://www.childtrends.org/Files/Parent_TeenRB.pdf.

Moore, T. M., Scarpa, A., & Raine, A. (2002). A meta-analysis of serotonin metabolite 5 HIAA and antisocial behavior. *Aggressive Behavior, 28*, 299–316.

Moreland, J. L., Dansereau, D. F., & Chmielewski, T. L. (1997). Recall of descriptive information: The roles of presentation format, annotation strategy, and individual differences. *Contemporary Educational Psychology, 22*, 521–533.

Morey, L. C. (2003). *Essentials of PAI assessment*. Hoboken, NJ: Wiley.

Morford, J. P. (2003). Grammatical development in adolescent first-language learners. *Linguistics, 41*, 681–721.

Morgan, A. H. (1973). The heritability of hypnotic susceptibility in twins. *Journal of Abnormal Psychology, 82*, 55–61.

Morgan, W. (1997). *Physical activity and mental health*. Philadelphia, PA: Taylor & Francis.

Morgan, W. P., Horstman, D. H., Cymerman, A., & Stokes, J. (1983). Facilitation of physical performance by means of a cognitive strategy. *Cognitive Therapy and Research, 7*, 251–264.

Morgenthaler, J., Wiesner, C. D., Hinze, K., Abels, L. C., Prehn-Kristensen, A., & Göder, R. (2014). Selective REM-sleep deprivation does not diminish emotional memory consolidation in young healthy subjects. *PLoS ONE 9*(2): e89849. doi:10.1371/journal.pone.0089849.

Morrell, M. J., Dixen, J. M., Carter, C. S., & Davidson, J. M. (1984). The influence of age and cycling status on sexual arousability in women. *American Journal of Obstetrics and Gynecology, 148*, 66–71.

Morris, D. (1967). *The naked ape: A zoologist's study of the human animal*. New York: McGraw-Hill.

Morris, J., & Dolan, R. (2001). The amygdala and unconscious fear processing. In B. De Gelder, E. H. F. De Haan, & C. A. Heywood (Eds.), *Out of mind: Varieties of unconscious processes*. London: Oxford University Press.

Morris, R., & Becker, J. (2005). *Cognitive neuropsychology of Alzheimer's disease*. New York: Oxford University Press.

Morris, R. K. (1994). Lexical and message-level sentence context effects on fixation times in reading. *Journal of Experimental Psychology: Learning, Memory and Cognition, 20*(1), 92–103.

Morrison, C. M., & Ellis, A. W. (1995). Roles of word frequency and age of acquisition in word naming and lexical decision. *Journal of Experimental Psychology: Learning, Memory and Cognition, 21*, 116–133.

Morrison, C. M., & Ellis, A. W. (2000). Real age of acquisition effects in word naming. *British Journal of Psychology, 91*, 167–180.

Morrison, S. (2006). *Hypothalamus: Brainstem interactions in homeostasis*. New York: Springer.

Morton, J., & Johnson, M. H. (1991). Conspec and Conlern: A two-process theory of infant face recognition. *Psychological Review, 98*, 164–181.

Moscovici, S. (1976). *Social influence and social change*. London: Academic.

Moscovici, S. (1985). Social influence and conformity. In G. Lindzey & E. Aronson (Eds.), *Handbook of social psychology* (3rd ed.). New York: Random House.

Moscovici, S., & Zavalloni, M. (1969). The group as a polarizer of attitudes. *Journal of Personality and Social Psychology, 12*, 124–135.

Moscovici, S., Lage, E., & Naffrechoux, M. (1969). Influence of a consistent minority on the responses of a majority in a color perception task. *Sociometry, 32*, 365–380.

Moskowitz, G. B., & Balcetis, E. (2014). The conscious roots of selfless, unconscious goals. *Behavioral and Brain Sciences, 37*, 151.

Moss, C. S. (1972). *Recovery with aphasia*. Urbana, IL: University of Illinois Press.

Mostofsky, D. I. (Ed.) (2014). *The handbook of behavioural medicine*. Oxford: Wiley-Blackwell.

Mowrer, O. H. (1947). On the dual nature of learning: A reinterpretation of 'conditioning' and 'problem solving'. *Harvard Educational Review, 17*, 102–150.

Mroczek, D. K., & Kolarz, C. M. (1998). The effect of age on positive and negative affect: A developmental perspective on happiness. *Journal of Personality and Social Psychology, 75*(5), 1333–1349.

Mukamel, R., Ekstrom, A. D., Kaplan, J., Iacoboni, M., & Fried, I. (2010). Single-neuron responses in humans during execution and observation of actions. *Current Biology, 20* (8), 750–756.

Mullainathan, S., & Washington, E. (2009). Sticking with your vote: Cognitive dissonance and political attitudes. *American Economic Journal: Applied Economics, 1*, 86–111.

Muramoto, Y. (2003). An indirect enhancement in relationship among Japanese. *Journal of Cross-Cultural Psychology, 34*, 552–566.

Murdin, L. (2010). *Understanding transference: The power of patterns in the therapeutic relationship*. London: Macmillan.

Murphy, S. L. (2000). Deaths: Final data for 1998. *National Vital Statistics Reports* (NCHS), pp. 26, 73.

Murray, C. (1998). *Income, inequality, and IQ*. Washington, DC: American Enterprise Institute.

Murray, H. A. ([1943] 1971). *Thematic apperception test manual*. Cambridge, MA: Harvard University Press.

Murray, R., Jones, P., Susser, E., van Os, J., & Cannon, M. (2003). *The epidemiology of schizophrenia*. New York: Cambridge University Press.

Murray, S. L., Griffin, D. W., Rose, P., & Bellavia, G. (2006). For better or worse? Self-esteem and the contingencies of acceptance in marriage. *Personality and Social Psychology Bulletin, 7*, 866–880.

Musek, J. (2007). A general factor of personality; Evidence for the Big One in the five factor model. *Journal of Research in Personality, 41*, 1213–1233.

Myin-Germeys, I., van Os, J., Schwartz, J. E., Stone, A. A., & Delespaul, P. A. (2001). Emotional reactivity to daily life stress in psychosis. *Archives of General Psychiatry, 58*, 1137–1144.

N

Nadler, A., & Ben-Slushan, D. (1989). Forty years later: Long-term consequences of massive traumatization as manifested by holocaust survivors from the city and the Kibbutz. *Journal of Consulting and Clinical Psychology, 57*, 287–293.

Nakayama, K., & Tyler, C. W. (1981). Psychophysical isolation of movement sensitivity by removal of familiar position cues. *Vision Research, 21*, 427–433.

Narrow, W. E., Rae, D. S., Robins, L. N., & Regier, D. A. (2002). Revised prevalence based estimates of mental disorders in the United States: Using a clinical significance criterion to reconcile 2 surveys' estimates. *Archives of General Psychiatry, 59*, 115–123.

Nash, R. A., & Wade, K. A. (2009). Innocent but proven guilty: Eliciting internalized

false confessions using doctored-video evidence. *Applied Cognitive Psychology, 23*, 624–637.

Nathan, P. E. (1985). Aversion therapy in the treatment of alcoholism: Success and failure. *Annals of the New York Academy of Sciences, 443*, 357–364.

National Center for Health Statistics (2004). *Health and longevity in the United States.* Retrieved from http://www.cdc.gov.

National Center for Health Statistics (2006). *Health in America, 2006.* Hyattaville, MD: Author.

National Center on Addiction and Substance Abuse (2005). *National survey of American attitudes on substance abuse X: Teens and parents.* Retrived from http://www. casacolumbia.org/Absolutenm/articlefiles/Teen_Survey_Report_2005.pdf.

National Evaluation of Sure Start (NESS) (2004). The impact of sure start local programmes on child development and family functioning: A report on preliminary findings. Retrieved from http://www.ness.bbk.ac.uk.

National Evaluation of Sure Start (NESS) (2005). Early impacts of sure start local programmes on children and families. Retrieved from http://www.ness.bbk.ac.uk.

National Institute for Health and Clinical Excellence (NICE) (2003 updated 2009). *Guidance in the use of electroconvulsive therapy* (Technology Appraisal Guidance 59). London: NICE.

National Institute for Health and Clinical Excellence (NICE) (2004). *Depression: Management of depression in primary and secondary care.* London: NICE.

National Institute of Clinical Excellence National Clinical Practice Guideline (2006) *Obsessive compulsive disorder: Core interventions in the treatment of obsessive- compulsive disorder and body dysmorphic disorder.* [CG31]. Published by the British Psychological Society and the Royal College of Psychiatrists.

National Institute of Health (2002). *Alzheimer's disease: Unraveling the mystery.* NIH Publication 02-3782. Bethesda, MD. Retrieved from http://www.alzheimers.org/unraveling/unraveling.pdf.

National Sleep Foundation (2002). *'Sleep in America' poll.* Washington, DC: National Sleep Foundation.

Natsoulas, T. (1999). An ecological and phenomenological perspective on consciousness and perception: Contact with the world at the very heart of the being of consciousness. *Review of General Psychology, 3*, 224–245.

Navon, D., & Gopher, D. (1979). On the economy of the human processing system. *Psychological Review, 86*, 214–253.

NCTC (2012). *2011 report on terrorism.* National Counterterrorism Center: United States of America.

Needham, A., Barrett, T., & Peterman, K. (2002). A pick me up for infants' exploratory skills: Early simulated experiences reaching for objects using 'sticky' mittens enhances young infants' object exploration skills. *Infant Behavior and Development, 25*, 279–295.

Neisser, U. (1967). *Cognitive psychology.* New York: Appleton-Century-Crofts.

Neisser, U., & Harsch, N. (1993). Phantom flashbulbs: False recollections of hearing the news about Challenger. In E. Winograd & U. Neisser (Eds.), *Affect and accuracy in recall: Studies of 'flashbulb' memories.* New York: Cambridge University Press.

Neisser, U., Bouchard, T. J., Jr, Boykin, A. W., Brody, N., Ceci, S. J., Halpern, D. F., … Sternberg, R. J. (1998). Intelligence: Knowns and unknowns. In M. E. Hertzig & E. A. Farber (Eds.), *Annual progress in child psychiatry and child development: 1997.* Bristol, PA: Brunner/Mazel.

Nelson, C. A., & Luciana, M. (Eds.) (2001). *Handbook of developmental cognitive neuroscience.* Cambridge, MA: MIT Press.

Nelson, K. (1993). The psychological and social origins of autobiographical memory. *Psychological Science, 4*, 7–14.

Nes, R. B., Roysamb, E., Harris, J. R., Czajkowski, N., & Tambs, K. (2010). Mates and marriage matter: genetic and environmental influences on subjective wellbeing across marital status. *Twin Research and Human Genetics, 13*(4), 312–321.

Nesbitt, E. B. (1973). An escalator phobia overcome in one session of flooding in vivo. *Journal of Behavior Therapy and Experimental Psychiatry, 4*, 405–406.

Nettle, D. (2006). The evolution of personality in humans and other animals. *American Psychologist, 61*, 622–631.

Neumäker, K. J. (2000). Mortality rates and causes of death. *European Eating Disorders Review, 8*, 181–187.

Neumeister, A. (2004). Neurotransmitter depletion and seasonal affective disorder: Relevance for the biologic effects of light therapy. *Primary Psychiatry, 11*, 44–48.

Neumeister, A., Young, T., & Stastny, J. (2004). Implications of genetic research on the role of the serotonin in depression: Emphasis on the serotonin type 1-sub(A) receptor and the serotonin transporter. *Psychopharmacology, 174*, 512–524.

Neuschatz, J. S., Lampinen, J., Preston, E. L., Hawkins, E. R., & Toglia, M. P. (2002). The effect of memory schemata on memory and the phenomenological experience of naturalistic situations. *Applied Cognitive Psychology, 16*, 687–708.

Newcombe, N. S., & Uttal, D. H. (2006). Whorf versus Socrates, round 10. *Trends in Cognitive Sciences, 10*, 394–396.

Newell, A., & Simon, H. A. (1972). *Human problem solving.* Englewood Cliffs, NJ: Prentice Hall.

Newlin, D. B., & Thomson, J. B. (1997). Alcohol challenge with sons of alcoholics: A critical review and analysis. In G. A. Marlatt & G. R. VandenBos (Eds.), *Addictive behaviors: Readings on etiology, prevention and treatment.* Washington, DC: American Psychological Association.

Newman, D. L., Caspi, A., Moffitt, T. E., & Silva, P. A. (1997). Antecedents of adult interpersonal functioning: Effects of individual differences in age 3 temperament. *Developmental Psychology, 33*, 206–217.

Newman, D. L., Moffit, T. E., Caspi, A., Magdol, L., Silva, P. A., & Stanton, W. R. (1996). Psychiatric disorder in a birth cohort of young adults: Prevalence, comorbidity, clinical significance, and new case incidence from ages 11–21. *Journal of Consulting and Clinical Psychology, 64*, 552–562.

Nezami, E., & Butcher, J. N. (2000). Objective personality assessment. In G. Goldstein & M. Hersen (Eds.), *Handbook of psychological assessment* (3rd ed.). New York: Elsevier.

Nezlek, J. B., Hampton, C. P., & Shean, G. (2000). Clinical depression and day-to-day

social interaction in a community sample. *Journal of Abnormal Psychology, 109*, 11–19.

Nezu, A. M., Nezu, C. M., & D'Zurilla, T. (2000). Problem-solving skills training. In G. Fink (Ed.), *Encyclopedia of stress*. San Diego, CA: Academic Press.

Ng, I. C. L., & Tseng, L. M. (2008). Learning to be sociable: The evolution of homo economicus. *American Journal of Economics and Sociology, 67*, 265–286.

NICHD Early Child Care Research Network (2001a). Child care and family predictors of preschool attachment and stability from infancy. *Developmental Psychology, 37*, 847–862.

NICHD Early Child Care Research Network (2001b). Child care and children's peer interaction at 24 and 36 months: The NICHD Study of Early Child Care. *Child Development, 72*, 1478–1500.

NICHD Early Child Care Research Network (2002). Early child care and children's development prior to school entry: Results from the NICHD Study of Early Child Care.

Nicholls, J. (1989). *The competitive ethos and democratic education*. Cambridge, MA: Harvard University Press.

Nichols, C. D., & Sanders-Bush, E. (2002). A single dose of lysergic acid diethylamide influences gene expression patterns within the mammalian brain. *Neuropsychopharmacology, 26*, 634–642.

Nichols, M. P. (2009). *Family therapy concepts and methods* (9th ed.). Harlow: Prentice Hall.

Nichols, P. L. (1984). Familial mental retardation. *Behavior Genetics, 14*, 161–170.

Nickerson, R. S., & Adams, M. J. (1979). Long-term memory for a common object. *Cognitive Psychology, 11*, 287–307.

Nicks, S. D., Korn, J. H., & Mainieri, T. (1997). The rise and fall of deception in social psychology and personality research, 1921 to 1994. *Ethics and Behavior, 7*(1), 69–77.

Nicolson, P., & Ussher, J. (Eds.). (2013). *Gender issues in clinical psychology*. London: Routledge.

Niedenthal, P. M. (2007). Embodying emotion. *Science, 316*, 1002–1005.

Niedenthal, P. M., Winkielman, P., Mondillon, L., & Vermeulen, N. (2009). Embodiment of emotion concepts. *Journal of Personality and Social Psychology, 96*(6), 1120–1136.

Nigg, J. T., Lohr, N. E., Westen, D., & Gold, L. J. (1992). Malevolent object representation in borderline personality disorder and major depression. *Journal of Abnormal Psychology, 101*, 61–67.

Nisbett, R. E. (2003). *The geography of thought: How Asians and Westerners think differently ... and why*. New York: Free Press.

Nisbett, R. E., & Wilson, T. D. (1977). The halo effect: Evidence for unconscious alteration of judgments. *Journal of Personality and Social Psychology, 35*, 250–256.

Nisbett, R. E., Peng, K., Choi, I., & Norenzayan, A. (2001). Culture and systems of thought: Holistic versus analytic cognition. *Psychological Review, 108*, 291–310.

Nishino, S., Mignot, E., & Dement, W. C. (2001). Sedative hypnotics. In A. F. Schatzberg & C. B. Nemeroff (Eds.), *Essentials of clinical psychopharmacology*. Washington, DC: American Psychiatric Association.

Noar, S. M. (2006). A 10-year retrospective of research in health mass media campaigns: Where do we go from here? *Journal of Health Communication, 11*, 21–42.

Noback, C. R., Strominger, N. L., & Ruggiero, D. A. (Eds.) (2005). *The human nervous system: Structure and function*. New York: Humana Press.

Noble, E. P. (1998). The D2 dopamine receptor gene: A review of association studies in alcoholism and phenotypes. *Alcohol, 16*, 33–45.

Noë, A. (2004) *Action in perception*. Cambridge, MA: MIT Press.

Noice, T., & Noice, H. (2002a). The expertise of professional actors: A review of recent research. *High Ability Studies, 13*, 7–20.

Noice, T., & Noice, H. (2002b). Very long-term recall and recognition of well-learned material. *Applied Cognitive Psychology, 16*, 259–272.

Nolen-Hoeksema, S. (1990). *Sex differences in depression*. Stanford, CA: Stanford University Press.

Nolte, J. (2002). *The human brain: An introduction to its functional anatomy*. London: Elsevier Science Health Science.

Noor, M. Z. H., Ismail, I., & Saaid, M. F. (2009). Signal processing and its applications. *CSPA 5th International Colloquium*, 247–249.

Noonan, J. P., Coop, G., Kudaravalli, S., Smith, D., Krause, J., Alessi, J., ... Rubin, E. M. (2006). Sequencing and analysis of Neanderthal genomic DNA. *Science, 314*, 1113–1118.

Normann, R. A., Maynard, E. M., Guillory, K. S., & Warren, D. J. (1996). Cortical implants for the blind. *IEEE Spectrum, 33*, 54–59.

Normann, R. A., Maynard, E. M., Rousche, P. J., & Warren, D. J. (1999). A neural interface for a cortical vision prosthesis. *Vision Research, 39*, 2577–2587.

Norris, J. (1994). Alcohol and female sexuality: A look at expectancies and risks. *Alcohol Health and Research World, 18*, 197–201.

Nosek, B. A., Hawkins, C. B., & Frazier, R. S. (2011). Implicit social cognition: From measures to mechanisms. *Trends in Cognitive Sciences, 15*, 152–159.

Nossal, C. J. V., & Hall, E. (1995). Choices following antigen entry: Antibody formation or immunologic tolerance? *Annual Review of Immunology, 13*, 171–204.

Nourkova, V., Bernstein, D. M., & Loftus, E. F. (2004). Altering traumatic memory. *Cognition & Emotion, 18*, 575–585.

Nowak, M. A., Tarnita, C. E., & Wilson, E. O. (2010). The evolution of eusociality. *Nature, 466*(7310), 1057–1062.

O

O'Connor, D. B., Archer, J., Hair, W. M., & Wu, F. C. W. (2002). Exogenous testosterone, aggression, and mood in eugonadal and hypogonadal men. *Physiology and Behavior, 75*, 557–566.

O'Connor, S. C., & Rosenblood, L. K. (1996). Affiliation motivation in everyday experience: A theoretical comparison.

Journal of Personality and Social Psychology, 70, 513–522.

O'Connor, P. J. (2006). Improving medication adherence: Challenges for physicians, payers, and policy makers. *Archives of Internal Medicine, 166*, 1802–1804.

O'Craven, K. M., Downing, P. E., & Kanwisher, N. (1999). fMRI evidence for objects as the units of attentional selection. *Nature, 401*, 584–587.

O'Keefe, D. J. (1990). *Persuasion: Theory and research.* Newbury Park, CA: Sage.

O'Leary, A., & The National Institute of Mental Health Multisite HIV Prevention Trial Group (2001). Social-cognitive theory mediators of behavior change in the National Institute of Mental Health Multisite HIV Prevention Trial. *Health Psychology, 20*, 369–376.

Oades, R. D., Roepcke, B., & Schepker, R. (1996). A test of conditioned blocking and its development in childhood and adolescence: Relationship to personality and monoamine metabolism. *Developmental Neuropsychology, 12*, 207–230.

Oakes, P. J., Haslam, S. A., & Turner, J. C. (Eds.) (1994). *Stereotyping and social reality.* Malden, MA: Blackwell.

Oakley, D. A., & Halligan, P. W. (2009). Hypnotic suggestion and cognitive neuroscience. *Trends in Cognitive Science, 13*(6), 264–270.

Oaksford, M. R., & Chater, N. (1994). A rational analysis of the selection task as optimal data selection. *Psychological Review, 101*, 608–631.

Oberman, L. M., Hubbard, E. M., McCleery, J. P., Altschuler, E. L., Ramachandran, V. S., & Pineda, J. A. (2005). EEG evidence for mirror neuron dysfunction in autism. *Cognitive Brain Research, 24*, 190–198.

Ockene, J. K., Emmons, K. M., Mermelstein, R. J., Perkins, K. A., Bonollo, D. S., Voorhees, C. C., & Hollis, J. F. (2000). Relapse and maintenance issues for smoking cessation. *Health Psychology, 19*, 17–31.

Office for National Statistics (2011). Retrieved on 23 October 2014 from http://www.ons.gov.uk/ons/index.html.

Office for National Statistics (2014). Measuring national well being: European comparisons, available from http://www.ons.gov.uk/ons/dcp171766_363811.pdf

Ohayon, M. M., & Lemoine, P. (2004). Sleep and insomnia markers in the general population. *Encephale, 30*, 135–140.

Ohayon, M. M., Guilleminault, C., & Priest, R. G. (1999). Night terrors, sleepwalking, and confusional arousals in the general population: Their frequency and relationship to other sleep and mental disorders. *Journal of Clinical Psychiatry, 60*, 268–276.

Öhman, A., & Mineka, S. (2001). Fears, phobias, and preparedness: Toward an evolved module of fear and fear learning. *Psychological Review, 108*, 483–522.

Öhman, A., & Soares, J. J. F. (1998). Emotional conditioning to masked stimuli: Expectancies for aversive outcomes following nonrecognized fear-relevant stimuli. *Journal of Experimental Psychology: General, 127*, 69–82.

Öhman, A., & Wiens, S. (2005). The concept of an evolved fear. In A. S. R. Manstead, N. H. Frijda, A. H. Fischer, & K. Oatley (Eds.), *Feelings and emotions: The Amsterdam Symposium.* New York: Cambridge University Press.

Okado, Y., & Stark, C. E. L. (2005). Neural activity during encoding predicts false memories created by misinformation. *Learning and Memory, 12*, 3–11.

Olds, J. (1958). Self-stimulation of the brain. *Science, 127*, 315–324.

Olds, J., & Milner, P. (1954). Positive reinforcement produced by electrical stimulation of septal area and other regions of rat brain. *Journal of Comparative and Physiological Psychology, 47*(6), 419.

Oleson, T. (2002). Auriculotherapy stimulation for neuro-rehabilitation. *NeuroRehabilitation, 17*, 49–62.

Ollendick, T. H., Davis III, T. E., & Sirbu, C. (2009). Specific phobias. In D. McKay & E. Storch (Eds.), *Cognitive behavior therapy for children: Treating complex and refractory cases.* New York: Springer.

Olness, K., & Ader, R. (1992). Conditioning as an adjunct in the pharmacotherapy of lupus erythematosus. *Journal of Developmental and Behavioral Pediatrics, 13*, 124–125.

Olsson, A., & Phelps, E. A. (2004). Learned fear of 'unseen' faces after Pavlovian, observational, and instructed fear. *Psychological Science, 15*, 822–828.

Olweus, D. (2004). Bullying at school. Prevalence estimation, a useful evaluation design, and a new national initiative in Norway. *Association for Child Psychology and Psychiatry Occasional Papers, 23*, 5–17.

Omarzu, J. (2000). A disclosure decision model: Determining how and when individuals will self-disclose. *Personality and Social Psychology Review, 4*(2), 174–185.

Onishi, K. H., & Baillargeon, R. (2005). Do 15-month-old infants understand false beliefs? *Science, 308*, 255–258.

Orbuch, T. L., House, J. S., Mero, R. P., & Webster, P. S. (1996). Marital quality over the life course. *Social Psychology Quarterly, 59*, 162–171.

Organization for Economic Development (2014). Retrieved from http://www.oecd.org/unitedkingdom/.

Orne, M. T. (1959). The nature of hypnosis: Artifact and essence. *Journal of Abnormal and Social Psychology, 58*, 277–299.

Orne, M. T. (1962). On the social psychology of the psychological experiment: With particular reference to demand characteristics and their implications. *American Psychologist, 17*, 776–783.

Orne, M. T., & Evans, F. J. (1965). Social control in the psychological experiment: Antisocial behavior and hypnosis. *Journal of Personality and Social Psychology, 1*, 189–200.

Orth, U., Robins, R. W., Trzesniewski, K. H., Maes, J., & Schmitt, M. (2009). Low self-esteem is a risk factor for depressive symptoms from young adult to old age. *Journal of Abnormal Psychology, 118*(3), 472–478.

Ortiz, J., & Raine, A. (2004). Heart rate level and antisocial behavior in children and adolescents: A meta-analysis. *Journal of the American Academy of Child & Adolescent Psychiatry, 43*, 154–162.

Osgood, C. E. (1969). Introduction. In J. G. Snider & C. E. Osgood (Eds.), *Semantic differential technique.* Chicago, IL: Aldine.

Ost, J., Granhag, P. A., Udell, J., & Roos af Hjelmsäter, E. (2008). Familiarity breeds distortion: The effects of media exposure on false reports concerning media coverage of the terrorist attacks in London on 7 July 2005. *Memory, 16*, 76–85.

Ost, J., Vrij, A., Costall, A., & Bull, R. (2002). Crashing memories and reality monitoring: Distinguishing between perceptions, imaginations and false memories. *Applied Cognitive Psychology, 16*, 125–134.

Ostatnikova, D., Celec, P., Putz, Z., Hodosy, J., Schmidt, F., Laznibatova, J., & Kudela, M. (2007). Intelligence and salivary testosterone levels in prepubertal children. *Neuropsychologia, 45*(7), 1378–1385.

Ostir, G. V., Markides, K. S., Peek, M. K., & Goodwin, J. S. (2001). The association between emotional well-being and the incidence of stroke in older adults. *Psychosomatic Medicine, 63*, 210–215.

Ostrom, T. M., & Sedikides, C. (1992). Out-group homogeneity effects in natural and minimal groups. *Psychological Bulletin, 112*, 536–552.

Ouellette, J. A., & Wood, W. (1998). Habit and intention in everyday life: The multiple processes by which past behavior predicts future behavior. *Psychological Bulletin, 124*, 54–74.

Ouyang, M., Hellman, K., Abel, T., & Thomas, S. A. (2004). Adrenergic signaling plays a critical role in the maintenance of waking and in the regulation of REM sleep. *Journal of Neurophysiology, 92*, 2071–2082.

Owen, P. R., & Laurel-Seller, E. (2000). Weight and shape ideals: Thin is dangerously in. *Journal of Applied Social Psychology, 30*, 979–990.

Oyserman, D., Coon, H. M., & Kemmelmeier, M. (2002). Rethinking individualism and collectivism: Evaluation of theoretical assumptions and meta-analyses. *Psychological Bulletin, 128*, 3–72.

Ozer, D. J., & Benet-Martinez, V. (2006). Personality and the prediction of consequential outcomes. *Annual Review Psychology, 57*, 401–421.

P

Paap, K.R. & Greenberg, G.Z.I. (2013). There is no coherent evidence for a bilingual advantage in executive processing. *Cognitive Psychology, 66*(2), 232–258.

Paffenbarger, R. S., Jr, Hyde, R. T., Wing, A. L., & Hsieh, C. C. (1986). Physical activity, all-cause mortality, and longevity of college alumni. *New England Journal of Medicine, 314*, 605–613.

Paivio, A. (1969). Mental imagery is associative learning and memory. *Psychological Review, 76*, 241–263.

Paivio, A., Khan, M., & Begg, I. (2000). Concreteness of relational effects on recall of adjective noun pairs. *Canadian Journal of Experimental Psychology, 54*, 149–160.

Palfai, T., & Jankiewicz, H. (1991). *Drugs and human behavior*. Dubuque, IA: Wm. C. Brown.

Palincsar, A. S., & Brown, A. L. (1984). Reciprocal teaching of comprehension-fostering and monitoring activities. *Cognition and Instruction, 1*, 117–175.

Palmer, J. (2003). ESP in the Ganzfeld: Analysis of a debate. In J. E. Alcock, J. E. Burns, & A. Freeman (Eds.), *PSI wars: Getting to grips with the paranormal*. Charlottesville, VA: Imprint Academic.

Palmer, J. A., & Palmer, L. K. (Eds.) (2002). *Evolutionary psychology: The ultimate origins of human behavior* (Vol. 15). Needham Heights, MA: Allyn & Bacon.

Palmer, S. E. (2002). Perceptual organization in vision. In H. Pashler & S. Yantis (Eds.), *Steven's handbook of experimental psychology: Vol. 1. Sensation and perception* (3rd ed.). New York: Wiley.

Palmere, M., Benton, S. L., Glover, J. A., & Ronning, R. (1983). Elaboration and recall of main ideas in prose. *Journal of Education Psychology, 75*, 898–907.

Panagopoulou, E., Maes, S., Rime, B., & Montgomery, A. (2006). Social sharing of emotion in anticipation of cardiac surgery – effects on preoperative distress. *Journal of Health Psychology, 11*, 809–820.

Panksepp, J. (2005). Basic affects and the instinctual emotion system of the brain: The primordial sources of sadness, joy and seeking. In A. S. R. Manstead, N. H. Frijda, A. H. Fischer, & K. Oatley (Eds.), *Feelings and emotions: The Amsterdam Symposium*. New York: Cambridge University Press.

Papadopoulos, F. C., Ekbom, A., Brandt, L., & Ekselius, L. (2009). Excess mortality, causes of death and prognostic factors in anorexia nervosa. *British Journal of Psychiatry, 194*(1), 10–17.

Papanicolaou, A. C. (1989). *Emotion: A reconsideration of the somatic theory*. New York: Gordon & Breach.

Papanicolaou, A. C. (1998). *Fundamentals of functional brain imaging: A guide to the methods and their applications to psychology and behavioral neuroscience*. Lisse: Swets & Zeitlinger.

Papanicolaou, A. C. (2007). What aspects of experience can functional neuroimaging be expected to reveal? *International Journal of Psychophysiology, 64*(1), 101–105.

Papies, E. K., & Hamstra, P. (2010). Goal priming and eating behavior: Enhancing self-regulation by environmental cues. *Health Psychology, 29*(4), 384–388.

Pappagallo, M. (2005). *The neurological basis of pain*. New York: McGraw-Hill.

Parati, G., Antonicelli, R., Guazzarotti, F., Paciaroni, E., & Mancia, G. (2001). Cardiovascular effects of an earthquake: Direct evidence by ambulatory blood pressure monitoring. *Hypertension, 38*, 1093–1095.

Parchman, S. W., Ellis, J. A., Christinaz, D., & Vogel, M. (2000). An evaluation of three computer-based instructional strategies in basic electricity and electronics training. *Military Psychology, 12*, 73–87.

Parent, M. B., Darling, J. N. & Henderson, Y. O. (2014). Remembering to eat: hippocampal regulation of meal onset. *American Journal of Physiology – Regulatory Integrative and Comparative Physiology, 306* (10), 701–713.

Paris, J. (1993). *Borderline personality disorder*. Washington, DC: American Psychiatric Press.

Park, C. L. (2010). Making sense of the meaning literature: An integrative review of meaning making and its effects on adjustment to stressful life events. *Psychological Bulletin, 136*, 257–301.

Park, C. L., Armeli, S., & Tennen, H. (2004). Appraisal-coping goodness of fit: A daily internet study. *Personality and Social Psychology Bulletin, 30*, 558–569.

Park, D. C., & Gutchess, A. H. (2005). Long-term memory and aging: A cognitive neuroscience perspective. In R. Cabeza, L. Nyberg, & D. Park (Eds.), *Cognitive neuroscience of aging: Linking cognitive and cerebral aging*. London: Oxford University Press.

Park, D. C., Smith, A. D., & Cavanaugh, J. C. (1990). Metamemories of memory researchers. *Memory and Cognition, 18*, 321–327.

Parke, R. D., & Gauvain, M. (2009). *Child psychology: A contemporary viewpoint* (7th ed.). New York: McGraw-Hill.

Parker, A. (2000). A review of the ganzfeld work at Gothenburg University. *Journal of the Society for Psychical Research, 64*, 1–15.

Parker, C. R., Bolling, M. Y., & Kohlenberg, R. J. (1998). Operant theory of personality. In D. F. Barone, M. Hersen, & V. B. Van Hasselt (Eds.), *Advanced personality*. New York: Plenum Press.

Parkin, A.J. (1996) *Explorations in Cognitive Neuropsychology*, Hove, UK: Psychology Press.

Parkinson, A. J., Parkinson, W. S., Tyler, R. S., Lowder, M. W., & Gantz, B. J. (1998). Speech perception performance in experienced cochlear-implant patients receiving the SPEAK processing strategy in the Nucleus Spectra-22 cochlear implant. *Journal of Speech, Language, and Hearing Research, 41*, 1073–1087.

Parrott, A. C. (2001). Human psychopharmacology of Ecstasy (MDMA): A review of 15 years of empirical research. *Human Psychopharmacology: Clinical and Experimental, 16*, 557–577.

Pascalis, O., & de Haan, M. (2002). Is face processing species-specific during the first year of life? *Science, 14*, 199–209.

Pascalis, O., de Haan, M., & Nelson, C. A. (2003). Is face processing species-specific during the first year of life? *Science, 296*, 1321–1323.

Pascalis, O., Scott, L. S., Kelly, D. J., Shannon, R. W., Nicholson, E., Coleman, M., & Nelson, C. A. (2005). Plasticity of face processing in infancy. *Proceedings of the National Academy of Sciences, USA, 102*, 5297–5300.

Pascual-Leone, A., Amedi, A., Fregni, F., & Merabet, L. B. (2005). The plastic human brain cortex. *Annual Review of Neuroscience, 28*, 377–401.

Pashler, H., & Yantis, S. (Eds.) (2002). *Stevens' handbook of experimental psychology, Volume 1: Sensation and perception* (3rd ed.). New York: Wiley-VCH.

Patel, G. & Fancher, T. (2013). Generalized anxiety disorder. *Annals of Internal Medicine, 159*(11), 1–12.

Patterson, C. (1998). *Evolution* (2nd ed.). London: Natural History Museum.

Patterson, D. R. (2004). Treating pain with hypnosis. *Current Directions in Psychological Science, 13*, 252–255.

Patterson, G. R., Littman, R. A., & Bricker, W. (1967). Assertive behavior in children: A step toward a theory of aggression. *Monographs of the Society for Research in Child Development, 32* (Whole No. 5).

Paul, G. L., & Lentz, R. J. (1977). *Psychosocial treatment of chronic mental patients: Milieu versus social learning programs*. Cambridge, MA: Harvard University Press.

Paul, R. (2009). Parents ask: Am I risking autism if I vaccinate my children? *Journal of Autism and Developmental Disorders, 39*(6), 962–963.

Paulson, T. (2004, December 14). Thought powers computer. *Seattle Post-Intelligencer*, p. A15.

Paunonen, S. V. (2003). Big Five factors of personality and replicated predictions of behavior. *Journal of Personality and Social Psychology, 84*, 411–424.

Pavlov, I. P. (1928). *Lectures on conditioned reflexes: Twenty-five years of objective study of the higher nervous activity (behaviour) of animals* (Trans. W. H. Gantt). New York: International Publishers. (Original work published 1923.)

Payne, B. K., Krosnick, J. A., Pasek, J., Lelkes, Y., Akhtar, O., & Tompson, T. (2010). Implicit and explicit prejudice in the 2008 American presidential election. *Journal of Experimental Social Psychology, 46*, 367–374.

Pearce, J. M., & Hall, G. (1980). A model for Pavlovian learning: Variations in the effectiveness of conditioned but not of unconditioned stimuli. *Psychological Review, 87*, 532–552.

Pearlin, L. I., & Schooler, C. (1978). The structure of coping. *Journal of Health and Social Behavior, 19*, 2–21.

Pearsall, M. J., Christian, M. S., & Ellis, A. P. J. (2010). Motivating interdependent teams: Individual rewards, shared rewards, or something in between? *Journal of Applied Psychology, 95*, 183–191.

Pedersen, W. C., Miller, L. C., Putcha-Bhagavatula, A., & Yang, A. (2002). Evolved gender differences in the number of partners desired? The long and short of it. *Psychological Science, 13*(2), 157–161.

Pedrotti, F. J., & Pedrotti, L. S. (1992). *Introduction to optics* (2nd ed.). Harlow: Prentice Hall.

Peleg, P., Ben-Zion, I. Z., Peleg, A., Gheber, L., Kotler, M., Weizman, Z., … Shvartzman, P. (2004). 'Bread madness' revisited; Screening for specific celiac antibodies among schizophrenia patients. *European Psychiatry, 19*(5), 311–314.

Pelletier, D. L., & Frongillo, E. A. (2003). Changes in child survival are strongly associated with changes in malnutrition in developing countries. *Journal of Nutrition, 133*, 107–119.

Pellino, T. A., & Ward, S. E. (1998). Perceived control mediates the relationship between pain severity and patient satisfaction. *Journal of Pain and Symptom Management, 15*, 110–116.

Peñate Castro, W., Roca Sáncheza, M. J., Pitti González, C. T., Bethencourt, J. M., de la Fuente Portero, J. A., & Marco, R. G. (2014). Cognitive-behavioral treatment and antidepressants combined with virtual reality exposure for patients with chronic agoraphobia. *International Journal of Clinical Health & Psychology, 14*(1).

Pendlebury, S. T. (2007). *Neurological case histories*. New York: Oxford University Press.

Penfield, W., & Jasper, H. (1954). *Epilepsy and the functional anatomy of the human brain*. Boston, MA: Little, Brown.

Pennebaker, J. W. (1995). *Emotion, disclosure and health*. Washington, DC: American Psychological Association.

Pennebaker, J. W. (1997). *Opening up: The healing power of expressing emotions*. New York: Guilford Press.

Penton-Voak, B., & Perrott, D. I. (2000). Consistency and individual differences in facial attractiveness judgements: An evolutionary perspective. *Social Research*, *67*, 219–244.

Peplau, L. A., Garnets, L. D., Spalding, L. R., Conley, T. D., & Veniegas, R. C. (1998). A critique of Bem's 'Exotic Becomes Erotic' theory of sexual orientation. *Psychological Review*, *105*, 387–394.

Pepperberg, I. M. (1987a). Evidence for conceptual quantitative abilities in the African grey parrot: Labelling of cardinal sets. *Ethology*, *75*, 37–61.

Pepperberg, I. M. (1987b) Interspecies communication: A tool for assessing conceptual abilities in the African grey parrot (Psittacus erithacus). In G. Greenberg & E. Tobach (Eds.), *Language, cognition consciousness: Integrative levels*. Hillsdale: Erlbaum.

Pepperberg, I. M. (1999). *The Alex studies: Cognitive and communicative abilities of grey parrots*. Cambridge,MA: Harvard University Press.

Pepperbeg, I.M. (2012). Numerical abilities of grey parrots: Comparisons with apes and children. *The Japanese Journal of Animal Psychology*, *62*(1), 27–39.

Perälä, J., Suvisaari, J., Saarni, S. I., Kuoppasalmi, K., Isometsä, E., Pirkola, S., … Lönnqvist, J. (2007). Lifetime prevalence of psychotic and bipolar I disorders in a general population. *Archives of General Psychiatry*, *64*, 19–28.

Perani, D., Paulesu, E., Galles, N. S., Dupoux, E., & Dehaene, S. (1998). The bilingual brain: Proficiency and age of acquisition of the second language. *Brain*, *121*, 1841–1852.

Perdue, C. W., Dovidio, J. F., Gurtman, M. B., & Tyler, R. B. (1990). Us and them: Social categorization and the process of intergroup bias. *Journal of Personality and Social Psychology*, *59*, 475–486.

Perner, J., & Ruffman, T. (2005). Infants' insight into the mind: How deep? *Science*, *308*, 214–216.

Perret-Clermont, A. N. (1980). *Social interaction and cognitive development in children*. London: Academic Press.

Perrett, D. I., Lee, K. J., Penton-Voak, I., Rowland, D., Yoshikawa, S., Burt, D. M., … Akamatsu, S. (1998). Effects of sexual dimorphism on facial attractiveness. *Nature*, *394*, 884–887.

Perrett, D. I., May, K. A., & Yoshikawa, S. (1994). Facial shape and judgments of female attractiveness. *Nature*, *368*(6468), 239–242.

Perrin, A. J. (2005). National threat and political culture: Authoritarianism, antiauthoritarianism, and the September 11 attacks. *Political Psychology*, *26*(2), 167–194.

Persson, I., Granath, F., Askling, J., Ludvigsson, J. F., Olsson, T., & Feltelius, N. (2014). Risks of neurological and immune-related diseases, including narcolepsy, after vaccination with Pandemrix: A population- and registry-based cohort study with over 2 years of follow-up. *Journal of Internal Medicine*, *275*(2), *172–190*.

Pert, C. B. (1986). The wisdom of the receptors: Neuropeptides, the emotions, and bodymind. *Advances*, *3*, 8–16.

Pert, C. B. (1997). *Molecules of emotion: Why you feel the way you feel*. New York: Simon & Schuster.

Pervin, L. A., Cervone, D., & John, O. (2005). *Personality: Theory and research*. New York: Wiley.

Peskin, M., & Newell, F. N. (2004). Familiarity breeds attraction: Effects of exposure on the attractiveness of typical and distinctive faces. *Perception*, *33*, 147–157.

Peters, G.-J. Y, Ruiter, R. A. C., & Kok, G. (2012). Threatening communication: A critical re-analysis and a revised meta-analytic test of fear appeal theory. *Health Psychology Review*, *7*(sup1), S8–S31.

Peterson, C., & Seligman, M. E. P. (2004). *Character strengths and virtues: A handbook and classification*. Washington, DC: American Psychological Association.

Peterson, C., & Whalen, N. (2001). Five years later: Children's memory for medical emergencies. *Applied Cognitive Psychology 15*, 7–24.

Peterson, C., Dowden, C., & Tobin, J. (1999). Interviewing preschoolers: Comparisons of yes/no and wh- questions. *Law and Human Behavior*, *23*(5), 539–555.

Peterson, L. R., & Peterson, M. J. (1959). Short-term retention of individual verbal items. *Journal of Experimental Psychology*, *58*, 193–198.

Petrill, S. (2003). The development of intelligence: Behavior genetics approaches. In R. J. Sternberg, J. Lautrey, & T. I. Lubart (Eds.), *Models of intelligence: International perspectives*. Washington, DC: American Psychological Association.

Petrovic, P., & Ingvar, M. (2002). Imaging cognitive modulation of pain processing. *Pain*, *95*, 1–5.

Petrovic, P., Kalso, E., Petersson, K. M., Andersson, J., Fransson, P., & Ingvar, M. (2010). A prefrontal non-opioid mechanism in placebo analgesia. *Pain*, *150*, 59–65.

Petrovic, P., Kalso, E., Petersson, M. K., & Ingvarm, M. (2002, February). Placebo and opioid analgesia: Imaging a shared neuronal network. *Science Express Reports*, 17–22.

Petrovich, G. (2013). Forebrain networks and the control of feeding by environmental learned cues. *Physiology & Behavior*, *121*, 10–18.

Petry, N., & Martin, B. (2002). Low-cost contingency management for treating cocaine-and opioid-abusing methadone patients. *Journal of Consulting and Clinical Psychology*, *70*, 398–405.

Pettigrew, T. F. (1979). The ultimate attribution error: Extending Allport's cognitive analysis of prejudice. *Personality and Social Psychology Bulletin*, *55*, 461–476.

Pettigrew, T. F., & Meertens, R. W. (1995). Subtle and blatant prejudice in western Europe. *European Journal of Social Psychology*, *25*, 57–76.

Pettigrew, T. F., & Tropp, L. R. (2006). A metaanalytic test of intergroup contact theory. *Journal of Personality and Social Psychology*, *90*, 751–783.

Pettigrew, T. F., & Tropp, L. R. (2013). *When groups meet: The dynamics of intergroup contact*. Hove: Psychology Press.

Petty, R. E., & Cacioppo, J. T. (1986). *Communication and persuasion: Central and peripheral routes to attitude change*. New York: Springer-Verlag.

Petty, R. E., Cacioppo, J. T., Strathman, A. J., & Priester, J. R. (2005). To think or not to think: Exploring two routes to persuasion. In T. C. Brock & M. C. Green (Eds.), *Persuasion: Psychological insights and perspectives* (2nd ed.). Thousand Oaks, CA: Sage.

Petty, R. E., Fleming, M. A., Priester, J. R., Feinstein, A. H. (2001). Individual versus group interest violation: Surprise as a determinant of argument scrutiny and persuasion. *Social Cognition, 19*, 418–442.

Petty, R. E., Haugtvedt, C. P., & Smith, S. M. (1995). Elaboration as a determinant of attitude strength: Creating attitudes that are persistent, resistant, and predictive of behavior. In R. E. Petty and J. A. Krosnick (eds.), *Attitude strength: Antecedents and consequences* (pp. 93–130). Hove: Psychology Press.

Pezdek, K. (2003). Event memory and autobiographical memory for the events of September 11, 2001. *Applied Cognitive Psychology, 17*, 1033–1045.

Pfeifer, M., Goldsmith, H. H., & Davidson, R. R. M. (2002). Continuity and change in inhibited and uninhibited children. *Child Development, 73*, 1474–1485.

Pfiffner, L. J., McBurnett, K., & Rathouz, P. (2001). Father absence and familial antisocial characteristics. *Journal of Abnormal Child Psychology, 29*, 357–367.

PGEU (2008). *Targeting adherence: Improving patient outcomes in Europe through community pharmacists' intervention.* Policy statement of the Pharmaceutical Group of the European Union. Retrieved from: http://www.pgeu.eu/policy/5-adherence.html.

Phelps, E. A. (2005). The power of the subliminal: On subliminal persuasion and other potential applications. In R. R. Hassin, J. S. Uleman, & J. A. Bargh (Eds.), *The new unconscious.* New York: Oxford University Press.

Piaget, J. (1926). *The language and thought of the child.* London: Routledge & Kegan Paul.

Piaget, J. (1970a). *Science of education and the psychology of the child.* New York: Viking.

Piaget, J. (1977). *The development of thought: Equilibration of cognitive structure.* New York: Viking.

Pickering, A. D., & Gray, J. A. (1999). The neuroscience of personality. In L. A. Pervin & O. P. John (Eds.), *Handbook of personality: Theory and research.* New York: Guilford Press.

Pickrell, J. E., Bernstein, D., & Loftus, E. F. (2009). The misinformation effect. In R. Pohl (Ed.), *Cognitive illusions: Fallacies and biases in thinking, judgment, and memory.* London: Psychology Press.

Pies, R. W. (1998). *Handbook of essential psychopharmacology.* Washington, DC: American Psychiatric Press.

Pike, K. M., Hilbert, A., Wifley, D. E., Fairburn, C. G., Dohm, F. A., Walsh, B. T., & Striegel-Moore, R. (2008). Toward an understanding of risk factors for anorexia nervosa: A case control study. *Psychological Medicine, 38*(10), 1443–1453.

Pilbeam, D. (1984). The descent of hominoids and hominids. *Scientific American, 250*, 84–97.

Pilcher, J. J., & Huffcutt, A. J. (1996). Effects of sleep deprivation on performance: A metaanalysis. *Sleep, 19*, 318–326.

Pilcher, J. J., & Walters, A. S. (1997). How sleep deprivation affects psychological variables related to college students' cognitive performance. *Journal of American College Health, 46*, 121–126.

Pilowsky, L. S., Bressan, R. A., Stone, J. M., Erlandsson, K., Mulligan, R. S., Krystal, J. H., & Ell, P. J. (2006). First in vivo evidence of an NMDA receptor deficit in medication-free schizophrenic patients. *Molecular Psychiatry, 11*(2), 118–119.

Pinker, S. (2000). Language as an adaptation to the cognitive niche. In M. Christiansen & S. Kirby (Eds.), *Language evolution: Reports from the research frontier.* New York: Oxford University Press.

Pinquart, M., & Sörensen, S. (2003). Differences between caregivers and noncaregivers in psychological health and physical health: Ameta-analysis. *Psychology & Aging, 18*, 250–267.

Pitman, R. K., Shalev, A. Y., & Orr, S. P. (2000). Posttraumatic stress disorder: Emotion, conditioning, and memory. In M. S. Gazzaniga (Ed.), *The new cognitive neurosciences* (2nd ed.). Cambridge, MA: MIT Press.

Pittman, T. S., & Zeigler, K. R. (2007). Basic human needs. *Social psychology: Handbook of Basic Principles, 2*, 473–489.

Pitz, G. F., & Sachs, N. J. (1984). Judgment and decision: Theory and application. *Annual Review of Psychology, 35*, 139–163.

Piven, J., Saliba, K., Bailey, J., & Arndt, S. (1997). An MRI study of autism: The cerebellum revisited. *Neurology, 13*, 546–551.

Plack, C. (2013). *The sense of hearing* (2nd ed.). Hove: Psychology Press.

Plant, E. A., & Peruche, B. M. (2005). The consequences of race for police officers' responses to criminal suspects. *Psychological Science, 16*, 180–183.

Plant, E. A., Peruche, B. M., & Butz, D. A. (2005). Eliminating automatic racial bias: Making race non-diagnostic for responses to criminal suspects. *Journal of Experimental Social Psychology, 41*, 141–156.

Pliny. (1952). *Natural history* (Vol. 9). Books XXXIII–XXXV. English translation by H. Rackham. London: Heinemann.

Plomin, R. (1997). *Behavioral genetics.* New York: St. Martin's Press.

Plomin, R., & Caspi, A. (1999). Behavior genetics and personality. In L. A. Pervin & O. P. John (Eds.), *Handbook of personality: Theory and research.* New York: Guilford Press.

Plomin, R., & Craig, I. (2002). 'Genetic research on cognitive ability': Author's reply. *British Journal of Psychiatry, 180*, 185–186.

Plomin, R., & Daniels, D. (1987). Why are children in the same family so different from each other? *Behavioral and Brain Sciences, 10*, 1–16.

Plomin, R., Haworth, C. M. A., Meaburn, E. L., & Price, T. S. (2013). Common DNA markers can account for more than half the genetic influence on cognitive abilities. *Psychological Science 20*(4), 562–568.

Plomin, R., & Spinath, F. M. (2004). Intelligence: Genetics, genes, and genomics. *Journal of Personality and Social Psychology, 86*, 112–129.

Plomin, R., DeFries, J. C., & Fulker, D. W. (2007). *Nature and nurture during infancy and early childhood*. New York: Cambridge University Press.

Plomin, R., Defries, J. C., McClearn, G. E., & McGuffin, P. (2001). *Behavioral genetics* (4th ed.). New York: Worth.

Plomin, R., DeFries, J. C., McClearn, G. E., & McGuffin, P. (2008). *Behavioral genetics* (5th ed.). Boston, MA: Worth.

Plomin, R., Fulker, D. W., Corley, R., & DeFries, J. C. (1997). Nature, nurture, and cognitive development from 1 to 16 years: A parent-offspring adoption study. *Psychological Science, 8*(6), 442–447.

Plotkin, S. A. (2006). The history of rubella and rubella vaccination leading to elimination. *Clinical Infectious Diseases, 43*, S164–S168.

Plotnik, J. M., de Waal, F. B. M., & Reiss, D. (2006). Self-recognition in an Asian elephant. *Proceedings of the National Academy of Sciences, USA, 103*, 7 November.

Plutchik, R. (1980). *Emotion: A psychoevolutionary synthesis*. New York: Harper.

Plutchik, R. (1994). *Psychology of emotion*. Reading, MA: Addison-Wesley.

Polanczyk, G., Silva de Lima, M., Lessa Horta, B., Biederman, J., & Rohde, L. A. (2007). The worldwide prevalence of ADHD: A systematic review and metaregression analysis. *The American Journal of Psychiatry, 164*, 942–948.

Poling, A., Weetjens, B., Cox, C., Beyene, N. W., Bach, H., & Sully, A. (2011). Using trained pouched rats to detect land mines: Another victory for operant conditioning. *Journal of applied behavior analysis, 44*(2), 351–355.

Pollack, I., & Pickett, J. M. (1964). Intelligibility of excerpts from fluent speech: Auditory vs. structural context. *Journal of Verbal Learning and Verbal Behavior, 3*, 79–84.

Pompili, M., Lester, D., Grispini, A., Innamorati, M., Calandro, F., Iliceto, P, De Pisa, E., Tatarelli, R., Girardi, P. (2009). Completed suicide in schizophrenia: Evidence from a case-control study. *Psychiatry Research, 167*, 251–257.

Poncin, P. (1994). Field observations of a mating attempt of a spawning grayling, *Thymallus thymallus* with a feeding barbel, *Barbus barbus. Journal of Fish Biology, 45*, 904–906.

Pool, R. (1994). *The dynamic brain*. Washington, DC: National Academy Press.

Poole, D. A., & Lamb, M. E. (1998). *Investigative interviews of children: A guide for helping professionals*. Washington, DC: American Psychological Association.

Poole, D. A., Lindsay, D. S., Memon, A., & Bull, R. (1995). Psychotherapy and the recovery of memories of childhood sexual abuse: US and British practitioners' opinions, practices and experiences. *Journal of Consulting and Clinical Psychology, 63*, 426–437.

Pornpitakpan, C. (2004). The persuasiveness of source credibility: A critical review of five decades' evidence. *Journal of Applied Social Psychology, 34*(2), 243–281.

Porter, J., Craven, B., Khan, R. M., Chang, S. J., Kang, I,, Judkewitz, B., … Sobel, N. (2007). Mechanisms of scent-tracking in humans. *Nature Neuroscience, 10*(1), 27–29.

Porter, N. P., & Geis, F. L. (1981). Women and nonverbal leadership cues: When seeing is not believing. In C. Mayo & N. M. Henley (Eds.), *Gender and nonverbal behavior*. New York: Springer-Verlag.

Porterfield S. P., & White, B. A. (2007). *Endocrine physiology*. St. Louis: Mosby.

Posada, G., Jacobs, A., Richmond, M. K., Carbonell, O. A., Alzate, G., Bustamante, M. R., & Quiceno, J. (2002). Maternal caregiving and infant security in two cultures. *Developmental Psychology, 38*, 67–78.

Posner, J., Russell, J. A., & Peterson, B. S. (2005). The circumplex model of affect: An integrative approach to affective neuroscience, cognitive development and psychopathology. *Development and Psychopathology, 17*, 715–734.

Posner, M. I. (1980). Orienting of attention. *Quarterly Journal of Experimental Psychology, 32*, 3–25.

Posner, M. I., & Rothbart, M. K. (2007a). Learning to look. In M. I. Posner & M. K. Rothbart (Eds.), *Educating the human brain*. Washington, DC: American Psychological Association.

Posner, M. I., & Rothbart, M. K. (2007b). *Educating the human brain*. Washington, DC: American Psychological Association.

Posthuma, D., & de Geus, E. J. C. (2006). Progress in the molecular-genetic study of intelligence. *Current Directions in Psychological Science, 15*, 151–155.

Postman, L., & Phillips, L. W. (1965). Short-term temporal changes in free recall. *Quarterly Journal of Experimental Psychology, 17*, 132–138.

Postman, L., & Underwood, B. J. (1973). Critical issues in interference theory. *Memory and Cognition, 1*, 19–40.

Postmes, T., & Spears, R. (1998). Deindividuation and antinormative behavior: A meta-analysis. *Psychological Bulletin, 123*, 238–259.

Potkin, S. G., Zetin, M., Stamenkovic, V., Kripke, D., & Bunney, W. E. (1986). Seasonal affective disorder: Prevalence varies with latitude climate. *Clinical Neuropharmacology, 9*, 181–183.

Potter, J., & Wetherell, M. (1987). *Discourse and social psychology: Beyond attitudes and behaviour*. London: Sage.

Powley, T. L., & Keesey, R. E. (1970). Relationship of body weight to the lateral hypothalamic feeding syndrome. *Journal of Comparative and Physiological Psychology, 70*, 25–36.

Pressman, J. D. (1998). *Last resort: Psychosurgery and the limits of medicine*. New York: Cambridge University Press.

Prestwich, A., Sniehotta, F. F., Whittington, C., Dombrowski, S. U., Rogers, L., & Michie, S. (2014). Does theory influence the effectiveness of health behavior interventions? Meta-analysis. *Health Psychology, 33*, 464–474.

Prigerson, H., Maciejewski, P. K, & Rosenheck, R. A. (2002). Population attributable fractions of psychiatric disorders and behavioral outcomes associated with combat exposure among U.S. men. *American Journal of Public Health, 92*(1), 59–63.

Priluck, R., & Till, B. D. (2004). The role of contingency awareness, involvement, and need for cognition in attitude formation. *Journal of the Academy of Marketing Science, 32*, 329–344.

Prior, H., Schwarz, A., & Güntürkün, O. (2008). Mirror-induced behavior in the magpie (*Pica pica*): Evidence of self-recognition. *PLoS Biology, 6*(8), e202.

Pritchard, R. M. (1961, June). Stabilized images on the retina. *Scientific American,* 72–78.

Prochaska, J., & DiClemente, C. (1984). *The transtheoretical approach: Crossing traditional boundaries of therapy.* Homewood, IL: Dow Jones-Irwin.

Prochaska, J. O., Norcross, J. C., & DiClemente, C. C. (1994). *Changing for good.* New York: Avon Books.

Project MATCH Research Group. (1997). Matching alcoholism treatments to client heterogeneity: Project MATCH posttreatment drinking outcomes. *Journal of Studies on Alcohol, 58,* 7–29.

Pruden, S. M., Hirsh-Pasek, K., & Golinkoff, R. M. (2006). The social dimension in language development: A rich history and a new frontier. In P. J. Marshall & N. A. Fox (Eds.), *The development of social engagement: Neurobiological perspectives.* New York: Oxford University Press.

Prüfer, K., Racimo, F., Patterson, N., Jay, F., Sankararaman, S., Sawyer, S. ... Pääbo, S. (2014). The complete genome sequence of a Neanderthal from the Altai Mountains. *Nature, 505,* 43–49.

Pryce, C. R., & Feldon, J. (2003). Long-term neurobehavioural impact of the postnatal environment in rats: Manipulations, effects and mediating mechanisms, *Neuroscience and Biobehavioral Reviews, 27,* 57–71.

Przybylski, A. K., Deci, E. L., Rigby, C. S., & Ryan, R. M. (2013). Competence-impeding electronic games and players' aggressive feelings, thoughts, and behaviors. *Journal of Personality and Social Psychology, 106,* 441–457.

Ptacek, J. T., Smith, R. E., & Zanas, J. (1992). Gender, appraisal, and coping: A longitudinal analysis. *Journal of Personality, 60,* 747–769.

Puhl, R. M., & Heuer, C. A. (2009). The stigma of obesity: A review and update. *Obesity, 17*(5), 941–964.

Punamäki, R. L., & Joustie, M. (1998). The role of culture, violence, and personal factors affecting dream content. *Journal of Cross-Cultural Psychology, 29,* 320–342.

Putman, P., van Honk, J., Kessels, R. P. C., Mulder, M., & Koppeschaar, H. P. (2004). Salivary cortisol and short and long-term memory for emotional faces in healthy young women. *Psychoneuroendocrinology, 29,* 953–960.

Putnam, F. W. (1989). *Diagnosis and treatment of multiple personality disorder.* New York: Guilford Press.

Putnam, F. W. (2000). Dissociative disorders. In A. J. Sameroff & M. Lewis (Eds.), *Handbook of developmental psychopathology* (2nd ed.). New York: Cambridge University Press.

Pylyshyn, Z. (2003). Return of the mental image: Are there really pictures in the brain? *Trends in Cognitive Sciences, 7,* 113–118.

Q

Qin, X., Phillips, M. R., Wang, W., Li, Y., Jin, Q., Ai, L., ... Liu, L. (2010). Prevalence and rates of recognition of anxiety disorders in internal medicine outpatient departments of 23 general hospitals in Shenyang, China. *General Hospital Psychiatry, 32*(2), 192–200.

Qu, T., Brannen, C. L., Kim, H. M., & Sugaya, K. (2001). Human neural stem cells improve cognitive function of aged brain. *Neuroreport: For Rapid Communication of Neuroscience Research, 12*(6), 1127–1132.

Quilty, L. C., Oakman, J. M., & Farvolden, P. (2007). Behavioural inhibition, behavioural activation, and the preference for familiarity. *Personality and Individual Differences, 42,* 291–303.

Quinn, J. M., Pascoe, A., Wood, W., & Neal, D. T. (2010). Can't control yourself? Monitor those bad habits. *Personality and Social Psychology Bulletin, 36,* 499–511.

Quintero, N. (1980). Coming of age the Apache way. *National Geographic, 157*(2), 262–271.

Quiroga, R. Q. (2012). Concept cells: The building blocks of declarative memory functions. *Nature Reviews Neuroscience, 13*(8), 587–597.

R

Rachman, S. (1998). *Anxiety.* Mahwah, NJ: Erlbaum.

Radley, K.C., Ford, W., Battaglia, A., & McHugh, M. (2014). The effects of a social skills training package on social engagement of children with autism spectrum disorders in a generalized recess setting. *Focus on Autism and Other Developmental Disabilities.* doi: 10.1177/1088357614525660.

Raeff, C. (2010). Independence and interdependence in children's developmental experiences. *Child Development Perspectives, 4*(1), 31–36.

Rahim-Williams, B., Riley, J. L., Williams, A. K., & Fillingim, R. B. (2012). A quantitative review of ethnic group differences in experimental pain response: Do biology, psychology, and culture matter? *Pain Medicine, 13,* 522–540.

Rahman, Q. (2005). Fluctuating asymmetry, second to fourth finger length ratios and human sexual orientation. *Psychoneuroendocrinology, 30,* 382–391.

Raine, A. (2002). Annotation: The role of prefrontal deficits, low autonomic arousal and early health factors in the development of antisocial and aggressive behavior in children. *Journal of Child Psychology and Psychiatry and Allied Disciplines, 43,* 417–434.

Raine, A. (2008). From genes to brain to antisocial behavior. *Current Directions in Psychological Science, 17*(5), 323–328.

Raine, A., Mellingen, K., Liu, J., Venables, P., & Mednick, S. A. (2003). Effects of environmental enrichment at ages 3–5 years on schizotypal personality and antisocial behavior at ages 17 and 23 years. *American Journal of Psychiatry, 160,* 1627–1635.

Raine, A., Venables, P. H., & Williams, M. (1996). Better autonomic conditioning and faster electrodermal half-recovery time at age 15 years as possible protective factors against crime at age 29 years. *Developmental Psychology, 32,* 624–630.

Raine, A., Lencz, T., Bihrle, S., LaCasse, L., & Colletti, P. (2000). Reduced prefrontal gray matter volume and reduced autonomic activity in antisocial personality disorder. *Archives of General Psychiatry, 57,* 119–127.

Rajah, M. N., & McIntosh, A. R. (2005). Overlap in the functional neural systems involved in semantic and episodic memory retrieval. *Journal of Cognitive Neuroscience, 17,* 470–482.

Ramachandran, V. S. & Hirstein, W. (1997). Three laws of qualia; What neurology tells us about the biological functions of consciousness. *Journal of Consciousness Studies, 4*(5–6), 429–457.

Ramchand, R., Schell, T. L., Karney, B. R., Osilla, K. C., Burns, R. M., & Caldarone, L. B. (2010). Disparate prevalence estimates of PTSD among service members who served in Iraq and Afghanistan: possible explanations. *Journal of Traumatic Stress, 23*(1), 59–68.

Ramey, C., & Ramey, S. (1998). Early intervention. *American Psychologist, 53*, 210–225.

Ramey, C. T., Ramey, S. L., & Lanzi, R. G. (1998). Differentiating developmental risk levels for families in poverty: Creating a family typology. In M. Lewis & C. Feiring (Eds.), *Families, risks, and competence*. Mahwah, NJ: Erlbaum.

Ramsey, J. L., Langlois, J. H., Hoss, R. A., Rubenstein, A. J., & Griffin, A. M. (2004). Origins of a stereotype: Categorization of facial attractiveness by 6-month-old infants. *Developmental Science, 7*, 201–211.

Randall, C., & Corp, A. (2014). Measuring National Well-being: European Comparisons Office for National Statistics. Retrieved from http://www.ons.gov.uk/ons/dcp171766_363811.pdf.

Rao, R. (2001). Cannabis: Some psychiatric aspects. *Primary Care Psychiatry, 7*, 101–105.

Rasch, B., & Born, J. (2013). About sleep's role in memory. *Physiological Reviews, 93*(2), 681–766.

Rasmussen, H. N., Scheier, M. F., & Greenhouse, J. B. (2009). Optimism and physical health: A meta-analytic review. *Annals of Behavioral Medicine, 37*, 239–256.

Ratcliff, R., Thapar, A., & McKoon, G. (2006). Aging and individual differences in rapid two-choice decisions. *Psychonomic Bulletin & Review, 13*, 626–635.

Raudenbush, B., & Meyer, B. (2003). Muscular dissatisfaction and supplement use among male intercollegiate athletes. *Journal of Sport & Exercise Psychology, 25*, 161–170.

Raven, J. (1962). *Colored progressive matrices*. New York: Psychological Corp.

Ray, E., & Heyes, C. (2011). Imitation in infancy: The wealth of the stimulus. *Developmental Science, 14*(1), 92–105.

Ray, O. S., & Ksir, C. J. (2004). *Drugs, society and human behavior* (9th ed.). Boston, MA: McGraw-Hill.

Raymaekers, L., Smeets, T., Maarten, J. V., & Merckelbach, H. (2010). Autobiographical memory specificity among people with recovered memories of childhood sexual abuse. *Journal of Behaviour Therapy and Experimental Psychiatry, 41*, 338–344.

Raz, A., & Shapiro, T. (2002). Hypnosis and neuroscience: A cross talk between clinical and cognitive research. *Archives of General Psychiatry, 59*, 85–90.

Reber, R., Schwarz, N., & Winkielman, P. (2004). Processing fluency and aesthetic pleasure: Is beauty in the perceiver's processing experience? *Personality and Social Psychology Review, 8*, 364–382.

Reeves, R. A. (2012). Introduction to the special issue: Psychology, marketing, and celebrities. *Psychology and Marketing, 29*, 637–638.

Regan, D. T., & Kilduff, M. (1988). Optimism about elections: Dissonance reduction at the ballot box. *Political Psychology, 9*, 101–107.

Regier, D. A., Narrow, W. E., Clarke, D. E., Kraemer, H. C., Kuramoto, S. J., Kuhl, E. A., & Kupfer, D. J. (2013). DSM-5 field trials in the United States and Canada, Part II: Test-retest reliability of selected categorical diagnoses. *American Journal of Psychiatry, 170*, 59–70.

Rehm, J., Mathers, C., Popova, S., Thavorncharoensap, M., Teerawattananon, Y., & Patra, J. (2009). Global burden of disease and injury and economic cost attributable to alcohol use and alcohol-use disorders. *The Lancet, 373*, 2223–2233.

Reicher, S., & Haslam, S. A. (2006). Rethinking the psychology of tyranny: The BBC prison study. *British Journal of Social Psychology, 45*, 1–40.

Reilly, R. G., & Radach, R. (2006). Some empirical tests of an interactive activation model of eye movement control in reading. *Cognitive Systems Research, 7*, 34–55.

Reisberg, D. (1997). *Cognition: Exploring the science of the mind*. New York: W.W. Norton.

Reisberg, D. (2001). *Cognition: Exploring the science of the mind* (2nd ed.). New York: W. W. Norton.

Rendell, P. G., & Thomson, D. M. (1999). Aging and prospective memory: Differences between naturalistic and laboratory tasks. *Journals of Gerontology: Series B: Psychological Sciences and Social Sciences, 54B* (4), 256–269.

Rensink, R. A. (2002). Change detection. *Annual Review of Psychology, 53*, 247–277.

Renzulli, J. S. (2002). Emerging conceptions of giftedness: Building a bridge to the new century, *Exceptionality, 10*, 67–75.

Reppucci, N. D., Wollard, J. L., & Fried, C. S. (1999). Social, community, and preventive interventions. *Annual Review of Psychology, 1*, 387–415.

Rescorla, R. A. (1968). Probability of shock in the presence and absence of CS in fear. *Journal of Comparative and Physiological Psychology, 66*, 1–5.

Rescorla, R. A., & Solomon, R. L. (1967). Two-process learning theory: Relationships between Pavlovian conditioning and instrumental learning. *Psychological Review, 74*, 151–182.

Rescorla, R. A., & Wagner, A. R. (1972). A theory of Pavlovian conditioning: Variations in the effectiveness of reinforcement and nonreinforcement. In A. H. Black & W. F. Prokasky (Eds.), *Classical conditioning: II. Current research and theory*. New York: Appleton-Century-Crofts.

Resick, P. (2005). *Stress and trauma*. San Francisco, CA: Taylor & Francis.

Resnick, S. M., Pham, D. L., Kraut, M. A., Zonderman, A. B., & Davatzikos, C. (2003). Longitudinal magnetic resonance imaging studies of older adults: A shrinking brain. *Journal of Neuroscience, 23*, 3295–3301.

Revonsuo, A. (2000). The reinterpretation of dreams: An evolutionary hypothesis of the function of dreaming. *Behavioral and Brain Sciences, 23*(6), 877–901.

Rey, J. M., & Walter, G. (1997). Half a century of ECT use in young people. *American Journal of Psychiatry, 154*, 595–602.

Rhadigan, C., & Huprich, S. K. (2012). The utility of the cognitive-affective processing system in the diagnosis of personality disorders: Some preliminary evidence. *Journal of Personality Disorders, 26*(2), 162–178.

Rhodes, G. (2006). The evolutionary psychology of facial beauty. *Annual Review of Psychology, 57,* 199–226.

Rhodes, G., Yoshikawa, S., Clark, A., Lee, K., McKay, R., & Akamatsu, S. (2001). Attractiveness of facial averageness and symmetry in non-Western cultures: In search of biologically based standards of beauty. *Perception, 30,* 611–625.

Rholes, W. S., & Simpson, J. A. (Eds.) (2006). *Adult attachment: Theory, research, and clinical implications.* New York: Guilford Press.

Rholes, W. S., Simpson, J. A., & Friedman, M. (2006). Avoidant attachment and the experience of parenting. *Personality and Social Psychology Bulletin, 32,* 275–285.

Richard, S., Davies, D. C., & Faure, J. M. (2000). The role of fear in one-trial passive avoidance learning in Japanese quail chicks genetically selected for long or short duration of the tonic immobility reaction. *Behavioural Processes, 48,* 165–170.

Richardson, D. R. (1991). Interpersonal attraction and love. In R. M. Baron, W. G. Graziano, & C. Stangor (Eds.), *Social psychology.* Fort Worth, TX: Holt, Rinehart & Winston.

Richerson, P. J., & Boyd, R. (2005). *Not by genes alone: How culture transformed human evolution.* Chicago, IL: University of Chicago Press.

Riesen, A. H. (1965). Effects of early deprivation of photic stimulation. In S. F. Osler & R. E. Cooke (Eds.), *The biosocial basis of mental retardation.* Baltimore, MD: Johns Hopkins University Press.

Rigato, S., Begum Ali, J., van Velzen, J., & Bremner, A. J. (2014). The neural basis of somatosensory remapping develops in human infancy. *Current Biology, 24,* 1222–1226.

Rilling, M. (1996). The mystery of the vanished citations: James McConnell's forgotten 1960s quest for planarian learning, a biochemical engram, and celebrity. *American Psychologist, 51,* 589–598.

Rimm, D. C., & Masters, J. C. (1979). *Behavior therapy: Techniques and empirical findings* (2nd ed.). New York: Academic Press.

Ringelmann, M. (1913). Recherches sur les moteurs animés: Travail de l'homme. *Annales de l'Institute National Agronomique, 12,* 1–40.

Rips, L. J. (1994). *The psychology of proof.* Cambridge, MA: MIT Press.

Rips, L. J. (1997). Goals for a theory of deduction: Reply to Johnson-Laird. *Minds and Machines, 7,* 409–424.

Ritblatt, S. N. (2000). Children's level of participation in a false-belief task, age, and theory of mind. *Journal of Genetic Psychology, 161,* 53–64.

Ritchie, C. W., Ames, D., Clayton, T., & Lai, R. (2004). Metaanalysis of randomized trials of the efficacy and safety of donepezil, galantamine, and rivastigmine for the treatment of Alzheimer disease. *American Journal of Geriatric Psychiatry, 12,* 358–369.

Ritter, R. C., Brenner, L., & Yox, D. P. (1992). Participation of vagal sensory neurons in putative satiety signals from the upper gastrointestinal tract. In S. Ritter, R. C. Ritter, & C. D. Barnes (Eds.), *Neuroanatomy and physiology of abdominal vagal afferents.* Boca Raton, FL: CRC Press.

Rivera, S. M., Wakeley, A., & Langer, J. (1999). The drawbridge phenomenon: Representational reasoning or perceptual preference? *Developmental Psychology, 35*(2), 427.

Roberts, B., Helson, R., & Klohnen, E. C. (2002). Personality development and growth in women across 30 years: Three perspectives. *Journal of Personality, 70,* 79–102.

Roberts, B. W., & Mroczek, D. (2008). Personality trait change in adulthood. *Current Directions in Psychological Science, 17*(1), 31–35.

Robertson, E. M., Pascual-Leone, A., & Miall, R. C. (2004). Current concepts in procedural consolidation. *Nature Reviews Neuroscience, 5,* 1–7.

Robins, L. N., & Regier, D. A. (Eds.). (1991). *Psychiatric disorders in America: The Epidemiological Catchment Area Study.* New York: Free Press.

Robins, R. W., Fraley, R. C., & Krueger, R. F. (2007). *Handbook of research methods in personality psychology.* New York: Guilford.

Robins, R. W., Gosling, S. D., & Craik, K. H. (1999). An empirical analysis of trends in psychology. *American Psychologist, 54,* 117–128.

Robinson, D. (1997). *Neurobiology.* New York: Springer-Verlag.

Robinson, M. D., Vargas, P. T., Tamir, M., & Solberg, E. C. (2004). Using and being used by categories. *Psychological Science, 15,* 521–526.

Robinson, O. C., & Wright, G. R. T. (2013). The prevalence, types and perceived outcomes of crisis episodes in early adulthood and midlife: A structured retrospective-autobiographical study. *International Journal of Behavioral Development, 37,* 407–416.

Robinson, P. A., Rennie, C. J., Rowe, D. L., O'Connor, S. C., & Gordon, E. (2005). Multiscale brain modelling. *Philosophical Transactions of the Royal Society. B 360,* 1043–1050.

Rochat, P. (2010). The innate sense of the body develops to become a public affair by 2–3 years. *Neuropsychologia, 48*(3), 738–745.

Rodham, K. (2010). *Health psychology.* Basingstoke: Palgrave Macmillan.

Rodin, J., & Salovey, P. (1989). Health psychology. *Annual Review of Psychology, 40,* 533–579.

Rodin, J., Bartoshuk, L., Peterson, C., & Schank, D. (1990). Bulimia and taste: Possible interactions. *Journal of Abnormal Psychology, 99,* 32–39.

Roebers, C. M. (2002). Confidence judgments in children's and adults' recall and suggestibility. *Developmental Psychology, 38,* 1052–1067.

Roediger, H. L., III, & McDermott, K. B. (1995). Creating false memories: Remembering words not presented in lists. *Journal of Experimental Psychology: Learning, Memory, and Cognition, 21,* 803–814.

Roediger, H. L., III, & McDermott, K. B. (2000). Tricks of memory. *Current Directions in Psychological Science, 9,* 123–127.

Roehling, M. V., Roehling, P. V., & Pichler, S. (2007). The relationship between body

weight and perceived weight-related employment discrimination: The role of sex and race. *Journal of Vocational Behavior, 71*, 300–318.

Roelofs, K., Hoogduin, K. A. L., Keijsers, G. P. J., Näring, G. W., Moene, F. C., & Sandijck, P. (2002). Hypnotic susceptibility in patients with conversion disorder. *Journal of Abnormal Psychology, 111*, 390–395.

Roffwarg, H. P., Muzio, J. N., & Dement, W. C. (1966). Ontogenic development of human dream-sleep cycle. *Science, 152*, 604.

Rogers, C. R. (1951). *Client-centered therapy*. Boston, MA: Houghton Mifflin.

Rogers, C. R. (1959). A theory of therapy, personality and interpersonal relationships, as developed in the client-centered framework. In S. Koch (Ed.), *Psychology: A study of a science* (Vol. 3). New York: McGraw-Hill.

Rogers, C. R. (1980). *A way of being*. Boston, MA: Houghton Mifflin.

Rogers, C. R. (Ed.) (1967). *The therapeutic relationship and its impact: A study of psychotherapy with schizophrenics*. Madison, WI: University of Wisconsin Press.

Rollman, G. (1998). Culture and pain. In S. S. Kazarian et al. (Eds.), *Cultural clinical psychology: Theory, research, and practice*. New York: Oxford University Press.

Rolls, B. J., Rolls, E. T., Rowe, E. A., & Sweeney, K. (1981). Sensory specific satiety in man. *Physiology and Behavior, 27*, 137–142.

Rolls, E. T. (2000). Memory systems in the brain. *Annual Review of Psychology, 5*, 599–630.

Rolls, E. T., & Deco, G. (2002). *Computational neuroscience of vision*. London: Oxford University Press.

Rolls, E. T., Murzi, E., Yaxley, S., Thorpe, S. J. & Simpson, S. J. (1986). Sensory-specific satiety: Food specific reduction in responsiveness of ventral forebrain neurons after feeding in the monkey. *Brain Research, 368*, 79–86.

Room, R., Babor, T., & Rehm, J. (2005). Alcohol and public health. *The Lancet, 365*, 519–530.

Rosch, E. (1973). On the internal structure of perceptual and semantic categories. In T. E. Moore (Ed.), *Cognitive development and the acquisition of language*. New York: Academic Press.

Rosch, E. (1977). Human categorization. In N. Warren (Ed.), *Advances in cross-cultural psychology* (Vol. 1). London: Academic Press.

Rosch, E., & Mervis, C. B. (1975). Family resemblances: Studies in the internal structure of categories. *Cognitive Psychology, 7*, 573–605.

Rosen, C. S. (2000). Integrating stage and continuum models to explain processing of exercise messages and exercise initiation among sedentary college students. *Health Psychology, 19*, 172–180.

Rosenberg, M. (1965). *Society and the adolescent self-image*. Princeton, NJ: Princeton University Press.

Rosenfarb, I. S., Goldstein, M. J., Mintz, J., & Nuechterlein, K. H. (1995). Expressed emotion and subclinical psychopathology observable within the transactions between schizophrenic patients and their family members. *Journal of Abnormal Psychology, 104*, 259–267.

Rosenhan, D. L. (1973). On being sane in insane places. *Science, 179*, 250–258.

Rosenhan, D. L., & Seligman, M. E. P. (1989). *Abnormal psychology* (2nd ed.). New York: Norton.

Rosenman, R. H., Brand, R. J., Jenkins, C. D., Friedman, M., Straus, R., & Wurm, M. (1975). Coronary disease in the Western Collaborative Group Study. Final follow-up experience of 8 1/2 years. *Journal of the American Medical Association, 233*, 872–877.

Rosenthal, N. E. & Benton, C. (2013). *Winter blues survival guide: A workbook for overcoming SAD*. New York: Guilford Press.

Rosenthal, N. E., Sack, D. A., Gillin, J. C., Lewy, A. J., Goodwin, F. K., Davenport, Y., & Wehr, T. A. (1984). Seasonal affective disorder: A description of the syndrome and preliminary findings with light therapy. *Archive of General Psychiatry, 41*, 72–80.

Rosenthal, N. E., & Wehr, T. A. (1992). Towards understanding the mechanism of action of light in seasonal affective disorder. *Pharmacopsychiatry, 25*, 56–60.

Rosenthal, R. (1985). From unconscious experimenter bias to teacher expectancy effects. In J. B. Dusek, V. C. Hall, & W. J. Meyer (Eds.), *Teacher expectancies*. Hillsdale, NJ: Erlbaum.

Rosenthal, R., Archer, D., DiMatteo, M. R., Koivumaki, J. H., & Rogers, P. L. (1974). Body talk and tone of voice: The language without words. *Psychology Today, 8*, 64–71.

Rosenzweig, M. R. (1984). Experience, memory, and the brain. *American Psychologist, 39*, 365–376.

Rosenzweig, M. R., & Bennett, E. L. (1996). Psychobiology of plasticity: Effects of training and experience on brain and behavior. *Behavioural Brain Research, 78*, 57–65.

Rosenzweig, S. (1992). Freud and experimental psychology: The emergence of idiodynamics. In S. Koch, & D. E. Leary (Eds.), *A century of psychology as science*. Washington, DC: American Psychological Association.

Rosqvist, J., & Hersen, M. (2006). *Exposure treatments for anxiety disorders*. New York: Brunner-Routledge.

Ross, L. (2001). Getting down to fundamentals: Lay dispositionism and the attributions of psychologists. *Psychological Inquiry, 12*, 37–40.

Ross, L., & Nisbett, R. E. (1991). *The person and the situation: Perspectives of social psychology*. New York: McGraw-Hill.

Ross, L., Lepper, M., & Ward, A. (2010). History of social psychology: Insights, challenges, and contributions to theory and application. In S. T. Fiske, D. T. Gilbert, & G. Lindzey (Eds.), *Handbook of social psychology* (5th ed., Vol. 1, pp. 3–50). Hoboken, NJ: Wiley.

Ross, M., & Wilson, A. E. (2003). Autobiographical memory and conceptions of self: Getting better all the time. *Current Directions in Psychological Science, 12*, 66–69.

Rossell, S. L., Bullmore, E. T., Williams, S. C. R., & David, A. S. (2002). Sex differences in functional brain activation during a lexical visual field task. *Brain and Language, 80*, 97–105.

Roth, A., & Fonagy, P. (2005). *What works for whom: A critical review of psychotherapy research* (2nd ed.). New York: Guilford Press.

Roth, G., & Ekblad, S. (2006). Longitudinal perspective on depression and sense of coherence in a sample of mass-evacuated adults from Kosovo. *Journal of Nervous Mental Disorders, 194* (5), 378–381.

Rothbaum, B. O., Hodges, L., Anderson, P. L., Price, L., & Smith, S. (2002). Twelve-month follow-up of virtual reality and standard exposure therapies for the fear of flying. *Journal of Consulting and Clinical Psychology, 70*, 428–432.

Rottenberg, J., & Johnson, S. L. (2007). *Emotion and psychopathology: Bridging affective and clinical science.* Washington, DC: American Psychological Association.

Rotter, J. B. (1954). *Social learning and clinical psychology.* Englewood Cliffs, NJ: Prentice Hall.

Rotter, J. B. (1966). Generalized expectancies for internal versus external control of reinforcement. *Psychological Monographs, 80* (Whole No. 609).

Rouw, R., & Scholte, H. S. (2007). Increased structural connectivity in grapheme-color synesthesia. *Nature Neuroscience, 10*(6), 792–797.

Rouhana, N. N., & Bar-Tal, D. (1998). Psychological dynamics of intractable ethnonational conflicts: The Israeli-Palestinian case. *American Psychologist, 53*, 761–770.

Rowe, D. C. (1999). Heredity. In V. J. Derlega, B. A. Winstead, & W. H. Jones (Eds.), *Personality: Contemporary theory and research.* Chicago, IL: Nelson Hall.

Rowley, J. T., Stickgold, R., & Hobson, J. A. (1998). Eyelid movements and mental activity at sleep onset. *Consciousness and Cognition: An International Journal, 7*, 67–84.

Roy, M. M., & Christenfeld, N. J. S. (2004). Do dogs resemble their owners? *Psychological Science, 15*, 361–363.

Rubenstein, H., Garfield, L., & Millikan, J. A. (1970). Homographic entries in the internal lexicon. *Journal of Verbal Learning and Verbal Behavior, 9*, 487–494.

Rubin, D. C., & Boals, A. (2010). People who expect to enter psychotherapy are prone to believing that they have forgotten memories of childhood trauma and abuse. *Memory, 18*(5), 556–562.

Rubin, D. C., & Kozin, M. (1984). Vivid memories. *Cognition, 16*, 81–95.

Rubin, R. T. (2000). Depression and manic depressive illness. In G. Fink (Ed.), *Encyclopedia of stress.* San Diego, CA: Academic Press.

Rubonis, A. V., & Bickman, L. (1991). Psychological impairment in the wake of disaster: The disaster-psychopathology relationship. *Psychological Bulletin, 109*, 384–399.

Ruffman, R., Perner, J., Naito, M., Parkin, L., & Clements, W. A. (1998). Older (but not younger) siblings facilitate false belief understanding. *Developmental Psychology, 34*, 161–174.

Rumbaugh, D. M. (1990). Comparative psychology and the great apes: Their competency in learning, language, and numbers. *Psychological Record, 40*, 15–39.

Rumelhart, D. E., & McClelland, J. L. (1981). An interactive model of context effects in letter perception: Part 1. An account of basic findings. *Psychological Review, 88*(5), 375–407.

Rumelhart, D. E., & McClelland, J. L. (1982). An interactive activation model of context effects in letter perception: Part 2: The contextual enhancement effect and some tests and extensions of the model. *Psychological Review, 89*, 60–94.

Rumelhart, D. E., McClelland, J. L., & the PDP Research Group (Eds.) (1986). *Parallel distributed processing* (Vol. 1). Cambridge, MA: MIT Press.

Rumstein, M. O., & Hunsley, J. (2001). Interpersonal and family functioning of female survivors of childhood sexual abuse. *Clinical Psychology Review, 21*, 471–490.

Rus-Calafel, M., Gutiérrez-Maldonado J., Ortega-Bravoa, M., Ribas-Sabatéb, J., Caqueo-Urízarc, A. (2013). A brief cognitive–behavioural social skills training for stabilised outpatients with schizophrenia: A preliminary study. *Schizoprenia Research, 143*(2–3), 327–336.

Rushton, J. P. (1989). Genetic similarity, human altruism, and group selection. *Behavioral and Brain Sciences, 12*, 503–559.

Rushton, J. P., & Irwing, P. (2008). The general factor of personality (GFP) from two meta-analyses of the Big Five: Digman (1997) and Mount, Barrick, Scullen, and Rounds (2005). *Personality and Individual Differences, 45*, 679–683.

Rushton, J. P., & Irwing, P. (2009). A general factor of personality (GFP) from the Multidimensional Personality Questionnaire. *Personality and Individual Differences, 47*, 571–567.

Rushton, J. P., Bons, T. A., & Hur, Y. M. (2008). The genetics and evolution of the general factor of personality. *Journal of Research in Personality, 42*, 1173–1185.

Russell, G. (2006). Review of understanding eating disorders: Conceptual and ethical issues in the treatment of anorexia and bulimia nervosa. *British Journal of Psychiatry, 189*, 288–289.

Russell, J. A. (1980). A circumplex model of affect. *Journal of Personality and Social Psychology, 39*, 1161–1178.

Russell, J. A. (1994). Is there universal recognition of emotion from facial expressions? A review of the cross-cultural studies. *Psychological Bulletin, 115*, 102–141.

Rutter, D., & Quine, L. (2002). Social cognition models and changing health behaviours. In D. Rutter & L. Quine (Eds.), *Changing health behaviour: Intervention and research with social cognition models.* Buckingham and Philadelpia, PA: Open University Press.

Rutter, M. (2000). Genetic studies of autism: From the 1970s into the millennium. *Journal of Abnormal Child Psychology, 28*, 3–14.

Rutter, M. L. (1997). Nature-nurture integration: The example of antisocial behavior. *American Psychologist, 52*, 390–398.

Ryan, R. M., & Lynch, J. (1989). Emotional autonomy versus detachment: Revisiting the vicissitudes of adolescence and young adulthood. *Child Development, 60*, 340–356.

Ryff, C. D., & Singer, B. (2003). Flourishing under fire: Resilience as a prototype of challenged thriving. In L. M. Keyes & J. Haidt (Eds.), *Flourishing: Positive*

psychology and the life well-lived. Washington, DC: American Psychological Association.

Rygula, R., Abumaria, N., Flugge, G., Fuchs, E., Ruther, E. and Havemann-Reinecke, U. (2005). Anhedonia and motivational deficits in rats: Impact of chronic social stress. *Behavioural Brain Research, 162,* 127–134.

S

Sabini, J., Siepmann, M., & Stein, J. (2001). The really fundamental attribution error in social psychological research. *Psychological Inquiry, 12,* 1–15.

Saby, N. J., Meltzoff, A., & Marshal, P. (2013). Infants' somatotopic neural responses to seeing human actions: I've got you under my skin. *PLoS One,* doi: 10.1371/journal.pone.0077905.

Sachse, R., & Elliott, R. (2002). Process-outcome research on humanistic therapy variables. In D. J. Cain (Ed.), *Humanistic psychotherapies: Handbook of research and practice.* Washington, DC: American Psychological Association.

Sack, A. T., Camprodon, J. A., Pascual-Leone, A., & Goebel, R. (2005). The dynamics of interhemispheric compensatory processes in mental imagery. *Science, 308,* 702–704.

Sack, R. L., Hughes, R. J., Edgar, D. M., & Lewy, A. J. (1997). Sleep-promoting effects of melatonin: At what dose, in whom, under what conditions, and by what mechanisms? *Sleep, 20,* 908–915.

Sacks, O. (1985). *The man who mistook his wife for a hat and other clinical tales.* New York: Summit Books and Simon & Schuster.

Sacks, O. (1999). *Awakenings.* Westminster, MD: Knopf.

Saczynski, J. S., Willis, S. L., & Schaie, K. W. (2002). Strategy use in reasoning training with older adults. *Aging, Neuropsychology and Cognition, 9,* 48–60.

Sadr, J., Jarudi, I., & Sinha, P. (2003). The role of eyebrows in face recognition. *Perception, 32,* 285–293.

Sage, C. E., Southcott, A. M., & Brown, S. L. (2001). The health belief model and compliance with CPAP treatment for obstructive sleep apnea. *Behaviour Change, 18,* 177–185.

Saklofske, D. H., Austin, E. J., Galloway, J., & Davidson, K. (2007). Individual difference correlates of health-related behaviours: Preliminary evidence for links between emotional intelligence and coping. *Personality and Individual Differences, 42,* 491–502.

Salize, H. J., & Dressing, H. (2005). Coercion, involuntary treatment and quality of mental health care: Is there any link? *Current Opinion in Psychiatry, 18,* 576–584.

Salovey, P., & Pizzaro, D. A. (2003). The value of emotional intelligence. In R. J. Sternberg, J. Lautrey, & T. I. Lubart (Eds.), *Models of intelligence: International perspectives.* Washington, DC: American Psychological Association.

Salthouse, T. A. (2004). What and when of cognitive aging. *Current Directions in Psychological Science, 13,* 140–144.

Salthouse, T. A. (2006). Mental exercise and mental aging. *Perspectives on Psychological Science, 1,* 68–87.

Sanchez-Armass, O., & Barabasz, A. (2005). Mexican norms for the Stanford Hypnotic Susceptibility Scale: Form C. *International Journal of Clinical and Experimental Hypnosis, 53,* 321–331.

Santiesteban, I., Banissy, M. J., Catmur, C., & Bird, G. (2012). Enhancing social ability by stimulating right temporoparietal junction. *Current Biology, 22*(23), 2274–2277.

Santonastaso, P., Scicluna, D., Colombo, G., Zanetti, T. & Favaro, A. (2006). Eating disorders and attitudes in Maltese and Italian female students. *Psychopathology, 39,* 153–157.

Saphier, D. (1992). Electrophysiological studies of the effects of interleukin-1 and interferon on the EEG and pituitary-adrenocortical activity. In J. J. Rothwell & R. D. Dantzer (Eds.), *Interleukin-1 in the brain.* Oxford: Pergamon Press.

Sarason, I. G., & Sarason, B. R. (1990). Test anxiety. In H. Leitenberg (Ed.), *Handbook of social and evaluation anxiety.* New York: Plenum Press.

Sarason, I. G., Sarason, B. R., Pierce, G. R., Shearin, E. N., & Sayers, M. H. (1991). A social learning approach to increasing blood donations. *Journal of Applied Social Psychology, 21,* 896–918.

Sargent, R. P., Shepard, R. M., & Glantz, S. A. (2004). Reduced incidence of admissions for myocardial infarction associated with public smoking ban: Before and after study. *British Medical Journal, 328,* 977–980.

Satcher, D. (1999). *Mental health: A report of the Surgeon General.* Washington, DC: US Department of Health and Human Services.

Satir, V. (1967). *Conjoint family therapy.* Palo Alto, CA: Sciences and Behavior Books.

Savage-Rumbaugh, E. S., McDonald, K., Sevcik, R. A., Hopkins, W. D., & Rupert, E. (1986). Spontaneous symbol acquisition and communicative use by pygmy chimpanzees (*Pan paniscus*). *Journal of Experimental Psychology: General, 115,* 211–235.

Savage-Rumbaugh, E. S., Murphy, J., Sevcik, R. A., Brakke, K. E., Williams, S. L., & Rumbaugh, D. M. (1993). Language comprehension in ape and child. *Monographs of the Society for Research in Child Development, 58*(233), 1–254.

Sawyer, K. M., Wechsberg, W. M., & Meyers, B. J. (2006). Cultural similarities and differences between a sample of Black/African and colored women in South Africa: convergence of risk related to substance use, sexual behavior, and violence. *Women and Health, 43,* 73–92.

Scarr, S. (1992). Developmental theories for the 1990s: Development and individual differences. *Child Development, 63,* 1–19.

Scarr, S., & McCartney, K. (1983). How do people make their own environments: A theory of genotype environment effects. *Child Development, 54,* 424–435.

Scarr, S., & Weinberg, R. A. (1977). Intellectual similarities within families of both adopted and biological children. *Intelligence, 32,* 170–190.

Schachter, S. (1959). *The psychology of affiliation: Experimental studies of the sources of gregariousness.* Stanford, CA: Stanford University Press.

Schachter, S. (1966). The interaction of cognitive and physiological determinants of emotional state. In C. D. Spielberger (Ed.), *Anxiety and behavior.* New York: Academic Press.

Seligman, M. E. P. (2002). *Authentic happiness: Using the new positive psychology to realize your potential for lasting fulfillment.* New York: Free Press.

Seligman, M. E. P. (2008). Positive health. *Applied Psychology: An International Review, 57*, 3–18.

Seligman, M. E. P., & Isaacowitz, D. M. (2000). Learned helplessness. In G. Fink (Ed.), *Encyclopedia of stress.* San Diego, CA: Academic Press.

Seligman. M. E. P., & Maier, S. F. (1967). Failure to escape traumatic shock. *Journal of Experimental Psychology, 74*(1), 1–9.

Seligman, M. E. P., & Peterson, C. R. (Eds.) (2004). *Human strengths: A classification manual.* New York: Oxford University Press.

Seligman, M.E.P, Steen, T.A., Park, N. & Peterson, C. (2005) Positive psychology progress: empirical validation of interventions, *American Psychologist, 60*, 5, 410-421.

Selye, H. (1976). *The stress of life* (rev. ed.) New York: McGraw-Hill.

Selzer, M. L., Vinokur, A., & van Rooijen, L. A. (1975). Self-administered Short Michigan Alcoholism Screening (SMAST). *Journal of Studies on Alcohol and Drugs, 36*, 117–126.

Semba, R. D., Ferrucci, L., Bartali, B., Urpí-Sarda, M., Zamora-Ros, R., Sun, K., ... & Andres-Lacueva, C. (2014). Resveratrol levels and all-cause mortality in older community-dwelling adults. *JAMA Internal Medicine* 174(7): 1077–1084.

Semple, R. J., Reid, E. F. G., & Miller, L. (2005). Treating anxiety with mindfulness: An open trial of mindfulness training for anxious children. *Journal of Cognitive Psychotherapy, 19*(4), 379–392.

Senden, M. von (1960). *Space and sight: The perception of space and shape in the congenitally blind before and after operation* (Trans. P. Heath). New York: Free Press.

Sergios, P. A., & Cody, J. (1985–86). Importance of physical attractiveness and social assertive-ness skills in male homosexual dating behavior and partner selection. *Journal of Homosexuality, 12*, 71–84.

Serpell, R. (2000). Intelligence and culture. In R. J. Sternberg (Ed.) (2000). *Handbook of intelligence.* New York: Cambridge University Press.

Sexton, M. M. (1979). Behavioral epidemiology. In O. F. Pomerleau & J. P. Brady (Eds.), *Behavioral medicine: Theory and practice.* Baltimore, MD: Williams & Wilkins.

Shaffer, D. R. (1989). *Developmental psychology: Childhood and adolescence* (2nd ed.). Pacific Grove, CA: Brooks/Cole.

Shallice, T., & Burgess, P. (1991). Higher-order cognitive impairments and frontal-lobe lesions in man. In H. S. Levin, H. M. Eisenberg, & A. L. Benton (Eds.), *Frontal lobe function and dysfunction.* New York: Oxford University Press.

Shanab, M. E., & Yahya, L. A. (1977). A behavioral study of obedience in children. *Journal of Personality and Social Psychology, 35*, 530–536.

Shanahan, M., & Baars, B. J. (2005). Applying global workspace theory to the frame problem. *Cognition, 98* (2), 157–176.

Shapiro, A. K., & Shapiro, E. (1997). *The powerful placebo: From ancient priest to modern physician.* Baltimore, MD: Johns Hopkins University Press.

Shapiro, C. M., Bortz, R., Mitchell, D., Bartel, P., & Jooste, P. (1981). Slow-wave sleep: A recovery period after exercise. *Science, 214*, 1253–1254.

Shapiro, J. R. (2011). Different groups, different threats: A multi-threat approach to the experience of stereotype threats. *Personality and Social Psychology Bulletin, 37*, 464–480.

Shapiro, J. R., Williams, A. M., & Hambarchyan, M. (2013). Are all interventions created equal? A multi-threat approach to tailoring stereotype threat interventions. *Journal of Personality and Social Psychology, 104*(2), 277.

Shaver, P. R., & Clark, C. L. (1996). Forms of adult romantic attachment and their cognitive and emotional underpinnings. In G. G. Noam & K. W. Fischer (Eds.), *Development and vulnerability in close relationships: The Jean Piaget symposium series.* Mahwah, NJ: Erlbaum.

Shaver, P., Hazan, C., & Bradshaw, D. (1988). Love as attachment: The integration of three behavioral systems. In R. J. Sternberg & M. L. Barnes (Eds.), *The psychology of love.* New Haven, CT: Yale University Press.

Shavit, Y. (1990). Stress-induced immune modulation in animals: Opiates and endogenous opioid peptides. In R. Ader, N. Cohen, & D. L. Felten (Eds.), *Psychoneuroimmunology II.* New York: Academic Press.

Sheehan, P. W., Green, V., & Truesdale, P. (1992). Influence of rapport on hypnotically induced pseudomemory. *Journal of Abnormal Psychology, 101*, 690–700.

Sheldon, K. M., & Kasser, T. (2001). Getting older, getting better? Personal strivings and psychological maturity across the life span. *Developmental Psychology, 37*, 491–501.

Sheldon, K. M., Joiner, T. E., Pettit, J. W., & Williams, G. (2003). Reconciling humanistic ideals and scientific clinical practice. *Clinical Psychology: Science and Practice, 10*, 302–315.

Shen, H., Wan, F., & Wyer Jr, R. S. (2011). Cross-cultural differences in the refusal to accept a small gift: The differential influence of reciprocity norms on Asians and North Americans. *Journal of Personality and Social Psychology,100*(2), 271.

Shepard, R. N., & Metzler, J. (1971). Mental rotation of three-dimensional objects. *Science, 171*, 701–703.

Shepherd, G. (1997). *The synaptic organizer of the brain.* New York: Oxford University Press.

Shepperd, J. A., Grace, J., Cole, L. J., & Kline, C. (2005). Anxiety and outcome predictions. *Personality and Social Psychology Bulletin, 31*, 267–275.

Sherif, M. (1935). A study of some social factors in perception. *Archives of Psychology* (No. 187).

Sherif, M. (1966). *In common predicament: Social psychology of intergroup conflict and cooperation.* Boston, MA: Houghton Mifflin.

Sherif, M., Harvey, O., White, B., Hood, W. R., & Sherif, C. W. (1961). *Intergroup conflict and cooperation: The Robbers Cave experiment.* Norman, OK: University of Oklahoma Press.

Sherwood, L. (2011). *Fundamentals of human physiology*, Andover: Cengage.

Shier, D., Butler, J., & Lewis, R. (2004). *Hole's essentials of human anatomy and physiology*. Maidenhead: McGraw-Hill.

Shiffrin, R. M., & Schneider, W. (1977). Controlled and automatic human information processing: II. Perceptual learning, automatic attending, and a general theory. *Psychological Review, 84*, 127–190.

Shiota, M.N., Campos, B., Keltner, D., Hertenstein, M.J. (2004) *Positive Emotion and the Regulation of Interpersonal Relationships: The Regulation of Emotion*. Lawrence Erlbaum.

Shneidman, E. S. (1976). A psychological theory of suicide. *Psychiatric Annals, 6*, 51–66.

Shneidman, E. S. (1998). *The suicidal mind*. New York: Oxford University Press.

Shoda, Y., & Mischel, W. (2000). Reconciling contextualism with the core assumptions of personality psychology. *European Journal of Personality, 14*, 407–428.

Shoda, Y., Mischel, W., & Wright, J. C. (1994). Intra-individual stability and patterning of behavior: Incorporating psychological situations into the idiographic analysis of personality. *Journal of Personality and Social Psychology, 67*, 674–687.

Shoda, Y., Wilson, N. L., Chen, J., Gilmore, A. K., & Smith, R. E. (2013). Cognitive-affective processing system analysis of intra-individual dynamics in collaborative therapeutic assessment: Translating basic theory and research into clinical applications. *Journal of Personality, 81*(6), 554–568.

Shorey, H. S., & Snyder, C. R. (2006). The role of adult attachment styles in psychopathology and psychotherapy outcomes. *Review of General Psychology, 10*, 1–20.

Short, M. A., Gradisar, M., Lack, L. C., Wright, H. R., Dewald, J. F., Wolfson, A. R., & Carskadon, M. A. (2013). A cross-cultural comparison of sleep duration between US and Australian adolescents: The effect of school start time, parent-set bedtimes, and extracurricular load. *Health Education & Behavior, 40*(3), 323–330.

Shorter, E. (1998). *A history of psychiatry: From the era of the asylum to the age of Prozac*. New York: Wiley.

Shultz, K. S., Morton, K. R., & Weckerle, J. R. (1998). The influence of push and pull factors on voluntary and involuntary early retirees' retirement decision and adjustment. *Journal of Vocational Behavior, 53*, 45–57.

Shumba, A. (2010). Resilience in children of poverty. *Journal of Psychology in Africa, 20*, 211–213.

Sia, C. L., Tan, B. C. Y., & Wei, K. K. (2002). Group polarization and computer mediated communication: Effects of communication cues, social presence, and anonymity. *Information Systems Research, 13*, 70–90.

Siegel, A. (2005). *Neurobiology of aggression and rage*. San Francisco, CA: Taylor & Francis.

Siegel, L.S. (1982). The development of quantity concepts: Perceptual and linguistic factors. In C.J. Brainerd (Ed.), *Children's logical and mathematical cognition*. Berlin: Springer-Verlag.

Siegel, S. (1984). Pavlovian conditioning and heroin overdose: Reports from overdose victims. *Bulletin of the Psychonomic Society, 22*, 428–430.

Siegel, S., & Allan, L. G. (1996). The widespread influence of the Rescorla-Wagner model. *Psychonomic Bulletin and Review, 3*, 314–321.

Siegel, S., Baptista, M. A. S., Kim, J. A., McDonald, R. V., & Weise-Kelly, L. (2000). Pavlovian psychopharmacology: The associative basis of tolerance. *Experimental and Clinical Psychopharmacology, 8*, 276–293.

Siegler, R. S. (1986). *Children's thinking*. Englewood Cliffs, NJ: Prentice Hall.

Siegler, R. S. (1998). *Emerging minds: The process of change in children's thinking*. Oxford: Oxford University Press.

Sigala, N., & Logothetis, N. K. (2002). Visual categorization shapes feature selectivity in the primate temporal cortex. *Nature, 415*, 318–320.

Silber, K. (2014). *Schizophrenia*. Basingstoke: Palgrave.

Silverman, L. H., & Weinberger, J. (1985). Mommy and I are one: Implications for psychotherapy. *American Psychologist, 40*(12), 1296–1308.

Simkin, L. R., & Gross, A. M. (1994). Assessment of coping with high risk situations for exercise relapse among healthy women. *Health Psychology, 13*, 274–277.

Simon, C. (2007). *Neurology*. New York: Oxford University Press.

Simon, H. A. (1990). Invariants of human behavior. *Annual Review of Psychology, 41*, 1–20.

Simons, D. J., & Chabris, C. F. (1999). Gorillas in our midst: Sustained inattentional blindness for dynamic events. *Perception, 28*(9), 1059–1074.

Simonton, D. K. (1999). Creativity and genius. In L. A. Pervin & O. P. John (Eds.), *Handbook of personality: Theory and research* (2nd ed.). New York: Guilford Press.

Simonton, D. K. (2001). Talent development as a multidimensional, multiplicative, and dynamic process. *Current Directions in Psychological Science, 10*, 39–43.

Simpaio, E., Maris, S., & Bach-y-Rita, P. (2001). Brain plasticity: 'Visual' acuity of blind persons via the tongue. *Brain Research, 908*, 204–207.

Simpson, J., & Kelly, J. P. (2011). The impact of environmental enrichment in laboratory rats – behavioural and neurochemical aspects. *Behavioural Brain Research, 222*(1), 246–264.

Singer, T., Seymour, B., O'Doherty, J., Kaube, H., Dolan, R. J., & Frith, C. D. (2004). Empathy for pain involves the affective but not sensory components of pain. *Science, 303*, 1157–1162.

Singer, T., Verhaeghen, P., Ghisletta, P., Lindenberger, U., & Baltes, P. B. (2003). The fate of cognition in very old age: Six-year longitudinal findings in the Berlin Aging Study (BASE). *Psychology and Aging, 18*, 318–331.

Single, E., Robson, L., Rehm, J., & Xie, X. (1999). Morbidity and mortality attributable to alcohol, tobacco and illicit drug use in Canada. *American Journal of Public Health, 89*, 385–390.

Sistler, A. B., & Moore, G. M. (1996). Cultural diversity in coping with marital stress. *Journal of Clinical Geropsychology, 2*, 77–82.

Siu, O. (2003). Job stress and job performance among employees in Hong Kong: The role of Chinese work values and organizational commitment. *International Journal of Psychology, 38,* 337–347.

Sjöström, M., Oja, P., Hagströmer, M., Smith, B. J. & Bauman, A. (2006). Health-enhancing physical activity across European Union countries: The Eurobarometer study. *Journal of Public Health, 14,* 291–300.

Skinner, B. F. (1938). *The behavior of organisms: An experimental analysis.* New York: Appleton-Century-Crofts.

Skinner, B. F. (1945). Baby in a box: The mechanical baby-tender. *The Ladies Home Journal, 62,* 30–31, 135–136, 138.

Skinner, B. F. (1948). *Walden two.* New York: Macmillan.

Skinner, B. F. (1953). *Science and human behavior.* New York: Macmillan.

Skinner, B. F. (1957). *Verbal behavior.* New York: Prentice Hall.

Skinner, B. F. (1971). *Beyond freedom and dignity.* New York: Knopf.

Skinner, B. F. (1989). Teaching machines. *Science, 243,* 15–35.

Skinner, B. F. (1990). Can psychology be a science of mind? *American Psychologist, 45,* 1206–1210.

Sklar, L. S., & Anisman, H. (1981). Stress and cancer. *Psychological Bulletin, 89,* 369–406.

Skotko, B. G., Kensinger, E. A., Locascio, J. J., Einstein, G., Rubin, D. C., Tupler, L. A., Krendl, A., & Corkin, S. (2004). Puzzling thoughts for H. M.: Can new semantic information be anchored to old semantic memories? *Neuropsychology, 18*(4), 756–769.

Skoyles, J. R. (1997). Evolution's 'missing link': A hypothesis upon neural plasticity, prefrontal working memory and the origins of modern cognition. *Medical Hypotheses, 48,* 499–501.

Slater, A. M., Morison, V., & Rose, D. (1983). Perception of shape by the newborn baby. *British Journal of Developmental Psychology, 1,* 135–142.

Slater, A., von der Schulenberg, C., Brown, G., Badenoch, M., Butterworth, G.,

Parsons, S., & Samuels, C. (1998). Newborn infants prefer attractive faces. *Infant Behavior and Development, 21,* 345–354.

Slater, C. L. (2003). Generativity versus stagnation: An elaboration of Erikson's adult stage of human development. *Journal of Adult Development, 10,* 53–65.

Slater, P. J. B. (1981). Chaffinch song repertoires: Observations, experiments and a discussion of their significance. *Zeitschrift fur Tierpsychologie, 56,* 1–24.

Sloan, D., & Marx, D. (2004). A closer examination of the structured written disclosure procedure. *Journal of Consulting and Clinical Psychology, 72,* 165–175.

Slotnick, S. D., Thompson, W. L., & Kosslyn, S. M. (2005). Visual mental imagery induces retinotopically organized activation of early visual areas. *Cerebral Cortex, 15,* 1570–1583.

Slovic, P., & Peters, E. (2006). Risk perception and affect. *Current Directions in Psychological Science. 15,* 322–325.

Slovic, P., Fischhoff, B., & Lichtenstein, S. (1988). Response mode, framing, and information-processing effects in risk assessment. In D. E. Bell & H. Raiffa (Eds.), *Decision making: Descriptive, normative, and prescriptive interactions.* New York: Cambridge University Press.

Smalley, S. L., McGough, J. J., Del'Homme, M., NewDelman, J., Gordon, E., Kim, T., Liu, A., & McCracken, J. T. (2000). Familial clustering of symptoms and disruptive behaviors in multiplex families with attention-deficit/hyperactivity disorder. *Journal of the American Academy of Child & Adolescent Psychiatry, 39,* 1135–1143.

Smart, R. G., & Ogbourne, A. C. (2001). Drinking and heavy drinking by students in 18 countries. *Drug Alcohol Dependence, 60,* 315–318.

Smillie, L. D., Cooper, A., Proitsi, P., Powell, J. F., & Pickering, A. D. (2010). Variation in DRD2 dopamine gene predicts extraverted personality. *Neuroscience Letters, 468,* 234–237.

Smillie, L. D., Cooper, A. J., & Pickering, A. D. (2011). Individual differences in reward–prediction–error: Extraversion

and feedback-related negativity. *Social Cognitive and Affective Neuroscience, 6*(5), 646–652.

Smith, B. D. (1998). *Psychology: Science and understanding.* New York: McGraw-Hill.

Smith, C. A., & Kirby, L. D. (2004). Appraisal as a pervasive determinant of anger. *Emotion, 4,* 133–138.

Smith, C. A. & Lazarus, R. S. (1993). Appraisal components, core relational themes, and the emotions. *Cognition and Emotion, 7,* 233–269.

Smith, C. S., Folkard, S., Schmieder, R. A., Parra, L. F., Spelten, E., Almiral, H., … Tisak, J. (2002). Investigation of morning-evening orientation in six countries using the preferences scale. *Personality and Individual Differences, 32,* 949–968.

Smith, C. T., Nixon, M. R., & Nader, R. S. (2004). Posttraining increases in REM sleep intensity implicate REM sleep in memory processing and provide a biological marker of learning potential. *Learning and Memory, 11,* 714–719.

Smith, D. (2002). The theory heard 'round the world. *Monitor on Psychology, 33* (9). Retrieved from http://www.apa.org/monitor/oct02/theory.html.

Smith, D. H. (2000). *Grassroots associations.* Thousand Oaks, CA: Sage.

Smith, D. V. and Seiden, A. M. (1991). *Olfactory dysfunction.* In D. G. Laing, R. L. Doty, & W. Breipohl (Eds.), *The human sense of smell.* New York: Springer-Verlag.

Smith, E. R., & Zarate, M. A. (1992). Exemplar-based model of social judgment. *Psychological Review, 99,* 3–21.

Smith, J. W., & Frawley, P. J. (1993). Treatment outcome of 600 chemically dependent patients treated in a multimodal inpatient program including aversion therapy and pentothal interviews. *Journal of Substance Abuse Treatment, 10,* 359–369.

Smith, M. C., & Phillips, M. R., Jr. (2001). Age differences in memory for radio advertisements: The role of mnemonic. *Journal of Business Research, 53,* 103–109.

Smith, M. L., & Glass, G. V. (1977). Metaanalyses of psychotherapy outcome studies. *American Psychologist, 32,* 752–760.

Smith, M.R., & Eastman, C. I. (2008). Improving night shift adaptation: Night shift performance is improved by a compromise circadian phase position: Study 3. Circadian phase after 7 night shifts with an intervening weekend off. *Sleep, 31*(12).

Smith, N., Young, A., & Lee, C. (2004). Optimism health-related hardiness and wellbeing among older Australian women. *Journal of Health Psychology, 9*, 741–752.

Smith, P., & Waterman, M. G. (2005). Sex differences in processing aggression words using the emotional Stroop task. *Aggressive Behavior, 31*, 271–282.

Smith, P. B., & Dugan, S. (1998). Individualism: Collectivism and the handling of disagreement: A 23 country study. *International Journal of Intercultural Relations, 22*, 351–367.

Smith, P. B., Bond, M. H., & Kagitcibasi, C. (2006). *Understanding social psychology across cultures: Living and working in a changing world.* London: Sage.

Smith, P. K., Cowie, H., & Blades, M. (2003). *Understanding children's development* (3rd ed.). Oxford: Blackwell.

Smith, R. E. (1989). Effects of coping skills training on generalized self-efficacy and locus of control. *Journal of Personality and Social Psychology, 56*, 228–233.

Smith, R. E. (1996). Performance anxiety, cognitive interference, and concentration enhancement strategies in sports. In I. G. Sarason, G. R. Pierce, & B. R. Sarason (Eds.), *Cognitive interference: Theories, methods, and findings.* Mahwah, NJ: Erlbaum.

Smith, R. E., Smoll, F. L., & Cumming, S. P. (2007). Effects of a motivational climate intervention for coaches on young athletes' sport performance anxiety. *Journal of Sport and Exercise Psychology, 29*, 38–58.

Smith, R. E., Smoll, F. L., & Schultz, R. W. (1990). Measurement and correlates of sportspecific cognitive and somatic trait anxiety: The Sports Anxiety Scale. *Anxiety Research* [now *Anxiety, Stress, & Coping*], *2*, 263–280.

Smith, S. M., & Vela, E. (2001). Environmental context dependent memory: A review and meta-analysis. *Psychonomic Bulletin and Review, 8*, 203–220.

Smith, S. M., McIntosh, W. D., & Bazzini, D. G. (1999). Are the beautiful good in Hollywood? An investigation of the beauty-and-goodness stereotype on film. *Basic and Applied Social Psychology, 21*, 69–80.

Smithson, J., Lewis, S., Cooper, C., & Dyer, J. (2004). Flexible working and the gender pay gap in the accountancy profession. *Work, Employment and Society, 18*, 115–135.

Smoll, F. L., Smith, R. E., & Cumming, S. P. (2007). Effects of a motivational climate intervention for coaches on young athletes' achievement goal orientations. *Journal of Clinical Sport Psychology, 1*, 23–46.

Smoll, F. L., Smith, R. E., Barnett, N. P., & Everett, J. J. (1993). Enhancement of children's self-esteem through social support training for youth sport coaches. *Journal of Applied Psychology, 78*, 602–610.

Smyth, J. M., Soefer, M. H., Hurewitz, A., & Stone, A. A. (1999). The effect of tape-recorded relaxation training on well-being, symptoms, and peak expiratory flow rate in adult asthmatics: A pilot study. *Psychology & Health, 14*, 487–501.

Snow, M. E., Jacklin, C. N., & Maccoby, E. E. (1983). Sex-of-child-differences in fatherchild interaction at one year of age. *Child Development, 54*, 227–232.

Snyder, C. R. (Ed.) (2001). *Coping with stress: Effective people and processes.* New York: Oxford University Press.

Snyder, C. R., & Lopez, S. J. (2007). *Positive psychology: The scientific and practical explorations of human strengths.* Thousand Oaks, CA: Sage Publications.

Snyder, M. (1987). *Public appearances/private realities: The psychology of self-monitoring.* New York: Freeman.

Snyder, M., Clary, E. G., & Stukas, A. A. (2000). The functional approach to volunteerism. In G. R. Maio & J. M. Olson (Eds.), *Why we evaluate: Functions of attitudes.* Mahwah, NJ: Erlbaum.

Snyder, S. H. (1977). Opiate receptors and internal opiates. *Scientific American, 236*, 44–56.

Soares, M. J., Macedo, A., Bos, S. C., Marques, M., Maia, B., Pereira, A. T., …

Azevedo, M. H. (2009). Perfectionism and eating attitudes in Portuguese students: A longitudinal study. *European Eating Disorders Review, 17*(5), 390–398.

Society for Personality Assessment. (2005). The status of the Rorschach in clinical and forensic practice: An official statement by the Board of Trustees of the Society for Personality Assessment. *Journal of Personality Assessment, 85*, 219–237.

Solberg Nes, L., & Segerstrom S. C. (2006). Dispositional optimism and coping: A meta-analytic review. *Personality and Social Psychology Review, 10*, 235–251.

Solms, M. (2002). Dreaming: Cholinergic and dopaminergic hypotheses. In E. Perry, H. Ashton, & A. Young (Eds.), *Neurochemistry of consciousness: Neurotransmitters in mind. Advances in consciousness research.* Amsterdam: Benjamins.

Solomon, R. L., & Wynne, L. C. (1953). Traumatic avoidance learning: Acquisition in normal dogs. *Journal of Abnormal and Social Psychology, 48*, 291–302.

Son, L. K., & Metcalfe, J. (2000). Metacognitive and control strategies in study-time allocation. *Journal of Experimental Psychology: Learning, Memory, and Cognition, 26*, 204–221.

Sorce, J. F., Emde, R. N., Campos, J., & Klinnert, M. D. (1985). Maternal emotional signalling: Its effect on the visual cliff behaviour of 1-year-olds. *Developmental Psychology, 21*, 195–200.

Soussignan, R. (2002). Duchenne smile, emotional experience, and autonomic reactivity: A test of the facial feedback hypothesis. *Emotion, 2*, 52–74.

Sowell, E. R., Thompson, P. M., Tessner, K. D., & Toga, A. W. (2001). Mapping continued brain growth and gray matter density reduction in dorsal frontal cortex: Inverse relationships during postadolescent brain maturation. *Journal of Neuroscience, 21*, 8819–8829.

Spanos, N. P. (1986). Hypnotic behavior: A social-psychological interpretation of amnesia, analgesia, and 'trance logic.' *Behavioral and Brain Sciences, 9*, 449–467.

Spanos, N. P. (1991). A sociocognitive approach to hypnosis. In S. J. Lynn & J. W. Rhue (Eds.), *Theories of hypnosis:*

responses in pediatric cancer patients receiving chemotherapy: Features of a classically conditioned response? *Brain, Behavior and Immunity, 14*, 198–218.

Stoker, B. (1897). *Dracula*. Hertfordshire: Wordsworth Classics

Stokstad, E. (2001). Development: New hints into the biological basis of autism. *Science, 294*, 34–37.

Stone, A. A., Shiffman, S. S., & DeVries, M. (2000). Rethinking our self-report assessment methodologies: An argument for collecting ecologically valid, momentary measurements. In D. Kahneman, E. Diener, & N. Schwarz (Eds.), *Understanding quality of life: Scientific perspectives on enjoyment and suffering*. New York: Russel Sage.

Stone, J., & Cooper, J. (2003). The effect of self-attribute relevance on how self-esteem moderates attitude change in dissonance processes. *Journal of Experimental Social Psychology, 39*, 508–515.

Stone, J., Warlow, C., & Sharpe, M. (2010). The symptom of functional weakness: A controlled study of 107 patients. *Brain, 133*(5), 1537–1551.

Stone, K., & Church, S. L. (1968). *Personality theories*. San Francisco, CA: Jossey-Bass.

Stone, M., Laughren, T., Jones, M. L., Levenson, M., Holland, P. C., Hughes, A., …, Rochester, G. (2009). Risk of suicidality in clinical trials of antidepressants in adults: Analysis of proprietary date submitted to US Food and Drug Administration. *British Medical Journal, 339*, b3066.

Stormshak, E. A., Bierman, K. L., McMahon, R. J., & Lengua, L. J. (2000). Parenting practices and child disruptive behavior problems in early elementary school. *Journal of Clinical Child Psychology, 29*, 17–29.

Stouffer, S. A., Lumsdaine, A. A., Lumsdaine, M. H., & Williams, R. M., Jr (1949a). *The American soldier: Combat and its aftermath*. Princeton, NJ: Princeton University Press.

Stouffer, S. A., Suchman, E. A., De Vinney, L. C., Star, S. A., & Williams, R. M. (1949b). *The American soldier: Adjustments during army life*. Princeton, NJ: Princeton University Press.

Støving, R. K., Andries, A., Brixen, K., Flyvbjerg, A., Hörder, K., &

Frystyk, J. (2009). Leptin, ghrelin, and endocannabinoids: Potential therapeutic targets in anorexia nervosa. *Journal of Psychiatric Research, 43*, 671–679.

Strack, F. (2009). The crisis in economics, a challenge for psychology. *Psychological Science in the Public Interest, 10*(1). doi: 10.1177/1529100610382386.

Strack, F., Martin, L. L., & Stepper, S. (1988). Inhibiting and facilitating conditions of facial expressions: A non-obtrusive test of the facial feedback hypothesis. *Journal of Personality and Social Psychology, 54*, 768–777.

Strand, S., Deary, I. J., & Smith, P. (2006). Sex differences in cognitive abilities test scores: A UK national picture. *British Journal of Educational Psychology, 76*, 463–480.

Stratton, G. M. (1896). Some preliminary experiments on vision without inversion of the retinal image. *Psychological Review, 3*(6), 611–617.

Straus, M. A., & Stewart, J. H. (1999). Corporal punishment by American parents: National data on prevalence, chronicity, severity, and duration, in relation to child and family characteristics. *Clinical Child and Family Psychology Review, 2* (2), 55–70.

Strauss, E., Sherman, E. M. S., & Spreen, O. (2006). *A compendium of neuropsychological tests: Administration, norms, and commentary*. New York: Oxford University Press.

Strawbridge, W. J., Shema, S. J., Cohen, R. D., Roberts, R. E., & Kaplan, G. A. (1998). Religiosity buffers effects of some stressors on depression but exacerbates others. *Journal of Gerontology, 53*, 118–126.

Streissguth, A. P. (1977). Maternal drinking and the outcome of pregnancy: Implications for child mental health. *American Journal of Orthopsychiatry, 47*, 422–431.

Streissguth, A. P. (1997). *Fetal alcohol syndrome*. New York: Oxford University Press.

Streissguth, A. P. (2001). Recent advances in fetal alcohol syndrome and alcohol use in pregnancy. In D. P. Agarwal & H. K. Seitz (Eds.), *Alcohol in health and disease*. New York: Marcel Dekker.

Streissguth, A. P. (2007). Offspring effects of prenatal alcohol exposure from birth to 25 years: The Seattle prospective longitudinal study. *Journal of Clinical Psychology in Medical Settings, 14*, 81–101.

Strentz, T., & Auerbach, S. M. (1988). Adjustment to the stress of simulated captivity: Effects of emotion-focused versus problem-focused preparation on hostages differing in locus of control. *Journal of Personality and Social Psychology, 55*, 652–660.

Striedter, G. F. (2005). *Principles of brain evolution*. Springfield, IL: Sinauer.

Stroebe, M., Stroebe, W., & Schut, H. (2001). Gender differences in adjustment to bereavement: An empirical and theoretical review. *Review of General Psychology, 5*, 62–82.

Stroebe, W. (2010). Majority and minority influence and information processing: A theoretical and methodological analysis. *Minority influence and innovation: Antecedents, processes and consequences*, 201–225.

Stroop, J. R. ([1935] 1992). Studies of interference in serial verbal reactions. *Journal of Experimental Psychology: General, 121*, 15–23.

Stroop, J. R. (1935). Studies of interference in serial verbal reactions. *Journal of Experimental Psychology, 18*, 643–662.

Stryer, L. (1987). The molecules of visual excitation. *Scientific American, 257*(1), 42–50.

Sturm, R. (2002). The effects of obesity, smoking, and drinking on medical problems and costs: Obesity outranks both smoking and drinking in its deleterious effects on health and health costs. *Health Affairs, 21*, 245–253.

Subramanian, K. N. S., Yoon, H., & Toral, J. C. (2002, October 31). *Extremely low birth weight infant*. Retrieved from http://www. emedicine.com/ped/topic2784.htm.

Sudhof, T. C. (2008). Neuroligins and neurexins link synaptic function to cognitive disease. *Nature, 455*, 903–911.

Sue, D. W., & Sue, D. (1990). *Counseling the culturally different: Theory and practice*. New York: Wiley.

Sue, S. (1998). In search of cultural competence in psychotherapy and counseling. *American Psychologist, 53,* 440–448.

Sue, S., & Chu, J. (2003). The mental health of ethnic minority groups: Challenges posed by the U.S. Surgeon General. *Culture, Medicine and Psychiatry, 27,* 447–465.

Sue, S., & Zane, N. (1987). The role of culture and cultural techniques in psychotherapy. *American Psychologist, 42,* 37–45.

Sue, S., Fujino, D., Hu, L., Takeuchi, D., & Zane, N. (1991). Community mental health services for ethnic minority groups: A test of the cultural responsiveness hypothesis. *Journal of Consulting and Clinical Psychology, 59,* 533–540.

Sugita, Y. (2004). Experience in early infancy is indispensable for color perception. *Current Biology, 14,* 1267–1271.

Suh, E., Diener, E., Oishi, S., & Triandis, H. (1998). The shifting basis of life satisfaction judgments across cultures: Emotions versus norms. *Journal of Personality and Social Psychology, 74,* 482–493.

Suinn, R. M., Osborne, D., & Winfree, P. (1962). The self-concept and accuracy of recall of inconsistent self-related information. *Journal of Clinical Psychology, 18,* 473–474.

Suls, J. M., & Wallston, K. A. (2003). *Social psychological foundations of health and illness.* New York: Blackwell.

Sun, M.-K. (Ed.) (2005). *Cognition and mood interactions.* Hauppauge, NY: Nova Science.

Sun, W. L., & Rebec, G. V. (2005). The role of prefrontal cortex D1-like and D2-like receptors in cocaine-seeking behavior in rats. *Psychopharmacology, 177,* 315–323.

Sunnafrank, M., Ramirez, A., Jr., & Metts, S. (Eds.) (2004). At first sight: Persistent relational effects of get-acquainted conversations. *Journal of Social and Personal Relationships, 21,* 361–379.

Super, D. E. (1957). *The psychology of careers.* New York: Harper & Row.

Sussman, N. M., & Rosenfeld, H. M. (1982). Influence of culture, language, and sex on conversational distance. *Journal of Personality and Social Psychology, 42,* 66–74.

Sutton, R., & Douglas, K. (2013) *Social psychology.* Basingstoke: Palgrave Macmillan.

Sutton, S. K. (2002). Incentive and threat reactivity: Relations with anterior cortical activity. In D. Cervone & W. Mischel (Eds.), *Advances in personality science.* New York: Guilford Press.

Sutton, R. M., & McClure, J. (2001). Covariational influences on goal-based explanation: An integrative model. *Journal of Personality and Social Psychology, 80,* 222–236.

Swain, J. C., & McLaughlin, T. F. (1998). The effects of bonus contingencies in a classwide token program on math accuracy with middle-school students with behavioral disorders. *Behavioral Interventions, 13,* 11–19.

Swann, W. B., Jr, Stein-Seroussi, A., & Giesler, R. B. (1992). Why people self-verify. *Journal of Personality and Social Psychology, 62,* 392–401.

Swartz, C. (1995). Setting the ECT stimulus. *Psychiatric Times, 12* (6). (Reprint edition.)

Swim, J. K., Clayton, S., Doherty, T., Gifford, R., Howard, G., Reser, J., Stern, P., & Weber, E. (2009). *Psychology and global climate change: Addressing a multi-faceted phenomenon and set of challenges. A report by the American Psychological Association's Task Force on the Interface between Psychology and Global Climate Change.*

Sylvius Interactive Brain Anatomy Dictionary (2014). Please visit the book's OLC site to access the Dictionary: http://www.mheducation.co.uk/textbooks/holt

Szadoczky, E., Papp, Z., Vitrai, J., & Füredi, J. (2000). A hangulat- és szorongásos zavarok előfordulása a felnőtt magyar lakosság körében. *Orvosi Hetilap, 141*(1), 17–22.

Szasz, T. (1963). *Law, liberty, and psychiatry: An inquiry into the social uses of mental health practices.* New York: Collier Books.

Szasz, T. S. (2004). *Faith in freedom: Libertarian principles and psychiatric practices.* Somerset, NJ: Transaction.

Szkrybalo, J., & Ruble, D. N. (1999). 'God made me a girl': Sex-category constancy judgments and explanations revisited. *Developmental Psychology, 35,* 392–402.

T

Taft, M. (1979). Lexical access via an orthographic code: The Basic Orthographic Syllabic Structure (BOSS). *Journal of Verbal Learning and Verbal Behavior, 18,* 21–39.

Taga, G., Watanabe, H., & Homae, F. (2011). Spatiotemporal properties of cortical haemodynamic response to auditory stimuli in sleeping infants revealed by multi-channel near-infrared spectroscopy. *Philosophical Transactions of the Royal Society A: Mathematical, Physical & Engineering Sciences, 369,* 4495–4511.

Tajfel, H., & Turner, J. C. (1979). An integrative theory of inter-group conflict. In W. G. Austin & S. Worchel (Eds.), *The social psychology of inter-group relations.* Monterey, CA: Brooks/Cole.

Tajfel, H., & Turner, J. C. (1986). The social identity theory of intergroup behavior. In S. Worchel & W. G. Austin (Eds.), *The psychology of intergroup relations* (2nd ed.). Chicago, IL: Nelson Hall.

Tajfel, H., & Wilkes, A. L. (1963). Classification and quantitative judgement. *British Journal of Psychology, 54,* 101–114.

Takahashi, Y. (1990). Is multiple personality disorder really rare in Japan? *Dissociation: Progress in the Dissociative Disorders, 3,* 57–59.

Talarico, J. M., & Rubin, D. C. (2003). Confidence, not consistency, characterizes flashbulb memories. *Psychological Science, 14,* 455–461.

Tamminga, C. A. (1997). The promise of new drugs for schizophrenia treatment. *Canadian Journal of Psychiatry, 42,* 265–273.

Tanaka-Matsumi, J. (1979). Taijin Kyofushu: Diagnostic and cultural issues in Japanese psychiatry. *Culture, Medicine, and Psychiatry, 3,* 231–245.

Tanaka-Matsumi, J., & Draguns, J. G. (1997). Culture and psychopathology. In J. W. Berry, M. H. Segall, & C. Kagitçibasi (Eds.), *Handbook of cross-cultural psychology* (Vol. 3). Boston, MA: Allyn & Bacon.

Tangney, C. C., Kwasny, M. J., Li, H., Wilson, R. S., Evans, D. A., & Morris, M. C. (2011). Adherence to a Mediterranean-type dietary

Treasure, J. (2005). *Essential handbook of eating disorders.* New York: Wiley.

Treisman, A. M. (1964). Selective attention in man. *British Medical Bulletin, 20,* 12–16.

Tremblay, L. K., Naranjo, C. A., Cardenas, L., Hermann, N., & Busto, U. E. (2002). Probing brain reward system function in major depressive disorder: Altered response to dextroamphetamine. *Archives of General Psychiatry, 59,* 409–417.

Trevarthen, C., & Aitken, K. J. (2001). Infant intersubjectivity: Research, theory, and clinical applications. *Journal of Child Psychology and Psychiatry, 42*(1), 3–48.

Trevethan, C. T., Sahraie, A., & Weiskrantz, L. (2004). Blindsight superior to 'sighted-sight'? *Journal of Vision, 4* (8), 204a.

Triandis, H. C. (1990). Cross-cultural studies of individualism and collectivism. In J. J. Berman (Ed.), *Nebraska symposium on motivation, 1989: Cross-cultural perspectives.* Lincoln, NE: University of Nebraska Press.

Triandis, H. C. (1994). *Culture and social behavior.* New York: McGraw-Hill.

Triandis, H. C. (1995). *Individualism and collectivism.* Boulder, CO: Westview.

Triandis, H. C., & Suh, E. M. (2002). Cultural influences on personality. *Annual Review of Psychology, 53,* 133–160.

Trimble, M. (2003). *Somatoform disorders.* New York: Cambridge University Press.

Triplett, N. (1898). The dynamogenic factors in pace-making and competition. *American Journal of Psychology, 9,* 507–533.

Trivers, R. (1971). The evolution of reciprocal altruism. *Quarterly Review of Biology, 46,* 35–57.

Trivers, R. L. (1972). Parental investment and sexual selection. In B. Campbell (Ed.), *Sexual selection and the descent of man.* Chicago, IL: Aldine-Atherton.

Tronick, E., Als, H., Adamson, L., Wise, S., & Brazelton, T. B. (1979). The infant's response to entrapment between contradictory messages in face-to-face interaction. *Journal of the American Academy of Child Psychiatry, 17*(1), 1–13.

Trottier, D., Roulear, J. Renaud, P., & Goyette, M. (2013). Using eye tracking to identify faking attempts during penile plethysmography assessment. *The Journal of Sex Research,* doi: 10.1080/00224499.2013.832133.

Trull, T. J., & Geary, D. C. (1997). Comparison of the Big-Five Factor structure across samples of Chinese and American adults. *Journal of Personality Assessment, 69,* 324–341.

Truscott, S. D., & Frank, A. J. (2001). Does the Flynn effect affect IQ scores of students classified as LD? *Journal of School Psychology, 39,* 319–334.

Trzesniewski, K. H., Donnellan, M. B., & Robins, R. W. (2003). Stability of self-esteem across the life span. *Journal of Personality and Social Psychology, 84,* 205–220.

Tsai, S. J., Yu, Y. W. Y., Lin, C. H., Chen, T. J., Chen, S. P. & Hong, C. J. (2002). Dopamine D2 receptor and N-methyl-D-aspartate receptor 2B subunit genetic variants and intelligence. *Neuropsychobiology, 45*(3), 128–130.

Tseng, W. S., Asai, M., Liu, J., Pismai, W., Suryani, L. K., Wen, J.-K., Brennan, J., & Heiby, E. (1990). Multi-cultural study of minor psychiatric disorders in Asia: Symptom manifestations. *International Journal of Social Psychiatry, 36,* 252–264.

Tucci, S., & Peters, J. (2008). Media influences on body satisfaction in female students. *Psicothema, 20*(4), 521–524.

Tucker, V. A. (2000). The deep fovea, sideways vision and spiral flight paths in raptors. *Journal of Experimental Biology, 203,* 3745–3754.

Tudor, M. (1939). *An experimental study of the effect of evaluative labeling of speech fluency.* Iowa City: University of Iowa Press.

Tuiten, A., Van Honk, J., Koppeschaar, H., Bernaards, C., Thijssen, J., & Verbaten, R. (2000). Time course of effects of testosterone administration on sexual arousal in women. *Archives of General Psychiatry, 57,* 149–153.

Tulsky, D. S., Saklofske, D. H., Chelune, G. J., Heaton, R. K., Ivnik, R. J., Bornstein, R., Prifitera, A., & Ledbetter, M. F. (Eds.) (2003). *Clinical interpretation of the WAIS-III and WMSIII.* San Diego, CA: Academic Press.

Tulving, E. (2002). Episodic memory: From mind to brain. *Annual Review of Psychology, 53,* 1–25.

Tulving, E., & Thomson, D. M. (1973). Encoding specificity and retrieval processes in episodic memory. *Psychological Review, 80,* 359–380.

Tupala, E., & Tiihonen, J. (2004). Dopamine and alcoholism: Neurobiological basis of ethanol abuse. *Progress in Neuro-Psychopharmacology & Biological Psychiatry, 28,* 1221–1247.

Turk, D. C. (2001). Physiological and psychological bases of pain. In A. Baum & T. A. Revenson (Eds.), *Handbook of health psychology.* Mahwah, NJ: Erlbaum.

Turk, D. C., & Melzack, R. (2001). *Handbook of pain assessment* (2nd ed.). New York: Guilford Press.

Turkheimer, E., Haley, A., Waldron, N., D'Onofrio, B., & Gottesman, I. I. (2003). Socioeconomic status modifies heritability of IQ in young children. *Psychological Science, 14,* 623–628.

Turkheimer, E., Pettersson, E., & Horn, E. E. (2014). A phenotypic null hypothesis for the genetics of personality. *Annual Review of Psychology, 65,* 515–540.

Turnbull, C. M. (1961). Some observations concerning the experiences and behavior of the BaMbuti Pygmies. *American Journal of Psychology, 74,* 304–308.

Turner, J. A., & Aaron, L. A. (2001). Painrelated catastrophizing: What is it? *Clinical Journal of Pain, 17,* 65–71.

Turner, J. A., Deyo, R. A., Loeser, J. D., Von Korff, M., & Fordyce, W. E. (1994). The importance of placebo effects in pain treatment and research. *Journal of the American Medical Association, 271,* 1609–1614.

Turner, J. C. (1991). *Social influence.* Milton Keynes: Open University Press.

Turner, J. C., Hogg, M. A., Oakes, P. J., Reicher, S. D., & Wetherell, M. S. (1987). *Rediscovering the social group: A self-categorization theory.* Oxford: Blackwell.

Turner, M. E., & Pratkanis, A. R. (1998). A social identity maintenance model of groupthink. *Organizational Behavior and Human Decision Processes, 73,* 210–235.

Turner, R. N., & Crisp, R. J. (2010). Imagining intergroup contact reduces implicit prejudice. *British Journal of Social Psychology, 49,* 129–142.

Tusing, K. J., & Dillard, J. P. (2000). The psychological reality of the door-in-the-face: It's helping, not bargaining. *Journal of Language and Social Psychology, 19*, 5–25.

Tversky, A., & Kahneman, D. (1982). Judgments of and by representativeness. In D. Kahneman, P. Slovic, & A. Tversky (Eds.), *Heuristics and biases.* Cambridge: Cambridge University Press.

Tversky, B., & Tuchin, M. (1989). A reconciliation of the evidence on eyewitness testimony: Comments on McCloskey and Zaragoza. *Journal of Experimental Psychology: General, 118*, 86–91.

Tyrka, A. R., Waldron, I., Graber, J. A., & Brooks-Gunn, J. (2002). Prospective predictors of the onset of anorexic and bulimic syndromes. *International Journal of Eating Disorders, 32*, 282–290.

Tzeng, O. J., Hung, W., Cohen, F. J., & Wang, P. (1979). Visual lateralization effect in reading Chinese characters. *Nature, 282*, 499–501.

Tzeng, S. F. (1997). Neural progenitors isolated from newborn rat spinal cords differentiate into neurons and astroglia. *Journal of Biomedical Science, 9* (1), 10–16.

U

Ungerleider, L. G., & Mishkin, M. (1982). Two cortical visual systems. In D. J. Ingle, M. A. Goodale, & R. J. W. Mansfield (Eds.), *Analysis of visual behavior.* Cambridge, MA: MIT Press.

Unkelbach, C., Forgas, J. P., & Denson, T. F. (2008). The turban effect: The influence of Muslim headgear and induced affect on aggressive responses in the shooter bias paradigm. *Journal of Experimental Social Psychology, 44*, 1409–1413.

United Nations. (2002). *Report on the global reach of AIDS.* New York: Editorinfo.

Unverzagt, F. W., Gao, S., Baiyewu, O., Ogunniyi, A. O., Gureje, O., Perkins, A., … Hendrie, H. C. (2001). Prevalence of cognitive impairment: Data from the Indianapolis Study of Health and Aging. *Neurology, 57*, 1655–1662.

US Census Bureau (2011). *American Community Survey* : Table C16001.

Language spoken at home by ability to speak English for the population 5 years and over. Retrieved from http://factfinder.census. gov/servlet/ DTTable?_bm=y&-geo_id=0100... lang=en&-mt_name=ACS_2005_EST_ G2000_C16001&-format=&-CONTEXT=dt.

US Census Bureau. (2011). Language Use in the United States: 2011: *American Community Service Reports.* Retrieved July 16th 2014, from http://www.census.gov/acs/www/ data_documentation/2011_release/

US National Institute of Mental Health (1992). *Psychiatric hospitalization in the United States.* Rockville, MD: Author.

US Public Health Service (1979). *Healthy people: The Surgeon General's report on health promotion and disease prevention.* Washington, DC: US Government Printing Office.

Usborne, D., & Taylor, D. M. (2010). The role of cultural identity clarity for self-concept clarity, self-esteem, and subjective well-being. *Personality and Social Psychology Bulletin, 36*(7), 883–897.

V

Valberg, A. (2006). *Light vision color.* New York: John Wiley & Sons.

Valent, P. (2000). Stress effects of the holocaust. In G. Fink (Ed.), *Encyclopedia of stress.* San Diego, CA: Academic Press.

Vallone, R. P., Griffin, D., Lin, S., & Ross, L. (1990). Overconfident prediction of future actions and outcomes by self and others. *Journal of Personality and Social Psychology, 58*, 582–592.

Valsiner, J., & Lawrence, J. A. (1997). Human development in culture across the life span. In J. W. Berry, P. R. Dasen, & T. S. Saraswathi (Eds.), *Handbook of cross-cultural psychology* (Vol. 2). Boston: Allyn & Bacon.

Van den Dries, L., Juffer, F., van IJzendoorn, M. H., & Bakermans-Kranenburg, M. J. (2009). Fostering security? A meta-analysis of attachment in adopted children. *Children and Youth Services Review, 31*(3), 410–421.

Van der Borght, K., Meerlo, P., Luiten, P., Eggen, B., & Van der Zee, E. A. (2005). Effects of active shock avoidance learning

on hippocampal neurogenesis and plasma levels of corticosterone. *Behavioural Brain Research, 157*, 23–30.

Van der Horst, F. (2011). *John Bowlby: From psychoanalysis to ethology.* Chichester: Wiley-Blackwell.

Van Der Werf, Y. D., Jolles, J., Witter, M. P., & Uylings, H. B. M. (2003). Contributions of thalamic nuclei to declarative memory functioning. *Cortex, 39*, 1047–1062.

Van Goozen, S., Snoek, H., Fairchild, G., & Harold, G. (2007). The evidence for a neurobiological model of childhood antisocial behavior. *Psychological Bulletin, 133*(1), 149–182.

Van Hemert, D. (2003). *Patterns of crosscultural differences in psychology: A metaanalytic approach.* Amsterdam: Dutch University Press FSW publicatiereeks.

Van IJzendoorn, M. (1995). Adult attachment representations, parental responsiveness, and infant attachment: A meta-analysis of the Adult Attachment Interview. *Psychological Bulletin, 117*, 387–403.

Van IJzendoorn, M. H., Bakermans-Kranenburg, M. J., Falger, P. R. J., De Ruiter, C., & Cohen, L. (1998). Type A behavior pattern in mothers of infants: An exploration of associations with attachment, sensitive caregiving, and life-events. *Psychology & Health, 13*, 515–526.

Van IJzendoorn, M. H., Moran, G., Belsky, J., Pederson, D., Bakermans-Kranenburg, M.J., Kneppers, K. (2000). The similarity of siblings' attachment to their mother. *Child Development, 71*, 1086–1098.

Van Knippenberg, A., & Wilke, H. (1988). Social categorization and attitude change. *European Journal of Social Psychology, 18*, 395–406.

Van Praag, H. M. (2004). *Stress, vulnerability and depression.* New York: Cambridge University Press.

Van Spronsen, M., & Hoogenraad, C. C. (2010). Synapse pathology in psychiatric and neurologic disease. *Current Neurology and Neuroscience Reports, 10*(3), 207–214.

Van Vugt, M., De Cremer, D., & Janssen, D. P. (2007). Gender differences in cooperation and competition the Male-Warrior hypothesis. *Psychological Science, 18*(1), 19–23.

Van Yperen, N. W. (2006). A novel approach to assessing achievement goals in the context of the 2 × 2 framework: Identifying distinct profiles of individuals with different dominant achievement goals. *Personality and Social Psychology Bulletin, 32,* 1432–1445.

Van Zomeren, A. H., & Brouwer, W. H. (1994). *Clinical neuropsychology of attention.* New York: Oxford University Press.

Vandell, D. L., Belsky, J., Burchinal, M., Vandergrift, N., & Steinberg, L. (2010). Do effects of early child care extend to age 15 years? Results from the NICHD study of early child care and young development. *Child Development, 81,* 737–756.

Vandell, D. L., Burchinal, M. R., & Belsky, J. (2005). Early child care and children's development in the primary grades: Follow-up results from the NICHD Study of Early Child Care. Paper presented at the biennial meeting of the Society for Research in Child Development, Atlanta, Georgia.

Vanman, E. J., Saltz, J. L., Nathan, L. R., & Warren, J. A. (2004). Racial discrimination by low-prejudiced whites: Facial movements as implicit measures of attitudes related to behavior, *Psychological Science, 15,* 711–714.

Varga, C. A., Sherman, G. G., & Jones, S. A. (2006). HIV-disclosure in the context of vertical transmission: HIV-positive mothers in Johannesburg, South Africa. *Aids Care, 18,* 952–960.

Vargha-Khadem, F., Gadian, D. G., Watkins, K. E., Connelly, A., Van Paesschen, W., & Mishkin, M. (1997). Differential effects of early hippocampal pathology on episodic and semantic memory. *Science, 277,* 376–380.

Vasilaki, E. I., Hosier, S. G., & Cox, W. M. (2006). The efficacy of motivational interviewing as a brief intervention for excessive drinking: A meta-analytic review. *Alcohol and Alcoholism, 41,* 328–335.

Vaughn, C., & Leff, J. (1976). The measurement of expressed emotion in the families of psychiatric patients. *British Journal of Social and Clinical Psychology, 15,* 157–165.

Vazire, S. (2010). Who knows what about a person? The self-other knowledge asymmetry (SOKA) model. *Journal of Personality and Social Psychology, 98,* 281–300.

Venn, O., Turner, I., Mathieson, I., De Groot, N., Bontrop, R. & McVean, G. (2014). Strong male bias drives germline mutation in chimpanzees. *Science, 344*(6189), 1271.

Verhulst, S., & Bolhuis, J. (2009). *Tinbergen's legacy: Function and mechanism in behavioural biology.* Cambridge: Cambridge University Press.

Verona, E., & Carbonell, J. L. (2000). Female violence and personality: Evidence for a pattern of overcontrolled hostility among one-time violent female offenders. *Criminal Justice and Behavior, 27,* 176–195.

Verona, E., Patrick, C., Curtin, J., Bradley, M. M., & Lang, P. J. (2004). Psychopathy and physiological response to emotionally evocative sounds. *Journal of Abnormal Psychology, 113,* 99–108.

Verplanken, B., & Holland, R. W. (2002). Motivated decision making: Effects of activation and self centrality of values on choices and behavior. *Journal of Personality and Social Psychology, 82,* 434–447.

Vertes, R. P., & Eastman, K. E. (2003). The case against memory consolidation in REM sleep. In E. F. Pace-Schott, M. Solms, M. Blagrove, & S. Harnad (Eds.), *Sleep and dreaming: Scientific advances and reconsiderations.* New York: Cambridge University Press.

Vetter, H. J. (1969). *Language behavior and psychopathology.* Chicago, IL: Rand McNally.

Victoir, A., Eertmans, A., Van den Bergh, O., & Van den Broucke, S. (2005). Learning to drive safely: Social-cognitive responses are predictive of performance rated by novice drivers and their instructors. *Transportation Research Part F: Traffic Psychology and Behaviour, 8,* 59–71.

Villarreal, D. M., Do, V., Haddad, E., & Derrick, B. E. (2002). NMDA receptor antagonists sustain LTP and spatial memory: Active processes mediate LTP decay. *Nature Neuroscience, 5,* 48–52.

Vinden, P. G. (2002). Understanding minds and evidence for belief: A study of Mofu

children in Cameroon. *International Journal of Behavioral Development, 26,* 445–452.

Vink, J. M., Groot, A. S., Derkhof, G. A., & Boomsma, D. I. (2001). Genetic analysis of morningness and eveningness. *Chronobiology International, 18,* 809–822.

Virnig, B., Huang, Z., Lurie, N., Musgrave, D., McBean, A. M., & Dowd, B. (2004). Does Medicare managed care provide equal treatment for mental illness across races? *Archives of General Psychiatry, 61,* 201–205.

Vitaliano, P. P., Young, H. M., & Zhang, J. (2004). Is caregiving a risk factor for illness? *Current Directions in Psychological Science, 13,* 13–16.

Vittengl, J. R., Clark, L. A., & Jarrett, R. B. (2009). Continuation-phase cognitive therapy's effects on remission and recovery from depression. *Journal of Consulting and Clinical Psychology, 77*(2), 367–371.

Vogel, D. D. (2005). A neural network model of memory and higher cognitive functions. *International Journal of Psychophysiology, 55*(1), 3–21.

Vogels, W. W. A., Dekker, M. R., Brouwer, W. H., & deJong, R. (2002). Age-related changes in event-related prospective memory performance: A comparison of four prospective memory tasks. *Brain and Cognition, 49,* 341–362.

Volkow, N. D., Wang, G. J., Fowler, J. S., & Tomasi, D. (2012). Addiction circuitry in the human brain. *Annual Review of Pharmacology and Toxicology, 52,* 321.

Von Bayern, A. M. P., Heathcote, R. J. P., Rutz, C., Kacelnik, A. (2009). The role of experience in problem solving and innovative tool use in crows. *Current Biology, 19*(22), 1965–1968.

Von Frisch, K. (1974). Decoding the language of the bee. *Science, 185,* 663–668.

Vurpillot, E. (1968). The development of scanning strategies and their relation to visual differentiations. *Journal of Experimental Child Psychology, 6,* 632–650.

Vygotsky, L. S. (1978). *Mind in society: The development of higher psychological processes.* Cambridge, MA: Harvard University Press. (Original work published 1935.)

W

Waaktaar, T., Christie, H. J., Borge, A. I. H., & Torgersen, S. (2004). How can young people's resilience be enhanced? Experiences from a clinical intervention project. *Clinical Child Psychology and Psychiatry, 9*, 167–183.

Wacker, H. R., Müllejans, R., Klein, K. H., & Battegay, R. (1992). Identification of cases of anxiety disorders and affective disorders in the community according to ICD-10 and DSMIII-R by using the Composite International Diagnostic Interview (CIDI). *International Journal of Methods in Psychiatric Research, 2*, 91–100.

Wadden, T. A., Brownell, K. D., & Foster, G. D. (2002). Obesity: Responding to the global epidemic. *Journal of Consulting and Clinical Psychology, 70*, 510–525.

Wade, P., & Bernstein, B. (1991). Culture sensitivity training and counselor's race: Effects on Black female client's perceptions and attrition. *Journal of Counseling Psychology, 38*, 9–15.

Waggoner, R. (2008). *Lucid dreaming: Gateway to the inner self*. Needham, MA: Moment Point Press.

Wagner, K. D., Ambrosini, P., Rynn, M., Wohlberg, C., Yang, R., Greenbaum, M. S., … Deas, D. (2003). Efficacy of sertraline in the treatment of children and adolescents with major depressive disorder: Two randomized controlled trials. *Journal of the American Medical Association, 290*(8), 1033–1041.

Wagstaff, G. F. (2008). Hypnosis and the law: Examining the stereotypes. *Criminal Justice and Behavior, 35*, 1277–1294.

Wagstaff, G., Brunas-Wagstaff, J., Cole, J., & Wheatcroft, J. (2004). New directions in forensic hypnosis: Facilitating memory with a focused meditation technique. *Contemporary Hypnosis, 21*, 14–27.

Wahlberg, K. E., Wynne, L. C., Oja, H., Keskitalo, P., Pykäläinen, L., Lahti, I., … Tienari, P. (1997). Gene-environment interaction in vulnerability to schizophrenia: Findings from the Finnish Family Study of Schizophrenia. *American Journal of Psychiatry, 154*, 355–362.

Wakefield, A. J., Murch, S. H., Anthony, A., Linnell, J., Casson, D. M., Malik, M., … Walker-Smith, J. A.. (1998).

Ileal-lymphoid-nodular hyperplasia, non-specific colitis, and pervasive developmental disorder in children. *The Lancet, 351* (9103), 637–641.

Wakefield, M., Reid, Y., Roberts, L., Mullins, R., & Gillies, P. (1998). Smoking and smoking cessation among men whose partners are pregnant: A qualitative study. *Social Science Medicine, 47*, 657–664.

Wakefield, M. A., Loken, B., & Hornik, R. C. (2010). Use of mass media campaigns to change health behaviour. *The Lancet, 376*, 1261–1271.

Wakeley, A., Rivera, S., & Langer, J. (2000). Can young infants add and subtract? *Child Development, 71*(6), 1525–1534.

Walen, S. R., & Roth, D. (1987). A cognitive approach. In J. H. Geer & W. T. O'Donohue (Eds.), *Theories of human sexuality*. New York: Plenum Press.

Walker, E. F., & Diforio, D. (1997). Schizophrenia: A neural diathesis-stress model. *Psychological Review, 104*, 667–685.

Walker, I. (2006). Time of day effects in drivers' overtaking of bicycles. *PHILICA. COM*, article number 24.

Walker, I. (2007). Drivers overtaking bicyclists: Objective data on the effects of riding position, helmet use, vehicle type and apparent gender. *Accident Analysis and Prevention, 39*, 417–425.

Walker, I., Holt, N., & Lewis, R. (Eds.) (2010). *Research methods and statistics*. Basingstoke: Palgrave Macmillan.

Walker, M. P., Brakefield, T., Morgan, A., Hobson, J. A., & Stickgold, R. (2002). Practise with sleep makes perfect: sleep-dependent motor skill learning. *Neuron, 35*, 205–211.

Walker M. P., &van der Helm, E. (2009). Overnight therapy? The role of sleep in emotional brain processing. *Psychological Bulletin, 135*(5), 731–748.

Walker, W. R., Skowronski, J. J., & Thompson, C. P. (2003a). Life is pleasant – and memory helps to keep it that way! *Review of General Psychology, 7*, 203–210.

Walker, W. R., Skowronski, J. J., Gibbons, J. A., Vogl, R. J., & Thompson, C. P. (2003b). On the emotions that accompany autobiographical memories: Dysphoria disrupts the fading affect bias. *Cognition & Emotion, 17*(5), 703–723.

Walker, W. R., Vogl, R. J., & Thompson, C. P. (1997). Autobiographical memory: Unpleasantness fades faster than pleasantness over time. *Applied Cognitive Psychology, 11*, 399–413.

Wallbott, H., & Scherer, K. (1988). How universal and specific is emotional experience? Evidence from 27 countries and five continents. In K. Scherer (Ed.), *Facets of emotion: Recent research*. Hillsdale, NJ: Erlbaum.

Walsh, B. T., & Devlin, M. J. (1998). Eating disorders: Progress and problems. *Science, 280*, 1387–1390.

Walsh, V., & Cowey, A. (2000). Transcranial magnetic stimulation and cognitive neuroscience. *Nature Reviews Neuroscience, 1*(1), 73–80.

Walster, E., Aronson, V., Abrahams, D., & Rottman, L. (1966). The importance of physical attractiveness in dating behavior. *Journal of Personality and Social Psychology, 4*, 508–516.

Walter, H., Bretschneider, V., Gron, G., Zurowski, B., Wunderlich, A. P,. Tomczak, R., & Spitzer, M. (2003). Evidence for quantitative domain dominance for verbal and spatial working memory in frontal and parietal cortex. *Cortex, 39*, 897–911.

Wang, A. Y., & Thomas, M. H. (2000). Looking for long-term mnemonic effects on serial recall: The legacy of Simonides. *American Journal of Psychology, 113*, 331–340.

Wang, P. S., Demler, O., & Kessler, R. C. (2002). Adequacy of treatment for serious mental illness in the United States. *American Journal of Public Health, 92*, 92–98.

Wang, Q. (2001). Culture effects on adults' earliest childhood recollection and self-description: Implications for the relation between memory and the self. *Journal of Personality and Social Psychology, 81*, 220–233.

Wang, Q. (2008). Being American, being Asian: The bicultural self and autobiographical memory in Asian Americans. *Cognition, 107*, 743–751.

Wang, Q. (2009). Are Asians forgetful? Perception, retention, and recall in episodic remembering. *Cognition, 111*(1), 123–131.

Wang, Q., & Conway, M. A. (2004). The stories we keep: Autobiographical memory in American and Chinese middle-aged adults. *Journal of Personality, 72*(5), 911–938.

Wang, S., Baillargeon, R., & Paterson, S. (2005). Detecting continuity violations in infancy: A new account and new evidence from covering and tube events. *Cognition, 95*, 129–173.

Wang, T., Brownstein, R., & Katzev, R. (1989). Promoting charitable behaviour with compliance techniques. *Applied Psychology: An International Review, 38*, 165–183.

Ward, A. J. (2012). Social facilitation of exploration in mosquitofish (Gambusia holbrooki). *Behavioral Ecology and Sociobiology, 66*(2), 223–230.

Ward, J. (2010). *The students guide to cognitive neuroscience* (2nd ed.). Hove: Psychology Press.

Ward, L. M., & Friedman, K. (2006). Using TV as a guide: Associations between television viewing and adolescents' sexual attitudes and behavior. *Journal of Research on Adolescence, 16*(1), 133–156.

Ward, S. L., & Overton, W. F. (1990). Semantic familiarity, relevance, and the development of deductive reasoning. *Developmental Psychology, 26*, 488–493.

Warga, C. (1987). Pain's gatekeeper. *Psychology Today, 21*, 50–59.

Warneken, F., & Tomasello, M. (2006). Altruistic helping in human infants and young chimpanzees. *Science, 311*(5765), 1301–1303.

Warneken, F., & Tomasello, M. (2007). Helping and cooperation at 14 months of age. *Infancy, 11*(3), 271–294.

Warneken, F., & Tomasello, M. (2009). The roots of human altruism. *British Journal of Psychology, 100*(3), 455–471.

Wason, P. C. (1966). Reasoning. In B. M. Foss (Ed.), *New horizons in psychology I*. Harmondsworth: Penguin.

Wasserman, D., & Wachbroit, R. (2001). *Genetics and criminal behavior*. New York: Cambridge University Press.

Watanabe, S., Sakamoto, J., & Wakita, M. (1995). Pigeon's discrimination of paintings by Monet and Picasso. *Journal of the Experimental Analysis of Behavior, 63*, 165–174.

Waterman, A. H., Blades, M., & Spencer, C. P. (2004). Indicating when you do not know the answer: The effect of question format and interviewer knowledge on childrens' 'don't know' responses. *British Journal of Developmental Psychology, 22* (3), 335–348.

Waters, A., Hill, A., & Waller, G. (2001). Bulimics' responses to food cravings: Is binge-eating a product of hunger or emotional state? *Behaviour Research and Therapy, 39*, 877–886.

Watkins, L. R., & Maier, S. F. (2003) When good pain turns bad. *Current Directions in Psychological Science, 12*, 232–236.

Watson, D., & Clark, L. A. (1992). Affects separable and inseparable: On the hierarchical arrangement of the negative affects. *Journal of Personality and Social Psychology, 62*, 489–505.

Watson, D. L., & Tharp, R. G. (1997). *Self-directed behavior: Self-modification for personal adjustment* (7th ed.). Belmont, CA: Brooks/Cole.

Watson, J. B. (1913). Psychology as the behaviorist views it. *Psychological Review, 20*, 158–177.

Watson, J. B. (1924). *Behaviorism*. New York: People's Institute.

Watson, J. B., & Rayner, R. (1920). Conditioned emotional reactions. *Journal of Experimental Psychology, 3*, 1–14.

Watson, J. C., & Greenberg, L. S. (1998). The therapeutic alliance in short-term humanistic and experiential therapies. In J. D. Safran & C. J. Muran (Eds.), *The therapeutic alliance in brief psychotherapy*. Washington, DC: American Psychological Association.

Wauterickx, N., Gouwy, A., & Bracke, P. (2006). Parental divorce and depression: Long-term effects on adult children. *Journal of Divorce & Remarriage, 45*, 43–68.

Weaver, C. A., III, & Krug, K. S. (2004). Consolidation-like effects in flashbulb memories: Evidence from September 11, 2001. *American Journal of Psychology, 117*, 517–530.

Webb, W. B. (1974). Sleep as an adaptive response. *Perceptual and Motor Skills, 38*, 1023–1027.

Webb, W. B. (1992). *Sleep: The gentle tyrant* (2nd ed.). Bolton, MA: Anker.

Webb, W. B. (1994). Prediction of sleep onset. In R. D. Ogilvie & J. R. Harsh (Eds.), *Sleep onset: Normal and abnormal processes*. Washington, DC: American Psychological Association.

Webster, D. M., Richter, L., & Kruglanski, A. W. (1996). On leaping to conclusions when feeling tired: Mental fatigue effects on impressional primacy. *Journal of Experimental Social Psychology, 32*, 181–195.

Weinberger, D. R., & McClure, R. K. (2002). Neurotoxicity, neuroplasticity, and magnetic resonance imaging morphometry: What is happening in the schizophrenic brain? *Archives of General Psychiatry, 59*, 553–559.

Weiner, B. (1992). *Human motivation: Metaphors, theories, and research*. Newbury Park, CA: Sage.

Weinert, F. E., & Hany, E. A. (2003). The stability of individual differences in intellectual development. In R. J. Sternberg, J. Lautrey, & T. I. Lubart (Eds.), *Models of intelligence: International perspectives*. Washington, DC: American Psychological Association.

Weingardt, K. R., & Marlatt, G. A. (1998). Harm reduction and public policy. In G. A. Marlatt (Ed.), *Harm reduction: Pragmatic strategies for managing high-risk behaviors*. New York: Guilford Press.

Weingarten, H. P. (1983). Conditioned cues elicit feeding in sated rats: A role for learning in meal initiation. *Science, 220*, 431–433.

Weinstein, N. D., & Sandman, P. M. (1992). A model of the precaution adoption process: Evidence from home radon testing. *Health Psychology, 11*, 170–180.

Weir, A. A. S., Chappell, J., & Kacelnik, A. (2002). Shaping of hooks in New Caledonian crows. *Science, 297*, 981.

Weiskrantz, L. (2002). Prime-sight and blindsight. *Consciousness and Cognition, 11*, 568–581.

Weiskrantz, L., Warrington, E. K., Sanders, M. D., & Marshall, J. (1974). Visual capacity in the hemianopic field following a restricted occipital ablation. *Brain, 97* (4), 709–728.

Weissman, M. M., Geshon, E. S., Kidd, K. K., Prusoff, B. A., Leckman, J. F., Dibble, E., ... Guroff, J. J. (1984). Psychiatric disorders in the relatives of probands with affective disorders. *Archives of General Psychiatry, 41,* 13–21.

Weissman, M. M., Markowitz, J. C., & Klerman, G. L. (2007). *Clinician's quick guide to interpersonal psychotherapy.* New York: Oxford University Press.

Weitlauf, J., Smith, R. E., & Cervone, D. (2000). Generalization effects of coping skills training: Influences of self-defense training on women's efficacy beliefs, assertiveness, and aggression. *Journal of Applied Psychology, 85,* 625–633.

Weitzenhoffer, A. M., & Hilgard, E. R. (1962). *Stanford Hypnotic Susceptibility Scale: Form C.* Palo Alto, CA: Consulting Psychologists.

Wells, A. (2000). *Emotional disorders and metacognition: Innovative cognitive therapy.* Chichester: Wiley.

Wen, L. M., Orr, N., Millett, C., & Rissel, C. (2006). Driving to work and overweight and obesity: Findings from the 2003 New South Wales Health Survey, Australia. *International Journal of Obesity, 30,* 782–786.

Wenzlaff, R. M., Wegner, D. M., & Roper, D. W. (1988). Depression and mental control: The resurgence of unwanted negative thoughts. *Journal of Personality and Social Psychology, 55,* 882–892.

Werker, J., & Tees, R. (1984). Cross-language speech perception evidence for perceptual reorganization during the first year of life. *Infant Behavior and Development, 7,* 49–63.

Werner, E. E., & Smith, R. S. (1982). *Vulnerable and invincible: A longitudinal study of resilient children.* New York: McGraw-Hill.

Wernig, M., & Brustle, O. (2002). Fifty ways to make a neuron: Shifts in stem cell hierarchy and their implications for neuropathology and CNS repair. *Journal of Neuropathology and Experimental Neurology, 61*(2), 101–110.

Werth, J. L., Jr., Blevins, D., Toussaint, K. L., & Durham, M. R. (2002). The influence of cultural diversity on end of life care and decisions. *American Behavioral Scientist, 46,* 204–219.

Wertheimer, M. (1912). Experimentelle studien über das Gesehen von Bewegung. *Zeitschrift fuer Psychologie, 61,* 161–265.

West, P. D., & Evans, E. F. (1990). Early detection of hearing damage in young listeners resulting from exposure to amplified music. *British Journal of Audiology, 24,* 89–103.

West, S. A., Pen, I., & Griffin, A. S. (2002). Cooperation and competition between relatives. *Science, 296,* 72–75.

Westen, D. (1998a). Implications of research in cognitive neuroscience for psychodynamic psychotherapy, reprinted in G. O. Gabbard, J. S. Beck, & J. Holmes (Eds.) (2005). *The Oxford textbook of psychotherapy.* Oxford: Oxford University Press.

Westen, D. (1998b). The scientific legacy of Sigmund Freud: Toward a psychodynamically informed psychological science. *Psychological Bulletin, 24,* 333–371.

Westen, D., & Morrison, K. (2001). A multidimensional meta-analysis of treatments for depression, panic, and generalized anxiety disorder: An empirical examination of the status of empirically supported therapies. *Journal of Consulting and Clinical Psychology, 69,* 875–899.

Westen, D., Novotny, C. M., & Thompson-Brenner, H. (2004). The empirical status of empirically supported psychotherapies: Assumptions, findings, and reporting in controlled clinical trials. *Psychological Bulletin, 130,* 631–663.

Wethington, E. (2000). Expecting stress: Americans and the 'midlife crisis.' *Motivation and Emotion, 24,* 85–103.

Whaley, C. P. (1978). Word-non-word classification time. *Journal of Verbal Learning and Verbal Behavior, 17*(2), 143–154.

Whalley, L. J., & Deary, I. J. (2001). Longitudinal cohort study of childhood IQ and survival up to age 76. *British Medical Journal, 322,* 819–822.

Wheeler, L., & Miyake, K. (1992). Social comparison in everyday life. *Journal of Personality and Social Psychology, 62,* 760–773.

Wheeler, M. E., & Fiske, S. T. (2005). Controlling racial prejudice: Social-cognitive goals affect amygdala and stereotype activation. *Psychological Science, 16,* 56–63.

Whitam, F. L., & Mathy, R. M. (1991). Childhood cross-gender behavior of homosexual females in Brazil, Peru, the Philippines, and the United States. *Archives of Sexual Behavior, 20,* 151–170.

White, K. M., Hogg, M. A., & Terry, D. J. (2002). Improving attitude behavior correspondence through exposure to normative support from a salient ingroup. *Basic and Applied Social Psychology, 24,* 91–103.

Whitson, J. A., & Galinsky, A. D. (2008). Lacking control increases illusory pattern perception. *Science, 322*(5898), 115–117.

Whorf, B. L. (1956). Science and linguistics. In J. B. Carroll (Ed.), *Language, thought and reality: Selected writings of Benjamin Lee Whorf.* Cambridge, MA: MIT Press.

Whyte, J., & Kavey, N. B. (1990). Somnambulistic eating: A report of three cases. *International Journal of Eating Disorders, 9,* 577–581.

Wiedenfeld, S. A., O'Leary, A., Bandura, A., Brown, S., Levine, S., & Raska, K. (1990). Impact of perceived self-efficacy in coping with stressors on components of the immune system. *Journal of Personality and Social Psychology, 59,* 1082–1094.

Wiederhold, B. K., & Wiederhold, M. D. (2005). *Virtual reality therapy for anxiety disorders.* Washington, DC: American Psychological Association.

Wiens, A. N., & Menustik, C. E. (1983). Treatment outcome and patient characteristics in an aversion therapy program for alcoholism. *American Psychologist, 38,* 1089–1096.

Wilbrecht, L., & Nottebohm, F. (2003). Vocal learning in birds and humans. *Mental Retardation and Developmental Disabilities Research Reviews, 9,* 135–148.

Wilcox, S., & Storandt, M. (1996). Relations among age, exercise, and psychological variables in a community sample of women. *Health Psychology, 15,* 110–113.

Wühr, P., & Huestegge, L. (2010). The impact of social presence on voluntary and involuntary control of spatial attention. *Social Cognition, 28*(2), 145–160.

Wurm, S., Tomasik, M. J., & Tesch-Römer, C. (2010). On the importance of a positive view on ageing for physical exercise among middle-aged and older adults: Cross-sectional and longitudinal findings. *Psychology and Health, 25,* 25–42.

Wyatt, T. D. (2003). *Pheromones and animal behaviour: Communication by smell and taste.* Cambridge: Cambridge University Press.

Wynn, K. (1992). Addition and subtraction by human infants. *Nature, 358,* 749–750.

Wynn, K. (1998). An evolved capacity for number. In D. D. Cummins & C. Allen (Eds.), *The evolution of mind.* New York: Oxford University Press.

Y

Yang, L., Krampe, R. T., & Baltes, P. B. (2006). Basic forms of cognitive plasticity extended into the oldest-old: Retest learning, age, and cognitive functioning. *Psychology and Aging, 21,* 372–378.

Yang, Y., Raine, A., Lencz, T., Bihrle, S., LaCasse, L., & Colletti, P. (2005). Volume reduction in prefrontal gray matter in unsuccessful criminal psychopaths. *Biological Psychiatry, 57,* 1103–1108.

Yau, J., & Smetana, J. (1996). Adolescent–parent conflict among Chinese adolescents in Hong Kong. *Child Development, 67,* 1262–1275.

Yen, S., Shea, T., Pagano, M., Sanislow, C. A., Grilo, C. M., McGlashan, T. H., … Morey, L. C. (2003). Axis I and Axis II disorders as predictors of prospective suicide attempts: Findings from the Collaborative Longitudinal Personality Disorders Study. *Journal of Abnormal Psychology, 112,* 375–381.

Yerkes, R. M., & Dodson, J. D. (1908). The relation of strength of stimulus to rapidity of habit-formation. *Journal of Comparative and Physiological Psychology, 18,* 459–482.

Yin, T. C. T., & Kuwada, S. (1984). Neuronal mechanisms of binaural interaction. In G. M. Edelman, W. M. Cowan, & W. E. Gall (Eds.), *Dynamic aspects of neocortical function.* New York: Wiley.

Young, E. (2009). Are bad sleeping habits driving us mad? *New Scientist, 2696.*

Young, L. R., & Joffe, R. T. (1997). *Bipolar disorder: Biological models and their clinical application.* New York: Marcel Dekker.

Youngstedt, S. D., O'Connor, P. J., & Dishman, R. K. (1997). The effects of acute exercise on sleep: A quantitative synthesis. *Sleep, 20,* 203–214.

Yudofsky, S. and Hales, R. (2008). *The American Psychiatric Publishing textbook of neuropsychiatry and behavioural neuroscience* (5th ed.). Arlington, VA. American Psychiatric Publishing.

Yzerbyt, V., Rocher, S., & Schadron, G. (1997). Stereotypes as explanations: A subjective essentialistic view of group perception. In N. Ellemers, S. A. Haslam, R. Spears & P. J. Oakes (Eds.), *The social psychology of stereotyping and group life.* Malden, MA: Blackwell.

Z

Zahava, S., Shklar, R., Singer, Y., & Mikulincer, M. (2006). Reactions to combat stress in Israeli war veterans twenty years after the 1982 Lebanon war. *Journal of Mental and Nervous Disease, 194,* 935–939.

Zajonc, R. B. (1965). Social facilitation. *Science, 149,* 269–274.

Zajonc, R. B. (1980). Feeling and thinking – preferences need no inferences. *American Psychologist, 35*(2), 151–175.

Zajonc, R. B. (1984). On the primacy of affect. *American Psychologist, 39*(2), 117–123.

Zajonc, R.B., Adelmann, P.K., Murphy, S.T., & Niedenthal, P.M. (1987). Convergence in the physical appearance of spouses. *Motivation and Emotion, 11,* 335–346.

Zajonc, R. B., Murphy, S. T., & Inglehart, M. (1989). Feeling and facial efference: Implications of a vascular theory of emotion. *Psychological Review, 96,* 395–416.

Zald, D., & Rauch, S. (Eds.) (2006). *The orbitofrontal cortex.* New York: Oxford University Press.

Zambelis, T., Paparrigopoulos, T., & Soldatos, C. R. (2002). REM sleep behaviour disorder associated with a neurinoma of the left pontocerebellar angle. *Journal of Neurology, Neurosurgery, and Psychiatry, 72,* 821–822.

Zampini, M., & Spence, C. (2004). The role of auditory cues in modulating the perceived crispness and staleness of potato chips. *Journal of Sensory Science, 19,* 347–363.

Zanarini, M. C., Frankenburg, F. R., Reich, D. B., & Fitzmaurice, G. (2010). The 10-year course of psychosocial functioning among patients with borderline personality disorder and axis II comparison subjects. *Acta Psychiatrica Scandinavica, 122,* 103–109. doi: 10.1111/j.1600-0447.2010.01543.

Zander, M. F. (2006). Musical influences in advertising: How music modifies first impressions of product endorsers and brands. *Psychology of Music, 34,* 465–480.

Zanker, J. (2010). *Sensation, perception, action – an evolutionary perspective.* London: Palgrave.

Zatzick, D. F., & Dimsdale, J. E. (1990). Cultural variations in response to painful stimuli. *Psychosomatic Medicine, 52,* 544–557.

Zavos, H. M. S., Rijsdijk, F. V., Gregory, A. M., & Eley, T. C. (2010). Genetic influences on the cognitive biases associated with anxiety and depression symptoms in adolescents. *Journal of Affective Disorders, 124* (1), 45–53. doi: 10.1016/j.jad.2009.10.030.

Zayas, V., & Shoda, Y. (2007). Predicting preferences for dating partners from past experiences of psychological abuse: Identifying the psychological ingredients of situations. *Personality and Social Psychology Bulletin, 33,* 123–138.

Zechner, U., Wilda, M., Kehrer-Sawatzki, H., Vogel, W., Fundele, R., & Hameister, H. (2001). A high density of X-linked genes for general cognitive ability: A runaway process shaping human evolution? *Trends in Genetics, 17,* 697–701.

Zeno, S. (Ed.). (1995). *The educator's word frequency guide.* Brewster, NJ: Touchstone Applied Science Associates.

Zevin, J. D., & Seidenberg, M. S. (2002). Age of acquisition effects in word reading and other tasks. *Journal of Memory and Language, 47*, 1–29.

Zhang, D., Zhang, X., Sun, X., Li, Z., Wang, Z., He, S., & Hu, X. (2004). Cross-modal temporal order memory for auditory digits and visual locations: An fMRI study. *Human Brain Mapping, 22*, 280–289.

Zhang, K., Sun, M., Werner, P., Kovera, A. J., Albu, J., Pi-Sunyer, F. X., & Boozer, C. N. (2002). Sleeping metabolic rate in relation to body mass index and body composition. *Journal of Obesity, 26*(3), 376–383.

Zhang, Y., Proenca, R., Maffei, M., Barone, M., Leopold, L., & Friedman, J. M. (1994). Positional cloning of the mouse obese gene and its human homologue. *Nature, 372*, 425–432.

Zhdanova, I. V., & Wurtman, R. J. (1997). Efficacy of melatonin as a sleep-promoting agent. *Journal of Biological Rhythms, 12*, 644–650.

Zhou, Z., Peverly, S. T., & Lin, J. (2005). Understanding early mathematical competencies in American and Chinese children. *School Psychology International, 26*, 413–427.

Ziermans, T. B., Schothorst, P. F., Schnack, H. G., Koolschijn, P. C. M. P., Kahn, R. S., van Engeland, H., & Durston, S. (2012).

Progressive structural brain changes during development of psychosis. *Schizophrenia Bulletin, 38*(3), 519–530. doi:10.1093/ schbul/sbq113.

Zimbardo, P. (1989). *Quiet rage: The Stanford prison study video*. Stanford, CA: Stanford University.

Zimbardo, P. G. (2004). A situationist perspective on the psychology of evil: Understanding how good people are transformed into perpetrators. In A. G. Miller (Ed.), *The social psychology of good and evil*. New York: Guilford Press.

Zimbardo, P. G., Haney, C., Banks, W. C., & Jaffe, D. (1973, April 8). The mind is a formidable jailer: A Pirandellian prison. *New York Times Magazine*, 38–60.

Zimmermann, P., & Thompson, R. A. (2014). New directions in developmental emotion regulation research across the life span: Introduction to the special section. *International Journal of Behavioral Development, 38(2)*, 139–141.

Zinbarg, R. E., Barlow, D. H., Brown, T. A., & Hertz, R. M. (1992). Cognitive-behavioral approaches to the nature and treatment of anxiety disorders. *Annual Review of Psychology, 43*, 235–268.

Zubieta, J.-K., Smith, Y. R., Bueller, J. A., Xu, Y., Kilbourn, M. R., Jewett, D. M.,… Stohler, C. S. (2001). Regional *mu* opioid

receptor regulation of sensory and affective dimensions of pain. *Science, 293*, 311–315.

Zucker, T. P., Flesche, C. W., Germing, U., Schröter, S., Willers, R., Wolf, H. H., & Heyll, A. (1998). Patient-controlled versus staffcontrolled analgesia with pethidine after allogeneic bone marrow transplantation. *Pain, 75*, 305–312.

Zuckerman, M. (1991). *Psychobiology of personality*. New York: Cambridge University Press.

Zuckerman, M. (2005). *Psychobiology of personality* (2nd ed.). New York: Cambridge University Press.

Zuckerman, M., Hall, J. A., DeFrank, R. S., & Rosenthal, R. (1976). Encoding and decoding of spontaneous and posed facial expressions. *Journal of Personality and Social Psychology, 34*, 966–977.

Zunft, H.-J. F., Friebe, D., Seppelt, B., Widhalm, K., Remaut de Winter, A. M., Vaz de Almeida, M. D., Kearney, J. M., & Gibney, M. (1999). Perceived benefits and barriers to physical activity in a nationally representative sample in the European Union. *Public Health Nutrition, 2*, 153–160.

Name index

Subject index